CONTEMPORARY
DRAMATISTS

Contemporary Writers of the English Language

Contemporary Poets

Contemporary Novelists
(including short story writers)

Contemporary Dramatists

CONTEMPORARY DRAMATISTS

SECOND EDITION

WITH A PREFACE BY
RUBY COHN

EDITOR
JAMES VINSON

ASSOCIATE EDITOR
D. L. KIRKPATRICK

ST. JAMES PRESS
LONDON

ST. MARTIN'S PRESS
NEW YORK

CONTENTS

PREFACE

This volume contains over three hundred entries for contemporary dramatists writing in English, thousands of miles apart. It might seem then that English drama is alive and well, but for that to be true, audiences should embrace drama. Do they? I have seen estimates ranging from one per cent of the population (of America) to five per cent (of England) who *ever* attend the theatre, but *regular* attendance thins down to decimals of decimals. Will three hundred dramatists continue to write for a diminishing audience?

How different from the burgeoning drama of the Elizabethans. And yet Burbage and Henslowe may also have worried about theatre attendance. No language seems to sport more than one great age of drama, and other periods of English language drama have looked pale by contrast with the Elizabethan. In later times English theatre came to be a fabulous invalid, enjoying its several prognoses, diagnoses, and forecasts of doom. Nevertheless I venture into these medical metaphors, not because our contemporary drama is less skillful than that of any age since the Elizabethan, nor even less plentiful. But because our drama, like that of no other period, has to survive in the noxious atmosphere of the mass media. Playwrights can defy the media, sidestep them, try to ignore them, or, as more often happens, use dramatic form as an entree into the media, notably films and television.

In English-speaking countries, with their meagre theatre subsidies and their major technical resources, drama abounds on film and television. (Dublin's Abbey Theatre in 1922 became the first nationally subsidized theatre in the English language, whereas the subsidized Comédie Française dates from 1680.) If today's writer is inadequately nurtured by theatre or publisher, he can turn to the media. But few media graduates have contributed significant dramas to live theatre. Mass media drama tends to appeal to the most facile reactions of an audience, and yet the techniques of the media can broaden the palette of the stage playwright. Since writing the Preface to the first edition of *Contemporary Dramatists,* I have become aware of media writers who return sporadically but significantly to the stage and of Heathcote Williams' *AC/DC* which grounds a frenzied strength in the weaknesses of a media civilization. The theatre has always drawn upon other arts, crafts, and technologies, and it may arrive at a *modus vivendi* with the media.

Perhaps the *drama* is dying in the form we have known for some four hundred years — a fairly inflexible prompt copy which is eventually printed. However, the *theatre* today — with or without promptbook — must recognize its uniqueness in that live actors play before live audiences. Each actor has a single instrument, the body that includes the voice. And for all the experimentation with non-verbal sounds, the voice has recourse to words, which are the province of the dramatist.

English drama is coeval with the printing press, and response to drama has for centuries been cumulative, as a reader-spectator travels from stage to page and, all the more receptive, to stage again. This itinerary may be less frequent for today's spectators. Contemporary stage dialogue may include primitive non-verbal sounds and electronic post-verbal devices, but new dramas of verbal distinction are nevertheless being written and played. As long as that continues, in the full awareness of live theatre as a minority art, drama will endure.

Prognosis pronounced, whom do we actually have in a volume on contemporary dramatists writing in English? Since "contemporary" has been defined (for this volume) as biologically alive, we find curious neighbors. Some dramatists have spent successful years appealing to middle-class entertainment-seekers; others have tried to entertain while supporting worthy causes or baring social problems. As has been true for four hundred years, certain plays were written to provide scope for the special talents of a particular actor. None of this sounds contemporary in an age when we take it for granted that we will fly faster than sound.

I have seen many, many plays, and many kinds of plays in nearly forty years of theatre-going. It seems only yesterday that I saw *The Iceman Cometh* in a production advised by Eugene O'Neill. (It was actually 1946). Or *The Apple Cart*, crackling wittily, only shortly after Bernard Shaw's witticisms had ceased to crackle. (It was actually 1953.) But yesterday is far away in contemporary theatre, so that Shaw and O'Neill belong to another age and another theatre language. And since this is true of master-playwrights, it is all the truer for their lesser colleagues. Even living playwrights are dead in today's theatre: a windy would-be Elizabethan, a once angry young man turned surly, a once fragile young lyricist turned coy, a reacher for tragedy resigned to routine comedy, or various squatters in the Abbey Theatre which nearly exploded under the impact of three different meteors. Such dramatists are less contemporary than Euripides or Shakespeare, not to mention John Whiting and Joe Orton, who died in mid-career. For there is no necessary convergence between biological and artistic life. I hope all playwrights live to be a hundred, but I cannot help exclaiming at some of the entries in this volume: "Is he still alive?"!

Since mid-century, we have seen specimens of English language theatre labelled epic, angry, kitchen sink, absurd, ridiculous, radical, third world, puppet, guerilla, fact, nude, improvisational, perspectivist, alternative—all soon exploited by the mass media. It is small wonder that many of the contemporary dramatists in this volume seem either uncontemporary or undramatic, regardless of chronology or biology.

To shift abruptly to a positive note, we have among contemporary dramatists one giant, Samuel Beckett, who writes sometimes in English, sometimes in French, always in his own distinctive dramatic idiom. Samuel Beckett's plays are enduring masterpieces. They are also a terminus to the Western dramatic tradition, dissecting the parts of a play so that they can never again articulate innocently. Through the tension of play, Beckett probes the bases of Western culture — faith, reason, friendship, family. Through the skills of play, Beckett summarizes human action — word and pause, gesture and stillness, motion rising from emotion. Beckett's most celebrated play, *Waiting for Godot,* is striking in its stage presence. As Brecht called attention to the theatre as theatre, Beckett calls attention to the play as play. Often pitched as polar opposites, Brecht and Beckett both reacted against the dominant illusionist drama of their time and ours, so that it is no longer so dominant. In spite of their differences, Beckett resembles Brecht in precision of language at the textural level, and in integration of verbal rhythms into an original scenic whole.

Relentlessly digging his own way, Beckett has inspired two English language playwrights, one on each side of the Atlantic, Harold Pinter and Edward Albee. From Beckett both younger dramatists have learned to convey the presence of stage action, without before or after, exposition or resolution. Pinter capitalizes on the unverifiability of a past, and Albee fits the past obliquely into the stage present. Both playwrights create the stage present through carefully crafted dialogue. Their characters speak in stylized patterns that draw upon colloquial phrases of contemporary speech. Unlike the realists with whom they are sometimes confused, they use repetition and cross-talk to probe beneath or beyond surface reality.

In their rejection of realism, other contemporary dramatists resemble Pinter and Albee. Since no stage designer can compete with the camera in photographic fidelity to surface appearance, many contemporary dramatists don't ask them to try. Departures from realism can be as diversified as John Arden's Brechtian songs in *The Ballygombeen Bequest,* Edward Bond's Ghost in *Lear,* the penitential geometry of Kenneth Brown's *Brig,* the seasonal symbolism of Ed Bullins' *In the Wine Time,* the eternal sparring in Irene Fornés' *Tango Palace,* the opportunity for improvisation in Paul Foster's *Tom Paine,* the drug metaphor in Jack Gelber's *Connection,* the mythic dimension in LeRoi Jones' *Dutchman,* the repetitive patterns of American history in Robert Lowell's *Old Glory,* the fadeout and spotlight of David Mercer's *After Haggerty,* the documentary absurdism of James Saunders' *Next Time I'll Sing to You,* the stretch toward Artaud in Peter Shaffer's *Royal Hunt of the Sun,* the manic rock monologues of Sam Shepard's *Tooth of Crime,* the tribal magic of Derek Walcott's *Dream on Monkey Mountain,* the play organically within the play in Patrick White's *Ham Funeral.* I am not saying that these plays are of equal quality, but I am saying that forays into non-realistic modes provide richer possibilities of theatricalizing the profundities of contemporary experience.

Provided that audiences come to see the plays.

*   *   *

This volume on *Contemporary Dramatists* is a companion to volumes on *Contemporary Poets* and *Contemporary Novelists*. My alarm about the state of the drama is matched by various alarms about the state of the novel or of lyric poetry. All literary genres are endangered by the mass media because, as any literate teacher knows, students read less today and less perceptively than they did a decade ago. People rarely acquire a reading habit after their student days, and one needn't swallow McLuhan whole to realize that films and television have displaced reading as a pastime. The medium may not be the message, but it has been pounding away at contemporary culture. The drama is particularly vulnerable because it suffers from the general erosion of reading habits *and* from direct competition of media drama.

Thus, *Contemporary Dramatists,* in contrast to *Poets* and *Novelists,* requires elucidation through Appendices. Three of this volume's six appendices document forms of drama on the media — film, radio and television. The other three appendices discuss live theatre, but musical libretto is a form in which the power of language is diluted into the pleasure of melody. Groups and Happenings both treat theatre as a medium in which the living actor blends body and voice to confront an audience. The appendices on Groups and Happenings highlight contemporary bifurcation of theatre and drama.

Though Happenings and counter-culture Groups are relatively new forms of theatre, they quite rightly belong in different rubrics. However, they share a few attitudes: both react against traditional theatre architecture and choose different spaces for performance. To different degrees and in different ways, they react against polished professionalism in the arts. They desire more intimate relationships between actor and audience, valuing spontaneity. Both seek to arouse new kinds of perception, and both de-emphasize language. Though Happeners and Group members see considerable overlap between art and life, they differ in their views of art and life. Group members tend to reject the various power packs of modern industrial society, favoring smaller ententes. Happeners tend to believe that all life is theatrical but that one has to see its stageability, which is enhanced by such techniques as slides, films, light shows, laser beams, Moog synthesizers, telephone switchboards, electrical control panels, and the mass media.

The word "happening" suggests chance — "It just happened" — but most happenings and events are prepared before chance is allowed to play its role. Developed mainly by visual craftsmen (Jim Dine, Allan Kaprow, Claes Oldenburg), Happenings were also influenced by John Cage's experiments with chance and silence. Coordinating people as part of plastic content, Happeners seek to elicit kinesthetic participation and response. As practitioners of music and the visual arts move increasingly into sophisticated technology, so Happeners have acquired skill in "mixed means," and the mixture is itself a form of non-utilitarian technical invention. Only occasionally are words one of the means to be mixed.

Ted Shank has traced Theatre Collective (or Group) ancestry to Artaud by way of the Living Theatre, which differs from Happenings in its pride in makeshift means. Many Groups have accepted Artaud's dictum, "No more masterpieces!" and they sometimes imply that they want no more masters either. As Artaud was inspired by the Balinese dances, New Theatre Groups attempt pre-theatre forms of tribal ritual, with accompanying incantation. For them as for Artaud and Stanislavski, the essence of theatre resides in the actor's body. Like these innovators, many new Groups embrace theatre in a missionary spirit, but their conversions tend to be more direct and sometimes violent.

Ted Shank suggest that New Theatre Groups are part of a counter-culture, but he does not suggest (as I do) that the media are greedily absorbing the counter-culture into mass culture; I believe the word is co-optation. Most Groups, aware of co-optation as a danger, resist a mass production society with its mass-produced attitudes. Certain Groups woo a specially designated audience — Blacks, women, Chicanos, homosexuals, emergent nationalities. But

ix

other Groups of this almost worldwide trend are unspecialized, and their work is often unpolished. Their productions may take the form of open rehearsals or of works in progress. Their performances may incorporate aspects of the actors' lives, or of audience biographies. Each Group member may try his hand at several of the theatre arts, sometimes mastering none. Performances always reflect the *raison d'être* of the Group.

In few cases is the *raison d'être* the exploration of a dramatic text as written, but Group attitudes towards texts vary. The Open Space, Freehold, and Performance Groups have worked variations upon well-known dramas. Playwrights – Jean-Claude van Itallie, Megan Terry, Susan Yankowitz – have participated in Open Theatre exercises, and produced scripts based on group dynamics. Several Groups evolve scripts collectively. The Performance Group has experimented with non-verbal sound, Peter Brook's International Company has invented a language, the Open Theatre has experimented with sign language. In most Group Performances, words are subordinated to movement. I have yet to see an English-speaking Group that approaches the skill of the Polish Laboratory Theatre or Danish Odin Teatret, though my lack of Polish and Danish may have compelled by closer focus on movement.

Jerzy Grotowski, Director of the Polish Laboratory Theatre, and one of the tutelary forces of the counter-culture Groups, has gathered his several essays under the title *Towards a Poor Theatre*. I respect what he means — rejection of all decorative accoutrements that distract from the actor. But audiences have wondered whether poor theatres need to be poor in craft.

The Living Theatre has made a mystique of the rough and spontaneous. Yet three of its widely toured productions did not improvise words, and the fourth did so only minimally. (Several spectators protested in Berkeley at the inflexibility of the *Paradise Now* chant: "I'm not allowed to smoke marijuana" when members of the audience had been tear-gassed that afternoon.) The Living Theatre uses words, and the words are commonplace. In general, undistinguished language proliferates in the New Theatre Groups. Perhaps it is paradoxical to ask for linguistic distinction, for colloquial elegance, from Groups committed to erode distinction and elegance.

But I ask it – in part because I admire the dedication of these Groups, in part because I think they herald the theatre of the problematic future, in which stars will be dissolved into sustained ensembles. Such solution (rather than dissolution) is evident in high quality performances of several subsidized Groups within the English establishment culture – Royal Shakespeare, Royal Court, Old Vic, Young Vic – which are hospitable to contemporary drama. In the United States, counter-culture drama has been blended with a verbal-gestural harmony in the now defunct Open Theatre, while the San Francisco Mime Troupe has achieved its own idiom of social caricature. I can only hope in ignorance about theatre groups in Canada, Australia, Africa.

The separation of popular theatre from a drama of distinctive language is not new. In the nineteenth century the mass media were popular theatre pieces of Boucicault, Kotzebue, Pixérécourt, and a host of others whose plays are fortunately lost, while Büchner went unperformed, and *Lorenzaccio* languished in mere print. At that time, too, there were spectacular mixed means – dogs, horses, floods, fires on stage. And there was body-worship, too, of the star. But serious exploration of human experience was channelled into fiction and poetry.

In our time, it is conceivable – if barely so – that such exploration will take place in the mass media. But only direct confrontation of actor and spectator can provide a totally personal interaction, and it is the personal that some of us need in theatre art. The Happeners have taught us to hone our perceptions, but what are we going to perceive with these sensitized instruments? The New Groups have emphasized the expressive potential of actors, but how can such potential be meaningfully actualized? English-speaking peoples have been highly verbal, and their dramas — on stage and page — have reflected human experience deeply and precisely. Now that the Poor Theatre has been enriched by painters, musicians, and even media technicians can we hope to hail the playwright?

RUBY COHN

EDITOR'S NOTE

The selection of dramatists included in this book is based upon the recommendations of the advisers listed on page xiii.

The entry for each dramatist consists of a biography, a full bibliography, a comment by the dramatist on his plays if he chose to make one, and a signed critical essay on his work.

Only those critical studies recommended by the entrant have been listed. British and United States editions of all books have been listed; other editions are listed only if they are the first editions. Data for plays first published in a magazine or anthology is not given if they have been later published as a separate book or in a collection of the author; acting editions of the plays are not listed unless there is no trade edition. Librettos are listed among the plays. The first production, first productions in both Great Britain and the United States, as well as subsequent productions in London and New York, if different, are listed. Reprints and revivals are not. Theatrical activities – acting and directing – have been summarized when the entrant requested it.

An appendix of entries has been included for some seven dramatists who have died since the 1950's but whose reputations are essentially contemporary. There is a Title Index of all plays (including screen, radio, and television plays) by the entrants, including those in the Supplement.

We would like to thank the entrants and contributors for their patience and cooperation in helping us compile this book.

ADVISERS

Arthur H. Ballet
Michael Benedikt
Eric Bentley
Herbert Blau
John Bowen
Harold Clurman
Ruby Cohn
John Robert Colombo
Albert Cook
Robert W. Corrigan
W. A. Darlington
John Elsom
Richard Gilman
Ronald Hayman
Stanley Kauffmann
Laurence Kitchin
Richard Kostelanetz

Frank Marcus
E. A. Markham
Benedict Nightingale
Richard Schechner
Alan Schneider
Michael Smith
John Spurling
Alan Strachan
J. L. Styan
Howard Taubman
John Russell Taylor
J. C. Trewin
Darwin T. Turner
Irving Wardle
Gerald Weales
B. A. Young

CONTRIBUTORS

Erica Aronson
Roger Baker
Arthur H. Ballet
David W. Beams
James Bertram
C. W. E. Bigsby
Michael Billington
Elmer Borklund
John Bowen
Gaynor F. Bradish
Katharine Brisbane
Connie Brissenden
John Russell Brown
Joseph Bruchac
Jarka M. Burian
Bernard Carragher
D. D. C. Chambers
Harold Clurman
Ruby Cohn
Robert W. Corrigan
W. A. Darlington
Reid Douglas
Arnold Edinborough
John Elsom
John V. Falconieri
Michael Feingold
Leonard Fleischer
Melvin J. Friedman
John Fuegi
S. R. Gilbert

Martin Gottfried
Anthony Graham-White
Jonathan Hammond
Ronald Hayman
Dick Higgins
Errol Hill
Morgan Y. Himelstein
Foster Hirsch
Harold Hobson
William M. Hoffman
Mervyn Jones
Burton Kendle
Laurence Kitchin
Richard Kostelanetz
John G. Kuhn
Michael T. Leech
Allan Lewis
Mary Lord
Frank Marcus
E. A. Markham
Thomas B. Markus
Thomas J. McCormack
George McElroy
Arthur E. McGuinness
Walter J. Meserve
Louis D. Mitchell
Christian H. Moe
Benedict Nightingale
Garry O'Connor
Marion O'Connor

Joseph Parisi
Dorothy Parker
Philip Purser
Henry Raynor
Nonnita Rees
John M. Reilly
John D. Ripley
James Roose-Evans
Arthur Sainer
Adele Edling Shank
Theodore Shank
Elaine Shragge
Michael Sidnell
Judith Cooke Simmons
P. Adams Sitney
Michael Smith

A. Richard Sogliuzzo
John Spurling
Carol Simpson Stern
Alan Strachan
J. L. Styan
Alrene Sykes
John Russell Taylor
J. E. P. Thomson
J. C. Trewin
Simon Trussler
Darwin T. Turner
David Wade
Gerald Weales
T. C. Worsley
B. A. Young

CONTEMPORARY
DRAMATISTS

George Abbott
Paul Ableman
Dannie Abse
Rodney Ackland
Ama Ata Aidoo
Edward Albee
William Alfred
Ted Allan
Robert Anderson
John Antrobus
Douglas Archibald
Jane Arden
John Arden
Robert Ardrey
George Axelrod
Alan Ayckbourn

Enid Bagnold
James Baldwin
Howard Barker
Djuna Barnes
Peter Barnes
Samuel Beckett
Saul Bellow
Alan Bennett
Eric Bentley
Barrie Bermange
Kenneth Bernard
George Birimisa
Bridget Boland
Carol Bolt
Robert Bolt
C. G. Bond
Edward Bond
Julie Bovasso
John Bowen
Howard Brenton
Brigid Brophy
Kenneth H. Brown
Ed Bullins
Abe Burrows
John Burrows
Alexander Buzo

David Campton
Denis Cannan
Lewis John Carlino
Lonnie Carter
David Caute
Mary Chase
Paddy Chayefsky
Alice Childress
Agatha Christie
Caryl Churchill
John Pepper Clark

Rick Cluchey
Barry Collins
Laurence Collinson
Stewart Conn
Marc Connelly
Michael Cook
Ron Cowen
David Cregan
Beverley Cross
Mart Crowley
Allen Curnow
Jackie Curtis

Robertson Davies
Ossie Davis
Joe DeGraft
Shelagh Delaney
Nigel Dennis
Keith Dewhurst
Charles Dizenzo
J. P. Donleavy
Rosalyn Drexler
Martin Duberman
Maureen Duffy
Ronald Duncan
Lawrence Durrell
Charles Dyer

R. Sarif Easmon
David Edgar
Obi Egbuna
Lonne Elder, III
Barry England
Stanley Eveling
Tom Eyen

Jules Feiffer
Lawrence Ferlinghetti
Richard Foreman
María Irene Fornés
James Forsyth
Paul Foster
Mario Fratti
Michael Frayn
David Freeman
David French
Bruce Jay Friedman
Brian Friel
Terence Frisby
Christopher Fry
Athol Fugard

Frank Gagliano
Tom Gallacher
Jack Gelber

William Gibson
Peter Gill
Frank D. Gilroy
James Goldman
Steve Gooch
Charles Gordone
Ronald Gow
Jack Gray
Simon Gray
Paul Green
Graham Greene
Trevor Griffiths
John Grillo
John Guare
A. R. Gurney, Jr.

Oliver Hailey
Wilson John Haire
John Hale
Willis Hall
David Halliwell
Christopher Hampton
James Hanley
William Hanley
John Harding
David Hare
Michael Hastings
John Hawkes
Joseph Heller
Lillian Hellman
Thomas Hendry
James Ene Henshaw
John Herbert
James Leo Herlihy
Dorothy Hewett
Jack Hibberd
Errol Hill
Robert Hivnor
William M. Hoffman
William Douglas Home
John Hopkins
Israel Horovitz
Roger Howard
Donald Howarth

Christopher Isherwood

Ann Jellicoe
Errol John
Denis Johnston
Keith Johnstone
LeRoi Jones

Lee Kalcheim
Garson Kanin

John B. Keane
Peter Kenna
Adrienne Kennedy
Sidney Kingsley
Kenneth Koch
Arthur Kopit
Bernard Kops
H. M. Koutoukas
Ruth Krauss

Kevin Laffan
David Lan
Arthur Laurents
Ray Lawler
Jerome Lawrence
John Howard Lawson
Robert E. Lee
Hugh Leonard
Doris Lessing
Henry Livings
Robert Lord
Robert Lowell
Charles Ludlam
Peter Luke

Roger MacDougall
Archibald MacLeish
Jackson Mac Low
Albert Maltz
Wolf Mankowitz
Frank Marcus
Bruce Mason
Ray Mathew
Mustapha Matura
Elaine May
Michael McClure
John McGrath
Terrence McNally
Murray Mednick
Mark Medoff
Leonard Melfi
David Mercer
Ronald Millar
Arthur Miller
Jason Miller
Ron Milner
Adrian Mitchell
Loften Mitchell
Michael Molloy
Mavor Moore
John Mortimer
Tad Mosel
David Mowat
Iris Murdoch
Arthur Lister Murphy

Thomas Murphy
Joseph Musaphia

Bill Naughton
James T. Ngugi
Peter Nichols
Lewis Nkosi
John Ford Noonan
Frank Norman
Elliott Nugent

Michael O'Neill
John Osborne
Lawrence Osgood
Alun Owen
Rochelle Owens

John Patrick
Robert Patrick
S. J. Perelman
David Pinner
Harold Pinter
Alan Plater
Stephen Poliakoff
Hal Porter
Dennis Potter
J. B. Priestley

David Rabe
Peter Ransley
Terence Rattigan
James Reaney
Dennis J. Reardon
Barry Reckord
Kenneth Rexroth
Ronald Ribman
Jack Richardson
Anne Ridler
David Rudkin
George Ryga

Howard Sackler
Arthur Sainer
William Saroyan
James Saunders
Dore Schary
James Schevill
Murray Schisgal
Jeremy Seabrook
David Selbourne
Alan Seymour
Anthony Shaffer
Peter Shaffer
Irwin Shaw
Robert Shaw

Wallace Shawn
Sam Shepard
Neil Simon
Beverley Simons
N. F. Simpson
Dodie Smith
Michael Smith
William Snyder
Wole Soyinka
Johnny Speight
Colin Spencer
John Spurling
David Starkweather
Barrie Stavis
Douglas Stewart
Tom Stoppard
David Storey
Mike Stott
Efua Sutherland

George Tabori
Ronald Tavel
Cecil P. Taylor
Megan Terry
Peter Terson
Gwyn Thomas
Ben Travers
William Trevor
Tsegaye Gabre-Medhin
David Turner

Peter Ustinov

Jean-Claude van Itallie
Gore Vidal
Kurt Vonnegut, Jr.

Derek Walcott
George F. Walker
Joseph A. Walker
Nancy Walter
Douglas Turner Ward
Keith Waterhouse
Leonard Webb
Jerome Weidman
Arnold Weinstein
Michael Weller
Arnold Wesker
Hugh Wheeler
John White
Patrick White
E. A. Whitehead
Thornton Wilder
Christopher Wilkinson
Emlyn Williams

Heathcote Williams
Tennessee Williams
David Williamson
Ted Willis
Lanford Wilson
Robert Wilson
Snoo Wilson

Charles Wood
Olwen Wymark

Susan Yankowitz

Paul Zindel

Supplement 1: Screen Writers

Robert Benton
Robert Bolt
Richard Brooks
John Cassavetes
Charlie Chaplin
Paddy Chayefsky
T. E. B. Clarke
Jules Dassin
Bryan Forbes
Carl Foreman
Christopher Fry
William Goldman
Graham Greene
Buck Henry
John Huston
Christopher Isherwood
Garson Kanin
Howard Koch

Stanley Kubrick
Joseph L. Mankiewicz
Elaine May
David Newman
John Osborne
Eleanor Perry
Harold Pinter
Abraham Polonsky
Michael Powell
Frederic Raphael
Terence Rattigan
Neil Simon
Terry Southern
Stewart Stern
Dalton Trumbo
Orson Welles
Billy Wilder

Supplement 2: Radio Writers

Rhys Adrian
John Arden
F. C. Ball
Howard Barker
Samuel Beckett
Frederick Bradnum
Caryl Churchill
Ian Dougall
John Fletcher
Shirley Gee
John George
David Halliwell
John Harrison
Don Haworth
Susan Hill
Gabriel Josipovici
Henry Livings
Tom Mallin
Philip Martin

Bill Morrison
Philip Oxman
Harold Pinter
Jonathan Raban
Derek Raby
Piers Paul Read
Henry Reed
David Rudkin
Michael Sadler
James Saunders
R. C. Scriven
N. F. Simpson
Tom Stoppard
Don Taylor
Peter Terson
Gwyn Thomas
William Trevor
Fay Weldon

Supplement 3: Television Writers

Jim Allen
Arthur Barron
John Bowen
Paddy Chayefsky
Donald Churchill
Brian Clark
Tom Clarke
Clive Exton
John Finch
Horton Foote
Michael Frayn
Wilfred Greatorex
Robert Holles

Arthur Hopcraft
Julia Jones
Nigel Kneale
Philip Mackie
Peter McDougall
Tad Mosel
Peter Nichols
John Osborne
Alun Owen
Dennis Potter
Jack Rosenthal
Fay Weldon
Colin Welland

Supplement 4: Musical Librettists

George Abbott
Don Appell
Lionel Bart
Michael Bennett
Guy Bolton
Caryl Brahms
William F. Brown
Abe Burrows
Truman Capote
Al Carmines
Michael Casey
Jerome Chodorov
Nevill Coghill
Betty Comden
C. C. Courtney
Beverley Cross
Gretchen Cryer
Ossie Davis
Howard Dietz
Donald Driver
Fred Ebb
Bob Fosse
George Furth
William Gibson
James Goldman
Adolph Green
Paul Green
E. Y. Harburg
Lillian Hellman
Jim Jacobs
Garson Kanin
Arthur Laurents
Jerome Lawrence

Robert E. Lee
Alan Jay Lerner
Joshua Logan
Stephen Longstreet
Joe Masteroff
Robert Nemiroff
Anthony Newley
S. J. Perelman
James Rado
Gerome Ragni
Bob Randall
Tim Rice
Peter Rose
Morrie Ryskind
Fred Saidy
Budd Schulberg
Ned Sherrin
Burt Shevelove
Neil Simon
Bella Spewack
Joseph Stein
Michael Stewart
Peter Stone
John-Michael Tabelak
Samuel Taylor
Peter Udell
Melvin Van Peebles
Dale Wasserman
Jerome Weidman
Meredith Willson
Sandy Wilson
Aubrey Woods
Charlotte Zaltzberg

Supplement 5: The Theatre of Mixed Means

George Brecht
John Cage
Merce Cunningham
Jim Dine
Richard Foreman
Red Grooms
Ann Halprin
Al Hansen
Dick Higgins
Allan Kaprow

Jackson Mac Low
Alwin Nikolais
Claes Oldenburg
Benjamin Patterson
Robert Rauschenberg
Carolee Schneemann
USCO
Robert Whitman
Robert Wilson
La Monte Young

Supplement 6: Theatre Collectives

The Alive and Trucking Theatre Company
Beggars Theatre
Belt and Braces Roadshow Company Ltd.
Bread and Puppet Theatre
Cartoon Archetypical Slogan Theatre
The Cockettes
The Company Theatre
The Free Southern Theatre
The Freehold
Hull Truck
Inter-Action Trust
It's All Right to Be Woman Theatre
John Bull Puncture Repair Kit
La Mama Experimental Theatre Club
The Living Theatre
Lumiere and Son
Mabou Mines
The Moving Being

The Natural Theatre
Negro Ensemble Company
New Lafayette Theatre
Open Theatre
Organic Theatre
The People Show
The Performance Group
Pip Simmons Theatre Group
The Play-House of the Ridiculous
Red Ladder Theatre
Ridiculous Theatrical Company
San Francisco Dancers' Workshop
San Francisco Mime Troupe
El Teatro Campesino
Theatre Workshop
Welfare State
Women's Theatre Group

Appendix

Brendan Behan
Giles Cooper
Lorraine Hansberry
N. C. Hunter

William Inge
Joe Orton
John Whiting

ABBOTT, George (Francis). American. Born in Forestville, New York, 25 June 1887. Educated at Hamburg High School, New York; University of Rochester, New York, B.A. 1911; Harvard University, Cambridge, Massachusetts, 1912–13. Married Ednah Levis in 1914 (died, 1930); Mary Sinclair, 1946 (marriage dissolved, 1951); has one child. Founder, with Philip Dunning, Abbott-Dunning Inc., 1931–34. Recipient: Donaldson Award, for directing, 1946, 1948, 1953, 1955; Tony Award, 1955, 1956, 1960, for directing, 1960, 1963; Pulitzer Prize, 1960; New York Drama Critics Circle Award, 1960. D.H.: University of Rochester, 1961. Address: 1 Rockefeller Plaza, New York, New York 10020, U.S.A.

PUBLICATIONS

Plays

> *The Head of the Family* (produced Cambridge, Massachusetts, 1912).
>
> *Man in the Manhole* (produced Boston, 1912).
>
> *The Fall Guy*, with James Gleason (produced New York, 1925; London, 1926).   New York, French, 1928.
>
> *A Holy Terror: A None-Too-Serious Drama*, with Winchell Smith (produced New York, 1925).   New York, French, 1926.
>
> *Love 'em and Leave 'em*, with John V. A. Weaver (also director: produced New York, 1926).   New York, French, 1926.
>
> *Cowboy Crazy*, with Pearl Franklin (produced New York, 1926).
>
> *Broadway*, with Philip Dunning (also director: produced New York and London, 1926). New York, Doran, 1927.
>
> *Four Walls*, with Dana Burnett (also director: produced New York, 1927).   New York, French, 1928.
>
> *Coquette*, with Ann Preston Bridgers (also director: produced New York, 1927; London, 1929).   New York, Longman, 1928.
>
> *Ringside*, with Edward A. Paramore, Jr., and Hyatt Daab (also director: produced New York, 1928).
>
> *Those We Love*, with S. K. Lauren (also director: produced New York, 1930).
>
> *Lilly Turner*, with Philip Dunning (also director: produced New York, 1932).
>
> *Heat Lightning*, with Leon Abrams (also director: produced New York, 1933).
>
> *Ladies' Money* (also director: produced New York, 1934).
>
> *Page Miss Glory* (also director: produced New York, 1934).
>
> *Three Men on a Horse*, with John Cecil Holm (also director: produced New York, 1935; London, 1936).   New York, French, 1935.
>
> *On Your Toes*, music and lyrics by Richard Rodgers and Lorenz Hart (also director: produced New York, 1936; London, 1937).
>
> *Sweet River*, adaptation of the novel *Uncle Tom's Cabin* by Harriet Beecher Stowe (also director: produced New York, 1936).
>
> *The Boys from Syracuse*, music and lyrics by Richard Rodgers and Lorenz Hart, adaptation of the play *A Comedy of Errors* by Shakespeare (also director: produced New York, 1938; London, 1963).
>
> *Best Foot Forward*, with John Cecil Holm (also director: produced New York, 1941).
>
> *Beat the Band*, with George Marion, Jr. (also director: produced New York, 1942).
>
> *Where's Charley?*, music by Frank Loesser, adaptation of the play *Charley's Aunt* by Brandon Thomas (also director: produced New York, 1948; London, 1958). London, French, 1965.
>
> *A Tree Grows in Brooklyn*, with Betty Smith, adaptation of the novel by Betty Smith (also director: produced New York, 1951).

The Pajama Game, with Richard Bissell, music by Richard Adler and Jerry Ross, adaptation of the novel *7¹/₂ Cents* by Richard Bissell (also co-director: produced New York, 1954; London, 1955).   New York, Random House, and London, Williamson Music, 1954.

Damn Yankees, with Douglass Wallop, music by Richard Adler and Jerry Ross, adaptation of the novel *THE Year the Yankees Lost the Pennant* by Douglass Wallop (also director: produced New York, 1955; London, 1957).   New York, Random House, 1956.

New Girl in Town, music and lyrics by Bob Merrill, adaptation of the play *Anna Christie* by Eugene O'Neill (also director: produced New York, 1957).   New York, Random House, 1958.

Fiorello!, with Jerome Weidman, music and lyrics by Sheldon Harnick and Jerry Bock (also director: produced New York, 1959; Bristol and London, 1962).   New York, Random House, 1960.

Tenderloin, with Jerome Weidman, music and lyrics by Sheldon Harnick and Jerry Bock, adaptation of the work by Samuel Hopkins Adams (also director: produced New York, 1960).   New York, Random House, 1961.

Flora, The Red Menace, with Robert Russell, music and lyrics by John Kander and Fred Ebb (also director: produced New York, 1965).

Anya, with Guy Bolton, music and lyrics by Robert Wright and George Forrest, adaptation of the play *Anastasia* by Marcelle Maurette and Guy Bolton (also director: produced New York, 1965).

Music Is, music by Richard Adler, lyrics by Will Holt, adaption of the play *Twelfth Night* by Shakespeare (produced Seattle, 1976).

Screenplays: *The Pajama Game*, 1957; *Damn Yankees*, 1958.

Other

Mister Abbott (autobiography).   New York, Random House, 1963.

Theatrical Activities:

Director: **Plays** — *Lightnin'* by Winchell Smith and Frank Bacon, New York, 1918; *Love 'em and Leave 'em*, New York, 1926; *Broadway*, New York, 1926; *Chicago* by Maurice Watkins, New York, 1927; *Spread Eagle* by George S. Brooks and Walter S. Lister, New York, 1927; *Four Walls*, New York, 1927; *Coquette*, New York, 1927; *Bless You, Sister* by John Meehan and Robert Riskin, New York, 1927; *Ringside*, New York, 1928; *Gentlemen of the Press* by Ward Morehouse, New York, 1928; *Jarnegan* by Charles Beahen and Garrett Fort, New York, 1928; *Poppa* by Bella and Samuel Spewack, New York, 1928; *Those We Love*, New York, 1930; *Louder, Please* by Norman Krasna, New York, 1931; *Lilly Turner*, New York, 1932; *The Great Magoo* by Ben Hecht and Gene Fowler, New York, 1932; *Twentieth Century* by Ben Hecht and Charles MacArthur, New York, 1932, 1971; *Heat Lightning*, New York, 1933; *The Drums Begin* by Howard Irving Young, New York, 1933; *John Brown* by Ronald Gow, New York, 1934; *Kill That Story* by Harry Madden and Philip Dunning, New York, 1934; *Small Miracle* by Norman Krasna, New York, 1934; *Ladies' Money*, New York, 1934; *Page Miss Glory*, New York, 1934; *Three Men on a Horse*, New York, 1935; *Jumbo* by Richard Rodgers and Lorenz Hart, New York, 1935; *Boy Meets Girl* by Bella and Samuel Spewack, New York, 1935; *On Your Toes*, New York, 1936, 1954; *Sweet River*, New York, 1936; *Brother Rat* by John Monks, Jr., and Fred F. Finklehoffe, New York, 1936; *Room Service* by John Murray and Allen Boretz, New York, 1937; *Angel Island* by Bernie Angus, New York, 1937; *Brown Sugar* by Bernie Angus, New York, 1937; *All That Glitters* by John Baragwanath and

Kenneth Simpson, New York, 1938; *What a Life* by Clifford Goldsmith, New York, 1938; *The Boys from Syracuse*, New York, 1938; *You Never Know* by Cole Porter, New York, 1938; *The Primrose Path* by Robert Buckner and Walter Hart, New York, 1939; *Mrs. O'Brien Entertains* by Harry Madden, New York, 1939; *Too Many Girls* by George Marion, Jr., New York, 1939; *Ring Two* by Gladys Harlbut, New York, 1939; *The White-Haired Boy* by Charles Martin and Beatrice Kaufman, Boston, 1939; *The Unconquered* by Ayn Rand, New York, 1940; *Goodbye in the Night* by Jerome Mayer, New York, 1940; *Pal Joey* by John O'Hara, New York, 1940; *Best Foot Forward*, New York, 1941; *Beat the Band*, New York, 1942; *Sweet Charity* by Irving Brecher and Manuel Seff, New York, 1942; *Kiss and Tell* by F. Hugh Herbert, New York, 1943; *Get Away Old Man* by William Saroyan, New York, 1943; *A Highland Fling* by J. L. Galloway, New York, 1944; *Snafu* by Louis Solomon and Harold Buchman, New York, 1944; *On the Town* by Betty Comden and Adolph Green, New York, 1944; *Mr. Cooper's Left Hand* by Clifford Goldsmith, Boston, 1945; *Billion Dollar Baby* by Betty Comden and Adolph Green, New York, 1945; *One Shoe Off* by Mark Reed, New Haven, Connecticut, 1946; *Beggar's Holiday* by John LaTouche (restaged), New York, 1946; *It Takes Two* by Virginia Faulkner and Sana Suesse, New York, 1947; *Barefoot Boy with Cheek* by Max Shulman, New York, 1947; *High Button Shoes* by Stephen Longstreet, New York, 1947; *Look Ma, I'm Dancin'* by Jerome Lawrence and Robert E. Lee, New York, 1948; *Where's Charley?*, New York, 1948; *Mrs. Gibbons' Boys* by Will Glickman and Joseph Stein, New York, 1949; *Tickets Please* (revue; restaged and rewritten), New York, 1950; *Call Me Madam* by Howard Lindsay and Russel Crouse, New York, 1950; *Out of This World* by Dwight Taylor and Reginald Lawrence (restaged), New York, 1950; *A Tree Grows in Brooklyn*, New York, 1951; *The Number* by Arthur Carter, New York, 1951; *In Any Language* by Edmund Beloin and Harry Garson, New York, 1952; *Wonderful Town* by Joseph Fields and Jerome Chodorov, New York, 1953; *Me and Juliet* by Richard Rodgers and Oscar Hammerstein II, New York, 1953; *The Pajama Game*, New York, 1954; *Damn Yankees*, New York, 1955; *New Girl in Town*, New York, 1957; *Drink to Me Only* by Abram S. Ginnes and Ira Wallach, New York, 1958; *Once upon a Mattress* by Jay Thompson and others, New York, 1959; *Fiorello!*, New York, 1959; *Tenderloin*, New York, 1960; *Take Her, She's Mine* by Phoebe and Henry Ephron, New York, 1961; *A Call on Kuprin* by Jerome Lawrence and Robert E. Lee, New York, 1961; *A Funny Thing Happened on the Way to the Forum* by Burt Shevelove and Larry Gelbart, New York, 1962, London, 1963; *Never Too Late* by Sumner Arthur Long, New York, 1962, London, 1963; *Fade Out–Fade In* by Betty Comden and Adolph Green, New York, 1964; *Flora, The Red Menace*, New York, 1965; *Anya*, New York, 1965; *Help Stamp Out Marriage* by Keith Waterhouse and Willis Hall, New York, 1966; *Agatha Sue, I Love You* by Abe Einhorn, New York, 1966; *How Now, Dow Jones* by Max Shulman, New York, 1967; *The Education of Hyman Kaplan* by Benjamin Zavin, New York, 1969; *The Fig Leaves Are Falling* by Allan Sherman, New York, 1969; *Norman Is That You* by Ron Clark and Sam Bobrick, New York, 1970. **Films** – *The Bishop's Candlestick*, 1928; *Why Bring That Up?*, 1929; *Halfway to Heaven*, 1929; *Manslaughter*, 1930; *All Quiet on the Western Front*, 1930; *The Sea God*, 1930; *Stolen Heaven*, 1931; *Secrets of a Secretary*, 1931; *My Sin*, 1931; *The Cheat*, 1931; *Too Many Girls*, 1940; *Kiss and Tell*, 1945; *The Pajama Game*, 1957; *Damn Yankees*, 1958. **Television** – *U.S. Royal Showcase*, 1952.

Actor: **Plays** – "Babe" Merrill in *The Misleading Lady* by Charles Goddard and Paul Dickey, New York, 1913; in *The Queen's Enemies* by Lord Dunsany, New York, 1916; Henry Allen in *Daddies* by John L. Hobble, New York, 1918; Sylvester Cross in *The Broken Wing* by Charles Goddard and Paul Dickey, New York, 1920; in *Dulcy* by Marc Connelly and George S. Kaufman, toured, 1921; Texas in *Zander the Great* by Salisbury Field, New York, 1923; Sverre Peterson in *White Desert* by Maxwell Anderson, New York, 1923; Sid Hunt in *Hell-Bent fer Heaven* by Hatcher Hughes, New York, 1924; Steve Tuttle in *Lazybones* by Owen Davis, New York, 1924; Dynamite Jim in *Processional* by John Howard Lawson, New York, 1925; Dirk Yancey in *A Holy Terror*, New York, 1925;

in *Cowboy Crazy*, New York, 1926; Frederick Williston in *Those We Love*, New York, 1930; title role in *John Brown* by Ronald Gow, New York, 1934; Mr. Antrobus in *The Skin of Our Teeth* by Thornton Wilder, New York, 1955.

*   *   *

George Abbott called his autobiography *Mister Abbott*, but *Mister Broadway* would have been more apt. Abbott notes: "From 1935 to this time [1963] I have, with the exception of a week or two, always had at least one play running on Broadway." Accepting without question the hit/flop mentality of the Broadway marketplace, Abbott is a professional showman whose canon is altogether undisturbed by the least suggestion of intellect. The Abbott production is a good show, a farce, a melodrama, a musical comedy; briskly paced, it is geared for the big laugh, the big climax, and its light-fingered, high-stepping rhythm naturally does not translate well to the library.

The Abbott play comes wrapped in two basic packages: the racy, slangy comedies and melodramas of the 1920's and 1930's, the musical comedies of the 1940's and 1950's. In both kinds of plays, the colorful details of a milieu or particular way of life offer the particular appeal. Abbott's plots (Abbott almost always worked with a collaborator) are neither especially compelling nor well-constructed. The "gimmick" is the milieu: the politics in *Fiorello!*, baseball in *Damn Yankees*, factory routine in *Pajama Game*, the red-light district in *Tenderloin*. Sports, politics, the working class: the Abbott musical takes for its field of action a significant aspect of American life, only to reinforce popular myths of Americana. Relentlessly unexploratory, the Abbott show is indebted almost exclusively to the conventions of Broadway folklore. Entertainments like *Pajama Game* and *Fiorello!* introduce a spurious kind of rebellious hero – a gal who wants the workers to get a raise, a mayor who tries to buck the compromises and corruptions of the political machine. But reinforcing rather than countering cliché, the shows ultimately leave the status quo unruffled. On the stage, aided by the music, and by the charm and élan of the Abbott direction, the weaknesses of the books are camouflaged; on the page, unadorned, the plays are dreary, devoid not only of "ideas" but of spirit as well.

Abbott's earlier collaborations are much more flavorful. *Broadway*, a melodrama that combines prohibition, gang warfare, and the clichés of the backstage musical, is a lively and engaging portrait of an era. The earthy dialogue captures the lingo of the gangster and the entertainer; the slang has its own peculiar kind of melody, and the story – murder and retribution – is comfortably situated against the prohibition nightclub setting. *Three Men on a Horse* does for bookies what *Broadway* does for hoods: gives them the status of popular myth. This time the genre is farce rather than melodrama, but the same perky, accurate yet subtly stylized dialogue prevails. In less successful, but equally "contemporary" plays like *The Fall Guy* and *Love 'em and Leave 'em*, Abbott and his collaborators regard from the same sly angle other scenes of the 1920's. The fall guy goes wrong with some hoods, is caught and reprimanded, and returns chastened to his long-suffering wife. *Love 'em and Leave 'em* is a harsh portrait of a dame on the make; she'll go out with the highest bidder, the one who can give her the most diamonds and furs. Her schemes of self-advancement are set against the problems of the tenants of a working-class rooming house. The plays seem quaint today, but these glimpses into an America of the past retain their undignified comic and melodramatic energy. Artifacts of popular culture, the plays record the values and the aspiration and the setbacks and the sins of various character types of a turbulent and appealing era.

A shrewd practical man of the theatre, George Abbott has given Broadway audiences what they wanted to see, and he has entertained them more often, and over a longer period of time, than any other professional in the history of the American theatre. That is a revealing if not an especially happy statistic.

—Foster Hirsch

ABLEMAN, Paul. British. Born in Leeds, Yorkshire, 13 June 1927; brought up in New York. Attended King's College, University of London. Military service: 3 years. Married; has one son. Agent: Jonathan Clowes Ltd., 19 Jeffrey's Place, London NW1 9PP. Address: Flat 37, Duncan House, Fellows Road, London N.W.3, England.

PUBLICATIONS

Plays

Letters to a Lady, with Gertrude Macauley (produced London, 1951).
Help! (revue; produced London, 1963).
One Hand Clapping (revue; produced Edinburgh, 1964).
Dialogues (produced London, 1965).
Green Julia (produced Edinburgh, 1965; London, 1967; Washington, D.C., 1968; New York, 1973). London, Methuen, and New York, Grove Press, 1966.
Tests (playlets). London, Methuen, 1966.
Emily and Heathcliff (produced London, 1967).
Blue Comedy: Madly in Love, Hank's Night (produced London, 1968). London, Methuen, 1968; Madly in Love published in Modern Short Comedies from Broadway and London, edited by Stanley Richards, New York, Random House, 1969.
The Black General, adaptation of Othello (produced London, 1969).
And Hum Our Sword (produced London, 1973).
Little Hopping Robin (produced London, 1973).
The Visitor (produced London, 1974).

Radio Play: The Infant, 1974.

Television Plays: Barlowe of the Car Park, 1961; That Woman Is Wrecking Our Marriage, 1969; Visits from a Stranger, 1970; The Catch in a Cold, 1970.

Novels

I Hear Voices. Paris, Olympia Press, 1958.
As Near as I Can Get. London, Spearman, 1962.
Vac. London, Gollancz, 1968.
The Twilight of the Vilp. London, Gollancz, 1969.

Verse

Bits: Some Prose Poems. London, Latimer Press, 1969.

Other

The Mouth and Oral Sex. London, Running Man Press, 1969; as The Mouth, London, Sphere, 1972; as The Sensuous Mouth, New York, Ace, 1972.

*   *   *

Paul Ableman's dramatic output so far is small, but striking, both for the unpretentious wit of its dialogue and for the moral concern implicit in its characterization and plot. It is obviously too early to talk of "overriding themes," but one would seem to be the difficulty of reconciling sexual fulfilment with good conscience and consideration for others. Certainly this is so in *Green Julia*, probably his most impressive piece to date, and as thoughtful a study of the hypocrisies of male sexuality as the modern theatre has produced.

There are only two characters onstage, Jake and Bob: the Julia of the title remains offstage throughout, a presence constantly invoked by them and, by the end of the play, a substantial one. Jake is leaving England, probably for a long time, and feels a faint guilt about Julia, the erratic, self-absorbed but generous divorcee he has made his mistress. Gradually, it becomes clear that he wants Bob, his best friend, to take her off his mind by taking her over. But Bob, who is the more morally pretentious of the two, affects both to despise her ("the most depraved old whore in Southern England") and to have a woman of his own. Not only will he reject the idea, he appears to resent it; and the verbal games the two men constantly play with each other (in which they imitate army officers, psychiatrists, university professors, anything capable of easy parody) become increasingly hostile. It is no longer possible to continue camouflaging their true feelings in such a way. Bob comes right out with: "What is your relationship with Julia? You never treat her, never help her or worry about her, hardly ever think about her except on the odd evenings when you happen to feel randy and she's available." This is clearly true; and yet, as we also gradually discover, Bob's stance is a fraud. He is inexperienced, anxious for sexual discovery, and likely to prove as unscrupulous as Jake in achieving it. The curtain falls on the arrival of Julia, who is evidently destined to be exploited by others until what promises to be a raddled and lonely old age.

By the end, the contrast between the jocular, harmless manner of these very ordinary young men and the callousness of their intentions is unmissable, and makes the play more than the light comedy it has at times pretended to be. With his other pieces on the same theme, however, there is no question of pretence. Both *Hank's Night* and *Madly in Love* leave a less bitter aftertaste, presumably because in each case mutual consent replaces exploitation and the tone can therefore remain good-humoured and amused. In *Madly in Love*, an eccentric poet poses as a psychiatrist in the hope of loving his virginity by seducing a girl whose quirk is to obey every order she is given: the irony is that the shock of being told "make love to me" cures her, whereupon she freely gives herself to him in gratitude for his help. In *Hank's Night*, two couples try to persuade themselves and each other to start an orgy, and fail lamentably until they give up the attempt, whereupon the thing actually happens, spontaneously and unselfconsciously. The moral of both plays, and perhaps also of *Green Julia*, may be that those who do not seek to manipulate others and bend them to their will may receive something the more satisfying for being offered freely and without constraint. In the most unpretentious way, Ableman's work is a criticism of the earnestness and anxiety that attaches to sex nowadays, with so many people regarding it, not as a means of cementing genuine relationships or even as a form of enjoyment, but as a mere proof of personal adequacy.

All these pieces are naturalistic, or nearly so: Ableman has also written some 50 surrealist sketches under the general title of *Tests*, some of which have been performed in *One Hand Clapping* and other revues, and most of which prove to have little more to offer than verbal invention and a vague aura of "absurdism." One speech, typical both in the apparent arbitrariness of its language and in its facetiousness, reads: "A mammal of an estuary saluted a kindly laundryman. With a yelp the match teetered. Pickle all laundrymen. Toast archipelagos as if to pronounce ronounce." A few "tests" do, however, seem to have a subject, notably *Johnson*, a parody of military conventions, *She's Dead*, in which two characters parrot cliché responses to violence and death, and *Another Lovely Day*, in which the speakers seek to fox each other by shifting their names and personae. However he develops as a dramatist (and recently he has applied himself more to the novel), it seems clear that Ableman is strongest when he is handling material that, at least to some extent, engages him as a moralist.

—Benedict Nightingale

ABSE, Dannie. Welsh. Born in Cardiff, Glamorgan, 22 September 1923. Educated at St. Illyd's College, Cardiff; University of South Wales and Monmouthshire, Cardiff; King's College, London; Westminster Hospital, London; qualified as physician, M.R.C.S., L.R.C.P. Served in the Royal Air Force, rising to the rank of Squadron Leader. Married Joan Mercer in 1951; has three children. Writer-in-Residence, Princeton University, New Jersey, 1973–74. Recipient: Foyle Award, 1960; Welsh Arts Council award, for verse, 1971. Agent: (drama) Margery Vosper Ltd., Suite 8, 26 Charing Cross Road, London WC2H 0DE; (literary) Anthony Shiel Associates Ltd., 52 Floral Street, London, WC2E 9DA. Address: 85 Hodford Road, London N.W.11, England.

PUBLICATIONS

Plays

Fire in Heaven (produced London, 1948). London, Hutchinson, 1956; revised version, as *Is the House Shut?* (produced London, 1964); revised version, as *In the Cage*, included in *Three Questor Plays*, 1967.
Hands Around the Wall (produced London, 1950).
House of Cowards (produced London, 1960). Included in *Three Questor Plays*, 1967; in *Twelve Great Plays*, edited by Leonard F. Dean, New York, Harcourt Brace, 1970.
The Eccentric (produced London, 1961). London, Evans, 1961.
Gone (produced London, 1962). Included in *Three Questor Plays*, 1967.
The Joker (produced London, 1962).
Three Questor Plays (includes *House of Cowards, Gone, In the Cage*). London, Scorpion Press, 1967.
The Dogs of Pavlov (produced London, 1969; New York, 1974). London, Vallentine Mitchell, 1973.
The Courting of Essie Glass (broadcast, 1975). Published in *The Jewish Quarterly* (London), 1972.
Funland (produced London, 1975).
Pythagoras (produced Birmingham, 1976).

Radio Plays: *Conform or Die*, 1957; *No Telegrams, No Thunder*, 1962; *You Can't Say Hello to Anybody*, 1964; *A Small Explosion*, 1964; *The Courting of Essie Glass*, 1975.

Novels

Ash on a Young Man's Sleeve. London, Hutchinson, 1954; New York, Criterion Books, 1955.
Some Corner of an English Field. London, Hutchinson, 1956; New York, Criterion Books, 1957.
O. Jones, O. Jones. London, Hutchinson, 1970.

Verse

After Every Green Thing. London, Hutchinson, 1949.
Walking under Water. London, Hutchinson, 1952.
Tenants of the House. London, Hutchinson, 1957; New York, Criterion Books, 1958.
Poems, Golders Green. London, Hutchinson, 1962.
Dannie Abse: A Selection. London, Studio Vista, 1963.

A Small Desperation.   London, Hutchinson, 1968.
Selected Poems.   London, Hutchinson, and New York, Oxford University Press, 1970.
Corgi Modern Poets in Focus 4, with others, edited by Jeremy Robson.   London, Corgi, 1972.
Funland and Other Poems.   London, Hutchinson, and New York, Oxford University Press, 1973.
Lunchtime.   London, Poem-of-the-Month Club, 1974.
Penguin Modern Poets 26, with D. J. Enright and Michael Longley.   London, Penguin, 1975

Recording: *Poets of Wales*, Argo, 1972.

Other

Medicine on Trial.   London, Aldus Books, 1967; New York, Crown, 1969.
A Poet in the Family: An Autobiography.   London, Hutchinson, 1974.

Editor, with Howard Sergeant, *Mavericks.*   London, Editions Poetry and Poverty, 1957.
Editor, *European Verse.*   London, Studio Vista, 1964.
Editor, *Corgi Modern Poets in Focus 1, 3, 5.*   London, Corgi, 1971–73.
Editor, *Thirteen Poets.*   London, Poetry Book Society, 1973.
Editor, *Poetry Dimension 2* and *3: The Best of the Poetry Year.*   London, Robson Books, 1974–75; New York, St. Martin's Press, 1975–76.

Critical Studies: reviews in *Tribune* (London), June 1967, and *Financial Times* (London), 18 June 1969; introductions to *Plays of the Year 23*, London, Elek, 1962; *Three Questor Plays*, 1967; *Twelve Great Plays*, 1970; *The Dogs of Pavlov*, 1973.

*   *   *

Dannie Abse is better known in Britain as a poet than a dramatist: and his work as a doctor prevents a full involvement with the theatre. In no disparaging sense, his plays can be described as non-professional, in that they make few concessions to the commercial theatre and reflect a training in literary, rather than theatrical skills. His first play, *Fire in Heaven*, was written in verse and received a successful rehearsed reading at the Institute of Contemporary Arts, London, in 1952. He then came into contact with the enterprising management of the West London amateur company, Questors. In 1960, Questors produced his first major stage play, *House of Cowards*, in their first New Plays Festival: and it was awarded the Charles Henry Foyle New Play award. In 1962, Abse wrote two further plays for Questors, the two-act tragi-comedy *The Joker* and the short curtain raiser *Gone*: and in 1964, he wrote a new version of *Fire in Heaven* (this time in prose), called *Is the House Shut?* which was also produced in the Questors New Plays Festival. His long association with this amateur company explains some features of his style. Questors was one of the first "fringe" theatres in London, whose achievements in an inadequate church hall encouraged its many supporters to build a costly new theatre. But Questors was never a student or underground theatre: it attracted many producers and directors from the BBC and elsewhere who used the theatre to try out plays of undoubted merit but of little commercial interest. It also attracted many professional and semi-professional actors who were prepared to work for nothing in order to extend the range of their talents. The atmosphere at Questors was one of high artistic idealism: and this quality too is reflected in Abse's work.

One aspect of this high-mindedness is shown by Abse's use of moral allegory. "*House of Cowards,*" he once wrote, "is concerned with a group of people in our time, in this country, who need to colour their unsatisfactory lives with gaudy dreams." It is rather like a semi-naturalistic *Waiting for Godot*. A town is caught up in a state of excitement because the Speaker is coming to the Sunshine Hall: everyone expects him to deliver some great and uplifting message to the world which will solve all their problems. Nobody knows who he is or what he will say: they invent their own images to fit their hopes and needs. But the Speaker fails to arrive and their expectations are dashed. At the end of the play, however, blaring loudspeakers from touring vans announce that He will come tomorrow – and the hopes begin anew. Although *House of Cowards* was praised when it appeared for being "compelling, modern and highly imaginative," it seems in retrospect to be Abse's least successful play. The theme is familiar enough – to be found in the plays of O'Neill, Beckett and Ionesco – and Abse can't prevent the story from seeming clichaic. But a worse fault is the uncertainty of style. The play is written in a naturalistic way: but the allegory prevents the naturalism from convincing. The mass gullibility of the town is implausible enough – because the Speaker is an unknown figure – and, when the expectations have been dashed, it seems even less likely that they can be so quickly revived. Symbolically, of course, the story represents the way in which frustrated lives are fired by one false dream after another: but in a naturalistic play this symbolism has to be rooted in careful and sympathetic observation. The Hicks family – around whom the plot revolves – are rather stock characters, examples of Average Men: and we know little about them beyond the fact that they're frustrated and unhappy. The naturalistic details – Hick's cough and Alf Jenkins' womanizing – are also familiar: and Abse relies too much on external dialogue, rather than internal inter-play between the characters which may be expressed verbally but equally may not.

Abse's early verse play, *Fire in Heaven*, and his prose version of the same story, *In the Cage*, are more successful. The theme is more original, although based on an anecdote from a short story by Honoré de Balzac: and the stylistic problems of *House of Cowards* aren't so noticeable. A small market town in an occupied country suffers from an excess of foreign soldiers. A partisan leader, David, takes part in a bomb attack on a munitions dump in which two of the enemy soldiers are killed. Reprisals are ordered: and David's family – his father and mother, his brother Christian and his sister Ruth – are captured. The executions take place in the town square: but to heighten the horror, the General of the occupying forces (instructing his Captain to make the reprisals terrible to deter others) insists that one member of the family should kill the others – and then be let free. David's elder brother, Christian, is the one chosen for this task: but Christian is an ardent pacifist, who has always shrunk from violence. Christian knows that if the orders aren't carried out, other families will suffer: and so he slaughters his family.

Both plays examine Christian's dilemma – which in turn reflects the wider problems of pacifism. Can a human being ever decide not to kill when circumstances exist where a limited killing will save other lives? *Fire in Heaven*, however, treats the theme solely from Christian's point of view. Christian is represented as a near-saint, from whom others expect miracles: and the awfulness of the massacre is increased by including a child with the family:

> The child's head rolled upon the floor.
> I saw its eyes staring at me, puzzled.
> The horror of it.
>
> Two fountains of blood, like red birds rising
> Spurted from the cut neck,
> and the little body walked some paces, headless,
> before it fell twitching on the ground.

In the Cage offers a wider treatment of the theme: even the enemy soldiers are shown to be caught in the escalating violence which nobody wants but nobody can stop. The General is someone who has deliberately repressed human feelings in order to command the war: but even he realizes the monstrosity of his deeds. The change from verse to prose in the later play prevents the dialogue from seeming somewhat narcissistic, but Abse even in the later play seems to give his characters too much to say.

Perhaps Abse's best single work is the one-act play, *Gone*, an exchange between a man, Peter, contemplating suicide, and his friend, Aubrey, who arrives to stop him. The dialogue is varied, amusing and easy to act: the action progresses to a tense climax, which is shot through with neat ironies. At his best, Abse combines the linguistic command of the post-war verse dramatists with an Absurdist realization of the importance of allegory: but his uneasy use of naturalism and his reluctance to give actors opportunities which are not expressed by the dialogue prevent his plays from achieving full impact in the theatre.

—John Elsom

ACKLAND, Rodney. British   Born in Westcliffe-on-Sea, Essex, 18 May 1908. Educated at Salesian College, 1915–16; Balham Grammar School, 1916–23; Central School of Speech Training and Dramatic Art, London. Married Mab Lonsdale in 1951 (died, 1972). Worked as a salesman for Swan and Edgar, London, 1924; in the Silks Department, Stagg and Mantles, London, 1925; in the Advertising Department, Vacuum Oil Company, London, 1925. Founder, with Roland Gillett, Kinsmen Pictures, 1946. Agent: Robin Dalton, 11 Hanover Street, London W.1, England.

PUBLICATIONS

Plays

    Improper People (produced London, 1929).   London, Heinemann, 1930.
    Marion-Ella (produced London, 1930).
    Dance with No Music (produced London, 1930).   London, Deane, and Boston, Baker, 1933.
    Strange Orchestra (produced London, 1931; New York, 1933).   London, Gollancz, 1932.
    Ballerina, adaptation of the novel by Eleanor Smith (produced London, 1933).
    Birthday (produced London, 1934).   London, French, 1935.
    The White Guard, adaptation of a play by Michael Bulgakov (produced London, 1934).
    The Old Ladies, adaptation of the novel by Hugh Walpole (produced London, 1935). London, Gollancz, 1935; as *Night in the House* (produced New York, 1935), New York, French, 1935.
    After October (produced London, 1936).   London, Gollancz, 1936.
    Plot Twenty-One (produced London, 1936).
    Yes, My Darling Daughter, adaptation of a work by Mark Reed (produced London, 1937).
    The Dark River (as *Remembrance of Things Past*, produced London, 1938; as *The Dark River*, produced London, 1941).   London, French, 1942.
    Sixth Floor, adaptation of a play by Alfred Ghéri (produced London, 1939).

Blossom Time, music by Franz Schubert (produced London, 1942).

The Diary of a Scoundrel, adaptation of a play by A. N. Ostrovsky (produced London, 1942; New York, 1956).   London, Sampson Low and Marston, 1948; New York, French, n.d.

Crime and Punishment, adaptation of the novel by Dostoevsky (produced London, 1946; New York, 1947).   London, Sampson Low and Marston, and New York, Holt, 1948.

Cupid and Mars, with Robert G. Newton, adaptation of a story by Robert G. Newton (produced London, 1947).

Before the Party, adaptation of a story by W. Somerset Maugham (produced London, 1949).   London, French, 1950.

A Multitude of Sins, with Robert G. Newton (produced London, 1951).

The Pink Room; or, The Escapists (produced London, 1952).

A Dead Secret (produced London, 1957).   London, French, 1958.

Farewell, Farewell Eugene, adaptation of a work by John Vari (produced London, 1959; New York, 1960).   London, French, 1960; New York, Dramatists Play Service, n.d.

The Other Palace (produced London, 1964).

Screenplays: *Number Seventeen*, with Alfred Hitchcock and Alma Reville, 1931; *Bank Holiday (Three on a Weekend)*, 1937; *Keep Smiling*, with Val Valentine, 1938; *Hatter's Castle*, 1941; *Rush Hour*, with Arthur Boys, 1941; *49th Parallel (The Invaders)*, with Emeric Pressburger, 1941; *Lady Be Kind*, with Arthur Boys, 1941; *Night Watch*, with Reg Groves, 1941; *Continental Express*, 1942; *The Hundred Pound Window*, with Albert Finkel and Brock Williams, 1943; *Thursday's Child*, 1943; *The School Teacher*, 1944; *George and Margaret*, 1944; *Uncensored*, with Terence Rattigan, 1944; *Wanted for Murder*, 1946; *Temptation Harbour*, 1949; *The Queen of Spades*, 1949; *Bond Street*, with Terence Rattigan, 1950.

Other

The Celluloid Mistress; or, The Custard Pie of Dr. Caligari, with Elspeth Grant (autobiography).   London, Wingate, 1954.

Critical Studies: "Rodney Ackland," in *Theatre World* (London), January 1939; Preface by Romain Fanvic to *The Dark River*, 1942; interview with Frank Granville-Barker, in *Plays and Players* (London), September 1957; "Rodney Ackland" by Norman Marshall, in *London Magazine*, April 1965; "Rodney Ackland" by Hilary Spurling in *The Spectator* (London), 22 November 1968; "Rodney Ackland" by Raymond Marriott in *The Stage* (London), November 1968.

Theatrical Activities

Director: **Plays** – *The Belle of New York* by Hugh Morton, London, 1942; *The Dark River*, London, 1943. **Films** – *Lady Be Kind*, 1941; *A Letter from Home*, 1942; *Thursday's Child*, 1943; *The School Teacher*, 1944.

Actor: **Plays** – Medvedieff in *The Lower Depths* by Gorky, London, 1924; roles with the Oxford Players, and Lubin, Zozim and The He-Ancient in *Back to Methusaleh* by Shaw, Edinburgh, in the late 1920's; title role in *Young Woodley* by John Van Druten, toured, 1929; in *Recipe for Murder* by Arnold Ridley, toured, 1932; Joseph in *Musical Chairs* by Ronald Mackenzie, toured, 1933; Paul in *Ballerina*, London, 1933; Tony Willow in

Birthday, London, 1934; Tony in *Battle Royal* by Kim Peacock, London, 1934; Oliver Nashwick in *After October*, London, 1936. **Films** – *The Case of Gabriel Perry*, 1935; *Alibi*, 1935.

Rodney Ackland quotes the programme note to the 1972 Gardner Centre production of *The Dark River*:

The idea of writing a play about women and men betrayed and destroyed by "remembrance of things past" first occurred to me during the summer of 1934 when I was working on the dramatization of a novel by Hugh Walpole and spending most of my time with Emlyn and Molly Williams in a huge ramshackle bungalow, the only human habitation on a small enchanted island midstream in the Thames near Wraysbury.

Returning to London ... and looking back on the whole of the rapidly receding but ever-to-be-remembered summer, I realized that all the time while I'd been adapting Walpole and enjoying the incomparable friendship and generosity of my hosts who, with or without the troops of friends who would regularly come down from London at weekends, made every occasion seem like the best kind of party, all this time there had been soaking into my consciousness the marvellously suggestive and evocative ambience of riverine life in which anything and everything becomes pregnant with symbolism as soon as you look at it, where the most trivial of happenings is liable to suggest an allegorical significance, where twilight – the quiet Thames flowing at one's feet and all the muted sounds and scents of Emlyn's enchanted island – could act like a mind-expanding drug revealing ... Swan Lake? Millais' Ophelia floating? The Lady of Shallot? or lurking in the shadows Jack the Ripper?

And now that I was away from it and the summer gone it suddenly struck me that all this would make the ideal setting and background for my new play, a play I had not done any concentrated thinking about as yet so that if I'd been forced to answer such a question as "What's the theme of your new play?" I could only have replied, "It's about the danger to foolish pedestrians of the swamps, morasses, quicksands, manholes, ambushes and booby-traps to be found from one end to another 'Down Memory Lane.'" An idea for a cautionary tale! Which, at this stage, was exactly what it was. I'd got no further than that. Then I saw that "an old house by the river" together with all that atmosphere I'd been recalling must inevitably emerge as of far more significance to the play than a mere "setting and background," must, in fact, be given equal importance with the leading characters, be integrated into the very fabric of the whole dramatic design.

In 1938 *The Dark River* went into production.... Rehearsals were resumed [after the Munich crisis].... But the play was different. Though the change was not in the piece itself but in the view taken of it by the audience. Munich had had the effect of seeming to undermine the play's foundation, had caused it, as it were, to slip sideways so that it seemed out of true. And yet *The Dark River* is not a political piece and was never meant to be. The fact that one of the characters foresees the imminence of Hitler's War and that the other characters refuse to is not what the play is about. And to describe them, in the words of one of the reviewers at the time, as "escaping into the past because they fear the future" is a great oversimplification....

And when at last *The Dark River* achieved the Commercial Theatre and commenced its run at the Whitehall, the grisly wheel had turned full circle, it was 1943, the "Little Blitz" was harrying London, curtains rang up at half past six to give the public a chance of reaching home before the bombs began to fall, and on certain nights, after the ALERT sign at the side of the proscenium had been switched on – generally during the climactic moments of Peggy Ashcroft's machless performance – it would sometimes be impossible to tell which was the stage-effect anti-aircraft practice that supplies a menacing *obbligato* to the closing passages of the play and which the ack-ack barrage against the German raiders exploding in the sky outside.

*   *   *

Rodney Ackland is one of those artists who, temporarily at least, lose on the swings what they have already lost on the roundabouts. In the 1930's when much of his best work was written and performed in small theatre-clubs or for short runs in West-End theatres, he was highly praised by critics, referred to as "the English Chekhov," but considered too highbrow to become a popular success. The enthusiastic notices for *Strange Orchestra* (directed by John Gielgud) cost Ackland his job with British International Pictures – the company saw no future in employing a serious writer. Now that fashions have changed and even Chekhov has become almost too respectable, Ackland is apt to be dismissed as "commercial," a practitioner of the "well-made play," for no better reason than that critics have learnt so to label a whole period in the English theatre.

His debt to Chekhov is unmistakable. Ackland's plays are organised as ant-heaps or hives in which a group of characters is arbitrarily gathered under one roof either by blood relationship (as in *Birthday* and *After October*) or by lodging together (as in *Strange Orchestra*), by belonging to the same club (*The Pink Room*), working on the same film (*The Other Palace*) or deliberately attempting to reconstruct the past (*The Dark River*). His characters have the same tendency as Chekhov's to follow separate lines of thought which surface abruptly in the middle of someone else's conversation, giving the same complex effect of mental isolation in the midst of physical conglomeration. And Ackland, like Chekhov, uses this effect to exploit the subtle range of emotional tones between comedy and tragedy – egotism, eccentricity, insensitivity, over-sensitivity shading down to loneliness, pathos and despair – intrinsic to the relationship between individuals and the more-or-less closed society of which they are part.

But the comparison with Chekhov will not go far beyond generalities. English middle-class metropolitan society of the period between the two World Wars had little in common with Russian rural society of the end of the nineteenth century and Ackland is a writer too faithful to his subject-matter to follow Chekhov where he cannot lead. Even to use the word "society" in connection with Ackland's work rings false, since his characters are almost without exception those who have been tossed off the central wheel of their time and left lying at the edges, slightly bruised and spattered with mud, likely if they try to stand up again, as they consistently do, to be flung down flatter than before.

In his early play *Strange Orchestra* this process is somewhat too crudely demonstrated: a pair of lovers whose mutual devotion amounts to narcissism try to gas themselves; a girl jilted by a con-man goes blind as well. But, behind the obtrusively engineered story-line, the insecure, neurotic atmosphere of genteel seediness in furnished rooms – the world of Eliot's Prufrock and of the typist in *The Waste Land* – is created by a careful accumulation of authentic detail. The play, like so many of Ackland's later and better ones, revolves around one of those elderly mother-figures, raffish, stalwart, broad-minded but none-too-bright, a giver and still more a taker of energy, who are perhaps his most recognizable contribution to the gallery of dramatic types.

His next play, *Birthday*, has no equal that I know of for its overtly humorous but finally savage portrait of a certain kind of English family life. The impenetrable selfishness of these people, the way they mask it as devotion to one another's interests, is expressed even in their appalling dog Jelly – surely the best part ever written for a dog – which has established such a tyranny of habit that its half-gnawed bones cannot be removed from the armchair without causing a scene. The play is weakened only by its heroine, whose attempt to escape from her family is too schematic, whose character is too unexplored, too fairy-tale, to stand up among so many realistic monsters.

No such weakness mars *After October*. It is the hero this time who has to bear the burden of a would-be escape, but although he is in himself a scarcely more realized character than the heroine of *Birthday*, his escape is altogether more tangible. The heroine of *Birthday* is dependent on love to take her away from lovelessness. The theatre is a good place for showing lovelessness and no one is better at it than Ackland, but love is another matter: even Shakespeare is apt to take refuge in formal passages about love rather than attempt a direct demonstration of the thing in action. But in *After October* the means of escape for the hero and all the other characters in his train is to be his success as a playwright. The essential tawdriness of this escape – to be rich and famous instead of poor and unknown – enables Ackland to treat his hero lightly and objectively, without in any way diminishing the pathos of his disillusionment. *After October* is alive with closely observed portraits of the hero's family and friends, including Oliver Nashwick, that doyen of surly poets, whose first words on entering through the window are: "You wish I hadn't come."

Ackland's masterpiece is undoubtedly *The Dark River*. Originally entitled *Remembrance of Things Past*, its themes and characters are easily recognizable from his earlier work, the plot still turns on a failed attempt at escape from a narrowly confined group of "throw-offs," but the play is somehow on a grander and more universal scale than his others. Is this simply because explosions and shouting Fascists are heard off-stage, because the little boy spells out "Guernica" from a newspaper headline, because the hero is obsessed with persuading the British Government to build deep air-raid shelters? Certainly one has more of a feeling of a large world beyong the wings than in his other plays. But the sense of sombre grandeur and universality is more intrinsic than this. The characters themselves, detailed, idiosyncratic portraits as always in Ackland's work, yet seem to cover more ground than before, to compose less a spectacle than an experience, drawing an audience into losses and defeats which temporarily stand for the audience's own, suggesting not simply that some unfortunates get caught in stagnant backwaters from which there is no escape, but that life itself is such a backwater when it is not infinitely worse, the approaching maelstrom that can be heard off-stage.

For all the vagaries of fashion, there is not an English playwright this century more certain of being understood and loved by posterity than Rodney Ackland.

—John Spurling

AIDOO, (Christina) Ama Ata.   Ghanaian.   Born in 1942. Educated at the University of Ghana, Legon, B.A. 1964; Stanford University, California. Recipient: Research Fellowship, Institute of African Studies, University of Ghana. Agent: c/o Longman, 5 Bentinck Street, London W1M 5RN, England.

PUBLICATIONS

Plays

> *The Dilemma of a Ghost.*   Accra, Longman, 1965; New York, Macmillan, 1971.
> *Anowa.*   London, Longman, and New York, Humanities Press, 1970.

Novel

> *Our Sister Killjoy, or, Reflections from a Blackeyed Squint.*   London, 1976.

Short Stories

No Sweetness Here.   London, Longman, 1970; New York, Doubleday, 1971.

*   *   *

Although she has published only two plays, Ama Ata Aidoo is one of Africa's most promising playwrights. In both, she handles situations which have become stock in African drama, but does so in such a way that the usual handling of them is unobtrusively shown to be shallow and conventional. Each goes beyond the commonplace opposition of European and African modes of life, of the modern and the traditional.

The stock situation in *The Dilemma of a Ghost* is the conflict between the "been-to" – the man who has gone to England – and the traditional ideas of his parents. The conflict is exacerbated by the ways of his American wife, Eulalie. An alien wife is also common in African drama, though usually white. Eulalie is black and her parents-in-law think it shameful that their son, Ato, has married the descendent of slaves. She finds the ways of his family rather primitive. Eulalie quarrels with her parents-in-law and both sides are increasingly humiliated. The parents, for example, cannot believe in contraception and try to make Eulalie undergo a ceremony to cure sterility. She takes to drink to escape her loneliness, and we expect Ato, who has been rather weakly trying to reconcile his wife and parents, to give her up and marry some girl from the village. This would be the standard pattern for the play to follow. Yet, in the end, it is the traditional ethic of hospitality that triumphs over other traditions that had led the family to take a hostile view of Eulalie. If blame is to be placed, it is upon Ato, for excusing each person's actions to the other instead of explaining them.

The writers of the colonial period, and many of their successors, proclaimed that the best of tradition should be matched with the best of modern ways. The significance of *Dilemma of a Ghost* is that tradition as a whole is not set against modernity as a whole, and that the capacity for solution to the conflict is found within tradition – which is not presented to us as a monolith.

The concern in Aidoo's first play with the adjustment between different ways of life necessary in day-to-day living – rather than with the presentation of arguments, allegories or demonstrations of rightness – prepares us for her second play. *Anowa* is perhaps the first historical play by an African in which the history is relegated to the background and made to serve the examination of a character. Anowa is a beautiful but wilful girl who refuses to marry the suitors of her parents' choice and marries a man whom they consider a good-for-nothing. The couple leave their home town and with her aid and ideas her husband, Kofi Ako, prospers mightily in trade with the British (who are represented in the play only by a picture of Queen Victoria). But Anowa finds wealth and the customary ideas of a woman's place confining, while Kofi finds his unconventional wife an increasing embarrassment. Finally, after a quarrel in which she guesses that the priest told Kofi that she had destroyed his manhood and that he half-believes her to be a witch – a quarrel which they become aware has been overheard by Kofi's slaves – he shoots himself, she drowns herself.

Anowa is set in the late nineteenth century and Aidoo uses the historical setting to give a fresh perspective to the call for a more liberated role for women in society. Anowa says,

I hear in other lands a woman is nothing. And they let her know this from the day of her birth. But here, O my spirit mother, they let a girl grow up as she pleases until she is married. And then she is like any woman anywhere: in order for her man to be a man, she must not think, she must not talk.

African dramatists have often attacked the lack of status of women, but in a contemporary setting their indignation usually delivers dramatic tension and subtlety over to righteousness. But in the context of the nineteenth century the modern woman (Anowa) appears as an eccentric and a dramatic balance is regained.

Though this theme is dominant, others are important: the tensions of a childless marriage in a traditional society, and the intimation that all wrongs in the African past cannot be blamed upon colonialism. Anowa is modern in her uneasiness at her husband's accumulation of slaves. She is, he tells her, "too fond of looking for the common pain and the general wrong." It is in part perhaps because several of the themes common to African drama are combined that the impression is given that the play turns not around any one of them but around the character of Anowa.

Aidoo's plays have their faults: the narrative framework of *Anowa* is at times clumsy; the Americanisms of Eulalie unconvincing; and the position of Ato, inactive between Eulalie and his parents, awkward. *The Dilemma of a Ghost* takes its title from a song sung by two children:

> One early morning,
> When the moon was up
> Shining as the sun,
> I went to Elmina Junction
> And there and there,
> I saw a wretched ghost
> Going up and down
> Singing to himself
>   "Shall I go
> To Cape Coast,
> Or to Elmina
> I don't know,
> I can't tell.
> I don't know,
> I can't tell."

The title of the play is quite enough of a hint that the song evokes the cultural tensions felt by the educated African; unfortunately Aidoo has Ato awake and tell how in his dream he saw himself as a small boy singing the song. Nevertheless, *Anowa* suggests that Aidoo is learning, as many of her fellow-dramatists need to do, that something should be left for the spectator to find in a play for himself, that like a good teacher the playwright should evoke a response rather than set out everything explicitly.

—Anthony Graham-White

ALBEE, Edward (Franklin).   American.   Born in Washington, D.C., 12 March 1928. Educated at Lawrenceville School; Valley Forge Military Academy; Choate School; Trinity College, Hartford, Connecticut. Served in the United States Army. Worked as a radio writer, WNYC, New York; office boy, Warwick and Legler, New York; record salesman, Bloomingdales, New York; book salesman, G. Schirmer, New York; counterman, Manhattan Towers Hotel, New York; Western Union Messenger, New York, 1955–58. Producer, with Richard Barr and Clinton Wilder, New Playwrights Unit Workshop, later Albarwild Theatre Arts, and Albar Productions, New York. United States Cultural Exchange Visitor to Russia. Recipient: Berlin Festival Award, 1959, 1961; Vernon Rice Award, 1960; Obie Award, 1960; Argentine Critics Award, 1961; Lola D'Annunzio

Award, 1961; New York Drama Critics Circle Award, 1964; Outer Circle Award, 1964; Tony Award, 1964; Pulitzer Prize, 1967, 1975. Litt.D.: Trinity College, 1974. Agent: William Morris Agency, 1350 Avenue of the Americas, New York, New York 10019. Address: Box 697, Montauk, Long Island, New York 11954, U.S.A.

PUBLICATIONS

Plays

The Zoo Story (produced Berlin, 1959; New York and London, 1960).   Included in *The Zoo Story, The Death of Bessie Smith, The Sandbox: Three Plays*, 1960.

The Sandbox (produced New York, 1960).   Included in *The Zoo Story, The Death of Bessie Smith, The Sandbox: Three Plays*, 1960.

The Death of Bessie Smith (produced Berlin, 1960; New York and London, 1961). Included in *The Zoo Story, The Death of Bessie Smith, The Sandbox: Three Plays*, 1960.

The Zoo Story, The Death of Bessie Smith, The Sandbox: Three Plays. New York, Coward McCann, 1960; as *The Zoo Story and Other Plays*, London, Cape, 1962.

Fam and Yam (produced Westport, Connecticut, and New York, 1960).   New York, Dramatists Play Service, 1961.

The American Dream (produced New York and London, 1961).   New York, Coward McCann, 1961; London, French, 1962.

Bartleby, with James Hinton, Jr., music by William Flanagan, adaptation of the story by Melville (produced New York, 1961).

Who's Afraid of Virginia Woolf? (produced New York, 1962; London, 1964).   New York, Atheneum, 1962; London, Cape, 1964.

The Ballad of the Sad Café, adaptation of the story by Carson McCullers (produced New York, 1963; Worcester, 1969).   New York and Boston, Atheneum-Houghton Mifflin, 1963; London, Cape, 1965.

Tiny Alice (produced New York, 1964; London, 1970).   New York, Atheneum, 1965; London, Cape, 1966.

Malcolm, adaptation of the novel by James Purdy (produced New York, 1966).   New York, Atheneum, 1966; London, Cape-Secker and Warburg, 1967.

A Delicate Balance (produced New York, 1966; London, 1969).   New York, Atheneum, 1966; London, Cape, 1968.

Breakfast at Tiffany's, music by Bob Merrill, adaptation of the story by Truman Capote (produced Philadelphia, 1966).

Everything in the Garden, adaptation of the play by Giles Cooper (produced New York, 1967).   New York, Atheneum, 1968.

Box-Mao-Box (produced Buffalo, 1968; as *Box and Quotations from Chairman Mao Tse-Tung*, produced New York, 1968).   Published as *Box and Quotations from Chairman Mao Tse-Tung: Two Inter-Related Plays*, New York, Atheneum, 1969; London, Cape, 1970.

All Over (produced New York, 1971; London, 1972).   New York, Atheneum, 1971; London, Cape, 1972.

Seascape (also director: produced New York, 1975).   New York, Atheneum, 1975; London, Cape, 1976.

Radio Play: *Listening*, 1976 (UK).

Bibliography: *Edward Albee at Home and Abroad: A Bibliography, 1958–June 1968* by Richard E. Amacher and Margaret Rule, New York, AMS Press, 1970.

Theatrical Activities:

Director: **Plays** – *Seascape*, New York, 1975; *Who's Afraid of Virginia Woolf?*, New York, 1976. **Radio** – *Listening* (co-director, with John Tydeman), 1976.

*   *   *

Seldom have reputations been as quickly won in the theatre as was that of Edward Albee. Despite his original difficulty in securing production for *The Zoo Story*, the powerful and impressive work which began his career, the appearance of that play, on a double bill with Samuel Beckett's *Krapp's Last Tape*, established him immediately as the best of the new generation of American dramatists then emerging. *The Zoo Story* is by no means the absurdist drama which several critics have suggested. Rather, it is a brilliantly orchestrated plea for human communication in a society growing daily more callous and materialistic – a theme which, essentially, runs through all of his work. Albee followed this with several more one-act plays, two of which, *The American Dream* and *The Sandbox*, seemed to draw heavily on absurdist techniques. But even here he was in fact a long way removed from the world as seen by Ionesco and Beckett.

His first three-act play, *Who's Afraid of Virginia Woolf?*, again encountered production problems. A number of managements refused to stage it, one, according to the play's director Alan Schneider, rejecting it as "a dull whiney play without a laugh in it." An attempt to cast Henry Fonda in the principal part foundered when his agent failed to forward the script. And even when the play's success and impressive integrity had made it an obvious candidate for the Pulitzer Prize, the drama sub-committee's nomination was rejected because a member of the full committee regarded it as a "dirty play."

With the exception of *Long Day's Journey into Night* few American plays have approached the emotional intensity of *Who's Afraid of Virginia Woolf?* Apparently a Strindbergian battle of the sexes, in fact it is an indictment of those who, on a personal and national level, choose to substitute illusion for reality. George and Martha, named after the first President and his wife, do battle with one another in an attempt to simulate meaning and purpose in a life which can have neither so long as they fail to confront the real nature of the world which they inhabit. Unable to have children, they have invented a fantasy child who, far from bringing them together, becomes the chief weapon with which they attack each other. But the play opens on the eve of his twenty-first birthday – his coming of age. It is a crucial moment and the final relinquishment of their fantasy marks a return to a genuine and simple relationship which is reflected in a language which moves from the complex exchanges of the earlier part of the play to the monosyllabic but real communication of the closing minutes. America has produced few plays of comparable stature and no dramatist with such a fine control of rhythm and language.

Despite affecting scorn for adaptations, Albee has curiously and, as it has transpired, unwisely turned his considerable talent to producing a number of them, from a version of Carson McCullers' *The Ballad of the Sad Café*, to James Purdy's *Malcolm* and Giles Cooper's *Everything in the Garden*. The first two of these are particularly unsuited for the stage and the third adds little to Cooper's somewhat lightweight drama of housewives who combine vocation with avocation and become part-time prostitutes.

His next original work, *Tiny Alice*, became something of a *cause célèbre* when a number of critics affected not to understand it and Albee himself conducted a somewhat uninformative dialogue with his audience following a performance of the play. It is a good deal more obscure than Albee has ever been willing to admit but essentially takes his concern with illusion and reality a stage further by investigating the nature and legitimacy of religious conviction. A baroque work, it turns on a conspiracy, reminiscent of Eliot's *The Cocktail Party*, designed to deliver Julian, a lay-brother, from his faith in an abstract God and to restore him to a direct relationship with reality and hence himself. The focus of the play is an architect's model which dominates the stage and the action. While an appropriate enough image of Albee's central contention that a reified reality is preferable to a more expansive illusion, the mannered metaphysics of the play failed to realize the promise of a brilliant opening scene.

A Delicate Balance returned to the metaphysical drawing room of *Who's Afraid of Virginia Woolf?* and though inferior to that work was ironically awarded the Pulitzer Prize denied to his earlier play. The delicate balance of the title refers to the precarious hold on sanity and reality which the individual must retain in the face of a threatening absurdity. Tobias and Agnes find their home invaded by friends who have glimpsed some spiritual terror beneath the routine of daily life. Faced with a choice between protective detachment and compassionate involvement Agnes retreats into a brutal self-concern. But Tobias confronts his personal failings and in doing so rises above them. To love is to be vulnerable – to commit oneself to obligations and responsibilities which may lead to pain. But he comes to feel that to evade such commitment is merely to buy an apparent and limited immunity whose cost is ultimately guilt, self-contempt and spiritual impotence.

The weakness of the play lies in the increasingly symbolic roles which Albee's characters are required to play. Where George and Martha were convincing in their own right, the characters in *A Delicate Balance* seem little more than ciphers – elements in a metaphysical debate which seems to lack an essential human dimension.

Albee's next work represented an abrupt change of direction. His two related plays, *Box* and *Quotations from Chairman Mao Tse-Tung*, were first performed at the Studio Arena Theatre, Buffalo, in 1968. *Box* has no characters. The stage is dominated by a cube, which provides the only visual focus while a voice from the back and sides of the theatre begins a monologue which rehearses the dilemma of the artist and of any individual in an age of crisis. The sibylline remarks seem to add up to an elegy on a civilization which perhaps has ceased to exist. The second play is enacted inside the cube. At first sight it is somewhat curious. Of the four characters one is silent, one reads lines taken directly from Mao's quotations, one recites a poem written by the nineteenth century popular poet Will Carleton and only one speaks dialogue written by Albee himself (only slightly more than half of the lines were actually written by him). Albee uses the speeches simply as "found" material, exploding the language so that "meaning" now relies on chance assonance. Yet, despite this rather esoteric method he succeeds in creating a play which captures not only the simultaneity of life – the complex interplay of public and private worlds – but also the fluid, evanescent and equivocal quality of any art which sets out to plot the decline of morality and morale in an age bereft of convictions which genuinely touch the quick of life. The surrealist method is applied, not to reveal the marvellous but to penetrate behind the bland façade of modern reality – personal, religious and political. The play is an experiment with language and theatrical form which raises intriguing questions about the nature of communication and art.

With *All Over* Albee returned once again to a theme implicit in most of his work from the early one-act plays through *Who's Afraid of Virginia Woolf?* and *A Delicate Balance* to the oblique insights of *Quotations from Chairman Mao Tse-Tung*. His central concern here is with those individual acts of cruelty and betrayal which litter everybody's lives – actions stemming from a self-concern which threatens the very personal alliances which are our only protection against a threatening absurdity. Like Arthur Miller in *After the Fall*, he sees personal treachery as containing the seeds of public callousness, the death of love in the family as an image of social anomie and that willing acquiescence in metaphysical despair which seems to characterize our age. This is a society of separate individuals linked only by mutual self-interest, wilfully blinding themselves to a fundamental unhappiness. Without some genuine love which can survive the knowledge of its own imperfection they can only evidence a declining humanity – a decline which is mirrored in the slow death of the play's central character.

Once again Albee's control of rhythm and tone and his meticulous orchestration of language create a work of considerable economy and power. And if he is moving towards an ever more stylized dialogue in which individual "arias" succeed one another in an over-elaborate structure of emotional and verbal excess, the pattern is itself sufficiently compelling to command respect. Yet, there is a sense in which Albee's work is becoming progressively more mannered; in which he has begun to parody himself as he allows autonomy to language, to tempo and to tone where he had previously subordinated these, with considerable effect, to a more sharply defined dramatic purpose. The febrile humor of *Seascape* lack precisely that passionate moral concern which gave such power to his early work. In this play his originality devolves into mere facility, his compelling metaphors into simplistic allegory. Of course every dramatist who commits himself to examining the potential of his craft runs the risk of self-indulgence and perhaps this is the price which must be paid for Albee's dedication not only to dramatic experimentation but also to the refinement of a sensibility which has won him such a dominant position in the American theatre. Certainly America has yet to produce a playwright with a greater sensitivity to the nature and possibilities of language and dramatic tension; it has produced few with his lucid wit or subtle intelligence.

—C.W.E. Bigsby

ALFRED, William. American. Born in New York City, 16 August 1922. Educated at Brooklyn College, B.A. 1948; Harvard University, Cambridge, Massachusetts, M.A. 1949, Ph.D. 1954. Served in the United States Army, 1943–46. Editor, *American Poet*, 1942–44. Instructor, 1954–57, Assistant Professor, 1957–59, Associate Professor, 1959–63, and since 1963, Professor of English, Harvard University. Member of the Dramatists Guild. Recipient, Booklyn College Literary Association Award, 1953; Amy Lowell Traveling Poetry Scholarship, 1956; Brandeis University Creative Arts Award, 1960; National Institute of Arts and Letters grant, 1965. Agent: Toby Cole, 234 West 44th Street, New York, New York 10036. Address: 31 Athens Street, Cambridge, Massachusetts 02138, U.S.A.

PUBLICATIONS

Plays

The Annunciation Rosary. New Jersey, Sower Press, 1948.
Agamemnon (produced Cambridge, Massachusetts, 1953). New York, Knopf, 1954.
Hogan's Goat (produced New York, 1965). New York, Farrar Straus, 1966; revised version, as *Cry for Us All*, with Albert Marre, music by Mitch Leigh (produced New York, 1970).

Other

Co-Editor, *Complete Prose Works of John Milton, Volume I.* New Haven, Connecticut, Yale University Press, 1953.

Translator, *Beowulf*, in *Medieval Epics*. New York, Modern Library, 1963.

*   *   *

William Alfred's prefatory remarks to his first produced play, *Agamemnon*, reveal that his focus will be on "lives full of moral responsibility for every previous action, lives in which justice works with brutal majesty." The observation applies not only to *Agamemnon* but also to Alfred's other, more widely known play, *Hogan's Goat*. In both poetic dramas, one with an ancient, the other with a modern setting, truths of events from the past have been suppressed. The result in both plays is a profound malaise, a corrupting sense of guilt that leads with relentless inevitability to suffering and disaster.

Agamemnon, one of many twentieth-century adaptations of classical prototypes, deals with activities behind the scenes on the eve and day of Agamemnon's homecoming. The crux of the situation is that Clytemnestra has remained unaware of Agamemnon's role in the sacrifice of Iphigenia. Employing a large number of characters and scenes in an essentially realistic format, Alfred provides alternating glimpses of Clytemnestra, Aegisthus, Agamemnon, and Cassandra as they approach their moment of truth. Alfred's play generates a considerable degree of power and suspense, largely as a result of his emotionally charged, idiomatic blank verse, yet at times this very strength of poetic utterance seems disproportionate to the action that prompts it; some speeches seem self-indulgently rhetorical, and the imagery occasionally borders on the precious. At times, moreover, character motivations and relationships seem ill-defined or blurred.

In *Hogan's Goat*, a more satisfactory dramatic balance is achieved among language, action, and character. Alfred sets the scene in Brooklyn in the 90's and centers the key issues within Irish power politics in a local campaign. His protagonist, Stanton, is torn between his hunger for power and his love for his wife. To satisfy both drives, Stanton has suppressed several crucial truths from both his wife and his political associates, truths which emerge in a powerfully rendered series of confrontations leading to a catastrophe that demolishes Stanton. Alfred joins a tightly knit, complex plot and a keen sense for the Irish ethnic milieu with language that moves readily from the bluntly idiomatic to the passionately eloquent. At times the action tips over into melodrama but on the whole *Hogan's Goat* is notable for the control and dramatic appropriateness with which Alfred exercises his poetic talent. Two other plays by Alfred have not yet received performance or been published at the time of this writing: *The Curse of an Aching Heart* and *Nothing Doing*.

—Jarka M. Burian

ALLAN, Ted.   Canadian.   Born in Montreal, Quebec, 25 January 1916. Educated at elementary schools and at Baron Byng High School, Montreal. Served in the International Brigade during the Spanish Civil War: Colonel. Married Kate Schwartz in 1939 (divorced, 1959); has two children. Has acted in radio and television plays. Member, Dramatists League of America, Screen Writers Guild of America, and of Great Britain, and League of British Dramatists. Recipient: Canada Council grant, 1956, 1970, Senior Arts Grant, 1974, and travel grant, 1974. Address: c/o Alvin Deutsch, Linden and Deutsch, 110 East 59th Street, New York, New York, U.S.A.

PUBLICATIONS

Plays

The Money Makers (produced Toronto, 1954; London, 1956).
The Ghost Writers (produced London, 1955).

Legend of Pepito, adaptation of a story by B. Traven (produced London, 1955).
Double Image (Gog and Magog), with Roger MacDougall, based on a story by Roy
    Vickers (produced London, 1956).   London, French, 1959.
The Secret of the World (produced London, 1962).
Oh What a Lovely War, with the Theatre Workshop, London (produced London and
    New York, 1964).   London, Methuen, 1965.
Chu Chem: A Zen Buddhist-Hebrew Musical, music and lyrics by Mitch Leigh, Jack
    Haines, and Jack Wohl (produced Philadelphia, 1966).
I've Seen You Cut Lemons (produced London, 1969).
My Sister's Keeper (produced Lennoxville, Quebec, 1974).   Toronto, Toronto
    University Press, 1976.

Screenplays: *Fuse*, 1970; *Lies My Father Told Me*, 1972; *Them Damned Canadians*,
1973.

Radio Plays: *Canadian Mental Health* series, 1953; *Coloured Buttons*, 1958; *The Good
Son*, 1969.

Television Plays: *Willie the Squowse*, 1954; *Go Fall in Love*, 1955; *Early to Braden*
series, 1957–58; *Legend of Paradiso*, 1960; *Flowers at My Feet*, 1968.

Novels

This Time a Better Earth.   London, Heinemann, 1939; New York, Morrow, 1940.
Quest for Pajaro (as William Maxwell).   London, Heinemann, 1961.
Chu Chem: A Zen Buddhist-Hebrew Novel.   Montreal, Editions Quebec, 1973.

Other

The Scalpel, The Sword: The Story of Dr. Norman Bethune, with Sydney Gordon.
    Boston, Little Brown, 1952; London, Hale, 1954; revised edition, New York,
    Monthly Review Press, 1973.

Critical Studies: reviews of *The Secret of the World* by Bernard Levin in the *Daily Express*
(London), 1962, by Mervyn Jones in the *Tribune* (London), 1962, and by Harold Hobson in
the *Sunday Times* (London), 11 March 1962.

Ted Allan comments:

I find it difficult to appraise my work. At some moments I think they are the most
underestimated plays of the 20th century. At other moments I think they all need to be
rewritten.

They have been praised and damned but have not attained the fame I sought for them,
with the exception of *Oh What a Lovely War*. But here my pleasure is mixed, for the
director-producer threw out my main plot, kept my peripheral scenes, rewriting most of
them, took my name off the play in England, and gave writing credits to a few hundred
people, to indicate that nobody *wrote* it. I consider my original version a theatrical *tour de
force* and hope to get it produced one day under a new title: *Smith and Schmidt*, directed by
someone who will do it as I wrote it.

Outside of *Gog and Magog*, which began life as *Double Image*, and which ran for a year in
London and almost five years in Paris, none of my plays ever achieved commercial success.

The Secret of the World (my major opus), which told the story of three generations of a Montreal family (the head of which goes mad), did get wild critical hosannas from most of London's critics, but was panned by Canadian critics when it was performed at Lennoxville in 1976.

I've Seen You Cut Lemons probed the problem of alleged insanity in those we, the so-called normal, like to call abnormal. It was cruelly savaged by most of London's critics. That sent me brooding for a few years and to writing screenplays. I will return to playwriting next year, after I finish a new screenplay, which will provide me with the wherewithal to write for the theatre.

I consider *Chu Chem* the happiest of my plays although it died an untimely death after six performances in Philadelphia. I keep hoping it will one day get the kind of imaginative production it needs. (We had an elderly and beloved lead who couldn't remember his lines. The poor man died soon after the play did.)

My wildest fantasy is called *Willie the Squowse*, which nobody wants to produce, although it's been done on both radio and television. I have a horrible feeling that my plays will start getting produced all over the world to be acclaimed with noisy popularity after I am dead. If that is the price I must pay to get my plays produced, I agree. I have decided to die before I am ninety. This is a concession, for I had planned to live to a hundred. When I finally go, I will let you know.

*   *   *

With his high octane forcefulness and his formidable technical expertise, Ted Allan is a playwright who has been undeservedly neglected in the London theatre since *The Secret of the World* was produced at Stratford East in 1962. His two-hander *I've Seen You Cut Lemons* is a far more interesting piece of theatrical writing than *Two for the Seesaw*, for instance, a two-character play which enjoyed considerable success.

The Secret of the World is rather like a Canadian *Death of a Salesman*, with the life of the central family set in a context of direct involvement in union politics during and after the upheaval caused by Krushchev's revelations about Stalin. Chris Alexander (or Sam Alexander as he became at Stratford East) is an idealistic union leader who fails to get re-elected when he breaks with the Communist Party, and, from being successful, busy and well-liked, declines further and further into loneliness, ineffectuality and near-madness. He is too honest to take advantage of an opportunity to get big money from a bus company in settlement of an accident claim, and hopes instead to make a fortune out of a crackpot invention – cufflinks joined by elastic, so that shirts can be put on without unfastening them.

The play's emotional brew is a very rich one. The interlocking emotional problems of Chris's father, wife, son, daughter and brother-in-law are all boiled up together, and the resulting soup would possibly be more digestible with a little more comedy and a little less meat. But there is an admirable sureness of touch in creating theatrical effects, even if this is done without letting the characters be conscious enough of their own theatricality. The old father is rather like a Montreal version of Ibsen's Old Ekdal. But the decline of Chris is powerfully plotted, and, even when it is too obvious that Ted Allan is trying to tug at the audience's heartstrings, the tugs are not usually fumbled.

Especially in family plays an over-rich emotional mixture is often due to the presence of too much autobiographical material and too much residue of the guilt that family pressures create. The suspicion one has that Ted Allan is drawing directly on his own experience is strengthened when we see how much Sarah in *I've Seen You Cut Lemons* resembles Susan in *The Secret of the World* and when we hear her recalling incidents we actually saw in the earlier play – the mother, for instance, shouting "I believe in God, I believe in God! Atheists. Communists," outside the door of a room in her house where the Young Communist League was holding a meeting.

I've Seen You Cut Lemons is a more controlled, more economical play, which succeeds in sustaining tension all through the action by focusing on different aspects and different phases of a semi-incestuous brother-sister relationship. The action is set in the London bachelor flat of a Canadian university lecturer. His sister is a few years younger than he is. Like Susan, Sarah is a painter but she blames the relationship with her brother for her partially deliberate failure to make more use of her talent, which they both regard as a very considerable one.

They both have children from broken marriages. As the action starts he is on the point of taking his son to Corsica for a holiday, when she arrives unexpectedly, discharged early from hospital. He lets her stay in the flat, judging her mental health to be sufficiently restored to stand up to a period of loneliness. Later, of course, he will regret this. When he returns she tries harder and harder to monopolise his life, untruthfully informing his girlfriend (who is also called Susan) that they are having an incestuous relationship, and going all out to convince him that this is what he really wants as much as she does. Ted Allan's dialogue measures up well to the difficult task of registering her oscillations between lucidity and hallucination, and it even convinces us that she could play on her brother's guilt feelings cleverly enough to make him believe that her sanity could be fully and permanently restored if only he would devote a month of his life to looking after her. The play ends touchingly as she voluntarily goes back to hospital and he emerges from the purgatory of their time together a wiser man than he was before.

Ted Allan has also written prolifically for the screen. Two original screenplays are *Seven Times a Day* and *Lies My Father Told Me*. His television plays include *Willie the Squowse*, and he collaborated with Roger MacDougall on the stage play *Double Image (Gog and Magog)*. He has also written *Chu Chem*, which he describes as a Zen Buddhist-Hebrew Musical Comedy. It owes as much to Brecht as to Zen Buddhism, and the ingredients do not quite jell, but there are some very amusing moments. The most inspired theatrical image is a seesaw with buckets attached to either end. A rock is put into one, and the villagers have to "balance the budget" by putting jewels and gold into the other.

—Ronald Hayman

ANDERSON, Robert (Woodruff).   American.   Born in New York City, 28 April 1917. Educated at Phillips Exeter Academy, New Hampshire, 1931–35; Harvard University, Cambridge, Massachusetts, 1935–42, A.B. (magna cum laude) 1939, M.A. 1940. Served as a Lieutenant in the United States Naval Reserve, 1942–46: Bronze Star. Married Phyllis Stohl in 1940 (died, 1956); the actress Teresa Wright, 1959; has two step-children. Actor, South Shore Players, Cohasset, Massachusetts, Summers 1937 and 1938. Assistant in English, Harvard University, 1939–42; Teacher, Erskine School, Boston, 1941; Teacher of Playwriting, American Theatre Wing, New York, 1946–51, and Actors Studio, New York, 1955; Member of the Faculty, Salzburg Seminar in American Studies, 1968; Writer-in-Residence, University of North Carolina, Chapel Hill, 1969. Member of The Playwrights Company, 1953–60; President, New Dramatists Committee, 1956, and the Dramatists Guild, 1971–73. Member of the Board of Governors, American Playwrights Theatre, since 1963; Member of the Council, Authors League of America, since 1965. Recipient: National Theatre Conference Prize (Best Play Written by Serviceman Overseas), 1945; Rockefeller Fellowship, 1946; Writers Guild of America Award, for screenplay, 1970. Agent: Audrey Wood, International Creative Management, 40 West 57th Street, New York, New York 10019. Address: Bridgewater, Connecticut, U.S.A.

PUBLICATIONS

Plays

> *Hour Town*, music by Robert Anderson (produced Cambridge, Massachusetts, 1938).
> *Come Marching Home* (produced Iowa City, Iowa, 1945; New York, 1946).
> *The Eden Rose* (produced Ridgefield, Connecticut, 1948).
> Sketches in *Dance Me a Song* (produced New York, 1950).
> *Love Revisited* (produced Westport, Connecticut, 1950).
> *All Summer Long*, adaptation of a novel by Donald Wetzel (produced Washington,
>   D.C., 1952; New York, 1954).   New York, French, 1955.
> *Tea and Sympathy* (produced New Haven, Connecticut, and New York, 1953; London,
>   1957).   New York, Random House, 1953; London, Heinemann, 1957.
> *Silent Night, Lonely Night* (produced New Haven, Connecticut, and New York, 1959).
>   New York, Random House, 1960.
> *The Days Between* (produced Dallas, 1965).   New York, Random House, 1965.
> *You Know I Can't Hear You When the Water's Running* (produced New York, 1967;
>   London, 1968).   New York, Random House, 1967.
> *I Never Sang for My Father* (produced Philadelphia, 1967; New York, 1968; London,
>   1970).   New York, Random House, 1968.
> *Solitaire/Double Solitaire* (produced New Haven, Connecticut, Edinburgh and New
>   York, 1971).   New York, Random House, 1972.

> Screenplays: *Tea and Sympathy*, 1956; *Until They Sail*, 1957; *The Nun's Story*, 1959;
> *The Sand Pebbles*, 1966; *I Never Sang for My Father*, 1970.

> Radio and Television Plays: *David Copperfield*, *Oliver Twist*, *Vanity Fair*, *The Glass
> Menagerie*, *Trilby*, *The Old Lady Shows Her Medals*, *The Petrified Forest*, *The Scarlet
> Pimpernel*, *A Farewell to Arms*, *Summer and Smoke*, *Arrowsmith*, and other
> adaptations, 1946–52.

Novel

> *After*.   New York, Random House, and London, Barrie and Jenkins, 1973.

Bibliography: *The Apprenticeship of Robert Anderson*, by David Ayers, unpublished
dissertation, Columbus, Ohio State University, 1969.

Manuscript Collection: Harvard University Theatre Collection, Cambridge, Massachusetts.

Critical Studies: Prefaces to *Best American Plays 1951–57, 1958–63, 1963–67*, edited by
John Gassner, New York, Crown, 1958, 1964, 1968; Prefaces to *Best Plays 1953–54,
1966–67, 1967–68*, edited by Otis Guernsey, New York, Dodd Mead, 1954, 1967, 1968;
"Robert Anderson, Playwright of Middle-Aged Loneliness" by Thomas P. Adler, in *Forum*
(Muncie, Indiana), Spring 1975.

Robert Anderson comments:

It is difficult and dangerous for a writer to talk about his own work. He should move on to
whatever he is impelled to write about next without looking back and trying to analyze his
work. Recently I read a doctoral thesis written about me and my plays. In many ways I

wish I hadn't read it. I don't think it is wise for a writer to think about his "continuing themes" and recurring attitudes.

When I was near the end of writing *Tea and Sympathy*, my first wife begged me to tell her something of the subject of my new play. (I never discuss my work with anyone while I am writing.) I gave in and simply told her it took place in a boys' school. She said, "Oh, my God, not another play about a boys' school!" This almost stopped me. At that moment I hadn't been consciously aware that I had written other (unproduced) work with a boys' school background. I simply knew that I wanted to write that play. My wife's making me aware that I had worked that vein before almost stopped me from finishing the play.

People sometimes say, "Why don't you write about something besides marriage?" Strangely, it is only after I have finished a play that I am aware that I have written again about marriage. Each time I start a play, I certainly don't have the feeling that I am going over old ground. I feel I have something new and different nagging at me to be written. I do not consciously say, "This is my theme. I have done it reasonably well before. Let's try it again."

And these "plays about marriage" are seldom just that. *Solitaire/Double Solitaire* was not about marriage in the present and in the future, as some critics described it. It was about the loneliness of being alone and the loneliness of marriage. *The Days Between* was not about an academic marriage on the rocks but about a man who was ruining his life and his marriage by being unable to live the ordinary, unexciting days of life, "the days between." Marriage is often the arena of the plays, but not always the real subject matter.

As a matter of fact, the plays are rarely "about" what critics say they are about. *Tea and Sympathy* has always been described as "a play about homosexuality." In effect, it has nothing to do with homosexuality. It has to do with an unjust charge of homosexuality and what follows such a charge. It has to do with responsibility, which must extend beyond giving tea and sympathy; it has to do again with loneliness; it has to do with questioning some popular definitions of manliness; and, most important, it has to do with judgment by prejudice ... and a great deal more, I hope.

You Know I Can't Hear You When the Water's Running was said to be "about" sex. The plays were told in terms of sex, but they were not about sex. As Elia Kazan said when he first read the manuscript, "They're about the same things as your other plays except this time it came out funny and sad." They are very sad plays. As Walter Kerr said of them, "Laugh only when it hurts."

I seem to have written largely about the family, or rather to have used the family as the arena. By and large English critics feel that American playwrights rather overwork this area of concern. Still, our three finest plays are, probably, *The Glass Menagerie, Death of a Salesman*, and *Long Day's Journey into Night*. I am glad that Williams, Miller and O'Neill didn't scare when and if someone said to them, "not another play about the family!"

I have been amused that I have sometimes been considered a "commercial" playwright. I am amused because each of my plays has had an enormous struggle to get on. Nobody has thought of them as "commercial" till after they were successful. *Tea and Sympathy* was turned down by almost every producer and was on its way back into my files when The Playwrights Company optioned it and started me on my career. *You Know I Can't Hear You When the Water's Running* was turned down by everyone until two new producers "who didn't know any better" took a chance on it. I waited something like seven years before someone "took a chance" on *I Never Sang for My Father*. I think I can't be blamed for being amused when I hear myself described as "commercial," especially inasmuch as three of my plays have premiered in very non-commercial regional theatres, one opened Off-Broadway, and one launched The American Playwrights Theatre, a project which seeks to get the plays of "established" playwrights into the regional and college theatres rather than into Broadway theatres.

At various times in my youth I wanted to be an actor and a poet. I acted in college and summer theatres, and I was elected Harvard Class Poet on graduation. I think it is only natural that with these two "bents" I should end up a playwright, because in playwriting one finds the same kind of compression and essentialization one finds in poetry. Poems and plays are both icebergs.

Finally, I admire form. I took a course at Harvard with Robert Frost. One evening he was asked why he didn't write free verse. He replied, "I don't like playing tennis with the net down." I think that a great deal of the excitement in the theatre comes from using the limitations of the theatre creatively. Most plays, when they are adapted as movies, "opened up", lose their effectiveness, because part of their attraction was the way the playwright had found intensity and a creative impulse in dealing with the limitations of the theatre. Compare the play and the film of *Our Town*. I believe that form can be challenged, changed, stretched. But some kind of form seems to me of the essence of theatre.

I would wish that a person coming on my plays for the first time would not have any preconceived idea as to what they are "about." Each reader or spectator is a new collaborator, and he will, in a sense, write his own play and arrive at his own meanings, based on his own experience of life.

*   *   *

Robert Anderson first received limited recognition as a playwright in 1945 when his play *Come Marching Home* was awarded first prize in a National Theatre Conference contest. This was followed five years later by *Love Revisited* which was performed at the Westport County Playhouse. But it was Alan Schneider's Washington Arena production of *All Summer Long* that really marked his emergence as a writer of genuine power and considerable subtlety. Though it was not particularly well received when it eventually reached Broadway two years later, the success of *Tea and Sympathy* had by then established his reputation as a skilful and impressive playwright.

All Summer Long is a sensitive if somewhat portentously symbolic play about the loss of illusions and the inevitable dissolution of beauty, love and innocence. The family, which is the focus for this elegy on human weakness, live beside a river which is slowly eroding the bank under their home – a none too subtle image of the collapse of genuine feeling within the family itself. Willie, the youngest boy, is on the verge of adolescence and his brother Don, a college sports star crippled in a motor accident, tries to protect him from his own emerging sexuality and from the cynicism and bitterness of the rest of the family, though ironically unable to come to terms with the change in his own life. Anderson piles on the agony, with parents who no longer care for each other or their children, and a girl who tries to produce an abortion by throwing herself on an electrified fence. Though Willie and Don spend the summer trying to build a wall to hold out the threatening floodwaters, the forces of nature can no more be controlled on this level than they can in the lives of individuals growing more self-centred and lonely as they grow older. The play ends as the house collapses – an obvious image of the family itself which has long since disintegrated in human terms.

Though he has never since relied on such a melodramatic climax Anderson's work is never entirely free of a certain dramatic overstatement. In *All Summer Long* Don is not only a crippled sports star, itself something of a cliché, but the accident which caused his injury had been a result of his father's inadequacy. Similarly, in a later play, *Silent Night, Lonely Night*, a child dies because her mother is at that very moment preoccupied with reading a letter which reveals her husband's adultery. Her subsequent plunge into insanity is, perhaps, understandable but serves to create a melodramatic setting for what is otherwise a subtle examination of human need. Nowhere, however, does he control this tendency better than in what remains his best play, *Tea and Sympathy*, though even here there is a certain lack of subtlety in his portrait of a callous father and a weak and therefore vindictive schoolmaster who may well share the very sexual deviancy which he denounces in others.

Tea and Sympathy was Robert Anderson's Broadway debut and earned him a deserved reputation for confronting delicate and even contentious issues with courage and effect – a reputation which he himself was to parody in his later *You Know I Can't Hear You When the Water's Running*. The play is concerned with the plight of a seventeen-year-old boy in a New England boarding school who is accused of being homosexual. Unsure of himself and tormented by his fellow pupils, be turns to his housemaster's wife, whom he loves with adolescent passion and anguish. Horrified by her husband's inhumanity and genuinely concerned for the fate of the young boy, she finally allows him to make love to her – the only way she can see him regaining his sexual self-confidence and his faith in other people. The boy's father, long since divorced, has never offered his son the slightest affection while his housemaster punishes the boy for his own suppressed fears. As a perceptive indictment of the witch hunt the play was produced at a particularly appropriate moment, the height of the McCarthy era. But it is a great deal more than this and despite the rather casual psychological assumptions which underlie his portrait of both father and housemaster the play was a perceptive comment on the failure of compassion in a society which demanded conformity as the price of acceptance.

Anderson's next play, *Silent Night, Lonely Night*, again dealt with the anguish of those who are deprived of the affection and understanding of those who should be closest to them. Katherine, temporarily separated from a husband whom she has just discovered to be unfaithful, finds herself alone in a New England inn on Christmas Eve. Upset and lonely she dines with another guest whose wife is in a nearby mental hospital – driven there by his own infidelity. For this one night they manage to overcome their sense of guilt and self-concern in order to offer one another the momentary consolation of true compassion. The simple symmetry of the structure underlines the justice of those who see Anderson primarily as a constructor of well-made plays, but despite this and despite the melodramatic nature of the man's personal history the play remains a delicate study which compares well with his earlier work.

His next production, four one-act comedies presented under the title *You Know I Can't Hear You When the Water's Running*, was not staged until eight years later. Lightweight sketches which partly depend on and partly satirize the new vogue for sexual explicitness, they show little of his earlier sensitivity or skill. The same nostalgic regret for the decay of love and the passing of youth is manifested in two of the plays, "The Footsteps of Doves" and "I'll Be Home for Christmas," but now it becomes the subject of rather tasteless jokes. The spectacle of Anderson mocking his earlier convictions is not an altogether attractive one, for the humour of the plays derives from precisely that cynical worldly-wise detachment which he had previously seen as the enemy of the human spirit. When he briefly comes close to a moment of true pathos, in "I'll Be Home for Christmas," the integrity of the scene is lost in the sophisticated banter of the rest of the play.

I Never Sang for My Father does little to redeem the weaknesses of this composite play. Centering on the almost neurotic need of a son to win the love of a bitter and virtually senile father, it reveals not only the terrifying gaps which can open up between those who should be drawn to one another by all the ties of natural affection and concern, but also the desperate absence of love in a world full of people who choose to shelter and exile themselves in the fragile shell of their own personalities. Yet, despite the emotive nature of his subject, Anderson fails, in the last resort, to establish the tension which he creates as anything more than a pathological study – a compassionate and detailed examination of individuals who, despite the familiarity of their situations, remain case studies rather than evocative projections of a universal state.

In some respects Anderson suggests comparison with dramatists like William Inge, Carson McCullers, and Tennessee Williams. Like them he has chosen to describe the plight of those whose romantic dreams founder on the harsh realities of modern life. Emotionally scarred and sexually vulnerable, his protagonists try to find their way in a world which frightens and dismays them. In *All Summer Long* and *Tea and Sympathy* the central figure, appropriately enough, is an adolescent – for the boy confronting sexuality and cruelty for the first time serves to emphasize simultaneously the ideals of youth and the cynicism and disillusionment of middle age. For Anderson this contrast constitutes the key to individual anguish and the mainspring of a pathos which he seems to regard as the truest expression of human experience. Clearly this is the stuff of which nostalgia and sentimentality are made and his work is open to both charges. Where Tennessee Williams balances his regret for the destruction of the innocent and the romantic with a grudging regard for the "Promethians" who dominate their surroundings, Anderson offers only a romantic regret that things cannot be other than they are. Where Inge and McCullers see the growth away from innocence into experience as a painful but necessary human process, Anderson tends to see it as the first stage in the extinction of genuine feeling and human compassion. If some people can sustain their innocence into maturity they do so, in his world it seems, only at the cost of their ability to act. It is a paradox which he is content to identify rather than examine with the kind of subtlety which Tennessee Williams had brought to *The Glass Menagerie* and *Orpheus Descending.*

—C. W. E. Bigsby

ANTROBUS, John. British Born in Woolwich, London, 2 July 1933. Educated at Bishop Wordsworth Grammar School, Salisbury; Selhurst Grammar School, Croydon; King Edward VII Nautical College; Sandhurst Military Academy. Served in the East Surrey Regiment, 1952–55. Married Margaret McCormick in 1958; has three children. Apprentice Deck Officer in the Merchant Navy, 1950–52; worked as a supply teacher and waiter. Since 1955, Freelance Writer. Recipient: George Devine Award, 1970. Agent: Blanche Marvin, Elspeth Cochrane Agency, 21a St. John's Wood High Street, London N.W.8, England.

PUBLICATIONS

Plays

> *The Bed-Sitting Room*, with Spike Milligan (also co-director: produced London, 1963). London, Jack Hobbs, 1970.
> *Royal Commission Review* (produced London, 1964).
> *You'll Come to Love Your Sperm Test* (also director: produced Edinburgh and London, 1965). Published in *New Writers 4*, London, Calder and Boyars, 1965.
> *Cane of Honour* (produced London, 1965).
> *The Missing Links* (televised, 1965). Included in *Why Bournemouth? and Other Plays*, 1970.
> *Trixie and Baba* (produced London, 1968). London, Calder and Boyars, 1969.
> *Why Bournemouth?* (produced London, 1968). Included in *Why Bournemouth? and Other Plays*, 1970.
> *Captain Oates' Left Sock* (produced London, 1969). London, French, 1974.
> *An Evening with John Antrobus* (produced London, 1969).
> *Why Bournemouth? and Other Plays: An Apple a Day, The Missing Links.* London, Calder and Boyars, 1970.
> *An Apple a Day* (televised, 1971; produced London, 1974). Included in *Why Bournemouth? and Other Plays*, 1970.
> *Stranger in a Cafeteria*, in *Christmas Present* (produced Edinburgh, 1971).
> *The Looneys* (produced Edinburgh, 1971; London, 1974).
> *Crete and Sergeant Pepper* (produced London, 1972).
> *The Dinosaurs, and Certain Humiliations* (produced Edinburgh, 1973; London, 1974).

The Illegal Immigrant (produced London, 1974).
Mrs. Grabowski's Academy (produced London, 1975).
They Sleep Together (produced Leicester, 1976).

Screenplays: *Idle on Parade*, 1960; *The Wrong Arm of the Law*, with others, 1963; *The Big Job*, 1965; *The Bed-Sitting Room*, with Charles Wood, 1970.

Radio Writing: *Idiot Weekly* and *The Goon Show* series.

Television Writing: *The Army Game* series; *Bootsie and Snudge* series; for Eric Sykes, Arthur Haynes, Frankie Howerd, Jimmy Wheeler shows; *Lenny the Lion Show*, 1957; *Variety Inc. Show*, 1957; *For the Children Show*, 1957; *Early to Braden* series 1957; *The April 8th Show (Seven Days Early)*, 1958; *The Deadly Game of Chess*, 1958; *The Missing Links*, 1965; *An Apple a Day*, 1971; *Don't Feed the Fish*, 1971; *Marty Feldman Show*, 1972; *Milligan in All Seasons*, with Spike Milligan, 1974.

Theatrical Activities:

Director: **Plays** – *The Bed-Sitting Room* (co-director, with Spike Milligan), London, 1963; *You'll Come to Love Your Sperm Test*, Edinburgh and London, 1965; *Savages* by Christopher Hampton, Aalsburg, Denmark, 1973.

Actor: **Plays** – *You'll Come to Love Your Sperm Test*, Edinburgh and London, 1965; *An Evening with John Antrobus*, London, 1969; Glendenning in *The Contractor* by David Storey, London, 1970. **Film** – *Raising the Wind (Roommates)*, 1961.

John Antrobus comments:

My life and therefore my work fall into two parts. It was in December 1968 that I found out I am an alcoholic, that I had a disease, "alcoholism," and that there was a path of recovery. I have not drunk since then and have slowly, "a day at a time," built a new life, involving the recovery of a bad marriage situation and being ready to look anew at the world, without worrying about my previous convictions (intellectual, not police!). From being in and out of mental hospitals and unable to cope with anything, I came to believe in God "as I understood him," not as a dogma might have me believe, and I put God to the test in my life. That might sound curious, but to trust this power beyond myself that could help and guide me, I had to go by results. Not dogma – results! The results have brought blessings in all departments of my life, and I have been able to make some sense of the rough bits too. *Captain Oates' Left Sock* was written between mental homes, without forethought, and first performed in the early months of my recovery from the booze. By the way, being an addict, I could not switch from alcohol to any other drug, and have not tried to. My dependency is absolute – on my faith and hope – and that has turned out to be Jesus. No dogma, no denomination – just Jesus.

*   *   *

At first sight it seems odd that John Antrobus, once an ex-Sandhurst army officer, should have primarily the reputation of being a scathing critic of the Establishment (with the Army as one of his favourite targets), and the anomaly, such as it is, has somewhat obscured the scope of his talent. Antrobus emerged as a dramatist during the 1960's when the so-called "satire boom" of that period, now a rather tattered memory, was at its peak; "satire" is something of a debased term now, but what emerges most powerfully in Antrobus's best work is a genuinely hard-edged, often brilliant satiric gift.

Antrobus began as a radio and T.V. scriptwriter at a time when radio and television comedy had a dazzling array of talent at its disposal before situation comedy declined into safe formulae. He was involved in *The Army Game* and *Bootsie and Snudge* on T.V., both series becoming part of the national folklore, and wrote for Eric Sykes, Arthur Haynes and Frankie Howerd among other comedians. On radio he was involved in *Idiot Weekly* and later gravitated to *The Goon Show* where his developing style of anarchic comedy found an ideal framework.

It is the *Goon Show* style which is most marked in Antrobus's first stage success, written in collaboration with Spike Milligan, one of the original Goons. *The Bed-Sitting Room* was very much their creation, for they also directed and designed it, and Milligan appeared in it. How it would revive without their participation is questionable, but it remains one of the funniest modern English plays. During its meandering progress, Lord Fortnum of Alamein turns into the bed-sitting room of the title and Harold Wilson becomes a parrot; it is a joyous collection of exuberant sketches, outrageously theatrical visual jokes and satirical barbs against the Church and T.V. – politicians who have sold St. Paul's to Onassis. What makes it more than a ragbag kind of stage Goon Show is the darker undercurrent forecast by its opening silent film of an H-Bomb explosion and the gradual realization that the mutations in the play are the result of radiation; the play is set during the first anniversary of the "Nuclear Misunderstanding" which led to World War III, and the movement of the play, for all its hilarious excursions, contains a premonition of doom, climaxing in cannibalistic rites (Fricassé of Lord Boothby on the menu at the Lord Mayor's Banquet) and partners being taken for the Extermination Waltz.

The enormous success of this play seems to have typed Antrobus as a zany comic ever since, and his widening range has been ignored. The world of lunatics and madness has been the strongest strain in his subsequent work. Both *Captain Oates' Left Sock* (to date only performed on the stage as a Sunday Night Royal Court production) which is set in a mental hospital and *The Looneys* (seen at the Edinburgh Traverse in 1971) explore this world, and while both are often wildly funny there is an edge to the comedy beyond revue-sketch humour. Joe Orton, another observer of lunacy on stage, once wrote: "Lunatics are melodramatic." Antrobus exploits this stage tradition and by linking his underlying serious treatment of madness to an essentially playful genre, his work gains an ironical dimension beyond either mere jokeyness or propaganda. *Captain Oates* in particular has a sense of pathos behind the abundant wit that reveals Antrobus as much more than an accomplished gag-writer.

This is particularly evident in two plays presented at the Royal Court. *Trixie and Baba* is essentially a character-comedy, exploring the world of a married couple – Baba, "just the right side of forty," a useless businessman-potter forever dreaming up new schemes and plans to abandon his responsibilities, and Trixie, a feckless housekeeper, the object of Baba's insults but who retorts with equal vigour and taunts of his sexual inadequacy. A young apprentice becomes the passive go-between in this relationship in which both Trixie and Baba use him as an ear for their respective complaints against each other and as a weapon of attack. The couple themselves are splendidly alive creations, and Antrobus scores their incessant rows with clever variation. The first act especially has an exhilarating energy, and although the second act, split into five short scenes, seems oddly-structured in comparison, its comic invention rarely flags. Always in focus, however, is the gulf between the couple (climaxing in a coda both shocking and hilarious as Baba realizes he has put their baby in the oven and their dinner-duck in the cot), as the play explores the strange and often unrecognized bonds which keep two seemingly incompatible people together.

Crete and Sergeant Pepper was generally critically seen as a rather old-fashioned comedy – yet another World War II satire in the manner of Charles Wood's film *How I Won the War*. Certainly its picture of a P.O.W. camp on Crete in 1941, with its escape plan during a Drag Ball, goose stepping Germans, a "Mad Major" fanatically guarding a huge safe containing the regimental papers, and a Corporal engraving the Beatitudes on a cherry pip, was familiar enough, but what was missed – partly due to a Royal Court production which concentrated on an exaggerated and rather heavy-handed comic-strip style – was not only much of the real fun of the play but also the strong current of irony at its core.

Antrobus has often been accused of lack of construction in his work, and perhaps his early scriptwriting days which necessarily concentrated on situation comedy for character-comedians, did lead to less concentration on plot. In his weakest work this can degenerate into aimless facetiousness (as in *You'll Come to Love Your Sperm Test*), but his best plays have an agility transforming the situations with a dialogue sense by which words become the principle activating the plays' movement. He uses a kind of Goonish brand of surrealism to create his own fast-moving fluid style of theatre which is one of the most individual among younger dramatists currently writing.

—Alan Strachan

ARCHIBALD, (Rupert) Douglas. Trinidadian. Born in Port of Spain, 25 April 1919. Educated at Queen's Royal College, Port of Spain, 1928–35; McGill University, Montreal, Bachelor of Engineering (Civil) 1946. Served in the 2nd Battalion, Trinidad Light Infantry, 1938–40: Sergeant; in the Canadian Army Reserve, 1943–45: 2nd Lieutenant. Married Maureen Wedderburn Berry in 1953; has two children. Student Engineer, Trinidad Government Railways, 1935–41; Riot Policeman, 1937, and Platoon Commander, 1940–41, Trinidad Special Police; Assistant Maintenance Engineer, Trinidad Government Railways, 1946–48; in private practice as a Consulting Civil Engineer, 1949–63; Editor, *Progress* magazine, 1952; Member of the Editorial Board, *Clarion* newspaper, 1954–56; General Manager, Trinidad and Tobago Telephone Service, 1963–68; Managing Director, Trinidad and Tobago Telephone Company Ltd., 1968–69; Chairman of the Railway Board, Trinidad, 1963–65; Chairman of the Central Water Distribution Authority, Trinidad and Tobago, 1964–65; Vice-Chairman of the Public Transport Service Corporation, Trinidad and Tobago, 1965–67. Since 1969, in private practice as a Consulting Civil Engineer; since 1970, Director, Trinidad Engineering and Research Ltd. Tutor in Creative Writing, University of the West Indies, St. Augustine, Trinidad, 1971, 1973, 1975. Founding Member, later Vice-President and President, Readers and Writers Guild of Trinidad and Tobago, 1948–54; Member, Engineering Institute of Canada, 1954; Founding Member, 1958, later Vice-President and President, Association of Professional Engineers of Trinidad and Tobago; since 1967, President, Historical Society of Trinidad and Tobago. Recipient: Theatre Guild Award, 1962. Address: 13 Elizabeth Street, St. Clair, Port of Spain, Trinidad and Tobago, West Indies.

PUBLICATIONS

Plays

Junction Village (produced Port of Spain, 1954; London, 1955). Mona, University College of the West Indies, 1958.
Anne Marie (produced Port of Spain, 1958; London, 1976). Mona, University College of the West Indies, 1967.
The Bamboo Clump (produced Port of Spain, 1962). Mona, University College of the West Indies, 1967.

The Rose Slip (produced Port of Spain, 1962).   Mona, University College of the West Indies, 1972.

Old Maid's Tale (produced Port of Spain, 1965).   Mona, University College of the West Indies, 1966.

Island Tide (produced San Fernando, Trinidad).   Mona, University College of the West Indies, 1972.

Radio Plays: *That Family Next Door* series and *Island Tide* series, 1973.

Television Play: *My Good Friend Justice*, 1974.

*   *   *

Douglas Archibald is concerned with the decay of rural society in Trinidad. We see something of the old bourgeois order in *Anne Marie*, set on an estate fifty miles from Port of Spain towards the end of the last century. Here, James Fanshawe and his Spanish-descended neighbour, Pedro Meijas, bemoan the fact that they are not the men their fathers were. Their estates are being run down, they've got no male heirs and if they make their housekeepers pregnant, it is not to perpetuate the old line. *Old Maid's Tale* is a sentimental extension of this world where "Aunt Hetty," last of the Macdougal's, brings romantic young lovers together over tea and cucumber sandwiches, recalling the lovers of her own youth – who exist only in her imagination.

Men in this society abdicate responsibility, and this is also the basic fact of life in the village, cut off equally from the town and from the plantation. In *The Bamboo Clump*, the hypochondriac Charles Mackenzie is master of the house in name only. He has ignored his family, neglected his 30-acre cocoa estate, and done little in the last five years but sit on a bench in his garden. As a result, his son Dennis, like every other West Indian youth unable to emigrate, adopts supposedly United States dress (this was before Black Power!) and drifts towards trouble with the police. His daughter Drina is an intolerable prude and is being trained for her projected school-teacher's career by the usual caricature spinster. When she fails her exams, there seems no way to stop Li Fat (the middle-aged Chinese shopkeeper from whom they'd been getting credit) claiming her as his wife. To stop the rot, Charles finally (and improbably) asserts himself.

But the men are fighting a losing battle. In *Junction Village*, the matriarchial society has arrived. The action centres round the household of Grannie Gombo who, past 90, is apparently dying. The neighbours (including Bobo and Lizzy, also in their 90's) gather for the wake, but are on their guard as Grannie has tried this trick before. As they wait, the grand-daughters discuss Grannie's money, and Bobo relives the many conquests of his youth – counting Granny and Lizzy among them. Bobo is now treated as a harmless nuisance, but when he echoes the dying cry of all the other nonagenarian men, from Baba in *Anne Marie* to Bucket in *The Rose Slip*, we are genuinely disturbed. Archibald shows us that their fear isn't only of a cold bath and the poor house, but of the loneliness and loss of power and respect which afflict the old. And they abound in these villages. Bobo reflects that

> dere was a time w'en Ah wus strong, an' me arm wus like iron. Den pipple use to fear me an' Ah use ter walk in an' out a whey Ah did want.... Ah had moh bed dan one to sleep in dose days. Now me strenk gorn. One day it leave me sudden, jus' like dat an' dey begin to push me aroun' an' aroun'. Dese days me bones hurtin' me somet'ing bad and me t'roat always dryin' up....

This is unsettling, also, because there seems so little compensating vitality among the youth. In the fishing village of *Island Tide* the three generation family of Mr. Paps, his son Copy Cat and his grandson Uncle Look Up, suggests a sort of evolution in reverse – somewhat like R. S. Thomas' hill farmers. Of the two young men in *Junction Village*, one is a fool addicted to long words, and the other is a violent lout who hides under the dying woman's bed to escape detection from the police – there is energy here but ill-directed. However, there is comic relief as Grannie Gombo returns to life and demands food. There's nothing like this to lighten the drudgery of the city dwellers in *The Rose Slip*. Men, young and old, have been reduced to children; the women are harassed by their landlord, and in spite of their prayer meetings, can't feed their children. There is no relief in sight.

Douglas Archibald's social concern is serious enough. The plays suggest that a lack of paternal grip in all its forms leads to disintegration, But there is a certain old-fashioned view of social order in that things are measured against the loss of past certainties rather than explored for their present potential. It is a determinism which eschews experiment, and is reflected at its worst in his characterization. The caricatures – of the spinster, the black Englishman, the druggist using long words, etc. – work beautifully; but when in play after play, *individuals* fail to break through this "type casting" either of their aspirations or of their diction, the result is an overall complacency that confirms old prejudices. Prejudices about the man who abdicates. Prejudices about the Chinese businessman (and they are interchangeable in Archibald) who comes to see the girl he has "bought":

> Li Fat: Clum ter slee lou.
> Louisa: You shoulden a com'.
> Li Fat: Ly not? Onlee plyin lil vlisit.
> Louisa: Sh-h-h! Doan talk so loud.
> Li Fat: (annoyed by her reception of him) Lot long?

—E. A. Markham

ARDEN, Jane.   British.   Born in Wales. Has two children. Director of the women's theatre company Holocaust, since 1970. Address: c/o Calder and Boyars Ltd., 18 Brewer Street, London W1R 4AS, England.

PUBLICATIONS

Plays

Conscience and Desire, and Dear Liz (produced London, 1954).
The Party (produced London, 1958).   London, French, 1958.
Vagina Rex and the Gas Oven (produced London, 1969).   London, Calder and Boyars, 1971.
A New Communion – for Freaks, Prophets and Witches (produced Edinburgh and London, 1971).

Screenplays: *The Logic Game*, 1966; *Separation*, 1968; *The Other Side of the Underneath*, 1973.

Theatrical Activities:

Director: **Film** – *The Other Side of the Underneath*, 1973.

Actress: **Plays** – Betty Lewis in *Dear Liz*, and Conscience in *Conscience and Desire*, London, 1954. **Films** – *The Logic Game*, 1966; *Separation*, 1968. **Television** – *Romeo and Juliet*, 1947; *The Logic Game*, 1965; Inez in *Huis Clos*, by Sartre.

Jane Arden comments:

Biology – physics – genetics – observation of phenomena – leading to self-discovery – opening of the inner world – books (rarely) – signpost the reader to a richer textured experience of the universe – arousing the reader from his slumber – awakening him to a more illuminating perception of "being" in the world.

Reading can be as paralysing an act (even absorbing so-called erudite works) as Bingo, if the information does not recreate the being and radicalize the behaviour. There are no such things as creative writers – some people have better radio-sets for tuning in to the only creation.

The world needs healers, not "artists." Some of my signposts: Gurdjieff: *All and Everything; Tibetan Book of the Dead;* Wilheim Reich's *Sexual Revolution*; C. Jung's *Psychology and Alchemy* and *Modern Man in Search of a Soul; I Ching*; Rumi (12th century Sufi poet-saint); writings of Malcolm X.

*   *   *

Jane Arden is an astonishing, and perhaps even unique, figure in contemporary drama. She is impossible to categorize, and would almost certainly rebel against any attempt to do so for her work is notable for its very wide range of technical resources harnessed to serve her one main theme, which is the oppression of women in our society.

She is a social-political writer. There are, of course, many dramatists whose motivation is primarily political and whose dynamic is derived from an urgent need to put across a particular message. But unlike them, Jane Arden has never tried to conform to the conventional structures of the theatre; the three-walled box set, the need for careful in-depth characterization, the beginning-middle-end construction are irrelevant to her. Instead she has drawn on techniques and influences from the cinema, television and other manifestations of contemporary media (light projection, pop music). Message and the way she puts it across are closely linked: she subverts the railway tracks of the mind and of theatrical expectations.

But this was not always so. Early in her career, as a dramatist in the most conventional manner possible, she wrote a play that is not only constructed with all the formality of conventional drama, but which was produced at a major London theatre with a major commercial cast that included Charles Laughton, Elsa Lanchester, Albert Finney and Joyce Redman. This was *The Party*, a penetrating and often touching exploration of adolescent conflicts, providing, incidentally, some very rewarding, if wordy, roles for the actors.

It would strain the use of hindsight beyond viability to detect in this play the seeds of Jane Arden's later development. Here her concern was with the conflict between reality and the fantasy-aspirations of the teenage heroine, Henrietta, who wishes to see herself as a glamorous, wealthy, perhaps even debby type of girl. Her family and circumstances deny her all of these aspirations; the father is an alcoholic just returned from a cure; the home is grim and dingy, the mother fighting a tough battle and taking in lodgers. The play shows Henrietta's cruelty in denying the reality of her existence and eventual reconciliation with a kind of truth.

It is indeed possible to see that the women in this play are oppressed, but this oppression is accepted and in the context of the play not overtly commented upon, though as a whole the play does make a strong comment on the way in which individuals are distorted, emotionally and socially, by attempting to conform to the expectations of society.

Jane Arden did not produce another stage work until more than ten years later. But in the intervening years she become well known as an actress, and also as a speaker on television programmes usually on women and politics. She also wrote screenplays. Her next stage play appeared in 1969, was in itself sensational, and revealed the radical change that had been going on. In 1966, Jane Arden had written a film called *The Logic Game* which is described as "a surrealist puzzle attempting to locate the isolation of woman in the context of bourgeois marriage," and this was the first creative result of her increasing interest in the position of women in society. A second film came in 1968 (directed by Jack Bond). This was *Separation*, in which "the nerve of exploitation [was] more exposed, as the woman's personal dilemma began to have a political context." In these works, or explorations, Jane Arden is revealed as one of the first major voices of Women's Liberation which began to take on coherence in the late 1960's.

Meanwhile, practical developments within the theatre itself had been happening. Writers, directors and actors were becoming increasingly discontented with the conventional theatrical forms; also with the financial/commercial situation of the theatre. And during the last years of the 1960's a number of experimental theatre groups came into being. The work shown in this context was at once more liberated politically and more liberated in form. In Jane Arden the two themes met with a production of her next play, *Vagina Rex and the Gas Oven*, which was given at the London Arts Laboratory, directed by Jack Bond.

This remains so far the most direct and intense expression of women's oppression in the theatre. Technically, it used one actress playing Woman (Sheila Allen) and one actor playing The Man (Victor Spinetti), plus a chorus of Furies, young actors and actresses who commented, took many parts and became a sort of choreographed background. There was a pop group and much use of projection, lights and varying sounds. Throughout, the techniques and images are used with a sound dramatic fluency that makes *Vagina Rex* outstanding as a political tract that is also extremely compelling theatre.

In *Vagina Rex*, Jane Arden exposes every nerve related to the inferior, passive position of women. It caused considerable comment, one of the most ironic being a trendy Sunday newspaper's piece called "Are Women Oppressed?" – "as though there was still some doubt about the matter," Jane Arden comments. In 1971, Jane Arden's next play *A New Communion – for Freaks, Prophets and Witches* was produced in Edinburgh and London. It had an all-female cast and explored the themes in more detail. *Vagina Rex* related women firmly to men and to the pre-ordained social role expected of women. *A New Communion* internalized the themes and the expression "women's rage" was made real.

Jane Arden's later work is excellent to read and gripping to watch when superbly performed, but it is doubtful whether it will be possible to perform *Vagina Rex* or *A New Communion* outside the context of a specialist and committed company of players. These plays are essentially products of a time and a place. Jane Arden is now concentrating more on film work, though her women's theatre company, called Holocaust, retains an existence.

—Roger Baker

ARDEN, John. British. Born in Barnsley, Yorkshire, 26 October 1930. Educated at Sedbergh School, Yorkshire; King's College, Cambridge, B.A. 1953; Edinburgh College of Art, diploma in architecture, 1955. Served as a Lance-Corporal in the Intelligence Corps, 1949–50. Married the actress Margaretta Ruth D'Arcy in 1957; has four children. Architectural Assistant, London, 1955–57. Fellow in Playwriting, Bristol University, 1959–60; Visiting Lecturer in Politics and Drama, New York University, 1967; Regents Lecturer, University of California, Davis, 1973; Writer in Residence, University of New England, Armidale, New South Wales, 1975. Co-founder, Corrandulla Arts Centre, County Galway, Ireland, 1973. Recipient: BBC Northern Region Prize, 1957; Encyclopedia

Britannica Prize, 1959; *Evening Standard* award, 1960; Trieste Festival Award, 1961; Vernon Rice Award, 1966; Arts Council award, 1973. Address: c/o Margaret Ramsay Ltd., 14a Goodwin's Court, London WC2N 4LL, England.

PUBLICATIONS

Plays

All Fall Down (produced Edinburgh, 1955).

The Waters of Babylon (produced London, 1957; New York, 1958).   Included in *Three Plays*, 1964.

When Is a Door Not a Door? (produced London, 1958).   Included in *Soldier, Soldier and Other Plays*, 1967.

Live Like Pigs (produced London, 1958; Boston, 1965).   Included in *New English Dramatists 3*, London, Penguin, 1961; in *Three Plays*, 1964.

Serjeant Musgrave's Dance: An Unhistorical Parable (produced London, 1959; San Francisco, 1961; New York, 1966).   London, Methuen, 1960; New York, Grove Press, 1962; revised version (produced London, 1972).

The Happy Haven, with the collaboration of Margaretta D'Arcy (produced Bristol and London, 1960; New Haven, Connecticut, 1966; New York, 1967).   Included in *New English Dramatists 4*, London, Penguin, 1962; in *Three Plays*, 1964.

Soldier, Soldier (televised, 1960).   Included in *Soldier, Soldier and Other Plays*, 1967.

The Business of Good Government: A Christmas Play, with Margaretta D'Arcy (also co-director: produced, as *A Christmas Play*, Brent Knoll, Somerset, 1960; New York, 1970).   London, Methuen, 1963; New York, Grove Press, 1967.

Wet Fish (televised, 1961).   Included in *Soldier, Soldier and Other Plays*, 1967.

Ironhand, adaptation of the play *Goetz von Berlichingen* by Goethe (produced Bristol, 1963).   London, Methuen, 1965.

The Workhouse Donkey: A Vulgar Melodrama (produced Chichester, Sussex, 1963).   London, Methuen, 1964; New York, Grove Press, 1967.

Three Plays: The Waters of Babylon, Live Like Pigs, The Happy Haven.   London, Penguin, 1964; New York, Grove Press, 1966.

Armstrong's Last Goodnight: An Exercise in Diplomacy (produced Glasgow, 1964; Boston, 1966).   London, Methuen, 1965; New York, Grove Press, 1967.

Ars Longa, Vita Brevis, with Margaretta D'Arcy (produced London, 1964).   London, Cassell, 1965.

Fidelio, adaptation of a libretto by Joseph Sonnleithner and Friedrich Treitschke, music by Beethoven (produced London, 1965).

Left-Handed Liberty: A Play about Magna Carta (produced London, 1965; Boston, 1968).   London, Methuen, 1965; New York, Grove Press, 1966.

Friday's Hiding, with Margaretta D'Arcy (produced Edinburgh, 1966).   Included in *Soldier, Soldier and Other Plays*, 1967.

The Royal Pardon; or, The Soldier Who Became an Actor, with Margaretta D'Arcy (also co-director: produced Beaford, Devon, 1966; London, 1967).   London, Methuen, 1966.)

Soldier, Soldier and Other Plays (includes *Wet Fish, When Is a Door Not a Door?* and *Friday's Hiding*).   London, Methuen, 1967.

The True History of Squire Jonathan and His Unfortunate Treasure (produced London, 1968; New York, 1974).   Included in *Two Autobiographical Plays*, 1971.

The Hero Rises Up: A Romantic Melodrama, with Margaretta D'Arcy (also co-director: produced London, 1968).   London, Methuen, 1969.

The Soldier's Tale, adaptation of a libretto by Ramuz, music by Stravinsky (produced Bath, 1968).

Harold Muggins Is a Martyr, with Margaretta D'Arcy and the Cartoon Archetypical
Slogan Theatre (produced London, 1968).

The Bagman; or, The Impromptu of Muswell Hill (broadcast, 1970).   Included in *Two
Autobiographical Plays*, 1971.

*Two Autobiographical Plays: The True History of Squire Jonathan and His Unfortunate
Treasure, and The Bagman; or, The Impromptu of Muswell Hill*.   London, Methuen,
1971.

The Ballygombeen Bequest, with Margaretta D'Arcy (produced Belfast and London,
1972).   Published in *Scripts 9* (New York), September 1972.

The Island of the Mighty: A Play on a Traditional British Theme, with Margaretta
D'Arcy (produced London, 1972).   London, Eyre Methuen, 1974; in *Performance*
(New York), 1974.

The Non-Stop Connolly Show, with Margaretta D'Arcy (also co-director: produced
Dublin, 1975; London, 1976).

Radio Plays: *The Life of Man*, 1956; *The Bagman*, 1970.

Television Plays: *Soldier, Soldier*, 1960; *Wet Fish*, 1961; *Sean O'Casey* (documentary),
with Margaretta D'Arcy, 1973 (Ireland).

Theatrical Activities:

Director, with Margaretta D'Arcy: **Plays** – *The Business of Good Government*, Brent
Knoll, Somerset, 1960; *Ars Longa, Vita Brevis*, Kirbymoorside, Yorkshire, 1965; *The
Royal Pardon*, Beaford, Devon, 1966; *The Hero Rises Up*, London, 1968; *The Non-Stop
Connolly Show*, with others, Dublin, 1975.

John Arden comments:

At the present time the gap between the playwright and the active life of the theatre
seems as wide as it has ever been: and it shows no sign of closing. Figures such as the
Director and the Scenic Designer, whose relevance to good dramatic writing is at best
marginal, have increased their power and influence in no small measure during the past few
years: and they stand ominously between playwright and actors, inhibiting proper
communication. The *content* of new plays is obscured and neutralized by over-emphasis on
aesthetic theatrical *form*. The dependence of the dramatic art upon subsidies from public
funds has given rise to a bureaucratic intransigence on the part of Directors, who are too
often Administrators as well, and are becoming less and less inclined to take the necessary
risks demanded by adventurous and expanding experiment. The problem is similar to that
faced by Ben Jonson in the 1620's, when he struck out against the dominance of Inigo Jones
as designer-director of court entertainment, and lost his battle. The result of Jones's victory
was the securing by the monarchy of the complete allegiance of the theatrical profession,
followed by the closure of the theatres during the Cromwellian Revolution. The
playwrights, as a trade-grouping, never again recaptured the position of artistic strength and
poetic potency which they had attained at the beginning of the 17th Century. To forestall an
equivalent disaster today, the modern dramatists must attempt two apparently
contradictory tasks. 1) They must abandon their solitary status and learn to combine
together to secure conditions-of-work and artistic control over the products of their
imagination. 2) They must be prepared to combine not only with their follows, but also with
actors. It is not enough for the occasional author to *direct*; playwrights should be members
of theatrical troupes, and take part in all aspects of production. In order to achieve goal 2),
goal 1) must first be arrived at. The authors together must establish the importance of their
written work as an essential *internal* element of the theatre, and then, individually, they

must become absorbed into the theatre themselves as co-workers.

I am aware that these requirements go against all current trends. But the current trends are running towards the complete death of the modern drama. Remember, Shakespeare and Molière regarded themselves as men of the theatre rather than *literary* figures: and I believe it to be no accident that their works remain unequalled in the Western tradition.

*   *   *

England has a counter-culture of its own, handed down from the industrial revolution and aligned on the coalfields. Writers like Storey, Sillitoe, Barstow and Bragg, following after D. H. Lawrence, carried an awareness of the key steam-age industry and its social pattern into the 1960's. Of this combative tradition, with its rugged energy and contempt for effete southern manners, John Arden is the playwright. "The Home Secretary's a Tory and he lives in bloody London" remarks his Alderman Butterthwaite, in conflict with the new Chief Constable who sees himself as an enemy alien in the North. When Skinner Normanton, thought to be the invention of a witty sports journalist, was suddenly revealed on television as a living person, he seemed to have materialized from *Waters of Babylon* or *The Workhouse Donkey* and had in fact played soccer for Barnsley where Arden was born. Too much of his dramatic work is what you might expect if Mr. Normanton had tried his hand at authorship; the best is as good as anything since Brecht.

A good deal has been said about Arden's "objectivity." On the contrary, his plays are suffused with a distinct personality, obstinate, eccentric, and verbose. The typically Yorkshire arrogance, which enabled him to persevere with live theatre when others were deflected to lucrative screen assignments, may also have been a brake on his progress. The West End audiences he has yet to reach might have led towards a taut narrative line and curbed the verbal self-indulgence. Indebted to coterie support, he is inclined to underrate the public and its intermediaries. Two London critics, for example, were honest enough to reverse their initial verdicts on *Serjeant Musgrave's Dance*, one of them after trailing the play through provincial theatres. Their reward was the equivalent of a B-minus in *Encore* from the author, for not decoding the message first time round.

When Arden's career began in the 1950's, the new drama was already taking parallel courses, one of literary fantasy, the other of political concern about imperialism and the social attitudes related to it. Anyone taking the second course had to come to terms with the increasing cult of Brecht. Since a great poet loses impact in translation and staging suffered from misuse of the master's theories, the result was confusion. It affected Arden adversely where directors besotted with the mannerisms of a new theatrical idiom threw his work out of focus and where similar mannerisms infected his writing. Ill-distributed ballads, sententious intrusive comment, are two of the legacies. On the other hand, to the best educated of the new dramatists Brecht had much of value to offer, including a shared admiration for the Elizabethans, seen as explorers of big issues in a popular stage idiom rather than intense poets. As a trained architect, Arden has also the capacity to supply structural backbone for offsetting prolixity and rhetoric. But if we are to estimate him accurately it is best to underline the differences from Brecht. First, he is an inferior poet, not in the same league as Auden in coping with the ballad and much of the time abysmal: "The lady's walls are large and high/The lady's grass is green and dry/The lady herself is green and blooming/And big fat Alfred, he's consuming...." And printed as verse: "You have drunk tea/Eaten cakes and toasted bread/And jam, and you yourself have talked to me/And I have been transported."

Second, Brecht's framework of Marxist dogma, heretical or not, exerts control on his anarchical pessimism and gives guidelines to the public. Third, he places song and commentary with careful precision, keeps all but a few characters within planned contours and tells a lucid theatrical story. Very rarely, and then triumphantly, does his follower achieve any of this, although the potential, except in poetry, is obviously there. Why has it not been more fully developed? Probably because of one crucial difference, that Brecht was not only a master dramatist but a great director. Without that advantage Arden has been a prey to the cults of mask, alienation, Kabuki, Pop satire, and comic strip history forced upon the live drama in desperate competition with the media. He has been a victim of the contemporary set-up as much as if he had served the conformist theatre itself.

Aside from some doubt about the integration of folk songs, shared by the playwright according to his introduction, none of these groping experiments applies to *Live Like Pigs* of 1958. It deals with a family of delinquents, evicted from a caravan site by the local authority and supplied with a council house which they promptly adapt to a slum. In the New Left atmosphere of that time (political "stance," commitment, etc.) it was easy to misread the approach as romantic travesty of a grave social problem. In fact it was prophetic, not only of one new housing estate where crime rose above the slum level, but of the hippy addiction to vagabondage and domestic squalor. The mode of the play is inverted domesticity of the kind attempted by Pinter, in a mannered idiom with too much contrivance, in *The Homecoming* seven years later. *Live Like Pigs* bulges with sardonic Rabelaisian scatology and its author's delight in the outrageousness of his own creation. The more conformist neighbours are summed up in one line: "Doreen, you forgot your plastic overshoes," as against "Rachel, ye bloody leprosy, come up to the bed."

The following year came the epic drama *Serjeant Musgrave's Dance*, an achievement to justify anyone's entire career. With sources in Brecht, the ballad tradition, Arden's own television play *Soldier, Soldier* (1960), modern Cyprus, Victorian imperialism, and Barnsley, it traces the impact of four enigmatic deserters on a snowbound colliery town. They bring home, literally, the reality of a distant war by exhibiting the skeleton of one of its local victims. They intend to execute leading civilians who bear the ultimate war guilt. But they themselves are tainted with it, and their leader, for all his religious fervour, is no fit emissary of retributive justice. The morality involved is outside the scope of limited "Roman" certainties, the soldier's code. When one of the deserters kills another in a brawl they lose face and their scheme misfires. They hang, but not without a tribute to the validity of their protest. Premature and muddled though it was, it had the seeds of human liberty at its core.

Musgrave has the complexity, the ambiguity and the involuted conflict riding a sinuous narrative line of major epic drama. Its relevance to Vietnam is instantly apparent to young Americans. Yet in spite of its knotty coherence it has brought out the worst of modish theatricalism in a succession of directors, and Arden was soon diverted into an approach as mannered as theirs. First there was *The Happy Haven,* in which his anxiety to avoid a stock sentimental response to discarded old people results in an over-correction. Passages of insight are neutralized by grotesque stylization. The tone devalues the message. Then, in *The Workhouse Donkey*, the promising theme of an incorruptible southern official adrift in northern local politics gets mislaid in facetious comedy. A tortuous plot ends up by stressing a boring physician and a veteran socialist alderman in a verbal idiom connoting Shaw, Barnsley and Brecht. To invoke Japanese popular drama, as Arden did by imagining nine to thirteen hours of performance to a drifting public, suggests lack of conviction. No doubt he was put off balance, too, by working with brilliant directors and a top-level company.

The next time that happened, however, he was back to the epic vein of *Musgrave*. *Armstrong's Last Goodnight* is less austere and controlled but even more adventurous, with layer upon layer of political tension ranging from Border chieftains at odds with an encroaching monarchy to analogy with feuds in Katanga. To say that the play stimulates cross-reference to Lukacs and Conor Cruise O'Brien would be complimentary but inadequate. In addition it throws off the Skinner Normanton/Barnsley syndrome by a shift to medieval Scotland. There Arden's ballad idiom becomes supple and to the point, his political intriguer no longer a provincial nonentity but a refined Machiavellian attached to the Scottish court. And the doomed, anarchical flamboyance of the Sawneys in *Live Like Pigs* is back again in the person of Armstrong.

Having for the third time achieved something which none of his contemporaries could rival, Arden then turned his back on the established theatre, and, in collaboration with Margaretta D'Arcy, has increasingly exploited the doggerel, slapstick, and grotesque elements of his earlier work.

—Laurence Kitchin

ARDREY, Robert, American   Born in Chicago, Illinois, 16 October 1908. Educated at
the University of Chicago, 1927–30, Ph.B. 1930 (Phi Beta Kappa). Married Helene Johnson
in 1938 (divorced, 1960); Berdine Grunewald, 1960; has three children. Theatre and film
writer until 1958. Since 1958, lecturer and consultant on the evolutionary origins of human
behaviour. Recipient: Sergel Drama Prize, 1935; Guggenheim Fellowship, 1937; Sidney
Howard Memorial Prize, 1940; Theresa Helburn Memorial Award, 1961; Willkie Brothers
grant, for anthropology, 1963. Fellow, Royal Society of Literature. Agent: Margery Vosper,
Suite 8, 26 Charing Cross Road, London WC2H 0DG, England; or, Brandt and Brandt, 101
Park Avenue, New York, New York 10017, U.S.A. Address: Via Garibaldi 89, Trastevere,
Rome, Italy.

PUBLICATIONS

Plays

> *Star-Spangled* (produced New York, 1936).   New York, French, 1936.
> *Casey Jones* (produced New York, 1938; London, 1946).
> *How to Get Tough about It* (produced New York, 1938).
> *Thunder Rock* (produced New York, 1939; London, 1940).   New York, Dramatists
>   Play Service, and London, Hamish Hamilton, 1940.
> *God and Texas.*   New York, Dramatists Play Service, n.d.
> *Jeb* (produced New York, 1946).   Included in *Plays of Three Decades*, 1968.
> *Sing Me No Lullaby* (produced New York, 1954).   New York, Dramatists Play
>   Service, 1955.
> *Shadow of Heroes* (produced London, 1958; as *Stone and Star*, produced New York,
>   1961).   London, Collins, 1958; in *Plays of Three Decades*, 1968.
> *Plays of Three Decades: Thunder Rock, 1939; Jeb, 1946; Shadow of Heroes, 1958.*
>   London, Collins, and New York, Atheneum, 1968.

> Screenplays: *They Knew What They Wanted,* 1940; *A Lady Takes a Chance,* 1943; *The
>   Green Years,* 1946; *The Three Musketeers,* 1948; *Madame Bovary,* 1949; *The Secret
>   Garden,* 1949; *Quentin Durward,* 1955; *The Power and the Prize,* 1956; *The Wonderful
>   Country,* 1959; *The Four Horsemen of the Apocalypse,* with John Gay, 1962; *Khartoum,*
>   1966; *The Animal Within* (documentary), 1975.

Novels

> *World's Beginning.*   New York, Duell, 1944; London, Hamish Hamilton, 1945.
> *The Brotherhood of Fear.*   New York, Random House, and London, Collins, 1952.

Other

> *African Genesis: A Personal Investigation into the Animal Origins and Nature of Man.*
>   London, Collins, and New York, Atheneum, 1961.
> *The Territorial Imperative: A Personal Inquiry into the Animal Origins of Property and
>   Nations.*   New York, Atheneum, 1966; London, Collins, 1967.
> *The Social Contract: A Personal Inquiry into the Evolutionary Source of Order and
>   Disorder.*   New York, Atheneum, and London, Collins, 1970.
> *Aggression and Violence in Man: A Dialogue Between Dr. Louis Leakey and Mr. Robert
>   Ardrey.*   Pasadena, California, Munger, 1971.

The Hunting Hypothesis: A Personal Conclusion Concerning the Evolutionary Nature of Man.   New York, Atheneum, and London, Collins, 1976.

Manuscript Collection: Boston University

Robert Ardrey comments:

Like any other dramatist, in my earliest writings I was fascinated by the central question, Why do we act as we do? From the time of Aeschylus through Shakespeare to the present, any dramatist worthy of the term has been preoccupied by the problem of motivation. Fashions have changed with the centuries. We have looked to the intervention of the gods, as in the time of the Greeks. We have looked to society as in Ibsen, to rationality as in Shaw. In my own time we looked to Freud and to Marx for the determinisms of sex and economics. Always we have had the question, Why do we *act* as we do? And that is why in theatre we have such terms as acts, actors, actresses. The dramatist, throughout all ages, has been the poet of principal responsibility in such human investigations. And perhaps that is why, dissatisfied with all contemporary fashions of sex and economics, I left the theatre to pursue my investigations of the evolutionary sources of human behaviour. That we are four-dimensional beings, in whom the past lives as a portion of the present, is a thesis brought alive by such dramatists of genius as Harold Pinter. But for definitive investigation one must turn to stages larger than those of the theatre, always with the hope that any new understanding of our nature will be as useful to the arts as to the sciences.

*   *   *

Any history of the American theatre would be deficient if it did not consider the plays of Robert Ardrey. His themes include many slices of American history and of the vast amalgam of cultures that America represents. But no playwright finds a place in history just for his themes and Ardrey's claim to acknowledgement must be attributed to his mastery over the components of dramatic literature. Settings are his particular forte, especially his native Midwest, but he has set plays and scenarios all over the world, and, in particular, Africa, which he has visited so often as an anthropologist and ethologist (remember *Khartoum*, cinematized, and *Out of Africa* – not filmed as yet). He is a playwright who visualizes staging problems long before the stage or movie director has seen them, and guides these generally distraught persons to easy functioning. No wonder he has been the golden boy of movie producers.

His characterizations – ordinary people in everyday situations – are made most convincingly real through his skill at recreating ethnic speech patterns such as the Polish-American jargon (*Star-Spangled*), Southern American Negro (*Jeb*), sub-standard speech of working class elements (*How to Get Tough about It, Casey Jones*), and so on. They are convincing and theatrically effective characters because Ardrey does not mimic them but represents them with a certain respect. This is because Ardrey respects all humanity and does not take up the clarion on behalf of the "down-trodden" or the underdog, but nurtures respect also for the anguished emotions of the powerful or the "overdog." Ardrey is not a political or even a social writer, but a writer about the human soul, in settings that are charged generally with social problems which, though interesting, are mere scaffolding. He is infinitely closer to Ibsen than to Shaw. If his themes of anguish are dealt with on a philosophic plane with dialogue alone furnishing the dramatic tension, he fails. He is no Pirandello or Unamuno; but Brechtian he is and he has demonstrated it in most of his plays. The exception – fundamental – is that Brecht takes historical themes from the past and far removed from the personal lives of his public. Ardrey always takes contemporary events, *current* events, thus risking the sympathy or antipathy of the public and its mood. If *Jeb*,

Shadow of Heroes, Star-Spangled and even *How to Get Tough about It* don't have the public following they deserve, it is the fault of the timing rather than of the plays. Let us examine several.

Thunder Rock is a fantastic-ontological play not too typical of Ardrey's repertoire. A man attempts to live in a fantastic world of his own ideation – and in isolation. He revives a group of immigrants who had lost their lives in a shipwreck ninety years earlier. The protagonist believes that he can create a better world through his fantasy only to come to realize through his resuscitated characters that the line betwixt real and fantasy is indeed thin, if existent at all. It is a Quixotic world and Ardrey succeeds in winning sympathy for his protagonist: this gives the play a certain charm. In its interplay of real and fanciful it will remind one of *Six Characters in Search of an Author* (in fact, Ardrey brings back from the dead exactly six people) in that the six do impart a sense of doom inherent in man, and an instinctual distrust in "progressivism." If there is a weakness in this subtly developed play it is the character of the protagonist who does not quite convince us that his anguish is endemic and that his idealist world is more than an experiment.

Jeb dealt with Negro social problems in the United States long before they reached their present exacerbated stage. The structure of the play is perfect, the characterization excellent, the theme alive, yet, all together this play would not find a public. The blacks would reject it because they want to bury that part of their history and the whites don't want a guilty conscience stirred up because of the behaviour (as tragic as that of the blacks) of the extreme elements portrayed here. Because of this *Jeb* may not see the stage but it remains superb dramatic literature. In *Thunder Rock* Ardrey demonstrated his skill in maintaining dramatic interest without a change of scenery, while in *Jeb* he ranges over half the United States, tying his shifting scenes together like a varied necklace.

Shadow of Heroes is the story of the Hungarian uprising and of the events leading to it. The characters are the historical figures that were actually involved, plus a light sprinkling of fictitious personages. Ardrey intended the play to be topical, to protest the tragic events of 1956. It is not surprising that this play would not be a box office success except during the moments of international concern concomitant with the events themselves. It would be very successful in present day Hungary, were this a political possibility, as *Jeb* would be popular in Harlem, were this a cultural possibility.

By focusing beyond current events, another theme in *Shadow of Heroes* emerges: the tragedy of Revolution – a transcendental tragedy which shows how Revolution eats its children; and, as Giuseppe Mazzini pointed out, all governments imposed by force cannot, by this very fact, be tolerant, democratic or free. Ardrey shows, unwittingly perhaps, what Revolution does to human relationships.

How to Get Tough about It is another piece of Americana, set in a Midwest steel town. Its action deals with strikes and strikebreaking in the "good ole days" when labor unions and management first sat down at the bargaining table for their game of Chinese wrestling, while under the table they kicked each other in the shins or any other vulnerable spot; but the real internal action deals with human values and sensibilities dear to Ardrey's heart: love, friendship, loyalty. But today's cynical mass-public is insensitive to these values, being more interested in spectacle (sexual preferably) than in drama. Ardrey sensed this and towards the end of the play, in order to rescue his characters from falling into trite types, he leans to farce. It is too little and too late to save the play; but it indicates that the play would have to be lifted entirely from the realistic mode and turned into complete farce or into a musical comedy or into ballet – something that would give backbone to the now flaccid (*o tempora, o mores*) human values.

Casey Jones is a tour de force for a scenographer, but Ardrey is up to it – he has the ability to convince any stage designer that *anything* can be represented on stage. *Casey Jones*, as the title indicates, is about the life of a man devoted to the god of progress symbolized in locomotives and train schedules. Having sold his soul to that particular god it stands to reason that trains travelling at eighty miles an hour are superior to those travelling at seventy miles an hour, thus Casey Jones becomes a devotee of the faster train, *no matter what*. "You're a good citizen," says one of the characters to Casey Jones; but as Casey wears out his body and those dear to him, Ardrey implies that behind each good citizen there must be a good man, and Casey slowly realizes that a man travelling eighty miles an hour is not necessarily superior to the one travelling fifty miles an hour. His god of progress is indeed a demon, a female witch that has raped his soul. All that remains to him now is his life; and in an effort to retrieve his soul, he gives that "bitch" of a locomotive his life. In addition to its very valid tragic base, *Casey Jones* is good drama because, just as *The Odyssey* and *Moby Dick* make good sea yarns, its superstructure makes a good ironhorse yarn.

—John V. Falconieri

AXELROD, George. American. Born in New York City, 9 June 1922. Served in the United States Signal Corps in World War II. Married Gloria Washburn in 1942 (divorced, 1954); Joan Stanton, 1954; has three children. Member, Dramatists Guild, and Authors League of America. Address: c/o The Viking Press, 625 Madison Avenue, New York, New York 10022, U.S.A.

PUBLICATIONS

Plays

Sketches, with Max Wilk, in *Small Wonder* (produced New York, 1948).
The Seven Year Itch: A Romantic Comedy (produced New York, 1952; London, 1953). New York, Random House, 1953; London, Heinemann, 1954.
Will Success Spoil Rock Hunter? (also director: produced New York, 1955). New York, Random House, 1956.
Goodbye Charlie (also director: produced New York, 1959). New York, French, 1959.

Screenplays: *Phffft*, 1954; *The Seven Year Itch*, with Billy Wilder, 1955; *Bus Stop*, 1956; *Breakfast at Tiffany's*, 1961; *The Manchurian Candidate*, 1962; *Paris When It Sizzles*, 1964; *How to Murder Your Wife*, 1965; *Lord Love a Duck*, with Larry H. Johnson, 1966; *The Secret Life of an American Wife*, 1968.

Radio Writer: *Midnight in Manhattan* program, 1940; material for *Grand Old Opry*, 1950–52.

Television Writer: for *Celebrity Time*, 1950.

Night Club Writer: *All about Love* (produced New York, 1951).

Novels

Beggar's Choice. New York, Howell Soskin, 1947; as *Hobson's Choice*, London, Elek, 1951.
Blackmailer. New York, Fawcett, 1952; London, Gold Medal, 1959.

> *Where Am I Now – When I Need Me?*   New York, Viking Press, and London, Deutsch, 1971.

Theatrical Activities:

Director: **Plays** – *Will Success Spoil Rock Hunter?*, New York, 1955; *Once More, With Feeling* by Harry Kurnitz, New York, 1958; *Goodbye Charlie*, New York, 1959; *The Star-Spangled Girl* by Neil Simon, New York, 1966.   **Films** – *Lord Love a Duck*, 1966; *The Secret Life of an American Wife*, 1968.

*   *   *

The playwriting career of George Axelrod well illustrates that dramatist of particular wit and imagination who manages to create marketable products for Broadway tastes and, for a brief period, enjoys the fame and fortune that successful commercial comedy brings. His brief period was the decade of the 1950's. Of his three plays – *The Seven Year Itch, Will Success Spoil Rock Hunter?, Goodbye Charlie* – the first one ran nearly three years in New York with 1,141 performances and the second lasted a year and had 444 performances. Prior to his first success he had learned his trade writing for radio and television. Since this decade of playwriting he has had some success as a director, effectively directing such plays as Neil Simon's *The Star-Spangled Girl* for an audience acceptance that he was no longer able to reach as a dramatist.

In the history of American comic drama Axelrod might be mentioned as the author of two plays which say something about American tastes and attitudes during that post-World War II decade when audiences enjoyed a semi-sophisticated joke along with a semi-realistic view of themselves. Although the period for this enjoyment continued under the aegis of Neil Simon, Axelrod's imagination for such playwriting dried up. A later novel, *Where Am I Now – When I Need Me?*, is an artless attempt to capitalize on current free expression in writing as well as a kind of pathetic admission. In the span of theatre history in America the decade of the 1950's will be of considerably diminished importance while Axelrod's contribution will be measured, if at all, in terms of conscious yet effective technique on the Broadway scale of carefully analysed entertainment.

Axelrod's success as a dramatist came with his ability to write clever, simply-structured comedy that seemed a bit outrageous or naughty at first but was generally acceptable and comforting. Liberal circles have labelled him a writer of right-wing comedy in which right-wing morality always triumphs and have considered his success a disturbing feature of American comedy. Such observations have their place in history, but it is nonetheless true that such conservative comedy has a rich reputation in American comedy and for a decade Axelrod's polished and carefully tailored plays were the most imaginative of those writing these slim pieces of professionally manufactured theatre. His plays satisfied an audience's needs. *The Seven Year Itch* tells of a New York businessman, Richard Shermans, who combines a humorous reluctance and eagerness as he spends a night with a girl after his wife has left the hot city for the summer months. *Will Success Spoil Rock Hunter?* toys with the Faustus theme as George MacCawley sells his soul ten percent at a time for fame, fortune, and certain pleasures. But Axelrod always emphasized a definite, if sometimes late, morality. Richard is funny because his reluctance, his ineptness, and his remorse contrast hilariously with his view of himself as a seducer. At the final curtain a likeable hero emerges from an educational experience; even the girl, who slept with him because he could not be serious with her, begins to think that marriage should be worth a try. George also eats his cake and has it to enjoy. His fantasies are dramatically fulfilled, and he does not lose his soul. In this manner Axelrod presented safe, conservative entertainment that would run for at least a year. A few years later it is out of date, and with another generation it has lost most of its appeal.

Technically, Axelrod used the accepted devices of unpretentious comic entertainment.

Verbal and visual jokes were a major part of a play's success with an audience. Perhaps that is why Axelrod has since substituted directing for playwriting. Topicality in the jokes was as much a part of a play's success as it was an appeal to snobbishness in the audiences. There are numerous local references to New York, while names were dropped in almost every scene. Obviously, Axelrod studied his audiences, considering them knowledgeable but not overly bright. Certain gags in *Will Success Spoil Rock Hunter?* – the positioning of the "Scarlet Letter" on a scantily clad model and the impossibility of making love in the sand – are repeated, and the staircase in *The Seven Year Itch*, described as giving "the joint a kind of Jean-Paul Sartre quality," is further explained as having "no exit." In *The Seven Year Itch* Axelrod enlivened his presentation with dramatic devices such as fantasy sequences, flashbacks, and soliloquies. Throughout all of his plays, ridiculing, making witty comments, and satirizing man and his society are standard ploys for humor. But Axelrod is neither innovator nor reformer, merely a professional entertainer. He satirized the usual things – the movies, psychiatrists, rental-novel sex, certain decadence, and so on. He had nothing to say to any thoughtful person, and he scarcely took himself seriously, suggesting as he did a thorough and comfortable acceptance of all that he ridiculed in his plays. John Gassner referred to his work as "imaginative fluff," and as such it has appeal for certain theatre audiences at certain times.

—Walter J. Meserve

AYCKBOURN, Alan.   British.   Born in London, 12 April 1939. Educated at Haileybury and the Imperial Service College, Hertfordshire, 1952–57. Married Christine Roland in 1959; has two sons. Stage Manager, Donald Wolfit's company, at Edinburgh, Worthing, Leatherhead, Oxford; Founding Member, Victoria Theatre, Stoke on Trent, 1962–64; Radio Drama Producer, BBC, Leeds, 1964–70. Currently, Artistic Director, Scarborough Theatre Trust Ltd. Recipient: *Evening Standard* award, 1974, 1975. Agent: Margaret Ramsay Ltd., 14a Goodwin's Court, London WC2N 4LL.

PUBLICATIONS

Plays

The Square Cat (as Roland Allen) (produced Scarborough, 1959).
Love after All (as Roland Allen) (produced Scarborough, 1959).
Dad's Tale (as Roland Allen) (produced Scarborough, 1961).
Standing Room Only (as Roland Allen) (produced Scarborough 1962).
Xmas v Mastermind (produced Stoke on Trent, 1963).
Mr. Whatnot (produced Stoke on Trent, 1963; London, 1964).
Relatively Speaking (as *Meet My Father*, produced Scarborough, 1965; as *Relatively Speaking*, produced London, 1967; New York, 1970).   London, Evans, and New York, French, 1968.
The Sparrow (produced Scarborough, 1967).
How the Other Half Loves (also director: produced Scarborough, 1969; London, 1970; New York, 1971).   London, Evans, and New York, French, 1972.
Countdown, in *We Who Are about to...*, later called *Mixed Doubles* (produced London, 1969).   London, Methuen, 1970.

Ernie's Incredible Illucinations (produced London, 1971).   Published in *Playbill One*, edited by Alan Durband, London, Hutchinson, 1969.

The Story So Far (also director: produced Scarborough, 1970).

Time and Time Again (also director: produced Scarborough, 1971; London, 1972). London and New York, French, 1973.

Absurd Person Singular (also director: produced Scarborough, 1972; London, 1973; New York, 1974).   London and New York, French, 1974.

Mother Figure, in *Mixed Blessings* (produced Horsham, Sussex, 1973).

The Norman Conquests: Table Manners, Living Together, Round and Round the Garden (also director: produced Scarborough, 1973; London, 1974; New York, 1975). London, Chatto and Windus, and New York, French 1975.

Absent Friends (also director: produced Scarborough, 1974; London, 1975).   London, French, 1975.

Confusions: Mother Figure, Drinking Companion, Between Mouthfuls, Gosforth's Fête, A Talk in the Park (also director: produced Scarborough, 1974; London, 1976).

Jeeves, music by Andrew Lloyd Webber, adaptation of works by P. G. Wodehouse (produced London, 1975).

Bedroom Farce (also director: produced Scarborough, 1975; London, 1976). Included in *Three Plays*, 1977.

Just Between Ourselves (also director: produced Scarborough, 1976).

Three Plays (includes *Absurd Person Singular, Absent Friends, Bedroom Farce*). London, Chatto and Windus, 1977.

Television Plays: *Service Not Included*, 1974; *Theatre*, 1976.

Critical Studies: *Theatre in the Round* by Stephen Joseph, London, Barrie and Rockliff, 1967; *The Second Wave* by John Russell Taylor, London, Methuen, 1971.

Theatrical Activities:

Director: **Plays** – Victoria Theatre, Stoke on Trent: *The Caretaker* by Harold Pinter, *Xmas v Mastermind* (co-director, with Peter Cheeseman), *The Referees, The Mating Season,* and *The Rainbow Machine* by Alan Plater, *Standing Room Only, Mr. Whatnot, Miss Julie* by Strindberg, and *The Glass Menagerie* by Tennessee Williams, 1962–64; The Library Theatre, Scarborough: many of his own plays, and *Wife Swapping – Italian Style* by Leon Katz and *The Shy Gasman* by Leonard Barras, 1970, *Carmilla* by David Campton, *Uncle Vanya* by Chekhov, and *Tom, Dick, and Harry* by Peter Blythe, 1972; *Away from It All* by Peter King, *The Breadwinner* by Somerset Maugham, *But Fred Freud Is Dead* by Peter Terson, and *Frost at Midnight* by André Obey, 1974; *Angels in Love* by Hugh Mills and *An Englishman's Home* by Stephen Mallatratt, 1975.   **Radio** – more than 100 productions, Leeds, 1964–70.

Actor: **Plays** – roles with Stephen Joseph's touring company; The Cook in *Little Brother, Little Sister* by David Campton, Newcastle under Lyme, 1961; Victoria Theatre, Stoke on Trent: Fred in *The Birds and the Wellwishers* and Robert in *An Awkward Number* by William Norfolk, Aston in *The Caretaker*, James in *The Collection*, and Ben in *The Dumb Waiter* by Harold Pinter, title role in *O'Flaherty, V.C.* by G. B. Shaw, Roderick Usher in *Usher* by David Campton, Bill Starbuck in *The Rainmaker* by N. Richard Nash, The Crimson Gollywog in *Xmas v Mastermind*, The Count in *The Rehearsal* by Anouilh, Vladimir in *Waiting for Godot* by Beckett, Thomas More in *A Man for All Seasons* by Robert Bolt, Jordan in *The Rainbow Machine* and Anderson in *Ted's Cathedral* by Alan Plater, Jerry Ryan in *Two for the Seesaw* by William Gibson, Mr. Manningham in *Gaslight* by Patrick Hamilton, The Interrogator in *The Prisoner* by Bridget Boland, and A Jew and Martin del Bosco in *The Jew of Malta* by Marlowe, 1962–64.

*   *   *

Alan Ayckbourn is an unusual figure amongst modern British dramatists in that his sole aim is to make us laugh. His plays contain no messages, offer no profound vision of the universe, tell us nothing about how to live our lives. Instead they are (for the most part) extremely ingenious farces based on a dazzling theatrical legerdemain. Such plays are often under-rated in their time; but they have a habit of getting a posthumous revenge by outlasting more serious contemporary work.

Mr. Ayckbourn, like so many of his contemporaries, did his basic theatrical training as an actor in provincial rep; and it was here that he obviously acquired his shrewd instinct for what would work in front of an audience. For instance his first main success as a writer, *Standing Room Only* (1961) presents us with an easily-foreseeable future in which London has become one great traffic-jam with people taking up permanent residence in marooned cars and buses. It's a good joke; and Mr. Ayckbourn just about manages to sustain it by contrasting people's pretence at suburban gentility with the outlandishness of the situation. But the most significant thing is that, whereas other writers might have used the basic idea to comment on the gradual fouling-up of our cities, Mr. Ayckbourn is solely interested in its comic possibilities.

Mr. Whatnot was again designed simply to make us laugh: heavily influenced by Tati and the Marx Brothers, it was a three-quarters mimed farcical comedy about a piano-tuner let loose in a stately home. But Ayckbourn's first West End success came with *Relatively Speaking* (1967) which, like all good farce, took an outlandish premise and then developed it with vertiginous skill. The premise was that an amiable young man could turn up at the country home of his girl-friend's former lover innocently believing it to be the residence of her parents. Every single misunderstanding sprang from that one idea and the enjoyment lay partly in seeing whether Mr. Ayckbourn could indefinitely sustain the situation. That he did so was due to his skill in making the hero totally unconscious of the mystification his presence caused, and in making the upper middle-class couple he landed on too polite or embarrassed to ask point blank who he was.

Even if Mr. Ayckbourn's plays depend heavily on their Chinese-box ingenuity, they are also rooted in a fairly precise observation of the English class structure. In *Relatively Speaking* the world of well-bred country life, with Sunday lunch on the patio and the morning devoted to hedge clipping, is very neatly conveyed. And in *How the Other Half Loves* Mr. Ayckbourn contrasts an upper middle-class couple (all bathroom stationery and sophisticated door-chimes) with a struggling young lower middle-class pair (who read *The Guardian* and have nappies all over the floor).

But although the class joke underpins the action, it is the sheer mechanical ingenuity that makes the play memorable. Mr. Ayckbourn's brilliant basic joke is not merely to put the two contrasted households on the same stage, but actually to superimpose one living-room on the other and to constantly intertwine the family conversations. And in one particular scene this reaches the heights of inspired lunacy: two dinner-parties are held simultaneously round the same table with an unfortunate couple, socially out of their depth, acting as guests at each. For sheer expertise, it's a scene hard to match outside *The Servant of Two Masters* where one man acts as waiter for two different dinner-parties.

Having established himself as an outstanding farce-writer, Mr. Ayckbourn in *Time and Time Again* slightly shifted his ground. Although the play bristles with farcical misunderstandings, Mr. Ayckbourn's chief interest seems to be in discovering how far you can go with a totally passive and inert hero. Leonard, the central character, is an ex-English teacher who chooses to work as a municipal gardener and who sees himself as one of life's sufferers rather than doers; yet although he is totally passive he still manages to become an agent of chaos.

The play has some beautifully funny scenes: one in particular shows the hero trying to field on the boundary in a cricket match while carrying on a passionate love scene with his girl-friend. And again he has caught accurately a particular suburban milieu where there are gnomes and a rockpool in the garden and battenburg for tea. But the play is less explosively funny than Mr. Ayckbourn's earlier successes and the reason, one suspects, is that he has concentrated more on the creation of character than on the manufacture of incident. To an Englishman, it would seem, pure farce can never be a self-sufficient genre: he must aim for the allegedly higher target of comedy. But one can only hope that Mr. Ayckbourn will stick in future to what he does best (sustaining ingenious situations, providing dazzling comic set-pieces, pin-pointing characters through their life-style) and will continue in his healthy resolve to do no more than make us laugh till it genuinely hurts.

—Michael Billington

BAGNOLD, Enid.   British.   Born in Rochester, Kent, 27 October 1889. Educated at Prior's Field, Godalming, and in Marburg, Lausanne, and Paris; studied painting with Walter Sickert. Widow of Sir Roderick Jones, for 25 years Chairman of Reuters; has four children. Served as a driver with the F.A.N.Y.'s in the French Army during World War I. Recipient: Arts Theatre Prize, 1951; American Academy of Arts and Letters Award of Merit, 1956. C.B.E. (Commander, Order of the British Empire), 1976. Agent: Harold Freedman, Brandt and Brandt, 101 Park Avenue, New York, New York 10017. Address: North End House, Rottingdean, Brighton, Sussex BN2 7HA, England.

PUBLICATIONS

Plays

> *Lottie Dundass* (produced Santa Barbara, California, 1942; London, 1943).   London, Heinemann, 1943; included in *Two Plays*, 1951.
> *National Velvet*, adaptation of her own novel (produced London, 1945).   New York, Dramatists Play Service, 1961.
> *Poor Judas* (produced London, 1951).   Included in *Two Plays*, 1951.
> *Two Plays* (includes *Lottie Dundass* and *Poor Judas*).   London, Heinemann, and New York, Doubleday, 1951.
> *Gertie* (produced New York, 1952; as *Little Idiot*, produced London, 1953).
> *The Chalk Garden* (produced New York, 1955; London, 1956).   New York, Random House, and London, Heinemann, 1956.
> *The Last Joke* (produced London, 1960).   Included in *Four Plays*, 1970.
> *The Chinese Prime Minister* (produced New York, 1964; London, 1965).   New York, Random House, and London, French, 1964.
> *Call Me Jacky* (produced Oxford, 1967).   Included in *Four Plays*, 1970; (revised version, as *A Matter of Gravity*, produced Washington, D.C., 1975; New York, 1976).
> *Four Plays* (includes *The Chalk Garden, The Last Joke, The Chinese Prime Minister, Call Me Jacky*).   London, Heinemann, 1970; Boston, Little Brown, 1971.

Novels

> *The Happy Foreigner*.   London, Heinemann, and New York, Century, 1920.
> *Serena Blandish; or, The Difficulty of Getting Married* (as A Lady of Quality).   London, Heinemann, 1924; New York, Doran, 1925; as Enid Bagnold, New York, Morrow, 1946.

National Velvet.   London, Heinemann, and New York, Morrow, 1935.

The Squire.   London, Heinemann, 1938; as *The Door of Life*, New York, Morrow, 1938.

The Loved and Envied.   London, Heinemann, and New York, Doubleday, 1951.

The Girl's Journey: Containing The Happy Foreigner and The Squire.   London, Heinemann, and New York, Doubleday, 1954.

Verse

The Sailing Ships and Other Poems.   London, Heinemann, 1918.

Other

A Diary Without Dates.   London, Heinemann, 1918; New York, Morrow, 1935.

Alice and Thomas and Jane (juvenile).   London, Heinemann, 1930; New York, Knopf, 1931.

Enid Bagnold's Autobiography: From 1889.   London, Heinemann, 1969; Boston, Little Brown, 1970.

Translator, *Alexander of Asia*, by Princess Marthe Bibesco.   London, Heinemann, 1935.

Enid Bagnold quotes her Foreword to *Serena Blandish*, 1946:

The Reader: This book of yours that you are now offering up again, when did you last read it?

The Author: I sent *Serena Blandish* to the publishers twenty-two years ago. On a day in November 1924 it came back to me, printed and bound. I handled it with rapture, with prayers for its success, with passionate self-pity that my father insisted on anonymity. I was too exhausted by having written it to read it.

The Reader: What happens when a book goes from its author? How soon, once more, do you receive pleasure from your work?

The Author: It left me as a wild animal leaves its mother, not again to be recognized: to be met, perhaps, as I meet it now, muzzle to stranger-muzzle, all thread of kinship snapped. For me, after that, it never freshened. The wind never blew in it. The angel never shouted in the landscape. I never read it — well I never read it for twenty-two years — not till this morning.

The Reader: Then what do you think of your work, Author?

The Author: That perhaps is a little private. But I reflect on it and how, by writing, one exorcises the devil or the angel in a stretch of life, till, the winged creature risen, the landscape which before had shaken with the bustle of his escape, is suddenly fixed, as with gum, unrevisitable. In the years preceding every book there's a hunt and a capture. But when the hunt is over the stirrup-cup is for the public. The Author cannot enjoy what he has caught. He must be off. He must shoot again. And when he shoots no more then he is old.

The Reader: But — some success — when he is old? Can't he sit back on that?

The Author: Success, to give pleasure, must be on the move. No, there's no laurel to wear that he notices is any different from his hat. And writing is like love: all that is past is ashes: and the thread snaps on every book that is done.

The Reader: The pleasure then is in the writing?

The Author (a little warm): Not at all! Writing is a condition of grinding anxiety. It is an operation in which the footwork, the balance, the knowledge of sun and shade, the alteration of slush and crust, the selection of surface at high speed is a matter of exquisite fineness. Heavens − a pleasure! When you are without judgement, and hallucinations look like the truth! When experience (which trails behind) and imagination (which runs in front) will only combine by a miracle! When the whole thing is an ambidexterity of memory and creation − of the front and back of the brain − a lethargy of inward dipping and a tiptoe of poise while the lasso is whirling for the words! (More heated.) It is a gamble, a toss-up, an unsure benevolence of God! No! It can't be called pleasure!

The Reader: One last obvious question. Why then do you write?

The Author (with a sigh): For the sake of a split second when I feel myself immortal...

The Reader: Yes? − And...

The Author: ...and just before the impact with my want of skill.

Miss Bagnold quotes Walter Kerr's review (New York *Herald-Tribune*, 3 January 1964) of *The Chinese Prime Minister*:

I find myself touched by *The Chinese Prime Minister*....I am touched, I think, because I have seen one whole play in which there is not a single careless line.

There are careless scenes, oh, yes. Quite a large portion of the middle act is taken up with a crossfire of family quarrelling that has as its purpose the badgering of Miss Leighton until Miss Leighton is pushed into a vital, and mistaken, decision. The sequence is ratchety enough to badger you, too, and to make you wonder whether the silken strands of the evening can be gathered into one steady hand again. But even here "carelessness" is not quite the right word. For playwright Enid Bagnold never does anything merely because she cannot think of anything better to do. Whatever she does, she does on impulse, inspiration, with a jump and with a dagger in her hand, eyes gleaming. The gleam, the mad glint of her inspiration, may indeed flash out of the untidiest of corners. But in itself it is marvelously pure.

The obvious word for a lofty, detached, unpredictably witty play of this sort is "civilized." But I think we should do Miss Bagnold the justice of trying to avoid obvious words. *The Chinese Prime Minister* might more nearly, more properly be called humanely barbaric.

Its comedy is barbaric in the sense that, for all the elegance of elbow-length blue gloves and for all the urbanity of precise syntax sounded against deep chocolate drapes, the minds of the people who make the comedy are essentially brutal minds, minds capable of caring for themselves.... All of the contestants who speak Miss Bagnold's brisk, knobby, out-of-nowhere lines somehow or other become admirable. For the lines are thoughts, not echoes, not borrowings. And they are so often so very funny because they come not from the stage or from remembered literature but from a head that has no patience with twilight cant.

Miss Bagnold does not construct a play that all audiences will settle to easily. That is clear enough.... It shimmers on the stage − and wavers there, too − like a vast, insubstantial spider's web, strung with bits of real rain. It is not conventional, and it is not altogether secure. But it is written. And what a blesing that is.

* * *

Enid Bagnold wrote four plays before *The Chalk Garden*, her first and only big success. They are *Lottie Dundass*, *National Velvet*, *Poor Judas* and *Gertie*; but in her autobiography Miss Bagnold speaks of *Lottie Dundass* as her first play and *Gertie* as her second, and as usual her discrimination is absolute. *National Velvet* is an adaptation of her successful novel; it was filmed (with the young Elizabeth Taylor) and gave birth to soap-opera spin-offs on radio and television, but the novel is the version to remember. *Poor Judas*, a play about a writer unable to come to terms with his own lack of talent, won a prize in 1951 but has not made a mark in the current repertory. *Lottie Dundass*, an anecdotal piece, had a five-month run during the War with Sybil Thorndike and Ann Todd in the cast. *Gertie*, a comedy, opened in New York on a Wednesday and came off the following Saturday; in England it was retitled *Little Idiot* but failed. To compensate for the disappointment, Miss Bagnold concentrated on *The Chalk Garden*, which she worked on for the next two years. It initiated the mandarin style that characterizes her last four plays, of which only *The Chalk Garden* has had a success befitting its merit.

The most immediately perceptible quality of *The Chalk Garden* is a rich suggestion of artificiality in the dialogue – "speech of an exquisite candour," Kenneth Tynan has called it, "building ornamental bridges of metaphor, tiptoeing across frail causeways of simile, and vaulting over gorges impassable to the rational soul." The whole play is in fact a metaphor, comparing the development of a child starved of mother-love with the development of plants starved of compost. Miss Bagnold claims to have been unaware of this parallel when she was writing the play, but it must have been lurking near the surface of her mind, for it is all-pervasive; the garden, never actually seen, is almost as much a character as the old retainer lying upstairs in whose amateur advice Mrs. St. Maugham, the aristocratic widow at the centre of the play, has placed her mistaken trust for so long.

There is something larger than life about all the people in the play; they are not caricatured in the manner of Rowlandson but elegantly exaggerated in the manner of El Greco. Miss Bagnold has lived most of her life among exceptional people and she can draw an exceptional character with confidence and consistency, though her success lies mostly in those who can be described, in the broadest possible sense, as aristocratic. Her themes are aristocratic too, themes like breeding and courage and resolution. Oddly enough, though, *The Last Joke*, in which the principal characters are Balkan princes drawn from life, is the least aristocratic of the four late plays. Perhaps this is due to the fact that these princes, Ferdinand Cavanati and his brother Hugo, are modelled on somewhat eccentric originals whom Miss Bagnold has revealed as Prince Antoine Bibesco and his brother Emmanuel. Reproducing a live eccentric is a harder task than creating one; and the provision of a plot in *The Last Joke* that seems almost as capricious as its executants does nothing to mend matters.

Nevertheless there is something to be admired in this play. The conception of the philosopher who has worked out so much about God that he is determined to hasten their meeting is potentially a brave one. It is a pity that more is not done with it than its incorporation into a melodramatic story about the stealing of a picture; or that the story, if this is to be the one, is not more straightforwardly told. But Miss Bagnold has had to include too much of real life in it, and the amalgam of life and romance has not worked out well. The play got poor notices when it opened in London and had only a short run. Its successor was in every way better; Miss Bagnold herself rates *The Chinese Prime Minister* more highly than *The Chalk Garden*. But this too, for reasons not entirely attributable to the qualities of the script, had only a modest success.

The Chinese Prime Minister is a play about the pleasures of old age (and to show that these are not available only to the wealthy the author has complemented her sixty-nine-year-old protagonist with a 100-year-old butler who dies twice during the play and finds the experience not at all unpleasant). "She" – the only name given to the heroine – is an actress on the verge of retiring who is suddenly reunited with the husband who left her many years before. She has a vision of retirement with a notional Chinese Prime Minister whose term of office is done, who writes poems to outlive his achievements, who goes up into the mountains with no baggage but a birdcage.... Her husband, having made a fortune in oil that has kept him permanently resident in Arabia, has other ideas; he thinks of summoning up anew all the joys of their youth. But oil calls him back to Arabia, and She is happily resigned to being her own Chinese Prime Minister and living her remaining years in the peaceful style she has mapped out for them.

There is a fine serenity about the play that is marred only by what seems to be Miss Bagnold's uncertainty about what to do with her batch of subsidiary characters – the heroine's children and their friends of their own generation, who never quite get integrated into the main scheme. In New York, where She was played by Margaret Leighton, it was a success; in London, where She was played by Edith Evans, the actress for whom it was written, it took on a sentimental patina foreign to the writing, and was not. Miss Bagnold is given to blaming producers for the artistic failures of her plays when they happen; of the four last plays *The Chalk Garden* is the only one (rightly or wrongly) that has acquired a stable reputation. Her rating of *The Chinese Prime Minister* as a better play than this is probably wrong; *The Chalk Garden* had the advantage of formidable discussions over a long period with Irene Mayer Selznick, a producer in whom Miss Bagnold had faith, and has emerged a dramatic jewel. But *The Chinese Prime Minister* has not deserved the neglect into which it has fallen.

Miss Bagnold's latest piece, *Call Me Jacky*, won its director a grudging "did his best" from the author, followed by a complaint that inadequate rehearsal time was given to it. Perhaps two years with Irene Selznick might have made something of it; but as played, and as published, the subtleties the author calls for seem to exist principally in her mind. Once more we have the rich old lady at the centre of the piece, playing on the destinies of the younger generation, represented by a cook extracted from a lunatic asylum (a reminiscence of *The Chalk Garden*), the lady's grandson, an Oxford student, and four friends of his, a male homosexual pair and a female. It seems to have been written to demonstrate how liberal this rich old lady (in which, as usual, a certain autobiographical element is unmistakable) can be when confronted with the problems that afflict the young.

Thus, she is undisturbed by the homosexual liaisons, or by her grandson's marriage to a black girl and siring of a black baby, or by communist accusations of depriving the poor of the use of her grounds to live in. But the theme appears to be that such open-mindedness is the result of the basically aristocratic nature of her character; and when, in the highly improbable conclusion, she asks to be admitted to the paying wing of the home where her cook comes from, and the cook asks her pathetically if she might then be called by her Christian name, she replies coldly "I'll be buggered if I do."

The combination of this attitude and this choice of words to express it in is characteristic of the generally muddled feeling of the play. The author claims that the piece works on two levels, but it is more truthful to say that it exists on two levels and works on neither of them, neither the surface frivolity nor the deeper implications. Miss Bagnold is accustomed to take years over the writing of her plays; that *Call Me Jacky* doesn't work suggests that the two years she worked on it and the time taken in production were neither of them enough, for the theme, a 20th-century version of *noblesse oblige*, is a characteristic one, worth developing, capable of development. In spite of Gladys Cooper's much-quoted judgement during the rehearsals for *The Chalk Garden*, Enid Bagnold is incapable of writing nonsense.

—B. A. Young

BALDWIN, James (Arthur).   American.   Born in New York City, 2 August 1924. Educated at P.S. 139, Harlem, and DeWitt Clinton High School, Bronx, New York. Lived in Paris, 1948–56. Member, Actors Studio, New York, National Advisory Board of CORE (Congress on Racial Equality), and the National Committee for a Sane Nuclear Policy. Recipient: Saxton Fellowship, 1945; Rosenwald Fellowship, 1948; Guggenheim Fellowship, 1954; *Partisan Review* Fellowship, 1956; National Institute of Arts and Letters grant, 1956; Ford Fellowship, 1958; National Conference of Christians and Jews Brotherhood Award, 1962; George Polk Award, 1963; Foreign Drama Critics Award, 1964. D.Litt.: University of British Columbia, Vancouver, 1964. Member, National Institute of Arts and Letters, 1964. Agent: Tria G. B. French, 118 rue la Boetie, Paris 75008, France. Address: 137 West 71st Street, New York, New York 10023, U.S.A.

PUBLICATIONS

Plays

The Amen Corner (produced Washington, D.C., 1955; New York, Edinburgh, and London, 1965).   New York, Dial Press, 1965.
Blues for Mr. Charlie (produced New York, 1964; London, 1965).   New York, Dial Press, 1964; London, Joseph, 1965.
One Day, When I Was Lost: A Scenario Based on "The Autobiography of Malcolm X." New York, Dial Press, and London, Joseph, 1972.
A Deed from the King of Spain (produced New York, 1974).

Screenplay: *The Inheritance*, 1973.

Novels

Go Tell It on the Mountain.   New York, Knopf, 1953; London, Joseph, 1954.
Giovanni's Room.   New York, Dial Press, 1956; London, Joseph, 1957.
Another Country.   New York, Dial Press, 1962; London, Joseph, 1963.
Tell Me How Long the Train's Been Gone.   New York, Dial Press, and London, Joseph, 1968.
If Beale Street Could Talk.   New York, Dial Press, and London, Joseph, 1974.

Short Stories

Going to Meet the Man.   New York, Dial Press, and London, Joseph, 1965.

Other

Notes of a Native Son.   Boston, Beacon Press, 1955; London, Mayflower, 1958.
Nobody Knows My Name: More Notes of a Native Son.   New York, Dial Press, 1961; London, Joseph, 1964.
The Fire Next Time.   New York, Dial Press, and London, Joseph, 1963.
Nothing Personal, with Richard Avedon.   New York, Atheneum, and London, Penguin, 1964.
A Rap on Race, with Margaret Mead.   Philadelphia, Lippincott, and London, Joseph, 1971.
No Name in the Street.   New York, Dial Press, and London, Joseph, 1971.
A Dialogue: James Baldwin and Nikki Giovanni.   Philadelphia, Lippincott, 1973; London, Joseph, 1975.
Little Man, Little Man (juvenile).   London, Joseph, 1976.
The Devil Finds Work: An Essay.   New York, Dial Press, and London, Joseph, 1976.

Bibliographies: "James Baldwin: A Checklist, 1947–1962" by Kathleen A. Kindt, and "James Baldwin: A Bibliography, 1947–1962" by Russell G. Fischer, both in *Bulletin of Bibliography* (Boston), January–April 1965; "James Baldwin: A Checklist, 1963–67" by Fred L. Standley, in *Bulletin of Bibliography* (Boston), May–August 1968.

Theatrical Activities:

Director: **Film** – *The Inheritance*, 1973.

*   *   *

One of the best known contemporary authors in the United States, James Baldwin is least known as a dramatist. He was admired in the 1950's for the style and thought of his novels, the semi-autobiographical *Go Tell It on the Mountain* and *Giovanni's Room*, and for his personal and literary essays, first published in "little" avant-garde magazines, then collected as *Notes of a Native Son*. During the early 1960's, as increased attention was directed to Afro-American quests for civil rights corresponding to those of other citizens of the United States, James Baldwin became recognized as a leading spokesman for black Americans. In a novel (*Another Country*) and two collections of essays (*Nobody Knows My Name* and *The Fire Next Time*), Baldwin seemed to articulate eloquently and persuasively the bitterness, the alienation, and the despair of Afro-Americans. Some critics felt that Baldwin's statements reached a pinnacle in his first widely known drama, *Blues for Mr. Charlie*. With an eye towards John Osborne and other British dramatists, some critics argued that Baldwin was "America's angriest young man." Just as few critics have recognized Baldwin's interest in drama, so most have missed the continuous message of the one-time preacher. In drama, as in his other writing, Baldwin repeatedly preaches that people must love and understand other people if they wish to save the world from destruction.

Born and reared in New York City, Baldwin, the eldest of nine children, suffered in childhood from the oppression of the poverty of the Depression and the religious enthusiasm of a fanatically devout father. During his youth, he wavered between the church and literature. Undoubtedly influenced by his stepfather, at least seeking to please him, Baldwin became a teen-aged minister in a faith which viewed romance (in literature or in life) as a snare for the godly. In junior high school, however, Baldwin had been a member of the literary society advised by Countee Cullen, a famous Negro poet and novelist. The opposing forces, Baldwin has written, met in a climactic confrontation when an excessively long sermon from the minister of Baldwin's church threatened to prevent Baldwin's attendance at a play for which he had tickets. When the minister chose to make an example of the quietly departing Baldwin, Baldwin became convinced that he could not endure the rigors of the faith. From this point Baldwin embraced literature as a faith with an emphasis upon the creed of love for fellow man.

After graduation from DeWitt Clinton High School, Baldwin worked as a waiter while he tried to write a novel. With assistance from Richard Wright, the most famous Afro-American novelist of the time, he secured a Saxton award, which temporarily relieved his financial needs. Despite occasional publication in little magazines, however, Baldwin increasingly despaired of his position as a black man and writer in the white-oriented United States of America. In 1948, he left for France, where, during the ten years following, he established a limited reputation as a creative writer and literary critic (the latter based partly on his rejection of Richard Wright, his former benefactor, as a novelist who sacrificed art to a message of social protest) and persuaded himself that he discovered his identity.

As early as 1957 Baldwin had made a dramatic adaptation of his novel *Giovanni's Room*, the story of a white American who discovers and surrenders to his latent homosexuality. Baldwin's recognition as a dramatist did not come until the season of 1963–64 when *Blues for Mr. Charlie* became the controversial sensation of the New York stage while the quieter *The Amen Corner*, first produced at a Negro college in Washington, D.C., was undergoing professional production on the West Coast. In both plays he tried to infuse the vitality of life which he felt to be missing from American drama.

Written after Baldwin had taken his first trip to Mississippi, to participate in Civil Rights demonstrations, *Blues for Mr. Charlie* is based in part on two actual incidents. In one, a fourteen-year-old Negro youth from Chicago was tortured and killed while visiting his grandparents in Mississippi. The reason given by one killer was that the youth allegedly had flirted with a white woman. Although one murderer freely admitted the crime and a second did not deny it, both were acquitted by an all-white jury. In a second incident, a Negro was killed by a white man. The reason was rumored to be the fact that the Negro protested against the white man's using the Negro's wife as a concubine.

In *Blues for Mr. Charlie*, Baldwin focused on Richard Henry, a young Negro entertainer, who, after succumbing to dope, has returned bitter and frustrated to his Mississippi home. Within a short period of time, Henry becomes involved in an altercation with Lyle Britton, a white man known to have killed another black who objected to surrendering his wife to Britton's sexual exploitation. Britton kills Henry, is tried, and is acquitted.

Although some critics denounced the play as melodramatic and excessively bitter, Baldwin's major theme – his recurrent theme – is found in the tragedy of two secondary figures, who see the destruction of their hope for love between the races. One is a white journalist who, unlike his neighbors, has no prejudices against Negroes. Once, in fact, he loved a Negro and wanted to marry her. At the critical moment in the play, however, this white "liberal" betrays himself and his black friends because, although he knows that Britton is guilty, he cannot force himself to testify that Lyle's wife – a Southern white woman – is lying. The second tragic figure is the Reverend Meridian Henry. All of his adult life, Henry has worked to improve the condition of his people by peaceful means. Even after his son's murder, he continues to urge black youths to limit themselves to non-violent protests in the manner of Mahatma Gandhi and Martin Luther King, Jr. After the acquittal of his son's murderer, however, the Christian minister decides that, in the future, he and other blacks need to carry their guns even to church to protect themselves from the savages in their community.

The Amen Corner is the story of a female minister who is forced to realize that love and compassion for human beings are more important than a fanatically rigid enunciation of God's law. After deserting her husband because he was inadequate to her needs after the death of their second child, Sister Margaret has become a minister who insists that members of her congregation and her son dedicate themselves to continuous sanctity. The return of her husband, who is dying, precipitates conflict by inspiring rebellion in her son and her congregation. By the end of the play, Margaret has been compelled to remember how human and loving she had been before the ministry. Now that she has regained compassion for human frailty, she is truly prepared for the first time to lead a congregation. But it is too late. Her son leaves her, her husband dies, and she can find no words to maintain her control over the faction of the congregation which has decided to replace her.

—Darwin T. Turner

BARAKA, Imamu Amiri.   See **JONES, LeRoi.**

BARKER, Howard.   British.   Born in London, 28 June 1946. Educated at Battersea Grammar School, London, 1958–64; Sussex University, Brighton, 1964–68, M.A. in history 1968. Married Sandra Law in 1972. Resident Dramatist, Open Space Theatre, London, 1974–75. Recipient: Arts Council bursary, 1971. Agent: Clive Goodwin Associates, 79 Cromwell Road, London S.W.7. Address: 23 Park Street, Brighton, Sussex, England.

PUBLICATIONS

Plays

    Cheek (produced London, 1970).   Published in *New Short Plays 3*, London, Eyre Methuen, 1972.
    No One Was Saved (produced London, 1971).
    Edward: The Final Days (produced London, 1971).
    Faceache (produced London, 1971).
    Alpha Alpha (produced London, 1972).
    Private Parts (produced Edinburgh, 1972).
    Skipper, and My Sister and I (produced London, 1973).
    Rule Britannia (produced London, 1973).
    Bang (produced London, 1973).
    Claw (produced London, 1975). Included in *Stripwell*, 1976.
    Stripwell (produced London, 1975). With *Claw*, London, John Calder, 1976.
    Wax (produced Edinburgh and London, 1976).

    Screenplays: *Made*, 1972; *Rape of Tamar*, 1973; *Aces High*, 1975.

    Radio Plays: *One Afternoon on the North Face of the 63rd Level of the Pyramid of Cheops the Great*, 1970; *Henry V*, 1971; *Herman, with Millie and Mick*, 1972.

    Television Plays: *Cows*, 1972; *The Chauffeur and the Lady*, 1972; *Mutinies*, 1974.

Howard Barker comments:

    The stage is the last remaining arena for the free assault of our society. It is the sump to which our poisons and our malices, our despairs and terrors, drain. It is not a place for reconciliation or relief. It is not a dark place rumbling with laughter or a padded private place for the touching of hands, but a granite crucible in which conflict and collision strike dangerous, disconcerting sparks. It is a world on a high gas. To shock the audience is not a worthwhile end. The theatre as hand-grenade is a sterile notion: it alienates, but does not penetrate; it warms the cockles of the dramtist's heart but creates a barrier to communication. Shock is a priceless moment but not the whole packet. The dramatist who wants to show the world in his form cannot become the victim of his own techniques or the moment of communication is lost. Nothing is unacceptable on the stage except the breakdown of communication. Nothing is incredible or unlikely. It is the world which is incredible and unlikely, and it is the business of the theatre to show the agony we experience in failing to come to terms with that. Because its form is unrestricted, because it has survived the market-slavery of the capitalist epoch, the stage is the last playground of the emotions, the last public place for a critical but humane judgement of a monstrous speculative society.
    To write for the theatre is to begin a process of definition of the world. When the definition has been reached, the dramatist stops. Sometimes, when the definition is acclaimed, the dramatist stops, or becomes a provider of relief, a reconciler of opposites. Every moment of reconciliation between the audience and its society is a misuse of the theatre, and a betrayal of its purpose.

*   *   *

    "We have to draw a line between what we feel ... here (He touches his heart) – our first impulse – and what is practical. (Pause) Don't we?"

The criminal, after a year in prison has broken into the judge's house with a sawn-off shotgun. The frightened judge tries to argue about the importance of compromise in a reasonable society and the question seems likely to win him his survival. After an almost intolerable pause, the thug wanders out through the French windows, only to return, shotgun levelled at the guardian of middle-class morality. "No," he yells, and shoots.

The question and the answer are both central not only to *Stripwell* but to Howard Barker's earlier work. Much of it focuses on the tug of war between individual libido and social super-ego. *Cheek*, his first play to be produced, justifies its title and sets up its tensions by taking its tone from the thrusting cockiness of the central character – outrageous by the standards of conventional behaviour, natural by the standards of a healthy boy's sexual appetite.

The next play was written in reaction against John Lennon's "Eleanor Rigby," which Barker regarded as a commercially successful exploitation of working-class loneliness. *No One Was Saved* is about an unmarried mother. It attracted the attention of director John Mackenzie and producer Joseph Janni, who filmed it, letting Barker write his own screenplay. But the Open Space production of *Alpha Alpha* did more to establish his reputation. It introduced Bernadette Devlin and a perverted peer into a story of two identical twins (criminals based on the Kray brothers) and their indulgent Jewish mother.

There has been nothing steady about Howard Barker's progress. Sometimes, as in *Edward: The Final Days*, he writes unimaginatively because his inventiveness has been clogged up with cheap indignation, cartoonish parody, and simplistic argument. But he has become a much better writer than he was. *Claw* is uneven and coarse-grained, but more sophisticated than any of his earlier plays in its treatment of the no-man's-land between private lust and public images. It was a good idea to make the central character a pimp, and an even better one to make him spectacled and virginal. The creation of Noel Biledew acted like a counterblast to the Jimmy Porter mythology: working-class boy makes middle-class girl, bold, sexy pleb versus timid, passive, effete female. Fed up with being victimised, Noel Biledew takes the name "Claw," but fails to learn from his mother's husband, a convert to communism, that he should save his anger for his class. His career as pimp begins badly. He offers a schoolgirl to a policeman, who buys her for a pound and then retrieves his money by punching Biledew in the stomach. After this he is very successful until he presses his luck too hard and a Cabinet Minister decides that he must be eliminated.

Much of the theatrical imagery is extremely vivid and much of the comedy is lively, especially in the second act, when the Cabinet Minister's ex-chorus-girl wife mischievously seduces the unattractive Biledew. The distended third act is the worst, resting – and nearly going to sleep – on the premise that the Establishment can survive only by employing ex-hangmen and ex-terrorists to staff a "mental hospital" where they rub out social misfits who could discredit the governing elite.

Stripwell has annoyed Marxist critics by failing to propose social remedies, but it is a much better play than *Claw*, less didactic, less dependent on stereotypes, better constructed. It is also more consistently entertaining because the comedy is more organic. Characteristically, Barker uses a criminal as an incarnation of the integrity that the judge lacks, and it is wise to keep the thug offstage throughout the central action, which occurs during the twelve months when he is safely in prison. If the writing is less heavy-handed than in *Claw*, it is partly because Howard Barker is now prepared to explore his ambivalence towards the main characters, though none of them is particularly likable. The old survivor of the first Labour government has no warmth or idealism left in him, Stripwell's wife is tiresomely fixated on her cynical son, the gogo dancer is loyal only to her own greed for experience and even Stripwell forfeits our sympathy when he informs the police that his son is smuggling drugs in elephants' vaginas.

—Ronald Hayman

BARNES, Djuna. American. Born in Cornwall-on-Hudson, New York, 12 June 1892. Educated privately, and at the Pratt Institute and the Art Students' League, New York. Journalist and Illustrator, 1913–31. Trustee, since 1961, Dag Hammarskjöld Foundation. Recipient: Merrill and Rothko grants. Member, National Institute of Arts and Letters. Address: 5 Patchin Place, New York, New York 10011, U.S.A.

PUBLICATIONS

Plays

Three from the Earth (produced New York, 1919). Included in *A Book*, 1923.
Kurzy of the Sea (produced New York, 1919).
An Irish Triangle (produced New York, 1919). Published in *Playboy* (New York), 1921.
To the Dogs, in *A Book*, 1923.
The Dove (produced New York, 1926). Included in *A Book*, 1923.
She Tells Her Daughter, in *Smart Set* (New York), 1923.
The Antiphon (produced Stockholm, 1961). London, Faber, and New York, Farrar Straus, 1958.

Novels

Ryder. New York, Liveright, 1928.
Nightwood. London, Faber, 1936; New York, Harcourt Brace, 1937.

Short Stories

The Book of Repulsive Women. New York, Bruno Chapbooks, 1915.
A Book (includes verse and plays). New York, Boni and Liveright, 1923; augmented edition, as *A Night among the Horses*, 1929; shortened version, stories only, as *Spillway*, London, Faber, 1962; New York, Harper, 1972.
Vagaries Malicieux: Two Stories. New York, Frank Hallman, 1975.

Other

Ladies Almanack: Showing Their Signs and Their Tides; Their Moon and Their Changes; The Seasons as It Is with Them; Their Eclipses and Equinoxes; As Well as a Full Record of Diurnal and Nocturnal Distempers Written and Illustrated by a Lady of Fashion. Paris, privately printed, 1928; New York, Harper, 1972.
Selected Works. New York, Farrar Straus, 1962.

Bibliography: *Djuna Barnes: A Bibliography* by Douglas Messerli, New York, David Lewis, 1976.

Manuscript Collection: University of Maryland, College Park.

Theatrical Activities:

Actress: **Plays** – in *Power of Darkness* by Tolstoy, New York, 1920; in *The Tidings Brought to Mary* by Paul Claudel, New York, 1922.

*   *   *

Best known as the author of the novel *Nightwood*, Djuna Barnes turned to drama early and late in her career. Three one-act plays were performed by the Provincetown Players and three published in *A Book*. In 1958 she published *The Antiphon*, a play that is Jacobean in feeling and language.

Two of her three one-act plays use that stock character, a Woman with a Past. In *Three from the Earth* such a woman is confronted by three brothers who ask for the return of their father's letters to her. The curtain falls on the revelation that the youngest brother is the woman's son. In *To the Dogs* such a woman denies love to the neighbor who vaults through her window. Cowed, the neighbor retreats, but the play is ambiguous as to which of the two is going "to the dogs." *The Dove* focuses on a young girl living with two old maid sisters who relish their collection of knives, guns, and romantic fantasies. The young girl taunts each of the old maids to use a weapon, but she alone shoots a gun – at a painting of prostitutes. None of these plays can be taken seriously, but *The Antiphon* is an astonishing if anachronistic achievement.

The title *The Antiphon* indicates its style; one verse speech seems to call forth its verse reply, in poetic rather than dramatic structure. The language is stiff and archaic on the lips of its twentieth-century characters. Set in 1939, on the eve of World War II, the play reveals sexual sin and a hint of expiation, as in Jacobean drama. To seventeenth-century Burley Hall in England come Miranda and her coachman companion from Paris. Her mother Augusta and her two merchant brothers have been summoned from America by a third and absent brother, Jeremy.

Act I reveals that Augusta has betrayed her aristocratic Burley lineage, marrying an American Mormon, Titus Higby Hobbs of Salem, by whom she has had four children. Titus has tortured his wife, brutalized his sons, offered his daughter Miranda for rape by a middle-aged Cockney. Though he has been dead some years, his memory is stronger in Burley Hall than that of the nobles who owned it. And his immortality is the heritage of his two merchant sons, who plan to murder their mother. Daughter Miranda has a checkered past as actress, writer, and woman of the world, and there are hints that she is having an affair with her coachman, Jack Blow. Only Augusta's brother Jonathan, who never left Burley Hall, is untainted by the life of Titus Higby Hobbs.

Though diction and verse of *The Antiphon* are Jacobean, the three-act structure has the tidiness of a well-made play. After the Act I exposition, Act II develops accusations and defence, climaxed when the merchant sons don masks of pig and ass in order to taunt Augusta and Miranda, mother and daughter. A grotesque masque is interrupted by the entrance of coachman Jack Blow with a doll's house, a minature of Hobbs' Ark, the family home in America, with its memories of Titus's seven mistresses, and the rape of the seventeen-year-old Miranda. Obliquely, the shared family past leads to the Act III confrontation between mother and daughter. Each woman recognizes herself in the other as they slowly mount the side staircase in an antiphon of accusation. At the top Augusta realizes that her sons have abandoned her in her ancestral home, but she refuses to accept the limitation of that home, and she drives her daughter down the stairs, accusing her of conspiracy. At the bottom of the staircase Augusta Burley Hobbs rings down a giant curfew bell, killing both women. Augusta's brother Jonathan and Miranda's erstwhile coachman, actually her brother Jeremy, gaze at the two dead women, and Jeremy muses: "But could I know/Which would be brought to child-bed of the other?" Through the rhythmed, imaged dialogue, the death of the women comes to symbolize the death of an aristocratic lineage, too easily seduced by the violence of a commoner.

—Ruby Cohn

BARNES, Peter.   British.   Born in London, 10 January 1931. Critic, *Films and Filming*, London, 1954; story editor, Warwick Films, 1956. Recipient: John Whiting Award, 1968; *Evening Standard* award, 1969. Agent: Margaret Ramsay Ltd., 14a Goodwin's Court, London WC2N 4LL. Address: 7 Archery Close, Connaught Street, London W.2, England.

PUBLICATIONS

Plays

> *The Time of the Barracudas* (produced San Francisco, 1963).
> *Sclerosis* (produced Edinburgh and London, 1965).
> *The Ruling Class: A Baroque Comedy* (produced Nottingham, 1968; London, 1969; Washington, D.C., 1971).   London, Heinemann, and New York, Grove Press, 1969.
> *Leonardo's Last Supper and Noonday Demons* (produced London, 1969).   London, Heinemann, 1970.
> *Lulu*, adaptation of plays by Frank Wedekind, translated by Charlotte Beck (also co-director: produced Nottingham and London, 1970).   London, Heinemann, 1971.
> *The Devil Is an Ass*, adaptation of the play by Ben Jonson (produced Nottingham, 1973).
> *The Bewitched* (produced London, 1974).   London, Heinemann, 1974.
> *The Frontiers of Farce*, adaption of plays *The Purging* by Georges Feydeau and *The Singers* by Frank Wedekind (also director: produced London, 1976).

Screenplays: *Violent Moment*, 1959; *The White Trap*, 1959; *Breakout*, 1959; *The Professionals*, 1960; *Off-Beat*, 1961; *Man with a Feather in His Hat*, 1961; *Ring of Spies* (*Ring of Treason*), 1964; *Not with My Wife You Don't*, 1966; *The Ruling Class*, 1972.

Critical Study: *Jenseits des Absurden* by Martin Esslin, Vienna, Europaverlag, 1973.

Theatrical Activities:

Director: **Plays** – *Lulu* (co-director, with Stuart Burge), Nottingham and London, 1970; *Frontiers of Farce*, London, 1976.

Peter Barnes quotes from his programme note for *The Ruling Class*, 1968:

The aim is to create, by means of soliloquy, rhetoric, formalized ritual, slapstick, songs and dances, a comic theatre of contrasting moods and opposites, where everything is simultaneously tragic and ridiculous. And we hope never to consent to the deadly servitude of naturalism or lose our hunger for true size, weight and texture.

*   *   *

Peter Barnes is the most viciously brilliant satirist to have emerged in British theatre since the war. He is also a superbly accomplished exponent of Gothic comedy and other surrealistic styles, which are always perfect expressions in his plays of their content. *The Ruling Class* is a profound and inventive attack on Toryism and the way it has blighted the life of Britain for centuries past, with an incandescent, vindictive and bloody-minded wit that sustains its comic course, just as funny as anything Shaw ever wrote with double the passion behind it.

The play revolves around the Gurney family, scions of the aristocratic landed gentry. The thirteenth Earl of Gurney accidentally kills himself while playing sexually perverse games with a hangman's rope. His son and heir, Jack, is mad; he believes he is God because every time he talks to Him he finds he is talking to himself. The surface plot is concerned with the efforts of the late earl's half-brother, Sir Charles, and Sir Charles' dim-witted son, Dinsdale (in line to be the next local Tory M.P.), to control the vast family fortune and prevent Jack from laying his hands on it. Sir Charles schemes to marry off his mistress to Jack, impregnate her himself and produce a male heir, after which Jack can safely be committed. But, under the ministrations of a German psychiatrist, Jack becomes "sane." He drops his assumption of divinity, murders Sir Charles' wife and makes a pro-hanging and flogging speech in the Lords which delights the Tory backwoodsmen. His psychosis, far from being cured, has merely been displaced to another part of his psychology, more socially acceptable to his upper-class colleagues and their allies. Apart from the various members of the Gurney family, there is one classic comic creation, Tucker, the family butler, an undercover card-carrying Communist, who symbolizes the deeply ambivalent attitudes of some English radicals to the class society they are supposedly committed to destroying.

The Ruling Class uses plot and incident unashamedly to make its points; indeed, it has the strongest story line in any major play I can think of in the last few years. It is consistently and hilariously funny, has a remorseless command of logic and, like all good satire, is informed by an absolute and uncompromising hatred for its subjects. Barnes is a great admirer of Ben Jonson, in particular the savagery and precision of his satire, and this seminal influence is very plain in *The Ruling Class*. The play makes clear the utter absurdity of a situation where a minute percentage of the population owns a huge proportion of its wealth, and the crippling distortions it imposes, not only on the people who are economically dependent, but also on people like the Gurneys, who go ga-ga because of the strains it imposes on them. In his preface to the published edition of the play, Harold Hobson is perfectly correct in stating that the play's original production was one of the four most important theatrical events in Britain since the war – the others being the productions of Beckett's *Waiting for Godot*, Osborne's *Look Back in Anger* and Pinter's *The Birthday Party*.

His two comedies, *Leonardo's Last Supper* and *Noonday Demons*, are masterly exercises in Gothic comedy, which show a brilliantly inventive and precise use of language. The first play shows the great Leonardo da Vinci, in a death-like trance, removed to a charnel-house as it is believed he is dead, while in fact he is undergoing a period of intense creative gestation. The vivid portrayal of the family who keep the charnel-house communicates imaginatively the seamy underside of the Renaissance, the dirt, the shit and the slime out of which geniuses like Leonardo evolved their ideas. At the play's climax, when the charnel-house family realize that Leonardo's greatness depends on the subjugation of people like themselves, they brutally murder him. The play's strong central image of decay is, again, an echo of Jonson. *Noonday Demons* is a scarcely less accomplished dramatic essay about two "saints" squabbling in a fourth-century Egyptian cave, showing the close relationship between religious fervour and crass egomania, just as *The Ruling Class* shows the link between unbridled political and economic power and insanity.

Sclerosis is an acute and savage demystification of the idea, accepted as conventional wisdom even by some political radicals, that the British colonial experience was somehow more humane and civilized in its effects than those of other European nations. About the Cypriots' struggle for freedom in the fifties, it juxtaposes, in a sharp, jagged style, waffling politicians, spouting vaguely liberal platitudes, in the House of Commons in 1954 and 1959, at the height of the EOKA freedom struggle and the decision to grant independence respectively, with the brutalities practised by the security forces against EOKA freedom fighters.

Barnes has also adapted Wedekind's "Lulu" plays, *Earth Spirit* and *Pandora's Box*, most concisely and powerfully into a single evening's entertainment. The plays essentially are about the real power of the sexual impulse, untrammelled by any moral inhibitions, and the cruel effects a lack of sexual freedom has on many different types of men and, ultimately, on Lulu herself (who is murdered by a sex maniac, Jack the Ripper). Lulu is one of the most memorable creations in dramatic literature in the last century; intensely earthy and human, she also symbolizes, for men anyway, the eternal fascination of women. Barnes has faithfully preserved this central core and, if anything, strengthened it by jettisoning some of the plays' dead wood.

In short, Barnes combines a savagery, precision and wit in his writing with a clarity about the basic political causes of the sickness in our modern society that make him a worthy follower of Jonson, and one of the most significant, as well as one of the most entertaining, British playwrights of the day.

—Jonathan Hammond

BECKETT, Samuel (Barclay).   Irish.   Born near Dublin, 13 April 1906. Educated at Portora Royal School, County Fermanagh; Trinity College, Dublin, B.A. in French and Italian 1927, M.A. 1931. Worked at the Irish Red Cross Hospital, St. Lô, France, 1945. Married Suzanne Dechevaux-Dumesnil in 1948. Lecturer in English, Ecole Normale Supérieure, Paris, 1928–30; Lecturer in French, Trinity College, Dublin, 1930–32. Closely associated with James Joyce in Paris in the late 1920's and the 1930's. Settled in Paris in 1938, and has written chiefly in French since 1945; translates his own work into English. Recipient: *Evening Standard* award, 1955; Obie Award, 1958, 1960, 1962, 1964; Italia Prize, 1959; International Publishers Prize, 1961; Prix Filmcritice, 1965; Tours Film Prize, 1966; Nobel Prize for Literature, 1969. D.Litt.: Dublin University, 1959. Address: c/o Editions de Minuit, 7 rue Bernard-Palissy, Paris 6, France.

PUBLICATIONS

Plays

> *Le Kid*, with Georges Pelorson (produced Dublin, 1931).
> *En Attendant Godot* (produced Paris, 1953).   Paris, Editions de Minuit, 1952; translated by the author as *Waiting for Godot: Tragicomedy* (produced London, 1955; Miami and New York, 1956), New York, Grove Press, 1954; London, Faber, 1956.
> *Fin de Partie; Suivi de Acte sans Paroles* (produced London, 1957).   Paris, Editions de Minuit, 1957; translated by the author as *Endgame: A Play in One Act; Followed by Act Without Words: A Mime for One Player* (*Endgame*, produced New York, 1958; *Act Without Words*, produced New York, 1960), New York, Grove Press, and London, Faber, 1958.
> *All That Fall* (broadcast, 1957).   New York, Grove Press, 1957; as *All That Fall: A Play for Radio*, London, Faber, 1957.
> *Krapp's Last Tape* (produced London, 1958; New York, 1960).   Included in *Krapp's Last Tape and Embers*, 1959; in *Krapp's Last Tape and Other Dramatic Pieces*, 1960.
> *Embers* (broadcast, 1959).   Included in *Krapp's Last Tape and Embers*, 1959; in *Krapp's Last Tape and Other Dramatic Pieces*, 1960.

Krapp's Last Tape and Embers.   London, Faber, 1959.

Act Without Words II (produced New York, 1959; London, 1960).   Included in *Krapp's Last Tape and Other Dramatic Pieces*, 1960; in *Eh Joe and Other Writings*, 1967.

Krapp's Last Tape and Other Dramatic Pieces (includes *All That Fall, Embers, Act Without Words I* and *II*).   New York, Grove Press, 1960.

Happy Days (produced New York, 1961; London, 1962).   New York, Grove Press, 1961; London, Faber, 1962.

Words and Music (broadcast, 1962).   Included in *Play and Two Short Pieces for Radio*, 1964; in *Cascando and Other Short Dramatic Pieces*, 1968.

Cascando (broadcast, in French, 1963).   Paris, Editions de Minuit, 1963; translated by the author as *Cascando: A Radio Piece for Music and Voice* (broadcast, 1964), included in *Play and Two Short Pieces for Radio*, 1964; in *Cascando and Other Short Dramatic Pieces*, 1968.

Play (produced Ulm-Donau, 1963; New York and London, 1964).   Included in *Play and Two Short Pieces for Radio*, 1964; in *Cascando and Other Short Dramatic Pieces*, 1968.

Play and Two Short Pieces for Radio (includes *Words and Music* and *Cascando*).   London, Faber, 1964.

Eh Joe (televised, 1966).   Included in *Eh Joe and Other Writings*, 1967; in *Cascando and Other Short Dramatic Pieces*, 1968.

Come and Go: Dramaticule (produced Paris, 1966; Dublin, 1968; London, 1970; New York, 1974).   London, Calder and Boyars, 1967; in *Cascando and Other Short Dramatic Pieces*, 1968.

Eh Joe and Other Writings (includes *Act Without Words II* and *Film*).   London, Faber, 1967.

Cascando and Other Short Dramatic Pieces (includes *Words and Music, Eh Joe, Play, Come and Go, Film*).   New York, Grove Press, 1968.

Film.   New York, Grove Press, 1969; London, Faber, 1971.

Breath (produced Oxford, 1970).   Included in *Breath and Other Shorts*, 1971.

Beckett 3 (includes *Come and Go, Cascando, Play*) (produced London, 1970).

Breath and Other Shorts (includes *Come and Go, Act Without Words I* and *II*, and the prose piece *From an Abandoned Work*).   London, Faber, 1971.

Not I (produced New York, 1972; London, 1973).   London, Faber, 1973; in *First Love and Other Shorts*, 1974.

That Time (produced London, 1976).   London, Faber, 1976.

Footfalls (also director: produced London, 1976).   London, Faber, 1976.

Ends and Odd: Dramatic Pieces.   New York, Grove Press, 1976.

Screenplay: *Film*, 1965.

Radio Plays: *All That Fall*, 1957; *Embers*, 1959; *The Old Tune*, 1960; *Words and Music*, 1962; *Cascando*, 1963.

Television Play: *Eh Joe*, 1966.

Novels

Murphy.   London, Routledge, 1938; New York, Grove Press, 1957.

Molloy.   Paris, Editions de Minuit, 1951; translated by the author and Patrick Bowles, Paris, Olympia Press, and New York, Grove Press, 1955; London, John Calder, 1959.

Malone meurt.   Paris, Editions de Minuit, 1951; translated by the author as *Malone Dies*, New York, Grove Press, 1956; London, John Calder, 1958.

L'Innommable.   Paris, Editions de Minuit, 1953; translated by the author as *The Unnamable*, New York, Grove Press, 1958; London, John Calder, 1959.

Watt (written in English).   Paris, Olympia Press, 1953; New York, Grove Press, 1959; London, John Calder, 1963.

Comment C'Est.   Paris, Editions de Minuit, 1961; translated by the author as *How It Is*, New York, Grove Press, and London, John Calder, 1964.

Mercier et Camier.   Paris, Editions de Minuit, 1970; translated by the author as *Mercier and Camier*, London, Calder and Boyars, 1974; New York, Grove Press, 1975.

Short Stories and Texts

More Pricks Than Kicks.   London, Chatto and Windus, 1934; New York, Grove Press, 1970.

Nouvelles et Textes pour Rien.   Paris, Editions de Minuit, 1955; translated by the author as *Stories and Texts for Nothing*, New York, Grove Press, 1967; included in *No's Knife: Selected Shorter Prose, 1945–1966*, 1967.

From an Abandoned Work.   London, Faber, 1958.

Imagination morte imaginez.   Paris, Editions de Minuit, 1965; translated by the author as *Imagination Dead Imagine*, London, Calder and Boyars, 1965.

Assez.   Paris, Editions de Minuit, 1966; translated by the author as *Enough*, in *No's Knife*, 1967.

Bing.   Paris, Editions de Minuit, 1966; translated by the author as *Ping*, in *No's Knife*, 1967.

Têtes-Mortes (includes *D'Un Ouvrage Abandonné, Assez, Bing, Imagination morte imaginez*).   Paris, Editions de Minuit, 1967; translated by the author, in *No's Knife*, 1967.

No's Knife: Selected Shorter Prose, 1945–1966 (includes *Stories and Texts for Nothing, From an Abandoned Work, Imagination Dead Imagine, Enough, Ping*).   London, Calder and Boyars, 1967.

L'Issue.   Paris, Georges Visat, 1968.

Sans.   Paris, Editions de Minuit, 1969; translated by the author as *Lessness*, London, Calder and Boyars, 1971.

Séjour.   Paris, Georges Richar, 1970.

Premier Amour.   Paris, Editions de Minuit, 1970; translated by the author as *First Love*, London, Calder and Boyars, 1973.

Le Dépeupleur.   Paris, Editions de Minuit, 1971; translated by the author as *The Lost Ones*, London, Calder and Boyars, 1972.

The North.   London, Enitharmon Press, 1973.

First Love and Other Shorts.   New York, Grove Press, 1974.

Fizzles.   New York, Grove Press, 1976.

For to End Yet Again and Other Fizzles.   London, John Calder, 1977.

Verse

Whoroscope.   Paris, Hours Press, 1930.

Echo's Bones and Other Precipitates.   Paris, Europa Press, 1935.

Gedichte (collected poems in English and French, with German translations).   Wiesbaden, Limes Verlag, 1959.

Poems in English.   London, John Calder, 1961; New York, Grove Press, 1963.

Other

"Dante...Bruno.Vico..Joyce," in *Our Exagmination round His Factification for Incamination of Work in Progress.*   Paris, Shakespeare and Company, 1929;

London, Faber, 1936; New York, New Directions, 1939.

Proust.   London, Chatto and Windus, 1931; New York, Grove Press, 1957; with
   Three Dialogues with Georges Duthuit, London, John Calder, 1965.

Bram van Welde, with others.   Paris, Georges Fall, 1958; translated by the author
   and Olive Classe, New York, Grove Press, 1960.

A Samuel Beckett Reader.   London, Calder and Boyars, 1967.

Collected Works.   New York, Grove Press, 1975.

I Can't Go On: A Selection from the Work of Samuel Beckett, edited by Richard Seaver.
   New York, Grove Press, 1976.

Translator, *Anthology of Mexican Poetry*, edited by Octavio Paz.   Bloomington,
   Indiana University Press, 1958; London, Thames and Hudson, 1959.

Translator, *The Old Tune*, by Robert Pinget.   Paris, Editions de Minuit, 1960; in
   Three Plays, by Robert Pinget, New York, Hill and Wang, 1966; in *Plays,* London,
   Calder and Boyars, 1966.

Bibliography: *Samuel Beckett: His Work and His Critics: An Essay in Bibliography* by
Raymond Felderman and John Fletcher, Berkeley, University of California Press, 1970
(through 1966).

Manuscript Collections: University of Texas, Austin; Ohio State University, Columbus;
Washington University, St. Louis, Missouri; Dartmouth College, Hanover, New
Hampshire; Reading University, England.

Theatrical Activities:

Director: **Plays** – *Come and Go*, Paris, 1966; *Endgame*, Berlin, 1967; *Krapp's Last Tape*,
Berlin, 1969; *Krapp's Last Tape* and *Act Without Words*, Paris, 1970; *Happy Days*, Berlin,
1971; *Waiting for Godot*, Berlin, 1975; *Krapp's Last Tape* and *Not I*, Paris, 1975; *Footfalls*,
London, 1976. **Television** – *Eh Joe*, 1966 (Germany).

* * *

Poet, novelist, playwright, Samuel Beckett is most widely celebrated for his drama. To
date he has written nineteen pieces in dramatic form – two mime plays, four radio plays,
one movie, one television script, one actorless play, and ten dramas for speaking actors in
the theatre. Seven pieces were written in French and five subsequently translated into
English by Beckett; the others were composed directly in English. In French or English,
Beckett's dramas condense human experience into theatrical metaphors.

Beckett's first play, *Le Kid* (not extant), parodied Corneille's *Cid* for a Trinity College
audience. Written sixteen years later, his second play, *Eleuthéria*, parodies the well-made
play with its three acts developed through climaxes to resolution. Act I satirizes the Krap
family with its several aches and pains, but their worst pain is their son Victor who has gone
to live in "sordid inertia." Victor's father dies between Acts I and II, and in Act II the Krap
family and friends try to lure Victor back to bourgeois respectability. In Act III
complications are resolved when Victor firmly declares his independence: "Liberty is seeing
yourself dead." For that unattainable liberty – the eleutheria of the title – Victor spurns both
middle-class life and romantic suicide. In dramatizing the familiar theme of a misunderstood
young man, Beckett stuffs his dialogue into a familiar structure. It is therefore astonishing
that within a year, Beckett penned *Waiting for Godot* (in French).

Waiting for Godot is divided into two acts, and the second seems to repeat the first: at dusk
Gogo and Didi meet to wait for Godot. Pozzo and Lucky arrive, stop a while, and then leave.
As night falls, a boy announces that Godot will come not today but tomorrow. This
"tragicomedy" rests on the account of the crucifixion in the gospel of St. Luke, as

summarized by St. Augustine: "Do not despair: one of the thieves was saved. Do not presume: one of the thieves was damned." The two thieves are Didi and Gogo; the two thieves are Pozzo and Lucky. And each spectator wonders whether he is saved thief or damned thief.

The four nationalities evoked by the characters' names – Slavic Vladimir, French Estragon, Italian Pozzo, English Lucky – suggest a composite portrait of an international Everyman. Though the printed text does not specify their costumes, Vladimir and Estragon wear the black suit and derby of music hall or silent films, and their antics arouse sympathetic laughter. The other couple, Pozzo and Lucky, wear elaborate but dated clothes, and their actions arouse horror as well as laughter. Grotesque Pozzo and Lucky confront endearing Didi and Gogo; for all the volumes of exegesis that have been written about the play, its theatricality rests on this confrontation of two couples during the endless wait for the mysterious Godot. While the two friends wait, their activities accumulate into a life, which mirrors and criticizes the activities of most lives. What is distinctively new about *Godot* is the inextricable union of its method and its madness; stage words and gestures are comically and excruciatingly concrete; stage words and gestures are metaphysically meaningful, though perhaps the play's main meaning is that life has no meaning.

After 1950 Beckett has found it increasingly difficult to write in any genre. His fourth play, *Endgame*, was nearly two years in the writing – again in French. Its single act takes place in a "shelter," a living and dying room of a family. In some ways the family is ordinary, with its quarrels and attachments; in most ways the family is extraordinary, being the last of the human race. The members of this family have no family name, but each of the four family members has a four-letter name meaning nail: Nell puns on English nail as Clov puns on French *clou*; Nagg abbreviates German *Nagel* as Hamm abbreviates Latin *hamus*. Nailhood seems to represent humanity, stick figures topped with a head. Hamm, however, is also an abridgement of hammer, which drives the nails on the stage board. He is chief actor and director of the sado-masochistic play of *Endgame*. Nagg and Nell are Hamm's parents, but Clov is variously called his son, menial, creature, and dog. After Clov claims to sight another character – a small boy – he prepares to leave the family shelter. At the end of the play, however, Clov stands in the doorway, as at the beginning. And Hamm curtains his face as at the beginning. The play plays full circle: the shelter still offers protection from world catastrophe, the endgame does not yet end, the stage lives are not quite finished, and the play will presumably be repeated on another night. More rigorous than *Godot*, with fewer music hall routines, *Endgame* rests more gravely on an economy of purposeless play. Words are echoic and actions are repetitive in the few moments before life fades into nothingness.

After the stringent suffering of *Endgame*, Beckett penned the mime play *Act Without Words I*, in which the mute figure painfully learns the futility of motion. The radio play *All That Fall* peoples the Irish town of Boggshill through sound alone. Experience with the mime play and radio play contributed to Beckett's next stage play, *Krapp's Last Tape*, his first theatre piece written directly in English. The invisible voice of radio is committed to tape in *Krapp's Last Tape*, while the lone character on stage plays much of his role in mime. At sixty-nine Krapp is addicted to bananas that constipate him, to alcohol that undermines him, to desire for women in fact and in fantasy. Sixty-nine year old Krapp listens to a tape recorded on his thirty-ninth birthday, in which he laments his addiction to bananas and alcohol, and lingers over his farewell to a loved woman. In that tape Krapp speaks of a tape made ten or twelve years earlier, in which he recalls his constipation and his weakness for alcohol and women. Finally, Krapp broods while the tape-recorder records silence. *Krapp's Last Tape* is a dramatic record of aging, with death imminent.

All Beckett's subsequent drama blends the familiar world into the context of an eternal void. *Happy Days* (written in English) shows Winnie literally sinking into her grave, returning to dust. And yet she prattles cheerfully under a blazing sun. Winnie uses four main resources in living through what she repeatedly designates as her happy day – the stage props, her husband Willie, the composition of a story, and the recollections that seem to be involuntary and through which thread fragments of quotations from English verse. By

Act II Winnie is buried up to her neck, and her resources are reduced; her face is her only prop, she tries to tell her story, she vainly addresses her husband, and she grasps for lines of verse. Indomitable, she is rewarded with the most startling climax in all Beckett's drama – the entrance of her husband Willie on all fours, in morning clothes. Despite Winnie's encouragement, Willie fails to reach her, but he does manage to utter a single syllable – "Win" – at once her name and a mockery of their lives of loss. In the final tableau Willie's hand is poised between Winnie and the revolver. Unsmiling, husband and wife look at one another as the curtain falls on this happy day that summarizes her life.

In shorter plays Beckett etches the human condition ever more sharply. The radio play *Embers* pits human embers against the inhuman timeless sea. The mime play *Act Without Words II* contrasts the slow gestures of a thinker with the swift movements of a doer, to show the same result or non-result. The stage play *Play* views a lovers' triangle from the perspective of eternity. *Words and Music* and *Cascando*, radio plays, play words and music against a creator who attempts to blend them meaningfully. *Film*, a movie, and *Eh Joe*, a television play, use and mock the camera upon which their genres depend. *Come and Go* plays the circularity of time in three minutes, and *Breath* plays the brevity of life in thirty seconds.

After several years of directing rather than writing plays, Beckett completed *Not I* in 1972. The title hints at the play's theme, the uncertainty of human identity, but it hardly hints at the melodic emotion uttered by a human mouth, the only speaking character. *That Time*, in contrast, intercalates phrases from three different stage directions, to assault the head of an old man. One voice speaks of childhood, the second of love, and the third of a derelict old age, but since the voices are the same voice, and since their phrases intermingle, each seemingly separate time – that time – merges into the next for the brevity of a human lifetime.

In his drama Beckett dramatizes the process of playing to suggest the process of living. But living is always dying. The living-dying play becomes poetic theater as Beckett's stage dialogue blends folly and philosophy, scatology and eschatology, humor and cruelty, passion and compassion. His plays are precisely worded parables, in which the characters are concrete universals, moving through time.

—Ruby Cohn

BELLOW, Saul. American. Born in Lachine, Quebec, Canada, 10 June 1915. Educated at the University of Chicago, 1933–35; Northwestern University, Evanston, Illinois, 1935–37, B.S. (honors) in sociology and anthropology 1937; University of Wisconsin, Madison, 1937. Served in the United States Merchant Marine, 1944–45. Married Anita Goshkin in 1937 (divorced); Alexandra Tschacbasov, 1956 (divorced); Susan Glassman, 1961; has three children. Teacher at the Pestalozzi-Froebel Teachers College, Chicago, 1938–42; Member of the Editorial Department, *Encyclopedia Britannica*, Chicago, 1943–46; Instructor, 1946, and Assistant Professor of English, 1948–49, University of Minnesota, Minneapolis; Visiting Lecturer, New York University, 1950–52; Creative Writing Fellow, Princeton University, New Jersey, 1952–53; Member of the English Faculty, Bard College, Annandale-on-Hudson, New York, 1953–54; Associate Professor of English, University of Minnesota, 1954–59; Visiting Professor of English, University of Puerto Rico, Rio Piedras, 1961. Since 1962, Professor, Committee on Social Thought, University of Chicago. Founding-Editor, *Noble Savage*, Chicago, 1960–62. Fellow, Branford College, Yale University, New Haven, Connecticut. Recipient: National Institute of Arts and Letters grant, 1952; National Book Award, for fiction, 1954, 1965, 1971; Ford grant, 1959, 1960; Friends of Literature award, 1960; James L. Dow Award, 1964; Prix

International de Littérature, 1965; Jewish Heritage Award, 1968; Pulitzer Prize, for fiction, 1976; Nobel Prize for Literature, 1976. D.Litt.: Northwestern University, 1962; Bard College, 1963. Member, National Institute of Arts and Letters. Agent: Harriet Wasserman, Russell and Volkening Inc., 551 Fifth Avenue, New York, New York 10017. Address: Committee on Social Thought, University of Chicago, 1126 East 59th Street, Chicago, Illinois 60637, U.S.A.

PUBLICATIONS

Plays

The Wrecker (televised, 1964). Published in *New World Writing 6*, New York, New American Library, 1954.
The Last Analysis (produced New York, 1964: Derby, 1967). New York, Viking Press, 1965; London, Weidenfeld and Nicolson, 1966.
Under the Weather (includes *Out from Under, A Wen,* and *Orange Soufflé*) (produced Glasgow and New York, 1966; as *The Bellow Plays*, produced London, 1966). *A Wen* published in *Esquire* (New York), January 1965; in *Traverse Plays*, London, Penguin, 1967; *Orange Soufflé* published in *Esquire* (New York), October 1965; in *Traverse Plays*, London, Penguin, 1967.

Novels

Dangling Man. New York, Vanguard Press, 1944; London, Weidenfeld and Nicolson, 1960.
The Victim. New York, Vanguard Press, 1945; London, Weidenfeld and Nicolson, 1965.
The Adventures of Augie March. New York, Viking Press, 1953; London, Weidenfeld and Nicolson, 1954.
Henderson the Rain King. New York, Viking Press, and London, Weidenfeld and Nicolson, 1959.
Herzog. New York, Viking Press, 1964; London, Weidenfeld and Nicolson, 1965.
Mr. Sammler's Planet. New York, Viking Press, and London, Weidenfeld and Nicolson, 1970.
Humboldt's Gift. New York, Viking Press, and London, Alison Press – Secker and Warburg, 1975.

Short Stories

Seize the Day, with Three Short Stories and a One-Act Play. New York, Viking Press, 1956; London, Weidenfeld and Nicolson, 1957.
Mosby's Memoirs and Other Stories. New York, Viking Press, 1968; London, Weidenfeld and Nicolson, 1969.

Other

Dessins, by Jess Reichek; text by Saul Bellow and C. Zervos. Paris, Editions Cahiers d'Art, 1960.
Recent American Fiction: A Lecture. Washington, D.C., United States Government Printing Office, 1963.

Like You're Nobody: The Letters of Louis Gallo to Saul Bellow, 1961–62, Plus Oedipus-Schmoedipus, The Story That Started It All.   New York, Dimensions Press, 1966.
The Future of the Moon.   New York, Viking Press, 1970.
The Portable Saul Bellow, edited by Gabriel Posipovici.   New York, Viking Press, 1974.
Technology and the Frontiers of Knowledge (lectures), with others.   New York, Doubleday, 1975.
To Jerusalem and Back: A Personal Account.   New York, Viking Press, and London, Secker and Warburg, 1976.

Editor, *Great Jewish Short Stories*.   New York, Dell, 1963; London, Vallentine Mitchell, 1971.

Translator, with others, *Gimpel the Fool and Other Stories*, by Isaac Bashevis Singer. New York, Farrar Straus, 1957; London, Peter Owen, 1958.

Bibliography: *Saul Bellow: A Comprehensive Bibliography* by B. A. Sokoloff and Mark E. Posner, Norwood, Pennsylvania, Norwood Editions, 1973.

*   *   *

Although Saul Bellow's deserved fame results from his achievements as a novelist, he has written one full length play and a number of one acts which are significant contributions to the repertoire of the contemporary theatre. This is particularly true of *The Last Analysis*, a work which revealed Bellow as one of the vanguard of mid-twentieth century writers who would lead the theatre to those frontiers beyond absurdity.

The play reminds one of Chekov. Like the great Russian playwright, Bellow is a comic artist. Comic, however, not in the sense that he pokes fun at humanity's shortcomings, but in that he sees the comic as the most appropriate weapon in man's struggle for survival in an absurd world. The characters in *The Last Analysis*, and especially its hero, Philip Bummidge, like so many of Chekov's memorable creations, are comedians by necessity, smitten with a tragic sense of life, and lyrically in love with the ideal in a world poorly equipped to satisfy such aspirations. And like his Russian predecessor, although more directly, Bellow reveals his belief that the only successful strategy for dealing with the absurd is to allow the actor in oneself to emerge; to play all of life's roles; to act furiously within the paradoxes of life in order to cope with our consciousness of its absurd terms.

On the surface, *The Last Analysis* appears to be a spoof of psychoanalytic methods and American popular taste; but its real subject, as Bellow indicates in his brief preface to the play, "is the mind's comical struggle for survival." Bummidge, a popular comedian of yesteryear, now fading, nearly broke and 60, has been struggling for self-mastery and self-definition by performing his own psychoanalysis. Playing the roles of both doctor and patient, he produces a kind of Freudian "This Is Your Life" show by re-enacting all of the psychic crises of his past.

The play opens as the analysis is in its final stages, and as a grand climax Bummidge is going to relive his life via closed-circuit television for an invited audience of distinguished psychiatrists using all of the people of his past – his wife, son, father, sister, girl friend, associates, friends, enemies, and even an old midwife who helped bring him into the world – as actors. The ensuing scenes are based on the archetypal pattern of life, death, and rebirth. The experiment is a smash hit (it has also been witnessed by TV executives and agency directors) and Bummy is offered the world. He declines the lucrative contracts, however, and marches off to the old theatre where he first got his start to establish the Bummidge Institute of Nonsense.

If this seems nonsensical, it is. But there is great sense in the nonsense. Like all great comic writers, Bellow uses comic techniques to serve serious ends. Life as revealed in *The*

Last Analysis is a grand guignol, but with less sense. To live is only to make the comic gesture, or what Pirandello called the comic grimace. This is not, however, cause for despair; for it is, after all, the only way of drawing life into a stalemate in our cold war with existence.

But Saul Bellow's greatest achievement in this play is finally his protagonist. Philip Bummidge is a modern day Hamlet, leavened with a liberal dose of the Quixotic. He is the prototype of the absurd man, and like Hamlet he comes to realize that only by becoming both the actor and the voyeur of his own life can he ever encompass the multiplication of paradox which defines his existence. Only as actors can we live with genuine commitment and without shame; only as actors can we have a sense of self-definition in a fragmented world; only as actors can we fail, and yet continue striving to build a better world without resorting to the insane illusion of success. The perfect society (The Bummidge Institute of Nonsense) can never exist for the absurd man, but when the final curtain comes down on Bummy as he exclaims "I am ready for the sublime," we believe that this little man, who – like each of us – can never quite trust the eccentricities he's born to, nonetheless has the courage of his hallucinations and is therefore a fitting Virgil to lead us toward the other side of despair.

—Robert W. Corrigan

BENNETT, Alan.   British.   Born in Leeds, Yorkshire, 9 May 1934. Educated at Leeds Modern School, 1946–52; Exeter College, Oxford, 1954–57 (Open Scholar in History), B.A. (honours) 1957. National Service: Joint Services School for Linguists, Cambridge and Bodmin. Recipient: *Evening Standard* award, 1961, 1968, 1971; Tony Award, 1963; Guild of Television Producers Award, 1967. Agent: Michael Linnit Ltd., 113–117 Wardour Street, London W.1, England.

PUBLICATIONS

Plays

Beyond the Fringe, with others (produced Edinburgh, 1960; London, 1961; New York, 1962).   London, Souvenir Press, 1962; New York, Random House, 1963.
Forty Years On (produced Manchester and London, 1968).   London, Faber, 1969.
Sing a Rude Song, by Carl Brahms and Ned Sherrin, additional material by Alan Bennett, music by Ron Grainer (produced London, 1969).
Getting On (produced Brighton and London, 1971).   London, Faber, 1972.
Habeas Corpus (produced Oxford and London, 1973; New York, 1975).   London, Faber, 1973.

Television Plays: On the Margin series, 1966; A Day Out, 1972; Sunset Across the Bay, 1975.

Theatrical Activities:

Actor: **Plays** – in *Better Late* (revue), Edinburgh, 1959; in *Beyond the Fringe*, Edinburgh, 1960, London, 1961, and New York, 1962; Archbishop of Canterbury in *Blood of the Bamburgs* by John Osborne, London, 1962; Reverend Sloley-Jones in *A Cuckoo in the Nest* by Ben Travers, London, 1964; Tempest in *Forty Years On*, London, 1968; Mrs. Swabb in *Habeas Corpus*, London, 1974. **Television** – Augustus Hare in *Famous Gossips*, 1965; in *On the Margin*, 1966.

*   *   *

...when we play language games, we do so rather in order to find out what game it is we are playing.

—*Beyond the Fringe*

The enticing deviousness of language, often objectified in the game metaphor, is the theme of Alan Bennett's plays. In the revue *Beyond the Fringe*, both his monologues and sketches with Cook, Miller and Moore play with the game figure, which trivializes the supposedly serious, yet suggests that even inane values are better than none. (This conservatism ballasts the Headmaster's epigram in *Forty Years On*: "Standards are always out of date. That is what makes them standards.") Bennett as the Duke of Edinburgh lecturing to Americans illustrates the precariousness of figurative language:

This business of international politics is a game.... It's a hard game, it's a rough game...sometimes, alas, it's a dirty game, but the point about a game, surely, is that there's no need to take it seriously.... Now let's try and find out where it is that you've been going wrong. Take all that Cuban business...oh dear, oh dear. No, no, no, no. Of course, one can see what you were trying to do...trying, I suppose, in your own way to emulate our splendid effort at Suez.

What emerges is neither British self-deprecation, nor fashionable anti-Americanism, but a sense of balance and an underlying desire for decency even in those like the Duke and the Headmaster who are Bennett's targets. This tolerance is unusual in what is basically an undergraduate revue; equally unusual is the stress on serious issues: Bennett as a prison governer tells a condemned man who rejects the analogy between capital punishment and a public school caning, "Come along, now, you're playing with words."

The comedy continually questions the limits of discourse. In a skit reminiscent of the speculations on the cow in Forster's *The Longest Journey*, Bennett's Cambridge Philosopher interprets a clerk's "I mean Yes" as "a splendid example in everyday life where two very ordinary people are asking each other what are in essence philosophical questions." Similarly, Bennett's preacher hears a rude "Where do you think you're going?" as a metaphysical question. And *Fringe* sketches often parody conventional figures of speech in sequences that suggest the mock-litanies in the plays of Auden and Isherwood: "... The huddled masses leapt at the opportunity. They came over in droves.... Bred like rabbits.... Died like flies.... And spread like wildfire...." Thus, in this context, only the image of the game, which denies its own significance ("there's no need to take it seriously"), is acceptable.

Just as the linguistic comedy of *Fringe* foreshadows the material of later plays like Hampton's *The Philanthropist* and Stoppard's *Jumpers*, "Aftermyth," an irreverent picture of Britain during the Blitz, seems the spiritual parent of the many parodies of wartime England in the London "Fringe" theatre of the early 1970's. Bennett's final lines reveal both the perversion of political rhetoric and the profound human need to find attractive equivalents for painful reality:

> But the tide was turning, the wicket was drying out. It was deuce, advantage Great Britain. Then America and Russia asked if they could join in and the whole thing turned into a free-for-all. So, unavoidably, came peace, putting an end to organized war as we knew it.

The Headmaster in *Forty Years On*, an ingenious play-within-a-play focusing on the annual performance by the boys and the faculty of Albion School, indulges in similar rhetoric:

> The more observant among you will have noticed that one of Bombardier Tiffin's legs was not his own. The other one, God bless him, was lost in the Great War. Some people lost other things, less tangible perhaps than legs, but no less worthwhile − they lost illusions, they lost hope, they lost faith....

Forty Years On organizes a series of skits, similar in tone to "Aftermyth," on the political and cultural history of the twentieth century. Wicked portraits of culture heroes like Virginia Woolf and T. E. Lawrence are both outrageously unfair and deadly accurate. The most successful of these interludes is the Wilde pastiche in which Lady Dundowne, played by one of the masters in drag, advises her nephew to marry his spinster mother: "the arrangement seems so tidy that I am surprised it does not happen more often in society" − a perfect spoof of the archetypal Wilde plot and wit. "But then all women dress like their mothers, that is their tragedy. No man ever does. That is his," a parody of the Wildean paradox, resonates with additional meaning from the elaborate pattern of homosexual allusion in the play; in this representative public school world, witty hyperbole equals literal statement.

In the same way, Bennett exposes the simultaneous idiocy and seductiveness of language on all levels, from the folk-wisdom of a typical nanny to the devious rhetoric of Chamberlain, while the rude rugby song of the school athletes both undercuts and elevates the idealized game metaphor of the school anthem. The Headmaster's final speech dramatizes this ambivalent role of language:

> Once we had a romantic and old-fashioned conception of honour, of patriotism, chivalry and duty. But it was a duty which didn't have much to do with justice, with social justice anyway. And in default of that justice and in pursuit of it, that was how the great words came to be cancelled out. The crowd has found the door into the secret garden. Now they will tear up the flowers by the roots, strip the borders and strew them with paper and broken bottles.

Thus, the play fuses pathos with the ridicule of a style of English life and men like the Headmaster who epitomize it. Though only the Headmaster achieves dimension as a character, the cast of stereotypes is suitable for what is essentially a comic allegory.

Getting On is an ambitious Chekhovian comedy involving a fortyish Labour MP, George Oliver, whose nostalgia for stability ("What we crave in life is order") and linguistic prowess link him with the Headmaster. George lives with his thirtyish second wife Polly, their two children who remain offstage but ominous ("children are anarchists"), and Andy, George's teenage son by a wife who apparently violated his conception of order. Brian Lowther, a Conservative MP whose homosexuality makes him a blackmail target, Geoff, a nineteen-year-old hippy with whom both Polly and Brian are having affairs, and Enid, Polly's mother, are the other key characters. Ironically, the temperaments of George and Brian are the complete antithesis of their political stances.

George's logorrhea offends almost everyone. (The stage directions state: "He is a deeply misanthropic man, hence his jokes.") Yet, since the play is ambiguous about the source of his compulsion, George remains primarily a man who can joke about anything, a facility useful for a politician but insufficient as an index to character. Though the play abounds in fine bits ("Can't have pouffs in the Conservative Party. No seat would be safe."), these are so funny they sometimes impede the dramatic tension (as Bennett's brilliant sexual explication of "Rock of Ages" broke the mood of the enjoyable but low-keyed musical *Sing a Rude Song*). For all his intelligence, the only thing George learns is that his envy of Andy's sexual prowess has no basis in fact; however, George merely replaces one over-simplified generalization with another: "Get through the haze of pot and cheap fellowship and underneath you're like everyone else, harsh, consorious bastards." George remains unaware of the Polly-Geoff-Brian triangle and the apparently fatal illness of Enid, to whom he is devoted. Though committed to his job, he discovers too late that his West Indian constituent who claimed neighbors were poisoning her dog was not mad, as he had thought. Reality seems too complex for his categorizing, analytical mind, and, despite his belief in logic and language, he concludes, after a hilariously unsuccessful attempt to order a cab, "Words fail me." This ironical treatment of George raises questions about the reliability of all his statements and their ultimate sources in his character, and he remains constant only in a discontinuity which provides brilliant revue repartee but not always insight.

Though continually confronted with signs of the pointlessness of work, he persists with the established order (his only radical action, from an English viewpoint, is throwing a bucket of water at a neighbor's dog that perpetually fouls his doorstep). Yet, as the punning title suggests, the reward for hard work is ageing and death. All the characters represent different stages of development/decay, sometimes a bit schematically – George has a young second wife primarily to provide an example of the bright thirty-year-old woman trapped in domesticity: "It's all been dealt and now all there is to do is to play it for, what? Thirty years?" Despite this most allegorical array of characters, the play falters only with Andy, whose unhygienic kitchen forays elicit approving chuckles from the audience but who represents an overly sentimentalized view of youth. (Bennett was much clearer-eyed with the young in *Forty Years On*.)

However, *Getting On* is a generally successful attempt to organize laughs for complex dramatic purposes. Bennett's progression in his three major works suggests a capacity for further development; even when he yields to the temptation to disrupt mood or theme with irrelevant laughter, this laughter stems from brilliant comedy.

—Burton Kendle

BENTLEY, Eric (Russell).   American.   Born in Bolton, Lancashire, England, 14 September 1916. Educated at Bolton School; Oxford University, B.A. 1938, B.Lit. 1939; Yale University, New Haven, Connecticut, Ph.D. 1941. Married Maja Tschernjakow (marriage dissolved); Joanne Davis in 1953; has twin sons. Taught at Black Mountain College, North Carolina, 1942–44, and University of Minnesota, Minneapolis, 1944–48; Brander Matthews Professor of Dramatic Literature, Columbia University, New York, 1952–69; Charles Eliot Norton Professor of Poetry, Harvard University, Cambridge, Massachusetts, 1960–61. Drama Critic, *New Republic*, New York, 1952–56. Recipient: Guggenheim Fellowship, 1948; Rockefeller grant, 1949; National Institute of Arts and Letters grant, 1953; Longview Award, for criticism, 1961; Ford grant, 1964; George Jean Nathan Award, for criticism, 1967. D.Litt.: University of Winsconsin, Madison, 1975. Address: 711 West End Avenue, New York, New York 10025, U.S.A.

PUBLICATIONS

Plays

A Time to Live, and A Time to Die, adaptations of plays by Euripides and Sophocles
   (produced New York, 1967).   New York, Grove Press, 1967.
Sketches in *DMZ Revue* (produced New York, 1968).
The Red White and Black, music by Brad Burg (produced New York, 1970). Published
   in *Liberation* (New York), May 1971.
*Are You Now or Have You Ever Been: The Investigation of Show-Business by the Un-
   American Activities Committee, 1947–1958* (produced New Haven, Connecticut,
   1972).   New York, Harper, 1972.
The Recantation of Galileo Galilei: Scenes from History Perhaps (produced Detroit,
   1973).   New York, Harper, 1972.
Expletive Deleted (produced New York, 1974).   Published in *Win* (New York). 6 June
   1974.
From the Memoirs of Pontius Pilate (produced Buffalo, 1976).

Other

*A Century of Hero-Worship: A Study of the Idea of Heroism in Carlyle and Nietzsche,
   with Notes on Other Hero-Worshipers of Modern Times.*   Philadelphia, Lippincott,
   1944; as *The Cult of the Superman*, London, Hale, 1947.
The Playwright as Thinker: A Study of Drama in Modern Times.   New York, Reynal
   and Hitchcock, 1946; as *The Modern Theatre: A Study of Dramatists and the Drama*,
   London, Hale, 1948.
Bernard Shaw: A Reconsideration.   New York, New Directions, 1947; London, Hale,
   1950; revised edition as *Bernard Shaw, 1856–1950*, New Directions, 1957; as
   Bernard Shaw, London, Methuen, 1967.
In Search of Theatre.   New York, Knopf, 1953; London, Dobson, 1954.
The Dramatic Event: An American Chronicle.   New York, Horizon Press, and London,
   Dobson, 1954.
What Is Theatre? A Query in Chronicle Form.   New York, Horizon Press, 1956;
   London, Dobson, 1957.
The Life of the Drama.   New York, Atheneum, 1964; London, Methuen, 1965.
The Theatre of Commitment and Other Essays on Drama in Our Society.   New York,
   Atheneum, 1967.
What Is Theatre? Incorporating "The Dramatic Event" and Other Reviews 1944–1967.
   New York, Atheneum, 1968; London, Methuen, 1969.
Theatre of War: Comments on 32 Occasions.   New York, Viking Press, and London,
   Eyre Methuen, 1972.

Editor, *The Importance of "Scrutiny": Selections from "Scrutiny," A Quarterly Review,
   1932–1948.*   New York, G. W. Stewart, 1948.
Editor and Part Translator, *From the Modern Repertory.*   Bloomington, Indiana
   University Press, series 1 and 3, 1949, 1965; Denver, University of Denver Press,
   series 2, 1952.
Editor, *The Play: A Critical Anthology.*   New York, Prentice Hall, 1951.
Editor, *Shaw on Music.*   New York, Doubleday, 1955.
Editor and Part Translator, *The Modern Theatre.*   New York, Doubleday, 6 vols.,
   1955–60.
Editor and Part Translator, *The Classic Theatre.*   New York, Doubleday, 4 vols.,
   1958–61.

Editor and Translator, *Let's Get a Divorce and Other Plays*.   New York, Hill and Wang, 1958.

Editor and Part Translator, *Works of Bertolt Brecht*.   New York, Grove Press, 1962–.

Editor and Part Translator, *The Genius of the Italian Theatre*.   New York, New American Library, 1964.

Editor, *The Storm over "The Deputy."*   New York, Grove Press, 1964.

Editor, *Songs of Bertolt Brecht and Hanns Eisler*....   New York, Oak Publications, 1966.

Editor, *The Theory of the Modern Stage : An Introduction to Modern Theatre and Drama*.   London, Penguin, 1968.

Editor and Part Translator, *The Great Playwrights : Twenty-Five Plays with Comments by Critics and Scholars*.   New York, Doubleday, 2 vols., 1970.

Translator, *The Private Life of the Master Race*, by Bertolt Brecht.   New York, James Laughlin, 1944.

Translator, *Parables for the Theatre : The Good Woman of Setzuan, and The Caucasian Chalk Circle*, by Bertolt Brecht.   Minneapolis, University of Minnesota Press, 1948; revised edition, 1965.

Translator, *Orpheus in the Underworld* (libretto) by Hector Cremieux and Ludovic Halévy.   New York, Program Publishing Company, 1956.

Recordings (all Folkways): *Bentley on Brecht; Brecht Before the UnAmerican Committee; A Man's A Man* (Spoken Arts); *Songs of Hanns Eisler; The Exception and the Rule; The Elephant Calf, Bentley on Biermann; Eric Bentley Sings The Queen of 42nd Street*.

Theatrical Activities:

Director: **Plays** – *Sweeney Agonistes* by T. S. Eliot, Salzburg, 1949; *Him* by E. E. Cummings, Salzburg, 1950; *The House of Bernarda Alba* by Lorca, Dublin, 1950; *The Iceman Cometh* (co-director) by Eugene O'Neill, Zurich, 1950; *Purgatory* by W. B. Yeats, and *Riders to the Sea* and *The Shadow of the Glen* by J. M. Synge, U.S. tour, 1951; *The Good Woman of Setzuan* by Brecht, New York, 1956.

Eric Bentley quotes from an interview with Jerome Clegg:

Clegg: Why on earth did you have to write a play? For you are nothing if not critical.

Bentley: Maybe the impulse was to write a counter-play.

Clegg: Counter to what?

Bentley: A (good) performance of the Anouilh Antigone – in its integrity, not in the Galantiere adaptation-distortion – had riled me. So I had to write a "correct" Antigone; set Anouilh straight. The same with Brecht.

Clegg: Meaning?

Bentley: He made such absurd demands upon his people. What else could Mother Courage have done?

Clegg: Galileo?

Bentley: Brecht wilfully chose to misunderstand him. The recantation could not possibly be taken as a betrayal of Marxism.

Clegg: So it was historical correctness you were after? Oh, you and your scholarly background!

Bentley: Rubbish. There would be no possible "historical correctness" for Antigone. It is a human correctness that interests me. Telling a story more honestly – truer to *our* time, if you will, not necessarily truer to some other time.

Clegg: Someone had called your dramatic works "no nonsense plays."

Bentley: Can one tell the Jesus story without nonsense? There would be no precedents.

Clegg: The New Testament nonsense?

Bentley: A very over-rated book

Clegg: "Better than the New Testament" – is that a good description of your Jesus-Pilate play?

Bentley: I hope so. Shaw spoke of himself as "better than Shakespeare" with something like that in mind.

Clegg: He also put a question mark after the phrase.

Bentley: As I do.

Clegg: What was your first play? I want to know how all this got started.

Bentley: Which is the wickedest of all your wicked questions.

Clegg: Answer it.

Bentley: My first play wasn't a play of mine at all, it was other people's plays.

Clegg: Especially Bertolt Brecht's.

Bentley: Actually, my first-play-that-was-really-someone-else's-play was not a Brecht, it was a Meilhac and Halévy.

Clegg: Who dey?

Bentley: Jacques Offenbach. The first time I launched out on my own was when I re-did the libretto to Offenbach's *Orpheus* for the New York City Opera Company.

Clegg: Everyone loved it.

Bentley: The press hated it. Except the communist paper.

Clegg: So you took up the Commie cause in *Are You Now or Have You Ever Been*?

Bentley: Well, that was some centuries later, and it wasn't the commie cause. Besides, that play is a documentary, the truth and nothing but the truth.

Clegg: How about the whole truth?

Bentley: I always save that for my next play.

Clegg: What's your Next Play about?

Bentley: The two other persons of the Trinity.

Clegg: Not Oscar Wilde?

Bentley: Same thing.

*   *   *

From a beginning as a theatre critic and as a translator not only of a large number of different dramatists but translator and adaptor of a considerable number of plays of Bertolt Brecht, Eric Bentley has emerged in the 1970's as an important playwright in his own idiom and right.

Though his libretto *Orpheus in the Underworld* had been published as early as 1956, it was not until the late 1960's in America that Eric Bentley began to find his own voice as a highly political playwright. *A Time to Live* (an adaptation of Euripides's *Andromache*) and *A Time to Die* (an adaptation of Sophocles's *Antigone*) were clearly related to the Algerian and Vietnamese conflicts when they were first produced in March of 1967 in New York. Equally political, but structurally much more daring than his Greek adaptations of the late 1960's is his 1970 work, *The Red White and Black*. Designed as a "stage show" rather than a traditional "play" as such, *The Red White and Black* requires a "rock group of 4 musicians and about 10 singing actors." In its intercutting of songs and political slogans and with its switches from dream to contemporary reality, Bentley's stage show carries us well beyond the rather traditional plot structure of Brechtian dramaturgy. We are carried back to the daring political spectacles of an earlier day, those of Piscator, Meyerhold, Tretiakov, and Hallie Flanagan. With music by Brad Burg, *The Red White and Black*, is a largely successful disruption of traditional dramaturgy. So technically daunting is this piece, however, that it is unlikely to be frequently performed.

Though less daring than *The Red White and Black*, the two plays Bentley published in 1972, *Are You Now or Have You Ever Been* and *The Recantation of Galileo Galilei*, are the ones on which his main reputation as a dramatist must rest. Written almost as a counter-play to Brecht's *Life of Galileo*, *The Recantation* sticks moderately closely to historical facts. Galileo's direct and private confrontation with the scientist-Pope, Urban VIII, is extremely successful as drama though Bentley does allow himself some factual liberty. Yet despite this single scene of great dramatic force, *The Recantation of Galileo Galilei*, in my view, is less successful as a stageable play than *Are You Now or Have You Ever Been*. In arranging and condensing the transcripts of the investigations of those "show-business" personalities interviewed by the UnAmerican Activities Committee between 1947 and 1958, Bentley has constructed a superb contribution to the modern art of documentary drama. The eighteen people Bentley has chosen to represnt the whole political and moral spectrum from the craven and obsequious (Jerome Robbins and José Ferrer) to the courageous and outspoken (Lillian Hellman and Paul Robeson), magnificently sum up a bleak political era. In a way similar to that Peter Weiss used in turning the lengthy and repetitious Auschwitz trial transcript into stunningly effective political drama, Bentley captures in *Are You Now or Have You Ever Been* the savage political crudity of an era shaped by the now dead Joseph McCarthy, the still alive but disgraced Richard Nixon, and the still alive and politically rampant Ronald Reagan.

Turning from the condensation of the transcript of the HUAC hearings, Bentley attempted in 1974 to construct a political drama in 1974 to construct a political drama out of the Nixon White House tape transcripts. Perhaps because he was still too close to the events themselves, he has not achieved in *Expletive Deleted* the same explosive force as he has in the HUAC play. Though one can hardly suggest lack of historical distance as the reason for the failure of his most recent play, *The Memoirs of Pontius Pilate*, nevertheless the play does somehow lack the vibrancy and political fireworks that distinguish Bentley's better works.

—John Fuegi

BERMANGE, Barry.   British.   Born in London, 7 November 1933. Studied at art school in Essex. National Service, 1952–54. Married the novelist Maggie Ross in 1961. Assistant Designer, Perth Repertory Company, 1955; Actor and Assistant Stage Manager, Swansea Repertory Company, 1956. Recipient: Arts Council drama bursary, 1964; Ohio State University Award, 1967; German Critics Award, for television play, 1968. Address: c/o Eyre Methuen Ltd., 11 New Fetter Lane, London EC4P 4EE, England.

PUBLICATIONS

Plays

No Quarter (broadcast, 1962; produced London, 1964).   Published in *New English Dramatists 12*, London, Penguin, 1968.
Nathan and Tabileth (broadcast, 1962; produced Edinburgh and London, 1967). Included in *Nathan and Tabileth, Oldenberg*, 1967.
The Cloud (produced London, 1964).
Four Inventions (includes *The Dreams, The Evening of Certain Lives, Amor Dei, The After Life*) (broadcast, 1964–65; as *Darkness Theatre*, produced London, 1969).

Oldenberg (televised, 1967; produced Edinburgh and London, 1967).   Included in *Nathan and Tabileth, Oldenberg*, 1967.

Nathan and Tabileth, Oldenberg.   London, Methuen, 1967.

The Interview (televised, 1968; produced London, 1969)   Included in *No Quarter and The Interview*, 1969.

Invasion (televised, 1969).   Included in *No Quarter and The Interview*, 1969.

No Quarter and The Interview (includes *Invasion*).   London, Methuen, 1969.

Scenes from Family Life (televised, 1969; produced Leatherhead, Surrey, 1974). Published in *Collection: Literature for the Seventies*, Boston, Heath, 1972.

Radio Plays: *The Voice of the Peanut*, 1960; *Never Forget a Face*, 1961; *No Quarter*, 1962; *Nathan and Tabileth*, 1962; *The Imposters* series, 1962; *Four Inventions*, 1964–65; *The Mortification*, 1964; *The Detour*, 1964; *Paths of Glory*, from the novel by Humphrey Cobb, 1965; *Letters of a Portuguese Nun*, 1966; *As a Man Grows Older*, 1967.

Television Plays: *Oldenberg*, 1967; *The Interview*, 1968; *Tramp*, 1968 (Germany); *Invasion*, 1969; *Scenes from Family Life*, 1969; *International*, 1976; *Stars*, 1976.

*   *   *

The most remarkable characteristic of Barry Bermange's style as a dramatist is his ability to convey a powerful, universal theme with the utmost economy of means. His early plays (originally written for the stage) were first produced on radio, a medium ideally suited to capture the full evocativeness of the language, the symbolic power of the stories and the graceful accuracy of each carefully calculated effect. Indeed a live audience sometimes seems to disturb the precise timing on which his plays depend: there is too little room for laughter or any other spontaneous reaction. Bermange has sometimes been compared to Beckett and Ionesco: and his plots are occasionally reminiscent of the Theatre of the Absurd. In *No Quarter*, for example, a fat man and a quiet man seek lodging in a mysterious collapsing hotel: and eventually huddle together in a dark upper storey room, hoping that nothing will happen to them if they stay quite still. But Bermange's dialogue, unlike Ionesco's, rarely exploits nonsense for its own sake. His images do not carry the logic-shattering irrelevance of Dadaism. The plain meaning of *No Quarter* is all too apparent: the fat man and the quiet man represent two recognizable human reactions to the fear that their world is disintegrating. Nor is Bermange an iconoclastic writer. The collapsing hotel is not symbolic, say, of religion falling apart. Unlike the writers of the Absurd, Bermange does not delight in pointing out the nonsense of cherished institutions: nor are his stories tantalizingly ridiculous. He doesn't attempt to give a pleasing *frisson* to the rational mind by rubbing it up the wrong way. The themes of his plays are usually coherent and indeed logical, although they may contain many ambiguities. Bermange is a writer who defies easy categorizing simply because he chooses each technique carefully to express most directly his underlying themes. His plays can be absurdist: they can be naturalistic: they can even include carefully manoeuvred "happenings." But the styles have always been selected for their appropriateness, not from any *a priori* assumptions about Theatre or Dramatic Art.

In the same way he chooses his different styles with care, so Bermange distils each effect to its essential elements. Like Marguerite Duras, he sometimes presents an apparently small incident observed in precise detail: and separates it from all the surrounding life until it exists in a significant isolation. In *The Interview*, eight men wait in an outer office, before being interviewed for a job. The audience never learns what the job is or who is finally selected. The play is solely concerned with the applicants' reactions to each other: and the small details – one man reading a newspaper, another looking at a picture – manage to convey an almost intolerable atmosphere of suspicion and rivalry. In *Nathan and Tabileth*, an elderly couple feed the pigeons in the park, return home and spend the evening by the fire. They are visited by a young man, Bernie, who says he is their grandson, although they do not recognize him, and who talks of relatives they have forgotten. When Bernie leaves, the couple go to bed: and "darkness comes." Bermange manages to capture in the rambling repetitive dialogue and in the intense short soliloquies the shifting concentration of the old. Certain details – the hired boats on the lake, the pigeons and the glowing fire – emerge in sharp focus: others slide into a grey and closing background. The timing of the play is calculated to break up the normal pace of events: the old people do not think consecutively and the audience is not allowed to do so. Sometimes they ramble on about the past: sometimes they try to cope with the present, with the breaking of a plate, with a scratched hand. No other contemporary play – with the possible exception of Beckett's *Happy Days* – conveys with such agonizing plausability the experience of old age.

The Interview and *Nathan and Tabileth* are both basically naturalistic plays: the observable details have been carefully selected and arranged to provide a particular impact – but these details are convincing on the level of external reality. In *Oldenberg*, however, Bermange caricatures the main characters. A man and a woman decide to let a room in their house. The tenant is a stranger, Oldenberg, whom they have never even met. At first they make considerable efforts to furnish the room comfortably: but then the possibility occurs to them that their tenant may not be *English*. In a fit of xenophobia, they destroy and desecrate the room they have so carefully prepared. But the stranger when he arrives is English – and blind. *Oldenberg* is an allegory about the way in which people long for change but are afraid of the unfamiliar – of invasion. By using some of the techniques of Absurdist writers, Bermange heightens the contradictory emotions caused by the intrusions of visitors.

But perhaps Bermange's most extraordinary achievement was to compile four "sound inventions," originally for radio, but which were afterwards presented at the Institute of Contemporary Art in London – through loudspeakers in a darkened auditorium. The inventions were recorded extracts of interviews with ordinary men and women – about their dreams, their reflections on old age, their beliefs or scepticisms about God and the After-life. The speeches were carefully edited into short revealing phrases, "orchestrated" with electronic music and finally presented as totally original music-drama works. In these inventions, Bermange's remarkable gifts for ordering sound effectively – both ordinary speech patterns and electronic effects – were allied to themes which could scarcely have been expressed effectively any other way. He invented a new form of radio and theatrical experience: and the only possible contemporary parallel would be with Berio's music-drama for Italian radio. With equal ingenuity, Bermange also wrote an improvisatory work for television, *Invasion*, where a dinner party is gradually submerged by the images of Vietnam, flickering across a television screen. Bermange's inventiveness, his assurance in handling different styles and media, and the powerful intensity of his chosen themes have won him a unique position among the younger British dramatists. No other writer can rival him for controlled daring and insight into the potentialities of experimental drama.

—John Elsom

BERNARD, Kenneth.   American (French, German, Italian).   Born in Brooklyn, New York, 7 May 1930. Educated at City College of New York, B.A. 1953; Columbia University, New York, M.A. 1956, Ph.D. 1962. Served in the United States Army, 1953–55: Private. Married Elaine Reiss in 1952; has three children. Taught in New York City high schools, 1956–58. Since 1959, member of the English Department, Long Island University, Brooklyn, New York: currently Professor of English. Recipient: Rockefeller grant

(University of Minnesota Office for Advanced Drama Research), 1971; Guggenheim Fellowship, 1972; Rockefeller grant, 1975; Creative Artists Public Service grant, 1976. Address: Department of English, Long Island University, Brooklyn, New York 11201; or, 788 Riverside Drive, New York, New York 10032, U.S.A.

PUBLICATIONS

Plays

> *The Moke-Eater* (produced New York, 1968).   Included in *Night Club and Other Plays*, 1971.
> *Marko's: A Vegetarian Fantasy*, in *Massachusetts Review* (Amherst), Summer 1969.
> *The Lovers*, in *Trace* (London), May 1969; in *Night Club and Other Plays*, 1971.
> *Night Club* (produced New York, 1970).   Included in *Night Club and Other Plays*, 1971.
> *The Monkeys of the Organ Grinder* (produced New Brunswick, New Jersey, and New York, 1970).   Included in *Night Club and Other Plays*, 1971.
> *The Unknown Chinaman* (produced Omaha, Nebraska, 1971).   Published in *Playwrights for Tomorrow: A Collection of Plays, Volume 10*, edited by Arthur H. Ballet, Minneapolis, University of Minnesota Press, 1973.
> *Night Club and Other Plays* (includes *The Moke-Eater, The Lovers, Mary Jane, The Monkeys of the Organ Grinder, The Giants in the Earth*).   New York, Winter House, 1971.
> *Mary Jane* (also director: produced New York, 1973). Included in *Night Club and Other Plays*, 1971.
> *Goodbye, Dan Bailey*, in *Drama and Theatre* (Fredonia, New York), Spring 1971.
> *The Magic Show of Dr. Ma-Gico* (produced New York, 1973).
> *How We Danced While We Burned* (produced New York, 1974).
> *King Humpy* (produced New York, 1975).
> *The Sensuous Ape*, in *Penthouse* (New York), September 1975.

Novel

> *The Maldive Chronicles*, in *The Minnesota Review* (Minneapolis), Summer 1970.

Short Stories

> *Two Stories*.   Mt. Horab, Wisconsin, Perishable Press, 1973.

Manuscript Collections: Lincoln Center Library of the Performing Arts, New York; University of Minnesota, Minneapolis.

Critical Study: Introduction by Michael Feingold to *Night Club and Other Plays*, 1971.

Theatrical Activities:

> Director: **Play** – *Mary Jane*, New York, 1973.

Kenneth Bernard comments:

I like to think of my plays as metaphors, closer to poetic technique (the coherence of dream) than to rational discourse. I am not interested in traditional plot or character development. My plays build a metaphor; when the metaphor is complete, the play is compléte. Within that context things and people do happen. I would hope the appeal of my plays is initially to the emotions only, not the head, and that they are received as spectacle and a kind of gorgeous (albeit frightening) entertainment. The characters in my plays can often be played by either men or women (e.g. *The Moke-Eater, Night Club*): only a living presence is necessary, one who reflects the character component in the play rather than any aspect of non-stage individuality: they are instruments to be played upon, not ego-minded careerists: they must "disappear" on stage. More important than technique, etc., are passion and flexibility. The defects of this preference are offset by strong directorial control: each play in effect becomes a training program. My plays utilize music, dance, poetry, rhetoric, film, sounds and voices of all kinds, costume, color, make-up, noise, irrationality and existing rituals to give shape (e.g., the auction, the magic show). The audience must be authentically pulled into the play in spite of itself. It must not *care* what it all means because it is enjoying itself and feels itself involved in a dramatic flow. What remains with the audience is a totality, the metaphor, from which ideas may spring – not ideas from which it has (with difficulty) to recreate the dramatic experience.

*   *   *

Kenneth Bernard's major plays have been produced mainly by the Play-House of the Ridiculous, under John Vaccaro's direction. This collaboration provides the best avenue of approach to an understanding of Bernard's plays. The "Ridiculous" style, with its shrilly pitched, frenzied extravagance, its compulsively and explicitly sexual interpretation of every action, the elaborate makeups and costumes that lend confusion to the antics of transvestites of both sexes, the general aura of bleakness and violence that adds despair to even the company's most optimistic productions – that style is a reasonable physicalization of the world Kenneth Bernard evokes.

The two interlocking themes of Bernard's drama are cruelty and entertainment. His characters are perpetually threatening each other with tortures, mutilations, particularly painful modes of execution, and these vicissitudes are constantly placed in a theatrical "frame" of some sort, as intended for the amusement of a group, or of the torture-master, or of the audience itself, implicated by its silent consent to the proceedings. In Bernard's first full-length work, *The Moke-Eater*, the setting is a prototypical American small town, the hero a stock figure of a traveling salesman, desperately ingenuous and jaunty, who suddenly finds himself, when his car breaks down, confronting the sinister, inarticulate townspeople and their malevolent boss, Alec. Alec alternately cajoles and bullies the salesman into submitting to an humiliating series of charades, nightmarish parodies of small-town hospitality, climaxing in his realization that he is trapped when he drives off in the repaired auto, only to have it break down outside the next town...which turns out to be exactly the same town he has just left. (In the Ridiculous production, an additional frisson was added to the salesman's re-entrance by having the townspeople, at this point, attack and eviscerate him – a fate which Alec describes earlier in the play as having been inflicted on a previous visitor.)

Later plays by Bernard present the spectacle of cruelty with the torturer, rather than the victim, as protagonist. *Night Club* displays Western civilization as a hideous, inept, cabaret show, controlled by an androgynous master of ceremonies named Bubi, who, like Alec in *The Moke-Eater*, cajoles and bullies both audience and performers into humiliating themselves. In fact, the theatre audience first sees the company performing the show as a parody of itself: the grotesque nightclub acts all emerge out of the "audience," which meanwhile cheers, catcalls, attacks the club's one waitress, and generally behaves boorishly. The acts themselves include a ventriloquist (male) trapped in a virulent love-hate relationship with his dummy (female), who spouts obscenities; a juggler (recalling the "Destructive Desmond" of Auden and Isherwood's *Dog Beneath the Skin*) who throws valuable antiques into the air and declines to catch them; an impersonator, obsessed with his own virility, whose imitations veer from a sex-starved Southern belle to a sadisitic Nazi; and "The Grand Kabuki Theatre of America," which lends the patina of Japanese ceremoniousness to a vulgar soap-opera-like story about a pregnant college girl. Eventually, the nightclub show culminates, at Bubi's behest, in mass copulation by the "audience," accompanied by the William Tell Overture; for a climax, the one member of the audience who declines to perform is summarily dragged onstage and decapitated, while he repeatedly screams, "The menu says there's no cover charge!" In a similar vein, Bernard's *The Magic Show of Dr. Ma-Gico* is a series of violent encounters, more courtly in tone but just as unpleasant, based on fairy-tale and romance themes. (A maiden, to test her lover's fidelity, transforms herself into a diseased old crone and forces him to make love to her; a king is challenged to pick up a book without dropping his robe, orb and scepter; in both cases the man fails.) *Auction* is a surreal, aleatory version of a rural livestock auction, whose items include a pig-woman and an invalid who sells off his vital organs one by one. The world-picture contained in these plays is essentially that of a continuous nightmare, and while the surface action and language changes (Bernard's language is exceptionally varied in texture, going from the loftiest politeness to the most degraded abuse), the emotional thrust of the material is constantly the same: towards revealing the sheer ludicrous horror of existence. In his collaboration with the Play-House of the Ridiculous, Bernard has carried the Artaudian project of raising and exorcizing the audience's demons about as far as it is likely to get through the theatrical metaphor.

—Michael Feingold

BIRIMISA, George.   Croatian-American.   Born in Santa Cruz, California, 21 February 1924. Attended school to the ninth grade; studied with Uta Hagen at the Herbert Berghof Studios, New York. Served in the United States Naval Reserve during World War II. Married Nancy Linden in 1952 (divorced, 1961). Worked in a factory, as a disc jockey, health studio manager, clerk, salesman, bartender, page for National Broadcasting Company, bellhop; counterman, Howard Johnson's, New York, 1952–56; typist, Laurie Girls, New York, 1969–70. Artistic Director, Theatre of All Nations, New York. Recipient: Rockefeller grant, 1969. Address: 1185 North Alexandria Avenue, Apartment 502, Los Angeles, California 90027, U.S.A.

PUBLICATIONS

Plays

> *Degrees* (produced New York, 1966).
> *17 Loves and 17 Kisses* (produced New York, 1966).
> *Daddy Violet* (produced Ann Arbor, Michigan, and New York, 1967).   Published in *Prism International* (Vancouver), 1968.
> *How Come You Don't Dig Chicks?* (produced New York, 1967).
> *Mister Jello* (produced New York, 1968; London, 1969; revised version, produced New York, 1974).

Georgie Porgie (produced New York, 1968).   Published in *More Plays from Off-Off-Broadway*, edited by Michael Smith, Indianapolis, Bobbs Merrill, 1973.
Adrian (produced New York, 1974).
Will the Real Yoganga Please Stand Up ? (produced New York, 1974).
A Dress Made of Diamonds (produced Los Angeles, 1976).
Pogey Bait! (produced Los Angeles, 1976).

Manuscript Collection: Joe Cino Memorial Library, Lincoln Center Library of the Performing Arts, New York.

Theatrical Activities:

Director: **Plays** – *The Bed* by Robert Heide, New York, 1966; *The Painter* by Burt Snider, New York, 1967; *Georgie Porgie*, New York, 1971; *A Buffalo for Brooklyn* by Anne Grant, Corning, New York, 1975.

Actor: **Plays** – title role in *Daddy Violet*, Ann Arbor, Michigan, and New York, 1967; Mr. Finley in *Georgie Porgie*, New York, 1968.

George Birimisa comments:

(1973) I write about the people I know. At this point in my life many of my friends are homosexual. I try to write honestly about them. In writing honestly about them I believe that my plays (in particular *Georgie Porgie*) mirror the terror of a schizophrenic society that is lost in a world of fantasy. In *Daddy Violet* I believe I showed how the individual's fantasy can lead to the burning of women and children in Vietnam. The problem with my plays is that many critics label them as homosexual plays. In the United States we live at the edge of a civilization that is near the end of the line. I feel that it is important for me to throw away every fantasy and get down into the total terror of this insane society. Only then can I truly write a play that is God-affirming, that is full of light. In my new play, tentatively titled *It's Your Movie*, I'm trying to write about the only alternative left in a demonic society – the nitty-gritty love of brother for brother and sister for sister. I know I must go through the passions of the flesh before I can break through to love my brother and sister. Anything else is an illusion. I also believe that the American male is terrified of his homosexuality and this is one of the chief reasons why he is unable to love his brother. His repression creates fires of the soul and this is translated into wars and violence. If all the "closet queens" would step out into the sunshine it would be a different country. I believe the above is what I write about in my plays.

(1977) At last I have discovered that four letter word LOVE. My early plays were screams of anger and rage. I was really screaming at myself because I was a microcosm of the good and evil of the western world, and I finally realize that it is possible to walk through death and destruction, and care ... really care.

*   *   *

George Birimisa's early play *Daddy Violet* is built on a series of cathartic acting exercises which, through a process of association and hallucinatory transformation, become an intense evocation of a battle in the Vietnam war. The cruelty and destruction of the war are connected, using a technique based on improvisation, with the actor's self-loathing and sexual immaturity.

Birimisa has acted in and directed his own plays. His major themes are the pain of human isolation and its economic and social roots. He is a fiercely moral writer; his plays are filled with compassionate rage against needless suffering, furious impatience with the human condition, desperately frustrated idealism. In several plays the defiant self-hatred of a man rejected by society is embodied in homosexual characters.

Mister Jello starts out with a mixed bag of characters: a waspish aging transvestite, a bitchy social worker, a dreamy boy flower child, a businesslike prostitute, and fat, foolish Mister Jello, who likes to pretend to be a little boy and have the prostitute as his mommy discipline him. The antagonisms between their various interests are set in perspective by reference to the social philosopher Henry George. Each of the characters has his own structure of action; each is in a place of his own and feels the others are intruding. At the end the whole group turns into a suburban family, the father a disappointed, pitiful Mister Jello pining away over the loss of his heroic elder son.

Birimisa's most popular play to date is *Georgie Porgie*, which is a series of vignettes about homosexual relationships, almost all bitter and ugly in tone, interspersed with choral episodes quoted from Friedrich Engels. The contrast between Engels's idealistic vision of human liberty and Birimisa's presentation of his variously stupid, contemptible, pitiful, self-despising characters, all imprisoned in their own compulsions, is powerful and painful. The writing is often crude, the language vulgar, the humor cruel, the events shocking; the author is preoccupied with an apparently needless but pervasive kind of suffering and the consequences of neurotic patterns, and his work makes up in self-examining integrity and emotional intensity what it eschews of seductiveness and beauty.

—Michael Smith

BOLAND, Bridget. British. Born in London, 13 March 1913. Educated at the Convent of the Sacred Heart, Roehampton, 1921–31; Oxford University, 1932–35, B.A. (honours) in politics, philosophy and economics, 1935. Served as a Senior Commander in the Auxiliary Territorial Service, 1941–46: produced morale-orientated plays for the troops, with three companies of actors, 1943–46. Film writer, since 1937. Agent: London Management, 235 Regent Street, London W1A 2JT. Address: Bolands, Hewshott Lane, Liphook, Hampshire, England.

PUBLICATIONS

Plays

    The Arabian Nights (produced Nottingham, 1948).
    Cockpit (produced London, 1948).   Published in *Plays of the Year 1*, London, Elek, 1949.
    The Damascus Blade (produced Edinburgh, 1950).
    Temple Folly (produced London, 1951).   London, Evans, 1958.
    The Return (as *Journey to Earth*, produced Liverpool, 1952; as *The Return*, produced London, 1953).   London, French, 1954.
    The Prisoner (produced London, 1954).   Published in *Plays of the Year 10*, London, Elek, 1954; New York, Dramatists Play Service, 1956.
    Gordon (produced Derby, 1961).   Published in *Plays of the Year 25*, London, Elek, 1962.

The Zodiac in the Establishment (produced Nottingham, 1963; as *Time Out of Mind*, produced Guildford, Surrey, 1970).   London, Evans, 1963.
A Juan by Degrees, adaptation of a play by Pierre Humblot (produced London, 1965).

Screenplays: *Laugh It Off*, 1939; *Spies of the Air*, 1939; *Gaslight*, 1940; *This England*, 1941; *Freedom Radio*, 1942; *He Found a Star*, 1942; *The Lost People*, 1950; *Prelude to Fame*, 1950; *The Voices in the Night*, 1951; *The Prisoner*, 1954; *War and Peace*, 1955; *Damon and Pythias*, 1962; *Anne of the Thousand Days*, 1969.

Radio Play: *Sheba*, 1954.

Television Play: *Beautiful Forever*, 1965.

Novels

The Wild Geese.   London, Heinemann, 1938.
Portrait of a Lady in Love.   London, Heinemann, 1942.
Caterina.   London, Souvenir Press, 1975; New York, St. Martin's Press, 1976.

Bridget Boland comments:

Although I hold a British passport I am in fact Irish, and the daughter of an Irish politician at that, which may account for a certain contrariness in my work. Many playwrights have become screenwriters: so I was a screenwriter and became a playwright. Most women writers excel on human stories in domestic settings: so I am bored by domestic problems and allergic to domestic settings. I succeed best with heavy drama (*The Prisoner*), so I can't resist trying to write frothy comedy (*Temple Folly*).

By the time you have written half a dozen plays or so you begin to realize you are probably still trying to write the one you started with. However different I begin by thinking is the theme of each, I find that in the end every play is saying: "Belief is dangerous" – the theme of *Cockpit*. In *The Damascus Blade*, which, produced by Laurence Olivier and with John Mills and Peter Finch in the cast, yet contrived to fold on its short pre-London tour, I tried to put across the theme by too complicated a paradox. An Irishman descended from a long line of soldiers of fortune holds that you must not kill for what you believe in, but that a man must be prepared to die for something, if only the belief of someone else. Having offered his sword to the foreign forces of extreme right and extreme left in turn, he ends by dying as bodyguard to the child of a prostitute, trying to keep it for her from its father – and realizes that in spite of all his/my theories he has come to believe in the justice of her cause: man – alas, thank God – is like that.

                                    *   *   *

In 1948 Bridget Boland was well ahead of her time as a playwright. *Cockpit* was one of the early forerunners of the vogue for environmental theatre which was to spread to England from Off-Broadway in the sixties. It was a play which boldly turned its back on everything that was normal in the English theatre of the time, including insularity. Its way of coming to grips with the problem of Displaced Persons in post-war Europe was to use the whole auditorium to create a theatrical image of a D.P. assembly centre, which itself served as an image of the chaos on the continent, with masses of bewildered hopeless people uprooted from where they belonged. Unsuspecting London theatregoers arriving at the Playhouse found themselves faced with a curtain painted in Germanic style and with notices in various European languages forbidding them to fight or carry firearms. The dialogue began incomprehensibly: a quarrel in Polish between two women fighting over a saucepan.

Two English soldiers take charge, appearing from the back of the stalls, shouting orders and questions, treating the whole audience like D.P.'s, forcing them to feel uncomfortably involved in the action.

The discomfort becomes most acute at the climax of the play. Behind the drawn curtains of one of the boxes a man is gravely ill. A Polish Professor tells the English Captain that it may be a case of bubonic plague. The theatre has to be sealed off. Armed guards are stationed at the exits and the suspense is sustained while they wait for a doctor to arrive and then while they wait for the news that it was a false alarm. If the play ran for only 58 performances it cannot have been because it failed to make an impact.

On the face of it, the subject of *The Return* could hardly have been more contrasted – a nun's return to the modern world after thirty-six years of seclusion in a convent. This is difficult material, but well-dramatized it could have produced fascinating insights both into the mind of the woman and into the changes which had overtaken the world that surrounded her since she last saw it – in 1913. The play is by no means a complete failure: it has some very touching moments. But it fails to do justice to its subject because, unlike *Cockpit*, it fails to find a way of making the audience participate in the raw experience. It relies too much on dialogue which analyses and describes.

The part of the nun is quite well-written, but on leaving the convent she goes to live with a nephew and his wife, who are both sentimentally and unconvincingly characterized, while the chaplain and the man who runs a youth club where the nun does voluntary work are seen very superficially. The problem of dramatizing the impact the modern world makes on the woman's mind is largely side-stepped. What we get instead is a plot in which a series of misunderstandings are peeled off to reveal an unrealistic core of human goodness.

In spite of several forays into the past (like *Gordon*, an old-fashioned drama about Gordon and the siege of Khartoum) Bridget Boland is at her best in writing about post-war Europe, and her best play is still *The Prisoner*, which seems to have been inspired partly by the trail of the Hungarian Cardinal Mindszenty and partly perhaps by Arthur Koestler's novel *Darkness at Noon*, which presents a similar relationship between a political prisoner in a Communist country and his interrogator, though in Koestler the sympathetic interrogator is replaced half way through the action by a callous and unintelligent party-liner of peasant stock. In *The Prisoner* it is the Cardinal whose origins are proletarian, while the Interrogator is a clever aristocrat who has joined the Party. The dialogue gives clear definition to the stages in the close personal relationship that develops between the two adversaries, who like and respect each other. Most of the cut and thrust is verbal, but there are some highly theatrical climaxes, as when a coffin is brought in containing the apparently dead body of the Cardinal's mother. The revelation that she has only been anaesthetized is followed by the threat that she will be killed if he does not sign the confession his captors want.

Not only the two central parts but also that of the main warder provide excellent opportunities for actors, and the physical breakdown of the Cardinal is particularly rewarding. The main flaw in the writing is a lapse into sentimentality when the Interrogator is made to repent, revealing that in destroying his victim he has also destroyed his faith in his own work. But the damage this does to the play is almost compensated by a fine twist at the end. The death sentence is repealed and the Cardinal, whose confession has discredited him, knows that it will be more difficult for him to live than to die.

—Ronald Hayman

BOLT, Carol. Canadian. Born in Winnipeg, Manitoba, 25 August 1941. Educated at the University of British Columbia, Vancouver, 1957–61, B.A. 1961. Married David Bolt in

1969; has one son. Dramaturge, 1972–73, and Chairwoman, Management Committee, 1973–74, Playwrights Co-op, Toronto; Dramaturge, Toronto Free Theatre, 1973. Recipient: Canada Council grant, 1967, 1972; Ontario Arts Council grant, 1972, 1973, 1974, 1975. Agent: Great North Agency, 345 Adelaide Street West, Toronto, Ontario M5V 1R5, Canada.

PUBLICATIONS

Plays

Daganawida (produced Toronto, 1970).
Buffalo Jump (as *Next Year Country*, produced Regina, Saskatchewan, 1971; as *Buffalo Jump*, produced Toronto, 1972).   Toronto, Playwrights Co-op, 1972.
My Best Friend Is 12 Feet High, music by Jane Vasey (produced Toronto, 1972). Toronto, Playwrights Co-op, 1972.
Cyclone Jack (produced Toronto, 1972).   Toronto, Playwrights Co-op, 1972.
The Bluebird (produced Toronto, 1973).
Gabe (produced Toronto, 1973).   Toronto, Playwrights Co-op, 1973.
Pauline (produced Toronto, 1973).
Tangleflags (produced Toronto, 1973).   Toronto, Playwrights Co-op, 1973.
Red Emma: Queen of the Anarchists (produced Toronto, 1974).   Toronto, Playwrights Co-op, 1974.
Maurice (produced Toronto, 1974).   Toronto, Playwrights Co-op, 1975.
Shelter (produced Toronto, 1974).   Toronto, Playwrights Co-op, 1975.
Finding Bumble (produced Toronto, 1975).
Bethune (produced Gravenhurst, Ontario, 1976).

Television Plays: *A Nice Girl Like You*, 1974; *Talk Him Down*, 1975.

Carol Bolt comments:

I've had a lot of opportunity to work in the theatre in the last four years, with twelve new plays commissioned. Much of this work has been inspired by the theatrical community, particularly work being done at the Toronto Free Theatre and the Théatre Passe Muraille.

The plays often deal with "political" subjects, the characters often want to change the world, but I think my preoccupation is with the adventure, rather than the polemic, of politics. I think a play like *Red Emma* is about as political as *The Prisoner of Zenda*.

I'm intersted in working in new forms of musical comedy and epic romance and in creating (or recreating) characters who are larger than life or mythic.

I'm also interested in exploring, recording, recreating, and defining Canadian concerns, characters, histories, cultures, identities. I want to create plays for this country, whether the plays are about the lost moments in Canada's past (like *Buffalo Jump*), whether they offer another view of an American mythic figure (like *Red Emma*), or whether they play at creating Canadian archetypes (*Shelter*).

I don't think this kind of cultural nationalism is parochial. I think our differences are our strengths, not our weaknesses, nationally and internationally, so I think the argument that if a Canadian play in any good the Americans or British will be happy to tell us via Broadway or the West End is specious and muddle-headed. I don't think Canadians will say anything of interest to the world until we know who Canadians are.

*   *   *

Carol Bolt's early work falls largely into two kinds – plays for children and political plays. There seems at first sight a pronounced divide between the two genres, but although all of the plays for children were commissioned for the Young People's Theatre in Toronto not all of them are strictly what would be called children's plays.

My Best Friend Is 12 Feet Tall and *Tangleflags* most exactly fit the convention of the children's play, and both suffer unfortunately from the kind of "cuteness" for which that genre is infamous. The kids in both plays seem to articulate, too hyped. We're not surprised when Bolt cautions the director about the dangers of kids in the audience getting involved. The world of talking dogs does not belong to imagination but derived whimsy. We are a thousand miles away from Reaney's *Colours in the Dark* or *Listen to the Wind*, in spite of the echo of both in King's remark in *My Best Friend*: "Stories won't keep you through the wintertime and if you think they will you're whistling in the dark."

The hero of *Cyclone Jack* is the sort of defeated-hero/hero that, perhaps as a Canadian paradigm (the literature of defeat), fascinates more playwrights than Bolt. Certainly he reappears in her plays *Gabe* and *Red Emma*. The dramatic problem of the anti-hero (or more properly ante-hero, for he never raises his consciousness to the struggle) is less than that of the villain, however. Duplessis in *Maurice*, like R. B. Bennett in *Buffalo Jump*, is too farcical.

It may well be that this Canadian sense of somehow always being just below the level of significant political confrontation is what Bolt best portrays. The enemy has no "edge." Bennett is not Hitler, he is not even Mussolini; the fascist tendencies of the population that he represented (and represents) are the more sinister for being so resolutely "nice."

In *Gabe*, it seems, Bolt brings to the surface that sense of life at two removes or the underwater sense of struggling upward for air but never breaking the surface. Joseph in *Buffalo Jump* says: "I'm getting out of next year country," and Rosie and Henry turn on Gabe in similar terms. "You got all your women dressed in silver paper in your head, speaking French," says Rosie, and Henry adds that Gabe's world is a "Goddamn fucking Louis Riel cowboy movie."

Of course this "cowboy movie" "silver paper" quality of life is something that fascinates Canadian playwrights as disparate as John Herbert, Michel Ondaatje, Hrant Alianak, George Walker, and Michael Tremblay (to name a few). It also shares with the important but unfortunately unscripted theatre of group creation (the works of Passe Muraille or Toronto Workshop) the influence of Brecht, both in the stress on "alienation" and in the epic sweep of political event.

In *Red Emma*, a play about Emma Goldman the so-called "Queen of the Anarchists" at the turn of the century, "alienation" is achieved in part by songs which seem overtly Brechtian. But like so many of Brecht's characters, Emma is no simple hero. "You are pure and fine and gullible" is her comrade Fedya's last remark on her, and our response is as ambiguous. As in *Shelter*, a play in which an M.P.'s widow decides to take on his life much to the condescending and mindlessly jovial disbelief of her friends, we are at first not sure what the import of the feminism is.

Red Emma's ironies are different in kind from those in *Shelter*, but both are preoccupied with the breaking out of plasticised and sentimentalised roles into a world where what is said might be taken seriously. Irony frames this vision as it frames Joyce's *Portrait*, but it is no diminution of the seriousness of that desire.

—D.D.C. Chambers

BOLT, Robert (Oxton).   British.   Born in Sale, Manchester, Lancashire, 15 August 1924. Educated at Manchester Grammar School; Manchester University, 1943, 1946–49,

B.A. (honours) in history 1949; Exeter University, 1949–50, teaching diploma 1950. Served in the Royal Air Force, 1943–44; in the Royal West African Frontier Force, 1944–46: Lieutenant. Married Celia Ann Roberts in 1948 (marriage dissolved, 1967); the actress Sarah Miles, 1967 (divorced, 1975); has four children. Worked as office boy, Sun Life Assurance Company, Manchester, 1942; Schoolmaster, Bishopsteignton, Devon, 1950–51, and Millfield School, Street, Somerset, 1952–58. Recipient: *Evening Standard* award, 1957; New York Drama Critics Circle Award, 1962; British Film Academy Award, 1962, 1966; Academy Award, 1966, 1967; New York Film Critics Award, 1966; Golden Globe Award, 1967. Agent: Margaret Ramsay Ltd., 14a Goodwin's Court, London WC2N 4LL, England.

PUBLICATIONS

Plays

> *A Man for All Seasons* (broadcast, 1954; produced London, 1960; New York, 1961).
> London, Heinemann, 1961; New York, Random House, 1962.
> *The Last of the Wine* (broadcast, 1955; produced London, 1956).
> *The Critic and the Heart* (produced Oxford, 1957).
> *Flowering Cherry* (produced London, 1957; New York, 1959).   London, Heinemann,
> 1958; New York, French, n.d.
> *The Tiger and the Horse* (produced London, 1960).   London, Heinemann, 1961; New
> York, French, n.d.
> *Gentle Jack* (produced London, 1963).   London, French, 1964; New York, Random
> House, 1965.
> *The Thwarting of Baron Bolligrew* (produced London, 1965; Chicago, 1970).   London,
> Heinemann, 1966; New York, Theatre Arts, 1967.
> *Doctor Zhivago: The Screenplay Based on the Novel by Boris Pasternak.*   London,
> Harvill Press, and New York, Random House, 1966.
> *Brother and Sister* (produced Brighton, 1967; revised version, produced Bristol, 1968).
> *Three Plays* (includes *Flowering Cherry, A Man for All Seasons, The Tiger and the
> Horse*).   London, Heinemann, 1967.
> *Vivat! Vivat Regina!* (produced Chichester and London, 1970; New York, 1972).
> London, Heinemann, 1971; New York, Random House, 1972.

> Screenplays: *Lawrence of Arabia*, 1962; *Doctor Zhivago*, 1965; *A Man for All Seasons*,
> 1966; *Ryan's Daughter*, 1970; *Lady Caroline Lamb*, 1972.

> Radio Plays: *The Master*, 1953; *Fifty Pigs*, 1953; *Ladies and Gentlemen*, 1954; *A Man
> for All Seasons*, 1954; *Mr. Sampson's Sundays*, 1955; *The Last of the Wine*, 1955; *The
> Window*, 1958; *The Drunken Sailor*, 1958; *The Banana Tree*, 1961.

Critical Study: *Robert Bolt* by Ronald Hayman, London, Heinemann, 1969.

Theatrical Activities:

> Director: **Film** – *Lady Caroline Lamb*, 1972.

* * *

Analysis of Robert Bolt's achievement in the British theatre since 1957, when his play *Flowering Cherry* was produced at the Theatre Royal in London, involves us willy-nilly in the general ambiance of theatre in the late fifties. His achievement is best understood as not only a regular absorption of major theatrical developments (particularly those associated with the aesthetics but *not* the politics of Bertolt Brecht), but also as a deliberate rejection of many facets of the kind of theatre practised by Bolt's contemporaries, playwrights such as John Osborne, John Arden, Arnold Wesker, and Harold Pinter in Great Britain and the Theatres of Cruelty and of the Absurd as practised in the English speaking world and very widely elsewhere. Through all the battles that have swirled around the standards of anger, cruelty, and the absurd, Robert Bolt has managed quietly but consistently to make his own very individual voice heard. On the stage he has been represented since *Flowering Cherry* by *The Tiger and the Horse, A Man for All Seasons, Gentle Jack, The Thwarting of Baron Bolligrew*, and *Vivat! Vivat Regina!* In addition, he has recently worked on an historical script on Byron's mistress, Caroline Lamb, and he completed in the early sixties two extremely successful screenplays, *Lawrence of Arabia* and *Doctor Zhivago*, both directed by David Lean.

It is probable that these two screenplays (and the screen version of his own *A Man for All Seasons*) served not only to make Robert Bolt's name known beyond the narrow confines of contemporary theatre audiences but helped him to break the bounds of the rather rigorous "fourth-wall" style dramaturgy which marked (by his own admission) his early stage plays. Robert Bolt is (and this is, of course, true of an extremely large majority of contemporary dramatists) uneasily aware of the enormous economic *and aesthetic* pressure placed on the style of contemporary drama by the very existence of the cinema as a competing form. Lest we move too rapidly, however, to the conclusion that the form of Bolt's best plays is a direct reflex of his own involvement with the cinema as a serious medium of expression, we shall need to pause to consider the well-documented and widely known fact that Bolt was at least as much influenced by "open" theatre techniques associated with the name of Brecht as he was by the pace and structure of the aesthetics of cinema. We must, therefore, relate Bolt's development as a playwright to two major influences: Brecht and the cinema.

Though *Flowering Cherry* was produced in 1957, a year after Brecht's death and the epochal appearance of his Berlin Ensemble in London, Robert Bolt's play is uncannily reminiscent not of Brecht and the European theatre of the mid-fifties but of Chekhov and the theatre of Stanislavski at the turn of the century. Jim Cherry's hopeless dream of returning to the orchard where be grew up too narrowly evokes the world of *The Cherry Orchard* (what's in a name?). With its tightly-knit cast of six, its remarkable unity of time and place, and its extremely conventional and operatic conclusion with Cherry's death and his wife's departure, the play is a model of competent but extremely conservative dramatic structure. Three years later, in his next play *The Tiger and the Horse* we find no major technical or structural breakthroughs. Again we have a cast of six closely-related characters. Again we have a remarkable unity of time and place with the place being an extremely conventional one that can be presented with ease in the "fourth-wall" manner. Finally, the play's conclusion is melodramatic with a highly conventional climax and a vaguely "off into the sunset" final curtain. My own dissatisfaction with these two extremely competent dramaturgic constructs is shared by Robert Bolt himself. In the preface to *A Man for All Seasons*, a remarkable piece of sustained and unbiased technical analysis, he writes:

> In the two previous plays..., I had tried, but with fatal timidity, to handle contemporaries in a style that should make them larger than life; in the first mainly by music and mechanical effects, in the second by making the characters unnaturally articulate and unnaturally aware of what they "stood for." Inevitably these plays looked like what they most resembled, orthodox fourth-wall dramas with puzzling, uncomfortable and, if you are uncharitable, pretentious overtones.

In contrast, as he then goes on to note, he made two major technical changes in writing his enormously successful *A Man for All Seasons*. First, he decided to treat an historical rather than a contemporary subject, and second, he consciously decided to get beyond the confines of fourth-wall style dramaturgy, and to write instead a play in the "open," "epic," or, in his own words, a "bastardized version" of a style "most recently associated with Bertolt Brecht." Bolt's own word choices here are extremely apt, since what he attempts in *A Man for All Seasons* is, in a political sense, hardly a legitimate issue of Brecht. Also, as Bolt is clearly aware, the style "most recently associated with Brecht" can with equal claim to legitimacy be traced either to Meyerhold in Russia or to the consciously theatrical tradition of the Elizabethan and/or Jacobean theatre in England. It is perhaps not pure coincidence that Bolt's choice of a 16th-century English subject should be couched in a somewhat modernized 16th-century British dramaturgical style.

When we consider the abrupt shift of style that obtains between Bolt's earlier plays and *A Man for All Seasons*, we can only wonder at how remarkably successful the playwright was writing in his wholly new style. We may be unhappy with the success of a specific character such as The Common Man, but the speed and vibrancy of this play with its rapid shifts in time and space must be judged a virtuoso performance in the epic or open dramatic mode. This is no timorous shift of mode but a play different in all major particulars from his earlier efforts. Gone completely is the fourth-wall style and in its place we see a major contribution to the "theatre theatrical." With a sovereign disregard of the hypnotic style of theatre beloved of Stanislavski and despised by people such as Meyerhold and Brecht, Bolt has his characters openly acknowledge their roles as players in an historical stage play. The Common Man, for instance, not only speaks about the play in the form of a preamble reminiscent of both the Brecht of *A Man's a Man* and the Shakespeare of *Henry V*, but plays all the different "servant" roles in the play, changing costume for each and commenting on each role in the full sight of the audience. Lest this then be insufficient to break the hypnotic mood of conjured-up historical reality that the contrasting fourth-wall style demanded, The Common Man also reads from 20th-century history texts that comment directly on and offer various interpretations of the 16th-century subject, Sir Thomas More. I would suggest that Robert Bolt has had the boldness and skill here to successfully carry Brecht's own theoretical pronouncements on Epic Theatre further than Brecht ever carried them himself in his major plays.

The technical skill exhibited in the use of devices drawn from the theatre theatrical is present again in Bolt's next play, *Gentle Jack*. A large cast is manipulated with great skill, but, I fear, to very little purpose. The play has been as unsuccessful in performance as *A Man for All Seasons* has been successful. Musing on this, and with his usual gift for highly accurate self-analysis, Bolt has written in the preface to the published version of *Gentle Jack*: "I do like plays in which the people have ideas as well as predicaments, but I think what happened with this play was that I became so interested in the ideas that the ideas rather than the people have the predicaments, clash, come to their climax, and so on." Read as a clash of the immoral world of monopoly capitalism with the amoral world of the ancient Jack-of-the-Green, we can follow the clash with considerable interest. However, the very qualities which strengthen *Gentle Jack* as a text for reading fatally weaken it as a text to be performed.

The clash of contrasting value systems which echoes so urgently through *Gentle Jack* is heard again, this time in a deliberately fairy-tale form in the children's play *The Thwarting of Baron Bolligrew*. Stated simply as a clash between the good Sir Oblong Fitz Oblong and the bad Baron Bolligrew, the play carries its metaphysical burden with sprightliness, grace, and a far-from-naïve charm.

With his return to the adult world in *Vivat! Vivat Regina!*, Bolt returns also to the historical distance afforded by the 16th-century and the dramaturgical freedom associated with the theatre theatrical. Borrowing as well as departing freely from earlier dramatic treatments of the clash of Elizabeth with Mary Stuart, Bolt plays a variation on a recurrent theme in his work, the clash of natural instinct with power invested in state, ecclesiastical, or corporate offices. In a suitably contemporary and frank treatment of the sex life of both monarchs Bolt demonstrates how that sexuality is deformed by state office. Mary, finally condemned by Elizabeth, defiantly declares as she approaches the block: "There is more living in a death that is embraced that in a life that is avoided across three score years and ten. And I embrace it – thus!" She then throws off her black cloak and is revealed as being dressed from head to foot in scarlet. There is Bolt's old penchant for melodrama in this gesture, of course, but it is melodrama largely justified in this mature play by the scale of the figures who indulge themselves in such gestures. It is a measure of the playwright's growth that this mature work is so ably plotted and the dialogue so well sustained that Mary's otherwise melodramatic gesture fits harmoniously into this richly dramatic and eminently successful treatment of her fate. *Vivat! Vivat Regina!*, though not in any sense a great play, is a meticulously crafted structure worthy of one of the most technically gifted playwrights now writing in English. There is much to be said for playwrights who possess such skills, for it is they, finally, who preserve whatever life there is on the contemporary stage.

—John Fuegi

BOND, C(hristopher) G(odfrey).   British.   Born in Sussex in 1945. Child actor; later studied at the Central School of Speech and Drama and the Drama Centre, London. Actor, 1968–70, and Resident Dramatist, 1970–71, Victoria Theatre, Stoke on Trent. Since 1976, Artistic Director, Everyman Theatre, Liverpool. Agent: Blanche Marvin, 21a St. John's Wood High Street, London N.W.8, England.

PUBLICATIONS

Plays

    Sweeney Todd: The Demon Barber of Fleet Street (produced Stoke on Trent, 1970; London, 1973).   London, French, 1974.
    Mutiny (produced Stoke on Trent, 1970).
    Downright Hooligan (produced Stoke on Trent, 1972).
    Tarzan's Last Stand (produced Liverpool, 1973).
    Judge Jeffreys (produced Exeter, 1973; London, 1976).
    The Country Wife, adaptation of the play by William Wycherley (produced Liverpool, 1974).
    Under New Management (produced Liverpool, 1975).
    The Cantril Tales, with others (produced Liverpool, 1975).
    George, in *Prompt One*, edited by Alan Durband.   London, Hutchinson, 1976.
    Scum: Death, Destruction and Dirty Washing, with Claire Luckham (produced London, 1976).

Novel

    You Want Drink Something Cold.   London, Joseph, 1969.

*   *   *

C. G. Bond is one of several young British dramatists to have grown up under the spell of Joan Littlewood's Theatre Workshop in Stratford, East London. In his case, however, a primary attraction to the theatre began almost from his cradle. His parents had run a touring company after the Second World War, and Bond himself was a child actor, playing at the Shakespeare Memorial Theatre, Stratford-upon-Avon from the age of eleven. He grew to love the rough-and-tumble of acting life, the performing skills and the ability to contact audiences at all levels of appreciation; and in his plays he loves to throw in effects which grab the attention – songs, dances, pieces of mime and simple stage tricks, such as the enlarged washing machine in *Under New Management* which "Harold MacMillan" mistakes for a Mini car and thus gets spun around with the rest of the laundry.

But the direction of his work, its more serious side, derives from Littlewood. Bond has written social and historical documentaries, such as *Under New Management* and *Judge Jeffreys*, and he seeks his audiences primarily from the young, working-class, left-wing public. Although not an overtly political writer, there is a strong vein of socialist thought within his work, which sometimes emerges into didactic messages but more normally is reflected in the handling of his themes – the caricatures of establishment authority, the sympathies with the under-privileged and downtrodden.

The clearest and most striking example of this tendency is *Downright Hooligan*, first produced at the Victoria Theatre, Stoke on Trent, where Bond was Resident Dramatist in 1972. The central character, Ian Rigby, is a sort of contemporary Woyzeck, whose eyes, deep-set beneath a granite forehead, suggest a Neanderthal mentality. Permanently out of work, a fixture in the betting shop, Ian is surrounded by a society whose logical illogicalities he cannot comprehend. His mother bawls at him for masturbating in his bedroom, while her lover winks at him and tells him dirty jokes. He accidentally kills the school hamster and sticks drawing pins in its eyes to decorate the body. His headmaster is appalled by the atrocity – but he doesn't know that Ian has just paid his last respects to his grandmother, whose dead drawn face has been padded out with clutches of her own hair. One form of decorating the dead is socially acceptable – Ian's treatment of the hamster is not. Confronted by the unpredictability of society, Ian asserts himself by hitting out savagely at an elderly man and is brought before the courts as a downright hooligan.

Thus, Bond, without glamourising his hero-victim, places the blame for his behaviour upon society at large; and some critics have claimed that his impression of the repressive social forces is simplistic, belonging too much to a "them" and "us" mentality. While his portrait of Ian Rigby's background was telling and convincing, and presented with marvellous detail by the Stoke company, *Under New Management* was almost a cartoon, agit-prop documentary, showing twelve cretinous general managers – one dressed as a schoolboy clutching a teddy bear – messing up the Fisher-Bendix factory on the outskirts of Liverpool, until the heroic workers, faced by mass redundancy, take over. It was a thoroughly lively, enjoyable production, but inevitably one-sided, partly because Bond had deliberately not interviewed anyone from the management while conducting his research.

By trying to make his plays immediately entertaining, Bond also falls into the trap which snared some of Littlewood's productions. There is too much outer fun, too little inner content. The scenes are short and sketch-like, sometimes extended by horseplay, separated by songs and little dances, and the connecting themes are either lost or so heavily stressed that they seem merely repetitive. In the hands of a highly disciplined company, such as that of Stoke or of the old Liverpool Everyman, where Bond became Artisitic Director, this music-hall mixture could be pulled into a tight shape. His plays usually require the concentration supplied by a firm director and an experienced team.

While striving for a casual, easy-going and lighthearted approach to the theatre, Bond in fact usually demands great restraint and professionalism from his performers – an apparent contradiction which not all directors have realised. There was a luckless production of *Judge Jeffreys* at Stratford East, where the script seemed as banal as the performances; and *Tarzan's Last Stand*, about Enoch Powell the "ape man," seemed to miss its very broad, satirical target by not taking Powell's arguments sufficiently seriously. Bond (like a somewhat similar writer of social documentaries, Alan Plater) has yet to find perhaps that dramatic structure within which his talents and social insights can be best expressed.

—John Elsom

BOND, Edward.   British.   Born in London, 18 July 1934. Educated at state schools to age 14. National Service: army. Married Elisabeth Pablé in 1971. Member of the Writers Group of the Royal Court Theatre, London. Recipient: George Devine Award, 1968; John Whiting Award, 1969. Agent: Margaret Ramsay Ltd., 14a Goodwin's Court, London WC2N 4LL. Address: Royal Court Theatre, Sloane Square, London S.W.1, England.

PUBLICATIONS

Plays

The Pope's Wedding (produced London, 1962).   Included in The Pope's Wedding and
   Other Plays, 1971.
Saved (produced London, 1965; New Haven, Connecticut, 1968; New York, 1970).
   London, Methuen, and New York, Hill and Wang, 1966.
The Three Sisters, adaption of the play by Chekhov (produced London. 1967).
Narrow Road to the Deep North (produced Coventry, 1968; London and New York,
   1969).   London, Methuen, and New York, Hill and Wang, 1968.
Early Morning (produced London, 1968; New York, 1971).   London, Calder and
   Boyars, 1968; New York, Hill and Wang, 1969.
Black Mass (produced for the Anti-Apartheid Movement, London, 1970).   Included in
   The Pope's Wedding and Other Plays, 1971; in The Best Short Plays 1972, edited by
   Stanley Richards. Philadelphia. Chilton, 1972.
Passion (produced for the Campaign for Nuclear Disarmament, London, 1971).
   Published in Plays and Players (London), June 1971; in The New York Times, 1971.
Lear (produced London, 1971; New Haven, Connecticut, 1973).   London, Methuen,
   and New York, Hill and Wang, 1972).
The Pope's Wedding and Other Plays (includes Mr. Dog, The King with Golden Eyes,
   Sharpville Sequence, Black Mass).   London, Methuen, 1971.
The Sea (produced London, 1973; New York, 1975).   London, Eyre Methuen, 1973;
   in Bingo, and the Sea, 1975.
Bingo: Scenes of Money and Death (and Passion) (produced Exeter, 1973; London,
   1974).   London, Eyre Methuen, 1974; in Bingo, and The Sea, 1975.
Spring's Awakening, adaptation of the play by Frank Wedekind (produced London,
   1974).
The Fool: Scenes of Bread and Love (produced London, 1975). Included in The Fool, and
   We Come to the River, 1976.
Bingo, and The Sea: Two Plays.   New York, Hill and Wang, 1975.
We Come to the River: Actions for Music, music by Hans Werner Henze (produced
   London, 1976).   London, Schott, 1976.
A-A-America : Grandma Faust, and The Swing (produced London, 1976). Included in
   Stone, and A-A-America, 1976.
The White Devil, adaptation of the play by Webster (produced London, 1976).
Stone (produced London, 1976).   Included in Stone, and A-A-America. 1976.
The Fool, and We Come to the River.   London, Eyre Methuen, 1976.
Stone, and A-A-America.   London, Eyre Methuen, 1976.

Screenplays: Blow-Up, 1967: Laughter in the Dark, 1969: The Lady of Monza (English
dialogue). 1970.

Radio Play: Badger by Owl-Light, 1975.

                              *   *   *

Edward Bond writes the most lapidary dialogue of today's English theater, absorbing popular locutions into its own mineral vein. Bond discarded over a dozen plays before sending *The Pope's Wedding* to George Devine's Royal Court in 1961. That drama is built with pithy phrases, swift scenes, and vivid characters. Bond has continued to use these building-blocks, styling them in three main ways – the surface realism of *The Pope's Wedding*, *Saved*, and *The Sea*; the invented or embellished history of *Early Morning*, *Black Mass*, *Bingo*, and *The Fool*; the war parables of *Narrow Road to the Deep North*, *Passion*, and *Lear*. Though Bond's reach occasionally exceeds his grasp, the reach itself is rare and exhilarating.

The plays of surface realism shock by their pointless murders: young Scopey throttles an old hermit at the end of *The Pope's Wedding*; a group of youths stone a baby to death in the middle of *Saved*; at the beginning of *The Sea* Colin drowns while Hatch watches idly from the shore. However, confrontation with these deaths involves radical action on the part of Bond's protagonists. Behind its provocative title *The Pope's Wedding* dramatizes a young man's vain effort to fully understand another human being. Step by step, Scopey abandons companions, wife, job, in order to spend his time with an old hermit to learn "What yoo 'ere for?" Even in the old man's coat, communing with his corpse, he never learns.

As the title *Saved* suggests, Len is more successful. A loner, Len does not share in the bored activities of London youths who game, steal, fornicate. They rub a baby's face in its diaper, then pitch stones into its carriage while Len, perhaps the baby's father, watches. The baby dies, and only later does Len admit: "Well, I should a stopped yer." Rejected by the baby's mother, flirting briefly with the grandmother, Len the loner is finally "saved" by the grandfather's barely articulate plea for him to remain in their household.

The Sea opens with Colin's drowning while his friend Willie pleads vainly for help from Evens a drunken recluse and Hatch a paranoid coast-guard watch. Later Willie barely escapes a murderous attack by Hatch, who believes him to be an enemy from outer space. Despite his grief at Colin's death, contrasted with the satirized indifference of the townspeople, Willie comes to see that "The dead don't matter." Persuading Colin's fiancée to leave the town with him, he swims in the sea after his dead friend's seaside funeral. Cumulatively, through these apparently realistic plays "Life laughs at death."

In the history-based plays such laughter is sporadic – riotously disrespectful in *Early Morning*, thinning toward zero in *Bingo*, and bordering on madness in *The Fool*. *Early Morning* puns on mourning, but the play is grotesquely hilarious. Proper Queen Victoria has Siamese twin sons, Crown Prince George and the protagonist Arthur. The Queen betroths the former to Florence Nightingale and then rapes her. Prince Albert, Disraeli, and Gladstone plot against the Queen. By mid-play the whole cast is dead in Heaven, where the main activity is cannibalism, with all flesh regenerating. Arthur alone refuses to accept heavenly habit, starving himself to a second death.

Suicide also closes the grimmer *Bingo*, whose protagonist is William Shakespeare in retirement at Stratford. Aware that the land enclosure spreads starvation, Shakespeare nevertheless fails to oppose it so long as his own investments are guaranteed. After a visit from drunk Ben Jonson, Shakespeare's disgust with the cruelties of his fellow-men shifts to self-disgust at failure to act: "How long have I been dead?" He answers the question with actual death by poison.

Like *Bingo*, *The Fool* indicts the cruelties of an acquisitive society. But unlike *Bingo*'s Shakespeare, The Fool who is poet John Clare is exploited by a new economic system. Not only does he lose money, his money-greedy love, and his poems, but also his sanity. Though Bond allows only sketchy development to his two protagonist poets, Shakespeare and Clare, he dramatizes their society with deft economy.

Of Bond's war parables, *Narrow Road to the Deep North* takes place in nineteenth-century Japan. Basho, the protagonist, follows the narrow road to the deep north in order to study solitude, but he learns that "enlightenment is where you are." And where he is necessitates a choice between two evils, an English invader or a homegrown warlord. Choosing the former, he obliquely causes the suicide of his young disciple. As the play ends, Basho is Prime Minister, his disciple falls disembowelled, and a stranger emerges from the river.

Each man must make his own decisions in a time of war.

Of all Bond's protagonists, his Lear experiences the hardest enlightenment. From Shakespeare Bond borrows the large tragic conception intensified by grotesque humor. By way of Shakespeare, Bond re-enforces his own dramatic concern with moral responsibility. As in Shakespeare, Lear is an absolute autocrat. Instead of dividing his kingdom, Bond's Lear encloses it within a wall built by forced labor. Lear's two daughters foment war, and both meet violent deaths. A composite of Kent and the Fool, Bond's Gravedigger's Boy has a wife named Cordelia. After the Boy is shot and his wife raped by the daughters' soldiers, his Ghost accompanies Lear on an infernal descent through madness and blindness. The Gravedigger's Boy's Ghost is slain, Lear attains wisdom, and Cordelia attains power as head of a new autocracy. At the old home of the twice killed Gravedigger's Boy, Lear speaks out against Cordelia's wall. In spite of his age, he then tries physically to dismantle the wall, but he is shot. Like Shakespeare's Lear, he has learned compassion, but he has also learned the necessity for socially responsible action.

Bond's violent scenes and cruel humor at first attracted attention rather than appreciation, but he has gradually gathered admirers of his moral commitment theatricalized with verve and economy. Speaking against the Theatre of the Absurd – "Life becomes meaningless when you stop *acting* on the things that concern you most" – Bond has called his work The Rational Theatre. Instead of preaching a rational gospel, however, he fills an almost bare stage with whole societies from which and against which heroes arise, who learn through their suffering to act responsibly. This resembles the *pathos-mathos* of classical tragedy, but it is translated into a modern godless world.

—Ruby Cohn

BOVASSO, Julie (Julia Anne Bovasso).   American.   Born in Brooklyn, New York, 1 August 1930. Educated at City College of New York, 1948–51. Married George Ortman in 1951 (divorced, 1958); Leonard Wayland, 1959 (divorced, 1964). Founder (director, producer, actress), Tempo Playhouse, New York, 1953–56. Taught at the New School for Social Research, New York, 1965–71; Brooklyn College, New York, 1968–69; since 1969, at Sarah Lawrence College, Bronxville, New York. President, New York Theatre Strategy, Inc. Recipient: Obie Award, Best Actress, and Best Experimental Theatre, 1956; Triple Obie Award, Best Playwright-Director-Actress, 1969; Rockefeller grant, 1969; New York Council on the Arts grant, 1970; Guggenheim Fellowship, 1971; Public Broadcasting Corporation award, 1972; Vernon Rice Award, for acting, 1972; Outer Circle Award, for acting, 1972. Agent: Helen Harvey Associates, 1697 Broadway, New York, New York 10019. Address: 14 West 10th Street, New York, New York 10011, U.S.A.

PUBLICATIONS

Plays

   The Moon Dreamers (also director: produced New York, 1967, and revised version, New York, 1969).   New York, French, 1972.

105

Gloria and Esperanza (also director: produced New York, 1968, and revised version, New York, 1970). New York, French, 1973.

Schubert's Last Serenade (produced New York, 1971). Published in *Spontaneous Combustion: Eight New American Plays*, edited by Rochelle Owens, New York, Winter House, 1972.

Monday on the Way to Mercury Island (produced New York, 1971).

Down by the River Where Waterlilies Are Disfigured Every Day (produced Providence, Rhode Island, 1972; New York, 1975).

The Nothing Kid, and Standard Safety (also director: produced New York, 1974). *Standard Safety* published, New York, French, 1976.

Super Lover, Schubert's Serenade, and The Final Analysis (also director: produced New York, 1975).

Theatrical Activities:

Director: **Plays** – many of her own plays; and at Tempo Playhouse, New York: *The Maids* by Jean Genet, 1953, *The Lesson* by Eugene Ionesco, 1955, and *The Typewriter* by Jean Cocteau, *Three Sisters Who Were Not Sisters* by Gertrude Stein, *Escurial* by Michel de Ghelderode, and *Amédée* by Eugene Ionesco, 1956; *Boom Boom Room* by David Rabe, New York, 1973.

Actress: **Plays** – A Maid in *The Bells* by Leopold Lewis, New York, 1943; Gwendolyn in *The Importance of Being Ernest* by Wilde, New York, 1947; title role in *Salome* by Wilde, New York, 1949; Belissa in *Don Perlimplin* by Lorca, New York, 1949; Lona Hessel in *Pillars of Society* by Ibsen, New York, 1949; title role in *Hedda Gabler* by Ibsen, New York, 1950; Emma in *Naked* by Pirandello, New York, 1950; Countess Geschwitz in *Earth Spirit* by Wedekind, New York, 1950; Zinida in *He Who Gets Slapped* by Andreyev, New York, 1950; title role in *Faustina* by Paul Goodman, New York, 1952; Anna Petrovna in *Ivanov* by Chekhov, San Francisco, 1952; Tempo Playhouse, New York: Margot in *The Typewriter* by Cocteau, 1953, Madeleine in *Amédée* by Eugene Ionesco, 1955, Claire, 1955, and Solange, 1956, in *The Maids* by Jean Genet, and The Student in *The Lesson* by Eugene Ionesco, 1956; Henriette in *Monique* by Dorothy and Michael Blankfort, New York, 1957; Luella in *Dinny and the Witches* by William Gibson, New York, 1959, The Wife in *Victims of Duty* by Eugene Ionesco, New York, 1960; Lucy and Martha in *Gallows Humor* by Jack Richardson, New York, 1960; Mistress Quickly in *Henry IV, Part One*, Stratford, Connecticut, 1963; Madame Rosepettle in *Oh Dad, Poor Dad...* by Arthur Kopit, Cincinnati, 1964; Mrs. Prosser in *A Minor Miracle* by Al Morgan, New York, 1965; Fortune Teller in *The Skin of Our Teeth* by Thornton Wilder, Cincinnati, 1966; Madame Irma in *The Balcony* by Jean Genet, Baltimore, 1967; Agata in *Island of Goats* by Ugo Betti, and Constance in *The Madwoman of Chaillot* by Giraudoux, Cincinnati, 1968; Gloria in *Gloria and Esperanza*, New York, 1970; The Mother in *The Screens* by Jean Genet, New York, 1971. **Television** – Rose in *From These Roots* series, 1958–60; Pearl in *The Iceman Cometh* by O'Neill, 1960, and other performances in *U.S. Steel Hour, The Defenders* and other series, 1958–63.

*   *   *

The Bovasso world is highly orchestrated; the work appears to be driven, indeed hounded, by an ideological aesthetic. Julie Bovasso, one of America's more interesting actresses, becomes as playwright a kind of mad mathematician, marshalling people and events into lunatic propositions and hallucinatory equations. The work sometimes marches to a drumbeat, sometimes sidles up to you, sometimes stridently calls out to the heavens, sometimes chuckles to itself. Throughout, there is the strong sense of the child infiltrating the grown-up theatre breathlessly, stealthily while the adults are asleep, relocating the furniture, putting bells on the cat, all to see how it will come out, to see whether the cunning proposition will prove itself.

The Moon Dreamers, one of the earlier Bovasso pieces, uses as the core of its narrative a simple situation in which life, husband and mistress can't agree as to who is to vacate the apartment. But into the situation, Miss Bovasso, with a sense of increasing lunacy, introduces the wife's mother (Jewish), a lawyer (specified as dark-haired) who turns out to be the wife's second cousin, a doctor who turns out to be a childhood admirer of the wife's, an Indian chief who turns out to be a Japanese Buddhist, and a chief of police who turns out to be a French midget. Doctor, Lawyer, Indian chief, as well as Jewish momma and Gallic Fuzz. All these argue and split hairs in an increasingly complicated situation that on its surface is humorous but nevertheless suggests it is going somewhere other than farce. Around this core, Miss Bovasso adds another layer, what she designates as an "Epic" world as opposed to the "Personal" world. The characters of the Epic world are in shadows, there is barely dialogue for them and they seem to exist principally as witnesses. But there are dozens of them, soldiers, Black stockbrokers, gangsters, belly dancers, snake dancers, Spanish royalty. The domestic squabble is thus both knotted with what we might call the presence of banal archetypes and overseen by graver archetypes until it simply ceases to be what it has been. That is, it seems to become nothing that we can intellectually comprehend – until the end when the appearance of the astronaut, a kind of deus ex machina, makes a comprehensive statement about humanity – but rather something that we must allow to wash over us if we want to continue sensing it at all. Any formation seems to be taken out of our hands and we must become like children or Martians witnessing an unknown world.

Monday on the Way to Mercury Island is filled with both dialogue and silent actions that recur numerous times, sometimes repeated identically, sometimes with variations. As in *Moon Dreamers*, these are sometimes banal and sometimes extraordinary. But even the banal elements usually suggest something beyond themselves. The repetition tends to ritualize these sounds and movements without providing a philosophical base. A formal, austere aesthetic seems to be at work. The ritual tends here to make the theatre more into play, a relentlessly earnest if also whimsical play.

But there appears to be a political thesis at work. Servants and peasants rise at last against socialite masters. The latter are painted as corrupt and soft, the former as steadfast and hard. But even here the intellectual content seems subordinate to the flowering theatrics, to the rhythms and colors of spectacle.

Down by the River Where Waterlilies Are Disfigured Every Day is another vast landscape, another epic with vivid theatrics. The Bovasso trait of mixed, merged or transferred identities is strong here. Phoebe and Clement, lovers for many years, exchange clothes and then sexes. Count Josef, leader of the established order, is at work on a statue of Pango, head of the revolutionary forces, breathing life and the qualities dear to him into the figure that is attempting to end his own life. Revolt is strong here. Overturned lives, overturned order. In *Monday* the peasants end by burying the aristocrat. In *Waterlilies* the children toss the old world on to a garbage heap in the town square. But again one has the sense that the playing out of the act takes precedence over the intellectual meaning of the act, that the logic of aesthetics and of form is ultimately the prime mover.

—Arthur Sainer

BOWEN, John (Griffith).   British.   Born in Calcutta, India, 5 November 1924. Educated at Pembroke College, Oxford, 1948–51; St. Anthony's College, Oxford (Frere Exhibitioner in Indian Studies), 1951–53, M.A., 1953; Ohio State University, Columbus, 1952–53. Served as a Captain in the Mahratha Light Infantry, 1943–47. Assistant Editor, *The Sketch* magazine, London, 1953–56; Copywriter, J. Walter Thompson Company, London, 1956–58; Head of the Copy Department, S. T. Garland Advertising, London, 1958–60; Script Consultant, Associated Television, London, 1960–67. Stage Director, at the London Academy of Dramatic Art, and elsewhere. Address: Old Lodge Farm, Sugarswell Lane, Edgehill, Banbury, Oxfordshire OX15 6HP, England.

PUBLICATIONS

Plays

> *The Essay Prize, with A Holiday Abroad and The Candidate: Plays for Television.* London, Faber, 1962.
> *I Love You, Mrs. Patterson* (produced Cambridge and London, 1964). London, Evans, 1964.
> *The Corsican Brothers*, based on the play by Dion Boucicault (televised, 1965; produced London, 1970). London, Methuen, 1970.
> *After the Rain*, adaptation of his own novel (produced London, 1966; New York, 1967). London, Faber, 1967; New York, Random House, 1968; revised version, Faber, 1972.
> *Fall and Redemption* (produced London, 1967; as *The Fall and Redemption of Man*, produced New York, 1974). London, Faber, 1969.
> *Silver Wedding* (televised, 1967; revised version, produced, in *We Who Are about to...*, later called *Mixed Doubles*, London, 1969). London, Methuen, 1970.
> *Little Boxes* (includes *The Coffee Lace* and *Trevor*) (produced London, 1968; New York, 1969). London, Methuen, 1968; New York, French, 1970.
> *The Disorderly Women* (produced Manchester, 1969; London, 1970). London, Methuen, 1969.
> *The Waiting Room* (produced London, 1970). London, French, 1970; New York, French, 1971.
> *A Woman Sobbing* (broadcast, 1972). Published in *The Television Play*, edited by Robin Wade, London, BBC, 1976.
> *Robin Redbreast* (televised, 1970; produced Guildford, Surrey, 1974). Published in *The Television Dramatist*, edited by Robert Muller, London, Elek, 1973.
> *Diversions* (produced London, 1973). Published in *London Magazine*, 1976.
> *Roger*, in *Mixed Blessings* (produced Horsham, Sussex, 1973).
> *Miss Nightingale* (televised, 1974; revised version, as *Florence Nightingale*, produced Canterbury, 1975).
> *Heil Caesar!* (televised, 1974; produced Birmingham, 1974). London, French, 1975.
> *Which Way Are You Facing?* (produced Bristol, 1976).
> *The Fortunate Conspiracy*, adaptation of a play by Marivaux (produced London, 1977).

Radio Plays: *Digby*, with Jeremy Bullmore (as Justin Blake), 1959; *Varieties of Love* (revised version of television play *The First Thing You Think Of*), 1968.

Television Plays: created the *Garry Halliday* series; episodes in *Front Page Story, The Power Game, The Guardians* (7 episodes), and *The Villains* series; *A Holiday Abroad*, 1960; *The Essay Prize*, 1960; *The Jackpot Question*, 1961; *The Candidate*, 1961; *Nuncle*, from the story by John Wain, 1962; *The Truth about Alan*, 1963; *A Case of Character*, 1964; *Mr. Fowlds*, 1965; *The Corsican Brothers*, 1965; *Finders Keepers*, 1967; *The Whole Truth*, 1967; *A Most Unfortunate Accident*, 1968; *Flotsam and Jetsam*, 1970; *Robin Readbreast*, 1970; *A Woman Sobbing*, 1972; *The Emergency Channel*,

1973; *Young Guy Seeks Part-Time Work*, 1973; *Miss Nightingale*, 1974; *Heil Caesar!*, 1974; *The Treasure of Abbot Thomas*, 1974; *The Snow Queen*, 1974; *A Juicy Case*, 1975; *Brief Encounter*, from the film by Noël Coward, 1976.

Novels

    The Truth Will Not Help Us: Embroidery on an Historical Theme.   London, Chatto and Windus, 1956.

    After the Rain.   London, Faber, 1958; New York, Ballantine, 1959.

    The Centre of the Green.   London, Faber, 1959; New York, McDowell Obolensky, 1960.

    Storyboard.   London, Faber, 1960.

    The Birdcage.   London, Faber, and New York, Harper, 1962.

    A World Elsewhere.   London, Faber, 1966; New York, Coward McCann, 1967.

Other

    Pegasus (juvenile).   London, Faber, 1957; New York, Day, 1958.

    The Mermaid and the Boy (juvenile).   London, Faber, 1958; New York, Barnes, 1960.

    Garry Halliday and the Disappearing Diamonds, with Jeremy Bullmore (as Justin Blake; juvenile).   London, Faber, 1960.

    Garry Halliday and the Ray of Death, with Jeremy Bullmore (as Justin Blake; juvenile). London, Faber, 1961.

    Garry Halliday and the Kidnapped Five, with Jeremy Bullmore (as Justin Blake; juvenile).   London, Faber, 1962.

    Garry Halliday and the Sands of Time, with Jeremy Bullmore (as Justin Blake; juvenile). London, Faber, 1963.

    Garry Halliday and the Flying Foxes, with Jeremy Bullmore (as Justin Blake; juvenile). London, Faber, 1964.

Manuscript Collections: Mugar Memorial Library, Boston University; Rare Book Department, Temple University, Philadelphia (television works only).

Critical Studies: *Writers on Themselves*, London, BBC Publications, 1964; "The Man Behind *The Disorderly Women*" by Robin Thornber, in *The Guardian* (London), 19 February 1969; "Like a Woman They Keep Coming Back To" by Ronald Hayman, in *Drama* (London), Autumn 1970; "Bowen on the Little Box" by Hugh Hebert, in *The Guardian* (London), 6 August 1971; "Author/Director" by the author, in *London Magazine*, December 1971; "*The Guardians*: A Post Mortem" by the author, in *Plays and Players* (London), January 1972.

Theatrical Activities:

    Director: **Plays** – at the London Academy of Music and Dramatic Art since 1967; *The Disorderly Women*, Manchester, 1969, London, 1970; *Fall and Redemption*, Pitlochry, Scotland, 1969; *The Waiting Room*, London, 1970.

    Actor: **Plays** – in repertory in North Wales, Summers 1950–51; Palace Theatre, Watford, Hertfordshire, 1965.

John Bowen comments:

    My plays, like my novels, are distinguished by a general preoccupation with myth (*The Truth Will Not Help Us, After the Rain, A World Elsewhere, Fall and Redemption, The*

Disorderly Women, Robin Redbreast), and mainly with one particular myth, that of the Bacchae, which in my reading represents the conflict between Apollonian and Dionysiac ways of living more than the mere tearing to pieces of a Sacred King. This theme, the fight in every human being and between beings themselves, rationality against instinct, is to be found somewhere in almost everything I have written.

Another common theme is of manipulation, one person using another or others, not always consciously, and sometimes "for their good." This theme has been most clearly expressed politically in the episodes I wrote for the television series, *The Guardians*, and in my novel *A World Elsewhere*. A third common theme, allied to the other two, is that of self-deceit.

I think of plays as constructions (as all literary forms are, but plays and poems perhaps most), and I enjoy theatricality. I like movement; plays are not talk, but action, though the talk may *be* action. I think that the cinema and television have helped the theatre in the 20th century to rediscover some of the mobility it had in the 16th. Though I like above all naturalistic acting, I hate naturalistic settings, and will try to avoid waits for scene changes: in most of my plays, the scenes flow into each other by a shift of light.

I have been influenced by Ibsen and Chekhov, probably by Coward. Anouilh, Pirandello and Shaw. Of 20th-century directors, I have most admired the late Sir Tyrone Guthrie.

*   *   *

When his first stage play, *I Love You, Mrs. Patterson*, opened in the West End in 1964, John Bowen was about forty and had considerable experience as a novelist, as a book reviewer, and as a broadcaster, but the medium with which he had most recently been involved was television. After writing a good many scripts, some of which derived from his own fiction, he wrote a novel about commercial television, *The Birdcage* (1962), and then went on to accept a job as script consultant for ATV.

His first attempt at a dramatization of his novel *After the Rain* was made in 1960 for Bryan Bailey of the Belgrade Theatre, Coventry, who died just after receiving the first draft. John Bowen himself was unhappy with it and his first play to be staged was therefore *I Love You, Mrs. Patterson*, a well carpentered play about a schoolboy's love affair with a teacher's wife. Both content and form were in line with his television plays.

Subsequently he has swung away from the naturalistic mode. The swing started in his 1966 version of *After the Rain*, which considerably enhanced his reputation but did not really do justice to its social, moral, philosophical and religious themes. It sets out ambitiously to satirize both 22nd century authoritarianism and our own antediluvian society. The story of the second Flood and the birth of the new society are narrated by a rather irritating lecturer and acted out by state prisoners who are under hypnosis to make them do what is required of them. John Bowen's considerable expertise as a story-teller is inadequate to sustain the tension as he shifts between the survivors' raft and the lecture hall where the story is being re-enacted two hundred years later, and many of his decisions about how to apportion the limited time the play can run seem to derive from the naturalistic habit. For instance, we get a leisurely build-up to the revelation that the muscle-man is impotent and only a sketchy treatment of huge themes like the return of the survivors to theocracy and the process by which their leader is elevated to the status of a god. Nor are the attempts at infusing comedy into the religious theme altogether successful, though one can see the kind of balance he is aiming at:

Gertrude –Oh Harold, I hope he will never appear to us in a frowning mask.
Muriel –   Not to us, but he may to some.
Lecturer – (to assistants) Bring on the god.
(Assistants go offstage. Characters face upstage in silence, and wait, lecturer continues)
They soaked pages of the Shell Guide to Bedfordshire in a pot with glue, and made a mask. The god kept to his own small room, and was

not seen outside.
(Assistants bring Arthur on. He is masked and his beard protrudes
outside the mask. He walks like a sleepwalker, guided by the Assistants
who stand him on a stool. While)
It was hot in the god's holy place, and close, and being a god, he could
not wash or visit the lavatory, except privately, so the atmosphere
became unpleasant.

Altogether the play is quite an inventive piece of writing but lacking in humour and
humanity, rather in the same way as the society he was attacking.

This could not be said of Bowen's 1968 double bill *Little Boxes*. The component plays *The
Coffee Lace* and *Trevor* were both amusing and warm, but more modest and more
naturalistic. The critics seemed disappointed at Bowen's failure to continue on an
experimental tack. Ronald Bryden complained of "a sacrifice of character to neatness,"
while Irving Wardle thought he detected an instance of "the well-made play's habit of
reducing a general theme to an artificially special case." The link between the two plays was
a concern for the isolation of city-dwellers in big cities. *The Coffee Lace* deals delicately –
though not altogether unsentimentally – with three married couples and the man who used
to be their manager when they worked together in a variety act. It could have been written
as a television play, but *Trevor* was highly theatrical, in the tradition of Goldoni and
Feydeau. It is about two Lesbian girls who are both going to be visited by their parents in
the flat they share. They employ an actor to double as two boyfriends, and the play works
amusingly to a hectic climax as he scampers from one part of the flat to another, going all
out to satisfy both sets of parents. The fun that John Bowen extracts from the situation is
legitimate enough, but the serious ending sits oddly on top of it.

Two of his subsequent plays, like his previous one, have been adaptations. *Fall and
Redemption*, which he staged himself in a 1967 production with students at LAMDA is a
reworking of mystery plays from the Chester, Coventry, Lincoln, Norwich, Wakefield and
York cycles into more-or-less modern English. But many archaisms remain and there is
considerable loss of vigour from the originals:

From forth her virgin womb shall come a child
Who will get for men more grace than ever they had.
Her maidenhead by no man shall be defiled.
She shall bear the son of Almighty God.
And for Adam, that now lies in sorrow's bane,
This glorious birth shall redeem him again
From bondage and thrall.
This deed shall be done in Israel, before my throne,
And shall delight you all.

Bowen again worked with LAMDA students in preparing *The Disorderly Women*, a version
of Euripides's *Bacchae* in verse and prose, which was staged at the Stables Theatre Club in
Manchester during February 1969. Some of the verse is thin and some is Audenesque, but
there are invigoratingly brisk modulations between cod-ancient and trivial-modern,
between narrative and dramatization, tragedy and comedy, myth and satire, serious theatre
and deliberate theatricality. The treatment of Agave's murder of her son, Pentheus, is
particularly clever.

The Corsican Brothers, which was produced at the Greenwich Theatre in 1970, was based
on a development of the same technique of mixing modes. Based on the story by Dumas
dramatized by Dion Boucicault, the adaptation introduced songs and masks – alienation
effects imposed wittily on the romantic plot though much of the dialogue might have
sounded better in French:

Chateau-Renaud –	Yes, you do. Oh, my dear Miss Saint-Bernard, what a come-on. All this talk about equality! Byron! Chateaubriand! Georges Sand! And at the end –
Melanie –	(near tears) Being free is more than a matter of...of...
Chateau-Renaud –	My dear, freedom for a woman begins in bed.
Melanie –	Monsieur, you know that I have enjoyed your company.
Chateau-Renaud –	Thank you.
Melanie –	It didn't seem wrong to me to...have friends...to talk about ideas...books....
Chateau-Renaud –	But why should you imagine that I am interested in such things? Except as a means to an end.

Robin Redbreast, produced first on television and then in Guildford, is as suspenseful as any thriller, but it is much more than a thriller, efficiently reworking the theme of human sacrifice for the sake of fertilising the land. Alone after the end of an eight-year long relationship, a sophisticated 35-year old woman buys an isolated cottage in the country. The unsophisticated man she takes as her lover for one night appears to be siding with the villagers against her, but he turns out to be the villagers' victim, and she survives.

Heil Caesar! was commissioned by a television producer who boasted of his inability to stay awake during a performance of Julius Caesar, arguing that Shakespeare's language prevents "ordinary" people from enjoying his plays. *Heil Caesar!* transposes most of the plot to the 20th century: Caesar is Commander-in-Chief of an army which is clearly not British, Brutus is Minister of the Interior in a coalition government, Cassius a young careerist politician, and Mark Antony a Colonel. The measure of Bowen's success in transposing the play to modern times comes in the equivalent of the "Friends, Romans, countrymen" speech, made in a television studio with the camera crew in view:

> I promised – well, I had to promise – that I wouldn't make any personal attacks, so I shan't. Anyway Brutus has already told you all about the people who murdered Caesar. Senators, bankers, directors of this and that, respected citizens. Top people, VIP's! Of course that makes a lot of difference, doesn't it? If anyone else stabbed an old man with a flick knife you might get indignant. When a VIP does it, that's a different matter.

—Ronald Hayman

BRENTON, Howard.   British.   Born in Portsmouth, Hampshire, 13 December 1942. Educated at Cambridge University, B.A. in English 1965. Married Jane Brenton in 1970. Stage Manager in several repertory companies. Since 1972, Resident Dramatist, Royal Court Theatre, London. Recipient: Arts Council bursary, 1969, 1970; John Whiting Award, 1970. Agent: Rosica Colin Ltd., 4 Hertford Square, London SW7 4TU, England.

PUBLICATIONS

Plays

Ladder of Fools (produced Cambridge, 1965).
Winter, Daddykins (produced Dublin, 1965).

It's My Criminal (produced London, 1966).

A Sky-Blue Life, adaptation of stories by Gorky (produced London, 1966; revised version, produced London, 1971).

Gargantua (produced Brighton, 1969).

Gum and Goo (produced Brighton, 1969; London, 1971).   Included in *Plays for Public Places*, 1972.

Revenge (produced London, 1969).   London, Methuen, 1970.

Heads, and The Education of Skinny Spew (produced Bradford, 1969; London, 1970). Included in *Christie in Love and Other Plays*, 1970.

Christie in Love (produced London, 1970).   Included in *Christie in Love and Other Plays*, 1970.

Christie in Love and Other Plays (includes *Heads* and *The Education of Skinny Spew*). London, Methuen, 1970.

Fruit (produced London, 1970).

Wesley (produced Bradford, 1970).   Included in *Plays for Public Places*, 1972.

Scott of the Antarctic; or, What God Didn't See (produced Bradford, 1971).   Included in *Plays for Public Places*, 1972.

Lay By, with others (produced Edinburgh and London, 1971).   London, Calder and Boyars, 1972.

Hitler Dances (produced London, 1972).

Plays for Public Places (includes *Gum and Goo*, *Wesley*, and *Scott of the Antarctic; or, What God Didn't See*).   London, Eyre Methuen, 1972.

How Beautiful with Badges (produced London, 1972).

England's Ireland, with others (produced Amsterdam and London, 1972).

Measure for Measure, adaptation of the play by Shakespeare (produced Exeter, 1972).

A Fart for Europe, with David Edgar (produced London, 1973).

The Screens, adaptation of a play by Jean Genet (produced Bristol, 1973).

Brassneck, with David Hare (produced Nottingham, 1973).   London, Eyre Methuen, 1974.

Magnificence (produced London, 1973).   London, Eyre Methuen, 1974.

Saliva Milkshake, adaptation of the novel *Under Western Eyes* by Joseph Conrad (televised, 1974; produced London, 1975).

The Churchill Play: As It Will Be Performed in the Winter of 1984 by the Internees of Churchill Camp Somewhere in England (produced Nottingham, 1974).   London, Eyre Methuen, 1974.

Government Property (produced Aarhus, Denmark, 1975).

Weapons of Happiness (produced London, 1976).   London, Eyre Methuen, 1976.

Screenplay: *Skin Flicker*, 1973.

Television Plays: *Lushly*, 1972; *Saliva Milkshake*, 1974; *The Paradise Run*, 1976.

Verse

Notes from a Psychotic Journal and Other Poems.   Brighton, privately printed, 1969.

Critical Study: Interview with Peter Ansorge, in *Plays and Players* (London), February 1972.

Theatrical Activities:

Actor: **Plays** – with the Brighton Combination, 1969.

*   *   *

Through his association with Portable Theatre, Howard Brenton was the first writer to develop its terse, concentrated, non-literary style which relies on speed of action, verbal and visual gags and sharpness of impression to make its points. A main theme of all his plays is the contrast, seen objectively, between the frequent, cruel sadism of people's fantasy lives and the irrelevant, inhuman, outmoded, external forms and restrictions of society that help both to intensify and invert these fantasies and deny them a real chance of expression.

Christie in Love, which won him the John Whiting Award in 1970, shows the mass-murderer Christie killing his victims and then making love to them, his necrophilia being the expression of his particular need and talent. There is no blockage between intention and action, so Christie is seen almost as an existential hero. The trouble begins when society, in the shape of the policeman, has to repress Christie's deviations in order to maintain a mythical, non-existent "normality." The Inspector and the Constable do their best to find a rational explanation for Christie's actions, without success. For it is they, in fact, who on one level are abnormal because they willingly subordinate their individual needs to those of society, while Christie just "does his own thing." Like many of his later plays, *Christie in Love* realizes the decay and irrelevance of society's outmoded moral code in physical and symbolic terms, in this case, putrid flesh, rotting corpses underneath the floorboards, horrible smells infecting Christie's house in Rillington Place.

Revenge explores the same area of an exhausted morality in another policeman versus criminal confrontation. Adam Hepple, a master criminal, vows revenge on Macleish, the policeman who put him away. Though they subjectively hate each other's guts, objectively they both play the game by recognizable rules, little realizing that these are no longer valid, as they are the product of a more settled society that is now rapidly changing. Seen against this perspective, their conflict is defunct, as a new phase of society's dialectic, dimly perceived by one of the ordinary coppers on the beat − "The times they are a-changing, to coin a phrase" − is in the process of creation. This irony is tartly expressed in the author's stage direction that the same actor should play Hepple and Macleish.

His trio of short plays about children, *Gum and Goo, The Education of Skinny Spew* and *Heads*, use a strip-cartoon style incisively and brilliantly, the first two to convey how adult emotional hang-ups originate in childhood, *Heads* to make an ironical comment on how society totally divorces and alienates our intellectual from our sensual needs. *Gum and Goo* enters the world of sado-masochistic children's games and shows how they are sparked off by children aping their parents' prejudices; *Skinny Spew* shows the progress of a juvenile delinquent from the cradle, through bumping off his parents, into an orphanage which is a symbol for the repressive forces of society as a whole, forcing Skinny to regress into infantilism; while *Heads* shows a girl torn between two boyfriends, one who is pure intellect, the other pure physique, grafting the head of one onto the body of the other, with disastrous results.

But though all of these plays make use of grotesque surrealistic images in an economical way originally forced on the plays by the conditions in which they were performed, they are far from being crude or one-dimensional. An astonishing compression and density of thought and imagination, along with a trenchant humour, characterize the best of Brenton's work, which all the plays so far mentioned are.

Skin Flicker, filmed in an appropriate neo-brutalistic style by Tony Bicat, starkly and effectively contrasts a pompous, phrase-making Cabinet Minister with three rather pathetic and inadequate deviants who kidnap and eventually kill him. Written in appropriately brutal and abrupt cinematic images, the script has many vital and interesting points to make about the total lack of connection between people's interior lives and the bureaucratic repressions placed on them by society. *How Beautiful with Badges* shows, with the author's customary sharpness and precision, how a young man fucked up by his bourgeois, right-wing background hangs on to his Maoist political beliefs as a lifeline to maintain some kind of balance and sanity. Politics as psychotherapy is also one of the strands in *Lushly*, a short television play, about some landlords' men and the strains imposed on them psychologically by the execution of their jobs. The characterization in this play is particularly effective.

Brenton has also written plays on more public themes which, however, represent the obverse side of the coin to his other work. *Fruit* is a stunning little play about corruption, specifically the fraudulence and pretence of Britian's "democratic," "two-party" political system. Disease of one kind or another is the central image of the play. The osteopath with grotesque physical and sexual deformities ministers to the needs of corrupt politicians like the homosexual Tory Prime Minister, interested only in personal power and its manipulation, and the boozy Labour ex-Minister, whose working-class origins got lost somewhere in the dim mists of antiquity. Private and public hypocrisy feed on each other in an escalating vicious circle of dishonesty and evasion. The osteopath's attempt to blackmail the Prime Minister on account of his sexual foibles founders in irrelevancy, as this has all been catered for in the idea of politics as "spectacle."

Scott of the Antarctic, written for a boozy late-night audience in the Bradford Ice Rink, savagely derides public school concepts of heroism in a series of crude hammer blows. *Wesley* is a giant blow-up account of the founder of Methodism and how his total commitment to his faith landed him in a mess of contradictions. *A Sky-Blue Life*, by contrast, is a subtle, sensitive examination of the interplay between Gorky's life and his art. Episodic in structure, it has a telling confrontation between Gorky and Lenin on the relation between politics and art.

Hitler Dances, created in conjunction with the Traverse Workshop Company, has as its theme the perennially relevant one of how war sanctifies the exercise of callous and sadistic instincts by the name of "patriotism." Principally, it does this by showing the career of Violette Szabo, heroine of the last war. But, despite many effective scenes, it does not really knit together as a whole, probably due in part to the artistic circumstances in which it was created.

Magnificence has many affinities with *Skin Flicker*. In both, we see young revolutionaries contrasted with the Establishment, in the form of Tory Cabinet ministers. The play begins with a squat, led by four young people, Jed, Mary, Will and Veronica. They bicker about the politics of what they are doing. Jed, Mary and Will are anarchists, while Veronica, who works for the BBC, is a *Guardian*-style liberal moralist. The action then cuts to Alice and Babs, a present and a former Tory minister, punting down the Cam. The best scene of the play in an artistic sense, it contrasts the Macmillanite paternalism of Babs, a superannuated statesman put out to grass, with the graceless, abrasive Heath-style Toryism of Alice. Despite its many virtues, the plays suffers from a lack of political clarity. Brenton seems to have a sneaking regard for the outmoded High Toryism of Babs, while his own politics are suspended between Jed's initial anarchism and its subsequent transformation into a half-baked version of Marxism.

Brassneck, written with David Hare, is an entertaining study of a cross-section of Nottingham society since the end of the war, in the often murky area where national and local politics and business interests intersect. The main action centres around three generations of the Bagley family, builders by trade. To get himself established, Alfred Bagley has to become a freemason; and a hilarious scene shows him going through the initiating ceremony. We see the opportunist wheeling-and-dealing, collaboration between Tories and Socialists, and general oiling of palms over a period of 30 years of public works. There is one particularly brilliant scene where Alfred imagines himself to be a new Borgia Pope. Artistically, the play is Brenton's most mature work to date and adds up to a convincing picture of capitalism in decline.

The Churchill Play is a further sign of the author's development. It shows Churchill and his ruling-class patriotism from the perspective of prisoners in a Fascist prison-camp in the Britain of 1984. In its totality, it shows the ideological struggle between the socialism we are painfully stumbling into and the positive political qualities of conservatism ossified into fascism.

—Jonathan Hammond

BROPHY, Brigid. British. Born in London, 12 June 1929. Educated at St. Paul's Girls'
School; St. Hugh's College, Oxford (Jubilee Scholarship), 1947–48. Married Michael Levey
in 1954; has one child. Collaborated with Maureen Duffy, *q.v.*, in making and exhibiting
Prop Art (3-D Construction), London, 1969. Vice-President, National Anti-Vivisection
Society of Great Britain, 1970; Co-Founder, Writers Action Group, 1972; Executive
Councillor, Writers' Guild of Great Britain, 1975. Recipient: Cheltenham Literary Festival
prize for a first novel, 1954; *London Magazine* prize for prose, 1962. Fellow, Royal Society of
Literature, 1973. Address: Flat 3, 185 Old Brompton Road, London S.W.5, England.

PUBLICATIONS

Plays

> *The Waste-Disposal Unit* (broadcast, 1964).   Published in *London Magazine*, April
>   1964; in *Best Short Plays of the World Theatre 1958–67*, New York, Crown, 1968.
> *The Burglar* (produced London, 1967).   London, Cape, and New York, Holt Rinehart,
>   1968.

> Radio Play: *The Waste-Disposal Unit*, 1964.

Novels

> *Hackenfeller's Ape.*   London, Hart Davis, 1953; New York, Random House, 1954.
> *The King of a Rainy Country.*   London, Secker and Warburg, 1956; New York,
>   Knopf, 1957.
> *Flesh.*   London, Secker and Warburg, 1962; Cleveland, World, 1963.
> *The Finishing Touch.*   London, Secker and Warburg, 1963.
> *The Snow Ball.*   London, Secker and Warburg, 1964.
> *The Snow Ball, with The Finishing Touch.*   Cleveland, World, 1964.
> *In Transit.*   London, Macdonald, 1969; New York, Putnam, 1970.
> *The Adventures of God in His Search for the Black Girl: A Novel and Some Fables.*
>   London, Macmillan, 1973; Boston, Little Brown, 1974.

Short Stories

> *The Crown Princess and Other Stories.*   London, Collins, and New York, Viking Press,
>   1953.

Other

> *Black Ship to Hell.*   London, Secker and Warburg, and New York, Harcourt Brace,
>   1962.
> *Mozart the Dramatist: A New View of Mozart, His Operas and His Age.*   London,
>   Faber, and New York, Harcourt Brace, 1964.
> *Don't Never Forget: Collected Views and Reviews.*   London, Cape, 1966, New York,
>   Holt Rinehart, 1967.
> *Religious Education in State Schools.*   London, Fabian Society, 1967.
> *Fifty Works of English and American Literature We Could Do Without*, with Michael
>   Levey and Charles Osborne.   London, Rapp and Carroll, 1967; New York, Stein
>   and Day, 1968.

Black and White: A Portrait of Aubrey Beardsley.   London, Cape, 1968.
The Longford Threat to Freedom.   London, National Secular Society, 1972.
*Prancing Novelist: A Defence of Fiction in the Form of a Critical Biography in Praise of
    Ronald Firbank.*   London, Macmillan, 1972; New York, Barnes and Noble, 1973.
Beardsley and His World.   London, Thames and Hudson, and New York, Crown,
    1976.

Critical Study: *Guide to Modern World Literature* by Martin Seymour-Smith, London,
Wolfe, 1973.

Brigid Brophy comments:

Between the ages of 6 and 10, I was a prolific playwright, mainly in blank verse. An
elderly widow in the London suburb where I lived, being anxious to foster the arts,
appointed herself my impresario. She assembled a cast (of local children) and a regular
audience (of their parents) and, season by season, mounted my *oeuvre* in her drawing room.

This excellent arrangement was, like much else, disrupted in 1939 by the war, and when I
eventually began my public literary career it was as an author of books. In 1961 or so I
reverted to my original vocation as dramatist by writing *The Waste-Disposal Unit*, a brief,
black and I hope funny *fleur du mal*, which I composed in two foreign languages (Italian and
American), with a touch of free verse, and through which I expressed my Baudelairean
fascination with the linguistic perversion that transforms English into American.

That was first performed, to approving notices, on BBC radio and has since been staged as
a one-act play, by students and other amateurs, in London, Cambridge and Hong Kong. In
1967 a full-length play of mine, *The Burglar*, was produced in the West End. It concerns the
plight of a burglar who, thinking to break into merely an empty household in order to filch
material objects, in fact irrupts into the close-woven relationships of four lovers. I hoped to
produce theatrical amusement, a pleasing formal pattern and some illumination of our
social morality by the shock confrontation of the burglar (an economic libertarian but a
sexual puritan) with the lovers, who are sexual libertarians but conventionalists on the
subject of property. The play displeased the London critics and was a moderately resounding
flop. (I believe, however, it fared more happily in Dortmund.) I subsequently published it
with a long preface which begins as an ephemeral defence of myself but continues, more
importantly, with a discussion of society's attitude, including its unconscious attitude,
towards the behaviour it labels crime.

The play's commercial failure understandably warned impresarios against me and
brought my public career as a dramatist to an end. I have naturally continued to pursue my
vocation, enlarging and varying my expressive use of the theatrical medium, first to create
an opera in words and then to incarnate, by expressionist means, a metaphor of the
unconscious wish to die. These experiments, however, remain private because of the present
shortage of elderly widows anxious to foster the arts.

                                *   *   *

Brigid Brophy's *The Burglar* is a very clever piece of writing which reads far better than it
plays. As Miss Brophy points out in the long Shavian preface, she learned her stagecraft
"from thinking hard about the form of great operas and not from ASMing for ten years in
provinical rep" and indeed the structure is more musical and logical than theatrical. As a
piece of argument for five voices it is witty and well constructed. As a radio play it might
work; in the theatre it is progressively disappointing after a highly theatrical opening – with
the stage almost in darkness, a ladder heaving into view outside the bedroom window, a
figure climbing stealthily into view and then into the room, a bigger man stepping out from
behind a curtain to seize the intruder and then the lights coming on.

The burden of the unanimously hostile reviews was that after this promising beginning there was a lot of talk and no action. This is not, in fact, what is wrong with the play. There is the burglar's amusing feebleness when Roderick manhandles him. There is the well-phased revelation that Roderick is not Edwina's husband. The sustained anti-climax of the lovers' inability to call the police is developed when the puritanic burglar seizes the moral advantage this gives him to justify his own immorality by savaging theirs. There is a well-contrived climax to Act One when Edwina's husband is heard letting himself into the flat. Roderick and the burglar hide and William comes into the room with an attractive girlfriend. Act Two is equally full of twists and surprises. Act Three culminates in a crash which indicates the burglar's off-stage death.

If, then, the play fails to involve an audience, it is not through lack of action but because the characters and the events fail to come theatrically to life. It is a very Shavian play: moral and social attitudes are dressed up as people, and Miss Brophy takes a Shaw-like delight in flaying the hide off sacred cows which are conventionally venerated. The burglar himself is descended from the burglar in *Heartbreak House* who makes the same point about the injustice of the equation between years of his life wasted in prison and the material value of what he steals. The four middle-class lovers are as wittily capable of stepping over the trip-wires of sexual jealousy as any Shaw hero, and as easy to make into mouthpieces for long arguments about social assumptions governing sex and property. Behind all this there is a Shavian balance in the play's moral structure which weighs the wrongness of stealing other people's property against the wrongness of sleeping with other people's marital partners. Miss Brophy is no more guilty than Shaw of using the stage as a platform for debate, but she is less expert at creating characters to involve an audience's emotions. There is no Captain Shotover, no Ellie Dunn to be saved from marrying a middle-aged industrialist, no Mazzini Dunn to be disabused from thinking himself to be in the industrialist's debt. If the cast of *Heartbreak House* were reduced to Hector and Hesiane, Randall and Ariadne, and the Burglar, no-one would be very involved.

It becomes clear quite early on that we are not watching a naturalistic play, that we are not being asked to believe that a burglar would be more interested in delivering moral diatribes about middle-class sexual morality than in making his escape, or that four lovers would behave with as much wit and poise when trapped into such an embarrassing situation. In making her characters almost vulnerable to anything except argument, Miss Brophy is creating a certain theatrical effect, but it is one which rules out a great many others. As the play proceeds we find that the surprises we are being given are all very much of the same quality and calibre, intellectual steps in an argument, musical modulations in a quintet. Theatrically, therefore, they are subject to a law of diminishing returns. This would matter less if it were a one-act play or even a two-act play, but to sustain an audience's interest over two intervals the play would need either to be more emotional or more farcical on a physical level to match up with Miss Brophy's description of it as "a bedroom farce."

On the other hand, her fifty-minute radio play, *The Waste-Disposal Unit*, is thoroughly successful as a farce within its own non-visual terms. As in her novel *In Transit*, which it prefigures, the comedy and the conflict are bedded in the language itself. The villain of the piece is the American idiom, which mangles the English language rather in the way that the waste disposal unit of the title, installed by visiting Americans in a 16th century Italian palazzo, finally crunches up the two American women, overwhelming mother and puritanic, sentimental daughter. La donn'e mobile, sing the men. E disponibile. But the triumph of the piece is to use both the medium and the abhorred idiom so very well, creating a bizarre farce of non-communication between Virgil Knockerbicker, the lethargic homosexual poet, Homer, his worried brother, Merry, the sweet young all-American wife, and Angelo Lumaca, the accredited agent of the Atlantic Seaboard Waste Disposal Unit Corporation. Having made the mistake of moving into three-dimensionality, Miss Brophy should have the courage to move back to radio, a medium in which her ingenuity comes near to genius.

—Ronald Hayman

BROWN, Kenneth H.   American.   Born in Brooklyn, New York, 9 March 1936. Educated at Brooklyn prep school. Served in the United States Marine Corps, 1954–57. Worked as a mail clerk, 1951–54, bartender and waiter, New York, and Miami, 1958–63; bank clerk, New York, 1960, cigarette salesman, New York, 1961. Resident Playwright, The Living Theatre, New York, 1963–67. Private Tutor, 1966–69, and Resident Playwright, 1968–69, Yale Graduate School of Drama, New Haven, Connecticut; Visiting Lecturer (improvisational acting), Hollins College, Virginia, 1969; Visiting Lecturer (history of theatre), Hunter College, New York, 1969–70, Associate Professor in Performance (theatrical production), University of Iowa, Iowa City, 1971. Recipient: Venice Film Festival Gold Medal, 1964; Rockefeller Fellowship, 1965, and grant, 1967; ABC-Yale Fellowship, 1966, 1967; Guggenheim Fellowship, 1966; Creative Artists Public Service grant, 1974. Agent: James Bohan, 27 West 96th Street, New York, New York 10025. Address: 150 74th Street, Brooklyn, New York 11209, U.S.A.

PUBLICATIONS

Plays

The Brig (produced New York, 1963; London, 1964).   London, Methuen, 1964; New
   York, Hill and Wang, 1965.
Devices (produced New York, 1965).
The Happy Bar (produced New York, 1967).
Blake's Design (produced New Haven, Connecticut, 1968; New York, 1974).
   Published in The Best Short Plays 1969, edited by Stanley Richards, Philadelphia,
   Chilton, 1969.
The Green Room (produced Iowa City, Iowa, 1971).
The Cretan Bull (produced Waterford, Connecticut, 1972; New York, 1974).
Nightlight (produced Hartford, Connecticut, 1973; London, 1974).   New York,
   French, 1973.

Screenplays: The Brig, 1965; Devices, 1967.

Novel

The Narrows.   New York, Dial Press, 1970.

Manuscript Collection: New York Public Library.

Kenneth H. Brown comments:

   I began as a playwright quite by accident. It was the best means to convey my experiences as a confined prisoner in a Marine Brig. All my plays since have been either direct or symbolic representations of my life experiences. As such, I have been classified by one theatre historian as an accidental playwright, a title I gladly accept since I adhere to the belief that all things of personal import in my life have come about as a result of pure chance. I do not take to writing as a daily chore that must be done. It is, for me, a labor of love and, as such, I engage in it only when moved to do so. As I get older, I am constantly amazed by the body of works accumulated through this philosophy.

*   *   *

Although Kenneth H. Brown has published poetry and a novel, *The Narrows*, his most significant achievements to date have been in drama. *The Brig*, a stark and appalling indictment of militarism, stamped Brown as one of the more gifted and experimental of the American dramatists. It placed him in a tradition with Artaud and proved him able to create what neither Artaud nor Ionesco accomplished, a "theatre of cruelty" complete with a metaphysics of language. His next published play, *Blake's Design*, gave further support to the belief that Brown was a dramatist who defied labels. Moving away from the stark, purposefully flat prose of *The Brig*, Brown played with the catchy rhythms of vaudeville, embellished his prose giving it a lyrical quality, and turned away from Naturalism to Expressionism. Of his recent play, *The Cretan Bull*, Brown says he has produced a "very funny play about complete strangers who meet in Central Park at dawn and confront a very odd set of circumstances." Again, Brown is going in new directions, experimenting with another style, and exploring different themes.

The elements his two very different published plays share in common are many. In both, an egalitarianism makes Brown select characters for his drama who reflect the ethnic and racial mix that makes up American society. In both Brown draws on music and popular songs: in *Blake's Design* the songs and dances are handled in a manner reminiscent of a vaudeville skit; in *The Brig* music is subverted from its high end and becomes an instrument of torture. The sarcastic, strident, sneering tone of a guard's voice is played contrapuntally against a clear, impersonal, unaffected voice. The barking of a command is answered by its own often inaudible flat echo. The hideous, dissonant, martial music that is the tool of the fascist or authoritarian state, the kind of music that breaks a man's mind and makes him crawl like a maggot at any command, is produced by clashing garbage can lids together as if they were cymbals. Yet more hellish music derives from the sound of a voice resonating against a toilet bowl as one of the prisoners, using the cubicle as his confessional, cries out his litany of wrongs in obedience to the guard's orders. Dance, too, figures in both plays. In *Blake's Design* Muvva and Zack sing of Zack's necrophilia with his dead, black wife while they do a soft shoe dance. In *The Brig* dance is a ritual in which the prisoners suffer repeatedly at the hands of the guards. The dance is one where men shrink, recoil, and double-over in response to the quick, sharp blows delivered by the truncheons of the Warden or the guards. This violent dance pattern is varied with a pattern of running across the stage and halting at every white line in conformity with the procedure outlined in the *Marine Corps Manual*. Finally, both plays employ a point of view that is reminiscent of the Naturalists. A dispassionate exact observer records precisely the world in all its minutiae as if the reality being depicted were a hard surface that can only be penetrated once it has been fully sounded. But for all these seeming similarities, the plays are, in fact, very different, both in style and in theme.

The Brig is a blatantly political play, or rather, "concept of theater," as Brown would have it called. A penal institute in Camp Fuji, the brig is the place where Marines are sent to be punished for any infraction of military orders. The set of the play duplicates as nearly as possible the specifications of the brig and its actions reenact the rules that govern its workings as set down in the *Marine Corps Manual*. The play opens with the waking of the prisoners at dawn and it closes with the putting out of the light at night. Between dawn and night, we see the prisoners repeat again and again the same gestures and motions as they are forced to dress and undress, eat and march, clean and stand at attention, for no other reason than to fulfill an order and submit to power. Nameless (they are called by number – only the guards have names), the prisoners grovel, crawl, abuse themselves, whimper silently, and try desperately to carry out any order to the letter while the military guards sadistically delight in finding new indignities for them to suffer and new punishments for their supposed failures. The discipline is without restraint or reason. Senselessly the prisoners are humiliated, beaten, and abused. The only logic that governs events is the relentless logic of power and physical force. In the course of the day, one prisoner is released, a new one enters, and a third is released to an even worse form of institutional imprisonment, the asylum. Number twenty-six, after two weeks in the brig which follows upon sixteen years of honorable military service, finds himself, against all orders and common sense, crying out his name, James Turner, and in so doing demonstrating that in the brig seemingly sane behavior is in fact insane. For two hours, the senses of the audience are assaulted as the prisoners are hollered at and harassed by the guards. Plot and character development in the ordinary sense of the words are absent from the play. Language, stripped of all warmth, finally negates itself. The members of the audience are left responding to sounds, intonations, incantations, and not denotative meanings. They experience an agony of feeling which derives from the immediacy of the violence unleashed both on the stage and in themselves and which has little reference to the world of reason that has systematically been destroyed by the extremes to which it has been pushed on the stage.

Blake's Design depicts Zack's struggle to free himself from both his past – the black woman whose dead body he has slept with for ten years – and his illusions – Blake, or call him God, is one of them – in order to tell his son the truth, live in the present and move out of his dark basement apartment upstairs and into the light. Zack's mulatto son, Sweek, and his two women, Muvva, with whom he has shared his bed, dead wife and son for ten years, and Modrigal, his half-oriental mistress, all talk rather self-consciously throughout the play about man's weakness, his lies, and that part of himself which he does not know or understand and so calls God, or Blake, in an effort to understand it. The play ends when Zack unburdens himself, tells the truth, closes the door on his past and mounts the stairs. The symbolism is rather obvious and the long talks about Blake tend to be tired; but the characters themselves are well imagined and the quick staccato exchanges between Sweek and Zack and the shuffling dances and songs save the play.

Brown's talents are considerable. It is too early to fix the parameters of his art, but it is late enough to recognize that he is one of the few genuinely original dramatists writing in America today.

—Carol Simpson Stern

BULLINS, Ed. Black American. Born in Philadelphia, Pennsylvania, 2 July 1935. Educated in Philadelphia public schools; William Penn Business Institute, Philadelphia; Los Angeles City College; San Francisco State College. Served in the United States Navy. Playwright-in-Residence, 1967–71, and since 1967, Associate Director, The New Lafayette Theatre, Harlem, New York. Editor, *Black Theatre* magazine, Harlem, 1969–74. Recipient: Rockefeller grant, 1968; Vernon Rice Award, 1968; American Place grant, 1968; Obie Award, 1971; Guggenheim grant, 1971; National Endowment for the Arts grant, 1974; New York Drama Critics Circle Award, 1975. D.L.: Columbia College, Chicago, 1976. Address: 932 East 212th Street, Brooklyn, New York 10469, U.S.A.

PUBLICATIONS

Plays

  Clara's Ole Man (produced San Francisco, 1965; New York, 1968; London, 1971). Included in *Five Plays*, 1969.
  How Do You Do: A Nonsense Drama (produced Boston, 1969). Mill Valley, California, Illuminations Press, 1965.
  Dialect Determinism (produced, 1965). Published in *Spontaneous Combustion: Eight*

New American Plays, edited by Rochelle Owens, New York, Winter House, 1972.

In New England Winter (produced New York, 1967).   Published in *New Plays from the Black Theatre*, edited by Ed Bullins, New York, Bantam, 1969.

In the Wine Time (produced New York, 1968).   Included in *Five Plays*, 1969.

A Son, Come Home (produced New York, 1968).   Included in *Five Plays*, 1969.

The Electronic Nigger (produced New York, 1968).   Included in *Five Plays*, 1969.

Goin' a Buffalo: A Tragifantasy (produced New York, 1968).   Included in *Five Plays*, 1969.

The Gentleman Caller (produced New York, 1969).   Published in *Illuminations 5* (Mill Valley, California), 1968.

Five Plays: Goin' a Buffalo; In the Wine Time; The Electronic Nigger; A Son, Come Home; Clara's Ole Man.   Indianapolis, Bobbs Merrill, 1969; as *The Electronic Nigger and Other Plays*, London, Faber, 1970.

The Game of Adam and Eve, with Shirley Tarbell (produced Boston, 1969).

It Has No Choice (produced Boston, 1969).

The Corner (produced Boston, 1969; New York, 1972).   Published in *Black Drama Anthology*, edited by Woodie King and Ron Milner, New York, New American Library, 1972.

Street Sounds (produced New York, 1970).

The Fabulous Miss Marie (produced New York, 1970).   Published in *The New Lafayette Theatre Presents*, edited by Ed Bullins, New York, Doubleday, 1974.

It Bees Dat Way (produced London, 1970).   Included in *Four Dynamite Plays*, 1971.

The Pig Pen (produced New York, 1970).   Included in *Four Dynamite Plays*, 1971.

Death List (produced New York, 1970).   Included in *Four Dynamite Plays*, 1971.

State Office Building Curse, in *The Drama Review* (New York), September 1970.

The Duplex: A Black Love Fable in Four Movements (produced New York, 1970). New York, Morrow, 1971.

The Devil Catchers (produced New York, 1971).

Night of the Beast (screenplay), in *Four Dynamite Plays*, 1971.

Four Dynamite Plays (includes *It Bees Dat Way, Death List, The Pig Pen, Night of the Beast*).   New York, Morrow, 1971.

The Psychic Pretenders (produced New York, 1972).

You Gonna Let Me Take You Out Tonight, Baby (produced New York, 1972).

House Party, music by Pat Patrick, lyrics by Ed Bullins (produced New York, 1973).

The Taking of Miss Janie (produced New York, 1975).

The Mystery of Phyllis Wheatley (produced New York, 1976).

Jo Anne!!! (produced New York, 1976).

Home Boy, music by Aaron Bell, lyrics by Ed Bullins (produced New York, 1976).

Screenplays: *Night of the Beast*, 1971; *The Ritual Masters*, 1972.

Novel

The Reluctant Rapist.   New York, Harper, 1973.

Short Stories

The Hungered One: Early Writings.   New York, Morrow, 1971.

Verse

To Raise the Dead and Foretell the Future.   New York, New Lafayette Publications, 1971.

Other

> Editor, *"Black Theatre Issue,"* of *The Drama Review* (New York), 1968.
> Editor, *New Plays from the Black Theatre.*   New York, Bantam, 1969.
> Editor, *The New Lafayette Theatre Presents: Plays with Aesthetic Comments by 6 Black Playwrights.*   New York, Doubleday, 1974.

Bibliography: in *Black Image on the American Stage* by James V. Hatch, New York, Drama Books, 1970.

Critical Studies: "The Polished Reality: Aesthetics and the Black Writer" in *Contact Magazine* (Sausalito, California), 1962; "The Theatre of Reality" in *Black World* (Chicago), 1966; "Up from Politics" in *Performance* (New York), 1972.

Ed Bullins comments:

I write plays for a number of reasons but the most simple and direct truth of the matter is that it is my work.

*   *   *

In his essay "The Negro Artist and the Racial Mountain" (1926) describing the arrival of Negro poets and novelists on the other side of the obstacles he termed the racial mountain, Langston Hughes said he anticipated next the arrival of a Negro theatre. It has been a long wait because, though literature can exist in tenuous relationship with the people who are its subject, sustaining itself by finding some sort of audience among an undifferentiated public, to build a theatre where none has previously existed requires a community of consciousness. Until recently that consciousness among blacks was fragmentary, finding expression in the church, numerous social organizations, or politics; but only with the advent of Black Power ("It's Nation Time") has Afro-America required and been ready to support the deliberate culture of theatre.

The prolific Ed Bullins introduces us fully to that theatre. His plays have been characterized variously as "theatre of reality," (that is his own term), "revolutionary drama," and "surnaturalism." Each description has validity, but the most meaningful term for Bullins' work may be nationalist. On one level the nationalism appears in a rejection of white American bourgeois culture. More profoundly, though, Bullins' plays are nationalist in the same way that Black music is nationalist. Like the blues writer, Bullins uses common life – troubles related to finding love or coping with frustration – as subject, the popular idiom for expression, and shapes his tales to reveal the moral significance of "gettin' it together" in the USA here and now.

Bullins' major project is a projected cycle of twenty plays. In each of the four cycle plays so far produced the focus is on urban blacks completely divorced from the Southern past, the soil, and traditional culture. They are neither the idealized folk primitives with whom twenties writers sought to identify, nor are they wishfully created agents of imminent revolution. They are, as Bullins himself might say, really the people, residing in the industrial slums of northeastern cities and the sunshine ghettoes of Southern California, deracinated as proletarians but marginal as the lumpen.

In the Wine Time, first in the cycle, develops from a prologue in which a young male narrator lyrically describes the beautiful woman who represents the fulfillment he innocently hopes to achieve in manhood. As counterpoint to the prologue the body of the play reveals through its slowly moving dialogue of a summer evening spent drinking wine the disappointments of the youth's exhausted aunt, the frustrated hopes of her husband, and the diversion of their ambitions into a contest over the boy. Structured as an initiation play, *In the Wine Time* carries the youth to the point where he begins taking on the character traits of older males, especially the anger with which they suppress more tender feeling. Since he is above all realistic, Bullins concludes the action with a pointless knifing that reveals the possible consequences of Derby Street adulthood.

In New England Winter picks up the leading adult male from the previous play, now freed from the prison sentence he received for the knifing and estranged from his wife, and juxtaposes him to yet another young man and a group of small-time hustlers. Scenes of a planned robbery intermix with memories of a young man's love idyll from five years before, an idyll at first attractive by its lyric telling and gradually revealed as a desperate escape. The human needs people have for each other issue in love-hate relationships, gratuitous brutality, and all demonstrate the incapacity for sustained feeling brought on by the American culture imaged in the title.

With *The Duplex*, subtitled *A Black Love Fable in Four Movements*, the theme of the cycle is fully established: the difficulties of love, and by implication group solidarity, and the complicity of people in disabling themselves. Again the movement is of a young man gaining experience in his social world. Steve Benson, also present in the previous play, hesitates between submission to the anodynes of alcohol and sex and the resolution to direct his own life. The forces for submission are so powerful that hesitation seems the only plausible action for him in the brief time of the play, for even if he strikes out on his own he must hurt others. It is a situation worthy of the blues, and it is part of Bullins' genius that he disavows either a strictly sociological or psychological presentation. He conveys clearly enough the fact that his characters are subject to socially caused conditions; yet his sympathy for them is so great, his identification with them so strong, that he rejects either a portrayal of them as victims or the easy sentiment of pity. Could any but the most sensitive black writer know that the people described in newspapers and public speeches as part of a "problem" know they actually perceive their experiences as personal troubles and doing so confront the troubles with dignity? Again it's the vision of the blues.

The Fabulous Miss Marie carries Bullins' cycle forward with a character who makes a brief appearance in *The Duplex*. Miss Marie, vital and vulgar, demonstrates the vigor that sustains humanity, even carries it to a level of achievement. As in each cycle play, though, a moral judgement is operative – not a condemnation and certainly nothing personally intended, but nonetheless a judgement that the Hollywood-debased life style presently confuses and must eventually destroy.

The dramaturgy of Bullins' cycle, as well as the pre-cycle play *Goin' a Buffalo*, exploits the entire theatrical ambience for effect. The decor of *Goin' a Buffalo* consists of all white walls and crimson carpet. The set of *The Duplex* is a non-realistic gradation of planes. Nearly all the plays call for musical accompaniment attuned to situation and shifting lighting effects to spot significant relationship; the stage directions suggest patterned movements. Such sensory attractions, along with the development of representative characters behaving in ways familiar to the audience, suggest adaptation of the theory of Antonin Artaud, though it must be insisted that where Bullins agrees with Artaud it is because of the demands of Black theatre for a way of uniting spectator and actor in a mutual reality.

Besides the cycle plays Bullins has written a number of short plays which are just as significant to audiences and other playwrights. *Clara's Ole Man* presenting the experience of a young man hoping to be with a woman when her "old man" is away shocks him with the discovery that the "old man" is another woman and provides the audience, which has sensed a menace in the strange household, the fascination of vital amoral personalities. *The Electronic Nigger* comically pits apparent stereotypes against each other in the setting of a college classroom devoted to a creative writing course. The standard-English-speaking black novelist is bested by the blustering Mr. Carpentier, a jargon spouting know-it-all. As the audience sympathizes first with one and then the other, its dependence upon *a priori* categories weakens. Every individual, each situation, Bullins seems to say, has a unique dimension.

As an exponent of community-based theatre Bullins is well-known for his production of short plays devoted to overt political statements as well as for his espousal of the politics of Black Theatre. Representative of the political plays brought together in the volume *Four Dynamite Plays* is *Death List*, dedicated to Al-Fatah. A character identified only as Blackman lines up bullets and loads his rifle while speaking indictments of black leaders who have signed a newspaper advertisement supporting Israel. As he intones the sentence of death for the alleged enemies of Black people, Blackwomen, the other character, indicates the extenuating circumstances for each case – the black leaders just have not caught up yet. Getting no response to pleas for mercy she asks if the potential assassin himself is not the actual enemy of black people. There is no resolution of the stated positions, and each is equally forceful. The action simply ends after Blackman exits with shots offstage.

Though the problem of reconciling vanguard actions with the ends of human liberation remains politically viable, for many reasons the theatre is taking a breather from militancy. So, too, Bullins recently has chosen to view politics indirectly through retrospect. *The House Party* satirizes political figures amidst a range of popular Black character types, and *The Taking of Miss Janie* uses political movements of the 1960's as the informing motives in a drama of inter-racial rape. The change is only one of mood in Bullins' plays, however, for like the cycle plays these recent works continue to represent their author's desire to create "a universe for future centuries," a spellbinding portrayal of life in our times.

Already the disposition of critical journalism to crown a champion has resulted in the declaration that Ed Bullins is the Best American Playwright now living. Not Best of Black, Best of all. Of course Bullins is prolific, bold, experimental, ambitious, consciously theatrical. In short he possesses the traits that promise greatness, but to set him off to be co-opted into the mainstream culture is a disservice. The intense dramatic situations and the human sympathy for the world of ignored common black people that mark his plays are the result of a consciousness that makes positive art out of estrangement from the dominant American way. That achievement must continue to be labeled what it is: Black National Theatre.

—John M. Reilly

BURROWS, Abe (Abram S. Burrows).   American.   Born in New York City, 18 December 1910. Educated at New Utrecht High School, Brooklyn, New York; City College of New York, 1928–29; New York University School of Finance, 1929, 1930, 1931. Married Carin Smith Kinzel in 1950; has two children. Worked for a Wall Street brokerage firm, 1931–34; in a paint business, and as a maple syrup salesman. Recipient: Radio Critics Award, 1947; New York Drama Critics Circle Award, 1951; Tony Award, 1951, 1962; Pulitzer Prize, 1962. Vice-President, Dramatists Guild, 1964. Agent: William Morris Agency, 1350 Avenue of the Americas, New York, New York 10019, U.S.A.

PUBLICATIONS

Plays

> *Guys and Dolls*, with Jo Swerling, music by Frank Loesser, based on a story and characters by Damon Runyon (produced New York, 1950; London, 1953). Published in *The Modern Drama, Volume 4*, edited by Eric Bentley, New York, Doubleday, 1956.

Three Wishes for Jamie, with Charles O'Neal (also director: produced New York, 1952).

Can-Can, music by Cole Porter (also director: produced New York, 1953; London, 1954). London and New York, Chappell, 1954.

Silk Stockings, with George S. Kaufman and Leueen MacGrath, music by Cole Porter, suggested by *Ninotchka* by Melchior Lengyel (produced New York, 1955). London and New York, Chappell, 1955.

Say, Darling, with Richard and Marian Bissell, music and lyrics by Betty Comden, Adolph Green, and Jule Styne, adaptation of the novel by Richard Bissell (also director: produced New York, 1958). London and New York, Chappell, 1958.

First Impressions, music by George David Weiss, adaptation of a work by Helen Jerome based on *Pride and Prejudice* by Jane Austen (also director: produced New York, 1959; Birmingham, 1971). New York, French, 1962.

How to Succeed in Business Without Really Trying, with Jack Weinstock and Willie Gilbert, music by Frank Loesser, adaptation of the book by Shepherd Mead (also director: produced New York, 1961; London, 1963). New York and London, Frank Music Company, 1963.

Cactus Flower, adaptation of a play by Pierre Barillet and Jean-Pierre Grédy (also director: produced New York, 1965; London, 1967). New York, French, 1968.

Four on a Garden, adaptation of a play by Pierre Barillet and Jean-Pierre Grédy (also director: produced New York, 1971). New York, French, 1973.

Screenplay: *The Solid Gold Cadillac*, 1956.

Radio Writer: *This Is New York*, 1938–39; *Texaco Star Theatre*, 1939; *Rudy Vallee-John Barrymore Show*, 1940; *Duffy's Tavern* program, 1940–45; *Dinah Shore Show*, 1945; *Joan Davis Program*, 1945; *Ford Program*, 1946; *Abe Burrows Show*, 1946–47; *Breakfast with Burrows*, 1948; *We Take Your Word*, 1950.

Television Writer: *Abe Burrows' Almanac*, 1950; *This Is Show Business*, 1950.

Other

Abe Burrows Song-Book. New York, Doubleday, 1955.

Recordings: *The Girl with the Three Blue Eyes*, 1946; *Abe Burrows Sings?*, 1950.

Theatrical Activities:

Director: **Plays** – *Two on the Aisle* by Betty Comden and Adolph Green, and others, New York, 1951; *Three Wishes for Jamie*, New York, 1952; *Can-Can*, New York, 1953; *Reclining Figure* by Harry Kurnitz, New York, 1954; *Happy Hunting* by Howard Lindsay and Russel Crouse, New York, 1956; *Say, Darling*, New York, 1958; *The Golden Fleecing* by Lorenzo Semple, Jr., New York, 1959; *First Impressions*, New York, 1959; *How to Succeed in Business Without Really Trying*, New York, 1961, London, 1963; *What Makes Sammy Run?* by Budd and Stuart Schulberg, New York, 1964; *Cactus Flower*, New York, 1965, London, 1967; *Forty Carats* by Jay Allen, New York, 1968; *Four on a Garden*, New York, 1971; *Good News* by Laurence Schwab and Buddy DaSylva, music by Ray Henderson, tour, 1974; *Hellzapoppin'* (revue), Baltimore, 1976, New York, 1977.

Abe Burrows comments:

Comedy is what I do. When I'm speaking in public, and ask for questions, the first question inevitably is "Mr. Burrows, haven't you ever wanted to do anything serious in the

Theatre?" My answer is always the same. "Everything I do is serious. It just turns out funny."

*   *   *

Abe Burrows never works alone; as co-author, play doctor, and director, he is adjusting and recasting someone else's original idea. Collaboration notwithstanding, the Burrows touch is clearly evident, the distinguishing trait being a Broadwaywise smart talk — New Yorkese laced with gags and wisecracks. The Burrows play is raffish, slangy; it has pace, animation. The best Burrows show, *Guys and Dolls*, represents exactly the sort of commodity Burrows is able to deliver: "low" comedy characters, a snappy farce plot, spicy colloquial dialogue. The Damon Runyon characters are in capable hands with Burrows, who has a real feel for the gamblers and the sharpshooters and the brassy dames. The play offers a typical Burrowslike contrast between the fast-lifers – the world of guys 'n dolls – and respectable society – here, the Salvation Army people. When the opposing groups are pushed into contact, the "proper" people loosen, pick up some pointers from the "low" people, who in turn acquire some (but not too much) class.

Can-Can follows the same pattern. The world of the nightclub is opposed to the world of the law; a representative from the latter softens and humanizes by prolonged exposure to characters from the former. As in *Guys and Dolls*, it is not the story or the individual characters that matter so much as it is the milieu against which the fragile stock plot and type characters are thrust. Because he is working on home territory in the Damon Runyon show, Burrows meets his material completely at ease. The inevitable New Yorkese of the Burrows touch is naturally less congenial in the context of fin de siècle Paris, which has been twisted and kneaded into sounding like guys 'n dolls New York, this being the only tone in which Burrows can work comfortably.

Can-Can was a hit because of a superior production (Lilo and Gwen Verdon as, respectively, a wise and triumphant madam and a high-stepping hoofer became instant celebrities). Behind the spectacular choreography and the giddy pace, the humdrum book remained unobtrusive. Burrows' inveterate New York mythologizing, however, was not so harmless for *First Impressions*, a musical adaptation of *Pride and Prejudice*. Jane Austen and Abe Burrows: an outrageous commingling. Cutting across the delicate surfaces and ironic depths of the Austen comedy like a bulldozer, Burrows reduces the story to the most obvious and threadbare essentials. Under his merciless snipping and shoving, *Pride and Prejudice* becomes merely another Broadway musical about the marriage market, a Gentile *Fiddler on the Roof* in which a pushy mother is anxious to marry off her bevy of daughters. The novel's most important "character" – the chiding, superbly ironic, superbly rhythmed voice of Jane Austen herself – has disappeared, and in its place – smart aleck jokes geared for the Borscht Belt.

In *Cactus Flower* (which he both adapted and directed) and *Forty Carats* (which he directed, though it certainly sounds as if he also participated in the writing), Burrows is successful in reworking for Broadway audiences two popular French farces by Barillet and Grédy. Both comedies about middle-aged women who get a second chance for romance are given a distinctly Manhattan shine; both are skilfully plotted; both are sustained by quick, wisecracking Burrows dialogue.

How to Succeed in Business Without Really Trying and *Say, Darling* are musical comedies about professions. *How to Succeed* looks wryly but affectionately at big business; *Say, Darling* looks saltily but fondly at Burrows' home territory – Broadway. Typically, the milieu is the true "star" of both shows: Madison Avenue shenanigans, the clashes of temperament involved in the production of a big-time musical. Both shows mock clichés of big business and show business, but both shows ultimately assume the point of view of what they are presumably ribbing: beneath the sarcastic glitter, *How to Succeed* really approves of big business, and *Say, Darling* is really a valentine to show business. Like everything else Burrows has worked on, these two musical comedies are conservative, amiable, slick Broadway entertainments.

—Foster Hirsch

BURROWS, John.   British.   Born in London, 19 November 1945. Educated at Manchester University, B.A. in drama. Married. Agent: Michael Imison, Dr. Jan Van Loewen Ltd., 81-83 Shaftesbury Avenue, London W1V 8BX, England.

PUBLICATIONS

Plays

> *For Sylvia*, with John Harding (produced London, 1972).
> *The Golden Pathway Annual*, with John Harding (produced Sheffield, 1973; London,
>   1974).   London, Heinemann, 1975.
> *Loud Reports*, with John Harding and Peter Skellern (produced London, 1975).
> *Dirty Giant*, with John Harding, music by Peter Skellern (produced Coventry, 1975).
> *The Manly Bit*, with John Harding (produced London, 1976).

Television Play: *Do You Dig It?*, with John Harding, 1976.

Theatrical Activities:

Director: **Play** – *Son of a Gun*, London, 1976.

Actor: **Plays** – several of his own plays.

*   *   *

John Burrows and John Harding are two actors who have evolved a distinctive revue-style to look at British class society and the effect its various myths have had on some of the inhabitants of that society. *For Sylvia* satirises gently and almost nostalgically the post-war myth-making of such 1950's epics as *The Dam Busters* and *Reach for the Sky*. John Burrows, in the original production, played the central part of the pilot hero while John Harding played everybody else. It was a very accurate re-creation and parody of that genre of film, performed with sensitivity and affection by the two actor/writers.

But *The Golden Pathway Annual* is a more considerable work. It revolves around Michael Peters, a member of the post-war grammar school generation, and traces him from his childhood, the son of working-class George and Enid, through primary school, the 11-plus examination, grammar school, university, and out to the prospect of graduate unemployment. Again, John Burrows played the central role in the first production, while Mark Wing-Davey and Maggie McCarthy played his parents and John Harding everybody else. It is written in a series of short scenes – "Dad comes home from the war," "Michael at school," "The Coronation," "The Famous Five." *The Golden Pathway Annual* is a motif for the whole play – an annual sold by a slick salesman to Michael's gullible parents for Michael's "education" and the trigger to Michael's fantasies, both in boyhood and early adolescence. We see him imagine himself as one of Enid Blyton's very middle-class "Famous Five" and then, a few years later, ironically realise this fantasy's bourgeois content. The play is a gently ironic satire on the rise of the post-war meritocracy and is beautifully evocative for anyone (like me) of that generation.

Their third play together, *Loud Reports*, done this time with pop singer Peter Skellern (of *Hold On to Love* fame), is about a blimpish brigadier, Corfe-Prater, and his resolute refusal to come to terms with modern-day social realities, whether it be the depression in the thirties, the advent of the Welfare State in the forties, or affluence in the fifties. Suez is a brief reminder of former glories, while he staggers on into the sixties. It is less original than *The Golden Pathway Annual*, though scarcely less entertaining.

—Jonathan Hammond

BUZO, Alexander. Australian. Born in Sydney, New South Wales, 23 July 1944. Educated at the Armidale School, 1956–60; International School of Geneva, 1962; University of New South Wales, Sydney, 1963–65, B.A. 1965. Married Merelyn Johnson in 1968; has one daughter. Salesman, David Jones Ltd., Sydney, 1960; Messenger, E.L. Davis and Company, Sydney, 1961; Storeman-Packer, McGraw-Hill Book Company, Sydney, 1967; Clerk, New South Wales Public Service, Sydney, 1967–68; Resident Playwright, Melbourne Theatre Company, 1972–73. Recipient: Australian Literature Society Gold Medal, 1972; Literature Board Fellowship, 1974. Agent: Howard Nicholson, 16 Taylor Street, Darlinghurst, Sydney, New South Wales 2010. Address: 14 Rawson Avenue, Bondi Junction, Sydney, New South Wales 2022, Australia.

PUBLICATIONS

Plays

> *Norm and Ahmed* (produced Sydney, 1968; London, 1974). Included in *Norm and Ahmed, Rooted, and The Roy Murphy Show*, 1973.
> *Rooted* (produced Canberra, 1969; London, 1973). Included in *Norm and Ahmed, Rooted, and The Roy Murphy Show*, 1973.
> *The Front Room Boys* (produced Perth, 1970; London, 1971). Melbourne, Penguin, 1970.
> *The Roy Murphy Show* (produced Sydney, 1971). Included in *Norm and Ahmed, Rooted, and The Roy Murphy Show*, 1973.
> *Macquarie* (produced Melbourne, 1972). Sydney, Currency Press, 1972.
> *Tom* (produced Melbourne, 1972). Sydney and London, Angus and Robertson, 1975.
> *Norm and Ahmed, Rooted, and The Roy Murphy Show: Three Plays.* Sydney, Currency Press, and London, Eyre Methuen, 1973.
> *Coralie Lansdowne Says No* (produced Adelaide, 1974). Sydney, Currency Press, and London, Eyre Methuen, 1974.
> *Martello Towers* (produced Sydney, 1976). Sydney, Currency Press, and London, Eyre Methuen, 1976.

> Screenplay: *Rod*, 1972.

Bibliography: in *Southerly 4* (Sydney), 1975.

Manuscript Collection: Mitchell Library, Sydney.

Critical Studies: introduction by Katharine Brisbane to *Norm and Ahmed, Rooted, and The Roy Murphy Show*, 1973; "Alexander Buzo: An Imagist with a Personal Style of Surrealism" by T.L. Sturm, and "Aggressive Vernacular" by Wendy Arnold, both in *Southerly 4* (Sydney), 1975; "Australian Drama" by Collin O'Brien, in *Westerly 4* (Nedlands, Western Australia), 1975.

Theatrical Activities:

> Director: **Plays** – *Care* by Daniel Hughes, Sydney, 1969; *Just Before the Honeymoon* by Jack Hibberd, Sydney, 1969.

> Actor: **Plays** – *The Alchemist* by Jonson, Sydney, 1966; *Macbird* by Barbara Garson, Sydney, 1967.

Alexander Buzo comments:

My plays are, I hope, realistic poetic comedies set in contemporary times. They are not naturalistic. The mentality behind them could be described as humanist-pacifist-socialist. Magritte is my favourite painter. When I started writing, the Theatre of the Absurd was a big influence. I place emphasis on verbal precision and visual clarity, and am not terribly interested in group anarchy. I believe in literacy, professionalism, and niceness. Nearly all my plays concentrate on one central character having problems with what's around and about.

*   *   *

Alexander Buzo's first short play, *Norm and Ahmed*, was something of a landmark on the route to the contemporary form of Australian play. It was only a decade from *Summer of the Seventeenth Doll* and seven years from *The One Day of the Year*, each of them regarded as quintessential Australian plays. But *Norm and Ahmed*, though not apparently revolutionary in form, gathered up a number of new popular influences which began to take the new writers in a different direction.

Norm, a middle-aged, lonely and unimaginative storeman, stops Ahmed, a Pakistani student, on a street corner one night and engages him in reluctant conversation. Norm's character has drawn on caricatures of the conservative returned serviceman and portraits like Barry Humphries' Sandy Stone and Alan Seymour's Alf Cook from *The One Day of the Year*. Buzo gives their xenophobia and their rigid daily rituals a new aspect by placing them in confrontation with an Asian hinterland. Norm's strikingly aggressive-defensive attitude, quite unprovoked by Ahmed, is crystallised in the final moment. Norm proffers his hand in farewell and when Ahmed takes it, Norm smashes his head.

This is the only real moment of violence in all of Buzo's writing. After that he moves into the middle-class for his context; the violence turns inward into verbal persecution.

In common with other playwrights, in the late 1960's Buzo was attracted by the variety of vernacular language and the loose rhythms of Australian life. Play by play he developed towards a comedy of manners which makes one listen afresh to familiar phrases and to his satirical embroidery of the colourful cliché. It has been said with justice that if his characters stopped talking they would scream: Buzo uses language both as a weapon against and as a shield between his people and an unpleasant or mundane reality.

For Buzo is more than a satirist. Behind the writing there are loneliness and a belief that in an older society with a stronger base of religious or social dogma things might be different. The absence of religious influence in Buzo's work is almost unique among the contemporary playwrights. In its place is a strong poetic response to nature which the characters express in unguarded moments. Without exception Buzo's figures are alienated. Both Norm and Ahmed are aliens in the same land, trying fruitlessly to understand it. Bentley, the timid but ambitious public servant in *Rooted*, is singled out for persecution in the schoolboy gang games of the young executives for no better reason than that he is a bore. Beneath the parody of adolescent manners, the comic-strip structure of the scenes, and the jargon of the beach, the art gallery, and the public service, *Rooted* is an allegory of every young man's sense of inadequacy in a society that has no roots but other people's acceptance. In *The Front Room Boys*, which satirically records in twelve scenes the tribal rituals of a city office, all the front room boys are hunted by the unexplained power of the back room boys and in turn hunt each other. In *Tom* Buzo gives us a manufactured hero, an oil exploration trouble-shooter who speaks in monosyllables and is surrounded by the camp followers of big business while his wife suffers suburban neurosis and toothache.

In *Macquarie* he abandons satire to deal with an early governor of New South Wales whose idealistic liberalism lead to his downfall at the hands of the conservative power group. And in *Coralie Lansdowne Says No*, his most serious comedy of manners, a high flying young rebel facing a bleak future on the other side of thirty settles for a tiresome public servant who offers durability. All of them are misfits, aliens like Norm in their own world, and they are swallowed up by the unquestioning values of their too-modern society.

This problem of rootlessness is most subtly investigated in his latest and most mature work to date, *Martello Towers*. The setting is an island holiday house on the Hawkesbury River, near Sydney, where Edward Martello and his estranged wife and their parents gather by accident. The family is aristocratic, two generations Australian, but still with roots in Trieste: old Martello has come to beg for a grandchild who will continue the family name. Edward says no, there are plenty of Martellos in the phone book. None of the family is happy, though they have their comforts and their brief contact with the earth and the water. The sense that no man is an island pervades them all.

—Katharine Brisbane

CAMPTON, David.   British.   Born in Leicester, 5 June 1924. Educated at Wyggeston Grammar School, 1935–41, matriculation 1940. Served in the Royal Air Force, 1942–44: in the Fleet Air Arm, 1944–46. Clerk for the City of Leicester Education Department, 1941–49; for the East Midlands Gas Board, Leicester, 1949–56. Member of the Board of Management, Scarborough Theatre Trust, and Stoke on Trent and North Staffordshire Theatre Trust. Recipient: Arts Council bursary, 1958. Agent: ACTAC (Theatrical and Cimematic) Ltd., 16 Cadogan Lane, London S.W.1. Address: 35 Liberty Road, Glenfield, Leicester LE3 8JF, England.

PUBLICATIONS

Plays

> *Going Home* (produced Leicester, 1950).   Manchester, Abel Heywood, 1951.
> *Honeymoon Express* (produced Leicester, 1951).   Manchester, Abel Heywood, 1951.
> *Change Partners* (produced Leicester, 1952).   Manchester, Abel Heywood, 1951.
> *Sunshine on the Righteous* (produced Leicester, 1953).   London, Rylee, 1952.
> *The Laboratory* (produced Leicester and London, 1954)   London, J. Garnet Miller, 1955.
> *The Cactus Garden* (produced Reading, Berkshire, 1955).   London, J. Garnet Miller 1967.
> *Dragons Are Dangerous* (produced Scarborough, 1955).
> *Idol in the Sky,* with Stephen Joseph (produced Scarborough, 1956).
> *Doctor Alexander.*   Leicester, Campton, 1956.
> *Cuckoo Song.*   Leicester, Campton, 1956.
> *The Lunatic View: A Comedy of Menace* (includes *A Smell of Burning, Then...,* *Memento Mori, Getting and Spending*) (produced Scarborough, 1957; New York, 1962). London, Studio Theatre, 1960; *A Smell of Burning and Then...,* New York, Dramatists Play Service, 1971.
> *Memento Mori and A Smell of Burning* (produced Boston, 1958).   Included in *The Lunatic View,* 1957.
> *Roses round the Door* (as *Ring of Roses,* produced Scarborough, 1958).   London, J. Garnet Miller, 1967.

Frankenstein: The Gift of Fire, adaptation of the novel by Mary Shelly (produced Scarborough, 1959). London, J. Garnet Miller, 1973.

Little Brother, Little Sister (produced London, 1966).   Leicester, Campton, 1960.

Mutatis Mutandis (produced London, 1972).   Leicester, Campton, 1960.

A View from the Brink (playlets; produced Scarborough, 1960).   Section entitled *Out of the Flying Pan* included in *Little Brother, Little Sister and Out of the Flying Pan*, 1966.

Four Minute Warning (includes *Little Brother, Little Sister, Mutatis Mutandis, Soldier from the Wars Returning, At Sea*) (produced Newcastle under Lyme, 1960). Leicester, Campton, 4 vols., 1960.

Soldier from the Wars Returning (produced London, 1961).   Leicester, Campton, 1960.

Funeral Dance (produced Dovercourt, Essex, 1960).   London, J. Garnet Miller, 1962.

Sketches in *You, Me and the Gatepost* (produced Nottingham, 1960).

Sketches in *Second Post* (produced Nottingham, 1961).

Passport to Florence (as *Stranger in the Family*, produced Scarborough, 1961). London, J. Garnet Miller, 1967.

The Girls and the Boys (revue; produced Scarborough, 1961).

Silence on the Battlefield (produced Dovercourt, Essex, 1961).   London, J. Garnet Miller, 1967.

Sketches in *Yer What?* (produced Nottingham, 1962).

Usher, adaptation of the story "The Fall of the House of Usher" by Poe (produced Scarborough, 1962; London, 1974).   London, J. Garnet Miller, 1973.

Incident (produced, 1962).   London, J. Garnet Miller, 1967.

A Tinkle of Tiny Bells (broadcast 1963; produced Cumbernauld, Dumbartonshire, 1971)

Comeback (produced Scarborough, 1963; revised version, as *Honey, I'm Home*, produced Leatherhead, Surrey, 1964).

Don't Wait for Me (broadcast, 1963; produced London, 1963).   Published in *Worth a Hearing: A Collection of Radio Plays*, edited by Alfred Bradley, London, Blackie, 1967.

Dead and Alive (produced Scarborough, 1964).

On Stage: Containing Seventeen Sketches and One Monologue.   London, J. Garnet Miller, 1964.

Resting Place (broadcast, 1964; in *We Who Are about to...*, later called *Mixed Doubles*, produced London, 1969).   London, Methuen, 1970.

The End of the Picnic (broadcast, 1964; produced Vancouver, British Columbia, 1973). Included in *Laughter and Fear*, 1969.

The Manipulator (broadcast, 1964; shortened version, as *A Point of View*, produced, 1964; as *The Manipulator*, produced, 1968).   London, J. Garnet Miller, 1967.

Cock and Bull Story (produced Scarborough, 1965).

Where Have All the Ghosts Gone? (broadcast, 1965).   Included in *Laughter and Fear*, 1969.

Split Down the Middle (broadcast, 1965; produced Scarborough, 1966).   London, J. Garnet Miller, 1973.

Little Brother, Little Sister and Out of the Flying Pan.   London, Methuen, 1966; New York, Dramatists Play Service, 1970.

Two Leaves and a Stalk (produced, 1967).   London, J. Garnet Miller, 1967.

Angel Unwilling (broadcast, 1967; produced, 1972).   Leicester, Campton, 1972.

More Sketches.   Leicester, Campton, 1967.

Ladies Night: Four Plays for Women (includes *Two Leaves and a Stalk, Silence on the Battlefield, Incident, The Manipulator*).   London, J. Garnet Miller, 1967.

The Right Place (produced, 1970).   Included in *Playbill One*, edited by Alan Durband, London, Hutchinson, 1969.

Laughter and Fear: 9 One-Act Plays (includes *Incident, Then..., Memento Mori, The End of the Picnic, The Laboratory, A Point of View, Soldier from the Wars Returning, Mutatis Mutandis, Where Have All the Ghosts Gone?*).   London, Blackie, 1969.

On Stage Again: Containing Fourteen Sketches and Two Monologues. London, J. Garnet Miller, 1969.

The Life and Death of Almost Everybody (produced London, 1970). Leicester, Campton, 1971, New York, Dramatists Play Service, 1972.

Now and Then (produced, 1970). London, French, 1976.

Timesneeze (produced London, 1970). London, Eyre Methuen, 1974.

Wonderchick (produced Bristol, 1970).

Jonah (produced Chelmsford, Essex, 1971). London, J. Garnet Miller, 1972.

The Cagebirds (produced Tunbridge Wells, Kent, 1971). Leicester, Campton, 1972.

Provisioning (produced London, 1971).

Us and Them (produced, 1972). Published in *The Sixth Windmill Book of One-Act Plays*, London, Heinemann, 1972.

Carmilla, adaptation of a story by Lefanu (produced Sheffield, 1972). London, J. Garnet Miller, 1973.

Come Back Tomorrow, Leicester, Campton, 1972.

In Committee. Leicester, Campton, 1972.

Three Gothic Plays (includes *Frankenstein, Usher, Carmilla*). London, J. Garnet Miller, 1973.

Eskimos, in *Mixed Blessings* (produced Horsham, Sussex, 1973).

Relics (produced Leicester, 1973). London, Evans, 1975.

An Outline of History (produced Bishop Auckland, County Durham. 1974).

Everybody's Friend (broadcast, 1974; produced Edinburgh, 1975). London, Evans, 1976.

Ragerbo (produced Peckleton, Leicestershire, 1975).

The Do-It-Yourself Frankenstein Outfit (produced Birmingham, 1975). Published in *The Eighth Windmill Book of One-Act Plays*, edited by E. R. Wood, London, Heinemann, 1975.

George Davenport, The Wigston Highwayman (produced Countesthorpe, Leicestershire, 1975).

What Are You Doing Here? Leicester, Campton, 1976.

No Go Area. Leicester, Campton, 1976.

One Possesed. Leicester, Campton, 1976.

Radio Plays: *A Tinkle of Tiny Bells,* 1963; *Don't Wait for Me,* 1963; *The Manipulator,* 1964; *Alison,* 1964; *Resting Place,* 1964; *End of the Picnic,* 1964; *Split Down the Middle,* 1965; *Where Have All the Ghosts Gone?,* 1965; *Angel Unwilling,* 1967; *The Missing Jewel,* 1967; *Parcel,* 1968; *Boo!,* 1971; *Now You Know,* 1971 (Italy); *Ask Me No Questions* (Germany); *Holiday, As Others See Us, So You Think You're a Hero, We Did It for Laughs, Deep Blue Sea?, Isle of the Free, You Started It, Good Money* (*Inquiry* series), 1971-75; *Everybody's Friend,* 1974.

Television Plays: *One Fight More,* with Stephen Joseph, 1956; *See What You Think* series, 1957; *Starr and Company* (serialization), 1958; *Tunnel under the World,* 1966; *Someone in the Lift,* 1967; *The Triumph of Death,* 1968; *A Private Place,* 1968; *Liar,* 1969; *Time for a Change,* 1969; *Slim John,* with others, 1971; *The Bellcrest Story,* 1972; *People You Meet,* 1972.

Other

Gulliver in Lilliput (English reader). London, University of London Press, 1970.

Gulliver in the Land of the Giants (English reader). London, University of London Press, 1970.

The Wooden Horse of Troy (English reader). London, University of London Press, 1970.

Modern Aesop Stories (English reader). Kuala Lumpar, Oxford University Press, 1976.

Critical Studies; *Anger and After* by John Russell Taylor, London Methuen, 1962: *The Disarmers* by Christopher Driver, London, Hodder and Stoughton, 1964; "Comedy of Menace" by Irving Wardle, in *The Encore Reader*, London, Methuen, 1965; *Laughter and Fear,* edited by Michael Marland, 1969; *Investigating Drama* by Kenneth Pickering, Bill Horrocks, and David Male, London, Allen and Unwin, 1974

Theatrical Activities:

Director: **Play**—*Usher*, Scarborough, 1962.

Actor: **Plays**—roles with Stephen Joseph's Theatre in the Round, Scarborough and on tour, 1957-63, including Petey in *The Birthday Party* by Harold Pinter, Birmingham, 1959, Old Man in *Memento Mori*, London, 1960, Polonius in *Hamlet*, Newcastle under Lyme, 1962, Noah in *The Ark* by James Saunders, Scarborough, 1962, and Harry Perkins in *Comeback*, Scarborough, 1963; Cinquemani in *The Shameless Professor* by Pirandello, London, 1959; Bread in *The Blue Bird* by Maeterlinck, London, 1963.

David Campton comments:

Realizing that a play in a drawer is of no use to anyone, and that, being an ephemeral thing, it will not wait for posterity to catch up with it, I have always written with a production in mind.

The circumstances of production have varied from the village hall, through radio and television, to the West End stage. (Though representation on that last has been confined to one-act plays and sketches.) This has also meant that my plays have varied in kind from domestic comedy, through costume melodrama to – as Irving Wardle coined the phrase – "comedy of menace."

My profession is playwriting, and I hope I approach it with a professional mixture of art and business. The art of playwriting is of prime importance; I hope I have never relegated it to second place. I have never written a play "because it might sell." Everything I have written has been clamouring to be written and as long as I have been able to make marks on paper, there has always been a queue of a dozen or more ideas waiting their turn to achieve solid form. But an idea can always be developed towards a particular medium, be it experimental theatre in the round or an all female group performing in a converted schoolroom.

I dislike pigeonholes and object to being popped into one. However, one label that might fit is the title of an anthology of my plays: *Laughter and Fear*. This is not quite the same as comedy of menace, which has acquired a connotation of theatre of the absurd. It is in fact present in my lightest domestic comedy. It seems to me that the chaos affecting everyone today – political, technical, sociological, religious, etc., etc. – is so all-pervading that it cannot be ignored, yet so shattering that it can only be approached through comedy. Tragedy demands firm foundations; today we are dancing among the ruins.

*   *   *

David Campton is one of the most prolific of the British dramatists who emerged at about the same time as Osborne and Pinter, and also one of the least-known. His plays have been performed widely in the regions, notably in the pioneering in-the-round theatres at Scarborough and Stoke on Trent, and also (significantly enough) to campaigners for nuclear disarmament on their annual marches from Aldermaston to London: London itself has scarcely seen him.

Much of his work is unremarkable, and could have been composed by any of a score of commercial playwrights: *Roses round the Door*, for instance, a romantic comedy in which a fireman and a young diplomat compete for the hand of a girl, while her mother makes off with the diplomat's old, rich father; *The Cactus Garden*, which shows how a neurotic young woman forces her elder sister to renounce a promising love-affair; *Funeral Dance, Going Home, Honeymoon Express, A Point of View, The End of the Picnic,* and others. Too often, Campton abjures hard thought, and becomes openly sentimental when confronted with young love or mature altruism. Indeed, even his best work ultimately tends to project a vague liberal humanism, facile and soft-centred by any rigorous emotional or intellectual standards.

His "positives" are somewhat unsatisfactory, then; but his satire, though sometimes veering from *saeva indignatio* towards mere facetiousness, shows considerable imaginative energy and pointedness. At his best, he takes the techniques of the "absurdists" and uses them to drive home his social criticism. This was perhaps most notable when Britain's possession of the H-bomb was politically controversial. In plays like *Mutatis Mutandis* (father reveals to mother that their new baby has three eyes, green hair and a tail), or *Then* (survivors of a nuclear holocaust fall in love, paper bags still over their heads), or *Little Brother, Little Sister*, he makes his opposition to the "deterrent" more than clear – and more clear than any other British playwright.

Little Brother, Little Sister is, indeed, probably his best and most characteristic play to date. It occurs deep underground, in a bunker, long after the world overhead has been ravaged by explosions and radiation. Helped by a gigantic cleaver, with which she threatens to turn them into "rissoles," the family cook holds sway over the two adolescent children of her dead master and mistress. Her wish is to perpetuate the more numb conventions of the old world; and she reacts splenetically to disobedience, the suggestion of sexuality and, especially the children's attempts to escape. The ending, as so often in Campton, may strike some as wrongheadedly optimistic, implying (as it does) that a better, more innocent world could emerge from the holocaust, and therefore somewhat undermining his opposition to the H-bomb; but the dialogue has enormous humour and verve, and the character of the cook, with her dour, plodding folk-wisdom, is marvellously drawn. This is a play one can imagine being revived with interest years hence.

But the present widespread public tolerance of the nuclear "deterrent," and the near-collapse of the Campaign for Nuclear Disarmament, appear to have silenced Campton on the subject. *Life and Death of Almost Everybody*, for instance, ignores such specific issues for more wide-ranging ones: it is partly about the limitations of the creative writer (shown when his characters insist on living their own lives in spite of his plans for them), partly about violence and oppression (shown by the type of lives the characters insist on living), and partly about man's need for God and God's need for man (shown by the relationship of the creative writer and his characters). It is a witty, intelligent piece but also overambitious and prolix. Campton is probably best when he concentrates his satire onto one object and his action into a single act, as in *Little Brother, Little Sister, Then, Mutatis Mutandis,* and a handful of other plays not connected with the H-bomb.

These include *Incident*, which imagines a world in which racial prejudice is directed at people called Smith; *Getting and Spending*, involving a couple which dreams so grandiloquently of the future that they fail to live out a satisfactory present; *A Smell of Burning*, an attack on the smug insularity of the average Englishman; *Soldier from the Wars Returning*, in which a triumphant hero gradually disintegrates into a maimed and bandaged parody of the men he has wounded and killed. Campton has not yet produced anything that marks him out as a writer of great originality or real importance; but he deserves more attention than he has had.

—Benedict Nightingale

CANNAN, Denis.   British.   Born in Oxford, 14 May 1919. Educated at Eton College, Buckinghamshire. Served in the Queen's Royal Regiment, 1939–45: mentioned in dispatches. Married Joan Ross in 1946 (marriage dissolved); Rose Evansky, 1965; has three children. Address: Godley's, Rudgwick, Horsham, Sussex RH12 3AJ, England.

PUBLICATIONS

Plays

> *Max* (produced Malvern, Worcestershire, and London, 1949).
> *Captain Carvallo* (produced Bristol and London, 1950).   London, Hart Davis, 1951.
> *Colombe*, adaptation of the play by Anouilh (produced London, 1951).   London, Methuen, 1952.
> *Misery Me! A Comedy of Woe* (produced London, 1955).   London, French, 1956.
> *You and Your Wife* (produced Bristol, 1955),   London, French, 1956.
> *The Power and the Glory,* with Pierre Bost, adaptation of the novel by Graham Greene (produced London, 1956; New York, 1958).   New York, French, 1959.
> *Who's Your Father?* (produced London, 1958),   London, French, 1959.
> *US*, with others (produced London, 1966).   Published as *US: The Book of the Royal Shakespeare Production US/Vietnam/US/Experiment/Politics...*, London, Calder and Boyars, 1968; as *Tell Me Lies: The Book of the Royal Shakespeare Production US/Vietnam/US/Experiment/Politics...*, Indianapolis, Bobbs Merrill, 1968.
> *Ghosts*, adaptation of the play by Ibsen (produced London, 1967).
> *One at Night* (produced London, 1971).
> *Les Iks*, with Colin Higgins, based on *The Mountain People* by Colin Turnbull (produced Paris, 1975; as *The Ik*, produced London, 1976).
> *Dear Daddy* (produced Oxford and London, 1976).

> Screenplays: *The Beggar's Opera*, 1953; *Alive and Kicking*, 1959; *Don't Bother to Knock (Why Bother to Knock)*, with Frederic Raphael, 1961; *Tamahine*, 1963; *The Amorous Adventures of Moll Flanders*, 1965 ; *Sammy Going South (A Boy Ten Feet Tall)*, 1965; *A High Wind in Jamaica*, 1965; *Tell Me Lies*, 1968; *Mayerling* (additional dialouge), 1968.

> Radio Plays: *Headlong Hall*, from the novel by Peacock, 1950, *The Moth and the Star*, from *Liber Amoris* by Hazlitt, 1950; *The Greeting*, from the work by Osbert Sitwell, 1964.

Theatrical Activities:

> Actor: **Plays** – Richard Hare in *East Lynne*, based on Mrs Henry Wood's novel, Henley on Thames, 1936; roles in repertory theatres, 1937–39; Citizens' Theatre, Glasgow: Hjalmar in *The Wild Duck* by Ibsen, Valentine in *You Never Can Tell* by G. B. Shaw, and Hsieh Ping Quei in *Lady Precious Stream* by S. I. Hsiung, and other roles, 1946–48; Sempronius in *The Apple Cart* by G. B. Shaw, Malvern, 1949; Kneller in *In Good King Charles's Golden Days* by G.B. Shaw, 1949; The Widower in *Buoyant Billions* by G. B. Shaw, Malvern and London, 1949; Oliver in *As You Like It*, Bristol, 1950; Julius Caesar and Octavius in *Julius Caesar*, Bristol 1950; Samuel Breeze in *A Penny for a Song* by John Whiting, London, 1951; Harold Trewitt in *All the Year Round* by N. Croft, London, 1951. **Television** – *The Rose Without a Thorn*, 1948; *Buoyant Billions*, 1949.

*   *   *

Denis Cannan is the kind of dramatist who always has a tough time of it in the English theatre: one who attempts to mix the genres. His forte, particularly in the early Fifties, was intelligent, satirical farce, much closer to the world of Giraudoux and Anouilh than that of Rattigan and Coward. After a period of prolonged silence, he dropped the comic mask and launched a couple of direct, frontal assaults on the values of our society; but he still seems a dramatist of manifest talent who has been critically undervalued and unfairly neglected by the public.

Like so many post-war English dramatists, he started out as an actor working his way round the quality repertory companies (Glasgow, Malvern, Bristol); and his first play, *Max*, was in fact staged at the 1949 Malvern Festival when he was also playing three key Shavian roles. The work is of interest now chiefly because it established the theme that was to preoccupy him for several years to come, the barren, life-destroying conflict between opposing ideologies. But it was an uncharacteristic work in that it explored the theme in slightly melodramatic terms.

Cannan really came into his own with *Captain Carvallo*, presented the following year at the St. James's under Laurence Olivier's management. This is an absolutely delightful play, a witty, bubbling farcical comedy about the absurdities of military conflict. Set behind the lines of an unspecified occupied territory, it confronts a pair of ineffectual, peace-loving partisans with a philandering enemy officer in a remote farm-house. The enemy Captain is interested only in suducing the farm-owner's wife: the partisans, though ordered to kill the Captain, are concerned only with keeping him alive. But, although the tone of the play is light and gay, it makes the perfectly serious point that the only sane attitude to life is to preserve it at all costs.

Misery Me!, which had a short run at the Duchess in 1955, is likewise the work of a man who, in Kenneth Tynan's words, "despises politics and is in no humour for war." And again Cannan puts to the test the English love of categorisation by encasing his theme within a light, semi-farcical framework. The setting is a moth-eaten Arcadian tavern: and the basic conflict is between a Communist and a Capitalist each determined to slay the other. Both hit on the idea of employing a suicidal young intellectual as a hired assassin and so we see two great powers forcing weapons on a man bent only on self-destruction: a resonant and neatly satirical idea in the cold-war atmosphere of mid-Fifties Europe. The weakness of the play is that the characters are abstractions invented to illustrate a theme and that the play's affirmation of life boils down in the end to an endorsement of romantic love: but again Cannan shows himself capable of satirising the contemporary condition and of expressing ideas within a popular format.

His other plays of the Fifties were rather less ambitious. *You and Your Wife* was about two fractious married couples trying to sort out their problems while held captive by a couple of gangsters; *The Power and the Glory* was a proficient adaptation (done in conjunction with Pierre Bost) of the Graham Greene novel about a whiskey-priest; and *Who's Your Father?* was an ingenious farce about a snobbish nouveau-riche couple and their daughter's irresponsible fiancé.

But, after a long absence from the theatre, Denis Cannan only surfaced again as part-author of the Royal Shakespeare Company's corporately devised Vietnam show, *US*. His precise contribution is difficult to disentangle. But we do know that he was author of Glenda Jackson's scorching and passionate indictment of the non-involvement of the English in anything happening outside their shores and that he wrote a very specific attack on the fact that Vietnam is a "reasonable" war. "It is," he said, "the first intellectuals' war. It is run by statisticians, physicists, economists, historians, psychiatrists, mathematicians, experts on everything, theorists from everywhere. Even the atrocities can be justified by logic." In the Fifties Cannan's attack on war had been comic and oblique: now it was impassioned and direct.

One at Night attacks certain aspects of our society with punitive vigour and sharp intelligence, if not with the greatest technical skill. Its hero is a middle-aged ex-journalist and advertising man seeking discharge from a mental institution to which he has been committed after having sexual relations with a girl under 16. He argues to the middle-class hospital tribunal that, far from corrupting an innocent, he has enlarged the girl's emotional experience: but he is steadfastly refused a discharge after shattering the tribunal's complacency by uncovering the hidden fears and frailties of its individual members. What gives the play its urgency is the feeling that Cannan isn't simply exploring a fashionable intellectual thesis (only the mad are sane) but that he is sharing with us a lived-through experience. And he makes, with some power, the point that in our society it is the scramble for wealth and material possessions that increases the incidence of insanity, but that it's the self-same scramble that produces the instant cure-alls and panaceas. It's precisely the point made, in fact, by Ken Loach's film, *Family Life*.

As a dramatist, Cannan has obviously changed course radically. Where once he wrapped his message up in farce and fantasy, he now lays it right on the line. Where once he adopted a deliberately apolitical stance, he now writes with a definite sense of commitment. But, whatever the profound changes in his style and attitude, he still writes with a bristling intelligence and pungent wit. For that reason one hopes the theatre will hear more from him in the Seventies than it has in the last decade.

—Michael Billington

CARLINO, Lewis John.   American.   Born in New York City, in 1932. Educated at El Camino College, California; University of Southern California, Los Angeles, B.A., M.A. in drama 1960. Served in the United States Air Force. Divorced; has three children. Member, Playwrights Unit, Actors Studio, New York. Member, New Dramatists Committee. Recipient: British Drama League prize, 1960; Huntington Hartford Fellowship; Yaddo Fellowship; Rockerfeller grant. Address: c/o Dramatists Play Service, 440 Park Avenue South, New York, New York 10016, U.S.A.

PUBLICATIONS

Plays

    The Brick and the Rose: A Collage for Voices (produced Los Angeles, 1957; New York, 1974).   New York, Dramatists Play Service, 1959.
    Junk Yard.   New York, Dramatists Play Service, 1959.
    Used Car for Sale.   New York, Dramatists Play Service, 1959.
    Objective Case (produced Westport, Connecticut, and New York, 1962).   With *Mr. Flannery's Ocean,* New York, Dramatists Play Service, 1961.
    Mr. Flannery's Ocean (includes *Piece and Precise*) (produced Westport, Connecticut, 1962).   With *Objective Case,* New York, Dramatists Play Service, 1961.
    Two Short Plays: Sarah and the Sax, and High Sign.   New York, Dramatists Play Service, 1962.
    The Beach People (produced Madison, Ohio, 1962).
    Postlude and Snowangel (produced New York, 1962).
    Cages: Snowangel and Epiphany (produced New York, 1963; Leicester, 1964; *Epiphany* produced London, 1974).   New York, Random House, 1964.
    Telemachus Clay: A Collage for Voices (produced New York, 1963).   New York, Random House, 1964.

Doubletalk: Sarah and the Sax, and The Dirty Old Man (produced New York, 1964; *Sarah and the Sax* produced London, 1971). New York, Random House, 1964.
The Exercise (produced Stockbridge, Massachusetts, 1967; New York, 1968). New York, Dramatists Play Service, 1968.

Screenplays: *Seconds*, 1966; *The Fox*, with Howard Koch, 1967; *The Brotherhood*, 1968; *The Mechanic*, 1972; *Reflection of Fear*, 1972; *Crazy Joe*, 1973; *The Sailor who Fell with Grace from the Sea*, 1976.

Television Plays: *In Search of America*, 1971; *Honor Thy Father*, 1972; *Doc Elliot* (pilot), 1972; *Where Have All the People Gone*, 1974.

Novels

The Brotherhood. New York, New American Library, 1968.
The Mechanic. New York, New American Library, 1972.

Theatrical Activities:

Director: **Film** – *The Sailor Who Fell from Grace with the Sea*, 1976.

*   *   *

Between June, 1963 and May, 1964 – less than a year's time – four one-act plays and one full length work by Lewis John Carlino were produced off-Broadway in New York. They ranged from the vast talent and imagination of *Telemachus Clay* to the burgeoning maturity of *Cages* to the unfulfilled *Doubletalk*. With these plays, Carlino established himself as an American playwright of exceptional quality and promise. The theatre did not hear from him again for four years, as he turned to screenwriting (*Seconds, The Brotherhood*). In 1968 he made his Broadway debut with the sloppy and self-indulgent *The Exercise*, and the catastrophe seems to have driven him permanently from the theatre.

If critics, financial uncertainty, and the unpredictable duration of a play's run are the theatre's risks, however, film writing has its own dangers. Like too many artistic writers caught up in the American commercial maelstrom, Lewis John Carlino was lost in the hurly-burly of a marketplace too busy to notice or care. Nevertheless, the originality and craftsmanship of his stage work endure. He is a playwright who should not forget or be forgotten.

His first notable New York production was a bill of one-act plays – *Cages*. The curtain raiser, *Snowangel*, is a minor look at a constricted intellectual and an earthy prostitute, spelling out the predictable point. The main work of the program, however, is devastating.

Called *Epiphany*, it is about an ornithologist who is discovered by his wife in a homosexual act. In reaction he turns into a rooster. The Kafkaesque metaphor is theatrically powerful, visually striking and provocative in context. But as he becomes that rooster, clucking and strutting, it turns out that he is laying eggs. Having really wanted to be a hen, he has suffered a breakdown only to find his wife all too willing to strip the coxcomb from the mask he has donned. He need no longer pretend to virility. She turns him into a female and stays to keep him that way.

Although the play came at a time when every other drama seemed to condemn women as man's arch-enemy, Carlino's imaginative story and powerful structure transcended the cliché. The dramatic scheme is faultless and the writing is for actors – something too few playwrights seem capable of doing.

As is often the case, a well-received play generates production of a writer's earlier work and, within six months, Carlino's *Telemachus Clay* was presented off-Broadway. One could only again ponder the judgment of producers for here was a drama of tremendous poetry, artistry and stage life – a drama that would never have been presented had it not been for the notices *Cages* received.

Like so many first plays, *Telemachus Clay* is a story of the artist as a young man, in this case drawn parallel to Odysseus' son. It is subtitled, *A Collage For Voices,* as indeed it is, the actors perched on stools, facing the audience. The eleven of them play a host of characters, changing time and location with the magic of poetry weaving the fabric of story, thought, event and emotion in overlapping dialogue and sound.

This is a device that risks pretension and artiness, but in *Telemachus Clay* it succeeds on the·sheer beauty of language and the structural control. There are thoughts and dreams, flashbacks, memories, overheard conversation – a score of effects beyond conventional structure and justifying the form. Like *Cages,* the play suffers from immature message making, but like it, too, there is a marvellous sense of theatre, of dialogue, of fantasy and of humor.

Doubletalk underlined these earlier plays' flaws rather than their strengths – instead of picking up on his technical finesse, strong dialogue and sense of stage excitement, Carlino stumbled on his inclination toward point-making and his trouble with plots. These two one-act plays used coy notions instead of stories – an old Jewish lady having a chance meeting with a black musician; a virgin having a chance meeting with an aged poet. This coyness came to a head with *The Exercise* – a play about actors, improvisations, reality and theatricality that threatened to bring Pirandello from his grave if only to blow up New York's Actors Studio, to which this play was virtually a bouquet.

The work output is slim, certainly inconsistent, and no peak of development was ever achieved. Yet, Lewis John Carlino's playwriting is unmistakably artistic. Its uncertain flowering is tragically representative of too many young American writers for the stage.

—Martin Gottfried

CARTER, Lonnie.   American.   Born in Chicago, Illinois, 25 October 1942. Educated at Loyola University, Chicago, 1960–61; Marquette University, Milwaukee, Wisconsin, B.A. 1964, M.A. 1966; Yale University Drama School, New Haven, Connecticut (Molly Kazan Award, 1967; Shubert Fellowship, 1968–69), M.F.A. 1969. Married Marilyn Smutko in 1966 (divorced, 1972). Taught English Composition, Marquette University, 1964–65, and Playwriting, Yale University Drama School, 1974–75. Recipient: Peg Santvoord Foundation Fellowship, 1969, 1970; Guggenheim Fellowship, 1971; National Endowment for the Arts grant, 1974; CBS Foundation grant, 1974. Address: Cream Hill Road, West Cornwall, Connecticut 06796, U.S.A.

PUBLICATIONS

Plays

    Adam (produced Milwaukee, 1966).
    Another Quiet Evening at Home (produced New Haven, Connecticut, 1967).
    If Beauty's in the Eye of the Beholder, Truth Is in the Pupil Somewhere Too (produced
       New Haven, Connecticut, 1969).

Workday (produced New Haven, Connecticut, 1970).

Iz She Izzy or Iz He Ain'tzy or Iz They Both, music by Robert Montgomery (produced New Haven, Connecticut, 1970; New York, 1972).   Published in *Scripts 7* (New York), May 1972.

More War in Store, and Time Space (produced New York, 1970).

Plumb Loco (produced Stockbridge, Massachusetts, 1970).

The Big House (produced New Haven, Connecticut, 1971).

Smoky Links (produced New York, 1972).

Watergate Classics, with others (produced New Haven, Connecticut, 1973). Published in *Yale/Theatre* (New Haven, Connecticut), 1974.

Cream Cheese (produced New York, 1974).

The Sovereign State of Boogedy Boogedy, in *Yale/Theatre* (New Haven, Connecticut), Fall 1976.

Critical Studies: by Richard Gilman in *The New York Times*, 22 September 1970; in *The National Observer* (New York), November 1971.

*   *   *

While Lonnie Carter was studying playwriting at Yale Drama School he spent most of his time not writing plays, but rather attending movie retrospectives of Buster Keaton, Charlie Chaplin, the Marx Brothers, and W. C. Fields. Spending hours watching these classic comedies, he saw something in the basic physiognomy of these characters that he was trying to do verbally in his plays. He then decided to write his own slap-stick farce using the Marx Brothers' film *The Big House* as a springboard.

Employing the original plot of *The Big House*, in which three con-men take over a prison and lock up the warden, he used the film's basic characters of Groucho, a cockney Chico, Harpo, and a minister made up to look like Chaplin. Carter's only additions were a few songs and dances. Basically what Carter ended up with was a hodge-podge of 20's and 30's movie comedies. The play is filled with low comedy hijinks, pratfalls galore, and very broad burlesque humor. The action proceeds at such a furious pace that by the middle of the second act the audience is out of breath and the playwright out of plot. The main trouble with Carter's *The Big House* lies in the plot and structure. It would have been fine as a one-act play or mini-musical, but in its present state, it needs further development.

The most popular play Carter has written is called *Iz She Izzy or Iz He Ain'tzy or Iz They Both*. It had its premiere at Yale in 1970, and has since been performed regularly by university and high school drama groups. *Izzy* is set in a chaotic contemporary courtroom where a schizoid judge (Justice "Choo-Choo" Justice; half-male and half-female) is on trial for having committed the premeditated murder of his female self. In *Izzy*, Carter once again uses many familiar movie gags, and supplements the action by songs with lovely lyrics that show off his audacious wit. A good example is the song sung by the frustrated Justice (Choo-Choo) Justice near the end of the play: "I'd like to have a baby/A lass or little laddie/But when it saw its mommy/Would it say 'Daddy'?"

Smoky Links, is about a revolution on a mythical Scotland golf course. The main revolutionary is a symbolic Oriental golf pro who threatens the whole club while turning the Scottish language around with his Oriental accent.

In *Smoky Links*, as in most of his plays, Carter wrestles with the subject of justice. All of his main characters, Wolfgang Amadeus Gutbucket in *The Big House*, Justice (Choo-Choo) Justice in *Izzy*, and the Oriental Golf Pro in *Smoky Links*, are in some way frustrated by the law. But the characters' attitude towards justice and the law remains mostly ambiguous, except in the case of the Marx Brothers in *The Big House*. The Marx Brothers are dyed in the wool anarchists and never offer any alternative except total disruption.

Except for the highly derivative *The Big House*, Carter's sharp humor and verbal sumersaults remind one more of Restoration comedy or the satires of Rabelais than the old-time Hollywood movie comedies. The influence of films is strong, but Carter has also a special, quite obvious talent that has yet to be developed to its fullest extent

—Bernard Carragher

CAUTE, (John) David.   British.   Born in Alexandria, Egypt, 16 December 1936. Educated at Edinburgh Academy; Wadham College, Oxford, M.A. in modern history, D.Phil. 1962; Harvard University, Cambridge, Massachusetts (Henry Fellow), 1960–61. Served in the British Army, in Africa, 1955–56. Married Catherine Shuckburgh in 1961 (divorced, 1970); has two sons. Fellow, All Souls College, Oxford, 1959–65; Visiting Professor, New York University and Columbia University, New York, 1966–67; Reader in Social and Political Theory, Brunel University, Uxbridge, Middlesex, 1967–70. Co-Organizer, Oxford Teach-In on Vietnam, 1965. Recipient: London Authors' Club Award, 1960; Rhys Memorial Prize, 1960. Lives in London, Address: c/o Elaine Greene Ltd., 31 Newington Green, London N16 9PU, England.

PUBLICATIONS

Plays

> *Songs for an Autumn Rifle* (produced Edinburgh, 1961).
> *The Demonstration* (produced Nottingham, 1969; London, 1970).   London, Deutsch, 1970. (With the novel *The Occupation* and the essay *The Illusion*, forms part of *The Confrontation: A Trilogy*.)
> *The Fourth World* (produced London, 1973).

> Radio Play: *Fallout*, 1972.

Novels

> *At Fever Pitch*.   London, Deutsch, 1959; New York, Pantheon Books, 1961.
> *Comrade Jacob*.   London, Deutsch, 1961; New York, Pantheon Books, 1962.
> *The Decline of the West*.   London Deutsch, and New York, Macmillan, 1966.
> *The Occupation*.   London, Deutsch, 1971; New York, McGraw Hill, 1972. (With the play *The Demonstration* and the essay *The Illusion*, forms part of *The Confrontation: A Trilogy*.)

Other

> *Communism and the French Intellectuals, 1914–1960*.   London, Deutsch, and New York, Macmillan, 1964.
> *The Left in Europe since 1789*.   London, Weidenfeld and Nicolson, and New York, McGraw Hill, 1966.

Fanon.   London, Fontana, and New York, Viking Press, 1970.

The Illusion,   London, Deutsch, 1971; New York, Harper, 1972. (With the novel *The Occupation* and the play *The Demonstration.* forms part of *The Confrontation: A Trilogy.*)

The Fellow–Travellers.   London, Weidenfeld and Nicholson, and New York, Macmillan, 1973.

Collisions: Essays and Reviews.   London, Quartet, 1974.

Cuba, Yes?   London, Secker and Warburg, and New York, McGraw Hill, 1974.

Editor, *Essential Writings of Karl Marx.*   London, MacGibbon and Kee, 1967; New York, Macmillan, 1968.

Critical Studies: *Anger and After* by John Russell Taylor, London, Methuen, 1962; "Rebels and Their Causes" by Harold Hobson, in *The Sunday Times* (London), 23 November 1969; "Keeping Our Distance" by Benedict Nightingale, in *The New Statesman* (London), 28 November 1969; in *Plays and Players* (London), February 1970; in *The Times* (London), 22 July 1971.

David Caute comments:

With one exception, my plays have all been public plays. A "public" play, like a "private" play, is of course populated by individual characters with distinctive personalities, but the real subject lies elsewhere, in some wider social or political issue. Obviously the most elementary problem for the public playwright is to present characters who are not merely ciphers or puppets – words much cherished by critics hostile to didactic theatre.

Songs for an Autumn Rifle, written in 1960, is shaped in the spirit of banal realism. By the time I wrote my next play, *The Demonstration*, seven years later, my attitude towards both fiction and drama had changed. While the necessity of commitment still imposed itself, the old forms of naturalism, realism and illusionist mimesis seemed incompatible with our present-day knowledge about language and communication. (These ideas are developed more fully in *The Illusion*, Deutsch, 1971.) One is therefore working to achieve a form of self-aware or dialectical theatre which is not only about a subject, but also about the play itself as a presentation – an inevitably distorting one – of that subject. The intention is to stimulate in the audience a greater critical awareness, rather than to seduce it into empathy and catharsis, In my view, for example, the lasting impact of Brecht's *Arturo Ui* consists less in what the play tells us about Hitler than what it tells us about *knowing about Hitler*.

The kind of writing I have in mind must pay far more attention to the physical possibilities of the theatre than did the old realism or well-made play. But whereas the author was once dictator, the modern playwright finds his supremacy challenged by directors or groups of actors. Up to a point this is healthy. But only up to a point! (See my "Author's Theatre," *The Listener,* 3 June 1971.)

One of my plays, *The Fourth World*, is different: a very private play, and, I hope a funny one. It was conceived and delivered all within a week.

*   *   *

While concern with social and political issues is no longer as rare among English dramatists as it was in the forties and early fifties, there are still very few who are as deeply committed as David Mercer and David Caute, or as deeply interested either in European politics or in committed European playwrights like Sartre. Caute's first play, *Songs for an Autumn Rifle*, was a direct response to the dilemma that the Russian treatment of the 1956 Hungarian uprising created for members of the Party. The central character is the editor of a

British Communist newspaper torn between his duty to the Party and his duty to the truth as relayed to him by an honest correspondent. On a personal level he is being pressured by his wife, who is not a Party member, by the doctrinaire daughter of a Party leader who works on his paper and is in love with him, and – indirectly – by his son, a National Serviceman who brings the Cyprus question into the plays, first going to military prison for refusing to serve there, then submitting to an Intelligence Officer's persuasions and later being killed.

The play plunges right into its subject-matter, with several scenes set in Hungary, showing the disillusioned correspondent of the English paper in argument not only with the Hungarian rebels but with Russian soldiers, whose attitudes are not altogether at one with the orders they have to carry out.

The Demonstration is a much more sophisticated piece of playmaking dramatising the problems of student revolution in terms of drama students at a university who rebel against the play their Professor gives them to perform, insisting on substituting a play about their own experience of repressive authoritarianism at the university. Their play has the same title as the play we are watching, and we are ofter jerked from one level of theatrical reality to another, when, for instance, a scene between the Women's Dean and a student turns out to be a scene between two students, on of whom is playing the Woman's Dean but can come out of character to make comments on her.

There is a very funny scene of rehearsing a sequence of the Professor's play ironically representing a confrontation between a bearded guerilla and a simple peasant, with interruptions from the students playing the parts, objecting that a bourgeois audience could take comfort from the satire. There is also an effective climax to the whole play when the police constables fail to respond to the Professor's orders to remove the handcuffs from the students they have arrested and the Superintendent's moustache fails to come off when he pulls at it. Reality has taken over.

But there is more theatrical exploitation than dramatic exploration of the no-man's-land between reality and illusion, and the play is not fuelled to fulfil the Pirandellian promise of its first few scenes. There are three main flaws. One is that the basic statement it is making seems to have been too rigidly pre-determined instead of being evolved during the course of the writing. The second is that while there is an admirable sympathy in general for the victims of our society – coloured women not admitted to hairdressing shops, students whose liberty is curtailed by rules that stem from pre-Victorian Puritanism – there is not enough sympathy for the private predicaments of the characters, who remain too much like stereotypes. This applies even to the central character, Professor Bright. David Caute (who himself resigned from All Souls the year after he helped to organise the Oxford Teach-In on Vietnam) has no difficulty in understanding the dilemma of a don who deplores the rule-worshipping bigotry of the university authorities but still cannot side with the rebellious students against them. So it may be a kind of personal modesty that makes him keep pulling Steven Bright away from the centre of the action. Or it may be the technical failure to provide a character Steven can confide in. Or it may be a determination to focus on social and political rather than personal problems. But his failure to project Steven's ambivalence results in the third flaw – the lack of a firm moral and structural centre. In Act Two Steven keeps disappearing to leave the stage free for the student actors. He makes two reappearances as an actor himself, in disguise. In the first he is not recognised until after he has made a long speech – an effective coup de théatre. But this does not reveal enough of what he is feeling. Instead he is crowded out by a host of peripheral characters. The stage direction at the beginning of Act Two Scene Two tells us that his "maliciously creative hand" can be detected in the presence on the stage of the hippies and drop-outs who reject the political aims of the student revolutionaries, and that he is seen prowling about taking occasional notes and photographs. This is not enough. He should be holding the play together and carrying it forward, even when he is left behind by the students who take the initiative away from him.

—Ronald Hayman

CHASE, Mary (Coyle).   American.   Born in Denver, Colorado, 25 February 1907. Educated in Denver public schools; Denver University, 1922–24; University of Colorado, Boulder, 1924–25. Married Robert Lamont Chase in 1928; has three children. Reporter, *Rocky Mountain News*, Denver, 1928–31; freelance correspondent, International News Service and the United Press, 1932–36; Publicity Director, NYA, Denver, 1941–42, and for Teamsters Union, 1942–44. Recipient: Pulitzer Prize, 1945. Litt.D.: University of Denver, 1947. Agent: Samuel French Inc., 25 West 45th Street, New York, New York 10036. Address: 505 Circle Drive, Denver, Colorado 80206, U.S.A.

PUBLICATIONS

Plays

   Me, Third (produced Denver, 1936; as *Now You've Done It*, produced New York, 1937).
   Sorority House (produced Denver, 1939).   New York, French, 1939.
   Too Much Business.   New York, French, 1940.
   A Slip of a Girl (produced Camp Hall, Colorado, 1941).
   Harvey (produced New York, 1944; London, 1949).   New York, Dramatists Play
      Service, 1944; London, English Theatre Guild, 1952.
   The Next Half Hour (produced New York, 1945).
   Mrs. McThing (produced New York, 1952),   New York, Oxford University Press,
      1952.
   Bernardine (produced New York, 1952).   New York, Oxford University Press, 1953.
   Lolita (produced Abington, Virginia, 1954).
   The Prize Play.   New York, Dramatists Play Service, 1961.
   Midgie Purvis (produced New York, 1961).   New York, Dramatists Play Service,
      1963.
   The Dog Sitters.   New York, Dramatists Play Service, 1963.
   Mickey.   New York, Dramatists Play Service, 1969.
   Cocktails with Mimi (produced Abington, Virginia, 1973).   New York, Dramatists
      Play Service, 1974.

   Screenplay: *Harvey*, 1950.

Other

   Loretta Mason Botts (juvenile).   Philadelphia, Lippincott, 1958.
   The Wicked Pigeon Ladies in the Garden (juvenile).   New York, Knopf, 1968.

*   *   *

   A comedy about a gentle alcoholic and his friend – who happens to be a six-foot-tall, invisible rabbit – made Mary Chase a significant name in the American theatre. *Harvey* won the Pulitzer Prize for the 1944–45 season and had one of the longest runs ever achieved on Broadway. It was made into a successful film and it has been successfully revived on American television.
   Harvey was Mrs. Chase's second play to be performed in New York. Her first, *Now You've Done It,* lasted only a few weeks back in 1937, giving little indication that her next comedy job in a brothel gives her a powerful hold on most of the male politicians in town. Mrs. Chase got a few good laughs out of her mischievous mixture of politics and prostitution.
   In *Harvey* (originally titled *The Pooka*), Mary Chase recounted the efforts of a widow, Veta Louise Simmons, to cure her alcoholic brother, Elwood P. Dowd, whose invisible

would be so popular. But in retrospect we can see the same setting in a western city, the same whimsy, and the same inverted morality that found fuller expression in *Harvey*. *Now You've Done It* is a comedy about a young man who seeks nomination to Congress. When he is opposed by the established party leaders, he is rescued by his mother's maid, whose former rabbit friend has become an embarrassment to the family. She takes Elwood to Dr. Chumley's Rest, a private psychiatric hospital, for shock treatment, but rescues him from the doctor because she fears that the cure will turn her harmless brother into an ogre.

The original production was a smash hit. Produced by Brock Pemberton – against the advice of his knowing Broadway friends – and staged with great fun and charm by Antoinette Perry, *Harvey* had an inspired cast. As Elwood P. Dowd, Frank Fay was making a Broadway comeback, having lost a fortune in Hollywood and having overcome – as rumor had it – his own problem with alcohol. New York audiences empathized nightly with his personal triumph as an actor almost as much as they cheered Elwood's quiet triumph over Dr. Chumley. Underplaying the role, Fay projected decency and gentleness along with a warm alcoholic glow, without ever descending to vulgarity or cuteness. Josephine Hull created Veta Louise with all her scatterbrained mannerisms but with the inner compassion that made her Elwood's sister beyond any doubt. These were two of the great American performances of the 1940's.

But even after Fay was succeeded by actors such as James Stewart, who did descend to cuteness, *Harvey* remained popular. The play had substance even without the great acting.

Harvey's strength derived from its highly theatrical use of illusion and reality. Mrs. Chase followed the tradition of plays like Thornton Wilder's *Our Town* that violated the laws of time and space, but she treated these dislocations of reality with a deadpan playfulness. Her comic motif of supernatural whimsy was like that of Noël Coward's *Blithe Spirit*, but she replaced his brittle sophistication with homespun compassion.

Though Harvey can hardly be regarded as a Christ symbol, Mary Chase dramatized a conflict between faith and disbelief. She suggested that the person who has faith in something invisible is mistakenly regarded as insane by "normal" society. Amid her comedy, she suggested further that faith and illusion should triumph over reality, that the psychiatrists were crazy, and that the abnormal were really sane. The punch line of the play is delivered by the cabby who warns Veta Louise about the shock teatment that Elwood is about to receive: "Lady, after this he'll be a perfectly normal human being, and you know what bastards they are!" Veta Louise pounds on the door of the treatment room and rescues her brother. Better a gentle alcoholic with faith in his invisible rabbit than a normal human bastard with no illusions and no ideals.

Audiences cheered Veta Louise on to her rescue of Elwood. Just as they applauded for Tinker Bell in *Peter Pan*, they gave Harvey an enthusiastic curtain call, one invisible paw held by Frank Fay and the other by Josephine Hull. The spectators may have been applauding the escape from reality to alcoholic illusion. But, on the other hand, they may have been cheering for the ideals of individualism, decency, and friendship.

Whatever audiences responded to Harvey's invisibility gave the play much of its humor as well as its meaning, During the Boston tryout an actor in a rabbit costume played the role for one performance. So great was the loss of laughs that Harvey was rendered invisible forever more.

A year after *Harvey*, Mary Chase tried a serious drama on a supernatural motif. In *The Next Half Hour* she wrote about an Irish immigrant woman who believed in little people and banshees. But the play failed quickly. Comedy was really her forte, she apparently decided, because her next three plays were comic treatments of illusion and reality.

In *Mrs. McThing*, produced in 1952, Mary Chase told the story of the wealthy Mrs. Howard V. Larue III, whose son is stolen away by a witch (Mrs. McThing) and replaced by a model boy. Aided by the witch's daughter, Mrs. Larue rescues her real son, who has become involved with a gang of comically incompetent gangsters. Like Harvey, the witch remained invisible, except for a moment in the last scene. Just as *Harvey* mixed real alcohol and whimsy, *Mrs. McThing* mixed whimsy with fake gangsters and fairy-tale witchcraft. This play was written for children, but it had a moderate success with adults who went to see Helen Hayes and Brandon de Wilde as mother and son. The Jean Arthur-Boris Karloff *Peter Pan*, a mixture of pirates and whimsy, had also been fairly popular with adults a few years earlier.

Later in 1952, Mary Chase brought her whimsy back to earth with *Bernardine*, a comedy about a group of teen-age boys who search without much success for sexual experience with "fast" women. They daydream of the accessible, but imaginary, Bernardine, who "lives" in Sneaky Falls. But since the sexual revolution, their fantacies seem quaintly dated.

No matter how sexual mores change, nothing remains so timely as a six-foot-tall invisible rabbit. In 1961 Mary Chase again tried the mixture of insanity and whimsy in *Midgie Purvis*, but, even with Tallulah Bankhead in the title role, the play failed, Mrs. Chase never succeeded in matching the comic perfection of *Harvey*. It is her classic.

—Morgan Y. Himelstein

CHAYEFSKY, Paddy. American. Born in the Bronx, New York, 29 January 1923. Educated at DeWitt Clinton High School, Bronx, graduated 1939; City College of New York, B.S. 1943. Served as a Private First Class in the United States Army, 4th Platoon of the 1st Company, 413th Regiment, 104th Battalion, 1943–45: Purple Heart. Married Susan Sackler in 1949; has one son. President. Sudan Productions. New York. 1956. and Carnegie Productions, New York, 1957. Since 1959, President of S.P.D. Productions, since 1967 of Sidney Productions, and since 1971 of Simcha Productions. all New York. Member of the Council of the Dramatists Guild. Recipient: Academy Award, 1955, 1972; New York Film Critics Award, 1956, 1971; Cannes Film Festival Award, 1955; Brussels, Venice and Edinburgh Film Festivals awards, 1958; Screen Writers Guild Best Screenplay Award, 1954, 1971. Agent: Maurice Spanbock. 10 East 40th Street. New York. New York. Address: 850 Seventh Avenue, New York, New York 10019, U.S.A.

PUBLICATIONS

Plays

Printer's Measure (televised, 1953). Included in *Television Plays*, 1955; in *On the Air*, edited by Percy R. Smith. London, Angus and Robertson, 1960.

Middle of the Night (televised, 1954; revised version, produced New York, 1956). New York, Random House, 1957.

Television Plays (includes *The Bachelor Party, The Big Deal, Holiday Song, Marty, The Mother*, and *Printer's Measure*). New York, Simon and Schuster, 1955.

The Bachelor Party (screenplay). New York, New American Library, 1957.

The Goddess (screenplay; stage version produced Edinburgh, 1971). New York, Simon and Schuster, 1958.

The Tenth Man (produced New York, 1959, London, 1961). New York, Randon House, 1960.

Gideon (produced New York, 1961). New York, Random House, 1962.

The Passion of Josef D (also director: produced New York, 1964). New York, Random House, 1964.

The Latent Heterosexual (produced Dallas and London, 1968). New York, Random House, 1967.

Screenplays: *Marty*, 1954; *The Bachelor Party*, 1957; *The Goddess*, 1958; *Middle of the Night*, 1959; *The Americanization of Emily*, 1964; *Paint Your Wagon*, 1969; *The Hospital*, 1971; *Network*,1975.

Television Plays: *Holiday Song*, 1952; *The Reluctant Citizen*, 1953; *Printer's Measure*, 1953; *Marty*, 1953; *The Big Deal*, 1953; *The Bachelor Party*, 1953; *The Sixth Year*, 1953; *Catch My Boy on Sunday*, 1953; *The Mother*, 1954; *Middle of the Night*, 1954; *The Catered Affair*, 1955.

Manuscript Collection: University of Wisconsin Theatre Center, Madison.

Theatrical Activities:

Director: **Play**–*The Passion of Josef D*, New York, 1964.

Paddy Chayefsky comments:

I suppose my primary concern is the preservation of humanity in an increasingly dehumanized world

*   *   *

Few American writers are able to devote themselves exclusively to writing for the theatre. Financial rewards are too hazardous and most professional playwrights turn to more lucrative fields, abandoning serious drama for the commercial requirements and artistic limitations of television and motion pictures. Yet for a brief spell in the early 1950's television prided itself on being the creative center of high-minded drama with original plays by Tad Mosel, Reginald Rose, Rod Serling and Gore Vidal, presented regularly on such programs as the Philco-Goodyear Playhouse. The boom did not last long and the total effect, in perspective, added little to the prestige of the American theatre. Many of the writers turned to the stage seeking fame rather than fortune and the satisfaction of literary prestige rather than the anonymity of the mass media. The most celebrated of the television graduates is Paddy Chayefsky.

He has had four plays produced on Broadway and a fifth, *The Latent Heterosexual*, was deliberately withheld from New York production but has been seen in London and several regional professional theatres in the United States. Chayefsky's best known work, *Marty*, an NBC production in 1953, and the first television script to be made into a motion picture, is characteristic of the playwright's later work. A Bronx butcher and a homely working girl, both lonely inarticulate people longing for love, discover happiness and emotional fulfilment in a proletarian romance that offsets the dull routine of their lives. His first Broadway play, *Middle of the Night*, an extended television script about middle-class Jewish people on New York's West Side, capitalized on *Marty's* fame. A widowed garment manufacturer seeking companionship with his secretary, a girl younger than his own daughter, has to overcome the objections of his children and his relatives. Sentimental and heartwarming, the play is the story of ordinary people who wrest few concessions from life and manage to achieve a happy adjustment. Filled with homespun humor, Jewish folklore, it offends no one and is a neatly tooled human comedy.

In his next two plays, Chayefsky attempted to deal with man's relation to God. *The Tenth Man*, a contemporary version of *The Dybbuk*. takes place in a shabby orthodox synagogue to the accompaniment of prayers and ceremonial ritual which proved extremely popular with the New York audience. The play is an attack on present-day intellectual cynicism, and offers instead the hallowed recipe of redemption through love. The language is a combination of demonology and Freud, fantasy and realism, but is weakened by the patter of Jewish whimsy, the stereotype of inverted sentence structure, and the juxtaposition of chant and wisecrack. A girl is to undergo the exorcism of the dybbuk which possesses her. A young lawyer, Arthur, with whom she falls in love, cannot accept faith in anything and certainly not the religious faith of his fathers, nor will he accept the reality of love. The most powerful scene of the play is the one in which the exorcism is performed. The Cabalist chants the prayer, blows the ram's horn and shouts for the excommunication from the world of the living and the dead of the being that inhabits the girl's soul. The girl remains untouched. Instead, the lawyer falls to the floor as the dybbuk of cynicism is removed from him. When he returns to consciousness, he has reason for living, a "desire to wake in the morning, a passion for the things of life."

The play is sensational in its setting, its use of folklore material, and the contrast of the acceptance of religion by the older people and its rejection by the young. Those with faith would defy the dybbuk; the lawyer would send the girl to a psychiatrist. However, the play never gets beyond the resolution of a young man in love finding a meaning for life. Boy meets girl in a synagogue and wins her by losing his dybbuk. Chayefsky pursued the religious theme in his next play, *Gideon*. God appears on stage but since the Hebraic God is the terrifying Unseen, save to a chosen few, Chayefsky used the Angel who forgets his role at times and calls himself God. He needs a messenger on earth and raises the simple peasant Gideon to leadership of the Israelites. The dull clod whom God has arbitrarily chosen to be a great leader grows with his responsibility and refuses blind obedience. As modern man has done, he attempts to discover himself instead. He put on the golden ephod and pleads with the Lord to release him from his contract saying, "I must believe in my own self and if you love me, God, let me do that." With God laughing in the background, Gideon turns to his people and offers a "historical, economic, sociopsychological and cultural" explanation of his victories.

The dialogue is often warm and touching, and occasionally poetic, but Chayefsky drips seriousness with sentiment and exploits all the commercially accepted topics: God, psychiatry, love and the petty problems of the middle class. The debate between God and Gideon often sounds like a discussion between two enterprising businessmen. At times a querulous tribal deity, God becomes almost comedic in his insistence on love, and only slightly larger than man. *Gideon* might well be termed a television writer's approach to God.

The Passion of Josef D deals with the Russian revolution and the role played by Stalin whose real name was Josef Dzhugashvili. Influenced by Bertolt Brecht, Chayefsky attempted a political burlesque comparable to those frequently seen in German nightclubs. The play is in the form of historical episodes often unrelated. Actors address the audience directly, and songs and comedy routines interrupt the action. The most successful scenes are those played in the manner of a nightclub revue.

The second half of the play avoids the broad satiric expressionistic tone and becomes a realistic story of Stalin who is pictured as a grim, tough, unsmiling bullyboy whose participation in the Revolution satisfies a religious craving. Christ's passion on the Cross and his love of mankind are converted into the bloody passion of Josef D. Once a seminary student who rejected the Christian God, Stalin finds a new God in Lenin, with himself as prophet. When his new God dies, he seeks another, but finding none turns into a wild beast and in Caligula fashion destroys everything that stands in his way.

The Latent Heterosexual deals with a successful author, happy, middle-aged and adjusted to his homosexual preferences. Upon the advice of his accountants, he marries to escape government taxes. To his amazement he finds himself falling in love with his wife. The play is witty, carefully avoids obscenity and is an extended development of a single conceit.

When he did not win full glory on Broadway, Chayefsky turned to Hollywood and has been responsible for such original screenplays as *The Goddess*, which deals with a declining motion picture actress, *The Hospital*, in which George C. Scott plays a doctor whose old fashioned liberalism is in conflict with the new radicalism, and *Network*, a critical account of the growing pains of the television industry.

Chayefsky turned to the theatre for greater freedom of expression, declaring that television was "not related to adult reality," but the television techniques pursued him. He has the courage to deal with grandiose themes, profound moral issues, and in his own words, "characters caught in the decline of their society." He is an excellent craftsman in the tight structure of psychological realism. His language captures the nervous, agitated, blunt speech of the lower middle class with moments of caustic wit and social insight. He follows in the tradition of Clifford Odets, Lillian Hellman and Arthur Miller, but has not as yet developed the vision and the poetry to reach beyond pat resolutions that are a bit too comfortable and reassuring.

—Allan Lewis

CHILDRESS, Alice. American. Born in Charleston, South Carolina, in 1920. Married to Nathan Woodard; has one daughter. Actress; Director, American Negro Theatre, New York, for twelve years. Scholar, Radcliffe Institute for Independent Study, Cambridge, Massachusetts, 1966–68. Recipient: Obie Award, 1956; Woodward School Book Award, 1975. Agent: Flora Roberts Inc., 65 East 55th Street, New York, New York 10022. Address: 800 Riverside Drive, New York, New York 10032, U.S.A.

PUBLICATIONS

Plays

Florence, in *Masses and Midstream* (New York), October 1950.
Trouble in Mind (produced New York, 1955). Published in *Black Theatre: A Twentieth-Century Collection of the Work of Its Best Playwrights*, edited by Lindsay Patterson, New York, Dodd Mead, 1971.
Wedding Band (produced Ann Arbor, Michigan, 1966; New York, 1972). New York, French, 1973.
The World on a Hill, in *Plays to Remember*. New York, Macmillan, 1968.
String (produced New York, 1969). Included in *Mojo, and String*, 1971.
Wine in the Wilderness (televised, 1969). New York, Dramatists Play Service, 1970.
Mojo, and String. New York, Dramatists Play Service, 1971.
When the Rattlesnake Sounds (juvenile). New York, Coward McCann, 1975.
Let's Hear It for the Queen (juvenile). New York, Coward McCann, 1976.

Television Play: *Wine in the Wilderness*, 1969.

Other Plays: *Gold Through the Trees; Just a Little Simple*, from stories by Langston Hughes; *Martin Luther King at Montgomery, Alabama*.

Other

Like One of the Family: Conversations from a Domestic's Life. New York, Independence Press, 1956.

150

A Hero Ain't Nothin' But a Sandwich (juvenile).   New York, Coward McCann, 1973.

Editor, *Black Scenes: Collections of Scenes from Plays Written by Black People about Black Experience.*   New York, Zenith, 1971.

*   *   *

The career of Alice Childress evidences the difficulty of earning major recognition in the world of theatre. Despite an Obie Award, international production of her work, collegiate and professional recognition of her play *Wedding Band*, and a Harvard appointment to the Radcliffe Institute, Alice Childress, a talented actress, director, and writer, has not received the attention lavished on some of her more sensational or more controversial contemporaries.

Born in Charleston, South Carolina, and reared in Harlem, she began her career in theatre by studying acting with the American Negro Theatre. During the twelve years she worked with that company as actress, director, and author, Alice Childress supported herself with a variety of jobs. The struggle to maintain the dream of a career in theatre forms the theme of *Florence*, a short story subsequently adapted into a drama. In the most telling incident of the play, an Afro-American mother, angered by a white woman's assumption that security as a domestic is ample opportunity for a black woman, encourages her daughter to continue to seek her dream regardless of the cost.

The best known of Alice Childress's other dramas are *Gold Through the Trees, Just a Little Simple, Trouble in Mind,* and *Wedding Band.* Her other work includes *Like One of the Family, Martin Luther King at Montgomery, Alabama, The African Garden,* and *Black Scenes.* Even a brief account of some of these reveals the variety of her interests. *Just a Little Simple* is a dramatic adaptation of Langston Hughes' *Simple Speaks His Mind,* a collection of dialogue narratives focused on Jesse B. Simple ("Simple"), a black man characterized by pride and keen insight into the follies of prejudice and hypocrisy. *Wedding Band*, the drama of an interracial romance, featured Ruby Dee in a Professional Theatre Production at the University of Michigan and Eartha Kitt in the New York production. *Like One of the Family* is a series of satiric monologues by a black domestic who, in temperament and character, might be considered a soul sister of Simple. *Black Scenes*, an anthology of scenes from plays by black authors, is a collection intended for people who wish to use scenes from black experience for auditions or classroom study.

In several respects, her most interesting drama in *Trouble in Mind*, which reveals the difficulties experienced by blacks as performers and as images in American theatre. The story takes place during a rehearsal of a play which the white director praises as a powerful and controversial protest against lynching. The director, who identifies himself as a liberal, does not perceive that the theme is outdated, the images of whites are polemically flattering, and the images of Blacks are demeaning. Consequently, the Black performers, seeking theatrical work to support themselves and further their dreams, must decide whether to withdraw from the play or to abet the perpetuation of derogatory stereotypes of Black people.

—Darwin T. Turner

CHRISTIE, Agatha (Mary Clarissa).   British.   Born in Torquay, Devon, 15 September 1890. Married Colonel A. Christie in 1914 (divorced, 1928); the archaeologist Sir Max Mallowan, 1932; has one daughter. Served as a volunteer nurse in the First and Second

World Wars. Has worked as an assistant to her husband on excavations in Iraq and Syria and on excavations of Assyrian ruins. Recipient: New York Drama Critics Circle Award. 1955. D. Litt.: University of Exeter, 1961. Fellow, Royal Society of Literature, 1950. C.B.E. (Commander, Order of the British Empire); 1956; D.B.E. (Dame Commander, Order of the British Empire), 1971 Agent: Hughes Massie Ltd., 69 Great Russell Street, London W.C.1. Address: Winterbrook House, Wallingford, Oxfordshire England. *Died 12 January 1976.*

PUBLICATIONS

Plays

Black Coffee (produced London, 1930).   London, Ashley, 1934.

Ten Little Niggers, adaptation of her own novel (produced Wimbledon and London, 1943).   London, French, 1944; as *Ten Little Indians* (produced New York, 1944), New York, French, 1946.

Appointment with Death, adaptation of her own novel (produced Glasgow and London, 1945).   London, French, 1945.

Murder on the Nile, adaptation of her own novel (produced Wimbledon, 1945; London and New York, 1946).   London and New York, French, 1946.

The Hollow, adaptation of her own novel (produced Cambridge and London, 1951; Princeton, New Jersey, 1952).   London and New York, French, 1952.

The Mousetrap (broadcast, 1952; revised version, produced Nottingham and London, 1952; New York, 1960).   London and New York, French, 1956.

Witness for the Prosecution, adaptation of her own story (produced Nottingham and London, 1953; New York, 1954).   London and New York, French, 1954,

The Spider's Web (produced Nottingham and London, 1954; New York, 1974).   London and New York, French, 1957.

Towards Zero, with Gerald Verner, adaptation of her own novel (produced Nottingham and London, 1956).   London, French, and New York, Dramatists Play Service, 1957.

Verdict (produced Wolverhampton and London, 1958).   London, French, 1958.

The Unexpected Guest (produced Bristol and London, 1958).   London, French, 1958.

Go Back for Murder, adaptation of her novel *Five Little Pigs* (produced Edinburgh and London, 1960).   London, French, 1960.

Rule of Three: Afternoon at the Seaside, The Patient, The Rats (produced Aberdeen and London, 1962; *The Rats* produced New York, 1973).   London, French, 1963.

Fiddlers Three (produced Southsea, 1971; London, 1972).

Akhnaton.   London, Collins, and New York, Dodd Mead, 1973.

Radio Plays: *The Mousetrap*, 1952; *Personal Call*, 1960.

Novels

The Mysterious Affair at Styles: A Detective Story,   London, Lane, and New York, Dodd Mead, 1920.

The Secret Adversary.   London, Lane, and New York, Dodd Mead, 1922.

The Murder on the Links.   London, Lane, and New York, Dodd Mead, 1923.

The Man in the Brown Suit.   London, Lane, and New York, Dodd Mead, 1924.

The Secret of Chimneys.   London, Lane, and New York, Dodd Mead, 1925.

The Murder of Roger Ackroyd.   London, Collins, and New York, Dodd Mead, 1926.

The Big Four.   London, Collins, and New York, Dodd Mead, 1927.

The Mystery of the Blue Train.   London, Collins, and New York, Dodd Mead, 1928.
The Seven Dials Mystery. London, Collins, and New York, Dodd Mead, 1929.
The Murder at the Vicarage.   London, Collins, and New York, Dodd Mead, 1930.
Giants' Bread (as Mary Westmacott).   London, Collins, and New York, Doubleday, 1930.
The Sittaford Mystery.   London, Collins, 1931; as *The Murder at Hazelmoor,* New York, Dodd Mead, 1931.
Peril at End House.   London, Collins, and New York, Dodd Mead, 1932.
Lord Edgware Dies.   London, Collins, 1933; as *Thirteen at Dinner,* New York, Dodd Mead, 1933.
Why Didn't They Ask Evans?   London, Collins, 1934; as *Boomerang Clue,* New York, Dodd Mead, 1935.
Murder on the Orient Express.   London, Collins, 1934; as *Murder on the Calais Coach,* New York, Dodd Mead, 1934.
Murder in Three Acts.   New York, Dodd Mead, 1934; as *Three Act Tragedy,* London, Collins, 1935.
Unfinished Portrait (as Mary Westmacott).   London, Collins, and New York, Doubleday, 1934.
Death in the Clouds.   London, Collins, 1935; as *Death in the Air,* New York, Dodd Mead, 1935.
The A.B.C. Murders: A New Poirot Mystery.   London, Collins, and New York, Dodd Mead, 1936.
Cards on the Table.   London, Collins, and New York, Dodd Mead, 1936.
Murder in Mesopotamia.   London, Collins, and New York, Dodd Mead, 1936.
Death on the Nile.   London, Collins, 1937; New York, Dodd Mead, 1938.
Dumb Witness.   London, Collins, 1937; as *Poirot Loses a Client,* New York, Dodd Mead, 1937.
Appointment with Death: A Poirot Mystery.   London, Collins, and New York, Dodd Mead, 1938.
Hercule Poirot's Christmas.   London, Collins, 1939; as *Murder for Christmas: A Poirot Story,* New York, Dodd Mead, 1939.
Murder Is Easy,   London, Collins, 1939; as *Easy to Kill,* New York, Dodd Mead, 1939.
Ten Little Niggers.   London, Collins, 1939; as *And Then There Were None,* New York, Dodd Mead, 1940.
One, Two, Buckle My Shoe.   London, Collins, 1940; as *The Patriotic Murders,* New York, Dodd Mead, 1941.
Sad Cypress.   London, Collins, and New York, Dodd Mead, 1941.
Evil under the Sun.   London, Collins, and New York, Dodd Mead, 1941.
N or M? The New Mystery.   London, Collins, and New York, Dodd Mead, 1941.
The Body in the Library.   London, Collins, and New York, Dodd Mead, 1942.
The Moving Finger.   New York, Dodd Mead, 1942; London, Collins, 1943.
Five Little Pigs.   London, Collins, 1942; as *Murder in Retrospect,* New York, Dodd Mead, 1942.
Death Comes as the End.   New York, Dodd Mead, 1942; London, Collins, 1945.
Towards Zero.   London, Collins, and New York, Dodd Mead, 1944.
Absent in the Spring (as Mary Westmacott).   London, Collins, and New York, Farrar and Rinehart, 1944.
Sparkling Cyanide.   London, Collins, 1945; as *Remembered Death,* New York, Dodd Mead, 1945.
The Hollow: A Hercule Poirot Mystery.   London, Collins, and New York, Dodd Mead, 1946.
Taken at the Flood.   London, Collins, 1948; as *There Is a Tide...,* New York, Dodd Mead, 1948.
The Rose and the Yew Tree (as Mary Westmacott).   London, Heinemann, and New

York, Rinehart, 1948.
Crooked House.   London, Collins, and New York, Dodd Mead, 1949.
A Murder Is Announced.   London, Collins, and New York, Dodd Mead, 1950.
They Came to Baghdad.   London, Collins, and New York, Dodd Mead, 1951.
They Do It with Mirrors.   London, Collins, 1952; as *Murder with Mirrors,* New York, Dodd Mead, 1952.
Mrs. McGinty's Dead.   London, Collins, and New York, Dodd Mead, 1952.
A Daughter's a Daughter (as Mary Westmacott).   London, Heinemann, 1952.
After the Funeral.   London, Collins, 1953; as *Funerals Are Fatal,* New York, Dodd Mead, 1953.
A Pocket Full of Rye.   London, Collins, 1953; New York, Dodd Mead, 1954.
Destination Unknown.   London, Collins, 1954; as *So Many Steps to Death,* New York, Dodd Mead, 1955.
Hickory, Dickory, Dock.   London, Collins, 1955; as *Hickory, Dickory, Death,* New York, Dodd Mead, 1955.
Dead Man's Folly.   London, Collins, and New York, Dodd Mead, 1956.
The Burden (as Mary Westmacott).   London, Heinemann, 1956.
4:50 from Paddington.   London, Collins, 1957; as *What Mrs. McGillicuddy Saw!,* New York, Dodd Mead, 1957.
Ordeal by Innocence.   London, Collins, and New York, Dodd Mead, 1958.
Cat among the Pigeons.   London, Collins, and New York, Dodd Mead, 1959.
The Pale Horse.   London, Collins, 1961; New York, Dodd Mead, 1962.
The Mirror Crack'd from Side to Side.   London, Collins, 1962; as *The Mirror Crack'd,* New York, Dodd Mead, 1963.
The Clocks.   London, Collins, 1963; New York, Dodd Mead, 1964.
A Caribbean Mystery.   London, Collins, 1964; New York, Dodd Mead, 1965.
At Bertram's Hotel.   London, Collins, and New York, Dodd Mead, 1965.
Third Girl.   London, Collins, 1966; New York, Dodd Mead, 1967.
Endless Night.   London, Collins, 1967; New York, Dodd Mead, 1968.
By the Pricking of My Thumb.   London, Collins, and New York, Dodd Mead, 1968.
Passenger to Frankfurt.   London, Collins, and New York, Dodd Mead,1970.
Nemesis.   London, Collins, and New York, Dodd Mead, 1971.
Elephants Can Remember.   London, Collins, and New York, Dodd Mead, 1972.
Postern of Fate.   London, Collins, and New York, Dodd Mead, 1973.
Murder on Board: Three Complete Mystery Novels (includes *The Mystery of the Blue Train, Death in the Air, What Mrs. McGillicuddy Saw!).*   New York, Dodd Mead, 1974.
Curtain: Hercule Poirot's Last Case.   London, Collins, and New York, Dodd Mead, 1975.
Sleeping Murder.   London, Collins, and New York, Dodd Mead, 1976.

Short Stories

Poirot Investigates.   London, Lane, 1924; New York, Dodd Mead, 1925.
Partners in Crime.   London, Collins, and New York, Dodd Mead, 1929.
The Underdog, with *Blackman's Wood,* by Phillips Oppenheim.   London, Reader's Library, 1929.
The Mysterious Mr. Quin.   London, Collins, and New York, Dodd Mead, 1930.
The Thirteen Problems.   London, Collins, 1932; as *The Tuesday Club Murders,* New York, Dodd Mead, 1933.
The Hound of Death and Other Stories.   London, Odhams Press, 1933.
Parker Pyne Investigates.   London, Collins, 1934; as *Mr. Parker Pyne, Detective,* New York, Dodd Mead, 1934.
The Listerdale Mystery and Other Stories.   London, Collins, 1934.

Murder in the Mews and Other Stories.   London, Collins, 1937; as Dead Man's Mirror
   and Other Stories, New York, Dodd Mead, 1937.
The Regatta Mystery and Other Stories.   New York, Dodd Mead, 1939.
The Labours of Hercules: Short Stories.   London, Collins, 1947; as Labors of
   Hercules: New Adventures in Crime by Hercule Poirot, New York, Dodd Mead, 1947.
Witness for the Prosecution and Other Stories.   New York, Dodd Mead, 1948.
Three Blind Mice and Other Stories.   New York, Dodd Mead, 1950.
Under Dog and Other Stories.   New York, Dodd Mead, 1951.
The Adventures of the Christmas Pudding, and Selection of Entrées.   London, Collins,
   1960.
Double Sin and Other Stories,   New York, Dodd Mead, 1961.
13 for Luck: A Selection of Mystery Stories for Young Readers.   New York, Dodd
   Mead, 1961; as 13 for Luck: A Selection of Mystery Stories, London, Collins 1966.
Star over Bethlehem and Other Stories (as A. C. Mallowan).   London, Collins, and
   New York, Dodd Mead, 1965.
Surprise! Surprize! A Collection of Mystery Stories with Unexpected Endings.   New
   York, Dodd Mead, 1965.
13 Clues for Miss Marple: A Collection of Mystery Stories.   New York, Dodd Mead,
   1965.
The Golden Ball and Other Stories.   New York, Dodd Mead. 1971.
Hercule Poirot's Early Cases.   London, Collins, and New York, Dodd Mead, 1974.

Verse

The Road of Dreams.   London, Bles, 1925.

Other

Come Tell Me How You Live (travel).   London, Collins, and New York, Dodd Mead,
   1946.

*   *   *

Agatha Christie is a seasoned and experienced spinner of webs and yarns. Like most
prolific and professional writers, the quality of her work varies considerably. A play like
Black Coffee is contrived, an obvious juggling of plot, while in a play like Verdict we see Miss
Christie, with the exception of one scene, at her worst, Of all her plays this is the most one-
dimensional in its characterization. The story concerns a crippled wife who whines so much
it is obvious she will be murdered: Karl, her husband, who is so saintly and forbearing it is
obvious he will be accused unjustly of her murder; and Helen, the daughter of a millionaire,
who is out to have an affair with Karl and who is so grotesquely drawn it is obvious she will
murder Lisa. The characters lurch clumsily about the stage of this creaking plot and yet, if
only on the level of crude melodrama, it does work. Just as the average Victorian novelist
knew how to keep the reader in suspense, how to wring an extra tear, Miss Christie even at
her lowest excels at telling a story. It is fashionable in intellectual circles to decry her as it
once was fashionable to dismiss Noël Coward. Yet even in a clumsy piece of stage craft like
Verdict, Miss Christie is capable of surprising writing as in the final scene (marred only by a
sentimental curtain) which is of an entirely different quality to the rest of the play, full of
insight. It is the scene in which Lisa, the lifelong friend who has always secretly loved him,
finally tells Karl the truth about himself, that he does not see people as they are but only as
concepts. "You put ideas first, not people; ideas of loyalty and friendship and pity, and
because of that people who are near suffer." Suddenly it is as though Miss Christie were
writing out of some personal experience so that the scene leaps off the page, as the

characters assume an extra dimension.

Certain of her plays are destined to become minor classics, perfect examples of a particular genre. *The Mousetrap* remains an oddity, a social, perhaps even sociological, phenomenon, but *Ten Little Niggers, Spider's Web,* and *The Unexpected Guest* are three good examples of her at her best.

In the latter play, the curtain rises on a man who that moment has been shot dead in his wheelchair. Nearby, hidden in the shadows, stands his wife. Is it she who has killed him? Through the french windows enters a motorist who has lost his way in the fog and proceeds at once to help the wife build up an alibi. Miss Christie, with a cool assurance, leads us swiftly past this improbable beginning, introducing her characters one after the other, each sharply etched (providing just enough for an actor to fill out). building up the suspense all round and skilfully levelling out a fair share of suspicion all round, so that the audience is so engrossed it does not have time to suspect that the murderer is in fact the intruder, the outsider, the uninvited guest.

Spider's Web is as stylishly constructed a thriller while at the same time a comedy of situation, of character. Clarissa, a scatty society woman, remarks how boring life is and says, jokingly, that one of these days she will surely walk into the drawing-room and find a corpse on the floor. Needless to say this is exactly what happens. The characters include a sinister figure involved with the international drug market; a small girl who is afraid of being kidnapped; a Lesbian-like housekeeper; and a butler with a past. Like those recipes for old-fashioned Christmas puddings full of nuts and fruit and brandy and beer and magic charms, Miss Christie's play is stuffed with all the right ingredients for a splendid evening out in the theatre. The essence of this particular play and its charm is perhaps best conveyed in the scene in which Clarissa's husband asks her what she has been doing all day, and when she replies, "I fell over a body," he answers, "Yes, darling, your stories are always enchanting, but really there isn't time now"

Clarissa —   But Henry, it's *true*. That's only the beginning. The police came and it
            was just one thing after another. There was a narcotic ring, and Miss
            Peake isn't Miss Peake, she's really Mrs. Brown, and Jeremy turned out
            to be the murderer and he was trying to steal a stamp worth £14,000.
Husband — Huh! Must have been a second Swedish yellow.
Clarissa —   That's just what it was!
Husband — The things you imagine, Clarissa!
Clarissa —   But darling, I didn't imagine it. How extraordinary it is; all my life
            nothing has really happened to me and tonight I've had the lot,
            murder, police, drug addicts, invisible ink, secret writing, almost
            arrested for manslaughter, and very nearly murdered. You know, in a
            way, it's almost *too* much all in one evening.
Husband — Do go and make the coffee, darling.

In that last speech of Clarissa is contained the secret of Agatha Christie's success as a writer. Her cosy, nice, middle-class audience (and they are not to be despised, fashionable though it is to decry the bourgeoisie) are able to identify with Clarissa. Their life, like that of Clarissa, is often full of boring routine and social trivia, and then after putting down the latest Agatha Christie thriller, or returning home to Forest Row after her latest play, they are able to say, Tonight I have had the lot: murder, police, drug addicts, etc. – It's almost too much in one evening!

—James Roose-Evans

CHURCHILL, Caryl.   British.   Born in London, 3 September 1938. Educated at Trafalgar School, Montreal, 1948–55; Lady Margaret Hall, Oxford, 1957-60, B.A. in English 1960, Married David Harter in 1961; has three sons. Resident Dramatist, Royal Court Theatre, London, 1974–75. Recipient: Richard Hillary Memorial Prize, 1961. Agent: Margaret Ramsay Ltd, 14a Goodwin's Court, London WC2N 4LL. Address: 12 Thornhill Square, London N.1, England.

PUBLICATIONS

Plays

Downstairs (produced Oxford, 1958; London, 1959).
Having a Wonderful Time (produced London, 1960).
Easy Death (produced Oxford, 1962).
The Ants (broadcast, 1962).   Published in *Penguin New English Dramatists 12*, London, Penguin, 1968.
Schreber's Nervous Illness (broadcast, 1972; produced London, 1972).
Owners (produced London, 1972; New York, 1973).   London, Eyre Methuen, 1973.
Perfect Happiness (broadcast, 1973; produced London, 1974).
Moving Clocks Go Slow (produced London, 1975).
Objections to Sex and Violence (produced London, 1975).
Light Shining in Buckinghamshire (produced London, 1976).

Radio Plays: *The Ants*, 1962; *Lovesick*, 1967; *Identical Twins*, 1968; *Abortive*, 1971; *Not, Not, Not, Not, Not Enough Oxygen*, 1971; *Schreber's Nervous Illness*, 1972; *Henry's Past*, 1972; *Perfect Happiness*, 1973.

Television Play: *The Judge's Wife*, 1972.

*   *   *

There is no simple answer to the question "How much radio experience should a playwright have?" Too much, obviously, is bad, but for each individual the optimum is different, and when one goes a long way beyond it, as Caryl Churchill has, it may be more a matter of not having had a good agent than of not having had enough talent. She made her debut with *Downstairs*, but made no mark, except on radio, until 1972 when *The Judge's Wife* was televised, *Owners* was produced at the Royal Court's Theatre Upstairs, and *Schreber's Nervous Illness* was put on at the King's Head. It was evident from her early radio play *The Ants* that she was an extremely fine writer. Even the more static of her stage plays are rich in moments when the characters come vibrantly to life, and she has acquired great skill in creating word-pictures but this advantage is offset by two bad habits: planning schematically in terms of themes and conceiving action in terms of speeches. Speech should be no more than a component part of a character's existence; her characters exist in order to talk, and talk in order to exist.

Her most theatrical play so far is *Owners*, which brings a story to organic life out of its carefully organised analysis of different attitudes to the idea of ownership. The characters are primarily exemplars, but whether their ideas are the cause or the result of the positions they have taken up, the confrontations produce effective action. The central character is a female property speculator. Her coarse husband, a butcher, who is no longer able to regard her as his property, fantasises about ending her growing independence by killing her. Alec, a young man who has transcended the possessive instinct, receives more sympathetic treatment than anyone else. Wanting nothing, he is free; fearing nothing, he is able to liberate his senile mother who still seems to *own* her meaningless, pleasureless, vegetable existence until he disconnects the hospital drip that is keeping her alive. His wife, in a desperate bid to regain possession of her flat, has been induced to sign away her baby to the childless property developer, who has a suicidal young man working for her winkling sitting tenants out of their homes.

The sexual meaning of the word "possess" is simultaneously explored in several relationships. The property developer wants the young man who wants nothing; her butcher husband sleeps vengefully with the young mother, who believes he will help her to regain possession of her baby. Characterisation is sometimes distorted to fit the schematic framework, but there is a strong verbal fibre running through the play; it also flashes out theatrical images of great power — the high meat being sold off cheaply in the butcher's shop, the randy butcher and the suicidal winkler in possession of the baby, the drip machinery that keeps the old lady in possession of her life.

The potentialities of the material of her next play, *Objections to Sex and Violence*, were enormous — too abundant, in fact. A divorcee who took a cleaning job has become involved in a sex-and-blackmail relationship with a rich man. Her other lover is obsessed with her younger sister, who has been married to a communist and is now involved with a group of terrorists. Her travelling companion turns out to be on the point of backing out. There are also three older characters, a demented spinster pathetically searching for the beach where she was once almost happy, a passion-starved husband who nearly assaults her, and the wife who is erotically less important to him than his daily diet of pornography.

The subject of the play was terrorism, but the violence remained notional, a theme for wordy variations, The speeches were extremely well-written, but they failed to animate the story. Instead of watching people living out their present tense, we were watching characters discussing their past and their future. In addition, the Royal Court management's decision to entrust the staging of the play to a radio producer may have looked like an inspired piece of malevolence, but it is doubtful whether even the most experienced and most theatrical of directors could have galvanised *Objections* into anything more than a conversation piece. Nonetheless, there is plenty of evidence that it might still not be too late for Caryl Churchill to make full use of the stage medium.

—Ronald Hayman

CLARK, John Pepper. Nigerian. Born in Kiagbolo, 6 April 1935. Educated at Warri Government College, Ughelli, 1948–54; Ibadan University, 1955–60, B.A. (honours) in English 1960; Princeton University, New Jersey (Parvin Fellowship), 1962–63; Ibadan University (Institute of African Studies Research Fellowship, 1961–64). Married; has one daughter. Nigerian Government Information Officer, 1960–61; Head of Features and Editorial Writer, *Daily Express*, Lagos, 1961–62. Founding–Editor, *The Horn* magazine, Ibadan. Since 1964, Member of the English Department, and currently Professor of English, University of Lagos. Founding Member, Society of Nigerian Authors. Agent: Curtis Brown Ltd., 1 Craven Hill, London W2 3EW, England. Address: Department of English, University of Lagos, Lagos, Nigeria.

PUBLICATIONS

Plays

Song of a Goat (produced Ibadan, 1961; London, 1965).   Ibadan, Mbari, 1961; in
Three Plays, 1964.
Three Plays: Song of a Goat, The Raft, The Masquerade.   London, Oxford University
Press, 1964.
The Masquerade (produced London, 1965).   Included in Three Plays, 1964.
The Raft (broadcast, 1966).   Included in Three Plays, 1964.
Ozidi.   Ibadan, London, and New York, Oxford University Press, 1966.

Screenplays (documentaries): The Ozidi of Atazi; The Ghost Town.

Radio Play: The Raft, 1966.

Verse

Poems.   Ibadan, Mbari, 1962.
A Reed in the Tide: A Selection of Poems.   London, Longman, 1965; New York,
Humanities Press, 1970.
Casualties: Poems 1966–1968.   London, Longman, and New York, Africana, 1970.

Other

America, Their America.   London, Deutsch-Heinemann, 1964; New York, Africana,
1969.
Example of Shakespeare: Critical Essays on African Literature.   London, Longman,
and Evanston, Illinois, Northwestern University Press, 1970.

*   *   *

There is in Africa today the opportunity – felt sometimes as an obligation – for those who
belong to the small élite of educated men to play more than one role in society. The same
was true of the European Renaissance, and, as the diversity of his activities and publications
indicates, John Pepper Clerk is a Renaissance man. He has not dedicated himself to the
theatre in the way that Wole Soyinka or Efua Sutherland has. Because his energies are
scattered, and because his most recent (and first full-length) play is unlike those before it, to
assess his work as a whole is difficult. It may even be that, when his writing career is over, it
will be as a poet rather than as a playwright that he seems important.
    Clark's best play is probably his first, Song of a Goat. The plot is simple: Zifa has lost his
virility and his wife Ebiere, in her frustration, turns to make love with his younger brother,
Tonye. Zifa is furious, seeking to kill Tonye, who, however, hangs himself. Shamed by his
own sterility and by his brother's death, Zifa walks into the sea, drowning himself.
    The virtues of the play flow directly from this strong situation. Unfortunately, Clark seeks
to shape the play along the lines of Greek tragedy. The self-consciousness of this attempt is
typified by the play's title and by the neighbours' function as a Greek chorus. This adds a
portentousness to the psychological restlessness of his characters that Clark, here and
elsewhere, can suggest so well.
    Clark's second play, The Masquerade, deals with the son whom Ebiere conceived with
Tonye. The son, Tufa, is to marry; as the marriage is about to be celebrated, his parentage is
disclosed; his strong-willed affianced, Titi, will not give him up and is shot by her father,

who mistakenly thinks she has given herself to Tufa before the marriage ceremony; and in a fight with her father Tufa is accidentally killed, too. Like Oedipus, Tufa is ignorant until half-way through the play of the circumstances of his parentage. Unlike him, however, he has committed no act which continues the crime of his parents' generation. And so the tragedy has a sense of arbitrariness about it. The sense of the author pushing beyond what a short play will bear is strongest in the character of the mother, whom events drive mad and who, cradling a cat, sings a ditty which sadly lacks the relevance of mad Ophelia's songs:

> Fresh fish at tuppence
> Who'll buy fresh, oh,
> Fresh fish at tuppence.

The play is full of echoes of Shakespeare's great lovers, and one suspects that the play was written as a sophisticated exercise – although any sense of irony remains the author's, uncommunicated to audiences.

The third of his short, poetic plays is *The Raft*. Here the flurry of onstage action of the earlier plays is abandoned. Four men float down a river on a raft of timbers over which they have no control. During the play, one gets chopped up by the propellers of a passing ship to which he swims, and another floats away when the raft splits. As the play ends, the last two are floating out of the mouth of the river in a thick fog. Whatever the characters symbolize – certainly the human condition, and perhaps the four Regions of which Nigeria was then composed – the play is largely an exercise in character revelation, abounding in set-piece descriptions of their past experiences.

Poetic adornment, in the form of set-pieces, increases in each of the short plays. The language itself, however, develops away from a poeticism reminiscent of Christopher Fry and Gerard Manley Hopkins. Clark has always been capable of simple diction which is yet rich with suggestions, as at the opening of *Song of a Goat*:

> Masseur – Your womb
>   Is open and warm as a room:
>   It ought to accomodate many.
> Ebiere – Well, it seems like staying empty.
> Masseur – An empty house, my daughter, is a thing
>   Of Danger. If men will not live in it
>   Bats or grass will, and that is enough
>   Signal for worse things to come in.
> Ebiere – It is not my fault. I keep my house
>   Open by night and day
>   But my lord will not come in.

Yet it is only in his most recent play, *Ozidi*, that he has resisted the temptation to embroider and has maintained rich but simple language throughout.

Ozidi is an adaptation of a traditional drama of the Ijaw – amongst whom all his plays are set. His other plays all have admirably tight structures, but this could hardly be expected of an adaptation from an epic that lasts seven days. It is Clark's first full-length play and he may be deliberately seeking a looser from; certainly, gone with the tight structure is the sense of the playwright's tight control over the characters.

Ozidi has links with Clark's earlier plays: a curse upon a family, bizarrely bloody events, a son obliged to pursue a fate determined by his father. Yet it is, one presumes, a transitional work – though transitional to what is unclear

—Anthony Graham-White

CLUCHEY, (Douglas) Rick(land).   American.   Born in Chicago, Illinois, 5 December 1933. Served in the United States Army, 1949–51. Married in 1951. Convicted of armed robbery in 1955: sentenced to life imprisonment at San Quentin State Prison, California; paroled, 1966. Founder and Executive Director, San Quentin Prison Theatre Group, 1957–66.

PUBLICATIONS

Plays

The Cage (produced San Quentin, California, 1965; New York, 1970; London, 1973).
The Wall is Mama (produced Edinburgh and London, 1974).
The Bug, with R. S. Bailey (produced Edinburgh, 1974).

Theatrical Activities:

Director: **Plays** – *In the Zone* by Eugene O'Neill, *Hughie* by Eugene O'Neill, *The Caretaker* by Harold Pinter, *Deathwatch* by Jean Genet, *Krapp's Last Tape* by Samuel Beckett, *The Cage, The Wall Is Mama, The Iceman Cometh* by Eugene O'Neill, *The Execution of Eddie Slovik, Escurial* by Michel de Ghelderode, and *Don Juan in Hell* by G. B. Shaw, 1957–75.

Actor: **Plays**—in his own directed plays, and in *Stalag 17* by Donald Bevan and Edmund Trzcinski, *Time Limit* by Henry Denker and Ralph Berkey, *Room Service* by John Murray and Allen Boretz, *Of Mice and Men* by John Steinbeck, *Inherit the Wind* by Jerome Lawrence and Robert E. Lee, *Brother Orchid, Waiting for Godot* by Samuel Beckett, *The Dock Brief* by John Mortimer, *Endgame* by Samuel Beckett, *The Advocate* by Robert Noah, *The Brig* by Kenneth H. Brown, *The Dumb Waiter* by Harold Pinter, *People Need People* by H. F. Greenberg, *Krapp's Last Tape* by Samuel Beckett, and *The Bug,* 1957–75.

Rick Cluchey comments:

I became involved with theatre while serving time at San Quentin. Prior to November 1957, no live drama had been seen within the walls of the prison since the turn of the century when Sarah Bernhardt's troupe entertained the convicts. Thus, when the San Francisco Actors Workshop production of Samuel Beckett's *Waiting for Godot* was staged in our North dining hall, the several hundred inmates who saw the play fairly howled their satisfaction, and the Warden gave his approval to the formation of our own drama group. Our theatrical program took time developing. Drama activity was in the main looked upon as something for sissies and homosexuals, child molesters and rapists. This attitude took time to overcome, but the program gradually gained acceptance and approval. Since no female was allowed to participate, and no inmates were allowed to impersonate females, we were limited to plays with all-male casts.

I began as an actor, and for several years (with the help of Al Mandell and, later, Ken Kitch of the San Francisco Actors Workshop) studied acting and directing. Since plays were difficult to find, I began to investigate possibilities of adapting plays for our use. I discovered that the plays of Beckett appeared void of any expository elements and seemed to take on wholly their own reality. There followed a period of several years when we experimented with the works of Beckett, producing *Waiting for Godot, Endgame,* and *Krapp's Last Tape.* We staged productions twice a year for the general public, and weekly for inmates. Martin

Esslin visited the workshop in 1963 and was impressed that we were preparing John Mortimer's *The Dock Brief* (the first American production), and sent us Mrozek's early play *Out at Sea*, which we also produced. Other productions were Solzhenitsin's *One Day in the Life of Ivan Denisovich* and Kenneth H. Brown's *The Brig*.

Throughout the decade of theatre activity at San Quentin, the inmates themselves were directly responsible for the total aspects of production. Outside professional assistance was welcome and warmly received, but only on an advisory level. As a theatre the workshop was committed to social and political themes; oddly the focus of much of this activity, although censored by the prison staff, seemed to point to conditions outside the walls of our own prison. But certainly prison as such was an on-going theme, although nothing could directly be said of our own four-walled hell.

Sadly the San Quentin workshop was closed down in 1967, though almost all of the convicts who'd worked to bring the program to fruition had already been paroled. In May 1967 the first outside production of the Quentin group was staged in Walnut Creek, California, the beginning of a ten-year journey.

*   *   *

Though Rick Cluchey has lived in relative freedom since December 1966, when he was paroled from his life sentence, he remains metaphorically in prison. Not only is the underworld the subject of the three plays, but he responds as director to confined spaces in which passions rise to explosion. Innocent of orthography and syntax, he writes of the world he knows in the idiom he knows.

While Cluchey was still in San Quentin prison, he composed *The Cage* for performance by the prison theatre group. "We asked the Warden for permission to perform the play," recalls Cluchey, "and he said fine – as long as it isn't about my prison." So Cluchey set his play in France, and the Warden exclaimed after the performance: "I had no idea French prisons were so bad." Though Cluchey had read Genet, the prison was his very own.

Cluchey has reworked the play, but the kernel remains invariant: Jive, a college graduate charged with murdering his girlfriend, is imprisoned in the same "cage" as three lifers – ex-prize fighter Doc, crippled homosexual Al, and mad Hatchet. Both Doc and Al make advances to the newcomer, but Hatchet, whose insanity takes a virulently religious form, places Jive on trial. Hatchet's two cell-mates are accustomed to lending themselves to his fixations, and they play Jive's defense counsel and prosecuting attorney. Hatchet is both judge and executioner, finally sentencing Jive to death and strangling him on stage. As Hatchet washes his murderous hands in the toilet-bowl, he addresses the gods: "I have done your will," but then points into the audience to conclude the play: "Your will."

The Wall Is Mama is nominally set outside prison, in the shady darkness of Mother's Bar on the Bowery in New York City. However, the characters have been in prison and are still caged by their criminal past. Duke, a black heroin user and dealer, claims to have kicked dope and is encouraged by his ex-mistress, bar owner Bea. However, two white members of the dope ring believe he has siphoned heroin for his own use, and they torture him to reveal its whereabouts. Nearly unconscious with pain, Duke nevertheless defies them until Bea seizes their gun and drives them from her bar. In Act 2, several hours later, a homosexual addict seduces a Marine in the presence of Duke, Bea, and a pseudo-preacher. The Marine addresses Duke much as did the gang killers. In a dope trance, Duke then reverts to childhood, seeing Bea as his mother. As she cuddles him, the white killers shoot both. For these rejects of society, the wall *is* mama.

The Bug, written with R. S. Bailey, a San Quentin colleague, is a work in progress. A woman is harrassed by obscene phone calls. Two policemen hide in an adjoining apartment, with electronic equipment that will ostensibly identify the source of the calls. But the play merges invasion of privacy into alleged obscenity.

Circumstances have walled Cluchey's life, but he has exchanged the enclosed space of prison for the enclosed space of theatre – an exchange that has liberated him and deepened public perception of prison-fostered brutalities.

—Ruby Colin

COLLINS, Barry. British. Born in Halifax, Yorkshire, 21 September 1941. Educated at Heath School, Halifax, 1953–61; Queen's College, Oxford. Married Anne Collins in 1963; has two sons and one daughter. Teacher, Halifax Education Committee, 1962–63; Journalist, *Halifax Evening Courier*, 1963–71. Recipient: Arts Council bursary. 1974, Agent: Sheila Lemon, Spokesmen, 1 Craven Hill, London W2 3EW. Address: 7 Golf Crescent, Highroad Well, Halifax, Yorkshire, England.

PUBLICATIONS

Plays

And Was Jerusalem Builded Here? (produced Leeds, 1972).
Beauty and the Beast (produced Leeds, 1973).
Judgement (produced Bristol, 1974; London, 1975). London, Faber, 1974.

Television Plays: *The Lonely Man's Lover*, 1974; *The Witches of Pendle, 1976.*

*   *   *

Judgement, Barry Collins's first play to be seen in London, gives a limited view of his potential as a dramatist. It is a monologue spoken on a bare stage by Andrei Vukhov, a Russian officer imprisoned for sixty days without food or water in the cellar of a monastery during the second world war. He tells of survival, how he and six other officers, abandoned as the battle moved away, decided to eat each other, casting lots as to the order in which this should be done. Vukhov asks the audience to be his judges, but he pleads guilty from the very start. Talking for two and a half hours, without intermission, he is concerned to know what should happen to him now. Only he and his brother, Rubin, have survived, and his brother is under care, heavily drugged in a hospital for the mad. What can happen after such an experience?

Barry Collins has given his hero a quiet and sustained sense of actuality, and not for a moment does the play rest in sensationalism. While the audience is drawn into imagining events that could never be enacted upon a stage, it is also alerted to ask how can society – how can each of them – live with such a man.

Judgement was first performed by Peter O'Toole at the Bristol Old Vic Theatre, but that was on one Tuesday afternoon only. The validity of the play and its hugely demanding role were established in Peter Hall's production with Colin Blakeley as Vukhov in a Studio Season given by the National Theatre at the small I.C.A. Terrace Theatre in 1975. Subsequently the production moved across the river to the Old Vic, and then back to the Royal Court for a short run.

With only a few, but notable, exceptions, the critics hailed Barry Collins as a master of narrative and intensely sober argument: his obvious theme was the survival of reason in an individual and in society. But there is more to the play than this. Barry Collins has imagined Vukhov coming to new relationships with his fellow officers and his memory of them, and giving more than his own life for his brother. It is a drama that discovers passionate conviction in the face of terrible suffering and despair. Its author is closer to Dostoevsky than to John Donne, or Sartre, with whom he has been compared. Those who saw Peter O'Toole's performance say that he played Vukhov as a saint.

It is this aspect of *Judgement* that links it most clearly with Barry Collins's other plays, not yet seen in London. His first was *And Was Jerusalem Builded Here?* written for Leeds Playhouse. Collins, as a journalist in Hallifax, had been asked to script a documentary about the Luddites, local weavers who had protested with growing violence against poverty and mechanisation in the Yorkshire mills in 1812–13. He provided no ordinary documentary, but an ambitious and extravagantly theatrical play which centered attention on John Booth, the son of a minister who joined the Luddites in a blood bond. Booth was a pamphleteer and does have one long story to tell that must have encouraged Barry Collins when he came to write *Judgement*, but there is much else besides verbal argument in the play: actors dressed as Tarot cards, a small band, simultaneity of setting through the use of moveable screens and projections, two choruses of rulers and of workmen, a juggler to act as narrator and clown, some lyrical and some tersely political songs. While the Luddites' attempt to burn down a mill is passed by in narration and a crucial murder occurs off-stage, Collins stages other scenes with realism and glowing economy of language. When Booth escapes from the arson fiasco, he meets his wife who has now been delivered of a still-born son and has gone mad. Booth's father and a midwife are also present and so the play's hero not only suffers but also questions his own responsibility.

Jerusalem is a first play powerful, like *Judgement,* in narrative and argument, but it also has lyricism and passion. Booth and his father are characters who change radically during the play, in ways that carry conviction and draw the audience into empathetic understanding and discovery. Some of the writing is lightly derivative – the juggler, the Shakespearian gaoler, the Sergeant who explains the general implications of his actions – but even some of these features may have been calculated. Collins has an eye for surprises that shift his audience's perception. When all seems set for a concluding trial scene in which the pamphleteer should defend himself eloquently or attack his prosecuters, this episode is quickly, almost mockingly, despatched: so the audience is led on to a further scene which his father tries to make Booth recite the Lord's Prayer. Here two irreconcilable impulses meet: a search for responsibility with compassion, and an awareness of political necessity and weakness. Before a bell tolls for his death, Booth is given a last word in a final scene with the juggler: "there's the agony: that I am what I am, knowing what I might be."

A children's play, *Beauty and the Beast*, and further stage plays that await performance, still further extend Barry Collins's range, notably into a fierce and contemporary social comedy. Meanwhile a television play has already been twice screened: in *The Lonely Man's Lover*, Collins exploits the televisual grandeur of the Yorkshire moors and the camera's ability to show the effects of slow-moving impulses that reach back in time in a man's inner life.

—John Russell Brown

———————

COLLINSON, Laurence (Henry). British. Born in Leeds, Yorkshire, 7 September 1925. Educated at various Australian primary schools; Brisbane State High School; Dalby High School, Queensland; University of Queensland, Brisbane; Julian Ashton Art School,

Sydney; Mercer House, Melbourne, teaching diploma 1955. Freelance radio, magazine and newspaper writer until 1954; English and Maths teacher in Victoria secondary schools, 1956–61; Editor, *The Educational Magazine,* Melbourne, teachers' journal of the Victorian Education Department, 1961–64. Also acted, directed and wrote for various Australian little theatres up to 1956. Sub-Editor, IPC Magazines Ltd., London, 1965–73. Recipient: Society of Australian Authors prize, London, 1969; Australian Council of the Arts special grant and fellowship, 1973. Agent: Margery Vosper Ltd., Suite 8, 26 Charing Cross Road, London WC2H 0DG.

PUBLICATIONS

Plays

    Friday Night at the Schrammers' (produced Brisbane, 1949).   Published in *Australian One-Act Plays, Book 2,* edited by Greg Branson, Adelaide, Rigby, 1962.
    No Sugar for George (produced Brisbane, 1949).
    The Zelda Trio (produced Melbourne, 1961; London, 1974).
    A Slice of Birthday Cake (broadcast, 1963).   Published in *Eight Short Plays,* Melbourne, Nelson, 1965.
    The Wangaratta Bunyip, in *Plays for Young Players,* edited by Colin Thiele and Greg Branson.   Adelaide, Rigby, 1970.
    Thinking Straight (produced London, 1975).   Published in *Homosexual Acts,* London, Inter-Action Imprint, 1975.

Screenplays: Two *Export Action* series documentaries, 1964.

Radio Plays: *A Slice of Birthday Cake,* 1963 (Australia); *The Slob on Friday,* 1969 (Canada).

Television Plays: *Uneasy Paradise,* 1963 (Australia); *Nude with Violin,* 1964 (Australia); *The Audition,* 1964 (Australia); *The Moods of Love,* 1964 (Australia); *Number Thirty Approximately,* 1968 (UK); *Loving Israel,* 1968 (UK); *The Girl from Upstairs,* 1971 (UK).

Novel

    Cupid's Crescent.   London, Grandma Press, 1973.

Verse

    Poet's Dozen.   Melbourne, privately printed, 1952.
    The Moods of Love.   Melbourne, Overland, 1957.
    Who Is Wheeling Grandma?   Melbourne, Overland, 1967.

Critical Studies: "Writer and Critic" by John Barnes, in *Westerly 3* (Perth), 1958; *Queensland and Its Writers* by Cecil Hadgraft, Brisbane, University of Queensland Press, 1959; "Place in Australian Plays" by Eunice Hanger, in *Australian Quarterly* (Sydney), June 1962; "The Zelda Trio" by Elizabeth Wolf, in *Overland 22* (Melbourne), 1962; "Australian Drama" by Eunice Hanger, in *The Literature of Australia,* edited by Geoffrey Dutton, Melbourne, Penguin, 1964; "Laurence Collinson: A Poet in Development" by Pauline M. Kirk, in *Overland 49* (Melbourne), 1971.

Laurence Collinson comments:

Primarily, my play-writing is based on subjective experience. Almost every play, in whatever medium, revolves around an incident or incidents from my own life, or contains people I have known, or myself in disguises which are sometimes transparent, sometimes – I trust – opaque. Most usually the plays are derived from a combination of all of these.

There is, in my plays, what some people might consider a contradiction – or a dichotomy, to use a fashionable word; a contradiction that I do not think is apparent to the reader or the audience, and that I personally doubt is a contradiction at all. But I raise this tenuous matter because of an opinion, much touted these days, that proclaims that form and content are indivisible. This I agree with, and cannot see that – provided the playwright knows his or her trade – the situation can be otherwise. Some of those holding this opinion, however, go on to assert that certain plays are "old fashioned" (a derogatory term), while others are "truly contemporary" or "avant-garde" (terms of praise). (A similar "predicament" prevails in the field of modern poetry.)

Since I regard many aspects of our present society as unnecessarily evil – war, poverty, hunger, bad housing, authoritarianism, for example – I believe that a society that permits such unspeakable crimes must be radically changed; and deem myself – in consequence – a radical. Nevertheless, in my writing I make use of all the conventional techniques: scenes, acts, blackouts, slow and fast curtains, business, invention, conflict, climax, characterisation, and so on. I may experiment, as every writer must, of necessity; but never for experiment's own sake. A number of writers today – or so it seems to me – assault their audience with the shape of a play rather than with its substance.

What little I know about the history of the theatre indicates that most surviving playwrights have used the conventions that were within easy reach, conventions that were either handed down to them from the past or were borrowed from other places; such formal mutations (sometimes seen as novelties, innovations, or even revolutionary techniques) as occurred were the result of interaction between, on the one hand, these conventions and, on the other, the forcefulness of the writer's subject-matter expressed through his personal style.

Terms such as "dated," "avant-garde," "old fashioned," "immediate," are instant vocabulary for instant critics, and should be irrelevant to the writer who is serious about his work. I trust I am not too presumptuous in hoping that the "conservatism" of my own plays is modified or transformed by what I have to say and the way I say it.

*   *   *

Laurence Collinson is, perhaps, best known as a poet admired for an ability to invest deeply personal lyrics with an awareness of social concern without objectifying the first or sentimentalizing the other. His output of plays reflects the same urgencies. The inter-personal behaviour of his characters is revealed as the result of certain social and political pressures, pressures more often than not either unthinkingly accepted, or even unrecognized by the characters themselves. Such themes include Zionism oppression within the family structure, the subliminal effect of advertising, homage to social conventions.

It would be correct to call him a political writer; but it would be misleading to suppose that this also implies didacticism or a sluggishness of dramatic charge. His plays are always tightly constructed; often one is ultimately concerned with the narrative point leaving the socio-political content to work its own message unconsciously. There are about a dozen plays (more are currently in progress) which include works for radio, for the stage (one-act and full-length) and for television. There is also a play for children which, like all good fairy-tales, has a back-taste for adults.

Collinson was born in England, but a year later his family moved to Australia where he grew up and was educated at Melbourne University. Many of his plays have, therefore, an authentically Australian accent. The situations are universal (or at least, universal in the Western world) but there is a feel, a smell, a pace which seems characteristically Australian.

This is most evident in *The Slob on Friday*, a sympathetically drawn slice from the life of a big-hearted slut, written for radio (Canadian Broadcasting Corporation, 1969). It is also unmistakable in *Uneasy Paradise* (ABC–TV, 1963) which attempts to understand the motivation of a compulsive gambler. Brenda (the slob) and Neville (the gambler) are different sides of the same coin: innocents in the world, following instinct but working from a position of rather simple-minded trust for society around them.

Opposition to Brenda and Neville comes from two fronts: from those who exploit them in their chosen worlds and from those who represent the uptight standards of conventional behaviour. Thus, Brenda'a generosity is exploited by her weak artist lover and treated with a faintly envious disdain by her typing-pool colleague who is saving (money and herself) for marriage. Neville becomes involved in the fringe world of illegal gambling and has responsibilities to his young wife and baby.

But in each case one's sympathies, a touch irritated now and then maybe, are with the protagonist. Laurence Collinson is arguing for the freedom of the spirit, for the virtues of generosity, intuition, emotion and creativity, and if pursuit of these things means rejection of conventional standards it also means awareness of the dangers of a fantasy world. This is acutely expressed, and perhaps rather too simplistically, in *Number Thirty Approximately* (BBC–2) in which an advertising executive, Clive, is allowed brief love-affairs by his wife. On these occasions he is able to fantasize himself as enjoying the sort of life projected by advertising. But his colour-supplement weekends are controlled by his realistic wife. This short play is distinguished for some sensitive and penetrating dialogue but rather marred by a too neat ending.

This quest for a personal liberation is seen over and over again. It receives its most complex expression in two plays which have a Jewish cultural background. *Friday Night at the Schrammers'* is a one-act stage play and is, therefore, dramatically restricted by the disciplines of its form. It is short, pointed and neat; its tension are quickly resolved but one is aware that the episode will be repeated and that the resolution is only temporary.

Superficially it may be seen as a typical family quarrel between son and daughter and their mother, the younger generation seeking freedom from parental bonds. But by setting it firmly during the Sabbath dinner and having the young people reject the staples of Jewish culture, the play has rather more depth. The children are showing dissatisfaction not just with their present circumstances but with history: "Children, kitchen and church. I wonder if the Jews realize they had one point in common with the Nazis," says the son, Mark, at one point.

Loving Israel is also set during the Friday evening of the Jewish Sabbath. The conflict here is more pointed. Tessa has invited her boyfriend Sam to dinner with her family. Sam is Jewish, but does not conform to the orthodoxy of Tessa's family. Mother and father might be happy to smooth things over, but Tessa's brother Marcus is a dedicated Zionist: "I don't eat with anti-Semites, Jewish or any other kind," he says. Sam's reply: "Because I disapprove of the ideology of Zionism, he thinks that automatically makes me anti-Israel, and thereby anti-Semitic...." Here again we see the forces ranged against expression of personal freedom within a clearly defined context. In form, setting and spring of dialogue, this television play (BBC–2) is probably Laurence Collinson's most accomplished piece.

Dependency and freedom, policital or personal, fight and drive a wedge in the conscience. In *A Slice of Birthday Cake* a mother clings blindly to her growing son failing to see that she could be stifling his development, bitter in her failure to adjust his needs to her own. In this radio play one finds again an awareness of the irritations, and compensating trivia that come from living in a close family environment. As in *Friday Night at the Schrammers'* one may take the boy's flight from mother at face value, or see it as representative of wider issues, a deeper need.

Jamie makes his decision and goes swimming with his friends, leaving his birthday cake untouched. But not all decisions are so intuitively easy to make. Jamie is only 15 and not yet fully aware of emotional blackmail. In *The Girl from Upstairs* (ATV, 1971). a middle-aged schoolmaster has left home and, in his bedsitter, is faced with a lively teenage girl. Their confrontation seems to offer an escape for each of them, he from his self-imposed loneliness, she from her confusing social life with boys of her own age. They come to see such freedom would be illusory, yet their dialogue leads them to another sort of freedom. Again, a neatly constructed, fluently written short play.

It is worth noting in conclusion that, throughout, Laurence Collinson displays remarkable sympathy for his female characters. Though we find, in the body of his plays, familiar figures such as the betrayed wife, the possessive mother, the prim and the puritan, none of these people is in any way a stereotype. In *The Slob on Friday* he introduces Miss Perfy, a brisk middle-aged spinster, a disciplinarian. It would be too easy to leave her at that; but she is given a short soliloquy offering unsights that ameliorate her image. The most ambitious portrait of a woman is in a full-length stage play called *The Zelda Trio* in which the heroine is seen at three ages (17, 27 and 37) at the same time. Technically the play is clearly a challenge for three actresses and the director; textually it demonstrates the inevitability of life; our beginnings do not know our ends and the moments when the bright, optimistic young Zelda fails to communicate with her older self are particularly poignant.

—Roger Baker

CONN, Stewart. British. Born in Glasgow, Scotland, 5 November 1936. Educated at Kilmarnock Academy and Glasgow University. National Service: Royal Air Force. Married Judith Clarke in 1963. Since 1962, Radio Drama Producer, BBC, Glasgow. Literary Adviser, Edinburgh Royal Lyceum Theatre, 1973–75. Recipient: Gregory Poetry Award, 1963; Scottish Arts Council Poetry Prize and Publication Award, 1968. Lives in Glasgow. Agent: Mrs. Nina Froud, Harvey Unna Ltd., 14 Beaumont Mews, Marylebone High Street, London W1N 4HE, England.

PUBLICATIONS

Plays

    Break-Down (produced Glasgow, 1961).
    Birds in a Wilderness (produced Edinburgh, 1964).
    I Didn't Always Live Here (produced Glasgow, 1967).   Included in *The Aquarium, The Man in the Green Muffler, I Didn't Always Live Here*, 1976.
    The King (produced Edinburgh, 1967; London, 1972).   Published in *New English Dramatists 14*, London, Penguin, 1970.
    Broche (produced Exeter, 1968).
    Fancy Seeing You, Then (produced London, 1974).   Published in *Playbill Two*, edited by Alan Durband, London, Hutchinson, 1969.
    Victims (includes *The Sword, In Transit,* and *The Man in the Green Muffler*) (produced Edinburgh, 1970).   *In Transit* published New York, Breakthrough Press, 1972; *The Man in the Green Muffler* included in *The Aquarium, The Man in the Green Muffler, I Didn't Always Live Here*, 1976.
    The Burning (produced Edinburgh, 1971).   London, Calder and Boyars, 1972.

A Slight Touch of the Sun (produced Edinburgh, 1972).
The Aquarium (produced Edinburgh, 1973).   Included in *The Aquarium, The Man in the Green Muffler, I Didn't Always Live Here,* 1976.
Thistlewood (produced Edinburgh, 1975).
Count Your Blessings (produced Pitlochry, Perthshire, 1975).
The Aquarium, The Man in the Green Muffler, I Didn't Always Live Here. London, John Calder, 1976.

Radio Plays: *Any Following Spring,* 1962; *Cadenza for Real,* 1963; *Song of the Clyde,* 1964; *The Canary Cage,* 1967.

Television Play: *Wally Dugs Go in Pairs,* 1973.

Verse

Thunder in the Air: Poems.   Preston, Lancashire, Akros, 1967.
The Chinese Tower.   Edinburgh, Macdonald, 1967.
Stoats in the Sunlight: Poems.   London, Hutchinson, 1968; as *Ambush and Other Poems,* New York, Macmillan, 1970.
Corgi Modern Poets in Focus 3, with others, edited by Dannie Abse.   London, Corgi, 1971.
An Ear to the Ground.   London, Hutchinson, 1972.

Other

Editor, New Poems 1973-74.   London, Hutchinson, 1974.

Manuscript Collection: Scottish National Library, Edinburgh.

Critical Studies: Interviews with James Aitchison in *Scottish Theatre* (Edinburgh), March 1969; with Allen Wright in *The Scotsman* (Edinburgh), 30 October 1971.

Theatrical Activities:

Director: **Radio**—*Armstrong's Last Goodnight* by John Arden, 1964; *The Anatomist* by James Bridie, 1965; *My Friend Mr. Leakey* by J. B. S. Haldane, 1967; *Mr. Gillie* by James Bridie, 1967; *Happy Days Are Here Again* by Cecil P. Taylor, 1967.

Stewart Conn comments:

My plays are about human beings, and about the dilemma of human choice. I interpret this dilemma in moral terms, and visualize the characters in the plays, and their relationships, as revolving around it. As Camus wrote (in *The Plague*), "On this earth there are pestilences and there are victims, and it's up to us, so far as possible, not to join forces with the pestilences." If there is a through line in what I have written so far, it might be a reminder that we do not live our lives in isolation — but that how we behave involves, and may cause hurt to, other people. At the same time the plays are explorations: they pose questions, rather than pretending to provide any easy answers. I do not wish to impose a set of values on an audience; but like to think what I write might induce them to reassess their own. At the same time I am concerned with theatricality and with the use of words in the theatre, as also with the attempt to provide an instructive metaphor for the violence and betrayal, large and small, with which we must come to terms, within ourselves and in our society. Playwrights with whose human statements I find myself in sympathy include Chekhov, Arthur Miller and Edward Bond. There is of course also Beckett!

*   *   *

Stewart Conn is a poet as well as a dramatist, and his best plays, like *The King, The Sword* and *The Burning*, reveal this lyrical side of him. Of his full-length plays *Broche* and *I Didn't Always Live Here* are little more than solid, competent pieces of dramatic craftsmanship; but *The Aquarium* and *The Burning* are both of considerable merit.

The Aquarium is set in a lower middle-class Scottish home and depicts a classical father-son confrontation. The father is imbued with the puritanical work ethic and has clearly defined attitudes and beliefs, based on an old-fashioned morality, that he attempts to impose on his teenage son. The son is restless, unsure of himself and tentative in his approach to life, an attitude which is reflected in his flitting from job to job. Not unnaturally, he resists his father's attempts to make him conform, and they needle and taunt each other, with the mother ineffectually intervening, until matters come to a head when the father attempts to give his son a beating. This action triggers the son into a final breakaway from his family environment. The oppressive family atmosphere is particularly well and truthfully observed in this play, and the characters have a depth and power to them that belies their slightly clichéd conception. Perhaps more than any other play of his, *The Aquarium* reveals the influence of Arthur Miller, a playwright he greatly admires.

The Burning is perhaps his most impressive work to date. It deals with the 16th-century power struggle between James VI of Scotland and his cousin, the Earl of Bothwell, and its theme can be deduced from Bothwell's line to James near the end of the play: "We are the upper and nether millstones, you and I. One way or another, it is those trapt in the middle must pay the price." The play is essentially about the brutality exercised toward those caught in the middle of any struggle for religious or political power, James standing for the divine right of kings, Bothwell for self-expression and individual freedom. But both treat the people under them as expendable and use them as pawns to advance their own positions. A subsidiary theme is that of witchcraft and superstition, but it is firmly placed within the context of the battle between authority and anarchy. The characters are vibrant with life, and reflect the underlying moral and ehtical problems posed by a commitment to one side or the other, in a powerful and an exact way. Another remarkable feature of the play is the hard, sinewy Scottish language, which cleverly contrives to give an impression of late 16th-century speech.

Count Your Blessings revolves around Stanley, a man on the brink of death looking back over his past life and regretting the lost opportunities for fulfilling his potentialities. A particularly powerful scene shows his as a boy berating his school master father for caving in to pressure from his headmaster employer and reneging on his commitment to address a Communist Party rally in the 1930's on the effect of Governmental cuts in education. *Thistlewood* is an impressionistic study of the 1820 Cato Street conspiracy of a group of radicals to assassinate the British Cabinet. The play draws modern parallels in the continuing struggle between conservatism and radicalism in our society.

Of his short plays, *The King* is a beautifully observed picture of two men fighting each other for the same girl, with a seduction scene between Attie and Lena that is replete with an unsentimental lyricism in the language. His trio of short plays, *Victims* (*The Man in the Green Muffler, In Transit,* and *The Sword*), are sharply and concisely drawn pictures of situations whose implications reverberate in the mind. The first play deals with an encounter between two pavement artists, one of whom has replaced someone who has died; the second is a macabre, Pinteresque exercise in violence, between two men and an intruder whom they slowly dominate; and *The Sword,* the best of the three, is a spooky psychological study of a man and a boy, both obsessed, for different reasons, with the idea of military glory. The characterisation in all of the plays is minutely and precisely accurate, qualities reflected in the taut dialogue, with strong undertones of lyricism (particularly in *The Sword*), and the craftsmanlike attention to form.

The metaphorical connotations of Conn's best plays are strengthened by his feeling for dramatic construction, his understanding of individual psychology and his basic interest in violence and its causes, both individual and in society at large. Allied with his quality of lyricism, these give his plays a peculiar power and depth.

—Jonathan Hammond

CONNELLY, Marc(us Cook).   American.   Born in McKeesport, Pennsylvania, 13 December 1890. Educated at Trinity Hall, Washington, Pennsylvania, 1902–07. Married Madeline Hurlock in 1930 (marriage dissolved). Reporter for the Pittsburgh *Press* and *Gazette-Times* and the New York *Morning Telegraph*, 1908–21. Associated with *The New Yorker* in the 1920's. Professor of Playwriting, Yale University Drama School, New Haven, Connecticut, 1947–52. United States Commissioner to UNESCO, 1951; Adviser, Equity Theatre Library, 1960. Recipient: Pulitzer Prize, 1930; O. Henry Award, for short story, 1930. Litt, D.: Bowdoin College, Brunswick, Maine, 1952; Baldwin-Wallace College, Berea, Ohio, 1962. Past President, Authors League of America; President, National Institute of Arts and Letters, 1953–56. Address: 25 Central Park West, New York, New York, U.S.A.

PUBLICATIONS

Plays

$2.50 (produced Pittsburgh, 1913).
The Lady of Luzon (lyrics only; produced Pittsburgh, 1914).
Follow the Girl (lyrics only, uncredited; produced New York, 1915).
The Amber Express, music by Zoel Joseph Parenteau (produced New York, 1916).
Dulcy, with George S. Kaufman (produced Indianapolis and New York, 1921; London, 1923).   New York, Putnam, 1921.
Erminie, revised version of the play by Henry Paulton (produced Boston and New York, 1921).
To the Ladies!, with George S. Kaufman (produced Rochester and New York, 1922; London, 1932).   New York, French, 1923.
Sketches in *No Sirree!* (produced New York, 1922).
Sketches in *The Forty-Niners* (produced New York, 1922).
West of Pittsburgh, with George S. Kaufman (produced New York, 1922; revised version, as *The Deep Tangled Wildwood*, produced New York, 1923).
Merton of the Movies, with George S. Kaufman, adaptation of the story by Harry Leon Wilson (produced New York, 1922; London, 1923).   New York, French, 1925.
A Christmas Carol, with George S. Kaufman, adaptation of the story by Dickens, in *Bookman* (New York), December 1922.
Helen of Troy, N.Y., with George S. Kaufman, music and lyrics by Harry Ruby and Bert Kalmar (produced New York, 1923).
Beggar on Horseback, with George S. Kaufman, music by Deems Taylor, suggested by a play by Paul Apel (produced Wilmington, Delaware, and New York, 1924; London, 1925).   New York, Liveright, 1925.

Be Yourself, with George S. Kaufman (produced New York, 1924).

The Wisdom Tooth: A Fantastic Comedy (produced Atlantic City, New Jersey, 1925, New York, 1926).   New York, French, 1927.

The Wild Man of Borneo, with Herman J. Mankiewicz (also director: produced New York, 1927).

How's the King? (produced New York, 1927).

The Green Pastures: A Fable Suggested by Roark Bradford's Southern Sketches "Ol' Man Adam an' His Chillun" (also director: produced New York, 1930).   New York, Farrar and Rinehart, 1929; London, Gollancz, 1930.

The Survey (skit), in *New Yorker*, 1934.

The Farmer Takes a Wife, with Frank B. Elser, adaptation of the novel *Rome Haul* by Walter Edmonds (also director: produced New York, 1934).   Abridgement published in *Best Plays of 1934–1935*, edited by Burns Mantle, New York, Dodd Mead, 1935.

Little David:...An Unproduced Scene from "The Green Pastures." New York, Dramatists Play Service, 1937; in *The Best One-Act Plays of 1937*, edited by J. W. Marriott, London, Harrap, 1938.

Everywhere I Roam, with Arnold Sundgaard (also director: produced New York, 1938).

The Traveler. New York, Dramatists Play Service, 1939.

The Mole on Lincoln's Cheek (broadcast, 1941).   Published in *The Free Company Presents*, edited by James Boyd, New York, Dodd Mead 1941.

The Flowers of Virtue (also director: produced New York, 1942).

A Story for Strangers (also director: produced New York, 1948).

Hunter's Moon (also director: produced London, 1958).

The Portable Yenberry (also director: produced Lafayette, Indiana, 1962).

Screenplays: *Whispers*, 1920; *The Bridegroom, The Burglar, The Suitor*, and *The Uncle* (film shorts), 1929; *The Unemployed Ghost* (film short), 1931; *The Cradle Song*, 1933; *The Little Duchess* (film short), 1934; *The Green Pastures*, 1936; *The Farmer Takes a Wife*, 1937; *Captains Courageous*, 1937; *I Married a Witch*, 1942; *Reunion* (*Reunion in France*), 1942; *The Imposter* (additional dialogue), 1944; *Fabiola* (English dialogue), 1951, *Crowded Paradise* (additional scenes), 1956.

Radio Play: *The Mole On Lincoln's Cheek*, 1941.

Novel

A Souvenir from Qam.   New York, Holt Rinehart, 1965.

Other

Voices Off-Stage: A Book of Memoirs.   New York, Holt Rinehart, 1968.

Manuscript Collection: University of Wisconsin, Madison,

Theatrical Activities:

Director: **Plays** – *The Wild Man of Borneo*, New York, 1927; *The Green Pastures*, New York, 1930, 1951; *Overture* by William Bolitho, New Haven, Connecticut, 1930; *Berkeley Square* by John L. Balderston, New York, 1930; *Anatol* by Schnitzler (co–director, with Gabriel Beer-Hofmann), New York, 1930; *Acropolis* by Robert

Sherwood, London, 1933; *The Farmer Takes A Wife*, New York, 1934; *Till the Cows Come Home* by Geoffrey Kerr, London, 1936; *Having Wonderful Time* by Arthur Kober, New York, 1937; *Everywhere I Roam*, New York, 1938; *The Two Bouquets* by Herbert Farjeon, New York, 1938; *The Happiest Days* by Charlotte Anderson, New York, 1939; *The Flowers of Virtue*, New York, 1942; *Hope for the Best* by William McCleery (co-director, with Jean Dalrymple), New York, 1945; *A Story for Strangers*, New York, 1948; *Hunter's Moon*, London, 1958; *The Portable Yenberry*, Lafayette, Indiana, 1962. **Film** —*The Green Pastures*, 1936.

Actor: **Plays** — in *No Sirree!*, New York, 1922; Compère in *The Forty-Niners*, New York, 1922; The Stage Manager in *Our Town* by Thornton Wilder, New York, 1944, London, 1946; Charles Osman in *The Tall Story* by Howard Lindsay and Russel Crouse, New York, 1959; Dr. Bingham in *The Portable Yenberry*, Lafayette. Indiana, 1962. **Films** — in *The Bridegroom, The Burglar, The Suitor*, and *The Uncle*, 1929; *The Unemployed Ghost*, 1934; *The Spirit of St. Louis*, 1957; *The Tall Story*. 1959   **Television** —*The Defenders* series, 1963; *The Borgia Stick*, 1967.

*   *   *

In his full-length study of the playwright Marc Connelly, Paul T. Nolan writes: "It is a rare study of American drama between the two world wars that is without some account of Marc Connelly; it is an equally rare study of American drama since 1945 that mentions him." Nolan is right of course. Though any respectable history of the American drama in the twentieth century makes at least a perfunctory bow to the place of *The Green Pastures* in that history, there always seems very little else that is worthy of note about Marc Connelly's career as a successful American playwright. It is possible, of course, that the very commercial success of his own plays, and his joint ventures with the even more successful George S. Kaufman, have caused critics (particularly those of an academic or purely textual persuasion) to dismiss all his work (with the exception of *The Green Pastures)* out of hand as cheeerful commercial fluff. This deprecating view of Connelly's frequently humorous constructs is not, of course, confined to Connelly but can trace its critical ancestry at least back to Aristotle and *The Poetics*. But such academic snobbism (however lofty its classical antecedents) does scant justice not only to Connelly's role in the technical development of the American drama but also to his contribution to the development of the American theatre.

An analysis of Connelly's contribution to the American stage might begin with *Dulcy*. written in conjunction with George S. Kaufman. In his preface to the book version of this commercially successful and richly humorous play about the scatter-brained Dulcy, Booth Tarkington reminds us of Walpole's harsh view of "that silly Dr. Goldsmith" and Walpole's equally harsh view of *She Stoops to Conquer*, a play seen by that less than astute critic as a piece of lightweight commercial trash. The warning is apt. As recent revivals of *Dulcy* have indicated, the play has worn a great deal better than most plays of 1921 (some highly praised by academic critics) and the character of Dulcy may be on her way to becoming a proverbial figure memorable in much the same way as Mrs. Hardcastle in Dr. Goldsmith's play, now granted (at this remove) academic respectability.

Though we may agree with Connelly's own assessment of *To the Ladies!*, written with George S. Kaufman in 1922 as a commercial star vehicle for Helen Hayes, it is less easy to dismiss *Merton of the Movies* written in the same year (again with Kaufman as co-author). The kind of rapid scene shifts required in this play constitute a real technical advance in America in 1922 and are an example of early use in theatre of "cutting" or editing techniques derived from the newly developed medium, the cinema. Equally important to the consolidation of a technical development in the American drama that was begun in 1923 with Elmer Rice's brilliant expressionist play, *The Adding Machine*, is another Connelly-Kaufman collaborative effort, *Beggar on Hourseback*, staged in 1924. Based on Paul Apel's *Hans Sonnenstoessers Hohlenfahrt* then running successfully in Berlin and seen there by

Connelly, *Beggar on Horseback* helped to establish an alternate mode of theatrical expression to that afforded by the devotees of Stanislavskian models of "fourth-wall" realism. Of perhaps equal importance as the innovational stuctural style of *Beggar on Horseback* is the play's carefully modulated commentary on a society dominated by money, bad taste, and mindless mass production. If one can justly argue that the play's conclusion is saccharine one might also remember Shaw's recipe for mixing social satire with a touch of sugar coating to help the audience swallow the bitter pill.

The mixture of subtle social commentary and innovational dramaturgical form that marks the major collaborative efforts of Connelly and Kaufman is nowhere more evident than in Connelly's major solo effort, the play that established his international fame and fortune, *The Green Pastures*. Adapted from Roark Bradford's negro folk version of the Bible, *Ol' Man Adam an' His Chillun*, the play not only was a major commercial success but it was a success despite the fact that it broke with a host of conventions of the standard American commercial theatre. With its large and all black cast it struck the first people who read it as totally lacking in any commercial possibilities. Not only would white people not pay to see an all black production of a play couched in contemporary black idiom, so it was argued, but these same white people would be outraged by the unorthodox theology of a black Jehovah and that Jehovah's intense and personal interest in the problems of impoverished and enslaved black men, women, and children. As though the commericial and theological arguments were not sufficient to damn the play, timorous producers could also point to the loose, episodic structure of the play with its radical shifts from the most holy to the profane and its free and deliberately anachronistic use of space and time. And to a certain extent these strictures were shown to be correct. Though the play was a gigantic success throughout the United States it sufficiently disturbed the Lord Chamberlain in England that it was promptly banned.

Though there is little doubt that Marc Connelly had reached his zenith as a highly influential playwright with the epochal 1930 production of *The Green Pastures*, there are three further contributions that he makes to the history of the American drama that deserve some brief mention here. *The Farmer Takes a Wife*, written in 1934 with Frank B. Elser, is a play well up to the standard of Connelly's earlier collaborative efforts. His radio play *The Mole on Lincoln's Cheek*, broadcast by the Free Company in 1941, is a carefully honed attack on the kind of "Americanism" that would later be practised in America under the patronage of Joseph McCarthy, Richard Nixon, and the House UnAmerican Activities Committee. Finally, it may be helpful for the historian to remember not only that the technical innovations in Connelly's plays helped prepare the way for "open" or "epic" theatre in America, but that Connelly's personal intercession on behalf of Thornton Wilder's *Our Town* helped lift that play from obscurity to the limelight it so richly deserves. In an apt conclusion of a career devoted not to texts *per se* but to dramatic texts in performance, our final view of Marc Connelly perhaps should be Marc Connelly as an actor playing the Stage Manager in the 1944 New York and 1946 London productions of *Our Town*. He remains as a man who has contributed significantly to the theatre of the contemporary world.

—John Fuegi

COOK, Michael.   Canadian.   Born in London, England, 14 February 1933.   Educated at Nottingham University College of Education, 1963–66, T.T.G. (honours) in English 1966. Served as a Staff Sergeant in the Royal Electrical and Mechanical Engineers, and later the Intelligence Corps, 1949–61. Married Muriel Horner in 1951 (marriage dissolved); Janis Jones in 1967 (marriage dissolved); Madonna Decker in 1973; has eleven children. Specialist in Drama, 1967–70, Lecturer, 1970–74, and since 1974, Assistant Professor of English,

Memorial University, St. John's, Newfoundland. Artistic Director, Newfoundland Summer Festival of the Arts, 1970–74; Director, Newfoundland Arts and Culture Centre productions, 1971–74; Host of the weekly television review "Our Man Friday," Canadian Broadcasting Corporation, St. John's, 1973; Governor, Canadian Conference of the Arts, Ottawa, 1975. Currently, Drama Critic, *Evening Telegram*, St. John's. Since 1973. Member of the Editorial Board, *Canadian Theatre Review*, Downsview, Ontario. Recipient: Canada Council Senior Arts grant, 1973. Agent: Renee Paris, 202/1019 East Cordova Street, Vancouver, British Columbia. Address: Box 327, R.R.1, Petley, Random Island, Newfoundland, Canada.

PUBLICATIONS

Plays

> *Colour the Flesh the Colour of Dust* (produced Ottawa, 1972).   Toronto, Simon and Pierre, 1972.
> *Tiln* (broadcast, 1971).   Published in *Encounter: Canadian Drama in Four Media*, edited by Eugene Benson, Toronto, Methuen, 1973.
> *The Head Guts and Soundbone Dance* (produced Montreal, 1974).   St. John's, Newfoundland, Breakwater, 1974.
> *Quiller* (produced Montreal, 1976).   Toronto, Playwrights Co-op, 1975.
> *Jacob's Wake* (produced Lennoxville, Ontario, 1975). Vancouver, Talonbooks, 1976.
> *Terese's Creed* (produced Montreal, 1976).   Toronto, Playwrights Co-op, 1976.
> *Not as a Dream* (produced Halifax, Nova Scotia, 1976).   Toronto, Playwrights Co-op, 1976.

Radio Plays; *He Should Have Been a Pirate*, 1967; *No Man Can Serve Two Masters*, 1967; *Or the Wheel Broken*, 1968; *A Walk in the Rain*, 1968; *The Concubine*, 1969; *A Time for Doors*, 1970; *The Truck*, 1970; *To Inhabit the Earth Is Not Enough*, 1971; *Tiln*, 1971; *Love Is a Walnut*, 1971; *A Walk into the Unknown*, 1972; *The Ballad of Patrick Docker*, 1972; *There's a Seal at the Bottom of the Garden*, 1973; *Apostles for the Burning*, 1974; *Travels with Aunt Jane*, 1974; *On the Rim of the Curve*, 1975; *Knight of Sorrow, Lady of Darkness*, 1975; *Ireland's Eye* (*The Best Seat in the House* series), 1976; *The Producer, The Director*, 1976.

Television Play: *In Search of Confederation*, 1969.

Michael Cook comments:

The basic source of inspiration for my stage plays has been, and I suspect will continue to be, the people and the environment of Newfoundland. The environment is startlingly dramatic; the people the inheritors of moral, social, and economic conflicts that have existed (in many instances, destructively) for three centuries. Specifically, the head-on conflict with technology has, in twenty years of Confederation with Canada, lifted the material prosperity and hopes of the nation but has undermined the fabric of community and social life which made survival possible and gave the island its unique identity. The people, mainly of Irish and West of England origins, maintained for centuries the rich dialects, the fatalistic humour, the careless command of a savage environment that historians might associate with their forebears, the sailors of Nelson's navy, the fodder of Wellington's army. Escaping the brutal caste system of Europe they developed, despite crippling economic circumstances,

175

a heroic individualism. Add to this a language colourful, rich, musical, scatological, varying in accent from Bay to Bay, full of the power of ancient metaphors, and I think it becomes obvious why, at times, I feel like a celebrant at a peculiarly rich, but obviously threatened, ceremony of a way of life in which individuals struggle with the timeless questions of worth and identity against an environment which would kill them if it could.

As in all such environments – the wild Coast of Clare, the weeping Hebrides, the granite coast of Cornwall – there is much in man that responds to the land in all its moods. There are, balancing energy and joy and spoken communion, madness and superstition and violence and repression and anger. There is an overwhelming sense of frustration as bureaucrats and technocrats condone the rape of the oceans.

It seems that what has occurred in Newfoundland has, or will, occur everywhere in North America. It is the continent in microcosm. And yet, because of this vastly reduced scale, it is still possible to conceive and portray men and women in the grip of great forces, changes, emotions that are in direct conflict with everything that they know and understand. There is no diffusion here through the silt of great cities. No. The changes occur where the sea still runs, where the land provides evidence of ancient struggles, and the aged provide eloquent testimony of traditional patterns of survival. I pay attention, therefore, to the realistic, the specific, the concern with the known identity and the agonised recognition of a different kind of survival. I like to think that my work speaks to the condition of all men who have only recently come to realise that somewhere in the transition between rural and industrial man they left behind a portion of their souls.

*   *   *

Michael Cook's plays are passionate, extravagant, intensely linked with his environment. His home is Newfoundland, a province that has always been and will always remain unconquerable. Nothing can stop the winds and tides which wrack its coastlines year in and year out. Its people must forever struggle against its unpredictable climate and unyielding nature. It is this struggle which gives Michael Cook his inspiration; he defines and hones it to a sharp, indelible edge.

Cook's heroes are often brutal, tough men. They would be despicable if the playwright did not delineate for us, in the most human of terms, their plight. They are brutal because the land is brutal, tough because that is the only way they can survive, In poetic terms, with the "million sea birds" screeching overhead, with the wind rising and falling, Michael Cook creates characters of passionate intensity.

In his first stage play, *Colour the Flesh the Colour of Dust*, the author looks to the historical past. Set in St. John's in 1762, it is the story of a garrison long forgotten· by England. The men are bitter and worn-out; the women coarsened by misery and want. The Captain, defeated by "the rock," reveals its power: "I've watched, year after year. People build. Then fire. Or drowning. Or famine. Or disease. Or just – failure of the spirit. Somebody else comes and carts the house away, for timber or firewood. The thin scrub marches across the cleared land. The flake rots into the sea... I have seen places where people once lived, where the land no longer bears the scar. It makes me frightened." The French come and go, the poor get poorer, the rich flourish, heroes die, the women remain to bear a new generation. The story is melodramatically predictable but the script is notable because it shows us, for the first time, both Cook's essential understanding and his sensitive poetic abilities.

In *The Head Guts and Soundbone Dance*, a splitting room, where fish are cut and cleaned, is the setting. Once the lively centre of Newfoundland industry, it has now become a mausoleum for three old die-hards, Skipper Pete, his retarded son Absalom, and his son-in-law John. They live in the past, knowing yet refusing to accept the truth...there are no more fish. The Skipper is intractable to the point of obsessiveness, but, in spite of the power of his refusal to let the past go and face the realities of the future, John has already begun to realize their fate. "Oh yis," he says to the unrelenting Skipper, "We'll go down round to St. John's and there we'll sell our season's catch. Six fish. It's alright to get drunk here because this is us. And I don't mind. But I'm dying, Skipper. And so is ye. And the trouble is the god damn place has died afore us. We can't git that out of our guts, can we?" When a young, bright boy falls off the dock, neither John nor Pete moves to save him, locked as they are in their dreams of the past. It is only the final cruel blow of this death, once comprehended, that compels John to leave. The Skipper refuses to acknowledge his departure; he remains stern and unforgiving, like "the rock."

The Head Guts and Soundbone Dance is not totally believable – once again because of its melodramatic overtones. Nevertheless, it can be played successfully. It moves well, heightened (as is *Colour the Flesh the Colour of Dust*) with song, ribald humour, and cathartic insight. And one can never ignore the language, with its colloquialisms and intimacy.

The past weighs heavily on all of Cook's characters. In both *Quiller* and *Tiln*, a pair of one-acts which follow *The Head Guts and Soundbone Dance*, the protagonists of the same names struggle with a tide of memories. Quiller, his wife and friend dead, lives on alone in his outport house. He rails against his neighbours, lusts comically but pathetically after a young widow, retraces his past, volubly communes with God and chats with his dead wife. Quiller's comprehension is slow in coming, but like John's, inevitable. "It's not the same," says John, and Quiller repeats the motif, "I'm still here. And they is still there, but it ain't the same." His monologue reveals the direction of his life, both to the audience and to himself and he finally comes to a holy realization – man is fire and water, not dust. He gives thanks for this insight which enables him to accept the tragedy of his son's death, "All dese years since Amos died I've been troubled. Didn't make sense ye see... We ain't dust, Lord. That's what it is. I've been foolish... Dat's a powerful piece of knowledge ye give me...."

Tiln also traces a life to a realization about death, but unlike Quiller's Tiln's is full of despair. The difference, perhaps, is that while Quiller talks to God, Tiln thinks he is God. He shouts at the seagulls overhead, "You may shit on my Kingdom, but I am still God. Tiln...God of the wilderness...I am Lord of the Universe still...." Tiln's Universe is the sea which surrounds the lighthouse where he has lived for an apparent eternity. But not completely alone. Ten years before, Fern came, a man half-dead, tossed up by the waves, to share Tiln's existence. Now Fern lies dying, begging Tiln for a few humble prayers from the Book to ease his passing. Tiln acts half-crazed, refusing Fern's request, packing him into a salt barrel to preserve his body before he's even dead, shooting off a rifle by his companion's head. "You were not listening Fern. Pay attention, I warn you." Then comes the shock of death... He roars in pain and cradles Fern's head in his arms, crying out in anguish, "You've cheated me Fern... You've cheated me..." as the lights fade. It is a moment as powerful in its despair as Quiller's was in its joy.

In spite of the dynamic poetry and indelible passions of the one-acts, Michael Cook's full-length play, *Jacob's Wake*, must be considered the tour de force of his work to date. Whereas the one-acts were virtual monologues, *Jacob's Wake* has a cast of seven. The occasion is Easter, and the sons – Brad, a defrocked Minister, Lonz, a local gambler and pimp, and Wayne, a politician whose government falls during the course of the play – join their parents, spinster Aunt, and bed-ridden Grandfather, the Skipper, to pass the holidays. There is nothing holy in this reunion. The Father agonizes over his failure as a son; the Aunt plots to get the Skipper into a mental institution; Lonz forges his Father's name on the interment certificate in return for governmental favours; Brad, crazed by the fact that he once seduced a girl who later killed herself and his baby, runs into a blinding snowstorm, coatless and hatless. The plot is complex and the agonies almost unrelenting but the playwright is in control, and the result is moving, detonating theatre. The home – the ship – is running aground, wracking itself on the ice, sinking with a roar.

What is remarkable about the play, indeed about all Cook's plays, is that the characters display a ribald, often wry humour which constantly challenges the grimness of their lives. This is the Newfoundlander's unfailing antidote to stress. The humour of Cook's plays, biting though it may be, makes the tragedy of his characters accessible. Life is a struggle, but what makes his people "Gods and Heroes" is that they can mock their fate. They are a strong people, caught by a strong yet sensitive writer.

—Connie Brissenden

COWEN, Ron(ald).   American.   Born in Cincinnati, Ohio, 15 September 1944. Educated at the University of California, Los Angeles, B.A. in English 1966; Annenberg School of Communications, University of Pennsylvania, Philadelphia, 1967–68. Taught classes in theatre at New York University, Fall 1969. Associate Trustee, University of Pennsylvania. Recipient: Wesleyan University Fellowship, 1968; Vernon Rice Award, 1968. Agent: Audrey Wood, International Creative Management, 40 West 57th Street, New York, New York 10019, U.S.A.

PUBLICATIONS

Plays

Summertree (produced Waterford, Connecticut, 1967; New York, 1968).   New York, Dramatists Play Service, 1968.
Valentine's Day (produced Waterford, Connecticut, 1968; revised version, music by Saul Naishtat, produced New York, 1975).
Saturday Adoption (televised, 1968).   New York, Dramatists Play Service, 1969.
Porcelain Time (produced Waterbury, Connecticut, 1972).
The Book of Murder (televised, 1974).   New York, Dramatists Play Service, 1974.
Lulu, adaptation of plays by Frank Wedekind (produced New York, 1974; as Inside Lulu, produced New York, 1975).

Television Plays: Saturday Adoption, 1968; The Book of Murder, 1974.

Ron Cowen comments:

In my plays I attempt to explore events associated with the basic social unit, the family, in a personal, stylized realism suitable for the stage, with the intention of creating certain responses in the audience. I also find some personal pleasure in creating an illusion of order for my feelings.

*   *   *

The ethical crisis arising from America's involvement in the Vietnamese war was a major concern for American writers in the 1960's. Summertree, the most successful American play of the decade to deal with this subject, was written by Ron Cowen at the age of twenty. (David Rabe's The Basic Training of Pavlo Hummel and Sticks and Bones may prove to be more significant works, but they appeared in the 1970's, after the initial national tension over the war had peaked.) Summertree, which has been widely produced in the U.S. and England and which has been made into a Hollywood film starring Michael Douglas and Brenda Vaccaro, was perhaps successful more because of its timeliness than its intrinsic worth.

The play is an excessively sentimental telling of an inconsequential young man's death and life in Vietnam. As the protagonist (Young Man) lies fatally wounded under a jungle tree, he hallucinates flashback episodes from his civilian and military experience: sometimes he is twenty, sometimes he is ten. The jungle tree becomes the backyard tree in which he once built a treehouse. His recollections are of his Mother and Father, his Girl and his Buddy (Soldier). These chaacters are drawn by Cowen in broad strokes that critics of the production were prone to see as American archetypes: the essential constellation of personae. A critic of a less emotionally charged era (now: only a few years later) is prone to see them as uninspired caricatures.

The play's most successful attribute is its three-act, cinematic structure which provides a degree of dramatic irony and gives the play substance. Its least successful is its banal dialogue. When the Young Man says to his father, late in the final act, "I want to tell the back yard goodbye," there is a cloying sentimentality which reduces the moment to bathos. Yet for an audience tired of both the brutality of the war and the hysteria of the anti-war protests which shook the land in 1967, the play (and even its dialogue) struck sympathetic chords.

The play is a product of its cultural climate in yet another sense. It was written by Cowen while he was a student at the University of Pennsylvania. When the play was first presented, in the summer of 1967 at the Eugene O'Neill Memorial Theatre Foundation in Waterford, Connecticut, it underwent major re-writings at the request of its director. As it was prepared for New York production by The Repertory Theater of Lincoln Center, additional changes were introduced. The play – far more than the average commercial project – became the reflection of many concerned persons' attitudes towards the war. Small wonder it found a receptive ear and was awarded the Vernon Rice Award for that turbulent year. (When the movie script was being prepared this procedure got out of control. Cowen wrote a first screenplay, Rod McKuen was hired to do a second, and the shooting script was finally the work of Hollywood pros Edward Hume and Stephen Yafa. The filmscript owes shockingly little to Cowen's initial intentions, images or characters.)

Cowen's subsequent career has not been impressive. In 1968 *Saturday Adoption* was telecast on CBS Playhouse and in 1974 ABC aired *The Book of Murder*. Both were critical failures. The first dealt with a socially conscious young man's failures to change the world through his father's money or his pupil's achievements; the second is a coy murder mystery. Cowen's trademarks are easily seen in both: the cinematic structure, the sentimental and nostalgic tone, the domestic circumstance, the conflict over money. His weaknesses are in evidence as well: the badly motivated actions, the clichéd characters, and the clumsy dialogue which the critic for *Variety* called "goody two-shoes language."

Cowen has completed subsequent stage scripts, but none has been given major production. He assisted on the "book" for *Billy* which flopped on Broadway in 1968. His musical *Valentine's Day* was show-cased at the Manhattan Theatre Club in 1975 but reviewed as an "unsatisfying experience." It included the Cowensque line, "I want to tell the apartment goodbye." *Inside Lulu* was a collaborative work of banality, loosely based on the Wedekind plays, and created by Section Ten, the off-off-Broadway improvisational group. Cowen was their literary collaborator.

In retrospect, *Summertree* appears very much to be in the tradition of TV "soap opera" and it is appropriate that Cowen should continue to write for the television medium. As long as his language, characters and situations remain banal, autobiographical, and domestic it is unlikely he will produce a major work. *Summertree* appears to have been less the work of a *wunderkind* than a timely reflection of a culture's anxieties.

—Thomas B. Markus

CREGAN, David (Appleton Quartus).   British.   Born in Buxton, Derbyshire, 30 September 1931. Educated at The Leys School, Cambridge, 1945–50; Clare College, Cambridge, 1952–55, B.A. in English 1955. Served as an Acting Corporal in the Royal Air Force, 1950–52. Married Ailsa Mary Wynne Willson in 1960; has three sons and one daughter. Head of English, Palm Beach Private School, Florida, 1955–57; Assistant English Master, Burnage Boys' Grammar School, Manchester, 1957; Assistant English Master and Head of Drama, 1958–62, and Part-time Drama Teacher, 1962–67, Hatfield School,

Hertfordshire; Salesman, and Clerk at the Automobile Association, 1958. Worked with Cambridge Footlights, 1953, 1954; The Royal Court Theatre Studio, London, 1964, 1968; the Midlands Arts Centre, Birmingham, 1971; conducted three-week studio at the Royal Shakespeare Company Memorial Theatre, Stratford upon Avon, 1971. Member of the Drama Panel, West Midlands Arts Association, 1972. Recipient: Arts Council bursary, 1966, and grant, 1971; Foyle Award, 1966. Agent: Margaret Ramsay Ltd., 14a Goodwin's Court, London WC2N 4LL. Address: 124 Briars Lane, Hatfield, Hertfordshire, England.

PUBLICATIONS

Plays

Miniatures (produced London, 1965).   London, Methuen, 1970.
Transcending, and The Dancers (produced London, 1966).   London, Methuen, 1967.
Three Men for Colverton (produced London, 1966).   London, Methuen, 1967.
The Houses by the Green (produced London, 1968).   London, Methuen, 1969.
A Comedy of the Changing Years (produced London, 1969).
Arthur, in Playbill One, edited by Alan Durband.   London, Hutchinson, 1969.
Tipper (produced Oxford, 1969).
Liebestraum and Other Pieces (produced Birmingham, 1970).   Included in The Land of Palms and Other Plays, 1974.
How We Held the Square: A Play for Children (produced Birmingham, 1971; London, 1974).   London, Eyre Methuen, 1973.
The Land of Palms (produced Dartington, Devon, 1972).   Included in The Land of Palms and Other Plays, 1974.
George Reborn (televised, 1972).   Included in The Land of Palms and Other Plays, 1974.
Cast Off (produced Birmingham, 1973).
Pater Noster, in Mixed Blessings (produced Horsham, Sussex, 1973).
The Land of Palms and Other Plays (includes Liebestraum; George Reborn; The Problem; Jack in the Box; If You Don't Laugh, You Cry).   London, Eyre Methuen, 1974.
The King (produced London, 1974).
Tina (produced London, 1975).
Poor Tom (produced Manchester, 1976).

Radio Play: The Latter Days of Lucy Trenchard, 1974.

Television Plays: That Time of Life, 1972; George Reborn, 1972; An Incident in Yorkshire, 1973; I Want to Marry Your Son, 1973; The Great Mouse Hunt, with Susan Pleat, 1974.

Novel

Ronald Rossiter.   London, Hutchinson, 1959.

Critical Study: The Second Wave by John Russell Taylor, London, Methuen, 1971.

David Cregan comments:

1. I am a socialist because there is no other reasonable thing to be. However, all problems, as well as all interesting thoughts, seem to stem from that one position. How much does the

individual matter and how much the community? Can a contemporary community ever avoid becoming systematized, and anyway how much less traumatic is it living unsystematically than systematically? How simplistic can a government be before it must be opposed totally? If material poverty produces spiritual poverty, which, with special exceptions, it does, can material wealth produce spiritual wealth? How important *is* spiritual wealth, and on what does its value depend? Can the elevation of one working class be justified if it is achieved at the expense of another working class? If freedom is no longer a meaningful conception (and it only achieves any meaning by being opposed to some form of tyranny), which qualified freedom is the most important? Of thought or from hunger? If leaders are bad, are institutions worse? What is the basic nature of man as opposed to the animals, and can it be improved?

I doubt if any of this appears overtly in any of my writing, though the head of steam is always provided by acute anxieties felt on one score or another among these and similar peculiarly twentieth-century questions.

2. Since for me the best plays seem to *be* rather than to be *about*, I personally prefer the episodic forms in which characters may be presented quickly and variously, so that the architecture provides the major insights.

3. Since I have this delight in form, I find no pleasure or virtue in personal rhetoric, self-indulgent self-revelation, or absolute naturalism.

4. Delight in construction also biases me against any form of expressionism or abstract symbolism, and increasingly I use songs, jazz, and a rough poetry spoken to music for various constructional purposes.

5. Since construction of the kind so far indicated is frequently a question of rhythm, there is a "playful" quality about my work. It has a musical quality, each scene sounding forward to another. This means the plays should be acted with a care for their surface, and anyone who acts them for any individual significance, the same shall surely lose it. There are frequently large alterations in emotional stance needed between the giving and receiving of the words, and there is much pleasure in watching this.

6. I have been much influenced by farce, Ibsen, Brecht, Beckett, and the directors I have been associated with at The Royal Court. Also by the intensely magical understanding of comedy shown by Keith Johnstone.

7. I am the fourth and youngest son of an Irish shirt manufacturer. My father fought and was gassed in the First World War, and sought peace and prosperity in a small Derbyshire town, where he pursued a quiet Protestant way of life. My brothers fought, and one died, in the Second World War. I was largely brought up by a young working-class nursemaid.

8. A writer's notes about himself are alas more revealing when they fail to confirm the impression of his work than when they succeed. This happens to more of us than is generally supposed.

*   *   *

David Cregan makes play with ideas, and yet he writes plays which cannot be summed up in a message or explanation. They are toys, in that although they are like life they could not be mistaken for anything outside the theatre; they are small, bright, amusing, and oddly challenging. Action is energetic and surprising. Characters are pampered so that they go quickly to extremes, and yet remain gay and comprehensible. Themes are supplied in plenty – education, money, marriage, religion, superstition, revolution, social change, psychology – but they are more like musical themes than the bases for an argument and demonstration, or the weapons for a fight.

In *The Houses by the Green*, Cregan's debt to classical or Plautine comedy and to *commedia dell'arte* techniques is obvious, and here he is abundantly successful in keeping a cast of four in busy action, with twin characterisations for each actor. The players are invited to elaborate entrances and exits, use two voices in a single scene, move ever more quickly on the single-set stage as they rise, eat, drink, play, argue, sing, act by stealth and by brazen confidence, dress, undress, pursue, retire and go to bed, and so on. Two characters are old (one rich and one poor) and two are young (one male and one female; both poor). As in classical comedy, the action is concerned with possessions (houses and money) and sex and marriage; but each of the two acts has an unclassical climax, the first when the girl raves to be a mother and enjoy multiple childbirths, and the second when after unmasking they all talk of love, and there are a kiss and a song.

The Houses by the Green, like Cregan's other plays, seems designed for a small group of lively actors who enjoy acting together, and for an audience who goes to the theatre for lively entertainment — lively in that this drama reflects life and has a life of its own, an irresistible "go." The reflection of life is that of good caricature, defined by the dialogue. Cregan has a keen ear for ordinary phrases that are revealing and for popular jargon, and he renders them musical by a sense of rhythm, climax and anti-climax.

In *Transcending*, Simon has the glib phrases of a sociology student and the thrust of a young cynical romantic. Father and Mother make a meal of trying to assert authority and romance; Lemester is smooth, adaptable and second-rate; the Girl takes herself seriously, finishing as a Nun singing a revivalist hymn. In simple cries, like "Rape, Rape!" from Mother or "Done it" from Father, and in long, involved and self-concerned attempts at justification, Cregan has given dramatic life to everyday words so that the audience will recognise them with a shock that alerts understanding. In *The King*, Arthur and his court are projected with similar clarity and lightness: the king pursues purity and order, but on his death the round table is replaced by a jolly picnic.

—John Russell Brown

CROSS, (Alan) Beverley.   British.   Born in London, 13 April 1931, son of the theatrical manager George Cross and the actress Eileen Williams. Educated at the Nautical College, Pangbourne, 1944–47; Balliol College, Oxford, 1952–53. Served in the British Army, 1948–50. Married Elizabeth Clunies–Ross in 1955 (marriage dissolved); Gayden Collins, 1965 (marriage dissolved); the actress Maggie Smith, 1974; has five children. Seaman in the Norwegian Merchant Service, 1950–52. Actor with the Royal Shakespeare Company, 1954–56; Production Assistant for Children's Drama, BBC Television, 1956. Since 1975, Drama Consultant to the Stratford Festival Theatre, Ontario. Recipient: Arts Council Award, 1957. Agent: Curtis Brown Ltd., 1 Craven Hill, London W2 3EW, England.

PUBLICATIONS

Plays

    One More River (produced Liverpool, 1958; London, 1959; New York, 1960). London, Hart Davis, 1958.
    The Singing Dolphin, based on an idea by Kitty Black (produced Oxford, 1959; London, 1963).   Included in *The Singing Dolphin and The Three Cavaliers*, 1960.
    Strip the Willow (produced Nottingham and London, 1960).   London, Evans, 1961.
    The Three Cavaliers (produced Birmingham, 1960).   Included in *The Singing Dolphin and The Three Cavaliers*, 1960.
    The Singing Dolphin and The Three Cavaliers: Two Plays for Children.   London, Hart Davis, 1960.

Belle; or, The Ballad of Dr. Crippen, with Wolf Mankowitz, music by Monty Norman (produced London, 1961.

Boeing-Boeing, adaptation of a play by Marc Camoletti (produced Oxford, 1961; London, 1962; New York, 1965).   London, Evans, 1965; New York, French, 1967.

Wanted on Voyage, adaptation of a play by Jacques Deval (produced Canterbury, 1962).

Half a Sixpence, music by David Heneker, adaptation of the novel *Kipps* by H. G. Wells (produced London, 1963; New York, 1965).   London, Chappell, 1963; Chicago, Dramatic Publishing Company, n.d.

The Mines of Sulphur, music by Richard Rodney Bennett (produced London, 1965; New York, 1968).   Published in *Plays of the Year 30*, London, Elek, 1965.

The Pirates and the Inca Gold (produced Sydney, 1966).

Jorrocks, music by David Heneker, adaptation of novels by R. S. Surtees (produced London, 1966).   London, Chappell, 1968.

All the Kings Men, music by Richard Rodney Bennett (produced Coventry and London, 1969).   London, Universal Editions, 1969.

Phil the Fluter, with Donal Giltinan, music and lyrics by David Heneker and Percy French (produced London, 1969).

Victory, music by Richard Rodney Bennett, adaptation of the novel by Joseph Conrad (produced London, 1970).   London, Universal Editions, 1970.

The Rising of the Moon, music by Nicholas Maw (produced Glyndebourne, Sussex, 1970).   London, Boosey and Hawkes, 1971.

Catherine Howard (televised, 1970).   Published in *The Six Wives of Henry VIII*, edited by J. C. Trewin, London, Elek, 1972; revised version (produced York, 1972), London, French, 1973.

The Crickets Sing (produced Devizes, Wiltshire, 1971).   London, Hutchinson, 1970.

The Owl on the Battlements (produced Nottingham, 1971).

Where's Winkle? (produced Liverpool 1972).

The Great Society (produced London, 1974).

Hans Anderson, music by Frank Loesser (produced London, 1974).

The Mask of Orpheus, music by Nicholas Maw.   London, Boosey and Hawkes, 1976.

Screenplays: *Jason and the Argonauts*, 1963; *The Long Ships*, with Berkley Mather 1964; *Genghis Khan*, 1965; *Half a Sixpence*, 1968; *The Donkey Rustlers*, 1969; *Mussolini: The Last Act*, with Carlo Lizzani, 1972; *Sinbad and the Eye of the Tiger*, 1976; *The Myth of Perseus*, 1976.

Television Plays: *The Nightwalkers*, 1960; *The Dark Pits of War*, 1960; *Catherine Howard*, 1970; *March On, Boys*, 1975; *A Bill of Mortality* 1975; *Miss Sugar Plum*, 1976 (Canada); *The World Turned Upside Down*, 1976 (USA); *Troubled Waters*, 1976 (Canada).

Novels

Mars in Capricorn: An Adventure and an Experience.   London, Hart Davis, and Boston, Little Brown, 1955.

The Nightwalkers. London, Hart Davis, and Boston, Little Brown, 1956.

Critical Studies: *Anger and After* by John Russell Taylor, London, Methuen, 1962; Introduction by J. C. Trewin, to *The Mines of Sulphur* in *Plays of the Year 30*, London, Elek, 1965.

Theatrical Activities:

Director: **Plays** – *Boeing-Boeing*, Sydney, 1964; *The Platinum Cat* by Roger Longrigg, London, 1965.

Actor: **Plays** – Agamemnon in *Troilus and Cressida*, Oxford, 1953; Soldier in *Othello*, Stratford upon Avon, 1954; Mr. Fox in *Toad of Toad Hall*, London, 1954; Balthazar in *Much Ado about Nothing*, London, 1955; Herald in *King Lear*, London, 1955.

Beverley Cross comments:

Three main divisions of work: (1) for the Commercial Theatre, viz, books for musicals, Boulevard Comedies (i.e., *Boeing-Boeing, Half a Sixpence*); (2) Libretti for Modern Opera (i.e., *Mines of Sulphur, Rising of the Moon*); (3) Comedies and Libretti for Children (i.e., *Three Cavaliers, All the King's Men, Owl on the Battlements*).

Due to illness – chronic insomnia and high blood-pressure – abandoned (1) in 1969, and has since lived abroad – mostly in Greece and in France – working on (2) and (3).

*   *   *

Beverley Cross has become best known as a writer of books for popular musicals (*Half a Sixpence, Jorrocks*) and of librettos for operas (*Victory, The Rising of the Moon*). He has also translated a highly successful boulevard farce (*Boeing-Boeing*), contributed one of the better episodes to a highly successful television series, *Henry VIII* (*Catherine Howard*), written several lively, if less obviously successful, plays for children, and a small number of commercially unsuccessful plays for adults. What generalisations can be made on the basis of such a spread of work?

First, that at his best he is capable of writing a vigorous, muscular, masculine dialogue which many more pretentious writers might envy. Second, that he is particularly interested in a spirit of adventure that (he feels) no longer exists in the contemporary world, and, consequently, in the character of the adventurer himself. It is significant that many of his works are set in other periods: the light children's play, *The Singing Dolphin*, among pirates in the 18th century, the serious opera, *The Mines of Sulphur*, in a remote country house at about the same time. This latter work, with its forceful language and vivid portrayal of a murderer who traps a troupe of wandering actors and is then trapped by them, shows Cross at his strongest. Another work is set in the future:

> No planes to spoil the view. No trippers to litter the grass. No stinking petrol
> fumes to poison the air. No silly women to bitch away your time with their gossip
> and intrigue Nothing to read, nothing to see. Complete freedom for the first time
> in my life. It's wonderful!

That is spoken by a character in *Strip the Willow*, a rather inconclusive quasi-Shavian comedy of ideas involving a tiny group of survivors of nuclear desolation, deep in the English countryside, living on their wits while the Russians and Americans divide the world between them; but the sentiment could be Cross's own.

He has written only one artistically successful play for adults; and that is his first, *One More River*, which occurs (characteristically) in a ship moored in a backwater on another continent and involves (characteristically) a mutiny. The seamen, among whom egalitarian notions have been circulating, turn on an unpopular officer and hang him, on false suspicion of having caused the death of one of their number. But they haven't the ability to exercise power, and are ignominiously forced to get an apprentice officer to navigate them upriver. The story is excitingly told, and some of the characterisation, notably of a self-satisfied, popularity-seeking bosun, is as good as some of it is melodramatic; but what makes the play interesting is its unfashionable viewpoint. Carefully, logically, it suggests that absolute democracy is mob-rule: some men are superior to others, and the others must submit to their authority . It is, of course, possible to pick holes in the argument as it emerges, for instance by pointing out that Cross does not face the possibility that the seaman's apparent inferiority may be less innate than the result of an unjust environment; but the achievement stands. *One More River* is one of the very few intelligent right-wing plays that the modern theatre has produced.

—Benedict Nightingale

CROWLEY, Mart.   American.   Born in Vicksburg, Mississippi, 21 August 1935. Educated at St. Aloysius High School, Vicksburg; Catholic University, Washington, D.C.; University of California, Los Angles. Secretary to the actress Natalie Wood for two years. Agent: Audrey Wood, International Creative Management, 40 West 57th Street, New York, New York 10019. Address: c/o Farrar Straus & Giroux Inc., 19 Union Square West, New York, New York 10003, U.S.A.

PUBLICATIONS

Plays

The Boys in the Band (produced New York, 1968; London, 1969).   New York, Farrar
     Straus, 1968; London, Secker and Warburg, 1969.
Remote Asylum (produced New York, 1970.)
A Breeze from the Gulf (produced New York, 1973).   New York, Farrar Straus, 1974.

*   *   *

Michael, the host of the homosexual birthday party in Mart Crowley's highly successful *The Boys in the Band*, through whose agency it becomes a shattering summation of all ironic birthdays, is also a character in Crowley's other two plays, *Remote Asylum* and *A Breeze from the Gulf*. In *The Boys in the Band*, in the aftermath of his drunken manipulation and mockery of his friends, Michael's hysterical guilt quiets into the memory of his father dying in his arms with the last words, "I don't understand any of it. I never did." In *Remote Asylum* this scene is re-enacted at an exotic clifftop mansion in Acapulco, where Michael is a guest. The wealthy American owner, Ray, mute from cancer and abjectly mothered by his wife, Irene, with furtive liquor and a shrine to the Madonna his sole remaining prerogatives, expires in Michael's arms as Michael speaks the confession-absolution for him. Finally, in *A Breeze from the Gulf* the original scene is enacted as Michael's father, Teddy, the insecure, conventionally Catholic owner of a pool hall who jocularly took a drink "just to be somebody," dies of alcoholism cradled in his son's arms. Since Michael's father is diminutive whether as "Daddy" or Teddy, his wife Loraine has taken to Demerol and to the protective and flirtatious smothering of her son, expressed in the adolescent Michael's asthma. Though Michael depends on Teddy and Teddy's God to keep his mother well, both let him down. At the climax of the first act, when Teddy threatens to have Loraine committed, Michael cracks a gin bottle over his head and curses God for betraying the bargain in which Michael stopped masturbating for his mother's sake. Thus Crowley's recurring image is of the death or bafflement of the masculine principle, not least in Michael himself.

The Boys in the Band was a sensational success in New York and was soon filmed. Although conventional in form, depending on a naturalistic verve in the styles with which the homosexual subculture disports itself, it marks a breakthrough in dramatizing that milieu from within. Its perspective of the comforting if not always comfortable camaraderie of a "gay" circle allows Crowley to project the internal conflict of the homosexual in the sphere and relationships in which it arises, besides exploiting the native mix of defiant role-playing and wry self-consciousness. Crowley may be said to invert the older pattern in that the outsider in this ensemble play is the one heterosexual character. Historically the importance of the play is that, in the idiom of its characters, it brings out of the "closet" the species of male bitch (in Eric Bentley's word) or that generic ambivalence notoriously felt but dissembled in the plays of Williams and Albee. Significantly these dramatists are integrated into Crowley's dialogue as the upper end of the "camp" culture with which his characters identify.

The homosexuals assembled in a smart New York duplex are demonstrative in several senses, ranging from giddy effeminacy through a pair of more masculine and stable lovers, a black, and a dumb hustler hired for $20 as a birthday present, to the host Michael, preoccupied with his thinning hair and feckless lifestyle, remembering his possessive mother and weak father, and drinking heavily until his self-hatred is turned on the others in the second-act "game." The unexpected presence of Michael's heterosexual college friend Alan focuses the fantasy of the "straight" man who can be had, and he is the intended victim of the game in which Michael compels the others to telephone the one individual they have truly loved. With surprising candor the game is evidence for a view of homosexuality as the dissimulated impulse to emasculate other men. The tables are turned on Michael when Alan calls his wife and when the lovers Hank and Larry repair the breach of jealousy by sentimentally phoning each other, but what lingers from this epiphany of love is the disembodiment of the telephone as an acute symbol of the severance of love and carnal expression which is the homosexual's plight, of the promiscuous Larry no less than the dehumanized hustler, Cowboy. Possibly the limitation of the play is that, beyond the desperate fraternity of the group, it finds no better image of love with which to transcend the self-centeredness and compulsion of sex. Michael says at the end, "You show me a happy homosexual and I'll show you a gay corpse." The dialogue preserves a witty flash and bite and refuses to solemnize the gambits of gay life, except for a persistent referent of self-pity, but intellectually, for all its epigrammatic edge and tartness, the camp ambience is a kind of glamorizing soft-focus suggestive of Hollywood models like Mankiewicz's *All about Eve* (which one of the boys can recite verbatim). In the end the dialogue is all about "Evelyn," the archetypal guilty mother who loved her son for his failures.

In *Remote Asylum* Michael depends on liquor and pills and a familial relationship with the lovers Diana and Tom, whom he accompanies to the Acapulco retreat of the older Americans Irene and Ray. Both Diana and Tom are flying from broken marriages, and the latter, a golden boy of tennis, is nearly as infantile as Michael. But the terrible example of the emasculating Irene, in whose barrenness and barren luxury the maternal haven is exposed for good and all, inspires Tom to a knowledge that responsibility as well as love is necessary for survival. And even Michael, after identifying with the dying Ray both as father and father confessor, flees the mad asylum of Irene. This play recalls Tennessee Williams in its vivid coastal scene and bizarre symbolism – the towers rising above the terrace set, the recurrent cry of a baby for which there appears to be no explanation (though Michael claims to be a ventriloquist), the magnified shadow of a rat, and the grotesquely cackling and jangling homosexual Mexican servants "La Damita" and "El Dorado," who cavort in obscene travesty of the Americans, of sex itself, and savagely beat Michael in the drained swimming pool. The pool, scene also of lovemaking between Diana and Tom in which Irene voyeuristically shares from atop her tower, is the ironic womb of Michael's yearnings. Simultaneously the audience hears Diana climaxing, the sleeping moans of the drunken Ray, and the cry of the baby. Set against masculine debility and the neuter freaks of Irene's household is the primitive virility of the native chauffeur Carlos who, besides befriending the helpless Ray, secretes and protects his peasant girl-wife and baby, and in the end coolly sells his body to Irene, meeting her on equal if ambiguous terms.

A Breeze from the Gulf, a three-character play spanning ten years of family life in a Mississippi town, also recalls Williams in the neurotic, drug-dependent Loraine, particularly in the final scene where she is being readied for the sanitarium and in her last speech about moments of happiness as "a breeze from the gulf." For that matter, in the miasma of alcohol and drugs, comparisons arise with O'Neill. And the familiarity of the basic situation lends itself to Michael's compact summary in the other two plays. The ineffectual Teddy censures his son's spelling and stands by while Loraine bathes, babies, and woos Michael. Loraine's own weakness – social insecurity, hypochondria, and dependence on drugs – becomes the classic feminine mode of domination.

But for all this, and the increasing extremities of conflict, the play has a remarkable integrity of felt experience owing to the naturalness, thrift, and energy of Crowley's dialogue. The first act is a lyric evocation of the family bond regardless of warps, of the intimate rites and instinctive if groping affirmations that, however universal, are *sui generis* in the matrix Michael "remembers." The irony of the second act is that Michael, out of his crucible of dependency and with now the addition of rankling resentments, must return from college to take bitter responsibility for both his parents. In the brutal duel of the final scene he compels Loraine to make her perennial trip to the sanitarium. Sex remains the fatality in Crowley's world, but here it is indivisible from love, and by that token the moral center passes from the self-pity of *The Boys in the Band* to the compassion of which Teddy speaks. This also he does not "understand," but where his last words have been objectified with harrowing and poignant force, it is the authentic form and distillate of Crowley's play.

—David W. Beams

CURNOW, Allen.   New Zealander.   Born in Timaru, 17 June 1911. Educated at Christchurch Boys High School, 1924–28; University of New Zealand, Canterbury, 1929–30, Auckland, 1931–38, B.A. 1938, Litt.D. 1966; St, John's College (Anglican theological), Auckland, 1931–33. Married Elizabeth J. LeCren in 1936; Jenifer Mary Tole, 1965; has three children. Cadet Journalist, *Sun*, Christchurch, 1929–30; Reporter and Sub-Editor, 1935–48, and Drama Critic, 1945–47, *The Press*, Christchurch; Member of the News and Sub-Editorial Staff, *News Chronicle*, London, 1949. Lecturer, 1951–53, Senior Lecturer, 1954–66, and since 1967, Associate Professor of English, University of Auckland. Recipient: New Zealand State Literary Fund travel award, 1949; Carnegie grant, 1950; New Zealand University Research Committee grant, 1957, 1966; Jessie Mackay Memorial Prize, for verse, 1957, 1962; Institute of Contemporary Arts Fellowship, Washington, D.C., 1961; Whittall Fund award, Library of Congress, for verse, 1966; New Zealand Poetry Award, 1975. Litt.D.: University of Canterbury, 1975. Address: 62 Tohunga Crescent, Parnell, Auckland, New Zealand.

PUBLICATIONS

Plays

>   *The Axe: A Verse Tragedy* (produced Christchurch, 1948).   Christchurch, Caxton Press, 1949.
>   *Moon Section* (produced Auckland, 1959).

The Overseas Expert (broadcast, 1961).   Included in *Four Plays,* 1972.
Doctor Pom (produced Auckland, 1964).
The Duke's Miracle (broadcast, 1967).   Included in *Four Plays,* 1972.
Resident of Nowhere (broadcast, 1969).   Included in *Four Plays,* 1972.
Four Plays (includes *The Axe, The Overseas Expert, The Duke's Miracle,* and *Resident of Nowhere*).   Wellington, Reed, 1972.

Radio Plays: *The Overseas Expert,* 1961; *The Duke's Miracle,* 1967; *Resident of Nowhere,* 1969.

Verse

Valley of Decision.   Auckland, University College Press, 1933.
Three Poems.   Christchurch, Caxton Press, 1935.
Enemies: Poems 1934–1936.   Christchurch, Caxton Press, 1937.
Not in Narrow Seas.   Christchurch, Caxton Press, 1939.
Recent Poems, with others.   Christchurch, Caxton Press, 1941.
Island and Time.   Christchurch, Caxton Press, 1941.
Verses, 1941–1942 (as Whim–Wham).   Christchurch, Caxton Press, 1942.
Sailing or Drowning.   Wellington, Progressive Publishing Society, 1943.
Jack Without Magic.   Christchurch, Caxton Press, 1946.
At Dead Low Water, and Sonnets.   Christchurch, Caxton Press, 1949.
Poems 1947–1957.   Wellington, Mermaid Press, 1957.
A Small Room with Large Windows: Selected Poems.   Wellington and London, Oxford University Press, 1962.
Whim Wham Land (as Whim–Wham).   Auckland, Blackwood and Janet Paul, 1967.
Trees, Effigies, Moving Objects: A Sequence of 18 Poems.   Wellington, Catspaw Press, 1972.
An Abominable Temper and Other Poems.   Wellington, Catspaw Press, 1973.
Collected Poems 1933–1973.   Wellington, Reed, 1974.

Other

Editor, *A Book of New Zealand Verse, 1923–1945.*   Christchurch, Caxton Press, 1945; revised edition, 1951.
Editor, *The Penguin Book of New Zealand Verse.*   London, Penguin, 1960.

Critical Study: "Allen Curnow's *The Axe*" by A. Krishna Sarma, in *The Achievement of Christopher Fry and Other Essays,* Visakhapatnam, India, M.S.R. Murty, 1970.

Allen Curnow comments:

If I am to be considered a dramatist, it must be in company with a very small handful of New Zealand writers who have turned to dramatic writing from time to time, though best known for their work in other forms. Among them are the novelist Frank Sargeson and my fellow-poet James K, Baxter. I suppose we have felt, as others have, that plays are a necessary medium for what we have tried to say in other ways; or better, for something we can say in no other way. One may well wonder how plays come to be written and performed at all, in a country almost totally lacking a theatre of its own, or the theatrical tradition which might sustain it. Yet this does happen, somehow; such beginnings are never spectacular. I think we are conscious (I know I am myself) that excellent plays of more than local interest, will hardly be written here unless we can master some part of our New Zealand subject: others will hardly want to know us until we know ourselves a little better – as well, at least, in drama as we have done in fiction or verse. We have yet established no theatre public of the kind that responds as a matter of course to *new* plays, close to their own concerns. I take this to be the mark of true theatre everywhere. I think of how it happened more than half a century ago, in Ireland, say, or the United States; though a New Zealander must scale down his expectations pretty radically if such comparisons are to be at all meaningful.

I began with *The Axe* 25 years ago. The subject could hardly be nearer home: the confrontation of European and Polynesian in this part of the world, early in the 19th century. A Christian missionary brings not peace, but war, to a Pacific island; a steel axe becomes a murder-weapon, the island is no longer "the hub/Of a sufficing... universe," it is cut adrift. In the later comedy *The Overseas Expert* the scene is a modern New Zealand suburb; a local business family are cut down by an English con man. "Always to islanders, danger/Is what comes over the sea," as I put it in a poem about Tasman's voyage to New Zealand in 1642. Navigator, missionary, con man, or British Resident – the last being the subject of *Resident of Nowhere*, about James Busby's years at Waitangi (1833–1840) – are all "overseas experts" in their dramatic roles. Whether they intend good or evil, they precipitate situations which neither they nor their victims really understand; I suppose this is the point of the plays, that (to quote another poem) what happens is "something different, something/Nobody counted on." I like to think something of the same sort goes on in *The Duke's Miracle*, but this is more than I should try to explain here. The 56 lines of Browning's "My Last Duchess" started me; but the play is quite long, and my Duke of Ferrara is hardly (as he develops) a Renaissance portrait in Browning's manner; he does murder his wife, if that is what Browning means to suggest. He certainly shares with my other "experts" the advantages of power and sophisticated intellect, as his doomed duchess has naturalness and naiveté in common with my Polynesians in *The Axe* – up to the point where none of them is as simple as that sounds. Very likely there is some New Zealand eccentricity between the lines of *The Duke's Miracle*; if it was not discerned, as such, by my Czech translators or listeners, I wonder if it was not (in part, however obscurely) a cause of the particular appeal it had for them. (The Czech version, translated by Josef Hirsal, was broadcast in the Czecho-Slovak Radio Festival of Foreign Plays, 1968.)

Only in what one calls weak moments (as Miss Compton-Burnett might remark, it's odd that we blame the moments) have I ever dreamt of writing a play that would hit Broadway or the West End. The best part of the success would be that New Zealand would swallow it whole, and the worst part, that they would do so without tasting it. It is not easy for us to realize how local even the great productive theatre centres are: and that the localness may be of the essence of the productiveness. In a pre-theatrical community like ours, the argument may apply *a fortiori*.

*   *   *

As poet, Allen Curnow has used a sophisticated technique to probe New Zealand attitudes towards the half-grasped national identity of islanders living in the Pacific in a particular place and time. His imagination works historically, and responds to certain moments or situations – discovery, the clash of cultures, "colonial mentality" and the search for independent social-aesthetic values – that inevitably plague the consciousness of many New Zealanders. The stages of his own career – he first studied for the Anglican priesthood, worked for many years on the editorial staff of *The Press*, Christchurch, and finally joined the English department of the University of Auckland – are reflected in his writing, and form a clear pattern in his drama.

An early publication, *Not in Narrow Seas*, is really a tentative poetic scenario for the prolonged exploration of New Zealand schizophrenia that was to follow. While Curnow was working on *The Press*, Ngaio Marsh undertook a remarkably successful series of productions with Canterbury University students in their Little Theatre. For this group

Curnow wrote his first full-scale poetic drama, *The Axe* (produced in Christchurch 1948, revived in Auckland 1953). The subject is the forcible conversion of the island of Mangaia to Christianity in 1824: the missionary agent is a sincere if limited Polynesian convert from Tahiti, but the new gospel is triumphant only by force of arms, and the tragic heroes are rather the old blind pagan chief Tereavi and the thwarted young lovers Hema and Hina, than the converted victorious chief Numangatini who is also killed. In form, *The Axe* is an austere verse drama complete with chorus and pervasive "island" imagery: the big scenes are well conceived for declamation, and the central symbol of the steel foreign weapon is dramatically effective. At its best the poetry is functional, not merely decorative:

> Tormented in the to and fro of tides,
> O inhabitants of the isle, think now:
> The world we know is a swaying disc of ocean
> With a scrap of green ground at the hub, the heart
> Of a sufficing ageless universe:
> But the old centre was shifting, shifting still;
> Sleeping, we fell apart in hostile camps,
> Each dreaming the other's nightmare....

The Axe, a big subject boldly and imaginatively treated, was a strikingly successful dramatic debut, and remains an impressive work in print.

It was not followed up for ten years. Curnow had moved to Auckland when he wrote *Moon Section*, a more complex treatment of New Zealand memory embodied in the consciousness of an eccentric old recluse, Thomas Judd. This play is in some ways Curnow's most original dramatic experiment: it was produced by Ronald Barker for the Community Arts Service Theatre, and for the 1959 Auckland Festival. The verse style is influenced by Christopher Fry, but the technique of self-stripping anticipates Pinter, and the play proved an effective vehicle for a most accomplished leading actor, Peter Varley. The character of Judd was acclaimed by Bruce Mason and a few other perceptive critics, but the poor public response seems to have wounded Curnow, who omits the work from his collected *Four Plays*.

Curnow's next play, *The Overseas Expert*, was "written in anger" as a satirical-comic response to the general incomprehension that had greeted *Moon Section*. Here, in a setting of pretentious suburban affluence, an Auckland family is all too easily and disastrously taken in by an English confidence man, a bogus baronet, who fleeces the father, seduces the daughter, is exposed by the son, but smoothly blackmails his host into keeping silence. This is a ready-made subject for the debunking of secondhand social values – indeed, it is notoriously the play-sterotype any New Zealand dramatist cuts his teeth on. Curnow has tailored his structure neatly enough, but the verse form he persists in is ill-suited to comedy, and the dialogue is often heavy-handed where it should be crisp and lightly ironic.

The Overseas Expert was produced for radio by William Austin in 1961 but never reached the stage. Curnow's two later plays – *The Duke's Miracle* and *Resident of Nowhere* – were commissioned for the NZBC, and first broadcast in 1967 and 1969. Both are accomplished and effective works for the medium; Curnow's mature poetic technique here comes fully into its own. *The Duke's Miracle*, "a play for radio from Browning's 'My Last Duchess,'" is a tour-de-force of scholarly poetic invention: its quality was recognized at least in Czechoslovakia, where it was translated by the poet Josef Hirsal and broadcast in Prague in 1968. *Resident of Nowhere*, a dramatic projection of the last days and obsessive memories of the first British Resident of New Zealand, captures with insight the difficult, ingenuous character of its protagonist, and reviews in tranquillity some of the colonial-missionary themes with which Curnow had begun.

It may well have been the example of T. S. Eliot that first turned Curnow towards poetic drama. His independent achievement in this lonely field, though uneven and in some ways thwarted, is surely of lasting significance, and will be increasingly appreciated by younger writers in his own country, and perhaps even by some "overseas experts."

—James Bertram

CURTIS, Jackie.   American.   Born in Stony Creek, Tennessee, 19 February 1947. Educated at the High School of Art and Design, New York; Hunter College, New York. Married Eric Emerson in 1969. Worked as a typist in New York, 1964; cloak room attendant and elevator operator in Broadway theatres during the runs of *Funny Girl*, *The Amen Corner* and *Foxy*, 1965–65. Recipient: three playwrights hororarium awards, from La Mama and other companies, 1971. Lives in New York. Address: c/o Dennis Spallina, 7606½ Fountain Avenue, West Hollywood, California 90046, U.S.A.

PUBLICATIONS

Plays

> *Glamour, Glory and Gold: The Life and Legend of Nola Noonan, Goddess and Star* (produced New York, 1967).
> *Lucky Wonderful: 13 Musicals about Tommy Manville* (also co–director: produced New York, 1968).
> *Heaven Grand in Amber Orbit* (produced New York, 1969).
> *Femme Fatale: The Three Faces of Gloria* (produced New York, 1970).
> *Vain Victory: The Vicissitudes of the Dammed* (produced New York, 1971).   Published in *The Great American Family*, New York, WNET–TV, 1972.
> *WR – Mysteries of the Organism* (screenplay).   New York, Avon, 1971.
> *Americka Cleopatra* (produced New York, 1972).

> Screenplays: *Flesh*, 1968; *Big Badge: The Brigid Polk Detective Story*, 1970; *Tits*, 1971; *Women in Revolt*, 1971; *WR – Mysteries of the Organism*, 1971.

Bibliography: in *Mug Shots: Who's Who in the New Earth* by Parker Hodges and others, Cleveland, World, 1972.

Manuscript Collection: Lincoln Center Library of the Performing Arts, New York.

Critical Studies: "Not a Boy, Not a Girl, Just Me" by Rosalyn Regelson, in *The New York Times*, 2 November 1969; "Jackie Curtis: The Victory Isn't Vain" by Raymond Macrino, in *The Herald* (New York), 6 June 1971; "Vulgarity Is Victorious" by Emory Lewis, in *The Record* (New York), 3 September 1971.

Theatrical Activities:

> Director: **Plays** – *Lucky Wonderful* (co–director, with Roz Kelly), New York, 1968; *Vain Victory*, New York, 1971.

> Actor: **Plays** – roles in *Scrooge*, based on Dickens's story, New York, 1965; Messenger in *Room Service* by John Murray and Allen Boretz, New York, 1966; Candy Butcher in *This Was Burlesque* by Ann Corio, New York, 1966; Ptolemy II in *Miss Nefertiti Regrets* by Tom Eyen, New York, 1967; Mickey East in *Glamour, Glory and Gold*, New York, 1967; Tommy Manville in *Lucky Wonderful*, New York, 1968; Catherine Kirkwood in *King of Spain* by Robert Wilson/Byrd Hoffman, New York, 1968; St. Frigid, Bijou and Mamona from Pomona in *Turds in Hell* by Charles Ludlam and Bill Vehr, New York, 1968; Nuns' Chourus and Lady Godiva in *The Life of Lady Godiva* by Ronald Tavel, New York and South Bend, Indiana, 1968–69; Usherette, the Angel Before Dawn, and A Screaming Woman in *The Moke Eater* by Kenneth Bernard, New York, 1969; "W" and the

Glamorous Medicine Woman in *Cock Strong* by Tom Murrin, New York, 1969; Irish Fairchild in *Femme Fatale,* New York, 1970; Warner Color, Blue Denim, Cal Task, and Pan and Donna Bella Beads in various versions of *Vain Victory,* New York, 1971; Court Musician in *Les Précieuses Ridicules* by Molière, New York, 1972; Ophelia in *A Modern Hamlet* by John Guenther, New York, 1972; Hera in *The Trojan Women* by Euripides, New York, 1972; Cleopatra in *Americka Cleopatra,* New York, 1972; Nola Noonan in *Glamour, Glory and Gold,* New York, 1974.   **Films** – *Flesh,* 1969; *Big Badge,* 1970; *Tits,* 1971; *Women in Revolt,* 1971; *WR – Mysteries of the Organism,* 1971.

Jackie Curtis comments:

I was a young Gary Cooper. I began writing plays out of desperation. I was being consumed by body worship. But no one would put me in a play. The energy being directed to me had to be re-directed so I could use it safely and survive. I created my own vehicles and found protection in a theatrical identity. The young Gary Cooper looked in the mirror and saw Greta Garbo. I first realized the strength within myself when I saw that whatever I chose to do soon became the thing that many chose to emulate. But being a trend-setter consumes even more of one than does mere body worship. People think they can become you by duplicating your image. Expending little creative energy, the duplicators were making all the money, but I retained my soul intact. Greta Garbo looked into the mirror and saw James Dean. The experimental theatre scene had brought me to my knees. I've paid my dues there and done my bit for Thespis. Now the world can be moved to its knees, moved to provide material rewards to an original, so I can survive and change and grow. I have this thing about being where the audience is, and I will not insult that audience with repetitions of my message when others have already heard it and are there saying it for me. I will follow the eternal will that governs my destiny and have found the strength to reveal much more of myself than I have ever before dared to. I look in the mirror and see Jackie Curtis. It is not comfortable to be constantly changing and searching. My work helps me to find the answers to my own questions, and I hope that through my work I can help others to look ahead and find comfort in the future that we create together.

*   *   *

Jackie Curtis for several years dressed as a woman, off and often on the stage. He has succeeded in making a public spectacle of himself, achieving some fame and notoriety in appearances in movies, on television, and in his own plays. His fantasy of himself seems to derive from the Hollywood of the 1940's, and his plays like his life have been an ironic mythologizing of what was a deliberately contrived myth to begin with.

Glamour, Glory and Gold: The Life and Legend of Nola Noonan, Goddess and Star is a direct presentation of the period image: conventional bathetic backstage melodrama about a chorine's rise through the usual tribulations and fall to the usual degradations. Curtis's basic thehnique is pastiche: the plays consist almost entirely of lines of dialogue lifted from movies shown on television. What redeems them is their outrageousness: Curtis recognizes no strictures to taste or logic, and though the work is often trashy and incoherent, it also has an authentic passion, a defiant commitment to its own idiosyncrasy. A talented and eccentric performer with a unique, compelling presence, he has brought to the stage an expressive vision and set of decadent values in which he is not alone. The decorative perversity, sexual mockery, and hysterical irreverence combine with tattered dreams into a touching image of innocence broken.

In his most striking play, *Heaven Grand in Amber Orbit,* the particular method creates a kaleidoscopic whirl of images around the central figure, a cinema star at the moment of her death. Deprived of their ordinary context, the clichés pay off afresh. In *Vain Victory,* an evocation of high school life in the 1950's, the technique seemed to reach nearly total incoherence, and the result was all but abstract, often wildly comical group scenes interspersed with solo turns and songs by the freaked-out, original performers.

—Michael Smith

DAVIES, Robertson. Canadian. Born in Thamesville, Ontario, 28 August 1913. Educated at Upper Canada College; Queen's University, Kingston, Ontario; Balliol College, Oxford, 1936–38, B.Litt. 1938. Married Brenda Mathews in 1940; has three children. Teacher and Actor, Old Vic Theatre School and Repertory Company, London, 1938–40; Literary Editor, *Saturday Night*, Toronto, 1940–42; Editor and Publisher, *Examiner*, Peterborough, Ontario, 1942–63. Since 1960, Professor of English, and since 1962, Master of Massey College, University of Toronto. Formerly, Governor, Stratford Shakespeare Festival, Ontario; Member, Board of Trustees, National Arts Centre. Recipient: Louis Jouvet Prize, Dominion Drama Festival, for directing, 1949; Leacock Medal, 1955; Lorne Pierce Medal, 1961; Governor-General's Award, for fiction, 1973. LL.D.: University of Alberta, Edmonton, 1957; Queen's University, 1962; University of Manitoba, Winnipeg, 1972; D.Litt.: McMaster University, Hamilton, Ontario, 1959, University of Windsor, Ontario, 1971; York University, Toronto, 1973; Mount Allison University, Sackville, New Brunswick, 1973; Memorial University of Newfoundland, St. John's, 1974; University of Western Ontario, London,1974; McGill University, Montreal, 1974; Trent University, Peterborough, Ontario, 1974; D.C.L.: Bishop's University, Lennoxville, Quebec, 1967; D.Univ.: University of Calgary, Alberta, 1975. Fellow, Royal Society of Canada, 1967. Companion of the Order of Canada, 1972. Address: Massey College, 4 Devonshire Place, Toronto, Ontario M5S 2E1, Canada.

PUBLICATIONS

Plays

> *Overlaid* (produced Peterborough, Ontario, 1947). Included in *Eros at Breakfast and Other Plays*, 1949.
> *Voice of the People* (produced Montreal, 1948). Included in *Eros at Breakfast and Other Plays*, 1949.
> *At the Gates of the Righteous* (produced Peterborough, Ontario, 1948). Included in *Eros at Breakfast and Other Plays*, 1949.
> *Hope Deferred* (produced Montreal, 1948). Included in *Eros at Breakfast and Other Plays*, 1949.
> *Fortune My Foe* (televised; produced Ottawa, 1948). Toronto, Clarke Irwin, 1949.
> *Eros at Breakfast* (produced Ottawa, 1948). Included in *Eros at Breakfast and Other Plays*, 1949.
> *Eros at Breakfast and Other Plays* (includes *Hope Deferred, Overlaid, At the Gates of the Righteous, Voice of the People*). Toronto, Clarke Irwin, 1949.
> *At My Heart's Core* (produced Peterborough, Ontario, 1950). Toronto, Clarke Irwin, 1950.
> *King Phoenix* (produced Peterborough, Ontario, 1950). Included in *Hunting Stuart and Other Plays*, 1972.
> *A Masque of Aesop* (produced Toronto, 1952). Toronto, Clarke Irwin, 1952.

A Jig for the Gypsy (broadcast; produced Toronto and London, 1954). Toronto, Clarke Irwin, 1954.

Hunting Stuart (produced Toronto, 1955). Included in *Hunting Stuart and Other Plays*, 1972.

Love and Libel; or, The Ogre of the Provincial World, adaptation of his own novel *Leaven of Malice* (produced Toronto and New York, 1960).

A Masque of Mr. Punch (produced Toronto, 1962). Toronto, Oxford University Press, 1963.

Four Favourite Plays (includes *Voice of the People, At the Gates of the Righteous, Fortune My Foe, Eros at Breakfast*). Toronto, Clarke Irwin, 1968.

Hunting Stuart and Other Plays (includes *King Phoenix* and *General Confession*). Toronto, New Press, 1972.

Question Time (produced Toronto, 1975). Toronto, Macmillan, 1975.

Radio Plays: *A Jig for the Gypsy*, and others.

Television Plays: *Fortune My Foe, Brothers in the Black Art*, and others.

Novels

Tempest Tost. Toronto, Clarke Irwin, 1951; London, Chatto and Windus, and New York, Rinehart, 1952.

Leaven of Malice. Toronto, Clarke Irwin, 1954; London, Chatto and Windus, and New York, Scribner, 1955.

A Mixture of Frailties. Toronto, Macmillan, London, Weidenfeld and Nicolson, and New York, Scribner, 1958.

Fifth Business. Toronto, Macmillan, and New York, Viking Press, 1970; London, Macmillan, 1971.

The Manticore. Toronto, Macmillan, and New York, Viking Press, 1972; London, Macmillan, 1973.

World of Wonders. Toronto, Macmillan, 1975; New York, Viking Press, 1976.

Other

Shakespeare's Boy Actors. London, Dent, 1939; New York, Russell, 1964.

Shakespeare for Young Players: A Junior Course. Toronto, Clarke Irwin, 1942.

The Diary of Samuel Marchbanks (essays). Toronto, Clarke Irwin, 1947.

The Table Talk of Samuel Marchbanks (essays). Toronto, Clarke Irwin, 1949.

Renown at Stratford: A Record of the Shakespeare Festival in Canada, 1953, with Tyrone Guthrie. Toronto, Clarke Irwin, 1953.

Twice Have the Trumpets Sounded: A Record of the Stratford Shakespearean Festival in Canada, 1954, with Tyrone Guthrie. Toronto, Clarke Irwin, 1954; London, Blackie, 1955.

Thrice the Brinded Cat Hath Mew'd: A Record of the Stratford Shakespearean Festival in Canada, 1955, with Tyrone Guthrie. Toronto, Clarke Irwin, 1955.

A Voice from the Attic. New York, Knopf, and Toronto, McClelland and Stewart, 1960.

The Personal Art: Reading to Good Purpose. London, Secker and Warburg, 1961.

Samuel Marchbanks' Almanack. Toronto, McClelland and Stewart, 1967.

Stephen Leacock: Feast of Stephen. Toronto, McClelland and Stewart, 1970.

The Revels History of Drama in English, vol. 7, with others. London, Methuen, 1975.

Manuscript Collection: Massey College, University of Toronto.

* * *

At the theatre, seated comfortably on the aisle, Robertson Davies is the kind of person one notices. Burly, broad of brow, neatly bearded, he is easily typed as the very model of a modern literary man. What other appellation can one give to a writer who is not only a playwright but also author, professor, editor and critic? Literature, in many of its aspects, is Mr. Davies' business *and* way of life. As playwright and critic he skates nimbly on both sides of the fence, writing amusingly and well on productions at Canada's Stratford, for example, often for his paper the Peterborough *Examiner*, while behind him is a body of work for the theatre that is considerable.

A Canadian bred, Mr. Davies bettered his education in Ontario and at Oxford University, later appearing at the Old Vic as an actor and as a writer. This early practical training shows up in much of his work – his theatre pieces are securely based on strong technical awareness of what makes a play work.

From early flirtations with TV and radio dramas on the Canadian Broadcasting Corporation network (once such a prodigious producer of original Canadian works as well as masterly productions of the classics) in plays such as *Fortune My Foe*, he went on to concentrate for a time on the difficult one-act form, publishing *Eros at Breakfast and Other Plays*. Early in the fifties an original radio play, *A Jig for the Gypsy*, was adapted for presentation at Toronto's Crest Theatre and later went to London to be presented by The Questors. Assured of a continued interest in his plays from a growing audience, and with the respectful attention of the critics, Mr. Davies presented several new titles at this time, including *At My Heart's Core* and *King Phoenix*, a rather heavy fantasy about Old King Cole, but during the early sixties seemed to veer away from the stage in favour of the novel. None of the plays of this period seems to have hit a major mark, and while on paper they seem well-written, somehow the effect onstage is often bloodless and life-lacking, the characters perhaps too much the creation of a fine intellectual mind rather than real and roundly fleshed.

In his latest plays, as in his novels, he has become increasingly involved with the workings of the psychoanalysts, most notably the one he dubs "that old fantastical duke of dark corners, C.G. Jung" and his obviously intriguing hypothesis of opposites, particularly the conscious and its opposing personal unconscious, or "the shadow" as Jung describes it. His recent novel, *Fifth Business*, is, in the words of the critic Gordon Roper, "a book whose form and substance is overwhelmingly Jungian." Mr. Davies himself applauds this writer's viewpoint, stating that all his plays have the same background of (Jungian) thought "and the one which is most recent, and puts forward this attitude of mind most strongly, is called *General Confession*." The impression that Jung, his own Wise Old Man, had on him by the sixties is indicated by this statement to students in 1968, entitled "The Conscience of the Writer":

> Freud...dealt more strikingly with problems of neuroses rather than with matters
> of aesthetics, and his cast of mind was powerfully reductive. After the Freudian
> treatment, most things look a little shabby – needlessly so. Jung's depth
> psychology, on the other hand, is much more aesthetic and humanistic in its
> effects on artistic experience. The light it throws on matters of literature and on
> the temperament of the writer is extremely useful and revealing.

And to take a second quote from the same talk which throws light on to Mr. Davies' work in his present middle-years as he increasingly ventures into spiritual realms:

> As Jung explains it, in the early part of life – roughly the first half of it – man's
> chief aims are personal and social. He must grow up, he must find his work, he
> must find out what kind of sexual life he is going to lead, he must achieve some
> place in the world and attempt to get security within it, or else decide that security
> is not important to him. But when he has achieved these ends, or come to some
> sort of understanding with this part of existence, his attention is turned to matters
> that are broader in scope, and sometimes disturbing to contemplate.... He finds

that, in Jung's phrase, he is not the master of his fate and that he is in fact the object of a supraordinate object. And he seeks wisdom rather than power – though the circumstances of his early life may continue to thrust power into his hands.... The values that are proper and all-absorbing during the first half of life will not sustain a man during the second half. If he has the courage and wisdom to advance courageously into the new realm of values and emotions he will age physically, of course, but his intellect and spiritual growth will continue, and will give satisfaction to himself and to all those associated with him.

Although he is far from giving up writing for the theatre, these roads are obviously taking him away from the theatre of the market-place to the kind of plays that, like those of Eliot, are better read than acted. Perhaps Mr. Davies has never wanted the common touch; perhaps the novel and his teaching at the University of Toronto are taking precedence. If so it is a pity. For with his driving interest in human personality, plus his many very real intellectual abilities, Robertson Davies could be a strong "shadow opposite" of so many pseudo-intellectual writers for the modern stage.

—Michael T. Leech

DAVIS, Ossie.   American.   Born in Cogdell, Georgia, 18 December 1917. Educated at Waycross High School, Georgia; Howard University, Washington, D.C., 1935–39. Married the actress Ruby Dee in 1948; has three children. Served in the United States Army as a Surgical Technician, 1942–45. Recipient: Frederick Douglass Award; Emmy Award, for acting, 1970. Address: 44 New Cortland Avenue, New Rochelle, New York 10801, U.S.A.

PUBLICATIONS

Plays

Goldbrickers of 1944 (produced in Liberia, 1944).
Alice in Wonder (produced New York, 1952; revised version, as The Big Deal, produced New York, 1953).
Purlie Victorious (produced New York, 1961).   New York, French, 1961; revised version, with Philip Rose and Peter Udell, music by Gary Geld, as Purlie (produced New York, 1970), New York, French, 1970.
Curtain Call, Mr. Aldridge, Sir (produced New York, 1963).   Published in The Black Teacher and the Dramatic Arts, edited by William R. Reardon and Thomas D. Pawley, Westport, Connecticut, Negro Universities Press, 1970.

Screenplays: Gone Are the Days!, 1963; Cotton Comes to Harlem, with others, 1970; Countdown at Kusini, with others, 1976.

Television Writing: Schoolteacher, 1963.

196

Theatrical Activities:

Director: **Films** – *Cotton Comes to Harlem*, 1970; *Kongi's Harvest*, 1970; *Black Girl*, 1972; *Gordon's War*, 1973; *Countdown at Kusini*, 1976.

Actor: **Plays** – in *Joy Exceeding Glory*, New York, 1941; title role in *Jeb* by Robert Ardrey, New York, 1946; Rudolf in *Anna Lucasta* by Philip Yordan, toured, 1947; Trem in *The Leading Lady* by Ruth Gordon, New York 1948; Lonnie Thompson in *Stevedore* by George Sklar and Paul Peters, New York, 1948; Stewart in *The Smile of the World* by Garson Kanin, New York, 1949; Jacques in *The Wisteria Trees* by Joshua Logan, New York, 1950, 1955; Jo in *The Royal Family* by George S. Kaufman and Edna Ferber, New York, 1951; Gabriel in *The Green Pastures* by Marc Connelly, New York, 1951; Al in *Remains to Be Seen* by Howard Lindsay and Russel Crouse, New York, 1951; Dr. Joseph Clay in *Touchstone* by William Stucky, New York, 1953; The Lieutenant in *No Time for Sergeants* by Ira Levin, New York, 1955; Cicero in *Jamaica* by E. Y. Harburg and Fred Saidy, New York, 1957; Walter Lee Younger in *A Raisin in the Sun* by Lorraine Hansberry, New York, 1959; Purlie in *Purlie Victorious*, New York, 1961; Sir Radio in *A Ballad for Bimshire* by Loften Mitchell, New York, 1963; in *A Treasury of Negro World Literature*, toured, 1964; Johannes in *The Zulu and the Zayda* by Howard DaSilva and Felix Leon, New York, 1965. **Films** – *No Way Out*, 1950; *Fourteen Hours*, 1951; *The Joe Louis Story*, 1953; *The Cardinal*, 1963; *Gone Are the Days!*, 1963; *Shock Treatment*, 1964; *The Hill*, 1965; *A Man Called Adam*, 1966; *The Scalphunters*, 1968; *The Slaves*, 1969; *Sam Whiskey*, 1969; *Countdown at Kusini*, 1976. **Television** – *The Emperor Jones*; *Seven Times Monday*; *The Defenders*, *The Doctors*, *The Nurses*, *The Fugitive*, and *Twelve O'Clock High* series; *Teacher*, 1969.

*   *   *

Ossie Davis is extraordinary on two accounts. Loften Mitchell says, in *Black Drama*, "For this tall, intelligent, graying, proud man came into the theater, interested in writing. Fortunately and unfortunately, it was learned that he is a good actor – a phenomenon rare for a writer, and detrimental as well. Mr. Davis went on to job after job working regularly as a Negro actor, never quite getting as much writing done as he wanted to do." However, although what he has lent to the performing arts as director and actor is widely acclaimed by both critic and playgoer, two of his plays are lasting contributions to dramatic literature.

The early 1950's were difficult years for black playwrights to have their works produced. One of the plays that happened to make the boards – directed and produced in September, 1952, in Harlem by the playwright and his friends, Maxwell Glanville, Julian Mayfield, and Loften Mitchell among others – was Ossie Davis's *Alice in Wonder*. The production, impoverished as it was, also included two of Mr. Mayfield's one-actors, *A World Full of Men* and *The Other Foot*. At the Elks Community Theater the talented group of spirited black artists "ushered in a hit show with few people in the audience" (Loften Mitchell in *The Crisis*, March 1972). Eventually Davis's charming play was optioned off to Stanley Greene and was produced successfully in downtown New York. Davis later expanded it into a full piece, *The Big Deal*.

Alice in Wonder – a reputable beginning of one of the most gifted men in the modern American Theatre – is a delightful piece. It is set in upper Harlem ("cadillac country," as Davis calls it). Alice (Ruby Dee in the original production) sees her husband Jay (Maxwell Glanville) given a sizeable contract by one of the leading television networks. In the meantime, Alice's brother (Ed Cambridge) has involved himself in a number of political affairs – one of which is to restore a passport to a militant Negro singer. The network director asks Jay to go to Washington to testify before a government committee and to denounce the singer. Complications arise and Alice – who refuses to compromise her principles – sees that Jay is about to "sell out." She packs up and leaves. The ethos of this play is racial tension and all that it means, providing the audience with a taste of what is to come from the talented playwright's pen.

Purlie Victorious – warmly received by the alert New York critics at the Cort Theater, 29 September 1961 – moved beyond an embryonic idea of a laugh to cure racial bigotry, a dramatic experiment, and artistic dream. At the very moment of its production, something grand happened, for *Purlie Victorious*, a comedy of manners (with author playing the title role, his talented wife, Ruby Dee, as Lutiebelle Gussiemae Jenkins, and Godfrey Cambridge as Gitlow Judson), not only reached a fine level of art but lifted its writer into the realm of playwrights where Plautus, Ben Jonson, Molière, and Sheridan can be found.

The play is farcical, mocking, sparkling, resounding in ethnic wit, rapid, and unyielding as satire. Purlie Judson, a man of impatience, with a flowery evangelical style, moved by messianic mission for his race ("Who else is they got?") goes South bent on returning Big Bethel (an old barn) back into a church as an integrated symbol of freedom. Every racial cliché of Southern life – and Northern life for that matter – is held up for Juvenalian attacks and rendered meaningless forever after. The white pro-Confederate Colonel, the Jim Crow System, the "colored" mammy and all that that image brings to mind, the Uncle Tom figures, the plantation store, the parochial cops, the stalking country sheriff, the NAACP, The Supreme Court, the church – and all that it symbolizes in both the white man's and the black man's psychology – integration, and constitutional rights are given a Swiftian examination.

Purlie Victorious is a series of irresistible mirrors in which men are forced to see the folly of hatred, the insanity of bigotry, and the fruitlessness of racial-supremacy theories. As Davis himself says (in *Contemporary Drama*, edited by Clinton T. Oliver and Stephanie Sills, 1971), "What else can I do but laugh?... The play is an attempt, a final attempt to hold that which is ridiculous up to ridicule – to round up all the indignities I have experienced in my own country and to laugh them out of existence."

The dialogue is scintillating, poetic, and realistic. There are many puns, ironic uses of idiomatic expressions, and an acute awareness of the American Negro's sense of melody and rhythm. The satire is sharply focused with the clever use of malapropisms and misnomers.

> Purlie –   This is outrageous – This is a catastrophe! You're a disgrace to the Negro profession!
>
> Lutiebelle – That's just what she said all right – her exactly words. (I,1)
>
> Ol' Cap'n – When I think of his grandpaw, God rest his Confederate soul, hero of the Battle of Chickamauga – ...(I,2) My ol' Confederate father told me on his deathbed: Feed the Negroes first – after the horses and cattle – and I've done it evah time! (I,2) You know something, I've been after these Negroes down here for years: Go to school, I'd say, first chance you get – take a coupla courses in advanced cotton picking. But you'd think they'd listen to me: No sireebob. By swickery! (II,1)

Like many other comic works – Molière's *Tartuffe*, Ben Jonson's *Volpone*, or Congreve's *Way of the World* – *Purlie Victorious* is an angry play. Like Dryden, Pope, or Lewis Carroll, Davis allows his anger to smolder through a gem-lit comedy, and, like Horace and Juvenal transported to America, he permits his work to romp and bound through Southern settings and bromidic racial situations of the most impoverished and demeaning variety. But Davis is ever in control. Like Molière he knows that people laugh at beatings, mistaken identities, disguises, clever repartee, buffoonery, indecency, and themselves when taken off guard. "There are many laughters," says J. C. Gregory, in *The Nature of Laughter* (1924) – and he cites both Hobbes and Fuller as finding great mirth in the fact of physical infirmity. "When the Philistine lords made sport of blind Samson, they were mocking an enemy. When the cynical bystanders challenged Christ to come down off the cross if He was divine, they were laughing at an apparent incongruity." Thus the satire – ever corrective in the hands of an artist (Davis is just that) – is both crude and polished in aiming its fire at both personal and general prejudices.

The struggle to keep the mask in place in comedy becomes a conflict between intelligence and character, craft and habit, art and nature. In Ossie Davis's principles of writing and performing there is a beautiful balance between poetry and realism.

—Louis D. Mitchell

DeGRAFT, Joe (Joseph Coleman DeGraft).   Ghanaian.   Director, Ghana Drama Studio. Address: c/o Oxford University Press, 37 Dover Street, London W1X 4AH, England.

PUBLICATIONS

Plays

Through a Film Darkly (as *Visitor from the Past*, produced Accra, 1962; as *Through a Film Darkly*, produced Accra, 1966).   Accra and London, Oxford University Press, 1970.
Sons and Daughters.   Accra and London, Oxford University Press, 1964.

Other Plays: *Ananse and the Glue Man*, 1961; *Old Kweku*, 1965.

Verse

Beneath Jazz and Brass.   London, Heinemann, 1975.

*   *   *

The first publication of Joe DeGraft's play *Sons and Daughters* and the mixed reception it received exemplify some of the problems involved in being an African writer. Eagerly snapped up by publishers, then run through the mill by critics, it is no wonder that some writers, such as DeGraft, have been slow about publishing second works.

Sons and Daughters has been described as a "model play." It presents us with the highly topical picture of generations in conflict: youth and a devotion to the arts versus age and a desire for money and position. This theme has been worked over many times in recent years, but in a West African context it takes on new freshness. So much emphasis has been placed on the idea of education being directly equal to affluence and a rise in social status that it must have been refreshing for West African producers and public alike to find a play of the nature of *Sons and Daughters* before them.

It seems, however, that *Sons and Daughters* may have been brought into print before the playwright had thought enough about it or done the kind of polishing and revision that would have made it more than just a good play. DeGraft is one of Ghana's finest poets, yet there is little "poetry" in the dialogue. Every writer does not have to be a Lorca or a Soyinka, but some of the speeches in *Sons and Daughters* are wooden and unwieldy. For instance, Aaron, the son who wishes to be a painter, says, "I'm fed up – fed up fit to burst! Why can't a chap do what he wants to do because he simply loves doing it? Why?" We may feel that his words are not that bad, but that they are somehow unsatisfying. The

199

language is too predictable, and both Aaron and his sister Manaan, the two rebels who chose art over wealth, seem to have too little of that art in their speech to express themselves in anything other than clichés. Ironically, it is their philistine father who comes up with some of the best lines in the play. The brief initial speech he makes while pouring libation offers us a real glimpse into the complexities of his nature. DeGraft allows us to see him not just as a villain, but as a representative of a generation which has seen the power of money and has vowed that his children will never experience the suffering he has had to go through because of it.

Perhaps the main problem with *Sons and Daughters* is haste. It is in so much of a hurry to reach a climax that a set of slightly unlikely coincidences are introduced. Lawyer Bonu sneaks into the house of his erstwhile friend to see the daughter he has supposedly been helping but actually wishes to seduce. The daughter is alone, the father conveniently within earshot, and Lawyer B, a paper character from the beginning, attacks her in the best melodramatic style hoarsely whispering: "I shall kiss you; I must kiss you."

I mention all this because the published version of his long-awaited play *Through a Film Darkly* shows us just how fine a playwright Joe DeGraft really is. Although it was first published in 1970, an earlier version entitled "Visitor from the Past" appeared in excerpt in 1965 in *Okyeame*, Ghana's literary magazine. A still earlier version was staged in September of 1962 in Accra, Ghana. Thus, *Through a Film Darkly* is a play which was almost a decade in the writing. This shows in the final result, for in language, character development, stagecraft and impact *Through a Film Darkly* is nothing short of superb.

If we compare the earlier versions with the final play we see how a simple confrontation between John, the Ghanaian student who has become a hater of whites, and Rebecca, the girl he jilted for an English lover, has been changed. A narrator-commentator (who describes himself as "the character the playwright wouldn't allow to appear in this play") has been added and certain devices (such as a false beginning which is also the end) have been deftly introduced. Fenyinka, the guitar playing narrator, comments not only on the action within the play, but also on the attitude of critics, a neat swipe on DeGraft's part at those who raked his earlier play over the coals. "Actually," says Fenyinka, "if I didn't know about the theatre and plays, I should label this one as a 'well-made play' and proceed straight away to damn it as a hopeless piece of drama."

Through a Film Darkly is an unusual play in both its freedom of form and its seriousness. It combines the author's commentary on theatre and contemporary critics with an intelligent plot which shows the results of racism and insensitivity. Fenyinka, the African married to an English girl, is like the African writer in English who is married to a language and a tradition which is beautiful and sensitive, yet an importation from another land. What DeGraft does in *Through a Film Darkly* is to show that such marriages can work.

—Joseph Bruchac

DELANEY, Shelagh.   British.   Born in Salford, Lancashire, 25 November 1939. Educated at Broughton Secondary School. Has one daughter. Worked as salesgirl, usherette, photographer's laboratory assistant. Recipient: Foyle New Play Award, 1959; Arts Council bursary, 1959; New York Drama Critics Circle Award, 1961; British Film Academy Award, 1962; Robert Flaherty Award, for screenplay, 1962; Encyclopedia Britannica Award, 1963; Writers Guild Award, for screenplay, 1969. Agent: CMA, 99 Park Lane, London W.1, England.

PUBLICATIONS

Plays

A Taste of Honey (produced London, 1958; New York, 1960).   London, Methùen, and
   New York, Grove Press, 1959.
The Lion in Love (produced Coventry and London, 1960; New York, 1963).   London,
   Methuen, and New York, Grove Press, 1961.

Screenplays: A Taste of Honey, with Tony Richardson, 1962; The White Bus, 1966;
Charley Bubbles, 1968.

Television Plays: Did Your Nanny Come from Bergen?, 1970; St. Martin's Summer,
1974.

Other

Sweetly Sings the Donkey.   New York, Putnam, 1963; London, Methuen, 1964.

*   *   *

Shelagh Delaney's first play has a single set of a room in a lodging house, and three main
characters, a mother, a schoolgirl daughter and a homosexual art student. Each woman has
an affair with a man. Helen, the mother, goes off with hers returning only when Jo, the
daughter, is about to give birth to the child of her boyfriend, a negro sailor who has long
since left without trace. In the last scene, Geoffrey, the art student who has been mothering
Jo, leaves the women alone together. Joan Littlewood first presented the play in 1958 at the
Theatre Royal, Stratford East, London, and provided the model for many subsequent
productions. There was a jazz trio who accompanied entrances and provided support for
songs. The actors played directly to the audience wherever possible, especially Avis Bunnage
as Helen. So the action had vitality and continuous interest, and the dialogue and
characterisation rang clearly; repetitions were strongly marked. So produced, the action
seems both lively and inevitable: and the audience is encouraged to see the implications
about education, housing, and need for affection that underlie the writing. The three main
characters have dialogue, especially in shorter speeches, that rings both true and
unexpectedly. More than this, Jo, who is portrayed as only a little younger than her nineteen
year-old creator, has speeches of sensitive irony: "I'm contemporary... aren't I, though,
Geoff? I really live at the same time as myself, don't I?"
   Shelagh Delaney's second play, The Lion in Love, followed two years afterwards and at
once her ambitions became clearer. The set is both a public place and the interior of a house.
The cast is large and is involved in many interwoven stories; at one time, the stage is busy
with buying and selling in a market. Almost all the characters are conscious of social change
and most have views to express about it. There is a bearded prophet who distributes
pamphlets. Some songs, dances and conscious joking again enliven the action, but the main
story-line is very slight – Frank may leave one woman for another, and doesn't – and the
author's sympathetic presentation of her characters can scarcely provide enough dramatic
interest and excitement. Again the presentation of a young girl is the most convincing
element, but Peg is not given a main part in the action: her story is simply that she falls into
a dazed love for a young boy and may go away with him.

—John Russell Brown

DENNIS, Nigel (Forbes).   British.   Born in Bletchingley, Surrey, 16 January 1912.
Educated at Plumtree School, Southern Rhodesia; Odenwaldschule, Germany. Married
Mary-Madeleine Massias; Beatrice Ann Hewart Matthew in 1959; has two children.
Secretary, National Board of Review of Motion Pictures, New York, 1935–36; Assistant
Editor, and Book Reviewer, *New Republic*, New York, 1937–38; Staff Book Reviewer, *Time*,
New York, 1940–59. Since 1960, Drama Critic, and Joint Editor, 1967–70, *Encounter*,
London; since 1961, Staff Book Reviewer, *The Sunday Telegraph*, London. Recipient:
Houghton Mifflin-Eyre and Spottiswoode Award, for fiction, 1950; Heinemann award, for
non-fiction, 1966. Fellow, Royal Society of Literature, 1966. Address: c/o A. M. Heath and
Company, 40–42 William IV Street, London WC2N 4DD, England.

PUBLICATIONS

Plays

> *Cards of Identity*, adaptation of his own novel (produced London, 1956).   Included in
> *Two Plays and a Preface*, 1958.
> *The Making of Moo* (produced London, 1957; New York, 1958).   Included in *Two
> Plays and a Preface*, 1958.
> *Two Plays and a Preface* (includes *Cards of Identity* and *The Making of Moo*).   London,
> Weidenfeld and Nicolson, 1958; New York, Vanguard Press, 1959.
> *August for the People* (produced Edinburgh and London, 1961).   London, French,
> 1962.

Novels

> *Boys and Girls Come Out to Play*.   London, Eyre and Spottiswoode, 1949; as *Sea
> Change*, Boston, Houghton Mifflin, 1949.
> *Cards of Identity*.   London, Weidenfeld and Nicolson, and New York, Vanguard
> Press, 1955.
> *A House in Order*.   London, Weidenfeld and Nicolson, and New York, Vanguard
> Press, 1966.

Verse

> *Exotics: Poems*.   London, Weidenfeld and Nicolson, 1970; New York, Vanguard
> Press, 1971.

Other

> *Dramatic Essays*.   London, Weidenfeld and Nicolson, 1962.
> *Jonathan Swift: A Short Character*.   New York, Macmillan, 1964; London,
> Weidenfeld and Nicolson, 1965.
> *An Essay on Malta*.   London, Murray, 1972.

*   *   *

Nigel Dennis has written only three plays: *Cards of Identity, The Making of Moo*, and
August for the People. This is regrettable since he specializes in satirical, dehumanized

comedy of a kind rare in modern English drama; and since, whatever the formal defects of his work, he at least has something to say. His output as a novelist and literary critic has been comparably slender; but, although the quantity is small, through all his work there can be heard the distinctive, iconoclastic tone of the funniest right-wing English satirist since Evelyn Waugh.

Underlying all his plays is a profound conviction that men are willing robots who can be readily manipulated. It first surfaced in *Cards of Identity* which he adapted from his own highly-acclaimed novel and which was one of the first works to be staged by George Devine when the English Stage Company began its historic tenancy of the Royal Court Theatre in 1956. The play's theme is the Pirandellian one that human personality is neither absolute nor immutable; and it's demonstrated through the activities of a fraudulent trio (reminiscent of the principal figures of Jonson's *The Alchemist*) who take over a vacant country-house in order to alter people's identities. Their weapon is the mumbo-jumbo of psychotherapy and hypnotism and their aim to cram the largest number of mutually exclusive qualities into the same new personality.

Like the novel, the play is full of dazzling set-pieces; but Dennis is unable to bind them together with a strong enough plot. The result is like looking at a collection of unstrung jewels. However one can almost forgive the invertebrate structure for the sake of a sub-Greene whisky-priest's soliloquy proving that religious experience is inseparable from the deepest debauchery and arriving at the conclusion "I stink, therefore I am"; or the Absurdist scene in which the Co-Wardens of the Badgeries discover that their only function is to parade an imaginary badger on state occasions. The play has all the heartlessness of good satire: what it lacks is the structure to support its attack on manipulable humanity.

By the time he wrote *The Making of Moo*, however, Mr. Dennis had clearly learned a good deal; for this attack on organized Christianity and the gullibility of its believers is neatly and ingeniously constructed. In the first act a civil engineer and his wife, situated in some colonial outpost, invent a new religion based on the Highway Code. In the second act the new religion of Moo has so asserted itself that its creators have become fanatical believers in it even to the extent of making human sacrifices. In the third act Moo is a successful, worldly, benign religion and it is up to the son of its creators to usher in another era of reformatory murder and bloodshed.

Historically the play is significant in that it was the first outright attack on religion ever to be presented on the English stage. And there is no gainsaying the sincerity of Mr. Dennis's belief that all religions are built on a foundation of pain, torture and blood: the second-act curtain involving the ritual slaughter of a pair of casual English visitors is meant in deadly earnest. But the play lacks the full blasphemous force of, say, Buñuel's *Viridiana* or Genet's *The Balcony* for the simple reason that Mr. Dennis denies the existence and power of God. Blasphemy, to be effective, paradoxically depends on belief. For a self-styled "history of religion" the play is also woefully incomplete, offering little more than three arbitrarily-chosen stages in the development of any religious cult. But even if the play is lightweight and elliptical, it still has a considerable power to shock (the substitution of toast and tomato juice for the bread and wine of Communion causes a particular frisson) and has the merit of being a genuine pioneering work. For all its faults, it occupies an important niche in the history of English drama.

Having attacked in his first two works people who readily change their personalities at anyone's bidding and those who happily follow any half-baked new religion, in *August for the People* Mr. Dennis went the whole hog and assaulted the democratic principle as such. His protagonist is a sceptical, ironic owner of a stately home who rudely attacks the average man at a public dinner and in consequence find his privacy invaded by an ever-swelling army of day-trippers and reporters. The more he abuses the common man and the hollowness of his illusions, the greater his notoriety and success until he too finds himself acting out a role for the benefit of the public. And the shame of this drives him mad.

Intellectually, the play is seriously flawed: it attacks the press, for instance, as an example of the abuse of democracy conveniently ignoring the fact that the British popular press is not democratically controlled. Theatrically, it is also weakened by the fact that it tries to contain a Shavian extravaganza inside a naturalistic framework. Yet once again Dennis shows considerable audacity in attacking deeply-cherished beliefs and proves that he is a considerable verbal stylist in the Coward tradition. Like his other work, *August for the People* had a short run at the Royal Court (with Rex Harrison in the principal role) but has not been much played elsewhere; and it seems a pity Dennis has been a theatrical exile ever since he provided a necessary satirical corrective to the sentimentality and woolly-mindedness of so much contemporary drama.

—Michael Billington

DEWHURST, Keith. British. Born in Oldham, Lancashire, 24 December 1931. Educated at Rydal School, 1945–50; Peterhouse, Cambridge, 1950–53, B.A. (honours) in English literature 1953. Married Eve Pearce in 1958; has three children. Yarn Tester, Lancashire Cotton Corporation, Romiley, Cheshire, 1953–55; Sports Writer, Manchester *Evening Chronicle*, 1955–59; Granada Television Presenter, 1968–69; BBC2 Television Presenter of *Review* arts programme, 1972. Since 1969, Arts Columnist for *The Guardian*, London. Recipient: Japan Prize, for educational television play, 1968. Agent: William Morris Agency, 147–149 Wardour Street, London W1V 3TB, England.

PUBLICATIONS

Plays

> *Running Milligan* (televised, 1965). Published in *Z Cars: Four Scripts from the Television Series*, edited by Michael Marland, London, Longman, 1968.
> *Rafferty's Chant* (produced London, 1967). Published in *Plays of the Year 33*, London, Elek, 1967.
> *The Last Bus* (televised, 1968). Published in *Scene Scripts*, edited by Michael Marland, London, Longman, 1972.
> *Pirates* (produced London, 1970).
> *Brecht in '26* (produced London, 1971).
> *Corunna!* (produced London, 1971).
> *Kidnapped*, adaptation of the novel by Stevenson (produced Edinburgh, 1972).
> *The Miser*, adaptation of a play by Molière (produced Edinburgh, 1973).
> *The Magic Island* (produced Birmingham, 1974).
> *The Bomb in Brewery Street* (produced Sheffield, 1975).
> *One Short* (produced Sheffield, 1976).

> Radio Plays: *Drummer Delaney's Sixpence*, 1971; *That's Charlie George Over There*, 1972.

> Television Plays: *Think of the Day*, 1960; *A Local Incident*, 1961; for *Z Cars* series, 1962–67; *Albert Hope*, 1962; *The Chimney Boy*, 1964; *The Life and Death of Lovely Karen Gilhooley*, 1964; *The Siege of Manchester*, 1965; *The Towers of Manhattan*, 1966; *Softly Softly* series, 1967, 1975–76; *The Last Bus*, 1968; *Men of Iron*, 1969; *Why Danny Misses School*, 1969; *It Calls for a Great Deal of Love*, 1969; *Helen*, from the play by

Eurpides, 1970; *The Sit-In*, 1972; *Lloyd George*, 1973; *Lost at Sea*, 1974; *End Game*, 1974; *The Great Alfred*, in *Churchill's People* series, 1975; *Our Terry*, 1975; *Just William* series, 1976; and for *Knight Errant, Skyport, Love Story, Front Page Story*, and *The Villains* series.

Keith Dewhurst comments:

My plays are written in several different styles. There are traditional North of England domestic comedies like *Albert Hope, It Calls for a Great Deal of Love, Why Danny Misses School*, and *Rafferty's Chant*. There are historical plays like *The Chimney Boy, The Seige of Manchester, Men of Iron, Drummer Delaney's Sixpence, Pirates* and *Corunna!*, all of them influenced to a greater or lesser degree by Marxist historical thought and by notions of continuing the epic drama after Brecht. This sounds too grandiose and probably is. Another group of plays, mainly short pieces written for TV, experiment with form: *Why Danny Misses School* is a multi-viewpoint play; in both *Karen Gilhooley* and *The Last Bus* the characters are asked about their motives by an interviewer; both *The Chimney Boy* and *Brecht in '26* create situations in which actors speak editorial material directly to the audience. Most recently there is a group of stage plays written with music for arena or at least frontal staging: *Brecht in '26, Corunna!*, an adaptation of *Kidnapped*, and *The Magic Island*. Another vein, that of modern naturalism showing people at very mundane crises in their lives, has been confined almost entirely to the episodes for TV drama serials from which for many years I earned most of my living. My ambition is to combine these various styles of writing in the one piece. This like the arena staging would refer perhaps to a very traditional English kind of construction with main and subsidiary story-lines and a spectrum of characters. So far I have only glimpsed this in historical plays like *Pirates, Corunna!* and *Men of Iron*, and in *The Bomb in Brewery Street*, a play about the British Army in Ulster. Of course having written all this I am well aware that it gives no idea of what my plays are actually like; perhaps in any case I am the last person to know. I hope that they are poetic — that is to say, that the various strands of interest indicated above are held together by the tone. I hope that the dialogue and the characters are written in a way that is personal to me; one can never be sure. I hope very much that the plays are entertaining. My interests are intellectual but I try to express them in simple human stories. *Drummer Delaney's Sixpence*, for example, is about a Crimean War drummer boy who while sheltering from the bombardment finds a sixpence under a bush but has it taken from him by a bullying sergeant. So there we all are and thank you.

*   *   *

Keith Dewhurst's plays are primarily entertainments but many carry an underlying theme: social injustice, the pressures of modern city life, the claims of the individual as against those of society. The dialogue is fast moving and often very funny; the characters and situations tend to be drawn from North of England working-class life.

Sometimes the humour is bitter. Like the novelist Alan Sillitoe, Dewhurst takes a gloomy view of the conditions created by the Industrial Revolution and perpetuated through two world wars. Life doesn't change much for those at the bottom of the ladder, he suggests; the characters in his plays may have resilience but this is not sufficient against the oppressions of poverty and power. A typical Dewhurst story is *Drummer Delaney's Sixpence*, a radio play. Delaney is a drummer boy serving in the Crimean War who, while sheltering from the bombardment, finds a sixpence under a bush; but even this is taken from him. The ideas expressed are relevant to a contemporary society but set in an historical context; this is also true of *The Siege of Manchester, The Chimney Boy* and *Men of Iron*.

The majority of Dewhurst's plays have been written for television, which gives them immediacy and bite. He contributed many scripts to the *Z Cars* series, a study of police work which often went beyond the simple formula of crime and detection and looked at such problems as the colour bar, loneliness, and changing attitudes to the law. One of Dewhurst's scripts, *Running Milligan*, raises many questions about the motives for crime and the adequacy of our penal system. Milligan is a convict, a weak, frightened man who is given parole to attend his wife's funeral. His grief and bewilderment become too much to bear and he breaks parole, though with no real intention of escaping; on the contrary, he wants to be given a longer sentence, since prison is the only place where he can feel secure. He is a pathetic figure, running from one bolt-hole to another until he meets a man more afraid of life than he is himself. This is a victim of shell-shock, an old meths drinker, hiding in a disused railway station. As the police close in on these two outcasts, Milligan is telling the tramp a fairy story to banish his nightmare memories of the trenches.

In contrast to the pathos of *Running Milligan, Rafferty's Chant* is a farce, describing "a middle-aged heavy in a Homburg hat," an amiable Manchester con-man. Rafferty's motto is "Human Nature May It Last For Ever"; he does quite well out of human nature, selling the same car to a string of dupes by playing on their weaknesses. It is the kind of play where the question "Where are you living?" is answered "Salvation Army." Rafferty is eventually found out and arrested but has one long speech on behalf of the judge who will sentence him "for heartless fraud upon people who asked only to be allowed to realize their dreams and indulge the simple pleasures for which they worked so hard and so honestly." He ends with a more direct expression of opinion, "I cock my hind leg up at the lot of you."

Keith Dewhurst's plays are written in a variety of styles and moods, ranging from compassion to broad comedy, from irony to indignation. His work for television has included experimental pieces such as *Why Danny Misses School*, a multi-viewpoint play, and two plays in which the characters are asked about their motives by an interviewer, *Karen Gilhooley* and *The Last Bus*. His recent work for the theatre is also experimental, in the tradition of Brechtian confrontation between the actors and the audience. *Corunna!*, for instance, is performed by five actors and a five-member folk-rock group; of its varied productions on different stages, Dewhurst preferred the "in the round" version. He himself described the opening of the play in a *Guardian* essay (16 June 1971):

> an opening number from the band followed by an opening number from the actors: a straight talk to the audience by Sir John Moore [the protagonist]. Then a song punctuated by narration with actors in view and by these degrees to an orthodox dramatic scene..., introduced by... alienation effects.

Works combining the strong social themes of his *Z Car* plays and *Rafferty's Chant* with the exhilarating experimentation of *Corunna!* would be welcome from a popular dramatist with Keith Dewhurst's range and professionalism.

—Judith Cooke Simmons

DIZENZO, Charles (John).   American.   Born in Hackensack, New Jersey, 21 May 1938. Educated at New York University, B.A. 1962. Married Patricia Hines in 1964. Instructor in Playwriting, New York University, 1970–71, and Yale University, New Haven, Connecticut, 1975–76. Recipient: Yale University-ABC Fellowship, 1966, and CBS Fellowship, 1975; Guggenheim Fellowship, 1967; National Endowment for the Arts grant, 1972. Agent: Helen Harvey, 110 West 57th Street, New York, New York 10019. Address: 106 Perry Street, New York, New York 10014, U.S.A.

PUBLICATIONS

Plays

> *The Drapes Come* (televised, 1965; produced New York, 1965; Liverpool, 1973). New York, Dramatists Play Service, 1966; in *Off-Broadway Plays*, London, Penguin, 1970.
>
> *An Evening for Merlin Finch* (produced New York, 1968; Coventry, 1969). New York, Dramatists Play Service, 1968; in *Off-Broadway Plays*, London, Penguin, 1970.
>
> *A Great Career* (produced New York, 1968). New York, Dramatists Play Service, 1968.
>
> *Why I Went Crazy* (produced Westport, Connecticut, 1969; New York, 1970; as *Disaster Strikes the Home*, produced Edinburgh, 1970; London, 1971).
>
> *The Last Straw, and Sociability* (produced New York, 1970). New York, Dramatists Play Service, 1970.
>
> *Big Mother and Other Plays* (includes *An Evening for Merlin Finch* and *The Last Straw*). New York, Grove Press, 1970).
>
> *Big Mother*, music by John Braden (produced New York, 1974). Included in *Big Mother and Other Plays*, 1970.
>
> *Metamorphosis*, adaptation of works by Kafka (produced New York, 1972).
>
> *The Shaft of Love* (produced New York, 1975).

Television Play: *The Drapes Come*, 1965.

Other

> *Phoebe*, with Patricia Dizenzo (juvenile). New York, Bantam, 1970.

Charles Dizenzo quotes the program note for the 1970 production of *The Last Straw*:

As a playwright I'm more interested in the typical than the atypical in life. I think it's more fruitful to try to see ordinary life freshly than to search out unusual situations and subjects and treat them in a conventional manner. I try to see ordinary situations stripped of preconceptions and let the emotional lives of the characters unfold.

Most new plays that get done in New York are still rather naturalistic in style and have a rather explicit meaning, even a moral — the current favorite being *We Are All Guilty*. When a playwright gives up either naturalism or moralizing he's in trouble and when he gives up both he's really in trouble.

When *A Great Career* and *An Evening for Merlin Finch* were done at Lincoln Center I was asked to write notes for the program and declined, thinking the plays should stand on their own. But something happened that made me decide to be less cavalier in the future. After a preview a woman buttonholed me, told me she'd been a practising psychologist for forty-five years and knew a lot about human nature and asked me what the final play meant. I said it was about how some parents destroy their children, and I could see her quickly review the play in the light of a simple interpretive sentence and saw that it changed a confusing experience into a satisfying one. "That's all I wanted to know," she said and walked away. Susan Sontag is right. Our kind of education ("Okay, kids, what does Hamlet mean?") tends to make us decipher art and not experience it. I think plays should be seen (and judged) as experiences of life, not as vehicles for "meaning," which popularly becomes "message" or "moral."

For me, writing is an attempt to see the world with new eyes. That's why I think naturalism no longer works. By now we're so used to seeing life represented naturalistically on film, TV and the stage, that we see life itself through naturalistic filters. We've almost forgotten that naturalism is just another stylized mode of perception. When a style of representing becomes as well-digested as naturalism is, it ceases to shed light on life and becomes a means of evading it. The tacit assumptions of a naturalistic play are now the audience's assumptions, so the audience faces very little that it doesn't already take for granted.

Painters are luckier than playwrights. They need just one buyer per painting ready to see things in a new way. A playwright needs hundreds every night or his play dies – which is why painting is way ahead of theatre.

Although my plays are not naturalistic, they usually start with commonplace situations often depicted in naturalistic plays – people at work in an office or families squabbling in living rooms.

*   *   *

Charles Dizenzo is a young American playwright who emerged out of the off-off Broadway workshop movement of the 1960's. His plays since have been presented by the Repertory Company of Lincoln Center, the David Merrick Arts Foundation, and the American Place Theater in New York, and in theatres in Europe.

The best example of Dizenzo's work so far has been a pair of one-act comedies presented at Lincoln Center's experimental Forum Theater under the umbrella title *An Evening for Merlin Finch*. The first play, *A Great Career*, is an office play built on the assumption that office life is impossible, but that for all the meaningless work and the petty quarrels among employees, the office is as much "womb as tomb," or, as the heroine snarlingly calls it as the play opens, "a home away from home." It is about a harried clerical worker named Linda who has a report to prepare. During the course of the action she explodes, gets herself fired and then realizing that there is no place else to go that is not the same she literally begs to be taken back. This description I realize makes the play sound more painful than funny, and it seems that Dizenzo obviously wants his audience to hang on to that side of the story. His ending points up this fact. We see Linda crawling around the stage picking up the papers that she scattered during her defiant scene, as a fellow employee tells her about the new book-keeper who tried to commit suicide unsuccessfully in the men's room. In *A Great Career* Dizenzo shows the emasculating nature of office life by having men play women and women turning out to be men.

In *An Evening for Merlin Finch*, the sterility of the office gives way to the silent violence of the home. Darlene Finch, an insensitive middle-class middle American housewife, is plagued by a vengeful mother who materializes in the shape of her son Merlin. This becomes her vision of hatred and guilt. As he demonstrates in all of his plays Dizenzo is fascinated with the normality within a sick society. His plays point up the compromises which sink the soul of modern man into a dismal acceptance of everyday predicaments. Merlin, the focus of concern, is forced to play his bassoon for company. Each observation his parents make is a body blow and each gesture of contact a refusal. Merlin's life turns out to be an eternal adolescence and as he blows away on his bassoon his slim identity evaporates before our eyes. His mother's ignorance and hostility continuously undercut the comic image of Merlin's silly instrument. Here Dizenzo's dry black humor together with a carefully constructed situation exposes and explodes the Finches' severely distorted family life.

Another Dizenzo play which in its own bizarre and comic way explodes the quiet violence of family life is *Disaster Strikes the Home* (also presented under the title *Why I Went Crazy*). In this play Dizenzo submerges his audience into a complete and outrageous comic world. Again the sex change idea is used. Wives are played by men, husbands by women. The reversal is not a gimmick, but a surrealistic view of sexual strangulation that exists in the American household. Dizenzo counterpoints these outlandish images with careful colloquial speech which points up the emptiness that exists. His basic hatred of the family unit and the violent role reversals that take place in weak marriages turns American family life into a vivid nightmare as frightening as a fire in the night.

Dizenzo's playwriting is always startlingly inventive and for the most part consistently amusing. Like an abstract artist, by distorting the real world he gets at the dark emotional silences between people which so many contemporary playwrights attempt but seldom achieve. Although his writing has none of the manicured edge of Albee or Ionesco, and in places is in serious need of tightening, he has a keen ear for the truthful phrase and a fine almost farceur's instinct for pace. His theatrical vision is controlled and iconoclastic, which places him far ahead of the many more fashionable playwrights of his generation. In his playwriting Dizenzo has imitated no one, relying totally on his own creative talents, thereby fostering a theatrical voice which is both unique and thoroughly American.

—Bernard Carragher

DONLEAVY, J(ames) P(atrick).   Irish.   Born in Brooklyn, New York, 23 April 1926; became an Irish citizen, 1967. Educated at preparatory school, New York; Trinity College, Dublin. Served in the United States Navy during World War II. Married Mary Wilson Price in 1970; has two children. Recipient: London *Evening Standard* award, 1961; Brandeis University Creative Arts Award, 1961; National Institute of Arts and Letters award, 1975. Address: Levington Park, Mullingar, County Westmeath, Ireland.

PUBLICATIONS

Plays

> *The Ginger Man*, adaptation of his own novel (produced London and Dublin, 1959; New
>   York, 1963).   New York, Random House, 1961; as *What They Did in Dublin, with
>   The Ginger Man: A Play*, London, MacGibbon and Kee, 1962.
> *Fairy Tales of New York* (produced Croydon, Surrey, 1960; London, 1961).   London,
>   Penguin, and New York, Random House, 1961.
> *A Singular Man*, adaptation of his own novel (produced Cambridge and London, 1964;
>   Westport, Connecticut, 1967).   London, Bodley Head, 1965.
> *The Plays of J. P. Donleavy* (includes *The Ginger Man, Fairy Tales of New York, A
>   Singular Man, The Saddest Summer of Samuel S*).   New York, Delacorte Press,
>   1972; London, Penguin, 1974.
> *The Saddest Summer of Samuel S*, adaptation of his own novel (produced London,
>   1976).   Included in *The Plays of J.P. Donleavy, 1972*.

Radio Play: *Helen*, 1956.

Novels

> *The Ginger Man*.   Paris, Olympia Press, and London, Spearman, 1955; New York,
>   McDowell Obolensky, 1958; complete edition, London, Corgi, 1963; New York,
>   Delacorte Press, 1965.
> *A Singular Man*.   Boston, Little Brown, 1963; London, Bodley Head, 1964.

The Saddest Summer of Samuel S.   New York, Delacorte Press, 1966; London, Eyre
and Spottiswoode, 1967.
The Beastly Beatitudes of Balthazar B.   New York, Delacorte Press, 1968; London,
Eyre and Spottiswoode, 1969.
The Onion Eaters.   New York, Delacorte Press, and London, Eyre and Spottiswoode,
1971.
A Fairy Tale of New York.   New York, Delacorte Press, and London, Eyre Methuen,
1973.

Short Stories

Meet My Maker the Mad Molecule.   Boston, Little Brown, 1964; London, Bodley Head,
1965.

Other

The Unexpurgated Code: A Complete Manual of Survival and Manners, drawings by the
author.   New York, Delacorte Press, and London, Wildwood House, 1975.

*   *   *

Although J. P. Donleavy is better known as a novelist, he has adapted his own novels, *The
Ginger Man* and *A Singular Man*, into plays which have received fairly successful
productions: while his original stage play, *Fairy Tales of New York*, won the *Evening
Standard* Most Promising Playwright Award for 1961. In adjusting to the medium of the
theatre, Donleavy faced two particular problems. His prose style is rich, idiosyncratic and of
a quality to encourage cult enthusiasms: but to what extent could this verbal power be
incorporated into stage dialogue without leaving the impression of over-writing? His novels
too are usually written from the standpoint of one man, an anti-hero such as Sebastian
Dangerfield or George Smith: but in a play the audience is necessarily aware of other
characters, simply because they're on the stage. If the central character talks too much, the
audience's sympathy may be drawn towards the reactions of other people to him. A single
angle of vision, easy to maintain in a novel, is often hard to achieve in the theatre, which is a
multi-dimensional medium.

His first play, *The Ginger Man*, revealed an uncertain control of these difficulties. The
story concerns Sebastian Dangerfield, an impoverished American living with his English
wife, Marion, in Dublin. He is supposedly studying law at Trinity College: but his main
efforts are directed towards staving off creditors, avoiding the responsibilities of fatherhood
and raking together enough money to get drunk. In the novel, Sebastian's sheer wildness, his
refusal to settle down, is exciting: it is an archetypal rebellion against dreary conformity.
But in the play, we are unavoidably aware of the pain Sebastian causes others – particularly
Marion who leaves him and the genteel spinster, Miss Frost, whom he seduces. And the fine
uninhibited imagination of Sebastian, which provides so much fun in the book, is in the play
relentlessly controlled by the physical surroundings of the set: the squalid flat at One
Mohammed Road, the prim suburban house at 11 Golden Vale Park. "*The Ginger Man*,"
concluded Richard Gilman, the American critic, "desperately requires: song, dance, lyrical
fragments, voices from nowhere, shapes, apparitions, unexplainable gestures——" In the
format of a naturalistic play, it lost many of the qualities which made the book so
remarkable. Even the theme seemed less original: the relationship between O'Keefe and
Sebastian recalled the boozing friendship between Joxer and "Captain" Boyle in O'Casey's
Juno and the Paycock.

Fairy Tales of New York was much more successful: a sequence of four related anecdotes,
which almost seems to continue the ginger man's career. An American returns to his home

city, with his English wife who dies on the voyage. Cornelius Christian is in the same state of desolation, harassed by poverty, guilty and grief-stricken, which faced Sebastian at the close of the previous play. The four scenes illustrate Cornelius's gradual rehabilitation: the burial of his wife and his job at the funeral parlour, his entry into the American business world, his work-outs at a gymnasium and finally his successful (though imaginary) conquest of a snobbish head-waiter and an embarrassed girl friend. Unlike Sebastian, however, Cornelius is a reserved quiet man − observing others and sometimes poking gentle fun at them: and this changed role for the central character, together with the much greater flexibility of play form, allows Donleavy's great gifts for caricature, witty dialogue and buoyant fun to be more evident. Nor are the episodes as unrelated and superficial as they may appear. Donleavy stresses the contrast between the democratic ideals of American society with the rigidly class-structured and snobbish habits: Christian is employed because he's been to Europe and acquired "breeding" − he dazzles the head-waiter, who refused to serve him because he wore peach shoes, by dressing as a visiting Eastern potentate wearing no shoes at all. The spurious emotionalism of the funeral parlour is related to Christian's moving grief: and the sheer falseness of an over-commercialized society is exposed with a delicate skill that only Evelyn Waugh and Edward Albee have matched.

Although *A Singular Man* lacks some of the moral seriousness (and fun) of *Fairy Tales of New York*, it too is a rewarding play: centered around the life of a fairly successful New York businessman, George Smith, his friendships and affairs with three girls, Ann Martin, Sally Tomson and Shirl. Smith is a fall guy, always missing out on the opportunities he dreams about. "The only time the traffic will stop for me," he confesses to Shirl, "is when I'm dead." His sexual fantasies focus on Sally Tomson, a gorgeous secretary, protected by her tough-guy brother and many other lovers. Her death at the end of the play, just before her marriage to a rich tycoon, crystallizes Smith's sense of cosmic defeat. But Smith never quite gives up hope: and his resilience through successive embarrassments and failures provides the mainspring for the play. *A Singular Man* is similar in construction to *Fairy Tales of New York*: a sequence of twelve anecdotal scenes, which work both on the level of isolated and very amusing revue sketches, and together as a group, the insights of one episode being carried forward to the next, until the full picture emerges both of the society and the central man. In the first scene, Smith opts out of conversation with a boring friend by answering just "Beep beep"; in the seventh, he tries the same tactics with Shirl, only to discover that his relationship with her is too charged and complex to admit such an evasion.

Donleavy's style of humour is reminiscent both of *New Yorker* cartoons and of his fellow American dramatist, Murray Schisgal, whose plays are also popular in Britain. But his jokes are never flippant − although they sometimes seem whimsical. They succeed because they're based on detailed observation and a rich command of language. Although as a dramatist, he may not yet have lived up to the promise of *Fairy Tales of New York*, he remains one of the most potentially exciting dramatists in the West.

—John Elsom

DREXLER, Rosalyn. American. Born in New York, 25 November 1926. Self-educated. Married Sherman Drexler in 1946; has two children. Also a painter, sculptor, singer, and wrestler. Member, The New Dramatists, New York Theatre Strategy, Dramatists Guild, P.E.N., Actors Studio. Recipient: Obie Award, 1965; two Rockefeller grants, 1965; *Paris Review* Fiction Prize, 1966; Guggenheim Fellowship, 1970. Agent: (drama) Helen Harvey, 110 West 57th Street, New York, New York 10019; (literary) Georges Borchardt, 145 East 52nd Street, New York, New York 10022. Address: 316 West 79th Street, New York, New York 10024, U.S.A.

PUBLICATIONS

Plays

> Home Movies, and Softly, and Consider the Nearness, music by Al Carmines (produced
>   New York, 1964).   Included in The Line of Least Existence and Other Plays, 1967.
> Hot Buttered Roll (produced New York, 1966; London, 1970).   Included in The Line of
>   Least Existence and Other Plays, 1967.
> The Investigation (produced Boston and New York, 1966; London, 1970).   Included in
>   The Line of Least Existence and Other Plays, 1967.
> The Line of Least Existence (produced New York, 1967; Edinburgh, 1968).   Included in
>   The Line of Least Existence and Other Plays, 1967.
> The Line of Least Existence and Other Plays: Home Movies; The Investigation; Hot
>   Buttered Roll; Softly, and Consider the Nearness; The Bed Was Full.   New York,
>   Random House, 1967.
> The Bed Was Full (produced New York, 1972).   Included in The Line of Least
>   Existence and Other Plays, 1967.
> Softly, and Consider the Nearness (produced New York, 1973).   Included in The Line
>   of Least Existence and Other Plays, 1967.
> Skywriting (produced New York, 1968).   Published in Collision Course, New York,
>   Random House, 1968.
> She Who Was He (produced New York, 1973).

Novels

> I Am the Beautiful Stranger.   New York, Grossman, 1965; London, Weidenfeld and
>   Nicolson, 1967.
> One or Another.   New York, Dutton, 1970; London, Blond, 1971.
> To Smithereens.   New York, New American Library, 1972; London, Weidenfeld and
>   Nicolson, 1973.
> The Cosmopolitan Girl.   New York, M. Evans, 1974.

Rosalyn Drexler comments:

I try to write with vitality, joy and honesty. My plays may be called absurd. I write to amuse myself. I often amuse others.

Almost all my reviews have been excellent, but I am not produced much. It seems that every theatre wants to premiere a play. (That's how they get grants.) Therefore, if a play is done once, good or bad, that's it for the playwright – unless she is Ibsen, Shaw...etc.

Playwriting is my first love. I'm considered established, but I have just begun.

*   *   *

Fun as Danger. Ms. Drexler swings the scythe in a generous arc, the cutting edge attacking all in its path, no preconceived plan but a natural urge to swing away. And the natural good health and good humor often resonate with fateful, sometimes awful incident. "I'll make him pay," we hear in Hot Buttered Roll:

Jewel – Through the nose!
Jordan – Through the eyes, ears, mouth and the South of him! Through Jan dear.

> (He caresses her.) And when he's through with her he'll be finished, done
> in, a panting, pitiful old man with just a bowl of soft, hot cream of farina
> to dip his finger into....
>
> Jewel — I'll take his teeth too. They make him look like a donkey anyway.

Awful incident, but all's well that ends well. The viciousness is in the utterance, we will do such things, as Lear mad on the moor utters. Banged by language, à la Lear and Groucho, with a vocal assist from Pa Ubu. In the end geniality reigns. *The Line of Least Existence* ends with Dr. Fraak genially signing himself and Mrs. Fraak into the looney bin. Fraak, the analyst, has also been pusher and pimp, he's been accused of white-slavery by an irate father who wants to kill him. But geniality takes over, shoulders are shrugged and the Fraaks do a kind of psychic soft-shoe out of the play into the mental hospital. And Pschug, the would-be killer, irately hounding Fraak the play long, goes off with them, too, for what does he have to do that's better? "I'll go quietly," says Fraak, "I've had a nap." And: "We'll meet for socials and make love on the grounds. I might even persuade her [Mrs. Fraak] to raid the pharmacy with me some night. It's my fault she never had any fun. I plan to change all that if we can synchronize our schedules."

A sense here of the old-fashioned, well-made play as well as of the partially well-made Hollywood film, where things in the end are patched up, where no real harm is done. What has been done is almost solely to the spectator, not to the characters. The spectator has been battered by the epigram, the pun, the metaphor, the obsessional song that comments on and rises above the action. The characters shrug or sing their way off as in *The Line of Least Existence* or as in *Home Movies*, where the Verduns sing and wrestle to the end.

The wrestling match appears to be a diversion except that diversion is one of the major traits of the Drexler comedies, so ingrained that it ceases to be diversion and becomes a motif within a generally bizarre pattern. The mainstream is thus colored by a lurching series of tributary streams which appear and disappear unexpectedly and rapidly. The narrative operates like a Marx Brothers film where Groucho's nose for the prurient takes him on unexpected journeys.

Sex in the Drexler world is open, blatant, a little bizarre — and genial. No mystery, no sense of the erotic. Sex is for buddies. The Verduns in *Home Movies* can either wrestle or make love, it hardly appears to matter which. Ibolya, the nubile young creature kept by Dr. Fraak, either wants sex or she wants to go shopping:

> Ibolya — (In Fraak's consulting room) I just saw a pair of knee high leather boots
> without seams that lace up the back, and you know what they cost?
>
> Fraak — An arm and a leg?
> (a little later:)
>
> Ibolya — Creeps! I hate creeps. Say, you don't want me now. Why am I here when
> I could be out shopping?

Fraak's value system tells him that a little love is better than paying through the nose and his peculiar sense of romance tells him that "Sex should have an air of mystery, or it will have the stink of familiarity." But his idea of mystery is to put Ibolya in a chair on his desk and pretend she's a whore working out terms with a potential client passing in the street.

In the Drexler plays, the male sex partner is often a middle-aged lecher like Fraak or an even dirtier old man like Corrupt Savage in *Hot Buttered Roll*, bedridden, with hair "a gray bush resembling Colette's."

But there is more talk than sex. The metaphors are rampant. Dr. Fraak, bargaining for Ibolya's favors, reminds her that "What I give you is priceless. I'm your supply depot, your armed guard, your ticket for a trip through inner space...." And the pun is always ready to be hurled in a breathless moment:

> Mrs. Fraak — (to her dog Andy) Are you rabid?
> Andy —   I don't belong to any faith.

213

The pun acts like a diversion and the characters are incorrigible; if the pun is potentially near they must sniff it out.

And there are the epigrams. "Don't you know," asked Dr. Fraak, "that appearance is everything and style is a way of living." And later, that "the line of least existence is preferable to going out of your way." The epigram appears to be a way of testing rather than affirming a vision, just as the plays are ways of testing. All things are being tried out, sniffed out, the implausible is being aired to see what's in it and also for its own sake. Perhaps nothing is in it but its appearance, but perhaps something is. The Drexler approach can have it both ways.

A recent Drexler work takes a radically different line from the earlier plays. *She Who Was He* leaves the modern and concrete for the ancient and mythical. Its tone is lofty and even autumnal. Wounds are real and the murder of Queen Hatshepsut is very real. Drexler has gone back into pre-Biblical times to introduce the spectre of death and the transcendence of myth into her work. Ephemeral hijinks have given way, at least for the moment, to the eternal seriousness of myth.

—Arthur Sainer

DUBERMAN, Martin. American. Born in New York City, 6 August 1930. Educated at Yale University, New Haven, Connecticut 1948–52, B.A. 1952; Harvard University, Cambridge, Massachusetts, 1952–57, M.A. 1953, Ph.D. 1957. Tutor, Harvard University, 1955–57; Instructor and Assistant Professor (Morse Fellow, 1961–62), Yale University, 1957–62; Assistant Professor, 1962–65, Associate Professor, 1965–67, and Professor of History, 1967–71, Princeton University, New Jersey. Since 1971, Distinguished Service Professor, Lehman College, City University of New York. Recipient: Bancroft Prize, for history, 1962; Vernon Rice Award, 1964; American Academy of Arts and Letters Award, 1971. Address: 70 Charles Street, New York, New York 10014, U.S.A.

PUBLICATIONS

Plays

> *In White America* (produced New York, 1963; London, 1964). Boston, Houghton Mifflin, and London, Faber, 1964.
> *Metaphors*, in *Collision Course* (produced New York, 1968). New York, Random House, 1968.
> *Groups* (produced New York, 1968).
> *The Colonial Dudes* (produced New York, 1969). Included in *Male Armor*, 1975.
> *The Memory Bank: The Recorder, and The Electric Map* (produced New York, 1970; *The Recorder*, produced London, 1974). New York, Dial Press, 1970.
> *Payments* (produced New York, 1971). Included in *Male Armor*, 1975.
> *Soon*, music by Joseph Martinez Kookoolis, adaptation of a story by Kookoolis and Scott Fagan (produced New York, 1971).
> *Dudes* (produced New York, 1972).
> *Elagabalus* (produced New York, 1973). Included in *Male Armor*, 1975.
> *Male Armor: Selected Plays 1968–1974* (includes *Metaphors, The Colonial Dudes, The*

Recorder, The Guttman Ordinary Scale, Payments, The Electric Map, Elagabalus).
New York, Dutton, 1975.
Kerouac (produced New York, 1976).

Screenplays: *The Deed,* 1969; *Mother Earth,* 1971.

Other

Charles Francis Adams, 1807–1886. Boston, Houghton Mifflin, 1961.
James Russell Lowell. Boston, Houghton Mifflin, 1966.
The Uncompleted Past (essays). New York, Random House, 1969.
Black Mountain: An Exploration in Community. New York, Dutton, 1972.

Editor, *The Antislavery Vanguard: New Essays on the Abolitionists.* Princeton, New
Jersey, Princeton University Press, 1965.

*   *   *

In White America was first produced in October of 1963, at a time of great optimism in
American social consciousness. It was the era of the New Frontier. The play was an
immediate, sustained, and internationally acclaimed success. Its author, however, was a
playwright by avocation only, and his subsequent theatrical productivity has proven to
reflect his true profession in subject matter, theory of communication, and evolution. Martin
Duberman is a Professor of History at Lehman College, a professional historian of
recognized accomplishment, and author of four major works in that field: *James Russell
Lowell, Charles Francis Adams, 1807–1886, The Uncompleted Past,* and *Black Mountain: An
Exploration in Community.*

In White America* is less a "play" in any traditional literary sense than it is an "evening of
theatre" – it is an *assemblage* of documents from the history of the American Negro's
experience of two hundred years' suffering. As an historical event reflecting the social fabric
of its time, the piece is significant, and at the time of its presentation it was a moving
experience for all audiences. It weaves together dialogues, documents, songs and narration
with impressive sensitivity for theatrical construction and it suggests a possible form for
playwrights to explore. In a 1963 essay "Presenting the Past," Duberman argued that "the
past has something to say to us...a knowledge of past experience can provide valuable
guidelines, though not blueprints, for acting in the present." Clearly his professional concern
for history provided him with a subject matter (he did not create material; he selected,
edited, and shaped it). His teaching duties, moreover, led him to a belief in the theatrical and
dramatic potential of oral communication: a lecturer can be more than informative. "The
benefits of a union between history and drama," Duberman wrote, "would not by any
means be all on one side. If theater, with its ample skill in communication, could increase
the immediacy of past experience, history, with its ample material on human behavior,
could broaden the range of theatrical testimony." In his preface to the printed play he added,
"I chose to tell this story on the stage, and through historical documents, because I wanted
to combine the evocative power of the spoken word with the confirming power of historical
fact." It was the assessment of critics of the time that Duberman had succeeded in all
respects. The play stimulated an awakening social consciousness, was vital in the
enactment, and communicated its thesis most effectively.

In the late 1960's Duberman's attitudes towards the uses of the past and the efficacy of
wedding history to theatre began to change. Perhaps the disenchantment of the New Left
that followed the Kennedy and King assassinations influenced his thinking. His work for the
theatre abandoned the path suggested by *In White America,* and he began to write fiction –
invented drama.

Male Armor collects seven plays written between 1968 and 1974. Two are full-length. Four

215

of the one-acts had been published previously. None had received successful production in the commercial theatre. In his introduction to the collection, Duberman professes that the plays explore a common theme, "What does it mean to be a 'man'?" The collection's title, he explains, is meant to recall Wilhelm Reich's concept of "character armor" – the devices we employ to protect ourselves from our own energy, particularly our sexual energy. Each of the plays investigates the way we build protective roles which then dominate us. For Duberman, the way to destroy these confining roles is, apparently, androgeny, either practiced or metaphorical.

Metaphors, The Electric Map, and *The Recorder* are all highly literate sparrings between consenting adults which explore the themes of power struggle and homosexuality. In *Metaphors* a young applicant to Yale University nearly seduces his admissions interviewer. *The Electric Map* and *The Recorder,* which had an unsuccessful off-Broadway production under the title *The Memory Bank,* are also duologues. The former is set before an elaborate, electrified map of the Battle of Gettysburg, and self-consciously uses this visual analogue to puff up a foolish domestic quarrel between two brothers into what the author hopes will be something akin to universality. There is a predictable undertone of latent homosexuality to the trite and poorly motivated action. *The Recorder* is an interview of the friend of a great man by an academician-historian. In it, Duberman is intrigued by the ineffectiveness and inaccuracy of historical inquiry, and the play unquestionably reflects his growing disenchantment with the study of history, as well as his growing use of sexuality as a dramatic subject. By the time of these plays, Duberman was referring to himself as "more a writer than a historian."

The newest play in *Male Armor* is *Elagabalus,* a six-scene realistic play about Adrian, a self-indulgent and affluent androgynist. Duberman writes, "Adrian is playful and daring. His gaity may be contaminated by petulance and willfulness, but he *is* moving toward an *un*-armored territory; moving out so far that finally he's left with no protection against the traditional weaponry brought to bear against him...other than the ultimate defense of self-destruction." In his quest for self, Adrian stabs himself fatally in the groin, and the final image the writer offers is a gratuitous freeze-frame from the porno film "Big Stick" in which a teenage girl sucks sensuously on a popsicle. This reader was reminded of the adage that many people (Adrian? Duberman?) who are looking for themselves may not like what they find. Adrian is a boring character whose self-destruction does not seem significant.

The Uncompleted Past is a collection of Duberman's critical and historical essays which concludes with an expression of his disenchantment with the study of history and reveals why his theatrical development had moved towards fiction (in which area he appears undistinguished) and away from the documentary (in which his initial acclaim was achieved). He writes,

> For those among the young, historians and otherwise, who are chiefly interested in changing the present, I can only say...they doom themselves to bitter disappointment if they seek their guides to action in a study of the past. Though I have tried to make it otherwise, I have found that a "life in history" has given me very limited information or perspective with which to understand the central concerns of my own life and my own times.

It seems probable that *In White America* will stand as Duberman's major writing for the theatre, and that it will prove more significant as an event of cultural history than as either an innovation in theatrical form or the first work in the career of a significant playwright – thus belying the very attitudes towards history and theatre which Duberman has recently held.

—Thomas B. Markus

DUFFY, Maureen.   British.   Born in Worthing, Sussex, 21 October 1933. Educated at the Trowbridge High School for Girls, Wiltshire; Sarah Bonnell High School for Girls; King's College, London, 1953–56, B.A. (honours) in English 1956. School teacher for five years. Collaborated with Brigid Brophy, *q.v.*, in making and exhibiting Prop Art (3-D Constructions), London, 1969. Recipient: City of London Festival Playwright's Prize, 1962; Arts Council Bursary, for drama, 1963, and for literature, 1966, 1975. Agent: Jonathan Clowes Ltd., 19 Jeffrey's Place, London NW1 9PP. Address: 8 Roland Gardens, London S.W.7, England.

PUBLICATIONS

Plays

The Lay Off (produced London, 1962).
The Silk Room (produced Watford, Hertfordshire, 1966).
Rites (produced London, 1969).   London, Methuen, 1969.
Solo, Olde Tyme (produced Cambridge, 1970).
A Nightingale in Bloomsbury Square (produced London, 1973).   Published in *Factions*, edited by Giles Gordon and Alex Hamilton, London, Joseph, 1974.

Television Play: *Josie*, 1961.

Novels

That's How It Was.   London, Hutchinson, 1962.
The Single Eye.   London, Hutchinson, 1964.
The Microcosm.   London, Hutchinson, and New York, Simon and Schuster, 1966.
The Paradox Players.   London, Hutchinson, 1967; New York, Simon and Schuster, 1968.
Wounds.   London, Hutchinson, and New York, Knopf, 1969.
Love Child.   London, Weidenfeld and Nicolson, and New York, Knopf, 1971.
I Want to Go to Moscow: A Lay.   London, Hodder and Stoughton, and New York, Knopf, 1973.
Capital.   London, Cape, 1975; New York, Braziller, 1976.

Verse

Lyrics for the Dog Hour: Poems.   London, Hutchinson, 1968.
The Venus Touch.   London, Weidenfeld and Nicolson, 1971.
Actaeon.   Rushden, Northamptonshire, Sceptre Press, 1973.
Evesong.   London, Sappho, 1975.

Other

The Erotic World of Faery.   London, Hodder and Stoughton, 1972.
The Passionate Shepherdess: Aphra Behn 1640–89.   London, Cape, 1977.

Translator, *A Blush of Shame*, by Domenico Rea.   London, Barrie and Rockliff, 1963.

Critical Studies: in *Transatlantic Review 45* (London), Spring 1973; *Guide to Modern World Literature* by Martin Seymour-Smith, London, Wolfe, 1973.

Maureen Duffy comments:

I began my first play in my third year at university, finishing it the next year and submitting it for *The Observer* playwriting competition of 1957/58. I had done a great deal of acting and producing at school and at this stage my aim was to be a playwright as I was already a poet. I wrote several more plays and became one of the Royal Court Writers Group which met in the late fifties to do improvisations and discuss problems. I have continued to write plays alternately with novels and every time I am involved in a production I swear I will never write anything else. From early attempts to write a kind of poetic social realism I have become increasingly expressionist. *Solo, Olde Tyme* and *Rites* are all on themes from Greek mythology. *Megrim*, the play I am working on at present, is a futurist study of racialism and the making of a society. I believe in theatrical theatre including all the pantomime elements of song, dance, mask and fantasy and in the power of imagery.

*   *   *

Maureen Duffy is firmly established as one of the foremost novelists of her generation. For the past fifteen years she has also written plays; the fact that these, with the possible exception of *Rites*, have not yet received the recognition they deserve is due quite as much to an absence of a fortuitous conjunction of circumstances typical of the theatre and necessary for the achievement of success, as to the demands made on the audience by the author.

Miss Duffy's plays are not "easy." They are densely written, pitched between fantasy and realism, and have allegorical undertones. At the centre of her work lie three short plays derived from Greek myths: The Bacchae (*Rites*), Narcissus (*Solo*), and Uranus (*Olde Tyme*).

Rites, which first appeared in an experimental programme of plays presented by the National Theatre, is set in a ladies' public lavatory, presided over by the monstrous Ada (Agave). Miss Duffy describes it as a black farce. She uses a chorus of modern prototypes – three office girls, a cleaner, an old tramp – and involves them in situations both modern (a girl's attempted suicide in a cubicle) and parallel to the myth. Her Dionysus is a boy doll, brought in by two women and examined with gloating curiosity; her Pentheus a transvestite Lesbian, dressed like a man. She is brutally murdered as a consequence of entering this exclusive women's domain, and disposed of in the incinerator for sanitary towels. It helps to know *The Bacchae*, but it is by no means essential. The strength of the play resides in the power of the writing, the violence of its situations, and the deliberate "Peeping Tom" element.

In *Solo*, her Narcissus is a man, reflecting on his image in a bathroom mirror: again a deft blending of the modern and the ancient mythical.

Olde Tyme, which deals with the castration of Uranus, is in many ways her most interesting and original play, but dramatically the least convincingly realized. It is studded with brilliant, Pirandellian ideas. Her hero is a television tycoon, keeping his employees in slavish dependence. He sustains his confidence with the help of cherished memories of his mother, a queen of the Music Halls. The slaves get their chance to revolt when he hires a derelict theatre and forces them to re-create an old Music Hall evening, with his mother as the star. This he plans to film and preserve for posterity.

Sexual fantasies are enacted, and at last his "mother" appears and punctures with her revelations the whole basis of the tycoon's life. He is destroyed ("castrated") and his minions take over. There are echoes here of *The Balcony*, but the play's effectiveness is undermined by the lack of credibility of the characters. To dehumanize a three-dimensional character and make him two-dimensional will engage an audience's emotions, but you cannot flatten caricatures.

Among Maureen Duffy's other work for the stage are *The Silk Room*, which chronicles the gradual disintegration of a pop group, and a play about François Villon.

More recently, *Megrim*, hitherto unperformed, is an expressionist, futuristic fantasy about a secluded society. It combines the nightmarish quality of Fritz Lang's film *Metropolis* with the intellectual daring of the discussions contained in Shaw's late extravaganzas. To these Miss Duffy has added a human, mainly sexual dimension of her own. It makes a rich but probably undigestible concoction.

More modestly, and entirely successfully, *A Nightingale in Bloomsbury Square* shows us Virginia Woolf going though a lengthy creative stocktaking prior to suicide before a spectral audience consisting of Sigmund Freud and Vita Sackville-West. It is an interrupted monologue, written with great sympathy and power.

Maureen Duffy is a recognized writer of fierce originality and imaginative depth; hopefully, she will have an opportunity before long to prove herself to a wider public as a dramatist, too.

—Frank Marcus

DUNCAN, Ronald (Frederick Henry).   British.   Born in Salisbury, Rhodesia, 6 August 1914. Educated in Switzerland and at Downing College, Cambridge, M.A. 1936. Married Rose Marie Theresa Hansom in 1941; has two children. Editor, *The Townsman*, London, 1938–46; Columnist ("Jan's Journal"), *Evening Standard*, London, 1946–56. Has farmed in Devon since 1939. Founder, Devon Festival of the Arts, Bideford, 1953; Co-Founder, English Stage Company at the Royal Court Theatre, London, 1955. Agent: David Higham Associates, 5–8 Lower John Street, Golden Square, London W1R 4HA. Address: Welcombe, Bideford, Devon, England.

PUBLICATIONS

Plays

Birth (produced London, 1937).

The Dull Ass's Hoof (includes *The Unburied Dead; Pimp, Skunk and Profiteer; Ora Pro Nobis*).   London, Fortune Press, 1940.

This Way to the Tomb: A Masque and Anti-Masque, music by Benjamin Britten (produced London, 1945; New York, 1961).   London, Faber, 1946; New York, Theatre Arts, 1967.

The Eagle Has Two Heads, adaptation of a play by Jean Cocteau (produced London, 1946; New York, 1947).   London, Vision Press, and New York, Funk and Wagnalls, 1948.

The Rape of Lucretia, music by Benjamin Britten, adaptations of a play by André Obey (produced Glyndebourne, Sussex, 1946).   London, Boosey and Hawkes, 1946; augmented edition, London, Lane, 1948.

Amo Ergo Sum (cantata), music by Benjamin Britten (produced London, 1948).

The Typewriter, adaptation of a play by Jean Cocteau (produced London, 1950). London, Dobson, 1948.

Stratton, music by Benjamin Britten (produced Brighton, 1949; London, 1950). London, Faber, 1950.

St. Spiv (as *Nothing up My Sleeve*, produced London, 1950; revised version, as *St. 'Orace*, music by Jerry Wayne, produced London, 1964).   Included in *Collected Plays*, 1971.

Our Lady's Tumbler, music by Arthur Oldham (produced Salisbury, Wiltshire, 1951). London, Faber, 1951.

Don Juan (produced Bideford, Devon, 1953; London, 1956).   London, Faber, 1954.

The Death of Satan (produced Bideford, Devon, 1954; London, 1956; New York, 1960). London, Faber, 1955; in *Satan, Socialities, and Solly Gold: Three New Plays from England*, New York, Coward McCann, 1961.

A Man Named Judas, adaptation of a play by C. A. Puget and Pierre Bost (produced Edinburgh, 1956).

The Cardinal, with Hans Keuls, adaptation of a play by Harold Brett (produced Cambridge, 1957).

The Apollo de Bellac, adaptation of a play by Jean Giraudoux (produced London, 1957). London, French, 1958.

The Catalyst (produced London, 1958; revised version, as *Ménage à Trois*, produced London, 1963).   London, Rebel Press, 1964; New York, Theatre Arts, 1967.

Christopher Sly, music by Thomas Eastwood (produced London, 1960).

Abelard and Heloise: A Correspondence for the Stage (produced London, 1960). London, Faber, 1961.

The Rabbit Race, adaptation of a play by Martin Walser (produced Edinburgh, 1963). Published in *Plays, vol. 1* by Martin Walser, London, John Calder, 1963.

O-B-A-F-G $\frac{K\text{-}M}{S^{R}\text{-}N}$ *: A Play in One Act in Stereophonic Sound* (produced Exeter, 1964).   London, Rebel Press, 1964; New York, Theatre Arts, 1967.

The Trojan Women, adaptation of a play by Jean-Paul Sartre based on the play by Euripides (produced Edinburgh, 1967).   London, Hamish Hamilton, and New York, Knopf, 1967.

The Seven Deadly Virtues: A Contemporary Immorality Play (produced London, 1968). Included in *Collected Plays*, 1971.

The Gift (produced Exeter, 1968).   Included in *Collected Plays*, 1971.

The Rehearsal (as *Still Life*, televised 1970).   Included in *Collected Plays*, 1971.

Collected Plays (includes *This Way to the Tomb, St. Spiv, Our Lady's Tumbler, The Rehearsal, The Seven Deadly Virtues, O-B-A-F-G, The Gift*).   London, Hart Davis, and New York, Theatre Arts, 1971.

Screenplay: *Girl on a Motorcycle*, 1968.

Television Plays: *The Portrait*, 1954; *The Janitor*, 1955; *Preface to America*, 1959; *Not All the Dead Are Buried*, 1960; *The Rebel*, music by Thomas Eastwood, 1969; *Still Life*, 1970; *Mandala*, 1972.

Novels

The Last Adam.   London, Dobson, 1952.
Saint Spiv.   London, Dobson, 1961.

Short Stories

The Perfect Mistress and Other Stories.   London, Hart Davis, 1969.
A Kettle of Fish.   London, Hart Davis, 1971.
A Tail of Tales.   London, Elephant Press, 1975.

Verse

Postcards to Pulchinella.   London, Fortune Press, 1941.
The Mongrel and Other Poems.   London, Faber, 1950.
The Solitudes.   London, Faber, 1960.
Judas.   London, Blond, 1960.
Unpopular Poems.   London, Hart Davis, 1969.
Man, part 1.   London, Rebel Press, 1970.
Man, part 2.   Welcombe, Devon, Rebel Press, 1972.
Man, part 3.   Welcombe, Devon, Rebel Press, 1972.
Man, parts 4 and 5.   Welcombe, Devon, Rebel Press, 1974.

Other

The Complete Pacifist.   London, Boriswood, 1937.
The Rexist Party Manifesto (as the Bishop of Marsland).   London, Townsman, 1937.
Strategy in War (as Major-General Marsland).   London, Townsman, 1937.
Journal of a Husbandman.   London, Faber, 1944.
Home-Made Home (on architecture).   London, Faber, 1947.
Jan's Journal 1.   London, William Campion, 1949.
Tobacco Growing in England.   London, Faber, 1950.
The Blue Fox (newspaper articles).   London, Museum Press, 1951; New York, Oxford
    University Press, 1952.
Jan at the Blue Fox (newspaper articles).   London, Museum Press, 1952.
Where I Live.   London, Museum Press, 1953.
Jan's Journal 2.   London, Museum Press, 1954.
All Men Are Islands: An Autobiography.   London, Hart Davis, 1964.
Devon and Cornwall.   London, Batsford, and New York, Hastings House, 1966.
How to Make Enemies (autobiography).   London, Hart Davis, 1968.
Obsessed (autobiography).   London, Joseph, 1975.

Editor, *Songs and Satires of John Wilmot, 2nd Earl of Rochester.*   London, Forge
    Press, 1948.
Editor, *Selected Poems,* by Ben Jonson.   London, Grey Walls Press, 1949.
Editor, *Selected Writings of Mahatma Gandhi.*   London, Faber, and Boston, Beacon
    Press, 1951.
Editor, with the Countess of Harewood, *Classical Songs for Children.*   London,
    Blond, and New York, Potter, 1965.
Editor, with Marion Harewood, *The Penguin Book of Accompanied Songs.*   London,
    Penguin, 1973.

Translator, *Diary of a Film: La Belle et le Bête,* by Jean Cocteau.   London, Dobson,
    1950.

Manuscript Collection: University of Texas, Austin.

Critical Studies: *Ronald Duncan* by Max Walter Haueter, London, Rebel Press, 1969
(includes bibliography); *Ronald Duncan* by William Wahl, Salzburg, Salzburg University
Press, 1973; *Tribute to Ronald Duncan* by Lord Harewood and others, London, Harton
Press, 1974.

Theatrical Activities:

Director: **Play** – *Abelard and Heloise*, London, 1973.

Ronald Duncan quotes his Introduction to *Collected Plays*, 1971 (reprinted by permission of Rupert Hart-Davis Ltd. and Theatre Arts Books):

Any dramatist finds that his plays fall into two categories: those for which he had some hopes but which went wrong either in the writing or in the production; and those for which he had none, and surprised him by achieving public approval. *This Way to the Tomb* fell into the latter category....

In the 1940's it was, as it still is to a large extent, a theatrical assumption that a character in a play should be a consistent type. I reacted strongly against this simplification. I knew of nobody who was consistent, including myself.

The other theatrical convention I was reacting against was the frivolity of the social and topical, and the triviality of the political theme, devoid of any universal application. I wanted to help break down the convention of naturalism in the theatre with all its clutter of box sets and papier maché props; naturalism which pretended to be realism but which, to my mind, was so far from reality as to be fantasy or pantomime. I maintain that all of us live at various levels at one and the same time. Although we may exchange inanities over the coffee-cups or sherry glasses, it is not the dramatist's job to reproduce life naturalistically, but to give it depth. And for a time in the 1940's, with the so-called revival of verse drama at the Mercury, it did seem that we had the theatre of "realism" on the run. But the victory was brief. Within a few years naturalism became the fashion again. The only change was that the convention of Shaftesbury Avenue duchesses fiddling with flower vases was replaced by Jimmy Porters picking their noses in public.

Whatever theories a dramatist may have, he has only words as tools. I decided to use verse for *This Way to the Tomb*, not to see whether I could write a poetic drama – a phrase which I have always disliked, because it puts the poetry before the drama – but because I wanted the language to carry the maximum charge. What is poetry but language at its most intense?...It was my ambition to forge a flexible verse which would contain the run and rhythms of everyday language and yet move on the muscles of thought. I wanted to write poetry that would carry the intensity I aimed at, but which would not be labelled poetic....

[*St. Spiv*] was a play I enjoyed writing, because in it I was able to draw on the Cockney character which I had known as a child. I lived in South London until I was sixteen, and before I was ten I had persuaded my mother to allow me to go to Covent Garden Market at 6 a.m. with a florist; to sit on a high, two-wheeled butcher's cart on his round; to serve behind a bar at the Union Arms; to spend many evenings selling newspapers at a newsagents; and even to take the pennies at a salad stall in Brixton Market. From this background I knew that the raciness of the Cockney's language had lost nothing since Elizabethan days, and in this comedy I tried to reproduce some of it.

I wrote *The Seven Deadly Virtues* in 1961. My purpose was to dramatise my belief that we cannot judge an act as either good or evil unless we know the circumstances and the person's intention. I therefore wrote two playlets in which the seven virtues are shown as vices and the seven vices as virtues. My intention was not to ridicule ethics, but perhaps to make people think again about what constitutes morality; and as in *St. Spiv* and other plays, I inclined to the view that there is often more virtue in the woman of easy virtue than there is in the chaste prig....

[In *The Rehearsal* (*Still Life*)], I was concerned with the problem that people are not only strangers to themselves, but to one another, however intimate their lives may superficially appear to be. In this play none of the four characters is aware of his own motives. I saw it as a play not of four characters, but eight: as each is both the character he thinks himself to be, and the character he really is....

The other theme running behind the play is one which I touched on in *Stratton*, and has to do with the way the young generation find their feet fitting into the previous generation's footsteps. It is about the tyranny of inherited limitations: the pattern repeats, and our only freedom resides in the acceptance of these limitations. In emphasising the power of inherited influences, I was making an unpopular comment in an age which believes that environment is the only factor. As a pig breeder I have never found that true.

*   *   *

Ezra Pound once called Ronald Duncan "the lone wolf of English letters," but it may be more apt to describe him as a surviving lamb. Duncan was one of several writers to follow T. S. Eliot into the field of poetic drama during and just after the Second World War. Eliot's *Murder in the Cathedral* (1935) convinced him (as it did others) that plays in verse were not only possible for modern theatre, but necessary. His best plays, *This Way to the Tomb*, *The Catalyst* and *Don Juan*, received substantial London productions: while his libretto for the Benjamin Britten opera, *The Rape of Lucretia*, and his inversion of traditional morality, *The Seven Deadly Virtues*, are also justifiably well known. During the early 1950's, however, his reputation tended to be overshadowed by Eliot and Christopher Fry, although his range as a dramatist was perhaps greater than either. His plays show considerable variety – ranging from taut sexual comedy to austere tragedy, from satire to farce – and his verse technique is subtle and skilful. But his somewhat bleak outlook, his didacticism and damning dismissal of all materialism prevented him perhaps from achieving popularity in the commercial West End theatres: while at the Royal Court (whose English Stage Company he helped to found) his opinions were considered too Christian and right-wing.

"Our most pressing problems," Duncan wrote in 1960, "are more in the realms of psychology and religion than materialism and sociological matters." Man now lives in a world where a belief in God has been systematically killed off: and Duncan, while not advocating a return to religious drama, sought to find some reconciliation between the prevailing scepticism and the innate human need to trust an authority above that of man's. He expressed this contrast between traditional faith and debased modernity most forcibly in his first major success, *This Way to the Tomb*, which is in the form of a masque and anti-masque. The Masque concerns the temptations of St. Antony of Santa Ferrata, a fourteenth-century mystic, who left his life as a prince of the Church to become a hermit. In form it is similar to the first act of *Murder in the Cathedral*: St. Antony is visited by three temptations, Gluttony, Lechery and Doubt, which he overcomes by the force of reasoning – only to find himself a victim of Pride, which only faith can conquer. The Masque ends with his assumption into paradise. The Anti-Masque is set in the twentieth century, where a T.V. company supposedly investigates the legend of St. Antony's tomb and the miraculous re-appearance of the saint on a certain night of the year. The modern setting gave Duncan the opportunity for some lively and forthright satirical sketches – of the Girl of Leisure, the revivalist sect known as the Astral Group, and television announcers: and the bouncy lyrics were heightened by Benjamin Britten's pastiche of popular music.

This Way to the Tomb, however, presented an over-simplified version of Duncan's rather complex thought: for he was neither dogmatically Christian – nor a total admirer of asceticism – nor a confirmed reactionary. Indeed the success of *This Way to the Tomb* (which ran for a year in London) may have distorted his reputation in the years to come. He was mainly concerned – not with damning the present – but with man's capacity for discovering substitutes for a love of God. In *Stratton*, the substitute is self-esteem. The central character, Sir Cory Stratton, is an eminent barrister who becomes a judge: Stratton is dimly aware that the crimes of his clients are ones which he is capable of committing. When he forgets this fact, the criminal side of his own nature takes over. He strangles his wife, commits incest with his daughter-in-law and shoots his son. The contrast between the somewhat melodramatic plot and the various moral lessons to be drawn from it did not find favour with the critics, who felt that there were simpler ways of pointing the dangers of hubris. *Don Juan* and *The Death of Satan* were more respectfully received at the Royal Court in 1956: a double-bill which arrived at the general conclusion that

> If we don't love something greater than ourselves
> We are incapable of loving one another.

Don Juan is a rake and an agnostic who seduces Donna Ana to win a bet – only to find that Ana fills the spiritual void in his character. He is damned to long for her eternally. *The Death of Satan* describes his future in hell – with Shaw, Wilde and Byron, each boring one another with brilliant conversation. Don Juan is allowed to return to earth, only to discover that women are now the seducers and virginal Anas no longer exist.

The Catalyst, Duncan's best play, moves away from the allegory and satire of his earlier works, although it retains some of the themes. The situation concerns a ménage à trois between Charles (a doctor), Therese (his wife) and Leone (his secretary): but the shock of the plot comes with the realization that Therese and Leone are also in love. The three are locked together in a manner reminiscent of Sartre's *Huis Clos*: they cannot escape from the obsessions which cause them pain. The dialogue is taut, funny and to the point: and the construction shows Duncan's command of the conventions of social comedy. It was also a mildly revolutionary play, the first to tackle openly the forbidden theme of lesbianism in a theatrical world still dominated by censorship. *The Seven Deadly Virtues* also defied the current moralities, by presenting a man, Christopher, whose merits of patience, tolerance and abstinence are shown to be the consequence of a damning spiritual pride – whereas his unfaithful wife, Melanie, redeems her "sins" by her generosity and charity.

Duncan's skill and technique as a dramatic poet rival that of Eliot himself: but he is always careful to prevent the felicities of his style from seeming obtrusive. Poetry "is not a mush of metaphor," he once wrote, "or rhetoric plastered on to the situation like stucco on the wall...it should evolve from the action and not impede it." He therefore chose originally to write in a stressed, colloquial verse, somewhat akin to Hopkins' sprung rhythm, using alliteration and assonance rather than rhyme:

> He fretted for fresh air and fields,
> For his father's father...
>
> – from *The Unburied Dead*

He used popular verse forms in the anti-masque of *This Way to the Tomb* for satiric effect: and in *The Catalyst* he breaks up and patterns the rhythms of normal conversation with great virtuosity.

Duncan's greatest misfortune perhaps was to live in an age when his particular moral preoccupations, much influenced by Christianity and Eastern mysticism, were considered old-fashioned. He was never sturdily opposed to socialism, as many of his critics implied: he founded a co-operative farm, was a friend of Gandhi, and once worked in the mines, gathering material for his first play, *The Unburied Dead*, which concerned an abortive strike. But he didn't support the revolutionary fervour of the new wave of British dramatists after the war: and felt that when all the social injustices were cleared away, man would still be confronted with an insoluble spiritual dilemma – that in a world without God, man was left alone and defenceless against despair.

—John Elsom

DURRELL, Lawrence (George).   British.   Born in Julundur, India, 27 February 1912. Educated at the College of St. Joseph, Darjeeling, India; St. Edmund's School, Canterbury, Kent. Married Nancy Myers in 1935 (divorced, 1947); Eve Cohen, 1947 (divorced); Claude

Durrell, 1961 (died, 1967); Ghislaine de Boysson, 1973; has two children. Has had many jobs, including jazz pianist (Blue Peter nightclub, London), automobile racer, and real estate agent. Lived in Corfu, 1934–40. Editor, with Henry Miller and Alfred Perles, *The Booster* (later *Delta*), Paris, 1937–39; Columnist, *Egyptian Gazette*, Cairo, 1941; Editor, with Robin Fedden and Bernard Spencer, *Personal Landscape*, Cairo 1942–45; Special Correspondent in Cyprus for *The Economist*, London, 1953–55; Editor, *Cyprus Review*, Nicosia, 1954–55. Taught at the British Institute, Kalamata, Greece, 1940. Foreign Press Service Officer, British Information Office, Cairo, 1941–44; Press Attaché, British Information Office, Alexandria, 1944–45; Director of Public Relations for the Dodecanese Islands, Greece, 1946–47; Director of the British Council Institute, Cordoba, Argentina, 1947–48; Press Attaché, British Legation, Belgrade, 1949–52; Director of Public Relations for the British Government in Cyprus, 1954–56. Andrew Mellon Visiting Professor of Humanities, California Institute of Technology, Pasadena, 1974. Recipient: Duff Cooper Memorial Prize, 1957; Prix du Meilleur Livre Etranger, 1959. Fellow, Royal Society of Literature, 1954. Has lived in France since 1957. Address: c/o National and Grindlay's Bank, 13 St. James's Square, London S.W.1, England.

PUBLICATIONS

Plays

Sappho: A Play in Verse (produced Hamburg, 1959; Edinburgh, 1961; Evanston, Illinois, 1964).   London, Faber, 1950; New York, Dutton, 1958.
Acte (produced Hamburg, 1961).   London, Faber, 1965; New York, Dutton, 1966.
An Irish Faustus: A Morality in Nine Scenes (produced Sommerhausen, Germany, 1966).   London, Faber, 1963; New York, Dutton, 1964.

Screenplays: *Cleopatra*, with others, 1963; *Judith*, with others, 1966.

Television Script: *The Lonely Road*, 1971.

Recording: *Ulysses Come Back: Sketch for a Musical* (story, music and lyrics by Lawrence Durrell), 1971.

Novels

Pied Piper of Lovers.   London, Cassell, 1935.
Panic Spring (as Charles Norden).   London, Faber, and New York, Covici Friede, 1937.
The Black Book: An Agon.   Paris, Obelisk Press, 1938; New York, Dutton, 1960; London, Faber, 1973.
Cefalù.   London, Editions Poetry, 1947; as *The Dark Labyrinth*, New York, Ace, 1958.
White Eagles over Serbia.   London, Faber, and New York, Criterion Books, 1957.
The Alexandria Quartet:
   Justine.   London, Faber, and New York, Dutton, 1957.
   Balthazar.   London, Faber, and New York, Dutton, 1958.
   Mountolive.   London, Faber, 1958; New York, Dutton, 1959.
   Clea.   London, Faber, and New York, Dutton, 1960.
The Revolt of Aphrodite.   London, Faber, 1974.
   Tunc.   London, Faber, and New York, Dutton, 1968.

Nunquam.   London, Faber, and New York, Dutton, 1970.
Monsieur; or, The Prince of Darkness.   London, Faber, and New York, Viking Press, 1975.

Short Stories

Esprit de Corps: Sketches from Diplomatic Life.   London, Faber, 1957; New York, Dutton, 1958.
Stiff Upper Lip: Life among the Diplomats.   London, Faber, 1958; New York, Dutton, 1959.
Sauve Qui Peut.   London, Faber, 1966; New York, Dutton, 1967.
The Best of Antrobus.   London, Faber, 1974.

Verse

Quaint Fragment: Poems Written Between the Ages of Sixteen and Nineteen.   London, Cecil Press, 1931.
Ten Poems.   London, Caduseus Press, 1932.
Bromo Bombastes.   London, Caduseus Press, 1933.
Transition: Poems.   London, Caduseus Press, 1934.
Proems: An Anthology of Poems, with others.   London, Fortune Press, 1938.
A Private Country.   London, Faber, 1943.
Cities, Plains and People.   London, Faber, 1946.
Zero, and Asylum in the Snow: Two Excursions into Reality.   Rhodes, privately printed, 1946; New York, Circle Editions, 1947.
On Seeming to Presume.   London, Faber, 1948.
Deus Loci.   Ischia, Italy, Di Mato Vito, 1950.
Private Drafts.   Nicosia, Cyprus, Proodos Press, 1955.
The Tree of Idleness and Other Poems.   London, Faber, 1955.
Selected Poems.   London, Faber, and New York, Grove Press, 1956.
Collected Poems.   London, Faber, and New York, Dutton, 1960; revised edition, 1968.
Penguin Modern Poets 1, with Elizabeth Jennings and R. S. Thomas.   London, Penguin, 1962.
Beccafico Le Becfigue (English, with French translation by F.-J. Temple).   Montpellier, France, La Licorne, 1963.
La Descente du Styx (English, with French translation by F.-J. Temple).   Montpellier, France, La Murène, 1964.
Selected Poems 1935–63.   London, Faber, 1964.
The Ikons: New Poems.   London, Faber, 1966; New York, Dutton, 1967.
The Red Limbo Lingo: A Poetry Notebook for 1968–1970.   London, Faber, 1971.
On the Suchness of the Old Boy.   London, Turret Books, 1972.
Vega and Other Poems.   London, Faber, 1973.
Plant-Magic Man.   Santa Barbara, California, Capra Press, 1973.
Lifelines.   Edinburgh, Tragara Press, 1974.

Other

Prospero's Cell: A Guide to the Landscape and Manners of the Island of Corcyra.   London, Faber, 1945; New York, Dutton, 1960.
A Landmark Gone.   Los Angeles, privately printed, 1949.
Key to Modern Poetry.   London, Peter Nevill, 1952; as *A Key to Modern British Poetry,*

Norman, University of Oklahoma Press, 1952.

Reflections on a Marine Venus: A Companion to the Landscape of Rhodes. London, Faber, 1953; New York, Dutton, 1960.

Bitter Lemons (on Cyprus).   London, Faber, 1957; New York, Dutton, 1958.

Art and Outrage: A Correspondence about Henry Miller Between Alfred Perles and Lawrence Durrell, with an Intermission by Henry Miller. London, Putnam, 1959; New York, Dutton, 1960.

Lawrence Durrell and Henry Miller: A Private Correspondence, edited by George Wickes.   New York, Dutton, and London, Faber, 1963.

Spirit of Place: Letters and Essays on Travel, edited by Alan G. Thomas.   London, Faber, and New York, Dutton, 1969.

Le Grand Suppositoire (a taped biographical interview with Marc Alyn).   Paris, Editions Pierre Belfond, 1972; as *The Big Supposer,* London, Abelard Schuman, 1973; New York, Grove Press, 1974.

The Happy Rock (on Henry Miller).   London, Village Press, 1973.

Editor, with others, *Personal Landscape: An Anthology of Exile.*   London, Editions Poetry, 1945.

Editor, *A Henry Miller Reader.*   New York, New Directions, 1959; as *The Best of Henry Miller,* London, Heinemann, 1960.

Editor, *New Poems 1963: A P.E.N. Anthology of Contemporary Poetry.*   London, Hutchinson, 1963.

Editor, *Lear's Corfu: An Anthology Drawn from the Painter's Letters.*   Corfu, Corfu Travel, 1965.

Editor, *Wordsworth.*   London, Penguin, 1973.

Translator, *Six Poems from the Greek of Sekilanos and Seferis.*   Rhodes, privately printed, 1946.

Translator, with others, *The King of Asine and Other Poems,* by George Seferis. London, Lehmann, 1948.

Translator, *The Curious History of Pope Joan,* by Emmanuel Royidis.   London, Verschoyle, 1954; revised edition, as *Pope Joan: A Personal Biography,* London, Deutsch, 1960; New York, Dutton, 1961.

Bibliography: by Alan G. Thomas, in *Lawrence Durrell: A Study* by G. S. Fraser. London, Faber, 1968.

Critical Studies: *The World of Lawrence Durrell,* edited by Harry T. Moore, Carbondale, Southern Illinois University Press, 1962; *Lawrence Durrell and the Alexandria Quartet* by Alan Warren Friedman, Norman, University of Oklahoma Press, 1970.

Lawrence Durrell comments:

After one is dead all one's work – good, bad and indifferent – comes together and one sees that it all forms part of a whole. But while one lives it irritates readers and publishers alike to tackle several forms, as D. H. Lawrence did, and Thomas Hardy. One didn't know how to take them: as poets or novelists.

This is rather a disingenuous way of saying that my plays are rather what one would have called "closet dramas" in the seventeenth century, but to my surprise they work quite well on the stage when tactfully put together by a great producer like the German Gustav Grundgens or John Hale, who took *Sappho* to Edinburgh with Margaret Rawlings in the part. But the plays were written in the wake and under the influence of the verse drama epoch launched by Eliot and ably backed up by Auden, Spender, MacNeice, Fry and so on. But verse plays are not "commercial" or indeed very modern, and it is only at Festivals that my sort of playwright gets a look in. But I am happy with this arrangement. I have learned how to write a play now, and prefer this rather cumbersome form in which words are paramount to the brilliant stammering and electronic shorthand of the great dramatists of today like Ionesco and Beckett. Ideally I would like to write a play in the tones of Valéry or Rilke. The only thing that stands in my way is the fact that I am neither of them but only L. Durrell Esq. Apprentice Sorcerer, and still learning.

*   *   *

Lawrence Durrell's plays explore the nature of love and the nature of reality and suggest that the two are interdependent. The protagonists of his poetic dramas love, suffer and speculate on the meaning of an absurd universe. They learn that all passion is suspect, all happiness fleeting and that a stoical acceptance of these truths may bring wisdom. Life cannot be understood but neither can it be evaded; Durrell's heroes are romantics, allowing themselves to feel acutely, in isolation.

All three plays centre on a search for absolute truth and suggest that it can be found only in the extremes of experience. Petronius Arbiter bleeds to death at the end of *Acte* and voices his contentment with suicide; it is for him the summation of philosophy. "Yes, it is possible to become an adept of reality." Similarly Faustus, returned from hell fire, describes its great attraction for him in the following terms:

> For the first time I knew I was in reality.
> Most of the time
> We are not, d'you see; life is a conditional state
> And reality prime.

Their attitudes suggest that an authentic statement about the human condition can be achieved but at a high cost, the total disintegration of accepted forms and beliefs. It is an idea which Durrell has expressed in his prose narratives, experimenting with style and structure in ways which reflect the bewildering contradictions of experience. His plays have a more formal framework, written in blank verse, based on classical myth and legend. They describe madness, vampirism, incest – morbid and fantastic subjects which are characteristic of his writing.

Sappho, Acte, Faustus: all are creatures of the ancient world, whose lives provide ample scope for the exuberance of Durrell's imagination. *Sappho* is a fine study of palace intrigue, an evocation of a past civilization and a credible portrait of a real woman. Sappho's origins are mysterious; we learn that she was orphaned in an earthquake, found by the philosopher Minos and educated by him to become the unacknowledged ruler of Lesbos. She is loved by twin brothers, Phaon, who retreats from the world, and Pittakos, who seeks to conquer it as a soldier. Neither can satisfy Sappho, who describes her nature, and that of all poets, as being beyond human love.

> Born old, we turn away from men and women;
> Hermaphrodites of conscience, copulating with ourselves.

Pittakos sends her a severed arm from battle, still bearing a golden bracelet; this is the only tribute that power can bring the artist. Phaon dives into the submerged city under the harbour of Lesbos and retrieves evidence which brings his mistress disaster; her parentage is discovered and it appears that she has married her own father, the punishment for which is exile. Pittakos, who becomes Tyrant, refuses to let Sappho's children accompany her from the island, and her son dies in his care. The action now resembles that of a Jacobean tragedy, dominated by the macabre and by the theme of revenge. Sappho brings about the death of both brothers but it is a bitter victory; she is elected Tyrant, thus losing her freedom as an artist but not the isolation of that role. She is reunited with her daughter and can only lament:

> Everyone is afraid of me
> All that I could not solicit of love
> I gained at last in fear

Durrell's *An Irish Faustus* is a reinterpretation of the Faust myth, unorthodox and in part comic, since this is Faust placed in County Galway. The traditional story is here reversed; Faustus sets the pace for the devil and goes to hell "dragging the cringing Mephisto with him." There is plenty of Gothic horror and melodrama but much of the dialogue is in a lighter vein as in the scenes with the pardoner, Martin, whose methods of selling relics differ little from the methods of the modern salesman:

> While nothing I ever say is quite true
> Nothing is quite false; I keep a sense of proportion
> I am what you might call a perfectly balanced man.

Faustus has certainly lost his soul by the end of the play but this is not expressed in terms of brimstone or heaven relinquished; he has to abandon the language of scientific enquiry for that of the card sharper. Magic becomes another confidence trick.

Acte is the story of a tragic passion, a love affair between a Scythian princess and the Roman general Fabius who takes her as hostage to Nero's Rome. Acte has been blinded by the conquerors and raped by a leader of her own primitive people; she has pathos and beauty and, it is hinted, a dark knowledge which can grow only from such extreme suffering. She resembles Justine and Clea, two characters from Durrell's *Alexandria Quartet*; indeed the whole play echoes that work. Acte and her lover are caught up in a political intrigue over which they have no control, pawns in a game, prisoners in a city of corruption. At night, the princess meets "the archpoet" Nero in the cellars of his palace, calms his fears and feeds him soup. The Emperor listens to her, as he listens to Petronius Arbiter, but their influence cannot restrain the excesses of his madness. Acte is doomed and her epitaph spoken by Petronius as he himself faces death:

> One could see that she would lose her life
> In some thoughtless and tragic pageant. She belonged to art!

Durrell's plays, like those of other post-war dramatists writing in blank verse, are not aimed at the commercial theatre; his interests in the bizarre and the grandiose places him outside the main current of contemporary drama. However, his themes are in many ways those of his contemporaries, although their expression is not. Durrell's luxuriance is the reverse coin to Samuel Beckett's brevity; but both playwrights are concerned with metaphysics, both appear deeply pessimistic, both write at opposite poles of the same tradition, that of debased romanticism.

—Judith Cooke Simmons

DYER, Charles (Raymond).   British.   Born in Shrewsbury, Shropshire, 17 July 1928. Educated at the Highlands Boys' School, Ilford, Essex; Queen Elizabeth's School, Barnet, Hertfordshire. Served as a Flying Officer in the Royal Air Force, 1944–47. Married Fiona

Thomson in 1959; has three sons. Actor and Director; Chairman and Artistic Director for Stage Seventy Productions Ltd. Address: Old Wob, Gerrards Cross, Buckinghamshire, England.

PUBLICATIONS

Plays

> Clubs Are Sometimes Trumps (as C. Raymond Dyer) (produced Wednesbury, Staffordshire, 1948).
> Who on Earth! (as C. Raymond Dyer) (produced London, 1951).
> Turtle in the Soup (as C. Raymond Dyer) (produced London, 1953).
> The Jovial Parasite (as C. Raymond Dyer) (produced London, 1954).
> Single Ticket Mars (as C. Raymond Dyer) (produced Bromley, Kent, 1955).
> Time, Murderer, Please (as C. Raymond Dyer) (produced Portsmouth, Hampshire, 1956).   London, English Theatre Guild, 1962.
> Wanted, One Body! (as C. Raymond Dyer) (produced on tour, 1956).   London, English Theatre Guild, 1961.
> Poison in Jest (as C. Raymond Dyer) (produced on tour, 1958).
> Prelude to Fury (as C. Raymond Dyer) (produced London, 1959).
> Red Cabbage and Kings (as R. Kraselchik) (produced Southsea, Hampshire, 1960).
> Rattle of a Simple Man (produced London, 1962; New York, 1963).   London and New York, French, 1963.
> Gorillas Drink Milk, adaptation of a play by John Murphy (produced Coventry, 1964).
> Staircase (produced London, 1966; New York, 1968).   London and New York, French, 1967.
> Mother Adam (produced York, 1971; also director: produced London, 1972). London, Davis Poynter, 1972.
> A Hot Godly Wind (produced Manchester, 1975).   Published in Second Playbill 3, edited by Alan Durband, London, Hutchinson, 1973.

> Screenplays: Rattle of a Simple Man, 1964; Staircase, 1969; Brother Sun and Sister Moon, 1970.

Novels

> Rattle of a Simple Man.   London, Elek, 1964.
> Charlie Always Told Harry Almost Everything.   London, W. H. Allen, 1969; as Staircase: or, Charlie Always Told Harry Almost Everything, New York, Doubleday, 1969.

Critical Studies: in Sunday Times (London), 14 April 1966, 5 December 1971, and 29 April 1973; Drama (London), Winter 1967; L'Avant Scène (Paris), 15 January 1968; New Yorker, 20 January 1968; Sipario (Rome), August 1969; Irish Tatler (Dublin), December 1969.

Theatrical Activities:

> Director: **Plays** – in London, Amsterdam, Rotterdam, Paris, Berlin; recently, Mother Adam, London, 1972, Stratford upon Avon, 1973.

Actor: **Plays** – roles in 250 plays; debut as Lord Harpenden in *While the Sun Shines* by Terence Rattigan, Crewe, Cheshire, 1947; Duke in *Worm's Eye View* by R. F. Delderfield, London and tour, 1948–50; Digger in *The Hasty Heart* by John Patrick, toured, 1950; Wilkie in *No Trees in the Street* by Ted Willis, toured, 1951; Turtle in *Turtle in the Soup*, London, 1953; Launcelot Gobbo in *The Merchant of Venice*, London, 1954; Maitre d'Hotel in *Room for Two* by Gilbert Wakefield, London, 1955; Syd Fish in *Painted Sparrow* by Guy Paxton and E. V. Hoile, Cork, Ireland, 1956; Flash Harry in *Dry Rot* by John Chapman, London and tour, 1958; Shylock in *The Merchant of Venice*, Bromley, Kent, 1959; Viktor in *Red Cabbages and Kings*, Portsmouth, Hampshire, and tour, 1960; Percy in *Rattle of a Simple Man*, London, 1963; Mickleby in *Wanted, One Body!*, Guildford, Surrey, 1966. **Films** – include *Cuptie Honeymoon*, 1947; *Naval Patrol*, 1959; *The Loneliness of the Long Distance Runner*, 1962; *Rattle of a Simple Man*, 1964; *The Knack*, 1965; *How I Won the War*, 1967.

Charles Dyer comments:

Outside bedtime, no one truly exists until he is reflected through the mind of another. We exist only as we think others think of us. We are not real except in our own tiny minds according to our own insignificant measurement of thought.

Animals adapt to their inadequacies without shame or discernible consciousness. Eventually, they wither to nothing, wagging their minds behind them, and die unsurprised – like frogs. Man is different, and is measured according to breadth of chest, amount of hair, inside leg, bosom and backside. He is insulted by death. He cares. And he cares more about what is seen than is hidden; yet unseen differences have greatest emotional effect.

Such as loneliness.

And I write about loneliness.

Obviously, Man is progressing towards a life, a world of Mind. Soon. Soon, in terms of creation. But with physicalities dismissed, the mind is lonelier than ever. Mind was God's accident. An unfortunate bonus. We should be more content as sparrows, spring-fluttering by the clock; a sudden day, tail-up; then the cock-bird, and satisfaction matter-of-factually; a search for straw; eggs and tomorrow automatic as the swelling of string in water. It happens for sparrows, that is all! Anything deeper is Mind. And Mind is an excess over needs. Therefore Mind is loneliness.

Rattle of a Simple Man and *Staircase* and *Mother Adam* form a trilogy of loneliness, three plays enacted on Sundays. Bells are so damned lonely. Duologues, they are, because two seems the most sincere symbolic number, especially as man plus woman may be considered physically One. My plays have no plots, as such. Action cannot heal loneliness; it is cured only by *sharing* an action, and is emphasized by reduction of plot. And reduction of stage setting – which should, I feel, be expendable once the play is written. I detail a setting for the preparation of each duologue, that its dialogue may relate to a particular room; then, as a casting reflects its mould, the setting becomes irrevocably welded into and between the lines. The potency of these duologues is greater in drapes.

They reprimand me, occasionally, for handicapping my characters either physically or mentally: Cyrenne the prostitute and Percy, male virgin, in *Rattle of a Simple Man*; schizophrenic Adam and arthritical Mammles in *Mother Adam*; homosexual Charlie and nakedly-bald Harry in *Staircase*. And as the Trilogy grew, I locked them into barber shops and attics, depriving them even of a telephone to outside realities. This was a private challenge; yet what interest in an even face? what fault in a crooked smile? I love the courage of my imperfect characters, I despair with them – so small in a world of mindless faces, and faceless minds driving science to God's borders. In *Staircase*, man plus man situation, Charlie and Harry are lost without one another. But Charlie is too proud to admit such a fatal interdependence. He patronises Harry, taunts him, and drops "exciting" names which are anagrams of his own; he refuses to reflect anything of Harry; thus, Harry

231

becomes an anagram, too; and even me, as their author. Charlie, Harry and me, become one: because there is no reality until we are reflected through someone else's eyes.

My characters have hope with their imperfections. They are dismayed by today's fading simplicity; today's lack of humility — no one ever wrong, always an excuse; kissing footballers without respect for the losers; and people who, from the safety of secret conscience, dismiss others as "them."

Man's disease is loneliness; God's is progress.

*   *   *

The opening performance of Charles Dyer's *Rattle of a Simple Man* was given at the Garrick Theatre on 19 September 1962. I had heard that it consisted of a dialogue between a mug and a tart, and, knowing nothing of Charles Dyer's delicacy and integrity, assumed it would be full of equivocal situations. Before the end of the first act I realized I was in the presence of a new and valid talent, possessed to an astonishing degree of the capacity to find pearls among swine. In drunken football fans, in middle-aged, failing homosexual hairdressers, and the half-paralysed relics of tambourine-banging religiosity, Charles Dyer finds not the débris of humanity, but unforgettable gleams of tenderness and self-sacrifice:

> Cyrenne – Been on holiday?
> Percy –   I went to Morecambe. There were lots of married couples at the digs.
>   They took a fancy to me. I was always making them laugh. It was
>   marvellous. I think I'll go somewhere else next year, though.

Dyer shows his skill in changing, by the simplest words, the whole mood of a scene. One can tell the very moment the light went out for Percy.

For many years Dyer travelled the country as an actor in provincial productions of London successes; and in Percy's unhappy seaside memories there may well be recollections of drab theatrical lodgings. The two homosexual barbers in *Staircase* are exceptionally bitter on this subject:

> Charlie – Even me honeymoon was a – a – a holocaust: one night/of/passion/and
>   food-poisoning for thirteen. Maggots in the haddock, she claimed.
>   (Harry giggles)
>   Oh, I was laughing, dear. Yes. What! Lovely – your blushing bride all
>   shivering and turgid in the promenade shelter; hurricanes whipping the
>   shingle. Couldn't even paddle for a plague of jellyfish.

Charles Dyer considers and reconsiders every aspect of his work, and does not let it go until he has got out of it everything that it contains. Unlike most other eminent contemporary dramatists he is ready, even delighted, to discuss his work, its meaning, and its origin. It is clear that what he puts into his plays is but a small part of his knowledge of the people he writes about. He has written two novels, which have had considerable success, and both are treatments of themes dealt with in his plays, *Rattle of a Simple Man* and *Staircase*. Most people suppose that the novels are rewritings of the plays, but this is not true. The novels are the original work, and the plays follow after.

Thus, though *Rattle of a Simple Man* has an effect similar to that of the *nouveau roman* in that it leaves the audience with a question unanswered, Dyer is really at the opposite pole from writers like Alain Robbe-Grillet and Marguerite Duras. They leave questions open because their philosophy tells them that human knowledge is limited, whereas Dyer ends with an uncertainty only because the wealth of information with which he could resolve it would blur the clear outline of what he wishes to say.

Long before the end of *Rattle* we understand and love Cyrenne and Percy. They are characters, bruised, resilient, and in their ridiculous way curiously dignified, who make for righteousness, because they manifest sympathy and consideration for others. They are in fact people of honour.

That they are so is the basis of Dyer's outlook on the drama. He writes his plays, which are spare and austere in form, according to a classic formula of abiding power. The question with Charles Dyer is not what his characters appear to be, but what they will do in the circumstances in which he places them. It is in my opinion a mistake to consider *Staircase* as primarily a study of homosexuality. Essentially it is a study of how under great stress a man's character may crumble, and then rebound to a level it never attained before.

Dyer is in fact the complement to Anouilh, whom in many ways he rivals in theatrical expertise. Whereas with bitter distress Anouilh discovers the sordidness of purity, Dyer – in this resembling Maupassant – comes upon purity in sordidness. Against dispiriting odds, people are capable of behaving unexpectedly well. This is one reason why Dyer's work is so much more exhilarating than that of most of even his most distinguished contemporaries. He is a dramatist who indulges neither in self-pity nor in recrimination.

In *Staircase*, presented by the Royal Shakespeare Company 1966–67, Dyer did a very curious thing. He gave his own name to the character played by Paul Schofield. This was the introduction of his theory that everybody is alone. He carries his theme into *Mother Adam*, but in *Staircase* all characters, on and offstage, are woven into patterns of the name Charles Dyer. It is a dramatic device to pinpoint the lack of substance in a man-man relationship where Charlie could not exist without Harry, nor Harry without Charlie. All is loneliness. And each without the other, says Dyer, would be like "a golfer holing-in-one by himself. Nobody to believe him. Nobody to prove his moment ever truly existed." Dyer is at his best when dealing with commonplace aspects of life, and discerning in them the emotional depths of their apparent shallowness. There is something both ludicrous and touching in the way Harry broods over the distresses he suffered as a scout master. Patrick Magee brought real humanity to his task of making tea for Scofield's Dyer, prissy, pampered, pomaded, a ruined god, awaiting a summons for indecent behaviour. To his lurking terror, Mr. Scofield gave a fine touch of injured vanity.

The actor who plays this splendid part – one of the best in modern drama – can be riveting, revolting, and masterly all at the same time: in his sudden bursts of panic, in his vain boastings of a largely imaginary past as a pantomime dame, in his irritability, and in his readiness, in his own terror, to wound his pitiably vulnerable companion.

Mother Adam, Dyer's recent play, is his most ambitious. Adam's paralysed mother is a tyrant of extreme power, and she brings it to bear on her son, who longs – he thinks – to escape and marry. Despite its consciousness that, in one of Dyer's shining phrases, "There aren't so many silk-loined years," the play is as full of laughter as it is of heartbreak. Its dialogue is rich in curious eloquence and stirring images.

Fine as these things are, it is not in them that Dyer's mastery is to be found, but in his capacity to hold in his mind two conflicting rights, and to see, with a true compassion, that their confrontation cannot be resolved. It is because of this capacity that he has written in *Mother Adam* one of the few real tragedies of our time. Adam cannot be free unless his mother is deserted; his mother cannot be cared for unless her son's life is ruined. It is this situation that Charles Dyer observes with a dancing eye and a riven heart.

I say, with the same absolute confidence with which I wrote of *The Birthday Party* in 1958, that in the history of the contemporary theatre *Mother Adam* will rank as a masterpiece.

Dyer has previously written two fine and successful plays: *Rattle of a Simple Man* and *Staircase*. Mother Adam is better than either. It is more disturbing; it has deeper resonances; it is more beautifully written, with an imagination at once exotic and desperately familiar; it has a profounder pity, and a more exquisite falling close.

Loneliness haunts Charles Dyer's imagination. Is there any solution of this terrible problem? Dyer says there is. Loneliness is the product of selfishness, and where no selfishness is, there is no loneliness. The condition of unselfishness is not easy to attain. It is within reach only of the saints. But sanctity is not an unattainable goal. We should all aim for it.

In *Mother Adam* Dyer seeks the continuing theme of Oneness. Man and mother, almost to the edges of Oedipus. The moment when Adam falls to his knees at the bedside, hugging his mother, dragging her crippled knuckles to his face, begging "Hug me! hug me! I dream of love. I need love," should represent the climax, not only of *Mother Adam*, but of the whole Loneliness Trilogy.

In two of his plays Charles Dyer deals with subjects which, when the plays were first produced, were considered daring. The Lord Chamberlain made twenty-six cuts in *Staircase*, including the scene in which Harry explains his hatred of the physical side of life. The *Report on Censorship 1967* mentioned *Staircase* throughout twenty-five of its two hundred pages. Dyer likes to feel he is ahead of trends, but not excessively so: "In terms of eternity, the interval between Adam and Eve's nakedness and the Moment when God cast them forth in animal skins is but a finger click. The serious, most important period is what happens *after* they put on clothes."

We clothe our inadequacies. This is what Charles Dyer's plays are all about.

—Harold Hobson

EASMON, R(aymond) Sarif.   Sierra Leonean.   Practising doctor. Address: 31 Bathurst Street, Freetown, Sierra Leone.

PUBLICATIONS

Plays

Dear Parent and Ogre (produced Lagos, Nigeria, 1961).   London and New York, Oxford University Press, 1964.
The New Patriots.   London, Longman, 1965.

Novel

The Burnt-Out Marriage.   London, Nelson, and New York, Humanities Press, 1967.

*   *   *

With his unfailing sense of the comic potential in any situation, it seems likely that R. Sarif Easmon is, as Bernth Lindfors puts it, "the first African offspring of Oscar Wilde and Noël Coward." His witty urbane plays deal with the romance of politics and the politics of romance – two areas dear to the heart of an African audience – and they move with the grace of a dancer from one finely choreographed scene to the next.

There has been some criticism of the language used by Easmon's "upper class" characters, a pure Oxford English of the type which has proven so satisfying to a generation of word-conscious and Western-educated Africans. Yet when one sees one of Easmon's plays in production there is no doubt that the language is perfectly suited to both the personalities and the social positions of the characters. After all, not all Africans speak continually in proverbs. Moreover, when Easmon introduces characters from different social backgrounds he fits their speech to their class. One need only compare the words of Dauda Touray, the "parent and ogre" of Easmon's first play – "Our gratitude shall transcend champagne, Saidu!" – with those of the hired ruffian Charles Randall – "Lord 'ave mercy – Oh! For de name way me daddy and mammy gave me!" – to see the difference.

There is nothing stock about the characters in Easmon's delightful comedies. The two roguish politicians of his second play, *The New Patriots*, who are struggling for the hand of the same woman are as alive as Dauda Touray, the main character of *Dear Parent and Ogre*, yet they are not in any way a copy of the earlier character. Easmon's figures have unorthodox turns to their nature. Sekou, the young hero of *Dear Parent and Ogre*, is a son of a Yalie, a class given over to singing (quite literally) the praises of the noble Touray family, yet he has found success in Europe as a recording star and returned, replete with impeccable French and Rolls-Royce, to claim the hand of Dauda's daughter.

Because they deal with the themes of a new Africa, an Africa where the two suitors for a daughter's hand can be a descendant from former slaves on the one hand and from a lowly class of minstrels on the other, an Africa where champagne, moonlight, Joloff rice and hired thugs can be blended into a scene of high comedy, R. Sarif Easmon's plays have attracted large audiences whenever they have been performed in West Africa. Because Easmon manages, while developing these themes, to present us with vital human characters and situations which have larger universal implications, it seems safe to say that his appeal will not be limited to only African audiences in the future.

—Joseph Bruchac

EDGAR, David. British. Born in Birmingham, Warwickshire, 26 February 1948. Educated at Manchester University, 1966–69, B.A. (honours) in drama 1969. Reporter, *Telegraph and Argus*, Bradford, Yorkshire, 1969–72; Resident Playwright, Birmingham Repertory Theatre, 1974–75. Currently, Lecturer in Playwriting, Birmingham University; Vice-Chairman, Writers' Section, Association of Cinematographic, Television, and Allied Technicians. Creative Writing Fellow, Leeds University, 1972–74. Agent: Michael Imison, Dr. Jan Van Loewen Ltd., 81–83 Shaftesbury Avenue, London W1V 8BX, England.

PUBLICATIONS

Plays

Two Kinds of Angel (produced Bradford, 1970; London, 1971). London, Burnham House, 1975.
A Truer Shade of Blue (produced Bradford, 1970).
Still Life: Man in Bed (produced Edinburgh, 1971; London, 1972).
The National Interest (produced on tour, 1971).
Tedderella (produced Edinburgh, 1971; London, 1973).
The Rupert Show (produced on tour, 1971).
Bloody Rosa (produced Edinburgh, 1971).
The End (produced Bradford, 1972).
Excuses Excuses (produced Coventry, 1972; London, 1973).
Rent; or, Caught in the Act (produced on tour and London, 1972).
State of Emergency (produced on tour and London, 1972).

Death Story (produced Birmingham, 1972; New York and London, 1975).
Road to Hanoi (produced London, 1972).
England's Ireland, with others (produced Amsterdam and London, 1972).
A Fart for Europe, with Howard Brenton (produced London, 1973).
Gangsters (produced London, 1973).
Up Spaghetti Junction, with others (produced Birmingham, 1973).
Baby Love (produced Leeds and London, 1973).
The Case of the Workers' Plane (produced Bristol, 1973).
Operation Iskra (produced on tour and London, 1973).
Liberated Zone (produced Cardiff, 1973; London, 1974).
The Dunkirk Spirit (produced on tour, 1974).
Dick Deterred (produced London, 1974).   New York, Monthly Review Press, 1974.
The...Show (produced Bingley, Yorkshire, 1974).
Fired (produced Birmingham, 1975).
O Fair Jerusalem (produced Birmingham, 1975).
Summer Sports (produced Birmingham and London, 1975).
The National Theatre (produced London, 1975).
Events Following the Closure of a Motorcycle Factory (produced Birmingham, 1976).
Destiny (produced Stratford upon Avon, 1976).   London, Methuen, 1976.
Blood Sports (produced London, 1976).
Saigon Rose (produced Edinburgh, 1976).

Television Plays: *The Eagle Has Landed*, 1973; *I Know What I Meant*, 1974; *Midas Connection*, 1975.

David Edgar comments:

There has been, in Britain, a deep-seated prejudice against political work. This is partly because of a general prejudice against politics ("politically-motivated" is, strangely, a pejorative), but also because of the particular class nature of the British theatre which has only recently started paying even lip-service to the idea of breaking down the barriers that keep working-class people out of the theatre. The stranglehold of middle-class themes performed by middle-class actors to middle-class audiences is still round our necks.

Radicals in the theatre must take account of this situation. Deliberately, the new Theatre must be almost everything the old Theatre is not. It must be serious in content, but accessible in form. It must be popular without being populist. It must be orientated towards a working-class audience. It must be temporary, immediate, specific, functional. It must get out of theatre buildings. It must be ideological, and proud of it. It must be celebratory (try to convince the Catholic Church that there's no function in "preaching to the converted"!). It must not be escapist; it must take our times by the throat.

I've tried to be some of these things in my work. A lot of its has been immediate and self-destructive, plays about current events that die with the events they portray. These have ranged from what I hope were serious and complex treatments of contemporary events (plays with the General Will, *The Case of the Workers' Plane* and *Events Following the Closure of a Motorcycle Factory*), to large scale comic parodies (*Tedderella* and *Dick Deterred*). I've also written straight plays for theatre and television, some on contemporary social themes (*Baby Love* and *Excuses Excuses*, both about types of social deviancy), and some theatre-plays on more general political themes (*Death Story* and *O Fair Jerusalem*).

My and other people's work in this field demonstrates that there are still huge problems. New styles have been found, but the progress towards finding new audiences is painfully slow. Writers, actors, and directors have realised that the central artistic problem is portraying people's behaviour as a function of their social nexus rather than individual psychology (and that's important); but the way of solving that problem is still far from clear.

But I hope that theatre workers in Britain have realised finally the untruth of perhaps the most famour post-war theatrical statements – that there is not "nothing to be done," there is in fact a lot to do, and it's time people set about doing it, in the Arts and in the society of which they are, whether they like it or not, an essential part.

* * *

David Edgar's plays have a brisk, brutal immediacy, as befits a playwright who started his career as a journalist. He is a prolific writer whose works have an economy and efficiency about them that derives from his experience of writing to strict deadlines.

His best work has been overtly political, around some topical theme – *The National Interest, Rent; or, Caught in the Act,* and *State of Emergency* (all for the General Will theatre company) and, more recently, *Dick Deterred* (about Nixon and Watergate) and *I Know What I Meant,* a TV play about Nixon and his self-destructive tapes (with Nicol Williamson as a memorably guilt-ridden President). *The National Interest* and *State of Emergency* were witty and polemical revues about the then Tory Government's crude and clumsy attempts to best the miners and other recalcitrant workers through such devices as the Industrial Relations Act and direct confrontation – while *Rent; or, Caught in the Act* was written as a Victorian melodrama and exposed the evil effects of private landlordism. *Dick Deterred* drew with a great deal of panache the obvious dramatic parallels between Nixon and an earlier Richard beset with troubles largely of his own making. In all the plays so far mentioned, Edgar's dramatic method has been essentially the same – a massive amount of research, which is then edited and arranged with a great sense of precision and effectiveness.

But Edgar also has another, more reflective, style, which was shown to its best effect in two plays that were performed at the Soho Poly, *Gangsters* and *Baby Love. Gangsters* was about three bank robbers, left over from the 1940's, whose exploits and methods are subtly shown to be dated in the 1970's of motorways and automatic machines. *Baby Love* is an intensely moving extended study in depth of a girl who battered her baby to death, the social, psychological and emotional pressures on her, and the efforts of various psychiatrists and probation officers to "help" her.

Edgar has also collaborated with Howard Brenton on an anti-EEC play called *A Fart for Europe* and the Portable Theatre's production of *England's Ireland.* His main dramatic style can best be described as "socialist polemicist," and this is seen to good effect in his latest work *Events Following the Closure of a Motorcycle Factory,* based on the attempts to close the Triumph Meriden factory at Coventry. In a recent interview in *Workers News,* he summed up his own philosophy of theatre thus: "The growth of political theatre since 1968 has been very encouraging. It was easier under the Tories but it becomes more complex with a Labour government. Images can often convey far more than the written word. I believe the political theatre has an important role to play as an element in working-class campaigns."

—Jonathan Hammond

EGBUNA, Obi (Benedict). Nigerian. Born in 1938. Lives in Nigeria. Address: c/o Oxford University Press, 37 Dover Street, London W1X 4AH, England.

PUBLICATIONS

Plays

The Anthill.   London and New York, Oxford University Press, 1965.
Wind Versus Polygamy (broadcast, 1966; produced Dakar, 1966).
Theatre of Power (produced Copenhagen, 1969).
The Agony (produced London, 1970).

Radio Plays: Divinity, 1965; Wind Versus Polygamy, 1966; Daughters of the Sun, 1970.

Novel

Wind Versus Polygamy: Where "Wind" Is the "Wind of Change" and "Polygamy" Is
the "Change of Eves."   London, Faber, 1964.

Short Stories

Daughters of the Sun and Other Stories.   London, Oxford University Press, 1970.
Emperor of the Sea and Other Stories.   London, Fontana, 1974.

Other

Destroy This Temple: The Voice of Black Power in Britian.   London, MacGibbon and
Kee, and New York, Morrow, 1971.
Menace of the Hedgehog.   London, Barrie and Jenkins, 1973.

*   *   *

Although Obi Egbuna's efforts as a dramatist include a number of radio dramas and a play entitled *Wind Versus Polygamy*, his light and frothy comedy *The Anthill* remains the only drama which he has published as such, his earlier works having been rewritten into short stories and a novel. It seems that Egbuna has chosen well, for of all his dramatic works *The Anthill* seems to be the most entertaining and the best constructed, displaying the sort of witty comedy which has made Wilde's *The Importance of Being Earnest* a perennial favorite.

In his tale of a young African painter, Bobo, who for some reason paints only anthills, Egbuna draws a number of characters (all of whom, except for Bobo, are British and White) who are just substantial enough to interest us and just stock enough to be taken less than seriously – which is necessary in any comedy which centers around a series of deaths, two real and one pretended. Even the landlady mother of the young British soldier, Tommy, who dies from a heart attack when confronted by Bobo, does not seem to be overly disturbed by her own son's death. She is more concerned that people admire her appendix, which she keeps in a jar on her mantel.

Egbuna presents us with a full house of coincidences – that the policeman who visits their room just happens to be the father of the girl who has matrimonial intentions on Bobo's friend Nigel, that Tommy dies because Bobo resembles a young African whose death Tommy caused while stationed in Tongo (Bobo's home country), that Bobo is the deceased African's twin brother, and so on. But such coincidences are as in keeping with this kind of frolic as are the puns, which flow fast and freely. The verdict of the judge that Tommy's death was his own fault – "All young British soldiers must behave like English gentlemen at home and abroad. Under no circumstances must you kill a man to whom you are not properly introduced" – is the perfect sort of climax to a story which another writer might have turned into a heavy-handed tragedy.

Underneath it all, of course, there is a deep undercurrent of seriousness. Comedy is the other side of the mask of tragedy. Egbuna himself is a serious writer – as his recent book, essays written while locked in an English prison, indicates. His other plays have dealt with the conflict between tribal ways and Christianity and the resultant agonies in the hearts of young men who are the sons of Christian Africans but advocates of Black Power themselves. When Egbuna has Bobo describe himself as "a typical Tongolese gentleman...a dedicated vindicator of African personality and I've got my Anglo-Saxon political and academic titles to prove it," the laughter is as bitter as it is sweet.

—Joseph Bruchac

ELDER, Lonne, III.   American.   Born in Americus, Georgia, 26 December 1931. Attended Yale University School of Drama, New Haven, Connecticut (John Hay Whitney Fellowship, and American Broadcasting Company Television Writing Fellowship, 1965–66; John Golden Fellowship, and Joseph E. Levine Fellowship in film-making, 1967). Served in the United States Army. Married Judith Ann Johnson in 1969; has two sons. Has worked as docker, a waiter, and a professional gambler. Coordinator of the Playwrights-Directors Unit, Negro Ensemble Company, New York, 1967–69; Writer, Talent Associates, New York, 1968; Writer/Producer, Cinema Center Films, Hollywood, 1969–70; Writer, Universal Pictures, Hollywood, 1970–71; Writer, Radnitz/Mattel Productions, Hollywood, 1971; Writer/Producer, Talent Associates, Hollywood, 1971; Writer, MGM Pictures and Columbia Pictures, Hollywood, 1972. Recipient: Stanley Drama Award, 1965; American National Theatre Academy Award, 1967; Outer Circle Award, 1970; Vernon Rice Award, 1970; Stella Holt Memorial Playwrights Award, 1970. Address: c/o New American Library, Box 120, Bergenfeld, New Jersey 07621, U.S.A.

PUBLICATIONS

Plays

> *Ceremonies in Dark Old Men* (produced New York, 1965; revised version produced New York, 1969).   New York, Farrar Straus, 1969.
> *Charades on East 4th Street* (produced Montreal, 1967).   Published in *Black Drama Anthology*, edited by Woodie King and Ron Milner, New York, New American Library, 1971.

Screenplays: *Sounder*, 1972; *Melinda*, 1972.

Television Plays: *Camera 3* series, 1963; *The Terrible Veil*, 1964; *NYPD* series, 1968; *McCloud* series, 1970–71.

Manuscript Collection: Boston University

Theatrical Activities:

Actor: **Plays** – Bob in *A Raisin in the Sun* by Lorraine Hansberry, New York, 1959; Clem in *Days of Absence* by Douglas Turner Ward, New York, 1965.

*   *   *

Lonne Elder III, an American Negro playwright, has involved himself in a sufficient variety of activities that his own career might serve as the subject of a drama. Born in Georgia, he has spent most of his life in New York and New Jersey, where he has supported himself by working on the docks, waiting tables, gambling professionally, and promoting political causes. Under the influence of Douglas Turner Ward, he abandoned interest in writing poetry and fiction to concentrate on drama.

The author of several stage plays, Elder has gained attention for the one-act *Charades on East 4th Street*, commissioned by New York City's Mobilization for Youth Inc., which was performed at Expo 67 in Montreal. A thesis drama, *Charades* urges young blacks to combat the oppression of corrupt police by legal means rather than by violence. Elder's best known stage drama, however, is *Ceremonies in Dark Old Men*, which was produced professionally in 1969 by the Negro Ensemble Company of New York City.

Elder, like Ward, articulates an argument of many Afro-American dramatists that, in order to develop fully as artists in professional theatre, they must be able to write for an audience sympathetic towards and informed about Negro life. Without the existence of such an audience, black dramatists are denied opportunity by producers who, believing that most American theatre-goers are indifferent or hostile to serious drama about Negroes, will risk money only on exotic or sensational presentations. Black dramatists are further restricted if they must write for an audience which, ignorant of actual Negro life, evaluates Afro-American plays according to their fidelity to clichés and false stereotypes. Like the serious white American playwright, the argument continues, the black dramatist desires to test his skill in revealing the nuances, the subtleties, and the complexities of the life he knows; he resents any effort to require him instead to write a primer for beginning readers.

Although his works have been presented before interracial groups, Elder has written them with the assumption that his audience is empathetic and informed. In *Ceremonies in Dark Old Men*, for instance, Elder did not follow the pattern of many Negro dramatists who write for uninformed, white audiences. Although he wrote *Ceremonies* in the midst of a period in which Afro-Americans actively crusaded for their rights as citizens, Elder did not plead the justice of their cause, nor did he capitalize upon the sensationalism of black-white confrontations. Unlike some of his contemporaries, he did not seek to promote integration by suggesting that his characters were identical to white Americans except for skin color. On the other hand, he did not try to exaggerate the differences between his characters and other Americans. Instead, he artistically created the story of the Parkers, a Negro family enervated by individual weaknesses and by a collective sense of the inability of Negroes to prosper in a white-oriented society.

The mother of the family has died from overwork. The father, Russell B. Parker, a former vaudeville entertainer, hides from the world while he relives the transitory successes of his earlier life. Theo, an academically talented son, has stopped attending school because he believes that education does not benefit black Americans; he hides in dreams of becoming an artist. A second son, Bobby, is a petty thief. The only full-time worker in the family, Adele, the daughter, bolsters her self-image of strength by complaining that she is the financial support of the family. Nevertheless, her failure to accept a challenge to leave the family reveals that her own insecurities cause her to prefer to cling to a crumbling household rather than face the responsibilities of an independent life outside the home.

When Adele Parker insists that the three males secure jobs, her father is forced to admit to himself that years of humiliation by whites when he was a performer have rendered him psychologically incapable of re-experiencing such humiliation as an employee. The family is further weakened by its decision to participate in a scheme to secure money by exploiting and defrauding the black community. Encouraged by having money to spend, Russell Parker seeks his lost youth in a young girl who eventually betrays him for a younger man. As the play ends, Parker, deaf to the reality that his son Bobby has been killed while attempting robbery, rejoices in his first victory in the checkers games which he has regularly lost to a friend.

—Darwin T. Turner

ENGLAND, Barry. British.   Born in London, 16 March 1934. Educated at Downside School, Bath. Served in the British Army, 1950–52. Married Diane Dirsztay in 1967; has one son and one daughter. Actor in provincial repertory companies, films, and television. Recipient: Arts Council grant; Author's Club Award, 1968. Agent: Patricia Macnaughton, M.L.R., 194 Old Brompton Road, London SW5 0AS, England.

PUBLICATIONS

Plays

End of Conflict (produced Coventry, 1961).   London, Evans, 1964.
The Big Contract (produced Coventry, 1963).
The Damn Givers (produced Coventry, 1964).
Conduct Unbecoming (produced Bristol and London, 1969; New York, 1970). London, Heinemann, and New York, French, 1971.

Television Plays: *The Sweet War Man*, 1966; *The Move after Checkmate*, 1966; *An Experience of Evil*, 1966; *You'll Know Me by the Stars in My Eyes*, 1966; *The Man Who Understood Women*, 1967.

Novel

Figures in a Landscape.   London, Cape, and New York, Random House, 1968.

Barry England comments:

I am a story-teller. I revere economy and precision.

*   *   *

Barry England is best known for one play, *Conduct Unbecoming*. The play's well-deserved success was no doubt partly due to its unfashionably gripping story, with some help perhaps from its fashionable period setting – British India in the 1880's – and its dashing red uniforms. But although England's approach to his subject-matter is a little reminiscent of the equally unfashionable Rattigan's in *The Winslow Boy* in that he treats a moral conflict in

241

which there is little doubt from the outset who is right and who is wrong, *Conduct Unbecoming* is more than a simple moral tract as it is more than a thriller.

England's dramatic method is that of "putting the screws on." The dramatist chooses a completely enclosed situation, fills it with mutually conflicting characters and then deftly tightens the situation until the pips squeak. In the form of plotting, this method is inevitably an ingredient in almost every sort of play. But it is a question of where the weight of the play finally rests. Do the characters, the stage images, the philosophical, political or social themes spill over the framework and more or less conceal it? Are they subservient to it, as in farces, thrillers and court-room dramas? Or almost miraculously created from it, as in Racine or middle-period Ibsen?

It is quite difficult to decide where the weight falls in *Conduct Unbecoming*. An image such as the pig-sticking episode in the second scene makes a most powerful impression in its own right, but loses force for being meticulously absorbed into the the final twists of the plot: there is not enough left over to expand in the mind of the audience. For all the subtlety and unexpectedness of the characters, the plot never ceases to contain them, and its neat finish seems to put them away in a box and shut the lid on them. As for England's theme, it is so much part and parcel of his method that one must ask whether he has chosen the method to explore the theme or the theme to suit the method.

His earlier plays *End of Conflict* and *The Damn Givers* argue for the primacy of the theme. *End of Conflict* is another army play, set in the New Territories of China at the time of the Korean War. Like *Conduct Unbecoming* its situation arises from the introduction of a new officer into the Mess. Its plotting is looser than that of the later play, but its theme is almost identical – the clash of an individual, still experimental code of behaviour with a traditional, collective code. For all its apparent rigidity, the army's code is shown to be flexible enough to allow good men to behave well. Indeed in *End of Conflict* the real hero is not the liberal-minded rebel who causes disaster by his inexperienced good intentions, but the liberal-minded and experienced conformist. In *Conduct Unbecoming* this clash and its outcome are more complex, but again it is the officer with "bourgeois principles" of honour who triumphs, saving the rebel from himself at the same time as restoring a true sense of honour to the regiment, whose collective pride and inflexibility had corrupted it.

The Damn Givers is a much less convincing piece, perhaps because a group of pleasure-loving socialites makes a less coherent collective than a regiment. The misfit here is a young sex-starved academic and the clash is between his awakened idea of lasting love – after he has slept with the voracious Lady Jane Moore-Fuller-Bracke – and the collective's idea of sex as one pleasure among others to be taken on the trot. England's own lack of conviction in this variation on his basic theme seems to be reflected both in the shadowy characters and the too predictable plot.

Nevertheless, it does seem clear that England's theme comes first. Because it is well defined – there is no suggestion of the infinite perplexities of life beyond the enclosed societies England studies – it is almost perfectly served by a tightly-geared plot. The characters too are emanations of the theme, in the sense that their passions stop at discovering the honourable mode of conduct within a given set of rules. But since, at least in the setting of an officers' Mess in the heyday of the British Raj such people are entirely credible, they can develop an individuality well beyond the limitations of the morality or the cliffhanger. The real strength of *Conduct Unbecoming* is in its delicately orchestrated character-studies. One would like to see what England could do with a contemporary story – there are after all plenty of enclosed collectives to choose from.

—John Spurling

EVELING, (Harry) Stanley. British. Born in Newcastle upon Tyne, Northumberland, 4 August 1925. Educated at Durham University (William Black Noble Student, 1950–51), B.A. (honours) in English 1950, B.A. (honours) in philosophy 1953; Lincoln College, Oxford, D.Phil. 1955. Served in the Durham Light Infantry, 1944–47. Assistant Lecturer, Department of Logic and Metaphysics, King's College, University of Aberdeen, 1955–57; Lecturer, Department of Philosophy, University College of Wales, Aberystwyth, 1957–60. Since 1960, Senior Lecturer in Philosophy, University of Edinburgh. Recipient: Earl Grey Fellowship, 1955. Agent: Harvey Unna Ltd., 14 Beaumont Mews, Marylebone High Street, London W1N 4HE, England. Address: 30 Comely Bank, Edinburgh EH4 1AS, Scotland.

PUBLICATIONS

Plays

The Balachites (produced Edinburgh, 1963). Included in The Balachites and The Strange Case of Martin Richter, 1970.

An Unspeakable Crime (produced London, 1963).

Come and Be Killed (produced Edinburgh, 1967; London, 1968). Included in Come and Be Killed and Dear Janet Rosenberg, Dear Mr. Kooning, 1971.

The Strange Case of Martin Richter (produced Glasgow, 1967; London, 1968). Included in The Balachites and The Strange Case of Martin Richter, 1970.

The Lunatic, The Secret Sportsman, and the Woman Next Door (produced Edinburgh, 1968; London, 1969). Included in The Lunatic, The Secret Sportsman, and the Woman Next Door, and Vibrations, 1970.

Dear Janet Rosenberg, Dear Mr. Kooning, and Jakey Fat Boy (produced Edinburgh and London, 1969; New York, 1970). Included in Come and Be Killed and Dear Janet Rosenberg, Dear Mr. Kooning, 1971.

Vibrations (produced Edinburgh, 1969; London, 1972). Included in The Lunatic, The Secret Sportsman, and the Woman Next Door, and Vibrations, 1970.

Dracula, with others (produced Edinburgh, 1969; London, 1973).

Mister (produced Edinburgh, 1970; London, 1971). London, Calder and Boyars, 1972.

The Balachites and The Strange Case of Martin Richter. London, Calder and Boyars, 1970.

The Lunatic, The Secret Sportsman, and the Woman Next Door, and Vibrations. London, Calder and Boyers, 1970.

Better Days, Better Knights (produced Edinburgh, 1971; London, 1972).

Our Sunday Times (produced Edinburgh and London, 1971).

Oh Starlings (produced Edinburgh, 1971). Published in Plays and Players (London), March 1971.

Sweet Alice (produced Edinburgh, 1971). Published in Plays and Players (London), March 1971.

The Laughing Cavalier (produced London, 1971).

Come and Be Killed, and Dear Janet Rosenberg, Dear Mr. Kooning (includes Jakey Fat Boy). London, Calder and Boyars, 1971.

He Used to Play for Hearts, in Christmas Present (produced Edinburgh, 1971).

Caravaggio, Buddy (produced Edinburgh, 1972).

Union Jack (and Bonzo) (produced Edinburgh and London, 1973).

Shivvers (produced London, 1974).

The Dead of Night (produced Edinburgh, 1975).

Radio Plays: Dance ti Thy Daddy, 1964; The Timepiece, 1965; A Man Like That, 1966;

The Devil in Summer, with Kate Eveling, 1971; *The Queen's Own*, 1976.

Television Play: *Ishmael*, 1973.

Verse

(Poems).   Oxford, Fantasy Press, 1956.

*   *   *

Stanley Eveling is a prolific and at first sight a somewhat baffling playwright: he writes in a variety of styles and almost always adopts a veiled, even blurred approach to his subject-matter. But although he is a professional moral philosopher as well as a playwright and although his characters often involve themselves in philosophical argument and speculation, his plays are by no means intellectual, in the sense of being elaborately constructed to act as working-models of some abstract thesis. Eveling's approach is veiled not because he is hiding the machinery, but on the contrary because he himself seems to write in the act of watching the machinery at work; he sits almost painfully close to the characters, feels them rather than thinks them, and uses one style or another, as he might use one stage or another, as at most a temporary accommodation for his stubborn and chaotic material.

This material is presented in its simplest versions in the two plays *Come and Be Killed* and *Dear Janet Rosenberg, Dear Mr. Kooning*. The first concerns an abortion, the second an abortive relationship between an ageing novelist and his female fan. The muddled, narrowly confined, squalid situations in which the characters find themselves in both plays are compounded by their own muddled, limited and selfish reactions. "You're not wicked, you're just ignorant," says one character to another in *Come and Be Killed*: this might be a motto for all Eveling's work. Creation in general is messy, cruel, blind, and the lords of creation are no more and no less: in *The Balachites*, Eveling shows a pair of innocents, a modern Adam and Eve, corrupted not by Satan but by the ghosts of dead men; in his nearest thing to an "absurdist" play *The Lunatic, The Secret Sportsman, and the Woman Next Door* he shows the pathetic innocence of mental and sexual aberration.

Naturally the idea of there being such creatures as "heroes" in such a world is a fruitful source of still further pain and confusion. The story of Donald Crowhurst, who made it appear that he was winning the *Sunday Times* single-handed yacht race round the world, but turned out to have disappeared, almost certainly overboard, without ever having sailed beyond the Atlantic, forms the basis of Eveling's play *Our Sunday Times*. But he extends the story, as the title implies, to cover a much more widespread form of bogus heroism, of cheaply-brought superiority over trivial circumstances, the vicarious act of reading newspapers or watching television. The play's effect is weakened by this attempt at generalisation; Eveling steps back too far from his characters. But *Mister*, in which he again treats a would-be sailor-hero, the owner of an antique-shop who acts out his fantasy of being Lord Nelson, with the unfortunate complication of having a Lady Hamilton on the premises who is not content with a sexual relationship confined to fantasy, is perhaps Eveling's best play. It is certainly his saddest and funniest, his finest example of what Janet Rosenberg calls "the curious mixture of farce and misery which is the slight ripple left by the receding impulse of tragedy."

Nevertheless, although Eveling's dramatic outlook is on the whole more sad than angry, reminiscent of those world-weary but intermittently kindly doctors in Chekhov's plays, he has written at least one play in which the mixture of farce and misery is replaced by that of savage humour and despair. In *The Strange Case of Martin Richter*, a German industrialist employs three ex-Nazis as household servants, not realising or not caring what this means for his butler, who is of "Swebish" origin and whose father was murdered during the Third Reich for being "Swebish." The butler's solution is to pretend that he himself was a prominent Nazi, claim acquaintance with Hitler, constitute himself "Leader" of a neo-Nazi party and pretend to eliminate the industrialist for being "Swebish." The play ends, after several twists of fortune and a marvellously composed drunken party, with everything as it was, the industrialist once more on top of the evil heap. *Martin Richter* is the nearest thing in Eveling's work to a straight political and moral fable. It is compact and clear, a powerful and bitterly comic outcry against the nastiness, brutishness and shortness of human life.

His recent plays – *Shivvers, Caravaggio, Buddy* and *The Dead of Night* – all deal with suicide in one form or another. The central character of *Shivvers*, having for a time assuaged his own sense of guilt by imposing vicious behaviour on a vicar and a whore, commits suicide when they shake off his domination. *Caravaggio, Buddy* is an ambitious comic fantasy – an episodic quest play somewhat reminiscent of *Peer Gynt* – whose hero fails in many attempts to commit suicide and ends up reconciled with society. The play's complex and carefully controlled shifts of style establish in dramatic rather than intellectual terms the reality and humanity of the misfit as against the unreality and inhumanity of the "organised." It is full of delightful comic inventions, such as the colloquy between Buddy and a Yeti on the slopes of Mount Everest, while just off-stage innumerable international expeditions make more or less disastrous assaults on the summit. *The Dead of Night* is a sombre piece – enlivened by a German general trying to disguise himself as a woman – set beside Hitler's bunker in Berlin and featuring the arch-suicide himself.

All three plays show Eveling sharpening his lines and clarifying his construction without losing his closeness to the characters. His themes remain the same, but his methods of exploring them are growing more precise and versatile.

—John Spurling

EYEN, Tom. American. Born in Cambridge, Ohio, 14 August 1941. Educated at Ohio State University, Columbus, 1957–61, B.A. in English 1961; American Academy of Dramatic Arts, New York, 1961–62. Married to Liza Giraudoux. Taught drama for Metropolitan Television Arts, New York, 1962; also worked as a publicity agent. Founder, Theatre of the Eye (affiliated with the La Mama group), New York, 1965; Director, sometimes under the pseudonym of Jerome Eyen or Roger Short, Jr. Recipient: Rockefeller grant, 1967; Guggenheim Fellowship, 1970. Agent: Bridget Aschenberg, International Creative Management, 40 West 57th Street, New York, New York 10019. Address: 41 Fifth Avenue, New York, New York 10003, U.S.A.

PUBLICATIONS

Plays

The White Whore and the Bit Player (produced New York, 1964; London, 1970). Included in *Sarah B. Divine! and Other Plays*, 1971.
Frustrata, The Dirty Little Girl with the Paper Rose Stuck in Her Head, Is Demented (produced New York, 1964).
My Next Husband Will Be a Beauty (produced New York, 1964). Included in *Sarah B. Divine! and Other Plays*, 1971.
Court (produced New York, 1965).
Why Hannah's Skirt Won't Stay Down (produced New York, 1965; London, 1970). Included in *Sarah B. Divine! and Other Plays*, 1971.

Can You See a Prince?, music by Bill Elliott (produced New York, 1965).
The Last Great Cocktail Party (produced New York, 1965).
The Demented World of Tom Eyen (produced New York, 1965).
Cinderella Revisited, music by Bill Elliott (produced New York, 1965).
Miss Nefertiti Regrets, music by Tom Eyen and Ilene Berson (produced New York, 1965).
Give My Regards to Off-Off-Broadway (produced New York, 1966; second edition, produced New York, 1966).
Sarah B. Divine!, music by Jonathan Kramer (produced Spoleto, Italy, 1967; London, 1973).   Included in *Sarah B. Divine! and Other Plays*, 1971.
Grand Tenement/November 22nd (produced New York, 1967).   Included in *Sarah B. Divine! and Other Plays*, 1971.
When Johnny Comes Dancing Home Again (produced New York, 1968).
The Kama Sutra [An Organic Happening] (produced New York, 1968).   Included in *Sarah B. Divine! and Other Plays*, 1971.
Who Killed My Bald Sister Sophie? (produced New York, 1968).   Included in *Sarah B. Divine! and Other Plays*, 1971.
Alice Through a Glass Lightly, music by Jonathan Kramer (produced New York, 1968).
Caution: A Love Story (produced New York, 1969).
4 Noh Plays (produced New York, 1969).
Lana Got Laid in Lebanon (produced New York, 1970).
Gertrude Stein and Other Great Men (produced New York, 1970).
Aretha in the Ice Palace; or, The Fully Guaranteed Fuck-Me Doll (produced New York, 1970; London, 1973).   Included in *Sarah B. Divine! and Other Plays*, 1971.
What Is Making Gilda So Gray? (produced New York, 1970).   Included in *Sarah B. Divine! and Other Plays*, 1971.
The Dirtiest Show in Town (produced New York, 1970; London, 1971).
Sarah B. Divine! and Other Plays (includes *Three Sisters from Springfield, Illinois*: I. *Why Hannah's Skirt Won't Stay Down*, II. *Who Killed My Bald Sister Sophie?*, III. *What Is Making Gilda So Gray?*; *Aretha in the Ice Palace*; *The Kama Sutra [An Organic Happening]*; *My Next Husband Will Be a Beauty*; *The Death of Off-Broadway [A Street Play]*; *The White Whore and the Bit Player*; *Grand Tenement/November 22nd*).   New York, Winter House, 1971.
Rachel Lily Rosenbloom and Don't You Ever Forget It, with Paul Jabara, music by Paul Jabara (also director: produced New York, 1973).
Ms. Nefertiti (also director: produced New York, 1973).
2008 1/2: A Spaced Oddity, music by Gary William Friedman (also director: produced New York, 1974).
Women Behind Bars (produced New York, 1974).   New York, French, 1975.

Television Plays: *Mary Hartman, Mary Hartman* series, 1976.

Theatrical Activities:

Director: **Plays** – most of his own plays.

*   *   *

Tom Eyen has perfected a unique style in which often corny, emotionally grotesque material is combined with sharply satirical humor and presented in a form that leaps about in time and space with great dexterity and ingenuity. For over a decade he has kept together a loose company of actors, the Theatre of the Eye, with himself as director. One of his characteristic themes has been the confrontation between the older, neurotic, sexually vivacious woman and the passive, narcissistic younger man. Beneath the often crass, brazenly trashy tone of most of the plays and their commitment to being entertaining at all costs is a sorrowing, even bitter view of the world and a deep compassion for its victims. Eyen's characters are lonely, reaching out to others with a desperation that usually frightens them away.

Why Hannah's Skirt Won't Stay Down is set in the "fun house" at Coney Island, where Hannah gets her thrills by standing over the air hole and Arizona, a handsome, vapid young man, admires himself in the multiple mirrors. Hannah lives alone and works as the cashier in a sleazy movie theatre, and the two of them make some contact through their fantasies. Hannah reappears in other Eyen plays including *Who Killed My Bald Sister Sophie?*, the story of a door-to-door cosmetics saleswoman.

Like many of his contemporaries, Eyen uses the Hollywood myths he grew up with as a basic imaginative resource. *The White Whore and the Bit Player*, an early work, explores the mind of a woman who was groomed by a movie studio for stardom and then relegated to bit parts. The play shows the woman as two, the beautiful, apparently virginal young woman whoring after fame, and her older self, dressed as a nun but crazy and corrupt within. The play occurs at the moment of her death and moves in a virtuoso flashback through the tragedy of her life. Eyen has staged the play in several versions. He has worked on several of his plays this way, rewriting and refining them through different presentations. Another preoccupation has been manifest in plays about famous people, including the Duke and Duchess of Windsor, Sarah Bernhardt, Lady Bird Johnson, and Santa Claus. Several of his plays have incorporated songs, and one of his projects is an entertainment to star the popular singer Tina Turner.

Eyen's greatest popular success so far is *The Dirtiest Show in Town*. The title is ironic, but then so is the whole show. In part a satirical response to the sex-oriented shows featuring nude actors that were prevalent in New York for a couple of seasons, it also was one of them. Its themes were sex and environmental pollution, but the presentation was strikingly bright and clean. The stage was all white, and the actors, wholesome looking, beautiful young men and women, were dressed all in white when not nude. The play substituted charm for Eyen's usual intensity of feeling, but its brilliance lay in his remarkable skill in creating multiple fictional realities and moving among them with exhilarating speed and freedom.

—Michael Smith

FEIFFER, Jules.   American.   Born in the Bronx, New York, 26 January 1929. Educated at the Arts Students League, New York, 1946; Pratt Institute, New York, 1947–48, 1949–51. Served as a cartoon animator in the United States Army Signal Corps, 1951–53. Married Judith Sheftel in 1961; has one child. Assistant to the cartoonist Will Eisner, 1946–51; drew cartoon *Clifford*, 1949–51; free-lance cartoonist and artist, 1951–56. Since 1956, Cartoonist, *Village Voice*, New York, and since 1959 syndicated in other newspapers and magazines. Faculty Member, Yale University Drama School, New Haven, Connecticut, 1973–74. Recipient: Academy Award, for cartoon, 1961; George Polk Memorial Award, 1962; London Theatre Critics Award, 1968; Obie Award, 1968; Outer Circle Award, 1969. Address: c/o Publishers-Hall Syndicate, 30 East 42nd Street, New York, New York, U.S.A.

PUBLICATIONS

Plays

The Explainers (produced Chicago, 1961; New York, 1964).
Crawling Arnold (produced Spoleto and London, 1961).   Published in *Best Short Plays of the World, 1958–1967*, edited by Stanley Richards, New York, Crown, 1968.
Little Murders (produced New Haven, Connecticut, 1966; London and New York, 1967).   New York, Random House, 1968; London, Faber 1970.
The Unexpurgated Memoirs of Bernard Mergendeiler (produced Los Angeles, 1967; New York, 1968; Glasgow, 1969; London, 1972).   Published in *Collision Course*, New York, Random House, 1968.
God Bless (produced New Haven, Connecticut, and London, 1968).
Feiffer's People. (produced Edinburgh and London, 1968; Los Angeles, 1971).
Dick and Jane, in *Oh! Calcutta!* (produced New York, 1969; London, 1970).   New York, Grove Press, 1970.
The White House Murder Case (produced New York, 1970).   New York, Grove Press, 1970.
Carnal Knowledge: A Screenplay.   New York, Farrar Straus, and London, Cape, 1971.
Watergate Classics, with others (produced New Haven, Connecticut, 1973).
Knock, Knock (produced New York, 1976).   New York, Hill and Wang, 1976.

Screenplays: *Munro* (animated cartoon), 1961; *Carnal Knowledge*, 1971; *Little Murders*, 1972.

Television Play: *VD Blues*, with others, 1972.

Novel

Harry, The Rat with Women.   New York, McGraw Hill, and London, Collins, 1963.

Other

Sick, Sick, Sick.   New York, McGraw Hill, 1958; London, Collins, 1959.
Passionella and Other Stories.   New York, McGraw Hill, 1959; London, Collins, 1960.
The Explainers.   New York, McGraw Hill, 1960; London, Collins, 1961.
Boy, Girl. Boy, Girl.   New York, Random House, 1961; London, Collins, 1962.
Hold Me!   New York, Random House, 1963.
Feiffer's Album.   New York, Random House, 1963.
The Unexpurgated Memoirs of Bernard Mergendeiler.   New York, Random House, 1965; London, Collins, 1966.
The Penguin Feiffer.   London, Penguin, 1966.
Feiffer on Civil Rights.   New York, Anti-Defamation League of B'nai B'rith, 1966.
Feiffer's Marriage Manual.   New York, Random House, 1967.
Pictures at a Prosecution: Drawings and Text from the Chicago Conspiracy Trial.   New York, Grove Press, 1971.
Feiffer on Nixon: The Cartoon Conspiracy.   New York, Random House, 1974.

Editor, *The Great Comic Book Heroes*.   New York, Dial Press, 1965; London, Allan Lane The Penguin Press, 1967.

*   *   *

Jules Feiffer is, first of all, a cartoonist. Long before he began to write plays, he had made a reputation as a satirist with an uncanny knack for catching the psychological, social and political clichés which are the refuge and the cross of the college-educated middle class that provides him with an audience as well as a subject matter. His talent has always been as much verbal as visual; his ear as good as his hand. His cartoons are ordinarily strips in which two characters pursue a conversation, panel by panel, until the congenial platitudes dissolve into open aggression, naked greed, impotence, ineffectuality, pain; a variation is the strip in which a single figure — I almost said performer — speaks directly to the reader. The line between this kind of cartoon and the revue sketch is a narrow one, and a great many of Feiffer's early cartoons have crossed that line. Most of the material in *Feiffer's People*, a collection of brief solo or duo bits subtitled "Sketches and Observations," presumably began as cartoon dialogue. Even those short works written for the theatre — *Dick and Jane*, the Feiffer sketch from *Oh! Calcutta!*, or the early one-actor *Crawling Arnold* — seem little more than extended cartoons with the stage directions standing in for the drawing.

Inevitably, Feiffer's full-length plays, *Little Murders* and *The White House Murder Case*, and his screenplay *Carnal Knowledge* have been viewed — and condemned in some cases — as the work of a cartoonist. There is justice in the viewing, if not in the condemnation, for — as so often with satirists — Feiffer works in terms of stereotypes, of those figures identified by a single idiosyncrasy or a pattern of related compulsions. Even the two young men in *Carnal Knowledge* are societal types rather than psychological studies, although the labels by which we identify them may be written in the kind of psychological language that one expects to find in the balloons of Feiffer's cartoons. Feiffer tends to see his figures as more realistic than my description suggests. Just before the off-Broadway revival of *Little Murders*, Feiffer told an interviewer (*New York Times*, 26 January 1969) that his characters "are very, very real to me. I care about them as people." Yet, elsewhere in the same interview, he identified the family in the play as "a nice, Andy Hardy type family," and the Hardy family films were straight stereotype. If we read *real* in the Feiffer quotation as *true* — that is, identifiable — then the characters are real, as Andy Hardy is, as the figures in his cartoons are; we look at them and say, *oh, yes, I know him*, meaning, *oh, yes, I know the type*. The concern in the second sentence of the quotation is less acceptable. It suggests not audience recognition of the characters, but identification with, sympathy for them, and it is difficult to imagine that kind of audience response without a concomitant violation of the satiric thrust of the play.

The important thing about Feiffer as a playwright is not that he creates characters for whom an audience can "care" in the conventional sense, but that he produces unified dramatic structures — related, in some of their elements, to his cartoons and to revue sketches — in which apparently disparate material is held together by a controlling idea, about violence (the two plays) and sex (the film) in our society. *Little Murders* is the best of his dramatic works to date. The random violence that is the ostensible subject of that play is simply the most obviously theatrical evidence of a general collapse that is reflected in technological malfunction (the failed electricity) and the impotence of traditional power-and-virtue figures (the comic turns of the judge, the detective, the priest). When Feiffer's nice American family begins to shoot people on the street, the event is not so much a culmination of the action as an open statement of what has been implicit all through the play. That last scene; the disintegration, physical and political, in *The White House Murder Case*; the sexual ignorance, and failure, that calls itself "Carnal Knowledge" — all these suggest that Feiffer has about as black a view of American society and of human possibility as one can find in the comtemporary theatre. The original satiric impulse is almost certainly a positive one, but in the artistic process the liberal reformer comes across as part Savonarola, part mourner. And, oh yes, often a very funny man, as well.

—Gerald Weales

249

FERLINGHETTI, Lawrence.   American.   Born in Yonkers, New York, 24 March 1919. Educated at the University of North Carolina, Chapel Hill, A.B.; Columbia University, New York, M.A. 1948; the Sorbonne, Paris, Doctorat de l'Université 1951. Served in the Naval Reserve, 1941–45: Lieutenant-Commander. Married Selden Kirby-Smith in 1951; has two children. Worked for *Time* magazine, New York, in the 1940's. Co-Founder, 1952, with Peter D. Martin, and since 1953, Owner and Editor-in-Chief, City Lights Books. Delegate, with Allen Ginsberg, to the Pan American Cultural Conference, University of Concepción, Chile, 1960. Address: City Lights Books, 1562 Grant Avenue, San Francisco, California 94133, U.S.A.

PUBLICATIONS

Plays

    The Alligation (produced San Francisco, 1962; New York, 1970).   Included in *Unfair Arguments with Existence*, 1963.
    Unfair Arguments with Existence: Seven Plays for a New Theatre (includes *The Soldiers of No Country, Three Thousand Red Ants, The Alligation, The Victims of Amnesia, Motherlode, The Customs Collector in Baggy Pants, The Nose of Sisyphus*).   New York, New Directions, 1963.
    The Customs Collector in Baggy Pants (produced New York, 1964).   Included in *Unfair Arguments with Existence*, 1963.
    The Soldiers of No Country (produced London, 1969).   Included in *Unfair Arguments with Existence*, 1963.
    3 by Ferlinghetti: Three Thousand Red Ants, The Alligation, The Victims of Amnesia (produced New York, 1970).   Included in *Unfair Arguments with Existence*, 1963.
    Routines (includes 13 short pieces).   New York, New Directions, 1964.

Novel

    Her.   New York, New Directions, 1960; London, MacGibbon and Kee, 1966.

Verse

    Pictures of the Gone World.   San Francisco, City Lights, 1955.
    A Coney Island of the Mind.   New York, New Directions, 1958.
    Tentative Description of a Dinner Given to Promote the Impeachment of President Eisenhower.   San Francisco, Golden Mountain Press, 1958.
    One Thousand Fearful Words for Fidel Castro.   San Francisco, City Lights, 1961.
    Berlin.   San Francisco, Golden Mountain Press, 1961.
    Starting from San Francisco: Poems.   New York, New Directions, 1961; revised edition, 1967.
    Penguin Modern Poets 5, with Allen Ginsberg and Gregory Corso.   London, Penguin, 1963.
    Where is Vietnam?   San Francisco, City Lights, 1965.
    To Fuck is to Love Again; Kyrie Eleison Kerista; or, The Situation in the West; Followed by a Holy Proposal.   New York, Fuck You Press, 1965.
    An Eye on the World: Selected Poems.   London, MacGibbon and Kee, 1967.
    After the Cry of the Birds.   San Francisco, Dave Haslewood Books, 1967.
    Moscow in the Wilderness, Segovia in the Snow.   San Francisco, Beach Books, 1967.

The Secret Meaning of Things.   New York, New Directions, 1969.
Tyrannus Nix?   New York, New Directions, 1969.
Back Roads to Far Places.   New York, New Directions, 1971.
Love Is No Stone on the Moon: Automatic Poem.   Berkeley, California, ARIF Press,
    1971.
The Illustrated Wilfred Funk.   San Francisco, City Lights, 1971.
Open Eye, Open Heart.   New York, New Directions, 1973.
Who Are We Now?   New York, New Directions, 1976.

Recordings: *Poetry Readings in "The Cellar,"* with Kenneth Rexroth, Fantasy, 1958;
Tentative Description of a Dinner to Impeach President Eisenhower and Other Poems,
Fantasy, 1959; *Tyrannus Nix? and Assassination Raga,* Fantasy, 1971; *The World's
Greatest Poets 1,* with Allen Ginsberg and Gregory Corso, CMS, 1971.

Other

The Howl of the Censor, edited by J. W. Ehrlich.   New York, Nourse, 1961.
The Mexican Night: Travel Journal.   New York, New Directions, 1970.

Editor, *Beatitude Anthology.*   San Francisco, City Lights, 1960.
Editor, with Michael McClure and David Meltzer, *Journal for the Protection of All
    Beings.*   San Francisco, City Lights, 1961.
Editor, *City Lights Journal.*   San Francisco, City Lights, 4 vols., 1963–73.
Editor, *Hunk of Skin,* by Pablo Picasso.   San Francisco, City Lights, 1969.
Editor, *Panic Grass,* by Charles Upton.   San Francisco, City Lights, 1969.
Editor, *City Lights Anthology.*   San Francisco, City Lights, 1974.

Translator, *Selections from Paroles by Jacques Prévert.*   San Francisco, City Lights,
    1958; London, Penguin, 1963.

Manuscript Collection: Columbia University, New York.

*   *   *

Poet of the Beat Generation, Lawrence Ferlinghetti has published two volumes of short
plays in prose. Ferlinghetti's plays, like his poems, are influenced by French Existentialist
attitudes to love and death, but, like his fellow Beats, he replaces French Existentialist
commitment by disaffiliation. Even before he turned to plays, Ferlinghetti "performed" his
poems, sometimes with jazz accompaniment. His first volume of plays, *Unfair Arguments
with Existence,* uses a casual American idiom for depicting existence as we know it in
modern industrial society. The progression of the seven plays in this volume is from the
roughly realistic to the distinctly symbolic. The next to last play is a monologue, and the last
play spurns all dialogue, striving for a more improvisational effect.

In the longest Argument with Existence, *The Soldiers of No Country,* a 60-year-old priest
and a 20-year-old deserter compete for the love of 35-year-old Erma. Watching this
grotesque triangle in a womblike cave are many silent people who fall, one by one, to the
ground. After the priest's victory, Erma stumbles out of the cave, and the deserter threatens
the priest. Though the play seems to end in ubiquitous death, a baby cries within the cave,
implying the possibility of rebirth.

Hope is fainter in the next two Arguments. *Three Thousand Red Ants* is an associational
conversation between Fat and Moth, a married couple in bed. At the end Fat turns
binoculars on the audience and exclaims that he sees a breakthrough, to which his wife
replies under the bedclothes: "Your own! Humpty Dumpty!" In *The Alligation* Ladybird is
fixated on her pet alligator, Shooky, though a Blind Indian warns her that this is dangerous.

When Ladybird stretches full length on Shooky, he rolls over on top of her, and the Blind Indian calls to the audience for help. Both plays pose audience help as an implicit question.

Influenced by the Theatre of the Absurd, the next Three Arguments are extended metaphors for the human condition. In *The Victims of Amnesia* a Night Clerk converses with a woman shown at four stages of diminishing age – Marie, Young Woman, Girl, Baby – all embraced in the name Mazda. At the play's end the Night Clerk *cum* Fate inveighs against all life, as the play explodes into smashing light bulbs of many sizes. But finally a single small bulb flickers in the dark before the theatre lights come up. Similarly, *Motherlode* theatricalizes the undimmed faith of a dying miner, even after the crass commercial Schmucks have despoiled the land. After the miner's death, with Schmuck triumphant, the birds still call "Love! Love!" *The Customs Collector in Baggy Pants* is set on a lifeboat "full of flush-toilets which we call civilization." Assailed by a storm outside and the storm of flushing toilets on the boat, the Customs Collector shouts his determination not to die or capitulate. Ferlinghetti punctuates the Absurd with hope.

In *The Nose of Sisyphus*, however, hope is all but extinguished. In a playground that is a metaphor for the world, Sisyphus uses his false nose to try to push a globe up a slide, while assorted human beings try to scale a jungle gym. Though Sisyphus cannot persuade the people to help him, he does succeed in leading their chants. But a whistle-blowing Big Baboon slides down the slide, toppling Sisyphus, frightening the people, and robbing Sisyphus of globe and nose. Alone on stage, the Big Baboon tosses the false nose into the audience. At best, one can hope for another Sisyphus to arise from the audience.

The Nose of Sisyphus is the last of the *Unfair Arguments with Existence*, and Ferlinghetti incorporates it as the last of the 13 pieces in his second volume of plays, *Routines*. He defines a routine as

> a song and dance, a little rout, a routing-out, a run-around, a "round of business or amusement": myriads of people, herds, flowerbeds, ships and cities, all going through their routines, life itself a blackout routine, an experimental madness somewhere between dotage and megalomania, lost in the vibration of a wreckage (of some other cosmos we fell out of).

All 13 Routines focus on visual metaphors, but they read rhythmically, with the free flexible rhythms of Ferlinghetti's poems. Their subjects are love, death, and the totalitarian establishment. Just before *The Nose of Sisyphus* appears *Bore*, a call to action: "Routines never end; they have to be broken. This little routine to end all routines requires the formation of a worldwide society dedicated to the non-violent disruption of institutionalized events." Play tries to infiltrate life in Ferlinghetti's final play.

—Ruby Cohn

FOREMAN, Richard. American. Born in New York City, 10 June 1937. Educated at Brown University, Providence, Rhode Island, 1955–59, B.A. 1959; Yale University Drama School, New Haven, Connecticut, 1959–62, M.F.A. 1962. Married Amy Taubin in 1961 (divorced, 1972). Associate Director, Film-Maker's Cinematheque, New York, 1966–68. Since 1968, Founding Director, Ontological-Hysteric Theatre, New York. Recipient: Obie Award, 1970, 1973; National Opera Institute grant, 1971; National Endowment for the Arts grant, 1972, 1974; Creative Artists Public Service grant, 1972, 1974; Rockefeller grant, 1974; Guggenheim Fellowship, 1975. Agent: Artservices, 463 West Street, New York, New York. Address: 152 Wooster Street, New York, New York 10012, U.S.A.

PUBLICATIONS

Plays

Angelface (also director: produced New York, 1968).

Ida-Eyed (also director: produced New York, 1968).

Elephant-Steps, music by Stanley Silverman (also director: produced Lenox, Massachusetts, 1968; New York, 1970).

Total Recall (also director: produced New York, 1970).

Dream Tantras for Western Massachusetts (also director: produced Lenox, Massachusetts, 1971).

Hotel China (also director: produced New York, 1971).   Excerpts published, as HCohtienla; or, Hotel China, in Performance 2 (New York), April 1972.

Evidence (also director: produced New York, 1972).

Dr. Selavy's Magic Theatre, music by Stanley Silverman, lyrics by Thomas Hendry (also director: produced Lenox, Massachusetts, and New York, 1972).

Sophia = (Wisdom): Part III (also director: produced New York, 1972).   Published in Performance 6 (New York), May–June 1973.

Particle Theory (also director: produced New York, 1973).

Honor (also director: produced New York, 1973).

Une Semaine sous l'Influence de... (also director: produced Paris, 1973).

Pain(t), and Vertical Mobility: Sophia = (Wisdom) Part IV (also director: produced New York, 1974).   Vertical Mobility published in Drama Review 63 (New York), June 1974.

RA-D-IO (Wisdom); or, Sophia: Part I, music by David Tice (produced New York, 1974).

Pandering to the Masses: A Misrepresentation (also director: produced New York, 1975).   Published in The Theatre of Images, edited by Bonnie Marrinca, New York, Drama Book Publishers, 1975.

Hotel for Criminals, music by Stanley Silverman (also director: produced New York, 1975).

15 Minutes of Evidence (produced New York, 1975).

Rhoda in Potatoland (Her Fall-starts) (also director: produced New York, 1975).

Le Théâtre de Richard Foreman, edited by Simone Benmussa.   Paris, Gallimard, 1975.

Plays and Manifestoes, edited by Kate Davey.   New York, New York University Press, 1976.

Manuscript Collections: Lincoln Center Library of the Performing Arts, New York; Anthology Film Archives, New York.

Critical Studies: "Richard Foreman's Ontological-Hysteric Theatre" by Michael Kirby, in Drama Review 58 (New York), June 1973; by Kate Davey, in Drama Review 62 and 65 (New York), June 1974 and March 1975.

Theatrical Activities:

Director: **Plays** – most of his own plays.

Richard Foreman comments:

In 1968 I began to write for the theatre which I wanted to see, which was radically different from any style of theatre which I had seen. In brief, I imagined a theatre which broke down all elements into a kind of atomic structure – and showed those elements of story, action, sound, light, composition, gesture, in terms of the smallest building-block units, the basic cells of the perceived experience of both living and art-making.

The scripts themselves read like notations of my own process of imagining a theatre piece. They are the evidence of a kind of effort in which the mind's leaps and inventions may be rendered as part of a process not unique to the artist in question (myself) but typical of the building-up which goes on through all modes of coming-into-being (human and non-human). I want to refocus the attention of the spectator on the intervals, gaps, relations and rhythms which saturate the objects (acts and physical props) which are the "givens" of any particular play. In doing this, I believe the spectator is made available (as I am, hopefully, when writing) to those most desirable energies which secretly connect him (through a kind of resonance) with the foundations of his being.

*   *   *

The theatre of Richard Foreman shares a broad aesthetic base with a constellation of radical artists working out of New York City, such as the musicians La Monte Young, Philip Glass, and Steve Reich, the dancer Yvonne Rainer, or the film-makers Michael Snow and Ken Jacobs. These artists, along with Foreman, tend to use *duration* aggressively, repudiate psychodynamics for perceptual psychology, and retard and elongate the few actions they employ. Their materials are deliberately limited (not diversified): extensive repetition is common, and, where it is not found, one can expect stasis. Foreman located the failure of contemporary theatre in its unwillingness to give up the idea of *moving* the audience, and to accept the idea of playwriting and direction as the making of a verbal performance object. The language of his plays superficially resembles that of Samuel Beckett: a description of the physical and mental states of the actors, as self-enclosed Cartesian units rather than characters in collisive relationships. Yet the thrust of his work is the inverse of Beckett's (who isolates his figures in an ironic panorama, as a metaphor for an existential alienation); and where Beckett's mode is irony, Foreman's is a strict formalism.

Foreman's distinction is twofold, as a writer and as a director. The functions have become inseparable in his work, but initially he was a writer. After graduating from the Yale Drama School in 1962, he attempted to reconcile his radicalism with the conventions and fashions of American play production. But after frustrated attempts to get his play *Harry in Love* produced in New York and London, he abandoned his hopes of working within the existing structures. The fashionable movement in play production of the mid-Sixties depended upon the tactics of audience rape, an acceleration of sever confrontations, as if a barrier had to be broken before the ancient relationship between audience and tragedy could be re-established. Foreman has always eschewed the tactics of direct attack. In 1968 when he founded his own "Ontological-Hysteric" Theatre, he turned his back to the audiences, ignored them. One feels as if the plays that he produces would go on if not a person showed up to see them. Like rivers they simply repeat their existence.

In founding his own theatre, without financial backing, Foreman was forced to invent new methods of production that would not require trained actors, expensive staging, or elaborate effects. His use of a tape recorder and minimal stage props in *Angelface*, his first production in 1968, was so effective that he was encouraged to assume the role of director as well as writer in his later productions. These roles have been fused together progressively in the subsequent productions he has mounted (including plays and operas). Yet in principle Foreman still conceives of his major contribution as the author of the text which is performed; and he looks forward to a time when his texts may be staged by other directors.

In calling his work the Ontological-Hysteric Theatre, Foreman alludes to the metaphysics of Being, the science of essence. His writing is ontological in its strategies of discarding the conventional attributes of drama: psychology, interaction of characters, plot, development. What, you may ask, can a play be after it has been stripped bare of these ontic elements? The relevation of a series of states of being, or a single static state of being disclosed by a series of slightly modified perspectives of consciousness. The plays themselves are exercises in the interpretation of something which never occurs on stage, presumably because it never can be staged.

Despite the severity of these aesthetic tactics, a Foreman play is not without emotional power; in fact, it is all the stronger because of its rejection of the formulae which we have come to think of as the bases of theatre. Like Bresson in his films, Foreman in his plays creates an emotional dynamic through the suppression of emotionalism. A single force mounts throughout the duration of each play. At the end it substitutes apotheosis for climax.

But to call this drama "hysterical" seems at first sight to be an identification through its opposite. Everything in his plays happens in slow motion, with repetition, so that the collapse of a chair or the opening of a window or the flickering of a light becomes a momentous event in context.

The ontology is direct; we see causality slowed down until it no longer can effect; the process of thought is dramatized. The hysteria is only implied. In all Foreman's plays a group of characters is postulated. Beyond the play, in the imagination of the spectator, there is set up an echo of the character on the stage. We are given enough evidence to image him or her in the mundane world. By hearing his deepest thought, we cannot help but fill in his more superficial desires, his daily disguises. What happens in this drama reverses a traditional process. We do not see the full-bodied character and fathom his soul: we observe the presence of the soul and imagine the character.

Foreman is conscious of the radical methodology of art in our time; his route has been through reading and seeing. One can extract from his work echoes of Descartes, Gertrude Stein, Gurdieff, Husserl and Kurt Weill. He obviously read Vsevelod Meyerhold's essay on theatre to good effect. Over all his works hover the Viennese ghosts of Robert Musil and Ludwig Wittgenstein. Yet his work is neither eclectic nor crushed by influence. There is an unmistakable identity to everything Foreman has done. Each actor speaks as he thinks, uttering an open interior monologue even when he seems to be talking to another. The dynamics of the play do not unravel from the rhythms of conversation or confrontation. These are structural plays, organized fugally, and their ultimate shape depends solely upon the orchestration of voices and appearances, repetitions and disappearances that the director has fashioned from his own text. In any Foreman play there are sure to be buzzers, collapsing furniture, doors, windows, and flickering lights.

—P. Adams Sitney

FORNÉS, María Irene.   American.   Born in Havana, Cuba, 14 May 1930; emigrated to the United States in 1945. Educated in Havana public schools. Painter, textile designer; costume designer for Judson Poets Theatre and New Dramatists Committee productions, 1965–70. Taught at the Judson Workshop, 1966, and the Teachers and Writers Collaborative, 1971–72, New York. President, New York Theatre Strategy, since 1973. Recipient: Whitney Fellowship, 1961; Centro Mexicano de Escritores Fellowship, 1962; Office for Advanced Drama Research grant, 1965; Obie Award, 1965; Cintas Foundation Fellowship, 1967; Yale University Fellowship, 1967, 1968; Boston University-Tanglewood Fellowship, 1968; Rockefeller Fellowship, 1971; Guggenheim Fellowship, 1972; Creative Artists Public Service grant, 1972, 1975; National Endowment for the Arts grant, 1974. Agent: Bertha Case, 42 West 53rd Street, New York, New York 10019. Address: 1 Sheridan Square, New York, New York 10014, U.S.A.

PUBLICATIONS

Plays

> *The Widow* (produced New York, 1961).   Published, as *La Viuda*, in *Cuatro Autores Cubanos*, Havana, Casa de las Americas, 1961.
> *Tango Palace* (as *There! You Died*, produced San Francisco, 1963; as *Tango Palace*, produced New York, 1964; revised version, also director: produced Minneapolis, 1965).   Included in *Promenade and Other Plays*, 1971.
> *The Successful Life of Three: A Skit for Vauderville* (produced Minneapolis and New York, 1965).   Included in *Promenade and Other Plays*, 1971.
> *Promenade*, music by Al Carmines (produced New York, 1965).   Included in *Promenade and Other Plays*, 1971.
> *The Office* (produced New York, 1966).
> *A Vietnamese Wedding* (produced New York, 1967).   Included in *Promenade and Other Plays*, 1971.
> *The Annunciation* (also director: produced New York, 1967).
> *Dr. Kheal* (produced New York, 1968; London, 1969).   Included in *Promenade and Other Plays*, 1971.
> *The Red Burning Light; or, Mission XQ3* (produced Zurich, 1968; New York, 1969). Included in *Promenade and Other Plays*, 1971.
> *Molly's Dream* (produced Lenox, Massachusetts, 1968; also director: produced New York, 1968).   Included in *Promenade and Other Plays*, 1971.
> *Promenade and Other Plays* (includes *A Vietnamese Wedding; The Red Burning Light; or, Mission XQ3; Dr. Kheal; Molly's Dream; Tango Palace; The Successful Life of Three)*.   New York, Winter House, 1971.
> *Baboon!!!*, with others (produced Cincinnati, 1972).
> *Aurora*, music by John FitzGibbon (also director: produced New York, 1974).
> *Cap-a-Pie*, music by Jose Raul Bernardo (also director: produced New York, 1975).

Manuscript Collection: Lincoln Center Library of the Performing Arts, New York.

Critical Study: "Cue the Giant Maraschino" by Phillip Lopate, in *Herald* (New York), 23 January 1972.

Theatrical Activities:

> Director: **Plays** – Several of her own plays, and *Dance* by Remy Charlip, London, 1972.

*   *   *

María Irene Fornés writes with a light, often whimsically satirical touch, yet there is a strong warmth of feeling in her plays. The characters are peculiarly on their own, each pursuing his own fantasy or destiny. There is a sense of fatality in her world, and the motive force of the plays is not sentiment or psychology, though the characters are well defined and sympathetic, but something more abstract, like the patterns of a dance. Fornés is Cuban by birth, and the fact that English is a second language may account in part for the delicate pungency of her verbal economy. More, it reflects her highly original turn of mind.

In the early, extraordinarily beautiful play *Tango Palace* the two characters are an androgynous clown and an earnest young man, their claustrally intense, strange relationship both cruel and tender, played out in a series of elusively symbolic games and word mockeries. *Dr. Kheal*, a monologue, presents a professor in a series of brief scenes, his subjects continually escaping his comprehension and control. The play is a satire of academic pomposity; but beyond that, giving it an unaccountable richness, are the characteristic Fornés intimations of contact with more sublime levels of perception and experience, intruding marvelously into the mundane.

Promenade, a play with songs (set to music by the Reverend Al Carmines), was a great success in its productions at a Greenwich Village church and later Off-Broadway. Within the frivolously loose narrative of two prisoners who escape from jail and are finally reunited with their mother, Fornés works some brilliant and charming social satire and coolly sentimental expressions of self-sufficiency and paradoxical well-being. The play's wit, inventiveness, and buoyancy of spirit are delicious and the song lyrics most refined and evocative. *The Successful Life of Three* is another play in which light-heartedness and a quizzical sense of the inevitability of romantic setbacks take the place of more tangible content. As elsewhere, Fornés puts charm at the service of a unique and honest sense of being, and the play goes deeper than its action or diverting surface implies.

Vietnamese Wedding, a documentary play in which actors and audience act out a traditional Vietnamese marriage ceremony, was widely presented as an act of protest against United States military and economic intrusion into Indochina and of solidarity with the Vietnamese people. More recent plays are *Molly's Dream*, set in a quasi-mythic Western saloon, and *Aurora*.

—Michael Smith

FORSYTH, James (Law). British. Born in Glasgow, 5 March 1913. Educated at Glasgow High School, graduated 1930; Glasgow School of Art, diploma in drawing and painting 1934. Married Louise Tibble (second marriage) in 1955; has two children. Served in the Scots Guards, 2nd Monmouthshire Regiment, 1940–46: Captain, Battalion Adjutant; Bronze Cross of the Netherlands. Worked with the General Post Office Film Unit, 1937–40; Dramatist-in-Residence, Old Vic Company: worked with the Old Vic School and the Young Vic, 1946–48; Dramatist-in-Residence, Howard University, Washington, D.C., 1962; Guest Director and Lecturer, Tufts University, Medford, Massachusetts, 1963; Distinguished Professor-in-Residence, Florida State University, Tallahassee, 1965; Director, Tufts University Program in London, 1967–71. Since 1972, Artistic Director, The Forsyths' Barn Theatre, Ansty, Sussex. Currently writing a commissioned biography of Sir Tyrone Guthrie. Since 1954, Member of the Executive Council, League of Dramatists and Radio Writers Association; Founding Member, Theatres Advisory Council. Agent: London Management, 235 Regent Street, London W1A 2JT; or Harold Freedman, Brandt and Brandt, 101 Park Avenue, New York, New York 10017, U.S.A. Address: "Grainloft", Ansty, Haywards Heath, Sussex, England.

PUBLICATIONS

Plays

> *Trog* (broadcast, 1949; produced Coventry, 1959; Tallahassee, Florida, 1964).
> *Brand*, adaptation of the play by Ibsen (broadcast, 1949; produced London, 1964). London, Heinemann, and New York, Theatre Arts, 1960.

The Medicine Man (produced London, 1950).

Emmanuel: A Nativity Play (broadcast, 1950; produced London and New York, 1960). London, Heinemann, 1952; New York, Theatre Arts, 1963.

Héloïse (broadcast, 1951; produced Southsea and London, 1951; New York, 1958). Included in *Three Plays*, 1956; New York, Theatre Arts, 1958.

Adelaise (broadcast, 1951; produced Ashburton, Devon, 1953).   Included in *Three Plays*, 1956.

The Other Heart (broadcast, 1951; produced London, 1952; also director: produced Medford, Massachusetts, 1963).   Included in *Three Plays*, 1956; New York, Theatre Arts, 1964.

Three Plays: The Other Heart, Héloïse, Adelaise.   London, Heinemann, 1956

The Pier (televised, 1957; produced Bristol, 1958).

The Road to Emmaus: A Play for Eastertide.   London, Heinemann, 1958; New York, Theatre Arts, n.d.

Joshua, music by Franz Waxman (produced Dallas, 1960).   New York, Ricordi, 1959.

Dear Wormwood, adaptation of *The Screwtape Letters* by C. S. Lewis (produced Brighton, 1965).   Chicago, Dramatic Publishing Company, 1961; as *Screwtape*, 1973.

Fifteen Strings of Money, adaptation of a play by Guenther Weisenhorn based on a story by Chu Su-Chen (produced Pitlochry, Perthshire, 1961).

Everyman (produced Coventry, 1962).

Defiant Island (produced Washington, D.C., 1962).   Chicago, Dramatic Publishing Company, 1975.

Seven Scenes for Yeni (produced Boston, 1963).

Cyrano de Bergerac, adaptation of the play by Edmond Rostand (produced Sarasota, Florida, 1963; London, 1967; New York, 1968).   Chicago, Dramatic Publishing Company, 1968.

If My Wings Heal (produced Stroud, Gloucestershire, 1966).

Lobsterback (produced Boston and Ansty, Sussex, 1975).

Four Triumphant (televised, 1966; as *Festival of Four*, produced Ansty, Sussex, 1976).

Screenplays: *The End of the Road* series, 1937–40; *Francis of Assisi*, 1961.

Radio Plays: *The Bronze Horse*, 1948; *Trog*, 1949; *Brand*, 1949; *Emmanuel*, 1950; *The Other Heart*, 1951; *Adelaise*, 1951; *Héloïse*, 1951; *The Nameless One of Europe*, 1951; *For He's a Jolly Good Fellow*, 1952; *Pig*, 1953; *Seelkie*, 1954; *The Festive Spirit*, 1955; *Lisel*, 1955; *Christophe*, 1958; *Every Pebble on the Beach*, 1963.

Television Plays: *The Pier*, 1957; *Underground*, 1958; *Old Mickmack*, 1961; *Four Triumphant*, 1966; *The English Boy*, 1969; *The Last Journey*, 1972; *The Old Man's Mountain*, 1972.

Manuscript Collection: Lincoln Center Library of the Performing Arts, New York.

*   *   *

Craft is fundamental to all art, although not all craftsmen are artists, any more than every artist is a craftsman. Indeed today, as artists are promoted by PRs, craft has become somewhat unfashionable. Hence the well-made play has, of recent years, come to be regarded as something slightly old-fashioned. Yet the virtue of a well-made play is that it knows how to tell a story, how to hold an audience, and this is an essential part of the dramatists's craft.

James Forsyth is such a playwright and this term is perhaps the most pat of all for an author who has himself said (January 1972): "I have yet to wright my best play. And 'wright' is right. I am not a 'dramatist,' I am a 'playwright.' Drama is the stuff, plays are the works, and I am professed to works."

His works are prolific, a steady output over the years, from the Old Vic production of *The Other Heart* to the recent commissioned television series on the patron saints of England, Scotland, Ireland and Wales. *The Last Journey*, a 90-minute television play on Tolstoy, was the ITV entry for the 1972 Italia Prize.

The Other Heart is one of James Forsyth's strongest and most powerfully constructed plays and full of excellent small character studies such as that of Marthe, the servant, who when asked why she risks her life in coming to Paris during the plague replies, "I need to help." In the character of the romantic poet, François Villon, Forsyth catches marvellously the impetuosity of young love, and the radiant recklessness of the visionary and poet. They are qualities that seem to attract him again and again. While he is drawn to "wrighting" plays about historical characters, it is noticeable how many of them are variations upon the theme of "a pair of starcrossed lovers." In this play we have Villon and Catherine de Vausselles; we have also Francis and Clare in *If My Wings Heal*, Héloïse and Abelard in *Héloïse*, while in *The Last Journey*, a study of the last days of Tolstoy, he has written brilliantly of the tragic gap between a husband and wife.

The clash of the idealist with reality is perhaps, however, the profoundest recurring theme in all James Forsyth's work. It has attracted him to a powerful adaptation of Ibsen's *Brand*, and in *If My Wings Heal* he sets out to explore the conflict between St. Francis of Assisi, the creative artist, poet, visionary, and Brother Elias, the ambitious administrative genius of the Franciscan Order. It was Brother Elias ʼvho wanted to turn the Friars Minor into the most powerful order within the Church, "for the sake of possession, for the possession of power." As one of the Friars remarks, "It was never Brother Francis's idea that we should be other than small bands, always on the move. We were to be the salt which is scattered."

This is a tougher and less sentimental rendering of the story of Francis of Assisi than the *Little Plays of St. Francis* by Laurence Housman, or the five-act devotional drama by Henri Ghéon, *The Marriage of St. Francis*. Only the scene of the stigmata fails. Perhaps it is an impossibility – to put on the stage a mystical experience. Perhaps only a major poet, such as T. S. Eliot, whose insight into the transcendental was close to that of the great mystics themselves, could really tackle such a scene. If James Forsyth is a playwright proven he is, I think, a poet *manqué*. His weakest writing stems almost always from a tendency to poeticize, to lapse into obvious rhyming blank verse. Yet in theatre terms one can see what he is about for the steady beat and rhythm of these passages serve to carry the story forward.

David, Andrew, Patrick and *George* are four full-length plays, envisaged as a cycle, to be performed over two days. They embody not merely the history of the four patron saints but are a study of the pioneers of Christianity. Each play is self-sufficient, and yet each gains from its relation to the others.

Perhaps James Forsyth's most memorable play is *Defiant Island*, the true story of Henri Christophe, the first negro king of Haiti. It is a deeply moving tragedy of an idealist who is led astray by his fanatical devotion to his own ideals, so that the man is destroyed at the expense of the image of himself as the first negro monarch. Finally, when Napoleon insists on "nothing less than the total extinction of every adult black, male and female," Henri Christophe, who had naively believed that all men could meet in equal justice, has to admit to himself, "I asked too much. It is a fault in me"

Henri Christophe, Brand, Abelard, Villon, Francis of Assisi are all portraits of men of thought suffused with passion; they are the solitary visionaries, the reckless romantics, the uncomfortable reformers; in the true sense of the word they are heroes. James Forsyth belongs to that great tradition of bardic poets, who sang the exploits and epics of heroes. It is a tradition that is at present a little out of fashion, but fashions change and the wheel comes full circle. When that happens James Forsyth will find he has wrought his best play.

—James Roose-Evans

FOSTER, Paul.   American.   Born in Pennsgrove, New Jersey, 15 October 1931. Educated at Rutgers University, New Brunswick, New Jersey, 1950–54, B.A. 1954; St. John's University Law School, New York, 1954, 1957, 1958. Served in the United States Naval Reserve, 1955–57. Since 1962, President, La Mama Experimental Theater Club, New York. Recipient: Rockefeller Fellowship, 1967, 1968; Irish Universities Play Award, 1967, 1971; New York Drama Critics Circle Award, 1968; New York State Council on the Arts grant, 1972, 1974; National Endowment for the Arts grant, 1973; Guggenheim Fellowship, 1974. Agent: John Calder, Calder and Boyars Ltd., 18 Brewer Street, London W1R 4AS, England. Address: 236 East 5th Street, New York, New York 10003, U.S.A.

PUBLICATIONS

Plays

Hurrah for the Bridge (produced New York, 1962; Edinburgh, 1967).   Bogota, Canal
    Ramirez, 1965; in Balls and Other Plays, 1967.
The Recluse (produced New York, 1964; Edinburgh, 1967).   Included in Balls and
    Other Plays, 1967.
Balls (produced New York, 1964; Edinburgh, 1967).   Included in Balls and Other
    Plays, 1967.
The Madonna in the Orchard (produced New York, 1965).   Published as Die Madonna
    im Apfelhag, Frankfurt, S. Fischer Verlag, 1968; as The Madonna in the Orchard,
    New York, Breakthrough Press, 1971; in Elizabeth I and Other Plays, 1973.
The Hessian Corporal (produced New York, 1966; Edinburgh, 1967).   Included in
    Balls and Other Plays, 1967.
Balls and Other Plays: The Recluse, Hurrah for the Bridge, The Hessian Corporal.
    London, Calder and Boyars, 1967; New York, French, 1968.
Tom Paine (produced New York, 1967; expanded version, produced Edinburgh and
    London, 1967; New York, 1968).   London, Calder and Boyars, 1967; New York,
    Grove Press, 1968.
Heimskringa; or, The Stoned Angels (televised, 1969; produced New York, 1970).
    London, Calder and Boyars, and New York, French, 1970.
Satyricon (produced New York, 1972).   Published in The Off-Off-Broadway Book,
    edited by Bruce Mailman and Albert Poland, Indianapolis, Bobbs Merrill, 1972; in
    Elizabeth I and Other Plays, 1973.
Elizabeth I (produced New York, 1972; London, 1973).   New York, French, 1972; in
    Elizabeth I and Other Plays, 1973.
Elizabeth I and Other Plays (includes The Madonna in the Orchard and Satyricon).
    London, Calder and Boyars, 1973.
Silver Queen Saloon (as Silver Queen, music by John Braden, produced New York,
    1973).   New York, French, 1975.
Rags to Riches to Rags (produced New York, 1974).
Marcus Brutus (produced Springfield, Massachusetts, 1975).   New York, French,
    1976.

Television Play: Heimskringa; or, The Stoned Angels, 1969.

Short Stories

Minnie the Whore, The Birthday, and Other Stories.   Caracas, Venezuela, Zodiac
    Editions, 1963.

Critical Studies: *The New Bohemia* by John Gruen, New York, Shorecrest, 1966; "The Theatre of Involvement" by Richard Atcheson, in *Holiday Magazine* (New York), October 1968; "The World's a Stage," in *MD Publications* (New York), October 1968; *Foster, Robbe-Grillet, Bergson: Teatro, Novela, Tiempo* by Gustavo Majia, unpublished doctoral dissertation, University of the Andes, Bogota, 1969; *Up Against the Fourth Wall* by John Lahr, New York, Grove Press, 1970; *Le Nouveau Théâtre Américain* by Franck Jotterand, Paris, Editions du Seuil, 1970; *Selvsyn-Aktuel Litteratur og Kulturdebat* by Elsa Gress, Copenhagen, Glydendal, 1970; *Now: Theater der Erfahrung: Material zur neuen amerikanischen Theaterbewegung* by Jens Heilmeyer and Pia Frolich, Cologne, Verlag M. Dumont Schauberg, 1971; *The Off-Off-Broadway Book*, edited by Bruce Mailman and Albert Poland, Indianapolis, Bobbs Merrill, 1972.

*   *   *

In the early 1960's, Paul Foster was one of the first playwrights to emerge on the off-off Broadway scene. His plays were presented at the Caffe Cino and he holds the distinction of being the first new playwright to have his work presented at the famous La Mama Experimental Theater Club. His best plays, *Tom Paine* and *Elizabeth I*, take the form of Brechtian chronicle plays. They are flamboyant historical pageants that view both the past and the present posing such age-old unanswerable questions as "What does it all mean? Why are we all here?"

In his early plays, such as *Balls, Hurrah for the Bridge, The Recluse* and *The Madonna in the Orchard*, we see Foster the young playwright casting around for styles, probing Brecht, Faulkner, Williams, Beckett, attempting to find where his individualism lies. *Balls* is perhaps the best example of his early work. Highly imitative of Beckett's *Play* and *Embers* there are only two ping-pong balls visible on the stage. They represent two dead men mind-tripping back through the memories of their past lives. Although there are constant echoes of Beckett, the play is highly imaginative and a feast of rich poetic language.

With *The Hessian Corporal* in 1966, Foster seemed to find the perfect artistic outlet for his playwriting talent in the historical play. Here we see the beginnings of *Tom Paine* and *Elizabeth I*. *The Hessian Corporal* is set near the barracks of George III's Hessian mercenaries on the eve of defeat in the Battle of Trenton, Christmas night 1776. The play is broken down into several fragmented scenes, but in theatrical terms it is most effective.

In *Tom Paine* which followed a year later, the playwright sets out to "expose the human weaknesses of the great man." We view the dual sides of Paine's personality (played by two actors), Paine the rationalist and Paine the alcoholic. Tom O'Horgan's production of *Tom Paine* was vividly theatrical, a fantasia of choral speeches, choreographed movements, singing and various gymnastic capers, though some critics felt that the seriousness of Foster's message got lost in the fervor. But subsequent revivals have shown Foster's portrait of Paine as both hero and outcast to be excellent.

In 1972 his chronicle play, *Elizabeth I*, was presented on Broadway for a limited run. This cock-eyed portrait of the public and private Elizabeth was in a Broadway house far too large for its intimate stage directions. This wild, disrespectful, song-filled cartoon look at Elizabeth I and her times was a relief from the serious treatments done recently. In it, Foster gave us a fascinatingly humane look at Elizabeth I.

—Bernard Carragher

FRATTI, Mario. American. Born in L'Aquila, 5 July 1927. Educated at Ca' Foscari University, Venice, 1947–51, Ph.D. in language and literature 1951. Served in the Italian Army, 1951–52: Lieutenant. Married Lina Fedrigo in 1953; Laura Dubman, 1964; has three children. Translator, Rubelli publishers, Venice, 1953–63; Drama Critic, *Sipario*,

Milan, 1963–66, *Ridotto*, Venice, 1963–73, *Paese Sera*, Rome, 1963–73, and *L'Ora*, Palermo, 1963–73. Professor, Columbia University, New York, 1967, Adelphi College, New York, 1967–68, and Hunter College, New York, 1967–73. Recipient: RAI-Television Prize, 1959; Ruggeri Prize, 1960, 1967, 1969; Lentini Prize, 1964; Vallecorsi Prize, 1965; Unasp-Enars Prize, 1968. Agent: Samuel French Inc., 25 West 45th Street, New York, New York, 10036. Address: 145 West 55th Street, Apartment 15D, New York, New York 10019, U.S.A.

PUBLICATIONS

Plays

 Il Campanello (produced Milan, 1958). Published in *Ridotto* (Venice), 1958; as *Doorbell* (produced New York, 1970; London, 1972), in *Ohio University Review* (Athens), 1971.

 La Menzogna (The Lie) (produced Milan, 1959). Published in *Cynthia* (Florence), 1963.

 A (produced Rome, 1965). Published in *Ora Zero* (Rome), 1959.

 La Partita (The Game) (produced Pesaro, 1960). Published in *Ridotto* (Venice), 1960.

 Il Rifiuto (produced Mantua, 1960). Published in *Dramma* (Turin) 1965; as *The Refusal* (produced New York, 1972; London, 1973), in *Races*, 1972.

 In Attesa (produced La Spezia, 1960). Rome, EIST, 1964; as *Waiting* (produced New York, 1970), in *Poet Lore* (Boston), 1968.

 Il Ritorno (produced Bologna, 1961). Published in *Ridotto* (Venice), 1961; as *The Return* (produced New York, 1963; London, 1972), in *Masterpieces of the Italian Theatre*, New York, Collier Macmillan, 1967.

 La Domanda (The Questionnaire) (produced La Spezia, 1961). Published in *La Prora* (Rome), 1962.

 Flowers from Lidice, in *L'Impegno* (Bari), 1961; in *Dramatics* (Cincinnati), 1972.

 L'Assegno. Cosenza, Pellegrini, 1961; as *The Third Daughter*, in *First Stage* (Lafayette, Indiana), 1966.

 Confidenze (produced Rome, 1962). Rome, EIST, 1964; as *The Coffin* (produced New York, 1967), in *Four Plays*, 1972.

 Gatta Bianca (produced Rome, 1962). Published in *Dramma* (Turin), 1962; as *White Cat*, in *Races*, 1972.

 Il Suicidio (produced Spoleto, 1962). Published in *Cynthia* (Florence), 1962; as *The Suicide* (produced New York, 1965; London, 1973), in *New Theatre of Europe II*, edited by Robert W. Corrigan, New York, Dell, 1964.

 La Gabbia (produced Milan, 1963). Published in *Cynthia* (Florence), 1962; as *The Cage* (produced New York, 1966), in *New Theatre of Europe II*, edited by Robert W. Corrigan, New York, Dell, 1964.

 The Academy (produced New York, 1963). As *L'Accademia*, Rome, EIST, 1964; as *The Academy*, in *Masterpieces of the Italian Theatre*, New York, Collier Macmillan, 1967.

 La Vedova Bianca (produced Milan, 1963). Published in *Ridotto* (Rome), 1972; as *Mafia* (produced Tallahassee, Florida, 1966), Newark, Delaware, Proscenium Press, 1971.

 La Telefonata (produced Rome, 1965). Rome, EIST, 1964; as *The Gift* (produced New York, 1966; London, 1972), in *Four Plays*, 1972.

 I Seduttori (produced Venice, 1972). Published in *Dramma* (Turin), 1964; as *The Seducers*, music and lyrics by Ed Scott (produced New York, 1974), in *The Roman Guest, and The Seducers*, 1972.

I Frigoriferi (produced Pistoia, 1965).   Published in *Ora Zero* (Udine), 1964; as *The Refrigerators* (produced New York, 1971), in *Modern International Drama* (University Park, Pennsylvania), 1970.

Le Spie (The Spies) (produced Pescara, 1967).

Eleonora Duse (produced Sarasota, Florida, 1967).   New York, Breakthrough Press, 1972.

Il Ponte (produced Pesaro, 1967).   Published in *Ridotto* (Rome), 1967; as *The Bridge* (produced New York, 1972), New York, McGraw Hill, 1970.

The Victim (produced Sacramento, California, 1968; New York, 1973).   As *La Vittima*, Rome, Lo Faro, 1972.

Che Guevara (produced Toronto, 1968; New York, 1971).   Published in *Enact* (New Delhi), 1970; in *Costume* (Bergamo), 1972.

Unique (produced Baltimore, 1968).   Published in *Ann Arbor Review* (Ann Arbor, Michigan), 1971.

L'Amico Cinese (produced Fano, 1969).   Published in *Ridotto* (Rome), 1969; as *The Chinese Friend* (produced New York, 1972), in *Enact* (New Delhi), 1972.

L'Ospite Romano (produced Pesaro, 1971).   Rome, ENARS, 1969; as *The Roman Guest*, 1972.

La Panchina del Venerdi (produced Milan, 1970); as *The Friday Bench* (produced New York, 1971), in *Four Plays*, 1972.

Betrayals.   Cosenza, Pellegrini, 1970; in *Drama and Theatre* (Fredonia, New York), 1970.

The Wish (produced Denton, Texas, 1971; London, 1972).   Included in *Four Plays*, 1972.

The Other One (produced New York, 1971).   Included in *Races*, 1972.

The Girl with a Ring on Her Nose (produced New York, 1971).   Published in *Janus* (Seaside Park, New Jersey), 1972.

Too Much (produced New York, 1971).   Published in *Janus* (Seaside Park, New Jersey), 1972.

Cybele (produced New York, 1971).

The Brothel (produced New York, 1972).   Published in *Mediterranean Review* (Orient, New York), 1971.

The Family (produced New York, 1972).   Published in *Enact* (New Delhi), 1971.

Four Plays (includes *The Coffin, The Gift, The Friday Bench, The Wish*).   Houston, Edgemoor, 1972.

Three Minidramas, in *Janus* (Seaside Park, New Jersey), 1972.

Rapes (produced New York, 1972).   Included in *Races*, 1972.

Races: Six New Plays (includes *Rapes, Fire, Dialogue with a Negro, White Cat, The Refusal, The Other One*).   Newark, Delaware, Proscenium Press, 1972.

Dialogue with a Negro (produced New York, 1975).   Included in *Races*, 1972.

The Roman Guest, and The Seducers.   Rome, Ora Zero, 1972.

Notti d'amore, in *Tempo Sensibile* (Novara), July 1972.

The Letter, in *Tempo Sensibile* (Novara), September 1972; in *Wind* (Kentucky), 1974.

Teatro Americano (includes *Fuoco, Sorelle, Violenze, Famiglia*).   Casale Monferrato, Tersite, 1972.

L'Ungherese (produced Florence, 1974).   Published in *Tempo Sensibile* (Novara), 1972.

The 75th (produced Florence, 1974).   Published in *Arcoscenico* (Rome), January 1972.

Dolls No More (produced London and Lafayette, Indiana, 1975).   Published in *Drama and Theatre* (Fredonia, New York), Winter 1973.

Chile 1973 (produced Parma and New York, 1974).   Published in *Enact* (New Delhi), 1973; in *Parola del Popolo* (Chicago), 1974.

New York: A Triptych (produced New York, 1974).

Patty Hearst, in *Enact* (New Delhi), 1975; in *Parola del Popolo* (Chicago), 1975.

Madam Senator, music and lyrics by Ed Scott (produced New York, 1975).

Originality (produced New York, 1975).   Published in *Romanica* (New York), 1975.
The Only Good Indian... (produced New York, 1975).
Tania, music by Paul Dick (produced New York, 1975).
Two Centuries, with Penelope Bradford (produced New York, 1976).
Kissinger (produced Rome, 1976).

Translations for Italian television: plays by David Shaw, Reginald Rose, Thomas W. Phipps, R. O. Hirson, J. P. Miller.

Verse

Volti: Cento Poesie (Faces: 100 Poems).   Bari, Edizione Mariano, 1960.

Bibliography: "Fratti" in *Ora Zero* (Udine), 1972; in *Four Plays*, 1972.

Manuscript Collection: Lincoln Center Library of the Performing Arts, New York.

Critical Studies: by Robert W. Corrigan, in *New Theatre of Europe II*, New York, Dell, 1964, and in *Masterpieces of the Modern Italian Theatre*, New York, Collier Macmillan, 1967; *Enciclopedia della Spettacolo*, Rome, Unione Editoriala, 1966; by Stanley Richards, in *The Best Short Plays 1968*, Philadelphia, Chilton, 1968; *A History of the Theatre* by George Freedley and John A. Reeves, New York, Crown, 1968; *Handbook of Contemporary Drama*, New York, Crowell, 1971; by Paul T. Nolan, in *Ora Zero* (Udine), 1972, and in *La Vittima*, 1972.

Mario Fratti quotes from *Masterpieces of the Modern Italian Theatre*, New York, Collier Macmillan, 1967:

I do not believe in composers who promise symphonies, painters who promise beautiful paintings, playwrights who promise plays. I do not believe in people who anticipate, explain, promise. I only believe in the given work which speaks for itself, explains by itself: I believe in the symphony, in the painting, in the play. Accordingly, when I am asked to explain my theatre, I immediately take a defensive attitude. It makes me nervous and upset. Nervous because I do not like to explain my plays – upset because I'm convinced they do not need any explanation.

When I am asked why I love the theatre, I have an instinctive desire to be rude. The answer seems obvious to me. Because I love life, I like people, I like "active" people. Only action is life. Theatre is and must be action. Accordingly, theatre is life. When I am asked why I insist on loving the theatre in spite of the fact that it is "dying," I smile. Theatre has supposedly been dying for centuries. It never did. It never will. As long as actors feel the need to act, to communicate their emotions to audiences and as long as audiences feel the need to live vicariously through actors' performances, theatre will be alive and needed.

There happens to be someone between the actor and the audience – the playwright. He must be clear to himself, clear to the actor, clear to the audience. The quintessence of clarity. Otherwise he is only an hysterical poet talking to himself in front of a mirror. Alone and sterile. Incapable of taking a stand in front of the actors and audiences who are waiting for his approach to life, for his clear thought. A human being should never try to resist the temptation of communicating as clearly as possible. After all, there is a reason why playwrights choose dialogue as their working tool. Dialogue means an attempt to reach another human being. That's my purpose in the theatre. At the risk of being considered conservative and traditional, my only purpose is to "communicate" my thoughts and emotions.

Does this mean that I deny the *avant garde*? I can't of course ignore it. But let me smile when I hear the expression. Pirandello, using traditional three acts, has put so much fire in his plays that he is to be considered the only true *avant garde* playwright of this century. Bertolt Brecht, giving us traditionally shaped fables with a beginning, a middle part and a moralistic ending is to be considered the first poet of the third millennium. The hallmark of the truly *avant garde* is not a twisted, absurd, incomprehensible pattern, nor is it some *new* form of theatre.

The contents of a play determine whether it is modern and valid. And there is nothing more revolutionary and modern than man, than the tragic reality of his life. I write about man, to be understood by men. My fundamental concern is human distress, the conflicts of every day, the reality of every day, the grotesque of human behavior in contemporary society.

A word about language. Our forefathers invented language to deceive, to conceal one's intimate sincerity, one's personal truth and belief. Must we continue on that path? Shall we go on lying? Let's at least use language to point out that man lies in order to survive (as in Pirandello). Let's point out that the future frightens every human being out of his wits. That's why he is cruel (temporarily – according to Brecht).

In all my plays there is a protagonist who seems a sly rascal or a monster of cruelty – the Professor in *The Academy*; Maso in *The Return*. They are not cruel. They are not responsible for what is happening around them. They only struggle to survive. Which is human, justifiable. They do not "see" that they spread grief around them, they do not realize that their victims are their friends: the beloved ones, the weakest, the oldest. If the protagonists of life (the characters) do not see, do not realize the harm they are doing, all the more reason why the average citizen does not see, does not realize this struggle to survive when he witnesses it in the streets around him. Cruelty and suffering do not move him. He can stop looking at them whenever he wants. He can escape. But when he becomes a member of an audience, he cannot escape. He is nailed down in his seat. He must look at the cruelty and the pain. He is moved and upset by what he sees because everything that happens on the stage is magnified and becomes important. It is like looking through a keyhole at the right moment. It is like spying from a window on the life of our neighbors. Theatre is a window open on the life of our fellow creatures – a window open on their secret, intimate behavior. Let's watch in silence from that window.

There is another important consideration. Since the playwright has such an interest for life – which is often prosaic – is he a poet in the accepted meaning of the word? At moments, unconsciously. The playwright is only a sensitive man among indifferent men. He sees, stresses, and points out what most watch with indifference. A playwright is only an "aware" man among careless people. I am aware. I believe in man's possibility of becoming aware. Writing plays, I hope to communicate my awareness because I believe in man – notwithstanding man.

*   *   *

Mario Fratti arrived in New York in 1963 as foreign correspondent for the Italian press. He had already achieved some distinction in Italy as a playwright, and made his American debut that same year with a production of *The Academy* and *The Return* at the Theatre De Lys, starring Ron Liebman. Although a critical success, this first production failed to establish Fratti as an important New York playwright. Undaunted, Fratti continued writing prolifically. Translations of his plays appeared in prominent American literary journals and anthologies; his works were produced throughout the United States and abroad, and were also the subject matter of several academic studies. Fratti was a phenomenon: a European playwright based in New York achieving national and international recognition without being produced in New York. While most playwrights struggled to "crack" the New York theatrical scene, Fratti imposed himself upon the city by the weight of his international success (more than 300 productions). By 1970 he became one of the most frequently produced playwrights in the Off-Off-Broadway Theatre (16 plays from 1970–72).

Fratti is fascinated with the idea of life as theatre. Existing in an unknowable universe, caught in social systems beyond his control, man becomes an actor wearing an endless array of public and private masks as a means of survival. In such a world, deceit, treachery, and violence are commonplace. While this theme is explored by other modern writers, Fratti is unique for embracing clarity rather than obscurity in the theatre, convinced that a playwright must be the "quintessence of clarity" both for the actor and the audience. Otherwise, he is only "an hysterical poet talking to himself in front of a mirror." Fratti's rich theatrical imagination and impeccable craftsmanship assure clarity.

Comparable to the plots of the commedia dell'arte, many of his plays hinge on a deception, but the results are frequently pathetic or tragic rather than comic. While the characters are passionate, and the situation tense, the structure is coldly logical and tight, progressing like a mystery thriller: the audience's sympathies shift from one character to another; each seems to be on the side of right and the truth is elusive. However, the conclusion is not the revelation of a murderer but a provocative idea regarding the human condition. "I want to open a door in the minds of the audience," states Fratti.

In *The Cage*, Cristiano's pessimism is convincing and his isolation seems justified. Ultimately, however, his moralizing proves destructive; his murder of Pietro, the presumably cruel husband, is the megalomaniacal act of a man who would play God with other peoples' lives. Sanguemarcio, the invalid degenerate of *The Coffin*, pays to hear lurid tales of violence and perversion, aided by his trusted friend, Paoletto, who provides him with storytellers. But the tales are lies; Paoletto is a thief and parasite using the old degenerate for profit. Sanguemarcio dies when he discovers that his one trusted friend was just another of life's frauds. Fratti, however, never moralizes: deceived and deceiver are caught in a hopeless struggle for survival.

The dominant metaphor in Fratti's plays is the trap: characters trapped in situations which they attempt to escape from by violence or deception. Most of the plays are set indoors: oppressive rooms, a cage: concretized images of entrapment. Even the short, percussive titles of his plays suggest traps that have been sprung. But Fratti is not another modern pessimist. While dramatizing life's *Inferno*, he believes in man's basic goodness: "I believe in man, man notwithstanding." In *The Bridge*, a courageous policeman risks his life to save potential suicide victims, recalling a biblical parable that it is better to save one lost sheep than keep a flock. The Priest of *The Roman Guest* learns a new liberalism in America, confronts a prejudiced mob, and returns to Italy with a more profound sense of Christianity. *Che Guevara* is a heroic yet realistic depiction of the Argentinean revolutionary, a man who views his actions as expedient rather than superhuman, necessary steps toward the positive evolution of society.

Fratti also has a subtle sense of comedy. Works such as *The Academy* and *Waiting* are humorous explorations of deceit and self deception. In *The Academy*, set in Post-War Italy, a Fascist attempts to revenge himself upon America by maintaining an academy for gigolos in pursuit of wealthy American women. The heroine of *Waiting* feigns docility in order to lure her seducer into marriage and then punish him by making his future life a hell. *The Refrigerators*, a dark comedy, is a bizarre parable of contemporary American life and technology, a unique departure from the essential realism of Fratti's drama. Transvestism and perversion are rampant, and the madcap events have a Marx brothers quality.

America has had a significant influence on Fratti: "This society with all its problems and conflicts is fascinating. It's the ideal society for a modern dramatist." He now writes in English as well as Italian, and evidences a remarkable ear for American dialogue: a terseness and directness that suit the compactness of his dramatic structure. Living in the heart of Manhattan's theatre district, Fratti is continually stimulated by the city, inspired by the most seemingly insignificant event or occurrence around him. "I am a great observer. Faces are incredibly revealing. Just an expression can give me an idea for a play." He describes the scene that provided him with the idea for *The Chinese Friend*, a one-act masterpiece of racial prejudice, filled with nuances regarding America's foreign policy in the Far East: "A very handsome, and elegantly attired American family passed me on the street. They seemed to be overly solicitous to a Chinese gentleman, who was, apparently, their guest. "

Deeply involved in the issues that confront America, Fratti focuses his American plays on racial prejudice, violence, and social oppression. However, he is never didactic. Rather than a call to political action, Fratti's drama is a plea for universal understanding and compassion, a philosophy which he not only espouses but practises. He is a committed playwright, committed to man and art, whose love of the theatre has always taken precedence over personal ambition, an inspiration to younger playwrights.

—A. Richard Sogliuzzo

FRAYN, Michael. British. Born in London, 8 September 1933. Educated at Kingston Grammar School, Surrey; Emmanuel College, Cambridge, B.A. 1957. Served in the Royal Artillery and Intelligence Corps, 1952–54. Married Gillian Palmer in 1960; has three children. Reporter, 1957–59, and Columnist, 1959–62, *The Guardian*, Manchester and London; Columnist, *The Observer*, London, 1962–68. Recipient: Maugham Award, 1966; Hawthornden Prize, for fiction, 1967· National Press Award, 1970; *Evening Standard* award, 1976. Address: c/o Elaine Greene Ltd., 31 Newington Green, London N16 9PU, England.

PUBLICATIONS

Plays

    Zounds!, with John Edwards, music by Keith Statham (produced Cambridge, 1957).
    The Two of Us (includes *Black and Silver, The New Quixote, Mr. Foot, Chinamen*) (produced London, 1970; Ogunquit, Maine, 1975). London, Fontana, 1970; *Chinamen* published in *The Best Short Plays 1973*, edited by Stanley Richards, Radnor, Pennsylvania, Chilton, 1973.
    The Sandboy (produced London, 1971).
    Alphabetical Order (produced London, 1975).
    Donkeys' Years (produced London, 1976).
    Clouds (produced London, 1976).

    Television Plays: *Jamie, On a Flying Visit*, 1968; *One Pair of Eyes* (documentary), 1968; *Birthday*, 1969; *Imagine a City Called Berlin* (documentary), 1975; *Making Faces*, 1975.

Novels

    The Tin Men. London, Collins, 1965; Boston, Little Brown, 1966.
    The Russian Interpreter. London, Collins, and New York, Viking Press, 1966.
    Towards the End of the Morning. London, Collins, 1967; as *Against Entropy*, New York, Viking Press, 1967.
    A Very Private Life. London, Collins, and New York, Viking Press, 1968.
    Sweet Dreams. London, Collins, 1973; New York, Viking Press, 1974.

Other

The Day of the Dog (Guardian columns).   London, Collins, 1962; New York, Doubleday, 1963.

The Book of Fub (Guardian columns).   London, Collins, 1963; as *Never Put Off to Gomorrah*, New York, Pantheon Books, 1964.

On the Outskirts (Observer columns).   London, Collins, 1964.

At Bay in Gear Street (Observer columns).   London, Fontana, 1967.

Constructions (philosophy).   London, Wildwood House, 1974.

Editor, *The Best of Beachcomber*, by J. B. Morton.   London, Heinemann, 1963.

*   *   *

A veteran columnist of *The Guardian* and *The Observer*, Michael Frayn has both extended and broadened his wit since his first West End play, *The Two of Us*. This enjoyed a successful run with Richard Briers and Lynn Redgrave playing the couple common to all four of the short plays that make up this work. The first three are duologues, the fourth, *Chinamen*, the longest and most substantial offering, has a host and hostess waiting for and receiving their dinner guests. This results in a farcical confusion that makes it the highlight of the quartet.

Frayn was clearly feeling his way in *The Two of Us*. The first duologue, in which a couple abroad on holiday take it in turn to be subjugated by their howling infant, is little more than an extended revue sketch, with the baby becoming like the proverbial hot brick being passed from hand to hand. The next is a spirited conversation piece between an electronics engineer and his girl-friend, where the frenzied talk is sometimes reminiscent of *Design for Living*, and where the plot's design is minimal. The third, *Mr. Foot*, has a middle-aged pair probing one another's mildly absurd anxieties, with more substance to the situation, possibly, than N.F. Simpson might have used.

Frayn's next play *The Sandboy*, produced at Greenwich with Joe Melia and Eleanor Bron playing, again, the omnipresent couple, has a more distinctive framework. A city planner's private life is invaded by an army of television cameras. They are symbolized by a fat slug of an electric cable which slides off the forestage and forms a kind of umbilicus joining the audience to the stage.

But the framework is little more than plasterboard for Frayn's wit to decorate. The subject is happiness. Phil always falls on his feet. Every phone call brings good news, and the television unit is an excuse for him to bounce into an apologia of good fortune. A woman from across the street disrupts this with a private marital grief. Phil becomes her grief's compère. Every time something might really happen, in he jumps with a clever inhibitory explanation. The conclusion would seem to be that happiness and unhappiness balance themselves out chemically, and people find out how happy they are by seeing how unhappy others are: a view depressingly limited, and to use a favourite word of Phil's, "metabolic." *The Sandboy*, like *The Two of Us*, is characterized by amusing and extremely well-observed bouts of repartee, but little by way of a reversal of fortune comes along to bring the play to a crisis, even a comic one. Repeated bouts of garrulity wear thin after a while.

Alphabetical Order is definitely the best expression of Frayn's theatrical talents to date, achieving resonance that owes a great deal to Frayn's own journalistic experience. The play is set in the cutting library of a small provincial newspaper, and at once the specialist wit Frayn brings to bear on the situation, lifts it quite out of the class of the other stage works.

The first act introduces a new arrival, Leslie, into the office, and in the tradition of occupational comedy, her acclimitization to the other members of the staff provides a breeding ground for fecund wit. There is Geoffrey, the messenger, "in and out all the time," who has a word for everybody, and insists on supplying Leslie with a clean hand towel. John, the leader writer from Oxford ("was it All Saints?"), takes a shine to Leslie, meanwhile turning every sentence he utters into a peroration. His parenthetic meanderings cover every subject under the sun from global density to local Indian nosh. "I'm merely being a channel through which an unasked question can get itself asked," he observes of himself. Finally, there is Lucy, the library chief, who keeps the place bungling along with happy ineptitude.

Leslie sets to and reforms the library, as well as the lives of those who work there, and when the job is nearing completion, the paper goes bankrupt and closes down. This gives rise to a splendid comic climax of frustration when the contents of files are scattered over the stage. "I can see I shall have to eat my words," one character remarks, and then chews cuttings. Here Frayn can indulge fully his gift for verbal high jinks.

The picture of newspaper life is faithful if anarchic, and, if the story remains slight, the parts of Lucy, Leslie, and John (played at Hampstead by Billie Whitelaw, Barbara Ferris, and Dinsdale Landen, respectively), provide material for some brilliant comic acting.

—Garry O'Connor

FREEMAN, David. Canadian. Born in Toronto, Ontario, 7 January 1945. Attended Sunnyview School, to grade 10; McMaster University, Hamilton, Ontario (News Features Editor, university newspaper, 1970), B.A. in political science 1971. Worked as a Public Relations Officer, I.B.M., Don Mills, Ontario, 1970. Recipient: Ontario Council for the Arts grant, 1971; Canada Council grant, 1972, 1974; Chalmers Award, 1973. Agent: John Goodwin and Associates, 3823 Melrose, Montreal Quebec H4A 2S3, Canada.

PUBLICATIONS

Plays

> *Creeps* (produced Toronto, 1971; Washington, D.C., and New York, 1973). Toronto, University of Toronto Press, and New York, French, 1972; London, French, 1975.
> *Battering Ram* (produced Toronto, 1972; New York, 1975). Toronto, Playwrights Co-op, 1972.
> *You're Gonna Be Alright, Jamie Boy* (produced Toronto, 1974). Vancouver, Talonbooks, 1974.
> *Flytrap* (produced Montreal, 1976).

David Freeman comments:

(1973) *Creeps* is an autobiographical play which takes place one afternoon in the men's washroom of a sheltered workshop for the cerebral palsied. It has basically four main characters: Tom, Jim, Pete, and Sam. The four congregate in the washroom in order to get away from such menial and boring tasks as sanding blocks, separating nuts and bolts, folding boxes, and weaving rugs. The main conflict is between Tom, who considers himself an abstract artist and wants to leave the workshop to devote more time to his painting, and Jim, who has recently been promoted to office work and would prefer that Tom stay in the workshop where life is less complicated. Pete is lazy and is content to let the world wait on

him, while Sam is bitter, cruel, foul-mouthed, and lecherous. This afternoon they talk about
sexual frustration, broken dreams, and rage at a society which has condemned them to the
mercy of false charity and at themselves for accepting it. The play came out of my own
experiences in such a place ten years ago, for I myself am afflicted with cerebral palsy. My
latest play, *Battering Ram*, also deals with a handicapped person, but is quite different is that
it deals with the problems of sexual frustration and loneliness more explicitly. At this
writing, I am at work on a screenplay, *The Poker Player*, which deals with handicapped
teenagers at camp. I hope you don't think I'm in a rut, because I intend soon to start work
on a play where the characters are only emotionally disabled – and not physically.

(1977) *You're Gonna Be Alright, Jamie-Boy* and *Flytrap* deal with emotionally
handicapped characters, not those who are physically handicapped.

*   *   *

David Freeman's world is one of cripples, both physical and psychological, and one which
mirrors the equally crippled morality, aspirations, and institutions of the "real" world
which surrounds his fictional one and which causes or assists in the deforming of his various
victims. It follows, therefore, that his characters and plots are naturalistic, although
dramatic hyperbole often breaks into the otherwise naturalistic conception in the form of
stereotype leading to caricature, as in *You're Gonna Be Alright, Jamie Boy*, or of intensely
theatrical and fantastic vignettes superimposed on the plot, as in the circus interludes of
Creeps.

The result in *Creeps* is the creation of a shockingly powerful dramatic vehicle for
Freeman's bitter but balanced attack on his audience, its physical normality, its ignorance of
the humiliation of life for an adult trapped in the crippled body and society of a hideous
child, and finally and most unrelentingly, on its pity. It is in the dramatic rather than
thematic elements that Freeman most devastatingly exposes the shallow and self-gratifying
attempts of the charitable institutions to invade this "sheltered" world. In its virtually
terroristic design, the play hurls its washroom set, sexual frustration, unremittingly obscene
language and grotesque mime at the audience in a *coup de théâtre* which the more
controlled and mature later plays cannot approach.

Battering Ram reworks the theme of sexual frustration, and in its removal of the
physically repulsive, loses much of the dramatic strength of *Creeps*. Still, the play makes an
arresting statement and, more importantly, builds it around a full characterization of the
protagonist. In this focus and its largely successful execution, Freeman evidences his growth
as a playwright, moving as he does into more literary and less personal devices.

In *You're Gonna Be Alright, Jamie Boy*, he continues this growth, creating a play in the
neo-naturalistic school becoming so popular in Canadian drama in the 1970's.
Unfortunately, in moving completely from his physically crippled familiars, Freeman has
created rather clichéd North American types working out a predictable pattern based on the
emptiness of television oriented lives. In this first attempt in the psychological, however, the
characterization holds together well and the dialogue picks up the brilliance of *Creeps*, often
leaping into moments of real comedy and pathos.

David Freeman shows enormous potential in his own maturation as a writer, to say
nothing of having produced a first play of staggering proportions. When he combines his
new control of the craft with his initial originality and energy, he will write a play of world
significance.

—S.R. Gilbert

FRENCH, David.   Canadian.   Born in Coley's Point, Newfoundland, 18 January 1939. Educated at Oakwood Collegiate High School, Toronto, graduated 1959; Pasadena Playhouse, California. Actor in Toronto, 1960–65. Recipient: Chalmers Award, 1973; Lieutenant-Governor's Award, 1974; Canada Council grant, 1974, 1975. Agent: Lois Berman, 156 East 52nd Street, New York, New York 10022, U.S.A. Address: c/o Tarragon Theatre, 30 Bridgman Avenue, Toronto, Ontario, Canada.

PUBLICATIONS

Plays

   Leaving Home (produced Toronto, 1972; New York, 1974).   Toronto, New Press, 1972; New York, French, 1976.
   Of the Fields, Lately (produced Toronto, 1973).   Toronto, New Press, 1975; New York, French, 1977.
   One Crack Out (produced Toronto, 1975).   Toronto, New Press, 1976.

   Radio Plays: *Angeline*, 1967; *Invitation to a Zoo*, 1967; *The Winter of Timothy*, 1968.

   Television Plays: *Beckons the Dark River*, 1962; *The Willow Harp*, 1963; *A Ring for Florie*, 1964; *After Hours*, 1965; *Sparrow on a Monday Morning*, 1965; *A Token Gesture*, 1970; *The Tender Branch*, 1972.

                        *   *   *

   The first of David French's three stage plays, *Leaving Home*, concerns the sense of displacement and frustration of a family of Irish immigrants who have been torn, not once, but twice from their roots, first from Ireland to Newfoundland and then from Newfoundland to Toronto. They carry with them the luggage of their past – Catholic-Protestant antagonisms, family loyalties amid bitter dissension, a salty vituperation, and a habit of convivial overdrinking. Because of the double displacement, the past has become meaningless, yet the older generation retain it and struggle to relate it to the future. The play's theme is the ancient one of a son's need to free himself from his father, paralleled and reinforced by the theme of the alienation of the immigrant from his children in the new land.
   The Mercer family organization is not unlike that in Arthur Miller's *Death of a Salesman*, with Mary Mercer loving but ineffectual in her efforts to keep the family peace and protect her husband, Jacob, and eldest son, Ben, from hurting each other. Jacob's life has been damaged by a brutal, uncaring father, the early death of his mother, and an interrupted education. In Ben, Jacob dreams of living again, successful in some socially esteemed profession and with a warm father-son relationship, yet sneers at the university education which is his son's path to a better life.
   The action of the play takes place in the Mercer kitchen and parlour, rendered with an effect of cramped and unlovely realism, on the wedding day of the younger son, Billy, who has gotten his high school girlfriend pregnant. Significantly, she is Catholic, and the daughter of Minnie Jackson, a sweetheart of Jacob's youth, a woman he did not marry because of her religion and because of her randy and slip-shod behaviour, which still both attracts and repels him. Instead he married Protestant Mary, pretty, austere, and middle class. The wedding triggers off a series of painful reminiscences and violent reactions in Jake, not against Billy, who is marrying a Catholic, abandoning school and the traditional prejudices of the Irish in general, but against Ben, whose leaving home Jacob regards with anguish as the death of all his hopes.

The sequel to this play, entitled *Of the Fields, Lately*, deals with Ben's return home after two futile years in the prairies, summoned ostensibly for the funeral of his aunt, but actually because of the growing frailty of his father. The play is permeated with the sense of death, but the funeral device does not create as tight a dramatic unity as the wedding in *Leaving Home*. The same temperamental antagonisms arise between Jacob and Ben, completing their alienation, shown by the use of soliloquies of reminiscence by both characters at the beginning of the play and by Ben alone after his father's death in the end. This single departure from realism frames the play declaring symbolically at the opening and reaffirming at the closing the sense of isolation felt by each character.

Yet rejection and alienation are not the whole story. Jake has a vitality lacking in his sons, although it has been warped into boasting, empty heroics at his job, and heavy drinking. Ben instinctively recognizes his father's superiority to him and feels a dogged sense of duty and even respect for Jacob, but cannot bear to be enslaved by Jacob's disappointments and dead values.

The realism of the first two plays is pushed to greater extremes in French's third, *One Crack Out*, which deals with the tawdry life of petty criminals and pool hall gamblers. The set is divided between the squalid pool hall and adjoining lavatory, and the equally squalid bed-sitting room of Charlie, a pool shark, and his wife, Helen, a stripper. These claustrophobic interiors, plus eleven short scenes tumbling upon one another, build up tension as the deadline approaches when Charlie must pay the Collector the $3,000 he owes or get his hands broken.

As all his efforts to raise the money by borrowing and hustling fail, Charlie emerges as not only devious and frantic, but also as one who is capable of loyalty and unselfish feeling. With his losing streak ended through an act of pure devotion by Helen, he is able to resolve his problem in his own terms by a duel of skill. In creating Charlie's dilemma and preventing any avenue of escape, French has over-plotted the play and its emotional power is diffused by melodramatic effects such as the breathlessly approaching deadline, the complication of Charlie's sexual impotence with his wife, and the unprepared-for conversion of the Collector to accepting Charlie's challenge debt. Despite the fact that this play is less strong than French's first two, it marks a forward step in his development by moving away from the autobiographical into an invented, objective world.

—Dorothy Parker

FRIEDMAN, Bruce Jay.   American.   Born in New York City, 26 April 1930. Educated at the University of Missouri, Columbia, Bachelor of Journalism 1951. Served in the United States Air Force, 1951–53: Lieutenant. Married Ginger Howard in 1954; has three children. Editorial Director, Magazine Management Company, publishers, New York, 1953–56. Address: c/o F. Levinson, 430 East 63rd Street, New York, New York 10021, U.S.A.

PUBLICATIONS

Plays

23 *Pat O'Brien Movies* (produced New York, 1966).
Scuba Duba: A Tense Comedy (produced New York, 1967).   New York, Simon and Schuster, 1968.

A Mother's Kisses, music by Richard Adler, adaptation of the novel by Bruce Jay
    Friedman (produced New Haven, Connecticut, 1968).
Steambath (produced New York, 1970).   New York, French, 1971.
First Offenders, with Jacques Levy (also co-director: produced New York, 1973).

Novels

Stern.   New York, Simon and Schuster, 1962; London, Deutsch, 1963.
A Mother's Kisses.   New York, Simon and Schuster, 1964; London, Cape, 1965.
The Dick.   New York, Knopf, 1970; London, Cape, 1971.
About Harry Towns.   New York, Knopf and London, Cape, 1974.

Short Stories

Far from the City of Class and Other Stories.   New York, Frommer-Posmantier, 1963.
Black Angels.   New York, Simon and Schuster, 1966; London, Cape, 1967.

Other

Editor, *Black Humor*.   New York, Bantam, 1965.

Theatrical Activities:

Director: **Play** – *First Offenders* (co-director, with Jacques Levy), New York, 1973.

           *   *   *

It has always been the temptation of fiction writers to turn to the theatre. From Balzac
through Henry James 19th-century novelists tried their hand at playwriting, with quite
mixed results. Most of us are now interested in only one of Balzac's plays, *Mercadet*, and
that probably because of its influence on *Waiting for Godot*. James's plays are readily
available in Leon Edel's fine edition but only specialists seem to bother to read them. The
same is true for most of the plays of the other 19th-century novelists-turned-dramatist. This
rule-of-thumb applies also to certain of our contemporaries: Saul Bellow and John Hawkes,
for example, have turned from first-rate fiction to the theatre; the results have been
somewhat frustrating and disappointing.

The case of Hawkes is instructive because his plays seem largely extensions of his novels
and elaborate on certain of their themes. Hawkes had already published four superb novels
by the time he brought out his collection of plays, *The Innocent Party*, in 1966. It would seem
that he turned to the theatre only after he felt his position as a novelist was fairly assured.
Bruce Jay Friedman appeared to follow the same pattern although he turned to playwriting
earlier in his career than Hawkes. The change from fiction to drama was also managed,
from all indications, with fewer problems. *Scuba Duba* and *Steambath* are clearly more
stageable, if less literary, than Hawkes's plays.

But like the plays in *The Innocent Party* Friedman's work for the theatre is thematically
very much tied to his fiction. *Scuba Duba* and *Steambath* use the ambience, character types,
and other literary props familiar to readers of Friedman's novels and collections of stories.
Guilt, failure, and frustration are words which come to mind when we look at any part of
his *oeuvre*.

Scuba Duba bears the subtitle "a tense comedy"; so might almost anything else he has
written because laughs come always at the expense of overbearing psychic pain in all of his

work. Harold Wonder, the thirty-five year old worrier who uses a scythe as a more aggressive kind of security blanket, has rented a chateau in the south of France. As the play opens he laments the fact that his wife has just run off with a black man. Harold's urban Jewish intonation is evident even in his first speech: "I really needed this. This is exactly what I came here for." He feels the need to communicate his *tsuris* to anyone who will listen. An attractive young lady, Miss Janus, is all too willing to help out, but Harold – like most of Friedman's other heroes – seems especially drawn to his psychiatrist and his Jewish mother. The former, aptly named Dr. Schoenfeld, who appears in the first act as a "cut-out" and returns in the flesh in Act II, warns him in accustomed psychiatric fashion: "...you've never once looked at life sideways...." Harold's mother seems cut from the same cloth as the mothers in Friedman's three novels, *Stern, A Mother's Kisses*, and *The Dick*. Harold speaks to her long-distance and the telephone conversation which follows should be familiar to readers of the fiction of Philip Roth, Wallace Markfield, Herbert Gold, and other American Jewish writers. Harold's mother's voice is perfectly tuned: "That's all right, Harold. I'll just consider that my payment after thirty-six years of being your mother."

As the play develops the stage gets more and more crowded. A namedropping French landlady, an American tourist who demands proximity to a Chinese restaurant, a thief with an aphoristic turn ("All men are thieves"), an anti-American gendarme, a "wild-looking blonde" named Cheyenne who prefers "Bernie" Malamud and "those urban Jews" to C. P. Snow – all appear at one time or other. The main confrontation occurs in the second act when Harold's wife appears, followed shortly by two Negroes, one of whom is her lover. Harold's reaction involves much of the ambivalence experienced by Friedman Jews when in the company of blacks. The hero of Friedman's first novel, for example, went out of his way to express an affection he was never certain was compelling enough: "...Stern, who had a special feeling for all Negroes, hugged him [Crib] in a show of brotherhood."

Harold, *schlemiel* that he is, ends up by losing his wife and vows to "get started in my new life." Stern and Kenneth LePeters (the hero of *The Dick*) make similar resolutions and LePeters even goes to the point of leaving his wife and planning an extended trip with his daughter.

Friedman has been grouped with the so-called black humorists on several occasions. In a foreword he wrote for a collection of stories, *Black Humor* (which included his own story "Black Angels"), he remarked: "There *is* a fading line between fantasy and reality...." This is evident in *Scuba Duba* but perhaps even more in *Steambath*. Almost half way through the first act, the protagonist Tandy makes the shocked discovery: "...We're dead? Is that what you were going to say? That's what I was going to say. That's what we are. The second I said it, I knew it. Bam! Dead! Just like that! Christ!" Until this point in the play all indications are of a *real* steambath; then everything suddenly dilates into symbol and "fantasy," with no noticeable change in the dramatic movement. (John Hawkes used the steambath in the fifth chapter of his novel *The Lime Twig* with somewhat the same symbolical intent.)

Tandy is clearly not quite ready for death and protests the Attendant's (read God) decision through the remainder of the play. He seems very like Kenneth LePeters at the end of *The Dick*. He is on the verge of doing things he likes – writing a novel about Charlemagne, working for a charity to help brain-damaged welders, courting a Bryn Mawr girl who makes shish kebab – after divorcing his wife and giving up his job "teaching art appreciation over at the Police Academy." Tandy shares his frustration with a blonde girl named Meredith in somewhat the way Harold Wonder shared his plight, conversationally, with Miss Janus in *Scuba Duba*.

Max Schulz, in a very good book on the American Jewish novel, *Radical Sophistication*, speaks of Friedman's manner as having something "of the stand-up comic." This is especially noticeable in *Steambath*. Its humor favors the incongruous and unlikely. One can almost hear Woody Allen pronouncing some of the lines with considerable relish, like Tandy's incredulous response when he realizes that God is a Puerto Rican steambath attendant or when he discovers what he stand to lose by being dead: "No more airline stewardesses... *Newsweek*...Jesus, no more *Newsweek*."

Much of the humor has to do with popular culture. Bieberman, who makes intermittent appearances, is very much taken with the actors and baseball players of the 1940's. Other characters refer to the impact made by such essentials of television as the David Frost Show and pro football (American style). Names of every variety, including those of defeated political candidates (Mario Procaccino) and editors of magazines (Norman Podhoretz), are introduced incongruously and irreverently in the conversations. Theodore Solotaroff believes that

> nostalgia has a particular attraction for many Jewish writers: some of them, like Gold or Bruce Jay Friedman or Wallace Markfield or Irwin Faust, seem to possess virtually total recall of their adolescent years, as though there were still some secret meaning that resides in the image of Buster Brown shoes, or Edward G. Robinson's snarl, or Ralston's checkerboard package.

How much to the point of this remark is *Steambath*!
There is a good deal of the spirit of the second-generation American Jew in Friedman's plays as well as in his novels. He has caught this verbal rhythm and pulse beat in much the way that Philip Roth and Woody Allen have.

—Melvin J. Friedman

FRIEL, Brian.   Irish.   Born in Omagh, County Tyrone, 9 January 1929. Educated at St. Columb's College, Derry, 1941–46; St. Patrick's College, Maynooth, 1946–49, B.A. 1949; St. Joseph's Training College, Belfast, 1949–50. Married Anne Morrison in 1954; has five children. School teacher in primary and intermediate schools in Derry, 1950–60. Since 1960, Full-time Writer. Observer, for five months in 1963, Tyrone Guthrie Theatre, Minneapolis. Recipient: Irish Arts Council Macauley Fellowship, 1963. D.Lit.: Rosary College, Chicago. Agent: Curtis Brown Ltd., 1 Craven Hill, London W2 3EW; or, Audrey Wood, International Creative Management, 40 West 57th Street, New York, New York 10019, U.S.A. Address: Ardmore, Muff, Lifford, County Donegal, Ireland.

PUBLICATIONS

Plays

   The Francophile (produced Belfast, 1960).
   The Enemy Within (produced Dublin, 1962).
   The Blind Mice (produced Dublin, 1963).
   Philadelphia, Here I Come! (produced Dublin, 1964; New York, 1966; London, 1967).
      London, Faber, 1965; New York, Farrar Straus, 1966.
   The Loves of Cass McGuire (broadcast, 1966; produced New York, 1966; Dublin, 1967;
      London, 1970).   London, Faber, and New York, Farrar Straus, 1967.
   Lovers: Part One: Winners; Part Two: Losers (produced Dublin, 1967; New York,
      1968; London, 1969).   New York, Farrar Straus, 1968; London, Faber, 1969.
   Crystal and Fox (produced Dublin, 1968; Los Angeles, 1970; New York, 1973).
      London, Faber, 1970; included in *Two Plays*, 1970.

The Mundy Scheme (produced Dublin and New York, 1969).   Included in *Two Plays*, 1970.
Two Plays: Crystal and Fox and The Mundy Scheme.   New York, Farrar Straus. 1970.
The Gentle Island (produced Dublin, 1971).   London, Davis Poynter, 1973.
The Freedom of the City (produced Dublin, London, and Chicago, 1973; New York, 1974).   London, Faber, 1974.
Volunteers (produced Dublin, 1975).
Faith Healer (produced New York, 1976).

Screenplay: *Philadelphia, Here I Come!*, 1970.

Radio Plays: *A Sort of Freedom*, 1958; *To This Hard House*, 1958; *A Doubtful Paradise*, 1962; *The Founder Members*, 1964; *The Loves of Cass McGuire*, 1966.

Short Stories

The Saucer of Larks.   London, Gollancz, and New York, Doubleday, 1962.
The Gold in the Sea.   London, Gollancz, and New York, Doubleday, 1966.
A Saucer of Larks: Stories of Ireland (selections from the two previous volumes). London, Arrow, 1969.

Critical Study: *Brian Friel* by D. E. S. Maxwell, Lewisburg, Pennsylvania, Bucknell University Press, 1973.

*   *   *

Brian Friel's first notable play, *Philadelphia, Here I Come!*, produced at the Dublin Theatre Festival in 1964, is ostensibly concerned with the pressures which lead a young Irishman to despair of his circumstances and contemplate emigration. Gareth O'Donnell, who has failed in love and sees himself as trapped in a humiliating job in his father's store, cut off from any real affection, responds to the notion of a new life in America with apparent enthusiasm. But beneath his gaudy images of a larger-than-life America is a more fundamental need. Indeed, the play's real concern is less with dissecting a particularly Irish dilemma than with examining the barriers of habit and self-consciousness which prevent people from offering the contact and consolation necessary to a meaningful existence. We are shown the two sides of Gareth O'Donnell's life, the public and the private, actually acted out by two different actors and much of the play's humour derives from the interplay between the two as well as from the comments which the invisible private personality makes about the other characters. But beneath this there is a touch of the sentimentality which is a mark both of his short stories and plays.

Reminiscent in some respects of the work of William Saroyan and Thornton Wilder, his plays are characterised by a bitter-sweet wistfulness as they plot the pathetic yet touching efforts of man to adjust his emotional responses to a world which seems designed to frustrate his desire for beauty and uncomplicated happiness. Friel traces this unequal struggle from the volatile adolescent love of *Lovers*, in which two young lovers are drowned, to the desperate retreat into illusion of an old woman disappointed by a life which could never quite match the magnificence of her dreams, in *The Loves of Cass McGuire*. Whether it is Fox, of *Crystal and Fox*, frantically trying to recapture the simplicity and happiness of his youth at the cost of those who look to him for help and encouragement in the present, or Gareth O'Donnell, trying to remind his father of a moment of shared intimacy in the past which may or may not have happened, we are confronted with individuals scrabbling away at the ashes of their lives in search of an ember which can be fanned into flames. That he manages to sustain pathos for the most part without collapsing into the worst excesses of sentimentality is a testament to his judgement; that his work at its best aspires to a poetic lyricism which nonetheless stops short of triteness is evidence of his genuine feeling for language and sensitivity to tone and rhythm — a sense of counterpoint which is emotional as well as verbal.

Friel's humour is never vicious. Though at times it exposes human inadequacy and deceit and though it has an admirable satirical edge, it is, finally, an indication of the indomitability of the human spirit rather than a means of mocking individual aspirations. For the characters themselves a joke becomes a protective device which is not without its dignity and courage. The sometimes bitter and painful experience of life are normally subsumed in a conviction that time can heal as well as injure. The brutal confusions of the political scene in Northern Ireland, however, as dramatised in *The Freedom of the City*, seem to threaten his earlier belief that illusions may sustain as well as destroy, that all experience is finally absorbed to become part of the bitter-sweet reality of human existence.

—C. W. E. Bigsby

FRISBY, Terence. British   Born in New Cross, London, 28 November 1932. Educated at Dartford Grammar School; Central School of Speech Training and Dramatic Art, London, 1955–57. Married Christine Vecchione in 1962 (divorced); has one son. Worked as a salesman, capstan lathe operator, factory hand, waiter, chauffeur, chucker-out at the Hammersmith Palais, etc.; since 1957, professional actor. Resident Director: New Theatre, Bromley, Kent, 1963–64. Agent: Harvey Unna, 14 Beaumont Mews, Marylebone High Street, London W1N 4HE. Address: 52 Cloncurry Street, London S.W.6, England.

PUBLICATIONS

Plays

   The Subtopians (also director: produced London, 1964).   London, French, 1964.
   There's a Girl in My Soup (produced London, 1966; New York, 1967).   London and
      New York, French, 1968.
   The Bandwagon (produced London, 1969).   London, French, 1973.

   Screenplay: *There's a Girl in My Soup*, 1970.

   Television Plays: *Guilty*, 1964; *Public Eye* Series, 1964; *Take Care of Madam*, 1965;
   Adam Adamant series, 1966; *More Deadly Than the Sword*, 1966; *Don't Forget the
   Basics*, 1967; *Lucky Feller* series, 1976.

Theatrical Activities:

   Director: **Plays** — in various repertory companies, including plays at Bromley, Kent,
   1963–64; *The Subtopians*, London, 1964.

Actor: **Plays** – over 200 roles in repertory theatres in Bromley, Guildford, Lincoln, Richmond, York; London debut as Charlie Pepper in *Gentleman's Pastime* by Marion Hunt, 1958; in *A Sense of Detachment* by John Osborne, London, 1973; *X* by Barry Reckord, London, 1974; other roles in London and on tour. **Television** – *Play School; It Must Be Something in the Water* by Alan Plater, 1973; *When the Boys Come Out to Play* by Richard Harris, 1974; *Leeds-United!* by Colin Welland, 1974.

*   *   *

Terence Frisby's first play, *The Subtopians*, was greeted with eulogies when, in 1964, it was seen for the first time. It was, critics decided, funny but complex, accurately worked out, deeply felt in spite of its genuine comedy, serious in intention but almost painfully hilarious, and it had an unbreakable grip on the realities of social life in the 1960's.

Frisby was 32 when *The Subtopians* arrived to signal a newcomer whose gifts were, to say the least, so interesting that his future activities were sure to demand close attention. Part at least of the technical neatness of his first play was due to his training at the Central School of Speech Training and Dramatic Art and to his work as an actor in repertory, musicals and films, as an entertainer in night clubs and cabaret, and as a director. There is a solid foundation of technique beneath the sometimes unkind observation and harsh comedy.

In 1966, *There's a Girl in My Soup* brought Frisby one of the greatest commercial successes in the modern theatre, running for six years in the West End and, at the same time, pleasing most of the critics. Like *The Subtopians*, it has beautifully efficient machinery and precision of observation. Its hero has the sort of position in life – he is an expert on food, writing for intellectual periodicals – which once would have pointed him out as a figure of fun but, in 1966, assured an audience that he was a leader of thought and fashion whose familiarity with the best restaurants is intrinsically romantic and enviable. Thus he is in a position to follow an exhausting, eventful career as an amorist whose endless successes are with the young who find his expertise, and the attitude towards him of those whose efforts he criticises, altogether glamorous. It is less the dialogue or anything explicit in the play than the form it takes and the succession of events which indicate that behind the parade of insatiable appetite for change and his pride in his sexual prowess he is at the same time both lonely and uncertain of his attractiveness to those whom he regards as victims. Frisby naturally chooses to study the girl whose victim he becomes, in whose life he is only a pleasant interlude. The "trendiness" and "contemporaneity" of *There's a Girl in My Soup* carried the play round a triumphal tour of the world's theatres, with productions not only throughout the English-speaking theatre but in most European countries as well as in Turkey, Israel and Mexico.

The course of events which led to the production of Frisby's third play, *The Bandwagon*, rose out of his success as a script writer. *Guilty*, a one-off piece for the BBC in 1964, was followed by a comedy, *Don't Forget the Basics*, for Independent Television and contributions to various series, notably to *Public Eye*, which at its best gave an almost continental seediness to the activities of a provincial private detective, and *Adam Adamant*, in which adventure stories which might almost have come to birth in a boys' comic were treated with ususual and preposterous elegancies and elaborations. *The Band Wagon*, originally *Some Have Greatness Thrust upon Them*, was to be one of BBC television's socially conscious Wednesday Plays. It chose to imagine the situation of a stupid, ugly, graceless teenage girl, a member of a family of almost appalling fecundity – her mother and her sister are both pregnant when the play begins – who discovers that, though unmarried, she is to become the mother of quintuplets. Her prolificness, before drugs inducing multiple births had won any special attention, reaches the ears of popular newspapers, who make her a heroine, and television, which interviews her. The interview comes to an end when Aurora (the most unfortunately named heroine) explains the physiological misinformation and ignorance that are responsible for her plight. Frisby's refusal to alter a line which, the BBC believed, would give unnecessary offence, led to the Corporation's refusal to produce the play.

The BBC was, perhaps, entirely wrong. The line – "My friend Syl told me it was safe standing up" – is all of a piece – with a matter-of-fact simplicity which makes Aurora almost unexploitable. The popular press, determined to make Aurora into a heroine of romance, finds the drab, nervous army cook who seduced her too soon for an evening at the theatre to end, so that, manoeuvred into marriage, Aurora has to be hurried from the church into childbed; and so have her mother and sister. The play belongs to the tradition of broad farce, and its final scene, as the women-folk depart from the altar in agonised haste, sacrifices the precarious dignity and simplicity which have won the sympathy of the audience. *The Bandwagon*, in the good old days of curtain-raisers, could have stopped at its natural end, the silent, almost unnerving confrontation of two essentially pathetic victims of exploitation, Aurora and her husband-to-be, and have retained its integrity.

Nevertheless, *The Bandwagon* seems likely to follow *There's a Girl in My Soup* into the cinema, and, like everything Frisby has so far done, points to an extension of his range. He is not, so to speak, a fundamentally cheerful writer, for his comedy so far is a response to painful experience. The offence of *The Bandwagon* is not the girl's admission of innocent ignorance but the grafting on of an ending which does not maintain the honesty which prevails through three-quarters of a play that disturbs while it amuses us.

—Henry Raynor

FRY, Christopher. British. Born in Bristol, 18 December 1907. Educated at Bedford Modern School, 1918–26. Served in the Non-Combatant Corps, 1940–44. Married Phyllis Marjorie Hart in 1936; has one son. Teacher, Bedford Froebel Kindergarten, 1926–27; Actor and Office Worker, Citizen House, Bath, 1927; Schoolmaster, Hazelwood School, Limpsfield, Surrey, 1928–31; Secretary to H. Rodney Bennett, 1931–32; Founding Director, Tunbridge Wells Repertory Players, 1932–35; Lecturer and editor of schools magazine, Dr. Barnardo's Homes, 1934–39; Director, 1939–40, and Visiting Director, 1945–46, Oxford Playhouse; Visiting Director, 1946, and Staff Dramatist, 1947, Arts Theatre Club, London. Recipient: Shaw Prize Fund Award, 1948; Foyle Poetry Prize, 1951; New York Drama Critics Circle Award, 1951, 1952, 1956; Queen's Gold Medal for Poetry, 1962; Heinemann Award, 1962. Fellow, Royal Society of Literature. Agent: ACTAC Ltd., 16 Cadogan Lane, London S.W.1. Address: The Toft, East Dean, near Chichester, Sussex, England.

PUBLICATIONS

Plays

    To Sea in a Sieve (as Christopher Harris) (produced Reading, 1935).
    She Shall Have Music, with F. Eyton and M. Crick (produced London, 1935).
    Open Door (produced London, 1936). Goldings, Hertfordshire, Printed by the Boys at
        the Press of Dr. Barnardo's Homes, n.d.
    The Boy with a Cart: Cuthman, Saint of Sussex (produced Coleman's Hatch, Sussex,
        1938; London, 1950; New York, 1953). London, Oxford University Press, 1939;
        New York, Oxford University Press, 1951.
    The Tower (pageant; produced Tewkesbury, 1939).
    Thursday's Child: A Pageant, music by Martin Shaw (produced London, 1939).
        London, Girls' Friendly Society, 1939.

A Phoenix Too Frequent (produced London, 1946; Cambridge, Massachusetts, 1948; New York, 1950).   London, Hollis and Carter, 1946; New York, Oxford University Press, 1949.

The Firstborn (produced Edinburgh, 1948).   Cambridge, University Press, 1946; New York, Oxford University Press, 1950; revised version (produced London, 1952; New York, 1958), London and New York, Oxford University Press, 1952, 1958.

The Lady's Not for Burning (produced London, 1948; New York, 1950).   London and New York, Oxford University Press, 1949; revised version, 1950, 1958.

Thor, With Angels (produced Canterbury, 1948; Washington, D.C., 1950; London, 1952).   Canterbury, H. J. Goulden, 1948; New York, Oxford University Press, 1949.

Venus Observed (produced London, 1950; New York, 1952).   London and New York, Oxford University Press, 1950.

Ring round the Moon: A Charade with Music, adaptation of a play by Jean Anouilh (produced London and New York, 1950).   London and New York, Oxford University Press, 1950.

A Sleep of Prisoners (produced Oxford, London and New York, 1951).   London and New York, Oxford University Press, 1951.

The Dark Is Light Enough: A Winter Comedy (produced London, 1954; New York, 1955).   London and New York, Oxford University Press, 1954.

The Lark, adaptation of a play by Jean Anouilh (produced London, 1955).   London, Methuen, 1955; New York, Oxford University Press, 1956.

Tiger at the Gates, adaptation of a play by Jean Giraudoux (produced London and New York, 1955).   London, Methuen, 1955; New York, Oxford University Press, 1956.

Duel of Angels, adaptation of a play by Jean Giraudoux (produced London, 1958; New York, 1960).   London, Methuen, 1958; New York, Oxford University Press, 1959.

Curtmantle (produced Tilburg, Holland, 1961; London, 1962).   London and New York, Oxford University Press, 1961.

Judith, adaptation of a play by Jean Giraudoux (produced London, 1962).   London, Methuen, 1962.

The Bible: Original Screenplay, assisted by Jonathan Griffin.   New York, Pocket Books, 1966.

Peer Gynt, adaptation of the play by Ibsen (produced Chichester, 1970).   London and New York, Oxford University Press, 1970.

A Yard of Sun: A Summer Comedy (produced Nottingham and London, 1970; Cleveland, 1972).   London and New York, Oxford University Press, 1970.

The Brontës of Haworth (televised, 1973).   London, Davis Poynter, 2 vols., 1975.

Cyrano de Bergerac, adaptation of the play by Edmond Rostand (produced Chichester, 1975).   London and New York, Oxford University Press, 1975.

Screenplays: *The Beggar's Opera*, 1953; *The Queen Is Crowned* (documentary), 1953; *Ben Hur*, 1959; *Barabbas*, 1962; *The Bible: In the Beginning*, 1966.

Radio Plays: for *Children's Hour* series, 1939–40.

Television Plays: *The Canary*, 1950; *The Tenant of Wildfell Hall*, 1968; *The Brontës of Haworth* (four plays), 1973; *The Best of Enemies*, 1976.

Other

An Experience of Critics, with *The Approach to Dramatic Criticism* by W. A. Darlington and others.   London, Perpetua Press, 1952; New York, Oxford University Press, 1953.

The Boat That Mooed (juvenile).   New York, Macmillan, 1966.

Translator, *The Boy and the Magic*, by Colette.   London, Dobson, 1964.

Bibliography: in *Tulane Drama Review* (New Orleans), March 1960.

Critical Studies: *Christopher Fry* by Derek Stanford, London, Longman, 1954; *The Drama of Comedy: Victim and Victor* by Nelson Vos, Richmond, Virginia, John Knox Press, 1965, *Creed and Drama* by W. M. Merchant, London, SPCK, 1965; *The Christian Tradition in Modern Verse Drama* by William V. Spanos, New Brunswick, New Jersey, Rutgers University Press, 1967; *Christopher Fry: A Critical Essay* by Stanley M. Wiersma, Grand Rapids, Michigan, Eerdmans, 1970.

Theatrical Activities:

Director: **Plays** – *How-Do, Princess?* by Ivor Novello, toured, 1936; *The Circle of Chalk* by James Laver, London, 1945; *The School for Scandal* by Sheridan, London, 1946; *A Phoenix Too Frequent*, Brighton, 1950; *The Lady's Not for Burning*, toured, 1971.

Actor: **Plays** – in repertory, Bath, 1937.

Christopher Fry comments:

The way a man writes for the theatre depends on the way he looks at life. If, in his experience, direction and purpose seem to be all-pervading factors, pattern and shape are necessary to his writing. The verse form is an effort to be true to what Eleanor, in *Curtmantle*, calls "the silent order whose speech is all visible things." No event is understandable in a prose sense alone. Its ultimate meaning (that is to say, the complete life of the event, seen in its eternal context) is a poetic meaning. The comedies try to explore a reality behind appearances. "Something condones the world incorrigibly" says Thomas Mendip in *The Lady's Not for Burning* – in spite of the "tragic" nature of life. The problem, a long way from being solved, is how to contain the complexities and paradoxes within two hours of entertainment: how to define the creative pattern of life without the danger of dogmatic statement. Dogma is static; life is movement. "La vérité est dans une nuance."

*   *   *

Christopher Fry's work was doubtless overrated in the fruitful years of *The Lady's Not for Burning* and *A Sleep of Prisoners*; it is most certainly underrated today. This is in part due to an integrity and consistency in the work of a playwright who has pursued his own style of the serio-comic and chosen to ignore fashion. It is as if Beckett and the theatre of the absurd had not existed, nor Brecht and the practice of epic theatre with its oblique devices of structure and technique, nor the socially and politically committed drama following Osborne's *Look Back in Anger*; and Fry's reputation has paid the price. His name is not even listed in the recent dictionary of dramatic literature by Gassner and Quinn. It remains to be seen whether his neglect of contemporary trends matters in the final verdict.

In his last play, *A Yard of Sun*, Fry is still writing in that highly idiosyncratic, all-but-verse idiom of loose pentameters which drew attention to his earliest plays. Characteristically mixing the colloquial and the allusive, a minor character can say, "I pick words gingerly like a rose out of thorns," and at a stroke equalize his role with that of a major, thus by prosaic kitchen-sink standards making all the parts equally literate and classless. Or Angelino Bruno, one of the two central characters whose families are unexpectedly united after World War II, can come out with a startling turn of expression which fixes and underscores the general statement of the stage:

> What a settling-up God's having this week!
> Both of us within two days. Well, once
> The bit's between His teeth things start to move.

Although it may not bear close analysis as poetry on the page, verbal panache of this kind keeps his stage alive even when a situation is static. It is often spendthrift with the necessary economy of the action, and the idiom which refreshed the grim post-war years and dazzled the critics can now seem irrelevant, even facile.

But Fry was seeking a spirited idiom for a contemporary and unobstrusively Christian verse drama after T. S. Eliot had prepared the ground with *Murder in the Cathedral* (1935) and *The Family Reunion* (1939). Where Eliot was concerned to find a spare and unobtrusive verse form designed to control the speech and movement on a stage of modern martyrs, Fry, in a less certain style but with more sense of the stage, aimed with abandon at a general mood to match his themes. There are moments in *A Sleep of Prisoners*, possibly the best anti-war play of its period, when the verse achieves the richness of both tonal and physical embodiment of the stage moment while exploring a verbal idea:

> How ceaseless the earth is. How it goes on.
> Nothing has happened except silence where sound was,
> Stillness where movement was...

These lines are spoken by the figure of Adam just after he has witnessed the murder of Abel his son, and they enact both the father's horror and the scene's meaning.

Where, however, Eliot's profundity of vision carried him through his own inadequacies as a dramatist – notably his inability to create character which did not suffer the atrophy of symbolism – Fry came to lean on an explosive central situation fruitful in itself. This situation might lack the qualities of conflict, tension and development, yet still be capable of holding attention. Thus *A Sleep of Prisoners* consists of a pattern of re-enacted Old Testament stories chosen to illustrate facets of the idea of violence. Each story is not only informed by the audience's own memories of the Bible, but also, because it is dreamed by a modern soldier held prisoner in a church, is automatically granted a contemporary relevance: within the structure of the play the spectator himself works to supply the missing factor in the dramatic equation, and the teaching element of a morality play is actively deduced by our application of the fiction to the fact. Nevertheless, this play suffers, as only morality plays can, from the static preconception by which morality characters tend to be fixed in their symbolic attitudes.

This play in its time startled and delighted audiences by the free use of its church setting, where at a glance the chancel could be Adam's jungle or the pulpit Abraham's mountain: as for *Murder in the Cathedral*, audiences were both theatregoers and congregation, and were unusually exercised by the multiplicity of association felt within the performance. There are no such props for a dramatic experience in Fry's other plays, although in *The Boy with a Cart*, a simple mystery play of spontaneous charm, *The Firstborn*, exploring the tragic dilemma of Moses and the Plagues, and *Curtmantle* he draws upon legend and history in parallel attempts to bring the remote closer to home. *Curtmantle*, too neglected a play, was his most sustained attempt at serious character study: this chronicle play of Henry II in conflict with his Archbishop Becket is set out in a sequence of vivid episodes more in the simple manner of Bolt's episodic *A Man for All Seasons* than with the prismatic counterpoint of Brecht's epic theatre, the scenes designed to illustrate the wit, the wisdom and the complex passions of the title part as Henry searches for a rational unity of divine and secular law.

Fry creates a drama of colour and flair, choosing a situation for its imaginative potential, often one of implicit crisis involving a clash of strong, bright personalities. His situation enables him to demonstrate a compassionate affirmation of life – an optimism which inevitably seemed escapist beside the bleak absurdist landscape of the post-war years, in spite of the tragic mode of *The Firstborn*, *Thor with Angels* (the 1948 Canterbury Festival play) and *The Dark Is Light Enough*, plays which exemplify Fry's philosophy of maturing through crisis:

> We reach an obstacle, and learn to overcome it;
> our thoughts or emotions become knotted, and we
> increase ourselves in order to unknot them; a
> state of being becomes intolerable, and, drawing
> upon a hidden reserve of spirit, we transform it.

But he is nevertheless remembered for those early comedies of mood touched with the wit and fantasy by which he could express his most gentle and humane thinking. The prototype for this kind of comedy, and still the most regularly revived, was the one-act *A Phoenix Too Frequent*. This was taken from the ancient tale of the young Roman widow romantically committed to a fast to the death in her husband's tomb, until she and an equally romantic young soldier agree to substitute the husband's body for the corpse the soldier was guarding with his life. With the lightest of touches, the widow decides for life, and youth and love supplant social convention and death: a joyful illustration of the life-force at work.

The spring-time comedy that made Fry's name and competed for London's attention with Eliot's *The Cocktail Party* in 1949 was his best-known play *The Lady's Not for Burning*, an extension of the style and spirit of *A Phoenix*. His verbal pyrotechnics were at their most assured, and the medieval colour on his stage lifted the play into a rarefied atmosphere that forced comparison with Giraudoux and the lighter Anouilh of *L'Invitation au château* (which Fry was later to translate beautifully as *Ring round the Moon*). A simple crisis again sets the play in motion, when one Thomas Mendip, desiring but denied death, is confronted with Jennet Jourdemayne, who wants to live but must die as a witch. She envies his death-wish, he her "damnable mystery," until, to test his sincerity and her courage, Fry impudently arranges for them one last "joyous" evening together before Jennet's execution. The result is to dramatize with graceful irony Fry's sense of cosmic purpose.

His other plays designed to celebrate the seasons followed irregularly in an unpredictable range of moods, some unexpectedly sombre: *Venus Observed* (autumn), *The Dark Is Light Enough* (winter) and *A Yard of Sun* (summer). *Venus Observed* was a comedy of middle-aged disillusionment, but pleasingly balanced and without fashionable cynicism. However, *The Dark Is Light Enough* selects the year of revolutions, 1848, for its darker setting, and secures its unity in the compassionate and gracious presence of an Austrian countess, a part created by Dame Edith Evans. With the Countess's "divine non-interference" it is demonstrated

> how apparently undemandingly
> She moves among us; and yet
> Lives make and unmake themselves in her neighbourhood
> As nowhere else.

Thus the theme is one of providence, and, through the wisdom of the Countess as she recognizes the imminence of death, embodies the necessity of our respect for every human personality in its touch of grace.

To set side by side plays as contrasting as *The Lady's Not for Burning* and *The Dark Is Light Enough* is inescapably to be impressed by Fry's versatility, and by the integrity of a writer who uses his chosen medium as a way of searching out his personal philosophy whether in the vein of farce or tragedy, spring or winter. Eliot notwithstanding, Fry's is the most sustained attempt in English to write an undogmatic Christian drama in modern times.

—J. L. Styan

FUGARD, Athol.   South African.   Born in Middleburg, Cape Province, 11 June 1932. Educated at Port Elizabeth Technical College; Cape Town University, 1950–53. Married Sheila Meiring in 1955; has one daughter. Worked as seaman, journalist, stage manager; since 1959, actor, director, playwright; Director, since 1965, Serpent Players, Port Elizabeth; Co-Founder, The Space experimental theatre, Cape Town, 1972. Recipient: Obie Award, 1971. Agent: William Morris Agency, 1350 Avenue of the Americas, New York, New York 10019, U.S.A. Address: P.O. Box 5090, Walmer, Port Elizabeth, South Africa.

PUBLICATIONS

Plays

No-Good Friday (also director: produced Cape Town, 1956; Sheffield, 1974).
Nongogo (also director: produced Cape Town, 1957; Sheffield, 1974).
The Blood Knot (also director: produced Johannesburg and London, 1961; New York, 1962).   Johannesburg, Simondium, 1963; New York, Odyssey Press, 1964; in *New English Dramatists 13*, London, Penguin, 1968.
Hello and Goodbye (also director: produced Johannesburg, 1965; New York, 1968; Leicester, 1971; London, 1973).   Cape Town, Balkema, 1966; in *Three Plays*, 1972.
People Are Living There (produced Glasgow, 1968; also director: produced Cape Town, 1969; New York, 1971; London, 1972).   Cape Town, Buren, 1969; New York and London, Oxford University Press, 1970.
The Occupation, in *Ten One Act Plays*, edited by Cosmo Pieterse.   London, Heinemann, 1968.
Boesman and Lena (also director: produced Grahamstown, 1969; New York, 1970; London, 1971).   Cape Town, Buren, 1969; London, Oxford University Press, 1972; in *Three Plays*, 1972.
Three Plays: The Blood Knot, Hello and Goodbye, Boesman and Lena.   New York, Viking Press, 1972; London, Oxford University Press, 1974.
Statements after an Arrest under the Immorality Act (also director: produced Cape Town, 1972; London, 1974).   Included in *Statements*, 1974.
Sizwe Bansi Is Dead, with John Kani and Winston Ntshona (also director: produced Cape Town, 1972; London, 1973; New York, 1974).   Included in *Statements*, 1974; in *Two Plays*, 1976.
The Coat, with *The Third Degree* by Don MacLennan.   Cape Town, Balkema, 1973.
The Island, with John Kani and Winston Ntshona (also director: produced London and New York, 1974).   Included in *Statements*, 1974; in *Two Plays*, 1976.
Statements: Two Workshop Productions devised by Athol Fugard, John Kani and Winston Ntshona, Sizwe Bansi Is Dead and The Island, and a New Play, Statements after an Arrest under the Immorality Act.   London, Oxford University Press, 1974.
Dimetos (also director: produced Edinburgh, 1975; London and New York, 1976).
Two Plays: Sizwe Banzi Is Dead and the Island, with John Kani and Winston Ntshona. New York, Viking Press, 1976.

Screenplay: *Boesman and Lena*, 1972.

Television Play: *Mille Miglia*, 1968.

Theatrical Activities:

Director: **Plays** – many of his own plays; *The Trials of Brother Jero* by Wole Soyinka, London, 1966.

Actor: **Plays** – roles in most of his own plays in South Africa; Morrie in *The Blood Knot*, New York, 1962, London, 1966. **Film** – *Boesman and Lena*, 1972. **Television** – *The Blood Knot* (UK).

*   *   *

Although the setting in Athol Fugard's plays may vary from a non-white location near Port Elizabeth to a cheap rooming house in Johannesburg, the landscape of all of them is the same. It is a grey bleak setting wherein the boredom and despair which lie at the edges of the human condition become all too real. In the harsh light of this setting, his characters are explored in painful depth, yet never without a respect for their basic humanity – the one ray of hope in all of his plays.

It is incontestable that Athol Fugard is South Africa's best-known playwright. It is also likely that he is one of the best younger playwrights in the English language today. Although his characters and plots are drawn from South African society – and usually from the edges of that society, from the outcasts, the poor whites, the blacks and the coloureds, from those who show most clearly the results of several decades of government sponsored racism – his South Africa has the same universality as the American south of Faulkner or Tennessee Williams. Fugard's stories have particular relevance to his own unhappy land, but the tragedies enacted are essentially those of humanity.

There are seldom more than a handful of characters in any of Fugard's plays. This is necessary for the sort of microscopic investigation of personality in which he deals. *People Are Living There*, one of his most recent plays, has four characters – the action centering on three of them for most of the play. *The Blood Knot*, his best known work, deals with only two people, the brothers Morrie and Zachariah.

The exact situation in *The Blood Knot* could only take place in South Africa today. Two brothers, one light-skinned and one dark, children of the same mother, try to relieve the boredom of the existence they are trapped in, in which the light-skinned Morrie sends the dark Zach out to work each day for the money they will use to buy a farm "out there" somewhere, away from the polluted lake and crumbling shacks of Korsten. Morrie has Zach buy a newspaper so that he can get Zach a pen-pal. Zach, however, is illiterate and brings back a white newspaper, a fact which Morrie only realizes when a pen-pal, Ethel, writes back enclosing a picture – and the information that her brother is a policeman. Morrie panics, but Zach forces him to continue to write. It is a dangerous game, yet it gives a meaning to their drab existence. Eventually, Ethel wishes to meet Zach and Zach forces Morrie, who can pass for white, to spend their hard-won savings on proper clothing which he will wear to take Zach's place. Before the meeting can happen, however, Ethel writes to inform Zach that she is engaged and must stop writing. Morrie is relieved, but Zach is downcast. In order to cheer him up Morrie agrees to put on the suit once more. Then, caught up in their game, the two brothers begin to enact the great drama of the colour barrier, of all the fears and hatred locked up in a suit and a different skin. They are at the point of physical violence when Morrie's alarm clock rings and Morrie strips off the suit, removing the extra skin and becoming the brother of a black man once more. When Zach asks, "What is it, Morrie? The two of us...you know...in here?" and Morrie answers, "Home," it should be clear that Fugard is not just speaking of the blood knot between the two brothers, but of the blood knot between all men which has been twisted or broken by the terrible consciousness of race and caste that has been the great problem of this century.

A group of three plays produced in the early 1970's has reinforced Fugard's reputation. Two of them, *Sizwe Bansi Is Dead* and *The Island*, written with the two actors who take the leading roles, John Kani and Winston Ntshona, are forceful representations of life in South Africa. The first involves the need for an identity card for a black migrant to a factory town; the second involves life in a South African prison. The third play, *Statements after an Arrest under the Immorality Act*, despite its documentary-like title, is a moving work about a white man and black woman.

Had Athol Fugard written only *The Blood Knot* his place in twentieth century theatre would have been secure. Yet he has written more and continues to write his chronicles of hope and despair from a land which, sadly enough, is not too unlike our own.

—Joseph Bruchac

GAGLIANO, Frank.   American.   Born in Brooklyn, New York, 18 November 1931. Educated at the University of Iowa, Iowa City, B.A. 1954; Columbia University, New York, M.F.A. 1957. Served in the United States Army, 1954–57. Married Sandra Gagliano in 1958; has one son. Free-lance copywriter, New York, 1958–61; Promotion Copywriter, McGraw-Hill Text-Film Division, New York, 1962–65. Associate Professor of Drama, Florida State University, Tallahassee, 1969–72; Lecturer in Playwriting and Director of the E. P. Conkle Workshop, University of Texas, Austin, 1972–75. Since 1975, Benedum Professor of Playwriting, University of West Virginia, Morgantown. Recipient: Rockefeller grant, 1965, 1966; Wesleyan University-O'Neill Foundation Fellowship, 1967; National Endowment for the Arts grant, 1973; Guggenheim Fellowship, 1974. Agent: Gilbert Parker, Curtis Brown Ltd., 60 East 56th Street, New York, New York 10021, U.S.A.; or, Dr. Jan Van Loewen Ltd., 81-83 Shaftesbury Avenue, London W1V 8BX, England.

PUBLICATIONS

Plays

> *Night of the Dunce* (as *The Library Raid*, produced Houston, 1961; revised version, as
>   *Night of the Dunce*, produced New York, 1966).   New York, Dramatists Play
>   Service, 1967.
> *Conerico Was Here to Stay* (produced New York, 1965).   Included in *The City Scene*,
>   1965.
> *The City Scene* (includes *Paradise Gardens East* and *Conerico Was Here to Stay*)
>   (produced New York, 1969).   New York, French, 1965.
> *Father Uxbridge Wants to Marry* (produced Waterford, Connecticut, and New York,
>   1967).   New York, Dramatists Play Service, 1968.
> *The Hide-and-Seek Odyssey of Madeleine Gimple* (produced Waterford, Connecticut,
>   1967).   New York, Dramatists Play Service, 1970.
> *The Prince of Peasantmania*, music by James Reichert (produced Waterford,
>   Connecticut, 1968; revised version, produced Milwaukee, 1970).
> *Big Sur* (televised, 1969; revised version, produced Tallahassee, Florida, 1970).   New
>   York, Dramatists Play Service, 1971.
> *In the Voodoo Parlour of Marie Leveau: Gris-Gris, and The Comedia World of Byron B*
>   (produced Waterford, Connecticut, 1973; as *Gris-Gris, and The Comedia World of
>   Lafcadio Beau*, produced New York, 1974).
> *Congo Square*, music by Claibe Richardson (produced Providence, Rhode Island, 1975).
> *The Resurrection of Jackie Cramer*, music by Raymond Benson (produced Providence,
>   Rhode Island, 1976).

Television Play: *Big Sur*, 1969.

Manuscript Collections: Lincoln Center Library of the Performing Arts, New York; The O'Neill Theatre Center Library, Waterford, Connecticut.

Critical Studies: *Stages: The Fifty-Year Childhood of the American Theatre* by Emory Lewis, Englewood Cliffs, New Jersey, Prentice Hall, 1969; *The Nature of Theatre* by Vera M. Roberts, New York, Harper, 1971.

Frank Gagliano comments:

1. The chief influence on me has been music; especially opera. All my plays end in a Verdian cabaletta. I wonder why no one has every pointed this out.

2. I've learned about characterization from actors. I try very hard to give my characters "spines of action"...in each scene...in each beat...as well as to give them the one major action that comprises the grand arc of their existence *within* the framework of the play. What does a character want? What is the obstacle to that want? When I've answered these two questions I've got conflict and the scene has been activated.

3. I always try to bring on my characters with strong attitudes already absorbed outside of the scene they are entering. These attitudes – if strong enough – invariably govern a character's behavior *within* the scene and, incidentally, give the actor something strong to "play" even before his main line of action begins.

4. I've learned not to worry too much about a character's bio until I've created a theatrical event for the character to exist within. The behavior of the character in an "event" is what's dramatic; the behavior is his bio.

5. In my opinion the greatest example of character fingerprinting in all dramatic literature is Shakespeare's introduction of Tybalt in *Romeo and Juliet*: (To Benvolio) "What, drawn, and talk of peace? I hate the word as I hate hell, all Montagues, and thee. Have at thee, coward" (I, 1, line 69). True, this is not a complex character. Still, the incredible compression that renders the absolute essence of this character (in three short sentences!) is brilliant, all that is necessary and what I should like to achieve. Sometime.

6. My point of attack is always arrived at after answering the question, "Why is this day different from any other?" Why does the curtain go up at this particular point in time rather than two minutes (hours, days) later? Or earlier? What is so different for these characters at this particular time that the curtain *must* go up then to let an audience in on it? My most successful point of attack is in my play *Father Uxbridge Wants to Marry*. The scene is an elevator where a passenger, Mrs. Bethnal-Green, is asking the elevator operator, "Well, Mr. Morden, and how do you like being replaced by an automatic elevator?" It's the first time Mr. Morden has heard of his dismissal and – womp! we and the play are off and running. For it is from this callous question of Mrs. Bethnal-Green that Morden's mind fragments and his past, present and future snowball into the abyss.

7. I don't always have to know where I'm headed in a play. In fact, I prefer not knowing (though, soon into it, I generally can glimpse the light at the end of the abyss). But I must, very soon into a work, create the atmosphere of the world of the play within which the characters walk, breathe and etc. Difficult to describe how I do it. Certainly I stage, light and design the play's world in my mind and that may have something to do with it. Sometimes it's a musical piece, the atmosphere of which I'm trying to recreate (as in my original TV play, *The Private Eye of Hiram Bodoni*, in which I tried to capture some of the feeling of Fauré's *Après une Rêve*). In any case, I've been told by lighting, stage and sound designers that I do achieve an almost palpable atmosphere in the text.

8. I have probably used sound to greater extent than most other contemporary dramatists. I do not think of sound as "effects." Rather, it is another scenic and atmospheric element and, quite often, the most important one. I have seen my plays performed in simple rooms under ordinary light bulbs without scenery. But the tape recorder with the sound score *had* to be there. I've been fortunate in working with one of the greatest sound composers in the

American theatre, James Reichert. He's scored most of my plays and, in *The Prince of Peasantmania*, achieved what in my opinion is his masterpiece.

9. Of my other plays, *Conerico Was Here to Stay* and *The Prince of Peasantmania* are my favorites. *Conerico* is a model of compressed character, event, mood, theatricality and violence. It will probably survive and transcend its time and locale (a NYC subway platform) because of the drawing of one character – a Puerto Rican boy – who is introduced in the last sequence of the play – and steals it; the play, I mean...and because the central problem, the search for self identity, will be with us a long, long time. *The Prince of Peasantmania* is a sprawling theatrical, operatic, pilgrims progress that many people dislike. On the other hand, many people like it. It contains some of my best lyrics and at least one scene that is touched with greatness, a scene in which a Cardinal of the church descends from arrogance and pomp into a drunken despair and rage against God. A dream of a tour de force for an actor.

10. Historically, I had the misfortune to arrive on the scene when craft was thought of as a sterile, unnecessary quality by the avant gardists and free form was looked down on by the traditionalists. Alas, my plays combined both and both sides condemned me for not being pure. Tough! My whole effort in dramatic writing has been to keep a center while allowing myself the freedom of following any absurd path that seems to make sense. Form and impulse; the artist's great tightrope act.

11. My favorite playwrights are Shakespeare, Georg Büchner, Mozart and Bach.

12. Basta!

*   *   *

Frank Gagliano describes the themes of his dramas as "the crisis of individual identity, the problems of a polluted society, the question of individual responsibility in a world where one is constantly facing violence." It is the drama not so much of the little man as of the inconspicuous man. His protagonists are usually the lost souls who dot the American landscape, suffering for want of meaning and love, best exemplified by Morden of *Father Uxbridge Wants to Marry*, condemned as the "lowest caste of all in an aristocracy of nothingness." Gagliano's drama is a prayer for the salvation of such unfortunates not by God but by man. "They are all Everyman journeys of one sort or another," he states. The odyssey format is a prevailing technique of Gagliano's dramatic structure. Most of his plays are literal or metaphorical journeys from darkness to light. The wisdom gained may, at times, be painful, but, despire the holocaust, existential man must survive.

Night of the Dunce (originally entitled *The Library Raid*) is Gagliano's most realistic and tightly structured work; but like all his plays it functions on a literal and symbolical level, a journey from apathy to involvement. The librarians and clerks of the Road's Ends Branch Library (an actual place inspired the play) are petty bureaucrats caught up in their squabbles, indifferent to the declining neighborhood around them. However, they are cruelly awakened to its reality when a pack of hoodlums, the Dunces, symbols of brute aggression, attempt to destroy the library. Ultimately, the staff decides to fight rather than yield, led into battle by their chief librarian, Mrs. Vickers. Having witnessed the Nazi onslaught, Vickers fully realizes the dangers of passivity; the library can no longer serve as an escape from reality. With sword in hand she marches out to meet the Dunces: "Dear Max, the ostrich game is over for both of us. I'll lop off a few heads for you." Violence must be crushed else the world of the future will be peopled by monsters. The play is deceptively simple. Set in a dilapidated library in a declining neighborhood, the play nevertheless conveys a universal theme with power and directness. One of the most fascinating characters is the Young Man, whose intelligent but twisted mind is focused on violence, deriving a perverse pleasure from terrorizing the staff and destroying the library. The union of the Young Man and the Dunces, intelligence and violence, represents the greatest threat to a healthy society.

Father Uxbridge Wants to Marry explores the mind and soul of a "non-man," Morden the elevator operator, threatened into extinction by automation. Beginning realistically, the play evolves into a nightmarish journey through Morden's past, the movements of the elevator symbolizing the ascent and descent of his soul, as he struggles with love, sex, and religion. Urged on by the sound of music which he believes to be the voices of angels, Morden attempts to smash through the roof of the building in a desperate attempt to reach heaven: "God the piper sounds like a violin....Did I smash through?" Structured like a dream, the plot progresses through a series of flashbacks into Morden's tormented unconscious, a hell of puritanical Catholicism. Two figures dominate his religious agony: Father Uxbridge, embodiment of traditional mediocrity in the Church, spewing meaningless aphorisms to save Morden's soul, and Father Ungar, Morden's distortion of religious liberalism, more Satan than priest, tormenting him with lurid rhetoric: "The truth being that we are made in God's image and so God is venal, spiteful and craves revenge; must get even, as must we all, and there he stands [points to Morden] victim of God's revenge; the God who made him and steered him to damnation."

As if to prove that even the insignificant Morden is capable of profound anguish, Gagliano fills Morden's nightmares with terrifying fantasies and dialogue. *Father Uxbridge Wants to Marry* is a contemporary morality play offering no possibility of salvation; its hero is condemned to the hell of his own psyche, a helpless victim of society and the Church.

In the two plays the comprise *The City Scene, Paradise Gardens East* and *Conerico Was Her to Stay*, Gagliano dramatizes the despair of life in an American metropolis. The more impressive of the two works in *Conerico*, a bitter parable of city life. The protagonist is Yam, an amnesiac whose only clues to his identity are the initials Y.A.M. The entire action of the play occurs on a subway station: several desperate and unfortunate characters appear on the platform imploring Yam for help. Frightened of involvement, Yam refuses to aid them, until he is befriended by a young Puerto Rican, Jesus (Conerico), whose life is threatened by a pack of hoodlums. At first, Yam struggles for detachment, "Please, please, Jesus. Must I get involved?" but finally friendship takes precedence over survival. He throws away the last vestiges of his former identity (credit cards, driver's license), and rushes into the subway tunnel to help Jesus in his battle against the thugs. Comparable to *Night of the Dunce*, *Conerico* is concerned with apathy in contemporary society, and also utilizes the odyssey format: a journey to self discovery. The subway is a symbol of city life traveled by unfortunates with no specific destination. The tunnel is the unknown, which Yam has always avoided, until friendship conquers fear. One of the most effective devices in the play is the use of a mysterious voice offering Yam synthetic salvation through the use of computers, a quack chorus echoing an insane society.

Big Sur is Gagliano's most obvious use of the odyssey format: Jeremy Chester travels out to Big Sur, California, in a combination car-covered wagon which he won in a raffle held in his home town. Sensing his isolation from his fellow man, Jeremy hopes to meet the people of America and establish a "dialogue" with them; but he encounters a host of characters whose problems and prejudices provide a microcosm of the ills of America. Gagliano's irony is evident. Like the pioneers of old, Jeremy seeks a new frontier but discovers, instead, a society dying from the pollution of its land and people. At the end, Jeremy and his hip Indian friend, Noble Savage, drive the wagon into Monterey Bay, the watery grave for two souls seeking hope for a better world, waiting until the garbage boats pass to enable them to continue their journey to Big Sur.

Although Gagliano's themes are repetitive, his plots, characters, and theatrical styles are varied, for he is indefatigably experimental. Art not success is his objective, and he relies on no easy formulas. His works range from realism to fantasy, but, whatever world is inhabited by his characters, they are usually given to elaborate flights of language: long soaring speeches, rhythmically rich and varied, like arias without music. This similarity to music is intrinsic to Gagliano's work. As a composer, he scores his plays with his own songs as well as classical pieces. Music is integral to theme, utilized, at times, with the unabashed sentimentality of the film melodramas of the 1930's.

There is an unresolved war between sentiment and embitterment raging within Gagliano's work that weakens their impact. His espousal of the simple virtues of love and compassion ofter results in didacticism, while his dramatization of evil is brilliantly theatrical. His plays are chamber works of sordid America: flawed but intriguing, indicative of a restless and rich theatrical imagination, and one of the most promising talents in the American theatre.

—A. Richard Sogliuzzo

GALLACHER, Tom.   British.   Born in Alexandria, Dumbartonshire, Scotland, 16 February 1934. Agent: Dr. Jan Van Loewen Ltd., 81-83 Shaftesbury Avenue, London W1V 8BX, England.

PUBLICATIONS

Plays

> *Our Kindness to Five Persons* (produced Glasgow, 1969).
> *Mr. Joyce Is Leaving Paris* (produced London, 1970; revised version produced Dublin, 1971; London, 1972).   London, Calder and Boyars, 1972.
> *Revival!* (produced Dublin, 1972; London, 1973).
> *Three to Play: Janus, Pastiche, Recital* (produced Montrose, Angus, 1972; *Recital* produced London, 1973).
> *Schellenbrack* (produced London, 1973).
> *Bright Scene Fading* (produced London, 1973).
> *The Only Street* (produced Dublin and London, 1973).
> *Personal Effects* (produced Pitlochry, Perthshire, 1974).
> *A Laughing Matter* (produced St. Andrews, Fife, 1975).
> *Hallowe'en* (produced Dundee; Angus, 1975).
> *The Sea Change* (produced Edinburgh, 1976).
> *A Presbyterian Wooing*, adaptation of the play *The Assembly* by Archibald Pitcairne (produced Pitlochry, Perthshire, 1976).

> Radio Play: *The Scar*, 1973.

Tom Gallacher comments:

Mainly, the plays deal with exceptions. Sometimes the exceptions are artists; sometimes it is another kind of outsider, a genius, a catalyst or a singular man. All of them are in some way seeking to extend the meaning of their lives or the boundaries of reality.

It will be readily admitted that artists cannot avoid being metaphysicians when they are about the business of creation. And the Seer is precisely he who identifies what was not visible before. Their ability to see what is ahead and to give it form and vitality is our only guarantee that human evolution will progress even one step more.

All the plays celebrate the individual. The protagonists are unmoved by Class, Party, or Movement but they are acutely conscious of the interior actions of emotion, spirit, and reason. The crises – whether sad or funny – are person to person. The conflict in comedy and drama arises from an effort to make a workable connection – between the accepted and the potential, between what we are and what we may be, between what is degrading and what is exalting.

"Only connect" was the motto which E.M. Forster placed as guardian over his novel *Howards End*. I can't think of a better motto for a writer because the motto leads to a concept of great courage and enterprise. The characters in my plays do not always master the concept or gain its acceptance by others. But if they go down they go down knowing which way is forward.

*   *   *

At the end of Tom Gallacher's first play, *Our Kindness to Five Persons*, an alcoholic Glaswegian author pours himself another drink and proposes a solitary toast : "Should auld acquaintance be forgot and *never* brought to mind ? Yes. Please God. Yes." The play has just demonstrated a denial of the prayer; but the question, and the artist's special rights of adjudication over it, are the constant threads through the ten full-length plays and several shorter pieces Gallacher has written since 1969.

Gallacher's preoccupation with art and artists is immediately obvious on the surfaces of his plays. Writers are the central characters of at least half of them, and Gallacher often points a passage of dialogue towards the epigrammatic use of a quotation, or builds a scene around the recitation of poetry or the singing of ballads. Literary sources and models are of even greater substantive and structural importance for some of Gallacher's work. *The Sea Change* and the short radio play *The Scar* are both dream-plays-within-plays in which the stuff of the central character's imagination comes from Shakespeare. *A Presbyterian Wooing* descends from literary obscurity: *The Assembly*, a Jacobite's dramatic satire on the ecclesiastical politics and personal morals of the Edinburgh Kirk. Trimmed and embroidered into a neo-Restoration comedy of sexual hypocrisy, *A Presbyterian Wooing* demonstrates Gallacher's sensitivity to earlier dramatic modes and his ability to tune his invention and idiom to the same key. The same knack belabours Ibsen's dramaturgy and Kierkegaard's ontology in *Revival!*, the aim of which seems to be to tease the audience into reading the complete works of both Scandinavians. In *Hallowe'en*, on the other hand, Fraser's account of that ritual in pagan times is compactly re-incarnated in contemporary Glasgow, and the literary *drame à clé* is cleanly unlocked in the dialogue.

The thematic purposes to which Gallacher puts these and other of his "auld acquaintance" in literature are remarkably repetitive, though the dramatic techniques he uses vary considerably. He is occupied unto the edge of obsession with the dual nature of the remembered past – omnipresent in influence and irretrievable in fact. Every one of his original plays is in large measure focussed upon the relationship between dramatic past and present. In some cases, a radical time change is built into the play, its point of departure being the out-of-time introduction of the central character. *The Sea Change, Bright Scene Fading*, and the unproduced *A Lady Possessed* are all constructed as flashbacks in time and space through the consciousness of that character, while *Mr. Joyce Is Leaving Paris* brings the personages of Joyce's past to the front of his present consciousness. The other plays, while preserving naturalistic time schemes and the convention of the fourth wall, investigate events and relationships anterior to the action of the play, re-enact them or exorcise them.

For Gallacher the memory that matters is the artistic statement of a perception about personal experience. Such a statement stands for him as evidence of the essentials of observed and observer, and as an imposition of order and connexion among these essentials. "Witness" and "pattern" are the terms which often turn up in the dialogue: another is "signpost," an indication of where someone has been and a directive to those who follow. When the plays incorporate such overt expositions of their author's understanding of art, it is not surprising that several draw attention to their own artificiality, nor that so many celebrate the triumph of artistic insight – over technology, biographical data, time, and the perceptions of the pedestrian majority of mankind.

Though the penultimate victory supplies him with some fairly strong stuff, Gallacher finds his best dramatic material in the last. Only here does he create any real competition, and only here are his aesthetic concerns communicated by more than interpretative glosses and plot gimmickry. The axis along which Gallacher most characteristically depicts these conflicts is that of an intense relationship between a gifted figure and a sympathetic sibling or comrade left behind: James and Stanislaus Joyce in *Mr. Joyce Is Leaving Paris*, Martin and Richard in *The Only Street*, and Otto and Steve in *Bright Scene Fading*. The high price of giftedness also hovers over the presentation of parent-child, husband-wife, and mentor-pupil relationships in these and other plays, but Gallacher plays a better game for higher stakes when he is dealing with doubles and shadows.

Gallacher's own practice of art as witness and as pattern is apparent in his plays and illuminates some of their more idiosyncratic aspects. His writing of dialogue is distinguished on the one hand by an accurate reproduction of spoken rhythms, with particularly precise variations for local, professional, social, and even situational idiom, and on the other hand by a wit which specializes in paradoxes, perfect squelches, and the literalisation of abstractions and figures of speech. Gallacher rarely loses this balance of an attentive ear and orderly invention.

Gallacher's patterning of his materials betrays a taste for symmetry, a mastery of plot mechanics, and an ability to exploit exposition, complication, reversal, and resolution in traditional well-made ways or to invert them for the sake of emphasis. (The exceptions to this rule of flexibility are found in his act-endings: he seems incapable of placing an interval anywhere but on the edge of a cliff in the plot.) His fascination with pattern is perhaps most easily perceived in miniature in the tidy and playful plots of his three one-acts for three players (*Janus, Recital*, and *Pastiche*). The patterning is, however, so apparent in the full-length plays as well that it is impressively ironic that Gallacher's best and best-known play should be, superficially, his most untidy: *Mr. Joyce Is Leaving Paris*. The second half of this play saw production first. Its order is not dictated by traditional dramaturgy but, as is pointed out by one of the figures which haunt the ageing Joyce, by the order of events at an Irish wake. That the "corpse" is the sole survivor of the wake is a good instance of how Gallacher can plot a joke to great thematic purpose. The order of the first half, set much earlier in Joyce's career but written slightly later in Gallacher's, is one of the playwright's confrontations of gifted and ungifted, moving from mutual challenge, through routines long familiar to both, towards acceptance. Though Stanislaus turns up, much muted, in the second half, the two patterns converge only through the consciousness of Joyce − formal confirmation of his (and, behind him, Gallacher's) claim to sole mastery of the remembered situations.

Mr. Joyce Is Leaving Paris in fact typifies Gallacher's dramatic writing as a whole as well as at its best. The qualitative difference between its parts is the difference between commendably accomplished craftsmanship and irresistibly imaginative insight. An analogous difference may be discerned in the use of theatrical resources. To these Gallacher is always attentive, using them to supplement the scripted action and dialogue in his fourth-wall dramas and pulling off some stunning isolated effects in the process. At best, however, Gallacher makes the technical parts of theatrical production indispensable to his dramatic statement. The lighting in the second half of *Mr. Joyce Is Leaving Paris*, for example, and the set for *The Sea Change* serve as visual indices to the central character's control of his memories and thus as evidence of the truth of his vision. In *The Sea Change* that vision, despite its ingenious presentation, remains derivative and diffuse. But when, as in the second half of *Mr. Joyce Is Leaving Paris*, Gallacher aligns tradition and his individual talent in perfect focus, he creates a signpost which will be well worth attention for some time.

—Marion O'Connor

GELBER, Jack. American. Born in Chicago, Illinois, 12 April 1932. Educated at the University of Illinois, Urbana, B.S. in journalism 1953. Married Carol Westenberg in 1957; has two children. Writer-in-Residence, City College of New York, 1965–66. Adjunct Professor of Drama, Columbia University, New York, 1967–72. Since 1972, Professor of Drama, Brooklyn College, City University of New York. Recipient: Obie Award, 1960, for directing, 1972; Vernon Rice Award, 1960; Guggenheim Fellowship, 1963, 1966; Rockefeller grant, 1972; National Endowment for the Arts grant, 1974. Agent: Ronald Konecky, 1 Dag Hammarskjold Plaza, New York, New York 10017. Address: 697 West End Avenue, New York, New York 10025, U.S.A.

PUBLICATIONS

Plays

The Connection (produced New York, 1959; London, 1961). New York, Grove Press, 1960; London, Faber, 1961.
The Apple (produced New York, 1961). New York, Grove Press, 1961.
Square in the Eye (produced New York, 1965). New York, Grove Press, 1966.
The Cuban Thing (also director: produced New York, 1968). New York, Grove Press, 1969.
Sleep (produced New York and Edinburgh, 1972). New York, Hill and Wang, 1972.
Barbary Shore, adaptation of the novel by Norman Mailer (also director: produced New York, 1973).
The Apple, and Square in the Eye. New York, Viking Press, 1974.
Rehearsal (produced New York, 1976).

Screenplay: The Connection, 1962.

Novel

On Ice. New York, Macmillan, 1964; London, Deutsch, 1965.

Critical Studies: Seasons of Discontent by Robert Brustein, New York, Simon and Schuster, 1965; Les U.S.A.: A la Recherche de Leur Identité by Pierre Dommergues, Paris, Grasset, 1967; Tynan: Right and Left by Kenneth Tynan, New York, Atheneum, 1968; Now: Theater der Erfahrung edited by Jens Heilmeyer and Pia Frolich, Cologne, Verlag M. Dumont Schauberg, 1971; The Living Theatre by Pierre Biner, New York, Avon, 1972; Theatricality by Elizabeth Burns, New York, Harper, 1972; Off Broadway by Stuart Little, New York, Coward McCann, 1972; People's Theatre in Amerika by Karen Taylor, New York, DBS, 1973; Introduction by Richard Gilman to The Apple, and Square in tthe Eye, 1974.

Theatrical Activities:

Director: **Plays** – works at Lincoln Center, New Theatre Workshop, and the American Place Theatre, including The Kitchen by Arnold Wesker, New York, 1966; Indians by Arthur Kopit, London, 1968; The Cuban Thing, New York, 1968; The Kid by Robert Coover, New York, 1972; Chickencoop Chinamen by Frank Chin, New York, 1972; Barbary Shore, New York, 1974.

*   *   *

American drama changed radically once Jack Gelber's *The Connection* opened at the Living Theatre in July 1959, and Edward Albee introduced *The Zoo Story* the following winter; for Tennessee Williams and Arthur Miller, though they remained much-produced, were no longer at the forefront of theatrical consciousness. Whereas Albee was clearly a master dramatist, whose verbal facility would sometimes transcend the necessities of sense and significance, the evaluation of Gelber's possible talent became more problematic. Since so much of the original production's success depended upon Judith Malina's stunning direction, as well as the Living Theatre's growing reputation, Gelber's contribution was critically slighted at the time. As he was then only 27, his youth, along with the limitations of his theatrical language, made critics also suspect *The Connection* might be "the only play he had in him." The subsequent publication of the work's text established, however, that Gelber was responsible for the play's theme and structure, and that he skilfully turned a naturalistic surface to non-naturalistic ends. For all of its anti-literacy, *The Connection* nonetheless echoed earlier plays by Gorky, Pirandello, O'Neill and Beckett. Just as the Living Theatre has since survived devastating misfortunes and artistically changed, so has Gelber continued to present new scripts, though none of them has been as successful, either critically or commercially, as his first. His theatrical activity is uneven, both in whole and in part, and his single novel, *On Ice*, is likewise intriguing, though flawed and finally unnclear.

A group of junkies are visible on stage before *The Connection* begins, suggesting that the situation existed before the audience entered the theatre and will probably continue to exist after it leaves. A better-dressed man, announcing that he is "Jim Dunn," the evening producer, steps off the stage and introduces "Jaybird, the author." Dunn explains that on stage are real addicts whom he has recruited to "improvise on Jaybird's themes" for a documentary motion picture. As two cameramen step forward, Jaybird starts to explain his play until Dunn interrupts him and then addresses the addicts, who in turn call him "Jim." By this time, much of the audience is successfully enticed into the authenticity of the scene before them.

All the pseudo-naturalistic devices are necessary, for only by breaking down the art-life barriers that customarily stand between spectator and performer can the audience fully confront the concerns of the play. The characters spend the first act waiting for a character name "Cowboy" to return from the "connection," where he has hopefully picked up some "horse." Beneath the boredom and general purposelessness, epitomized by Beckettish waiting, run several lines of tension. (The play's title has a double meaning, referring both to the man who sells heroin to the addict, and to the act of plunging a heroin-filled needle into a human arm.) During the only intermission, some of the performers follow the audience into the lobby and try to panhandle. Once the second act begins, Cowboy enters, wearing the all-white of an emissary of mercy, to give each of the waiting men what he calls a "baptism." Out of the audience comes one of the two "photographers" announcing that he too wants a shot. Jaybird, the putative author, tries to dissuade him but becomes convinced that he too must undergo the authentic experience. Whereas the drunks of O'Neill's *The Iceman Cometh* converse with suspicious coherence through their stupor, Gelber wisely lets improvised jazz dominate their narcotic euphoria.

The question is thus posed to the audience – do you want a "connection" too? You see a world lacking in purpose, where the highest goal is individual happiness. You are presented with heroin, which represents a quick and easy way to achieve contentment. It may be illegal, but the morality of heroin is scarcely different from that of other pleasurable stimulants. Sam, an oversized Negro, articulates the ethical center of the play: "People who worry so much about the next dollar, the next new coat, the chlorophyll addicts, the aspirin addicts, the vitamin addicts, those people are hooked worse than me. Worse than me." They are "hooked worse," it can be reasoned, because they must go through so many more steps, some of them demeaning, to achieve the happiness that Sam gets in a single shot. Another, more intellectual character, Solly, voices the contrary position that dope is ultimately self-annihilating. Nonetheless, of the four characters in the audience, two of them ask Cowboy for their "baptism," thus suggesting that, if given the chance, half the audience might do likewise. The point is that heroin exemplifies a possible life-choice which reflects certain values and which is freely, existentially made. However, the result of one's choice can determine his way of life, or to what kinds of goods he becomes addicted; and this theme of drug-induced escape continued to have much relevance through the sixties.

Gelber's next work, *The Apple*, is in many ways his most difficult; it is surely his most misunderstood. All but totally panned in its opening production, even by critics previously enthusiastic about *The Connection*, it suffers from a sense of chaos that is more intentional than accidental, and finally more cunning than obscuring. Once again in Gelber's work, worldly absurdity is assumed, and the absence of a protagonist means that key lines are distributed among several characters, one of them muttering, at the beginning, "Up here or down here, in here or out there, we are not all here." As before, the particular situation determines the play's subject and themes, as a disparate collection of stereotypes come together to make a performance. These people are also identified as actors, who sometimes use their real names and thus make a play-outside-a-play (echoing Pirandello again). Many themes are broached in the course of their conflicts, only to be dropped; and the dialogue is filled with hipsters' platitudes. What happens is very confusing, and the play's title is no help, as several symbolic associations for apples are announced, and one character says, in passing, "I'm whatever you want me to be....I'm your apple, baby," such arbitrariness suggesting not only multiple possibility and relativity, but also a comic updating of Ecclesiastes. The most reasonable interpretation of this confusion comes from the late mixed-means creator, Ken Dewey, who directed a production in Los Angeles in 1962. As Dewey describes his experience in my book, *The Theatre of Mixed Means* (1968, 1971), the play is "talking about democracy as opposed to dictatorships." A group comes together and tries to improvise a result without acknowledging a leader or a plan; and in this respect, *The Apple* deals with certain radical theatrical processes (based upon process, rather than product), as well as becoming a prophetic commentary upon the subsequent development of "The Living Theatre," to whom it is explicitly dedicated.

Gelber's third play, *Square in the Eye*, received a more conventional off-Broadway production. Marked by great shifts in tone and style, as well as a garbled chronology, it portrays Ed Stone, a failed painter turned schoolteacher, whose wife suddenly dies of peritonitis. Typically, the end of act one, in which Ed Stone remarries, takes place several weeks after the play's concluding scene. Not much of importance is revealed. Gelber's next production, *The Cuban Thing*, which closed after a single Broadway performance, deals with the various effects that Castro's Revolution had upon a single Cuban family; and although the playwright reportedly did his homework the result seemed terribly artificial. Since Gelber also directed this production, the critic Richard Gilman quipped that it "should never have been allowed by its author to publicly embarrass him the way it did." (His other directorial credits include a New York production of Arnold Wesker's *The Kitchen* and a Royal Shakespeare premiere of Arthur Kopit's *Indians*.) It seems symbolic, in retrospect, that soon after *The Cuban Thing* opened on Broadway and then quickly disappeared, The Living Theatre returned from exile, performing far off-Broadway to the best kind of controversy and enthusiastic audiences.

Sleep, presented in New York in 1972, forebodes a comeback. For one thing, Gelber's writing has become better, as lines are beginning to stand above their declamation, and certain technical feats are impressive. For the first time, his work is based not upon a situation but a character, who seems something of a protagonist. "Sleep scientists" subject a *moyen* Jewish *homme* to psychological testing. They analyze his dreams, repeatedly asking questions that are either stupid or vulgar, until he rebels against such gross invasions of his privacy. What is technically clever is Gelber's management of the audience's shifting perspective − from observing the protagonist's revolt to participating in his fantasies. His dreams become the occasion for reviving that favorite Gelberian device of a play-within-a-play and thus the pet theme of illusion-reality contradictions − the realities-of-illusion vs. the illusoriness of "reality." (Another repeated theme is the contradictions inherent in anti-bourgeois life-styles.) For once, the work does not suffer from excessive incoherence, and the execution is superior to the theme, which is indeed surprisingly familiar. At minimum, Gelber has survived not only professional misfortune but the stigma of precocity; and in certain respects, including authentic adventurousness, he now seems a more interesting playwright than Albee.

—Richard Kostelanetz

GIBSON, William. American. Born in New York City, 13 November 1914. Educated at the City College of New York, 1930–32. Married Margaret Brenman in 1940; has two children. Recipient: Harriet Monroe Memorial Prize (*Poetry*, Chicago), 1945; Sylvania Award, for television play, 1957. Address: Stockbridge, Massachusetts 01262, U.S.A.

PUBLICATIONS

Plays

I Lay in Zion (produced Topeka, Kansas, 1943). New York, French, 1947.
Dinny and the Witches: A Frolic on Grave Matters (produced Topeka, Kansas, 1945; revised version, produced New York, 1959). Included in *Dinny and the Witches and The Miracle Worker*, 1960.
A Cry of Players (produced Topeka, Kansas, 1948; New York, 1968). New York, Atheneum, 1969.
The Ruby (as William Mass), libretto based on a work by Lord Dunsany, music by Norman Dello Joio. New York, Ricordi, 1955.
The Miracle Worker: A Play for Television (televised, 1957). New York, Knopf, 19575; stage version (produced New York, 1959; London, 1961), included in *Dinny and the Witches and The Miracle Worker*, 1960; London, French, 1960.
Two for the Seesaw (produced New York and London, 1958). Published as *The Seesaw Log: A Chronicle of the Stage Production with the Text of "Two for the Seesaw,"* New York, Knopf, 1959; London, Corgi, 1962.
Dinny and the Witches and The Miracle Worker. New York, Atheneum, 1960.
Golden Boy, with Clifford Odets, adaptation of the play by Clifford Odets, music by Charles Strouse (produced New York, 1964). New York, Atheneum, 1965.
American Primitive (produced Stockbridge, Massachusetts, 1969). New York, Atheneum, 1972.
The Body and the Wheel: A Play Made From the Gospels. New York, Dramatists Play Service, 1975.
The Butterfingers Angel, Mary and Joseph, Herod the Nut, and the Slaughter of 12 Hit Carols in a Pear Tree: A Christmas Entertainment. New York, Dramatists Play Service, 1975.

Screenplays: *The Cobweb*, 1954; *The Miracle Worker*, 1962.

Television Play: *The Miracle Worker*, 1957.

Novel

The Cobweb. New York, Knopf, and London, Secker and Warburg, 1954.

Verse

Winter Crook.   New York, Oxford University Press, 1948.

Other

A Mass for the Dead.   New York, Atheneum, 1968.
A Season in Heaven: Being a Log of an Expedition after that Legendary Beast, Cosmic Consciousness.   New York, Atheneum, 1974.

*   *   *

William Gibson, the playwright, began as a novelist and a poet. He published verse in various literary magazines and in his own collection entitled *Winter Crook*; and earned a reputation with a best-selling novel called *The Cobweb*, which later was made into a motion picture. An early interest in dramatic writing resulted in *I Lay in Zion*, a published one-act verse play well-tailored for production by church groups. The story centers on the Apostle Peter's denial of Christ, his subsequent self-condemnation and resolve to found the Church in Rome where crucifixion awaits him. Larger dramas were to come.

Gibson's first success on the Broadway stage came in 1958 with *Two for the Seesaw*, a two-character drama about an embittered Nebraska lawyer in New York, lonely in self-imposed exile from his wife, and his affair with a generous-hearted Bronx gamine down on her luck as a dancer. Although mutual love and dependency develop between these two disparate people, the lawyer's home ties are strong enough ultimately to draw him back to his wife. The drama's chief appeal lies in its engaging portrait of the Bronx girl, a role which brought recognition to the actress Anne Bancroft, who was thereafter to portray many other Gibson heroines. She is the more dimensional of the two characters, and her colorful individuality and guileless generosity in the face of what she realizes is a doomed relationship strike one's attention and mark the author as one of the few contemporary American dramatists writing strong roles for women. The critics generally praised the play, which enjoyed a substantial Broadway run resulting in a film contract for the author.

In *The Seesaw Log*, Gibson relates the biography of *Two for the Seesaw* from inception through production and furnishes a lively account of preparing a new play for New York. The chronicle also reveals its author's disenchantment and dismay with the processes of professional production, but not without respect for the contribution to his plays of his professional collaborators.

In 1959, Gibson was represented by an off-Broadway production of *Dinny and the Witches*, a satirical fantasy with song which was a refurbished version of an earlier script. The title character, Dinny Jones, is a bumptious young musician who mysteriously finds himself the possessor of the power of the world previously exercised by three witches. He immediately attempts to correct the witches' mismanagement of human affairs by granting the desires of three unhappy people, but is unsuccessful. Realizing that happiness is not effected by changing conditions external to those within man himself, the sobered hero returns his power to the witches and seeks his own earthly joy in marriage. The play's good intentions exceeded its effectiveness and it closed after a few performances.

Also produced in 1959 was Gibson's greatest success, *The Miracle Worker*. Originally written as a television script, the biography-drama portrays teacher Anne Sullivan's turbulent but triumphant struggles with her savagely recalcitrant pupil, Helen Keller, in freeing the child from the prison of a sightless and soundless body. The action encompasses the time it takes the young Boston Irish teacher to gain mastery over the seemingly ungovernable, blind, deaf-mute child in order to teach her language. The play is brought to a poignant resolution when Helen, having had her hand repeatedly doused under the water pump, excitedly discovers the connection between words and things as she writes the word "water" in the palm of her teacher's hand. Somewhat uneven and clumsy structure results from an insufficient transformation of the drama from its television form. Although critics faulted *The Miracle Worker* for its sentimentality and deficiencies in craftsmanship, they and the public agreed on its theatrical impact in presenting a compassionate portrait of a heroic teacher who helped make possible the greatness of Helen Keller. The play's success led to a 1962 film for which Gibson wrote the script.

A further extension of the writer's experience came in 1965 when he collaborated on the book of a musical version of Clifford Odets' *Golden Boy*. The musical follows closely the action of the original, with the chief exception that Odets' white violinist-turned-pugilist hero is transformed into a black boxer with no propensity toward music. Surviving sizeable problems before reaching Broadway, *Golden Boy* became a moderately successful musical utilizing the talents of Sammy Davis, Jr. And the author's contribution of a well-adapted "book" substantially influenced the final result.

In *A Cry of Players* Gibson dramatized the story of a troubled young man named William and his older wife Anne residing in "an obscure town in England in the 1580's." Without mentioning his hero's surname, the author characterizes Shakespeare as a free-spirited near-profligate frustrated by the limitations of his town and the constricting ties of his family. Young Will endures a poaching sentence in the stocks, a whipping, and a humiliating trial to join Will Kemp's troupe of players and leave family and town for the destiny that awaits in London. The play won insufficient critical or popular approval to sustain a long run. Gibson, although able to exercise his natural gifts for poetic speech, was accused by critics of lapses into either pretentious or unimaginative dialogue. However, Will's wife Anne becomes a full-bodied figure enlisting our compassion and demonstrating once more the author's adept creation of substantial women's roles.

Turning again to biography in 1969, Gibson put the letters of John and Abigail Adams into theatrical form in *American Primitive*. The script furnishes an effective documentary of the two remarkable Adamses in the stormy Revolutionary period from 1774 to 1777.

A novelist and poet, a film writer and playwright, William Gibson possesses both literary and dramatic gifts. His major plays can be applauded for their sensitivity, substance of subject, and stageworthiness. Particularly successful in dramatizing actual figures, William Gibson promises to secure his place in American letters as an effectual writer of biography-drama.

—Christian H. Moe

GILL, Peter. British. Born in Cardiff, 7 September 1939. Educated at St. Illtyd's College, Cardiff. Actor, 1957–65. Associate Artistic Director, Royal Court Theatre, London, 1970–72. Recipient: Belgrade International Theatre Festival prize, for directing, 1968; George Devine Award, 1968. Agent: Margaret Ramsay Ltd., 14a Goodwin's Court, London WC2N 4LL, England.

PUBLICATIONS

Plays

The Sleepers' Den (produced London, 1965; revised version, also director: produced London, 1969). Included in *The Sleepers' Den and Over Gardens Out*, 1970.

A Provincial Life, adaptation of *My Life* by Chekhov (also director: produced London, 1966).

Over Gardens Out (also director: produced London, 1969).   Included in *The Sleepers' Den and Over Gardens Out*, 1970.

The Sleepers' Den and Over Gardens Out.   London, Calder and Boyars, 1970.

The Merry-Go-Round, adaptation of the play by D.H. Lawrence (also director: produced London, 1973).

Small Change (also director: produced London, 1976).   Published in *Plays and Players* (London), August–September 1976.

Theatrical Activities:

Director: **Plays** – *A Collier's Saturday Night* by D. H. Lawrence, London, 1965, 1968; *The Ruffian on the Stair* by Joe Orton, London, 1966; *O'Flaherty, V.C.* by G. B. Shaw, London, 1966; *A Provincial Life*, London, 1966; *The Local Stigmatic* by Heathcote Williams, London, 1966; *The Soldier's Fortune* by Thomas Otway, London, 1967; *The Daughter-in-Law* by D. H. Lawrence, London, 1967, 1968; *Crimes of Passion* by Joe Orton, London, 1967; *June Evening* by Bill Naughton, on tour, 1967; *The Widowing of Mrs. Holroyd* by D. H. Lawrence, London, 1968; *Over Gardens Out*, London, 1969; *Life Price* by Michael O'Neill and Jeremy Seabrook, London, 1969; *Much Ado about Nothing*, Stratford, Connecticut, 1969; *The Sleepers' Den*, London, 1969; *Hedda Gabler* by Ibsen, Stratford, Ontario, 1970; *Landscape and Silence* by Harold Pinter, New York, 1970; *The Duchess of Malfi* by Webster, London, 1971; *Macbeth*, Stratford, Ontario, 1971; *Crete and Sergeant Pepper* by John Antrobus, London, 1972; *The Merry-Go-Round*, London, 1973; *Twelfth Night*, Stratford upon Avon, 1974; *Fishing* by Michael Weller, New York, 1975; *The Fool* by Edward Bond, London, 1975; *As You Like It*, Nottingham and Edinburgh, 1975. **Television** – *Grace* by David Storey, from the story by James Joyce, 1974; *Fugitive* by Sean Walsh, 1974; *Hitting Town* by Stephen Poliakoff, 1976.

Actor: **Plays** – Plato in *The Trial of Cob and Leach* by Christopher Logue, London, 1959; Mangolis in *The Kitchen* by Arnold Wesker, London, 1959; Marcus and A Postcard Seller in *This Way to the Tomb* by Ronald Duncan, London, 1960; Silvius in *As You Like It*, London, 1962. **Films** – *H.M.S. Defiant (Damn the Defiant!)*, 1962; *Zulu*, 1964.

*   *   *

Peter Gill's reputation rests on his directing rather than his writing, but it would be a mistake to consider his two original short plays produced to date – *The Sleepers' Den* and *Over Gardens Out* – as mere director's exercises.

The two activities are, however, not unconnected. His triumphant realization of the D. H. Lawrence trilogy, which established belatedly Lawrence's unquestioned stature as a major dramatist, rested on qualities which are also discernible in Gill's own work: a meticulous eye for detail, a totally truthful evocation of working class environments, and a deep compassion.

Over Gardens Out is written impressionistically in short scenes, using staccato dialogue. Everything is implied; very little is stated. The effect is not unlike looking at slightly blurred childhood snapshots. This technique suits his subject excellently: his heroes are two boys living not only in the limbo of pubescence but also in a social, moral, and psychological no-man's land. Reality and fantasy overlap; their families offer little security and no understanding; inevitably, this leads to gratuitous violence. Genet's definition – "I give the name violence to a boldness lying idle and hankering for danger" – describes their state exactly.

The Sleepers' Den is a more substantial work. It shows the harrowing mental disintegration and collapse into madness of a very ordinary housewife harassed by poverty, the demands of a bedridden mother, the desperate search for contact of her growing daughter, and the indifference of a brother who takes refuge in drink. Everybody leans on Mrs. Shannon, and she is too frail to carry the burden. "You asleep, Mam?" asks her daughter when she sinks exhausted into bed: even sleep is an insufficient form of oblivion.

Except for Mrs. Shannon's final demented soliloquies, which seem to me too self-consciously written and a mistake stylistically, Peter Gill does not stray from the path of veracity. The debt collector and the lady from the Mission of Mercy try their impotent best to help, but this problem family is beyond reach. Gill's absence of indignation at the plight of these victims of society makes his play all the more affecting.

Last but not least, he demonstrates in *The Sleepers' Den* his ability to create with the most economical of means an acting part of heroic dimensions. Those fortunate enough to have seen Eileen Atkins as Mrs. Shannon will not forget the performance.

Actions speak louder than words in these plays: a lesson learned no doubt from his experiences as a director. But his sensitivity and his grasp of dramatic nuances proclaim a playwriting talent that cries out to be pursued and developed. We must hope that he will be able to accommodate it within his other creative and valuable work in the theatre.

—Frank Marcus

GILROY, Frank D(aniel).   American.   Born in New York City, 13 October 1925. Educated at DeWitt Clinton High School, Bronx, New York; Dartmouth College, Hanover, New Hampshire, B.A. (magna cum laude) 1950; Yale University Drama School, New Haven, Connecticut, 1950–51. Served in the United States Army, 1943–46. Married Ruth Dorothy Gaydos in 1954; has three sons. Since 1964, Member of the Council, and President, 1969–71, Dramatists Guild, New York. Recipient: Obie Award, 1962; Pulitzer Prize, 1965; New York Drama Critics Circle Award, 1965; Berlin Film Festival Silver Bear, 1971. Address: c/o Random House Inc., 201 East 50th Street, New York, New York 10022, U.S.A.

PUBLICATIONS

Plays

A Matter of Pride, adaptation of the story "The Blue Serge Suit" by John Langdon (televised, 1957).   New York, French, 1970.

Who'll Save the Plowboy? (produced New York, 1962; London, 1963).   New York, Random House, 1962.

The Subject Was Roses (produced New York, 1964).   New York, French, 1962; included in *About Those Roses; or, How Not to Do a Play and Succeed, and the Text of "The Subject Was Roses,"* New York, Random House, 1965.

Far Rockaway (televised, 1965).   Included in *That Summer – That Fall, and Far Rockaway*, 1967.

That Summer – That Fall (produced New York, 1967).   Included in *That Summer — That Fall, and Far Rockaway*, 1967.

That Summer — That Fall, and Far Rockaway.   New York, Random House, 1967.

The Only Game in Town (produced New York, 1968).   New York, Random House, 1968.

Present Tense (includes Come Next Tuesday, Twas Brillig, So Please Be Kind, Present Tense) (produced New York, 1972).   New York, French, 1973.

Screenplays: Fastest Gun Alive, 1956; The Gallant Hours, 1960; The Subject Was Roses, 1968; The Only Game in Town, 1969; Desperate Characters, 1971; From Noon till Three, 1976.

Television Plays: A Matter of Pride, 1957; Far Rockaway, 1965; Gibbsville series, from stories by John O'Hara, 1976; Burke's Law series; and since 1952 plays for U.S. Steel Hour, Omnibus, Kraft Theatre, Studio One, Lux Video Theatre, and Playhouse 90.

Novels

Private.   New York, Harcourt Brace, 1970.
From Noon till Three: The Possibly True and Certainly Tragic Story of an Outlaw and a Lady Whose Love Knew No Bounds.   New York, Doubleday, 1973. as For Want of a Horse, London, Coronet, 1975.

Other

Little Ego (juvenile), with Ruth G. Gilroy.   New York, Simon and Schuster, 1970.

Theatrical Activities:

Director: **Films** – Desperate Characters, 1971; From Noon till Three, 1976. **Television** – Gibbsville series, 1976.

*   *   *

In his Foreword to That Summer – That Fall, Frank D. Gilroy writes that he intended his play to work "realistically and as a ritual. Unfortunately, the latter element has, so far, escaped detection, and the play is taken as further evidence of my exclusive dedication to the 'real.'" Gilroy is here claiming a double allegiance that marks all his work, for his plays, subtly and quietly, make rituals of the realistic textures of American family life. Gilroy's stylistic heightening – the repetition of words and phrases, the rapid exchange of very short lines of dialogue – is so unobtrusive that his work has been catalogued as strict Broadway naturalism, which it decidedly is not: Gilroy's complaint of critical mishandling is entirely justified.

The inevitably spare conception of the Gilroy play is matched by its lean, taut style: simple ideas, simply done. Gilroy works with standard Broadway subjects – the domestic drama, the sex comedy – and he manages, with modest grace and style, to elaborate his small sketch-like concepts into surprisingly sturdy full-length plays. Only his first stage play, Who'll Save the Plowboy?, is propelled by a conventional plot. The other plays, mere wisps of ideas, are novelettish character studies.

His first play, then, is his most "dramatic" piece. Its frame, the reunion of army buddies, is altogether standard. Familiar, too, are the unhappy consequences of the reunion: the disillusionments, the admissions of loss of youth and of fellow feeling. The soldier who saved his friend's life (and is now, improbably, dying as a result of the bullet wound he suffered as a reward for his heroism) visits his buddy, after an absence of many years, to see if he sacrificed his life for a good cause. He finds out, of course, that he has not: his friend's

301

child, named after him, is a monster, closeted in an institution; his friend's marriage is a failure, both husband and wife are adulterous; his friend's career, once so eagerly anticipated, has been frustrated. These accumulated horrors are revealed piece by piece through intricate and neatly handled exposition. The play is melodrama, sure enough; its characters' burden of suffering is contrived, overdone. But even here Gilroy's writing is so low-key, his characters converse so quietly and casually that the melodramatic excess is considerably softened; the play's stock theatrical revelations and climaxes even begin to assume a naturalistic texture. ·

In his most successful play, *The Subject Was Roses*, Gilroy pares away the plotty and keyed-up framework, thereby allowing his particular strengths (clipped dialogue and perceptive "small" characterization) central stage. Again, the basic design is thoroughly conventional. A son returns home after several years in the army, and he confronts the inevitable problems of readjustment. His father is a man's man, robust and gregarious out in the business world, awkward, unable to express his real feelings in the home, and covering up his embarrassment behind a noisy assertiveness. He's stubborn, miserly, too emphatically authoritative. His mother aligns herself with her son against his father. Married to the wrong man and knowing it, she depends on her son for more than he can give and more than she has any right to expect. Wiser now than when he left home, the son is nonetheless trapped at first by the old family structure, but he manages after a week-end to be both reconciled to and freed from his loving, damaging parents. Gilroy's story is embroidered with details – what's for breakfast, family gossip, discussions about the quality of the coffee, remembrance of things past: all the tricks of the trade, in short – and it works, it works: *The Subject Was Roses* is a lovely "little" play, moving and true.

That Summer – That Fall is another domestic drama, only this time the tensions lead to tragic consequences. The aura of ritual is more pronounced here than in *Roses*; in terms of a New York Italian family, the play retells the Phaedra story: a woman falls passionately, helplessly in love with her unknowing stepson. Here as elsewhere, Gilroy's writing is austere. Gilroy works for subtextual resonance, the Thing Left Unsaid, as a means of heightening the mythic thrust of his material, but the rigorously plain language, for all its formal beauty, is not full enough to contain the energy of character and situation.

The Only Game in Town is a Broadway love story about two charming losers, a compulsive gambler and a dancer no longer young. He's a shifty guy who doesn't want to be tied down, and of course the woman is crazy about him, gives up her long-time fiancé for him. They meet (the play is set in Las Vegas), they flirt, they go to bed, they argue (mostly about his gambling habit), they make up, they plan to marry. As light as – no, lighter than – air, the play is aggressively inconsequential, but it has those two slightly soiled and appealing characters and the trim, rhythmic, antiphonal Gilroy dialogue.

—Foster Hirsch

GOLDMAN, James. American. Born in Chicago, Illinois, 30 June 1927; brother of the writer William Goldman. Educated at the University of Chicago, Ph.B 1947, M.A. 1950; Columbia University, New York, 1950–52. Served in the United States Army, 1952–54. Married Marie McKeon in 1962 (divorced 1973); has two children. Since 1966, Member of the Council, Dramatists Guild, and since 1967, Member of the Council, Authors League of America. Recipient: Academy Award, 1968. Agent: Creative Management Associates, 600 Madison Avenue, New York, New York, U.S.A.

PUBLICATIONS

Plays

They Might Be Giants (produced London, 1961).
Blood, Sweat and Stanley Poole, with William Goldman (produced New York, 1961).
   New York, Dramatists Play Service, 1962.
A Family Affair, with William Goldman and John Kander (produced New York, 1962).
The Lion in Winter (produced New York, 1966; Pitlochry, Perthshire, 1970). New
   York, Random House, 1966; London, French, 1970.
Follies, music and lyrics by Stephen Sondheim (produced New York, 1971). New
   York, Random House, 1971.

Screenplays: *The Lion in Winter*, 1968; *They Might Be Giants*, 1970; *Nicholas and
Alexandra*, 1971; *Robin and Marian*, 1976.

Novels

Waldorf. New York, Random House, 1965; London, Joseph, 1966.
The Man from Greek and Roman. New York, Random House, 1974; London,
   Hutchinson, 1975.

*   *   *

James Goldman at his best is a second-rate Neil Simon: both are dramatists who entertain
rather than engage their audiences. Whether he is writing situation comedies (in
collaboration with his brother), *A Family Affair* and *Blood, Sweat and Stanley Poole*,
historical dramas, *The Lion in Winter* and *Nicholas and Alexandra*, or a musical, *Follies*, his
work is always predictable, never ranging outside of the already-tested limits of the form.
Only his skillful handling of dialogue occasionally redeems his plays, but even it cannot
compensate for his deficiency in imagination, nor can it conceal that his characters are
stock, plots mechanical, and themes imperfectly realized.
   A Family Affair and *Blood, Sweat and Stanley Poole* play like the pseudo-comedies that
could be seen between six and ten p.m. any week-night on American television throughout
the late fifties and early-to-middle sixties. One concerns itself with the bustle and bickering
that typically occurs when two families attempt to plan a wedding and the guardian of the
bride wants a simple, elegant "family affair" while the mother of the groom longs for
something a bit fancier. The other involves an army officer, 1st Lieutenant Stanley Poole,
who has been bribing the education officer, Malcolm, with goods from the supply room to
pass him on the army proficiency tests. The hero-of-the-day is Private Robert Oglethorpe
who runs a "cram" course for the army officers, making it possible for Poole to replace the
pilfered supplies, free himself from his bondage to Malcolm, and retain his military rank by
passing the proficiency exams. The plot is mechanical, the jokes are stale, the characters too
familiar, and the situation – Oglethorpe's classroom for the army's dunderheads – plays like
a classroom scene from *Our Miss Brooks* or *Sergeant Bilko*, replete with all the cute
gimmicks and mnemonics that teach the adult student to learn the names of the five Great
Lakes or to recognize "the Symphony that Schubert wrote and never finished." Even the
two Goldmans' sense of theatricality falters in this play. The slap-stick accident where the
good guys mangle and mutilate the villainous Captain Malcolm's coveted Jag takes place
off-stage and can only be recounted, supposedly hilariously, by the conspirators on the stage.
The climax of the play comes when the clumsy Private Oglethorpe, who previously got
headaches whenever even the word "bayonet" was mentioned, catches the rifle Malcolm
throws at him and brilliantly executes the manual of arms. The first action better fits a

movie or television program than a play; the second simply lacks enough intrinsic importance to carry even the climax of a silly piece of canned comedy.

Goldman finds better success in another genre, the history or chronicle play, which had its revival in the sixties with *Luther, Beckett, Lawrence of Arabia*, and, most successfully, *A Man for All Seasons*. Well done, the chronicle play examines and revitalizes characters from the past whose significance is unchallenged. It brings the past to life and, more importantly, it shows how the present has worked upon the past making it relevant. Goldman, however, seems to have overlooked this most important aspect of historical drama. It is not surprising that the dramatist of *They Might Be Giants* left the contemporary world and looked to the past to supply him with the heroes he sought, but it is regrettable that he only went to the past to acquire material and not to relate it to modern concerns. In *The Lion in Winter* Henry II of England and Eleanor of Aquitaine engage in a battle of wits as each attempts to outdo the other and settle the questions of succession, which son will marry the king's mistress, and which son will inherit the Vexin and Aquitaine. Henry, the aging monarch, still the roaring, regal lion, seeks to possess both his mistress and his wife and both their lands in order to pass England and that portion of France which is England's to John, his youngest and weakest son. Eleanor fights fiercely to hold Henry, and, failing that, to guarantee that England and her precious Aquitaine are willed to Richard Coeur de Lion. Geoffrey, the middle and cleverest son, plays brother against brother and son against father as he, too, struggles to protect what he believes should be his own. Alais, the lovely mistress, is pawn to Henry and his aged and imprisoned wife throughout the play. The dialogue in the play is witty, intelligent, pithy, and often mercurial. Henry and Eleanor alternately rage at each other and ask each other for pity in a manner reminiscent of George and Martha's quarrels in *Who's Afraid of Virginia Woolf?* But finally, the play is too contrived, the games of one-upmanship grow stale, and the audience begins to doubt that anything so real as the fate of the kingdom is at stake. The Christmas Court ends in a stalemate; the question of succession is postponed to another year; Eleanor and Henry conclude acknowledging to each other that their real enemy is time and that it will win. Goldman, meanwhile, seems to have forgotten that there was ever a real historical question raised in the play. History, and not the play, is left to tell us how the question of succession was resolved. The natures of the regal pair and not succession seem to have been the stuff of the play, but Goldman never demonstrates why these natures matter or who this King and Queen are.

Recently, Goldman has tried his hand at musical comedy; but he seems no more likely to be successful with this form than with the others. The script of *Follies* suffers from the same flaws that plagued his earlier works. It is *déjà vu*. The occasion is a reunion called by an Impresario of the Weismann Follies' girls. Back to the crumbling music hall that had its heyday thirty years earlier come the showgirls who had danced for the era between the two wars. Among the guests are two girls, Sally and Phyllis, and their husbands, Buddy and Ben. As the evening progresses, we watch these pairs when they were young and in love, thirty years ago, and now, when they are old and discontent and flirting with the possibility that they can undo time and their marriages and return to the men who had jilted them before they married so long ago. The soap opera tale can be guessed. After an evening in which the couples dance and sing down memory lane and exorcize their regrets in a Follies Loveland, the couples leave their fancied past and return to drab realities and each other. The lyrics do much to redeem the play and the gauzy interplay of past and present, shadows and substance, is visually well-handled and extremely well-suited to a musical that has taken sentimentality and nostalgia for its theme. Nonetheless, all this really says is that the form camouflages some of Goldman's limitations. His inability to create fully realized characters of his own fresh imagining, his dependence upon a mechanical plot that repeats with slight variation the same situations, and his lack of a significant theme continue to plague his work.

—Carol Simpson Stern

GOOCH, Steve. British. Born in Surrey, 22 July 1945. Educated at the Emanuel School, London, 1956–63; Trinity College, Cambridge, 1964–67, B.A. (honours) in modern languages 1967; St. John's College, Cambridge (Harper-Wood Scholar), 1967; Birmingham University, 1968–69. Assistant Editor, *Plays and Players* magazine, London, 1972–73; Resident Dramatist, Half Moon Theatre, London, 1973–74, and Greenwich Theatre, London, 1974–75. Recipient: Arts Council bursary, 1973; Thames Television Award, 1974. Agent: Margaret Ramsay Ltd., 14a Goodwin's Court, London WC2N 4LL. Address: 18 Vauxhall Grove, London S.W.8, England.

PUBLICATIONS

Plays

The NAB Show (produced Brighton, 1970).
Great Expectations, adaptation of a novel by Charles Dickens (produced Liverpool, 1970).
Man Is Man, adaptation of the play by Bertolt Brecht (produced London, 1971).
It's All for the Best, adaptation of the novel *Candide* by Voltaire (produced Stoke on Trent, 1972).
Big Wolf, adaptation of a play by Harald Mueller (produced London, 1972). London, Davis Poynter, 1972.
Will Wat; If Not, What Will? (produced London, 1972). London, Pluto Press, 1975.
Prison (produced Exeter, 1972).
The Mother, adaptation of a play by Bertolt Brecht (produced London, 1973).
Female Transport (produced London, 1973; New York, 1976). London, Pluto Press, 1975.
Dick (produced London, 1973).
The Motor Show, with Paul Thompson (produced Dagenham, Essex, and London, 1974). London, Pluto Press, 1975.
Cock-Artist, adaptation of a play by R.W. Fassbinder (produced London, 1974).
Strike '26, with Frank McDermott (produced London, 1975).
Made in Britain, with Paul Thompson (produced Oxford, 1976).
Our Land Our Lives (produced London, 1976).

Theatrical Activities:

Director: **Plays** – *Work Kills!* by Bruce Birchill, London, 1975; *Consensus* by Michael Gill, London, 1976.

Steve Gooch comments:

My work is mainly about working-class experience and history, and for a working-class audience and readership. Its intention is to align itself with the most developed and progressive sections of the working-class movement in Britain and elsewhere. To this end it draws on traditions of thought from the working-class movement, both in Britain and abroad. It also draws freely on innovations in style and dramatic technique from working-class culture everywhere, in an experimental attempt to find a new socialist, humanist theatre.

*   *   *

Steve Gooch is one of the most skilful and prolific writers to have emerged through British fringe theatres. His reputation is two-fold. He read French and German at Cambridge University, and has become a skilful translator/adaptor of works from both these languages. He adapted Voltaire's *Candide* for the Victoria Theatre, Stoke on Trent (under the title of *It's All for the Best*); and has translated two of Brecht's plays, *Man Is Man* and *The Mother*, together with Harald Mueller's *Big Wolf*. The flair and wit of these translations, however, reflect the other side of Gooch's work, as a straight dramatist, whose social documentaries have been among the most successful of this now familiar genre and whose fictional plays reveal an unusual tact, understanding and sympathy.

This sympathy can be one-sided. Gooch is a socialist, further to the left than is customary in the British Labour Party, but orthodox, coherent and not wildy radical. He therefore tends to see society in terms of class-warfare, the exploiters versus the exploited, choosing his examples from history accordingly and leaving little doubt where his own loyalties lie. His documentary, *The Motor Show*, written with Paul Thompson about the Ford factory at Dagenham, was compiled with the help of shop stewards, but not that of the management. The "show" of the title suggests the style: bright, cartoon-like (Henry Ford is shown as Mr. Big, wheeling and dealing over a Big City pool table), rising to a climax in which the Ford workers are urged to rise up and seize the means of production.

Although the "exploiters" are often caricatured, Gooch has the ability to present working-class men and women more naturalistically, without too much sentimentality but with a realistic appraisal of their needs and hopes. In *Female Transport*, he showed six female convicts on a nineteenth-century prison ship, bound for Australia. Through the voyage and their suffering, these six, thrown together as the result of different "crimes," learn to know each other and unite in a common cause, the hatred and outwitting of their oppressors. Like Edward Bond, Gooch has the power to reinforce his arguments with startling images of cruelty and violence which avoid the charge of melodrama by the restraint of the sober realism of their contexts. In *Female Transport*, one convict commits suicide and her body is left hanging on the stage. In his translation of Fassbinder's *Katzelmacher* (*Cock-Artist*), Gooch shows how a foreign worker in a small country town becomes the object of unreasoning fears and jealousies from the locals. This hatred develops into a violent brawl where the "guest worker" is beaten up; but Gooch skilfully builds up the tense atmosphere by short elliptical scenes, fragmented conversations and a deliberately restrained, almost monosyllabic vocabulary. The violence derives from the culture.

Cock-Artist was presented in the small fringe theatre, the Almost Free, on a bare arena stage: similarly, *Female Transport*, *The Mother* and *Will Wat; If Not, What Will?* were first shown at the little Half Moon Theatre, a converted synagogue in East London. It is in such bare surroundings that Gooch's work is perhaps seen at its best, for his dialogue is strong enough to hold the attention, his situations are presented with a firm grasp of their dramatic essentials, and he handles the close proximity of the audience with imagination. In *Will Wat*, for example, a historical documentary about the Peasants' Revolt of 1381, a knight in full armour is swung up on a trapeze and mounted on two actors, while the audience is warned that one in every three will shortly die of the Black Death. Members of the public were examined for signs of the disease.

If such forms of audience-involvement seem now almost conventional in fringe theatres, Gooch has the taste to use them discreetly. In handling the wide-ranging but quickly told plot of *Candide*, Gooch showed his capacity to reduce the story to its essentials, often choosing surprising ways of doing so. The old woman's tale of rape and cannibalism across at least two continents becomes a music-hall monologue in doggerel verse; while the massacre of two armies is presented by the sound of a fusillade and four soldiers meeting across a stage – and crawling off, lights dimmed. Gooch uses quick images to present arguments, such as the ridiculous optimism of Pangloss or the wide-eyed naivety of Candide.

These talents of dialogue skill, use of theatrical effects from music-hall to sombre realism, audience involvement and clear story-telling make Gooch one of Brecht's best translators, capable of finding a dramatic energy in English to match the original. They also indicate that Gooch has the makings of a major dramatist, a fact which has not been overlooked by leading companies in Britain. Both the Royal Court and the Royal Shakespeare Company have used his translation of *Man Is Man*. But Gooch so far has stayed with the fringe theatres and small touring companies whom he has served so well. Their limited resources appeal to his austere outlook.

—John Elsom

GORDONE, Charles. American. Born in Cleveland, Ohio, 12 October 1925. Educated at Elkhart High School, Indiana; University of California, Los Angeles; Los Angeles State College. Served in the United States Air Force. Married to Jeanne Warner; has one daughter. Co-Founder, with Godfrey Cambridge, The Committee for the Employment of Negro Performers. Recipient: Obie Award, for acting, 1964; Pulitzer Prize, 1970; New York Drama Critics Circle Award, 1970; Vernon Rice Award, 1970; National Institute of Arts and Letters grant, 1971. Agent: William Morris Agency, 1350 Avenue of the Americas, New York, New York 10019, U.S.A.

PUBLICATIONS

Plays

> *No Place to Be Somebody: A Black-Black Comedy* (produced New York, 1969). Indianapolis, Bobbs Merrill, 1969.
> *Gordone Is a Muthah* (miscellany; produced New York, 1970). Published in *The Best Short Plays 1973*, edited by Stanley Richards, Radnor, Pennsylvania, Chilton, 1973.
> *The Last Chord* (produced New York, 1976).

Critical Study: "Yes, I Am a Black Playwright, But..." by the author, in *The New York Times*, 25 January 1970.

Theatrical Activities:

Director: **Plays** – about 25 plays, including *Tobacco Road* by Erskine Caldwell, *Detective Story* by Sidney Kingsley, *Hell Bent fer Heaven* by Hatcher Hughes, Eugene O'Neill's "Sea Plays," and *Faust* by Goethe, New York, 1959.

Actor: **Plays** – in *Fortunato*; George in *Of Mice and Men* by John Steinbeck; in *Mrs. Patterson* by Greer Johnson and Charles Sebree; in *The Climate of Eden* by Moss Hart, New York, 1952; The Valet in *The Blacks* by Jean Genet, New York, 1961; Jero in *The Trials of Brother Jero* by Wole Soyinka, New York, 1967; in *Gordone Is a Muthah*, New York, 1970.

*   *   *

307

Charles Gordone's *No Place to Be Somebody* is a stunning play. An introductory course in various types of black-white confrontations, it is a packed play, a busy play, that sacrifices individual characters for the general social context formed by their interaction. Pressed for time, Gordone relies on short-hand methods of characterization, but for all the stereotyping and the crowded structure, his is a consistently challenging drama.

The setting, a bar, allows for the easy introduction of many characters. The focus in the creation of the characters is color, and a unifying theme is the desire of black and white characters to exchange roles. Johnny Williams, proprietor of the bar, wants to form his own Mafia syndicate. He has been waiting for an old friend, a patriarchal figure, to be released from jail, but the old man, changed by his experience, points out to Johnny that the dream of success in the underworld is only an attempt to compete with the white man on his own terms. Shanty, a white boy who works for Johnny, wants to be as good as a black drummer, and Shanty's black girl wants white respectability. Johnny's white girl, in a jealous rage, puts on black face, a moment that epitomizes the double-stranded theme.

The play is not so schematic as this sounds, however. Gordone's perspective is complicated, shifting; he has not written a black protest play or a conventional thesis play. Gordone allows for no heroics, and he has not written his play on the glib theme of oppression and defeat. His criticisms are double-edged; though *No Place to Be Somebody* belongs to what is by now the convention of the angry black play, Gordone's anger, unlike, say, LeRoi Jones', is not directed solely at a vicious and smug white world, but also at an embittered and uninstructed and violent black world as well.

A main axis of the play, in fact, is the division between two different kinds of black man. The action is presided over by a playwright-narrator, Gabe Gabriel, who sets the characters in motion, and who drops in on the bar to listen and to comment when he feels like it. He opens each act with a showy set-piece which is similar in function to the Greek chorus, serving as a general commentary on the world of the play and, more particularly, mocking white conceptions of blacks and black conceptions of themselves. In the bizarre finale, he comes on in drag, mourning for his people who are "dying into a new life." In creating his hero, Johnny Williams, Gabe has created his opposite. Gabe, a would-be actor, is cautious, practical, so nearly white in appearance that he has trouble getting black roles. Johnny is hard, militant; he operates a prostitution ring, and he treats the white prostitute who falls in love with him as callously as he treats a naive liberal white college girl. Gabe disapproves of Johnny's desperation and bitterness, and when Johnny is determined to take on the Mafia, after having killed some of its members, Gabe kills Johnny: the playwright kills his erring hero and so ends the play.

Gordone's large concerns help him over the rough spots, the leisurely pacing, the awkward management of plot, the reversion to melodrama in the plot-heavy third act. In the first two acts, the action is constructed as a series of encounters between characters who express opposing notions about how to live. Act III springs a conventional story on us; there are secret files, bribes, shoot-outs, and, by the end, as many corpses as in a bloody Jacobean revenge tragedy.

What helps move the play along — and what holds it together — is the terrific energy generated by Gordone's handling of the black idiom. The dialogue has a seemingly reportorial authenticity, yet in its rhythmic, insistent pulse, the language has a charged, incantatory, poetic intensity. Frank, caustic, tangy, the language is a torrent of black anger and black humor.

No Place to Be Somebody isn't a "promising" play: the author is already there.

—Foster Hirsch

GOW, Ronald. British. Born in Heaton Moor, near Manchester, Lancashire, 1 November 1897. Educated at Altrincham Grammar School, Cheshire; Manchester University, B.Sc. 1922. Served in the army, 1918–19. Married the actress Wendy Hiller in 1937; has two children. Worked as a chemist and schoolmaster; produced educational films for the Historical Association. Agent: Laurence Fitch, 113 Wardour Street, London W.1. Address: 9 Stratton Road, Beaconsfield, Buckinghamshire, England.

PUBLICATIONS

Plays

Breakfast at Eight (produced Altrincham, 1920). London, French, 1921.

The Sausage (produced Altrincham). London and New York, French, 1924.

Under the Skull and Bones: A Piratical Play with Songs (produced Altrincham). London, Gowans and Gray, and Boston, Baker, 1929.

Higgins: The Highwayman of Cranford (produced Altrincham). London, Gowans and Gray, and Boston, Baker, 1930.

Henry; or, The House on the Moor (produced Altrincham). London, Gowans and Gray, and Boston, Baker, 1931.

Five Robin Hood Plays (includes *The King's Warrant, The Sheriff's Kitchen, All on a Summer's Day, Robin Goes to Sea, The Affair at Kirklees*). London, Nelson, 1932.

The Golden West (produced Altrincham). London, Gowans and Gray, and Boston, Baker, 1932.

The Vengeance of the Gang (produced Altrincham). London, Gowans and Gray, and Boston, Baker, 1933.

Plays for the Classroom (text). London, Murray, 1933.

O.H.M.S. London, Deane, 1933.

Gallows Glorious (produced London, 1933; as *John Brown*, produced New York, 1934). London, Gollancz, 1933.

My Lady Wears a White Cockade (produced London, 1934). London, Garamond Press, 1935.

Love on the Dole, with Walter Greenwood, adaptation of the novel by Walter Greenwood (produced Manchester, 1934; London, 1935; New York, 1936). London, Cape, 1935; New York, French, 1936.

Compromise. London, Deane, and Boston, Baker, 1935.

The Marrying Sort. London, Garamond Press, and Boston, Baker, 1935.

The Miracle on Watling Street: A Play for the Open Air. London, Dickson and Thompson, 1935.

Men Are Unwise, adaptation of the novel by Ethel Mannin (produced London, 1937).

Ma's Bit o' Brass, based on the screenplay *Lancashire Luck* (produced Colwyn Bay and London, 1938; as *Lovejoy's Millions*, produced London, 1938). London, Deane, and Boston, Baker, 1938.

Scuttleboom's Treasure. London and New York, French, 1938.

Grannie's a Hundred. London, Deane, and Boston, Baker, 1939.

The Lawyer of Springfield (broadcast, 1940). Boston, Baker, 1949.

Jenny Jones, music by Harry Parr Davies, adaptation of stories by Rhys Davies (produced London, 1944).

Tess of the D'Urbervilles, adaptation of the novel by Thomas Hardy (produced London, 1946).

Jassy, adaptation of the novel by Norah Lofts (produced Wimbledon, 1947).

Ann Veronica, adaptation of the novel by H. G. Wells (produced London, 1949).

London, French, 1951; revised version, with Frank Wells, music by Cyril Ornadel (produced London, 1969).

The Full Treatment, with Robert Morley (produced London, 1953).

The Edwardians, adaptation of the novel by V. Sackville-West (as *Weekend in May*, produced Windsor, 1959; as *The Edwardians*, produced London, 1959). London, French, 1960.

Mr. Rhodes (produced Windsor, 1961).

A Boston Story, adaptation of the novel *Watch and Ward* by Henry James (as *Watch and Ward*, produced Windsor, 1964; revised version, as *A Boston Story*, produced London, 1968). London, Theatre Guild, 1969.

This Stratford Business, adaptation of stories by Henry James (produced Cheltenham, 1971).

The Friendship of Mrs. Eckley (produced Cheltenham, 1975).

Screenplays: *Lancashire Luck*, 1937; *Mr. Smith Carries On*, 1938; *Jig Saw*, 1942.

Radio Plays: *The Lawyer of Springfield*, 1940; *Enter, Fanny Kemble*, 1940; *Front Line Family* series, during World War II; *Darwin Comes Ashore*, 1941; *Patience on a Monument*, 1944; *Westward Ho* (serialization), from the novel by Charles Kingsley, 1953; *Lorna Doone* (serialization), from the novel by R. D. Blackmore, 1954.

Television Play: *Trumpet in the Clouds*, 1955.

Ronald Gow comments:

The question I am being asked is "what makes me tick as a playwright?" I was brought up near Manchester with the strong belief that the Gaiety Theatre was the greatest thing that ever happened there – even greater than the Hallé – and that Brighouse, Monkhouse and Houghton were not only household words but shining examples. We knew them all and I had even acted with the author of *Hindle Wakes*. I was definitely stage-struck and when we built a theatre in my home town I cared little whether I shifted scenery or acted or took tickets at the door. After many one-act plays and a desperate wish to be a shining example I began to look around for something to be angry about. Most of my plays had some compelling obsession in them. When I wrote about Bonnie Prince Charlie it became anti-war and anti-romantic. Result, a mere six weeks at the Embassy. Next play about John Brown, whose soul went marching on, brought the audience cheering to their feet at the old Shaftesbury. But a bitter anti-slavery bias and an austere title (*Gallows Glorious*) were no good in that temple of musical comedy. Two weeks. (Two nights in New York.) I was trying to write an anti-unemployment play (three million of them) but fortunately read Walter Greenwood's *Love on the Dole* and decided to dramatize that instead. Marriage necessitated making money, with no axes to grind, resulting in comedies like *Ma's Bit o' Brass* and various film scripts and a great deal of propaganda radio and film work during the war (*Front Line Family*). Success with adapting novels led to London productions of *Tess of the D'Urbervilles*, *Ann Veronica*, *The Edwardians*, and *A Boston Story* from a Henry James novel.

*   *   *

Ronald Gow is a very modest man. Questioned about his work, he will say that any claim to distinction as a playwright that he may have achieved is due rather to his ability as an adaptor of borrowed plots to stage production than as an inventor of original stories. He will say this with a deprecating air, as of one ready to admit that he is operating on an artistic level rather below the highest.

How he can take this view, seeing that he is following the lead given by the most inveterate plot-borrower of them all, William Shakespeare, is not clear. One suspects Gow of being over-modest; and suspicion becomes certainty when a close critical look at his whole range of dramatic writings reveals that his early original plays were no less distinguished than his subsequent adaptations. Simply, they were less popular.

A reason for this can easily be found. Gow was educated at the grammar school at Altrincham in Cheshire, a town with easy access to Manchester. His subject was science, and his objective a B.Sc. degree at Manchester University; but during his schooldays the institution in that city which chiefly excited his interest was the Gaiety Theatre, where Miss Horniman had installed her famous regime and a whole group of angry young men were writing for her a whole series of realistic plays about social injustices of the time.

Gow, violently stage-struck, worshipped at the feet of these dramatists, came to know some of them (Harold Brighouse, Stanley Houghton, and the older Alan Monkhouse), and made up his mind that when the time came he would follow their example; meanwhile he became an enthusiastic amateur actor.

Fortunately for him, there lay at his very door the means to make the theatre an absorbing hobby without too much encroachment on the more serious business of earning a living. An amateur dramatic society at Altrincham, the Garrick, was fast becoming (and, incidentally, is still) one of the leaders in its own field. In the period after World War I when the professional stage was given over almost wholly to glittering frivolity and the general playgoing public asked for nothing better, the task of keeping a more serious theatre alive fell to amateurs who, organised and led by the newly formed British Drama League, rose nobly to the call.

As the movement gathered force and a large public responded, men like Gow found their hobby growing into something very like a profession. He himself, now a young man with his science degree behind him, working first as research chemist and then as schoolmaster, was in his spare time wholly at the Garrick Theatre's service. He acted for it, wrote for it, shifted scenery, took money at the doors. For several years he was its secretary; and when it decided to build itself its own playhouse, he even laid bricks for it. By the time when, at 33 or so, he decided to try his luck as a professional dramatist, he had had a fuller training for the craft than most.

True to the principles he had learnt as a boy, he now looked for social injustices to write about. This was easy enough so far as themes went, for he had as sharp a sense of the follies and injustices of human life as any of the Horniman dramatists whose disciple he was. Unlike them, however, he had a natural sense of period, and was apt to look to the past for his plots.

From the first, there was no question of the excellence of his writing, and he soon had a play accepted for West End production. This was *Gallows Glorious*, which told the story of that John Brown whose soul, in the song, goes marching on. It was produced at the old Shaftesbury Theatre in 1933, and the first-night audience received it with raptuous applause and a standing ovation. But the Shaftesbury (destroyed by German bombs in World War II) was a big house to fill, and the general public, which was not in the mood for period pieces anyhow, showed no interest in John Brown whatever. The play limped along for two weeks and then had to be taken off.

A rather similar experience in the following year with an anti-romantic and anti-war play about Bonnie Prince Charlie must have taught him the lesson that a man writing a play-with-a-purpose should choose to set his action in the immediate present, for he next sat down to write about unemployment, the chief problem of the moment. While engaged on this he happened to read Walter Greenwood's novel *Love on the Dole*, and decided to dramatise Greenwood's story instead of going on with his own.

The great success of this play changed Gow's whole life. It made a name not only for him but for Wendy Hiller, the aspiring young actress who played his heroine and whom, in 1937, he married. It also brought him sharply to the notice of Pinewood film studios and the BBC, with the ironic result that he was, practically speaking, lost to the stage for nine years or so. Indeed, his next two stage plays, *Ma's Bit o' Brass* and *Tess of the D'Urbervilles* were both adapted to the stage from film-scripts of his own.

311

The first-named of these two, a light-hearted exercise in the Lancashire idiom, ranks rather uneasily among Gow's original pieces. It never quite reached the West End, but it toured successfully and became a favourite among "Reps" and amateurs. Its author now regards it with a kind of rueful gratitude.

He wrote the film version of *Tess* for his wife, who during the war was invited to play this part in Hollywood. He himself did not quite "see" her in the part, and advised her against taking it – and, indeed, it was not one of her greatest successes. But she did well enough for John Burrell to want her to do it on the London stage, and to invite Gow to write the play. His next three West End productions — *Ann Veronica, The Edwardians* and the very delightful *A Boston Story* — were adaptations but his latest piece, *The Friendship of Mrs. Eckley*, is an original story about the Brownings.

—W. A. Darlington

GRAY, Jack. Canadian. Born in Detroit, Michigan, United States, 7 December 1927. Educated at primary and secondary schools in Ontario; Queen's University, Kingston, Ontario; University of Toronto, B.A., M.A. Married Araby Lockhart in 1952; has five children. Assistant Editor, *Maclean's Magazine*, Toronto, 1953–57; Executive Director and Resident Playwright, Nepture Theatre, Halifax, 1963; Professor of Integrated Studies, University of Waterloo, Ontario, 1969–71; Secretary General, Canadian Theatre Centre, Toronto, 1971–73. Since 1970, Member of the Executive Board, and Chairman of the Writers Council, Association of Canadian Television and Radio Artists (ACTRA). President, International Writers Guild. President of John Gray Productions Ltd. Editor of the Canadian Play Series, University of Toronto Press. Agent: Blanche Marvin, Elspeth Cochrane Agency, 1 The Pavement, London SW4 0HY, England. Address: 32 Binscarth Road, Toronto, Ontario M4W 1Y1, Canada.

PUBLICATIONS

Plays

    Bright Sun at Midnight (produced Toronto, 1957).
    Ride a Pink Horse, music by Louis Applebaum (produced Toronto, 1958).
    The Teacher (produced Stratford, Ontario, 1960).
    Chevalier Johnstone (as *Louisbourg*, produced Halifax, 1964). Toronto, Playwrights Co-op, 1972.
    Emmanuel Xoc (produced Toronto, 1965).
    Godiva (produced Coventry, 1967).
    Susannah, Agnes and Ruth (broadcast 1969). Toronto, Playwrights Co-op, 1972.
    Striker Schneiderman (produced Toronto, 1970). Toronto, University of Toronto Press, 1973.

    Radio Plays: *To Whom It May Concern*, 1958; *The Lost Boy*, 1959; *Susannah, Agnes and Ruth*, 1969; *The Cracker Man*, 1970; *And I Mayakovsky*, 1976.

    Television Plays: *The Ledge*, 1959 (UK); *The Glove*, 1961 (UK); *Man in Town*, 1962; *The Enemy*, 1962 (UK); *The Guard*, 1963; *Miss Hanago*, 1964 (UK).

Manuscript Collection: Metropolitan Toronto Library.

Theatrical Activities:

Director: **Play** – *Clap Hands* (revue), London, 1962.

*   *   *

Jack Gray is a Shavian with a taste for the baroque. Most of his plays inhabit the world of witty altercation – to the detriment, occasionally, of their dramatic form. But they are on the whole well made, and the aphoristic quality of many of the speeches indicates more than superficial wit. In *Susannah, Agnes and Ruth* (the first of six projected plays to be called *Six Summers*) the repartee is brittle:

> Ian –   He'll never get over it.
> Susannah – He never got over being born.

But it is more than brittle. Gray has listened to the ghastly maxims of middle-class Methodism with an attentive ear. "Don't be smart" or "A responsible parent can never be said to be interfering." Both speak for the world of *Ah, Wilderness!* with all the exuberance removed – a world in which we expect to hear that "the Attorney-General says that dancing on Sunday must stop in Ontario." This is only just the day before yesterday, and it does Gray credit not only that he can capture it so exactly without cause or rancour but that he can give to Susannah (the grandmother figure who is its spokesman) a toughness and a life that even the men in the play have missed. In a passage reminiscent of Strether's impassioned speech to Little Bilham in *The Ambassadors*, Bob, one of the uncles, says to Ruth: "We've evaded life – sidestepped it – it's like a dance – one-two-sidestep – one-two-step aside.... Don't be like we are, Ruth – take hold of life." But it is Susannah more than the rest who realizes the importance of seizing upon life and denying death. She rebukes the simpering vicar who speaks of her son and others as having died heroic deaths in France in the First World War:

> They did not. They died dirty, lonely blasphemous deaths. Each year on that anniversary, Mr. Smith, I take off my mourning, I wear my gayest clothes. It's all I can do to protest the shallow sham you men make of life. It's how I would meet God – singing! We must never celebrate such deaths.

It is this festivity in the face of bleakness and heroism in spite of itself that characterize the lead in Gray's later play *Striker Schneiderman* – probably his best-known work. But there is a set-piece quality about the play, a sense of its being written for an occasion or to a prescription that does not allow it to be much more than an entertaining piece of theatre. Its elements are too predictable, even down to the tailor joke from *Endgame*.

This criticism is valid to some degree for *Chevalier Johnstone* as well, but although it too seems very much written for an occasion (not to say for television) it has a greater toughness about it, and the ending seems somehow less forced. Part of this is due to the hard-headedness of the dialogue – the absence of sentimentality and Jewish melodrama – and part to a sense that the world described, though it is two centuries away from our own, is closer to our preoccupations than are those of Schneiderman. The play has a curiously Brechtian quality – partly the result no doubt of the rapid shifting of scenes and the extravagant stage directions: "We lose the woods and stream and follow them as they walk back to, and then through, the fortress." But this Brechtian character is most obvious in the restraint of sentiment by a wit that keeps us off. This wit is directed against our prejudices – of flabby democracy and literary superstition, for instance. "I'm an Indian, not a gentleman," says Samuel, the scout who attaches himself to Johnstone while repulsing any foolish notion of mere equality. And in response to Johnstone's explanation that he reads for his recreation, "Pascal...Molière. And, of course, Voltaire," Drucour, his superior, asks "What do you do for healthy recreation?"

Emmanuel Xoc and *The Teacher* both suffer from flaws not so evident in the other plays. In fact, in spite of some turns of phrase in *Emmanuel Xoc* – "fifty years' caution in a man is a kink" – the play is not a good onem It is like a combination of *Gianni Schicchi* and *The Milk Train Doesn't Stop Here Any More*. But its host of characters – Tweedie, Xoc, Baptist, Fink, Fingers, Arnold and Morgan – is too much like something out of an old Bowery Boys film for us to take the play as more than a sort of baroque exercise.

There is a similar element of fantasy in *The Teacher* (like *Emmanuel Xoc*, it has a ghost), though the fantasy is not grotesque but lyrical in a way that easily becomes sentimental. Indeed there is a studied quality about the play that, coupled with the absence of the sort of wit so evident in the later plays, gives it an unfortunate flatness. Its gestures are both towards *Under Milk Wood* and Joyce's *The Dead*, but it fails to get beyond the sort of artificial melodrama – complete with folksongs – that used to be the favorite of the CBC.

Fortunately Gray has come a great way since then. His later plays show both an eye for detail and an ear for wit that are badly needed. None of his plays so far is great, but some of them are very good indeed.

—D. D. C. Chambers

GRAY, Simon. British.   Born on Hayling Island, Hampshire, 21 October 1936. Educated at Dalhousie University, Halifax, Nova Scotia, Canada, 1954–57. B.A. (honours) in English 1957; Trinity College, Cambridge, 1958–61, B.A. (honours) in English 1961. Married Beryl Mary Kevern in 1965; has two children. Harper-Wood Student, St. John's College, Cambridge, 1961–62; Research Student, Trinity College, Cambridge, 1962–63; Lecturer in English, University of British Columbia, Vancouver, 1963–64; Supervisor in English, Trinity College, Cambridge, 1964–66. Since 1966, Lecturer in English, Queen Mary College, London. Since 1964, Editor of *Delta* magazine, Cambridge. Recipient: *Evening Standard* award, 1972, 1976. Address: 70 Priory Gardens, London N.6, England.

PUBLICATIONS

Plays

> *Wise Child* (produced London, 1967; New York, 1972).   London, Faber, 1968.
> *Sleeping Dog* (televised, 1967).   London, Faber, 1968.
> *Spoiled* (televised, 1968; produced Edinburgh, 1970; London, 1971).   London, Methuen, 1971.
> *Dutch Uncle* (produced London, 1969).   London, Faber, 1969.
> *The Idiot*, adaptation of a novel by Dostoevsky (produced London, 1970).   London, Methuen, 1971.
> *Butley* (produced Oxford and London, 1971; New York, 1972).   London, Methuen, 1971; New York, Viking Press, 1972.
> *Dog Days* (produced Watford, Hertfordshire, 1975).
> *Otherwise Engaged* (produced Oxford and London, 1975).   London, Eyre Methuen, 1975.

Screenplay: *Butley*, 1975.

Television Plays: *The Caramel Crisis*, 1966; *Death of a Teddy Bear*, 1967; *A Way with the Ladies*, 1967; *Sleeping Dog*, 1967; *Spoiled*, 1968; *Pig in a Poke*, 1969; *The Dirt on Lucy Lane*, 1969; *Style of the Countess*, 1970; *The Princess*, 1970; *The Man in the Sidecar*, 1971; *Plaintiffs and Defendants*, 1975; *Two Sundays*, 1975.

Novels

Colmain.   London, Faber, 1963.
Simple People.   London, Faber, 1965.
Little Portia.   London, Faber, 1967.
A Comeback for Stark (as Hamish Reade).   London, Faber, 1969.

Other

Editor, with Keith Walker, *Selected English Prose*.   London, Faber, 1967.

*   *   *

Simon Gray made his debut as a dramatist for the stage in October 1967 with *Wise Child*. Since then he has produced three further stage plays (not counting an adaptation of Dostoevsky's *The Idiot* for the National Theatre), of which the latest, *Butley*, has achieved the highest regard and certainly the biggest popular success. At this time, Gray was also an established television playwright and had published several novels.

Wise Child was a somewhat sensational debut on the London stage. Among other things it required its leading actor (in this case Sir Alec Guinness) to spend all but the last moments of the play disguised as a rather prim, middle-aged, middle-class woman. Elderly people tended to make noisy exits from the stalls of Wyndham's Theatre when they realized this oddity. The play handled two forms of transvestism, included a strong homosexual theme and used variants of carnality to prove inter-personal relationships. It was fairly freaky, even for a London on the pendulum turn from the frantic search for permissiveness that characterized the mid-60's.

Most were impressed. The play was well-constructed, witty, expressed in interestingly strange syntactical rhythms and had, naturally, a thrillingly sexy undertow.

Harold Hobson, the always unpredictable drama critic of *The Sunday Times*, was impressed. "The theatre has discovered a writer of quality and consequence," he wrote. The quality is indisputable; always, Simon Gray's writings is vivid, spikey, sometimes eccentric and possesses, too, a sort of esoteric literary quality which reached a new force in *Butley*.

The Royal Shakespeare Company was impressed. For it was that company which mounted the next stage play *Dutch Uncle* with a cast that included Warren Mitchell and the astonishing Frances de la Tour. A strange one, this, and not a popular success. But it did reiterate, in a quite different way, some of the themes that had been expressed in *Wise Child*.

Simon Gray's next play to appear on the stage was *Spoiled*, and was an expanded version of a television play. And it seemed very different from the previous pair. For one thing it was set in a comfortable middle-class intellectual household whereas the others had been set in rooms constructed from the imagination, rooms which one would recognize possibly but never feel immediately at home with, and therefore personally related to. The characters, too, were accessible: a French teacher, his pregnant wife, a schoolboy taking private tuition before an exam. Domestic drama.

Spoiled made no demands on its audience; one was not required to make a conscious effort to understand the events on stage as in the previous plays. It was as cosy and as comfortable to settle down to as any ordinary West End offering. But the bombs go off effectively enough and that comfortable audience is reasonably discomforted. Another new element Gray introduced in *Spoiled* was the academic theme. Its main character is a teacher, a born teacher as they say, and Gray draws the character well; it is clearly something he knows about. The theme is the totality in *Butley*, which takes place in the room of a university lecturer and which is, therefore, academic/literary throughout.

In a programme note he wrote to accompany his adaptation of *The Idiot*, Simon Gray has a phrase which leads us neatly into the themes he explores in his plays. He refers to "the futility of a world gone made with convention." The maintenance of convention involves the necessity of everyone observing, and keeping to, their assigned roles. Furthermore, it means that some people are going to be stronger, more powerful, smarter, richer than others. But this quality of being stronger, more powerful, etc., does not necessarily derive from the ability of the individual, from his own personality, but is put on him by others and, like it or not, he must play the role to maintain the convention.

Gray's characters have rebelled from, or have been forced to contest, this. The central character in *Wise Child* – called "Mrs. Artminster" – is a man who has suffered a radical change of role. He is a criminal on the run. To avoid detection he has disguised himself as a woman. From his natural role, that of tough, inventive criminal he has had to assume the role of gracious, timid middle-aged woman. A lot of the comedy in the play stems from this. At the time Sir Alec Guinness was quoted as saying that he regarded *Wise Child* as a sort of updated *Charley's Aunt*, and, in that the motivation for cross-dressing is pretty much the same, he was right.

But *Wise Child* contains a scene that rather devalues this view. Mrs. Artminster persuades the coloured maid, Janice, to strip for her and here we see the creepy spectacle of a kindly woman and a lubricious man fighting for dominance in the same person. Moreover, Mrs. Artminster is accompanied by a young criminal, Jerry, passed off as her son. In the final scene when Mrs. Artminster returns to male dress and male role, Jerry now appears in drag. If he cannot be a son, then he must be a daughter.

In *Dutch Uncle* we find the central character in rebellion against his own dominating role – rebelling against being a husband (he will not have sexual intercourse with his wife) and against his job. He wishes to occupy another role and insists on being a victim, revealed in his slavish servility to the police.

Domination/submission themes are clearly expressed in these plays, and presented through the media of interesting and wayward plots and language which has wit, style and comic force. In *Spoiled* the theme is presented in, as I have suggested, accessible domestic circumstances. Here the child, Donald, is victim, of his excessively loving mother, of the examination system and, in the foreground, of his teacher. That the pupil-teacher relationship should culminate in a homosexual experience is significant. Homosexual themes recur in Gray's work and his use of them seems to be rather more as an illustrative image than a realistic concern. For the success of male-female relationships in a conventional society depend on both partners accepting their different roles. Single-sex partnerships contest this in a more basic way.

Ben Butley is Simon Gray's most fully-fleshed character so far. And, in dramatic terms, probably at the expense of the other characters who seem to come, say their pieces, and go away again. But Butley stays in full spate throughout the play. In the programme note referred to above, Gray writes that he "noted in the university at which I was an undergraduate those poseurs who had already thrown fits in lecture rooms, and just outside them, and whose dreadful sufferings their gentle smiles had made famous in that world...."

This could be Butley, a lecturer in English, oppressive and bullying, laying about him with a brilliant but cutting wit and yet hurt and surprised when all around him – wife, colleagues, friends – get fed up, bored and impatient. Butley wants more than he gives and sooner or later his victims rebel. In many ways a cruel and defeatist play, it nevertheless works through its acute observation of the academic world and its superb leading role.

Simon Gray has always been fortunate to have his plays presented by the best actors with the best directors. Good as they are to read, they do not possess on the page the vitality brought to them by Alec Guinness, Jeremy Kemp, Simon Ward, Alan Bates and Warren

316

Mitchell. Plays are, of course, meant to be performed, not read. But one does wonder whether Simon Gray has the "consequence" that Harold Hobson predicted. He is a skilful and successful playwright but whether, in deeper terms, his work is more than a product of the idiom and terms of reference of the 1960's and 1970's must remain a matter for debate. In either case the multi-layered explorations of *Wise Child* and the splendid language of *Butley* are extremely influential.

—Roger Baker

GREEN, Paul (Eliot).   American.   Born in Lillington, North Carolina, 17 March 1894. Educated at Buies Creek Academy, North Carolina, graduated 1914; University of North Carolina, Chapel Hill, A.B. 1921; graduate study, 1921–22, Cornell University, Ithaca, New York, 1922–23. Served in the United States Army Engineers, 1917–19: Lieutenant. Married Elizabeth Atkinson Lay in 1922; has four children. Lecturer, then Associate Professor of Philosophy, 1923–39, Professor of Dramatic Arts, 1939–44, and Professor of Radio, Television and Motion Pictures, 1962–63, University of North Carolina. Editor, *The Reviewer* magazine, Chapel Hill, 1925. President, National Folk Festival, 1934–35; President, National Theatre Conference, 1940–42; President, North Carolina State Literary and Historical Association, 1942–43; Member of the United States Executive Committee, and Member of the National Commission, UNESCO, 1950–52; United States Delegate to the UNESCO Conference, Paris, 1951; Director, American National Theatre Company, 1959–61; Delegate to the International Conference on the Performing Arts, Athens, 1962. Recipient: Pulitzer Prize, 1927; Guggenheim Fellowship, 1928, 1929; Claire M. Senie Drama Study Award, 1939, Freedoms Foundation George Washington Medal, 1951, 1956, 1966; Susanne M. Davis Award, 1966. Litt.D.: Western Reserve University, Cleveland, 1941; Davidson College, North Carolina, 1948; University of North Carolina, 1956; Berea College, Kentucky, 1957; University of Louisville, Kentucky, 1957; Campbell College, Buies Creek, North Carolina, 1969; Moravian College, Bethlehem, Pennsylvania, 1976; D.F.A.: North Carolina School of the Arts, Winston-Salem, 1976. Member, National Institute of Arts and Letters, 1941. Agent: Samuel French Inc., 25 West 45th Street, New York, New York 10036. Address: Old Lystra Road, Chapel Hill, North Carolina 27514, U.S.A.

PUBLICATIONS

Plays

The Forest Warder, adaptation of a play by Otto Ludwig, in *Poet Lore* (Boston), Summer 1913.

Surrender to the Enemy (produced Chapel Hill, 1917).

The Last of the Lowries (produced Chapel Hill, 1920).   Included in *The Lord's Will and Other Carolina Plays*, 1925.

The Long Night, in *Carolina Magazine* (Chapel Hill), 1920.

Granny Boling, in *Drama* (Chicago), August–September 1921.

Old Wash Lucas (The Miser) (produced Chapel Hill, 1921).   Included in *The Lord's Will and Other Carolina Plays*, 1925.

The Old Man of Edenton (produced Chapel Hill, 1921).   Included in *The Lord's Will and Other Carolina Plays,* 1925.

The Lord's Will (produced Chapel Hill, 1922).   Included in *The Lord's Will and Other Carolina Plays,* 1925.

Blackbeard, with Elizabeth Lay Green (produced Chapel Hill, 1922).   Included in *The Lord's Will and Other Carolina Plays,* 1925.

White Dresses (produced White Plains, New York, 1923).   Included in *Lonesome Road,* 1926.

Wrack P'int (produced Chapel Hill, 1923).

Sam Tucker, in *Poet Lore* (Boston), Summer 1923; revised version, as *Your Fiery Furnace,* included in *Lonesome Road,* 1926.

Fixins, with Erma Green (produced Chapel Hill, 1924).   New York, French, 1934.

The No 'Count Boy (produced Dallas and New York, 1925, London, 1960).   Included in *The Lord's Will and Other Carolina Plays,* 1925; in *Fifty One-Act Plays: Second Series,* edited by Constance M. Martin, London, Gollancz, 1940; revised (white) version, New York, French, 1953.

In Aunt Mahaly's Cabin: A Negro Melodrama (produced Baltimore, 1925).   New York, French, 1925.

The Lord's Will and Other Carolina Plays (includes *Blackbeard, Old Wash Lucas (The Miser), The No 'Count Boy, The Old Man of Edenton, The Last of the Lowries*).   New York, Holt, 1925.

Quare Medicine (produced Chapel Hill, 1925).   Included in *In the Valley and Other Carolina Plays,* 1928.

The Man Who Died at Twelve O'Clock (produced Thermopolis, Wyoming, 1925).   New York, French, 1927.

In Abraham's Bosom (produced New York, 1926).   Included in *The Field God and In Abraham's Bosom,* 1927; published separately, London, Allen and Unwin, 1929.

Lonesome Road: Six Plays for the Negro Theatre (includes *In Abraham's Bosom,* one-act version; *White Dresses; The Hot Iron; The Prayer Meeting; The End of the Row; Your Fiery Furnace*).   New York, McBride, 1926.

The Hot Iron in *Lonesome Road,* 1926; revised version, as *Lay This Body Down* (produced Berea, Kentucky, 1972), included in *Wings for to Fly,* 1959.

The Field God (produced New York, 1927, London, 1928).   Included in *The Field God and In Abraham's Bosom,* 1927.

The Field God and In Abraham's Bosom.   New York, McBride, 1927.

Bread and Butter Come to Supper.   New York, McBride, 1928; as *Chair Endowed* (produced New York, 1954).

In the Valley and Other Carolina Plays (includes *Quare Medicine, Supper for the Dead, Saturday Night, The Man Who Died at Twelve O'Clock, In Aunt Mahaly's Cabin, The No 'Count Boy, The Man on the House, The Picnic, Unto Such Glory, The Goodbye*).   New York, French, 1928.

Supper for the Dead (produced New York, 1954).   Included in *In the Valley and Other Carolina Plays,* 1928.

Unto Such Glory (produced New York, 1936; London, 1958).   Included in *In the Valley and Other Carolina Plays,* 1928.

The Goodbye (produced New York, 1954).   Included in *In the Valley and Other Carolina Plays,* 1928.

Blue Thunder; or, The Man Who Married a Snake, in *One Act Plays for Stage and Study.*   New York, French, 1928.

Old Christmas.   New York, McBride, 1928.

The House of Connelly (produced New York, 1931).   Included in *The House of Connelly and Other Plays,* 1931; revised version (produced New York, 1959), included in *Five Plays of the South,* 1963.

The House of Connelly and Other Plays (includes *Potter's Field* and *Tread the Green Grass*).   New York, French, 1931.

Potter's Field (produced Boston, 1934).   Included in *The House of Connelly and Other Plays,* 1931; revised version, as *Roll Sweet Chariot: A Symphonic Play of the Negro*

People, music by Dolphe Martin (produced New York, 1934), New York, French, 1935.

Tread the Green Grass, music by Lamar Stringfield (produced Iowa City, Iowa, 1932). Included in *The House of Connelly and Other Plays*, 1931.

Shroud My Body Down (produced Chapel Hill, 1934).   Iowa City, Iowa, Clio Press, 1935, revised version, as *The Honeycomb*, New York, French, 1972.

The Enchanted Maze: The Story of a Modern Student in Dramatic Form (produced Chapel Hill, 1935).   New York, French, 1939.

Hymn to the Rising Sun (produced New York, 1936).   New York, French, 1936; in *Contemporary One Act Plays from Nine Countries*, edited by Percival Wilde, London, Harrap, 1936.

Johnny Johnson: The Biography of a Common Man, music by Kurt Weill (produced New York, 1936).   New York, French, 1937; revised version, 1972.

The Southern Cross (produced Dallas, 1936).   New York, French, 1938; in *The Best One-Act Plays of 1938*, edited by J. W. Marriott, London, Harrap, 1939.

The Lost Colony (produced Roanoke Island, North Carolina, 1937).   Chapel Hill, University of North Carolina Press, 1937; revised version, 1939, 1946, 1954, 1962.

Alma Mater, in *The Best One-Act Plays of 1938*, edited by Margaret Mayorga.   New York, Dodd Mead, 1938.

Out of the South: The Life of a People in Dramatic Form (includes *The House of Connelly, The Field God, In Abraham's Bosom, Potter's Field, Johnny Johnson, The Lost Colony, The No 'Count Boy, Saturday Night, Quare Medicine, The Hot Iron, Unto Such Glory, Supper for the Dead, The Man Who Died at Twelve O'Clock, White Dresses, Hymn to the Rising Sun*).   New York, Harper, 1939.

The Critical Year: A One-Act Sketch of American History and the Beginning of the Constitution.   New York, French, 1939.

Franklin and the King.   New York, Dramatists Play Service, 1939.

The Highland Call: A Symphonic Play of American History (produced Fayetteville, North Carolina, 1939).   Chapel Hill, University of North Carolina Press, 1941.

Native Son, with Richard Wright, adaptation of the novel by Richard Wright (produced New York, 1941; London, 1948).   New York, Harper, 1941.

A Start in Life (broadcast, 1941).   Published in *The Free Company Presents*, edited by James Boyd, New York, Dodd Mead, 1941; as *Fine Wagon* in *Wings for to Fly*, 1959.

The Common Glory: A Symphonic Drama of American History (produced Williamsburg, Virginia, 1947).   Chapel Hill, University of North Carolina Press, 1948; revised version, New York, French, 1975.

Faith of Our Fathers (produced Washington, D.C., 1950).

Peer Gynt, adaptation of the play by Ibsen (produced New York, 1951).   New York, French, 1951.

The Seventeenth Star (produced Columbus, Ohio, 1953).

Serenata, with Josefina Niggli (produced Santa Barbara, California, 1953).

Carmen, adaptation of the libretto by H. Meilhac and L. Halévy, music by Bizet (produced Central City, Colorado, 1954).

Salvation on a String (includes *The Goodbye, Chair Endowed, Supper for the Dead, The No 'Count Boy*) (produced New York, 1954).

Wilderness Road: A Symphonic Outdoor Drama (produced Berea, Kentucky, 1955; revised version, produced 1972).   New York, French, 1956.

The Founders: A Symphonic Outdoor Drama (produced Williamsburg, Virginia, 1957).   New York, French, 1957.

The Confederacy: A Symphonic Outdoor Drama Based on the Life of General Robert E. Lee (produced Virginia Beach, Virginia, 1958).   New York, French, 1959.

The Stephen Foster Story: A Symphonic Drama Based on the Life and Music of the Composer (produced Bardstown, Kentucky, 1959).   New York, French, 1960.

Wings for to Fly: Three Plays of Negro Life, Mostly for the Ear But Also for the Eye (includes *The Thirsting Heart, Lay This Body Down, Fine Wagon*).   New York, French, 1959.

The Thirsting Heart (produced Orangeburg, North Carolina, 1971). Included in
  Wings for to Fly, 1959.
Five Plays of the South (includes *The House of Connelly, In Abraham's Bosom, Johnny
  Johnson, Hymn to the Rising Sun, White Dresses*). New York, Hill and Wang, 1963.
Cross and Sword: A Symphonic Drama of the Spanish Settlement of Florida (produced
  St. Augustine, Florida, 1965). New York, French, 1966.
The Sheltering Plaid. New York, French, 1965.
Texas: A Symphonic Outdoor Drama of American Life (produced Canyon, Texas, 1966).
  New York, French, 1967.
Sing All a Green Willow (produced Chapel Hill, 1969).
Trumpet in the Land (produced New Philadelphia, Ohio, 1970). New York, French,
  1972.
*Drumbeats in Georgia: A Symphonic Drama of the Founding of Georgia by James
  Edward Oglethorpe* (produced Jekyll Island, Georgia, 1973).
*Louisiana Cavalier: A Symphonic Drama of the 18th Century French and Spanish
  Struggle for the Settling of Louisiana* (produced Natchitoches, 1976).
*We the People: A Symphonic Drama of George Washington and the Establishment of the
  United States Government* (produced Columbia, Maryland, 1976).

Screenplays: *Cabin in the Cotton*, 1932; *State Fair*, 1933; *Dr. Bull*, 1933; *Voltaire*,
1933; *The Rosary*, 1933; *Carolina*, 1934; *David Harum*, 1934; *Time Out of Mind*, 1947;
Roseanna McCoy, 1949; *Broken Soil*, 1949; *Red Shoes Run Faster*, 1949; *Black Like
Me*, 1963.

Radio Play: *A Start in Life*, 1941.

Novels

The Laughing Pioneer: A Sketch of Country Life. New York, McBride, and London,
  Gollancz, 1932.
This Body the Earth. New York, Harper, 1935; London, Heinemann, 1936.

Short Stories

Wide Fields. New York, McBride, 1928; London, Gollancz, 1929.
Salvation on a String and Other Tales of the South. New York, Harper, 1946.
Dog on the Sun: A Volume of Stories. Chapel Hill, University of North Carolina Press,
  1949.
Words and Ways: Stories and Incidents from My Cape Fear Valley Folklore Collection.
  Raleigh, North Carolina Folklore Society, 1968.
Home to My Valley. Chapel Hill, University of North Carolina Press, 1970.
Land of Nod and Other Stories: A Volume of Black Stories. Chapel Hill, University of
  North Carolina Press, 1976.

Verse

The Lost Colony Song-Book. New York, Fischer, 1938.
The Highland Call Song-Book. Chapel Hill, University of North Carolina Press, 1941.
Song in the Wilderness. Chapel Hill, University of North Carolina Press, 1947.
The Common Glory Song-Book. New York, Fischer, 1951.
Texas Song-Book. New York, French, 1967.
Texas Forever. New York, French, 1967.

Other

> Contemporary American Literature: A Study of Fourteen Outstanding American Writers, with Elizabeth Lay Green.   Chapel Hill, University of North Carolina Press, 1925; revised edition, 1927.
> The Hawthorn Tree: Some Papers and Letters on Life and the Theatre.   Chapel Hill, University of North Carolina Press, 1943.
> Forever Growing: Some Notes on a Credo for Teachers.   Chapel Hill, University of North Carolina Press, 1945.
> Dramatic Heritage (essays).   New York, French, 1953.
> Drama and the Weather: Some Notes and Papers on Life and the Theatre.   New York and London, French, 1958.
> Plough and Furrow: Some Essays and Papers on Life and the Theatre.   New York and London, French, 1963.

Manuscript Collection: University of North Carolina Library, Chapel Hill.

Critical Studies: *Paul Green* by Barrett H. Clark, New York, French, 1928; *Paul Green of Chapel Hill* by Agatha Boyd Adams, Chapel Hill, University of North Carolina Press, 1951; *Paul Green* by Walter S. Lazenby, Austin, Texas, Steck Vaughn, 1970; *The Dream Still Lives* (television documentary), 1971; *Paul Green* by Vincent S. Kenny, New York, Twayne, 1972.

Paul Green comments:

For several decades now my main efforts have been toward the establishing in the United States of a truly strong and representative people's theatre.

*   *   *

As a dramatist, Paul Green has had three careers. He first emerged in the 1920's as a writer of one-act plays emphasizing the local color and cruelty of his native South. Later in the decade he arrived on Broadway with full-length dramas, still for the most part South-oriented, but occasionally advancing into a more national and even international drama. Finally in the 1930's he began to write historical pageants designed for regional production each summer, largely in the Southern states.

Green's early one-act plays, designed for little theatres rather than Broadway, were published in three volumes – *The Lord's Will and Other Carolina Plays, Lonesome Road: Six Plays for the Negro Theatre*, and *In the Valley*. Notable in these collections were *No 'Count Boy* (a delicate folk drama), *White Dresses* (a play rich in pathos), and *Unto Such Glory* (a farce about religious zealots). Green constructed these works compactly, using essential details of folklore and local color. He also revealed a great compassion for society's underdogs without wearing his social conscience on his sleeve. In these plays, and in his full-length dramas too, he recalled the locale of his childhood which he described as "a place of sandy roads, crude and cruel doctors, maladjusted and lonely children, weary housewives, ignorance, pain, and cheap religion."

Green's best one-act play, *Hymn to the Rising Sun*, was written in the 1930's. It was first presented by the left-wing New Theatre League in 1936, which was also responsible for the premières of the other one-act Depression masterpieces – Clifford Odets' *Waiting for Lefty* and Irwin Shaw's *Bury the Dead*. Set in a Southern prison camp, ironically on the Fourth of July, *Hymn to the Rising Sun* recounted the brutal life of a chain gang tormented by its sadistic guards. The audience witnessed the horror of the Captain whipping a sick young White man and felt the shock of discovering a Black prisoner dead in a "sweat box."

Without explicitly denouncing chain gangs, Green used strong irony, graphic stage images, and sharp characterizations to expose the violence inherent in all prisons. *Hymn to the Rising Sun* transcended its own local color.

Paul Green's first full-length play, *In Abraham's Bosom*, reached New York in 1926. Produced by the Provincetown Players and staged by Jasper Deeter, this "folk tragedy" won the Pulitzer Prize, much to the surprise of the commercial theatre community. Using material from several of his one-act plays, Green told the story of a self-educated Black man who wants to open a school in rural North Carolina. He kills his White half-brother and is lynched by a posse of Whites. Green wrote with both sympathy and despair about the plight of Blacks, but, except for the protagonist, the other characters – Blacks and Whites – were familiar sterotypes. In his next full-length play, *The Field God*, Green wrote about poor Whites down South with the same mixture of sterotypes, sympathy, and despair. This play failed in New York.

In 1931 Green offered more hope – at least for Southern Whites – in *The House of Connelly*, the first play produced independently by the Group Theatre. Originally his script called for a tragic ending, but, while it was being transferred to the stage by Lee Strasberg and Cheryl Crawford, Green added some hope at the end with the marriage of a Southern aristocrat to a poor White woman. As the curtain fell, the couple planned to carry on despite past hostility and adversity. Green wrote poignantly of the dying White aristocracy, but not too far in the background he suggested the horrible violence of Black life and death. The performance made the Group Theatre famous, but the play, too serious and too subtle for Broadway, was not a commercial success.

Nor was *Johnny Johnson*, his next collaboration with the Group. First performed in 1936, this comedy with music by Kurt Weill was Green's most imaginative full-length work and one of the outstanding anti-war plays in the American theatre. Green told the episodic story of a young soldier who tries to stop World War I. Arrested by the military and committed for a time to an insane asylum, he tearfully manages to keep his pacifism and hope intact. Green attacked war directly by satirizing the military establishment and indirectly by his ironic juxtaposition of idealism and violence. Weill's sweetly melodic music underscored the irony. So did Lee Strasberg's staging, which was in the epic theatre style of Bertolt Brecht (whose *Die Mutter* had been seen as *Mother* in New York one year earlier). But the Group, noted for its highly emotional realism, did not take well to the stylized kind of performance that *Johnny Johnson* needed.

Paul Green's full-length works also included two adaptations. The first was *Native Son*, which he and Richard Wright based on Wright's novel. Directed by Orson Welles and produced by the Mercury Theatre in 1941, the play concerned a Black man who murders a White girl in blind revenge for the social, economic, and psychological wrongs done to his race. Green wrote the first drafts of the play, making good use of his long experience as a playwright and his sympathetic attitude toward Blacks. But the essential power of the drama came from Wright's final revision, which reflected his own more revolutionary attitude toward the repression of American Blacks. Green's other adaptation – *Peer Gynt*, produced by ANTA in 1951 – was a shortened and dulled version of Ibsen's poetic fantasy.

In 1937 Paul Green began his third theatrical career by writing *The Lost Colony*, a "symphonic drama" about the first British settlement in America. This pageant was presented in an outdoor theatre at Roanoke Island, North Carolina, the site of the colony, and has been repeated there almost every summer since. For other outdoor regional theatres, Green has written many pageants glorifying the American past. During the summer of 1972, seven of them were revived in various places from Virginia to Texas.

Although Green's "symphonic dramas" are still revived, his real importance in the American theatre has been his treatment of Black themes. While any White writer on the Black experience is suspect in our time, from the 1920's to the 1940's Paul Green came closer to an inside understanding of Black life in America than any other White writer.

—Morgan Y. Himelstein

GREENE, Graham.   British.   Born in Berkhamsted, Hertfordshire, 2 October 1904. Educated at Berkhamsted School; Balliol College, Oxford. Served in the Foreign Office, London, 1941–44. Married Vivien Dayrell-Browning in 1927; has two children. Staff Member, *The Times*, London, 1926–30; Movie Critic, 1937–40, and Literary Editor, 1940–41, *Spectator*, London. Director, Eyre and Spottiswoode, publishers, London, 1944–48, and The Bodley Head, publishers, London, 1958–68. Recipient: Hawthornden Prize, 1941; Black Memorial Prize, 1949; Shakespeare Prize, Hamburg, 1968; Thomas More Medal, for fiction, 1973; Mystery Writers of America award, 1976. Litt.D.: Cambridge University, 1962; D.Litt.: Edinburgh University, 1967. Honorary Fellow, Balliol College, 1963. Companion of Honour, 1966. Chevalier of the Legion of Honour, 1969. Address: c/o The Bodley Head, 9 Bow Street, London WC2E 7AL, England.

PUBLICATIONS

Plays

The Living Room (produced London, 1953, New York, 1954).   London, Heinemann, 1953; New York, Viking Press, 1954.

The Potting Shed (produced New York, 1957; London, 1958).   New York, Viking Press, 1957; London, Heinemann, 1958.

The Complaisant Lover (produced London, 1959; New York, 1961).   London, Heinemann, 1959; New York, Viking Press, 1961.

Carving a Statue (produced London, 1964; New York, 1968).   London, Bodley Head, 1964.

The Third Man: A Film, with Carol Reed.   New York, Simon and Schuster, 1968; London, Lorrimer Films, 1969.

Alas, Poor Maling, adaptation of his own story (broadcast, 1975).   Published in *Shades of Greene*, London, Bodley Head-Heinemann, 1975.

The Return of A.J. Raffles: An Edwardian Comedy Based Somewhat Loosely on E. W. Hornung's Characters in "The Amateur Cracksman" (produced London, 1975). London, Bodley Head, 1975; New York, Simon and Schuster, 1976.

Screenplays: *21 Days*, 1938; *The Green Cockatoo*, 1938; *The New Britain*, 1940; *Went the Day Well?*, 1942; *Brighton Rock*, with Terence Rattigan, 1946; *The Fallen Idol*, 1949; *The Third Man*, 1950; *Saint Joan*, 1957; *Our Man in Havana*, 1960; *The Comedians*, 1967.

Radio Play: *Alas, Poor Maling*, 1975.

Novels

The Man Within.   London, Heinemann, and New York, Doubleday, 1929.

The Name of Action.   London, Heinemann, 1930; New York, Doubleday, 1931.

Rumour at Nightfall.   London, Heinemann, 1931; New York, Doubleday, 1932.

Stamboul Train: An Entertainment.   London, Heinemann, 1932; as *Orient Express: An Entertainment*, New York, Doubleday, 1933.

It's a Battlefield.   London, Heinemann, and New York, Doubleday, 1934.

England Made Me.   London, Heinemann, and New York, Doubleday, 1935.

A Gun for Sale: An Entertainment.   London, Heinemann, 1936; as *This Gun for Hire: An Entertainment*, New York, Doubleday, 1936.

Brighton Rock.   London, Heinemann, 1938; as *Brighton Rock: An Entertainment*, New York, Viking Press, 1938.

The Confidential Agent.   London, Heinemann, and New York, Viking Press, 1939.

The Power and the Glory.   London, Heinemann, 1940; as *The Labyrinthine Ways*, New York, Viking Press, 1940.

The Ministry of Fear: An Entertainment.   London, Heinemann, and New York, Viking Press, 1943.

The Heart of the Matter.   London, Heinemann, and New York, Viking Press, 1948.

The Third Man: An Entertainment.   New York, Viking Press, 1950.

The Third Man and The Fallen Idol.   London, Heinemann, 1950.

The End of the Affair.   London, Heinemann, and New York, Viking Press, 1951.

Loser Takes All: An Entertainment.   London, Heinemann, 1955; New York, Viking Press, 1957.

The Quiet American.   London, Heinemann, 1955; New York, Viking Press, 1956.

Our Man in Havana: An Entertainment.   London, Heinemann, and New York, Viking Press, 1958.

A Burnt-Out Case.   London, Heinemann, and New York, Viking Press, 1961.

The Comedians.   London, Bodley Head, and New York, Viking Press, 1966.

Travels with My Aunt.   London, Bodley Head, 1969; New York, Viking Press, 1970.

The Honorary Consul.   London, Bodley Head, and New York, Simon and Schuster, 1973.

Short Stories

The Basement Room and Other Stories.   London, Cresset Press, 1935.

The Bear Fell Free.   London, Grayson, 1935.

Twenty-four Stories, with James Laver and Sylvia Townsend Warner.   London, Cresset Press, 1939.

Nineteen Stories.   London, Heinemann, 1947; New York, Viking Press, 1949; augmented edition, as *Twenty-one Stories*, London, Heinemann, 1954.

A Visit to Morin.   Privately printed, 1959.

A Sense of Reality.   London, Bodley Head, and New York, Viking Press, 1963.

May We Borrow Your Husband? and Other Comedies of the Sexual Life.   London, Bodley Head, and New York, Viking Press, 1967.

The Collected Stories of Graham Greene.   London, Heinemann-Bodley Head, 1972; New York, Viking Press, 1973.

Verse

Babbling April: Poems.   Oxford, Blackwell, 1925.

Other

Journey Without Maps: A Travel Book.   London, Heinemann, and New York, Doubleday, 1936.

The Lawless Roads: A Mexican Journey.   London, Longman, 1939; as *Another Mexico*, New York, Viking Press, 1939.

British Dramatists.   London, Collins, 1942; included in *The Romance of English Literature*, New York, Hastings House, 1944.

The Little Train (published anonymously; juvenile).   London, Eyre and Spottiswoode, 1946; New York, Lothrop, 1958.

Why Do I Write? An Exchange of Views Between Elizabeth Bowen, Graham Greene and V. S. Pritchett.   London, Marshall, 1948.

After Two Years.   Privately printed, 1949.
For Christmas.   Privately printed, 1950.
The Little Fire Engine (juvenile).   London, Parrish, 1950; as *The Little Red Fire Engine,* New York, Lothrop, 1952.
The Lost Childhood and Other Essays.   London, Eyre and Spottiswoode, 1951; New York, Viking Press, 1952.
The Little Horse Bus (juvenile).   London, Parrish, 1952; New York, Lothrop, 1954.
The Little Steam Roller. A Story of Mystery and Detection (juvenile).   London, Parrish, 1953; New York, Lothrop, 1955.
Essais Catholiques, translated by Marcelle Sibon.   Paris, Editions de Seuil, 1953.
In Search of a Character: Two African Journals.   London, Bodley Head, and New York, Viking Press, 1961.
The Revenge: An Autobiographical Fragment.   Privately printed, 1963.
Victorian Detective Fiction: A Catalogue of the Collection Made by Dorothy Glover and Graham Greene, Introduced by John Carter.   London, Bodley Head, 1966.
Collected Essays.   London, Bodley Head, and New York, Viking Press, 1969.
A Sort of Life (autobiography).   London, Bodley Head, and New York, Simon and Schuster, 1971.
The Pleasure-Dome: The Collected Film Criticism of Graham Greene, 1935–1940, edited by John Russell Taylor.   London, Secker and Warburg, 1972; as *Graham Greene on Film,* New York, Simon and Schuster, 1972.
The Portable Graham Greene, edited by Philip Stratford.   New York, Viking Press, 1973.
Lord Rochester's Monkey: Being the Life of John Wilmot, Second Earl of Rochester.   London, Bodley Head, and New York, Viking Press, 1974.

Editor, *The Old School: Essays by Divers Hands.*   London, Cape, and New York, Peter Smith, 1934.
Editor, *The Best of Saki.*   London, British Publishers Guild, 1950.
Editor, with Hugh Greene, *The Spy's Bedside Book: An Anthology.*   London, Hart Davis, 1957.
Editor, *The Bodley Head Ford Madox Ford.*   London, Bodley Head, 4 vols., 1962, 1963.
Editor, *An Impossible Woman: The Memories of Dottoressa Moor of Capri.*   London, Bodley Head, 1975; New York, Viking Press, 1976.

Bibliography: *Graham Greene* by J.D. Vann, Kent, Ohio, Kent State University Press, 1970.

*   *   *

Graham Greene was approaching his 50th birthday and generally accepted as one of the few outstanding novelists of the age when, in 1953, his first play, *The Living Room,* was produced. Three years later, John Osborne's *Look Back in Anger* inaugurated a revolution in the English theatre, but Greene's later plays, *The Potting Shed, The Complaisant Lover,* and *Carving a Statue,* were obviously uninfluenced by the outburst of new activity and the exploration of new styles and themes.

As a novelist, Greene has developed new and effective narrative techniques, but his almost cinematic cutting and timing of scenes have been fed into the tradition. When he turned to the theatre, fulfilling ambitions which (he explained in the Preface to *Three Plays*) had been with him since his schooldays, he turned to the traditional disciplines of the "well-made play." He found "a fascination in unity" and designed his plays to preserve traditional theatrical virtues. The results are elegantly made for all their harshness, economical and precise; their interest is always in the matter expressed, not in the development of new means of expression.

Greene's range has always been limited; he has a few obsessive themes to which he tends to return always with new and sharper intensities. He is concerned primarily about the relation of man – not generalised, abstract man but whatever individual happens to demand his attention – to God, and secondly about men's relationship to each other. *The Complaisant Lover*, which is a comedy, restricts itself to his secondary theme; its tone is not happy but, at times, distressing; its solution to a difficult moral problem is by no means conventional and its observation of average sensual life is not designed to comfort an audience. For all her clandestine love affair with a possessive bookseller, Mary Rhodes loves her dentist husband (the domestic clown, the practical joker who is most at home in the mental world of his prep-school son) no less than she loves her lover.

The play might easily become a commonplace domestic tragedy; Rhodes might carry out his suicide plan, but it is his wife's needs which persuade him to abandon it: if she wants a husband and a lover, she must have both for the sake of her happiness; it is the adulterer who finds the solution outrageous until Rhodes persuades him that to love is to give the beloved what she needs.

The Complaisant Lover is Greene's *Comédie humaine*; in his first play, *The Living Room*, he returns to the idea of a Catholic suicide without repeating the ideas of his novel *The Heart of the Matter*. Rose Pemberton, who kills herself because her life can bring only unhappiness to the people she loves, is the centre round which others – her old aunts and her crippled uncle who can no longer function as a priest – revolve in a life which rejects the truth and refuses to acknowledge the fact of death. Rose's suicide compels them to do so; in a sense, it offers them salvation. The rules, the crippled priest explains, are man's rules, man's attempt to make God's will into comprehensible law; decisions rest ultimately with God. It is not only *The Heart of the Matter* but *Brighton Roack* and *The Power and the Glory* which are somehow involved in *The Living Room*, but it is a remarkably gentle, emotionally simple work to have come from a writer so wittily harsh as Greene.

The Potting Shed is harsh in Greene's accustomed way, and it seems that it won less respect than it deserves because it is rooted in a supernatural event. Its central character, as a boy, hanged himself but was restored to life because a priest sacrificed his faith to being the boy back. Greene's own unsparing criticism of the play is that the "hollowness" of the man who had been dead is less convincingly treated than the "hollow man" he had explored in the novel *A Burnt-Out Case*, but nothing in the novel compares with the tragedy of the priest who found that God took him quite seriously and destroyed his capacity for faith when the boy was given life again. Greene could have quoted again the line of the old priest at the end of *Brighton Rock*, and offered another reflection on "the appalling strangeness of the mercy of God." Nothing in *A Burnt-Out Case* is so moving as the prospect of warmth returning to the play's spiritually dead central figure.

Carving a Statue, Greene told the world in the Preface to its published version, is neither "symbolic" nor "theological," and he has some caustic fun at the expense of critics who found its symbolism and theology obscure while they should have been regarding it as a play of direct statements which means no more than is seen and heard on the stage. A bad sculptor – the author was thinking, he wrote, of Benjamin Robert Hayden, who killed himself when he awoke from a dream of impossible greatness – has given his life to the making of a statue to God the Father. Everything except his dreams is sacrificed to his task; he knows that his work – though he does not realize its worthlessness – is a refuge from the pressures he would suffer if he abandoned a task he has no notion of how to complete. His friends, his adolescent son's happiness, dumb girl's life, are all destroyed. Greene draws no moral and offers no comment.

The Return of A.J. Raffles came as a disappointment after these plays. Witty and lightly treated, almost a sub-Wildean pastiche, its sets E.W. Hornung's upper-class burglar into more imposing social circumstances than his creator envisaged for him; Raffles is involved in the quarrel of Lord Alfred Douglas with the Marquess of Queensberry; Edward VII appears as an unconscious *deus ex machina*. But there is no sense, in this play, that the Society burglar is blaspheming the standards by which he lives; the late-twentieth century, perhaps, sees nothing outrageous in the idea of a gentleman-thief, and the seamier side of

Edwardian society, thus exposed, turns Raffles from a kind of unaltruistic Robin Hood into one of the corrupt in a corrupt society.

If the plays are not notable for any technical or stylistic experiments but live as their author's expression in traditional dramatic form of the essential preoccupation of all his work, one thing – and again it is traditional – should be said of them. They create personalities – the crippled priest of *The Living Room*, the hollow man who returned from the dead in *The Potting Shed*, and the sculptor of *Carving a Statue* – which demand and reward fine acting, as do the husband and lover of *The Complaisant Lover*. They translate into terms of theatre the strangeness and haunting power which belong to Greene's novels. Inescapably, they are religious plays in which men are able to see that they live inescapably and often terrifyingly in the presence of God.

—Henry Raynor

GRIFFITHS, Trevor. British. Born in Manchester, Lancashire, 4 April 1935. Educated at St. Bede's College, Manchester, 1945–52; Manchester University, 1952–55, B.A. in English language and literature 1955. Served as an Infantryman in the Manchester Regiment, 1955–57. Married in 1960; has three children. Teacher and lecturer for eight years; BBC Education Officer, 1965–72. Agent: Clive Goodwin, 79 Cromwell Road, London S.W.7, England.

PUBLICATIONS

Plays

The Wages of Thin (produced Manchester, 1969; London, 1970).
The Big House (broadcast, 1969). Included in *Occupations and The Big House*, 1972.
Occupations (produced Manchester, 1970; London, 1971). Included in *Occupations and The Big House*, 1972.
Apricots (produced London, 1971).
Thermidor (produced Edinburgh, 1971).
Lay By, with others (produced Edinburgh and London, 1971). London, Calder and Boyars, 1972.
Sam Sam (produced London, 1972). Published in *Plays and Players* (London), April 1972.
Occupations and The Big House. London, Calder and Boyars, 1972.
The Party (produced London, 1973). London, Faber, 1974.
All Good Men (televised, 1974; produced London, 1975).
Comedians (produced Nottingham and London, 1975; New York, 1976). London, Faber, and New York, Grove Press, 1976.

Radio Plays: *The Big House*, 1969; *Jake's Brigade*, 1971.

Television Plays: *Such Impossibilities; All Good Men*, 1974; *Absolute Beginners*, in *Fall of Eagles* series, 1975; *Through the Night*, 1975, *Bill Brand* series, 1976.

Other

Tip's Lot (juvenile).   London, Macmillan, 1972.

*   *   *

Trevor Griffiths is a Marxist writer whose political commitment pours out of his plays, whether they are on demonstrably public themes, as in *Occupations*, or cover more private, personal areas, as in his short play *Apricots*.

The theme of *Occupations* is a perennially relevant one for socialists, whether to be content with reforming the present capitalist system or whether to work for a revolutionary change in the ownership of production, distribution and exchange. The setting is the 1920 Fiat motor strike in Italy. The problem is posed in the conflict between Antonio Gramsci, the brilliant Marxist theoretician, and the Soviet agent Kabak (based on Kabakchiev, a Comintern agent of that period). Gramsci's commitment to revolution is total, as is evidenced by his passionate speeches to the workers warning them of the dangers of compromise; his concept of revolution is based on his love for the workers and his subjective identification with their needs. Kabak's idea of revolution is a more mechanistic one. The motives for his machinations gradually become apparent; he sees each potentially revolutionary situation within the context of Soviet needs and, if it cannot be achieved, will compromise with the existing situation. Though the characters, situations and dialogue seem to be naturalistic (and certainly the London production was played in this way), they are not really. The dialectic between the two protagonists' different concepts of revolution is the play's core; and, interspersed with that, are symbolic figures such as Kabak's mistress, an aristocrat dying of womb cancer, and Valletta, a Fiat chief executive, who represents capitalism's ability to adapt to potentially revolutionary situations. In formal terms, it could be said that an expressionist play is bursting to emerge from a naturalistic framework.

The play graphically shows that the workers' lack of nerve in settling for a compromise hastened the Fascist counter-revolution of a few years later. It has been criticized by certain Marxist critics for its historical incorrectness in its depiction of Gramsci's character and attitudes, and for its pessimistic tone regarding the likely outcome of an attempt at revolution; but, when Tom Nairn made these points in the paper *7 Days*, Griffiths convincingly rebutted them by quoting from Gramsci's writings and impressions of his character by colleagues and friends, and by also quoting his maxim "It is a revolutionary duty to tell the truth." A more valid criticism has been that, by dealing with a 50-year-old situation instead of one that is happening now, Griffiths has placed the whole problem in a false perspective, by romantically distancing it and not relating it strongly enough to present situations. But imperfect though it is, the play is remarkable for discussing revolution from a Marxist standpoint, in healthy contrast to the bourgeois social democracy of writers like Osborne and Wesker.

While *Occupations* is an analytical play, *Sam Sam* is descriptive and, to a large extent, autobiographical. Its theme is how modern industrial capitalism dehumanises people in subtly different ways. The two Sams of the title are working-class brothers; Sam 1 is tied to his upbringing, is of minimal education, unemployed and with a nagging shrew of a wife, whom he treats in an openly sexist way. But though he is at the bottom of the social heap, and in that sense a loser, yet in many ways he is quite happy. He accepts his limitations and at least has the benefit of the warmth and cohesion an old-style working-class family situation can give him. Sam 2 has undergone a process of *embourgeoisment*, through rising up the educational ladder. He is in line for a safe Labour seat, has a middle-class wife, daughter of a bank manager, and is materially well off. But the process of being uprooted from his background has made him lonely and dissatisfied. His marriage is unhappy, having a strong sado-masochistic element, based on class; and he has a running conflict with his wife's snobbish parents. The root problem (as Griffiths makes clear) is that the educational system is geared to capitalist ends. The play, by its nature, is less rich in ideas than *Occupations* but, nevertheless, a valuable piece of dramatic sociology.

The Party, much panned by most of the critics when it first appeared at the National Theatre, is one of the most important plays of the last fifteen to twenty years, being about the impotence of the British revolutionary left and its inability to take advantage of the crisis of modern industrial capitalism. Set at the time of the May 1968 uprising in Paris, it takes place in the Kensington flat of a trendy and successful TV producer, Joe Shawcross, who has been asked by John Tagg, an ageing Glaswegian Trotskyist, to convene a meeting of representatives of the British revolutionary left, to see if any meaningful "dialogue" can be established between them. The producer is of working-class origin but suffers from guilt feelings at enjoying a life-style that betrays his class. The play's main dialectic consists of the political argument between Tagg, leader of the "Revolutionary Socialist Party," and Andrew Ford, a "New Left" professor at the LSE. The intellectual conflict between the two main antagonists is consistently stimulating and interesting. But the real protagonist of the play is Joe Shawcross. His own uncertainty as to what direction Marxism should be going to take advantage of a deep world-wide crisis – an uncertainty reflected at another level in his life-style – mirrors the author's own.

Comedians centres around a class of aspiring comics, taught by Eddie Waters, a disillusioned former stand-up comedian. The class consists of two cross-talking brothers, Phil and Ged Murray; a Jewish club-owner, Sammie Samuels; two Irishmen, George McBrain, who panders in his act to English prejudices about the Irish, and Mick Connor, who by contrast exposes his own insecurity as an expatriate living among not particularly friendly Mancunians; and finally Gethin Price, who lets his imagination run riot around the searing class hatred at the centre of his personality. The play is an analysis of humour and the social forces that give rise to it. It is also political, in the sense that it is about the nature of compromise, capitulation, and standing out for what you believe.

Griffiths, however, regards himself primarily as a TV dramatist because of its more immediate impact on the working-class people he is trying to reach. Among his recent efforts in this direction has been an episode in the series *Fall of Eagles* called *Absolute Beginners*, showing the painful growth of the Russian Bolshevik movement in the early years of the century. Also there has been the quite remarkable and harrowing *Through the Night*, about a woman who goes into hospital for an apparently routine check-up on a lump on her breast, senses that the medical staff are keeping things from her, and wakes up to find that one of her breasts has been removed. The play is a savage indictment of the grotesque lack of communication between medical staffs and patients.

If he can solve the problem that has met other committed socialist dramatists – that his very success could cut him off from the roots of the society he is examining – Griffiths' future as a writer who, as he says, "shows the way society is moving" could be a great one.

—Jonathan Hammond

GRILLO, John. British. Born in Watford, Hertfordshire, 29 November 1942. Educated at Watford Boys Grammar School, 1954–61; Trinity Hall, Cambridge, 1962–65, B.A. in history 1965. Professional Actor: in Lincoln, Glasgow, Farnham, Brighton, London. Resident Dramatist, Castle Theatre, Farnham, Surrey, 1969–70. Since 1971, Literary Associate, Soho Theatre Club, London. Recipient: Arts Council bursary, 1965. Agent: Marjorie Clayton, International Copyright Bureau Ltd., 53a Shaftesbury Avenue, London W.1, England.

PUBLICATIONS

Plays

> *Gentlemen I...* (produced Cambridge, 1963; London, 1968).
> *It Will Come or It Won't* (produced Dublin, 1965).
> *Hello Goodbye Sebastian* (produced Cambridge, 1965; London, 1968). Published in *Gambit 16* (London), 1970.
> *The Downfall of Jack Throb* (produced London, 1967).
> *The Fall of Samson Morocco* (produced London, 1969).
> *Oh Everyman Oh Colonel Fawcett* (produced Farnham, Surrey, 1969).
> *Mr. Bickerstaff's Establishment* (produced Glasgow, 1969; expanded version, produced London, 1972).
> *History of a Poor Old Man* (produced London, 1970).
> *Number Three* (produced Bradford and London, 1970). Included in *New Short Plays*, London, Methuen, 1972.
> *Blubber* (produced London, 1971).
> *Zonk* (produced London, 1971).
> *Food* (produced London, 1971).
> *Will the King Leave His Tea Pot* (produced Edinburgh and London, 1971).
> *George and Moira Entertain a Member of the Opposite Sex to Dinner* (produced Edinburgh and London, 1971).
> *The Hammer and the Hacksaw*, in *Christmas Present* (produced Edinburgh, 1971).
> *Christmas Box, and Civitas Dei* (produced London, 1972).
> *Snaps* (*Civitas Dei, Days by the River, MacEnery's Vision of Pipkin*) (produced London, 1973).
> *Crackers* (produced London, 1973).
> *Mr. Ives' Magic Punch and Judy Show* (produced London, 1973).

Television Play: *Nineteen Thirty Nine*, 1973.

Critical Study: by Germaine Greer, in *Cambridge Review*, 29 May 1965.

Theatrical Activities:

Actor: **Plays** – Theatre Royal, Lincoln: Dabble in *Lock Up Your Daughters* by Bernard Miles, Billy Bones in *Treasure Island* by Jules Eckert Goodman, Poet in *Five to a Flat* by Valentine Kataev, Ingham in *Little Malcolm and His Struggle Against the Eunuchs* by David Halliwell, roles in *Beyond the Fringe*, Andrei in *The Three Sisters* by Chekhov, Clarence in *Henry IV, Part II*, Max in *The Homecoming* by Harold Pinter, Jopplin in *A Shouting in the Streets* by Elizabeth Dawson, and Rusty Charley in *Guys and Dolls* by Abe Burrows and Jo Swerling, 1966–67; Brighton Combination: Old Man in *Hello Goodbye Sebastian* and Rasputin in *The Rasputin Show* by Michael Almaz, 1968; Royal Court Theatre, London: Verlaine in *Total Eclipse* by Christopher Hampton, 1968, roles in *Erogenous Zones* by Mike Stott, 1969, Perowne in *AC/DC* by Heathcote Williams, 1970, Reporter and Deaf and Dumb Man in *Lulu* by Peter Barnes, 1971, and Marx in *Anarchist* by Michael Almaz, 1971; Glendower in *Henry IV, Part I*, Glasgow, 1969; Castle Theatre, Farnham: Eddy in *Tango* by Mrozek, Millionaire in *Cliffwalk* by Sebastian Shaw, Fawcett in *Oh Everyman Oh Colonel Fawcett*, and Don Pedro in *Much Ado About Nothing*, 1969–70; Soho Theatre Club, London: Nurse in *Number Three*, 1970, Thug in *Dynamo* by Christopher Wilkinson, 1971, and Recorder in *Inquistion* by Michael Almaz, 1971; Mr. Bickerstaff in *Mr. Bickerstaff's Establishment*, London, 1972; in *The Tooth of Crime* by

Sam Shepard, London, 1972; Sergeant Kite in *The Recruiting Officer* by Farquhar, Hornchurch, Essex, 1972; Dr. Rank in *A Doll's House* by Ibsen, Greenwich, 1972. **Films** – *The F and H Film; Dynamo.*

John Grillo comments:

Aspects of my work include (1) A writing out of private obsessive fantasies and an attempt to excite the audience by parading on the stage that which is forbidden. (2) The plays are firmly based in the lower middle class morality and culture of my childhood. (3) Influence of theatrical innovators and fantasists such as Ionesco and Jarry. (4) Influence of television and film. Before the age of twenty I had visited the theatre perhaps half a dozen times. (5) I do not know how my work will develop but I hope it will become more public, less private, more realistic, less fantastic.

*   *   *

John Grillo is the Alfred Jarry of modern British theatre: a clown dramatist whose plays mingle outrageous solemnity with knockabout comedy and a Rabelaisian relish for dirty jokes. His stories have the simplicity of Punch and Judy shows. Bickerstaff (in *Mr. Bickerstaff's Establishment*) murders his sleep-walking wife as an alternative to committing suicide. Emboldened by this desparate deed, he tries to take over the underworld of pimps, thugs and prostitutes: but finally the Forces of the Law – and his wife's ghost – catch up with him and condemn him to death. Bickerstaff (like Punch) escapes and decides to "emigrate – to Beirut ": where his yearning for the fleshpots of the East can be satisfied. The Nurse (in *Number Three*) is a male fascist orderly in a mental hospital, preserving a solemn repressive dignity before a torrent of sexual insults from his worst patient, Three. The King (in *Will the King Leave His Tea Pot*) retires from the Affairs of State – and his frustrated thinning wife – into a huge womb-like tea-pot: thus causing the utmost outrageous consternation among his subjects, who lose all sense of protocol. These outrageous anecdotes are also told in the style of children's stories. The characters are dressed like cartoons: Bickerstaff is a "fat man with a drooping bedraggled moustache " – like Crippen. The Queen (in *Will the King Leave His Tea Pot*) "wears a long silver dress, which is frayed at the edges, a necklace of pearls, several of which are missing and two or three of which are molars. " The dialogue mainly consists of torrential speeches, where wild puns, extreme thought-associations and an almost innocent scatology provide a buoyant, idiosyncratic fun. The characters talk at each other – rather than to or with – and any change in mood is underlined by asides to the audience. When the Nurse, who is trying to persuade Three to go to bed, changes his tactics, he tells the audience that he is doing so. "Poor Nurse is worried because Number Three is such a bad boy. Nurse is a very sensitive man and he cries when Number Three plays him up.... (aside) This is called 'Making the patient feel guilty.'"

This overtness in handling the story, the dialogue, the bawdiness and the characters gives Grillo's plays an ingenuous charm. Grillo is an actor – as well as a dramatist – and he has a performer's instinct for bizarre, shock tactics. As an actor, he has worked extensively with fringe theatre in Britian: in the rudimentary pub theatres of London and the student theatre clubs. His plays are designed to require little in the way of staging, but to rely on actor-audience contact, in the style of music hall. He is one of the rare dramatists to exploit the essential roughness, the slapdash circumstances of fringe theatre: and therefore his plays work particularly well in pubs. Nor is the humour as unsophisticated as may appear. Grillo delights in choosing apparently "serious" themes and placing them in comic-strip settings. In his longest, and perhaps most ambitious play, *Hello Goodbye Sebastian*, Grillo tells the story of an apprentice gravedigger, Sebastian, who longs for a better life and refuses to fill in a grave, because the old man whose wife occupies it believes in the resurrection of the dead. Sebastian's home life however is an unhappy one. His mother, Mary, and the lodger,

Charlie, are living off his earnings: and their sex life dominates the household arrangements. Sebastian can't leave his job – to become a barber – because his mother doesn't want him to: it would destroy the precarious balance of her affair. And so Sebastian finally resigns himself to being a gravedigger: and in the final scene, he fills in the grave of the old man's wife. Grillo has therefore selected a story which has allegorical overtones – similar to the Theatre of the Absurd and to Ionesco's plays in particular. The suppression of innocence and adolescent hope leads to a death-centredness. Sebastian at the end of the play fills up the grave with unnecessary relish: "Half a pound of worms, landlord, down the hatch. Pound of filth, landlord. Coming, sir, down the hatch!" But this "serious" theme is handled with a flippant lightness, which does not however prevent the allegory from being both noticeable and important to the success of the play.

Grillo's cheerful irreverence has a habit of misfiring in the wrong surroundings. Grillo was once the resident dramatist/actor with the Farnham Repertory Theatre, in a quiet country town in the South of England. His comic-strip version of the Everyman story caused the greatest possible local consternation. "They called the play," remembers Grillo, "lavatorial, smutty, schoolboyish, nihilistic, unnecessarily cruel and what's more my acting stank." Nor was he at ease in the portentous atmosphere of avant-garde theatre clubs, which may be one reason why his plays have been under-rated by British critics. His best productions have perhaps come with the talented fringe group, Portable Theatre, who included *Zonk* and *Food* in their 1971 repertoire. *Zonk* is an extraordinary family comedy, involving a mother, Dora (a man in drag), a domineering father, Bone, a son, and a substitute Dora (an attractive woman in her early forties). The son's antagonism towards his father and his yearnings for sex with his mother provide a comic interpretation of Oedipalism. The son eventually disgusts the father by sucking milk from his mother's artificial penis. Not all of Grillo's plays are however equally extreme. His *History of a Poor Old Man* is a mock-melancholic monologue of an old man arrested for soliciting in a lavatory.

Grillo's great quality as a dramatist is that his sense of fun is infectious. The jokes tumble over each other to be said: and the uninhibitedness of the bawdry creates an easy relaxation in the theatre. He breaks down the over-solemn atmosphere of playgoing and brings back a childlike delight in trying anything once. His plays are unlike any others being written by dramatists in Britain today: and seem fresh and exuberant. His technical range is severely limited, but within these limits his imagination is exhilarating.

—John Elsom

GUARE, John.   American.   Born in New York City, 5 February 1938. Educated at Georgetown University, Washington, D.C., A.B. 1960; Yale University Drama School, New Haven, Connecticut, M.F.A. 1963. Member, Dramatists Guild Council. Recipient: Obie Award, 1968, 1971; *Variety* award, 1969; New York Drama Critics Circle Award, 1971, 1972; Tony Award, 1972. Agent: R. Andrew Boose, Greenbaum Wolf and Ernst, 437 Madison Avenue, New York, New York, U.S.A.

PUBLICATIONS

Plays

Did You Write My Name in the Snow? (produced New Haven, Connecticut, 1962).

To Wally Pantoni, We Leave a Credenza (produced New York, 1964).

The Loveliest Afternoon of the Year, and Something I'll Tell You Tuesday (produced New York, 1966; *The Loveliest Afternoon of the Year* produced London, 1972).   New York, Dramatists Play Service, 1968.

Muzeeka (produced Waterford, Connecticut, 1967; New York and Edinburgh, 1968; London, 1969).   Included in *Muzeeka and Other Plays*, 1969; in *Off-Broadway Plays*, London, Penguin, 1970.

Cop-Out (includes *Home Fires*) (produced Waterford, Connecticut, 1968; New York, 1969).   Included in *Muzeeka and Other Plays*, 1969; *Cop-Out* published in *Off-Broadway Plays*, London, Penguin, 1970.

Kissing Sweet (televised, 1969).   With *A Day for Surprises*, New York, Dramatists Play Service, 1970.

A Day for Surprises (produced London, 1971; New York, 1975).   With *Kissing Sweet*, New York, Dramatists Play Service, 1970.

Muzeeka and Other Plays (includes *Cop-Out* and *Home Fires*).   New York, Grove Press, 1969.

The House of Blue Leaves (produced New York, 1971).   New York, Viking Press, 1972.

Two Gentlemen of Verona, with Mel Shapiro, music by Galt MacDermot, lyrics by John Guare, adaptation of the play by Shakespeare (produced New York, 1971; London, 1973).   New York, Holt Rinehart, 1973.

Taking Off (screenplay), with Milos Forman.   New York, New American Library, 1971.

Optimism; or, The Misadventures of Candide, with Harold Stone, based on the novel by Voltaire (produced Waterford, Connecticut, 1973).

Marco Polo Sings a Solo (produced 1973).

Rich and Famous (produced Academy Theatre, Illinois, 1974; New York, 1976).

Screenplay: *Taking Off*, with Milos Forman, 1971.

Television Play: *Kissing Sweet*, 1969.

*   *   *

John Guare is the most successful and promising American playwright to forge to the front of the public's attention since Edward Albee. Guare's early plays, brief sketches done at the Caffe Cino in 1966 (*Something I'll Tell You Tuesday* and *The Loveliest Afternoon of the Year*) and the Obie-winning *Muzeeka*, introduced a witty, exuberant, and perceptive playwright to an ever-growing audience. With *The House of Blue Leaves* and *Two Gentlemen of Verona* Guare achieved national prestige – the cover story for *Saturday Review* – and critical acclaim – *Blue Leaves* won both an Obie and the New York Drama Critics Circle Award for the Best New Play of the Year; *Two Gentlemen* was named the Best Musical of 1971–72 by the same Circle.

From its beginnings, Guare's writing has reflected that same intense brand of urban paranoia which is identified with the humor of Philip Roth, Jules Feiffer, Joe Orton and Edward Albee. "The impossible is made casual," one critic observed of Guare's world, in which a 28,000 pound stone lion walks through the Public Library without attracting attention (*A Day for Surprises*), in which murder silently disrupts an idyllic afternoon stroll in the park (*The Loveliest Afternoon of the Year*), and in which a zany, frightened New Yorker says earnestly to his beloved, "you're from Ohio...you don't understand the weirdness, the grief that people can spring from." Guare finds the extremity of pain to be the source of laughter and so he writes a form of savage farce, he tells us,

> because it's the most abrasive, anxious form and I'm trying to extend its boundaries because I think the chaotic state of the world demands it. Who says I have to be confined and show a guy slipping on a banana peel? Why can't I take him to the next level and show him howling with pain because he's broken his ass?

Guare's plays are vitally theatrical. They erupt through the conventions of realistic theatre with asides, monologues, songs and mimes. And underneath the craft, which sometimes appears as self-consciously cute, there is a unique vision – the clearest indication of a writer's talent. "Why shouldn't Strindberg and Feydeau get married, at least live together?" Guare has queried. In the savage and domestic conflicts which fascinate both Strindberg and Guare, this playwright has found the oblique and foolish human activities which entertain both Feydeau and himself. Guare's mature, full-length play, *The House of Blue Leaves*, is filled with aberrant comic characters, bustling entrances through a myriad of doors, and is best described by *New York Post* critic Jerry Tallmer who called it as "wildly implausible and slam-bang hilarious as anything in the George Abbott days of the 1930's. But more serious."

The situations in Guare's plays are frequently domestic, and it is not surprising to find that he draws his subject matter directly from his own experience. The plays are frankly autobiographical. But what an autobiography! Such wildly comic passages as young Ronnie Shaughnessy's audition for the film role of Huck Finn (*Blue Leaves*), Guare tells us, is almost a literal recording of his own eight-year-old encounter with his talent-scout uncle, Billy Grady. The circumstance of *Cop-Out* was suggested by the expression on the face of a New York cop at the moment his horse kicked Guare in the head during a Times Square peace demonstration. The policeman-ancester who raided a "cat-house" and discovered and adopted a midget named Billy Rhodes, who later went into the circus, suggests that Guare has much to draw from in his quest for circumstances and characters for his plays. Unlike many autobiographical writers who indulge themselves in nostalgia, Guare finds the bizarre and comic in his experience and extracts from it the germ for his writing. Of *Blue Leaves* he has written, "The play is autobiographical in the sense that everything in the play happened in one way or another over a period of years, and some of it happened in dreams and some of it could have happened and some of it, luckily, never happened. But it's autobiographical all the same."

Guare has been able to turn his fantasies of autobiography into material of general and sometimes social and political interest. "I think most concerned writers are political in one way or another," Guare has stated. His satiric statements are found in such works as *Kissing Sweet*, his contribution to *Foul!* – a TV anthology of short plays protesting the world's pollution – in *Muzeeka*, and even in the lyrics he has written for the delightful musical adaptation of *Two Gentlemen* in which a black Duke of Milan, seeking re-election, sings his promise to "Bring all the boys back home." It is this socially conscious side of Guare's thinking that has led him to contribute to Milos Forman's satiric film on American life, *Taking Off*, and to the aborted musical adaptation of Brecht's *The Exception and the Rule* which was planned by Leonard Bernstein and Jerome Robbins as a vehicle for Zero Mostel.

Guare continues to write energetically. His two most recent plays are still "in-progress." They have had production outside New York, but Guare is still re-working them. *Marco Polo Sings a Solo* is an eight character morality play set in 1999. Each character represents one of the major foibles of the 20th century. Critic Henry Hewes called it an "extremely ambitious but quite disorderly masterwork." *Rich and Famous* is an autobiographical play about a young playwright, Bing Ringling, who seeks success through writing an autobiographical play. Two additional actors present a matrix of characters who assist and hinder the protagonist. Both of these works retain Guare's sharp wit and explosive sense of theatrical form, the attributes which will certainly see him contribute major works to the American theatre during the next decade. His diversity is perhaps his strength, and his attitude towards writing is found in his preface to the published version of *Blue Leaves:* "I think the only playwrighting rule is that you have to learn your craft so that you can put on the stage plays you would like to see." Happily, what John Guare likes to see and what his audiences like to see appear to be the same.

—Thomas B. Markus

GURNEY, A. R., Jr.   American.   Born 1 November 1930. Educated at St. Paul's School, Concord, New Hampshire, 1944–48; Williams College, Williamstown, Massachusetts, 1948–52; Yale University Drama School, New Haven, Connecticut, 1955–58. Served in the United States Navy, 1952–55: Korean Service Medal. Married Mary Goodyear in 1957; has four children. Since 1960, Professor of Literature, Massachusetts Institute of Technology, Cambridge. Recipient: Drama Desk Award, 1971. Agent: Gilbert Parker, Curtis Brown Ltd., 60 East 56th Street, New York, New York 10022. Address: 20 Sylvan Avenue, West Newton, Massachusetts 02165, U.S.A.

PUBLICATIONS

Plays

> *Three People*, in *The Best Short Plays 1955–56*, edited by Margaret Mayorga.   Boston, Beacon Press, 1956.
> *Turn of the Century*, in *The Best Short Plays 1957–58*, edited by Margaret Mayorga. Boston, Beacon Press, 1958.
> *Love in Buffalo* (produced New Haven, Connecticut, 1958).
> *The Bridal Dinner* (produced Cambridge, Massachusetts, 1962).
> *The Comeback* (produced Cambridge, Massachusetts, 1965).   New York, Dramatists Play Service, 1967.
> *The Rape of Bunny Stuntz* (produced Cambridge, Massachusetts, 1966; New York, 1967; Richmond, Surrey, 1976).   London, French, 1976.
> *The David Show* (produced Tanglewood, Massachusetts, 1966; New York, 1968). New York, French, 1968.
> *The Golden Fleece* (produced New York, 1968).   Published in *The Best Short Plays 1969*, edited by Stanley Richards, Philadelphia, Chilton, 1970.
> *The Problem* (produced Boston, 1969; London, 1973).   New York, French, 1968; London, French, 1972.
> *The Open Meeting* (produced Boston, 1969).   New York, French, 1969.
> *The Love Course* (produced Boston, 1970; London, 1974; New York, 1976). Published in *The Best Short Plays 1970*, edited by Stanley Richards, Philadelphia, Chilton, 1971; published separately, London, French, 1976.
> *Scenes from American Life* (produced Tanglewood, Massachusetts, 1970; New York, 1971).   New York, French, 1976.

The Old One-Two (produced Waltham, Massachusetts, 1973; London, 1974).   New
    York, French, 1971; London, French, 1976.
Children, suggested by the story "Goodbye, My Brother" by John Cheever (produced
    London, 1974; Richmond, Virginia, 1976).   London, French, 1975.
Who Killed Richard Cory? (produced New York, 1976).   New York, Dramatists Play
    Service, 1976.

Screenplay: *The House of Mirth*, 1972.

Novel

The Gospel According to Joe.   New York, Harper, 1974.

*   *   *

A.R. Gurney, Jr., is in the curious position for an American dramatist of being relatively
well-established in both the U.S. and the U.K. without as yet achieving a major
breakthrough in either country. To some extent this is a reflection on the lack of continuum
in the U.S. between theatres and playwrights not writing exclusively for Broadway. Gurney
had two early pieces tried out by Edward Albee's playwrights' workshop in New York and
his first full-length play, *Scenes from American Life*, was produced at the Forum Theatre at
Lincoln Center in 1971. But when the new regime at the Center seemed less interested in his
work, Gurney had really nowhere to go with future work, while in England he remains best
known for his short plays, whose small casts and simple sets have made them ideal fare for
lunchtime theatres in London and provincial studio theatres. To a perhaps greater extent,
his ambivalent standing may also be due to his main concern – analysis of WASP attitudes –
which at first sight may seem somewhat conventional. But this would be to overlook not
only his irony but also the oblique and often fascinating viewpoint of his work, not to
mention his technical skill which enables song, music, and offstage characters to give a
resonance and flexibility to his work.

Scenes from American Life is, as the title implies, a kind of montage of Americana. With a
small cast including an on-stage pianist linking scenes, it uses an almost cinematic technique
of dissolving and overlapping scenes to build up a series of vignettes of WASP life from the
1930's to the immediate future – a 1930's aristocratic christening, a 1940's debutante dance,
a bitingly funny meeting between a Society mother and her daughter in the Plaza Hotel tea-
room in 1948, a modern Encounter Therapy session and so on. There is no linear plot-
progression as the play swings to and fro through time, and the result, although ingenious
and extremely assured, remains somewhat slight and occasionally self-consciously clever. In
its use of basic essentials to create a sense of scene and period, it recalls Thornton Wilder,
but in its concern with archetypal American attitudes towards the family-unit and children,
not to mention the device of an offstage character (the omnipresent Snoozer), the play
indicates that Gurney has his own characteristic tone.

Offstage characters dominate his one-act plays to a great extent; *The Golden Fleece* is
about a suburban couple, friends of Jason and Medea whom the audience never in fact see,
and, in the very funny *The Open Meeting*, a discussion-group discover startling new
relationships while awaiting the arrival of a mysteriously-vanished fourth member. Both the
latter play and *The Rape of Bunny Stuntz* (again using the situation of a discussion-meeting,
in which a new chairwoman is reduced to crack-up under the influence of a looming
offstage presence) play interesting variations on the audience-cast relationship – as the
theatre audience is presumed to be the audience attending the meetings – with richly comic
rewards. The shorter plays derive much of their edge and power from characters who never
appear; as in Greek plays, the Gods often remain offstage but people are influenced by them
(or, as Gurney has said "One way of looking at it might be to say that people find their Gods
in other people") and Gurney often uses and adapts classical motifs. *The Love Course* and

The Old One-Two are both sharp satires on academic-liberal attitudes, but *The Old One-Two* develops a deeper strain of almost Plautine farce as a hip young college Dean discovers that he is the son of his adversary, an old-fashioned Professor, and that his adultery with the Professor's wife has been an incestuous affair.

Gurney's most satisfying play to date remains *Children*, which was premiered in London to widely-opposed critical reactions, ranging from acclaim as the best mainstream American play to arrive in London since Arthur Miller to dismissals with faint praise as mildly old-fashioned, a view perhaps influenced by the fact that *Children* was "suggested by" a 1940's short story by John Cheever. In fact Gurney's play is only very loosely derived from the original story, "Goodbye, My Brother," which likewise takes place in a New England summer home and has a violent confrontation between two brothers, an offstage event in the play. In structure, *Children* is much tighter than *Scenes from American Life*, covering one Saturday of a July 4th weekend in the lives of a well-to-do WASP family vacationing at their Massachusetts summer home. Since the play concerns people who shape and contain themselves, the spare and unrestrained structure is highly appropriate, although Gurney gives it a further atmosphere of suggestion through the offstage close-harmony campfire songs linking the scenes and the dance-music in a beautifully-balanced scene in which the younger son and his wife re-create their first meeting. The play is a deceptively simple study of the tensions in the family caused by the presence of the eldest son, Pokey, who contrives to rule his family as an offstage presence, a kind of avenging fury stirring old resentments and rivalries, only one of the offstage "Gods" in the piece; the widowed Mother has her old admirer (her great "Gatsby") who could take her away, the daughter has her truck-driver lover, while the dead father is also a kind of god to them all. In a long and moving final speech, Mother reverses her decision to re-marry and escape and talks to Pokey (finally visible through the screen-door of the house shadowing the terrace on which the whole play passes), rejecting him and casting him out to preserve the family. The scene is a fitting summation to the play which subtly exposes (not least in its sparse, dry dialogue, devoid of metaphor) a culture in erosion as his people begin to realise their limitations.

Gurney's latest full-length play, *Who Killed Richard Cory?*, is an exploration around a central middle-class lawyer-hero, who in middle age begins to explore the idea of freedom and "Liberation." Its world and themes recall *Children* while in structure it is much more open-ended, a more confident and deeper handling of the techniques of *Scenes from American Life*. It confirms Gurney's special ability to suggest a world of distress and unease under the surface of average American life and an even surer sense of the interest of cultural crisis on the stage.

—Alan Strachan

HAILEY, Oliver.   American.   Born in Pampa, Texas, 7 July 1932. Educated at the University of Texas, Austin, B.F.A. 1954; Yale University Drama School, New Haven, Connecticut (Phyllis S. Anderson Fellowship, 1960, 1961), M.F.A. 1962. Served in the United States Air Force; Captain in the Reserve. Married Elizabeth Ann Forsythe in 1960; has two daughters. Story Editor for *Macmillan and wife* television series, 1972–74. Recipient: Vernon Rice Award, 1963. Agent: Robert Lantz, 114 East 55th Street, New York, New York 10022. Address: 11747 Canton Place, Studio City, California 91604, U.S.A.

PUBLICATIONS

Plays

Hey You, Light Man! (produced New Haven, Connecticut, 1962; New York, 1963;
     Bromley, Kent, 1971).   Published in *The Yale School of Drama Presents*, edited by
     John Gassner, New York, Dutton, 1964.
Child's Play: A Comedy for Orphans (produced New Haven, Connecticut, 1962).
Animal (produced New York, 1965). Included in *Picture, Animal, Crisscross,* 1970.
Picture (produced New York, 1965).   Included in *Picture, Animal, Crisscross,* 1970.
First One Asleep, Whistle (produced New York, 1966).   Frankfurt, S. Fischer Verlag,
     1967.
Who's Happy Now? (produced Los Angeles, 1969; New York, 1969).   New York,
     Random House, 1969.
Crisscross (produced Los Angeles, 1969).   Included in *Picture, Animal, Crisscross,*
     1970.
Picture, Animal, Crisscross: Three Short Plays.   New York, Dramatists Play Service,
     1970.
Continental Divide (produced Washington, D.C., 1970).   New York, Dramatists Play
     Service 1973.
Father's Day (produced Los Angeles, 1970; New York, 1971).   New York, Dramatists
     Play Service, 1971.
For The Use of the Hall (produced Providence, Rhode Island, 1974).   New York,
     Dramatists Play Service, 1975.
And Where She Stops Nobody Knows (produced Los Angeles, 1976).

Television Plays: 9 episodes for *Macmillan and Wife* series, 1971–74.

Critical Study: *Showcase One* by John Lahr, New York, Grove Press, 1969

Oliver Hailey comments:

My plays are primarily the attempt to take a serious theme and deal with it comedically.
Though the idea for a particular play often begins as something quite serious, I try not to
start writing until I have found a comic point of view for the material.
    In the case of my play that is most autobiographical, *Who's Happy Now?*, it took ten years
to find that comic attitude. There had been nothing particularly funny about my childhood –
and yet I felt that to tell the story without a comic perspective was to put upon the stage a
story too similar to many that had been seen before. With the comic perspective came the
opportunity for a much fresher approach to the material – and also, strangely, it allowed me
to deal with the subject on a much more serious level than I would have risked otherwise.
    Because, finally, my plays are an attempt to entertain – and when they cease to entertain
– no matter how "important" what I am trying to say – they fail as plays.

*   *   *

Despite considerable early promise Oliver Hailey has yet to achieve either critical or
commercial success in the theatre. While some of his plays have been well received in
university and regional playhouses, the four full-length works presented in New York City
all had brief runs.
    Hey You, Light Man!, written and first produced at Yale Yniversity, contrasts the reality-

stained world of banal domesticity with the more glamourous role-playing offered by the stage. Hailey's hero, an unhappily-married actor named Ashley Knight, flees from his dreadful family to live on a stage set. There meets a lonely young widow who has fallen asleep during a performance and is locked in the theatre. Lula Roca's husband, a stage hand, was accidentally killed by some falling equipment and her three children were all lost at a national park. One fell into a waterfall at the same time that another fell off a mountain. A third was taken by a bear. Ashley and Lula, an unlikely pair, change the direction of each other's life. Lula's experience with the illusory world of the stage permits her to develop her imaginative powers so as to face the future with new hope. Ashley, on the other hand, for whom reality could only be dreary, sees in Lula new possibilities in life off the stage and is able to make a final excape from his domestic prison. Much of the play's humor and charm stems from Lula's endearing innocence, but Hailey's somewhat redundant elaboration of his illusion vs. reality theme weakens the play. A number of oddball characters appear, but the playwright's straining for an eccentric originality is apparent. At times, however, his dialogue achieves the intended poetic effect, and his tender concern for his odd couple results in some touching moments.

   First One Asleep, Whistle, which had only one performance on Broadway, reflects some of the same concerns as *Hey You, Light Man!* but lacks its offbeat charm. The milieu is again theatrical, the heroine an actress in television commercials. She has a daughter by a man not her husband and during the course of the play has an affair with a married man. This time her lover is an emotionally immature actor who is separated from his wife. As in *Light Man* the lovers eventually part, the actor returning to his wife, unaware that his mistress is pregnant. Elaine, the actress, has somehow been strengthened by this latest affair and remains confident that she will survive without a man. The ill-fated romance is complicated by the presence of Elaine's seven-year-old daughter whose innocent responses to her mother's unconventional life is the principal source of the play's occasional humor. While Hailey avoids a sentimental "happy" ending, his characters are never very interesting and the play remains at the level of semi-sophisticated soap opera.

   Who's Happy Now? also deals with domestic difficulties, but the setting is far removed from the urbane New York scene. The play takes place in Texas during the years 1941–1955 and focuses on the confused reactions of a young man to the bizzare relationship between his parents. His father, a strong-willed and crude butcher, has managed to keep both his wife and mistress happy, despite the efforts of his son to alter the situation. The mistress, a waitress named Faye Precious, has lost her husband as a result of a freak accident and respects her butcher/lover (aptly names Horse) despite his continuing affection for his wife. The hero is an aspiring songwriter, his ambition inspiring disgust in Horse, and the play is a kind of comic variation of the Oedipal struggle. *Who's Happy Now?* contains some diverting musical numbers, but the mixture of irony and sentiment results in a confused tone. The frame of the play involves the hero attempting to explain to his mother, through the medium of drama, what he really felt about his parents. Such a device seems intended to point out the disparity between actual experience and its painful, often inaccurate, re-creation on stage, a theme Hailey deals with elsewhere. There are other theatrical techniques that serve to distance the audience from potentially mawkish material, but the effects, while at times inventive, ultimately manage to make the play too diffuse in impact. Despite Hailey's genuine ironic gifts, his play suffers from the lack of a firm larger design.

   Continental Divide, which has not appeared in New York, is closer to pure farce as it broadly contrasts a wealthy couple from Long Island with the down-at-heel parents of their future son-in-law. The latter couple are visitors from their native Arkansas and the juxtaposition of rich and poor in mined of its limited potential for original insight and humor. Mr. John, the father of the groom, had killed his first wife and during the course of the play manages to wound his host twice. There are other farcical events, and whatever satiric thrusts intended by the playwright are subordinated to the broad comic effects.

   Hailey's best play, *Father's Day,* despite some highly favorable reviews, ran for only one performance on Broadway. It marks a return to the urbane New York scene, and the dialogue has a pungency and bite. The characters are three divorced couples briefly reunited on Father's Day. The play focuses primarily on the complex feelings of the women, as it uncovers their ambivalent desires for both independence and security. The comic tone on the surface barely conceals the pathos of their situation, and the play has a toughminded quality normally absent in a conventional sex comedy. The characters, especially the women, are sharply drawn and while *Father's Day* at times suffers from an overly eager attempt to be topical, the playwright's verbal energy is sufficient to sustain the work. Hailey demonstrates his usual compassion and refusal to impose standard moral judgments. Here he has avoided his tendency to employ striking, if redundant or irrelevant, theatrical effects. At the close of the play, there is a reference to Chekhov's *The Three Sisters* suggesting that Hailey saw a parallel to his unhappy trio in the Russian classic. While *Father's Day* lacks the depth and resonance of Chekhov's work its tenderness and its willingness to understand the bitterness and frustration of unfulfilled lives make the parallel not altogether inapt.

In addition to the above full-length plays, Hailey has written several shorter works. *Picture,* a laboured one-act play or "demonstration" is similar to *Who's Happy Now?* in its concern with the problems in recreating the past through the medium of drama. *Crisscross* is a strained sketch in which Santa Claus is crucified by his father, a carpenter resentful of his son's desire for independence. *Animal* is a brief, but effective, monologue by a mother desparately struggling to impose her will on her rebellious daughter.

It is perhaps too early to make any definitive judgment on Hailey's playwriting career. What does seem evident at this point is that he has failed in his efforts at employing conventional commercial formulas to sustain an often original point of view. Despite his refusal to provide emotionally satisfying conclusions to his plays, his dramas seem too designed to please, too eager to be charming and clever. His major themes appear rooted in the dislocations of family life and while he is often adept in revealing the sadness beneath the laugh, the shifting tone of his plays results in uncertain dramatic effects. In his four major plays, the characters are ultimately "liberated" although their freedom contains no guarantee of happiness or security. Hailey's fondness for obvious comic devices prevents the emergence of the genuine artist he at times reveals himself to be.

—Leonard Fleischer

HAIRE, Wilson John.   British.   Born in Belfast, Northern Ireland, 6 April 1932. Educated at Clontonacally Elementary School, Carryduff, County Down, 1939–46. Married Rita Lenson in 1955 (marriage dissolved); Sheila Fitz-Jones in 1974; has five children and two stepchildren. Actor, Unity Theatre, London, 1962–67; Co-Director, Camden Group Theatre, London, 1967–71; Resident Dramatist, Royal Court Theatre, London, 1974 and Lyric Theatre, Belfast, 1976.   Recipient: George Devine Award, 1972; *Evening Standard* award, 1973; Thames Television Award, 1974; Leverhulme Fellowship, 1976.   Agent: Margaret Ramsay Ltd., 14a Goodwin's Court, London WC2N 4LL.   Address: 26 Denning Road, London N.W.3, England.

Publications

Plays

Clockin Hen (produced London, 1968).

340

The Diamond Bone and Hammer, and Along the Sloughs of Ulster (produced London, 1969).
Within Two Shadows (produced London, 1972; New York, 1974).   Published in *Scripts 9* (New York), September 1972; published separately, London, Davis Poynter, 1973.
Bloom of the Diamond Stone (produced Dublin, 1973).
Echoes from a Concrete Canyon (produced London, 1975).

Television Plays: *Letter from a Soldier*, 1975; *The Dandelion Clock*, 1975; *The Pact*, 1976.

Wilson John Haire comments:

I am a late starter: having had my first play produced professionally when I was forty. Now, at the age of fourty-four, I have to discard much of my earlier theories on the craft of playwriting (gleaned mostly from the works of Beckett, Arthur Miller, and Chekhov), because of the rapid change in world conditions by which civil unrest on a universal scale is liable to effect immediately the individual in his private life. Escapist drama and the constant West End revivals are filling a temporary void until such time as the British dramatist once again finds the right road for his new journey.

*   *   *

Wilson John Haire, born in the Shankill Road, Belfast, from a Catholic mother and a Protestant father, has drawn much of the background material for his plays from that stark area of a tortured city. Even when the actual turmoil of Northern Ireland is not part of a play, as in *Echoes from a Concrete Canyon*, we can still feel the claustrophobic atmosphere of an unfriendly town beyond the walls of a lonely flat. Four of his plays, however are set against the background of sectarian violence, bigotry and loneliness. He conveys the tragedy of Ulster more directly and vividly than any other contemporary writer, drawing upon memories which reach far back into his childhood.

Haire is not a polemical writer. Political ideas interest him, particularly as part of the environment from which they come, but he is concerned more with the nature and extent of Ulster's suffering than with easy moralising. His best-known play, *Within Two Shadows*, is also the most autobigraphical. It deals with a working-class Belfast family, dog-eared with poverty, and torn apart by predjuces which they try to exclude but which gradually eat into their lives. In the play, the mother is a Protestant, the father a Catholic, and we feel that both, at some time in their lives, have made conscientious efforts to leap over the religious barriers which divide them. But the pressure of events, the opinions of their neighbours, and the growing violence are too much for them. They try to stay away from conflict, if only to protect their children; but the children are growing up, now teenagers, and quick to enter into the rivalries, as part of their puppy-play but with fangs bared.

In *Bloom of the Diamond Stone*, Haire shows what could almost have been the beginnings of that marriage, a Romeo and Juliet love affair, where the young couple from opposite sides fall in love and then have to battle against their families, the restrictions set at work, and the rigid outlooks of their former friends. In both plays, Haire conveys a sense of inner honesty and goodness corruped by circumstance. In that way, he can be an optimistic writer. His characters are not vicious in themselves, only made so by a historical backlog of revenge, fear, and defensiveness. To that extent, Ulster's torment seems the result of a curable mixture of follies, rather than the dark nightmare of the soul as other dramatists, including Rudkin, have sometimes presented it. The British soldier searching for a "terrorist" in *Bloom of the Diamond Stone* is shown to be a likable human being, until his fears and his job prompt him to be otherwise.

But the follies extend in all direction. They are sometimes rooted in sheer lack of understanding of the awfulness of the situation. In his first television play, *Letter from a Soldier*, Haire merely describes a soldier's effort to make his family in England understand what a tour of duty in Ulster is like, while his second, *The Dandelion Clock*, concerns the particular problems facing a young girl growing up in Belfast. What sort of future can she plan for herself? The problems, however, are not just ones of comprehension. They also stem from the social organisation which is out of touch with the lives people lead.

Clockin Hen, his first stage play, concerns a court case in which two shipyard workers of different religions are put on trial, following a Paisleyite demonstration in 1966. How do they react to the presence of the Law? Do they regard Law in any meaningful sense? And if they do not, where does an Ulsterman go? "Emotionally," Haire has said, "I am a Catholic, but intellectually I am a Protestant." This conflict is reflected in his plays. Haire perceives the need for a formal social order, but is sympathetic to the resentments caused by the existing one. To be out of touch with society, to defy, ignore, or simply have an engrained distrust of the ordering forces which are there, is equivalent to "dropping out." Haire's sympathy with Irish drop-outs, tramps, and drunkards is shown in *The Latchicoes of Fort Camden*, an unperformed play set in a London dosshouse.

Haire's skill as a dramatist reveals the strength and weaknesses of someone who chooses subjects so close to his personal experience. He can write vigorously and directly, usually naturalistically, but without the detachment needed to ensure that his plays have a clear form and that each point is made dramatically and concisely. He has indicated an intention to break away from his concentration on Northern Ireland; but in *Echoes from a Concrete Canyon*, which concerns the mental breakdown of a woman living with her daughter in a block of flats and estranged from her husband, the clotted verbosity which often accompanies autobiography is still present. Lightening touches of humour are rare; and the frequent poeticisms add heaviness rather than variety to the language. Haire in time may gain maturity as a dramatist by becoming less dependent on his background, but he may lose the force of reality which adds power to his Ulster plays. He speaks as a witness and a survivor of a continuing drama of stupidity, cruelty and resentment. That, so far, has been his main role, and not an insignificant one, in contemporary British theatre.

—John Elsom

HALE, John, British. Born in Woolwich, Kent, 5 February 1926. Educated at army schools in Egypt, Ceylon and Malta; Borden Grammar School, Sittingbourne, Kent; Royal Naval College, Greenwich. Served in the Fleet Air Arm, 1941–51: boy apprentice to petty officer, later commisioned. Married Valerie June Bryan in 1950; has two children. Stage hand, stage manager, electrician, in variety, touring and repertory companies. Founder, and Artistic Director, Lincoln Theatre, 1955–58; Artistic Director, Arts Theatre, Ipswich, 1958–59; Artistic Director, Bristol Old Vic, 1959–61; free-lance director, 1961–64; Member of the Board of Govenors, 1963–71, and Associate Artistic Director, 1968–71, Greenwich Theatre. Since 1964, free-lance writer and director. Representative: Laurence Harbottle, Harbottle and Lewis, 34 South Molton Street, London W1Y 2PB, England.

PUBLICATIONS

Plays

The Black Swan Winter (as *Smile Boys, That's the Style*, produced Glasgow, 1968; as
    The Black Swan Winter, also director: produced London, 1969).   Published in *Plays
    of the Year 37*, London, Elek, 1970
It's All in the Mind (also director: produced London, 1968).
Spithead (also director: produced London, 1969).   Published in *Plays of the Year 38*,
    London, Elek, 1971.
Here Is the News (produced Beaford, Devon, 1970).
Lorna and Ted (also director: produced London, 1970).
Decibels (produced Liverpool, 1971).   Published in *Prompt Three*, edited by Alan
    Durband, London, Hutchinson, 1976.
The Lion's Cub (televised, 1971).   Published in *Elizabeth R*, London, Elek, 1971.
In Memory of...Carmen Miranda (also director: produced London, 1975).
Love's Old Sweet Song (also director: produced London, 1976).

Radio Writing: *Micah Clarke* series, 1966.

Television Plays: *The Rules that Jack Made*, 1965: *The Noise Stopped*, 1966; *Light the
Blue Touch Paper*, 1966; *Thirteen Against Fate* series, 1966; *The Queen's Traitor* (5
parts), 1967; *Retreat*, 1968; *The Picnic*, 1969; *The Distracted Preacher*, 1969; *The
Lion's Cub*, 1971; *The Bristol Entertainment*, 1971; *Anywhere But England*, 1972; *Ego
Hugo: A Romantic Entertainment*, 1973, *The Brotherhood*, 1975; *An Impeccable
Elopement*, 1975; *Goodbye America*, 1976.

Novels

Kissed the Girls and Made Them Cry.   London, Collins, 1963; Englewood Cliffs, New
    Jersey, Prentice Hall, 1966.
The Grudge Fight.   London, Collins, 1964; Englewood Cliffs, New Jersey, Prentice
    Hall, 1967.
A Fool at the Feast.   London, Collins, 1966.
The Paradise Man.   London, Rapp and Whiting, and Indianapolis, Bobbs Merrill,
    1969.
The Fort.   London, Quartet Books, 1973.
The Love School.   London, Pan, 1974; New York, St. Martin's Press, 1975.
Lovers and Heretics.   London, Gollancz, 1976.

Theatrical Activities:

Director: **Plays** – about 150 plays in Lincoln, Ipswich, Bristol and elsewhere, including
An Enemy of the People by Arthur Miller, Lincoln, 1958; *Cyrano de Bergerac* by Edmond
Rostand, Bristol, 1959; *The Merry Wives of Windsor*, London, 1959; *The Tinker* by
Laurence Dobie and Robert Sloman, Bristol and London, 1960; *The Rehearsal* by
Anouilh, Bristol and London, 1961; *The Killer* by Ionesco, Bristol, 1961; *Sappho* by
Lawrence Durrell, Edinburgh, 1961; *Mother Courage* by Brecht, Hiram, Ohio, 1966; *It's
All in the Mind*, London, 1968; *The Black Swan Winter*, London, 1969; *Spithead*, London,
1969; *Lorna and Ted*, London, 1970; *In Memory of...Carmen Miranda*, London, 1975;
Love's Old Sweet Song, London, 1976. **Television** – about 16 plays, 1961–64, including
The Fruit at the Bottom of the Bowl by Ray Bradbury, and *Drill Pig* by Charles Wood; *The*

Rules That Jack Made, 1965. **Recordings** – 13 Shakespeare plays, including *The Taming of the Shrew, Richard II* and *Henry V,* FCM Productions.

John Hale comments:

Until I was asked to write this introduction I had not considered what, if anything, my plays have in common. On the face of it – not much.

Once, in the first flush of being published, I was incautious enough to write earnestly about my motives and aims as a writer. It is painful even at this distance to read that piece. So having considered the plays and come to some conclusions I shall keep them to myself and try to avoid repeating the error of that first article.

I am both a playwright and a novelist. The plays and novels were written alternately when I could afford the luxury of the time. I bought the time with television plays and film scripts. If I have anything to say only part of it is in the plays: all of it, whatever it is, is in the plays and the novels taken together.

Much of contemporary drama deals with the extreme situation. The reasons are fairly obvious, and music and art go that way too. I do not subscribe to the extreme situation and am drawn to a balance of passion and intellect. I enjoy the company of women and write for them as often as for men. *It's All in the Mind* and *Lorna and Ted* reflect this.

I sometimes write what are, on the face of it, historical or period pieces – like *Spithead.* In fact they are contemporary and permit me to permit the characters to express freely emotions and ideas generally believed (and falsely believed) not to be part of our time. *Spithead* is a political or, if you wish, a social play. So is *It's All in the Mind.*

The Black Swan Winter is a requiem for my father.

It also reflects the fact that, at the time, literally every forty-ish man that I knew with any intimacy was in a mess either sexually or professionally or spiritually and going under. Nothing new in that except it did not seem to me to be quite the way the cliché has it about the male change of life.

You can't run theatres for a decade and ignore the hopes and needs of an audience. There is a conscious effort to see that when they come to the stage the plays have a life of their own; a world of their own.

And humour: with luck the characters quite often make a joke, mock themselves, are wry or ironic where conventions suggest they might be solemn.

I worked for five years on and off to get *Spithead* and four years for the final version of *Black Swan Winter.* I had *Lorna and Ted* in mind for years and wrote it in a month between drafts of a film because the theatre at Greenwich had been let down over a promised two-handed play for the autumn of 1970.

Later when the play opened the new theatre at Wythenshawe (the partner to the Library Theatre, Manchester) the people packed in off the housing estates on the word of mouth: and because no one had told them that there is no such thing as a funny tragedy about ordinary unfashionable people they laughed so you could hear it outside; like the Ghurkas make a joke with the dead – even when under fire they may shake the hand of a passing friend, covered on a stretcher, and gee him up to paradise.

If I am writing for anybody it is for people with that view of life.

*   *   *

As a playwright, John Hale seems to share what is a common quality of actors, the ability to take up a theme, immerse himself in it, work it out, and leave it: recognizably the same actor is performing, if your concern is to look for him, yet the characters are different creations. Where other writers may work through and within an obsession, in some cases (Strindberg and Tennessee Williams) becoming trapped by it, so that the plays are like a series of studies of some vast central object too large to be contained in any one play, John

Hale seems to make a fresh start in each case, as if he were to say, "Here is my subject. I give myself to it. I use *this* particular piece of my own experience for it. I build it from inside, and shape it from the outside. I have made a play. I move on."

The Black Swan Winter, his first stage play, was written after his own father's death, and uses memories of his father and himself. In a later play, *Love's Old Sweet Song*, Hale and his father appear again, and his grand-father also, but as supporting characters in what seems to be primarily an appaled examination of two castrating women, mother and daughter jointly devoted to the destruction of all the men around them. His novel *The Grudge Fight* used his experience of the navy, and when he wanted to return to the subject in *Spithead* he used instead the secondary experience of history. *It's All in the Mind* is only excursion into politics. *Lorna and Ted* the only one into Suffolk, and his one-act monologue *In Memory of...Carmen Miranda* the only one into Samuel Becket country, which is just as well since he seems not to be happy there.

Yet there is a moral being, Hale himself, who made all this work, even though he is modest as well as moral, and requires one to search for him. *Kissed the Girls and Made Them Cry*, *The Black Swan Winter*, and *Love's Old Sweet Song* all share a theme, the attempt to get back into one's past and find out what went wrong. The shadow of his father, a warrant officer in the Regular Army, lies upon his work and is shown in Hale's concern for fairness and his admiration of discipline, most of all self-discipline: if Forster can be boiled down to "Only connect," then John Hale's two words are "Soldier on." Fairness for him means most of all fairness to other people, a decent recognition of the right to difference, but it can also mean (*Lorna and Ted*) fairness to oneself, an assertion of one's own rights, and an acceptance of responsibility.

Hale's plays are well-made in the manner, nowadays common, of a television play or a play by Shakespeare, with a number of scenes running into each other, and a fragmented set. They are thoughtful, observed, humane, and only rarely self-indulgent. Their fault (commonly found in company with these virtues) is an occasional over-explicitness: Hale's characters, like Priestley's, too often say what they should only mean, though this is not a fault of *Lorna and Ted*, which is his most interesting play so far. He seems always to have been happiest when writing duologues (too many characters at once appear to worry him,) and in this two-hander, with only a non-speaking voluptuous lady in support, his construction has been most at ease, most relaxed, least stiff.

—John Bowen

HALL, Willis.   British.   Born in Leeds, Yorkshire, 6 April 1929. Educated at Cockburn High School, Leeds. National Service: radio playwright for the Chinese Schools Department of Radio Malaya. Has four children. Agent: London Management, 235–241 Regent Street, London W.1., England.

PUBLICATIONS

Plays

Final at Furnell (broadcast, 1954).   London, Evans, 1956.

Poet and Pheasant, with Lewis Jones (broadcast, 1955; produced Watford, Hertfordshire, 1958).   London, Deane, 1959.

The Gentle Knight (broadcast, 1957; produced London, 1964).   London, Blackie, 1966.

The Play of the Royal Astrologers (produced Birmingham, 1958; London, 1968). London, Heinemann, 1960.

Air Mail from Cyprus (televised, 1958).   Published in *The Television Playwright: Ten Plays for BBC Television*, edited by Michael Barry, London, Joseph, and New York, Hill and Wang, 1960.

The Long and the Short and the Tall (produced, Edinburgh, 1958; London, 1959; New York, 1962).   London, Heinemann, 1959; New York, Theatre Arts, 1961.

A Glimpse of the Sea and Last Day in Dreamland (produced London, 1959).   Included in *A Glimpse of the Sea: Three Short Plays*, 1960.

Return to the Sea (televised, 1960).   Included in *A Glimpse of the Sea: Three Short Plays*, 1960.

A Glimpse of the Sea: Three Short Plays (includes *Last Day in Dreamland* and *Return to the Sea*).   London, Evans, 1960.

Billy Liar, with Keith Waterhouse, adaptation of the novel by Keith Waterhouse (produced London, 1960; Los Angeles and New York, 1963).   London, Joseph, and New York, Norton, 1960.

Chin-Chin, adaptation of the play by François Billetdoux (produced London, 1960).

Celebration: The Wedding and The Funeral, with Keith Waterhouse (produced Nottingham and London, 1961).   London, Joseph, 1961.

Azouk, with Robin Maugham, adaptation of a play by Alexandre Rivemale (produced Newcastle upon Tyne, 1962).

England, Our England, with Keith Waterhouse, music by Dudley Moore (produced London, 1962).   London, Evans, 1964.

Squat Betty, with Keith Waterhouse (produced London, 1962; New York, 1964). Included in *The Sponge Room and Squat Betty*, 1963.

The Sponge Room, with Keith Waterhouse (produced Nottingham and London, 1962; New York, 1964).   Included in *The Sponge Room and Squat Betty*, 1963; in *Modern Short Plays from Broadway and London*, edited by Stanley Richards, New York, Random House, 1969.

All Things Bright and Beautiful, with Keith Waterhouse (produced Bristol and London, 1962).   London, Joseph, 1963.

Yer What?, with others, music by Lance Mulcahy (revue; produced Nottingham, 1962).

The Sponge Room and Squat Betty, with Keith Waterhouse. London, Evans, 1963.

The Days Beginning: An Easter Play.   London, Heinemann, 1963.

The Love Game, adaptation of a play by Marcel Achard, translated by Tamara Lo (produced London, 1964).

Come Laughing Home, with Keith Waterhouse (as *They Called the Bastard Stephen*, produced Bristol, 1964; as *Come Laughing Home*, produced Wimbledon, 1965). London, Evans 1965.

Say Who You Are, with Keith Waterhouse (produced London, 1965).   London, Evans, 1967; as *Help Stamp Out Marriage* (produced New York, 1966), New York, French, 1966.

Joey, Joey, with Keith Waterhouse, music by Ron Moody (produced London, 1966).

Whoops-a-Daisy, with Keith Waterhouse (produced Nottingham, 1968).

Children's Day, with Keith Waterhouse (produced Edinburgh and London, 1969). London, French, 1975.

Who's Who, with Keith Waterhouse (produced Coventry, 1971; London, 1973). London, French, 1974.

The Railwayman's New Clothes (televised, 1971).   London, French, 1974.

They Don't All Open Men's Boutiques (televised, 1972).   Published in *Prompt Three*,
    edited by Alan Durband, London, Hutchinson, 1976.
Saturday, Sunday, Monday, with Keith Waterhouse, adaptation of a play by Eduardo
    de Filippo (produced London, 1973).   London, Heinemann, 1974.
The Card, with Keith Waterhouse, music and lyrics by Tony Hatch and Jackie Trent,
    adaptation of the novel by Arnold Bennett (produced Bristol and London, 1973).
Walk On, Walk On (produced Liverpool, 1975).   London, French, 1976.
Kidnapped at Christmas (produced London, 1975).   London, Heinemann, 1975.
Stag-Night (produced London, 1976).
Christmas Crackers (produced London, 1976).

Screenplays: *The Long and the Short and the Tall* (additional dialogue), 1961; with
Keith Waterhouse: *Whistle Down the Wind*, 1961; *A Kind of Loving*, 1961; *The Valiant*,
1962; *Billy Liar*, 1963; *West Eleven*, 1963; *Man in the Middle*, 1964; *Pretty Polly (A
Matter of Innocence)*, 1968; *Lock Up Your Daughters*, 1969.

Radio Plays: *Final at Furnell*, 1954; *The Nightingale*, 1954; *Furore at Furnell*, 1955;
Frenzy at Furnell, 1955; *Friendly at Furnell*, 1955; *Fluster at Furnell*, 1955; *Poet and
Pheasant*, with Lewis Jones, 1955; *One Man Absent*, 1955; *A Run for the Money*, 1956;
Afternoon for Antigone, 1956; *The Long Years*, 1956; *Any Dark Morning*, 1956; *Feodor's
Bride*, 1956; *One Man Returns*, 1956; *A Ride on the Donkeys*, 1957; *The Calverdon
Road Job*, 1957; *The Gentle Knight*, 1957; *Harvest the Sea*, 1957; *Monday at Seven*,
1957; *Annual Outing*, 1958; *The Larford Lad*, 1958; *The Case of Walter Grimshaw*,
with Leslie Halward, 1958.

Television Plays: *Air Mail from Cyprus*, 1958; *Return to the Sea*, 1960; *On the Night of
the Murder*, 1962; *The Ticket*, 1969; *The Railwayman's New Clothes*, 1971; *The Villa
Maroc*, 1972; *They Don't All Open Men's Boutiques*, 1972; *Song at Twilight*, 1973;
Friendly Encounter, 1974; *The Piano-Smashers of the Golden Sun*, 1974; *Illegal
Approach*, 1974; *Midgley*, 1975; *Match-Fit*, from a story by Brian Glanville, 1976; with
Keith Waterhouse: *Happy Moorings*, 1963; *How Many Angels*, 1964; *Inside George
Webley* series 1968; *Queenie's Castle* series, 1970; *Budgie* series, 1971–72; *The Upper
Crusts* series, 1973; *Three's Company* series, 1973; *By Endeavour Alone*, 1973; *Billy
Liar* series, 1973–74.

Other

They Found the World, with I. O. Evans (juvenile).   New York, Warne, 1959;
    London, Warne, 1960.
The Royal Astrologers: Adventures of Father Mole-Cricket or the Malayan Legends
    (juvenile).   London, Heinemann, 1960; New York, Coward McCann, 1962.
The A to Z of Soccer, with Michael Parkinson.   London, Pelham, 1970.
The A to Z of Television, with Bob Monkhouse.   London, Pelham, 1971.
My Sporting Life.   London, Luscombe, 1975.
Incredible Kidnapping (juvenile).   London, Heinemann, 1975.

Editor, with Keith Waterhouse, *Writers' Theatre*.   London, Heinemann, 1967.
Editor, with Michael Parkinson, *Football Report: An Anthology of Soccer*.   London,
    Pelham, 1973.
Editor, *Football Classified: An Anthology of Soccer*.   London, Luscombe, 1975.
Editor, *Football Final*.   London, Pelham, 1975.

*   *   *

Willis Hall and Keith Waterhouse have written so many stage plays and television and film scripts over the past fifteen years that critics are wont to regard them as the stand-by professionals of British theatre. Their technical skill has never been doubted – but their artistry and originality often have. They were both born in Leeds in 1929 and have therefore shared a similar Yorkshire background. Both were successful individually before their long-standing collaboration began. Hall's *The Long and the Short and the Tall* was premiered by the Oxford Theatre Group in 1958: and was described by Kenneth Tyan as "the most moving production of the [Edinburgh] festival." Waterhouse's novel, *Billy Liar*, was well-received in 1957. The stage version of *Billy Liar* was their first joint effort, and its success in London (where it helped to establish the names of the two actors who played the title role, Albert Finney and Tom Courtenay) encouraged them to continue in the vein of "purely naturalistic provincial working class comedy," to quore T. C. Worsley's description. *Celebration, All Things Bright and Beautiful* and *Come Laughing Home*, together with the one-act plays *The Sponge Room* and *Squat Betty*, allowed critics to regard them as the true successors of Stanley Houghton and Harold Brighouse: and this convenient label stuck to their work, until 1965, when their farce, *Say Who You Are*, set in Kensington, London, and concerning a middle-class *ménage à quatre*, proved an unexpected success of the season. This lively and (in some respects) ambitious sexual comedy demonstrated that their talents were not confined to one style of humour nor their sense of place to the North of England. When this barrier of mild prejudice was broken, it was remembered that Hall was responsible for perhaps the best British adaption of a contemporary French comedy, Billetdoux' *Chin-Chin* (1960), that both had contributed widely to revues and satirical programmes (such as the BBC's *That Was the Week That Was)* and had written modern versions of Greek tragedies (such as Hall's *Afternoon for Antigone)*. Their range as writers and their sophistication obviously extended beyond the narrow limits which brought them their reputations.

Not is technical skill so common a quality among contemporary dramatists that it can be dismissed as unimportant. Hall and Waterhouse have the merits of good professionals. When they write satirically, their polemic is sharp, witty and to the point. When they write naturalistically – whether about a provincial town in Yorkshire, a seaside amusement arcade, the war in Malaya or Kensington – they take the trouble to know the surroundings in detail: and this groundwork enables them to discover possibilities which other writers overlook. *Celebration*, for example, presents two contrasting family events – a marriage and a funeral set in a working class suburb of a Yorkshire town. There is no main story to hold the episodes together, nor a theme, nor even a clearly indentifiable climax. But the play triumphs because the distinctive flavour of each "celebration" is captured and because the fifteen main characters are each so well-drawn. The slender threads of continuity which bind the episodes together reveal a sensitive insight into the nature of the society. The first act is about the wedding preparations in the backroom of a pub: Rhoda and Edgar Lucas are determined to do well by their daughter, Christine, who is marrying Bernard Fuller. But Rhoda has decided to economize by not employing Whittaker's, the firm in the town who specialize in weddings. Her efforts to ensure that the wedding breakfast doesn't let her daughter down are helped and hindered by the other members of the family: but despite the tattiness of the scene, the collapsible tables, the grease-proof paper and the dirty cups, the audience eventually is drawn to see the glowing pride and family self-importance which surround the event. Christine and Bernard survey the transformed room at the end of the act: and their contented happiness justifies the efforts. The second act is about the funeral of Arthur Broadbent, Rhoda's great-uncle and the best-known eccentric of the family, who has been living in sin for years with May Beckett. The funeral is over and the pieties continue in the living-room of the Lucas's house. But the family don't wish to aknowledge May Beckett, until she invades the house both physically (since they try to prevent her from coming) and emotionally, by expressing a grief which the conventional sentiments of the family cannot match. May's nostalgic tribute to her lost lover – so carefully prepared for in the script and emerging with an easy naturalness – is one of the truly outstanding moments of post-war British naturalistic drama: to rank with Beatie's speech at the end of Wesker's *Roots*.

This assured handling of naturalistic details is a feature of all their best plays. What other writers would have used the pub and the telephone box as so important a part of a sex comedy, replacing the more familiar stage props of a settee and a verandah? Or caught the significance of a back yard for a lonely introvert like Billy Liar? Or surrounded the pregnant unmarried girl, Vera Fawcett, in *Come Laughing Home*, with a family whose stultifying complacency offered a convincing example of the waste land from which she is trying unsuccessfully to escape? With this unusual skill in capturing an exact *milieu*, Hall and Waterhouse are also adept at writing those single outstanding roles which actors love to play. The part of Private Bamforth in *The Long and the Short and the Tall* gave Peter O'Toole his first opportunity – which he seized with relish: Hayley Mills was "discovered" in their film, *Whistle Down the Wind*, with the then underrated actor, Alan Bates. Hall and Waterhouse were once criticised for writing "angry young man" parts without providing the psychological insight or rhetoric of Osborne's Jimmy Porter. John Russell Taylor wrote that

> the central characters, Bamforth and Fentrill [in *Last Day in Dreamland*], are almost identical: the hectoring angry young man who knows it all and stands for most of the time in the centre of the stage, aquiver as a rule (whether the situation warrants it or not) with almost hysterical intensity, berating the other characters, who in each case, rather mysteriously, accept him as a natural leader and the life and soul of the party. The indebtedness to *Look Back in Anger* is unmistakable ....

This description may apply to Fentrill, whose anger at the run-down amusement arcade seems somewhat strained since he's not forced to stay there: less so to Bamforth, whose bitterness derives from the claustrophobic jungle war: and scarcely at all to the other main characters of their plays. The distinctive strength of their protagonists lies not in their volubility nor their character complexities, but in their reactions to unsympathetic surroundings. Vera Fawcett is not a stock rebel: Billy Liar doesn't rebel at all – he's too satisfied with fantasies about escape. Unlike John Osborne, Hall and Waterhouse rarely offer "mouthpiece" characters, people whose insight and rhetoric about their own problems justify their presence on the stage. Their central characters emerge from their surroundings: the environment shapes the nature of their rebellion. Their dilemmas are a typical part of their societies: and are not superimposed upon their families as a consequence of too much intelligence or education.

A fairer criticism of their work might run along these lines: that while their dialogue is always lively and accurate, it rarely contains flashes of intuition. Much of the humour of *Celebration, Billy Liar* and *Say Who You Are* depends upon carefully calculated repetition. The characters are sometimes given verbal catch-phrases – Eric Fawcett teases his son Brian endlessly for ordering "whisky and Scotch" in a pub – but more frequently are given habits which become irritating after a time. Eric Fawcett's life centres around making model boats (in *Come Laughing Home*): Edgar continually chides Rhoda for not arranging the wedding through Whittaker's, while his son Jack greets every newcomer with the same question, "Lend us a quid?" Often the reiteration makes a valid dramatic point – if only to illustrate the poverty of the relationships: but sometimes it seems just an easy way of establishing a person, by constantly reminding the audience of an obsession. Hall and Waterhouse often fail to reveal any deeper cause behind the nagging habit: and this lack of depth prevents the characters from seeming sympathetic. In *Say Who You Are*, the two men, David and Stuart, are both self-opinionated male chauvinists: credible enough but rather uninteresting because they have so little self-knowledge. Valerie, who invents a marriage so that she can have an affair without getting too involved, is a more engaging creation – but she too seems superficial when we learn that her objections to marriage rest on a dislike of "togetherness" – "toothbrushes nestling side by side" – and on little else. Sometimes when Hall and Waterhouse try to give an added dimension to their characters, the effect seems strained: when Vera Fawcett resigns herself to an arid future with her family from whom she cannot escape, she says "I wanted to reach out for something, but I couldn't reach far enough. It's

349

something you need – for living – that I haven't got. I haven't really looked, but I wanted to, I was going to." This statement of her defeat doesn't dramatically match or rise to the opportunity which the play provides for her.

This superficiality has often been explained as the reverse side of the authors' facility: writers who produce so many scripts can't be expected to be profound as well. But there may be another reason. Hall and Waterhouse share a remarkable sense of form and timing, which partly accounts for the success of *Say Who You Are* and *Celebration*. David and Sarah go to two different telephones at the same time, intending to ring each other up – with the result that the numbers are always engaged and they jump to the wrong conclusion. The scenes are based on a clever use of parallels and counterpoint: but this also depends on the characters behaving with a mechanical predictiveness. We know what they're really going to do, and the fun comes from seeing their stock reactions fail to achieve the expected results. The formalism of the scripts, in short, sometimes prevents the characters from having an independent life: and this is the result, not so much of technical facility, as of an over-zealous care in construction which shortsightedly ignores other possibilities. Despite these limitations, however, Hall and Waterhouse have an expertise which few other writers of the new wave of British drama can match and which accounts for the continuing popularity of their best plays.

—John Elsom

HALLIWELL, David (William).   British.   Born in Brighouse, Yorkshire, 31 July 1936. Educated at Bailiff Bridge Elementary School; Victoria Central Secondary Modern School, Rastrick; Hipperholme Grammar School; Huddersfield College of Art; Royal Academy of Dramatic Art, London, graduate. Since 1966, Director, and since 1971, Committee Member, Quipu group, London. Visiting Fellow, Reading University, 1969–70. Recipient: *Evening Standard* award, 1967. Agent: Sheila Lemon, Spokesmen Ltd., 1 Craven Hill, London W2 3EW. Address: 28 Chepstow Court, Chepstow Crescent, London W11 3ED, England.

PUBLICATIONS

Plays

    Little Malcolm and His Struggle Against the Eunuchs (produced London, 1965). London, French, 1966; as *Hail Scrawdyke!* (produced New York 1966), New York, Grove Press, 1966.

    A Who's Who of Flapland (broadcast, 1967; produced London, 1969). Included in *A Who's Who of Flapland and Other Plays*, 1971.

    The Experiment, with David Calderisi (also co-director: produced London and New York, 1967.

    A Discussion (produced Falmouth, 1969).   Included in *A Who's Who of Flapland and Other Plays*, 1971.

    K. D. Dufford Hears K. D. Dufford Ask K. D. Dufford How K. D. Dufford'll Make K. D. Dufford (produced London, 1969).   London, Faber, 1970.

    Muck from Three Angles (produced Edinburgh and London, 1970).   Included in *A Who's Who of Flapland and Other Plays*, 1971.

The Girl Who Didn't Like Answers (produced London, 1971).

A Last Belch for the Great Auk (produced London, 1971).

A Who's Who of Flapland and Other Plays (includes *A Discussion* and *Muck from Three Angles*).   London, Faber, 1971.

An Amour, and A Feast (produced London, 1971).

Bleats from a Brighouse Pleasureground (broadcast, 1972; also director: produced London, 1972).

Janitress Thrilled by Prehensile Penis (also director: produced London, 1972).

An Altercation (also director: produced London, 1973).

Sketch, in *Off The Bus* (also director: produced London, 1974).

The Freckled Bum (also director: produced London, 1974).

Minyip (also director: produced London, 1974).

Progs (also director: produced London, 1975).

A Process of Elimination (also director: produced London, 1975).

Radio Plays: *A Who's Who of Flapland*, 1967; *Bleats from a Brighouse Pleasureground*, 1972.

Television Plays: *A Plastic Mac in Winter*, 1963; *Cock, Hen and Courting Pit*, 1966; *Triptych of Bathroom Users*, 1972; *Blur and Blank via Checkheaton*, 1972; *Steps Back*, 1973, *Daft Mam Blues*, 1975; *Pigmented Patter* (*Crown Court* series), 1976; *Meriel the Ghost Girl* (*The Mind Beyond* series, 1976.

Theatrical Activities:

Director: **Plays** – Quipu group: many of his own plays and *The Dumb Waiter* by Harold Pinter, *Keep Out, Love in Progress* by Walter Hall, *The Stronger* by Strindberg, and *A Village Wooing* by G. B. Shaw, 1966; *A Day with My Sister* by Stephen Poliakoff, 1971; *The Hundred Watt Bulb* by George Thatcher, *I Am Real and So Are You, A Visit from the Family*, and *Crewe Station at Two A.M.* by Tony Connor, 1972; *The Only Way Out* by George Thatcher and *Spayed Bitch* by Frank Dux, 1973; *The Experiment* (co-director, with David Calderisi), London and New York, 1967; *We Are What We Eat* by Frank Dux, *The Knowall* by Alan C. Taylor, and *The Quipu Anywhere Show* (co-director, with Gavin Eley), London, 1973; *The Last of the Feinsteins* by Tony Connor, London, 1975.

Actor: **Plays** – Vincentio in *The Taming of the Shrew* and Seyton in *Macbeth*, Nottingham, 1962; Hortensio in *The Taming of the Shrew*, Leicester, 1962; Sydney Spooner in *Worn's Eye View* by R. F. Delderfield, Colchester, 1962; General Madigan in *O'Flaherty, V. C.* by G. B. Shaw, and Jim Curry in *The Rainmaker* by N. Richard Nash, Stoke on Trent, 1962; Hero in *The Rehearsal* by Anouilh, Pozzo in *Waiting for Godot* by Beckett, and The Common Man in *A Man for All Seasons* by Robert Bolt, Stoke on Trent, 1963; Scrawdyke in *Little Malcolm and His Struggle Against the Eunuchs*, London, 1965; Jackson McIver in *The Experiment*, London, 1967; Policeman in *An Altercation*, London, 1973; Botard in *Rhinoceros* by Ionesco, London, 1974; Frankie in *Birdbath* by Leonard Melfi, Bristol, 1975.

David Halliwell comments:

When I wrote a statement for the last edition of this book, I said very firmly that I would write only multiviewpoint plays in future. I spoke with the desperate certainty of a man about to crumble. The obsession with multiviewpoint was a product of severe identity disturbances which came to a climax early in 1974. I stopped writing completely and sought other means of resolving my conflicts. One of these, putting plays together by means of improvisation, was very salutary in that it was extremely social. In my new writing, I wish to develop a style of my own which will be organic, which will juxtapose different levels of human activity and which will be entertaining. A style which to some extent has evolved through multiviewpoint but is not multiviewpoint. A style achieved through the precise voicing of each character and each modality of character. The text of the play being a score from which actors perform. I feel an analogy with jazz, particularly jazz since the pop revolution of the early 1940's. What I have in mind is very much a performer's style which can, if necessary, be presented anywhere with absolutely no mechanical equipment.

*   *   *

David Halliwell's dramatic territory is Flapland; his perennial subject, the Hitler syndrome; the motive force of his central characters, that childish outburst of King Lear's: "I will do such things,/What they are, yet I know not, but they shall be/The terrors of the earth." Malcolm Scrawdyke, the hero of *Little Malcolm and His Struggle Against the Eunuchs,* models himself explicitly on the early Hitler, except that he wears a Russian anarchist's greatcoat in place of Hitler's raincoat. Expelled from Art School, Scrawdyke enlists three variously inadequate siblings into his Party of Dynamic Erection, plans a ludicrous revenge (which never gets beyond the fantasy stage) on the man who expelled him, and succeeds only in two petty, but nonetheless unpleasant, acts of terror: the "trial" of his most articulate and independent sibling, and the beating-up of a girl who has taunted him with sexual cowardice. Scrawdyke is only a phantom Hitler, his rabble-rousing speeches are confined to the inside of his Huddersfield garret and his grasp of reality so tenuous as to constitute little danger even to his specific enemies, let alone the community at large. But the hero of Halliwell's other full-lengh play, *K. D. Dufford Hears K. D. Dufford Ask K. D. Dufford How K. D. Dufford'll Make K. D. Dufford,* who actually wears a raincoat, sets his sights lower than Scrawdyke: his recipe for instant notoriety is to murder a child and he is entirely successful. Halliwell makes an ambitious attempt in this play not simply to suggest the imterplay between fantasy and reality, but actually to display it, chapter and verse, on the stage, with several different versions of each scene – the real event compared with the event as imagined to his own advantage by K. D. Dufford and by each of the other main characters.

Halliwell explores the possibilities and limitations of this device in a series of short plays – *Muck from Three Angles, A Last Belch for the Great Auk, Bleats from a Brighouse Pleasureground* and *Janitress Thrilled by Prehensile Penis.* The effect is often clumsy and ultimately superfluous since the shades of fantasy and reality pursue one another with such unerring clarity through his virtuoso monologues, that an audience must grow restive at being told by means of explicit technical devices what it has already grasped implicitly through intense dramatic sympathy.

For, however faceless, talentless, witless, loveless, lacking in courage and moral compunction these characters may be, Halliwell's comic view of them makes them irresistibly sympathetic. Something similar happens in the plays of Halliwell's contemporary Joe Orton, as well as in those of the master from whom they both learnt, Samuel Beckett. The fact that these characters would be, if met in real life, virtually sub-human, certainly pitiable or despicable to an extreme degree, is beside the point. In Halliwell's, as in Orton's and Beckett's plays, they are exaggerated dramatic representations of universal human weaknesses; and Halliwell has found and shown that, in this age of overpopulation and social disorientation, we are peculiarly vulnerable to paranoia. In *The Experiment,* partly devised by himself, partly improvised by the actors, Halliwell acted an avant-garde theatrical director "of international repute" rehearsing his company in "a modern epic translated from the Icelandic entitled *The Assassination of President Garfield.*" The efforts of this director to drive his cast towards the nadir of art, to discover in the purposeless murder of a forgotten American politician deeper and deeper levels of insignificance, satirized the gullibility of audiences as much as the inflated self-admiration of certain members of the theatrical profession, but they were above all a direct demonstration of Halliwell's own special subject: the banal striving to be the unique, the insignificant the significant, the squalid reality the dream of power.

In his lightest and most charming play, *A Who's Who of Flapland*, originally written for radio but successfully translated to lunch-time theatre, Halliwell closes the circle by confronting one paranoiac with another, his equal if not his master at the gambits and routines of Flapland. Here, as in *Little Malcolm*, Halliwell relies entirely on his mastery of dramatic speech, using his native industrial Yorkshire idiom as a precision instrument to trace complex patterns of aggression, alarm, subterfuge, humiliation, triumph, surrender. When *Little Malcolm* appeared on the West End stage, the audience stopped the play to applaud two speeches; it was one of the first signs that the fourth wall was really coming down, that there was to be a new relationship – or rather an old one revived – between stage and audience. It was also perhaps a recognition that on his chosen ground David Halliwell has no need of any cruder methods of innovation than words to make himself fully understood.

—John Spurling

HAMPTON, Christopher (James).   British.   Born in Fayal, the Azores, 26 January 1946. Educated at Lancing College, Sussex, 1959–63; New College, Oxford, 1964–68, B.A. in modern languages and literature (French and German) 1968. Married Laura de Holesch in 1970; has one daughter. Resident Dramatist, Royal Court Theatre, London, 1968–70. Recipient: *Evening Standard* award, 1970. Agent: Margaret Ramsay Ltd., 14a Goodwin's Court, London WC2N 4LL, England.

PUBLICATIONS

Plays

> *When Did You Last See My Mother?* (produced Oxford and London, 1966; New York, 1967).   London, Faber, and New York, Grove Press 1967.
> *Marya*, adaptation of a play by Isaac Babel, translated by Michael Glenny and Harold Shukman (produced London, 1967).   Published in *Plays of the Year 35*, London, Elek, 1969.
> *Total Eclipse* (produced London, 1968; Washington, D.C., 1972; New York, 1974). London, Faber, 1969; New York, French, 1972.
> *Uncle Vanya*, adaptation of a play by Chekhov, translated by Nina Froud (produced London, 1970).   Published in *Plays of the Year 39*, London, Elek, 1971.
> *The Philanthropist: A Bourgeois Comedy* (produced London, 1970; New York, 1971). London, Faber, 1970; New York, French, 1971.
> *Hedda Gabler*, adaptation of a play by Ibsen (produced Stratford, Ontario, 1970; New York, 1971).   New York, French, 1971.
> *A Doll's House*, adaptation of a play by Ibsen (produced New York, 1971; London, 1973).   New York, French, 1972.
> *Don Juan*, adaptation of a play by Molière (broadcast, 1972; produced Bristol, 1972). London, Faber, 1974.

Savages (produced London, 1973).   London, Faber, 1974.

Treats (produced London, 1976).   London, Faber, 1976.

Signed and Sealed, adaption of a play by Georges Feydeau and Maurice Desvallieres (produced London, 1976).

Screenplay: *A Doll's House*, 1973.

Radio Plays: *2 Children Free to Wander*, 1969; *Don Juan*, 1972.

Critical Study: interview in *Theatre Quarterly 12* (London), 1973.

*   *   *

To make more than the most tentative assessment of Christopher Hampton's work, even though there are five plays to consider, must be previous; he is still only in his thirties. His first, second, third and fifth plays (*When Did You Last See My Mother?*, *Total Eclipse*, *The Philanthropist* and *Treats*) have a preoccupation with emotional isolation and emotional self-sufficiency. His fourth play, *Savages*, is present out on its own.

Hampton is a traditional playwright, and skillful. He has a strong sense of shape, though his construction is not yet assured enough to match it, and a fluent command of dialogue: in this he is close to Osborne. In *When Did You Last See My Mother?*, the influence of Osborne and the sense of shape may both be noticed in Hampton's use of the twice-told story of the woman lecturing on modern sculpture at the Sorbonne: she uses lantern slides, and in the dark one by one her audience leaves until the lights come up at the end, and she has no audience left. As Ian first tells this story, it is a mere invention to feed his own self-pity, but as he begins to face a kind of truth about himself, he is able to tell the story again, and the truth is not pitiful. The same sort of repetition is used in *Total Eclipse*. This time it is a repetition of incident, not anecdote, and the order is reversed. Sitting at a café table, Rimbaud asks Verlaine, "Do you love me?" "Yes." To prove it, Verlaine must put his hands, palms upwards, on the table, and Rimbaud stabs them with a clasp knife. At the end of the play, soggy with absinthe and self-delusion, Verlaine remembers the incident, but in his memory, Rimbaud kisses his hands instead of stabbing them.

Most shapely of all, most contrived, and most satisfying is the repetitive use of the revolver in *The Philanthropist*. At the very beginning of the play, one man faces two others trying to convince them of his seriousness. At the end of his argument, he places a revolver to his head – and says "Bang!": we discover he has been reading a play to them. But at the end of that scene, to convince them that suicide can be justified, he places the same revolver to his mouth and pulls the trigger, and the revolver is loaded, and he most spectacularly kills himself. And at the end of the play, Philip takes a pistol from a drawer of his desk, and for a moment we believe that he will also commit suicide, but the pistol is a cigarette lighter, and all he does is light a cigarette – except that we know that he has given up smoking because he fears death by lung cancer, so that to begin smoking again is a symbolic suicide, which is the only kind of suicide of which Philip is capable.

In *Treats*, the formalism becomes almost obviously neat. The opening of both the first and last scenes are identical. A man is listening to music, and paying no attention to the woman in whose flat he is living. They are interrupted by the woman's discarded lover, breaking a window. The lover in the first scene is the discarded lover in the last, and vice versa. Both the men, Patrick and Dave, are devourers. Patrick (kin to Philip of *The Philanthropist*) is a leech, dependent, unable to make decisions; Dave is a piranha, voracious and selfish. Both need a woman as food, and that is the role of Ann, the third side of the triangle – to be eaten. Though she is the most fully drawn of any of Hampton's women so far, she remains a patient, not an agent. Dave wins. The play, though comic, is not a comedy.

Treats is slight as well as neat, but slight plays may be satisfying; it is more economical and more clear-sighted than Coward's *Design for Living*, to which it has a family resemblance. *Savages* is not economical and in many ways unsatisfying, but it is also Hampton's most rewarding play so far, inasmuch as it has a much wider concern. That concern is with the genocide of the tribal Indians of the South American jungles; his original inspiration was an article in *The Sunday Times*. The *story* of the play, however, is the kidnapping of West, a minor Embassy official (British Council?) by urban guerillas as a hostage for the release of prisoners. West has a sentimental interest in the Indians: he reduces their myths to a "slim volume" of his own verse. His kidnappers have no interest in any such bourgeois notion as the duty to protect a self-sufficient but alien culture. Everyone loses. West is shot, his kidnappers (one assumes) captured, an Indian tribe wiped out by bombing. Because the scheme of the play is so large with three different strands – the Indians, West's interest in them, West's kidnapping, the three intertwining but never brought together – nothing is fully developed; the characters are less "real" than those of Hampton's other plays, and exist to be displayed, not explored. Yet I feel that this is the way – or at least *a* way – in which Hampton may go further, and grow. He has the time and talent to be one of the most important playwrights of his generation.

—John Bowen

HANLEY, James. British.   Born in Dublin, in 1901; brother of the novelist Gerald Hanley. Served in the Canadian Navy during World War I. Married to Dorothy Enid Heathcot; has one son. Merchant seaman and journalist. Has lived in Wales since 1931. Agent: David Higham Associates, 5–8 Lower John Street, Golden Square, London W1R 3PE, England. Address: The Cottage, Llanfechain, Gwent, Wales.

PUBLICATIONS

Plays

> *Say Nothing* (broadcast, 1961; produced London, 1962; New York, 1965).   Published in *Plays of the Year 27*, London, Elek, 1963.
> *The Inner Journey* (produced Hamburg, 1967; New York, 1969).   London, Black Raven Press, and New York, Horizon Press, 1965.
> *Forever and Ever* (produced Hamburg, 1966).
> *Plays One* (includes *The Inner Journey* and *A Stone Flower*).   London, Kaye and Ward, 1968.
> *It Wasn't Me* (produced London, 1968).
> *Leave Us Alone* (produced London, 1972).

> Radio Plays: *S.S. Elizabethan*, 1941; *Freedom's Ferry* series, 1941; *Open Boat* series, 1941; *Return to Danger*, 1942; *A Winter Journey*, 1958; *I Talk to Myself*, 1958; *A Letter in the Desert*, 1958; *Gobbet*, 1959; *The Queen of Ireland*, 1960; *Miss Williams*, 1960; *Say Nothing*, 1961; *A Pillar of Fire*, 1962; *A Walk in the World*, 1962; *A Dream*, 1963; *The Silence*, 1968; *Sailor's Song*, 1970; *One Way Only*, 1970; *A Terrible Day*, 1973; *A Dream Journey*, 1974.

> Television Plays: *The Inner World of Miss Vaughan*, 1964; *Another Port, Another Town*,

355

1964; *Mr. Ponge,* 1965; *Day Out for Lucy,* 1965; *A Walk in the Sea,* 1966; *That Woman,* 1967; *Nothing Will Be the Same Again,* 1968.

Novels

Drift.   London, Joiner and Steele, 1930.
Boy.   London, Boriswood, 1931; New York, Knopf, 1932.
Ebb and Flood   London, Lane, 1932.
Captain Bottell.   London, Boriswood, 1933.
Resurrexit Dominus.   Privately printed, 1934.
The Furys:
    The Furys.   London, Chatto and Windus, and New York, Macmillan, 1935.
    The Secret Journey.   London, Chatto and Windus, and New York, Macmillan, 1936.
    Our Time Is Gone.   London, Lane, 1940; with *The Furys* and *The Secret Journey,* New York, Dent, 1949.
    Winter Song.   London, Phoenix House, and New York, Dent, 1950.
    An End and a Beginning.   London, Macdonald, and New York, Horizon Press, 1958.
Stoker Bush.   London, Chatto and Windus, 1935; New York, Macmillan, 1936.
Hollow Sea.   London, Lane, 1938.
The Oceam.   London, Faber, and New York, Morrow, 1941.
No Directions.   London, Faber, 1943.
Sailor's Song.   London, Nicholson and Watson, 1943.
What Farrar Saw.   London, Nicholson and Watson, 1946.
Emily.   London, Nicholson and Watson, 1948.
The House in the Valley (as Patric Shone).   London, Cape, 1951.
The Closed Harbour.   London, Macdonald, 1952; New York, Horizon Press, 1953.
The Welsh Sonata: Variations on a Theme.   London, Verschoyle, 1954.
Levine.   London, Macdonald, and New York, Horizon Press, 1956.
Say Nothing.   London, Macdonald, and New York, Horizon Press, 1962.
Another World.   London, Deutsch, 1972.
A Woman in the Sky.   London, Deutsch, and New York, Horizon Press, 1973.
A Dream Journey.   London, Deutsch, and New York, Horizon Press, 1976.

Short Stories

The German Prisoner.   Privately printed, n.d.
A Passion Before Death.   Privately printed, 1930.
The Last Voyage.   London, W. Jackson-Joiner and Steele, 1931.
Men in Darkness: Five Stories.   London, Lane, 1931; New York, Knopf, 1932.
Stoker Haslett.   London, Joiner and Steele, 1932.
Aria and Finale.   London, Boriswood, 1932.
Quartermaster Clausen.   London, Arlan, 1934.
At Bay.   London, Grayson, 1935.
Half an Eye: Sea Stories.   London, Lane, 1937.
People Are Curious.   London, Lane, 1938.
At Bay and Other Stories.   London, Faber, 1944.
Crilley and Other Stories.   London, Nicholson and Watson, 1945.
Selected Stories.   Dublin, Fridberg, 1947.
A Walk in the Wilderness.   London, Phoenix House, and New York, Dent, 1950.
Collected Stories.   London, Macdonald, 1953.
Darkness.   London, Covent Garden Press, 1973.

Other

> *Broken Water: An Autobiographical Excursion.*   London, Chatto and Windus, 1937.
> *Grey Children: A Study in Humbug and Misery.*   London, Methuen, 1937.
> *Between the Tides.*   London, Methuen, 1939.
> *Don Quixote Drowned* (essays).   London, Macdonald, 1953.
> *John Cowper Powys: A Man in the Corner.*   Loughton, Essex, Ward, 1969.
> *The Face of Winter* (sketch).   Loughton, Essex, Ward, 1969.
> *Herman Melville: A Man in the Customs House.*   Loughton, Essex, Dud Noman Press, 1971

*   *   *

Diary entry: "Going to visit James Hanley for the first time − 'Come at 11 and I'll brew you a strong cup of tea.' As I approach the house in Camden Town I look up at the topmost window and observe the pale smudge of a face, like some look-out in a lonely lighthouse. I sense that it is Hanley. A hand waves and then the face disappears. I wait at the front door. He is dressed formally in a suit but wears brown carpet slippers. His blue eyes gleam from under wild eyebrows and soft untidy hair which he keeps brushing back off his forehead. He chuckles as though we are about to take part in a conspiracy and then leads me up stairs to the small front room where he hibernates."

Since that first visit I have often looked back over my many meetings with this unique and lonely artist and I have thought of the words of Antaeus in his play *The Inner Journey,* "My living dream is for the wastes of some high up, remote, lost, shut in and forgotten room. How I love silence. Peace." as well as of the words of another of his characters, Gareth, in *A Stone Flower,* "I'll find you a nice quiet place at the top of a house, and there'll be a window there, and when you look out you will see the sea and it will be very near."

So many of Hanley's novels are concerned with the sea but increasingly over the past years he has turned inland, and inward. Again, as Antaeus says, "I want to live on myself now, with myself, in myself." Yet Hanley is no pale introvert or self-indulgent narcissist. As a novelist he has long been recognised as a major writer − "Too long!" he might grunt. E. M. Forster called him a writer of distinction and originality; John Cowper Powys described him as a genius; and C. P. Snow rated him as one of the most important living authors, unsurpassed in qualities of compassion, humility and sheer power.

Then, for eight years, he stopped writing novels and turned to writing plays for the radio, television and theatre. Yet he regards the period of writing plays as a delusion. In a *Sunday Times* interview (12 May 1972), he said "Now I know I'm not [a playwright] and I'd better get back to the job that I know doing best."

Although his radio and television plays (bar one) have all been performed, Hanley has been singularly unlucky in the theatre. I tried at one point in the history of the Hampstead Theatre Club to mount a season of three of his plays; I also tried unsuccessfully, to cast his play *The Inned Journey,* and I commissioned a stage play from the television script, *A Stone Flower.* His best known play remains *Say Nothing.* Staged at the Theatre Royal, Stratford East, it was highly praised by critics, notably B. A. Young and John Russell Taylor, the latter subsequently describing it as "the most neglected play of the past two decades."

In this wild and fantastical black comedy he portrays three people in the North of England whose attitudes are so fixed that they are incapable of change. They take in a young lodger, Charlie. He tries to draw them out but comes, painfully, to realise that "nothing will get in, and nothing will get out." Mr. Baynes dreams of escaping from Mrs. Baynes but, as she tells him, "I know even about your dreams." As Hanley himself says, "*Say Nothing* is a total and final situation for three people lying on the rack of their own limitations is a moral morass − the character of these people is itself their fate. The moral right to drive them an inch further than this (as Charlie attempts to do) does not exist. They dream, but their dreams smoulder, and never catch fire." Yet it is not a dead household. Like Sartre in *Huis Clos,* Hanley portrays a living hell in which these people (as in so many of his plays) are their own judges, prisoners, and warders, unable to climb beyond their own natures. Charlie departs, saddened and bewildered, his idealism shaken. "Nobody can do anything for anybody," he cries. The others remain "drowned in the grey monotones of their tight and hidden lives." Some people belong inside, nourished by their hate, by their pride (like Mair, the young wife in *A Stone Flower*). These are the characters Hanley brilliantly portrays.

In *Say Nothing* Mrs. Baynes says at one point, "I never said this to you before, Baynesy, but sometimes I have a dread of the words that will come out of one's mouth – you never know where their journey ends." And in Hanley's plays people do say terrible and forbidden things, they wound and savage each other, scarring for life.

A Stone Flower is a dramatic poem on pride, carved as it were on a granite and slate. Set in mid-Wales at the turn of the century, it is the story of a young wife who will not forgive her husband, a sailor, who has, unwittingly, poxed her. Hanley is brilliant in his creation of smaller characters, and in this play he paints a powerful portrait of Mair's mother, a proud and lonely woman, as well as of the twisted bitterness of the chapel minister, Moesen Davies, who still lusts after her daughter – "she lives in my skull, old woman, and I remember once I split myself wide open so she can look inside." In a superb scene, set in the chapel by night, Hanley brings together Moesen Davies and Gareth, the young sailor husband, pain confronting pain. It has always suprised me that no one has thought of filming this play.

Of his other plays, *The Inner Journey* (which has been staged in America) is an extraordinary work of flawed genius. I say flawed because in it Hanley has created not merely a play requiring titanic actors but written one of the roles for a dwarf. It is therefore practically unstageable, at least until such time as a dwarf who is also an actor of magnitude can be found. It is said that at one point Scofield thought of doing the play and then chose to do King Lear instead. Perhaps the Royal Shakespeare Company will one day invite Scofield to reconsider it and bring over the American dwarf actor, Michael Dunne, to recreate his performance of Antaeus.

The story concerns a 70-year-old vaudeville artist (had it been written earlier here would have been a role for that great actor, Wilfred Lawson), his dypsomaniac wife, and their embittered dwarf son who is made to pose as a ventriloquist doll in a savage ventriloquist act. Of this play Hanley writes, "The journeys of Antaeus and Christian are always inward. Their dreams are as desperate as their hopes. Their love/hate relationship will flower either side of the grave, and the chain that holds them will always clang. They are people crucified by their imagination." Once again the play is rich with minor characters, Dickensian in their detail and richness of comedy. For though Hanley may write savagely – "Would you like me to draw my fingernail slowly round his skull and open the windows in his head?" – he has also a pungent, mordant, earthy sense of humour.

Few know that it was James Hanley who discovered the poet R. S. Thomas, and sent his poems to publisher after publisher until they were finally accepted by Rupert Hart-Davis. That first volume is dedicated to James Hanley. It is not suprising that Hanley, living for many years in a lonely Welsh valley, was drawn to Thomas and his poetry, such as the following, from *The Minister*, a radio play:

> "Beloved, let us love one another." The words are blown
> To pieces by the unchristened wind
> In the chapel rafters, and love's text
> Is riddled by the inhuman cry
> Of buzzards circling about the moor.

Like Thomas, James Hanley is an original whose intense and lonely vision burns as fiercely and as proudly as that of another great Welsh artist, David Jones, the poet and artist. Though Liverpool-Irish in origin, Hanley regards himself as wholly Welsh by adoption.

When finally the Welsh National Theatre comes to be built, it could do well to stage the works of James Hanley.

—James Roose-Evans

HANLEY, William. American.   Born in Lorain, Ohio, 22 October 1931. Educated at Cornell University, Ithaca, New York, 1950–51; American Academy of Dramatic Arts, New York, 1954–55. Served in the United States Army, 1952–54. Married Shelley Post in 1956 (divorced, 1961); Patricia Stanley in 1962; has two children. Recipient: Vernon Rice Award, 1963; Outer Circle Award, 1964. Agent: Georges Borchardt, 145 East 52nd Street, New York, New York 10022. Address: 190 Lounsbury Road, Ridgefield, Connecticut 06877, U.S.A.

PUBLICATIONS

Plays

> *Whisper into My Good Ear* (produced New York, 1962; London, 1966).   Included in
>   *Mrs. Dally Has a Lover and Other Plays*, 1963.
> *Mrs. Dally Has a Lover* (produced New York, 1962).   Included in *Mrs. Dally Has a
>   Lover and Other Plays*, 1963.
> *Conversations in the Dark* (produced Philadelphia, 1963).
> *Mrs. Dally Has a Lover and Other Plays* (includes *Whisper into My Good Ear* and *Today
>   Is Independence Day*).   New York, Dial Press, 1963.
> *Today Is Independence Day* (produced New York, 1965).   Included in *Mrs. Dally Has a
>   Lover and Other Plays*, 1963.
> *Slow Dance on the Killing Ground* (produced New York, 1964).   New York, Random
>   House, 1964.
> *Flesh and Blood* (televised, 1968).   New York, Random House, 1968.
> *No Answer*, in *Collision Course* (produced New York, 1968).   New York, Random
>   House, 1968.

> Screenplay: *The Gypsy Moths*, 1969.

> Radio Play: *A Country Without Rain*, 1970.

> Television Play: *Flesh and Blood*, 1968.

Novels

> *Blue Dreams; or, The End of Romance and the Continued Pursuit of Happiness*.   New
>   York, Delacorte Press, and London, W. H. Allen, 1971.
> *Mixed Feelings*.   New York, Doubleday, 1972.

*   *   *

With a trio of one-act plays and one full-length drama William Hanley achieved a reputation in American drama which seems to have satisfied him. During a three year period he made his appearance, created a play – *Slow Dance on the Killing Ground* – which not only reflected relevant contemporary issues but provided three acting vehicles, and disappeared from the New York theatre scene.

In spite of some serious dramaturgical weaknesses in his work Hanley was one of the few American playwrights who infused a certain amount of vitality into American drama of the early 1960's. His one-act plays are somewhat unstructured, talky, two-character plays. They are essentially conversations, but they involve perceptive thought, poetic tenderness, and the problems and feelings of generally believable people. Hanley's major concern is communication, that sometimes impossible connection between two people. Language, therefore, is important to him and his plays occasionally show a too luxuriant use of it, just as these same plays become overly concerned with discussion. Understandably, then, his sense of humanity, which is allied to his feelings for communication, frequently erupts in a distasteful sentimentality. He believes in the optimism which such sentiment suggests, however; and although his characters would seem to stumble around in an unhappy world, they do see something better. It is this vague idea of something better which he once explained as the major thought he wished his audiences for *Slow Dance on the Killing Ground* would take with them. It was a shrewd comment, however, for throughout man's history such points of view have not only been acceptable but ardently desired, especially in the theatre.

Whisper into My Good Ear presented the conversation of two old men who are contemplating suicide but change their minds. One can find a good ear for his problems; friends have value. Hanley's most popular one-act play, *Mrs. Dally Has a Lover*, is a conversation between a middle-aged Mrs. Dally and her 18-year-old lover. Before they part as the curtain falls and their affair ends the difficulty of conversation is dramatized as they are drawn in and out of their respective psychological shells. The sympathy created in this play for Mrs. Dally is further explored in *Today Is Independence Day* where she talks with her husband Sam who almost leaves her but decides to stay. Mrs. Dally also makes decisions about her own attitudes, and, although the ending of the play is sad and essentially unhappy, it is an affirmation of living.

The same comment can be made for *Slow Dance on the Killing Ground*, his only full-length Broadway Success. (*Conversations in the Dark*, a discussion of the problems of husband-wife infidelity, closed in Philadelphia.) At the end of Act I of *Slow Dance* Hanley introduced his third character. None of the three – a young Negro genius, a middle class white girl, a Jew who has denied his heritage and his family – can escape the violence of the world, that killing ground. In Act II each is unmasked, and in Act III a mock trial shows each one guilty. Although the play suggests that nothing can be done, there is a cohesiveness among the characters, a joint decision toward commitment and responsibility on this "killing ground," which tends to remove the play from sentimental and simply clever melodrama. Instead Hanley's insight into his characters and his obvious theme of contemporary significance have challenged critics to see *Slow Dance* as a quite substantial theatre piece of the past decade.

—Walter J. Meserve

HARDING, John.   British.   Born in Ruislip, Middlesex, 20 June 1948. Educated at Manchester University, 1966–69, B.A (honours) in drama 1969. Married to Gillian Harding. Agent: Michael Imison, Dr. Jan Van Loewen Ltd., 81–83 Shaftesbury Avenue, London W1V 8BX, England.

PUBLICATIONS

Plays

> *For Sylvia*, with John Burrows (produced London, 1972).
> *The Golden Pathway Annual*, with John Burrows (produced Sheffield, 1973; London, 1974).
> *Loud Reports*, with John Burrows and Peter Skellern (produced London, 1975).
> *Dirty Giant*, with John Burrows, music by Peter Skellern (produced Coventry, 1975).
> *The Manly Bit*, with John Burrows (produced London, 1976).

> Television play: *Do You Dig It?*, with John Burrows, 1976.

Theatrical Activities:

> Actor: **Plays** – all his own plays, and *My Fat Friend* by Charles Laurence, London, 1972; *Donkeys' Years* by Michael Frayn, London, 1976.

*   *   *

See the essay on John Burrows and John Harding on page 128.

HARE, David. British. Born in Sussex, in 1947. Educated at Lancing College, Sussex, and Cambridge University. Director, Portable Theatre, Brighton and London, 1968–71; Literary Manager, 1969–70, and Resident Dramatist, 1970–71, Royal Court Theatre, London; Resident Dramatist, Nottingham Playhouse, 1973. Recipient: *Evening Standard* award, 1971; Rhys Memorial Prize, 1975. Agent: Margaret Ramsay Ltd., 14a Goodwin's Court, London WC2N 4LL. Address: 39 Richborne Terrace, London S.W.8, England.

PUBLICATIONS

Plays

> *Inside Out*, with Tony Bicat, adaptation of the diaries of Kafka (also director: produced London, 1968).
> *How Brophy Made Good* (production Brighton, 1969).   Published in *Gambit* (London), 1970.
> *What Happened to Blake?* (produced London, 1970).
> *Slag* (produced London, 1970; New York, 1971).   London, Faber, 1971.
> *The Rules of the Game*, adaptation of a play by Pirandello (produced London, 1971).
> *Deathsheads*, in *Christmas Present* (produced Edinburgh, 1971).
> *Lay By*, with others (produced Edinburgh and London, 1971).   London, Calder and Boyars, 1972.
> *The Great Exhibition* (produced London, 1972).   London, Faber, 1972.
> *England's Ireland*, with others (also director: produced Amsterdam and London, 1972).

Brassneck, with Howard Brenton (also director: produced Nottingham, 1973). London, Eyre Methuen, 1974.

Knuckle (produced London, 1974; New York, 1975).   London, Faber, 1974.

Fanshen, from a book by William Hinton (produced London, 1975).   London, Faber, 1976.

Teeth 'n' Smiles (also director: produced London, 1975).   London, Faber, 1976.

Television Play: *Man above Men,* 1973.

Critical Study: by John Simon, in *Hudson Review* (New York), 1971.

Theatrical Activities:

Director: **Plays** – *Inside Out,* London, 1968; *Christie in Love* by Howard Brenton, Brighton, 1969, London, 1970; *Purity* by David Mowat, Canterbury, 1969; *Fruit* by Howard Brenton, London, 1970; *Blow Job* by Snoo Wilson, Edinburgh and London, 1971; *England's Ireland,* Amsterdam and London, 1972; *The Provoked Wife* by Vanbrugh, Watford, Hertfordshire, 1973; *Brassneck,* Nottingham, 1973; *The Pleasure Principle* by Snoo Wilson, London, 1973; *The Party* by Trevor Griffiths, tour, 1974; *Weapons of Happiness* by Howard Brenton, London, 1976.

*   *   *

David Hare's first dramatic effort with the Portable Theatre, a collaboration with Tony Bicat on an adaptation of Kafka's diaries called *Inside Out,* was, according to him, "a long steady stream of neurosis ... bashed out at our audiences." Essentially, it is about a young man freeing himself from the repressions of his bourgeois background; the adaptation is pleasingly modest and unpretentious in form and already has in embryo the down-to-earth qualities of clarity and tough-mindedness that characterise the author at his best.

Then followed two solo plays, again for Portable, which were full of talented ideas but did not really have the technique to sustain them convincingly. *How Brophy Made Good* is a slick, funny but finally disposable little piece about a would-be revolutionary corrupted by his success as a TV celebrity. It has a youthful energy and vitality but is only really interesting for its theme, the absurdity of any idealism that does not take into account the corrupt nature of our society, one that recurs in all his later plays. However, it contains shafts of the satirical, tongue-in-cheek wit that is Hare's particular forte and is certainly enjoyable, despite its ephemerality.

What Happened to Blake? is an intellectually and imaginatively ambitious exercise which remains no more than that, despite its undoubted cleverness. Blake's visionary quality as an artist is something that Hare half-admires and half-dismisses as something irrelevant to a modern society that catalogues "art" as just another consumer good. The spiritual purity of the poet's vision is evoked by throwing him and his work into surrealistic relationships with Pope, Eliot, Jane Austen, Wordsworth, Dr. Johnson and others who are more down-to-earch and rationally inclined than he.

In both these plays, then, we see ideals failing through not connecting with the real world of shabby, mean compromise. This theme becomes even more clearly marked in his two major works so far, the award-winning *Slag* and *The Great Exhibition. Slag* is about three teachers at a girl's boarding school who vow to abstain from sexual intercourse as a protest against male-dominated society, and as a start toward building an "ideal" community of their own. They become progressively more cranky, obsessed with their relationships with each other and correspondingly jealous of any contacts the others have with the outside world; and while this goes on, lose all their pupils. In the end, Elise, the most in touch with reality at any level, deflates their pretensions by announcing that the hysterical pregnancy she has manufactured to hold the relationship together has gone "like a great wet fart."

The Great Exhibition is technically a very accomplished piece of writing and takes the satirising of attitudes based on unreality a stage further. Its "hero" is Charlie Hammett, a disillusioned middle-class Labour M.P. in his early thirties who wants to opt out of his parliamentary world of "walking wounded, geriatrics." So he incarcerates himself in his flat for six weeks, while employing a seedy private detective to spy on his casting director wife, who is having an affair with a zombie, drug-crazy Australian. His wife leaves him, he spends his evenings "flashing" on Claphan Common and picks up Catriona, a former lesbian friend of his wife's. Hare's withering contempt for his characters' capacity for deluding themselves seems to exclude any compassion for a real understanding of their problems; this was also apparent in *Slag*, but there the novelty of the play's central situation disguised this contempt more effectively. So the overall feeling one gets from the play is a negative one despite its many good points.

Hare was also one of the seven writers of *Lay By*, a compelling little study of the sub-culture of pornography, based on a real-life rape case. It is impossible, though, for an outsider to disentangle who was responsible for what on this project, particularly as the play has an amazing stylistic unity.

Knuckle is another study of the futility of any kind of idealism that does not take into account the corrupt nature of our society. Curly, its kind-of-hero, is a hard-boiled cynic on the surface. Yet he cares enough about the mysterious death of his sister to want to investigate the murky truth about it. Hare's most daring conceit is to transpose the seedily romantic world of the Los Angeles private eye, to be found in the thrillers of Raymond Chandler and Ross Macdonald, to suburban Surrey, and to re-work the genre with his own distinct brand of wry, cool, deflating irony. On the face of it, there don't seem to be many cultural affinities between downtown L.A. and similar areas of Guildford; but Hare's main achievement is to make you see the comfortable complacencies of middle-class Home Counties life in a totally new light. The link between the two cultures is, of course, provided by the merchant capitalism that motivates the people in one as much as it does in the other. Curly's sister's demise is shown to be directly affected by the way that capitalism has distorted her personal relationships.

Brassneck, written with Howard Brenton, is a powerful and entertaining study in depth of a cross-section of Nottingham society since the end of the war, in the often murky area where national and local politics and business interests intersect. The play adds up to considerably more than the sum totaly of the two authors' individual talents.

Fanshen, on the other hand, displays the obverse side of the author's obsession with true and false idealism. It is an adaptation of William Henton's superb documentary study of the effect of the Chinese revolution on a small village in the late 1940's. "Fanshen" is a Chinese word meaning "to transform"; and Hare's play shows in microcosm the whole process of land reform as a small first step towards the achievement of socialism in this society. In a series of scenes, we see land being taken away from the old landlords and re-distributed to poor and middle peasants and the role of the Communists Party in raising the consciousness of the masses. Hare observes the process of revolutionary change meticulously and sympathetically. By inference, we feel that he believes the Chinese revolution to be an example of true idealism, based as it was on the reality of the corrupt Kuomintang regime that preceded it and not on an idealised version of what people should be.

Teeth 'n' Smiles, set during a May Ball in Cambridge in 1969, is described by its author as a "history play." It centres around Maggie Frisby's touring rock group. Maggie, a singer with superficial resemblances to the late Janis Joplin, knows instinctively that the pop culture of the middle and late 1960's is about to dissolve and drowns her knowledge in whisky, deliberately wrecking performances which have become no more than ego-trips. Before the ball ends, she burns down the wine tent. The play is essentially about how pop culture was absorbed by the Establishment and how its initial challenge to Establishment values did not have the political stamina to sustain itself.

From his last three plays, different as they are, it seems that Hare is groping toward a socialism that takes a complete account of the corruption that late capitalist society has forced on us.

—Jonathan Hammond

HASTINGS, Michael (Gerald).   British.   Born in London, 2 September 1938. Educated at the Imperial Services College, Windsor, Berkshire, 1944–46; Dulwich College Preparatory School, 1946–49; Alleyn's College, 1949–53. Recipient: Arts Council award, 1956; Encyclopedia Britannica Award, 1965; Maugham Award, 1972; Writers Guild Award, 1972; Emmy Award, 1972. Address: c/o National Westminster Bank, 1 Kensington High Street, London W.8, England.

PUBLICATIONS

Plays

   Don't Destroy Me (produced London, 1956; New York, 1957).   London, Nimbus, 1956.
   Yes, and After (produced London, 1956; New York, 1957).   Included in *New English Dramatists 4*, London, Penguin, 1962.
   The World's Baby (produced London, 1965).   Included in *Three Plays*, 1966.
   The Silence of Lee Harvey Oswald (produced London, 1966).   London, Penguin, 1966.
   Three Plays (includes *Don't Destroy Me; Yes, and After; The World's Baby*).   London, W. H. Allen, 1966.
   The Silence of Saint-Just (produced Brighton, 1971).   London, Weidenfeld and Nicolson, 1970.
   The Cutting of the Cloth (produced London, 1973).

Screenplay: *The Nightcomers*, 1971.

Television Plays: *For the West*, 1957; *Sucker*, 1961; *The Game*, 1961, revised version, 1973; *Confidence Class*, 1964; *Blue as His Eyes the Tin Trumpet He Wore*, 1967; *Camille '68*, 1968; *Ride, Ride*, 1970; *The Search for the Nile*, with Derek Marlowe (documentary in 6 parts), 1971

Novels

   The Game.   London, W. H. Allen, 1957; New York, McGraw Hill, 1958.
   The Frauds. London, W. H. Allen, 1960; New York, Orion Press, 1961.
   Tussy Is Me: A Romance.   London, Weidenfeld and Nicolson, 1970; New York, Delacorte Press, 1971.
   The Nightcomers.   New York, Delacorte Press, 1972; London, Pan, 1973.

Verse

Love Me Lambeth and Other Poems.   London, W. H. Allen, 1961.

Other

The Handsomest Young Man in England: Rupert Brooke: A Biographical Essay.
London, Joseph, 1967.

Manuscript Collections: Princeton University, New Jersey; University of Texas, Austin.

Critical Studies: *The Angry Decade* by Kenneth Allsop, London, Peter Owen, 1958; *Curtains*
by Kenneth Tynan, London, Longman, 1961; *Anger and After* By John Russell Taylor,
London, Methuen, 1962.

*   *   *

What is most remarkable about Michael Hastings' development is the total dissimilarity
of the later plays. Not that any playwright who makes his debut with a play written at the
age of 17 would be expected to go on quite in the way he started, but re-reading *Don't
Destroy Me* (staged in 1956) and *Yes, and After* (1957) today, it is hard to find any common
multiple with *The Silence of Lee Harvey Oswald* (1966) and *The Silence of Saint-Just* (1971).

Don't Destroy Me shows a tremendous fluency and flair for the kind of dialogue that
vividly projects a character and an emotional atmosphere, dragging an audience's sympathy
into a situation in which the self-pity of youngsters is justified by the pain inflicted on them
by the emotional clumsiness of the parents and step-parents. The basic conception is
sentimental, but only just, and the poetic monologues are overwritten, but not unbearably.
The young girl is particularly touching, and the construction is impressive not so much for
its handling of the plot as for dividing the focus between the characters in a way that
sustains interest in all of them.

Yes, and After tackles an intractable subject – the immediate aftermath of the rape of a 14-
year-old girl. Again the elephant-footed gaucherie of the parents in handling the situation is
used to great emotional effect, and the sensitivity of the boy and girl in *Don't Destroy Me* is
combined in the figure of the destroyed girl, who is very touching, particularly in her
fantasizing speeches about the "flower tree" in the garden.

The World's Baby, which was finally produced at the Embassy in 1965 with Vanessa
Redgrave in the lead, is highly ambitious, and fails not so much because Michael Hastings
was over taxing his talent as because of the diffusion which results from spreading the
action over 17 years. There are five acts, the first and last being set in 1959, the middle three
representing a long flashback showing the characters first at Cambridge in 1936, then in
Spain during the Civil War, then in England during and just after the World War. The
inevitable perfunctoriness of the backgrounds might have been acceptable if the device of
showing the girl and the two main men in her life at different ages had produced a series of
deep insights into their developing characters, but in fact the whole conception of their
development is fairly superficial.

The Silence of Lee Harvey Oswald is less obviously ambitious, but the intention was to
present all the available facts about him with "no intended prejudice at to whether he killed
Kennedy or not." If Oswald's wife and mother both emerge more vividly than the man
himself, the failure to bring him into focus seems inevitable in view of the task Michael
Hastings had set himself.

The play-in-production at the Hampstead Theatre Club was better than the play-in-script
that was published by Penguin. Besides cutting down on the amount of discussion, the

rewriting added to the amount of specific dramatic detail, as well as to the number of filmed inserts, though Oswald's humourless, heavyweight mother, whom we saw on the clips from newsreels, was worryingly different from Bessie Love's satirical performance in the part. The treatment of his wife, Marina, by both script and actress – Sarah Miles – was more successful. We saw how the shy, long-haired, naive Russian girl that Oswald brought to America became sly, hard-eyed and materialistic.

But "Theatre of Fact" is a contradiction in terms and the play fell between the unwieldy mass of factual material that was available and the central riddle that it was trying not to answer. Not that analysis of the facts in theatrical terms could have gone very far towards solving the mysteries, but it is impossible to put Oswald on stage and remain totally non-committal about what kind of man he was. Michael Hastings shows him as a man fond of weaving mysteries about himself to make himself interesting. We see him beating up his wife, battling with his formidable mother and withdrawing into reading biographies of American statesmen. He fails not only with both women but in his political love-affairs with Cuba and the Soviet Union. He escapes into fantasies and self-importance: "There's no reason why I shouldn't be President of the United States in twenty years." When we see him cleaning his rifle, he is like a child playing with a new toy, or like one of the destroyed adolescents of the early plays. His sulks, his sudden rages, his jealousy of his wife's friends are equally immature. If he killed Kennedy, these factors would be relevant. But did he? Michael Hastings neither believes in the single assassin theory nor that Oswald was the sort of man to join a conspiracy. But the play is not based on a belief in his innocence. It limits itself to collecting some biographical jigsaw pieces which, as the actor found, cannot possibly be fitted together into a satisfactory performance.

Even in 1971, when *The Silence of Saint-Just* was staged at the Gardner Centre at Sussex University, Michael Hastings had not altogether abandoned the idea of Theatre of Fact, and he incorporated into his play some of the speeches that the revolutionary leaders made at the assembly. The documentary material assorts very oddly with the invented dialogue, which presents them as sadistic and their women as masochistic.

As in the previous play, Michael Hastings had to face the problem of bridging private lives and public actions. The dialogue needs to convince us that these young men – Saint-Just was only 26 when he died, Robespierre 36 – were capable of doing what the history books tell us they did. The title refers to Saint-Just's depressive silence during his thirty-hour confinement in the Hotel de Ville before his execution, and Michael Hastings had the right instinct in wanting to make this into the play's crucial anti-climax. But by then too many of the climaxes have misfired. The treatment of Saint-Just's relationship with Louise Thorin is unashamedly romantic and most of the love scenes are embarrassing.

The Cutting of the Cloth is a play which draws directly on Michael Hastings' boyhood experience. When he left school he was apprenticed to a bespoke tailor for four years. The whole action of the play is set in the work-room of a Dover Street tailor between 1953 and 1955. The main characters are a 16-year-old Jewish apprentice and a 55-year-old Jewish tailor. Technical knowledge and terminology are put to good use but the pace is too leisurely to be effective.

—Ronald Hayman

HAWKES, John (Clendennin Burne, Jr.).   American.   Born in Stamford, Connecticut, 17 August 1925. Educated at Trinity School, 1940–41; Pawling High School, 1941–43;

Harvard University, Cambridge, Massachusetts, 1943–49, A.B. 1949. Served as an ambulance driver with the American Field Service in Italy and Germany, 1944–45. Married Sophie Goode Tazewell in 1947; has four children. Assistant to the Production Manager, Harvard University Press, 1949–55; Visiting Lecturer, 1955–56, and Instructor in English, 1956–58, Harvard University. Assistant Professor, 1958–62, Associate Professor, 1962–67, and since 1967, Professor of English, Brown University, Providence, Rhode Island. Special Guest, Aspen Institute for Humanistic Studies, Colorado, 1962; Visiting Professor of Creative Writing, Stanford University, California, 1966–67; Visiting Distinguished Professor of Creative Writing, City College of the City University of New York, 1971–72. Member, Panel on Educational Innovation, Washington, D.C., 1966–67. Recipient: National Institute of Arts and Letters grant, 1962; Guggenheim Fellowship, 1962; Ford Fellowship, 1964; Rockefeller Fellowship, 1968; Prix du Meilleur Livre Etranger, 1973. Agent: Harold Ober Associates Inc., 40 East 49th Street, New York, New York 10017. Address: 18 Everett Avenue, Providence, Rhode Island 02906, U.S.A.

PUBLICATIONS

Plays

  The Wax Museum (produced Boston, 1966).   Included in The Innocent Party: Four
    Short Plays, 1966
  The Questions (produced Stanford, California, 1966).   Included in The Innocent Party:
    Four Short Plays, 1966.
  The Innocent Party: Four Short Plays (includes The Wax Museum, The Questions, The
    Undertaker).   New York, New Directions, 1966; London, Chatto and Windus,
    1967.
  The Undertaker (produced Boston, 1967).   Included in The Innocent Party: Four Short
    Plays, 1966.
  The Innocent Party (produced Boston, 1968).   Included in The Innocent Party: Four
    Short Plays, 1966.

Novels

  The Cannibal.   New York, New Directions, 1949; London, Spearman, 1962.
  The Beetle Leg.   New York, New Directions, 1951; London, Chatto and Windus,
    1967.
  The Lime Twig.   New York, New Directions, 1961; London, Spearman, 1962.
  Second Skin.   New York, New Directions, 1964; London, Chatto and Windus, 1966.
  The Blood Oranges.   New York, New Directions, and London, Chatto and Windus,
    1971.
  Death, Sleep, and the Traveler.   New York, New Directions, 1974; London, Chatto
    and Windus, 1975.
  Travesty.   New York, New Directions, and London, Chatto and Windus, 1976.

Short Stories

  The Goose on the Grave and The Owl: Two Short Novels.   New York, New Directions,
    1954.
  Lunar Landscapes: Stories and Short Novels 1949–1963.   New York, New Directions,
    1969; London, Chatto and Windus, 1970.

Other

> Editor, with others, *The Personal Voice: A Contemporary Prose Reader*, Philadelphia, Lippincott, 1964.
> Editor, with others, *The American Literary Anthology 1: The 1st Annual Collection of the Best from the Literary Magazines.* New York, Farrar Straus, 1968.

Manuscript Collection: Houghton Library, Harvard University, Cambridge, Massachusetts.

Critical Studies: by Webster Schott in *The New York Times Book Review,* 1966; *The Fabulators* by Robert Scholes, New York, Oxford University Press, 1967; "Necessary Landscapes and Luminous Deteriorations" by Tony Tanner, in *Tri-Quarterly* (Evanston, Illinois), Winter 1971.

John Hawkes comments:

I discovered the theatre quite by accident, thanks to a Ford Foundation Fellowship for Poets and Fiction Writers which enabled me to work briefly with the Actor's Workshop in San Francisco in 1964–65. Under the stimulus of Herbert Blau and Jules Irving and their theatre company, I wrote four short plays in which I hoped to bring to the stage something of the language and vision of my novels. I am still interested in trying to satisfy this ambition.

*   *   *

John Hawkes, a fiction writer who received a Ford Foundation grant to work with the San Francisco Actor's Workshop, has produced four plays. Like his fiction, Hawkes' drama portrays the decline of Protestant white America. Unlike his fiction, however, Hawkes' plays focus on a confrontation of mounting intensity.

The Innocent Party is a punning title which refers at once to a tequila party and to an innocent victim. A millionairess visits her brother, his wife, and their daughter who live in an abandoned motel. The daughter is described in the Cast List as "part tomboy and part Aphrodite-as-young-girl, and as such approaches a mythic force." Desired by her rich aunt, surrendered by her impoverished parents, Jane seems to be the innocent victim of both, but she gradually gains control of all relationships. Hawkes' title finally implies that these are no innocent parties.

In *The Wax Museum* Bingo, a young female attendant, fondles the wax figures of a Royal Canadian Mountie, but she is interrupted by a museum visitor, the virgin Sally Ann. The play then traces the erotic education of Sally Ann by Bingo, using the wax museum figures as props: "Blood and ecstasy, that's the ticket." Bingo compares the wax figure to Sally Ann's absent but living fiancé. By the end of the play the two young women change clothes, and it is Bingo who answers the offstage call of Sally Ann's fiancé, while Sally Ann fondles the wax figure, murmuring the same endearments with which Bingo opened the play. There is, finally, little to chose between wax figures and flesh we mould into wax figures.

The Undertaker is based on an incident in Hawke's novel, *Second Skin* – the father's suicide. More vividly than fiction, however, the play juxtaposes presence and memory, since father and son are both in their mid-forties. The father, a small-town undertaker, shoots himself while sitting on a toilet lid, and the son recalls this event which took place when he was twelve years old. Desperately playing Brahms on his cello, the boy tried to ward off the suicide, but for the adult son the playing becomes a "phantom accomplice to his brutal act." The boy tries other ruses to prevent the suicide, but the father finally sits on the toilet lid and places the revolver against his temple. In a mixture of fear, desire, and re-enactment, the son comments on this scene, recalling that he has relived it for thirty years. On stage the undertaker completes his undertaking.

The Questions, Hawkes' best-known play, is also a dialogue between two people – a dialogue riddled with questions. In spite of questions, through questions, a Man and a Girl reconstruct a family – a Southern couple and their adolescent daughter. The interrogator seems to be the father, and the one who answers the daughter. But neither of them seems to know the fate of the mother and an Englishman who may have been her lover. Death hovers in the air as both Man and Girl talk about "the kill," which is the end of a foxhunt they intermittently describe. Though questioner and questioned give different accounts of that hunt, they seem to agree on the kill, And the Girl emphasizes this: "listen – my story was just as good as yours. I mean, they were the same, weren't they?" Questions and answers delineate the breakdown of the father's Puritan, humanitarian traditions before the triple threat of the foreign, the native foreign (Negro), and the animal. The playlong anguish of the questioning Man establishes him as the victim of "the kill." However, the theatricality of Hawkes' play arises from the relentless crescendo of suggestive questions, building a fatal foursome whose relationship comments upon a way of life – the passing of the genteel tradition.

—Ruby Cohn

HELLER, Joseph. American. Born in Brooklyn, New York, 1 May 1923. Educated at New York University, B.A. 1948; Columbia University, New York, M.A. 1949; Oxford University (Fulbright Scholar), 1949–50. Served in the United States Army Air Force in World War II. Married Shirley Held in 1945; has two children. Instructor in English, Pennsylvania State University, University Park, 1950–52. Advertising Writer, *Time* magazine, New York, 1952–56, and *Look* magazine, New York, 1956–58; Promotion Manager, *McCall's* magazine, New York, 1958–61. Recipient: National Institute of Arts and Letters grant, 1963. Address c/o Alfred A. Knopf Inc., 201 East 50th Street, New York, New York 10022, U.S.A.

PUBLICATIONS

Plays

    We Bombed in New Haven (produced New York, 1967; London, 1971). New York, Knopf, 1968; London, Cape, 1969.
    Catch–22, adaptation of his own novel. New York French, 1971; London, French, 1973.
    Clevinger's Trial, adaptation of chapter 8 of his own novel *Catch–22* (produced London, 1974). New York, French. 1973; London, French, 1974.

    Screenplay: *Sex and the Single Girl,* with David R. Schwartz, 1964; *Casino Royale* (uncredited), 1967; *Dirty Dingus Magee,* with others, 1970.

369

Novels

Catch–22. New York, Simon and Schuster, 1961; London, Cape, 1962.
Something Happened. New York, Knopf, and London, Cape, 1974.

*   *   *

You five idiots are either very smart or very
dumb. If you're very smart, you wouldn't be
here with us. But you are here with us, so that
means you're very dumb. But we're not very
dumb, are we, and we're here with you.
We're pretty bright, in fact. We're much
smarter than you but here we are *with* you. So
that means we may be much dumber than
you after all, doesn't it?

—*We Bombed in New Haven*

The witty self-contradiction, the Catch-22 that becomes an insanely logical trap, shapes
the grotesque military world of Joseph Heller's two plays. The prophetic daring of the
punning *We Bombed in New Haven* (the play unfortunately did "bomb" in that city and
New York) seems a flippant attempt to forestall criticism, like Warhol's titling his film
Trash. Lines like "If it's Pirandello, it's lousy Pirandello" further suggests that *We Bombed*
may be failing dramatically in order to work as propaganda, that an audience satisfied
emotionally and aesthetically would be incapable of responding to its anti-war message.
This Brechtian distancing cleverly keeps the audience aware that it is seeing a theatrical
presentation; the curtain, in fact, rises before the actors are in their places, and, in a puzzling
violation of Equity policy, are still arranging the sets. The action occurs at an Air Force base
from which pilots bomb not only distant targets like Constantinople, but also those
frighteningly closer to home like Minnesota, apparently the entire state. Such exaggerations,
and the frequent intrusions of actors dissatisfied with their roles create a mood of comic
dislocation gradually turning sinister because of the "real" disappearance of the actor
playing a soldier killed in an air raid. The conclusion of Act I destroys any vestiges of humor
with a lethal basketball game the officers use to condition the men. As one of the balls,
tossed offstage, explodes violently, and Captain Starkey teasingly threatens the audience
with another, the distinction between player and spectator vanishes permanently. War may
merely be a form of theatre, but theatre is potentially fatal to both actor and spectator.

Starkey, who insincerely talks to the rebellious Sgt. Henderson "like a father to a son,"
ironically confronts his own son at the end of Act II while selecting a conscript for a certain-
death bombing assignment. Though he helps his son escape, the son keeps returning under
different names – Brandwine, Mendoza (all children are presumably everyone's children).
Unable to save his son, Starkey tries desperately to return to the mood of the play's
beginning and declares he is only an actor playing a part: "There is no war taking place
now! There has never been a war." This ominous reference to the undeclared Vietnamese
war exposes the murderousness of what is officially non-existent, of the role that traps the
actor.

Though this climax effectively reinforces the theme, the ideological basis of the play is not
always convincing. Since Starkey's son begs his father to act like a loving parent and "smash
[the] face" of the Major in charge of the base, the play implies that some violence, even
carried to the point of murder, is justifiable. Admittedly, there is a vast difference between
the passionate defense of an offspring and the abstract destruction of Minnesotans, but the
latter atrocity may stem from a concatenation of motives deriving from feelings as profound
as the concern for a child. Having posited the polar opposites of violence, the play fails to

explore the middle area linking these extremes.

Another partly ideological, partly dramatic, weakness is the colorless character of the Major. Though the insane General Dreedle and Colonel Cathcart of the novel *Catch-22* were perhaps too hilariously lunatic (like vaudeville versions of Caligula) to seem as evil as the book demanded, they nonetheless dramatized the power that is a prison both for those giving and those receiving orders. Perhaps the approximately ten years separating the novel from *We Bombed* have made comic bureaucracy an unviable propaganda concept. Also, though the stage directions endow the Major with "a knowledge and authority that are ominous and inscrutable," and he enigmatically alludes to "the Colonel," the Major evades Starkey's question about the source of power: "Instead of replying the Major smiles slightly again, looks at the clock on the wall, then at his wristwatch." If, as these actions suggest, an inevitable time-table controls the universe of the play, then to what end does Heller stress the lethal aspects of an unassailable system?

Certainly the impossibility of rebellion in *We Bombed* contrasts with the optimistic picture of Yossarian's escape from the military trap in both the novel and play versions of *Catch-22*, which epitomize the hopeful anti-authoritarianism of the early 60's. Though superior to Mike Nichols' film adaptation, which turned the book into an anti-capitalist nightmare dominated by the sinister Milo Minderbinder, Heller's dramatization lacks the resonance of the novel. However faithful in spirit (sometimes the dialogue is a direct transcription from the novel), the play is primarily a series of amusing skits that fail to explode with the cumulative impact of the book. The Chaplain's reading of a letter to his wife frames the action of the play but is an inadequate substitute for the rich context which gives meaning to the individual episodes of the novel. The play also deprives Major-Major, the most brilliant creation in the novel, of his bizarre family background, and he emerges as a cartoon figure with no roots in an authenticating past. In the play's final scene he subsumes the role of the novel's Major Danby: "I'm a college professor who's trying to serve his country." Heller's consistent attack on the well-intentioned, but impotent intellectual is inevitable in a universe dominated by perverted logic which creates the insidious Catch-22 and the whole machinery of militarism.

A more serious character truncation weakens Nately's Whore in the play; without the novel's background of her initial cruelty to Nately that changes to love, her violent grief at his death seems inexplicable. However, she is still a terrifying Nemesis, whose murderous pursuit of Yossarian suggests not only humanity's irrational reaction to the trap of war, but also Yossarian's own image of guilt/involvement that triggers his defection. In dropping Yossarian's sentimentalized desire to rescue Nately's Whore's Kid Sister from the iniquities of Rome to a new life in Sweden, the play improves on the novel.

The play's nightmare recreation of Snowden's death, which haunts Yossarian in a series of images fusing only when he is ready to face the full meaning of the horror of war, is more vivid and thematically appropriate than the surrealistic episode in the novel. His refrain-like "There, there. There, there," to the grotesquely-mutilated Snowden, conveys simultaneously the profound need to express compassion through language when action is impossible, and the ultimate inadequacy of language to deal with suffering. However, since the play provides no real substitute for the third person voice of the novel, the supremely human and colloquial Yossarian becomes an uncomfortable spokesman for the stylized, godlike summation of the scene: "Man was matter, that was Snowden's secret. Drop him out a window and he'll fall. Set fire to him and he'll burn. Bury him and he'll rot, like other kinds of garbage. The spirit gone, man is garbage." These lines convey the force both of the play and of Heller's work in general. Men misuse language and logic to articulate causes like war or freedom, all ironically enbodying Catch-22. Man may be garbage without the human spirit, but this spirit, in turn, depends upon human feelings having their origin in man's physical nature: the passion and compassion that can destroy Catch-22 vivify Heller's plays. *We Bombed* is often technically brilliant, and the adaptation of *Catch-22*, though interesting primarily as an index to the force of the novel, also reveals a dramatic talent Heller should pursue.

—Burton Kendle

HELLMAN, Lillian (Florence).   American.   Born in New Orleans, Louisiana, 20 June 1907. Educated at New York University, 1923–25; Columbia University, New York, 1926. Married the writer Arthur Kober in 1925 (divorced, 1932). Reader, Horace Liveright, publishers, New York, 1924–25; Reviewer, New York *Herald-Tribune,* 1925–28; Theatrical Play Reader, 1927–30; Reader, MGM, 1930–32. Taught at Yale University, New Haven, Conneticut, 1966; and at Harvard University, Cambridge, Massachusetts; Massachusetts Institute of Technology, Cambridge; and the University of California, Berkeley. Recipient: New York Drama Critics Circle Award, 1941, 1960; Brandeis University Creative Arts Award, 1960; National Insitute of Arts and Letters Gold Medal, 1964; Paul Robeson Award, 1976. M.A.: Tufts College, Medford, Massachusetts, 1940; LL.D.: Wheaton College, Norton, Massachusetts, 1961; Rutgers University, New Brunswick, New Jersey, 1963; Brandeis University, Waltham, Massachusetts, 1965; Yale University, 1974; Smith College, Northampton, Massachusetts, 1974; New York University, 1974; Franklin and Marshall College, Lancaster, Pennsylvania, 1975; Columbia University, 1976. Member, National Institute of Arts and Letters; American Academy of Arts and Sciences. Agent: Don Congdon, c/o Harold Matson Company, 22 East 40th Street, New York, New York 10017. Address: 630 Park Avenue, New York, New York, 10021, U.S.A.

PUBLICATIONS

Plays

> *The Children's Hour* (produced New York, 1934; London, 1936).   New York, Knopf, 1934; London, Hamish Hamilton, 1937.
> *Days to Come* (produced New York, 1936).   New York and London, Knopf, 1936.
> *The Little Foxes* (produced New York, 1939; Sutton Coldfield, Warwickshire, 1946). New York, Random House, and London, Hamish Hamilton, 1939.
> *Watch on the Rhine* (produced New York, 1941; London, 1942).   New York, Random House, 1941; London, English Theatre Guild, 1946.
> *Four Plays* (includes *The Children's Hour, Days to Come, The Little Foxes, Watch on the Rhine*).   New York, Random House, 1942.
> *The North Star: A Motion Picture about Some Russian People.*   New York, Viking Press, 1943.
> *The Searching Wind* (produced New York, 1944).   New York, Viking Press, 1944; in *Collected Plays,* 1972.
> *Another Part of the Forest* (also director: produced New York, 1946; Liverpool, 1953). New York, Viking Press, 1947; in *Collected Plays,* 1972.
> *Montserrat,* adaptation of a play by Emmanuel Roblès (also director: produced New York, 1949; London, 1954).   New York, Dramatists Play Service, 1950; in *Collected Plays,* 1972.
> *Regina,* music by Marc Blitzstein (produced New York, 1949).
> *The Autumn Garden* (produced New York, 1951).   Boston, Little Brown, 1951; in *Collected Plays,* 1972.
> *The Lark,* adaptation of a play by Jean Anouilh (produced New York, 1955).   New York, Random House, 1955; in *Collected Plays,* 1972.
> *Candide,* music by Leonard Bernstein, lyrics by Richard Wilbur, John LaTouche and Dorothy Parker, adaptation of the novel by Voltaire (produced New York, 1956; London, 1959).   New York, Random House, 1957; in *Collected Plays,* 1972.
> *Toys in the Attic* (produced New York and London, 1960).   New York, Random House, 1960; in *Collected Plays,* 1972.
> *Six Plays.*   New York, Modern Library, 1960.
> *My Mother, My Father and Me,* adaptation of the novel *How Much?* by Burt Blechman

(produced New York, 1963).   New York, Random House, 1963; in *Collected Plays*,
1972.
The Collected Plays of Lillian Hellman (includes *The Children's Hour, Days to Come, The
Little Foxes, Watch on the Rhine, The Searching Wind, Another Part of the Forest,
Montserrat, The Autumn Garden, The Lark, Candide, Toys in the Attic, My Mother,
My Father and Me).*   Boston, Little Brown, and London, Macmillan, 1972.

Screenplays: *The Dark Angel*, 1935: *These Three*, 1936; *Dead End*, 1937; *The Little
Foxes*, 1941; *Watch on the Rhine*, 1943; *The North Star*, 1943; *The Searching Wind*,
1946; *The Chase*, 1966.

Other

An Unfinished Woman: A Memoir.   Boston, Little Brown, and London, Macmillan,
1969.
"Pentimento": A Book of Portraits.   Boston, Little Brown, 1973; London, Macmillan,
1974.
Scoundrel Time.   Boston, Little Brown, and London, Macmillan, 1976.

Editor, *The Letters of Anton Chekhov.*   New Yorh, Farrar Straus, 1955.
Editor, *The Big Knockover*, by Dashiell Hammett.   New York, Random House, 1966;
as *The Dashiell Hammett Story Omnibus*, London, Cassell, 1966.

Manuscript Collection: University of Texas, Austin.

Theatrical Activities:

Director: **Plays** – *Another Part of the Forest*, New York, 1946; *Montserrat*, New York,
1949.

Narrator – *Marc Blitzstein Memorial Concert*, New York, 1964.

*   *   *

Lillian Hellman's excellent dialogue is astringent. In *Toys in the Attic* one of the characters
says, "Everybody talks too much, too many words, and gets them out of order." Miss
Hellman's avoidance of inflated rhetoric is not stylistic idiosyncrasy; it is a form of moral
control (almost a repression) which instructs her not to say more than what she thinks is
true, precise, just. This characteristic leads to a notable scrupulousness in dramatic diction
and meticulous logic of dramatic construction.

What Miss Hellman "represses" is excess of sentiment, a fault which leads to disaster
through self-deception as well as to deception of others. The want of justness becomes
injustice, hence something which verges on crime. She expresses this in another speech in
Toys in the Attic: "The pure and innocent sometimes bring harm to themselves and those
they love and, when they do, for some reason that I do not know, the injury is very great."
One cannot help appreciating the modesty and balance suggested by the phrase, "for some
reason that I do not know."

Miss Hellman's suspicion of sentimentality – she often exorcises it by humorous contempt
– is at the root of such plays as *The Autumn Garden* and *Toys in the Attic*. In these somewhat
acrid comedies (not without their pathos) the characters – by no means evil – fool
themselves with dreams they will not fulfill or even attempt to fulfill. Their spiritual
prevarication makes them waste their or other people's lives and sometimes both.

Self-delusion is of many kinds. Amorousness, often depicted as a superlative blessing, may become overwhelming and destructive; it often stems from an incapacity to deal with other realities as fateful as love itself. Love doesn't necessarily conquer all! Lily in *Toys in the Attic* spreads havoc through a fierce attachment to her husband. A comfortable, cosy life may have its own sentimentality and is not infrequently the source of social inanition and hence disaster. That is the case in *The Searching Wind*. Mushy sentiment prevents us from recognizing the nature of our own motives; it beclouds reason and is a betrayal of justness. *The Children's Hour*, the dramatization of a personal tragedy, adumbrates the larger calamity in all manner of wich-hunting. Here sentimentality takes on the guise of righteous responsibility which destroys everyone.

The composition of Miss Hellman's artistic traits lends a certain pristine hardness to her work. This might arouse a suspicion of coldness were it not for her no-nonsense humor and, more especially, for her only half-declared but unmistakable admiration for every kind of excellence: self-discipline, loyalty, the determination never to injure others, and, most important, the unselfish persuit of humanly valid ideals.

One has only to read her letter to the House UnAmerican Activities Committee, a letter which is a model of tempered force and utterly probity, to discern how the qualities which I have noted as attributes of her dramaturgy have become integral with her total personality. Many of these same qualities are also evident in the final pages of *An Unfinished Woman*. They reveal her unremitting effort to be objective about herself. She is ever unsure that she knows the truth or even what the truth is. One thing is certain: she has an immense scorn of the phony in life or in art. She is hardheaded but never hardhearted.

Her "toughness" is a quest for the just. Most moralists are inclined to retreat from the consequences of their position. The one positive hero in all her plays in Kurt Muller in *Watch on the Rhine*, who is forced to kill in order to continue his fight against the curse of Nazism. Kurt must also leave his beloved family to fulfill his mission, knowing that he may never be able to return from it. Miss Hellman is in entire accord with the holy injunction to love one's fellow men, but she also understands the severe realism of "an eye for an eye." That is the harshest justice and she is prepared to accept it.

Miss Hellman has few peers in our country in the mastery of her craft. But her spirit is alien to the theatre. She cannot abide the truth of what Pirandello once set down in a paradoxical apothegm: "In the theatre the work of the author does not exist any longer." The theatre is nothing if it is not the art of collaboration and Miss Hellman has no talent for collaboration. She is a strong individual and a staunch individualist. She is first and foremost a writer, and it has always been a kind of martyrdom to her that after the arduous task of completing a script it must be taken over by those "intrusive strangers" – the actors, the directors, the scene designer, and others. One had only to hear her pronounce the words "a good writer" as if she were savoring a choice dish to sense her almost physical appreciation for the art of writing.

She is, above all, an admirable citizen in the realm of American letters and, what is perhaps even more rare, a clean and upright person.

—Harold Clurman
(First appeared as the Introduction to *Lillian Hellman: Playwright* by Richard Moody, 1972; reprinted by permission of The Bobbs-Merrill Co., Inc.)

HENDRY, Thomas. Canadian. Born in Winnipeg, Manitoba, 7 June 1929. Educated at Kelvin High School, Winnipeg, graduated 1947; University of Manitoba, Winnipeg,

1947; Manitoba Institute of Chartered Accountants, admitted to membership 1955. Married Irene Chick in 1958 (divorced, 1963); Judith Carr, 1963; has three children. Owner, Thomas Hendry, C.A., 1956–58, and Partner, Hendry and Evans, 1958–61, Winnipeg. Founder and Partner, Theatre 77, 1957–58, Winnipeg; Manager and Producer, Rainbow Stage, Winnipeg, 1958–60; Founder and Producer, Manitoba Theatre Centre, Winnipeg, 1958–63; Secretary-General, Canadian Theatre Centre, Toronto, 1964–69; Editor and Contributor, *The Stage in Canada*, Toronto, 1965–69; Literary Manager, Stratford Festival, Ontario, 1969, 1970. Since 1971, Founding Director, Playwrights Co-op and the Toronto Free Theatre, Toronto. Playwright-in-Residence, Banff Centre, Alberta, 1975–76. Recipient: Centennial Medal, 1967; Ontario Governor-General's Medal, 1969; Canada Council Senior Arts Grant, 1973. Agent: Playwrights Co-op, 8 York Street, Toronto M5J 1R2. Address: 34 Elgin Avenue, Toronto 5, Ontario, Canada.

PUBLICATIONS

Plays

> *Do You Remember* (televised, 1954; produced Winnipeg, 1956).
> *Trapped!* (for children; produced Winnipeg, 1961).
> *Do Not Pick the Flowers* (mime play; produced Winnipeg, 1962).
> *All about Us*, with Len Peterson (produced Winnipeg and tour, 1964–65).
> *15 Miles of Broken Glass* (televised, 1966).   Toronto, Nelson, 1968; revised version
>   (produced Toronto, 1969), Toronto, Playwrights Co-op, 1972.
> *Satyricon*, music by Stanley Silverman, adaptation of the work by Petronius (produced
>   Stratford, Ontario, 1969).
> *How Are Things with the Walking Wounded?* (as *The Walking Wounded*, produced
>   Lansing, Michigan, 1970; as *How Are Things with the Walking Wounded?*, produced
>   Toronto, 1972).   Toronto, Playwrights Co-op, 1974.
> *That Boy – Call Him Back* (produced Lansing, Michigan, 1970; Toronto, 1971).
>   Toronto, Playwrights Co-op, 1972.
> *You Smell Good to Me, and Séance* (produced Toronto, 1972).   Toronto, Playwrights
>   Co-op, 1972.
> *The Missionary Position.*   Toronto, Playwrights Co-op, 1972.
> *Dr. Selavy's Magic Theatre* (lyrics only), with Richard Foreman, music by Stanley
>   Silverman (produced Lenox Massachusetts, and New York, 1972).
> *Gravediggers of 1942*, music by Stephen Jack, lyrics by Thomas Hendry (produced
>   Toronto, 1973).   Toronto, Playwrights Co-op, 1973.
> *Aces Wild*, music and lyrics by Thomas Hendry (produced Toronto, 1974).
> *The Dybbuk* (lyrics only), book by John Hirsch, music by Alan Laing, adaptation of the
>   play by S. Ansky (produced Manitoba, 1974).
> *Naked at the Opera* (produced Banff, Alberta, 1975).   Toronto, Co-opera, 1976.
> *A Memory of Eden* (produced Banff, Alberta, 1975).
> *Byron* (produced Toronto, 1976).   Toronto Playwrights Co-op, 1976.
> *Confidence* (produced Banff, Alberta, 1976).

> Screenplays: *Box Car Ballet* (documentary), 1955; *A City in White* (documentary),
> 1956; *A House Divided* (documentary), 1957; *The Day the Freaks Took Over*, 1972; *Aces
> Wild*, 1974; *Private Places*, with Ron Kelly, 1976.

> Television Plays: *Do You Remember*, 1954; *The Anniversary*, 1955; *15 Miles of Broken
> Glass*, 1966; *Last Man on Horseback*, 1968; *I Was Never In Kharkov*, 1972; *Pickles*,
> 1976; *Royal Whee*, 1976; *Santa Claus from Florida*, 1976.

Other

The Canadians (on English-Canadian theatre).   Toronto, Macmillan, 1967.

Manuscript Collection: Toronto Public Library.

Thomas Hendry comments:

I cannot explain why I write plays, or why I choose the subjects that I do. The people in the plays reflect the people in my life – mostly they are outsiders. Paradoxically, I believe that if you examine anyone closely you will find that in some important area of his life he is an outsider, a non-participant. I believe that civilized society is a system of institutionalized violence directed at the individuals who make it up, and that to some extent each of us is aware of and opposes this violence. I believe that how people behave is as important as why they behave as they do. I believe that the damage we do to each other will only abate and finally cease when more perfect forms of communication – akin to ESP – are discovered and taught to everyone. Therefore I believe that dreams and nightmares and fairy tales are the only things worth writing or writing about. My plays say what I have to say.

*   *   *

Thomas Hendry fills his plays with articulate and urban characters, with artists, models, *literati* and successful businessmen. His is a world of chic parties, brittle dialogue, liquor and drugs and of sexual freedom of a marked homosexual ambiance – a world of falsity. In this world of stereotypes, the very shallowness of these fictional personalities is true to the real world they represent and which Hendry obviously knows well. Hendry's world is less erudite than is Waugh's but it is also mercifully less guilty than is Mart Crowley's and, therefore, more credible. At times, in fact, Hendry draws elements out of even these predictable characters that make them refreshingly full. Nevertheless, the strains of *Boys in the Band* and Albee are more than reminiscent and, when Hendry is imitative, he is as shallow as his characters and as boring. In a play like *How Are Things with the Walking Wounded?*, an unevenness arises between those sections which are original and contribute to the working out of a pattern, and those which seem superimposed snatches of Noël Coward, a difficulty in integrating material (especially lyrics) which persists in the later *Gravediggers of 1942*. This is unfortunate, as a very definite maturation can be traced from the early radio play *15 Miles of Broken Glass* to *How Are Things with the Walking Wounded?* and apart from the feeling of *deja vu* which besets it, *Wounded* is a fine play. Unfortunately also, Simone is correct in remarking of herself and her fellow characters, "we do tend to talk a lot, darling."

All the plays are concerned with human relationships based upon prostitution; it is the recurrent theme and the only motivation. Whether it is the often violent struggle between a civil servant and his mistress as in *You Smell Good to Me* or the bitter exchanges between a businessman and his beautiful, younger lover as in *How Are Things with the Walking Wounded?* and *The Missionary Position*, or the capitulation of the ingenue to Hitler's offers of wealth and power in *Gravediggers*, the love/hate/self-hate dualities are reworked with growing craftsmanship from play to play. Indeed, perhaps the most significant echo in each play is not to other writers, but to the earlier plays themselves, especially to the plays of the prolific period of publishing around 1972. Seen from various vantages, Albert-Steven-Willy is the same character, and Regan-Rene-Barbara, although they display different external characteristics and even genders, are simply facets of the hustler figure.

The cast of *How Are Things with the Walking Wounded?* is described by its *provocateur* as "a group of irresponsible children." It appears that throughout 1972, Hendry was becoming more and more responsible in his handling of these children. Unfortunately, his later play

Gravediggers of 1942 is less well handled in many respects. The thesis is a more intellectual statement of the Hendry theme, with the prostitution symbolically extended to a willing self-destruction of the Canadian psyche and the design enhanced by a counter-plot of campy, musical comedy satire. The problem lies in the often amateurish handling of the relation of song to plot and character and the clumsiness of the lyrics. This Toronto Free Theatre co-operative project was an exciting experiment and a major step for Hendry but it remains only an experiment in need of revision and completion. The play is, however, a statement of a growing sense of theatricality and of a larger vision and again convinces the reader of the possibility of Tom Hendry's writing a truly excellent play.

—S. R. Gilbert

HENSHAW, James Ene.   Nigerian.   Born in Calabar, in 1924. Educated at Christ the King College, Onitsha; National University of Ireland, Dublin, M.D. Married; has five children. Writes in Efik and English. Recipient: Henry Carr Memorial Cup, 1952. Address: c/o University of London Press, Warwick Lane, London, EC4P 4AH, England.

PUBLICATIONS

Plays

>   *This Is Our Chance : Plays from West Africa* (includes *The Jewels of the Crown, A Man of Character, This is Our Chance*).   London, University of London Press, 1957.
>   *Children of the Goddess and Other Plays* (includes *Companion for a Chief* and *Magic in the Blood*).   London, University of London Press, 1964.
>   *Medicine for Love.*   London, University of London Press, 1964.
>   *Dinner for Promotion.*   London, University of London Press, 1967.
>   *Enough Is Enough : A Play of the Nigerian Civil War* (produced Benin City, Nigeria, 1975).   Benin City, Ethiope Publishing House, 1976.

*   *   *

Although James Ene Henshaw has been criticized for the "simplicity" of his plays, he is undoubtedly one of the most frequently produced playwrights in West Africa. Part of the reason for this may be found in his statement that he has chosen to write "to the African audience," feeling that "the problem of how to get African countries or tribes to understand each other" is far more important that "explaining the African to the non-African." Like George Bernard Shaw, Henshaw envisions his entertaining plays as having a positive impact on his society. (Also, like Shaw, Henshaw prefaces his plays with long introductions which are more essay that introduction.)

Presenting us with situations drawn from the head of contemporary Africa, Henshaw invariably manages to bring off his comic confrontations in such a way that the good are rewarded, the wrong are both chastened and instructed and the audiences are sent home remembering the uproarious scenes Henshaw is so adept at staging. His characters win immediate recognition and response from his audiences and range from juju priests and old maiden aunts who attempt to use magic in order to ensure success in a nephew's bid for political office to two friends who cheerfully employ all manner of treachery against each other to win promotion and the hand of the boss's daughter.

True, Henshaw's plays do not delve into the psychological depths or the metaphysical speculations of a Soyinka, but this is part of the reason for Henshaw's success – he knows his depth and keeps to it, writing competent, well-staged, sophisticated African comedies. In his own way, Henshaw is an important to the dramatic diversity and liveliness of Africa as is a genius such as Soyinka.

Moreover, like a number of other African writers, Henshaw is developing new directions in the use of the English language by non-westerners. He mentions his concern with the use of "mixed English" and employs it in his plays. Pidgin English, ungrammatical (but quite understandable) popular usages, phrases which result from the transliteration of African idioms into English and the Queen's speech itself are all a vital part of the language Henshaw ably employs.

Since his early plays were written primarily for use by schools, James Ene Henshaw has been a popular and influential dramatist throughout most of anglophone Africa. There seems little doubt that this will continue to be so in the future.

—Joseph Bruchac

HERBERT, John.   Pseudonym for John Herbert Brundage.   Canadian.   Born in Toronto, Ontario, 13 October 1926. Educated in public schools, 1932–43; Art College of Ontario, 1947–49; New Play Society School of Drama, 1955–58; National Ballet of Canada School, 1958–60. Artistic Director, Adventure Theatre, Toronto, 1960–62, and New Venture Players, Toronto, 1962–65; Artistic Director and Producer, Garret Theatre Company, Toronto, 1965–70; Lecturer in Drama, Ryerson Polytechnical School, Toronto, Summers 1969–70, and York University, Toronto, Summer 1972. Actor, set and costume designer, prop man, lighting, stage and house manager, New Play Society, Toronto; dancer with Garbut Roberts' Dance Drama Company; actor and dancer with other companies. Lecturer in Drama, New College, University of Toronto, Summers 1973–76; Lecturer in Writing, Three Schools of Art, Toronto, 1975–76. Associate Editor, *Onion* magazine, Toronto, 1975–76. Recipient: Dominion Drama Festival's Massey Award, 1968 (refused). Agent: Mrs. Ellen Neuwald, 905 West End Avenue, New York, New York, U.S.A. Address: Apartment 1A, 1050 Yonge Street, Toronto, Ontario, Canada.

PUBLICATIONS

Plays

    A Marshmallow Drama (produced Canoe Lake, Ontario, 1942).
    Private Club (also director: produced Toronto, 1962).
    A Household God (also director: produced Toronto, 1962).
    A Lady of Camellias, adaptation of a play by Dumas (also director: produced Toronto, 1964).
    Closer to Cleveland (also director: produced Toronto, 1967).
    Fortune and Men's Eyes (produced New York, 1967; London, 1968).   New York, Grove Press, 1967; in *Open Space Plays*, edited by Charles Marowitz, London, Penguin, 1974.

World of Woyzeck, adaptation of the play by Büchner (also director: produced Toronto, 1969).

Close Friends (produced Toronto, 1970).

Born of Medusa's Blood (also director: produced Toronto, 1972).

Omphale and the Hero (produced Toronto).   Published in *Canadian Theatre Review 3* (Toronto), 1974.

Some Angry Summer Songs (includes *The Pearl Divers, Beer Room, Close Friends, The Dinosaurs*) (produced Toronto, 1974).   Vancouver , Talonbooks, 1976

Critical Studies: by Nathan Cohen, in *Canadian Writing Today*, London, Penguin, 1970; by Neil Carson, in *Twentieth Century Literature* (Los Angeles), July 1972; *Dramatists in Canada* by Ann P. Messenger, Vancouver, University of British Columbia Press, 1972.

Theatrical Activities:

Director: **Plays** – *Mourning Becomes Electra* by O'Neill, Toronto, 1957; Adventure Theatre, Toronto: *The Chalk Garden* by Enid Bagnold, 1961, and *Dear Brutus* by James Barrie, 1962; New Venture Players, Toronto: *Private Club* and *A Household God*, 1962, and *A Lady of Camellias*, 1964; Garret Theatre, Toronto: *The Maids* by Jean Genet and *Escurial* by Michel de Ghelderode, 1965, *The Sea Gull* by Chekhov, 1966, *Closer to Cleveland*, 1967, *Doberman* by David Windsor and *Gin Rummy* by S. Bordenvik, 1968, and *World of Woyzeck*, 1969; *Born of Medusa's Blood*, Toronto, 1972; *Some Angry Summer Songs*, Toronto, 1974; *The Gnädiges Fräulein* by Tennessee Williams, Toronto, 1976.

Actor: **Plays** – Shylock in *The Merchant of Venice*, Toronto, 1939; Thisbe in *A Midsummer Night's Dream*, Toronto, 1939; Juliet in *Romeo and Juliet*, Toronto, 1940; Father in *The Monkey's Paw* by W. W. Jacobs and L. N. Parker, Toronto, 1941; Farmer in *The Arkansas Traveller*, Toronto, 1942; Singer in *The Rising of the Moon* by Lady Gregory, Canoe Lake, Ontario, 1942; Carmen in *A Marshmallow Drama*, Canoe Lake, Ontario, 1942; Dancer in *Paris after Midnight* by Betty Rohm, Canadian tour, 1953; Tom in *The Glass Menagerie* by Tennessee Williams, Toronto, 1956; Octavius and Doctor in *The Barretts of Wimpole Street* by Rudolph Besier, Toronto, 1957; Orin in *Mourning Becomes Electra* by O'Neill, Toronto, 1957; Trigorin in *The Sea Gull* by Chekhov, Toronto, 1958; Dr. Sloper in *The Heiress* by Ruth and Augustus Goetz, Toronto, 1958; Professor Tobin in *The Druid Circle* by John Van Druten, Toronto, 1959; Mental Patient in *The Wall* by Vyvyan Frost, Toronto, 1960; Rhangda in *A Balinese Legend* by Garbut Roberts, Toronto, 1967; title role in *The Gnädiges Fräulein* by Tennessee Williams, Toronto, 1976.

John Herbert comments:

My life in theatre goes back as far as I can remember, for I fell in love with the art as a small child. I saw Leonide Massine dance the Cuban Sailor in a production of *Gaîté Parisienne* with a touring company. I saw and heard some of the greatest artists of the theatre at Toronto's Royal Alexandra, in the days when all artists of magnitude travelled the world for us, and I have never lost my passion as a member of the audience. I visit the theatre constantly to see and hear what others are thinking, feeling, and doing. Occasionally, the original thrilling convulsion of surprise returns, as when the Bolshoi Ballet dances, or when Laurence Olivier plays the father in O'Neill's *Long Day's Journey into Night*, or whenever I encounter a new young voice in the theatre, whether it be playwright, director, or player. I cannot say that I care more about writing a play than for directing, acting, designing, or dancing. I try to live in the theatre as one would revel as a swimmer in the ocean. The tides must always be felt, powerful, endless, timeless, and terrible as life itself.

*   *   *

John Herbert's reputation as the *enfant terrible* of Canadian drama arose almost entirely from the acclaim with which his *Fortune and Men's Eyes* was first greeted. That it was well written and without the worst aspects of nationalistic theatre recommended it highly to audiences weary of the sentimental quest for the great Canadian play.

Having said that, though, it is necessary to say that *Fortune and Men's Eyes* is not a great play. Its attractions are that it can easily be performed by a small cast with a modest competence and few resources for sets. Its weakness is that, for all its Sartrean setting, it is sentimental in another way – in its depictions of good and evil in "Western" terms. Smitty, the first-time criminal, who is at the center of the play, is essentially a Victorian character. He is corrupted not by defects present in his own character but by the circumstances of his confinement. In fact, we have very little sense of what sort of person he is, and in that sense his transformation from bewildered innocence to black awareness is artificial. His last speech – "I'll pay you all back" – reminds us of Malvolio's "I'll be revenged on the whole pack of you." But the comparison reveals the thinness of the conflict.

Something of this artifice is manifested in Smitty's diction. To Mona, the Blanche Dubois of this underworld whose brutalization is the moment of Smitty's awakening, he says, "You keep your secrets, like Greta Garbo – under a hat." And his revulsion from Mona is too articulate for the character that he is meant to be: "Let me out of here! I'll go to the bloody concert – anywhere – where there is life."

It is the tendency toward caricature that weakens the play and exposes it as trading both in a fashionable subject and on the need for social reform. Neither of these things would in itself have prevented the play from retaining some permanent stature – Ibsen's *Ghosts* is an example of similar defects – were it not for the fact that the characters seem manufactured. Mona is too weak, and "her" penchant for great books too exaggerated. (It is from "her" attempt to make analogies between the banal life of Kingston Pen. and Shakespeare's relation to Southampton that the somewhat precious title comes.) Queenie is credible enough as a caricature queen but not as a person. "Her" vocabulary is just not credible. "Does Macy's bother Gimbel's?" is not a phrase that we believe he, as a Canadian, in a Canadian prison, would use. The author is coming through. It is, in fact, in precisely this absence of particular places and definable voices that the play is weakest. To be everywhere is to be nowhere.

This is not to say that the play is without dramatic force. In its first production (in Toronto, not New York as the publishers wrongly claim) and again in its London premiere, it was shocking in the forthrightness of its language and action. But more than shock and a passable narrative are required in a play of stature. And not even these are present in his subsequent play *Omphale and the Hero*, where an archetypal whore-meets-hustler situation is the venue for a great deal of bathetic language and a plot that creaks at every joint. It is sad to see Herbert's talent wasted on bad Tennessee Williams.

—D. D. C. Chambers

HERLIHY, James Leo.   American.   Born in Detroit, Michigan, 27 February 1927. Educated at Black Mountain College, North Carolina, 1947–48; Pasadena Playhouse, California, 1948–50; Yale University Drama School, New Haven, Connecticut. Served in the United States Navy, 1945–46. Taught playwriting at City College of New York,

1967–68. Agent: Jay Garon-Brooks Associates Inc., 415 Central Park West, New York, New York 10025, U.S.A.

PUBLICATIONS

Plays

> *Streetlight Sonata* (produced Pasadena, California, 1950).
> *Moon in Capricorn* (produced New York, 1953).
> *Blue Denim*, with William Noble (produced New York, 1958; Swansea, Wales, 1970). New York, Random House, 1958.
> *Crazy October* (also director: produced New Haven, Connecticut, 1958).
> *Stop, You're Killing Me* (includes *Terrible Jim Fitch, Bad Bad Jo-Jo*, and *Laughs, Etc.*) (produced Boston, 1968; New York, 1969; *Terrible Jim Fitch* and *Laughs, Etc.*, produced London, 1973). New York, Simon and Schuster, 1970.

Novels

> *All Fall Down*. New York, Dutton, 1960; London, Faber, 1961.
> *Midnight Cowboy*. New York, Simon and Schuster, 1965; London, Cape, 1966.
> *The Season of the Witch*. New York, Simon and Schuster, and London, W. H. Allen, 1971.

Short Stories

> *The Sleep of Baby Filbertson and Other Stories*. New York, Dutton and London, Faber, 1959.
> *A Story That Ends with a Scream and Eight Others*. New York, Simon and Schuster, 1967; London, Cape, 1968.

Theatrical Activities:

Director: **Play** – *Crazy October*, New Haven, Connecticut, 1958.

Actor: **Plays** – roles at the Pasadena Playhouse, California; in *The Zoo Story* by Edward Albee, Boston and Paris, 1961. **Film** – *In the French Style*, 1963.

*   *   *

> So I'll get on a bus to Hell. Which will probably be another San Pedro – or Times Square or Tia Juana or Dallas – and I'll make out all right. I can make out in places like Hell. I've had practice.
>
> —*Terrible Jim Fitch*

Embattled innocence and vulnerable corruption, often shading into each other, define the limits of James Leo Herlihy's drama. The innocent, struggling in a hostile society they inadvertently threaten, sometimes perish, sometimes triumph, and occasionally become embodiments of the corruption they once challenged. In Herlihy's unpublished fantasy *Moon in Capricorn*, Jeanne Wilkes has an actual star in her heart, a condition producing untrammelled happiness, often objectified in her tendency toward impromptu dancing. Such behavior causes incomprehension, pain, and hostility in those around her (including a typical Herlihy psychotic cripple), and ultimately Jeanne's own death. Another unpublished play, *Crazy October*, derived from Herlihy's story "The Sleep of Baby Filbertson," focuses on a mother who tyrannizes over her simple-minded son until he unearths a literal family skeleton that could destroy her, a reversal suggesting both the victory of innocence and its transmutation into corrupt power. Despite the presence of Tallulah Bankhead in a showy role, the play failed to reach New York, perhaps because the conventional plotline, which punishes the wicked Mrs. Filbertson, lacked an irony consistent with the black-comic atmosphere and characterizations.

Herlihy's least representative play, *Blue Denim*, written in collaboration with William Noble, was both a critical and financial success and became a popular film. In some ways the archetypal version of the misunderstood adolescent theme of the 50's, *Blue Denim* partially transcends the genre through clever scenic symbolism and a sympathetic portrait of the adults. The setting, the Detroit home of Major Bartley, his wife, their 23 year old daughter Lillian, and 15 year old son Arthur, provides simultaneous views of both the main-floor existence of the family and the basement refuge of Arthur and his friends, Janet and Ernie, a combination hideaway and copy of the adult world upstairs (the boys' beer parodies the Major's serious brandy drinking). Though the play fails to explore the full possibilities of the semi-underground life of the adolescents, the setting suggests that their rebellion (the sexual union of Janet and Arthur, Janet's abortion, the boys' forgery to help pay for the abortion) will be short-lived. The young are already aping their elders.

The blue jeans of the title, a familiar image in Herlihy, stress Arthur's sexual vulnerability (in Herlihy's novels like *Midnight Cowboy* and *All Fall Down* the garment displays sexual aggressiveness or commercial availability). The innocence of Arthur and Janet causes her pregnancy and encounter with a shady abortionist. However, the painful experience does not destroy the youngsters, nor turn them into variants of the abortionist of Lillian's gangster suitor. Ultimately, Arthur and Janet will become part of the world of the Major, a muted version of Herlihy's familiar grotesque, whose "game leg" results not from eighteen years army service but from a ludicrous fall on a department store escalator. Though Arthur seems the logical protagonist and achieves an insight into his relationship with his parents, Janet's plight generates more interest; unfortunately, most of her anguish occurs offstage, and Arthur's once-removed reactions seem too inarticulate to reveal either his own feelings or to echo Janet's. Thus, in a sense, Major Bartley, the faintly ridiculous, faintly grotesque personification of the American Legion outlook, emerges as the focal figure and the catalyst in Arthur's maturation. Though the Major's sudden prominence unbalances the play, his changing role seems designed less to please a predominantly middle-aged Broadway audience than to convey the decency latent in such a man: his belief that feeding Arthur huge quantities of food will effect the desired reconciliation may be simplistic, but works convincingly in the play and amusingly underscores Arthur's youthfulness.

Herlihy's next dramatic work, *Stop, You're Killing Me*, is a collection of three one-act plays that experiment in varying ways with the monologue and attempt to create a nightmare vision of a violent America. In *Laughs, Etc.*, a single-character play in the Ruth Draper tradition, Gloria, the middle-aged wife of a lawyer, reminisces to unseen friends and husband about her recent party at which she fed vicariously off the lives of some East Village neighbors and the young female addict they had befriended. Gloria's nastiness inadequately disguises a vulnerability stemming from her childlessness, the source of her quasi-sexual, quasi-maternal obsession with her "safe" homosexual neighbors. Gloria's stress on her essential purity, as she describes the effect of a popular song heard across the courtyard, is predictably ludicrous: "It was as if we were all seven again, and taking our first Holy Communion together. There was this feeling of the oneness of humanity, the sort of thing Dostoevski raved about." However, the irony becomes obtrusive when Gloria, having spent generously for the party, refuses to provide $35 in drug money for the girl, who dies the next day from the forced withdrawal. Not only is it difficult to understand why none of the men living in an expensive building could find the necessary money, but it is also difficult to accept the play's assessment of the girl as a violated innocent whom only Gloria sees as grotesque: "Then Michael said, Gloria, I hope you'll try to bring her out, will ya? Try to get to know her a little? She's very worthwhile, she has all kinds of original thoughts, insights, ideas, she has her own little window on the world." This view seems as falsely sentimentalized as Gloria's reaction to the song. Despite Gloria's shallowness and bitchery, it is easy to share her indignation at the charge that "...this same dreadful Gloria is responsible for shelling out thirty-five smackeroos to save the life of every drug fiend in Manhattan." The play fails to make a $35 drug purchase an index either to the girl's purity or Gloria's compassion, and seems a rigged attempt to flay the would-be hip bourgeois. Since Gloria's auditors apparently respond to her lines, the monologue does not intensify her sense of isolation and remains merely a technical exercise.

Bad Bad Jo-Jo begins with what is essentially a telephone monologue by Kayo Hathaway, creator of the pop novel and movie figures, Bad Bad Jo-Jo and Mama, allegorical right-wing dispensers of violent law and order in a mother-dominated society. A poster depicts them as "a little old lady with tiny eyeglasses and sensible shoes leading an enormous apelike young man by a chain. The young man wears an Uncle Sam hat that is too small for him." The play parodies the Frankenstein myth when two young men invade Kayo's home and don the garb of Jo-Jo and Mama in order to murder their creator ritualistically. Though Kayo protests, "Is it really and truly necessary to point out to you that I do not kill people? I am in show business," he is responsible for the violence he commercializes. The play, least effective of the three because of its predictable conclusion and use of camp humor to satirize a camp culture hero like Kayo, merely dwells on varieties of corruption and creates neither a sense of justice at Kayo's death, nor sufficient irony to define the climax as more than an exercise in sadism.

Terrible Jim Fitch, Herlihy's best play, focuses on a man who robs churches, a character with rich folklore resonance and the allegorical dimensions of Spenser's Kirkrapine. In a variation of Strindberg's method in *The Stronger*, Jim addresses his monologue to the silent, but responsive Sally Wilkins, a former singer whose face he once scarred in a fit of rage. The motel room setting helps build a powerful sense of Jim's loneliness and frustration, as he half-threatens, half-begs a reaction from Sally:

> What am I talking about, Sal, something about sleeping in cars? Help me! Answer
> me, goddam you....Some day, some day, lady, you are not gonna answer me, and
> God help — I got it! Sleeping in cars! One night in a saloon in Key West, I got in a
> fistfight and when it was daylight I went to sleep in a car and had this dream
> about philosophy. There! I remembered — without anybody helping me.

Jim eventually loses his battle for control in the face of loneliness heightened by Sally's unspoken hostility (her behavior underlines the effectiveness of the monologue); but Jim is sometimes capable of raw tenderness: "If I was God, I'd hear you." However, his final plea apparently goes unanswered and leads to Sally's death: "Come on Sally, let me quit now. I'm beggin you. What's my name? Just say what my name is. You don't have to call me darling with it, but just say that one thing. Say my name. Once." The play illuminates Jim's blend of "criminal mentality" and vulnerability, and implies their genesis without sociological jargon or condescension. The inevitability of the conclusion heightens the tension and helps create that fusion of corruption and innocence toward which all Herlihy's plays aspire.

—Burton Kendle

HEWETT, Dorothy (Coade).   Australian.   Born in Wickepin, Western Australia, 21 May 1923. Educated at Perth College; University of Western Australia, Perth, 1941–42, 1959–63, B.A. 1961, M.A. 1963. Married Lloyd Davies in 1944 (marriage dissolved, 1949); Les Flood in 1950 (marriage dissolved), three sons; Merv Lilley in 1960, two daughters. Millworker, 1950–52; advertising copywriter, Sydney, 1956–58; Senior Tutor in English, University of Western Australia, 1964–73; Writer in Residence, Monash University, Melbourne, 1975. Poetry Editor, *Westerly* magazine, Nedlands, Western Australia, 1972–73. Since 1970, Member of the Editorial Committee, *Overland* magazine, Melbourne. Since 1975, Chairwoman, Australian Playwrights Conference, Sydney. Recipient: Australian Broadcasting Corporation Poetry Prize, 1945, 1965; Australia Council grant, 1973; Australian Writers Guild award, 1974; International Women's Year grant, 1976. Address: 49 Jersey Road, Woollahra, New South Wales 2025, Australia.

PUBLICATIONS

Plays

>   *This Old Man Comes Rolling Home* (produced Perth, 1968).   Sydney, Currency Press, 1976.
>   *Mrs. Porter and the Angel* (produced Sydney, 1970).
>   *The Chapel Perilous; or, The Perilous Adventures of Sally Banner*, music by Frank Arndt and Michael Leyden (produced Perth, 1971).   Sydney, Currency Press, 1972; London, Eyre Methuen, 1974.
>   *Bon-Bons and Roses for Dolly* (produced Perth, 1972).   Included in *Bon-Bons and Roses for Dolly, and The Tatty Hollow Story*, 1976.
>   *Catspaw* (produced Perth, 1974).
>   *Miss Hewett's Shenanigans* (produced Canberra, 1975).
>   *Joan* (produced Canberra, 1975).
>   *The Tatty Hollow Story* (produced Sydney, 1976).   Included in *Bon-Bons and Roses for Dolly, and The Tatty Hollow Story*, 1976.
>   *Bon-Bons and Roses for Dolly, and The Tatty Hollow Story*.   Sydney, Currency Press, 1976.

Screenplays: *Five Acts of Violence*, with Tom Cowan, 1976; *For the First Time*, with others, 1976.

Novel

>   *Bobbin Up*.   Sydney, Australasian Book Society, 1959.

Short Stories

>   *The Australians Have a Word for It.*   Berlin, Seven Seas, 1964.

Verse

>   *What about the People*, with Merv Lilley.   Sydney, Realist Writers, 1962.
>   *Windmill Country*.   Sydney, Edwards and Shaw, 1968.
>   *The Hidden Journey*.   Newnham, Tasmania, Wattle Grove Press, 1969.

> *Late Night Bulletin.*   Newnham, Tasmania, Wattle Grove Press, 1970.
> *Rapunzel in Suburbia.*   Sydney, New Poetry, 1975.

Other

> Editor, *Sandgropers: A Western Australian Anthology.*   Nedlands, University of
> Western Australia Press, 1973.

Manuscript Collections: Australian National Library, Canberra; Fisher Library, University of Sydney; Flinders University, Adelaide, South Australia.

*   *   *

It is hard to be indifferent to the work of Dorothy Hewett. Everything she has goes into it, provoking in the observer anger, distaste, admiration, extravagant praise and partisanship and, on two occasions, threat of court action. Firstly a poet, author of one novel and much left-wing journalism, she turned to playwriting in 1965 and since then has written seven plays. Her materials are the female psyche and the burden that men and society lay on the romantic imagination and the artistic soul. She disclaims any autobiographical intention, bending her mind as she does to the universal experience of the artist as woman through her own painful experience of the role; but it is nevertheless true that most of her characters can be identified by a style of language and imagery that refers noticeably to her own life and literary experience.

The progress of her work shows a steady motion from dramatic narrative to ritual poetry; and much of the discomfort she causes stems from her defiant intrusion of the private nature of the poetic experience into the naked public arena of the theatre.

Her first play, *This Old Man Comes Rolling Home*, remains her most immediately accessible and contains some of her best dramatic writing. It is the story of a household of Communist activists in Redfern, an inner Sydney suburb, in the early 1950's, the fierce time of the unsuccessful attempt by Sir Robert Menzies to ban the Communist Party. The play was a response to her own time in Redfern and is an acknowledgement of what she calls her "love affair with the working class."

Two early dramatic influences were Patrick White and Tennessee Williams, both of them moving out of realism towards a poetic interpretation of the ordinary man. Like them but in her own way she has since progressed into a landscape not "real" in the accepted sense but born of and reflecting the mind and sensibilities of the author and her characters. She made a leap into this landscape with *Mrs. Porter and the Angel*, a play in which a deranged woman teacher wanders through the gathering dark to the houses of her colleagues in search of an imaginary dog. The play is replete with black dog images of impotence and closet sexuality, of men and women destroying each other out of their own fantasies. And yet the play adds up to a kind of celebration of the good and evil in them all: it shares the optimism of *This Old Man*, a comedy of poverty which pays tribute to the force of life and laughter.

Journeys are endemic to Dorothy Hewett's writing. The major journey to date is that taken by Sally Banner in *The Chapel Perilous*, her most widely-performed play. In it she audaciously compares to the questing of Mallory's heroes a woman's search for spiritual truth through literary striving, sexual adventures, marriage, Communism, and public acknowledgement. In *Bon-Bons and Roses for Dolly* her heroine is a teenager of the 1940's, indulged by her emotionally-starved parents and grandparents and fed on the fairy floss of the Hollywood movie. In Act 2 Dolly returns, middle-aged, to the now crumbling Crystal Palace – a meeting of two empty and neglected monuments to second-hand dreams.

Her rock opera *Catspaw* in different style offers a drop-out guitar player in search of the real Australia. In a ribald grand parade of legendary characters the author postulates that most of these enlightened minds were stick-in-the-mud conservatives.

The Tatty Hollow Story and *Joan* return to the theme of the female predicament and demonstrate how women rise to the roles men create for them. The former ritually brings together the five lovers of the mysterious Tatty Hollow, whom each remembers in a different fantasy. At last, in retaliation for what she sums up as a wasted life, Tatty takes revenge on them and dissolves – and the play with her – into a poetic madness. *Joan* is the Joan of Arc story as a rock opera with four eponymous heroines – Joan the peasant, Joan the soldier, Joan the witch, and Joan the saint.

Dorothy Hewett's work is informed by a strongly literary background and an incorrigible romanticism which contrasts oddly with her critical armoury. Part of the romanticism is an attention-getting daring and a determination to prove that life can be beautiful – a desire so strong in some plays that the energy consumes an often-shaky structure. The source of her romanticism can be traced to the artistic isolation of her girlhood in Western Australia and her long allegiance to the Communist Party. It is reflected in the defiance of her heroes and in the strain often placed on them by the conflict between the author's life experience and her faith in a better world to come. She left the Party soon after writing *This Old Man* and Marxism leaves little trace in her writing for the theatre. Perhaps the weakness of her writing finally is that the goal of her poetic journeys remains undefined and the lack of definition in itself leads to failure. The great credo at the centre is always the force of the creative life of which poetry and sexuality are her principal images. The theme, recurrently and inevitably, is disappointment.

—Katharine Brisbane

HIBBERD, Jack. Australian. Born in Warracknabeal, Victoria, in 1940. Educated at Marist Brothers College, Bendigo, Victoria; University of Melbourne, M.D. 1964. Married; has one daughter and one son. Practising physician. Lives in Melbourne. Address: 87 Turner Street, Abbotsford, Victoria 3067, Australia.

PUBLICATIONS

Plays

> *Brain Rot* (produced Carlton, 1967; augmented version produced Melbourne, 1968).
> Section entitled *Who* published in *White with Wire Wheels*, 1970; *One of Nature's Gentlemen* in *Three Popular Plays*, 1976.
> *White with Wire Wheels* (produced Melbourne, 1967). Published with *Who*, London, Penguin, 1970.
> *Dimboola: A Wedding Reception Play* (produced Carlton, 1969). London, Penguin, 1974.
> *Customs and Excise* (also director: produced Carlton, 1970; augmented version, as *Proud Flesh*, produced Carlton, 1972).
> *Klag* (produced Melbourne, 1970).
> *Marvelous Melbourne*, with John Romeril (produced Melbourne, 1970).
> *Aorta* (produced Melbourne, 1971).
> *A Stretch of the Imagination* (also director: produced Carlton, 1972). Sydney, Currency Press, 1973; London, Eyre Methuen, 1974.

Women!, adaptation of the play by Aristophanes (produced Carlton, 1972).

Captain Midnight VC (produced Carlton, 1973).

The Architect and the Emperor of Assyria, adaptation of a play by Fernando Arrabal (produced Carlton, 1974).

The Les Darcy Show (produced Adelaide, 1974). Included in *Three Popular Plays*, 1976.

Peggy Sue (produced Carlton, 1974).

A Toast to Melba (also director: produced Adelaide, 1976). Included in *Three Popular Plays*, 1976.

The Overcoat, adaptation of a story by Nikolai Gogol (produced Carlton, 1976).

Three Popular Plays (includes *One of Nature's Gentlemen, A Toast To Melba, The Les Darcy Show*).   Melbourne, Outback Press, 1976.

Critical Studies: "Snakes and Ladders" by Margaret Williams, in *Meanjin* (Melbourne), no. 2, 1972; "Assaying the New Drama" by A. A. Phillips, in *Meanjin* (Melbourne), no. 2, 1973.

Theatrical Activities:

Director: **Plays** – several of his own plays, and *Bedfellows* by Barry Oakley, Carlton,1975.

Jack Hibberd comments:

I have striven over the last ten years to write specifically of an Australian experience on matters of social aberration and folly, history, politics, popular myth, and individual torment. As a playwright, I believe implacably in the necessity for practical involvement in theatre. Though my plays do not evolve out of laboratory and workshop situations, I believe theatre is the best context in which to attempt dramaturgical diversity and innovation.

*   *   *

Jack Hibberd, a foundation member of the influential Australian Performing Group, is a highly prolific writer whose reputation rests on a handful of plays: *White with Wire Wheels, Dimboola, A Stretch of the Imagination, Captain Midnight VC*, a few short plays, and his most recent success, a lively reconstruction of the life of the famous Australian singer, *A Toast to Melba*.

Hibberd's plays are for the most part vigorous, amusing satires on contemporary Australian society; individual psychology interests him less than observation of social patterns. Hibberd's most frequently performed theatre piece (it is not precisely a play) is *Dimboola*, which takes the audience, as guests, to a country wedding reception, with bad food, excruciating vocal renditions, lewd telegrams, and a bridal party which manages to become inebriated in record time. (The play is normally performed in theatre restaurants.) In *Dimboola*, Hibberd shows two complementary facets of social ritual: ritual as a trap, and ritual providing us with a role to play and a sense of community; *Dimboola* is both social celebration and social satire. Social ritual and social conformity are dominant subjects in Hibberd's plays, and in his first full-length play, *White with Wire Wheels* (still one of his best), he uses deliberately stereotyped characters to demonstrate individuality submerged in role-playing. Through the rituals of their obsession with cars and beer, his three "young executive" male characters preserve their superficial mateship, while they attempt to hide their basic fear of women beneath a contemptuous, off-hand attitude towards their girlfriends – all four female roles being played by the same actress: "Women are basically all the same."

Hibberd's most important play is the monologue *A Stretch of the Imagination*. The one character is an old man, Monk O'Neill, who lives alone in a dilapidated corrugated iron hut on top of One Tree Hill, apparently near to death. He acts out a series of fantasy-memories – it is hard to tell sometimes if he is remembering or imagining his encounters with a variety of men, women, and animals. These encounters, in which Monk is, of course, always the hero, cover a wide range of Australian myth. Critic Margaret Williams says in her introduction to the Currency edition of the play that he is "a distillation of the Australian legend of pioneer, old fossicker, footie hero, womaniser, and of solitary hero pitted against the land," and to these I would add, man about town and scholar. Once again social ritual is a major theme: Monk performs a whole series of superficially meaningless tasks, changing his clothes, fussing with the clock, altering his will, going through his possessions; he seems to be trapped by ritual, even though he is no longer part of society – but at the same time, kept alive by it. Monk is not a lovable character, but Hibberd, while undercutting his pretensions, rouses respect for his genuine stoicism and sympathy for his plight. He is modern Everyman, facing death without his predecessor's consolations of religion.

In recent years, the Australian Performing Group has been increasingly concerned with women's liberation. Hibberd's *Peggy Sue* was a rather uncritically feminist play which had to battle against the fundamental unlikelihood, or at best triteness, of its central situation; that is, three women, abandoned by their men, having to turn to prostitution to support themselves and their families. More successful and less self-conscious is *A Toast to Melba*, a cheerfully iconoclastic but genuinely admiring piece about one of Australia's few cultural heroines.

Jack Hibberd has a wide-ranging vocabulary and a love of words which ranges through appreciation of subtle, precise meaning to deliberately appalling puns. ("Conjunctivitis. As they say at funerals.") He has a Pinter-like appreciation of place names, and the ability to invest the most banal with a sense of mystery: Ultima, Echuca, Bundaberg, Sunraysia, Leongatha. A good deal of his humour is verbal, sometimes based on unexpected alliteration. In the end, the plays are, paradoxically, highly physical; there is in them (as in most contemporary Australian drama) a good deal of violence – someone normally gets knocked down at least once in a Hibberd play. There is also a good deal of knockabout farce. Particularly characteristic of Hibberd is the humour which is at the same time funny, and terribly painful. One startling example is the moment in *Captain Midnight VC* (a fiercely pro-Aborigine play) in which Ruby, an old aboriginal woman, is shot. Ruby is a sympathetic character with a touch of Mother Courage dignity; at one moment in the play, a character kicks away her crutch (she has only one leg) so that she falls to the ground, and then shoots her in the foot. The moment is horrifying, but audiences seem to be torn between the indrawn breath of horror, and at the same time, laughter: not I think for release of tension only, but because it looks funny. In the end, the shock of horror normally wins the day.

—Alrene Sykes

HILL, Errol (Gaston). Citizen of Trinidad and Tobago. Born in Trinidad, 5 August 1921. Educated at the Royal Academy of Dramatic Art, London, graduate diploma 1951; London University (British Council Scholarship), diploma in dramatic art 1951; Yale University, New Haven, Connecticut, B.A., M.F.A., D.F.A. 1966. Married Grace L. E. Hope in 1956; has four children. Drama Tutor, University of the West Indies, Kingston, Jamaica, 1952–58; Creative Arts Tutor, University of the West Indies, Trinidad, 1958–65; Teaching Fellow in Drama, University of Ibadan, Nigeria, 1965–67; Associate Professor of Drama, City University of New York, 1967–68. Associate Professor of Drama, 1968–69, and since 1969, Professor of Drama and Chairman of the Drama Department, Dartmouth College,

Hanover, New Hampshire. Founder, The Whitehall Players, Trinidad. Editor, Caribbean Plays series, University of the West Indies, 1954–65. Since 1971, Editor of the *ATA Bulletin of Black Theatre*, Washington, D.C. Recipient: Rockefeller Fellowship, 1958, 1959; Theatre Guild of America Playwriting Fellowship, 1961; Rockefeller Teaching Fellowship, 1965–67. Address: Hopkins Center, Dartmouth College, Hanover, New Hampshire 03755, U.S.A.

PUBLICATIONS

Plays

Oily Portraits (as *Brittle and the City Fathers*, produced Trinidad, 1948).   Trinidad, University of the West Indies, 1966.
Square Peg (produced Trinidad, 1949)   Trinidad, University of the West Indies, 1966.
The Ping Pong: A Backyard Comedy-Drama (broadcast, 1950; produced Trinidad, 1953).   Trinidad, University of the West Indies, 1955.
Dilemma (produced Jamaica, 1953).   Trinidad, University of the West Indies, 1966.
Broken Melody (produced Jamaica, 1954).   Trinidad, University of the West Indies, 1966.
Wey-Wey (produced Trinidad, 1957).   Trinidad, University of the West Indies. 1958.
Strictly Matrimony (produced New Haven, Connecticut, 1959).   Published in *Black Drama Anthology*, edited by Woodie King and Ron Milner, New York, New American Library, 1971.
Man Better Man, (produced New Haven, Connecticut, 1960; London, 1965; New York 1969).   Published in *The Yale School of Drama Presents*, edited by John Gassner, New York, Dutton, 1964.
Dimanche Gras Carnival Show (produced Trinidad, 1963).
Whistling Charlie and the Monster (carnival show; produced Trinidad, 1964).
Dance Bongo (produced New York, 1965; Ibadan, 1966).   Published in *Caribbean Literature: An Anthology*, edited by G. R. Coulthard, London, University of London Press, 1966.

Radio Play: *The Ping Pong*, 1950 (UK).

Other

The Trinidad Carnival: Mandate for a National Theatre.   Austin, University of Texas Press, 1972.
Why Pretend? A Conversation about the Performing Arts, with Peter Greer. San Francisco, Chandler and Sharp, 1973.

Editor and Contributor, *The Artist in West Indian Society: A Symposium*.   Trinidad, University of the West Indies, 1964.
Editor, *A Time and a Season: 8 Caribbean Plays*.   Trinidad, University of the West Indies, 1976.

Theatrical Activities:

Director: **Plays** – over 100 plays and pageants in the West Indies, England, the United States, and Nigeria.

Actor: **Plays** – over 40 roles in amateur and professional productions in the West Indies, England, the United States and Nigeria.

Errol Hill comments:

I was trained first as an actor and play director. I began writing plays when it became clear to me, as founder of a Trinidad theatre company (The Whitehall Players, later merged with The New Company to become The Company of Players), that an indigenous West Indian theatre could not exist without a repertoire of West Indian plays. The thrust of my work as playwright has been to treat aspects of Caribbean folk life, drawing on speech idioms and rhythms, music and dance, and to evolve a form of drama and theatre most nearly representative of Caribbean life and art. As Drama Tutor for the West Indies University I have carried this message to every part of the Caribbean and have written plays by way of demonstrating what could be done to provide a drama repertoire for Caribbean theatre companies.

*   *   *

Like Ben Jonson, William Congreve, and George Bernard Shaw, Errol Hill demonstrates a remarkable talent in two separate but closely associated artistic fields – namely, playwriting and literary criticism. Presently Chairman of the Department of Drama at Dartmouth College, Hanover, New Hampshire, he is the author of eight one-act plays and three full length dramas – the unproduced *The Silver Palace* (1948) and *What Price a Slave; or, Freedom Brothers Is ...* (1970), and his most famous *Man Better Man* (1954, revised with calypso verse in 1960). As a critic, Hill has edited the Caribbean Plays series and is the author of many articles and reports. *The Trinidad Carnival: Mandate for a National Theatre* is a definitive contribution to the study of rich folklore.

Man Better Man, Hill's most outstanding theatrical success, tells of a young suitor for the hand of Petite Belle Lily. His method is to challenge the village stick-fighting champion to a decisive duel. To the grand end of the colorful West Indian-setting the young lover resorts to the supernatural means of his vibrant culture. The suitor goes to the village obeahman, Diable Papa, and is subsequently cheated by the quack magician. He receives an herb, "Man Better Man" – a known cure for all which guarantees invincibility.

With characteristic humility Dr. Hill once wrote to me the following explanation:

It [*Man Better Man*] was for me little more than an experiment in integrating music, song, and dance into dramatic action, and using the calypso form with its rhymed couplets to carry the rhythm and make the transitions occur more smoothly....I never had an orchestral score of the music for the play. Since most of it is traditional-based, with a few numbers "composed by me,"...I simply provided a melodic line and left it to each production to create their own orchestration. Much of the music should appear to be improvised anyway with, ideally, the musicians carrying their instruments as part of the chorus on stage.

Hill's play, produced at the Yale School of Drama (1960 and 1962), in Trinidad (1965) England (1965) and New York (1969), celebrates, with ritualistic overtones, the triumphal pleasure of comedy. Richard F. Shepard says in the *New York Times* (July 3, 1969): "Mr. Hill has encapsuled an authentic folk tale flavor, letting us know something about a people, his people, whose history antedates steel drum bands. It is quaint, yet not condescending; ingenuous, yet not silly." On the surface the musical play gleams with a tropical panache; beneath are threatened subtleties and hidden meanings. Thus that magic, that mystery which the festive Greeks knew very well, which Plautus and Terence employed, which Shakespeare and Corneille explored, which Ibsen, Chekhov, and Willians understood, is engaged – no, released – by Hill on a richly set Caribbean stage. The connection between the author's skill in portraying effects obtained by the juxtaposition of the real with the assumed – one of the several functions of comedy – and his symbolic comic vision is the dynamic element of his chief work. The Dramatist, like Molière and Wilde before him, has arranged – through Mediaeval dramatic techniques, functional improvisation, the use of folk drama devices, and a mixture of fundamental Christianity and black magic – situations in which the two views clash and amuse by the abruptness of the contrast. However, let us proceed from the mask to the comedy.

C. L. R. James was deeply moved when Hill produced and directed a lengthy skit in Trinidad of dramatic, musical, festive, and political impact. He observed that the audience enjoyed it while "the authorities" did not approve. This venture to me is completely West Indian, and completely Greek. Sir William Ridgeway in *The Origin of Tragedy* (1910) and *The Dramas and Dramatic Dances of Non-European Races* (1915) could have been speaking of West Indian drama as well as Greek tragedy when he states that the heavy emphasis on ghosts, burial rites, and ancestor worship could not be derived from such a deity as Dionysus alone. The art must be related to hero and ancestor worship and the cult of the dead. For example, in *Man Better Man* Hannibal, Calypsonian, enjoys a position roughly analogous to the Anglo-Saxon court scop. He immortalizes the Island's heroes in song, and his repertoire constitutes a veritable oral chronicle. Pogo's homeric cataloguing of famous stick-fighters (p. 45) displays a continuity of an heroic tradition. Villagers manifest an awareness that they see tradition-in-the-making. "Excitement for so/More trouble and woe/A day to recall/When you grow old" (p. 47).

Mediaeval courtly conventions are carried off to the Caribbean setting in the most graceful and lyrical moods. Courtly love comes forward and all action stems from Tim Riscoe's desire to win a woman's affection through a demonstration of physical prowess. He expresses his longing in courtly love terms (pp. 51–2) for Petite Belle Lily. Tim displays those familiar symptons of "heroes" – the conventional lover's malady – when he says "I cannot eat by day, come the night/Cannot sleep, what a plight." Petite Belle Lily shows her indifference – perhaps Mediaeval, perhaps Petrarchan – to her lover's sorry state which is so fitting and proper to her courtly heroine-like state. Then the stick-fight – traditionally accompanied by a calinda – between Tim and Tiny Sata is reminiscent of a Mediaeval tournament whose proceedings are governed by ritualistic rigid customs. Aspects of trial-by-combat are ever present, along with the strong emphasis on personal honor and its defence. Indeed, stick-fighting is envisioned among these Island dwellers as a folk-institution. The fighter is a true folk-hero, like Beowulf or Achilles, who embodies not only the primitive drive of the Islanders, but also the qualities which they esteem most highly – physical courage, prowess in battle, personal honor. The reigning champion becomes a personification of the communal ideal.

The tension between Diable Papa – a fake and a counterfeit who, by means of voodoo, makes money from the primitive fears of the people – and Portagee Joe, supplies the intellectual focus of the drama. The obeahman – the holder of all the local rituals, spells, and incantations – represents the power of illusion and mass deception. Portagee Joe, who successfully challenges Diable Papa's authority, is the typical "village atheist" – whose cynicism or rationalism keeps him outside the circle of communal belief. "The social significance of the play lies in the relationship between Portagee Joe and his customers: They were not 'niggers' to him and he is not 'white' to them," writes Mrs. Stanley Jackson, in a letter to the *New York Times*. "A man could be judged as a man seventy years ago in Trinidad....The author of *Man Better Man* knew his material extremely well."

Lastly, Diable Papa, who is a fraud, nevertheless reflects some picaresque influences. He is somewhat reminiscent of the Mediaeval and Tudor horrific-comic depiction of stock diabolic figures. But the obeahman is balanced against a broader irony of the play's resolution. Tim Briscoe qua anti-hero, although defeated, emerges as a hero in spite of himself. Diable Papa, confounded by supposedly "supernatural" happenings and spectral visitations, is actually victimized by the very beliefs he has fostered in the villagers.

The drama is a picture of thoughtful delight. The audience becomes, even while reading

Man Better Man, an extension of the stage. One cannot help recalling throughout the work Michael Rutenberg's advice to directors: "Break through the proscenium!" The ceremonial interaction of chorus, dancers, actors, and calypsonian sequences – responsorial in nature (counter-melodies are used by Diable Papa and Minee, p. 64) – and the lively verse – incantatorial in quality and reflecting the natural rhythmic delivery of the West Indian speech pattern – all go to picture and re-emphasize the profundity of life, dying, and existence when tragic and comic values meet in confrontation. And, as Alvin Kernan says of Molière (in *Introduction to Drama,* 1963), one may say of Hill that his play, "...Like all comedies [shows] the value of *what works in life.*"

—Louis D. Mitchell

HIVNOR, Robert.   American.   Born in Zanesville, Ohio, in 1916. Educated at the University of Akron, Ohio, A.B. 1936; Yale University, New Haven, Conneticut, M.F.A. 1946; Columbia University, New York, 1952–54. Served in the United States Army, 1942–45. Married Mary Otis in 1947; has three children. Political cartoonist and commercial artist, 1934–38; Instructor, University of Minnesota, Minneapolis, 1946–48; Instructor, Reed College, Portland, Oregon, 1954–55; Assistant Professor, Bard College, Annandale-on-Hudson, New York, 1956–59. Recipient: University of Iowa Fellowship, 1951; Rockefeller grant, 1968. Address: 420 East 48th Street, New York, New York 10028, U.S.A.

PUBLICATIONS

Plays

> *Martha Goodwin,* adaptation of the story "A Goat for Azazel" by Katherine Anne Porter (produced New Haven, Connecticut, 1942; revised version, broadcast, 1959).
> *Too Many Thumbs* (produced Minneapolis, 1948; New York, 1949; London, 1951). Minneapolis, University of Minnesota Press, 1949.
> *The Ticklish Acrobat* (produced New York, 1954).   Published in *Playbook: Five Plays for a New Theatre,* New York, New Directions, 1956.
> *The Assault upon Charles Sumner* (produced New York, 1964).   Published in *Plays for a New Theatre: Playbook 2,* New York, New Directions, 1966.
> *Love Reconciled to War* (produced Baltimore, 1968).   Published in *Breakout! In Search of New Theatrical Environments,* edited by James Schevill, Chicago, Swallow Press, 1973.
> *"I" "Love" "You"* (produced New York, 1968).   Published in *Anon* (Austin, Texas), 1971.
> *DMZ* (includes the sketches *Uptight Arms, How Much?, "I" "Love" "You"*) (as Osbert Pismire and Jack Askew; produced New York, 1969).
> *A Son Is Always Leaving Home,* in *Anon* (Austin, Texas), 1971.

Critical Studies: by Saul Bellow in *Partisan Review* (New Brunswick, New Jersey), 1954; *The Theatre of the Absurd* by Martin Esslin, London, Methuen, 1961; *American Drama since*

World War II by Gerald Weales, New York, Harcourt Brace, 1962; *The New American Arts* by Richard Kostelanetz, New York, Horizon Press, 1965; by Albert Bermel, in *The New Leader* (New York), 1966; by A. W. Staub, in *Southern Review* (Baton Rouge, Louisiana), Summer 1970.

*   *   *

The economics of theatre are all too cruel to art, as a play costs so much more to produce than, say, a novel that many important texts are rarely, if ever, presented. Those particularly vitimized by such economic discrimination include older playwrights who have neither the time nor energy necessary to launch non-commercial productions on their own. There is no doubt, in my judgement, that Robert Hivnor has written two of the best and most original American post-war dramas, but it is lamentable that our knowledge of them, as well as his reputation, must be based more upon print than performance and that lack of incentive keeps yet other plays half-finished. The first, called *Too Many Thumbs* (1948), is more feasible, requiring only some inventive constuming and masks to overcome certain difficulties in artifice. It tells of an exceptionally bright chimpanzee, possessed of a large body and a small head, who in the course of the play moves up the evolutionary ladder to become, first, an intermediate stage between man and beast, and then a normal man and ultimately a god-like creature with an immense head and a shrivelled body. The university professors who keep him also attempt to cast him as the avatar of a new religion, but unending evolution defeats their designs. Just as Hivnor's writing is often very funny, so is the play's ironically linear structure also extremely original (preceding Ionesco's use of it in *The New Tenant*), for by pursuing the bias implicit in evolutionary development to its inevitable reversal, the play coherently questions mankind's claim to a higher state of existence. Hivnor's second play, *The Ticklish Acrobat*, strikes me as a lesser work, nonetheless exhibiting some true originality and typically Hivnorian intellectual comedy; but here the practical difficulty lies in constructing a set whose period recedes several hundred years in time with each act.

Hivnor is fundamentally a dark satirist who debunks myths and permits no heroes; but unlike other protogonist-less playwrights, he is less interested in absurdity than comprehensive ridicule. *The Assault upon Charles Sumner*, his third published work is an immensely sophisticated history play, regrettably requiring more actors and scenes than an unsubsidized theatre can afford, and an audience more literate than Broadway has. Its subject is the supreme example of liberal intellectuality in American politics – the nineteenth-century Senator from Massachusetts, Charles Sumner, who had been a distinguished proponent of abolition and the Civil War. Like the eminent historian David Donald, whose recent two-volume biography was well-received, Hivnor finds that Sumner, for all his saintliness, was politically ineffectual and personally insufferable. The opening prologue, which contains some of Hivnor's most savage writing, establishes the play's tone and thrust, as it deals with the funeral and possible afterlife of the last living Negro slave. "Sir, no American has ever been let into heaven." "Not old Abe Lincoln?" the slave asks. "Mr. Lincoln," Sumner replies, "sits over there revising his speech at the Gettysburg...."

Extending such negative satire, Hivnor feasts upon episodes and sumbols of both personal and national failure, attempting to define a large historical experience in a single evening. While much of the imagery is particularly theatrical, such as repeating the scene where Preston Brooks assaults Sumner with a cane, perhaps the play's subject and scope are finally closer, both intrinsically and extrinsically, to extended prose fiction.

—Richard Kostelanetz

HOFFMAN, William M.   American.   Born in New York City, 12 April 1939. Educated at the City University of New York, 1955–60, B.A. (cum laude) in Latin 1960 (Phi Beta Kappa). Assistant Editor, later Drama Editor, Hill and Wang, publishers, New York, 1960–67; Literary Adviser, *Scripts* magazine, New York, 1971–72; Playwright-in-Residence, Lincoln Center Student Program, New York, 1971–72; Playwright-in-Residence, Changing Scene Theatre, Denver, 1972; Artistic Director, Extension Theatre, New York, 1972; Visiting Lecturer and Artist-in-Residence, University of Massachusetts, Boston, Spring 1973. Member, New York Theatre Strategy. Recipient: MacDowell Colony Fellowship, 1971; Colorado Council on the Arts and Humanities grant, 1972; P.E.N. grant, 1972; Guggenheim Fellowship, 1974; National Endowment for the Arts grant, 1975, 1976. Agent: Helen Merrill, 337 West 22nd Street, New York, New York 10011. Address: 199 Prince Street, New York, New York 10012, U.S.A.

PUBLICATIONS

Plays

> *Thank You, Miss Victoria* (produced New York, 1965; London, 1970).   Published in *New America Plays 3*, edited by William M. Hoffman, New York, Hill and Wang, 1970.
> *Saturday Night at the Movies* (produced New York, 1966).   Published in *The Off-Off-Broadway Book*, edited by Albert Poland and Bruce Mailman, Indianapolis, Bobbs Merrill, 1972.
> *Good Night, I Love You* (produced New York, 1966).
> *Spring Play* (produced New York, 1967).
> *Three Masked Dances* (produced New York, 1967).
> *Incantation* (produced New York, 1967).
> *Uptight!* (produced New York, 1968).
>   *XX*
> *X X* (produced New York, 1969; as *Nativity Play*, produced London, 1970).
>   *X*
>   Published in *More Plays from Off-Off-Broadway*, edited by Michael Smith, Indianapolis, Bobbs Merrill, 1972.
> *Luna* (also director: produced New York, 1970).   As *An Excerpt from Buddha*, published in *Now: Theater der Erfahrung: Material zur neuen amerikanischen Theaterbewegung*, edited by Jens Heilmeyer and Pia Frolich, Cologne, Verlag M. Dumont Schauberg, 1971.
> *A Quick Nut Bread to Make Your Mouth Water* (also director: produced New York, 1970).   Published in *Spontaneous Combustion: Eight New American Plays*, edited by Rochelle Owens, New York, Winter House, 1972.
> *From Fool to Hanged Man* (produced New York, 1972).   Published in *M.E.A.L.* (New York), 1970.
> *The Children's Crusade* (produced New York, 1972).
> *Gilles de Rais* (also director: produced New York, 1975).

> Television Plays: *Notes from the New World: Louis Moreau Gottschalk*, with Roger Englander, 1976; *The Last Day of Stephen Foster*, 1976.

Verse

> *The Cloisters: A Song Cycle,* music by John Corigliano.   New York, G. Schirmer, 1968.

Other

Editor, *New American Plays 2,3*, and *4*.   New York, Hill and Wang, 1968, 1970, 1971.

Manuscript Collections: University of Winconsin, Madison; Lincoln Center Library of the Performing Arts, New York.

Theatrical Activities:

Director: **Plays** – *Thank You, Miss Victoria*, New Brunswick, New Jersey, 1970; *Luna*, New York, 1970; *A Quick Nut Bread to Make Your Mouth Water*, New York, 1970, Denver, 1972; *XXX*, New York, 1970; *First Death* by Walter Leyden Brown, New York, 1972; *Gilles de Rais*, New York, 1975.

Actor: **Plays** – Frank in *The Haunted Host* by Robert Patrick, New York, 1964; Cupid in *Joyce Dynel* by Robert Patrick, New York, 1969; Twin in *Huckleberry Finn*, New York, 1969.   **Film** – *Guru the Mad Monk*, 1970.

William M. Hoffman comments:

Until now the themes that have interested me have been concerned with what might be called "oneliness," the singularity of people, the consequences of that singularity.

In my first plays I dealt with requited and unrequited love, the distances between people that remain dark and unbridgeable. In *Thank You, Miss Victoria* I portrayed a man trying to reach his love oned through abject servility. In *Good Night, I Love You* the lovers communicate through a shared fantasy. In *Spring Play* couples strive for closeness by means of drugs, children, and suicide. In my early plays joy was to be obtained in the almost hopeless struggle of people finding each other.

Later I became interested in people who have abandoned hope in romantic love and who instead attempt a spiritual attainment. In *XXX* I depict Jesus as a man seeking to break the communal bonds that hold us to false values. In *A Quick Nut Bread to Make Your Mouth Water*, my contemplation takes place within the framework of a bread-baking lesson, in which two men and a woman withdraw from false relationships to maintain a positive though painful individuality.

But what about the not-so-innocent or the downright criminal? What about those *other* great individualists Adolf Hitler, Jack the Ripper, or Gilles de Rais? My last play is about Gilles, the sadistic child murderer who somehow in popular imagination became attached to the legend of Bluebeard. A dream of sincerity and serenity has given way for the moment to a curiosity about people any society would declare outlaw.

Was Gilles a thwarted lover, a mystic following a bloody left-hand path, or a man who just happened to develop a taste for murder as one might acquire a taste for vanilla ice cream? I guess my interest in "oneliness" has remained constant, although the kind of people I write about has changed considerably.

*   *   *

Willaim M. Hoffman's early work, *Spring Play*, is about a young man leaving home, girlfriend, and innocence and coming to New York City, where he meets a variety of exciting, corrupting people and experiences and comes to some grief in his growing-up. The style of the play is romantic and poetic, a kind of hallucinatory naturalism. Since then Hoffman has edited several anthologies of new American plays, and his awareness of contemporary styles and modes of consciousness is reflected in his own work. *Thank You, Miss Victoria* is a brilliant monologue in which a mother-fixated young business executive gets into a bizarre sado-masochistic relationship on the telephone. *Saturday Night at the Movies* is a bright, brash comedy, and *Uptight!* a musical revue. The eccentrically titled play *X X* has as characters Jesus, Mary, Joseph, the Holy Ghost, and God. It retells the story of Jesus's life in a personal, free-form, associative, hip, provocatively beautiful fashion. The play is conceived as an ensemble performance for five actors, and the Xs of the title designate their essential positions in the stage space. *Luna* is a light show. *A Quick Nut Bread to Make Your Mouth Water* is an ostensibly improvisatory play for three actors constructed in the form of a recipe, and the nut bread is served to the audience at the finish of the performance. In one production the author himself directed, he incorporated a group of gospel singers into the play.

Hoffman has continually explored forms other than drama, seeking a renewal of dramatic energies, attempting to expand theatrical possibilities and the audience's awareness. *From Fool to Hanged Man*, done in New York in 1972, is not a play at all but a scenario for pantomime, produced in collaboration with a choreographer, a musician and a lighting designer, based on imagery from the Tarot. By contrast with much of Hoffman's prior work, which make a point of the possibility of enlightenment, in which innocence was rewarded at least with edifying experience, in *From Fool to Hanged Man* the innocent hero moves blindly, almost passively through a bleak succession of destructive encounters and is finally hanged. Characteristically, the forces at work are not worldly or political but seem to exist in the individual state of mind. The beauty of the work only emphasizes its despair. *The Children's Crusade* is similar, another dance-pantomime of naive and sentimental innocence brought down by the mockery and hostility of the corrupt, historically worn out world. The new theme parallels a widespread shift of attitude among the younger generation in the United States, and to follow Hoffman's work is to observe a representative contemporary consciousness.

—Michael Smith

HOME, William Douglas. British. Born in Edinburgh, 3 June 1912. Educated at Eton College, Buckinghamshire; New College, Oxford, B.A. in history 1935; Royal Academy of Dramatic Art, London, 1935–37. Served in the Royal Armoured Corps, 1940–44: Captain. Married Rachel Brand in 1951; has four children. Progressive Independent Candidate for Parliament, Cathcart Division, Glasgow, April 1942, Windsor Division of Berkshire, June 1942, and Clay Cross Division of Derbyshire, April 1944; Liberal Candidate, South Edinburgh, 1957. Agent: Christopher Mann Ltd., 140 Park Lane, London W1Y 4BU. Address: Drayton House, East Meon, Hampshire, England.

PUBLICATIONS

Plays

Great Possessions (produced London, 1937).
Passing By (produced London, 1940).
Now Barabbas...(produced London, 1947).   London, Longman, 1947.

The Chiltern Hundreds (produced London, 1947).   London, French, 1949; as *Yes, M'Lord* (produced New York, 1949), New York French, 1949.

Ambassador Extraordinary (produced London, 1948).

Master of Arts (produced Brighton and London, 1949).   London, French, 1950.

The Thistle and the Rose (produced London, 1949). Included in *The Plays of William Doublas Home*, 1958.

Caro William (produced London, 1952).

The Bad Samaritan (produced Bromley, Kent, 1952; London, 1953).   London, Evans, 1954.

The Manor of Northstead (produced London, 1954).   London, French, 1956.

The Reluctant Debutante (produced London, 1955; New York, 1956).   London, Evans, 1956; New York French, 1957.

The Iron Duchess (produced Brighton and London, 1957).   London, Evans, 1958.

The Plays of William Douglas Home (includes *Now Barabbas...*, *The Chiltern Hundreds*, *The Thistle and the Rose*, *The Bad Samaritan*, *The Reluctant Debutante*).   London, Heinemann, 1958.

Aunt Edwina (produced Eastbourne, Sussex and London, 1959).   London, French, 1960.

Up a Gum Tree (produced Ipswich, 1960).

The Bad Soldier Smith (produced London, 1961).   London, Evans, 1962.

The Cigarette Girl (produced London, 1962).

The Drawing Room Tragedy (produced Salisbury, Wiltshire, 1963).

The Reluctant Peer (produced London, 1964).   London, Evans, 1964; New York, French, 1965.

Two Accounts Rendered: The Home Secretary and Lady M.P.? (produced London, 1964).

A Friend Indeed (produced Windsor, 1965; London, 1966).   London, French, 1966.

Betzi (produced Salisbury, Wiltshire, 1965; London, 1975).

The Queen's Highland Servant (produced Salisbury, Wiltshire, 1967; London, 1968).

The Secretary Bird (produced Manchester and London, 1968).   London, French, 1968.

The Grouse Moor Image (produced Plymouth, 1968).

The Bishop and the Actress (televised, 1968).   London, French, 1969.

Uncle Dick's Suprise (produced Salisbury, 1970).

The Jockey Club Stakes (produced London, 1970; Washington, D.C., 1972; New York, 1973).   London, French 1973.

The Douglas Cause (produced London, 1971).

Lloyd George Knew My Father (as *Lady Boothroyd of the By-Pass*, produced Boston, Lincolnshire, 1972; as *Lloyd George Knew My Father*, produced London, 1972). London, French, 1973.

The Bank Manager (produced Boston, Lincolnshire, 1972).

At the End of the Day (produced Guildford, Surrey, 1973; London, 1974).

The Dame of Sark (produced Oxford and London, 1974).

The Lord's Lieutenant (produced Farnhan, Surrey, 1974).

Screenplays: *Now Barabbas*, 1949; *The Amazing Mr. Beecham (The Chiltern Hundreds)*, 1949; *The Colditz Story*, 1957; *The Reluctant Debutante*, 1959; *Follow That House*, with others, 1960.

Television Plays: *The Bishop and the Actress*, 1968; *The Editor Regrets*, 1970; *On Such a Night*, 1974.

Verse

Home Truths.   London, Lane, 1939.

Other

Half-Term Report: An Autobiography.   London, Longman, 1954.

Theatrical Activities:

Actor: **Plays** – with the Brighton Repertory Company, 1937; Brian Morellian in *Bonnet over the Windmill* by Dodie Smith, London, 1937; Johnny Greystroke in *Plan for a Hostess* by Thomas Browne, London, 1938; Pym in *The Chiltern Hundreds,* London, 1948; Jimmy Broadbent in *The Reluctant Debutante,* London, 1955; Colonel Ryan in *Aunt Edwina,* Brighton, 1960.

*   *   *

Like any other writer who makes his home in the West End Theatre and lives there comfortably, William Douglas Home is often condemned for his failure to write the type of plays which belong to a stage quite different from that of which he is indubitably master. The son of an Earl and brother of an ex-Prime Minister, educated at Eton and New College, it might for a start be foolish to expect from him the sort of social actuality achieved by the playwrights most admired since the 1950's; the post-Osborne revolution made it perhaps too easy for its supporters to decide that some brands of reality are somehow more real than others; the reforming zeal of the revolutionary converts long ago decided that nothing good can be said of the light entertainment which is the real theatrical pursuit in the West End.

The judgement is unfair to Douglas Home; *Now Barbbas...,* his third play and first great success, was something of a revolution itself. A cleverly worked out study of a prison during the brief time between a condemned murderer's arrival and excution, it discreetly indicates the strains between warders and prisoners, the development of a homosexual friendship, the day-to-day existence of a variety of inadequates and the closeness of the criminal to the average, decent member of society. Oddly enough – for Douglas Home tends to write sentimentally – *Now Barabbas...*rises to the turning-point at which the murderer hears that his appeal has been dismissed.

From time to time, Home has turned from the neat flippancies with which he indulges conventional audiences. *The Thistle and the Rose,* a chronicle play nearer to the style of Gordon Daviot than that of William Shakespeare, studies the events that led to the destruction of a Scottish army at the Battle of Flodden, seeing the Scottish tragedy as that of a king who continued to live in the age of chivalry after the age of power politics had dawned. *The Thistle and the Rose* is neatly built and moves fluently; its dialogue is easy and natural; plainly its author knew exactly what he wanted to do and how to do it, working exactly within the limitations which deny him eloquence and depth. When, as in *The Bad Samaritan,* he attempts to exceed his limitations, the elegance of his design is weakened by the way in which chatacters slip through his fingers into sentimentality. He can convince us that an easy-going "bad" brother might marry the girl to whom his good, priest-to-be brother has made love to save her child from bastardy, but he cannot quite convince us that they would express themselves in terms that, despite their claim to intensity of emotion, are easy-going enough to sound glib.

The Queen's Highland Servant, his next successful serious play, deals with the strange, not quite comic friendship between Queen Victoria and the Scottish gillie, John Brown. Douglas Home's explanation of the incongruous association goes behind the scandalous stories to which it gave rise and thinks simply of a lonely widow who found a friend capable of treating her not as a Queen but as a little woman who liked to be looked after and mildly bullied. Because Brown could do this, her affection for him never noticed his coarseness. The play is a finely balanced, smoothly working machine; if we feel that Queen Victoria was a difficult, neurotically unbalanced woman and if, as the play monentarily suggests, Brown's feeling for her was more than simple, comradely frienship, the play avoids any consideration of the pain involved in the association; we can only say that the writer has precisely marked out the area in which he knows he can work most effectively, and he has not once set a foot outside it.

The Dame of Sark, a play about the German occupation of the Channel Islands, and At the End of the Day were greeted with limited enthusiasm, but there seems to be no reason why they should have scored fewer points than Lloyd George Knew My Father. As always the correspondence between the writer's aims and his techniques was complete. Betzi, reaching London ten years after its provincial premiere, left Home's admirers relatively cool, in spite of its tactful handling of the exiled Napoleon's final love affair and a masterly modulation from cheerful comedy into seriousness.

The rest of William Douglas Home's work is comedy, smart, brightly fluent, precisely timed to give each snappy answer some appearance of wit, and designed with considerable elegance. We notice that it finds its subjects in the stratum of society in which he was born, but that he finds the English upper classes, with their eccentricities, preconceptions and inherited way of life, to be as funny as they are charming.

The Earl's son, having failed to win a parliamentary seat – the family's seat – as a Conservative, is converted and fights it again (the victor having been shunted off to the Lords) as a Socialist. He is beaten by his father's butler, temporarily loses an American girl-friend who sees him as a traitor to the English tradition, and is, equally temporarily, loved by a Socialist housemaid. Only his father refuses to take any notice of the political excitements. The Chiltern Hundreds, which told this story in 1947 and was a great success on the stage before it became an almost equally neat film, grew, apparently, from the intense political involvement of its author's father's butler, whose relinquishing of the seat in The Manor of Northstead brought the same characters back to the theatre in 1954 in an equally easy-going, charmingly neat play. Family history, and Douglas Home's brother's renunciation of a peerage and tenure of the Prime Ministry apparently sparked off The Reluctant Peer on an equally successful career. The Reluctant Debutante finds its comedy in the splendours and miseries of a London "season," the fluttering possessiveness of a mother whose daughter, taking no pleasure in being "brought out," seem likely to chose the wrong husband, and her father's gently sophisticated method of solving the problem.

Even Douglas Home, however, has his misses. A Friend Indeed has a group of adults appalled by the progress of a love affair between a couple of nice young innocents who do not know that they are half-brother and half-sister; its less than total success is, perhaps, the result of the social tact in which the characters on the stage swathe the dangerous situation. The Secretary Bird was not only a standard Douglas Home box-office success; it is a play in which his natural easy comedy comes to grips with a serious theme – the probable destruction of a marriage – and controls it with as precise a sense of style as it had controlled the toothlessly enjoyable "political" comedies. Neatness and precision still make less than witty lines appear as masterpieces of brilliant repartee; the stylistic limitations are still both observed and exploited; it is the underlying seriousness of the theme that counts. Lloyd George Knew My Father moves further into the realm of serious comedy, dealing with a marriage that was worn out into dependence on a habitual boredom in which husband and wife no longer listen to each other until the wife plans her suicide; the laughter is, at times, both harsh and embarrassed. Between the two "serious" comedies, however, an unregenerate Douglas Home, in The Jockey Club Stakes, organised a pleasant tale of upper-class skullduggery and tergiversation to demonstrate that St. Paul was far too narrow-minded when he was shocked by the notion of doing evil that good may come.

The rejection of the type of play of which William Douglas Home is master, because it uses traditional ideas in a traditional form and is resolutely upper class, is as foolishly prejudiced as any other refusal to accept a body of work on its own terms. The theatre is, or should be, a home for all, including those who ask for little more than a peasant evening out; invariably to provide this in works that are honest, elegantly made and worthy of the attention of fine actors is to give the theatre notable service.

—Henry Raynor

HOPKINS, John (Richard).   British.   Born in London, 27 January 1931. Educated at Raynes Park County Grammar School; St. Catharine's College, Cambridge, B.A. in English. National Service, 1950–51. Married Prudence Balchin in 1954; the actress Shirley Knight, 1970; has two children. Worked as television studio manager; writer for BBC Televison, 1962–64. Since 1964, Free-lance Writer. Recipient: two Screenwriters Guild Awards. Agent: William Morris Agency, 4 Saville Row, London W.1. Address: 24 Malmains Way, Beckenham, Kent, England.

PUBLICATIONS

Plays

   A Place of Safety (televised, 1963).   Published in *Z Cars: Four Scripts from the Televison Series,* edited by Michael Marland, London, Longman, 1968.
   Talking to a Stranger: Four Televison Plays (includes *Anytime You're Ready I'll Sparkle, No Skill or Special Knowledge Is Required, Gladly My Cross-Eyed Bear, The Innocent Must Suffer*) (televised, 1966).   London, Penguin, 1967.
   A Game – Like – Only A Game (televised, 1966).   Published in *Conflicting Generations: Five Television Plays,* edited by Michael Marland, London, Longman, 1968.
   This Story of Yours (produced London, 1968)   London, Penguin, 1969.
   Find Your Way Home (produced London, 1970; New York, 1974).   London, Penguin, 1970; New York Doubleday, 1975.
   Economic Necessity (produced Leicester, 1973).
   Next of Kin (produced London, 1974.).

   Screenplays: *Thunderball,* 1965; *The Virgin Soldiers,* 1969; *Divorce – His, Divorce – Hers,* 1972; *The Offence,* 1973.

   Televison Plays: *Break Up,* 1958: *After the Party,* 1958; *The Small Back Room,* 1959; *Dancers in Mourning,* 1959; *A Woman Comes Home,* 1961; *A Chance of Thunder* (6 parts), 1961; *By Invitation Only,* 1961; *The Second Curtain,* 1962; *Look Who's Talking,* 1962; *Z Cars* series (53 episodes), 1962–65; *The Pretty English Girls,* 1964; *I Took My Little World Away,* 1964; *Parade's End* (serialization), from the novel by Ford Madox Ford, 1964; *Time Out of Mind,* 1964; *Houseparty* (ballet scenario), 1964; *The Make Believe Man,* 1965; *Fable,* 1965; *Horror of Darkness,* 1965; *A Man Like Orpheus,* 1965; *Talking to a Stranger* (4 parts), 1966; *Some Place of Darkness,* music by Christopher Whelen, 1966; *A Game – Like – Only a Game,* 1966; *The Gambler* (serialization), from the novel by Dostoevsky, 1968; *Beyond the Sunrise,* 1969; *The Dolly Scene,* 1970; *Some Distant Shadow,* 1971; *That Quiet Earth,* 1972; *Walk into the Dark,* 1972; *The Greeks and Their Gifts,* 1972; *A Story to Frighten the Children,* 1976; *Double Dare,* 1976.

*   *   *

   With well over 50 scripts for the TV series, *Z Cars,* and several short TV plays behind him, John Hopkins is not primarily a writer for the stage. It was on the newer medium that his reputation was made, and continues to stand at its highest. Indeed, one important critic called his tetralogy, *Talking to a Stranger,* "the first authentic masterpiece written directly for television," and there must be many others who, though perhaps charier of the word "masterpiece," would agree that no finer dramatic work has yet been seen on it. It is undeniably impressive in itself: it also makes a helpful introduction to the plays Hopkins was subsequently to write for the theatre, *This Story of Yours* and *Find Your Way Home.*
   Each of the four plays involves approximately the same day, and each is written from the

stance of a different member of the same family, the father, the mother and their two grown-up children, Alan and Teresa. All are characterised in striking depth; all, with the possible exception of the son, are thoroughly self-absorbed, more inclined to talk in monologue than dialogue; all, again except for him, stand in danger of being overwhelmed by their own self-destructive feelings; all, including him, are lonely and dissatisfied. The tetralogy opens with Teresa, bustling with frantic neurosis, and ends with the mother, dead by her own hand, and, between the two, Hopkins avoids none of the emotional collisions and unpleasantnesses that his plot throws up. Where most contemporary writers would hedge, or tread warily, or retreat into irony, he strides wholeheartedly and sometimes repetitively in, using straightforward, unpretentious, naturalistic language. Not suprisingly, he has been accused of dramatic overstatement, even melodrama.

But "melodrama" occurs when a writer presents extremes of feeling which are neither justified by his material nor empathetically understood by himself. In *Talking to a Stranger* the emotions on display are no more than the "objective correlative" of the dramatic situation, so painstakingly assembled; and, equally, Hopkins has a thorough grasp of the people he has created. He gives the impression of knowing, instinctively, how they would react to any new event. The question is: can we say as much for his stage plays? And the proper answer would seem to be: not quite.

This Story of Yours seems almost to be accusing Hopkins's scripts for *Z Cars* of romanticizing their subject, the police (though in fact they were widely admired for their wry realism). It is a study of the mind of Dectective-Sergeant Johnson, trapped in an unfulfilling marriage and at once disgusted and facinated by work that, characteristically, Hopkins describes in lurid detail. He breaks, and, in a scene of considerable dramatic intensity, beats to death an alleged child rapist: an act that is doubly self-destructive, since it wrecks his career and since it is clearly a way of sublimating his loathing for his own hideous thoughts and corrupt desires. *Find Your Way Home* mainly concerns two homosexuals, one young, unhappy and apparently a part-time prostitute, the other a married man, and ends with them settling down seriously to live together, having confessed their mutual love. By bringing on a distraught wife, and by accentuating the crudity and sadness of the homosexual subculture, Hopkins is at pains to make this decision as difficult as possible. But his view evidently is that it is the right one. The older man has "found his way home," to a more honest and fulfilling way of life.

From this, it will be seen that Hopkins's view of the world is bleak; and what seems "melodramatic" in his work is often only his way of emphasizing his belief that people are lonely and perverse, full of black thoughts and longings. If a relationship is capable of any success at all, which is doubtful, it can be only after each partner has accepted his own and the other's emotional inadequacies, as the protogonists of *Find Your Way Home* are beginning to do. It is an outspoken, unfashionable moral stance which, to be persuasive, may need the more thorough characterisation we find in *Talking to a Stranger*. There are psychological gaps left open in both Hopkins's stage plays, and notably in *Find Your Way Home*, whose scheme forces him to the dubious assumption that a young man who has gone very far in self-destructive promiscuity may be capable of sustained affection in a relationship as mature as any homosexual one can be. Hopkins achieves his effects by accumulating the emotional evidence as thickly as he can, and may therefore need more space, more time, than other contemporary writers in order to do so.

—Benedict Nightingale

HOROVITZ, Israel. American. Born in Wakefield, Massachusetts, 31 March 1939. Educated at Harvard University, Cambridge, Massachusetts, A.B. 1961; Royal Academy of Dramatic Art, London, M.A. equivalent 1963; City University of New York, M.A., Ph.D.

1972. Married Elaine Abber in 1959 (divorced, 1960); Doris Keefe, 1960 (divorced, 1972); has three children. Stage Manager, in and around New York, 1961–67; Playwright-in-Residence, Royal Shakespeare Company, London, 1965; Professor of Playwriting, New York University, 1967–69; Professor of English Literature, City College of New York, 1968–73. Since 1973, Fanny Hurst Professor of Theatre Arts, Brandeis University, Waltham, Massachusetts. Since 1968, regular contributor to the *Village Voice,* New York; since 1971, Columnist ("Words from New York"), *Magazine Littéraire,* Paris. Recipient: Obie Award, 1969, 1970; Rockefeller Fellowship, 1969; Vernon Rice Award, 1969; *Jersey Journal* Award, 1969; Cannes Film Festival award, 1971; New York State Council of the Arts Fellowship, 1971, 1975; American Academy of Arts and Letters Award in Literature, 1972; National Endowment for the Arts grant, 1974. Agent: Mary Dolan, Safier Office, 667 Madison Avenue, New York, New York 10021; or, Margaret Ramsay Ltd., 14a Goodwin's Court, London, WC2N 4LL, England. Address: c/o Safier Office, 667 Madison Avenue, New York, New York 10021, U.S.A.

PUBLICATIONS

Plays

    The Comeback (produced Boston, 1958).
    The Hanging of Emanual (produced South Orange, New Jersey, 1959).
    This Play Is about Me (produced South Orange, New Jersey, 1960).
    The Killer Dove (produced West Orange, New Jersey, 1963).
    The Indian Wants the Bronx (produced Waterford, Connecticut, 1966; New York and Watford, Hertfordshire, 1968; London, 1969). Included in *First Season,* 1968; in *Off-Broadway Plays,* London, Penguin, 1970).
    Line (produced New York, 1967; London, 1970). Included in *First Season,* 1968.
    It's Called the Sugar Plum (produced Waterford, Connecticut, 1967; New York and Watford, Hertfordshire, 1968; Lodnon, 1971). Included in *First Season,* 1968; in *Off-Broadway Plays,* London, Penguin, 1970.
    Acrobats (produced New York, 1968). New York, Dramatists Play Service, 1971.
    Rats (produced New York, 1968; London, 1969). Published in *Collision Course,* New York, Random House, 1968.
    Morning (produced Spoleto, Italy, and New York, 1968). Published in *Morning, Noon and Night,* New York, Random House, 1969.
    First Season: Line, The Indian Wants the Bronx, It's Called the Sugar Plum, Rats. New York, Random House, 1968.
    Leader (produced New York, 1969). With *Play for Trees,* New York, Dramatists Play Service, 1970.
    Play for Trees (televised, 1969). With *Leader,* New York, Dramatists Play Service, 1970.
    The Honest to God Schnozzola (produced New York, 1969). New York, Breakthrough Press, 1971.
    Shooting Gallery (produced New York, 1971). With *Plays for Germs,* New York, Dramatists Play Service, 1973.
    Dr. Hero (as *Hero,* produced New York, 1971; revised version, as *Dr. Hero,* produced Great Neck, New York, 1972; New York City, 1973). New York, Dramatists Play Service, 1973.
    The Wakefield Plays:
        1. *Alfred the Great* (produced Paris and Great Neck, New York, 1972; New York City, 1973). New York, Harper, 1974.
        2. *Our Father's Failing* (produced Waterford, Connecticut, 1973; New York 1974).

3. *Alfred Dies* (produced New York, 1976).

Clair-Obscur.   Paris,_Gallimard, 1972.

Play for Germs, with others (as *VD Blues,* televised, 1972).   With *Shooting Gallery,* New York, Dramatists Play Service, 1973.

The First, The Last, and the Middle: A Comedy Triptych (produced New York, 1974).

Spared, and Hopscotch (also director: produced New York, 1974).   *Spared* published in *The Best Short Plays 1975,* edited by Stanley Richards, Radnor, Pennsylvania, Chilton, 1975.

Turnstile (produced Hanover, New Hampshire, 1974).

The Primary English Class (produced Waterford, Connecticut, 1975; also director: produced New York, 1975).

Uncle Snake: An Independence Day Pageant.   New York Dramatists Play Service, 1976.

Screenplays: *Machine Gun McCain* (English adaption), 1970; *The Strawberry Statement,* 1970; *Believe in Me (Speed Is of the Essence),* 1970; *Acrobats,* 1972.

Televison Plays: *Play for Trees,* 1969; *VD Blues,* with others, 1972; *Start to Finish,* 1975; *The Making and Breaking of Splinters Braun,* 1976.

Novels

Cappella. New York Harper, 1973.

Nobody Loves Me.   Paris, Editions de Minuit, 1975; New York, Braziller, 1976.

Verse

Spider Poems and Other Writings.   New York, Harper, 1973.

Manuscript Collection: Lincoln Center Library of the Performing Arts, New York.

Critical Studies: *Thirty Plays Hath November* by Walter Kerr, New York, Simon and Schuster, 1969; *Opening Nights* by Martin Gottfried, New York, Putman, 1970; *The Playmakers* by Stuart W. Little and Arthur Cantor, New York, Dutton, 1970; in *Etudes Anglaises* (Paris), Summer 1975.

Theatrical Activities:

Director: **Plays** — *The Indian Wants the Bronx, It's Called the Sugar Plum,* and *Chiaroscuro: Morning, Noon and Night,* by Israel Horovitz, Leonard Melfi, and Terrence McNally, Spoleto, Italy, 1968; *Line* and *The Honest to God Schnozzola,* Paris, 1972; *Spared, and Hopscotch,* New York, 1974; *The Primary English Class,* New York, 1975. **Film** — *Acrobats,* 1972. **Television** — *VD Blues,* 1972.

Actor: **Film** — *The Strawberry Statement,* 1970.

Israel Horovitz comments:

All of my plays are flawed, none are to be taken seriously. The few shards of prose I've managed to print are altogether hopeless and should be erased.

*   *   *

Israel Horovitz had been working as a writer for a number of years, but it seemed as if he suddenly burst upon the New York scene in 1967 when the successful productions of four of his one-act plays established him as a brilliant new American playwright, and a socially commited artist. Like several other off-off-Broadway playwrights of the 1960's, Horovitz worked closely with actors and profited from their experimentation and dedication to ensemble productions. His plays were ensemble pieces, not star vehicles.

Although intensely concerned about the social issues facing America, Horovitz remains objective about the playwright's art. "If a play has pristine concept – if you have a clear concept of what the hell you're writing about before you sit down to write, you have a chance of writing a good play." His structure is clear, compact, and logical. Theme is implicit and didacticism is eschewed. His plays are impact not message plays, brutally realistic in their exposure of the American malaise. Even his two parable plays, *Line* and *Rats*, are basically realistic in style. Horovitz has an extraordinary ear for dialogue and has found poetry in the harsh language of the slum dweller and juvenile delinquent.

His play *Line* is a grotesque allegory of the American success myth; five characters struggle by the use of force or guile to gain first place on a line leading nowhere. In the course of their struggles, each alternately gains and loses first place. The mad contest in perpetuated by the young man, Stephen, who delights in belittling the combatants. He has an insane desire to die younger than his idol, Mozart, and is forever singing Figaro's aria from *The Marriage of Figaro*: "Cleverly, hitting, planning, and scheming, I'll get the best of the hypocrite yet." Like the wily barber, Stephen is not above using a little deception himself in his battle against hypocrisy. Ultimately, in an attempt to commit suicide and defeat his opposition, Stephen eats the line, but retches it up involuntarily. Each of the combatants grabs the pieces from his mouth, and rush to separate parts of the stage to be first on their own individual lines, a vivid stage metaphor of isolation and meaningless power struggles. Stephen rushes off in a fit of joy, liberated by a renewed sense of the absurdity of the human condidtion.

The only jarring moment in this otherwise imaginative allegory is Stephen's monologue revealing his inner conflict – a conventional bit of psychological realism, but too brief to weaken the play. Steven's bathetic monologue is quickly terminated by the promiscuous Molly, who scorns his need for a "mommy." Molly has used sex as a means of tormenting her husband, and also winning the game. She coarsely declares that she had "them" (the men), thus maintaining her dominance in the battle of the sexes, which is as meaningless as the desire to be first.

The work that overwhelmed the critics and achieved fame for Horovitz was *The Indian Wants the Bronx,* a genre classic of violence. It was one of the most gripping productions of the off-Broadway theatre of the 1960's, introducing the brilliant young actor, Al Pacino, and offering a stirring performance by John Cazale as the Indian.

A non-English speaking East Indian is lost somewhere in the city and is attempting to get to his son's home in the Bronx. Two juvenile delinquents discover the Indian, and proceed to tease, torment, and beat him. They have a strange mixture of love and hatred for the Indian : pity for his helplessness and contempt for him as a foreigner, referring to him as "Turkie" and "elephant." He becomes a convenient scapegoat for their own self hatred. Their treatment of the Indian is terrifying, leading to what seems to be his inevitable murder. The Indian's frantic pleadings in his native language intensify the diabolical mood of the play.

Ultimately, the two youths cut the wire of the telephone receiver as well as the Indian's hand and then run off. The play ends on a tableau – the Indian holding the receiver toward the audience, sobbing and uttering his few words of English: "How are you? You're welcome. Thank you. Thank you" – a more effective piece of business than actually murdering the Indian. His pathetic appeal to the audience is a grim reminder of the city's apathy toward violence.

It's Called the Sugar Plum is a cynical one-act situation comedy: a slight work with some funny lines and two zany characters. Zuckerman has accidentally killed a fellow Harvard student. He is aquitted by the court, but the deceased's fiancée (or so she claims), Joanna, calls upon Zuckerman and accuses him of murder. Initially agonizing over her lover's death, Joanna soon rhapsodizes over Zuckerman's romantic occupation as a part-time butcher in a slaughterhouse. Ultimately, the masks are removed: both characters had hoped the accident would bring them notoriety, but were dissapointed by the minimal coverage they received in the local papers. The play satirizes the self-righteousness of certain young people who are as fundamentally self-seeking as the rest of crass America. Despite the revelation of the actual motivations, Zuckerman and Joanna begin romanticizing their relationship. With the flicker of a light bulb, lust in converted into true love.

The Honest to God Schnozzola is somewhat of a departure from the fundamental realism of Horovitz' drama: an unnerving study of fantasy and reality set in a German bar, and adorned with suitably decadent trimmings – a smoke filled atmosphere, a dwarf, a whore, a male transvestite, and two American T.V. executive types. The style is presentational: asides to the audience, songs, dances and a filmic plot structure utilizing flashbacks, blackouts, tableau freezes, and a flexible use of lighting reminiscent of a camera cut.

The two executives are on a brief European vacation, and have left their wives at home. Although the men dislike each other, their jobs force them into an artificial friendship. Emotionally weak and insecure, they make the conventional declaration of virility of immature American males. One of the men, Jimmy, described as "a small man with a large nose" maintains Jimmy Durante as an alter ego (hence the title of the play): "I wanted to be something special. I became Jimmy Durante."

The plot has a bizarre twist. On the previous evening, Jimmy has been duped into having anal intercourse with the transvestite, Athenia, believing he was female. Tourtured by this experience, Jimmy is determined that his associate, Johnny, should experience the same degradation. Johnny is comparably deceived, and Jinny later maliciously reveals Athenia's sexual identity.

There is a deliberate ambiguity inherent in the plot. Were the men ignorant of Athenia's sexual identity? Is their suffering actually a guilt reaction for having fulfilled their own homosexual desires? Is the play allegorical – post-war Germany's revenge on the American supermen – or a commercially appealing tale of perversion cloaked in seriousness?

Horovitz' description of *Line* as "comedy of displacement" provides a key to his dramatic technique: situations in which characters cleverly or brutally attempt to displace their competition in a vicious game of survival. Most of his plays begin in a mood of relative calm (except *Rats*) which is quickly shattered by the arrival of another character. Fleming is contentedly singing and sitting on his line when Stephen arrives and begins the insane game of displacement. Joanna invades Zuckerman's privacy and accuses him of murder, but the play really deals with a success struggle in which each character believes himself to have been displaced by the press notoriety of the other. Murphy and Joey torment the Indian as a means of vindicating themselves for their own displacement from society. Jebbie and Bobby, the two Harlem rats, battle for territory, each attempting to dispace the other. Jimmy and Johnny veer from the "straight" world by a fleeting homosexual experience, a displacement effected through clever disguise.

Horovitz' recent work evidences a departure from his somewhat formalized technique of displacement, being more experimental in form and style. Rather than realistic or parable plays of social malaise, Horovitz focuses on plays of character introspection and mental disorientation: dark chamber pieces of fragmented dialogue, staccato rhythms, monologues, or silent interaction. His characters are impelled helplessly into the vortex of their own mental disorientation.

In the Wakefield trilogy, Horovitz probes into the roots of his own psyche by dramatizing the adventures of Alfred, a celebrated citizen of Wakefield, Massachusetts, who returns to this small town to unravel the confusing narrative of his past. *Alfred the Great*, the first play of the trilogy, is a complex dramatic structure uniting farce, allegory, and psychoanalysis. Alfred encounters his childhood sweetheart, Margaret, in her sitting room, resulting in a painful yet amusing situation of nostalgia, awkwardness, and ultimately diabolical revenge effected by her jealous husband, Will.

In *Our Father's Failing*, Alfred visits his aged Father in an insane asylum and discovers the dark secret of his past: as a boy he stabbed and murdered his mother and her lover. In order to protect his son, Alfred's father declared himself the murderer; the court pronounced him insane and committed him to the asylum. Despite this somewhat melodramatic revelation, the play avoids the pitfalls of stock psychological drama: it is a dark comedy, exploring the complex undercurrents of love and hostility existing between a father and son. The most inspired aspect of the play is Horovitz' comic treatment of the hostile relationship existing between the father and his old crony Sam: a badinage of insult, innuendo, and nonsequiturs.

Alfred reappears as the character merely described as "The Man" in the one act monologue, *Spared,* another dark comedy, in which he narrates his bizarre, unsuccessful attempts at suicide or euthanasia. Despite his longing for death, fate keeps him alive.

Horovitz' outstanding recent success is *The Primary English Class*, a zany farce set in a classroom where a sexually repressed and highly neurotic young woman attempts to teach English to a group of foreigners. Two narrators translate the foreign dialogue, revealing the absurdity of the young teacher's dark suspicions of her students' innocent motivations and sincere desire to understand and communicate with her.

—A. Richard Sogliuzzo

HOWARD, Roger. British.   Born in Warwickshire, 19 June 1938. Educated at Dulwich College, London; Royal Academy of Dramatic Art, London; Bristol University. National Service: sentenced to imprisonment for refusal to wear uniform: dishonourable discharge. Married; has one son. Teacher, Nankai University, Tientsin, China, 1965–67; worked at Collets Bookshop, Peterborough, 1967–68, and Bookshop 85, London, 1968–72. Teacher, Peking University, 1972–74. Member, Council of Management, Society for Anglo-Chinese Understanding, and Editorial Committee, *China Now* magazine, 1970–72. Recipient: Arts Council bursary, 1975. Address: c/o Allen and Unwin, 40 Museum Street, London WC1A 1LU, England.

PUBLICATIONS

Plays

> *Bewitched Foxes Rehearsing Their Roles* (produced London, 1968).
> *Fin's Doubts* (produced London, 1969).   London, privately printed, 1968.
> *The Love Suicides at Havering* (produced London, 1969).   Included in *A Methuen Playscript*, 1968.
> *The Carrying of X from A to Z* (produced New Guinea/Papua, 1971).   Included in *A Methuen Playscript*, 1968.
> *Dis* (produced New York, 1971).   Included in *A Methuen Playscript*, 1968.
> *Seven Stages on the Road to Exile* (produced Carlisle, 1970).   Included in *A Methuen Playscript*, 1968.
> *A Methuen Playscript*, with others (includes *The Carrying of X from A to Z, Dis, The Love*

Suicides at Havering, Seven Stages on the Road to Exile).   London, Methuen, 1968.
Season (produced London, 1969).
Simon Murdering His Deformed Wife with a Hammer (produced London, 1969).
The Meaning of the Statue (produced London, 1971).   Included in *Slaughter Night and Other Plays,* 1971.
Writing on Stone (produced London, 1971).   Included in *Slaughter Night and Other Plays,* 1971.
Episodes from the Fighting in the East, in *Slaughter Night and Other Plays,* 1971; in *Scripts 4* (New York), February 1972.
Returning to the Capital, in *Slaughter Night and Other Plays,* 1971; in *Scripts 4* (New York), February 1972.
The Travels of Yi Yuk-sa to the Caves at Yenan (produced Colchester, 1976).   Included in *Slaughter Night and Other Plays,* 1971; in *Scripts 4* (New York), February 1972.
Slaughter Night and Other Plays: The Meaning of the Statue, The Travels of Yi Yuk-sa to the Caves at Yenan, Returning to the Capital, Writing on Stone, Korotov's Ego-Theatre, Report from the City of Reds in the Year 1970, The Drum of the Strict Master, The Play of Iron, Episodes from the Fighting in the East, A New Bestiary.   London, Calder and Boyars, 1971.
The Drum of the Strict Master (produced Colchester, 1976).   Included in *Slaughter Night and Other Plays,* 1971.
The Auction of Virtues (produced London, 1972).
Sunrise.   Peking, Peking University, 1973.
Klöng 1, Klöng 2, and the Partisan (produced Colchester, 1976).
Notes for a New History (produced Colchester, 1976).
The Mao Play (The Tragedy of Mao in the Lin Piao Period) (produced London, 1976).
The Great Tide (produced Colchester, 1976).
History of the Tenth Struggle (produced London, 1976).

Novels

A Phantastic Satire.   Bala, Merioneth, Chapple, 1960.
From the Life of a Patient   Bala, Merioneth, Chapple, 1961.

Short Stories

Four Stories, with *Twelve Sketches,* by Tony Astbury.   London, Mouthpiece, 1964.

Verse

To the People....   London, Mouthpiece, 1966.
Praise Songs.   Tientsin, Tianjin Ribao, and London, Mouthpiece, 1966.

Other

The Technique of the Struggle Meeting.   London, Clandestine, 1968.
The Use of Wall Newspapers.   London, Clandestine, 1968.
The Hooligan's Handbook (political essay).   London, Action Books, 1971.
Method for Revolutionary Writing.   London, Action Books, 1972.
Mao Tse-tung and the Chinese People.   London, Allen and Unwin, 1976.
Contemporary Chinese Theatre.   Brussels, La Renaissance du Livre, and London, Heinemann, 1976.

Editor, *Culture and Agitation: Theatre Documents.*   London, Action Books, 1972.

Roger Howard comments:

(1973) In revolutionary war, plays are performed to show scenes of the struggle in which fighters who actually took part replay their "parts" as examples to other fighters. Their short, instructional plays go back over the battle just ended in order to point out the lesson to be learnt for the next round. They educate by showing the audience – other fighters – the significance of their actions.

Such drama is deeply rooted in the day-to-day work experience of the people. It captures their imagination because it closely expresses themselves. At the same time it is a higher form of artistic expression than mere realism, because it shows the people's actions in their relationship to the new, evolving and advancing socialist morality. Their plays are agitation in the service of the people's advance and an aid in the overthrow of the old society.

My short plays are part of the same process. Preparing for the situation where there will be open military warfare, they are agitational plays in the wider war which engulfs us all, the war between classes which takes many forms and which will not cease until classes cease. Each play is located at a point where a certain stage of development in struggle has been reached, and where the choices are open as to what the following stage should be.

The point reached at the opening of each play may be either a victory or a defeat for revolutionary advance. The body of the play then develops the initial point by showing the contending sides and conflicting interests, giving visual and verbal guidelines from the particular instance to the wider significance in the form of interpolated screen captions, extended sound words, lyrical or didactic verses or actual physical combat.

The characters are shown in their class as well as in their individual roles; they are individuals who express class positions in the way they think, speak, act and interact. Their conflicts therefore elicit humour, grotesquery, poetry, reason, tragedy and decision.

The resolution of the conflicts between the characters, as of those within one character, is resolution not of a "personality" to his "destiny" or of the "mind" to the "universe," still less of the "underdog" to his "station in life." It is a resolution that will give the revolutionary protagonist, the positive character, his due as the man who has history on his side in an era when capitalism in in decline and the many forces of socialism are in the ascendant. It is therefore a resolution of *ideas*, by which the conscious, active man triumphs over the slave in man, whether it be in himself or in others. For some, the resolution comes as a condemnation: they are the negative characters, the reactionaries, backward rejects of history. For others, the resolution comes too late; for them, they have their message to pass on to a new generation. For all our mistakes, man is learning to advance. The point of resolution in each play is therefore an ideological point, to be perceived as such by the audience.

So the characters of the plays are representations of contradictory class position as they appear in individual human beings. This gives the positive characters greater dimensions than those of mere self-contained, alienated individuals at odds with society for their own sake, just as in life itself the activists of revolution are so much greater figures than those who merely talk about it or those who use socialism for their personal advantage.

Our oppression will last for as long as we remain afraid; if only we act, we lose our fear. Oppressors tremble when they lose their grip on our terror. The revolutionary characters in my plays are heroic because they are no longer afraid. And they are no longer afraid because they have become conscious. They know that as active workers, conscious of class, they hold the future in their hands. I warm to those men and women in our century who, raising the people to raise themselves, and growing thus in stature, have reminded mankind of its dignity. My heart is stung when I hear of their deeds; they are few of them famous and most suffered great privation and even death. My plays can hardly emulate their lives but they are some sort of small monuments, not for us to gaze at and pity, but to stir us to action. They rescue from the great killings some memorials of actions that teach us to kill more precisely in future: our killers.

(1977) The idea of people as doers, as much as sufferers, has been pushed into the background in much of recent drama that has become academically respectable, from Ibsen to Beckett. The idea that people are capable of directing their future more completely has been neglected.

In my short plays I have introduced prototypes of such representative men and women. The transition I am now making from short to full-length plays will give the idea of renewal more scope. The first long play, *The Tragedy of Mao in the Lin Piao Period*, is a 19-scene construction of the shifts in the relationship between two men striving to remake men and themselves. Then follows a trilogy on turning points in English history, from tribalism to feudalism, to capitalism, and to socialism.

*   *   *

Roger Howard is a genuine original, whose plays combine an essentially Maoist political stance with a range of diverse and eclectic styles, including Brechtian epic theatre, slapstick, music hall and cartoon theatre. In his introductory essay to his volume of plays, *Slaughter Night*, he makes the point that, in the present political situation, it is the playwright's task to divide and agitate, not to help in the creation of culture, which is part of the "deep sleep" our rulers want to impose on us. His plays, which are all short in length, are sharp, clear and carry out this task of division with an admirable precision, though their form is very far from being conventional agitational socialistic realism. This essay, which of necessity considers the plays more as cultural objects than as means of heightening political consciousness, is an exercise in contradictions, an example of the dialectical relationship between politics and art; but it's true to say that the best of the plays do work on an artistic and aesthetic level over and above their directly political one.

His plays fall into three distinct phases. First, there are the lyrical pre-China pieces, like *Season* and *Simon Murdering His Deformed Wife with a Hammer*, which propagate a William Morris-type socialism through semi-abstract poetic characters and language. *Season* shows the struggle between urban and rural values; while *Simon* shows a young man trying to educate his wife to his own level of political consciousness, failing and murdering her as a result. Then come more complex plays, like *The Love Suicides at Havering*, which shows a group of people attempting to overcome their psychological inhibitions as a necessary precondition to achieving a revolutionary situation, and *Fin's Doubts*, which shows in symbolist form the full cycle of a revolution. A group of revolutionaries overthrow an era of reactionary repression, achieve the first stages of a revolution, and impose temporary authoritarian measures to consolidate its achievements; by a process of bureaucratic ossification this authoritarianism becomes permanent, and the whole cycle starts off again.

Howard went to China as a teacher for two years and the result can be seen in the plays in his volume *Slaughter Night*, artistically and politically his most mature achievements to date. The title play juxtaposes Sauer, the Dog King, and the Writer, a nice, cosy arrangement with the Writer reflecting Sauer's interests through his works until two Wolves and an Outlaw show him the error of his ways. *The Meaning of the Statue* shows a young man in conversation with the statue of a general. Essentially, it is about the loss of spontaneity and fluidity in a revolutionary situation occasioned by its bureaucratic organisation, symbolised by the youth being shot by the statue and being put, in the same fixed position, in his place. *Returning to the Capital* uses the characters of Seami Motokiyo and his son, the fashioners of the first Noh plays, to point the differences between and consequences of being a reformist, like Seami, and a revolutionary. *Writing on Stone* is about a couple romanticising the past in lyrical images and being afraid to face up to the implications of the present. *Korotov's Ego-Theatre* shows the irrelevance and sterility of individualist concepts of art in a revolutionary situation; *Episodes from the Fighting in the East*, the erratic progress of a revolution and the shifts of power that take place within it;

while *A New Bestiary* hilariously satirises, through animal imagery, types of people pretending to be revolutionaries who are in fact, without realizing it, on the revolutionaries' side. They all use language and sound in a most original way.

He has recently made a new departure and written a full-length play entitled *The Tragedy of Mao in the Lin Piao Period*. This examines the ideological differences between Mao and the PLA commander-in-chief Lin (who was killed in an air crash in 1971 while fleeing to Moscow) and their origins in the civil war struggles of the 1930's. It is a subtle stylistic mixture of realism and a kind of heightened poetry, which in its totality gives some idea of how China's peasant-based socialism has evolved.

Howard has been little performed as yet; his plays are, however, eminently actable and stageable. They condense more into their brief spans, both in thought and style, than most full-length plays.

—Jonathan Hammond

HOWARTH, Donald.   British.   Born in London, 5 November 1931. Educated at the Grange High School for Boys, Bradford; Esme Church Northern Children's Theatre School, 1948–51. Stage Manager and Actor in various repertory companies, 1951–56. Since 1975, Literary Manager, Royal Court Theatre, London, Recipient: Encyclopaedia Britannica Award, 1961; George Devine Award, 1971. Agent: Margaret Ramsay Ltd., 14a Goodwin's Court, London WC2N 4LL, England.

PUBLICATIONS

Plays

> *Lady on the Barometer* (also co-director: produced London, 1958; as *Sugar in the Morning*, produced London, 1959).
> *All Good Children* (produced Bromley, Kent, 1960; also director: produced London, 1964).   London, French, 1965.
> *Secret of Skiz*, adaptation of a play by Zapolska (produced Bromley, Kent, 1962).
> *A Lily in Little India* (televised, 1962; also director: produced London, 1965). London, French, 1966.
> *Ogodiveleftthegason* (also director: produced London, 1967).
> *School Play*, in *Playbill One*, edited by Alan Durband.   London, Hutchinson, 1969.
> *Three Months Gone* (produced London, 1970).   London, French, 1970.
> *Othello Sleges Blankes*, adaptation of the play by Shakespeare (also director: produced Cape Town, 1972).
> *Scarborough* (also director: produced Cape Town, 1972).
> *The Greatest Fairy Story Ever Told*, adaptation of a play by Kathleen Housell-Roberts (also director: produced New York, 1973).
> *Meanwhile, Backstage in the Old Front Room* (produced Leeds, 1975).

Screenplay: *Gates to Paradise*, 1968.

Television Plays: *A Lily in Little India*, 1962; *Scarborough*, 1972; *Stanley*, 1972.

Critical Study: Introduction by Michael Billington, to *New English Dramatists 9*, London, Penguin, 1966.

Theatrical Activities:

Director: **Plays** — *Lady on the Barometer* (co-director, with Miriam Brickman), London, 1958; *This Property Is Condemned* by Tennessee Williams, London, 1960; *All Good Children*, London, 1964; *A Lily in Little India*, London, 1965; *Minatures* by David Cregan, London, 1965; *Ogodiveleftthegason*, London, 1967; *Othello Sleges Blankes* and *Scarborough*, Cape Town, 1972; *The Greatest Fairy Story Ever Told*, New York, 1973; *Play Mas* by Mustapha Matura, London, 1974; *Mama, Is Terry Home for Good?* by James Edward Shannon, Johannesburg, 1974; *Parcel Post* by Yemi Ajibade, London, 1976.

Actor: **Plays** — roles in repertory, 1951–56; Salvation Army Captain in *Progress to the Park* by Alun Owen, London, 1959.

Donald Howarth comments:

When I started to write plays I tried to catch the "literature of conversation" rather than make what the characters said have literary value.

Novels and poems are best read to oneself. Plays are best when heard and seen — with good actors. Lately I've been more interested in what characters (people?) do, how they feel and behave rather than in what they say. A group of people (characters?) will still do things and react to each other, in spite of what they say or talk about. Words, dialogue are/is parasitic, living off human beings and the way they are. The best parts aren't always the ones with most to say, though the audience and the actors usually think so.

*   *   *

One of the pleasures of reading through Donald Howarth's earlier plays in sequence — *Sugar in the Morning, All Good Children, A Lily in Little India, Ogodiveleftthegason*, and *Three Months Gone* — is the pleasure of seeing a playwright finding his way to an individual and successful compromise between naturalism and freewheeling expressionism by dint of returning again and agian to the same themes and the same characters but never to the same style. He has worked hard, and at its worst his writing is laborious, but he has been capable from the beginning of sustaining passages of comedy which deftly combine truthfulness with elegant and compelling theatrical rhetoric. Finally, in *Three Months Gone*, he has achieved a sureness of touch that enables him to tie fantasy material down to solid surfaces and to draw dividends from all his earlier stylistic experiments. *Ogodiveleftthegason* is the play in which he takes the most expressionistic short cuts and spans over the greatest amount of human experience. It is his least successful play, though, not because it is the least comic or the least realistic, but because it is the most shapeless and the least able to gain an audience's sympathy for the characters or sustain its interest in them. Partly because their identity keeps changing. *Three Months Gone*, while no less remote from the slow development of the conventional naturalistic three-act play, has a story-line strong enough to keep the colourful balloons of fantasy that both main characters fly tethered securely to a solid matter-of-factness.

Mrs. Broadbent, the sexually frustrated landlady in *Sugar in the Morning*, and Grannie Silk, her obstinately vulgar, cheerful, warm-hearted, interfering mother, are both rough prototypes of Mrs. Hanker in *A Lily in Little India* and *Three Months Gone*, who combines the main characteristics of both of them without having Mrs. Broadbent's pretensions to gentility or her ineptness at finding food for her sexual appetites. A clear picture of suburban life emerges in *Sugar in the* Morning but much of the basic energy is spent on drawing it. Decisions about which lodgers to take, clipping the privet hedge, arguments about noisy radios and washing hung up outside windows, rent collecting, drinking cups of tea in the landlady's room, hurrying for the twenty-to-eight bus, finding a shilling for the gas meter, discussing whether to have a baby – in using episodes like these as its currency, the play makes them all seem equally important. None of the characters in *Sugar in the Morning* reappears in *All Good Children* but Rev. Jacob Bowers and his son and daughter, Anna and Maurice, are in both *All Good Children* and *A Lily in Little India*, which introduces Mrs. Hanker and her son Alvin, who are to reappear in *Three Months Gone,* together with Anna and Maurice. The whole of the action of *All Good Children* is set in a converted farmhouse in South Yorkshire, but the 60-year-old minister is about to retire and to move his family to the suburb where we find them in the two subsequent plays. The new theme introduced in *All Good Children,* which will recur persistently in the later work, is the relationship between Protestant morality and sexual deprivation. Jacob Bowers, now a devout anti-sensualist, has been very different when younger, and became a minister only because of guilt-feelings after his affair with a minister's daughter had caused the old man's death. Unlike his younger brother, Clifford, who has been more of a conformist, Maurice has reacted violently against his Puritanic upbringing and become a sailor. His letters, with their juicy descriptions of local brothels, have been Anna's main life-line, and the love she feels for Maurice verges on the incestuous, but after her mother's death, caused by an on-stage fall down a staircase, she rejects her chance of breaking out of the family cage and condemns herself, after twenty years of imprisonment, to staying with her father.

The plot of *All Good Children* is developed mostly through speeches that rake over the past. *A Lily in Little India* is a less Ibsenite play, and physical action bulks larger in it. The action, like the stage, is divided between the Bowers' house and the Hankers'. We see Anna waiting on the old father who has spoiled her life by his narrowness, and writing letters to the brother through whom she is still vicariously living; in the other house a selfishly sensual landlady is trapping a reluctant postman into an affair regardless of the harm done to her sensitive son, who finds happiness only in growing a lily and in his encounters with Anna. When his mother, poised on a ladder outside his bedroom window, threatens to destroy his beloved lily, he throws water in her face causing her to fall backwards, and moves into Anna's house when she is moved into hospital. The characters win considerable sympathy and interest, and there are some very funny and some very touching moments but the comedy and the seriousness do not quite balance or reinforce each other as one comes to feel they should and, though the dialogue has been praised by Michael Billington (in his Introduction to the Penguin *New English Dramatists 9)* as "a just sufficiently heightened version of ordinary speech," it sinks sometimes into self-consciousness and just occasionally into sentimentality.

But the dialogue of *Three Months Gone* is virtually unflawed. The rapid shifts in and out of Anna's fantasies, and later Alvin's, give Donald Howarth the opportunity to penetrate funnily but compassionately their private views of themselves, each other, and the two other main characters, Maurice and Mrs. Hanker, who are sexually so much more robust. There is a hilarious scene in which Mrs. Hanker, bullying Alvin to find the pluck to make Anna marry him, makes him propose to her while she pretends to be Anna, and this is followed by a sequence in which Maurice makes a pass at him under guise of teaching him how to make a woman submit. The audience's uncertainty about which sequence represents fantasy, which reality, is often an advantage.

The recent plays are different and less successful. *The Greatest Fairy Story Ever Told* is a skittish pantomime full of arch chinoiserie. There are characters called Much Too Yin and Too Much Yang and jokes about Pon-Tings fabric hall and the Royal Courtyard. *Meanwhile, Backstage in the Old Front Room* is highly serious, ambitiously moving further away from naturalism than any of his earlier works. It leans on both Beckett and Genet: *Endgame* is feminised in the relationship between the dominating old woman who never leaves her wheelchair and the blind younger women, possibly her daughter, who lives with her. The power games and the extremism in making the characters speak out their thoughts are reminiscent of Genet's *The Maids*. The influence is domesticated into a family setting, but not altogether digested.

—Ronald Hayman

ISHERWOOD, Christopher. American. Born in High Lane, Cheshire, England, 26 August 1904. Settled in the United States in 1939; became an American citizen, 1946. Educated at Repton School, 1919–22; Corpus Christi College, Cambridge, 1924–25, King's College, London, as a medical student, 1928–29. Private Tutor, and Secretary to André Mangeot and His Music Society String Quartet, London, 1926–27. Taught English in Berlin, 1930–33. Travelled in Europe, 1933–37; in China, with W. H. Auden, 1938; in South America, 1947–48. Worked in films, in England, for Gaumont-British; and since 1939 in Hollywood for M.G.M., Warner Brothers and Twentieth Century Fox. Worked with the American Friends Service Committee, Haverford, Pennsylvania, 1941–42. Resident Student, Vedanta Society of Southern California, Hollywood; Editor, with Swami Prabhavananda, *Vedanta and the West*, Hollywood, 1943–44. Guest Professor of Modern English Literature, Los Angeles State College, and the University of California at Santa Barbara, 1959–62, Regents Professor, University of California at Los Angeles, 1965–66, and University of California at Riverside, 1966–67. Member, National Institute of Arts and Letters, 1949; Member, Academy of Motion Picture Arts and Sciences. Address: 145 Adelaide Drive, Santa Monica, California 90402, U.S.A.

PUBLICATIONS

Plays

The Dog Beneath the Skin; or, Where Is Francis?, with W. H. Auden (produced London, 1936; revised version, produced London, 1937). London, Faber, and New York, Random House, 1935.
The Ascent of F6, with W. H. Auden (produced London, 1937, New York, 1939). London, Faber, 1936; revised version, New York, Random House, and Faber, 1937.
On the Frontier, with W. H. Auden (produced Cambridge, 1938; London, 1939). London, Faber, 1938; New York, Random House, 1939.
The Adventures of the Black Girl in Her Search for God, adaptation of the novel by G. B. Shaw (produced Los Angeles, 1969).
A Meeting by the River, with Don Bachardy, adaptation of the novel by Christopher Isherwood (produced Los Angeles and New York, 1972).
Frankenstein: The True Story (screenplay), with Don Bachardy, based on the novel by Mary Shelley. New York, Avon, 1973.

Screenplays: *Diane*, 1955; *The Loved One*, with Terry Southern, 1965; *Frankenstein: The True Story*, with Don Bachardy, 1972.

Novels

All the Conspirators. London, Cape, 1928; New York, New Directions, 1958.
The Memorial: Portrait of a Family. London, Leonard and Virginia Woolf, 1932;

New York, New Directions, 1946.

Mr. Norris Changes Trains. London, Hogarth Press, 1935, as *The Last of Mr. Norris,* New York, Morrow, 1935.

Sally Bowles. London, Hogarth Press, 1937.

Goodbye to Berlin. London, Hogarth Press, and New York, Random House, 1939.

Prater Violet. New York, Random House, 1945; London, Methuen, 1946.

The Berlin Stories (includes *Mr. Norris Changes Trains, Sally Bowles,* and *Goodbye to Berlin*). New York, New Directions, 1946, as *The Berlin of Sally Bowles,* London, Hogarth Press, 1975.

The World in the Evening. New York, Random House, and London, Methuen, 1954.

Down There on a Visit. New York, Simon and Schuster, and London, Methuen, 1962.

A Single Man. New York, Simon and Schuster, and London, Methuen, 1964.

A Meeting by the River. New York, Simon and Schuster, and London, Methuen, 1967.

Other

Lions and Shadows: An Education in the Twenties. London, Hogarth Press, 1938; New York, New Directions, 1948.

Journey to a War, with W. H. Auden (on China). New York, Random House, and London, Faber, 1939.

The Condor and the Cows: A South American Travel Diary. New York, Random House, and London, Methuen, 1950.

An Approach to Vedanta. Hollywood, Vedanta Press, 1963.

Ramakrishna and His Disciples. New York, Simon and Schuster, and London, Methuen, 1965.

Exhumations: Stories, Articles, Verse. New York, Simon and Schuster, and London, Methuen, 1966.

Essentials of Vedanta. Hollywood, Vedanta Press, 1969.

Kathleen and Frank (autobiographical). New York, Simon and Schuster, and London, Methuen, 1971.

Christopher and His Kind (autobiography). New York, Farrar Straus, 1976.

Editor, *Vedanta and the Western World.* Hollywood, Marcel Rodd, 1946; London, Allen and Unwin, 1948.

Editor, *Vedanta for Modern Man.* New York, Harper, 1951; London, Allen and Unwin, 1952.

Editor, *Great English Short Stories.* New York, Dell, 1957.

Translator, *Intimate Journals,* by Charles Baudelaire. London, Blackamore Press, and New York, Random House, 1930.

Translator (verse only), *Penny for the Poor,* by Bertolt Brecht. London, Hale, 1937, New York, Hillman Curl, 1938, as *Threepenny Novel,* New York, Grove Press, 1956.

Translator, with Swami Prabhavananda, *Bhagavad-Gita: The Song of God.* Hollywood, Marcel Rodd, 1944, London, Phoenix House, 1947.

Translator, with Swami Prabhavananda, *Crest-Jewel of Discrimination,* by Shankara. Hollywood, Vedanta Press, n.d.

Translator, with Swami Prabhavananda, *How to Know God: The Yoga Aphorisms of Patanjali.* New York, Harper, and London, Allen and Unwin, 1953.

Bibliography: *Christopher Isherwood: A Bibliography, 1923–1967* by Selmer Westby and Clayton M. Brown, Los Angeles, California State College, 1968.

Critical Studies: *Christopher Isherwood* by Carolyn G. Heilbrun, New York, Columbia University Press, 1970; *Christopher Isherwood* by Alan Wilde, New York, Twayne, 1971.

Christopher Isherwood comments:

I have always regarded the three Auden-Isherwood plays as being works by Auden rather than by me, since their literary merit belongs almost entirely to their passages of poetry. I merely helped in the construction and in writing the larger part of the prose-dialogue.

A Meeting by the River is, in my opinion, much more than a dramatization of my novel; it carries the story further in several directions and is a more completely realized piece of work.

I have written many other screenplays [than the ones listed here], but the ones I liked best were never produced and the rest aren't worth remembering.

*   *   *

Though both W. H. Auden and Christopher Isherwood have written plays without the collaboration of the other, their main contribution to dramatic literature is usually associated with their inextricably entwined collaborative efforts. This should not perhaps surprise us as we must remember that the educational, poetic, political, and religious lives of the two men cross at so very many points. Both studied at British elitist universities: Auden at Oxford and Isherwood at Cambridge. Both were attracted to Marxism in the late twenties and early thirties and both resided in Berlin for extended periods. Both men moved in the thirties from committed Marxism to other and more overt forms of religiosity, as they paralleled their spiritual-political movement with physical movement from Europe to residence in the United States (Isherwood to California and Auden to New York).

Before proceeding to an examination of the collaborative efforts of these two authors in the mid and late thirties, Auden's own "dramatic poem," *The Dance of Death* deserves separate consideration. It must be stressed that to view this play — or any of his solo and joint playwriting ventures — merely as a written text is to fail to understand the necessity of relating these texts to actual performance. As we read *Dance of Death* we must attempt to imaginatively project the play as a full aesthetic construct *requiring* the use of dance and song. Fairness to Auden and to Auden-Isherwood requires that we not dismember his (their) aesthetic constructs by reducing them to words on flat pages. Many of these plays are as heavily dependent on music and deliberately tawdry stage effects as the operas of Brecht to which they obviously owe so much. If Auden and Isherwood are as heavily influenced by Brecht as Eric Bentley has long since suggested, then it might help us to see the particular Brecht of *Mahagonny, The Threepenny Opera*, and *Lucullus* as the closest aesthetic parallel to their work. Our viewing the Auden-Isherwood plays as being perhaps more operatic than dramatic is given considerable support by Auden's essay, "The World of Opera," in his book of essays, *Secondary Worlds*. It may not be wholly far-fetched to see the Auden-Isherwood plays of the thirties as a preface to Auden's later works that are specifically labelled as libretti: his *The Rake's Progress*, written for Stravinsky, and *Elegy for Young Lovers* and *The Bassarids*, both written for Hans Werner Henze. I believe it proper to see a very real link between the early *Dance of Death* and the "late" libretto, *The Rake's Progress*. In both instances Auden attempts to project humdrum, everyday events on a mythic plane. Auden said specifically of his view of the Rake: "If he was to have any mythical resonance, though setting, costumes and diction might be eighteenth century, he would have to be an embodiment of Everyman, and the libretto a mixture of fairy-story and medieval morality play." This description, it seems to me, is as readily applicable to *The Dance of Death* as it is to *The Rake's Progress*. There is rather obviously something of the myth, the medieval morality play, and the fairy story in a play that begins with a statement by the Announcer: "We present to you this evening a picture of the decline of a class, of how its members

dream of a new life, but secretly desire the old, for there is death in them. We show you that
death as a dancer." Such a text establishes itself at the outset as overtly theatrical or, if you
will, operatic, and depends for its major effect on our recognition of the total artificiality of
this "secondary world." As with Brecht, every effort must be made to stress the unreality of
this world. The main staging note on the play might, in fact, be drawn directly from Brecht.
It reads: "The stage is bare with a simple backcloth, in front of which are the steps on which
the Announcer sits, like the umpire at a tennis tournament. Down stage is a small Jazz
orchestra. In front of the conductor a microphone." Only if we can catch some sense of the
impact of this jazz orchestra, and of the major role of song and dance, and of the parodies of
the radio announcer that are central to the performance, can we begin to appreciate this
remarkable and considerably underrated play. And, lest we jump too quickly to the
conclusion that *Dance of Death* is but warmed-over Brecht, it may be worth noting that not
only did Brecht very much appreciate Auden's work (they worked jointly on an adaptation
of *The Duchess of Malfi* in the mid-forties), but Brecht might be seen as having, in a sense,
presented warmed-over Auden in his own post-World War II play, *The Salzburg Dance of
Death*. It would be perhaps fairest, therefore, simply to note here that in the 1930's, and
later, stage innovations in one country were very quickly picked up by the *avant-garde* in
other theatre centres and that mutual borrowing was the rule rather than the exception.
Neither Brecht nor Auden and Isherwood were exceptions to this rule.

The bitter commentary on the European bourgeoisie that forms the heart of Auden's
Dance of Death is repeated with a specific British focus in Auden and Isherwood's first
collaborative effort, the play *The Dog Beneath the Skin*, written in 1935, and first produced
in 1936. The plot of this play turns around the "impenetrable disguise" of a massive dog
which is finally discovered to have been human and to have been observing for several years
the vicious foibles of its ostensibly decorous masters. The play is made up entirely of type
characters (a general, a vicar, a financier, etc., etc.) and is designed to deliberately exaggerate
everything silly, tragic, and hideous in the behaviour of these characters. With its use of a
chorus, cabaret announcer, and a chorus line, the play is similar in tone to Auden's own
Dance of Death. The play closes with an explicit exhortation to seek new modes of social
behaviour and organization more civilized and humane than those exposed in the body of
the play itself.

The extreme and explicit social, indeed socialist commentary which totally permeates
every line of *Dance of Death* and *The Dog Beneath the Skin* is somewhat modified in Auden
and Isherwood's *The Ascent of F6*. Though the play clearly does attempt to expose once
again bourgeois hypocrisy in government, in national states, and in capitalism, the play's
hero, Michael Ransom, anticipates Auden and Isherwood's own later shift from politics to
metaphysics in his flirtation with Far Eastern mysticism. Our final impression is one of the
unmitigated shabbiness of the various Western ideologies competing to exploit Ransom,
when these ideologies are compared with that of the Far Eastern Abbot met by Ransom
during his ascent of the unnamed peak, F6.

The drift towards religion and away from politics that is evident in *The Ascent of F6* is
somewhat less apparent in the next joint effort of the two playwrights, *On the Frontier*,
written in 1938 as Europe and the world teetered on the edge of war. Set somewhere in
Europe, the action of the play takes place literally on the frontier of "Ostnia" and
"Westland." Though we can at times seem to identify Ostnia with the Soviet Union and
Westland with Hitler's Germany, such identification is surely undercut by the fact that in
both Ostnia and Westland the soldiers smoke Woodbines and ostentatiously declare them to
be "the only brand." Further, any audience tendency to make a one-to-one identification of
stage reality with any specific country is undercut by the deliberate conjuring up of a dream-
like quality of behaviour on both sides of the frontier. As war finally does break out despite
vacuous declarations of a wish for peace made on both sides, the dream of peace of the
young lovers (Eric in Westland and Anna in Ostnia) is pushed into the future as Eric
declares: "But in the lucky guarded future/Others like us shall meet, the frontier gone,/And
find the real world happy." Finally in an amazingly optimistic view of what they apparently
see as the outcome of the holocaust that is to consume them, Eric and Anna recite together:

"Dry their imperfect dust,/The wind blows it back and forth./They die to make man just/ And worthy of the earth." At our present remove it is a little difficult to share this view of World War II as expressed in this last collaborative effort of Auden and Isherwood in the field of drama.

Of plays written since their collaborative efforts of the thirties, Isherwood's adaptation of Shaw's *Adventures of the Black Girl in Her Search for God*, his stage adaptation of his own novel *A Meeting by the River*, and his screenplay *Frankenstein*, deserve mention.

—John Fuegi

JELLICOE, Ann.   British.   Born in Middlesbrough, Yorkshire, 15 July 1927. Educated at Polam Hall, Darlington; Queen Margaret's, Castle Howard, Yorkshire; Central School of Speech and Drama (Elsie Fogarty Prize, 1947), 1944-47. Married C. E. Knight-Clarke in 1950 (marriage dissolved, 1961); Roger Mayne, 1962; has two children of the second marriage. Actress, Stage Manager, Director, in London and the provinces, 1947–51; Founding Director, Cockpit Theatre Club, London, 1950–53; Lecturer and Director, Central School of Speech and Drama, 1953–55; Literary Manager, Royal Court Theatre, London, 1973–75. Committee Member, League of Dramatists. Agent: Margaret Ramsay Ltd., 14a Goodwin's Court, London WC2N 4LL, England.

P<small>UBLICATIONS</small>

Plays

> *Rosmersholm*, adaptation of the play by Ibsen (also director: produced London, 1952; revised version, produced London, 1959).   San Francisco, Chandler, 1960.
> *The Sport of My Mad Mother* (also co-director: produced London, 1958).   Published in *The Observer Plays*, London, Faber, 1958; revised version, London, Faber, 1964; in *Two Plays*, 1964.
> *The Lady from the Sea*, adaptation of a play by Ibsen (produced London, 1961).
> *The Knack* (also co-director: produced Cambridge, 1961; London, 1962; Boston, 1963; New York, 1964).   London, Encore, and New York, French, 1962.
> *The Seagull*, with Ariadne Nicolaeff, adaptation of a play by Chekhov (produced London, 1964).
> *Der Freischütz*, translation of the libretto by Friedrich Kind, music by Weber (produced London, 1964).
> *Two Plays: The Knack and The Sport of My Mad Mother*.   New York, Dell, 1964.
> *Shelley; or, The Idealist* (also director: produced London, 1965).   London, Faber, and New York, Grove Press, 1966.
> *The Rising Generation* (produced London, 1967).   Published in *Playbill 2*, edited by Alan Durband, London, Hutchinson, 1969.
> *The Giveaway* (produced Edinburgh, 1968; London, 1969).   London, Faber, 1970.
> *You'll Never Guess* (also director: produced London, 1973).   Included in *3 Jelliplays*, 1975.
> *Two Jelliplays: Clever Elsie, Smiling Jack, Silent Peter, and A Good Thing and a Bad Thing* (also director: produced London, 1974).   Included in *3 Jelliplays*, 1975.
> *3 Jelliplays* (includes *You'll Never Guess; Clever Elsie, Smiling Jack, Silent Peter; A Good Thing and a Bad Thing*).   London, Faber, 1975.

Other

> *Some Unconscious Influences in the Theatre.*   London and New York, Cambridge
>   University Press, 1967.
> *Devon: A Shell Guide,* with Roger Mayne.   London, Faber, 1975.

Theatrical Activities:

> Director: **Plays** – *The Confederacy* by Vanbrugh, London, 1952; *The Frogs* by
> Aristophanes, London, 1952; *Miss Julie* by Strindberg, London, 1952; *Rosmersholm* by
> Ibsen, London, 1952; *Saints' Day* by John Whiting, London, 1953; *The Comedy of Errors,*
> London, 1953; *Olympia* by Ferenc Molnar, London, 1953; *The Sport of My Mad Mother*
> (co-director, with George Devine), London, 1958; *For Children* by Keith Johnstone,
> London, 1959; *The Knack* (co-director, with Keith Johnstone), London, 1962; *Skyvers* by
> Barry Reckord, London, 1963; *Shelley,* London, 1965; *You'll Never Guess,* London, 1973;
> *Two Jelliplays,* London, 1974; *A Worthy Guest* by Paul Bailey, London, 1974; *Six of the
> Best,* London, 1974.

Ann Jellicoe has condensed the Preface to *Shelley; or, The Idealist* (reprinted by permission
of Faber and Faber Ltd.):

In my first play *The Sport of My Mad Mother* character and motive were shown in action
not described in words; to give a simple example instead of a man saying "I'm angry," he
was angry. This seems more obvious now than it did some years ago when theatre was still
much influenced by Shaw and T. S. Eliot, both extremely literary dramatists. *The Sport of
My Mad Mother* began with a fragment I wrote in which youngsters cavorted around a
college-bred American teasing, tormenting, losing control and finally, as their ecstasy rose to
a climax, passing out with hysteria: the words they used were meaningless sounds to release
emotion. I looked at the fragment and asked: "What sort of people would behave like this?"
and so began to build character and then: "What would such people do?" And began to
build situation. I was interested in piling up patterns of sound and releasing them, and this
taste dictated the play: it was about people who behaved like that because that was the way
I wanted to write.

The Knack, like my first play, was written from the inside, character determining
situation, situation defining character. The principle that action is not *narrated* was
developed further. In *The Sport of My Mad Mother* the characters were incapable of
understanding their own motives; in *The Knack* Tom sees clearly what motivates him and
the others. Speech rhythms are more subtly used than in *The Sport of My Mad Mother*; but
there are interlocking rhythms which, with the youth of the characters and their zest, give
the play its bounce. I was, however, beginning to be bored with verbal rhythms used in an
obvious, musical way as they were in the first play, and to feel they were a mannerism.

"Theatrical" began to have a further meaning for me. It used to mean tinsel, glitter,
artificiality; it had come to mean in my first two plays the tension that arises from the
conflict between what people say and what they do; but now "theatrical" began to mean,
purely and simply, the actors catching the audience's imagination and the effects that
follow.

It was becoming clear that I wanted to write a play that would have a strong narrative. I
wanted to do without vocal rhythms. Although in my earlier plays vocal rhythms were an
organic part of character and situation, they seemed now to betray an anxiety to hold the
audience's attention, and I wanted to see if I could hold it without them.

A combination of circumstances led me to read a biography of Shelley. I found that his
life illustrates certain problems which fascinate me; particularly the problems of goodness

which are so much more interesting than those of evil. Evil tends to run in grooves, evil men more or less conform in their evil; but goodness can be very subtle once you concede that goodness doesn't begin with a set of rules but with the search to define its own nature. Shelley's life involves, too, the problems of the creative artist rejected by his time, of the position of women, of the teacher who projects his own standards on his pupils and is disturbed when they don't live up to his image.

The search into his life was delightful; at first through biographies but soon entirely from original sources. There was, too, a real delight in finding how English was this man who battled against what he disliked in England; and so a rediscovery of one's own Englishness. Selecting the episodes of his life and arranging them dramatically implies stress and bias, and so it should; this is a play not a work of scholarship.

My ideas continued to change and develop – not, one hopes, for the sake of change, but because it's rather boring to know what one will do next. I write slowly and my plays appear at fairly widely-spaced intervals; I tend to cover a lot of ground in my theatrical thinking between plays and I suppose it must be disconcerting to find that I don't pick up where the last play left off but a bit further on.

I expect I shall go on exercising my freedom to write serious plays or frivolous plays, to develop or consolidate. I write for four reasons: for the pleasure of creating something, for the exhileration of defining and trying to answer certain questions, because writing is a process of self-discovery and self-enrichment, for the sake of communication.

*   *   *

Most of the dramatists in that motley assemblage known as the New Drama in Britain can, whatever their extreme differences of style and temperament, be fitted in somewhere according to allegiance: as Absurdists, Brechtians, traditional exponents of the well-made play or whatever. But Ann Jellicoe has from the beginning gone her own way, not like anyone else either in her approach to dramatic form or in the way she has developed from play to play. The key to her uniqueness may perhaps be found in her theatrical background: her ambitions were never primarily as a writer, and almost throughout her career she had worked as and planned to be a director. She studied at the Central School of Speech and Drama, and joined the staff there as a director in 1953. She also founded and ran an open-stage theatre club (for which she wrote her first play, a one-act indiscretion in the style of Christopher Fry), and at the onset of the New Drama in 1956 all her ambitions were set on becoming a director in the professional London theatre. Rather naively, as she subsequently came to realize, she thought a way in might be to write a play which, if it met with any sort of response from managements, she might get to direct herself.

The play was *The Sport of My Mad Mother*, which was entered for a competition of new drama organized by the *Observer* newspaper in 1956, and won joint third prize. It was hardly the sort of thing to rejoice the hearts of any commercial management: a wild, whirling, free-ranging fantasy about a group of teddy-boys who behave throughout in a spirit of casual, apparently unmotivated violence, a couple of outsiders (a wandering young American and a 13-year-old retarded girl) who get involved with them, and their spiritual leader, Greta, who seems to represent a sort of Earth-mother goddess figure of destruction and finally, when she gives birth to a child, of creation. (The title of the play comes from Indian mythology: "All creation is the sport of my mad mother Kali.") As a text for reading it makes little sense, unless one can at once begin to exercise a director's creative imagination on it: it is the equivalent of a short score from which a full orchestral sound can be conjured by a skilled musician, a sort of aide-memoire for its deviser-director in realizing on stage her own initial conception, in which the actual words are only a part of the larger, more intricate pattern of lights and sounds and movements.

In other words, as well as being director's theatre to the nth degree, *The Sport of My Mad Mother* can be seen as a sort of visceral theatre, rather like that advocated by Antonin Artaud under the label "theatre of cruelty": it seeks to bypass our intellects and play instead upon our instincts, using more than the normal theatrical channel of verbal communication to make its effect. This line of approach is in fact more or less dictated by the play's subject-matter: if it would be hard to produce a formal paraphrase of its action, it is easy to say what in a simpler subtler sense it is about. The total gesture of the play is clear, despite its very complex means: it is about people who are inarticulate and uncommunicative, and instead of trying to externalise their emotions in words which would necessarily seem strained and artificial, it sets out to create a sort of symbolic equivalent of the mental climate in which they live and then plunges us helplessly, unarguably into it.

The play was produced by the English Stage Company at the Royal Court Theatre, home of so much that was most enterprising and creative in British Theatre at that time. (Ann Jellicoe did get to co-direct it with the company's director, George Devine.) Shortly afterwards she received, despite its total commercial disaster and the general critical incomprehension it provoked, a commission from an unlikely quarter, the Girl Guides' Association. For them she wrote a show intended for spectacular staging with a cast of around a thousand, *The Rising Generation*. Not surprisingly, the Association baulked when it received the text, a terse extravaganza much in the style of *The Sport of my Mad Mother* in which hundreds of girls are urged on by a monstrous Mother-figure to reject man in the best Women's Lib manner, announcing that "Shakespeare was a woman. Milton was a woman ... Newton was a woman" until finally they are defeated by the spirit of youthful open-mindedness and cooperation, which carries a mixed group of boys and girls off to colonise new worlds in space. The play was not staged by the Girl Guides.

With her next play, *The Knack*, Ann Jellicoe unexpectedly scored one of the most resounding popular successes of the New Drama, particularly when the play was transferred to film. And this, without sacrificing anything of her own individuality. *The Knack* is a comedy about three men, respectively very successful, moderately successful and entirely unsuccessful with girls, and the oddly knowing innocent girl who wanders accidentally into the house they all share. There is a minimum of plot; simply a pattern of relationships, a precarious balance of emotional power which is adjusted in the course of the play as much by action, by what happens among the characters between, around and in spite of the words, as through what is actually said. What is actually said in fact often reduces itself to an ordered pattern of sound, most obviously in a key scene in which Colin and Tom (the two less successful members of the triumvirate) gradually draw the hesitant Nancy over to their side by involving her in their fantasy that the bed on stage is actually a piano – a scene which in the published script consists of some three pages of "Pings" and "Plongs" variously distributed and virtually uninterrupted by deviations into more literary sense.

It was four years before Ann Jellicoe came forward with another play, and this, *Shelley; or, The Idealist*, could hardly have been more different, or a more unexpected development. It is a very verbal play, a sober, deliberately documentary reconstruction of Shelley's life from his first getting into trouble at university for atheistical pamphleteering to his death as described by Trelawny. It is constructed in a series of terse, scrupulously unmelodramatised scenes which mark the successive stages of his romantic and literary career neatly off one from another and build up to a composite picture of a group almost universally unsympathetic; for if Shelley himself does come over more than a little like a male chauvinist pig, it can hardly be claimed that either of the principal ladies in his life is proffered much more sympathy. A strange, almost wilfully unappealing play, which yet gives the impression of determined honesty and accuracy, and sends one out of the theatre feeling that one knows more about a number of historical characters, one has been interested along the way, and that one would (which is very rare in the theatre of illusions) be inclined to trust in the reasonableness and accuracy of the conclusions which the play, without drawing them itself, forces one to.

Shelley seemed in some ways like a conscious reaction to the earlier plays, a demonstration by Ann Jellicoe for her own benefit that she could write a wholly verbal play if she wanted to. At any rate her next play, *The Giveaway*, did return more to the country of *The Knack*, though its form of expression was considerably less extreme. The framework is a popular, relatively conventional farce about a family who have won a ten years' supply of breakfast cereal, palpably present on stage in eight enormous crates. There is a little plot revolving round the son of the house and a romantic triangle consisting of him, a lodger he fancies, and a neighbour who fancies him. It was light and agreeable enough, but seemed to suffer from some forms of compromise, perhaps enforced by commercial pressures and a bumpy provincial tour. *You'll Never Guess* explores rather similar territory, and the two short plays she has had produced since give rather the impression of marking time. Now perhaps we may hope that she will return to a subject within the centre of her most personal style and range – that area where she is just not at all like anyone else.

—John Russell Taylor

JOHN, Errol.   Trinidadian.   Recipient: Guggenheim Fellowship, 1958. Agent: Fraser and Dunlop Ltd., 91 Regent Street, London W1R 8RU, England.

PUBLICATIONS

Plays

Moon on a Rainbow Shawl (produced London, 1958; revised version, produced New York, 1962).   London, Faber, 1958; revised version, 1963.
Force Majeure, The Dispossessed, Hasta Luego: Three Screenplays.   London, Faber, 1967.

Television Plays: *For the Children* series, 1952; *The Emperor Jones*, 1953; *Teleclub*, 1954; *Dawn*, 1963; *The Exiles*, 1969.

Theatrical Activities

Actor: **Plays** – roles in many plays, including Lester in *Anna Lucasta* by Philip Yordan, London, 1953; Paul Prescott in *Local Colour* by Joan Sadler, London, 1954; The Negro in *The Respectable Prostitute* by Jean-Paul Sartre, London, 1954; Nubian Slave in *Salome* by Oscar Wilde, London, 1954; Jeremy in *South* by Julien Green, London, 1955; Honey Camden Brown in *Member of the Wedding* by Carson McCullers, London, 1957; at the Old Vic Theatre, London: Prince of Morocco in *The Merchant of Venice*, 1962, title role in *Othello*, 1962, and Barnardine in *Measure for Measure*, 1963. **Films** – *The Nun's Story*, 1959; *The Sins of Rachel Cade*, 1961; *PT 109*, 1963; *Man in the Middle*, 1964; *Guns at Batasi*, 1964; *Assault on a Queen*, 1966.

*   *   *

Errol John's main theme is escape, and in *Moon on a Rainbow Shawl*, as well as the screenplays *The Dispossessed* and *Hasta Luego*, we see the various traps which destroy those who remain. These Caribbean plays come from a world of linguistic vitality, of improvised music and assorted animal noises all seeming to wage war on nature.

The trap in *Moon on a Rainbow Shawl* is the Trinidad backyard of a prostitute exhibiting her American sailors; of a poor "respectable" woman who goads her broken husband into theft and jail; and of the pregnant girl now abandoned, who settles for the protection of an old rack-renting landlord. From this mess Ephraim escapes. Ephraim is a young handsome trolley-bus driver in line for promotion as inspector, but who rejects this way out as illusory. His single-mindedness causes him to brush aside the girl he's just made pregnant, recalling the time he put his foster-mother in a home to die after she had got in the way.

But at least he gets out, which is more than those on the run in the Spanish-Caribbean pressure-cooker of *The Dispossessed* achieve. The religious strangle-hold is fiercer here and thus the extended family becomes one of the main battlefields. For a fisherman's son like Lou Delvado, who doesn't want to take over his father's boat, the only outlet, apart from crime, seems to be to put "classy" girls on their backs to prove he is as good as they are. But there is a limit to this. He organizes a robbery which results in the death of an old woman, and is eventually stabbed by his crippled father before he can escape. The number of fatherless children who blight the lives of young girls in these plays cannot be dismissed as a pre-pill relic, but is more part of the general lack of tidiness in human relationships prevalent in the society.

In three other plays, *Force Majeure, Dawn* and *The Exiles*, Errol John shows us the effects of having escaped the trap. There is no continuation of the Ephraim story of *Moon on a Rainbow Shawl*. Those who make it into exile are fairly successful artists and academics: the implication must be that the numerous Ephraims will sink without a trace. John now widens the area of rootlessness to include American blacks. In *Force Majeure*, we meet the ex-bus driver who, having adopted the literary name of Robert Rademaeker, has risen to New York glossy magazine fame, and is brought to London by his new agent Scott Linehard to conquer the film world. (Here he meets his ex-wife, now a successful singer living in Rome.) Everything is provided for Rademaeker's comfort in England, including Scott's Mustang, Scott's flat and Scott's fiancée, Christa. It all turns out to be a big con, of course, for Scott is white and Jewish, and wants to destroy the arrogance of the black Rademaeker for the smugness of all blacks who've climbed out of the gutter (there is no film contract) and he also wants to punish his German girlfriend (and her aunt) by letting a black loose in the house. As Scott reveals this, he escapes being murdered by Rademaeker only by the discovery of Christa's suicide. In *The Exiles*, it is middle-class West Indians who are trying to adapt to new surroundings – Kester McWilliams, white-looking Trinidad Professor of History on an exchange to Keele telling his students how it really happened with the slaves; his artist sister attempting suicide in a London flat (which she shares with a French-Sicilian model) because her lover called her a black woman; and their dark-skinned cousin, retracing his steps to the last war with his wife's $60,000 insurance money. More interesting is *The Dawn* where the Ivy League All-American writer Wayne Coty actually finds roots in Africa. Wayne is on a Manhattan assignment to an Africa on the verge of revolution. At an awkward party of German and Portuguese residents, he meets Salena (American friend of his earlier days in Paris). On their visit across country to Salena's Dutch farmer-employer, Erik Van Den Hoorn, they run into Africans being shot; and Wayne is insulted by the police. All this makes him more receptive to the servant in the Van Den Hoorn's household who takes Wayne to a village and shows him evidence of white brutality (an old man with an arm chopped off and tongue torn out, etc.). From here on, however, the play collapses under much talk about roots and then limps on to the contrived disclosure that Salena is really black; that it is time for them both to stop running, and return to fight in their own country.

Middle-class West Indians (and that includes the artists) have always had a certain amount of mobility. That's probably the strongest theme of romance in West Indian fiction. But what of the poor man who insists on being treated like a human being, and who finds it impossible to live either at home, or to escape abroad? Is there any answer but revolution?

—E. A. Markham

JOHNSTON, (William) Denis. British. Born in Dublin, 18 June 1901. Educated at St. Andrew's College, Dublin; Merchiston Castle, Edinburgh; Christ's College, Cambridge, 1919–23, M.A., LL.M. 1926; Harvard Law School, Cambridge, Massachusetts (Pugsley Scholar), 1923–24; Barrister, Inner Temple, London, 1925, and King's Inns, Dublin, 1925. Married Shelah Richards in 1928; Betty Chancellor, 1945; has four children. Producer, Dublin Drama League, Abbey Theatre, and Dublin Gate Theatre, 1927–36; Member of the Board of the Dublin Gate Theatre, 1931–36. Features Producer, BBC, Belfast, 1936–38; Television Producer, BBC, London, 1938–39; BBC Correspondent, in the Middle East, Italy, France, and Germany, 1942–45; mentioned in despatches, O.B.E. (Officer, Order of the British Empire), 1946; Director of Television Programmes, BBC, London, 1945–47. Visiting Director of the Kirby Memorial Theatre, Amherst, Massachusetts, 1950; Professor of English, Mount Holyoke College, South Hadley, Massachusetts, 1950–60; Chairman of the Department of Theatre and Speech, Smith College, Northampton, Massachusetts, 1960–66; Visiting Professor, Amherst College, Massachusetts, 1966–67, University of Iowa, Iowa City, 1967–68, and the University of California, Davis, 1970–71; Berg Professor, New York University, 1971–72; Arnold Professor, Whitman College, Walla Walla, Washington, 1972–73. Literary Editor, Abbey Theatre, Dublin, 1975. Recipient: Guggenheim Fellowship, 1955. Address: 8 Sorrento Terrace, Dalkey, County Dublin, Ireland.

PUBLICATIONS

Plays

The Old Lady Says "No!" (produced Dublin, 1929; Amherst, Massachusetts, and London, 1935; New York, 1948). Included in The Moon in the Yellow River and The Old Lady Says "No!", 1932; in The Old Lady Says "No!" and Other Plays, 1961.

The Moon in the Yellow River (produced Dublin, 1931; New York, 1932; London, 1934). New York, French, 1931; in The Moon in the Yellow River and The Old Lady Says "No!", 1932.

The Moon in the Yellow River and The Old Lady Says "No!": Two Plays. London, Cape, 1932.

A Bride for the Unicorn (produced Dublin, 1933; Cambridge Massachusetts, 1934; London, 1936). Included in Storm Song and A Bride for the Unicorn, 1935.

Storm Song (produced Dublin, 1934; Cambridge, 1935; London, 1936). Included in Storm Song and A Bride for the Unicorn, 1935.

Storm Song and A Bride for the Unicorn: Two Plays. London, Cape, and New York, Smith, 1935.

Blind Man's Buff, with Ernst Toller, adaptation of a play by Ernst Toller (produced Dublin, 1936; London, 1938). London, Cape, 1938.

The Golden Cuckoo (produced Dublin, 1938; London, 1939; New York, 1950). Included in The Golden Cuckoo and Other Plays, 1954; revised version, Newark, Delaware, Proscenium Press, 1971.

The Dreaming Dust (as Weep for Polyphemus, broadcast, 1938; revised version, as The Dreaming Dust, produced Dublin, 1940; Bristol, 1946; New York, 1954; London, 1962). Included in The Golden Cuckoo and Other Plays, 1954.

A Fourth for Bridge (as The Unthinking Lobster, televised, 1948). Included in The Golden Cuckoo and Other Plays, 1954; in The Old Lady Says "No!" and Other Plays, 1961.

Six Characters in Search of an Author, adaptation of the play by Pirandello (produced South Hadley, Massachusetts, 1950); revised version, music by Hugo Weisgall (produced New York, 1956). New York, Presser, 1957.

The Golden Cuckoo and Other Plays (includes The Dreaming Dust and A Fourth for

Bridge).   London, Cape, 1954.

Strange Occurrence on Ireland's Eye (produced Dublin, 1956).   Included in *Collected Plays*, 1960.

Tain Bo Cuailgne (pageant; produced Dublin, 1956).

The Scythe and the Sunset (produced Cambridge, Massachusetts, and Dublin, 1958; London, 1959).   Included in *Collected Plays*, 1960; in *The Old Lady Says "No!" and Other Plays*, 1961.

Ulysses in Nighttown, adaptation of parts of *Ulysses* by James Joyce (produced New York, 1958).

Finnegans Wake, adaptation of the novel by James Joyce (produced New Haven, Connecticut, 1959).

Collected Plays:

    I. *The Old Lady Says "No!", The Scythe and the Sunset, A Fourth for Bridge.* London, Cape, 1960

    II. *The Moon in the Yellow River, The Dreaming Dust, Strange Occurrence on Ireland's Eye.*   London, Cape, 1960.

The Old Lady Says "No!" and Other Plays (includes *The Scythe and the Sunset* and *A Fourth for Bridge*).   Boston, Little Brown, 1961.

Nine Rivers from Jordan, music by Hugo Weisgall (produced New York, 1969).   New York, Presser, 1969.

Screenplays: *Guests of the Nation,* 1933; *River of Unrest,* 1937; *Ourselves Alone,* 1937.

Radio Plays: *Death at Newtownstewart,* 1937; *Lillibulero,* 1937; *Weep for Polyphemus,* 1938; *Multiple Studio Blues,* 1938; *Nansen of the "Fram,"* 1940; *The Gorgeous Lady Blessington,* 1941; *The Autobiography of Mark Twain,* 1941; *Abraham Lincoln,* 1941; *In the Train,* 1946; *Verdict of the Court* series, 1960.

Television Plays: *The Last Voyage of Captain Grant,* 1938; *The Parnell Commission,* 1939; *Weep for the Cyclops,* 1946; *The Unthinking Lobster,* 1948; *The Call to Arms,* 1949; *Siege at Killyfaddy,* 1960.

Ballet: *The Indiscreet Goat,* Dublin, 1931.

Other

Nine Rivers from Jordan: The Chronicle of a Journey and a Search (wartime autobiography).   London, Verschoyle, 1953; Boston, Little Brown, 1955.

In Search of Swift.   Dublin, Figgis, 1959.

John Millington Synge.   New York, Columbia University Press, 1965.

The Brazen Horn (autobiographical).   Privately printed, 1968; revised edition, Dublin, Dolmen Press, 1976.

Manuscript Collections: Boston University; New University of Ulster, Coleraine; Dublin University.

Critical Study: *Denis Johnston's Irish Theatre* by Harold Farrar, Dublin, Dolmen Press, 1975.

Theatrical Activities:

Director: **Plays** – *King Lear*, Dublin, 1927; *From Morn to Midnight* by Georg Kaiser, Dublin, 1927; *The Fountain* by Eugene O'Neill, Dublin, 1928; *Hoppla* by Ernst Toller,

Dublin, 1928; *Happy Families* by Mary Manning, Dublin, 1934; *The Moon in the Yellow River*, London, 1934; *A Bride for the Unicorn*, London, 1936; *Ah, Wilderness!* by Eugene O'Neill, London, 1936; *Finnegans Wake* by Mary Manning, New Haven, Connecticut, 1957; *The Scythe and the Sunset*, Toronto, 1976. **Film** – *Guests of the Nation*, 1934.

Actor: **Plays** – King Gustavus Adolphus in *The School of Princesses* by Jacinto Benavente, Dublin, 1925; Duvallet in *Fanny's First Play* by Shaw, Dublin, 1925; Cusins in *Major Barbara* by Shaw, Dublin, 1925; Ulysses in *Cyclops* by Euripides, Dublin, 1926; Roberto in *The Constant Nymph* by Margaret Kennedy and Basil Dean, Dublin, 1927; Guido Venanzi in *The Game As He Played It* by Pirandello, Dublin, 1927; Nojd in *The Father* by Strindberg, Dublin, 1927; The Student in *The Chief Thing* by Evreinov, Dublin, 1927; Terence in *Youth's the Season* by Mary Manning, Dublin, 1933; An Lu-Shan in *Armlet of Jade* by Lord Longford, London, 1936.

*   *   *

Denis Johnston's plays have never had either the wider exposure or critical attention outside his native Ireland which they merit. As the wryly witty Prefaces to his *Collected Plays* admit, he is thought of as quintessentially Irish except in Ireland, an attitude not much helped by what he calls "the widespread impression, put about by unscrupulous enemies, that I died of some unspecified disease in the summer of 1933, and have never written anything since." Only one of his plays – *The Moon in the Yellow River* (1931) – has achieved any international currency, and this play, although set in Ireland, takes international industrialism for its theme and has a German protagonist. Even then, as his amusing account of its exposure on Broadway shows, it was thought "too Irish" to travel without alteration.

Johnston's career did in fact begin with a play the point of which can be fully appreciated only in Ireland. *The Old Lady Says "No!"* makes its full effect only with an audience which can understand its complex layers of allusion, parody, irony and historical and political satire. Taking the story of Robert Emmett as its starting-point and juxtaposing the romantic legend with the harsher facts, it is, ironically, a subtly anti-Irish play, although in Ireland it has always been seen as a strongly nationalistic piece. It was an early production of the enterprising avant-garde Gate Theatre Company in Dublin of which Johnston, with Michael MacLiammoir and Hilton Edwards, was a moving spirit (there is a story that the play's title refers to Lady Gregory, director of the more established Abbey Theatre to which the play was offered) – a company fired with new ideas. As Johnston put it:

> we were tired of the conventional three-act shape ... and we wanted to know whether the emotional appeal of music could be made use of in terms of theatrical prose, and an opera constructed that did not have to be sung .... Could dialogue be used in lieu of some of the scenery, or as a shorthand form of character-delineation? Could the associations and thought-patterns already connected with the songs and slogans of our native city be used deliberately to evoke a planned reaction from a known audience?

With this in mind, the play is packed with motifs of common Irish currency: the high romantic opening between Emmett and his sweetheart is made up of lines from the familiar nineteenth century Irish romantic poets, and the final section contains easily-recognizable (in Ireland) sections of Pearse's funeral oration for O'Donovan Rossa, quotations from Shaw's *John Bull's Other Island*, and sections of Emmett's actual speech at his trial. This in its day was innovatory enough, but the play was also technically a novelty – one of the first examples of an Expressionist comedy, using expressionism allied to orchestral scoring to create an abstract impression akin to music. With little conventional plot the events are seen through the distorted vision of its central character, with the Chorus of "Forms" taking on specific character only when they impinge on the consciousness of the central

Speaker-figure. The influence of the German Expressionists and also of *Finnegans Wake* has often been mentioned, but this is only incidental – a deeper influence, as Johnston acknowledges, was the example of Kaufman and Connelly's *Beggar on Horseback*, another instance of popular satirical expressionism.

Johnston mined the vein again in *A Bride for the Unicorn*, a version of the Jason legend, a development of *The Old Lady*'s symphonic form in its use of counterpointed themes. But he was not content to remain in one mode for long; *Storm Song* is by contrast a strongly naturalistic play about the making of a film on the West Coast of Ireland, although it is an oddly laboured piece for Johnston. The early 1930's was his most prolific period; in 1931 his most famous and most enduring play was first produced. *The Moon in the Yellow River* is an extraordinarily resonant play. Although it is thought of outside Ireland as a modern Irish masterpiece, its title is from Pound's translation from the Chinese and its theme is international in application, while although it contains incidents drawn from the background of the conflict between Free Stater and Irregular, in Ireland it has always been suspected of "harbouring a superior ascendancy smile at the expense of the native Irish." This anomaly is partly due to the structure of irony within the play, its inversion of the clichés of melodrama and its balance of brilliantly intelligent argument and wit with harsh political realities. The play is only outwardly an attack on the menace of international industrialism, and even this argument is many-sided; to the rebel Blake the industrialist German Tausch has outraged the sacred person of Cathleen ni Houlihan, whereas a more subtle line is taken by the play's central character, the ex-engineer Dobelle who describes Tausch's kind of progress as "the fruit of evil men with sinister motives." Entwined with this main theme is the wider issue of the ethics of revolution, again summed up by Dobelle's warning to Tausch: "In most countries the political idealist is merely a bore, but here he has a disconcerting tradition of action." And when Tausch attacks the Irish as being only talkers, the very next line sees the rebel calmly shot dead by his Free Stater opponent. Often the play has been described as "difficult," which might better be taken to mean that it is too uncomfortably intelligent and uncompromisingly dispassionate for the average commercial theatre.

Certainly, after *The Moon in the Yellow River*, few of Johnston's plays have travelled abroad, which is particularly unfortunate in the case of *The Scythe and the Sunset* which is overdue for revival. Set in Dublin during Easter Week 1916, its title is an obvious parody of (and homage to) O'Casey's *The Plough and the Stars* which Johnston regards as O'Casey's masterpiece, and, although Johnston claims that the resemblance ends there, his play does share O'Casey's gift for sudden and dramatic changes of mood – the interruption of the dancing and festivities in Act III by Tetley (Johnston's Pearse-figure) bringing in his dying fellow-rebel recalls O'Casey's gear-change in *Juno and the Paycock* when Mrs. Tancred shatters the mood of the Boyle celebrations. Johnston describes his play as an "antimelodrama" on what has become a sacred subject, questioning the "shopsoiled axioms" of the romantic glory of embattled rebels. Although his play is by no means a debunking of the Easter Week events, its clear-eyed presentation of its (disguised) leaders and issues, its refusal to romanticise the role played by embattled womanhood during the Maud Gonne era (his heroine is a killer) or to depict the forces of oppression as totally in the wrong, make it a tense and disturbing play, allied to a sure sense of the theatre, that deserves to be more widely seen. Only a rather strained and over-inflated final scene between the two protagonists on either side somewhat mars its final effect.

Johnston's other plays include an intriguing play about Swift – *The Dreaming Dust* – a highly theatrical play beginning as a Masque on the Seven Deadly Sins in St. Patrick's Cathedral which then assumes the form of an exploration of Swift as the Masquers assume other roles as each searches for the nature of the sin which nurtured Swift's *saeva indignatio*. Its fluid construction gives a multi-faceted picture of Swift more revealing than any of the so-called "authoritative" biographies. He has also written a gripping play updating a nineteenth-century murder trial – *Strange Occurrence on Ireland's Eye* (produced at the Abbey in 1956) – which avoids the usual high melodrama of courtroom-plays and turns instead to an examination of the ethics of justice.

Why Johnston remains so little-known outside Ireland is something of a puzzle; his intelligence, wit and sense of theatre add up to a rare combination.

—Alan Strachan

JOHNSTONE, Keith. British. Born in Brixham, Devon. Married to Ingrid Johnstone. Worked at the Royal Court Theatre, London, in various capacities: Director of the Theatre Studio, 1965–66; Associate Director, 1966. Director of the Theatre Machine Improvisational Group. Taught at the Royal Academy of Dramatic Art, London, and at Calgary University, Alberta. Address: Statens Teaterskole, Holger Danskes Vej, Copenhagen, Denmark.

PUBLICATIONS

Plays

Brixham Regatta, and For Children (produced London, 1958).
Gloomy Go Round (produced London, 1959).
Philoctetes, adaptation of the play by Sophocles (produced London, 1964).
Clowning (produced London, 1965).
The Performing Giant, music by Marc Wilkinson (also co-director: produced London, 1966.
The Defeat of Giant Big Nose (for children; also director: produced on Welsh tour, 1966).
Instant Theatre (produced London, 1966).
Caught in the Act (produced London, 1966).
The Time Machine (produced London, 1967).
The Martians (produced London, 1967).
Moby Dick: A Sir and Perkins Story (produced London, 1967).
Wakefield Mystery Cycle (also director: produced Victoria, British Columbia, 1968).
Der Fisch (also director: produced Tübingen, 1971).
The Last Bird (produced Aarhus, Denmark, 1973).
Shot by an Elk (produced Kingston, Ontario, 1974).
Robinson Crusoe (produced Calgary, Alberta, 1976).

Other Plays: The Nigger Hunt, 1959; The Cord, Home.

Theatrical Activities:

Director: **Plays** – Eleven Plus by Kon Fraser, London, 1960; The Maimed by Bartho Smit, London, 1960; The Triple Alliance by J. A. Cuddon, London, 1961; Sacred Cow by Kon Fraser, London, 1962; Day of the Prince by Frank Hilton, London, 1962, 1963; The Pope's Wedding by Edward Bond, London, 1962; The Knack by Ann Jellicoe (co-director, with Ann Jellicoe), London, 1962; Edgware Road Blues by Leonard Kingston, London, 1963; The Cresta Run by N. F. Simpson, London, 1965; The Performing Giant (co-director, with

William Gaskill), London, 1966; *The Defeat of Giant Big Nose*, Welsh tour, 1966; *Wakefield Mystery Cycle*, Victoria, British Columbia, 1968; *Der Fisch*, Tübingen, 1971; *Waiting for Godot* by Samuel Beckett, Alberta, 1972.

Keith Johnstone comments:

I began writing plays when the Royal Court commissioned me in '57. They were about physical sensations, often sensations experienced in infancy, expressed in visual images.

When I began writing again in '66 it was only to provide suitable scripts for improvisors and short "entertainment" pieces. Most of my work from '65 to '70 was with my group Theatre Machine. We toured in many parts of England, gave demonstrations to teachers and trainee teachers, and hammered out an effective formula. *Instant Theatre* was the Theatre Machine in an early show. We were the only British group to be invited to Expo 67 in Montreal, and toured in Denmark, Germany, Belgium, Yugoslavia, and Austria.

I am at present writing an account of my improvisational methods, and am returning to writing "real" plays. *Brixham Regatta* was given a Sunday night production at the Mermaid in about '69 and it looked O.K. to me. This has made me feel that there might be some point in trying a serious work again.

I dislike "sets." I think theatre should be popular. I think theatre should "freak-out" the audience rather than offer conversation pieces. Favourite play − *Do It* performed by the Pip Simmons Group.

*   —   *   *

Keith Johnstone's work has been relatively little-exposed and it can hardly be claimed that he has had much direct influence on the British theatre; but in a more subtle and pervasive manner, his work has played an important role in the British theatre of the 1960's. To a large extent this was initially confined to his work at the Royal Court for the English Stage Company during one of its most creative periods. Associated with the Court since 1957, he was a co-director of the 1965−66 season and director of the Theatre Studio, from which emerged Johnstone's Theatre Machine group, whose work, based on improvisations, has influenced a large number of younger English actors and writers.

The first efforts of the Court Studio to gain widespread attention consisted of a 1965 Christmas show, *Clowning*. Designed for both children and adults, each performance was unpredictable and different, basing itself on mime and improvisation exercises originated in the Court's acting classes. Its theme, broadly, was the making of clowns examining whether and how they can be trained. Taking a few basic situations from which the actors could take off into improvisation, the show intriguingly experimented with that sense of the unexpected and dangerous which Johnstone evidently sees as a major clowning skill, in its concentration on the immediacy of the theatrical moment. Some aspects of this work were elaborated in Johnstone's most interesting play to date, *The Performing Giant*, produced in a double-bill with Cregan's *Transcending* at the Court in 1966. The play received a poor reception at the time; critics seemed to lack a critical vocabulary with which to cope with a kind of theatre which later many other experimental groups were to make easier for them. Basically the play is an allegory of the adolescent's attempt to understand the mysteries and puzzles of the outside world as well as the processes of the developing body; a group of pot-holers encounter a giant and explore the terrain of his inside as a potential tourist Disneyland only to have the giant rebel and defeat them with the aid of the female pot-holer with whom he falls in love. To most critics the play seemed merely strange and extravagant; charging it with whimsical obscurity in its initial premise, they missed the denseness of the developing fantasy and the way in which Johnstone's allegory worked, not as a planned series of concepts but as an immediate theatrical experience, using a loose basic structure as a starting-point in a manner parallel to the work of another Court dramatist, Ann Jellicoe, in *The Sport of My Mad Mother*. It would be interesting to see *The Performing Giant* revived, for it is a more important play than was noticed at the time.

Johnstone's other work in England has been mainly in the shape of further Theatre Machine shows, each one progressively more adventurous, or of adaptations (such as his excellent version of Sophocles' *Philoctetes*). He has said that he intends to return to more serious work, and it is to be hoped that this will be soon. His sense of the possibilities of theatre, coupled with his ability to work within the terms of fantasy without sentimentality or whimsy, marks him as an original voice too rarely heard.

—Alan Strachan

JONES, (Everett) LeRoi. Pseudonym: **Imamu Amiri Baraka.** American. Born in Newark, New Jersey, 7 October 1934. Educated at Central Avenue School and Barringer High School, Newark; Rutgers University, Newark; Howard University, Washington, D.C., B.A. 1954; New School for Social Research, New York; Columbia University, New York, M.A. Served in the United States Air Force, 1954–56. Married Hettie Cohen in 1958 (divorced, 1965); Sylvia Robinson (Bibi Amina Baraka), 1966; has five children. Taught at the New School for Social Research, 1961–64; State University of New York, Buffalo, Summer 1964; Columbia University, 1964; Visiting Professor, San Francisco State College, 1966–67. Founder, *Yugen* magazine and Totem Press, New York, 1958; Co-Editor, with Diane di Prima, *Floating Bear* magazine, New York, 1961–63. Founding Director, Black Arts Repertory Theatre, Harlem, New York, 1964–66. Since 1966, Founding Director, Spirit House, Newark. Involved in Newark politics: Member of the United Brothers, 1967; Committee for Unified Newark, 1968. Member of the International Coordinating Committee, Congress of African Peoples; Chairman, Congress of Afrikan People; Secretary-General, National Black Political Assembly. Recipient: Whitney Fellowship, 1961; Obie Award, 1964; Guggenheim Fellowship, 1965; Dakar Festival Prize, 1966; National Endowment for the Arts grant, 1966. Address: C. A. P., 13 Belmont Avenue, Newark, New Jersey 07103, U.S.A.

PUBLICATIONS

Plays

A Good Girl is Hard to Find (produced Montclair, New Jersey, 1958).
Dante (produced New York 1961; as The 8th Ditch, produced New York, 1964). Included in The System of Dante's Hell, 1965.
Dutchman (produced New York, 1964; London, 1967). Included in Dutchman and The Slave, 1964.
The Slave (produced New York, 1964; London, 1972). Included in Dutchman and The Slave, 1964.
Dutchman, and The Slave. New York, Morrow, 1964; London, Faber, 1965.
The Baptism (produced New York, 1964; London, 1971). Included in The Baptism and The Toilet, 1967.
The Toilet (produced New York, 1964). Included in The Baptism and The Toilet, 1967.
Jello (produced New York, 1965). Chicago, Third World Press, 1970.

Experimental Death Unit #1 (produced New York, 1965).   Included in *Four Black Revolutionary Plays*, 1969.

A Black Mass (produced Newark, 1966).   Included in *Four Black Revolutionary Plays*, 1969.

The Baptism and The Toilet   New York, Grove Press, 1967.

Arm Yrself and Harm Yrself (produced Newark, 1967).   Newark, Jihad Publications, 1967.

Slave Ship: A Historical Pageant (produced Newark, 1967; New York, 1969).   Newark, Jihad Publications, 1969.

Madheart (produced San Francisco, 1967).   Included in *Four Black Revolutionary Plays*, 1969.

Home on the Range (produced Newark and New York, 1968).   Published in *Drama Review* (New York), Summer 1968.

Police, in *Drama Review* (New York), Summer 1968.

The Death of Malcolm X, in *New Plays from the Black Theatre*, edited by Ed Bullins. New York, Bantam, 1969.

Great Goodness of Life (A Coon Show) (produced New York, 1969).   Included in *Four Black Revolutionary Plays*, 1969.

Four Black Revolutionary Plays (includes *Experimental Death Unit #1, A Black Mass, Great Goodness of Life (A Coon Show), Madheart*).   Indianapolis, Bobbs Merrill, 1969; London, Calder and Boyars, 1971.

Junkies Are Full of (SHHH . . .), and Bloodrites (produced Newark, 1970; *Junkies Are Full of (SHHH . . .)* produced New York, 1972).   Published in *Black Drama Anthology*, edited by Woodie King and Ron Milner, New York, New American Library, 1971.

BA-RA-KA, in *Spontaneous Combustion: Eight New American Plays*, edited by Rochelle Owens.   New York, Winter House, 1972.

Sidnee Poet Heroical (also director: produced New York, 1975).

S-1 (also director: produced New York, 1976).

Screenplays: *Dutchman*, 1967; *A Fable*, 1971.

Novel

The System of Dante's Hell   New York, Grove Press, 1965; London, MacGibbon and Kee, 1966.

Short Stories

Tales.   New York, Grove Press, 1967; London, MacGibbon and Kee, 1969.

Verse

Preface to a Twenty Volume Suicide Note.   New York, Totem Press, 1961.

The Dead Lecturer.   New York, Grove Press, 1964.

Black Art.   Newark, Jihad Publications, 1966.

A Poem for Black Hearts.   Detroit, Broadside Press, 1967.

Black Magic: Poetry 1961–1967.   Indianapolis, Bobbs Merrill, and London, MacGibbon and Kee, 1969.

It's Nation Time.   Chicago, Third World Press, 1970.

Spirit Reach.   Newark, Jihad Publications, 1972.

Hard Facts.   Newark, Peoples War Publications, 1976.

Other

Blues People: Negro Music in White America.   New York, Morrow, 1963; London,
   MacGibbon and Kee, 1965.
Home: Social Essays.   New York, Morrow, 1966; London, MacGibbon and Kee,
   1968.
Cuba Libre   New York, Fair Play for Cuba Committee, 1966.
Black Music.   New York, Morrow, 1967.
In Our Terribleness: Some Elements and Meaning in Black Style, with Fundi (Billy
   Abernathy).   Indianapolis, Bobbs Merrill, 1970.
A Black Value System.   Newark, Jihad Publications, 1970.
Raise Race Rays Raze: Essays since 1965 (as Imamu Amiri Baraka).   New York,
   Random House, 1971.
The Creation of the New Ark.   Washington, D.C., Howard University Press, 1975.

Editor, Four Young Lady Poets.   New York, Corinth Books, 1962.
Editor, The Moderns: New Fiction in America.   New York, Corinth Books, 1964;
   London, MacGibbon and Kee, 1965.
Editor, with Larry Neal, Black Fire: An Anthology of Afro-American Writing.   New
   York, Morrow, 1968.
Editor, African Congress: A Documentary of the First Modern Pan-African Congress.
   New York, Morrow, 1972.
Editor, with Diane di Prima, The Floating Bear: A Newsletter, Numbers 1-37.   La
   Jolla, California, Laurence McGilvery, 1974.

Bibliography: "LeRoi Jones: A Checklist to Primary and Secondary Sources" by Stanley
Schatt, in Bulletin of Bibliography (Westwood, Massachusetts), April-June 1971.

Theatrical Activities:

Director: **Plays** – Sidnee Poet Heroical, New York, 1975; S-1, New York, 1976.

*   *   *

The debut of LeRoi Jones on the New York stage was an enviable personal success for the
young playwright. In March 1964 when three one-act plays at different off-Broadway
locales introduced Jones to city audiences, black theatre in America knew it had found a
compelling voice summoning black playwrights to a new and urgent mission.

The first of these plays, The 8th Ditch (staged semi-professionally at the New Bowery
Theatre), closed by action of civic authorities after a few days. Its fate foretold the
playwright's continuing quarrel with officialdom. His second play, The Baptism (given two
performances at the Writers' Stage), with its deliberate satire of subjects held sacred and
taboo, served notice of Jones's determination ruthlessly to strip the hypocritical masks that
society wears to protect its vested interests. But it was in his third play and first professional
production, Dutchman (presented at the Cherry Lane Theatre), that LeRoi Jones found his
authentic voice to delineate a clearly perceived mission. That mission is nothing less than the
cultural liberation of the black man in white America.

Dutchman, hailed by critic Clayton Riley as "the finest short play ever written in this
country," spoke lucidly to black Americans of the savage destruction of their cultural
identity should they continue to imitate or to flirt with an alien, though dominant, white
lifestyle. White establishment critics, impressed with the power of the play but largely
ignoring its fundamental revolutionary message, praised Jones's "fierce and blazing talent";
The Village Voice awarded Dutchman an Obie as the best American play of the season.

Overnight LeRoi Jones became the top cultural freedom-fighter of black America. Before he could properly assume this role, however, Jones had to win credibility by first liberating himself. Aged 29, a graduate of Howard and Columbia universities, and an airforce veteran, Jones belonged to a group of young Greenwich Village intellectuals, the beat generation of the troublesome sixties, influenced by writers like Allen Ginsberg and Jack Kerouac. He was already a published poet, essayist, and sometime editor of an underground literary journal. He had married a Jewess, Hettie Cohen, and the marriage had produced two daughters. Paradoxically, the acknowledged new leader of the black cultural revolution had elected to share his life with a representative of the decaying and corrosive white culture which he condemned. The dilemma had to be speedily resolved.

Jones's next professional production consisted of two plays, *The Slave*, a two-act drama, and *The Toilet*, another one-acter, staged at the St. Mark's Playhouse in December 1964. *The Slave*, although it purports to speak of a coming race war between black and white and is called by Jones "a fable," is frankly autobiographical in intent. Walker Vessels, a tall, thin Negro leader of a black army, enters the home where his former white wife, their two children, and her second husband are living together, apparently quite happily. The husband is a white liberal-minded professor who had taught Vessels in college. After a long, excoriating harangue in which he renounces his former life, Vessels shoots the white man, watches with indifference as his ex-wife is hit by a falling beam, and departs as shells from his black revolutionary forces demolish the house while the cries of children in an upstairs room mingle with the boom of guns and the shriek of falling debris. *The Toilet*, a curious work of teenage brutality and homosexual love set in a school lavatory, hints at the possibility of black and white coming together at some future time after the black man has earned his manhood and self-respect by defeating the white.

These two revolutionary plays were followed by an even more lurid and propagandistic work when *Experimental Death Unit # 1* was staged at the St. Mark's Playhouse in New York in March 1965. In this short play Jones concentrates on a night-time encounter between two white homosexuals and a black whore in a seamy section of the city. The climax occurs when a death unit of marching black militants enters and executes the three degenerates. The men are beheaded and their heads stuck on pikes at the head of the procession. The black liberation army, Jones seems to say, has a duty to rid society not only of the oppressor but also of the collaborator. Skin colour is not enough to escape due penalty for betraying the revolution.

Writing of this second group of plays, white critics who a few months ago had hailed the rising star of playwright Jones were now confounded. He had rejected the blandishments of popular (white) success held out to him and had become, to them, a bitter dramatist and violent propagandist preaching race hatred in virulent terms. Their attitude in the main confirmed Jones's suspicions that the white culture would allow nothing but what it approved of to have credence and value.

Having declared his artistic independence, Jones was now ready to deal with his personal life. A month after the production of *Experimental Death Unit # 1*, he imitated the actions of his fictitious character, Walker Vessels, by breaking with his past life. He left his white wife and two children, moved to Harlem, and founded what he called the Black Arts Repertory Theatre School. The aim of the School was to train and showcase black theatrical talent, as well as teach classes in remedial reading and mathematics. It lasted for only a short time. Supportive funding from the U.S. Office of Economic Opportunity ceased once the initial grant was exhausted and this setback coupled with internal problems forced an early closing of the theatre. But the idea of a black arts movement did not die. In its short life in Harlem, LeRoi Jones's Black Arts Group proved, in the words of critic Larry Neal, "that the community could be served by a valid and dynamic art [and] that there was a definite need for a cultural revolution in the black community."

Similar black arts groups were formed on the West Coast; the idea sparked movements in Detroit, Philadelphia, Jersey City, New Orleans, and Washington, D.C. On many college campuses across the nation, black arts programs were started and festivals held. The black cultural revolution was in fact taking place. In a forum on Black Theatre held at the Gate

Theatre, New York, in 1969, LeRoi Jones articulated the philosophic premise of this movement, giving credit to Ron Karenga of San Francisco for having helped in its formulation. Black art, he affirmed, is collective, functional, and committed since it derives from the collective experience of black people, it serves a necessary function in the lives of black people (as opposed to the useless artifacts of most white art that adorns museums), and is committed to revolutionary change.

The shortlived Harlem-based theatre produced only one new play by Jones called *Jello*, a hard-hitting satire on the once popular Jack Benny radio program advertising this product. The play, rejected by at least one established publisher because of its attack on a well-lnown stage personage, was performed on the streets of Harlem by the Black Arts Group. The straightforward plot casts Rochester, Benny's chauffeur and stereotype black handyman as a militant who demands and gets full redress for years of subservience and oppression. In this play Jones is less interested in attacking the white man than in erasing the myth of black inferiority which decades of white-controlled entertainment have helped to perpetuate. Hereafter, Jones will be more conscious of addressing a black audience in his plays. His main characters will be black, and whitey will become either the symbolic beast whose ritualistic death is necessary for the emergence of black consciousness and nationhood, or else whitey will be pilloried mercilessly as completely irrelevant to the black struggle. Jones declared:

> The artist must represent the will, the soul of the black community. [His art] must represent the national spirit and the national will .... We don't talk about theatre down here, or theatre up there as an idle jest but because it is necessary to pump live blood back into our community.

When the Black Arts Repertory Theatre closed in 1966, Jones transferred the operational base of his cultural movement from Harlem to his native Newark in New Jersey. He rented a three-story building on Stirling Street, known as Spirit House, and formed the Spirit House Movers, a group of non-professional actors who perform his plays as well as the plays of other black writers. Jones spent a year teaching at San Francisco State College where he was exposed to the influence of the young black nationalist, Ron Karenga. Then he returned to Newark determined to practice some of the liberating ideas which he advocated in his works.

In January 1968 he formed the Committee for Unified Newark dedicated to the creation of a new value system for the Afro-American community. Aspects of this new system of values are evidenced in the wearing of traditional African dress, the speaking of Swahili language as much as English, the rejection of Christianity as a Western religion that has helped to enslave the minds of black people and the adoption of the Kawaida faith in its stead, and finally the assumption of Arabic names in place of existing Christian names. Jones became a minister of the Kawaidi faith, adopted his new name of Amiri Baraka prefixed by the title Imamu (Swahili for Spiritual Leader) and continues to live in Newark with his present wife, Amina, and their children.

Jones's work continues to dwell on themes of black liberation and the need to create a new black sensibility by alerting audiences to the reality of their lives in a country dominated by a culture that Jones passionately believes to be alien and hostile to Blacks. The urgent need to root out white ways from the hearts and minds of black people is constantly reiterated. White error is seen in *A Black Mass* as the substitution of thought for feeling, as a curiosity for anti-life. In *Home on the Range* the white family speaks a gibberish of unintelligible sounds and gazes glasseyed at the television box like robots of the computer society they have created. The devils in *Bloodrites* eat of the host and chant a litany of love immediately after attempting to shoot Blacks in a glaring indictment of the hypocrisy of Christianity.

Jones graphically dramatizes the problem by personifying the evil white lifestyle in the form of a devil or beast that must be slain if Blacks are to gain their freedom. In *A Black Mass*, a play based on an Islamic fable, one of a trio of magicians persists in creating a wild white beast that he believes he can tame through love. The beast goes on a rampage and destroys everything in sight, including the magicians. *Madheart* has a Devil Lady that keeps a mother and sister of the Black Man in thrall, worshipping whiteness. In *Bloodrites*, whites are gun-toting devils that masquerade as artists, musicians and hipsters to seduce Blacks struggling towards spiritual reconstruction.

Jones has been accused of preaching race hatred and violence as a way of life. In 1967 he was given the maximum sentence of three years in prison by a county judge for possession of revolvers during the Newark riots, a conviction that was condemned as victimization by the American Council of Civil Liberties and was later overturned by a higher court. It is true that violence permeates his plays, that Jones seems to revel in bloodletting, but the intensity of his feeling and the power of his language have the effect of lifting violence to the level of a holy war against evil forces of supernatural potency. When the Devil Lady in *Madheart* boasts that she can never die, the Black Man responds "you will die only when I kill you" whereupon he stabs her several times, impales her with a stake and arrows, abuses her, stomps on her dead face, and finally drops her body into a deep pit from which smoke and light shoot up. Such needless overkill can only be understood in terms of magic and ritual.

Ritual, in fact, is the crucible that helps to transform the melodramatic incident in LeRoi Jones's plays into significant drama. Clay, the young Black hounded by the vampire Lula in a subway train in *Dutchman*, realizes that the murder of a white is the only cure for the black man's neuroses, but he is too ingrained in white middleclass values to perform the rite that will liberate him. He dies as a result. Not so Walker Vessels in *The Slave*. When he shoots Easley, the white liberal professor, the latter's last words are "Ritual drama, like I said, ritual drama." Similarly, when Court Royal, the weak-kneed assimilationist in *Great Goodness of Life* is forced to shoot his militant son, this too is a rite that must be performed, "a rite to show that you would be guilty, but for the cleansing rite." In keeping with his philosophy that black theatre must be functional, Jones has sought to make his plays identify with his audiences in form as well as content. Thus, *Bloodrites* calls for the sacrifice of a chicken whose blood is sprinkled into the audience. In *Police*, the white cops are required to eat chunks of flesh from the body of the black policeman who has killed a member of his race and is forced by the black community to commit suicide. Such ritualistic acts reinforce the magical dimension of the struggle in which black people are engaged.

A second medium of identification is language. Jones, the poet and litterateur, deliberately reaches for the vernacular and idiom of the urban Black to pound home his message. *The Slave* is a fine example of the way in which college-educated Walker Vessels rejects the elegant but alienating discourse of which he is capable for the unifying language of the ghetto. The language in *Police* is pruned and compressed to a single drumbeat, with the syncopation and lyricism associated with that pervasive black musical instrument. The process of creating a new and appropriate language for black drama is pushed further in *Slave Ship* where the narrative element relies heavily on action and music rather than language, and where Yoruba instead of English was used in the first part of the production.

Finally, in his capacity as Spiritual Leader, Jones uses the stage as a pulpit from which he exhorts his audiences to carry his message for revolutionary thinking and action into their daily lives. The Black Man in *Madheart* urges the audience to "think about themselves and about their lives when they leave this happening." A concluding narration in *A Black Mass* reminds the audience that the beasts are still loose in the world and must be found and slain. *Junkies* begins with an address by an Italian dope dealer who informs the audience that he succeeds by getting "niggers to peddle dope." The audience at *Police* are expected to leap on stage at one point of the play and join the characters in demanding vengeance on the black cop who shot and killed a black brother.

Jones's theatre is blatantly agit/prop drama exalted to an elemental plane. Apart from *Slave Ship* the structure of his plays remains conventional but the dynamic of message, the boldness of conception, and the lyricism of language give his dramas a fierceness on the stage that defies complacency. Critics may praise or damn him, but Jones is no longer writing for critical acclaim. Neither does he write for posterity, so it is irrelevant to conjecture whether his plays will last. That they have brought hope and a vision of a better life to millions of Americans, that they have infused the theatre with a new vitality and veered it closer to the lives of people, such achievements are enough to win LeRoi Jones a permanent place in the annals of the American and world theatre.

—Errol Hill

KALCHEIM, Lee.   American.   Born in Philadelphia, Pennsylvania, 27 June 1938. Educated at Trinity College, Hartford, Connecticut, B.A.; Yale University Drama School, New Haven, Connecticut, one year. Recipient: Rockefeller grant, 1965; Emmy Award, 1973. Agent: Audrey Wood, International Creative Management, 40 West 57th Street, New York, New York 10019. Address: 31 West 9th Street, New York, New York 10011, U.S.A.

PUBLICATIONS

Plays

A Party for Divorce (produced New York, 1963).
Match Play (produced New York, 1964).   Published in New Theatre in America, edited
    by Edward Parone, New York, Dell, 1965.
...And the Boy Who Came to Leave (produced Minneapolis, 1965; New York, 1973).
        Published in Playwrights for Tomorrow: A Collection of Plays, Volume 2, edited by
    Arthur H. Ballet, Minneapolis, University of Minnesota Press, 1966.
An Audible Sigh (produced Waterbury, Connecticut, 1968).
The Surprise Party (produced New York, 1970).
Who Wants to Be the Lone Ranger (produced Los Angeles, 1971).
Hurry, Hurry, with Jeremiah Morris and Susan Perkins, music by Bill Weeden, lyrics
    by David Finkle (produced New York, 1972).
The Prague Spring (produced Providence, Rhode Island, 1975; New York, 1976).
Win with Wheeler (produced Waterford, Connecticut, 1975).

Television Plays: Reunion, 1967; Let's Get a Closeup of the Messiah, 1969; Trick or Treat, 1970; All in the Family series, 1971–72; Is (This) Marriage Really Necessary, 1972; The Class of '63, 1973; The Bridge of Adam Rush, 1974.

Lee Kalcheim comments:

I am a realist. So, my plays are realistic. Comic. Dramatic. Strongly based on characters. I grew up with the realistic writers of the 1950's. Found myself sitting in the middle of the Avant Garde movement with an inherited style. And then as the theatre began to be less faddish (in N.Y.) it became apparent that I could indeed maintain my love of character – of reality – and survive as a playwright. My work in improvisational theatre and film began to broaden my work. My later work becoming more fragmented or filmlike. Less ... livingroomish. But I realized that for all the excitement of theatrical effects (I have tried various experiments with mixed media), the thing that still moved me most, standing in rehearsal watching my plays, were those one to one scenes. Those scenes where two people faced each other, wanting something from each other. Those scenes where something happened between people. They washed out all the media effects, or unusual transitions, or whatever. They were theatre at its strongest. And I suppose I keep coming back to those in my plays. I do write film. But I keep coming back to the theatre for the excitement of those live, vibrant scenes – that put flesh and blood out there in front of you.

*   *   *

"It makes me very sad and very happy to be a playwright," was Lee Kalcheim's answer to a request for a statement which could introduce this piece about him. It serves well. Kalcheim is indeed a melancholy and a joyful chronicler. But what makes him almost unique among the younger crop of dramatists in the United States has been his ability to bustle, hustle, and earn his own way *as a writer*. While most "young playwrights" are weaving their tortured ways through the mazes of foundations and endowments and theatre boards seeking grants, honoraria, subsistences, and other encouraging hand-outs, Kalcheim has energetically and quite successfully gone into the *business* of writing.

He has a good mind and that intelligence which reflects both cool observations and warm insights into the characters he creates. More than storytelling, Kalcheim is people-telling. His plays, he says, are about "human ideas," and I think I know what he means; he's right. As a playwright, he is less concerned with the usual ideas *per se* than he is with the humanness of those ideas, with the humanity which generates those ideas.

Moreover, as even a quick reading or viewing of his work for the stage reveals, Kalcheim is fascinated by human loneliness. What for other, more abstract writers is a concern with the condition of loneliness, for Kalcheim becomes both a compassionate and an uninvolved concern for the human being as an alone creature: yes, both passionate and uninvolved, both sad and happy. People trying – desperately, lazily, sadly, hopefully, hilariously, pathetically, ridiculously – to make contact with other people is what his plays not only are but are about.

At the end of *An Audible Sigh*, one of the characters, Gale, says, "You see ... I want to be loved, but I don't want to have strings attached." And there, indeed, is the rub. Kalcheim's people are lonely, loving but afraid of being loved and even of being un-lonely. They sometimes seem to enjoy their loneliness and find sanctuary in their states of not being loved. Driven in part by fear of being possessed and by desire to possess, the characters are intensely vulnerable. Their bulwarks seem all terribly sturdy and well-planned but facing in the wrong direction.

In play after play, Lee Kalcheim examines these qualities. Even more personally, he exhibits a unique ability to watch and be part of the action *and*, to double the effect, to watch the watchers (himself included) and the actors. Again and again, Kalcheim seems to be writing much the same play – each time in a different guise but each time about the same qualities, sensibilities. If these feelings and events are indeed his own experiences (love, divorce, joining, separation, regret, hope, need, fear, tenacity, escape), he is quite excellent at turning that experience into theatrical action, because Kalcheim the writer is a very astute observer of Kalcheim the man.

Moreover, his technique works unusually well: he justapositions comedy and drama with almost metronomic regularity, but at the critical heart of the matter is a much more important and profound juxtaposition: The Fear of Death poised against An Immortality Assured, if one may capitalize such sentiments anymore.

He has been writing since he was eleven years old, and he says that when his first playlet was produced, he wept at the recognition of his own voice "up there." If he has turned now more and more to film and television to earn a living, his first and enduring love is perhaps not a person (ironically) but the theatre. As with many media writers, Kalcheim plays the game of running down his own television writing, but nonetheless he speaks with justified pride about the way his voice is now heard "up there."

As with many new writers, his dissatisfaction with present theatrical systems is deep and revolutionary. He would eliminate, if he could, the producer altogether and do his plays himself in New York, in Los Angeles, wherever there are audiences. But he realizes too that then he would himself become that terrible tyrant, the producer, and the cycle would continue.

—Arthur H. Ballet

KANIN, Garson. American. Born in Rochester, New York, 24 November 1912. Left school at age 15; later attended the American Academy of Dramatic Arts, New York, 1932–33. Served in the United States Army Signal Corps, 1941–42: Private; Air Force, 1942–43, and the Office of Strategic Services, 1943–45: Captain, on Staff of SHAEF (European Theatre Operations). Married the actress and playwright Ruth Gordon in 1942. Worked as a jazz musician, Western Union messenger, stock boy and advertising proof-reader at Macy's, New York, burlesque comedian, summer camp social director. Assistant to the playwright and director George Abbott, *q.v.*, 1935–37; radio interviewer and actor; on Production Staff, Samuel Goldwyn Productions, Hollywood, 1937–38. Free-lance Director, Producer, since 1938. Recipient: New York Film Critics Circle Award Citation, 1945; Academy Award, for documentary, 1946; Sidney Howard Memorial Award, 1946; Donaldson Award, for play and direction, 1946; American Academy of Dramatic Arts Award of Achievement, 1958. Agent: William Morris Agency, 1350 Avenue of the Americas, New York, New York 10019. Address: P.O. Box 585, Edgartown, Massachusetts 02539, U.S.A.

PUBLICATIONS

Plays

> *Born Yesterday* (also director: produced New York, 1946; London, 1947).   New York, Viking Press, 1947.
> *The Smile of the World* (also director: produced New York, 1949).   New York, Dramatists Play Service, 1949.
> *The Rat Race* (also director: produced New York, 1949).   New York, Dramatists Play Service, 1950.
> *The Live Wire* (also director: produced New York, 1950).   New York, Dramatists Play Service, 1951.
> *The Amazing Adèle*, adaptation of a play by Pierre Barillet and Jean-Pierre Grédy (also director: produced Westport, Connecticut, 1950).
> *Fledermaus*, adaptation of the libretto by Haffner and Genée, music by Johann Strauss (also director: produced New York, 1950).   New York, Boosey and Hawkes, 1950.
> *The Good Soup*, adaptation of a play by Felicien Marceau (also director: produced New York, 1960).
> *Do Re Mi*, music and lyrics by Jule Styne, Betty Comden and Adolph Green, adaptation of his own novel (also director: produced New York, 1960, and London, 1961).
> *A Gift of Time*, adaptation of *Death of a Man* by Lael Tucker Wertenbaker (also director: produced New York, 1962).   New York, Random House, 1962.
> *Come On Strong*, based on his own stories (also director: produced New York, 1962).   New York, Dramatists Play Service, 1964.

Remembering Mr. Maugham, adaptation of his own book (produced New York, 1966).
Adam's Rib, with Ruth Gordon (screenplay).   New York, Viking Press, 1972.

Screenplays: *The More the Merrier*, with Bob Russell (not credited), 1943; *Born Yesterday*, with others (not credited), 1950; *It Should Happen to You*, 1954; *The Rat Race*, 1959; *High Time*, 1960; *The Right Approach*, 1961; *Where It's At*, 1969; *Some Kind of Nut*, 1969; with Ruth Gordon: *From This Day Forward*, 1946; *A Double Life*, 1948; *Adam's Rib*, 1949; *The Marrying Kind*, 1952; *Pat and Mike*, 1952.

Television Plays: *An Eye on the Family*, 1963; *The He-She Chemistry*, 1963; *Something to Sing About* (*Mr. Broadway* series), 1964.

Novels

Do Re Mi.   Boston, Little Brown, 1955.
Blow Up a Storm.   New York, Random House, 1959; London, Heinemann, 1960.
The Rat Race.   New York, Pocket Books, and London, Ace, 1960.
Where It's At.   New York, New American Library, 1969.
A Thousand Summers.   New York, Doubleday, 1973; London, Hart Davis, 1974.
One Hell of an Actor.   New York, Harper, 1976.

Short Stories

Cast of Characters: Stories of Broadway and Hollywood.   New York, Atheneum, 1969.

Other

Remembering Mr. Maugham.   New York, Atheneum, and London, Hamish Hamilton, 1966.
Tracy and Hepburn: An Intimate Memoir.   New York, Viking Press, 1971; London, Angus and Robertson, 1972.
Hollywood: Stars and Starlets, Tycoons and Flesh-Peddlers, Movie-Makers and Moneymakers, Frauds and Geniuses, Hopefuls and Has-Beens, Great Lovers and Sex Symbols.   New York, Viking Press, 1974; London, Hart Davis MacGibbon, 1975.

Theatrical Activities:

Director: **Plays** – assistant director, to George Abbott, of *Three Men on a Horse* by George Abbott and Cecil Holm, New York, 1935, *Boy Meets Girl* by Bella and Samuel Spewack, New York, 1935, *Brother Rat* by John Monks, Jr., and Fred F. Finklehoffe, New York, 1936, and *Room Service* by John Murray and Allen Boretz, New York, 1937; director of *Hitch Your Wagon* by Sidney Holloway, New York, 1937; *Too Many Heroes* by Dore Schary, New York, 1937; *The Rugged Path* by Robert E. Sherwood, New York, 1945; *Years Ago* by Ruth Gordon, New York, 1946; *Born Yesterday*, New York, 1946; *How I Wonder* by Donald Ogden Stewart, New York, 1947; *The Leading Lady* by Ruth Gordon, New York, 1948; *The Smile of the World*, New York, 1949; *The Rat Race*, New York, 1949; *The Amazing Adèle*, Westport, Connecticut, 1950; *The Live Wire*, New York, 1950; *Fledermaus*, New York, 1950, 1966; *Into Thin Air* by Chester Erskine, London, 1955; *The Diary of Anne Frank* by Frances Goodrich and Albert Hackett, New York, 1955; *Small War on Murray Hill* by Robert E. Sherwood, New York, 1957; *A Hole in the Head* by Arnold Schulman, New York, 1957; *The Good Soup*, New York, 1960; *Do Re Mi*, New

York, 1960, London, 1961; *Sunday in New York* by Norman Krasna, New York, 1961; *A Gift of Time*, New York, 1962; *Come On Strong*, New York, 1962; *Funny Girl* by Isobel Lennart, New York, 1964; *I Was Dancing* by Edwin O'Connor, New York, 1964; *A Very Rich Woman* by Ruth Gordon, New York, 1964; *We Have Always Lived in the Castle* by Hugh Wheeler, New York, 1966; *Remembering Mr. Maugham*, Los Angeles, 1969; *Idiot's Delight* by Robert E. Sherwood, Los Angeles, 1970. **Films** – *A Man to Remember*, 1938; *Next Time I Marry*, 1939; *The Great Man Votes*, 1939; *Bachelor Mother*, 1939; *My Favorite Wife*, 1940; *They Knew What They Wanted*, 1940; *Tom, Dick and Harry*, 1941; *Night Shift, Fellow Americans*, and *Ring of Steel* (documentaries), 1942; *Woman of the Year*, 1942; *Battle Stations* (documentary), 1944; *The True Glory*, with Carol Reed (documentary), 1945; *Spars Salute to France*, 1946; *Where It's At*, 1969; *Some Kind of Nut*, 1969. **Television** – *Born Yesterday*, 1956.

Actor: **Plays** – Tommy Deal in *Little Ol' Boy* by Albert Bein, New York, 1933; Young Man in *Spring Song* by Bella and Samuel Spewack, New York, 1934; Red in *Ladies' Money* by George Abbott, New York, 1934; Al in *Three Men on a Horse* by George Abbott and Cecil Holm, New York, 1935; Izzy Cohen in *The Body Beautiful* by Robert Rossen, New York, 1935; Green in *Boy Meets Girl* by Bella and Samuel Spewack, New York, 1935; Vincent Chenevski in *Star Spangled* by Robert Ardrey, New York, 1936; Garson Kanin in *Remembering Mr. Maugham*, Los Angeles, 1969. **Radio** – *March of Times* news re-enactments, *The Goldbergs, Aunt Jenny's Real Life Stories, The Theatre Guild on the Air, Five-Star Final, The NBC Theatre, The Honeymooners* – *Grace and Eddie*, 1935–37.

*   *   *

For the critic of American theatre Garson Kanin remains a dramatist of a single play. After gaining some reputation as an actor and as a director, he wrote *Born Yesterday*, his first and only successful play. Mainly, the play is hokum and sweet sentiment, the stock-in-trade of the commercial comic dramatist, but in this work Kanin also showed perception as a comic satirist which he, unfortunately, never repeated. In *Born Yesterday* the traditional dumb blonde is provided with a variant reading which gives her a substance that one accepts even when recognizing the play's flimsy quality. Educated by a *New Republic* correspondent, she realizes that the junk-man tycoon who keeps her is endangering the country. And with her teacher, she defeats him, providing a memorable stage exit in such a way that the play makes a comment on the state of the nation.

Never again has Kanin found the right combination for an effective theatre piece. Generally, he has employed the same devices as his colleagues writing comedies for the New York stage, but his tricks have not worked properly, and he has not provided good or interesting story lines or carefully created characters. Topicality and local color have been major devices in his plays – name dropping of places, movie stars, dramatists, and so on. He likes the stage joke, usually visual as well as verbal, as well as the quick one-line gag. As a good director of his own plays as well as plays by others, he emphasizes stage business, prop gimmicks, and well-paced dialogue. None of these techniques is, of course, unusual even in good plays, but without interesting characters and plots and some good wit such devices or techniques become ineffective.

In 1949 Kanin wrote and directed both *The Rat Race*, the rather tired story of a beaten down dancer and an optimistic saxaphone player, and an equally tepid play called *The Smile of the World*. The next year he offered *The Live Wire*. In this play he shows how a pretty good fellow is unintentionally saved from marrying a gold digger by a loud-mouthed, self-indulgent heel who makes everyone hate him and yet reaches the success that they all want. If there were a serious note in the play, one might call the dramatist bitter, but it is all patently thin and meaningless. At this point Kanin began to spend his time directing or writing stories. Then in 1962 he provided New York audiences with two plays – both characteristically his and both too slight to be considered by historians of the drama. *A Gift of Time* was a dramatization of a novel. A man discovers that he has an inoperable cancer, and Kanin dramatizes that "gift of time" the man is given before death takes him. Although the action is not completely sentimentalized, the thinness of the characters and the ineffective episodic narrative make that action meaningless and the climax, as the wife helps her husband slash his wrists, both improbable and theatrically unpleasant. *Come On Strong* brings only a slight twist to the tired plot: boy meets girl but girl marries other man who dies, later boy meets girl who has now become hard and commercial, boy meets girl again in the third act, convinces her of her original charm, and all ends happily.

More than most American dramatists Garson Kanin has divided his career between writing (fiction, plays, essays) and practical theatre (acting and directing). But he has been truly outstanding in neither art. Rather, he merges with the mass of dramatists who produce the daily theatrical fare, rising to recognizable height only in *Born Yesterday*.

—Walter J. Meserve

KEANE, John B(rendan).   Irish.   Born in Listowel, County Kerry, 21 July 1928. Educated at Saint Michael's College, Listowel, graduated 1946. Married Mary O'Connor in 1955; has four children. Worked as a chemist's assistant, 1946–51; moved to England in 1951 and worked as a street sweeper and furnace operator. Currently, pub owner-operator, Listowel. Weekly Columnist for *Limerick Leader* and *Dublin Evening Herald*. Since 1973, President, Irish P.E.N. Agent: May Bleazard, 32 Great Windmill Street, London W.1, England. Address: 37 William Street, Listowel, County Kerry, Ireland.

PUBLICATIONS

Plays

> *Sive* (produced Listowel, County Kerry, 1959; London, 1961).   Dublin, Progress House, 1959; Elgin, Illinois, Performance, n.d.
> *Sharon's Grave* (produced Cork, 1960; New York, 1962).   Dublin, Progress House, 1960; in *Seven Irish Plays 1946–1964*, edited by Robert G. Hogan, Minneapolis, University of Minnesota Press, 1964.
> *The Highest House on the Mountain* (produced Dublin, 1961).   Dublin, Progress House, 1961.
> *Many Young Men of Twenty* (produced Cork, 1961).   Dublin, Progress House, 1961.
> *No More in Dust* (produced Dublin, 1962).
> *Hut 42* (produced Dublin, 1963).   Dixon, California, Proscenium Press, 1963.
> *The Man from Clare* (produced Cork, 1963).   Cork, Mercier Press, 1963.
> *The Year of the Hiker* (produced Cork and Chicago, 1964).   Cork, Mercier Press, 1964.
> *The Field* (produced Dublin, 1965; New York, 1976).   Cork, Mercier Press, 1967.
> *The Roses of Tralee* (produced Cork, 1966).
> *The Rain at the End of the Summer* (produced Cork, 1967).   Cork, Mercier Press, 1967.
> *Big Maggie* (produced Cork, 1969; Los Angeles, 1976).   Cork, Mercier Press, 1969.
> *The Change in Mame Fadden* (produced Cork and Chicago, 1971).   Cork, Mercier Press, 1973.
> *Moll* (produced Killarney, County Kerry, 1971).   Cork, Mercier Press, 1971.
> *The One-Way Ticket* (produced Listowel, County Kerry, 1972).
> *Values: The Springing of John O'Dorey, Backwater, and The Pure of Heart* (produced Cork, 1973).   Cork, Mercier Press, 1973.
> *The Crazy Wall* (produced Waterford, 1973).   Cork, Mercier Press, 1974.

Matchmaker (produced Dublin, 1975).
The Good Thing (produced Limerick, 1976).   Cork, Mercier Press, 1976.

Radio Plays: *Barbara Shearing*, 1959; *A Clutch of Duckeggs*, 1969; *The War Crime*, 1976.

Short Stories

Death Be Not Proud.   Cork, Mercier Press, 1976.

Verse

The Street and Other Poems.   Dublin, Progress Publications, 1961.

Other

Strong Tea.   Cork, Mercier Press, 1963.
Self-Portrait.   Cork, Mercier Press, 1964.
Letters of a Successful T.D.   Cork, Mercier Press, 1967.
Letters of an Irish Parish Priest.   Cork, Mercier Press, 1972.
Letters of an Irish Publican.   Cork, Mercier Press, 1973.
The Gentle Art of Matchmaking.   Cork, Mercier Press, 1973.
Letters of a Love-Hungry Farmer.   Cork, Mercier Press, 1974.
Letters of a Matchmaker.   Cork, Mercier Press, 1975.
Letters of a Civic Guard.   Cork, Mercier Press, 1976.
Is the Holy Ghost Really a Kerryman. Cork, Mercier Press, 1973.

Critical Studies: in *Seven Irish Plays 1946–1964*, edited by Robert G. Hogan, Minneapolis, University of Minnesota Press, 1964; *After the Irish Renaissance* by Robert G. Hogan, London, Macmillan, and Minneapolis, University of Minnesota Press, 1968.

John B. Keane comments:

I regard the playwright of today as a man who must speak for his people, to speak up and to speak out, to say what vested interests, politicians, and big business are afraid to say. I believe that men should be tried for not speaking out when doing so would benefit their fellows and ultimately save lives. Those guilty of not doing so are criminals in every sense of the word. Most men have moral courage, but moral courage without skill to impose one's views is like a steed without a rider. I feel strongly about exploring the ills of modern Ireland and the world, for the anguish of our times is the Frankenstein monster that has been created by our convenient and long silences. We reap this anguish because we have encouraged its growth by pulling the bedclothes over our heads, hoping that the ogres might go away and that dawn might purify all. That is why we are fast approaching a post-Christian era. This is why speaking out early and often is so essential if there is to be a decent quality of life. I look to life as it is lived around me and listen to a language that is living. It would be against my nature to ignore a living speech and a living people. I sometimes feel I would die without these to sustain me. Playwriting is my life. Just as a tree spreads its roots into the earth, I spread my recording impulses around the breasts of my people and often into their very cores. People need to be recorded, to be witnessed; they expect and deserve it. I feel a responsibility to my people, a duty to portray them accurately and with dignity lest they are falsely delineated. There is a lot of love and humour in my plays, for without love and humour there is nothing. Where there is love there is every virtue you care to think of: love begets all that is great and constant. Think of that word "constant." That's what love is. That is the rock to which I have anchored myself, and I think my best is to come.

*   *   *

Despite his reputation in Ireland as a dramatist, essayist, publican, and raconteur, John B. Keane is little known outside Ireland. Unlike many other Irish writers, Keane has chosen not to leave home but to remain in Listowel, the small market town in rural North Kerry where he was born and educated and where he has for twenty years operated "John B. Keane's Public House." Not surprisingly, his best plays, *Sive, Sharon's Grave, The Field*, and *Big Maggie*, are those which deal with rural Irish experience. The nightly drama at his pub provides a rich source of situation, character, and theme. Keane possesses a natural understanding of Irish countrymen. He knows the rhythm of their language and their lives. One never doubts that the problems he dramatizes are real problems in rural Ireland — emigration (*Many Young Men of Twenty*), arranged marriages (*Sive*), class conflict (*The Rain at the End of the Summer*), the breakdown of families (*Big Maggie, The Crazy Wall*), the disposition of land (*Sharon's Grave*), and the conflict of tribal and national loyalties (*The Field*).

In nearly all his plays Keane is concerned with the intimidation and exploitation of the weak by the strong, and with the insensitive, brutal, and often terrifying nature of this exploitation. In his earlier plays, perhaps up to *The Rain at the End of the Summer*, the power of violence and intimidation is limited by the greater power of a Christian providence which judges evil acts and promises justice, if not in this world, then in the next. The brutalization of the young orphan Sive by those who would force her into an unwanted arranged marriage with the doddering lecher Sean Dota will be punished. The tinkers Pats Bocock and Carthalawn lament Sive's untimely death and their choric songs promise the ultimate justice which Keane's Irish Catholic audience would have expected.

Similarly, in *Sharon's Grave*, the bullying Dinzie Conlee, who tries to sieze the land from his defenseless cousin, meets a horrible but "just" fate at the end of the play. Even in Keane's most violent play, *The Field*, in which "The Bull" McCabe beats to death a young stranger who has outbid him for title to a four-acre field, there is the sense that justice will prevail. The murderer survives, but so does his conscience: "That's the way of the world. The grass won't be green over his grave when he'll be forgot by all...forgot by all except me!"

Keane's more recent plays have taken a darker, more ironic, and therefore more modern view of exploitation and violence. *Big Maggie*, opens in a graveyard with Maggie sitting on a gravestone listening to the sound of the dirt being thrown down on her husband's coffin. Keane is suggesting here the finality of death and in the play he offers no traditional palliatives for the inevitability of age and for the mulish actions of a mother who drives away her four grown children in the name of domestic economy. Big Maggie prevails; she has her possessions intact. But her things mean nothing. She is alone and she has willed it so.

The Rain at the End of the Summer and *Moll* both suggest the darker moral vision of *Big Maggie*. Moll, housekeeper in an Irish rectory, has the tenacity and self-centeredness of Maggie. She copes with a succession of venal pastors in a Christian house which is indifferent to God. *Rain*, one of John B. Keane's best-made plays, is a domestic tragedy which developes with a *Lear*-like inevitability the change in fortune of an old man who begins utterly confident of his family's love and ends rejected and defeated, muttering empty commands to a daughter who has given up her religious vocation to remain with him. The play in no way provides an ultimate justice which would make sense of such human suffering. Joss O'Brien, like Lear, has experienced "this tough world."

In a recent play, *The Crazy Wall*, Keane seems to be moving in new directions, but he remains preoccupied with the breakdown of traditional Christian values. More obviously autobiographical than any of his earlier plays – the central figure is a schoolmaster and one of his sons wants to be an actor – *The Crazy Wall* is set in rural Ireland during World War II. Michael Barnett, convinced that the stone wall which he is building will gain him the privacy he desires, becomes instead more exposed and more vulnerable. He cannot maintain the psychological walls which he has built against human relations. His vulnerability results in a powerful and cathartic encounter with his wife at the end of the play in which truths are told and possibilities develop for a deeper and more genuine love. Keane develops these human possibilities in a context which rejects pious platitudes. Michael Barnett's final line, the last line of the play – "God always comes up trumps in the morning" – is surely ironic. Much closer to the moral center of *The Crazy Wall* and very likely to John B. Keane's own values are the words of Moses McCoy, a poor wanderer who has lost his wife and two sons and who will not be appeased by traditional Christian consolation, "What fool says God is good? God is no damned good, never was and never will be world without end."

—Arthur E. McGuinness

KENNA, Peter (Joseph).   Australian.   Born in Sydney, New South Wales, 18 March 1930. Educated at the Christian Brothers' School, Lewisham, New South Wales. Radio actor and singer; formerly member of the Australian Elizabethan Theatre Trust; has worked as a salesman. Recipient: Australia Council grant, 1973, 1975. Agent: Howard Nicholson (Australia) Ltd., 17/29–B Nelson Street, Woollahra, New South Wales 2025, Australia.

PUBLICATIONS

Plays

    The Slaughter of St. Teresa's Day (produced Sydney, 1959).   Sydney, Currency Press, 1972; London, Eyre Methuen, 1973.
    Talk to the Moon (produced London, 1963).
    Muriel's Virtues? (produced Sydney, 1966).
    Listen Closely (produced Sydney, 1972).
    A Hard God (produced Sydney, 1973).   Sydney, Currency Press, and London, Eyre Methuen, 1974.
    Mates (produced Sydney, 1975; London, 1976).

Theatrical Activities:

    Actor: **Radio** – *Portia Faces Life* and *Life Can Be Beautiful* series.

*   *   *

The work of Peter Kenna spans two movements in Australian playwriting and expresses the radical changes which took place in that country's theatre between the fifties and the seventies. From childhood a working actor and a private writer, he first came to national notice as a playwright in 1958 with *The Slaughter of St. Teresa's Day*. At that time he was one of a cluster of new playwrights, among them Ray Lawler, Alan Seymour, Ric Throssell, Ru Pullan, and Richard Beynon, who reflected the flush of hope accorded by the establishment of Australia's first subsidising body for the performing arts, the Australian Elizabethan Theatre Trust.

The Slaughter of St. Teresa's Day is a comedy drama about an underworld party that ends in violence. It was inspired by the then queen of the Sydney madams, Tilly Devine, but its style owes more to the Hollywood movies and to Tennessee Williams, whose influence on the Australian theatre in the fifties and sixties was significant. The play survives today, despite its theatrical contrivances, for the warm Irish exuberance of its characterisation.

The true source of this play and of all his work to date has been Peter Kenna's family. Eleventh of 13 children of a Sydney carpenter, Kenna stems from Irish farming stock who settled in New South Wales at the beginning of the century. Kenna grew up within the sound of stories of country and urban working class life as the relatives came and went. These people inspired *Talk to the Moon*, an urban drama about a disappointed woman whose restlessness places strain on her children and on her dying husband. They inspired *Listen Closely*, a comedy of country manners in which the conventions of the teenage generation confront those of their parents.

Kenna spent most of the 1960's in Britain; it was when he returned home to settle in 1971 that his work developed to its present maturity. The new playwrights by this time had discarded the conventions in which the plays like *The Slaughter of St. Teresa's Day* had been bred in favour of looser, more personal dramatic structures based on rhythms more familiar to Australian life and language. Out of this climate Kenna wrote three largely autobiographical plays about a working class Catholic family, the Cassidys.

In the first play, *A Hard God* (the only play of the trilogy yet produced), set in 1945, the home of Dan and Aggie Cassidy is invaded by Dan's brothers, Martin, an eccentric poet and anti-Communist activist, whose estranged wife has "got religion," and Paddy, a weak charmer whose rebellious wife Sophie is pursuing him with a razor. Dan's painful, ultimately terminal illness is forced to take second place to the absurd domestic problems of his feckless family. And in contrapuntal movement is a brief, guilt-ridden affair between 16-year-old Joe Cassidy and his friend Jack Shannon. The play is about time, which hurts and heals, about dislocation from ancestral roots, and is an indictment of a superstitious form of Catholicism that lacks compassion.

In the second play, *Unrequited Passions*, the time is the 1950's and Joe an established actor, playwright, and homosexual in a company exhausted at the end of a long tour. The sense of uprootedness that pervades *A Hard God* is here channelled into an investigation of personal identity expressed through the image of the itinerant actor. As their disbandment approaches, the company clings together, their predicament personified in the character of the amnesiac Ned, who keeps his biography, cut out of a theatre programme, in his pocket to remind himself. The play ends with the taking of a group photograph, which confirms their need to capture the image of themselves before they dissolve into vacancy.

While Joe is the constant in the three plays he is the observer rather than the protagonist. In the third play, *In Captivity*, Joe is in his thirties, his health failing from incipient kidney disease as he tries to pull together his new play. As his fortune wanes, that of his charming and worthless brother rides high. *In Captivity* is Kenna's hard submission to a hard God. Joe's time, he says at the end of the play, is not yet come.

Kenna's plays are about love, particularly familial bonds in their variety: possessiveness, self-sacrifice, a reluctance to tell the truth and face the truth. Pivotal to most of his work is a maternal figure whose life force, for good or evil, dominates the action. The finest of these creations is Aggie Cassidy in the centre of *A Hard God* and *In Captivity* – a loving, pragmatic woman who believes first in her family and secondly in her God.

His short play *Mates* is a light comment on aspects of love which brings into perspective the self-deception behind the lost souls who people Kenna's world. An old shearer on holiday in the city is led in the pre-dawn hours by a dream of lost youth to the site of a former brothel, now a night club. The old man, a transvestite singer, his footballer friend, and a retired prostitute expose by degrees that their varied sexual relations have taught them nothing about human relationships: four uncomprehending souls in a house of illusion. If one can sum up the themes of Kenna's work to date, they turn on the delicate balance between the need to exploit others for comfort against the world and the need to give comfort and make one's peace with God.

—Katharine Brisbane

KENNEDY, Adrienne.   American.   Born in Pittsburgh, Pennsylvania, 13 September 1931; grew up in Cleveland, Ohio. Educated in Cleveland public schools; Ohio State University, Columbus, B.A. in education 1953; Columbia University, New York, 1954–56. Married in 1952; has two children. Joined Edward Albee's workshop in 1962. Lecturer in Playwriting, Yale University, New Haven, Connecticut, 1972–74. Recipient: Obie Award, 1965; Guggenheim Fellowship, 1967; Rockefeller grants, 1967, 1969, 1973; New England Theatre Conference grant; National Endowment for the Arts grant, 1972; Creative Artists Public Service grant, 1974. Agent: Bridget Aschenberg, 40 West 57th Street, New York, New York 10019. Address: 172 West 79th Street, Apartment 8C, New York, New York 10024, U.S.A.

PUBLICATIONS

Plays

Funnyhouse of a Negro (produced New York, 1964; London, 1968).   New York, French, 1969.

The Owl Answers (produced Westport, Connecticut, and New York, 1965).   Included in Cities of Bezique, 1969.

A Beast's Story (produced New York, 1965).   Included in Cities of Bezique, 1969.

The Lennon Play: In His Own Write, with John Lennon and Victor Spinetti, adaptation of works by John Lennon (produced London, 1967; revised version, produced London, 1968).   London, Cape, 1968.

A Lesson in Dead Language (produced New York and London, 1968).   Published in Collision Course, New York, Random House, 1968.

A Rat's Mass (produced New York and London, 1970).   Published in New Black Playwrights, edited by William Couch, Jr., Baton Rouge, Louisiana State University Press, 1968.

Boats (produced Los Angeles, 1969).

Sun: A Poem for Malcolm X Inspired by His Murder (produced London, 1969). Published in Scripts 1 (New York), November 1971.

Cities of Bezique: 2 One-Act Plays: The Owl Answers and A Beast's Story.   New York, French, 1969.

An Evening with Dead Essex (produced New York, 1973).

445

Adrienne Kennedy comments:

My plays are meant to be states of mind.

*   *   *

Adrienne Kennedy is the most complex contemporary American Negro dramatist and certainly one of the most complex of all contemporary dramatists. Influenced by American dramatists Tennessee Williams and Edward Albee, she writes surrealistic and expressionistic avant-garde drama, characterized by lyric dialogue and penetrating insights. Since 1965, when she received an Obie (Off-Broadway) Distinguished Play Award for *Funnyhouse of a Negro,* her rapidly growing reputation has earned for her two Rockefeller grants, a Guggenheim Award, and commissions to write plays for the New York Shakespeare Festival and the Royal Court's Theatre Upstairs.

Although interest in Tennessee Williams influenced her to consider theatre, her career as a dramatist was more directly stimulated by Edward Albee. While she was a member of his Playwriting Workshop in New York City's Circle in the Square, the workshop produced her drama *Funnyhouse of a Negro.*

Because of its subject, artistry, and frequent publication, *Funnyhouse of a Negro* is probably the best-known of Adrienne Kennedy's dramas. A one-act play, *Funnyhouse* expresses the neuroses and psychic dilemmas of Sarah, an American mulatto who hangs herself because she cannot resolve problems related to her identity, her attitudes towards her parents, and her existence as a Negro. Living with Raymond, a Jewish poet, in a boarding house run by a sympathetic white landlady, Sarah spends her days writing poetry in imitation of Edith Sitwell, yearning for a life of European culture and white intellectual friends, and fantasizing herself to be Queen Victoria, the Duchess of Hapsburg, Patrice Lumumba, and Jesus. No matter which role she assumes, she professes a hatred for her dark-skinned father, a missionary teacher in Africa, who betrayed three women in his life. By marrying a white woman, he destroyed his Negro mother's hopes that he would become a Christ, a Messiah, to return to Africa, the land of beginnings, and rescue his people from the cross of oppression. By taking his white wife to Africa, where he sought to transform his mother's dream into partial reality, he caused his wife to lose her sanity. By raping his wife, who denied him access to the wedding bed, he brought into a white-skinned, straight-haired world a sallow-skinned, frizzy-haired misfit, Sarah herself.

Because of her hatred, Sarah says, she killed her father. Sarah's confession of murder, however, is denied by her landlady, who recalls how the father came to the house to beg Sarah to forgive him for being black and to return with him to Africa to try to save the Negro race. The landlady insists that Sarah's father hanged himself in a Harlem hotel on the day he learned of the murder of Lumumba, the African revolutionary leader. After Sarah has killed herself, partly because she cannot effect reconciliation between her Jesus-self and her Lumumba-self, both of whom she identifies with her father, Raymond informs the audience that Sarah's father is not dead – he is a Negro doctor married to a white whore and living in a setting of European culture.

The title "Funnyhouse," Adrienne Kennedy has explained, derived from her recollection of an amusement park that she frequented during her childhood in Cleveland. On either side of the entrance to the park towered a gigantic, laughing, white-faced figure (Raymond and The Landlady) who symbolized for her White America, ridiculing and mocking American Negroes.

—Darwin T. Turner

KINGSLEY, Sidney. American. Born in New York City, 22 October 1906. Educated at Townsend Harris Hall, New York, 1920–24; Cornell University, Ithaca, New York, 1924–28, B.A. 1928. Served in the United States Army, 1939–43. Married Madge Evans in 1939. Past President, Dramatists Guild. Recipient: Pulitzer Prize, 1934; New York Theatre Club Medal, 1934, 1936, 1943; New York Drama Critics Circle Award, 1943, 1951; New York Newspaper Guild Front Page Award, 1943, and Page One Citation, 1949; Edgar Allan Poe Award, 1949; Donaldson Award, 1951; American Academy of Arts and Letters Award of Merit Medal, 1951. Address: c/o Dramatists Play Serivce, 440 Park Avenue South, New York, New York 10016, U.S.A.

PUBLICATIONS

Plays

> *Men in White* (produced New York, 1933; also director: produced London, 1934). New York, Covici Friede, 1933; London, Gollancz, 1934.
> *Dead End* (also director: produced New York, 1935). New York, Random House, 1936.
> *Ten Million Ghosts* (also director: produced New York, 1936).
> *The World We Make*, adaptation of the novel *The Outward Room* by Millen Brand (also director: produced New York, 1939). New York, Dramatists Play Service, 1939.
> *The Patriots* (produced New York, 1943). New York, Random House, 1943.
> *Detective Story* (also director: produced New York, 1949; London, 1950). New York, Random House, 1949.
> *Darkness at Noon*, adaptation of the novel by Arthur Koestler (also director: produced New York, 1951). New York, Random House, 1951.
> *Lunatics and Lovers* (also director: produced New York, 1954). Condensed version published in *Theater 1955*, New York, Random House, 1955.
> *Night Life* (also director; produced New York, 1962). New York, Dramatists Play Service, 1966.

Theatrical Activities:

Director: **Plays** – all his own plays except *The Patriots*.

*   *   *

In his first play, *Men in White*, Sidney Kingsley startled New York with his strong sense of exciting theatre. He knew how to contrive a powerful melodramatic plot with socially significant overtones. He also knew how to capture his audience with graphic details and memorable characters. As a tabloid realist writing about city life, Kingsley can be compared to Sean O'Casey and Clifford Odets. He surpassed them in neatness and objectivity of detail, but he fell behind in poetry and feeling. Putting aside his graphic melodramas from time to time, Kingsley also experimented with plays on historical themes.

Produced in 1933 by the Group Theatre, *Men in White* was directed by Lee Strasberg, using his own version of the Stanislavsky Method. The cast included such later-to-be-famous names as Luther Adler, Morris Carnovsky, Elia Kazan, and Clifford Odets. The play won the Pulitzer Prize and the Group Theatre scored its first big hit. The conflict concerned an intern who had to choose between an easy life married to a wealthy young woman and the hard life of a dedicated surgeon. But his choice of surgery was overshadowed by the sensational details of the drama. In the operating room, for example, as the surgeons scrubbed up for a seemingly real operation, Kingsley artfully revealed the secret sexual affair between the intern and the nurse (about to die because of an abortion). The melodramatic situation seemed natural because its medical details were so skilfully presented.

Two years later, Kingsley repeated his theatrical success with *Dead End*, which he himself directed. It was produced by Norman Bel Geddes, who also designed the set that juxtaposed the terrace of a luxury apartment house and the slum tenements on a dead end street near the East River. The play started with a shocking view of boys – some wearing ragged bathing trunks and some nude – swimming in the river and playing on the wharf. Their language, Kingsley wrote, was a "shocking jargon that would put a truck-driver to blush." The plot involved a love triangle, the killing of a gangster, and the arrest of a poor boy for attacking a rich man. As in *Men in White* the plotting, carefully crafted though it was, was secondary to the spectacular slice of life, especially the playing and fighting of the unforgettable "Dead End Kids" (who later moved on to their own career in Hollywood). Kingsley's theme – that poverty and slums breed crime – was also secondary to the ugly facts of slum life.

Kingsley's next play, his first experiment with historical drama, failed. *Ten Million Ghosts*, which he produced and directed in 1936, was a semi-expressionistic expose of the international military-political-industrial complex during World War I. Though the professional theatre was not able to cope with the experimental style, Kingsley continued to try his hand at historical drama now and again.

In his next play, a dramatization of Millen Brand's novel *The Outward Room*, Kingsley returned to his factual forte. The play, which he produced and directed in 1939 as *The World We Make*, told the romantic story of a mentally ill rich girl who regains her health by keeping house for a handsome young laundry worker. Kingsley provided graphic details and fascinating characters for his scenes in the psychiatric hospital, the laundry, and the worker's tenement. But unfortunately the romance and the oversimplified view of mental health overshadowed the documentary elements in the play.

In 1943, again experimenting with historical drama, Kingsley wrote *The Patriots*, a pageant-like chronicle that focused on Thomas Jefferson's struggle with Alexander Hamilton. Kingsley suggested that both men were patriots and that both the left and right wings in American politics had much to contribute to national unity, even in 1943. But the play was chiefly notable for its personal portraits of Jefferson, Hamilton, and Washington. It won the Drama Critics Circle Award for 1942–1943.

In 1949, Kingsley returned to his tabloid realism with *Detective Story*, a melodrama with such superb documentary detail that one did not mind the contrived plot. Just as Kingsley had taken his audience to the operating room and the dead end street, he took them into a New York City police station – still another unfamiliar but intriguing locale to Broadway's middle-class theatre-goers. He told the story of an honest but zealous detective who attacks an abortionist only to discover that this "doctor" once performed an abortion on the detective's wife. The story was suspenseful, but the real excitement came from the brilliant characters like the detective (played by Ralph Bellamy), the hysterical burglar (played by Joseph Wiseman), and the feather-brained shoplifter (played by Lee Grant) pathetically in search of a husband.

Turning again to history in 1951, Kingsley wrote and staged his dramatization of Arthur Koestler's novel, *Darkness at Noon*. But the playwright, overlooking the novelist's psychological probing, produced a simplistic political attack on Stalinism. The play was popular but it missed the humanity of *The Patriots*.

In 1954, Kingsley produced a pure farce, *Lunatics and Lovers*, which was devoid of his usual "important" theme and sensational story. But his talent for construction, detail and character sketches stood him in good stead as cops, robbers, fast women, and slow wives raced across the Broadway hotel setting amid ringing doorbells and telephones.

Kingsley tried to recapture his earlier sensational realism in 1962 with *Night Life*, a play set in a New York City key club, but he failed. Admirable though this style was from the 1930's to the 1950's, it was passé after *Detective Story*. With the advent of television as a medium for documentary reporting and with the growing cynicism of the audience,

Kingsley's melodramatic stories of social injustice were no longer shocking. Even the language and shadowed nudity of *Dead End* seemed mild by 1970, and his social ideas had become commonplace. What remained? The memorably detailed roles he created. While *Dead End* may be forgotten, the Dead End Kids have remained alive.

—Morgan Y. Himelstein

KOCH, Kenneth. American. Born in Cincinnati, Ohio, 27 February 1925. Educated at Harvard University, Cambridge, Massachusetts, A.B. 1948; Columbia University, New York, M.A. 1953, Ph.D. 1959. Served in the United States Army, 1943–46. Married Mary Janice Elwood in 1955; has one daughter. Lecturer in English, Rutgers University, New Brunswick, New Jersey, 1953–54, 1955–56, 1957–58, and Brooklyn College, 1957–59; Director of the Poetry Workshop, New School for Social Research, New York, 1958–66. Since 1959, Member of the English Department, and since 1970, Professor of English, Columbia University. Associated with the magazine *Locus Solus*, 1960–62. Recipient: Fulbright Fellowship, 1950; Guggenheim Fellowship, 1961; National Endowment for the Arts grant, 1966; Ingram Merrill Foundation Fellowship, 1969; Harbison Award, for teaching, 1970; Frank O'Hara Prize (*Poetry*, Chicago), 1973; National Institute of Arts and Letters award, 1976. Address: Department of English, Columbia University, New York, New York 10027, U.S.A.

PUBLICATIONS

Plays

Bertha (produced New York, 1959; revised version, music by Ned Rorem, produced New York, 1973). Included in *Bertha and Other Plays*, 1966.

The Election (also director: produced New York, 1960). Included in *A Change of Hearts*, 1973.

Pericles (produced New York, 1960). Included in *Bertha and Other Plays*, 1966.

George Washington Crossing the Delaware (produced New York, 1962). Included in *Bertha and Other Plays*, 1966.

The Construction of Boston (produced New York, 1962). Included in *Bertha and Other Plays*, 1966.

Guinevere; or, The Death of the Kangaroo (produced New York, 1964). Included in *Bertha and Other Plays*, 1966.

The Tinguely Machine Mystery; or, The Love Suicides at Kaluka (also co-director: produced New York, 1965). Included in *A Change of Hearts*, 1973.

Bertha and Other Plays (includes *Pericles, George Washington Crossing the Delaware, The Construction of Boston, Guinevere; or, The Death of the Kangaroo, The Gold Standard, The Return of Yellowmay, The Revolt of the Giant Animals, The Building of Florence, Angelica, The Merry Stones, The Academic Murders, Easter, The Lost Feed, Mexico, Coil Supreme*). New York, Grove Press, 1966.

The Gold Standard (produced New York, 1975). Included in *Bertha and Other Plays*, 1966.

The Moon Balloon (produced New York, 1969). Included in *A Change of Hearts*, 1973.

The Artist, music by Paul Reif, adaptation of the poem "The Artist" by Kenneth Koch (produced New York, 1972).   Poem included in *Thank You and Other Poems*, 1962.

A Little Light (produced Amagansett, New York, 1972).

A Change of Hearts: Plays, Films, and Other Dramatic Works 1951–1971 (includes the contents of *Bertha and Other Plays*, and *E. Kology; The Tinguely Machine Mystery; The Moon Balloon; Without Kinship; Ten Films: Because, The Color Game, Mountains and Electricity, Sheep Harbor, Oval Gold, Moby Dick, L'Ecole Normale, The Cemetery, The Scotty Dog*, and *The Apple; Youth*; and *The Enchantment*).   New York, Random House, 1973.

Rooster Redivivus (produced Garnerville, New York, 1975).

Novel

The Red Robins.   New York, Random House, 1975.

Verse

Poems.   New York, Tibor de Nagy Gallery, 1953.

Ko; or, A Season on Earth.   New York, Grove Press, 1960.

Permanently.   New York, Tiber Press, 1960.

Thank You and Other Poems.   New York, Grove Press, 1962.

Poems from 1952 and 1953.   Los Angeles, Black Sparrow Press, 1968.

When the Sun Tries to Go On.   Los Angeles, Black Sparrow Press, 1969.

Sleeping with Women.   Los Angeles, Black Sparrow Press, 1969.

The Pleasures of Peace and Other Poems.   New York, Grove Press, 1969.

Penguin Modern Poets 24, with Kenward Elmslie and James Schuyler.   London, Penguin, 1973.

The Art of Love: Poems.   New York, Random House, 1975.

The Duplications.   New York, Random House, 1977.

Other

Wishes, Lies and Dreams: Teaching Children to Write Poetry.   New York, Random House, 1970.

Rose, Where Did You Get That Red? Teaching Great Poetry to Children.   New York, Random House, 1973.

Editor, with David Shapiro, *Learn Something America*.   Bedford, Massachusetts, Bedford Museum, 1968.

Theatrical Activities:

Director: **Plays** – *The Election*, New York, 1960; *The Tinguely Machine Mystery* (co-director, with Remy Charlip), New York, 1965.

*   *   *

Kenneth Koch is a genuine man of letters, though that epithet seems inappropriate for a writer whose natural instincts are comic and parodic. In addition to writing much first-rate poetry and some striking fiction, he has been one of America's best teachers of writing – not only inspiring several promising younger poets, but also popularizing the idea of poetry writing in elementary education. His book *Wishes, Lies and Dreams* details his own experience in the New York City public schools, and thus establishes a pedagogical example that is currently imitated all over the United States. Koch has also written short plays over the past two decades, most of which originated as responses to his personal experience as a graduate student of literature, a college professor, a serious poet, and a participant in the New York art scene. Perhaps because of their occasional inspiration, many of these shorter works remained too attached to their original circumstances to be presented again. His second collection, *A Change of Hearts*, includes several new pieces, all of which are typically Kochian, none of which are particularly better than his past work.

On one hand, Koch is an absurdist and a giggler, incapable of taking anything too seriously, whose plays exploit situations and/or subjects for their available humor. On the other, he is a "New York School" poet capable of extraordinary acoherent (as distinct from incoherent) writing, such as the marvelous nonsense of these concluding lines from his earliest published play, *Pericles*:

> And we stood there with pure roots
> In silence in violence one two one two
> Will you please go through that again
> The organ's orgasm and the aspirin tablet's speechless spasm.

In structure, his plays tend to be collections of related sketches, strung together in sequences of varying duration, allowing imaginative leaps between the scenes. The best also reveal his debt, both as playwright and as poet, to the French surrealists and dadaists.

Bertha and Other Plays collects most of his early works in chronological order. The very best, *George Washington Crossing the Delaware*, originated as a response to Larry Rivers' painting of the same title (and the play is appropriately dedicated to the artist). Koch's compressed historical play ridicules several kinds of clichés: the myths of American history, the language of politicians, war films, military strategies, patriotism, and much else. The theme of Koch's multiple burlesques, here and elsewhere, is that the accepted familiar versions are no more credible than his comic rewritings. The play also reveals Koch's love of Apollinaire's great poem *Zone* (1918) by scrambling space and time. The British general refers at one point to "the stately bison," which did not enter popular mythology until the nineteenth century and certainly could not be seen on the East Coast; and the play takes place in "Alpine, New Jersey," which is nowhere near the Delaware River.

In the ten short-short scenes of his earlier mini-epic, *Bertha*, whose text runs less than ten pages, Queen Bertha of Norway uses power to assuage her evident madness, attacks Scotland only to halt at the frontier, shoots lovers for their sins, and much else, only to win the confidence, nonetheless, of both her armies and their captives. (The historical source of this burlesque is less obvious than for *George Washington*, but several possibilities come to mind.) Koch's book also includes *Guinevere*, an early work with some marvelous nonsense writing; and "Six Improvisational Plays," four of which are prose texts that suggest a performance (much like a script for a "happening"); and the book closes with scenes from *Angelica*, an opera about nineteenth-century French poetry that was written for the American composer Ben Weber but never performed.

These plays suggest a huge dramatic capability that none of them fully realizes. Neither as a fictionist nor as a playwright has Koch written the epic masterpiece his imagination hints at – the equal in their genres of his two great book-length poems, *When the Sun Tries to Go On* (written in 1953, but not published until 1969) and *Ko; or, A Season on Earth* – but symptoms of such ambition abound in his work. It should also be noted that Koch, like his poetic colleagues John Ashbery and the late Frank O'Hara (both of whom also wrote plays), belongs to the counter-tradition of American playwriting – a theatre of poets and novelists that emphasizes not naturalism but fantasy; not character but circumstance; not events but essence.

—Richard Kostelanetz

KOPIT, Arthur (Lee).   American.   Born in New York City, 10 May 1937. Educated at Lawrence High School, New York, graduated 1955; Harvard University, Cambridge, Massachusetts, B.A. (cum laude) 1959 (Phi Beta Kappa). Married to Leslie Ann Garis. Recipient: Vernon Rice Award, 1962; Outer Circle Award, 1962; Guggenheim Fellowship, 1967; Rockefeller grant, 1968; National Institute of Arts and Letters award, 1971; National Endowment for the Arts grant, 1974; Wesleyan University Center for the Humanities Fellowship, 1974. Lives in Connecticut. Agent: Audrey Wood, International Creative Management, 40 West 57th Street, New York, New York 10019, U.S.A.

PUBLICATIONS

Plays

The Questioning of Nick (produced Cambridge, Massachusetts, 1957; New York, 1974). Included in *The Day the Whores Came Out to Play Tennis and Other Plays*, 1965.
Gemini (produced Cambridge, Massachusetts, 1957).
Don Juan in Texas, with Wally Lawrence (produced Cambridge, Massachusetts, 1957).
On the Runway of Life, You Never Know What's Coming Off Next (produced Cambridge, Massachusetts, 1957).
Across the River and into the Jungle (produced Cambridge, Massachusetts, 1958).
To Dwell in a Place of Strangers, Act I published in *Harvard Advocate* (Cambridge, Massachusetts), May 1958.
Aubade (produced Cambridge, Massachusetts, 1959).
Sing to Me Through Open Windows (produced Cambridge, Massachusetts, 1959; revised version, produced New York, 1965; London, 1976).   Included in *The Day the Whores Came Out to Play Tennis and Other Plays*, 1965.
Oh Dad, Poor Dad, Mama's Hung You in the Closet and I'm Feelin' So Sad: A Pseudoclassical Tragifarce in a Bastard French Tradition (produced Cambridge Massachusetts, 1960; London, 1961; New York, 1962).   New York, Hill and Wang, 1960; London, Methuen, 1962.
Mhil'daim (produced New York, 1963).
Asylum; or, What the Gentlemen Are Up To, and And As for the Ladies (produced New York, 1963; *And As for the Ladies* produced, as *Chamber Music*, London, 1971). *Chamber Music* published in *The Day the Whores Came Out to Play Tennis and Other Plays*, 1965.
The Conquest of Everest (produced New York, 1964).   Included in *The Day the Whores Came Out to Play Tennis and Other Plays*, 1965.
The Hero (produced New York, 1964; London, 1972).   Included in *The Day the Whores Came Out to Play Tennis and Other Plays*, 1965.
The Day the Whores Came Out to Play Tennis (produced New York, 1965).   Included in *The Day the Whores Came Out to Play Tennis and Other Plays*, 1965.
The Day the Whores Came Out to Play Tennis and Other Plays (includes *Sing to Me Through Open Windows, Chamber Music, The Conquest of Everest, The Hero, The Questioning of Nick*).   New York, Hill and Wang, 1965; as *Chamber Music and Other Plays*, London, Methuen, 1969.
Indians (produced London, 1968; Washington, D.C., and New York, 1969).   New York, Hill and Wang, 1969; London, Methuen, 1970.
An Incident in the Park, in *Pardon Me, Sir, But Is My Eye Hurting Your Elbow?*, edited by Bob Booker and George Foster.   New York, Geis, 1968.
What's Happened to the Thorne's House (produced Peru, Vermont, 1972).
Louisiana Territory; or, Lewis and Clark – Lost and Found (also director: produced Middletown, Connecticut, 1975).

Critical Study: review of *Indians* by John Lahr, in *Evergreen Review* (New York), January 1969.

Theatrical Activities:

Director: **Plays** – *Oh Dad, Poor Dad, Mama's Hung You in the Closet and I'm Feelin' So Sad*, Paris, 1963; *Louisiana Territory*, Middletown, Connecticut, 1975. **Television** – *The Questioning of Nick*, 1959.

*   *   *

When Arthur Kopit came to international attention with *Oh Dad, Poor Dad, Mama's Hung You in the Closet and I'm Feelin' So Sad* – productions in New York, London, Paris, over forty productions in West Germany alone – it was clear that a major new dramatist had announced himself. But to those who knew his previous work the excitement caused by *Oh Dad*, even its extraordinary title, were not surprising. He had begun his playwriting career as a sophomore at Harvard College with a prize-winning one-act play, *The Questioning of Nick*, written for the Dunster House Drama Workshop, and he followed this play with six others, most of them written for the Workshop, including *Sing to Me Through Open Windows*, which was produced later off-Broadway. Since *Oh Dad* he has written several plays, with *Chamber Music, The Day the Whores Came Out to Play Tennis*, and especially *Indians* the most significant.

Perhaps Kopit's most important gift is his ability first to select central images from American life and then to transform them by means of his own highly personal imagination into a dramatic world uniquely his own. The result is plays strikingly original in conception, which are nevertheless, by the indirection appropriate to art, plays of powerful social comment. In *Oh Dad*, for example, he presents in an exotic Caribbean world dominated by the larger-than-life mother, Madame Rosepettle, and decorated by Venus'-flytraps and Rosalinda the piranha fish, a bizarre and brilliant parody of the Oedipus complex, which has been an American preoccupation from Sidney Howard's *The Silver Cord* to *Portnoy's Complaint*. As the "babysitter" Rosalie tries to seduce the son Jonathan on his "mother's bed" and the stuffed corpse of his father falls out of the closet on top of them, Kopit creates one of the most frighteningly hilarious scenes in modern drama. In *Chamber Music* a group of women confined to an asylum, with the double meaning of the word intended, believe themselves to be such famous women from history and popular culture as Susan B. Anthony, Gertrude Stein, Amelia Earhart, Pearl White, and Osa Johnson. The mad women, who feel a sense of threat and kill Amelia Earhart as a sacrifice and a warning, present a paranoiac exaggeration which is psychologically timeless, but their terror is also a deliberate reflection of the nuclear terror so strongly felt in the 50's and early 60's.

In *The Day the Whores Came Out to Play Tennis* the focus of attention is the country-club, social-climbing aspirations of all new American wealth. But the most vivid example of Kopit's method is provided by the more recent *Indians*, an eloquently passionate play which is also his finest. Here Kopit transfigures the familiar territory of the American West into an eerily revealing dreamscape of his own, and in his hero Buffalo Bill, with his willingness to forget the blundering destroyer of the Indians for the fake self of his own wild west show, Kopit personifies the American impulse to invent an imagined past and a romanticized identity. The metaphor has multiple application – to the Indians, to the blacks, to the war in Vietnam – and this play, one of the two or three most important American plays of the 60's, represents more powerfully than any other play the painful soul-searching and awakening that have characterized a troubled decade.

Kopit's plays, which began securely with the realism of *The Questioning of Nick*, are distinguished as well by his virtuosity in the handling of dramatic form. In *Oh Dad*, for example, tragicomedy is developed contrapuntally in terms both of tone and of time as wild comedy and pathos, and the son's present and the mother's past, are played against one another. *Chamber Music*, as the title suggests, is specifically musical in formal inspiration, and, in a very different vein, *Whores* parodies the social realism of O'Casey and Arthur Miller. *Indians* presents retrospective action ordered not by historical chronology but by the psychologically significant sequential pattern of a dream, and the play is also consciously contrapuntal in structure with the United States Commission's hearings into Indian affairs and Bill's more personal memories, his career and the Indians' destruction, simultaneously developed.

There is, finally, Kopit's concern with a heightened, almost mythic human identity. From *Nick* to *Indians* his characters seek, like the mad women in *Chamber Music*, to claim a pretended self, and like Buffalo Bill, they ultimately fail. But the attempt serves as a catalyst for the transformation of Kopit's shock-of-recognition, everyday images into the splendor of the plays' imaginative private worlds, and the failure provides a measure of their impulse toward tragedy. And it is primarily to Kopit's pervasive concern with failed identities, and the psychological forces responsible that we owe his Madam Rosepettle, his Amelia Earhart, his Buffalo Bill, characters who will linger long to trouble the American dream.

—Gaynor F. Bradish

KOPS, Bernard. British.   Born in London, 28 November 1926. Educated in London elementary schools to age 13. Married Erica Gordon in 1956; has four children. Has worked as a docker, chef, salesman, waiter, lift man, and barrow boy. Recipient: Arts Council bursary, 1957. Agent: David Higham Associates, 5–8 Lower John Street, Golden Square, London WIR 4HA. Address: Flat 1, 35 Canfield Gardens, London N.W.6, England.

PUBLICATIONS

Plays

> *The Hamlet of Stepney Green* (produced Oxford, 1957; London and New York, 1958). London, Evans, 1959.
> *Goodbye World* (produced Guildford, Surrey, 1959).
> *Change for the Angel* (produced London, 1960).
> *The Dream of Peter Mann* (produced Edinburgh, 1960).   London, Penguin, 1960.
> *Enter Solly Gold*, music by Stanley Myers (produced Wellingborough, Northamptonshire, and Los Angeles, 1962; London, 1970).   Published in *Satan, Socialites, and Solly Gold: Three New Plays from England*, New York, Coward McCann, 1961; in *Four Plays*, 1964.
> *Home Sweet Honeycomb* (broadcast, 1962).   Included in *Four Plays*, 1964.
> *The Lemmings* (broadcast, 1963).   Included in *Four Plays*, 1964.
> *Stray Cats and Empty Bottles* (televised, 1964; produced London, 1967).
> *Four Plays* (includes *The Hamlet of Stepney Green, Enter Solly Gold, Home Sweet Honeycomb, The Lemmings*).   London, MacGibbon and Kee, 1964.
> *The Boy Who Wouldn't Play Jesus* (juvenile; produced London, 1965).   Published in *Eight Plays: Book 1*, edited by Malcolm Stuart Fellows, London, Cassell, 1965; Chicago, Dramatic Publishing Company, n.d.
> *David, It is Getting Dark* (produced Rennes, France, 1970).   Paris, Gallimard, 1970.

Radio Plays: *Home Sweet Honeycomb*, 1962; *The Lemmings*, 1963; *Born in Israel*, 1963; *The Dark Ages*, 1964; *Israel: The Immigrant*, 1964.

Television Plays: *I Want to Go Home*, 1963; *Stray Cats and Empty Bottles*, 1964; *The Lost Years of Brian Hooper*, 1967; *Alexander the Greatest*, 1971; *Just One Kid*, 1974; *Why the Geese Shrieked*, and *The Boy Philosopher*, from stories by Isaac Bashevis Singer, 1974; *It's a Lovely Day Tomorrow*, 1975; *Moss*, 1975; *Rocky Marciano Is Dead*, 1976.

Novels

Awake for Mourning.   London, MacGibbon and Kee, 1958.
Motorbike.   London, New English Library, 1962.
Yes from No-Man's Land.   London, MacGibbon and Kee, 1965; New York, Coward McCann, 1966.
The Dissent of Dominick Shapiro.   London, MacGibbon and Kee, 1966; New York, Coward McCann, 1967.
By the Waters of Whitechapel.   London, Bodley Head, 1969; New York, Norton, 1970.
The Passionate Past of Gloria Gaye.   London, Secker and Warburg, and New York, Norton, 1971.
Settle Down Simon Katz.   London, Secker and Warburg, 1973.
Partners.   London, Secker and Warburg, 1975.

Verse

Poems.   London, Bell and Baker Press, 1955.
Poems and Songs.   Lowestoft, Suffolk, Scorpion Press, 1958.
An Anemone for Antigone.   Lowestoft, Suffolk, Scorprion Press, 1959.
Erica, I Want to Read You Something.   Lowestoft, Suffolk, Scorpion Press, and New York, Walker, 1967.
For the Record.   London, Secker and Warburg, 1971.

Other

The World Is a Wedding (autobiography).   London, MacGibbon and Kee, 1963; New York, Coward McCann, 1964.

*   *   *

Since he is much the same age, has a strikingly similar East End/Jewish background, and emerged as a playwright at about the same time, Bernard Kops tends too often and easily to be compared with Arnold Wesker. In fact, he has an exuberance, an instinctive sense of life, quite lacking in Wesker: he also has much less ability (and desire) to reflect, reason and philosophise. The more "intellectual" Kops becomes, the less successful he customarily is; and, though his earlier plays often invoke the hydrogen bomb, reflecting the anxieties of the period when the Campaign for Nuclear Disarmament was a potent force, he has, unlike Wesker, no great political sophistication and no special ideological views to impose on his audience. The Bomb is, rather, simplistically seen as the last throw of a society already destroying itself in numerous smaller ways. At times it almost seems to be welcomed, as a quick and dramatic escape from the paucity of contemporary life. Many of Kops's characters are attracted by suicide, and they are, significantly enough, often those who seem to be most capable of full and responsive lives. Indeed, the essential conflict at the centre of all his work is between a life-wish and a death-wish.

Sometimes one side triumphs, sometimes the other. Kops moves from an extreme of elation to an extreme of alienation, like a manic depressive. *The Hamlet of Stepney Green* involves a young dreamer whose father is "poisoned," not directly by his wife and the old friend she marries after his death, but by the unrewarding quality of his life: by the "self-deception, the petty lies and silly quarrels." His son swears revenge, but, instead falls in love with the local Ophelia; and the play ends on scenes of reconciliation and rejoicing, with his father's ghost satisfied by his survivors' common determination to "commit arson every day in your imagination, burn down the previous day's lies, have a little revolution now and again in your heart." But contrast the optimism of this with *Home Sweet Honeycomb* or *The Lemmings*. In each, we meet a characteristic Kops creation, the mother who wishes to crush the spirits of her children, and, indeed, would rather see them dead than defying the conventions of a world where (in Kops's satiric view) everything comes in plastic cartons and a population of zombies spends its time chanting advertising slogans. Life, it seems, is crude, stupid and desperately uniform. *The Lemmings* ends when the British nation, including the young couple who appear to be the only people left with any vestige of life-wish, has walked into the sea. *Home Sweet Honeycomb* ends with his young rebel-hero reclaimed for "normality" by his mother and equally emasculating fiancée: he joins the firing squad which is just lining up to shoot another, still unrepentant outsider.

Kops may be thought sentimental in his idealisation of young love, sensational in his treatment of contemporary reality, and ingenuous in each. But what his accusers miss is the energy, fun and humour of much of his work, notably, perhaps, of *Enter Solly Gold*, his best play to date. This concerns a conman who, disguised as a rabbi, invades a materialistic, bored household, briefly convinces the master he is the Messiah, and, finally, leaves him and all his other victims happier and more alive than when he came. The message, again, is: try harder to distinguish virtue from convention, true value from false, solid reality from mere illusion, and *carpe diem*. This is not, of course, particularly original or very penetratingly explored, but it is put across with a verve that is all Kops's own, and may hence be more effective than what is much the same moral in the better-known, but more solemn *The Dream of Peter Mann*: an updating of the Peer Gynt story in which the hero discovers the sterility of his search for riches, and accordingly reconciles himself to hearth, home, and the warmer, more genuine and less glamorous of his two girl-friends. This play, with its dream-picture of a world devoting all its resources to making shrouds in preparation for nuclear war, also suffers at times from Kops's weakness for emotional exaggeration and dramatic overstatement.

In recent years, Kops has largely deserted the theatre for novels and TV, to the regret of those who originally saw, in his simplicity and natural intelligence, a corrective to the regenerate British theatre's tendency to address itself too exclusively to the more educated and sophisticated. Unfortunately, his only recent stage play is one of his weakest: the story (characteristically) of how a suicidal would-be poet accepts his own inadequacies and the love of a good woman, but (uncharacteristically) set largely in a non-East End, non-Jewish milieu and full of wooden, English upper-crust dialogue. In it, he also deserts the freewheeling style of most of his plays for a narrow naturalism, another error. The true line of his literary development, one feels, is not in this direction.

—Benedict Nightingale

KOUTOUKAS, H. M.   Hellenic-American.   Born in Athens. Educated at Harpur College, Binghamton, New York; at the Maria Ley-Piscator Dramatic Workshop, New School for Social Research, New York; Universalist Life Church, Modesto, California, Ph.D. Associated with The Electric Circus and other theatre groups in New York; Founder of the Chamber Theatre Group, New York. Recipient: Obie Award, 1966; National Arts Club Award; Professional Theatre Wing Award. Agent: Madame Nino Karlweis, 250 East 65th Street, New York, New York. Address: c/o Judson Church, Washington Square, New York, New York, U.S.A.

PUBLICATIONS

Plays

> *The Last Triangle* (produced New York, 1965).
> *Tidy Passions; or, Kill, Kaleidoscope, Kill* (produced New York, 1965).   Published in *More Plays from Off-Off Broadway*, edited by Michael Smith, Indianapolis, Bobbs Merrill, 1972.
> *All Day for a Dollar* (produced New York, 1966).
> *Medea* (produced New York, 1966).
> *Only a Countess* (produced New York, 1966).
> *A Letter from Colette* (also director: produced New York, 1966).
> *Pomegranada*, music by Al Carmines (produced New York, 1966).
> *With Creatures Make My Way* (produced New York, 1967).
> *When Clowns Play Hamlet* (also director: produced New York, 1967).
> *View from Sorrento* (produced New York, 1967).
> *Howard Kline Trilogy* (produced New York, 1968).

> Other Play: *Christopher at Sheridan Squared.*

Theatrical Activities:

> Director: **Plays** – *A Letter from Colette*, New York, 1966; *When Clowns Play Hamlet*, New York, 1967; *Two Camps by Koutoukas: The Last Triange (An Embroidered Camp)* and *Only a Countess May Dance When She's Crazy (An Almost Historical Camp)*, New York, 1968.

*   *   *

H. M. Koutoukas wrote a very large number of plays – several dozen – in the decade beginning about 1963. Most of them he produced himself in a wide variety of situations. He is the quintessential Off-Off-Broadway dramatist: in addition to showing his work in the usual coffee houses, churches, and lofts, he put on plays in art galleries, concert halls, movie theatres, and, on commission, at parties as private entertainment for the rich. He gained a considerable though largely underground following, but this did not bring him readier access to stages. The theatre scene has changed, there is less personal rapport between producers and artists, more commercial pressure, and in the past few years Koutoukas's output has declined.

His plays have a special tone and flavor that are all his own and immediately recognizable. He often writes in verse, and the characters and situations are the product of a highly fanciful imagination and an elaborately refined sensibility. Most of his plays are designated "camps" rather than dramas or comedies, and the style is flamboyantly romantic, idiosyncratic, sometimes self-satirizing, full of private references and inside jokes, precious, boldly aphoristic, and disdainful of restrictions of sense, taste, or fashion. Koutoukas is perhaps the last of the aesthetes. Underlying the decoration, his characteristic themes concern people or creatures who have become so strange that they have lost touch

457

with ordinary life, yet their feelings are all the more tender and vulnerable – the deformed, the demented, the rejected, the perverse.

Medea is an adaptation of the Greek play in which the action is set in a laundromat, and in the author's production Medea was played by a man. On the surface a ridiculous notion, the play vividly articulates the situation of a woman from a more primitive, natural, expressive culture trapped among the overcivilized, calculating Greeks and conveys a sympathetic insight into her desperation. The characters in *Tidy Passions; or, Kill, Kaleidoscope, Kill* include a high priestess and several witches of a broken-down cobra cult, a dying dove, Narcissus, and Jean Harlow, who proclaims, "Glamour is dead." *With Creatures Make My Way* is set in a sewer where the single character, neither man nor woman, finally consummates an eternal love with a passing lobster. *A Letter from Colette*, in the naturalistic mode, sweetly tells of romance between an aging woman and a handsome young delivery boy. *Pomegranada* opens in the Garden of Eden and is about tarnish. *Christopher at Sheridan Squared* is an hallucinatory documentary about the Greenwich Village street where Koutoukas has lived for years.

These are some of the exotic and poignant special worlds that Koutoukas creates and explores. His plays are heroic in spirit and fiercely compassionate. He is likely to be remembered as one of the most original dramatist of his time.

—Michael Smith

KRAUSS, Ruth. American. Born in Baltimore, Maryland, in 1911. Educated in public elementary schools; Peabody Institute of Music, Baltimore; poetry workshops at the New School of Social Research, New York; Maryland Institute of Art, Baltimore; Parsons School of Art, New York, graduate. Married Crockett Johnson in 1941. Address: 24 Owenoke, Westport, Connecticut 06880, U.S.A.

PUBLICATIONS

Poem-Plays

> *The Cantilever Rainbow.* New York, Pantheon Books, 1965.
> *There's a Little Ambiguity Over There among the Bluebells and Other. Theatre Poems.* New York, Something Else Press, 1968.
> *If Only.* Eugene, Oregon, Toad Press, 1969.
> *Under Twenty.* Eugene, Oregon, Toad Press, 1970.
> *Love and the Invention of Punctuation.* Lenox, Massachusetts, Bookstore Press, 1973.
> *This Breast Gothic.* Lenox, Massachusetts, Bookstore Press, 1973.
> *Under Thirteen.* Lenox, Massachusetts, Bookstore Press, 1976.

> Productions include *A Beautiful Day, There's a Little Ambiguity Over There among the Bluebells, Re-Examination of Freedom, Newsletter, The Cantilever Rainbow, In a Bull's Eye, Pineapple Play, Quartet, A Show, A Play – It's a Girl!, Onward, Duet* (or *Yellow Umbrella*), *Drunk Boat, If Only, This Breast*, many with music by Al Carmines, Bill Dixon, and Don Heckman, produced in New York, New Haven, Boston, and other places, since 1964.

Other

A Good Man and His Good Wife (juvenile).   New York, Harper, 1944; revised edition, 1962.
The Great Duffy (juvenile).   New York, Harper, 1945.
The Carrot Seed (juvenile).   New York, Harper, 1946.
The Growing Story (juvenile).   New York, Harper, 1947.
Bears (juvenile).   New York, Harper, 1948.
The Happy Day (juvenile).   New York, Harper, 1949.
The Backward Day (juvenile).   New York, Harper, 1950.
The Bundle Book (juvenile).   New York, Harper, 1951.
A Hole Is to Dig: A First Book of First Definitions (juvenile).   New York, Harper, 1952.
I Can Fly (juvenile).   New York, Golden Press, 1952.
The Big World and the Little House (juvenile).   New York, Harper, 1952.
A Very Special House (juvenile).   New York, Harper, 1953.
I'll Be You and You Be Me (juvenile).   New York, Harper, 1954.
The Birthday Party (juvenile).   New York, Harper, 1955.
Charlotte and the White Horse (juvenile).   New York, Harper, 1955.
How to Make an Earthquake (juvenile).   New York, Harper, 1956.
I Want to Paint My Bathroom Blue (juvenile).   New York, Harper, 1956.
Monkey Day (juvenile).   New York, Harper, 1957.
Is This You? (juvenile).   New York, Scott, 1958.
Moon or a Button (juvenile).   New York, Harper, 1959.
Somebody Else's Nut Tree (juvenile).   New York, Harper, 1959.
Open House for Butterflies (juvenile).   New York, Harper, 1960.
"Mama, I Wish I Was Snow" "Child, You'd Be Very Cold" (juvenile).   New York, Atheneum, 1962.
A Bouquet of Littles (juvenile).   New York, Harper, 1963.
Eye Nose Fingers Toes (juvenile).   New York, Harper, 1964.
The Little King, The Little Queen, The Little Monster (juvenile).   New York, Scholastic Press, 1967.
Everything under a Mushroom (juvenile).   New York, Farrar Straus, 1967.
This Thumbprint (juvenile).   New York, Harper, 1967.
I Write It (juvenile).   New York, Harper, 1970.
Little Boat Lighter Than a Cork.   Weston, Connecticut, Magic Circle Press, 1976.

Manuscript Collection: Dupont School, Wilmington, Delaware.

Ruth Krauss comments:

All the "works" – or "plays" – are essentially poems – with an approach from the words themselves, rather than ideas, plot, etc. (This division cannot be made in so cut-and-dried a fashion.) The interpretation is *mostly* left completely to the director – i.e., one line can be made to take dozens of forms in actual presentation.

Part of the philosophy behind this is: say *anything* – and leave it to the director to see what happens. This does not always work out for the best – depending on the director.

*   *   *

Ruth Krauss has always seemed to me a fine, vigorous lady writing from the vegetable patch. That is, the nature of the work is that it is bursting with health, bursting with greenery, with fresh promise. This nutritional assault, this vitality asserts itself beyond all the emotions of the day, all of which, sadness, wistfulness and hilarity, appear ephemeral beside the steady residue of glowing good health.

But this health seems to issue from a steadying optimism and a kind of bravery, an ability to look the universe in the eye. Nothing cannot be looked at, nothing is so awful that it cannot be faced, perhaps mended, always accepted.

But the world that she sees appears to be without serious menace, without horror; it appears to be essentially benign, so that in effect what Krauss faces is what she perhaps nearsightedly envisions.

The bursting sense to her work is matched by a quieter sense, one of comic wistfulness. And one of whimsy. The world viewed in comic tranquillity.

I recall a series of Krauss whimsies. A number of years ago the Hardware Poets, long since gone not only from Manhattan but from the planet, presented an evening of her works which, if memory doesn't betray me, had the generic term of seven-second plays. I may be inventing this name but they certainly *felt* like seven-second plays. They were little, exploding, comic pellets which appeared, exploded and disappeared in dazzling succession for many long minutes. Or what appeared to be many long minutes. They were delightful charmers, about nothing that I can now possibly recall, except the essential sense of them — comic energy organisms, dramatic meteorites which lasted long enough to be retained forever in the spirit.

My sense of Krauss's work is that it consists of fragmented interruptions in the more sombre concourse of human events, healthy winks from over the fence. Health — a recurring term, it appears, in this critique. The fragments give off the sense also of interrupting shards of sunlight in a universe grown perceptibly greyer as the years go on. Here are excerpts from a Krauss fragment, a monologue called *If Only* which Florence Tarlow, a performer with an especially dry wit, delivered with comic gravity at the Judson Poets Theatre in New York some years back:

> If only I was a nightingale singing
> If only I was on my second don't-live-like-a-pig week
> If only the sun wasn't always rising behind the next hill
> If only I was the flavor of tarragon
> If only I was phosphorescence and a night phenomena at sea
> If only Old Drainpipe Rensaleer as we used to call him hadn't hit bottom in Detroit
>   the time he made a fancy dive and got absentminded and forget to turn and all
>   his shortribs got stove in he got sucked down the drainpipe because the grate
>   wasn't on
> If only I didn't have to get up and let our dog out now
> If only the glorious day in April because it has no beginning or end that all
>   Flatbush had awaited impatiently between creation and construction had come
> If only I was James Joyce and had written Finnegans Wake only then I'd be gone
>   . . . .
> If only somebody would kiss me on the back of the neck right now
>   . . . .
> If only those degraded bastards hadn't monkeyed around with the Oreo Sandwich
>   pattern

If only Ruth Krauss would make plays happen around my house when both the flesh and spirit grow weak.

—Arthur Sainer

LAFFAN, Kevin (Barry). British. Born in Reading, Berkshire, 24 May 1922. Married Jeanne Lilian Thompson in 1952, has three children. Repertory Actor and Director until 1950. Director of Productions, Pendragon Company, Reading, 1950–52, and Everyman Theatre Company, Reading, 1953–58. Recipient: ATV Television Writers Award, 1959; Irish Life Theatre Award, 1969; National Union of Students Award, 1969; *Sunday Times* Award, 1970. Agent. ACTAC (Theatrical and Cinematic) Ltd., 16 Cadogan Lane, London S.W.1. Address: The Grange, Colworth, Chichester, Sussex, England.

PUBLICATIONS

Plays

Angie and Ernie, with Peter Jones (produced Guildford, Surrey, 1966).
Zoo Zoo Widdershins Zoo (produced Leicester, 1969). London, Faber, 1969.
It's a Two-Foot-Six-Inches-above-the-Ground World (produced Bristol, 1969; London, 1970). London, Faber, 1970.
The Superannuated Man (produced Watford, Hertfordshire, 1971).
There Are Humans at the Bottom of My Garden (produced London, 1972).
Never So Good (produced London, 1976).

Screenplays: *It's a Two-Foot-Six-Inches-above-the-Ground World*, 1971; *The Best Pair of Legs in the Business*, 1972.

Radio Play: *Portrait of an Old Man*, 1961.

Television Plays: *Lucky for Some*, 1969; *The Best Pair of Legs in the Business*, 1969; *You Can Only Buy Once*, 1969, *Castlehaven* series, 1970; *Kate* series, 1970; *A Little Learning*, 1970; *The Designer*, 1971; *Decision to Burn*, 1971; *Fly on the Wall* (trilogy), 1971; *The General*, 1971, *Emmerdale Farm*, 1972; *Justicer* series, 1973; *The Reformer*, 1973; *Getting Up*, 1973; *Beryl's Lot* series, with Bill McIlwraith, 1973; *After the Wedding Was Over*, 1975; *It's a Wise Child*, 1975; for Bud Flanagan programme.

*   *   *

Anybody leaving the theatre after the first performance of Kevin Laffan's *Zoo Zoo Widdershins Zoo* would probably have been amazed to discover that the writer was a man in his forties. Laffan's study of a group of young people – the eldest are in their early twenties – sharing a house and everything in it while refusing to work and turning to petty crime – shop-lifting, the robbing of telephone booths and the cheating of gas meters – when money is scarce, seems to have come exactly out of the way of life it re-creates.

Laffan, however, was born in 1922 and *Zoo Zoo Widdershins Zoo* was his first real success. It won an award from the National Union of Students, which wanted a play for production in universities. If the occasion of the play suggested its theme, only a complete understanding of the people he had created, not only their idioms, but their attitudes and their rejection of social responsibility, can account for its authenticity and for its cool, morally neutral sympathy with its people. It captures and makes comprehensible a gaiety which seems to grow out of the apparently depressing life-style these people have adopted. Cleverly, it is a play entirely about a minute community, and there is a feeling that the audience, as well as the shiftless parasites of the *dramatis personae*, is betrayed when the couple whose house has become a home for the group manoeuvre the others out and, suddenly, revert to conventional bourgeois habits.

Zoo Zoo Widdershins Zoo is almost plotless, carefully designed to seem as aimless as the way of life it observes, and its alternations of intensity and relaxation are all conveyed in the limited, inexplicit dialogue which exploits its young people's idiom.

This was by no means Laffan's first play. He began his career in the theatre as an actor; with others, he helped to found the Everyman Theatre Company in Reading and in 1959 won an award from ATV for a television play *Cut in Ebony* which was never produced because it deals, in terms of comedy, with problems of race and colour. Laffan, abandoning acting and direction, earned the time to write plays by undertaking any other writing that would pay, including a not very successful series of television programmes for the comedian Bud Flanagan. His television plays, *Lucky for Some, You Can Only Buy Once* and *The Best Pair of Legs in the Business*, however, established him as a television playwright, and *Castlehaven*, a television serial doing for a Yorkshire community what *Coronation Street* does for Lancashire, became a fixed part of commercial television schedules outside London.

Laffan's stage-play, *Angie and Ernie*, was produced outside London. *The Superannuated Man* won an Irish Life award in 1969 but was produced only in 1971. But *Zoo Zoo Widdershins Zoo*, after its university production, was given a successful commercial production in London and impressed the critics, with the result that *It's a Two-Foot-Six-Inches-above-the-Ground World*, first seen at the Theatre Royal, Bristol, was able to travel to London and make a distinct impression there; it considers, in a very individual tone of toughly angry, affectionate hilarity, the effects on a young Catholic husband and wife of their Church's refusal to permit any means of birth control; Catholics have complained that Laffan's play misstates the Church's attitude, but in its own terms, as a work for the theatre, it is entirely successful.

The marriage of a young Liverpool Catholic is falling into ruins; his wife, a Protestant girl who was converted to Catholicism only so that she could marry him, has provided him with three sons, another child would probably kill her, while sexual abstinence, which suits the wife even less than it suits the husband, is destroying the marriage. The voice of the Church is transmitted by a young priest who expresses the Catholic prohibition at its most extreme and unyielding. A totally permissive view is offered by an outsider – a van driver making a delivery at the middle son's Catholic primary school. The father's prudery had prevented him from teaching his children anything about their physical functions, so that the van driver's use of the school lavatory, arousing the child's interest in an adult masculine body, had cost the unfortunate driver – an energetic and undeviating lecher – his job.

These people argue the case with great energy, and the play dresses the situation in continual high spirits. When all else fails, the wife's surreptitiously acquired and so far unused collection of contraceptive pills comes in useful; they can, for example, be mistaken for aspirins. It would not be fair to accuse Laffan of pulling his punches in the interests of good taste or of scrupulous intellectual fairness in his presentation of opposed points of view. He is, however, far more deeply involved through his emotions than through any desire to solve intellectual arguments, and under the hard-edged hilarity of its presentation, there is a touching awareness of the painful situation of two simple, good, likeable people trapped by the husband's earnest conviction.

Laffan's progress has been slow. *There Are Humans at the Bottom of My Garden* did not rival the success of its predecessor, and his later work for television, notably the skillfully written *Emmerdale Farm* and the more predicable *Justicer* series, won a loyal television following without suggesting any of the tougher moral and social implications of his work for the theatre. A handful of television plays and two unusual comedies, differing so widely in tone and aim as *Zoo Zoo Widdershins Zoo* and *It's a Two-Foot-Six-Inches-above-the-Ground World*, suggest that his other plays deserve careful study by some enterprising theatre manager.

—Henry Raynor

LAN, David. South African. Born in Cape Town, 1 June 1952. Educated at the University of Cape Town, 1970–72, B.A. in English 1972; London School of Economics, 1973–76, B.Sc. in social anthropology 1976. Puppeteer and magician, Cape Town, 1966–69. Agent: Margaret Ramsay Ltd., 14a Goodwin's Court, London WC2N 4LL, England.

PUBLICATIONS

Plays

    Painting a Wall (produced London, 1974).
    Bird Child (produced London, 1974).
    Paradise (produced London, 1975).
    Homage to Been Soup (produced London, 1975).

Theatrical Activities:

Director: **Play** – *The Sport of My Mad Mother* by Ann Jellicoe, Cape Town, 1972.

David Lan comments:

I find it difficult to talk about my plays. There aren't too many of them to talk about. I wrote elsewhere, "The lowest common denominator is pretty far down. My plays are attempts to crack the social code, to find the hidden alternatives. But what good plays aren't?" I still think that.

Painting a Wall lasts an hour, during which time four black South Africans paint a wall. *Bird Child* is about a pregnant white South African girl who can't bear the thought that her child will grow up in an unjust world, and tries to do something about it. *Paradise* is set in Spain during the Napoleonic Wars. Eight people, in different and opposed ways, try to work out a method of living that seems to them both just and satisfactory. In *Homage to Been Soup*, a middle-aged woman and a girl sit and talk in the sun, near the sea. This goes on for half an hour and then stops.

When I wrote them I thought they were extremely interesting, better than most, that they might be useful and therefore ought to be done everywhere. I still think that.

*   *   *

David Lan is a young South African, so he begins with a subject. His one-acter, *Painting a Wall*, and his full-length play, *Bird Child*, both deal with aspects of South African life – which is to say, with aspects of *apartheid*. The first is slight, impressionistic, a short story. Two coloured men and an Indian paint a wall, helped by a coloured boy. The Indian has lost his child, and makes a botched attempt at suicide by drinking paint. The boy runs away. The men paint pictures on the wall, but must paint over them. They talk, and paint. The wall is finished. They leave. In *Bird Child*, all but one of the characters (and that a small part) are white, quasi-hippy, students and friends of students, in collision with the police. In protesting against the denial of freedom to her mother's maid, the heroine discovers the nature of freedom for herself. All the other protagonists of the play are locked by the system into sets of predetermined attitudes. Though the structure falls to pieces by the end, this is Lan's most successful play, particularly in his handling of Krou, the Colonel of Police, an intelligent, logical, and resourceful man, by no means a target for the scoring of easy liberal points.

But a single subject will not do for a serious artist, and Lan's next two plays, *Homage to Been Soup* and *Paradise*, both presented by the Theatre Upstairs at the Royal Court in 1975, represent his attempt to find a way on. The first is again a one-acter only twelve manuscript pages long, a mere technical exercise, sterile except in so far as it has allowed its author to grow. *Paradise* is more ambitious, his most interesting play so far, though botched in the execution. He appears to have been inspired by Goya's *Horrors of War*, and has set the play in Northern Spain in 1808, the year of Bonaparte's invasion, but his research has been sadly slapdash; an important strand of the plot requires that potatoes (which can be dented by a thumb-nail) should be mistaken for stones and that, although potatoes were introduced into Spain in 1580, they should still be objects of ignorance and wonder in 1808. His characters — deserters from the French army, Spanish peasants and their landlord, his wife and school-mistress daughter — have no particularity of time and place, and the play might more suitably have been set in a non-particular Whiting-land, into which his two most successful images, a simpleton who teaches the others his private unintelligible non-language, and the birds which move their nests from trees about to be chopped down, might more successfully fit. Nevertheless, again Lan's concern with the nature of freedom ("You begin by giving people their freedom. Then you pick up a gun, if they won't voluntarily do what you want." – my paraphrase) is noble, his images striking, and his own search for a language, fuller than the stylised short sentences of the two earlier plays to allow him to express more complex ideas, is admirable.

—John Bowen

LAURENTS, Arthur.   American.   Born in Brooklyn, New York, 14 July 1918. Educated at Cornell University, Ithaca, New York, B.A. 1937. Served in the United States Army, rising to the rank of Sergeant, 1940–45; Radio Playwright, 1943–45 (Citation, Secretary of War, and *Variety* Radio Award, 1945). Director, Dramatists Play Service, New York, 1961–66. Since 1955, Member of the Council, Dramatists Guild. Recipient: National Institute of Arts and Letters grant, 1946; Sidney Howard Memorial Award, 1946; Tony Award, 1967. Agent: Shirley Bernstein, Paramuse Artists, 745 Fifth Avenue, New York, New York. Address: Quogue, New York 11959, U.S.A.

PUBLICATIONS

Plays

> *Now Playing Tomorrow* (broadcast, 1939).   Published in *Short Plays for Stage and Radio*, edited by Carless Jones, Albuquerque, University of New Mexico Press, 1939.
> *Western Electric Communicade* (broadcast, 1944).   Published in *The Best One-Act Plays of 1944*, edited by Margaret Mayorga, New York, Dodd Mead, 1944.
> *The Last Day of the War* (broadcast, 1945).   Published in *Radio Drama in Action*, edited by Erik Barnouw, New York, Farrar and Rinehart, 1945.
> *The Face* (broadcast, 1945).   Published in *The Best One-Act Plays of 1945*, edited by Margaret Mayorga, New York, Dodd Mead, 1945.
> *Home of the Brave* (produced New York, 1945, as *The Way Back*, produced London, 1946).   New York, Random House, 1946.

Heartsong (produced New Haven, Connecticut, 1947).

The Bird Cage (produced New York, 1950).   New York, Dramatists Play Service, 1950.

The Time of the Cuckoo (produced New York, 1952).   New York, Random House, 1953.

A Clearing in the Woods (produced New York, 1957).   New York, Random House, 1957.

West Side Story, music by Leonard Bernstein (produced New York, 1957; London, 1958).   New York, Random House, 1958; London, Heinemann, 1959.

Gypsy, music by Jule Styne, lyrics by Stephen Sondheim, adaptation of a book by Gypsy Rose Lee (produced New York, 1959; also director: produced London, 1973).   New York, Random House, 1960.

Invitation to a March (also director: produced New York, 1960; Hereford, 1965).   New York, Random House, 1961.

Anyone Can Whistle, music by Stephen Sondheim (also director: produced New York, 1964).   New York, Random House, 1965.

Do I Hear a Waltz?, music by Richard Rodgers, lyrics by Stephen Sondheim (produced New York, 1965).   New York, Random House, 1966.

Hallelujah, Baby!, music and lyrics by Jule Styne, Betty Comden and Adolph Green (produced New York, 1967).   New York, Random House, 1967.

The Enclave (also director: produced Washington, D.C., and New York, 1973).   New York, Dramatists Play Service, 1974.

Screenplays: *The Snake Pit*, 1948; *Rope*, 1949; *Anna Lucasta*, 1949; *Caught*, 1949; *Bonjour Tristesse*, 1955; *Anastasia*, 1956; *The Way We Were*, 1973.

Radio Plays: *Now Playing Tomorrow*, 1939; *Hollywood Playhouse, Dr. Christian, The Thin Man, Manhattan at Midnight*, and other series, 1939–40; *The Last Day of the War, The Face, Western Electric Communicade*, 1944, and other plays for *The Man Behind the Gun, Army Service Force Presents* and *Assignment Home* series, 1943–45; *This Is Your FBI* series, 1945.

Novel

The Way We Were.   New York, Harper, 1972; London, W.H. Allen, 1973.

Manuscript Collection: Brandeis University, Waltham, Massachusetts.

Theatrical Activities:

Director: **Plays** – *Invitation to a March*, New York, 1960; *I Can Get It for You Wholesale* by Jerome Weidman, New York, 1962; *Anyone Can Whistle*, New York, 1964; *The Enclave*, Washington, D.C. and New York, 1973; *Gypsy*, London, 1973, New York, 1974.

Arthur Laurents comments:

Too much of today's theatre brings "The Emperor's New Clothes" to my mind. Style is considered content; formlessness is considered new technique; character is reduced to symbol and/or type; and story has been banished – not necessarily a loss – in favor of incident which is usually too thin and too undramatic to fuse an entire play. Moreover, the

465

dominent tone is modish pessimism or militancy, both of which can be as sentimentally romantic as effulgent optimism.

All a matter of taste, of course. My own is for a heightened theatricality and for new forms – but I still believe that form is determined by content and requires control. I want characters in a play, I want to be emotionally involved; I want social content; I want language and I want a *level* of accessibility. (I suspect obscurantism of being the refuge of the vague, the uncommitted and the chic.) Although I do not demand it, I prefer optimism – even if only implied. For I think man, naturally evil or not, is optimistic. Even the 'bleakest has hope: why else does he bother to write?

For the United States, for New York, I want subsidized theatres with permanent companies playing repertory. I think that is the most important need of the American playwright and would be of the greatest aid in his development.

*   *   *

One of the most promising dramatists appearing immediately after World War II was Arthur Laurents. His first success in New York, *Home of the Brave* showed both his skill as a dramatist and his insight into human nature as he dramatized the ethnic and individual problems of a Jewish soldier in a battle situation. During the following fifteen years Laurents wrote four plays – *The Bird Cage, The Time of the Cuckoo, A Clearing in the Woods*, and *Invitation to a March* – which continued to demonstrate his theatrical powers and his inclination to write serious drama. Unfortunately, in neither area – theatricality or intellectual penetration – was he able to sustain or develop a first-rate drama for the American commercial theatre. Perhaps he recognized either the personal or public impasse. At any rate, toward the end of this period Laurents had begun to devote more of his talents to musical comedy with considerable success. His creation of the books for *West Side Story* and *Gypsy* gave these musicals the careful integration and character development which distinguish them among modern musicals. During the next decade he collaborated on musicals but without significant success, and seemed to abandon his career in legitimate drama – a disappointment for critics who had felt his promise twenty-odd years in the past.

Laurents' seriousness as a dramatist was most evident in the themes that he chose to develop. The fearful uncertainties of the lonely person trying to find a meaningful identity in a world full of frustrations and strangers – this is a dominant theme in his works. Generally, his major character was trying to discover the essentials of love which Laurents seemed to believe would lead to a revelation of self. Although his psychological penetration into his major characters suggests a generally acute perception of humanity, his dramatized solutions tend more consistently toward theatricality than a probing concern for mankind. In other words, the problems of man that he considers – his fears, frustrations, feeling of alienation – place Laurents among those seriously concerned with modernity, but his insistence that sex is fundamental to all such problems limits both his psychology and his insight into modern man.

In three of his four plays since his initial success his major characters have been women whose psychological problems have driven them toward disaster. (The other play, *The Bird Cage*, tells the story of Wally, a vicious egomaniac and owner of a night club, whose abuse of everyone stems from his own sexual frustrations.) In *The Time of the Cuckoo* Leona Samish is that warm but lonely woman whose pathos rests in her inability to know and have faith in herself or accept the love of others. Sorry for herself and bitter towards life and thus unable to get what she most desires, she is that dangerous person who destroys. Virginia, the heroine of *A Clearing in the Woods*, sees herself as that destroyer although she wants desperately to be loved. Discovering that someone does truly care, she can work toward a position where she accepts both herself and the real world around her. *Invitation to a March* tells of a girl who, at first, wants to "march" along with the ordinary world and its seemingly inherent problems of love, sex, and divorce. But she changes, rejects the "march" and finds love with one who said "come dance with me." Unlike other Laurents plays a strongly made decision becomes the climax of this play, and perhaps both the author and his characters abandon the ordinary world as idealism seems a possible alternative to drudgery. Unfortunately, no further step has been dramatized.

Although Laurents has not been an innovator in technical theatre, he has courageously employed distinctive techniques in his plays. While *The Bird Cage* employs a rather obvious use of theatrical symbol, the "clearing in the woods" with its "magic circle" is well integrated into the structure of the play where three characters – Ginna, Nora, Jigee – act out particular ages in the heroine's life and tease her with her inability to accept what "they" contribute to her present problems. The frequent "front" delivery to the audience in an attempt to indicate unspoken and personal feelings was unsuccessful even in a semi-fantasy such as *Invitation to a March*. Music becomes a dominant part of several of his plays, as might be expected of a dramatist interested in musical comedy. In all of Laurents' theatre works his care in the creation of his characters is a major asset. Whether in musical comedy or straight drama, through an integration of theme and theatrical technique Laurents has tried to express his views on psychological and social man in the modern world.

—Walter J. Meserve

LAWLER, Ray(mond Evenor).   Australian.   Born in Footscray, Melbourne, Victoria, in 1921. Left school at age 13. Married to Jacklyn Kelleher; has three children. Worked in a factory; then as an actor in variety, Brisbane; as actor and producer, National Theatre Company, Melbourne; and as Director, Melbourne University Repertory Company. Recipient: *Evening Standard* award, 1958. Agent: M.C.A. (England) Ltd., 139 Piccadilly, London W.1, England.

PUBLICATIONS

Plays

Cradle of Thunder (produced Melbourne, 1949).
Summer of the Seventeenth Doll (produced Melbourne, 1955; London, 1957; New York, 1958).   London, Angus and Robertson, and New York, Random House, 1957.
The Piccadilly Bushman (produced Melbourne, 1959; Liverpool, 1965).   London, Angus and Robertson, 1961.
The Unshaven Cheek (produced Edinburgh, 1963).
A Breach in the Wall (televised, 1967; produced Canterbury, Kent, 1970).
The Man Who Shot the Albatross (produced Melbourne, 1972).
Kid Stakes (produced Melbourne, 1975).

Television Plays: *A Breach in the Wall,* 1967; *Cousin Bette* (serialization), from the novel by Balzac, 1971; *The Visitors* (serialization), from the novel by Mary McMinnies, 1972; *Two Women* (serialization), from the novel by Alberto Moravia, 1972; *Mrs. Palfrey at the Claremont,* from the novel by Elizabeth Taylor, 1973; *Seeking the Bubbles,* in *The Love School* series, 1975; *True Patriots All,* 1975; *Husband to Mrs. Fitzherbert,* 1975.

Theatrical Activities:

Actor: **Play** – Barney Ibbot in *Summer of the Seventeenth Doll*, Melbourne, 1955, London, 1957.

*   *   *

With the production of Ray Lawler's *Summer of the Seventeenth Doll* in 1955, the Australian theatre emerged from its prolonged adolescent dependence on imported commercial successes, and from its patronising attitude to the local product. Here, at last, was a play which showed a mature concern with the contemporary Australian experience. *The Doll* was the first successful Australian play which attacked, rather than extolled, some of the most hallowed beliefs of its audience and showed them to be illusions. In the course of the play two Queensland cane-cutters and a Sydney barmaid discover that they are victims of a sentimental attachment to each other that has been destroyed by time and circumstance: it belonged to their youth. In a broader sense the play coolly appraised the shallowness of firmly held national sentiments about the impregnable loyalty of mates, the superiority of outback workers over soft city slickers, the submissiveness of women to the muscular male: these too were shown to be notions which may have been true in the early days of settlement, but were unreliable guides to conduct or expectation in present-day urban Australia.

The effect on the theatre was cataclysmic. A flood of new plays on contemporary subjects, or attacking other myths, followed. The best enjoyed a commercial success which would have been impossible before *The Doll*, but this success was not merely due to the fact that Lawler opened up a new and rich vein of subject-matter for local playwrights. His more impressive achievement lay in his abandoning the clichés which had typified the "Aussie" in earlier dramatic literature, and his inventing of a dramatically viable equivalent of the ordinary speech of real, as opposed to imaginary, working-class Australians. There is not a "Struth" or a "fair dinkum" in *The Doll*, nor indeed are there many of the other hackneyed expletives or phrases which, before Lawler, were thought to be as essential to the stage Australian as "Begorrah" was to the stage Irishman. Instead, Lawler captured the directness, simplicity, and studied understatement of the Australian vernacular. He used this new and entirely realistic dramatic idiom to explode the traditional image of the indomitable bushman in dialogue which avoided artifice and had, instead, the unmistakable ring of authenticity.

By comparison Lawler's later plays have been disappointing. *The Piccadilly Bushman* mocks Australian middle-class pretentiousness and crudeness, but the satire lacks subtlety and the plot has none of the startling originality of *The Doll*. Again Lawler attacks a myth, this time the ludicrous and sentimental attachment of Australians to England as "home" or "our mother-country." Although *The Piccadilly Bushman* is a carefully written, well-constructed play, Lawler's attack misfires because the myth was moribund, if not dead, long before his play appeared. His principal character, the Australian who went to London and made good as an actor, became more English than the English, and developed a neurotic abhorrence for all things Australian, is a credible enough individual, as Lawler draws him, but few Australians could see anything of themselves in him; he is too flaccid and inconsequential a personality to arouse either sympathy or contempt. Where *The Doll* moves close to tragedy – the myth it destroyed had heroic proportions – *The Piccadilly Bushman* merely raises non-issues.

Lawler's recent play, *The Man Who Shot the Albatross*, is his most important work since *The Doll* and his most ambitious. This play is quite distinct both in subject and in style: he has moved from the contemporary to the historical to offer a dramatic re-appraisal of one of Australia's most notorious founders, Captain William Bligh of the *Bounty*, who was governor of New South Wales from 1806 to 1808. As the title suggests, the play explores the effects of the mutiny on Bligh's personality when he is once again in a position of considerable authority over a faction-ridden community. Lawler here abandons the conventional realistic setting for a skeletal arrangement of rostrums on several levels, which allows great fluidity in the action. The play moves backwards and forwards through a number of scenes both present and past and in and out of Bligh's mind which is haunted by memories of the mutiny and fantasies surrounding it. This is a play of considerable power and psychological penetration, factually accurate, exploring but not resolving one of Australia's most enigmatic historical figures. While the influence of Arthur Miller's *Death of a Salesman* is clearly apparent in Lawler's handling of an impressionistic set to allow free movement through time and space, and to translate Bligh's imaginings into visual terms, his own mastery of authentic-sounding dialogue (here with a necessarily antique flavour) and his sure sense of the essence of conflict in drama make this play a real contribution to Australia's increasing body of serious dramatic liberature.

The Man Who Shot the Albatross received a mixed critical reception when it was first produced in Australia in 1972 with Leo McKern in the demanding role of Bligh. Later performances of the same production showed how much the play was strengthened by extensive but judicious pruning. But, for all its strength, this play is unlikely to have the dynamic effect on local playwrights and audiences that *Summer of the Seventeenth Doll* produced. While it shows Lawler's continuing concern with Australia's historical and legendary past, historical re-assessment is an interesting exercise whereas reappraisal of myth is deeply disturbing, and it is for this reason the *The Doll* remains Lawler's most significant and influential achievement.

—Mary Lord

LAWRENCE, Jerome. American. Born in Cleveland, Ohio, 14 July 1915. Educated at Ohio State University, Columbus, B.A. 1937; University of California, Los Angeles, 1939–40. Director of summer stock, Connellsville, Pennsylvania, then Pittsfield, Massachusetts, Summers 1934–37; Reporter and Telegraph Editor, Wilmington, Ohio, *News-Journal,* 1937; Editor, New Lexington, Ohio, *Daily News,* 1937–38; Continuity Editor, Radio Station KMPC, Beverly Hills, California, 1938, 1939; Senior Staff Writer, Columbia Broadcasting System, Hollywood and New York, 1939–41; Scenario Writer, Paramount Pictures, Hollywood, 1941. Expert Consultant to the Secretary of War during World War II: Co-Founder of Armed Forces Radio Service, and Radio Correspondent in North Africa and Italy (wrote and directed the official Army-Navy Programs for D-Day, VE Day and VJ Day). Since 1942, Partner, Lawrence and Lee, and since 1955, President, Lawrence and Lee Inc., New York and Los Angeles. Founder and National President, Radio Writers Guild; Co-Founder and President, American Playwrights Theatre; Co-Founder and Judge, Margo Jones Award; Founder and Board Member, Writers Guild of America; Member of the Council, Dramatists Guild and Authors League of America; Member of the Advisory Board, Eugene O'Neill Foundation, American Conservatory Theatre, Board of Standards of the Living Theatre, and Ohio University School of Journalism. Member of the United States State Department Cultural Exchange Panel, 1962–70. Professor, Banff School of Fine Arts, Alberta, Canada, 1950–53; Master Playwright, New York University, 1967, 1968; Visiting Professor of Playwriting, Ohio State University, 1969; Lecturer, Salzburg Seminar in American Studies, 1972. Recipient: New York Press Club Award, 1942; *Radio-TV Life* Award, 1948, 1952; Peabody Award, 1949, 1952; *Radio-TV Mirror* Award, 1952, 1953; *Variety* Showmanship Award, 1954, and Critics Poll Award, 1955; Donaldson Award, 1955; Outer Circle Award, 1955; Tony Award, 1955, 1966; British Drama Critics Award, 1960; Moss Hart Memorial Award, 1967. D.H.L.: Ohio State University, 1963; D.Litt.: Fairleigh Dickinson University, Rutherford, New Jersey, 1968; D.F.A.: Villanova University, Pennsylvania, 1969. Agent: Harold Freeman, Brandt and Brandt Inc., 101 Park Avenue, New York, New York 10017. Address: 21056 Las Flores Mesa Drive, Malibu, California 90265, U.S.A.

PUBLICATIONS

Plays

Laugh, God!, in *Six Anti-Nazi One-Act Plays.*   New York, Contemporary Play Publications, 1939.

Tomorrow, with Budd Schulberg, in *Free World Theatre*, edited by Arch Oboler and Stephen Longstreet.   New York, Random House, 1944.

Inside a Kid's Head, with Robert E. Lee, in *Radio Drama in Action*, edited by Erik Barnouw.   New York, Farrar and Rinehart, 1945.

Look, Ma, I'm Dancin', with Robert E. Lee, music by Hugh Martin, conceived by Jerome Robbins (produced New York, 1948).

The Crocodile Smile, with Robert E. Lee (as *The Laugh Maker*, produced Hollywood, 1952; revised version, as *Turn on the Night*, produced Philadelphia, 1961; revised version, as *The Crocodile Smile*, also director: produced Flatrock, North Carolina, 1970).   New York, Dramatists Play Service, 1972.

Inherit the Wind, with Robert E. Lee (produced New York, 1955; London, 1960). New York, Random House, 1955; London, Four Square, 1960.

Shangri-La, with Robert E. Lee and James Hilton, music by Harry Warren, adaptation of the novel *Lost Horizon* by James Hilton (produced New York, 1956).   New York, Morris Music, 1956.

Auntie Mame, with Robert E. Lee, adaptation of the work by Patrick Dennis (produced New York, 1956; London, 1958).   New York, Vanguard Press, 1957; revised version, music by Jerry Herman, as *Mame* (produced New York, 1966; London, 1969), New York, Random House, 1967.

The Gang's All Here, with Robert E. Lee (produced New York, 1959).   Cleveland, World, 1960.

Only in America, with Robert E. Lee, adaptation of the work by Harry Golden (produced New York, 1959).   New York, French, 1960.

A Call on Kuprin, with Robert E. Lee, adaptation of the novel by Maurice Edelman (produced New York, 1961).   New York, French, 1962.

Sparks Fly Upward, with Robert E. Lee (as *Diamond Orchid*, produced New York, 1965; revised version, as *Sparks Fly Upward*, produced Dallas, 1967).   New York, Dramatists Play Service, 1967.

Live Spelled Backwards (produced Beverly Hills, California, 1966).   New York, Dramatists Play Service, 1970.

Dear World, with Robert E. Lee, music by Jerry Herman, based on *The Madwoman of Chaillot* by Giraudoux (produced New York, 1969).

The Incomparable Max, with Robert E. Lee (also director: produced Abingdon, Virginia, 1969; New York, 1971).   New York, Hill and Wang, 1972.

The Night Thoreau Spent in Jail, with Robert E. Lee (produced Columbus, Ohio, and 140 other theatres, 1970).   New York, Hill and Wang, 1970.

Jabberwock: Improbabilities Lived and Imagined by James Thurber in the Fictional City of Columbus, Ohio, with Robert E. Lee (produced Columbus, Ohio, 1972).   New York, French, 1974.

First Monday in October, with Robert E. Lee (produced Cleveland, 1975).

Screenplays, with Robert E. Lee: *My Love Affair with the Human Race*, 1962; *The New Yorkers*, 1963; *Joyous Season*, 1964; *The Night Thoreau Spent in Jail*, 1972.

Radio Plays: *Junior Theatre of the Air* series, 1938; *Under Western Skies* series, 1939; *Nightcap Yarns* series, 1939 1940; *Stories from Life* series, 1939, 1940; *Man about Hollywood* series, 1940; *Hollywood Showcase* series, 1940, 1941; *A Date with Judy* series, 1941, 1942; *They Live Forever* series, 1942; *Everything for the Boys* series, 1944;

I Was There series; with Robert E. Lee: *Columbia Workshop* series, 1941–42; *Armed Forces Radio Service Programs*, 1942–45; *The World We're Fighting For* series, 1943; *Request Performance* series, 1945–46; *Screen Guild Theatre* series, 1946; *Favorite Story* series, 1946–49; *Frank Sinatra Show*, 1947; *Dinah Shore Program*, 1948; *The Railroad Hour*, 1948–54; *Young Love* series, 1949–50; *United Nations Broadcasts*, 1949–50; *Halls of Ivy* series, 1950–51; *Hallmark Playhouse* series, 1950–51; *Charles Boyer Show*, 1951; other free-lance and special programs, 1941–50.

Television Plays: *Lincoln, The Unwilling Warrior*, 1975; with Robert E. Lee: *The Unexpected* series, 1951; *Favorite Story* series, 1952–53; *Song of Norway*, 1957; *West Point*, 1958.

Other

Oscar the Ostrich (juvenile).   New York, Random House, 1940.
Off Mike (radio writing).   New York, Duell, 1944.
Actor: The Life and Times of Paul Muni.   New York, Putnam, 1974; London, W. H. Allen, 1975.

Manuscript Collections: Lawrence and Lee Collection, Lincoln Center Library of the Performing Arts, New York; Ohio State University, Columbus; Kent State University, Ohio; Ziv-United Artists film and transcription library.

Theatrical Activities:

Director: **Plays** – *You Can't Take It with You*, by George S. Kaufman and Moss Hart, *The Imaginary Invalid* by Molière, *Anything Goes* by Howard Lindsay and Russel Crouse, *The Green Pastures* by Marc Connelly, *Boy Meets Girl* by Bella and Samuel Spewack, *H.M.S. Pinafore* and *The Pirates of Penzance* by Gilbert and Sullivan, and *Androcles and the Lion* by G. B. Shaw, in summer stock, 1934–37; *Mame*, Sacramento, California, 1969; *The Incomparable Max*, Abingdon, Virginia, 1969; *The Crocodile Smile*, Flatrock, North Carolina, 1970; *The Night Thoreau Spent in Jail*, Dublin, 1972; *Jabberwock*, Dallas, 1974; *Inherit the Wind*, Dallas, 1975; *First Monday in October*, Cleveland, 1975.

Jerome Lawrence comments:

Robert E. Lee and I have been called by various critics: "the thinking man's playwrights." In our plays and in our teaching we have attempted to be part of our times. We have done all we can to encourage truly national and international theatre, not confined to a few blocks of real estate in Manhattan or London's West End. Thus, we have sought to promote the growth of regional and university theatres through the formation of American Playwrights Theatre, to bring new and vital and pertinent works to all of America and all of the world.

It has been my privilege to travel to more than a hundred countries, often on cultural-exchange missions. In 1964 I went completely around the world, studying theatre and meeting with theatre people in Japan, Thailand, Egypt, Greece, France and England. In October and November of 1971, Robert E. Lee and I were guests of the Ministry of Culture of the Soviet Union and we exchanged ideas with leading Russian playwrights, directors, actors, and theatre-workers. In March of 1972, I had the joy of directing our play, *The Night Thoreau Spent in Jail*, in its 142nd production at the Dublin Theatre Festival.

We have tried to encourage and aid new and untried playwrights, stimulating their work through teaching and through the annual Margo Jones Award.

In our plays we have hoped to mirror and illuminate the problems of the moment – but we have attempted to grapple with universal themes, even in our comedies. We have tried for a blend between the dramatic and the entertaining: our most serious works are always leavened with laughter (*Inherit the Wind* is an example) and our seemingly frivolous comedies (*Auntie Mame, Mame, Jabberwock*) have sub-texts which say something important for the contemporary world.

We are lovers of the living theatre and hope to continue working and living in it.

*   *   *

"Eatable things to eat and drinkable things to drink," comments a shocked character in Dickens' short story "Mugby Junction," describing a visit to France. The British railway station buffet is the object of Dickens' scorn, and the news that French railways provide edible and easily assimilated food causes the staff of Mugby Junction's restaurant to come close to catatonic fits.

Many a critic, professional *or* amateur, might, in snobbish chorus, make similar comments about the works of collaborators Jerome Lawrence and Robert E. Lee. "Playable plays to play – or readable plays to read!" might be their disbelieving cry if satirized. The expressions of disapproval and disdain might be almost as extreme as those of the 19th century railway grotesques, for both playability and readability are cardinal points of the works of Lawrence and Lee. Their plots are tight, their characters cleanly developed, their dialogue smooth. Actors like them for they present strong speeches and well developed scenes, and although this might be considered old-fashioned playwriting it is clear that audiences like it too. Their most successful work, *Inherit the Wind* (first presented at the National Theatre in New York, April, 1955, after a run in Dallas, Texas, under a great encourager of new talent, Margo Jones) was the third longest-running serious play in the history of Broadway. It is based on the famous Scopes Trial in Tennessee (the "Monkey Trial") when Darwinism and traditional religion had a head-on crash in a rural American setting. It featured Paul Muni and Ed Begley, who made the dialogue of this solid courtroom drama flow back and forth like a mounting tide. The script is very readable and with little imagination the drama can play itself again in your own living room as you sit in your favourite armchair. Although not deep it is most engaging in a theatrical, if not an intellectually involving way. The effect of putting two great contemporary orators, pitted one against the other, as the core of the play makes for compelling speeches, and the device of the trial itself provides a rounded dramatic vehicle, still open-ended enough to allow one of the protagonists to stand at the end weighing copies of the Bible and Darwin while planning the appeal. Today's audience (even though we would like to think ourselves beyond quaint beliefs) can still become emotionally involved over God versus gorilla. Good and forceful fare, it has been produced around the world, and the authors feel "it has many important things to say for our time."

Many of the works of Lawrence and Lee are lighter, mirroring their ability to zero in on the essentially sentimental underbelly of the average Broadway audience. Their evident enjoyment of the sentimental is one of their secrets. By far the largest part of the Broadway audience is out for fun, a pleasurable look at the land of never-never, which is why the musical when successful is always such a huge money-spinner. The collaborators pull off a clever trick with *Inherit the Wind* for it has many elements of the musical, yet gives patrons the self-importance of feeling they have seen something serious. They are also at home in creating an impossible character like *Auntie Mame*, first produced in New York in 1952. This giddy American dame was adored onstage, although she probably would not have been tolerated for more than a moment beyond Manhattan or Wiltshire Boulevard. Many of the members of the audience would have come from suburban patios like the satirized Upsons (whose house in Connecticut is called "Upson Downs" – Lawrence has a weakness for rather ponderous puns in conversation and his own California house is called "Writers to the Sea") but the social comment is kept gentle and the medicine is never too strong. An amusing evening and intended to be nothing more no doubt, yet for this writer the play only sparked into life when Beatrice Lillie played the part in the London production. But perhaps then the vehicle was less Auntie Mame than Auntie Bea, a true eccentric.

Auntie Mame became the very successful musical *Mame* (May 1966) which the co-authors also wrote, featuring the then relatively unknown Angela Lansbury. Their collaboration on a monolithic musical called *Dear World* based on the Giraudoux play *The Madwoman of Chaillot* was less successful. However it's hard to find fault with writers when faced with the complexities of producing musicals in New York City where music, lyrics, choreography, special songs, production numbers, direction, elaborate costumes and staggering scenery – along with equally staggering costs – seem often to overwhelm the basic book.

Nevertheless Lawrence and Lee seem happier when they are away from the big-time musical stage, as witness their commitment to a play entitled *The Night Thoreau Spent in Jail*. This last title, presented first at Ohio State University in April, 1971, is an interesting experiment. Some years ago, intent on trying to circumvent the sterile Broadway scene where serious plays are concerned, the partners set up American Playwrights Theatre in Columbus, Ohio. It was a deliberate move away from New York in a laudable attempt to develop new audiences for serious drama, with the plays of dramatists, known and unknown, presented in a new "circuit" – the network of resident and university theatres across America. Each writer was guaranteed a number of *different* productions in various spots on this new circuit and many were produced before Lawrence and Lee launched one of their own – *Thoreau*, a subject of particular interest to young audiences, for it deals with one of the first cases of civil disobedience in America. Later collaborations include *Jabberwock* and *First Monday in October*.

Their hand with humour can, unfortunately, be a little heavy, and when tackling such a delicate exponent of the art as Max Beerbohm in *The Incomparable Max* they became caught in a morass that was anything but Maxian. There are times when the pair cleaves dangerously close to the jungle of clichés.

Lawrence and Lee collaborate easily – each has a veto, "but it's a positive one" says Lawrence. They both feel they can, and do, learn from criticism. Their contribution to American drama is perhaps most significant when one looks at the number of nations that know them from the many translations of their principle works. *Inherit the Wind* has been translated into 28 different tongues, while the citizens of Ireland, Israel, Holland, Germany, Bangladesh, and Russia, among others, have been given an eye-opening view of a Yankee philosopher's protest in *Thoreau*. If this play alone conveys the authors' real concern and attempt to fathom American problems, it is a considerable achievement.

—Michael T. Leech

LAWSON, John Howard.   American.   Born in New York City, 25 September 1894. Educated at Yonkers High School, New York; Cutler School, New York, graduated 1910; Williams College, Williamstown, Massachusetts, B.A. 1914. Served in the American Ambulance Service in France and Italy during World War I. Married Katharine Drain in 1918 (divorced, 1923); Susan Edmond, 1925; has three children. Cable Editor, Reuters Press Cables, New York, 1914–15. Council Member of the Authors League of America, 1930–40; Founding President, 1933–34, and Member of the Executive Board, 1933–40, Screenwriters Guild. Served one-year sentence for contempt of the House Un-American Activities Committee, 1948.

PUBLICATIONS

Plays

Servant-Master-Lover (produced Los Angeles, 1916).
Standards (produced Syracuse, 1916).
Roger Bloomer (produced New York, 1923).   New York, Seltzer, 1923.
Processional: A Jazz Symphony of American Life (produced New York, 1925).   New York, Seltzer, 1925.
Nirvana (produced New York, 1926).
Loudspeaker (produced New York, 1927).   New York, Macaulay, 1927.
The International (produced New York, 1928).   New York, Macaulay, 1928.
Success Story (produced New York, 1932).   New York, Farrar and Rinehart, 1932.
The Pure in Heart (produced New York, 1934).   Included in With a Reckless Preface: Two Plays, 1934.
Gentlewoman (produced New York, 1934).   Included in With a Reckless Preface: Two Plays, 1934.
With a Reckless Preface: Two Plays (includes The Pure in Heart and Gentlewoman). New York, Farrar and Rinehart, 1934.
Marching Song (produced New York, 1937).   New York, Dramatists Play Service, 1937.

Screenplays: Dynamite (dialogue only), 1929; The Sea Bat (dialogue only); Blushing Brides (dialogue only); Success at Any Price (dialogue only), 1934; Blockade, 1938; Algiers, 1938; They Shall Have Music, 1939; Four Sons, 1940; Action in the North Atlantic, with W. R. Burnett, 1943; Sahara, 1943; Counter-attack, 1945; Smashup: The Story of a Woman, 1947.

Other

Theory and Technique of Playwriting.   New York, Putnam, 1936; revised edition, as Theory and Technique of Playwriting and Screenwriting, 1949.
The Hidden Heritage: A Rediscovery of the Ideas and Forces That Link the Thought of Our Time with the Culture of the Past.   New York, Citadel, 1950.
Film in the Battle of Ideas.   New York, Masses and Mainstream, 1953.
Film: The Creative Process: The Search for an Audio-Visual Language and Structure. New York, Hill and Wang, 1964; revised edition, 1967.

*   *   *

The plays of John Howard Lawson reflect both a political radicalism and a penchant for theatrical experimentation. His first major work, Roger Bloomer, is an early example of American expressionism. Its plot is conventional – almost archetypal – as it chronicles the journey of a naive idealistic youth from Iowa to the hard reality of New York City. Roger's father is a smug, anti-intellectual businessman who ultimately fails to impose his own materialistic values upon his son. In New York, Roger becomes involved with a girl from his home town and their relationship constitutes the emotional center of the play. She commits suicide – for which Roger is temporarily imprisoned – but in a highly stylized dream sequence replete with sexual imagery she reappears to liberate him from his fears and guilt and inspires his birth into maturity. Although much of the material is dated, the play is significant because of its attempts at objectifying the inner turmoil of the hero. In the dream sequence, characters from Roger's past appear in a distorted and fragmented manner to reveal the nightmare aspects of American life. In previous scenes Lawson's satiric attack on the hollow values of business is conveyed through characters whose mechanical and artificial behavior mirrors their commitment to an inhuman materialistic ethic. The language of *Roger Bloomer* is self-consciously poetic and the rather forced optimism with which the play concludes seems overly contrived.

Processional also borrows techniques from the expressionists, but the play is deeply rooted in the reality of American experience. Subtitled "a jazz symphony of American life," the play attempts to merge the popular arts of jazz and vaudeville with a sardonic critique of American ills. Lawson's work is set in a West Virginia mining town where labor disputes have sharply divided the community. The protagonist of the play, Dynamite Jim Flimmins, is no unworldly innocent like Roger Bloomer, but is rather a tough and courageous worker who, after defying the local capitalists, politicians and bigots is blinded for his rebelliousness. *Processional*, in its desire to mirror the American scene, employs the familiar crude stereotyped stage Negro and Jew. While such portrayals seem offensive today, Lawson was utilizing them to demonstrate America's diversity. The play has an undeniable theatricality, despite its somewhat broadly conceived characters. Lawson's drama examines such aspects of American life as the Ku Klux Klan and yellow journalism, but, like *Roger Bloomer*, contains a sentimental romance at its core. At the conclusion of *Processional* the sightless Jim Flimmins weds the pregnant Sadie Cohen. While there is no doubting the seriousness of Lawson's social criticism, his play seems more concerned with demonstrating the buoyant vitality of the country – as expressed through popular culture – than with the radical ideas that characterize his later works.

Loudspeaker is another attempt at employing a form of popular art – here the farce – to structure a critical examination of American institutions. The focus here is politics and the manner is highly stylized to reveal the essential absurdity of the political scene. The hero is an unethical businessman with gubernatorial ambitions. He ultimately succeeds, but not before his apparently idyllic family life is exposed for the sham it is. There is another cliché-ridden romance, this time between the governor's daughter and a brash young newspaperman. The tone of the work is slangy and cynical and its cartoon-like characters seem even more unreal with the passage of time.

The International, set in Tibet, is perhaps the most extravagant of Lawson's plays, certainly the least coherent. Abandoning a linear plot sequence for a structure that would permit the use of song, dance, and choral movement, Lawson proves unable to shape his materials to any clear end. Some elements are characteristic of the playwright: the assault on an acquisitive society that abandons human values; the sentimental romance here involving a businessman's son who is radicalized as a result of his love for a Soviet agent and dies a martyr's death for a noble cause; and the humorless rhetoric which lacks any semblance of real speech.

In his later plays Lawson abandoned much of the technical experimentation that marked his plays of the 1920's. His thematic concerns, however, remained the same despite the shift to realism. *Success Story* is a tightly-organized account of the rise and fall of a young Jewish radical from the Lower East Side of New York City. Sol Ginsberg forsakes his left-wing beliefs for a successful career in advertising. His intense desires for wealth and power destroy him as Lawson demonstrates in rather obvious terms the corrupting effects of the capitalistic ethic. The hero further demonstrates his betrayal by abandoning his loving Jewish girl friend for the coldly materialistic mistress of his employer.

The Pure in Heart, like *Roger Bloomer*, traces the fortunes of a small-town girl in the big city. The heroine is determined to succeed in the New York theatre, but her innocence causes her to get involved with some hardened sophisticates, one of whom has just been released from a prison. Although love does blossom between the would-be actress and the ex-convict, the romance ends in death. Back-stage life becomes in effect a microcosm of the larger world dominated by a callous inhumanity, and innocence is ultimately destroyed.

Gentlewoman focuses on the milieu of upper-class society as it dramatizes the ineffectual sterility of the rich and well-educated. Into this decadent society bursts Rudy Flannigan, a variant of Lawson's familiar proletarian hero. Gwyn Ballantine, the polished and wealthy title character, is attracted to the rough-hewn, but vital Flannigan, but their relationship soon ends. She is too much a prisoner of her ingrained values to accept him for what he is. Flannigan similarly realizes that his commitment to radical causes would be compromised if he should remain with Gwyn.

Marching Song, written after Lawson's conversion to Communism, is the most didactic and emtionally charged of his plays, the one most clearly designed to galvanize an audience. It preaches the need for group solidarity – a common theme in nearly all of Lawson's work – and does so in a highly tendentious manner with all nuance eliminated. As in *Processional* the locale is a company town in the midst of labor troubles, but *Marching Song* eschews the vaudeville hijinks of his earlier work. Here he is far more intense in his account of capitalist cruelty and exploitation, not to mention the determined heroism and nobility of the workers. One labor organizer dies after being brutally tortured; a worker's child is even killed as Lawson spares no sympathy for his ideological enemies. At the conclusion, the striking workers have seized a power station and have won a victory over their bosses.

There seems little likelihood of Lawson's work surviving in the theatre. While *Roger Bloomer* and *Processional* are interesting because of their innovative techniques – some of which are much in vogue today – his plays are either overstated expressions of by now stale ideas or confused attempts to wed a variety of theatrical effects. For all of his declared sympathy for the working class, Lawson fails to convince that he is aware of how they speak or act. His language is often stilted and artificial, and his attempts at an Odets-like prose-poetry generally miss the mark. Lawson's firm ideological commitments prevented him from creating believable human beings while his artistic experiments – daring and controversial in his own day – are by now familier staples of the nonrepresentational theatre.

—Leonard Fleischer

LEE, Robert E(dwin).   American.   Born in Elyria, Ohio, 15 October 1918. Educated at Northwestern University, Evanston, Illinois; Drake University, Des Moines, Iowa; Ohio Wesleyan University, Delaware, Ohio, 1935–37. Served in the United States Army, 1942–45: Expert Consultant to the Secretary of War, 1942; Co-Founder, with Jerome Lawrence, Armed Forced Radio Service; Writer-Director, Armed Forces Radio Service, Los Angeles, 1942–45: Special Citation, Secretary of War, 1945. Married Janet Waldo in 1948; has two children. Astronomical Observer, Perkins Observatory, Delaware, Ohio, 1936–37; Director, Radio Station WHK-WCLE, Cleveland, 1937–38; Director, Young and Rubicam, New York and Hollywood, 1938–42; Professor of Playwriting, College of Theatre Arts, Pasadena Playhouse, California, 1962–63. Since 1942, Partner, Lawrence and Lee, and since 1955, Vice-President, Lawrence and Lee Inc., New York and Los Angeles; since 1966, Lecturer, University of California at Los Angeles. Co-Founder and Judge, Margo Jones Award; Co-Founder, American Playwrights Theatre. Recipient: New York Press Club Award, 1942; City College of New York Award, 1948; *Radio-TV Life* Award, 1948, 1952; Peabody Award, 1949, 1952; *Radio-TV Mirror* Award, 1952, 1953; *Variety* Showmanship Award, 1954, and Critics Poll Award, 1955; Donaldson Award, 1955; Outer Circle Award, 1955; Tony Award, 1955, 1966; British Drama Critics Award, 1960; Moss Hart Memorial Award, 1967. Lit.D.: Ohio Wesleyan University, 1962; M.A.: Pasadena Playhouse College of Theatre Arts, 1963. Agent (Attorney): Martin Gang, 6400 Sunset Boulevard, Hollywood, California 90028. Address: 15725 Royal Oak Road, Encino, California 91436, U.S.A.

PUBLICATIONS

Plays

Inside a Kid's Head, with Jerome Lawrence, in Radio Drama in Action, edited by Erik
   Barnouw.   New York, Farrar and Rinehart, 1945.
Look, Ma, I'm Dancin', with Jerome Lawrence, music by Hugh Martin, conceived by
   Jerome Robbins (produced New York, 1948).
The Crocodile Smile, with Jerome Lawrence (as The Laugh Maker, produced
   Hollywood, 1952; revised version, as Turn on the Night, produced Philadelphia,
   1961; revised version, as The Crocodile Smile, produced Flatrock, North Carolina,
   1970).   New York, Dramatists Play Service, 1972.
Inherit the Wind, with Jerome Lawrence (produced New York, 1955; London, 1960).
   New York, Random House, 1955; London, Four Square, 1960.
Shangri-La, with Jerome Lawrence and James Hilton, music by Harry Warren,
   adaptation of the novel Lost Horizon by James Hilton (produced New York, 1956).
   New York, Morris Music, 1956.
Auntie Mame, with Jerome Lawrence, adaptation of the work by Patrick Dennis
   (produced New York, 1956; London, 1958).   New York, Vanguard Press, 1957;
   revised version, music by Jerry Herman, as Mame (produced New York, 1966;
   London, 1969), New York, Random House, 1967.
The Gang's All Here, with Jerome Lawrence (produced New York, 1959).   Cleveland,
   World, 1960.
Only in America, with Jerome Lawrence, adaptation of the work by Harry Golden
   (produced New York, 1959).   New York, French, 1960.
A Call on Kuprin, with Jerome Lawrence, adaptation of the novel by Maurice Edelman
   (produced New York, 1961).   New York, French, 1962.
Sparks Fly Upward, with Jerome Lawrence (as Diamond Orchid, produced New York,
   1965; revised version, as Sparks Fly Upward, produced Dallas, 1967).   New York,
   Dramatists Play Service, 1969.
Dear World, with Jerome Lawrence, music by Jerry Herman, based on The Madwoman
   of Chaillot by Giraudoux (produced New York, 1969).
The Incomparable Max, with Jerome Lawrence (produced Abingdon, Virginia, 1969;
   New York, 1971).   New York, Hill and Wang, 1972.
The Night Thoreau Spent in Jail, with Jerome Lawrence (produced Columbus, Ohio,
   and 140 other theatres, 1970).   New York, Hill and Wang, 1970.
Jabberwock: Improbabilities Lived and Imagined by James Thurber in the Fictional City
   of Columbus, Ohio, with Jerome Lawrence (produced Columbus, Ohio, 1972).
   New York, French, 1974.
Ten Days That Shook the World, based on reports from Russia by John Reed (produced
   Los Angeles, 1973).
First Monday in October, with Jerome Lawrence (produced Cleveland, 1975).
Sounding Brass (produced New York, 1975).   New York, French, 1976.

Screenplays, with Jerome Lawrence: My Love Affair with the Human Race, 1962; The
New Yorkers, 1963; Joyous Season, 1964; The Night Thoreau Spent in Jail, 1972; with
John Sinn: Quintus, 1971.

Radio Plays: Empire Builders series, 1938; Opened by Mistake, 1940; Flashbacks series,
1940–41; Three Sheets to the Wind, 1942; Task Force, 1942; Ceiling Unlimited, 1942;
Meet Corliss Archer, 1942; Suspense, 1943; The Saint, 1945; with Jerome Lawrence:
Columbia Workshop series, 1941–42; Armed Forces Radio Service Programs, 1942–45;
The world We're Fighting For series, 1943; Request Performance series, 1945–46;
Screen Guild Theatre series, 1946; Favorite Story series, 1946–49; Frank Sinatra Show,

1947; *Dinah Shore Program*, 1948; *The Railroad Hour*, 1948–54; *Young Love* series, 1949–50; *United Nations Broadcasts*, 1949–50; *Halls of Ivy* series, 1950–51; *Hallmark Playhouse* series, 1950–51; *Charles Boyer Show*, 1951; other free-lance and special programs, 1941–50.

Television Plays: *A Colloquy with Paul*, 1961; with Jerome Lawrence: *The Unexpected* series, 1951; *Favorite Story* series, 1952–53; *Song of Norway*, 1957; *West Point*, 1958.

Other

Television: The Revolutionary Industry.   New York, Duell, 1944.

Manuscript Collections: Lawrence and Lee Collection, Lincoln Center Library of the Performing Arts, New York; Ohio State University, Columbus; Kent State University, Ohio.

Theatrical Activities:

Director: **Plays** – *Only in America*, Los Angeles, 1960; *The Night Thoreau Spent in Jail*, Los Angeles, 1970; *The Gang's All Here*, Los Angeles, 1972; *Ten Days That Shook the World*, Los Angeles, 1973.

Robert E. Lee comments:

The devil's name is Dullness. An eraser is sometimes more essential than a pencil. But merely to entertain is fatuous. Writing for today is really writing for yesterday; I try to write for tomorrow.

*   *   *

See the essay on Jerome Lawrence and Robert E. Lee on page 472.

LEONARD, Hugh.   Pseudonym for John Keyes Byrne.   Irish.   Born in Dublin, 9 November 1926. Educated at Presentation College, Dun Laoghaire, 1941–45. Married Paule Jacquet in 1955; has one daughter. Civil Servant, Dublin, 1945–59; Script Editor, Granada Television, Manchester, 1961–63; Free-lance Writer, London, 1963–70. Since 1976, Literary Editor, Abbey Theatre, Dublin. Recipient: Italia Prize, 1967; Writers Guild of Great Britian Award of Merit, 1967. Agent: Harvey Unna, 14 Beaumont Mews, Marylebone High Street, London W1N 4HE, England. Address: Killiney Heath, Killiney, County Dublin, Ireland.

PUBLICATIONS

Plays

The Italian Road (produced Dublin, 1954).
The Big Birthday (produced Dublin, 1956).

A Leap in the Dark (produced Dublin, 1957).

Madigan's Lock (produced Dublin, 1958; London, 1963).

A Walk on the Water (produced Dublin, 1960).

The Passion of Peter McGinty (produced Dublin, 1961).

Stephen D, adaptation of the works *A Portrait of the Artist as a Young Man* and *Stephen Hero* by James Joyce (produced Dublin, 1962; London, 1963; New York, 1967). London, Evans, 1962.

Dublin One, adaptation of the stories *Dubliners* by James Joyce (produced Dublin, 1963).

The Poker Session (produced Dublin, 1963; London, 1964; New York, 1967). London, Evans, 1963.

The Family Way (produced Dublin, 1964; London, 1966).

The Late Arrival of the Incoming Aircraft (televised, 1964).   London, Evans, 1968.

The Saints Go Cycling In, adaptation of the novel *The Dalkey Archives* by Flann O'Brien (produced Dublin, 1965).

All the Nice People (as *Mick and Nick*, produced Dublin, 1966).   Published in *Plays and Players* (London), December 1966.

The Quick, and The Dead (produced Dublin, 1967).

The Au Pair Man (produced Dublin, 1968; London 1969; New York, 1973). Published in *Plays and Players* (London), December 1968; New York, French, 1974.

The Barracks (produced Dublin, 1969).

The Patrick Pearse Motel (produced Dublin and London, 1971; Washington D.C., 1972).   London, French, 1972.

Da (produced Dublin and Washington, D.C., 1973).   Published in *Plays and Players* (London), December 1973; Newark, Delaware, Proscenium Press, 1976.

Summer (produced Dublin, 1974).

Irishmen: A Suburb of Babylon (Irishmen, Nothing Personal, The Last of the Last of the Mohicans) (produced Dublin, 1975).

Some of My Best Friends Are Husbands, adaptation of a play by Eugene Labiche (produced London, 1976).

Liam Liar, adaption of the play *Billy Liar* by Keith Waterhouse and Willis Hall (produced Dublin, 1976).

Screenplays: *Great Catherine*, 1968; *Interlude*, 1968; *Whirligig*, 1970; *Percy*, 1971; *Our Miss Fred*, 1972.

Television Plays: *The Irish Boys* (trilogy), 1962; *Saki* series, 1962; *A Kind of Kingdom*, 1963; *Jezebel Ex-UK* series, 1963; *The Second Wall*, 1964; *A Triple Irish*, 1964; *Realm of Error*, 1964; *My One True Love*, 1964; *Second Childhood*, 1964; *The Late Arrival of the Incoming Aircraft*, 1964; *Do You Play Requests?*, 1964; *The View from the Obelisk*, 1964; *The Hidden Truth* series, 1964; *Undermind* series, 1964; *I Loved You Last Summer*, 1965; *Great Big Blond*, 1965; *Blackmail* series, 1965; *Public Eye* series, 1965; *Simenon* series: *The Lodger* and *The Judge*, 1966; *Insurrection* (8 parts), 1966; *The Retreat*, 1966; *Silent Song*, 1966; *The Liars* series, 1966; *The Informer* series, 1966; *Out of the Unknown* series, 1966–67; *A Time of Wolves and Tigers*, 1967; *Love Life*, 1967; *Great Expectations* (serialization), from the novel by Dickens, 1967; *Wuthering Heights* (serialization), from the novel by Emily Brontë, 1967; *No Such Things as a Vampire*, 1968; *The Corpse Can't Play*, 1968; *A Man and His Mother-in-Law*, 1968; *Assassin*, 1968; *Nicholas Nickleby* (serialization), from the novel by Dickens, 1968; *Conan Doyle* series: *A Study in Scarlet* and *The Hound of the Baskervilles*, 1968; *Hunt the Peacock*, with H. R. Keating, 1969; *Talk of Angels*, 1969; *The Possessed* (serialization), from the novel by Dostoevsky, 1969; *Dombey and Son* (serialization), from the novel by Dickens, 1969; *Somerset Maugham* series: *P & O*, 1969, and *Jane*, 1970; *A Sentimental Education* (serialization), from the novel by Flaubert, 1970; *The Sinners* series, 1970–71; *Me Mammy* series, 1970–71; *White Walls and Olive Green Carpets*, 1971; *The*

Removal Person, 1971; *Pandora*, 1971; *The Virgins*, 1972; *The Ghost of Christmas Present*, 1972; *The Trugh Game*, 1972; *Tales from the Lazy Acres* series, 1972; *The Moonstone* (serialization), from the novel by Wilkie Collins, 1972; *The Sullen Sisters*, 1972; *The Watercress Girl*, from the story by H. E. Bates, 1972; *The Higgler*, 1973; *High Kampf*, 1973; *Milo O'Shea*, 1973; *Stone Cold Sober*, 1973; *The Bitter Pill*, 1973; *Another Fine Mess*, 1973; *Judgement Day*, 1973; *The Travelling Woman*, 1973; *The Hammer of God, The Actor and the Alibi, The Eye of Apollo, The Forbidden Garden, The Three Tools of Death*, and *The Quick One* (*Father Brown* series), 1974.

Theatrical Activities:

Actor: **Play** – in *A Walk on the Water*, Dublin, 1960.

Hugh Leonard comments:

Being an Irish writer both hampers and helps me: hampers, because one is fighting the preconceptions of audiences who have been conditioned to expect feyness and parochial subject matter; helps, because the writer can utilise a vigorous and poetic idiom which enables him to combine subtlety with richness. Ireland is my subject matter, but only to the degree in which I can use it as a microcosm; this involves choosing themes which are free of Catholicism and politics, both of which I detest, and which deprive one's work of applicability outside Ireland.

For many years I was obsessed with the theme of betrayal (*A Walk on the Water* and *The Poker Session*) – its effects and its inevitability. My work then began to reflect a preoccupation with defining and isolating the essence of the new prosperity, which I used as the subject for satire (*The Patrick Pearse Motel* and *Thieves*, as yet unproduced). By and large – and after the event – my work reflects Ibsen's observation that to be a writer is to sit in judgment on oneself; and perhaps for this reason I now want to write a play which, like *A Walk on the Water* and *Pandora*, is autobiographical. Like most writers I am involved in seeking a form. A play takes me a long time to write, and my methods involve – partly deliberately, partly because of how I work – various subterranean levels. At times this leads to an excess of cleverness, stemming perhaps from a lack of faith in one's own powers. Now that I have learned both the requirements and the uses of the dramatic form I would like to use a simplicity of style combined with visual situations – the image in my mind is the scene in which Lavinia confronts her mother across her father's corpse in *Mourning Becomes Electra*.

Like all writers who achieve middle-age, I am conscious of having wasted time, and also of having at last arrived at a sense of identity. Ideally, I would now like to write my "failures": i.e., plays written as pure acts of self-expression, without any hope of their being staged. I am conscious that my main faults are the cleverness (in the structural sense) which I have mentioned and at times irresponsible sense of comedy, which is not so much out of place as inclined to give my work an unintended lightness. These faults at least I know and can guard against. I regard myself as an optimist, and the theme that emerges from my plays is that life is good if it is not misused. But this is only an impression which – again after the event – I have gleaned from revisiting my work. As Moss Hart has said, one begins with two people on a stage, and one of them had better say something pretty damn quick! One starts to write, and one's own character and beliefs – not consciously defined – shapes, limits, enriches, pauperises and defines one's work. Choice of subject and form are the cartridge case which contains the bullet. A play is an accident: often one writes the right play at the wrong time in one's life, and vice-versa; often one begins to write it that vital fraction in time before it has ripened in one's skull – or a moment too late, when it has gone cold. One goes on trying.

*   *   *

Hugh Leonard is the best living Irish dramatist. Not only that: he also merits a special Lope de Vega prize for sheer creative abundance. He has written over 20 stage plays, an enormous number of one-shot plays and serial adaptations for television and several film scripts. On top of all this, he has been a regular drama critic for *Plays and Players*. Whatever faults he may have as a writer, lack of industry is certainly not amongst them.

Not unnaturally for a Dublin-based writer, Leonard is chiefly concerned in his plays with explorations of the contemporary Irish scene and with the attempt to put the greatest Irish writers on the stage. Thus his first international success as a writer (though it was very far from being his first play) came in 1962 with *Stephen D*, adapted from Joyce's *A Portrait of the Artist as a Young Man* and *Stephen Hero*. Like most of Leonard's plays, it first appeared at the Dublin Theatre Festival; but it soon transferred to London and New York because, as Bernard Levin said, it really took us inside Joyce's mind and "the excitement, passion and colour of so great a mind are fine things to be among."

Leonard's skill as an adaptor should not be underrated. He drew the first act from *The Portrait*, Joyce's spiritual autobiography: the second from *Stephen Hero*, which stuck closer to the objective facts. But he gave the material unity by turning it into a memory play with the distant past seen, at first, in a slightly hazy perspective and with the narrator, Stephen, gradually stepping into the action as the sequences became longer and more sharply defined. With great skill, he also showed Joyce cutting loose from the restrictive bonds of family loyalties, patriotism and religion and ended the play on a fine note of exultant defiance with the hero going into permanent exile.

The following year he had two plays done at the same fesitval: *Dublin One* (adapted from Joyce's *Dubliners*) and *The Poker Session*, a sour and savage original comedy. The first work was much more than a straight piece of adaptation: it ran the stories together in pairs neatly contrasting the Dubliner in private with the Dubliner in public and in some cases ("A Little Cloud" for instance) altered Joyce's narrative with shattering effect. *The Poker Session* (which later came to London) was perhaps more significant in that it displayed Mr. Leonard's own eloquence at work. Set in the outskirts of Dublin, it showed a boy returning to his family after a spell in a lunatic asylum and bringing with him a middle-aged, red-haired, bowler-hatted chum to help discover who or what drove him mad. The stranger who proceeds to uncover a family's sinister web of guilt is a well-tried dramatic device; but what gave the play its vitality was the sheer linguistic exuberance of the raffish intruder and Mr. Leonard's own rather black and bilious wit.

The next play of his to make the transition from Dublin to the West End, *The Au Pair Man*, was more ambitious in its aim but much more limited in its achievement. It was intended as an irreverent allegorical attack on Britain's fading imperial grandeur, its remote, over-privileged monarchy and its indestructible class system; but what made it unconvincing was that the allegory never seemed to grow out of a plausible realistic situation. The play showed us, in fact, an ardent lady royalist (initial E. R.) taking a plebeian debt collector (initials E.H. and with a predecessor called Wilson) into her home and eventually confronting him with a choice between her elegant graciousness and the democratic world outside: needless to say, he chose the former. Some of the dialogue had a splendid sub-Wildean quality ("At its worst, rape is no more than pressing an unwanted gift on another person") but Mr. Leonard's analysis of Britain's troubles seemed oversimplified and his satire slightly toothless.

He made brilliant amends, however, with his next transfer, *The Patrick Pearse Motel*, which broke all the established theatrical rules by proving that farce could be used as a vehicle for social satire. The play is simultaneously an act of conscious homage to Feydeau and a pungent, witty, acerbic attack on the Irish *nouveau riche*: in particular, on their exploitation of their country's political and folk heritage as a tourist attraction. Set in Dublin's vodka-and-bitter-lemon belt, the first act deftly punctures the pretensions of the expense-account suburbanites with their stereo ping-pong and decorated sauna baths and the dialogue is full of sharp asides about the twin Irish obsessions of sex and religion ("She's an Irish Catholic wife and mother – the only thing she has left is her virginity"). In the second act we get closer to the door-banging, bedroom-hopping Feydeau prototype but again the unifying factor is the vanity and greed of the thriving Irish middle-classes. It's rare to find a farce as literate as this.

The question now is whether Mr. Leonard, who has enjoyed a great deal of critical acclaim both for his original plays and for his adaptations, can achieve the complete popular success that so far seems to have eluded him. Irish plays traditionally do badly in London; but if there is any writer around today who deserves to break the spell then it is surely the indefatigable, resourceful Mr. Leonard.

—Michael Billington

LESSING, Doris (May). British. Born in Kermanshah, Persia, 22 October 1919. Married Frank Charles Wisdom in 1939 (divorced, 1943); Gottfried Lessing, 1945 (divorced, 1949); has three children. Lived in Southern Rhodesia, 1924–49; came to England in 1949. Recipient: Maugham Award, 1954. Address: c/o Curtis Brown Ltd., 1 Craven Hill, London W2 3EW, England.

PUBLICATIONS

Plays

Before the Deluge (produced London, 1953).
Mr. Dolinger (produced Oxford, 1958).
Each His Own Wilderness (produced London, 1958). Included in *New English Dramatists*, London, Penguin, 1959.
The Truth about Billy Newton (produced Salisbury, Wiltshire, 1960).
Play with a Tiger (produced London, 1962; New York, 1964). London, Joseph, 1962.
The Storm, adaptation of the play by Alexander Ostrowsky (produced London, 1966).
The Singing Door, in *Second Playbill 2*, edited by Alan Durband. London, Hutchinson, 1973.

Television Plays: *The Grass Is Singing*, 1962; *Please Do Not Disturb*, 1966; *Care and Protection*, 1966; *Between Men*, 1967.

Novels

The Grass Is Singing. London, Joseph, and New York, Crowell, 1950.
Children of Violence:
  Martha Quest. London, Joseph, 1952.
  A Proper Marriage. London, Joseph, 1954; with *Martha Quest*, New York, Simon and Schuster, 1964.
  A Ripple from the Storm. London, Joseph, 1958.
  Landlocked. London, MacGibbon and Kee, 1965; with *A Ripple from the Storm*, New York, Simon and Schuster, 1966.
  The Four-Gated City. London, MacGibbon and Kee, and New York, Knopf, 1969.

Retreat to Innocence.   London, Joseph, 1956.
The Golden Notebook.   London, Joseph, and New York, Simon and Schuster, 1962.
Briefing for a Descent into Hell.   London, Cape, and New York, Knopf, 1971.
The Summer Before the Dark.   London, Cape and New York, Knopf, 1973.
The Memoirs of a Survivor.   London, Octagon Press, 1974; New York, Knopf, 1975.

Short Stories

This Was the Old Chief's Country: Stories.   London, Joseph, 1951; New York,
    Crowell, 1952.
Five: Short Novels.   London, Joseph, 1953.
The Habit of Loving.   London, MacGibbon and Kee, 1957; New York, Crowell, 1958.
A Man and Two Women: Stories.   London, MacGibbon and Kee, and New York,
    Simon and Schuster, 1963.
African Stories.   London, Joseph, 1964; New York, Simon and Schuster, 1965.
Nine African Stories.   London, Longman, 1968.
The Story of a Non-Marrying Man and Other Stories.   London, Cape, 1972.
The Temptation of Jack Orkney and Other Stories.   New York, Knopf, 1972.
Collected African Stories:
    1. *This Was the Old Chief's Country.*   London, Joseph, 1973.
    2. *The Sun Between Their Feet.*   London, Joseph, 1973.

Verse

Fourteen Poems.   Lowestoft, Suffolk, Scorpion Press, 1959.

Other

Going Home.   London, Joseph, 1957.
In Pursuit of the English: A Documentary.   London, Joseph, 1960; as *In Pursuit of the
    English*, New York, Simon and Schuster, 1961.
Particularly Cats.   London, Joseph, and New York, Simon and Schuster, 1967.
A Small Personal Voice: Essays, Reviews, Interviews, edited by Paul Schlueter. New
    York, Knopf, 1974.

Bibliographies: *Doris Lessing* by C. Ipp, Johannesburg, University of the Witwatersrand
Department of Bibliography, Librarianship and Typography, 1967; "Doris Lessing Issue" of
Contemporary Literature (Madison, Wisconsin), Autumn 1973.

*   *   *

In any theatre, a deal of talent must go to waste, especially among playwrights, but it is a
great pity that Doris Lessing's career as a playwright should have been abortive. One of the
failures of George Devine's successful regime at the Royal Court was its failure to help her
to go on from *Each His Own Wilderness*, which was given a Sunday night production in
1958. Though it was dismissed by many of the critics as a novelist's play can so readily be
dismissed, simply be describing it as "a novelist's play," in fact it was remarkably free from
the flaws that might have been expected – flat characters, over-leisurely development, verbal
analysis written out as dialogue, lack of dramatic drive. Doris Lessing had, on the contrary,
a very keen instinct for how to ignite a situation theatrically.

By building the play around a mother-son conflict and empathising successfully with the son, she steered clear of the pitfall of subordinating all the other characters to the woman she could most easily identify with. Myra Bolton is an attractive, middle-aged campaigner for Left Wing causes, warm, well-meaning, but gauche in human relationships, liable to inflict unintended pain not only on her son but on the three men in the play she has had relationships with – two of her own generation, one of her son's. The muddles and misunderstandings of these involvements are all developed in a way that contributes richly to the play's dramatic texture, and the untidiness we see on the set – the hall of her London house – contributes visually to the impression of an inability to keep things under control.

The men are all well characterised – the sad, ageing, lonely politician, the architect trying to embark on a new marriage with a young girl, the opportunistic 22-year-old son of a woman friend, and above all Tony, the son, who returns from National Service to find Myra did not know which day to expect him. His pained anger at his own inability to commit himself to any outside reality and at the lack of understanding between them mounts effectively through the play, reaching a climax when he discovers that she has sold the house he loves more than anything, intending to help him by raising money to set him up on his own in a flat. It may be a well-made play but it is made remarkably well, with an unusual talent for keeping a number of relationships simultaneously on the boil, and it catches the flavour of the life of Left Wing intellectuals in the fifties. Showing private people devoting their lives protesting about public issues, Doris Lessing successfully merges personal and political themes. Like the characters in John McGrath's recent work, these people are all "plugged in to history."

Doris Lessing had started writing for the theatre five years earlier, in 1953, and of the three plays she turned out *Mr. Dollinger* was also produced in 1958, earlier in the year, at the Oxford Playhouse, and *The Trugh about Billy Newton* was produced in 1960 at Salisbury. But the only play of hers to receive a full-scale London production was *Play with a Tiger* which was written in 1958 and had a seven-and-a-half week run at the Comedy in 1962 with Siobhan McKenna as the central character, who is, unfortunately, very much more central than any of the characters in *Each His Own Wilderness*.

Doris Lessing was determined to turn her back on both naturalism and realism. "It is my intention," she wrote in a 1963 note on the play,

> that when the curtain comes down at the end, the audience will think: Of course!
> In this play no one lit cigarettes, drank tea or coffee, read newspapers, squirted soda into Scotch, or indulged in little bits of "business" which indicated "character." They will realize, I hope, that they have been seeing a play which relies upon its style and its language for its effect.

But it starts off naturalistically in an underfurnished room with a litter of books and cushions, paraffin heaters, a record player and a telephone. There are also sound effects of traffic noises. Anna Freeman is a woman of "35 or so" who lives as a literary freelance, has a son by a broken marriage and has recently decided not to marry an Englishman who is about to settle for a safe job on a woman's magazine. She is in love with an American Jew who would never settle and if she had been entertaining ideas of marrying him, these would be killed off in Act One by the visit of a nice young American girl who announces that she is going to have Dave's baby.

The play's starting points, in other words, are all naturalistic and there is even a naturalistic cliché neighbour who fusses about an invisible cat. But towards the end of Act One the walls disappear, and though the neighbour is going to reappear and the play is still going to make gestures towards satisfying the audience expectations that its first half-hour has aroused, its centre has been shifted. With only a few interruptions from other characters, about 62 pages of the 92 page script are taken up with a dialogue between Anna and Dave. But the language and the style cannot depart completely from those of the naturalistic beginning. Some of the writing in it is very good, some of it bad and embarrassing, expecially when they play games reminiscent of the psycho-analytical situation.

Even the best sections of the dialogue, which make a defiant and articulate declaration of rights on behalf of the woman against the male predator, tend to generalise the play away from its roots in the specific predicament of a specific woman. In reacting against naturalism, Doris Lessing is renouncing all its disciplines, some of which were very useful to her in *Each His Own Wilderness*. *Play with a Tiger* may look more like a public statement and it has been seized on by Women's Lib groups, whose performances have unbalanced the central relationship by failing to give Dave equal weight with Anna. Doris Lessing complains about this in a 1972 postscript, but the fault is basically in the play, which is really more private than *Each His Own Wilderness*, and more self-indulgent, in that the dialogue is spun too directly out of personal preoccupations.

—Ronald Hayman

LIVINGS, Henry.   British. Born in Prestwich, Lancashire, 20 September 1929. Educated at Park View Primary School, 1935–39; Stand Grammar School, Prestwich (scholarship), 1940–45; Liverpool University, 1945–47, read Hispanic studies. Served in the Royal Air Force, 1948–50. Married Fanny Carter in 1957; has two children. Associated with the BBC programme *Northern Drift*. Recipient: *Evening Standard* award, 1961; Encyclopedia Britannica Award, 1965; Obie Award, 1966. Agent: Harvey Unna Ltd., 14 Beaumont Mews, Marylebone High Street, London W1N 4HE. Address: 33 Woods Lane, Dobcross, Oldham, Lancashire, England.

PUBLICATIONS

Plays

> *Stop It Whoever You Are* (produced London, 1961).   Published in *New English Dramatists 5*, London, Penguin, 1962.
> *Big Soft Nellie* (as *Thacred Nit*, produced Keswick, Cumberland, 1961; as *Big Soft Nellie*, produced London, 1961).   Included in *Kelly's Eye and Other Plays*, 1964.
> *Nil Carborundum* (produced London, 1962).   Published in *New England Dramatists, 6*, London, Penguin, 1963.
> *Kelly's Eye* (produced London, 1963).   Included in *Kelly's Eye and Other Plays*, 1964.
> *There's No Room for You Here for a Start* (televised, 1963).   Included in *Kelly's Eye and Other Plays*, 1964.
> *The Day Dumbfounded Got His Pylon* (broadcast, 1963; produced Stoke on Trent, 1965).   Published in *Worth a Hearing: A Collection of Radio Plays*, edited by Alfred Bradley, London, Blackie, 1967.
> *Kelly's Eye and Other Plays* (includes *Big Soft Nellie* and *There's No Room for You Here for a Start*).   London, Methuen, and New York, Hill and Wang, 1964.
> *Eh?* (produced London, 1964; Cincinnati and New York, 1966).   London, Methuen, 1965; New York, Hill and Wang, 1967.
> *The Little Mrs. Foster Show* (produced Liverpool, 1966).   London, Methuen, 1968.
> *Brainscrew* (televised, 1966; produced Birmingham, 1971).   Published in *Second Playbill 3*, edited by Alan Durband, London, Hutchinson, 1973.
> *Good Grief!* (includes *After the Last Lamp, You're Free, Variable Lengths, Pie-Eating*

Contest, Does It Make Your Cheeks Ache?, The Reasons for Flying) (produced Manchester, 1967).   London, Methuen, 1968.

Honour and Offer (produced Cincinnati, 1968; London, 1969).   London, Methuen, 1969.

The Gamecock (produced Manchester, 1969).   Included in *Pongo Plays 1–6*, 1971.

Rattel (produced Manchester, 1969; London, 1974).   Included in *Pongo Plays 1–6*, 1971.

Variable Lengths and Longer: An Hour of Embarrassment (includes *The Reasons for Flying, Does It Make Your Cheeks Ache?*) (produced London, 1969).

The Boggart (produced Birmingham, 1970).   Included in *Pongo Plays 1–6*, 1971.

Conciliation (produced Lincoln, 1970; London, 1971).   Included in *Pongo Plays 1–6*, 1971.

The Rifle Volunteer (produced Birmingham, 1970; London, 1971).   Included in *Pongo Plays 1–6*, 1971.

Beewine (produced Birmingham, 1970; London, 1971).   Included in *Pongo Plays 1–6*, 1971.

The Ffinest Ffamily in the Land (produced Lincoln, 1970; London, 1972).   London, Eyre Methuen, 1973.

You're Free (produced London, 1970).

GRUP (televised, 1970; produced York, 1971).

Mushrooms and Toadstools (produced London, 1970).   Included in *Six More Pongo Plays*, 1974.

Tiddles (produced Birmingham, 1970).   Included in *Six More Pongo Plays*, 1974.

Pongo Plays 1–6 (includes *The Gamecock, Rattel, The Boggart, Beewine, The Rifle Volunteer, Conciliation*).   London, Methuen, 1971.

This Jockey Drives Late Nights, adaptation of a play by Tolstoy (produced Birmingham, 1972).   London, Eyre Methuen, 1972.

Daft Sam (televised, 1972; produced London, 1976).   Included in *Six More Pongo Plays*, 1974.

The Rent Man (produced Stoke on Trent, 1972).   Included in *Six More Pongo Plays*, 1974.

Cinderella, adaptation of the story by Perrault (produced Stock on Trent, 1972).   London, Dobson, 1976.

The Tailor's Britches (produced Stoke on Trent, 1973).   Included in *Six More Pongo Plays*, 1974.

Glorious Miles (televised, 1973; produced Sheffield, 1975).

The Cross-Buttock Show (produced Durham, 1973).

Jonah (produced Manchester, 1974).   London, Pulpit Press, 1975.·

Six More Pongo Plays Including Two for Children (includes *Tiddles, The Rent Man, The Ink-Smeared Lady, The Tailor's Britches, Daft Sam, Mushrooms and Toadstools*).   London, Eyre Methuen, 1974.

Jack and the Beanstalk, music by Alex Glasgow (produced London, 1974).

Jug, adaptation of a play by Heinrich von Kleist (produced Nottingham, 1975).

Radio Plays: *After the Last Lamp*, 1961; *The Weavers*, from the play by Hauptmann, 1962; *The Day Dumbfounded Got His Pylon*, 1963; *A Public Menace*, from the play by Ibsen, 1964; *Nelson Cape Requests the Pleasure*, 1967; *The Government Inspector*, from the play by Gogol, 1969; *The Dobcross Silver Band*, 1971; *The Red Cockerel Crows*, from the play by Hauptmann, 1974; *A Most Wonderful Thing*, 1976.

Television Plays: The Arson Squad, 1961; *Jack's Horrible Luck*, 1961; *There's No Room for You Here for a Start*, 1963; *A Right Crusader*, 1963; *Brainscrew*, 1966; *GRUP*, 1970; *Daft Sam*, 1972; *Glorious Miles*, 1973; *Shuttlecock*, 1976; *The Game*, 1976.

Other

That the Medals and the Baton Be Put on View: The Story of a Village Band 1875–1975.
Newton Abbot, Devon, David and Charles, 1975.

Critical Study: *Anger and After* by John Russell Taylor, London, Methuen, 1962.

Theatrical Activities:

Actor: **Plays** – with the Century Theatre, the Midland Theatre Company, Coventry,
Theatre Workshop, Stratford East, and other repertory and London theatres. **Radio** –
Northern Drift (miscellany). **Television** – *Cribbins, Livings and Co.*, 1976; *Get the Drift*,
1976.

Henry Livings comments:

To me, a show is an opportunity for communal imaginings, actors and audience together,
for which I provide the material. When I first wrote plays, I felt there weren't enough plays
which were fun, and that plot and naturalism were overwhelming the other aspects (fun,
magic, social observation, the sculptural kinetics, the social connection that can be set up in
a theatre); I now feel that I neglected story too much: I still feel it's better to know the story
beforehand – if we're wondering what happens next, how can we pay attention to what's
happening now? – but I try to steal a good story as well. I would like to make plays that are
neither a simple narrative nor a flat picture, but a complete experience to carry out of the
building, so that we could look around us with new eyes and say "Oh yes, that's right." For
this I go mostly for laughter, because for me laughter is the shock reaction to a new way of
looking at something: even a pun questions our security in the solidity of words. I also
believe that we are what we do, rather than having some kind of permanent identifiable
reality: the materials of art, observation, ritual, symbol, gesture, community, give us a
chance to focus for a moment, and then go forward with fresh hope that we matter and that
what we do signifies. For this reason again I try to choose as a principal character or
characters someone who isn't normally big deal in our thinking – not that I'm not interested
in power, as we all are, but that I want to see how it works and on whom. I have only once
had the worm turning (in *Stop It*), and then only on Mrs. Warbeck, the scold, which is a
good gag; but have frequently shown the humble to be indestructible – which I consider to
be a fair observation of what goes on: we do survive, in our millions, in spite of famine, war
and pestilence.

*   *   *

An actor with Joan Littlewood's Theatre Workshop, as well as numerous repertory
companies throughout the country, Henry Livings has had plays produced by the English
Stage Company, the Royal Shakespeare Company and Theatre Workshop itself. His first
play, *Stop It Whoever You Are*, misleadingly described as a "North Country farce" in the
Penguin Dictionary of the Theatre, is in fact a mixture of farce and fantasy with social
overtones – a combination which has characterized most of his work. In plays like *Big Soft
Nellie*, his television play *There's No Room for You Here for a Start, Eh?*, and *Honour and
Offer*, he pitches a bewildered and socially inept individual against the forces of authority
and permits him a minor victory. But this is not the conventional social battlefield and the
victory is doubtful and even ironic. The issues are trivial and absurd, the characters are
reduced to caricature and the farcical elements permitted to extend into a fantasy which

subverts any social commitment. If this is social drama it is social drama refracted by the surreal. The settings are recognisably real; the characters who inhabit them are unreal, parodies of the social types which they represent. Indeed, far from insisting on humanist values in these plays, Livings seems to regard man as irretrievably ridiculous. His moments of fulfilment are brief and farcically trivial; his claims for dignity derisively ironic. In *Big Soft Nellie*, Stanley, a partly demented television mechanic, is given a lyrical speech in which he describes the progress of the Royal Highlander train towards London, a train which seems to shout "this is what it's for" as it surges down the main line. But when this miracle of engineering reaches the capital "who gets out?...Fellers! That's all...Crumpled, little people!" It is these very crumpled little people who are the subject of his plays and, with the exception of his more realistic work, he deals with them in a way which they cannot understand, waging battles which only serve to underline their own insignificance.

As a social dramatist, he offers no solutions except an anarchic resistance to any authority – a refusal to serve the machine. But the individuals who do resist tend to be portrayed, as is William Warbeck in *Stop It Whoever You Are*, Valentine Brose in *Eh?*, Len in *There's No Room for You Here for a Start*, and Stanley in *Big Soft Nellie*, as at least marginally deranged. The fact that they nonetheless constitute a contrast with the self-important representatives of the Establishment indicates Livings' social objectives but fails, finally, to validate them. The ending of *Eh?*, in which the machine explodes while everyone sits around eating narcotic mushrooms, typifies the collapse of this social dimension. Livings seems unwilling to concede any potential for meaningful action or to grant any substance to character. If everything is equally absurd then there is no room for social commitment and no point in distinguishing the vitally subversive from the debilitatingly conformist. The ruler and the ruled are ultimately interchangeable – as they had seemed clearly enough to the Samuel Beckett of *Waiting for Godot*. And yet Livings seems to see a distinction while proving unable to define the nature of that distinction or to grant it any real significance. As a result his characters constantly threaten to become merely figures of fun – wholly so in a play like *The Ffinest Ffamily in the Land*, in which the humour derives in part from the middle class pretensions of working class characters (itself a patronising form of humour), and in part from the willing acquiescence of these characters in the most outrageous of suggestions – an echo of *The Homecoming*, which underlines Livings' debt to Pinter as his earlier work had emphasized the influence of N.F. Simpson. But where Simpson is a farceur with no real social pretensions, and Pinter a metaphysician intent on examining the nature of human relationships and the pressure of existence itself, Livings is too content to play for laughs while implying a satirical dimension which could be sustained only if there was some evidence of the dramatist himself occupying an identifiable moral world of his own. The evidence that he does indeed grant value to integrity and humanity, that he does regard the individual who sustains his own values in the face of authority as being potentially heroic, is clear enough from plays like *Nil Carborundum* and *Kelly's Eye* and from the satirical energy of *The Little Mrs. Foster Show*. But his reliance, elsewhere, on characters who are little more than music hall patsies creates a drama which, while astute in its use of linguistic incongruities and visual humour, lacks the fundamental seriousness which distinguishes the work of writers like Beckett and Pinter.

The Little Mrs. Foster Show is an exception because here the elements of fantasy, the music hall format, the savage caricatures, become totally functional, for the play is a pitiless examination of human nature and an attack on the tasteless display of brutality for public entertainment. When a member of the audience walked out of the Nottingham Playhouse production complaining that, "It's not a play at all! It's a nightmare," he came remarkably close to stating the play's central theme and method. As Livings himself remarked,

> It's no pleasure to me so to offend a customer that he leaves his seat; but I'm bound to feel a little proud that I could tell a story of our time in such a way that, in spite of having repellent atrocity and horror daily under our satiated noses, at least one man felt its impact afresh.... Reading a newspaper or listening to radio or watching television, we guzzle in horror, boredom, jokes etc as they come; by setting these experiences on the stage we made quite a lot of people take notice.

The play presents the experiences of a white mercenary in Africa as a stage show, complete with atrocity photographs hired at £20 a set. But the violence of the war itself, briefly sketched but familiar enough to a modern audience even in the theatrical form in which it is presented, is finally secondary to Livings' contempt for those who display their inhumanity through a seemingly limitless ability to absorb horror as though it were designed for its entertainment value. Indeed here, and in later short plays like *Pie-Eating Contest* and *Does It Make Your Cheeks Ache?*, he denounces those who contrive to create spectacle out of human anguish. If this raises questions about his own art this play remains, nonetheless, one of his more effective and consistent works.

It is, indeed, in military conflict that human nature is seen at its most naked and it is perhaps not without significance that one of his earliest plays, *Nil Carborundum*, a basically naturalistic play produced in 1962 by the Royal Shakespeare Company, should have been set in an RAF camp. But his concern here is less with man's capacity for brutality than with the pointless waste of a life designed to serve the interests of authority without questioning its purpose. It is a play, moreover, which shows a compassionate understanding even of the weakest and most vacillating characters virtually absent from all of his work with the exception of the lyrical *Kelly's Eye*. His theme is expressed in the typically humorous title, *Nil Carborundum* – don't let them grind you down. And if this is essentially the motto of all of his work it has a validity here which it is difficult to maintain in plays which see no real human resource for such resistance. Of course the inanities of service life, the strict delineation of social position, the harnessing of human energy to serve the interests of a self-justifying system arguably constitute an appropriate image of society at large and Livings' play should not be seen as a comment only on the nature of military service. When he describes the patent absurdities of a military exercise in which people perform their prescribed roles with no clear understanding of the purpose or progress of the attack, he is equally describing a society in which individuals are likewise required to conform to socially defined identities. The only possible response is that offered by the unit cook who is described as "cockily cheerful" and "resilient" and who continues to cook his chips as the battle rages around him.

The following year *Kelly's Eye*, performed by the Royal Court Theatre, offered another portrait of resilience, but his view of human nature in this play is already considerably darker and the resilience now simply a form of desperate resistance. It is a demonstration of his growing conviction that "inside we are scarlet, raw, bloody." The play is set in 1936 and 1939, a time which Livings describes as "an evil time" when men demonstrated "apathy in the face of cruelty and the will to destroy." Kelly himself is a murderer but a man who has come to understand both himself and his society, which seems infected with the same spirit which had led him to kill his best friend. His own youthful conviction that "if I hit the first feller hard enough the others'd lie down by themselves" is clearly now enshrined in the principles of a nation which is itself on the verge of war. That Kelly comes to learn the need for compassion suggests little hope, for he in turn is destroyed by the single-minded and callous vengefulness of society. We are left with the narrator's observation that "Kelly is hollow, inferior and evil" and that "the only thing that can recommend him to us is his humanity, which we share and so must love."

The play is a powerful work, combining a lyric subtlety with emotional force. Nothing he has written since has approached this level of explicit statement. The confident humanism of *Nil Carborundum* has dissipated and this perhaps explains the apparent contempt which seems implicit in the caricatures of his other plays – a contempt never entirely neutralised by his humour or by the anarchic eccentricity which seems to be the only strategy which the individual can adopt in the face of social pressure. Indeed, the eccentricity is perhaps itself a product of that pressure and the caricature as much a consequence of the deadly power of an inhuman society. The high rise apartment block which is the setting of *The Ffinest Ffamily in the Land* is an entirely appropriate setting for a family so totally detached from all conventional values and isolated from other human contact.

His recent series of "Pongo plays," short works based on Japanese Kyogen plays and stories culled from folklore, suggests a continuation of his moral ambivalence. These delightfully humorous sketches feature Sam Pongo, a cunning Lancashire weaver, who scores a series of victories over authority, in the person of the Master, and over anyone else gullible enough to be taken in by his quick wits and plausible patter. Livings creates a hero, in other words, who can successfully challenge the system only because he is aware of human fallibility and can manipulate it to his advantage.

Whether it be with the participant of a pie-eating contest who competes in order to forget her lost lover, or a ventriloquist who is controlled by his dummy, Livings creates a disconcerting world in which the pain of living is embodied in distorted characters. If the humour of his plays is never quite sufficient to neutralise a more fundamental sense of despair, nevertheless the resulting tension expresses essentially the same sense of ambivalence which one finds in other contemporary writers from Wesker to Orton, from Pinter to Bond. Livings' particular gift to the English theatre lies in his capacity to reproduce on stage the colour and energy of the comic strip. His work has all the virtues and vices of the form.

—C. W. E. Bigsby

LORD, Robert. New Zealander. Member of the Editorial Board, *Act* magazine, Wellington, 1970–74. Recipient: Katherine Mansfield Award, for short story, 1969; Arts Council of New Zealand Travel Bursary, 1974. Agent: Gilbert Parker, Curtis Brown Ltd., 60 East 56th Street, New York, New York 10022. Address: 43 West 93rd Street, Apartment 12, New York, New York 10025, U.S.A.

PUBLICATIONS

Plays

It Isn't Cricket (produced Wellington, 1971). Published in *Act 15* (Wellington), November 1971.
Moody Tuesday (broadcast, 1972). Wellington, New Zealand Broadcasting Corporation, 1972.
Meeting Place (produced Wellington, 1972; New York, 1975). Published in *Act 18* (Wellington), December 1972.
Balance of Payments (produced Wellington, 1972). Brisbane, University of Queensland Press, 1976.
Nativity (produced Auckland, 1973).
Well Hung (produced Wellington and Providence, Rhode Island, 1974).
Heroes and Butterflies (produced Auckland, 1974).
Glitter and Spit, in *Act 27* (Wellington), May 1975.

Screenplay: *The Day We Landed on the Most Perfect Planet in the Universe*, 1971.

Radio Plays: *Moody Tuesday*, 1972; *Friendship Centre*, 1972; *Blood on My Sprigs*, 1973; *Body in the Park*, 1973.

*   *   *

The 1970's have been the best years ever for local dramatists in New Zealand. A number of small professional theatres have been established, with some show of permanence, in various parts of the country, and they have built up loyal audiences which have evinced an unprecedented degree of interest in the work of local playwrights. Robert Lord, who won a short story competition in 1969 and who would still like to write novels, has candidly confessed his recognition that there was more money in the theatre – perhaps even a livelihood. In 1970 he was part-time promotions officer for Downstage Theatre in Wellington, he has had a year as resident playwright at the Mercury Theatre in Auckland, and he is now living in the United States. In this short period he has had four full length and two shorter plays produced, most of them several times; some have had runs in Australia and New York.

Commentators have distinguished two types of Robert Lord play. There is the exaggerated farce, with a touch of the macabre (Joe Orton's name has been mentioned), of which *Balance of Payments* and *Well Hung* are examples; and there is the play, much more original in method, which explores the way personality is affected by varying human relationships, as happens in *It Isn't Cricket* and *Meeting Place*.

Well Hung, Lord's most popular piece so far, is not altogether characteristic. It was written, in part, to prove to himself and to his critics that he could handle conventional plot, but it is also clearly a commercial piece and was influenced by the kind of comedy Lord found popular in Australia when he attended a Playwrights' Conference there in 1973. It makes fun out of the sexual exploits and problems of officers in a small country police station whose activities are endangered by outside investigation of a local murder. The quite amoral capital made of double entendre, from the title of the piece on, hardly pretends to offer more than easy entertainment, but the effect is almost destroyed by the late introduction of melodrama with its simple but insistent black and white morality, when the police are shown attempting to secure an improper conviction by underhand methods. It is an unsettling turn; Lord is not a satirist, nor a champion of a better way of life. He has said he does not believe the theatre to be the vanguard of revolution, and in any case his more serious purpose in writing plays has been to heighten one's perceptions of one's relations with others, an aim difficult (though not impossible) to reconcile with farce. So while a recent script like *Glitter and Spit* shows Lord toying with such a reconciliation, one looks elsewhere for more truly original qualities.

When he reviewed Donald Howarth's play *Three Months Gone* in 1970, Lord noted approvingly how this work existed beyond the bounds of formal unities, and said, "It is the realisation that Alvin never really decided where he was at or who he was that lingers, and of course these are decisions that very few of us make." Both comments could stand as epigraphs to *It Isn't Cricket* and *Meeting Place*.

It Isn't Cricket presents a middle class couple and their friends talking to one another about one another, and reveals how they describe things differently in differing circumstances. It isn't cricket to cheat at games, but do the same rules apply in the much more complex game of life? Only one lie is shown up in the course of the play to be a socially unacceptable falsehood, but there is a whole range of usually barely conscious prevarication, employed according as the speaker wants to please, or win sympathy from, or indeed give hurt to his or her auditor. Lord is less interested than, say, Pinter in why people lie and does not build a plot out of what they try to gain by it; he simply shows what an entertaining pattern can be made of demonstrating how it goes on.

Pattern rather than plot also shapes *Meeting Place*, a play which has so far proved difficult to present convincingly to an audience, but which is undoubtedly Lord's most ambitious and intriguing piece. The difficulties lie in the abandoning of a defined locality for the action, and more importantly, of a precise chronological sequence – breaks with convention which time and further plays may well clarify. What interests him here is the way people's personalities can be affected, and perhaps even defined, by their relationship to others; how in extreme emotional circumstances (in this play it is sexual assault of one sort or another), character can for a while alter beyond recognition. What seems to remain constant is the cycle, set in motion as pairs of characters group and regroup. This is a play which more than any of the others "exists beyond the bounds of formal unities."

There is perhaps little distinction in Lord's use of language. His characters fall back endlessly on the common clichés of conversation in their attempts to handle new and unexpected relationships, and the life of the plays depends upon his ability to maintain unceasingly this incongruity. His great strength lies, as this suggests, in his exploitation of the possibilities of stage presentation. Robert Lord may have begun as a writer; he has become a man of the theatre.

—J. E. P. Thomson

LOWELL, Robert (Traill Spence, Jr.). American. Born in Boston, Massachusetts, 1 March 1917. Educated at St. Mark's School; Harvard University, Cambridge, Massachusetts, 1935–37; Kenyon College, Gambier, Ohio, A.B. (summa cum laude) 1940 (Phi Beta Kappa). Conscientious objector during World War II: served prison sentence, 1943–44. Married the writer Jean Stafford in 1940 (divorced, 1948); the writer Elizabeth Hardwick, 1949, has one daughter; third marriage, has one daughter. Worked for Sheed and Ward, publishers, New York, 1941–42. Taught at the University of Iowa, Iowa City, 1949–50, 1952–53; Salzburg Seminar on American Studies, 1952; Boston University; New School for Social Research, New York; Harvard University. Consultant in Poetry, Library of Congress, Washington, D.C., 1947–48; Visiting Fellow, All Souls College, Oxford, 1970. Since 1970, has taught at Kent University, Canterbury. Recipient: Pulitzer Prize, 1947; National Institute of Arts and Letters grant, 1947; Guggenheim Fellowship, 1947, 1974; Harriet Monroe Poetry Award, 1952; Guinness Prize, 1959; National Book Award, for poetry, 1960; Harriet Monroe Memorial Prize, 1961, and Levinson Prize, 1963 (*Poetry*, Chicago); Bollingen Poetry Translation Award, 1962; New England Poetry Club Golden Rose, 1964; Ford grant, 1964; Obie Award, 1965; Sarah Josepha Hale Award, for poetry, 1966; Copernicus Award, 1974. Member, American Academy of Arts and Letters. Address: 15 West 67th Street, New York, New York 10023, U.S.A.

PUBLICATIONS

Plays

> *Phaedra*, adaptation of the play by Racine (produced London 1961). Included in *Phaedra and Figaro*, New York, Farrar Straus, 1961; as *Phaedra*, London, Faber, 1963.
> *The Old Glory* (*Benito Cereno* and *My Kinsman, Major Molineux*) (produced New York, 1964; *Benito Cereno* produced London, 1967). New York, Farrar Straus, 1964; expanded version, including *Endecott and the Red Cross* (produced New York, 1968), London, Faber, 1966; Farrar Straus, 1968.
> *Prometheus Bound*, adaptation of a play by Aeschylus (produced New Haven, Connecticut, 1967; London, 1971). New York, Farrar Straus, 1969; London, Faber, 1970.

Verse

The Land of Unlikeness.   Cummington, Massachusetts, Cummington Press, 1944.
Lord Weary's Castle   New York, Harcourt Brace, 1946.
Poems 1938–1949.   London, Faber, 1950.
The Mills of the Kavanaughs.   New York, Harcourt Brace, 1951.
Life Studies.   London, Faber, 1959; augmented edition, New York, Farrar Straus,
    1959; Faber, 1968.
Imitations.   New York, Farrar Straus, 1961; London, Faber, 1962.
For the Union Dead.   New York, Farrar Straus, 1964; London, Faber, 1965.
Selected Poems.   London, Faber, 1965.
Near the Ocean.   New York, Farrar Straus, and London, Faber, 1967.
The Voyage and Other Versions of Poems by Baudelaire.   New York, Farrar Straus,
    and London, Faber, 1968.
Notebook 1967–1968.   New York, Farrar Straus, 1969; augmented edition, as
    Notebook, London, Faber, and Farrar Straus, 1970.
For Lizzie and Harriet.   London, Faber, and New York, Farrar Straus, 1973.
History.   London, Faber, and New York, Farrar Straus, 1973.
The Dolphin.   London, Faber, and New York, Farrar Straus, 1973.
Poems: A Selection, edited by Jonathan Raban.   London, Faber, 1974.
Selected Poems.   New York, Farrar Straus, 1976.

Other

Editor, with Peter Taylor and Robert Penn Warren, *Randall Jarrell 1914–1965.*   New
    York, Farrar Straus, 1967.

*   *   *

Robert Lowell is the most considerable American poet of his generation to write for the
stage. His first play was a verse translation of Racine's *Phèdre*, and though it is faithful to
the French text, Lowell's imagery and energy seep into the English. Similarly, Lowell's
translation of Aeschylus' *Prometheus Bound* shows his modern existential awareness of
man's precarious fate. These translations have invigorated two classical tragedies into
English, but Lowell's most important achievement in drama is the three plays of *The Old
Glory*. Dramatizing stories of Hawthorne and Melville, Lowell has refracted America's past
through the lens of the present. His plays are linked by the theme of revolution and the
image of the American flag, the Old Glory. The three plays show that every declaration of
independence is grounded in violence, however lofty the banner.

Based on Hawthorne stories, the first two plays of Lowell's trilogy are set in American
colonial times, but for Lowell the seed of imperial America is already present in seventeenth-
century Puritan Massachusetts and in eighteenth-century Boston. Lowell's third play, based
on Melville's novella *Benito Cereno*, foreshadows the Civil War and contemporary racial
conflict. In all three dramas a single act of rising tension explodes into violence. Far from
patriotic celebration, these three plays underline the ambiguities and cruelties of
revolutionary action.

Endecott and the Red Cross, the first play of the trilogy, takes its subject and title from a
Hawthorne short story, but Lowell also uses another Hawthorne story about Endecott,
"The Maypole of Merry Mount," as well as Thomas Morton's *New English Canaan*.
Morton's account serves as background for the two Hawthorne stories. Unlike Hawthorne,
Lowell provides his Puritan protagonist Endecott with an Anglican antagonist Morton, and
the play implies that Endecott's Puritans and Morton's Anglicans shared a taste for
commerce. Economic competition sharpens ideological conflict, and during the course of the
play that conflict becomes irreconcilable, erupting into Endecott's rebellion against English
rule.

Lowell's Endecott can remember his courtly youth, before the death of his wife turned him into a soldier needing a stern faith. Highly self-conscious, Lowell's Endecott understands his own Puritanism, and he is still prey to gentle memories, so that he countermands the punitive dicta of Elder Palfrey. And yet, he recounts to Elder Palfrey a dream in which he, Endecott, is Elder Palfrey, preacher and executioner. That dream, invented by Lowell, portrays men who commit cruelties in the name of rigid religions. Even as Endecott narrates the dream, he perceives its symbolic prophecy: a rigid English ruler will force upon the colony his governor and his religion, and an equally rigid opponent will have no recourse but rebellion.

By the end of the play, Endecott as Endecott acts out his dream: opposing the king's rule in Morton, he addresses his soldiers in words that are "half truth, half bombast." Originally as moderate as Morton, he has acquired the cruel rigidity of Elder Palfrey. "A Bible in his left hand and a loaded pistol in his right," he orders Merry Mount destroyed and captive Indians executed. In cutting the Red Cross flag of England from its staff, Endecott has takeen the first violent step that will result in the supremacy of the Old Glory.

The second play of Lowell's trilogy, based on Hawthorne's "My Kinsman, Major Molineux," takes place a century and a half later, on the eve of the American Revolution. The protagonist, eighteen-year-old Robin, comes to Boston to seek his fortune, hoping for favor from his kinsman, Major Molineux, British governor. Within the few hours that Robin spends in the city, his country innocence gradually gives way to complicity in the lynching of his kinsman.

Lowell emphasizes the impact of events upon Robin by giving him a younger brother, who is at once more innocent and more self-absorbed during their long day in the city, in which they are initiated into corruption and rebellion. In the play's last scene Robin and his brother finally see their kinsman, Major Molineux, tarred and feathered by the rebels. Even as Robin pities his kinsman, Robin "unconsciously" waves the rebel Rattlesnake flag in his face as his brother "unthinkingly" offers dirt to be flung at the Major. The latter remains courageously loyal to the English king, and is finally silenced by Lowell's infernal figures, the Ferryman knocking him senseless with an oar and a masked colonel stabbing him with his sword. When the Major is dead, the crowd cries: "Long live the Republic! Long live the Republic!" Slowly, the crowd disperses until Robin and his brother are alone. But they are immutably tainted. Robin's brother echoes the words he has heard: "Major Molineux is dead." Robin, leading his brother back to the city, affirms: "Yes, Major Molineux is dead." They are independent now, and neither of them mentions that the Major was their kindly kinsman.

As in *Endecott and the Red Cross* the flag emerges as the central image. In *My Kinsman, Major Molineux* the Union Jack is emblematic of British authority, and the Rattlesnake flag of the Boston rebellion. Endecott had to cut down the Red Cross to prepare the way for the Old Glory, and the Boston rebels have to raise their Rattlesnake in the same cause. The Old Glory will wave over gory ground.

In *Benito Cereno* Lowell follows the events of the Melville novella, to subvert its intention. Only in this third play does the Old Glory actually appear, as the standard of Yankee Captain Delano's ship. Lowell's play opens with a "machinelike" salute to the American flag, which will soon be opposed by the pirateflag on the slave-ship San Domingo – a black skull and crossbones on white ground. But slavery as piracy is a metaphor of implicit and gradual meaning in Lowell's play about white slavers and black slaves, which takes place, ironically, on American Independence Day.

When Lowell's Captain Delano boards the San Domingo captained by Don Benito Cereno, he disapproves of the dirt and lack of discipline. Once aboard, Delano is almost hypnotized by the heat and the buzzing insects, the rambling Captain Cereno and the unctuous slaves. Patronizing and friendly to Spanish Benito Cereno, Delano is patronizing and oppressive to the Negro Babu. While Don Benito is taking his siesta, Babu shows Captain Delano four brief plays within the play, symbolizing the cruel complexity of racial relations. Later Delano is a spectator at scenes that stage like plays within the play: an African king festooned with chaines, Babu shaving Cereno with the Spanish flag as towel, a formal dinner with "La Marseillaise" as background music.

When Delano's boatswain Perkins (invented by Lowell) warns Delano that the Negroes are the masters of Cereno's slave ship, the Yankee captain is incredulous but courageous. With the Negroes in open and vengeful command, Delano watches with disapproval as Don Benito is forced to walk across the Spanish flag to kiss a skull, as his boatswain takes the same path. When his own turn comes, Delano points his gun at Babu. American seaman arrive in the nick of time, and Babu raises a white handkerchief but cries out: "The future is with us." Delano retorts: "This is your future," and shoots him dead. Melville's Delano is a man of good will with limited perceptions. Lowell's Delano is a man whose good will is eroded by his limited perceptions. Behind his smoking gun, the Old Glory is not visible, but its presence is felt.

The Old Glory is an unglorious view of American history. Lowell's dramatizations rely on imagery and analogy rather than conventional characters. *Endecott and the Red Cross* incorporates an aborted Maypole ritual; *My Kinsman, Major Molineux* is a voyage through an Inferno; *Benito Cereno* is mesmerizing in its plays within plays within the play of black and white. Each member of the trilogy lives in its own theatrical atmosphere, but Robert Lowell's language provides dramatic dialogue that is highly imaged and rhythmed, relevant and resonant.

—Ruby Cohn

LUDLAM, Charles.   American.   Co-Founder of the Play-House of the Ridiculous, New York, 1966; then Founder, Ridiculous Theatrical Company, New York. Recipient: Obie Award, for acting, 1973. Address: Gotham Art Theatre, 455 West 43rd Street, New York, New York, U.S.A.

PUBLICATIONS

Plays

> *When Queens Collide* (produced New York, 1967).
> *Big Hotel* (produced New York, 1967).
> *Conquest of the Universe* (produced New York, 1967).
> *Turds in Hell*, with Bill Vehr, in *Drama Review* (New York), September 1970.
> *Bluebeard* (produced New York, 1970; London, 1971).   Published in *More Plays from Off-Off Broadway*, edited by Michael Smith, Indianapolis, Bobbs Merrill, 1972; revised version (produced New York, 1975).
> *The Grand Tarot* (produced New York, 1972).
> *Eunuchs of the Forbidden City* (produced New York, 1972).   Published in *Scripts 6* (New York), April 1972.
> *Corn*, music by Virgil Young (also director: produced New York, 1972).
> *Camille: A Tear-Jerker*, adaptation of a play by Dumas (also director: produced New York, 1973).
> *Stage Blood* (also director: produced New York, 1974).
> *Hot Ice* (also director: produced New York, 1974).

Theatrical Activities:

Director: **Plays** – *Whores of Babylon* by Bill Vehr, New York, 1968 and several of his own plays.

Actor: **Plays** – Norma Desmond in *Big Hotel*, New York, 1967; in *Eunuchs of the Forbidden City*, New York, 1972. **Film** – *Lupe*, 1966.

*   *   *

Charles Ludlam has won no playwriting prizes; he has had no long-running success, on or off-Broadway; magazines and Sunday newspapers do not print studious analyses of his accumulated plays, nor do they publish picture-essays of his dinner parties. In short, he possesses none of the symptoms of the celebrated playwright. Yet he is not merely the passing fancy of an elite minority. Ludlam is a superb comic playwright, excluded from mainstream American theatre because his work is too zany and *outré*, and from underground American theatre because he chose to be literary when everyone else wanted the actors to roll around on the floor. Undaunted, he established his own company – the Ridiculous Theatrical Company (not to be confused with the Play-House of the Ridiculous, the New York troupe he co-founded and then left).

Ludlam's style has been casually included in the overall genre of *camp*, and while there is no gainsaying its flamboyant homosexuality and inclination toward the effete-bizarre, there is considerably more to it than that. Ludlam has managed to be very funny at a time when art is terribly serious; he has managed to remember story-telling and general decoration at a time when plots and styles are minimal. His is the grand manner, the theatre of display, and it is tonic.

Ludlam's major works are *Bluebeard, The Grand Tarot* and *Eunuchs of the Forbidden City*. They have in common a simultaneous satire and earnestness. *Bluebeard* is an appreciation of (and likewise a deviation from) an old Charles Laughton film, *Island of Lost Souls*. It typifies his style of faithful paraphrase despite the most outlandish alteration. In this case, the mad scientist has become Baron Khanazar von Bluebeard (with beard and pubic hair of bright blue) who calls his laboratory "The House of Pain" and is dedicated to the invention of a new genital. He has practised this operation on his employees – the half-monster Sheemish; Lamia the Leopard Woman; and the housekeeper, Mrs. Maggot. Now, in fez and bathrobe (though sometimes in bottomless panties), he is intent on perfecting it upon the latest visitors, a couple imported from a Victorian operetta.

The Grand Tarot found Ludlam in a less frivolous state of mind, searching for Christian principles in the Tarot card deck, but with *Eunuchs of the Forbidden City* he once more found his Baroque stride. The script and production were based on the Hollywood-style Oriental epic and consequently resembled Brecht's Eastern plays (as well as, or perhaps including, Edward Bond's *Narrow Road to the Deep North*). The play is filled with the sort of story detail most contemporary playwrights do not accumulate in an entire career: an emperor who wants a son; a consort who cannot give him one; a concubine who does; a royal murder; a fork-tongued lieutenant; escape to the forbidden city.

These details are worked out with logic as impeccable as it is absurd, amid dialogue of stylistic incongruities ("I don't know what the forbidden city is coming to"); underlined clichés ("Sign, seal and deliver this document"); straightfaced banalities ("So – it was war, not love we made in bed"); and classic Ludlamisms ("Boredom is absence of yumyum").

Though the play has a paucity of the author's usual genital humor, it is not entirely impoverished ("I don't think of myself as being castrated – I think of myself as being extremely well circumcised") and the evening's comic peak has the chief eunuch drop his pants to reveal himself intact, only to be promptly castrated.

Because his approach is so special (to say the least), Ludlam is not well known, and his plays are given threadbare productions which lend them a bracing tackiness. They have about them a shabby opulence that is not inappropriate. Unfortunately, the plays have won

496

an obscure chic rather than a deserved public appreciation, and they are seldom reviewed. Nevertheless, Ludlam does survive, providing an endearing and ultrasophisticated highbrow-lowbrow comedy of considerable literariness (he is as prone to spoof 16th Century drama as 20th Century Fox movies). As a manager, director, actor and playwright, he is doubtless the contemporary theatre person of whom Shakespeare would have been fondest.

—Martin Gottfried

LUKE, Peter (Ambrose Cyprian). British. Born in St. Albans, Hertfordshire, 12 August 1919. Educated at Eton College, Buckinghamshire; Byam Shaw School of Art, London; Atelier André Lhote, Paris. Served in the Rifle Brigade, in the Western Desert, Italy, Northwest Europe, 1940–46: Military Cross. Married the actress June Tobin in 1963; has seven children. Sub-Editor, Reuters, 1947; worked in the wine trade, 1947–57; Book Critic, *Queen* magazine, London, 1957–58; Story Editor, ABC Television, London, 1958–60; Editor, *Bookman*, ABC-TV, 1960–61; Editor, *Tempo* arts programme, ABC-TV, 1961–62; Drama Producer, BBC Television, London, 1963–67. Since 1967, free-lance writer, producer and director. Recipient: Italia Prize, for television production, 1967; Tony Award, 1969. Agent: Harvey Unna Ltd., 14 Beaumont Mews, Marylebone High Street, London W1N 4HE, England. Address: La Almona, El Chorro, Malaga, Spain.

PUBLICATIONS

Plays

Hadrian VII, based on *Hadrian the Seventh* and other works by Frederick Rolfe, "Baron Corvo" (produced Birmingham, 1967; London, 1968; New York, 1969). Published as *The Play of Hadrian VII*, London, Deutsch, 1968; New York, Knopf, 1969.
Bloomsbury (produced London, 1974).

Television Plays: *Small Fish Are Sweet*, 1959; *Pig's Ear with Flowers*, 1960; *Roll On, Bloomin' Death*, 1961; *A Man on Her Back*, from story by William Sansom, 1966; *The Devil a Monk Wou'd Be*, 1967. Films for Television: *Anach Cuan: The Music of Sean O Riada*, 1967; *Black Sound – Deep Song: The Andalusian Poetry of Federico García Lorca*, 1968.

Other

Siysphus and Reilly: An Autobiography. London, Deutsch, 1972.

Critical Studies: by Ronald Bryden in *The Observer* (London), 21 April 1968; by Harold Hobson in *The Sunday Times* (London), 21 April 1968; "Peter Luke Used to Be a Television Producer. Then He Escaped" by the author, in *The Listener* (London), 12 September 1968; by Clive Barnes in *The New York Times*, 9 January 1969; "*Hadrian VII* Is Alive and a Hit" by John Chapman, in *The San Francisco Examiner*, 5 October 1969.

Theatrical Activities:

Director: **Play** – *Hadrian VII*, Dublin, 1970. **Television** – *Hamlet at Elsinore*, 1963; *A Passage to India*, 1966; *Silent Song*, 1967; films for television – *Anach Cuan: The Music of Sean O Riada*, 1967; *Black Sound – Deep Song: The Andalusian Poetry of Federico García Lorca*, 1968.

Peter Luke comments:

To write an introduction to my work as a playwright is difficult because to date there is relatively little of it. I did not write my first play until I was nearly forty. The *oeuvre*, such as it is to date, consists of four original plays for television and one dramatisation of a novel by William Sansom for the same medium. In addition there are two films d'auteur commissioned by the BBC. They are respectively, and perhaps significantly, about a musician and a poet. Then there is the stage play, *Hadrian VII*, which was first written in 1961 but was not produced until 1967. *Bloomsbury*, produced by Richard Cottrell in 1974, ran for only five weeks due to the American recession as it affected Throgmorton Street and the tourist trade and a petulant notice from the late [sic] Harold Hobson.

I would like to be able to give some indication of the direction in which I think I am going, but this is difficult. Certainly I am more than ever interested in poetry, which is not to say that I am immediately contemplating a play in verse. But if I can see a development in my work, it is towards the articulate. Language is my preoccupation and I feel that the theatre, now as in the past, and quite irrespective of present day vogues and trends, should be the place to use it in.

The choice of medium was made for me. My father, Harry Luke, was a writer but early on I decided that I wanted to paint and I had already spent two years studying when the war broke out in 1939. Nineteen – nearly twenty – years later, in 1959, my first television play, *Small Fish Are Sweet*, starring Donald Pleasence and Katherine Blake, was produced. Several others followed hard upon. What happened in between is told in an essay in autobiography, *Sisyphus and Reilly*, published recently by André Deutsch.

I did not intend to become a playwright. It happened by accident. I do not even now consider myself to be solely a writer of plays, though I suppose few men can have been so fortunate as to have had an international success on the scale of *Hadrian VII*. Indeed, how many playwrights have had a major success which began as a flop? Thanks to Hadrian, however, I am now free to write what I want to and my intention for the foreseeable future is to alternate plays with books. This I find very therapeutic and my one concern now is that the results will justify the therapy, and that the therapy will give me a long life in which to write a great deal more.

*   *   *

At the end of Peter Luke's play, the bailiff removing the furniture from Baron Corvo-alias-Frederick Rolfe's room, picks up the manuscript of the novel, *Hadrian the Seventh*.

"What's this then?" he asks.
"It's about a man," replies Rolfe, "who made the fatuous and frantic mistake of living before his time."
"Any value?"
"It's a masterpiece," replies Rolfe, "and therefore probably not worth twopence. At the same time it is possibly beyond price."

It is one of the ironies of life that Rolfe was to die virtually unknown and that Luke has become famous as a result of his play based upon Rolfe's novel.

One day, in 1959, I set out to adapt two books for the theare, Laurie Lee's *Cider with Rosie*, and Frederick Rolfe's *Hadrian the Seventh*. Both seemed unlikely books for adaptation was the general reaction. Then I met Peter Luke, at that time working as Head of Scripts for ABC Armchair Theatre Television who said how much he longed to write for the theatre. I realized I could not adapt two books simultaneously and so told him about my projects and invited him to choose the one that appealed to him and I would complete the one he did not chose.

He replied, "My father knew Rolfe. Rolfe invested him as Grand Master of the Order Santissima Sophia. There were only ever three members!"

Having just launched the Hampstead Theatre Club I was able to get Peter Luke a modest grant and during the summer of 1960 we worked on the play as author and director. The subsequent history of the play is well known.

Reading the published version after so many years I am reminded afresh of the clarity and sweep of Peter Luke's treatment. It is a text pared down to the essential story; the magnificent set pieces of the novel could only be caught in a film.

Luke's play is, of course, more than an adaptation of the novel. By drawing upon the story of Rolfe's own life and his other writings he has written a play about the man himself. This is important because a full appreciation of the novel can only come from the knowledge that it is a wish-fulfilment fantasy on the part of the penniless Rolfe.

Skilfully Luke leads us into the fantasy by the simple device of having the two bailiffs reappear as Talacryn and Courtleigh, the two ecclesiastics whom Rolfe imagines as coming to offer him ordination as a priest, and by this means, he is then eligible to be voted as the next successor to the Papacy. The question – "Reverend Father, the Sacred College has elected thee to be the successor of St. Peter. Wilt thou accept pontificality? The response is Volo or Nolo," to which Rolfe replies, "Volo...I will," – forms the brilliant curtain to the end of the first act.

The weakest character in the novel is Jerry Sant who finally assassinates Hadrian. He is therefore essential to the plot but in Rolfe's hands he remains a one-dimensional melodramatic figure. Luke has had the imaginative idea of turning him from a Scot into a Belfast Fenian, singing "The Sash my Father wore." When he says, "It's the smell of the Papist I can't abide. I'll not stand for an Englishman giving out the orders, Pope or not," and Mrs. Crowe, his paramour, replies, "Oh, I'll never understand Irish politics as long as I live," suddenly the play leaps into theatrical topicality, even more now than when it was first staged.

Although the story of Hadrian is intensely theatrical and Rolfe's style unique and baroque, the story is none the less strangely prophetic of the winds of change that were to sweep through the Vatican some fifty years later. It was this, as well as a strong affection for the novel, that first tempted me to adapt it for the stage.

To a gathering of Cardinals, Hadrian says,

> Venerable Fathers, ask yourselves whether we really are as successful as we think we are, whether in fact we are not abject and lamentable failures in the eyes of God. We have added and added to the riches, pomp and power of the Church, and yet everywhere there is great wealth alongside dire poverty....Let us now try the road of Apostolic simplicity... the simplicity of Peter the Fisherman. Let us at least try!

Always this reminded me of those little known words of Pope Pius XII, recorded by Christopher Hollis, to a gathering of Cardinals shortly before his death, as startling as anything Rolfe puts into the mouth of his central character: "The Roman Church must not seek to embrace the entire world. It must learn to accept that there are other faiths and other creeds and other temperaments."

After the Martyrdom of Hadrian, Luke brings Rolfe's alter ego, George Arthur Rose, on to the stage to deliver a speech in memoriam:

Have any of you ever dissected a crab? Under its hard shell your crustacean is a labyrinthine mass of most sensitive nerves for the defence of which it is armed with crookedly curving, ferociously snapping claws....Similarly, Frederick William Rolfe, Baron Corvo, as hard as adamant outside, was, within, the tenderest, the most sensitive, the cleverest, the unhappiest, the most dreadful of all creatures....Let us pray for the repose of his soul.

With another coup de théâtre Luke has Rolfe standing at the side of the stage, watching the funeral cortège of Hadrian, smoking a cigarette and holding the manuscript of his novel.

Peter Luke's second stage play is an attempt to portray the Bloomsbury group on stage, seen through the eyes of Virginia Woolf who appears, speaking in soliloquies, as a linking narrator but never a participant, which makes for a major weakness in the play's structure. The chief protagonists are Lytton Strachey, Lady Ottoline Morell, Carrington, Partridge and Gertler. "I have created an art form out of them all," says Virginia Woolf towards the end; "I have conducted their gyrations, their rise and fall. I have orchestrated their movements like the waves." The play ends with Carrington's suicide, the increasing madness and incipient suicide of Verginia Woolf. Whether it is possible to create a successful play about real literary figures is a matter of opinion but it is probable that a subject such as this is better suited to a film treatment.

—James Roose-Evans

MacDOUGALL, Roger.   British.   Born in Bearsden, Dumbartonshire, Scotland, 2 August 1910. Educated at Bearsden Academy; Glasgow University. Married to Renée Dunlop. Composer of film music and documentary film director. Crippled by multiple sclerosis in 1955. Address: 8 Willow Road, London N.W.3, England.

PUBLICATIONS

Plays

Macadam and Eve (produced London, 1950).   London, Evans, 1951.
The Gentle Gunman (produced Cambridge and London, 1950).   London, Evans, 1951.
To Dorothy, A Son (produced London, 1950; New York, 1951).   London, Evans, 1952.
Escapade (produced London and New York, 1953).   London, Heinemann, 1953.
The Facts of Life (produced Blackpool and London, 1954).   London, French, 1955.
The Man in the White Suit (produced Pitlochry, Perthshire, 1954).
The Delegate (produced Manchester, 1955).
Double Image (Gog and Magog), with Ted Allan, based on a story by Roy Vickers (produced London, 1956).   London, French, 1957.
Hide and Seek, with Stanley Mann (produced New York, 1957).
Trouble with Father (produced Northampton, 1964).
Jack in the Box (produced London, 1971).

Screenplays and Documentaries: *This Man Is News*, with Allan Mackinnon, 1938; *This Man in Paris*, with Allan Mackinnon, 1939; *Spare a Copper*, with others, 1940; *The*

Foreman Went to France (Somewhere in France), with others, 1942; *The Bells Go Down*, with Stephen Black, 1943; *Law and Disorder*, 1946; *As Others See Us*, 1947; *The Man on the Beat*, 1947; *Country Policeman*, 1947; *T for Teacher*, 1947; *The Man in the White Suit*, 1951; *The Mouse That Roared*, with others, 1959; *A Touch of Larceny*, with others, 1959.

Radio Plays: *This Man Is News*, 1940; *Close Relations*, 1958.

Theatrical Activities:

Director: **Films** (documentaries) – *Back to Normal*, 1944; *Teaching*, 1946; *As Others See Us*, 1947; *The Man on the Beat*, 1947; *The Casual Caller*, 1948.

*   *   *

Roger MacDougall is a dramatist who may still have much to give, though his middle-period plays fell below his early ones. Later, a crippling illness of many years' duration from which he emerged in the mid-1970's, bravely ready to begin again, prevented him from following his craft.

Combining ready invention with an uncommon verbal gift, he once described how he worked: "My method, when I have an idea that seems suitable for a play, is to sit down and write, not knowing what will come next. To me there is nothing creative in the carefully-planned, neatly-built play; this sort of work is no more than adaptation. I never know how my plays will end. I find that if my idea is good enough in the first place, and I work as best as I can from the 'inside' of my characters and situations as they arise, the whole thing will develop quite naturally."

Within three years in the early 1950's he had four plays staged in London, and they remain his most telling work: it was a sudden exciting efflorescence by a dramatist who was already 40 years old but who had gone through the testing disciplines of a screenwriter. The first of the plays is the least; having had a potentially good idea, the creation of an immortal, the Old Adam who has been in his time – not that it matters – both the wandering Jew and Shakespeare, MacDougall goes on to labour the joke: possibly the title, *Macadam and Eve*, should be a warning. Macadam turns up in the rain at the Scottish resort of Tillyfruin, still recalling Eden and still tortured by Eve: the development is too protracted and too self-indulgent.

At the time it was clear that MacDougall would be a dramatist to watch. Presently we recognised his talents more fully in the argumentative comedy *The Gentle Gunman*, a perilous play for the current Irish situation but, in the text, both wise and cogent. If we are hardly persuaded that things can happen as they do, we are glad enough to let them happen. The play is lively with debate: the gentle gunman of the title, who tries to explain to more orthodox members of the I.R.A. why violence can only be futile, has blarney enough to set the mountains of Mourne dancing; and behind the blarney there is very often the sharpest truth. Even if MacDougall wants us to believe that his Mr. Justice Truethorn, scourge of the I.R.A., is likely to spend his summer holidays on the Ulster border, asking to be kidnapped, we cannot object too loudly; there are ideas, there is a narrative, and the dramatist has an almost Galsworthian way (though he might not admit the likeness) of letting us hear both sides of an argument.

After this it was another leap to MacDougall's third play of 1950, *To Dorothy, A Son*. By then it was obvious that no pigeon-hole would do. This was a dramatist who refused to repeat himself: not, maybe, the best of tactics in a world where repetition can be sovereign. *To Dorothy, A Son* is probably MacDougall's best play yet; within its limits it is precisely designed and carried out. Agreed, at its first production it was lucky enough to have Yolande Donlan, an actress always adept at wide-eyed wonder, but the text fortified her and the author's share was under-valued. One must tremble even at suggesting the plot: it has something to do with the International Date Line and Greenwich Mean Time. In performance – and this is the main thing – MacDougall gets it across easily – to everyone, that is, except the girl Myrtle who may or may not qualify for a bequest of a million dollars. "Well, what should I do?" she exclaims when faced with the time problem, "Go out and look at the sun? Where would that get me? You're up to no good." But the author is; it is an enchantingly absurd scene, and MacDougall sustains the nonsense throughout.

To Dorothy, A Son is a better play, though less ambitious, than *Escapade*. There, as in *The Gentle Gunman*, MacDougall, in his idiosyncratic way, is again speaking for peace; the trouble is that he allows himself to wander, Bridie-fashion. An audience's concentration can waver, even if there is more thought behind the piece than behind half-a-dozen goldfish-bowl comedies. The main visible character is a pacifist in difficulties. Really, the principal figure (who does not appear) is the man's sixteen-year-old son – named Icarus – who "borrows" an aircraft with his brothers and carries a peace manifesto from his school to a U.N.O. conference at Venice. The message, we gather, is that a child's vision is clearer than an adult's: the sagest folk are the child and the aged. *Escapade* contains so much that it is a pity MacDougall shifts the mood so often. He is too apparently in charge of his characters, too obviously ventriloquising, cheerfully anxious to see what may come next.

Not many dramatists could have had a start more promising than MacDougall had with these four plays. His later work was less assured. In *The Facts of Life* we have a contrast between wisdom and folly, the wisdom of a seraphic schoolboy allegedly a "failure," and the folly of his probing relatives. In effect, it is a joke teased out to full-length with a steady snip-snap of question and answer.

MacDougall's only other West End play has been *Double Image*, which he and Ted Allan based on a story by Roy Vickers. Roughly, did Julian or David kill Uncle Ernest? And is there a David? Or, for that matter – so confused do we become – is there indeed a Julian? Are we, in fact, identical twins ourselves? The play ends in one of those genuinely taut scenes inescapable from a "perfect murder" problem, but until then one is less absorbed than bewildered.

Now, after two decades beset by multiple sclerosis, MacDougall is returning to the stage. With his fine mind and steady determination, it may well be that the dramatist of those fruitful years of the early 1950's will find himself again; and for the theatre that should be a bonus.

—J. C. Trewin

MacLEISH, Archibald.   American.   Born in Glencoe, Illinois, 7 May 1892. Educated at the Hotchkiss School, Lakeville, Connecticut; Yale University, New Haven, Connecticut, A.B. 1915; Harvard University, Cambridge, Massachusetts, LL.B. 1919. Served in the United States Army, 1917–19: Captain. Married Ada Hitchcock in 1916; has three children. Lecturer in Government, Harvard University, 1919–21; Attorney, Choate, Hall, and Stewart, Boston, 1920–23; Editor, *Fortune* magazine, New York, 1929–38; Curator of the Niemann Foundation, Harvard University, 1938; Librarian of Congress, Washington, D.C., 1939–44; Director, United States Office of Facts and Figures, 1941–42, Assistant Director of the Office of War Information, 1942–43, and Assistant Secretary of State, 1944–45, Washington, D.C. Chairman of the United States Delegation to the UNESCO drafting conference, London, 1945, and Member of the Executive Board, UNESCO, 1946. Rede Lecturer, Cambridge University, 1942; Boylston Professor of Rhetoric and Oratory, Harvard University, 1949–62; Simpson Lecturer, Amherst College, Massachusetts, 1964–67. Recipient: Shelley Memorial Award, 1932; Pulitzer Prize, for verse, 1933, 1953, for drama, 1959; New England Poetry Club Golden Rose, 1934; Levinson Prize, (*Poetry*, Chicago), 1941; Bollingen Prize, 1952; National Book Award, 1953; Sarah Josepha Hale Award, 1958; Tony Award, 1959; National Association of Independent Schools Award, 1959; Academy of American Poets Fellowship, 1965; Academy Award, 1966. M.A.: Tufts University, Medford, Massachusetts, 1932; Litt.D.: Wesleyan University, Middletown, Connecticut, 1938; Colby College, Waterville, Maine, 1938; Yale University, 1939; University of Pennsylvania, Philadelphia, 1941; University of Illinois, Urbana, 1947; Rockford College, Illinois, 1952; Columbia University, New York, 1954; Harvard University, 1955; Carleton College, Northfield, Minnesota, 1956; Princeton University, New Jersey, 1965; University of Massachusetts, Amherst, 1969; York University, Toronto, 1971; LL.D.: Dartmouth College, Hanover, New Hampshire, 1940; Johns Hopkins University, Baltimore, 1941; University of California, Berkeley, 1943; Queen's University, Kingston, Ontario, 1948; University of Puerto Rico, Rio Piedras, 1953; Amherst College, Massachusetts, 1963; D.C.L.: Union College, Schenectady, New York, 1941; L.H.D.: Williams College, Williamstown, Massachusetts, 1942; University of Washington, Seattle, 1948. Commander, Legion of Honor; Commander, El Sol del Peru. President, American Academy of Arts and Letters, 1953–56. Address: Conway, Massachusetts 01341, U.S.A.

PUBLICATIONS

Plays

> *Nobodaddy.* Cambridge, Massachusetts, Dunster House, 1926.
> *Union Pacific* (ballet scenario; produced New York, 1934). Published in *The Book of Ballets*, New York, Crown, 1939.
> *Panic: A Play in Verse* (produced New York, 1935). Boston, Houghton Mifflin, 1935; London, Boriswood, 1936.
> *The Fall of the City: A Verse Play for Radio* (broadcast, 1937). New York, Farrar and Rinehart, and London, Boriswood, 1937.
> *Air Raid: A Verse Play for Radio* (broadcast, 1938). New York, Harcourt Brace, 1938; London, Lane, 1939.
> *The States Talking* (broadcast, 1941). Published in *The Free Company Presents*, edited by James Boyd, New York, Dodd Mead, 1941.
> *The American Story: Ten Radio Scripts* (includes *The Admiral; The American Gods; The American Name; Not Bacon's Bones; Between the Silence and the Surf; Discovered; The Many Dead; The Names for the Rivers; Ripe Strawberries and Gooseberries and Sweet Single Roses; Socorro, When Your Sons Forget*) (broadcast, 1944). New York, Duell, 1944.
> *The Trojan Horse* (broadcast, 1952). Boston, Houghton Mifflin, 1952.
> *This Music Crept by Me upon the Waters* (broadcast, 1953). Cambridge, Massachusetts, Harvard University Press, 1953.
> *J.B.: A Play in Verse* (produced New Haven, Connecticut, and New York, 1958; London, 1961). Boston, Houghton Mifflin, 1958; London, Secker and Warburg, 1959.
> *The Secret of Freedom* (televised, 1959). Included in *Three Short Plays*, 1961.
> *Three Short Plays: The Secret of Freedom, Air Raid, The Fall of the City*. New York, Dramatists Play Service, 1961.
> *Our Lives, Our Fortunes, and Our Sacred Honor* (as *The American Bell*, music by David Amram, produced Philadelphia, 1962). Published in *Think* (Armonk, New York), July–August 1961.
> *Herakles: A Play in Verse* (produced Ann Arbor, Michigan, 1965). Boston, Houghton Mifflin, 1967.

An Evening's Journey to Conway, Massachusetts: An Outdoor Play (produced Conway, *1967*).   Northampton, Massachusetts, Gehenna Press, 1967.

Scratch, suggested by *The Devil and Daniel Webster* by Stephen Vincent Benet (produced New York, 1971).   Boston, Houghton Mifflin, 1971.

The Great American Fourth of July Parade (produced Pittsburgh, 1975).   Pittsburgh, University of Pittsburgh Press, 1975.

Screenplays: *Grandma Moses*, 1950; *The Eleanor Roosevelt Story*, 1965.

Radio Plays: *The Fall of the City*, 1937; *Air Raid*, 1938; *The States Talking*, 1941; *The American Story* series, 1944; *The Son of Man*, 1947; *The Trojan Horse*, 1952; *This Music Crept by Me upon the Waters*, 1953.

Television Play: *The Secret of Freedom*, 1959.

Verse

Songs for a Summer's Day (A Sonnet-Cycle).   New Haven, Connecticut, Yale University Press, 1915.

Tower of Ivory.   New Haven, Connecticut, Yale University Press, and London, Oxford University Press, 1917.

The Happy Marriage and Other Poems.   Boston, Houghton Mifflin, 1924.

The Pot of Earth.   Boston, Houghton Mifflin, 1925.

Streets in the Moon.   Boston, Houghton Mifflin, 1926.

The Hamlet of A. MacLeish.   Boston, Houghton Mifflin, 1928.

Einstein.   Paris, Black Sun Press, 1929.

New Found Land: Fourteen Poems.   Boston, Houghton Mifflin, and Paris, Black Sun Press, 1930.

Before March.   New York, Knopf, 1932.

Conquistador.   Boston, Houghton Mifflin, 1932; London, Gollancz, 1933.

Frescoes for Mr. Rockefeller's City.   New York, Day, 1933.

Poems, 1924–1933.   Boston, Houghton Mifflin, 1933; as *Poems*, London, Boriswood, 1935.

Public Speech: Poems. New York, Farrar and Rinehart, and London, Boriswood, 1936.

Land of the Free – U.S.A.   New York, Harcourt Brace, and London, Boriswood, 1938.

America Was Promises.   New York, Duell, 1939; London, Lane, 1940.

Actfive and Other Poems.   New York, Random House, 1948; London Lane, 1950.

Collected Poems, 1917–1952.   Boston, Houghton Mifflin, 1952.

Songs for Eve.   Boston, Houghton Mifflin, 1954.

Collected Poems.   Boston, Houghton Mifflin, 1963.

"The Wild Old Wicked Man" and Other Poems.   Boston, Houghton Mifflin, 1968; London, W. H. Allen, 1969.

The Human Season: Selected Poems 1962–1972.   Boston, Houghton Mifflin, 1972.

New and Collected Poems 1917–1976.   Boston, Houghton Mifflin, 1976.

Recording: *Archibald MacLeish Reads His Own Poetry*, Caedmon.

Other

Housing America, by the Editors of *Fortune*.   New York, Harcourt Brace, 1932.

Jews in America, by the Editors of *Fortune*.   New York, Random House, 1936.

Background of War, by the Editors of *Fortune*.   New York, Knopf, 1937.

The Irresponsibles: A Declaration.   New York, Duell, 1940.

The Next Harvard, As Seen by Archibald MacLeish. Cambridge, Massachusetts, Harvard University Press, 1941.

A Time to Speak: The Selected Prose of Archibald MacLeish. Boston, Houghton Mifflin, 1941.

The American Cause. New York, Duell, 1941.

American Opinion and the War: The Rede Lecture. Cambridge, University Press, and New York, Macmillan, 1942.

A Time to Act: Selected Addresses. Boston, Houghton Mifflin, 1943.

Poetry and Opinion: The Pisan Cantos of Ezra Pound: A Dialogue on the Role of Poetry. Urbana, University of Illinois Press, 1950.

Freedom Is the Right to Choose: An Inquiry into the Battle for the American Future. Boston, Beacon Press, 1951; London, Lane, 1952.

Poetry and Journalism. Minneapolis, University of Minnesota Press, 1958.

Emily Dickinson: Papers Delivered at Amherst College, with others. Amherst, Massachusetts, Amherst College Press, 1960.

Poetry and Experience. Boston, Houghton Mifflin, and London, Bodley Head, 1961.

The Dialogues of Archibald MacLeish and Mark Van Doren, edited by Warren V. Busch. New York, Dutton, 1964.

The Eleanor Roosevelt Story. Boston, Houghton Mifflin, 1965.

Remarks at the Dedication of the Wallace Library, Fitchburg, Massachusetts. Worcester, Massachusetts, A. J. St. Onge, 1967.

A Continuing Journey. Boston, Houghton Mifflin, 1968.

The Great American Frustration. Stamford, Connecticut, Overbrook Press, 1968.

The University – The Library: Papers..., with Samuel Rothstein and Richard Blackwell. Oxford, Shakespeare Head Press, 1972.

Editor, *Law and Politics*, by Felix Frankfurter. New York, Capricorn Press, 1962.

Bibliographies: *A Catalogue of the First Editions of Archibald MacLeish* by Arthur Mizener, New Haven, Connecticut, Yale University Press, 1938; *Archibald MacLeish: A Checklist* by Edward J. Mullahy, Kent, Ohio, Kent State University Press, 1973.

Manuscript Collections: Library of Congress, Washington, D.C.; Yale University, New Haven, Connecticut; Harvard University, Cambridge, Massachusetts.

*   *   *

Were it not for the success of *J.B.*, Archibald MacLeish would be another of the many modern poets who yearned to hear their verse in the theatre without accommodating that verse to the exigencies of the theatre. MacLeish has been sporadically drawn to the theatre over four decades, since he published his first play *Nobodaddy* in 1926. Of his plays, two are drawn from classical myth, two from the Bible, one from a modern American story.

Nobodaddy is a biblical play, but the title is an invention of the poet, William Blake, who designated the God of orthodox religion by this word composed of "nobody" and "daddy." In MacLeish's play God is absent from the three acts resting on Genesis – the fall of Adam in Acts I and II, Cain's murder of Abel in Act III. In the absence of God, Eve offers her human love first to Adam and then to Cain. Father and son are men who pit their questioning minds against an indifferent universe, and human love does not fulfill them.

Ie the socially conscious 1930's MacLeish shifted his attention from the universe to society. While the 1929 financial crash was fresh in people's minds, MacLeish wrote *Panic*, a verse play about the panic produced by the bank failures. The play is influenced by German Expressionist contrast between the caricature protagonist-banker McGafferty and the mass of men whom he wrongs. Though McGafferty refuses to panic at the bank failure, he finally shoots himself rather than face the accusations of those he has ruined.

MacLeish's next two plays (written for radio but also produced on the stage) contain the collective protagonist and social resonances of Expressionist drama. In *The Fall of the City* the city falls because it will not defend itself against invaders. In *Air Raid* the village inhabitants are destroyed because they will not take shelter from enemy planes in the early days of air-raids. In each play the collective victim cannot believe in the dangerous reality of destructive war.

Though MacLeish's play *The Trojan Horse* was written over a decade after the radio plays, it too uses a collective protagonist that consents to its own destruction. Disregarding warnings, the people of Troy admit the deadly horse, and the play ends on Cassandra's prophecies of doom for the city. A year later, however, MacLeish wrote a verse play in a quite different key, *This Music Crept by Me upon the Waters*. The Shakespearian title already suggests a mood play, where the drama lies largely in the music of the lines. A moonrise on the Caribbean is of such exquisite beauty that two of the ten characters are inspired to base a new, shared life on its enchantment. Elizabeth and Peter plan to leave their respective husband and wife, but they do not wish to injure them. Faced with the sudden disappearance of Peter's wife, the romantic couple renounce their hope of a new union. At the plays's end, Peter's wife is found prosaically cooking potatoes, but the poetic inspiration has "crept by," never to return.

By the time MacLeish dramatized the Job story in his *J.B.*, he had experimented with mood play, Expressionist play, and modern relevance of myth in a variety of meters. *J.B.* is a composite of earlier MacLeish techniques, and the new whole coheres through the playlong viability of a play within the play. MacLeish's inner play is the Job story, but his frame draws upon an area that has fascinated modern artists – the circus. "A traveling circus...has been on the roads of the world for a long time," and "the raking of the rings and the hang of the canvas give a sense that the audience too is inside the huge, battered, ancient tent."

In the acting version of *J.B.* (unfortunately less widely distributed than the reading version), the play opens as two nameless Roustabouts finish putting up the circus tent, and two circus vendors enter with their wares. Frame and inner play are joined when the Roustabouts take minor roles in the play within the play: soldiers who announce the war death of Job's son, reporters who bring the news of the automobile accident in which two more children die, policemen who describe the rape and murder of Job's youngest daughter, and finally Civil Defense officers during an atomic war.

More important is the consistent framing role of the circus vendors, Zuss and Nickles, who feel impelled to stage the Job story. A little uneasily, they don the masks of God and Satan, and they later register surprise at the biblical words they emit through their masks. But they frequently remove the masks, to comment on the story that they witness. Paradoxically, they become more involved in the story as their roles diminish, and their involvement is consistent in viewpoint – Zuss speaking for orthodox acceptance of God's will and Nickles for rebellious and sometimes cynical youth.

What Zuss and Nickles half create and half observe is the Job story in a modern American setting. J.B. is first seen as a successful businessman, surrounded by a loving family at a Thanksgiving dinner. But soon, as in the Bible, disaster descends: J.B. loses his children, his fortune, his home, and his health. At the end of Act I he pleads: "Show me my guilt, O God!" But God remains mysterious, as in the Bible. Job's biblical comforters appear in contemporary guise – Freudian, Marxist, and clergyman – who yield no more comfort than their ancestors. Uncomforted, deserted by his wife, J.B. offers to repent. Finally, however, J.B. asserts his innocence and his dignity, rejecting the attitudes of both Zuss and Nickles, rejecting both "Yes in ignorance" and "No in spite." Toward the end of MacLeish's *J.B.* Zuss and Nickles exit separately. The frame dissolves into the Job story, which becomes the portrait of Everyman. J.B. is beaten but not vanquished, and his wife returns to him in love. Frail human love is J.B.'s answer to the Voice out of the Whirlwind.

MacLeish's *J.B.*, a humanized Job play, was followed by his *Herakles*, a humanized Greek tragedy, based on *Mad Herakles* of Euripides. Like the Greek tragedy, the American play splits in two. Euripides shows the triumphant return of Herakles in time to rescue wife and sons from their enemy, but, mad, Herakles himself then slays wife and sons. MacLeish writes about a proud, monomaniacal American scientist who visits Athens after receiving the Nobel Prize. In the second half of MacLeish's play the scientist's wife and child visit Delphi, where they witness Herakles' story as a play within the play. The relationship of Herakles and Megara reflects that of the scientist and his wife. Like J.B.'s wife, Megara pleads for human love, but the ancient hero is no humanist, and Herakles spurns Megara in order to vie with the gods, as did Adam and Cain in MacLeish's first play, *Nobodaddy*. The implication is that such heroic hubris is also the sin of modern American science.

Through various verse forms and settings, MacLeish has espoused a simple dignified humanism in the face of disaster. And this persistent optimism, couched in a rhythmic and readily apprehended language, embellished with a setting at once colorful and meaningful, has made for his unusual success on the commercial stage – in *J.B.*

—Ruby Cohn

MAC LOW, Jackson.   American.   Born in Chicago, Illinois, 12 September 1922. Educated at the University of Chicago, 1939–43, A.A. 1941; Brooklyn College, New York, 1955–58, A.B. (cum laude) in philosophy 1958. Married to the painter Iris Lezak; has two children. Free-lance music teacher, English teacher, translator and editor, 1950–66; reference book editor, Funk and Wagnalls, 1957–58, 1961–62, Unicorn Books, 1958–59; copy editor, Alfred A. Knopf, 1965–66. Member of the editorial staff, and Poetry Editor, 1950–54, *Why?*, later *Resistance*, a pacifist-anarchist magazine. Since 1966, Instructor, American Language Institute, New York, and Poetry Editor of *WIN* magazine, New York. Address: 42 North Moore Street, New York, New York 10013, U.S.A.

PUBLICATIONS

Plays

 Biblical Play (produced New York, 1955).
 The Marrying Maiden: A Play of Changes, music by John Cage (produced New York, 1960).
 Verdurous Sanguinaria (produced New York, 1961).   Act I published in *Tulane Drama Review* (New Orleans, Louisiana), Winter 1965.
 Thanks: A Simultaneity for People (produced Wiesbaden, 1962).
 Letters for Iris, Numbers for Silence (produced Wiesbaden, 1962).
 A Piece for Sari Dienes (produced Wiesbaden, 1962).
 Thanks II (produced Paris, 1962).
 The Twin Plays: Port-au-Prince and Adams County Illinois (produced New York, 1963). New York, Something Else Press, 1966.
 Questions and Answers: A Topical Play (produced New York, 1963).
 Play (produced New York, 1965).
 Asymmetries No. 408, 410, 485 (produced New York, 1965).
 Asymmetries, Gathas and Sounds from Everywhere (produced New York, 1966).

 Composer: incidental music for *The Age of Anxiety* by W. H. Auden, produced New York, 1954; for *The Heroes* by John Ashbery, produced New York, 1955.

507

Verse

The Pronouns: A Collection of 40 Dances – for the Dancers – 6 February–22 March 1964.
   New York, Jackson MacLow, 1964; London, Tetrad Press, 1970.
Manifestos.   New York, Something Else Press, 1966.
August Light Poems.   New York, C. Eshleman, 1967.
22 Light Poems.   Los Angeles, Black Sparrow Press, 1968.
23rd Light Poem: For Larry Eigner.   London, Tetrad Press, 1969.
Stanzas for Iris Lezak.   New York, Something Else Press, 1970.
36th Light Poem: In Memoriam Buster Keaton.   New York, Permanent Press, 1975.
21 Matched Asymmetries.   London, Aloes Books, 1976.

Recordings: *A Reading of Primitive and Archaic Poems*, with others, Broadside; *From a Shaman's Notebook*, with others, Broadside.

Theatrical Activities:

Actor: **Plays** – in *Tonight We Improvise* by Pirandello, New York, 1959, and other plays.

*   *   *

In recent years Jackson Mac Low has been recognized as America's leading dramatist of the aleatoric school, which uses chance-structured materials and is best known by its principal musical exponent, John Cage. Mac Low's works for theatre have been performed in the U.S.A., Canada, West Germany, Brazil and England, although except for *The Twin Plays* (1963, published by Something Else Press, 1966) none has ever been commercially published in a complete form.

Mac Low's original interest was musical composition, though after 1939 he became increasingly involved in poetry. During the 1940's Mac Low contributed to such anarchist publications as *Now, Why?* (later called *Resistance*) and to this day he edits poetry for *WIN*, for the Workshop In Nonviolence. Most of his poems are, however, designed for live performance and Mac Low has described himself as a "Writer and Composer of Poetry, Music, Simultaneities, and Plays."

The most active phase of his theatre activity begins with Prester Jo in's Company in New York in 1949 (one of the most interesting early Off-Off-Broadway groups), as co-director and actor in various Paul Goodman plays, and continues in a long association with The Living Theater beginning in 1952, originally as composer for productions of John Ashbery's *The Heroes*, W. H. Auden's *The Age of Anxiety*, etc., but also as an actor, and eventually as dramatist.

The major phase of his dramatic corpus begins also with his association with The Living Theater and, at about the same time, with John Cage. There are two sets of "Biblical Poems" and a "Biblical Play," performed in 1955, and a major play called *Lawrence*, based on writings by D. H. Lawrence. These pieces are extremely static and resemble Gagaku oratorios of words. The climax of this group of works is *The Marrying Maiden* (1958–59) performed in repertoire by The Living Theater in 1960–61 with a sound score by John Cage. This play is totally lyrical and abstract, and it includes actions to be determined by the performers using a randomizing process. The Living Theater's production was extremely conventional and inappropriate; it failed to bring out the uniqueness of the piece which was, as a result, unpublished except as an acting scipt and has not been performed since. About the works of this time, Mac Low has written:

> All during the 1940's and 1950's, many poems of mine in all modes express a pacifistic and libertarian political viewpoint strongly related to religious attitudes derived from Taoism, Buddhism, amd mystical Judaism (Chassidism and

Cabala).... These religious and political views, along with the more libertarian schools of psychotherapy [e.g., Paul Goodman], helped make me receptive to the use of chance operations and to the interpenetration of art works and the environment....

Mac Low's performance works are structured as social models in which each participant participates as a co-equal and direction is by self-guidance and by working-out, rather than being along doctrinaire, authoritarian or imposed-visionary lines. The sound of the lines is as important as the sense (the sound often *is* the sense), resulting in a uniquely musical theatre experience.

After *The Marrying Maiden* the plays become more choric – there is action, usually in unison and repetitive – though the texts remain more musical than semantic. As with *Lawrence*, the pieces take their names from some aspect of their source material. For instance, one major work of this period is *Verdurous Sanguinaria* (from which an excerpt appeared in the *Tulane Drama Review* for Winter, 1965). which is derived from a botanical text on wild flowers. Another is *The Twin Plays*, mentioned before, two plays with identical action in all respects, but one of which uses combinations of the letters in the name "Port-au-Prince" and the other proverbs collected from "Adams County Illinois" which become the names for their respective plays. Another of these works is *Questions and Answers Incredible Statements the Litany of Lies Action in Freedom Statements and Questions All Round Truth and Freedom in Action; or, Why Is an Atom Bomb Like a Toothbrush? A Topical Play* (1963). which takes political texts reflecting Mac Low's views, treats it as a litany, then randomizes the actions.

Simultaneous with Mac Low's theatre work (and not necessarily completely separate from it) Mac Low's poems wre developing in parallel blocks. There are early works such as *Peaks and Lamas* (1957, included in *Abyss*, Spring 1971). There are the *Stanzas for Iris Lezak* (1960–62, published by Something Else Press, 1972), a massive cycle of over 400 pages, written more or less immediately after *The Marrying Maiden* and in some ways paralleling it. And at the end of the *Stanzas*, the work develops into the *Asymmetries*, another large cycle (unpublished in any complete form but like the stanzas, often performed). These poems are overwhelmingly ear-oriented. They include long silences, difficult to approximate on a printed page apart from performance. They may be "poetry" but they partake of theatre, especially of the heard elements. Many are "simultaneities," by Mac Low's term, but theatre in fact.

Starting in the late 1950's the theatre of Happenings began to develop, with its emphasis on the simple image. The acme of Happenings was the Fluxus group, which performed in Europe, Japan and the U.S.A. many works by George Brecht, Ben Vautier, Ay-o, Dick Higgins, Bob Watts, Wolf Vostell, Yoko Ono, Chieko Shiomi and others. In 1962 and the years immediately following, the Fluxus group published and performed a number of Mac Low pieces. Mac Low's third major body of performance works relates to the Fluxus kind of piece. Many of these pieces, such as *Thanks* (1960) or *Questioning* (1967), have sets of directions and intentions as scripts, and these are filled in improvisatorially by the performer. Others, such as the *Gathas* (a series begun in 1961), are purely choric "simultaneities," in which the readers read the sounds in any direction. Still other performance pieces are "buried" in other cycles, such as the *8th Light Poem* (1962) which is a scenario, written in a fairly typical Happenings vein. There also exist film scenarios from this period and in this style, the best known of which is *Tree* (1961?) in which the camera man is asked to photograph a tree, unmoving and static, through a day.

Currently Mac Low's major work is a new cycle called *The Odes*, highly personal poems in classical form which do not use chance in any direct way. If he is working on any theatre pieces they have not yet surfaced. However, the *Odes* take Mac Low into a more direct and semantic phase of his work and one would imagine that any new Mac Low theatre pieces would reflect this movement.

—Dick Higgins

MALTZ, Albert.   American.   Born in Brooklyn, New York, 28 October 1908. Educated at Erasmus High School, Brooklyn, graduated 1926; Columbia University, New York, A.B. 1930 (Phi Beta Kappa); Yale University Drama School, New Haven, Connecticut, 1930–32. Married Margaret Larkin in 1937 (divorced, 1964); Rosemary Wylde, 1964 (died, 1968); Esther Engelberg, 1969; has two children. Instructor in Playwriting, New York University 1937–41; Writers Conference in the Rocky Mountains, Boulder, Colorado, 1939, 1940. Editor, *Equality* magazine, New York, 1939, 1940. Co-Founder, and Member of the Executive Board, Theatre Union, 1933–37; Member of the Council, Authors League of America, 1936–41. Recipient: O. Henry Award, for short story, 1938, 1941; Academy Award, 1946. Agent: Roslyn Targ Literary Agency Inc., 250 West 57th Street, New York, New York 10019. Address: c/o Authors League of America, 234 West 44th Street, New York, New York 10036, U.S.A.

PUBLICATIONS

Plays

>   *Merry-Go-Round*, with George Sklar (produced New York, 1932).
>   *Peace on Earth: An Anti-War Play*, with George Sklar (produced New York, 1933). New York, French, 1934.
>   *Black Pit* (produced New York, 1935).   New York, Putnam, 1935.
>   *Private Hicks* (produced New York, 1935; London, 1936).   Published in *The Best Short Plays of the Social Theatre*, edited by William Kozlenko, New York, Random House, 1939.
>   *Red-Head Baker* (broadcast, 1937).   Published in *100 Non-Royalty Radio Plays*, edited by William Kozlenko, New York, Greenberg, 1941.
>   *Rehearsal* (produced New York and London, 1938).   Published in *One-Act Play Magazine* (New York), March 1938.
>   *Mr. Tojo and His Friends*, in *Plays* (New York), December 1942.

>   Screenplays: *This Gun for Hire*, 1942; *Moscow Strikes Back* (commentary), 1942; *Destination Tokyo*, with Delmer Daves, 1943; *Seeds of Freedom* (commentary), 1943; *Pride of the Marines*, 1945; *The House I Live In*, 1945; *Cloak and Dagger*, with Ring Lardner, Jr., 1946; *The Naked City*, 1948; *Two Mules for Sister Sara*, 1970.

>   Radio Play: *Red-Head Baker*, 1937.

Novels

>   *The Underground Stream: An Historical Novel of a Moment in the American Winter*. Boston, Little Brown, 1940.
>   *The Cross and the Arrow*.   Boston, Little Brown, 1944; London, Harrap, 1946.
>   *The Journey of Simon McKeever*.   Boston, Little Brown, and London, Gollancz, 1949.
>   *A Long Day in a Short Life*.   New York, International Publishers, and London, John Calder, 1957.
>   *A Tale of One January*.   London, Calder and Boyars, 1966.

Short Stories

>   *The Way Things Are and Other Stories*.   New York, International Publishers, 1938.
>   *Afternoon in the Jungle: The Selected Short Stories of Albert Maltz*.   New York, Liveright, 1971.

Other

> The Citizen Writer: Essays in Defense of American Culture.   New York, International
> Publishers, 1950.

Manuscript Collections: Columbia University, New York; Boston University; University of Wisconsin, Madison.

> Critical Study: "Hoover, Maltz, and the Literary Left" by Jack Salzman, in *Journal of Human Relations* (Wilberforce, Ohio), 1967.

*   *   *

Born in New York City to immigrant parents, Albert Maltz is a writer whose career was forged in the Great Depression. In a collection of essays entitled *The Citizen Writer*, he testifies that the responsible writer must forsake impartiality toward social issues for an active awareness of contemporary ills. His own plays reflect social protest within Marxist themes.

Merry-Go-Round, Maltz's first major play and written in collaboration with fellow Yale Drama School student George Sklar, was produced at New York's Provincetown Playhouse in 1932. An attack on machine politics and police corruption, the story centers on a hotel bellhop forced by police to falsely confess to a murder all know as been committed by an influential gangster controlling politicians who in turn control the constabulary. The latter, given orders from above, feign a suicide by hanging the scapegoat bellhop in his cell when he resolves to identify the real murderer. The fast-moving action permits a few major characters to achieve individuality. During its short run, the drama's muckraking intent caused the administration of New York City Mayor Jimmy Walker some uneasiness.

Continuing his partnership with Sklar, Maltz helped found in 1933 the Theatre Union, a left-wing production group dedicated to presenting at low-scale prices plays treating contemporary social and economic problems that would attract a proletarian audience.

The Theatre Union opened its first season in 1933–34 with a second Maltz and Sklar effort, *Peace on Earth*. Attacking war as the inevitable outcome of the capitalist system, the episodically structured play depicts a workers' strike against the shipment of munitions to Europe. A progressive young university professor, given to thought rather than to action, is pulled into the struggle on the side of the workers. His decision to act subsequently destroys his family life and engenders the enmity of university colleagues. The professor is falsely accused and convicted of a killing when police attack him and other demonstrators protesting the honoring of a munitions-making industrialist at a university comncement. Imprisoned and awaiting execution, he envisions the machinations that promote war in an expressionistic montage sequence that includes events from his trial. A victim of jingoists, the protagonist walks to his execution while strking workers demonstrate against his death and war. The play explicates the theme that all should join the vanguard of the working class against war and its promoters.

Judged from the perspective of its time, *Peace on Earth* is a powerful social drama not without application today. Its chief shortcoming is one often found in didactic drama of social protest: the sacrifice of full characterization to action and thesis. The characters tend toward the polarity of melodrama – e.g., most workers are heroes and most Establishment figures are either villains or moral cowards – and function more as personified social ideas than as individuals. While the proffesor presents the interesting dilemma of the intellectual preferring to be observer but challenged to become activist, the swiftness of his transformation from a passive to active social role stretches credibility. The play, despite mixed critical reactions, was popular and provided an auspicious beginning for the Theatre Union.

Maltz was the sole author of *Black Pit*, produced by the Theatre Union in 1935. Set in a

West Virginia coal camp, the action portrays in many scenes the plight of the miners and the tragedy of one worker compelled to betray his companions in order to provide a living for his family. Protagonist Joe Kovarsky returns to his wife and friends after serving a prison term for participating in a miners' strike. Blacklisted as a union agitator, he is unable to find work unless he turns informer for the coal company. When he learns his pregnant wife cannot have medical care unless her husband is a company employee, Kovarsky reluctantly consents to be a stool pigeon, but promises himself not to convey significant information. However, he is forced to reveal the identity of the chief union organizer, who is subsequently beaten and fired. Kovarsky's betrayal is discovered and he is cast out in disgrace by his fellow miners. The central idea expressed is that the worker gains no hope for a better life unless he puts his class above his own personal welfare and joins in the class struggle. The strength of *Black Pit* lies not as much in its theme as in its well-drawn characterization of Joe Kovarsky; and, for the most part, the play's other characters are more individualized than in many other dramas of this genre. Theatrically effective, *Black Pit* stands as its author's strongest dramatic work. However, Maltz's two plays produced by the short-lived Theatre Union had neither long runs nor their intended attraction for a working-class audience, a fate typical of the leftist social drama which reached its zenith in the thirties.

In 1939 also appeared *Private Hicks*, a one-act play whose title character is a National Guardsman who defiantly goes to prison rather than fire on strikers. It forcefully repeats the theme that proletarian solidarity must not be denied. Other short plays which followed this one were *Rehearsal; Red-Head Baker*, a radio play; and *Mr. Tojo and His Friends*, a patriotic propaganda piece.

During World War II Maltz also wrote such popular patriotic screenplays as *Pride of the Marines* and *Destination Tokyo* (with Delmer Daves). His film-writing career unfairly suffered when, with several other writers, he was investigated by the Un-American Activities Committee in the late forties and subsequently blacklisted by the film studios.

Unyieldingly concerned with the issues of his time, Albert Maltz merits a strong position in the history of American social drama.

—Christian H. Moe

MANKOWITZ, Wolf. British. Born in London, 7 November 1924. Educated at East Ham Grammar School, London; Downing College, Cambridge, M.A. (English tripos) 1946. Married Ann Margaret Seligman in 1944; has four children. Producer, with Oscar Lewenstein, 1955–60; independent producer, 1960–70; producer, with Laurence Harvey, 1970–72. Recipient: Society of Authors Award, for poetry, 1946; Venice Film Festival prize, 1955; British Film Academy Award, 1955, 1961; Academy Award, 1957; Film Council of America Golden Reel, 1957; *Evening Standard* award, 1959; Critics Prize, Cork Film International, 1972; Cannes Film Festival Grand Prix, 1973. Address: The Bridge House, Ahallista, County Cork, Ireland.

PUBLICATIONS

Plays

Make Me an Offer, adaptation of his own novel (televised, 1952; produced London, 1959).

The Bespoke Overcoat (produced London, 1953). London, Evans, 1954; New York, French, n.d.

The Baby, adaptation of a work by Chekhov (televised, 1954). Included in *Five One-Act Plays*, 1955.

The Boychik (produced London, 1954).

It Should Happen to a Dog (televised, 1955; produced Princeton, New Jersey, 1967). Included in *Five One-Act Plays*, 1955.

Five One-Act Plays (includes *The Bespoke Overcoat, The Baby, It Should Happen to a Dog, The Last of the Cheesecake, The Mighty Hunter*). London, Evans, 1955; New York, French, n.d.

The Mighty Hunter (produced London, 1956). Included in *Five One-Act Plays*, 1955.

The Last of the Cheesecake (produced London, 1956). Included in *Five One-Act Plays*, 1955.

Expresso Bongo, with Julian More, music and lyrics by David Heneker and Monty Norman (produced London, 1958). London, Evans, 1960.

Belle; or, The Ballad of Doctor Crippen, with Beverley Cross, music by Monty Norman (produced London, 1961).

Pickwick, music and lyrics by Cyril Ornadel and Leslie Bricusse, adaptation of the novel by Dickens (produced London, 1963).

Passion Flower Hotel, music and lyrics by Trevor Peacock and John Barry, adaptation of thg novel by Rosalind Erskine (produced London, 1965).

The Samson Riddle (produced Dublin, 1972). London, Vallentine Mitchell, 1972.

Jack Shepherd, music by Monty Norman (produced Edinburgh, 1972; as *Stand and Deliver*, produced London, 1972).

Dickens of London (televised, 1976). London, Weidenfeld and Nicolson, 1976.

Screenplays: *Make Me an Offer*, 1954; *A Kid for Two Farthings*, 1955; *The Bespoke Overcoat*, 1955; *Trapeze*, 1955; *Expresso Bongo*, 1959; *The Two Faces of Dr. Jekyll (House of Fright)*, 1960; *The Long and the Short and the Tall* , 1960; *The Millionairess*, with Ricardo Aragno, 1960; *The Day the Earth Caught Fire*, 1961; *The Waltz of the Toreadors*, 1961; *Where the Spies Are*, 1966; *Casino Royale*, 1967; *The Twenty-fifth* 1967; *Assassination Bureau*, 1969; *Bloomfield*, 1970; *Black Beauty*, 1970; *Treasure Island*, 1971; *The Hebrew Lesson*, 1972; *The Hireling*, 1973.

Television Plays: *Make Me an Offer*, 1952; *The Baby*, 1954; *The Girl*, 1955; *It Should Happen to a Dog*, 1955; *The Killing Stones*, 1958; *Love Is Hell*, 1966; *Dickens of London* series, 1976.

Novels

Make Me an Offer. London, Deutsch, and New York, Dutton, 1952.

A Kid for Two Farthings. London, Deutsch, 1953; New York, Dutton, 1954.

Laugh Till You Cry: An Advertisement. New York, Dutton, 1955; included in *The Penguin Wolf Mankowitz*, 1967.

My Old Man's a Dustman. London, Deutsch, 1956; as *Old Soldiers Never Die*, Boston, Little Brown, 1956.

Cockatrice. London, Longman, and New York, Putnam, 1963.

The Biggest Pig in Barbados: A Fable. London, Longman, 1965.

Short Stories

The Mendelman Fire and Other Stories. London, Deutsch, and Boston, Little Brown, 1957.

Expresso Bongo: A Wolf Mankowitz Reader.   New York, Yoseloff, 1961.
The Blue Arabian Nights: Tales of a London Decade.   London, Vallentine Mitchell, 1973.
The Day of the Women and the Night of the Men: Fables.   London, Robson Books, 1976.

Verse

XII Poems.   London, Workshop Press, 1971.

Other

The Portland Vase and the Wedgwood Copies.   London, Deutsch, 1952.
Wedgwood.   London, Batsford, and New York, Dutton, 1953.
Majollika and Company (juvenile).   London, Deutsch, 1955.
ABC of Show Business.   London, Daily Express Book Department, 1956.
A Concise Encyclopaedia of Pottery and Porcelain, with R. G. Haggar.   London, Deutsch, and New York, Hawthorn Books, 1957.
The Penguin Wolf Mankowitz.   London, Penguin, 1967.

Wolf Mankowitz comments:

There have been some quite good notes and notices on odd works of mine from time to time, but I really could not give details. Let's just say that they all agreed that I was somewhat over-diversified and altogether too varied, and generally speaking, pragmatic, which means, I suppose, opportunistic in the way one tends to be if one is a professional writer.

*   *   *

In his novels and short stories, Wolf Mankowitz displayed a sure grasp of the dramatic, that sense of character and situation which makes for good theatre. *Make Me an Offer* and *A Kid for Two Farthings* are both simple, direct narratives, sensitive and funny; it was natural enough to see them transcribed for the stage and the screen. Since then, Mankowitz has joyfully embraced show biz at all levels; he has become an impresario, he is a screenwriter who adapts his own scripts and those of others, and he has put every form of popular entertainment on celluloid. The films to which he has contributed range in their appeal from the glamorous (*The Millionairess*) to the horrific (*The Two Faces of Dr. Jekyll*), from adventure (*The Day the Earth Caught Fire*) to schmaltz (*Black Beauty*).

Mankowitz has certainly found his spiritual home in Shaftesbury Avenue but that hasn't shaken his allegiance to the basic principles of story-telling first learnt in the East End; he still employs a powerful mixture of cynicism and sentiment, still reveres the past, still delights in patterns of speech and idiosyncrasies of behaviour. At a guess, his central character in *Make Me an Offer* is something of a self-portrait. "Who knew better than he that nothing is given, that everything passes, the woods decay. He was the ultimate human being. He resigned himself to make a profit." *Expresso Bongo* is a further comment on commercialisation, a musical set in Soho, where the promoters of pop live in the continued hope of overnight successes, sudden fortune.

Of his one-act plays, *The Bespoke Overcoat* has always attracted praise for its technical skill and depth of feeling. It is published together with four smaller pieces, one entitled *It Should Happen to a Dog*, another, *The Last of the Cheesecake*. As one might expect, these are anecdotes of Jewish life, poignant, comic and shrewd. *The Bespoke Overcoat* is something more, a celebration of that stubborn reverence for life which the good adhere to, however desperate their circumstances. Morry the tailor ("a needle like Paganini") can never give his friend the longed-for overcoat, since Fender has died in poverty. But human values are not negated by death: this truth is triumphantly stated in Morry's speeches and, at the close of the play, in his chanting of the Kaddish. Pathos is the dominant mood in another early play, *The Boychik*; this is a study of hopeless ambition, that of an elderly actor who, with his son, dreams of reopening the decaying theatre where he was once a star.

Mankowitz has made an important contribution to post-war drama, which is not always acknowledged by those who distrust box office success. His picture of Jewish life is convincing for its realism and memorable for its use of symbolism, as in *A Kid for Two Farthings*. He eschewed the avant garde but is nevertheless a highly sophisticated playwright who understands the traditions of the European theatre and has worked against the parochialism of the English stage.

—Judith Cooke Simmons

MARCUS, Frank.   British.   Born in Breslau, Germany, 30 June 1928; emigrated to England in 1939. Educated at Bunce Court School, Kent (evacuated to Shropshire), 1939–43; St. Martin's School of Art, London, 1943–44. Married Jacqueline Sylvester in 1951; has three children. Secretary, Salesman, Manager, T.M.V. Ltd., London, 1944–54; Manager, Marshal's Antiques (Silver), London, 1954–65. Actor, Director, Scenic Designer, Unity Theatre, Kensington, London; Founder, International Theatre Group. Since 1968, Theatre Critic, *The Sunday Telegraph*, London. Regular contributor to *Plays and Players, London Magazine*, both in London, and *The Dramatists' Guild Quarterly*, New York. Recipient: *Evening Standard* award, 1965; *Plays and Players* award, 1965; *Variety* award, 1966. Agent: Margaret Ramsay Ltd., 14a Goodwin's Court, London WC2N 4L!.. Address: 42 Cumberland Mansions, Nutford Place, London W1H 5ZB, England.

PUBLICATIONS

Plays

    Minuet for Stuffed Birds (also director: produced London, 1950).
    Reigen (La Ronde), adaptation of the play by Arthur Schnitzler (produced London, 1952).   Published as *Merry-Go-Round*, London, Weidenfeld and Nicolson, 1953.
    The Man Who Bought a Battlefield (produced London, 1963).
    The Formation Dancers (produced London, 1964; revised version, produced London, 1971).   London, Elek, 1964.
    The Killing of Sister George (produced Bristol and London, 1965; New York, 1966). London, Hamish Hamilton, 1965; New York, Random House, 1966.
    Cleo (produced Bristol, 1965).   Excerpt, as *Cleo and Max*, published in *London Magazine*, 1966.
    The Window (televised, 1966; produced London, 1970; New York, 1973).   London and New York, French, 1970.
    Studies of the Nude (produced London, 1967).

Mrs. Mouse, Are You Within? (produced Bristol and London, 1968).   Published in
   Plays of the Year 35, London, Elek, 1969.
The Guardsman, adaptation by a play by Ferenc Molnar (produced Watford,
   Hertfordshire, 1969; London, 1976).
Blank Pages: A Monologue (televised, 1969; also director: produced London, 1972;
   New York, 1973).   London, French, 1973; in *The Best Short Plays 1974*, edited by
   Stanley Richards, Radnor, Pennsylvania, Chilton, 1974.
Notes on a Love Affair (produced London, 1972).   Published in *Plays of the Year 42*,
   London, Elek, 1973.
Christmas Carol (produced London and New York, 1973; as *Carol's Christmas*,
   produced London, 1975).
Keyholes (produced New York, 1973).
Beauty and the Beast (produced Oxford, 1975).
Anatol, adpatation of the play by Arthur Schnitzler (produced London, 1976).
From Morning to Midnight, adaptation of a play by Georg Kaiser (produced London,
   1977).

Television Plays: *Liebelei*, 1954; *The Window*, 1966; *A Temporary Typist*, 1966; *The
Glove Puppet*, 1968; *Blank Pages*, 1969.

Screenplays: *The Snow Tiger*, 1966; *The Formation Dancers*, 1972.

Manuscript Collection: Boston University Libraries.

Critical Studies: "The Plays of Frank Marcus" by Irving Wardle, in *London Magazine*,
March 1966; "The Comedy Is Finished" by the author, in *London Magazine*, June–July
1971.

Theatrical Activities:

   Director: **Plays** – *House of Regrets* by Peter Ustinov, London, 1948; *The Servant of Two
   Masters* by Carlo Goldoni, London, 1949; *Minuet for Stuffed Birds*, London, 1950; *The
   Broken Jug* by Heinrich Von Kleist, London, 1950; *Husbands and Lovers* by Ferenc
   Molnar, London, 1950; *The Man of Destiny* by G. B. Shaw, London, 1950; *Reigen (La
   Ronde)* by Arthur Schnitzler, London, 1952; *Georges Dandin* by Molière, London, 1953;
   This Property Is Condemned by Tennessee Williams, London, 1953; *The Killing of Sister
   George*, toured, 1967; *Blank Pages*, London, 1972.

   Actor: **Plays** – The General in *House of Regrets* by Peter Ustinov, London, 1948; Silvio in
   The Servant of Two Masters by Carlo Goldoni, London, 1949; title-role in *The Man with
   the Flower in His Mouth* by Pirandello, London, 1950; Priest in *The Broken Jug* by
   Heinrich Von Kleist, London, 1950; Napoleon in *The Man of Destiny* by G. B. Shaw,
   London, 1950; Orlando in *Angelica* by Leo Ferrero, London, 1951; The Son in *My Friend,
   The Enemy* by Sheila Hodgson, London, 1952.

Frank Marcus quotes from his article "I Ask Myself" in *Transatlantic Review* (London and
New York), Spring 1966:

The very term comedy was ripe for re-definition. Until quite recently, it suggested
laughter and a happy end but, unlike farce, an underlying seriousness or social criticism.
"Happy End" usually meant the hero marrying the heroine, but that notion of happiness

was demolished years ago by Ibsen. What is there to put in its stead?...The only honest conclusion to a comedy is the sense of life going on. What more *dare* one suggest?...in the sense in which I write my plays, comedy is the very last alternative to despair.

I feel close – really personally close – to the great writers of comedy: from Molière, Goldoni and Nestroy down to Chekhov, Wedekind, Schnitzler, Molnar and Pirandello in this century. I share their attitudes and I admire their courage. And the clowns, too, and those who could laugh even at Hitler.... Using comedy as a weapon; laughing cruelty and oppression out of existence! The greater the menace, the more potent and important the function of comedy.... I still regard Authority as the Enemy.

All my plays are about illusion and reality: about the impossibility of living either with or without illusions.... That's why I love the theatre: because it's illusion made real – or is it the other way round? Because there's a shape, a form to a play that you cannot get in real life....

Sad and funny at the same time. Is that deliberate? No, it's natural. That's how I see people and events. Sometimes it's a great effort to wrench myself away from a painful situation and force myself to see it from a detached (comical) point of view, but I'd hate to be accused of self-indulgence.

*   *   *

A quality that has distinguished all Frank Marcus's mature plays is his sympathetic, though not sentimental, understanding of the behaviour of women in love, using the word "love" in its widest possible sense. The examination of feminine amatory practice in its various forms has been his theme in play after play. In two of them, *Cleo* and *Notes on a Love Affair*, it furnishes virtually the whole material of the plot.

Marcus's first play to achieve any kind of commercial success was *The Formation Dancers*, a light-hearted foursome in which one man borrows another man's mistress for a brief episode. His wife, to reclaim his fidelity, feigns an affair with this other man. The plot, in fact, is triviality itself; but two points are worth observing. One is the insistence that it is the two women who are always in command. The other is the drawing of the mistress, a Chelsea demi-beatnik of a type more common in 1964 (the date of the play) than now, who recurs several times in later work.

A much more detailed portrait of what is pretty well the same character appears in *Cleo* in 1965. *Cleo* is a theme and variations; the protagonist, that same demi-beatnik, as intelligent as she is footloose, is observed in a series of encounters with assorted men. (It may be significant that in 1953 Marcus published a translation of Schnitzler's *Reigen*, best known as the film *La Ronde*.) In this play it is clear that woman is unarguably the dominant sex, even if her dominance cannot always insure her against disaster. A later play, *Studies of the Nude*, was a developed version of one of the episodes from *Cleo*.

Between *The Formation Dancers* and *Cleo* came what is certainly Marcus's most imaginative play so far, *The Killing of Sister George*. This is a penetrating study of a lesbian love-affair. The "masculine" woman of the association is a once-successful actress whose career has dwindled to a steady part in a radio soap-opera from which the producers now intend to drop her. She shares her life with a girl who appears to be merely young and silly, but who is later revealed as not so young and mentally retarded, the object not only of love but of a genuinely charitable beneficence. It is the younger girl, however, who at the end of the play has moved into a greater happiness and left the older woman on the brink of despair: the dominance is once again attributed to the weaker vessel. This play, in which the events mark an almost uninterrupted sequence of sadness, is nevertheless hilariously funny throughout: an imaginative masterpiece. Its sensitivity was somewhat obscured in a subsequent film version, in which Marcus did not work on the script.

After *Sister George*, Frank Marcus's next piece dealt with characters almost defiantly ordinary. This was *Mrs. Mouse, Are You Within?*, once more a comedy of which the story-line is unrelieved tragedy. It is set among mildly trendy middle class people in London, and once again there is a strong female part at the core, though on this occasion, for once, she is a character to whom things happen rather than a character who makes things happen.

What happens is that she becomes pregnant by a passing association with a Negro neighbour. The Negro decamps; the boring man to whom she has been engaged for eight years is so stuffy that she sends him away; and her Marxist landlord, in whom she has never felt much interest, makes a proposal of marriage to which she agrees from the depths of her despair.

The ordinariness of the characters is an asset to the play, in that vast misfortunes seem vaster when they light on little people. But *Mrs. Mouse* has not quite the imaginative spark of *Sister George* nor the wit of *the Formation Dancers*, though there is plenty of good comedy and real pathos in it. The *Cleo* character is once more recognisable in the heroine's younger sister.

Notes on a Love Affair is more romantic and less comic than any of Marcus's previous work. In this, a woman novelist stuck on a play sets up a love-affair between a former lover of hers and a colourless girl who works for her dentist, so that she may observe their mutual reactions. As so often, the experiment progresses through realms of comedy to final heartbreak. The play does not mark any advance on Marcus's part, unless in his willingness to adopt the Pirandellian shift of having his heroine explain directly to the audience what she is doing. But it is a moving play, and contains two fine parts for actresses.

Marcus has also made a stylish translation of Molnar's *The Guardsman* and written several plays for television, one of which, a short two-hander called *The Window*, has also been seen in the theatre. There is some significance in the Molnar translation. If there is any detectable influence in Marcus's work, it is in Molnar and Schnitzler that you will find it.

—B. A. Young

MASON, Bruce (Edward George).   New Zealander.   Born in Wellington, New Zealand, 28 September 1921. Educated at Takapuna Grammar School, Auckland; Wellington Boys' College; Victoria University College, now Victoria University of Wellington, B.A. 1945. Served in the New Zealand Army, 1941–43; Royal New Zealand Naval Volunteer Reserve, 1943–45: Sub-Lieutenant. Married Diana Manby Shaw in 1945; has three children. Research Assistant, War History Branch, Wellington, 1946–48; Assistant Curator of Manuscripts, Alexander Turnbull Library, Wellington, 1948–49; travelled in Europe, 1949–51; Public Relations Officer, New Zealand Forest Service, Wellington, 1951–57; Radio Critic, 1955–61, Record Critic, 1961–62, and Music Critic, 1964–69, *New Zealand Listener*, Wellington; Senior Journalist, Tourist and Publicity, Wellington, 1957–58; Drama Critic, *Dominion*, Wellington, 1958–60; Editor, *Te Ao Hou* (Maori Affairs), Wellington, 1960–61; Editor, *Act*, Wellington, 1967–70; Senior Copywriter, Wood and Mitchell Advertising, Wellington, 1969–71. President, Secretary, and Committee Member, Unity Theatre, Wellington, 1948–60. New Zealand Delegate, International Drama Conference, Edinburgh, 1963. Full-time Actor, Producer and Director: has directed first productions of most of his own plays, operas for the New Zealand Opera Company, and revues for the Unity Theatre and Downstage, Wellington. Recipient: British Drama League Playwriting Competition prize, five times; Auckland Festival Society National Playwriting Competition prize, 1958; State Literary Fund Scholarship in Letters, 1973. Agent: John Johnson, 51–54 Goschen Buildings, 12–13 Henrietta Street, London WC2E 8LF, England. Address: 14 Henry Street, Wellington 3, New Zealand.

PUBLICATIONS

Plays

The Bonds of Love (also director: produced Wellington, 1953).
The Evening Paper (also director: produced Wellington, 1953).
The Verdict (also director: produced Wellington, 1955).
The Licensed Victualler, music by Bruce Mason (also director: produced Wellington, 1955).
A Case in Point (also director: produced Wellington, 1956).
Wit's End (revue; also director: produced Wellington, 1956).
The Pohutukawa Tree (also co-director: produced Wellington, 1957).   Wellington, Price Milburn, 1960.
Birds in the Wilderness (also director: produced Auckland and London, 1958).
The End of the Golden Weather (for solo actor; also director: produced Wellington, 1960; Edinburgh and London, 1963).   Wellington, Price Milburn, 1962.
We Don't Want Your Sort Here, music by Bruce Mason (cabaret; also director: produced Wellington, 1961).
The Counsels of the Wood (for solo actor; also director: produced Wellington, 1965).
The Hand on the Rail (produced Wellington, 1965).
Swan Song (produced Wellington, 1965).
The Waters of Silence, adaptation of a work by Vercors (for solo actor; also director: produced Wellington, 1965).
Awatea (produced Wellington, 1968).   Wellington, Price Milburn, 1969.
Hongi (broadcast, 1968; produced Wellington, 1968).   Published in Contemporary New Zealand Plays, edited by Howard McNaughton, Wellington, Oxford University Press, 1974.
Zero Inn (produced Christchurch, 1970).   Christchurch, New Zealand Play Library, 1970.
Not Christmas, But Guy Fawkes (for solo actor; also director: produced Rotorua, 1976).
Courting Blackbird (for solo actor; also director: produced Christchurch, 1976).

Radio Plays: The Cherry Orchard, from the play by Chekhov, 1960; Hongi, 1968.

Verse

We Don't Want Your Sort Here: A Collection of Light Verse.   Hamilton, Paul's Book Arcade, 1963.

Other

Theatre in Danger, with John Pocock.   Wellington, Paul's Book Arcade, 1957.
New Zealand Drama: A Parade of Forms and a History.   Wellington, Price Milburn, 1972.

Bibliography: in Act (Wellington), 1967–70.

Manuscript Collection: Alexander Turnbull Library, Wellington.

Critical Studies: articles and reviews in Landfall (Christchurch), March 1954, September 1958, June 1960, September 1961, March 1964, and September 1965; essay by the author in

The Pattern of New Zealand Culture, Ithaca, New York, Cornell University Press, 1968;
Bruce Mason by Howard McNaughton, Wellington, Oxford University Press, 1975.

Theatrical Activities:

Director: **Plays** – those listed above and many others. **Opera** – *The Medium* by Gian-Carlo Menotti, Wellington, 1955; *Le Nozze di Figaro* by Mozart, Wellington, 1958.

Actor: in four solo plays above and others.

Bruce Mason comments:

At the Edinburgh International Drama Festival of 1963, to which I was a New Zealand Delegate, I heard a West Indian novelist declare that "to be a writer in the Caribbean is to be a shoemaker where everyone goes barefoot." To be a playwright in New Zealand has sometimes seemed as meaningless and aimless as this, writing away in a country with no theatrical tradition of its own, with no living native theatre at all until after the First World War, when the amateur theatrical movement began in most large New Zealand cities. Even then, this theatre was mostly given over to nostalgic recall of the culture the actors and audiences had left behind, in the West End comedy or thriller, the midly teasing, mildly diverting pot-boiler, allowing third generation New Zealanders to project themselves imaginatively into a situation where there were servants, women could sometimes have lovers, or where someone outwardly bland and innocent would reveal his true colours and come to a sticky end in Act III. By the time I began to write plays in 1953, the situation had changed a great deal. We were part of a wider world, had lost more men per capita in the Second World War than any other Commonwealth country, and the younger portion of the population would no longer put up with imported tosh. The more adventurous amateur groups now began to produce plays of much wider provenance and resonance. Theatre audiences made their first acquaintance with the later Bernard Shaw (clever), J. M. Synge (quaint) and Sean O'Casey (strong meat). Unity Theatre, Wellington, of which I was President, Secretary, and a long-committed and committee-member, produced almost the entire corpus of modern drama between 1948 and 1960, in a programme that would have been unheard of 15 years before. I wrote my first plays for the annual festivals of the British Drama League (now absorbed in New Zealand into a composite body, The New Zealand Theatre Federation). These gigantic *fest-spiels* occupied more than 1,000 actors, all over the country every year, in local festivals, regional festivals, elimination festivals, and grand finales, when the four best plays were presented for expert adjudication. My first play, *The Bonds of Love*, was written for a BDL Festival. The British Drama League, though some have smiled or sneered at its pretensions, was the first body in New Zealand theatre actively concerned to sponsor New Zealand plays, though the conditions of presentation and performance decreed that they be only a single act.

Also in 1953, New Zealand made its first sustained attempt at professional theatre. The country's most gifted young director, Richard Campion, and his wife Edith, both graduates of the Old Vic School led by George Devine and Michel St. Denis, returned to New Zealand, devoted (and lost) a sizeable private fortune to founding the New Zealand Players, recruiting the best amateur actors in the country, giving three exhausting touring productions a year in twelve-week stints from end to end of the country. In seven years, The Players performed to a million and a half people, no mean audience in a community totalling less than three million. At their best, in some Shakespeare, in programmes popular but never base, they stood strict comparison with good English repertory. I wrote my best-known play, *The Pohutukawa Tree*, for the

New Zealand Players and Richard Campion and I produced it jointly in a workshop production which, alas, never toured, though the play has now had over fifty New Zealand productions, been telecast by the BBC, and played in several European countries. By 1960, the New Zealand Players collapsed, crippled and broken by the astronomical costs of constant touring. Since then, there has been no further sustained attempt at a national theatre company (New Zealand responding nationally only for football, the budget and the threat of war), and what professional experiments there have been are regional, devoted to a city, at widest a province. Downstage, Wellington (1964–) where several of my plays have been presented, and The Mercury, Auckland (1968–) are both healthy and lively, serving their cities and regions.

My most successful work has been occupied with the theme of culture clash or attempted resolution between Europeans and the resonant Polynesian culture they displaced a century and a half ago. I have now written five plays on various aspects of this theme, and hope eventually to have them published in one volume. The coming of television in 1960, to saturation point by 1970, has proved at once baneful and stimulating to New Zealand theatre, virtually extinguishing the "gentleman amateur," but giving professional companies an enormous spur, not only by affording them the sight of the best actors in the English-speaking world night by night on their screens, but offering at first intermittent and now, for a few, regular employment in television plays and series.

An actor also, I tried to turn my country's greatest advantage – that whatever you try, there is no one to say no – to good purpose, by writing for solo theatre and arrogantly taking all the parts. The most successful of these essays has been *The End of the Golden Weather* – a voyage into a New Zealand childhood, which I have performed more than 500 times, in every town in my own country in five gruelling years of touring, at the Edinburgh Festival of 1963, and in London the same year. I also prepared for presentation at Downstage, Wellington, a solo evening called *The Counsels of the Wood*, in which I made use of my experience as a cultural delegate to the USSR, and this I toured, though less massively, in 1965–66. A third piece, *The Waters of Silence*, I adapted from *Le Silence de la Mer* of Vercors, for solo theatre, re-translated it into French, and engaged in extensive school tours in 1967, playing successively in both languages. I have also served my theatre as a critic for over twenty years, and still do; like most New Zealanders engaged in theatre, I have humped scenery round and painted it: in fact, have tried everything at least once.

My future work must acknowledge that the regional phase of New Zealand drama is over; to take world attention we must move out into it, not in any spirit of faceless internationalism, but in the knowledge that, if the threat of chaos can be interrupted – the supreme task of creation in the next generation, or less – then we all have work to do. I have recently been enormously refreshed and stimulated by the theories and practices of Jerzy Grotowski and his theatre, and am now exploring how I may use his insights.

*   *   *

After youthful activities in student drama groups, Bruce Mason in 1944 found himself serving in the navy at Portsmouth: he showed his first play to J. B. Priestley in London and was told it had promising dialogue. Back in New Zealand after the war, he attached himself to Unity Theatre, a lively "progressive" drama group in Wellington, and gained considerable experience both as actor and producer. He won his first literary reputation with a number of strikingly original short stories, often featuring eccentric characters and elements of "the wild" impinging on the placid surface of normal small-town life.

Over the years since then, Bruce Mason has been a distinguished critic of music and drama for *The Dominion* and the *New Zealand Listener*, and has edited the journal of Maori life, *Te Ao Hou*. He has written more than thirty plays, ranging from revues and short pieces for radio and television to full-scale "big theatre" productions: today he is certainly the best known and most experienced New Zealand playwright.

His approach to drama, and his hopes for an indigenous professional theatre in his own country, are outlined in a revealing exchange of letters with the critic John Pocock, published in 1957 under the title *Theatre in Danger*. Mason's first two plays to make an impact both use English immigrants to highlight, by contrast, distinctive New Zealand attitudes. *The Bonds of Love*, a tart and concentrated piece, exposes in a sleazy hotel setting the progress in "love" of two sisters, married and unmarried, who have come to New Zealand after the war; its unsparing realism and crisp dialogue gave it something of a *succès de scandale*. *The Evening Paper* is a more ambitious attack on "nice" New Zealanders, in particular on the crippling effect of the typical matriarich on the emotional life of husband and daughter. The young English cousin who acts as catalyst is perhaps too idealistic and considerate to be convincing, but the play cuts close to the bone in its unsparing treatment of the women. A shorter play, *The Verdict*, takes as its starting point a spectacular local scandal – the apparently motiveless murder of a parent by a teenage girl – and skilfully uses this incident to provoke two originally scornful middle-class couples into exposing the motes, if not the beams, in their own eyes. This is another tautly constructed play in which some rhythmical heightening of language is attempted.

With *The Pohutukawa Tree* (written 1955, produced 1957; BBC television 1959) Bruce Mason suddenly reached a new dimension. The subject is highly coloured and melodramatic; the precarious survival, on their ancestral cliff-site, of a single Maori family – mother, son and daughter – who try hard to resist assimilation into the common flux of modern materialism, but in their separate ways inevitably fall victim to it. The girl is seduced by a pakeha youth who refuses to marry her; the boy runs amok and earns a gaol sentence; only the mother holds out, renouncing the fervent Christianity she had once embraced, wills her own death in the traditional Maori code of the defeated. Here Mason has grasped a theme of true tragic potential, and is able to bring it off by an effective counterpointing of noble Christian-pagan motifs with the rough and inarticulate sympathy of decent middle-of-the-road New Zealanders. The role of the Maori mother, Aroha Mataira (brilliantly realised in the first stage performance, and for the BBC, by the actress Hira Tauwhare), is the outstanding "big part" hitherto conceived by any New Zealand dramatist: Mason has found for her speech of remarkable eloquence and authority, and the play's impact in the theatre can be quite shattering. Like the elms in O'Neill's American tragedy, the sagging pohutukawa tree of the title dominates the stage setting and strongly symbolises the central theme.

Other plays of the 1960's include a number of operettas; a grim little one-act play on nineteenth-century English justice; and the successful light comedy in three acts, *Birds in the Wilderness*, in which a more exotic team of immigrants help to enliven the New Zealand scene. But Mason's chief effort in this period was in "solo theatre": most notably in *The End of the Golden Weather* (worked up from two earlier short stories, and presented by the author on tour through New Zealand, in London, and at the Edinburgh Festival); but also in a lively if extravagant Russo-American political satire. *The Counsels of the Wood*, and in an adaptation of *Le Silence de la Mer*, the study of a German officer during the French occupation by Vercors. Mason, an accomplished linguist, has also done his own translation of Chekhov's *The Cherry Orchard*.

The return to New Zealand in 1965 of the celebrated Maori bass singer, Inia te Wiata, led to a number of plays specially designed to provide a vehicle for this accomplished performer. The biggest in scale was *Awatea*, an improbably plotted but theatrically effective show piece which was given a full-dress performance in the Wellington Town Hall. *Awatea* was much criticised by experts for its straining of the traditional customs of *Maoritanga*; no such charge can be levelled against *The Hand on the Rail*, a less ambitious and totally convincing play on the dangers of urban life for the unsophisticated young Maori, and one which creates a movingly authentic part for an old Maori father. *Swan Song*, another tragi-comedy melodrama which explores the clash of Maori-pakeha cultures and frustrated ambitions, is like *Awatea* suspect in some of its material, but has real dramatic pathos. *Hongi*, another "big" historical part developed for radio/television with Inia te Wiata in mind, is something of an historical pageant play, but contains a good deal of robust humour. *Zero Inn* uses Brechtian techniques to weave its own variations on the contemporary generation gap.

Clearly, throughout his career Bruce Mason has resolved to be one New Zealand dramatist whose plays would be acted: whether this has in practice driven him increasingly towards obviously popular subjects and some vulgarisation of treatment remains an open question. He is a writer of almost too many talents who may yet succeed in bringing them all into dramatic focus; meantime, with *The Pohutukawa Tree* he has written the one New Zealand play that has some claim to being regarded as a classic.

—James Bertram

MATHEW, Ray(mond Frank).   Australian.   Born in Sydney, New South Wales, 14 April 1929. Educated at Sydney Boys' High School; Sydney Teachers College, 1947–49. Schoolteacher in New South Wales, 1949–51; Free-lance Journalist, 1951–52; staff member, Commonwealth Scientific and Independent Research Organisation, Sydney, 1952–54; Tutor and Lecturer, Workers Education Association, University of Sydney, 1955–60. Recipient: Commonwealth Literary Fund grant, 1951, 1956; Arts Council of Great Britain bursary, 1960. Address: c/o Mrs. E. Kollsman, Apartment 38-H, Waldorf Towers, 100 East 50th Street, New York, New York 10022, U.S.A.

PUBLICATIONS

Plays

    Church Sunday (produced Ballarat, Victoria, 1950).
    We Find the Bunyip (produced Sydney, 1955).   Adelaide, Branson, 1959; in *Three Australian Plays*, edited by Eunice Hanger, Minneapolis, University of Minnesota Press, 1969.
    Lonely Without You (produced Hobart, 1957).
    The Bones of My Toe (produced Brisbane, 1957).   Published in *Australian One-Act Plays, Book One*, edited by Eunice Hanger, Adelaide, Rigby, 1962.
    A Spring Song (produced Brisbane, 1958; Edinburgh and London, 1964).   Adelaide, Branson, 1959.
    Sing for St. Ned: An Entertainment for the Theatre (produced Brisbane, 1960). Adelaide, Branson, 1962.
    The Life of the Party (produced London, 1960).   Adelaide, Branson, 1965.

    Radio Plays: *The Love of Gotama*, 1952; *The Medea of Euripides*, 1954.

Novel

    The Joys of Possession.   London, Chapman and Hall, 1967.

Short Stories

    A Bohemian Affair: Short Stories.   Sydney, Angus and Robertson, 1961.
    The Time of the Peacock, with Mena Abdullah.   Sydney, Angus and Robertson, 1965; New York, Roy, 1968.

Verse

With Cypress Pine.   Sydney, Lyre-Bird Writers, 1951.
Song and Dance.   Sydney, Lyre-Bird Writers, 1956.
South of the Equator.   Sydney, Angus and Robertson, 1961.

Other

Miles Franklin.   Melbourne, Lansdowne Press, 1963.
Charles Blackman.   Melbourne, Georgian House, 1965.

*   *   *

By the time Ray Mathew had his first play produced he had been a schoolteacher, radio scriptwriter, university tutor, poet. Before leaving Australia to live in Italy five years later he had published his second and third volumes of poetry, one minor and three full-length plays, as well as having written most of the short stories later collected in *A Bohemian Affair*. The fourth major play was written a year later, the novel in 1965–66. He now lives in New York.

One of the dimensions used in surveying a playwright's work is the breadth of his technical resource, another the innovations which arose from his experimental structures. On both Ray Mathew scores unusually well.

Technically he is the most sophisticated playwright Australia has produced. His range of dramatic devices, most particularly in the area of dialogue, is remarkable and it is difficult to find any instance where a structure obtrudes or is used merely as dramatic ornamentation. Even in *Sing for St. Ned*, which uses some of the Expressionistic devices to achieve alienation, the technical means to Mathew's end remain in control, always revealing rather than distracting from his sub-text.

Mathew's work as a poet has had material influence on his drama, many of his more interesting sequences using modes common to both. His dialogue is based on idiomatic syntax, built into rhythmical blocks with caesurae and stresses placed as they are by the sub-group to which each character belongs. This leaves the impression of real speech but creates a denser texture and much broader emotional range.

Repetition is a favourite device, sometimes used to reinforce the texture of ostensibly colloquial chatter, sometimes to establish his key phrases without obvious emphasis, frequently to restore significance to devalued words. In *We Find the Bunyip* the key word "happy" occurs thirty times, in as many emotional colours, on a side and a half of dialogue – its original coinage is re-established and it takes a final, ironic, value with considerable impact. In performance the point of the sub-text is clearly established but both the use of the device and the rather formal structure of the sequence go unnoticed.

Mathew's ability to create freshly observed characters, his avoidance of stereotype and his lack of condescension give him much in common with those older playwrights, Lawler, Seymour, Beynon and Summer Locke-Elliot who, using more conventional moulds, were working in Australia during the same period.

Both *Spring Song* and *We Find the Bunyip* are closely related to biographical sources, a point which perhaps gives each its authoritative, unforced grasp of the value systems in Australian provincial life. In each play the young middle-class schoolmaster is plummeted among those with whom he appears to have little in common: instead of using them to look on in anger or play the quasi-narrator, Mathew has both characters interact with their new setting, sometimes in wry puzzlement, always with compassion and delight. The myth of Australian egalitarianism is not invoked, neither is there a single extraneous gag for the benefit of the middle-class audience at the expense of the humble.

The very rapid modification of emotional colour necessary in Mathew dialogue is typical of a rather late period of playwriting than that in which it was conceived. What might now be dismissed as "pinteresque" was written before Pinter was published. Equally innovatory in the middle fifties, when it was written, was *Sing for St. Ned*, one of the earliest plays to use extensive sequences where the cast was encouraged to use the techniques of improvisation.

Originally intended for college and university use, it developed a number of devices now taken for granted in educational theatre. Simultaneous discovery is as common in the arts as in science,'logical innovations often arising from experiments in several test-tubes.

Mathew's plays do not "read" well, largely because they depend more on the Chekhovian interaction of characters than upon a strong plot line and resolution. On the printed page his deliberately unsensational vocabulary (much closer to Australian reality than to stereotype stage-Australian vernacular) and the subtle flexibility of his emotional colours both contribute to the same difficulty.

The doyen of Australian drama critics, Eunice Hanger, was the first to perceive Mathew's substantial technical resource, other commentators having often missed the carefully concealed technique. Some find the plays unattractive because Mathew does not attempt to capitalize, as a later crop of playwrights have, on the popular Australian sociological and psychological myths.

Ray Mathew's work was not maximised, either quantitatively or qualitatively, at its point of origin. His characteristic qualities needed to be confirmed and consolidated by major Australian directors and actors. When staged in England, with that form of Cockney-cum-Loamshire which passes there for an Australian dialect, the plays – perhaps predictably – failed.

His work remains one of the many basic resources which Australian's heavily subsidized non-commercial management has failed to exploit. He remains abroad, in company with the aforementioned Lawler, Seymour, Beynon and Sumner Locke-Elliot.

—Reid Douglas

MATURA, Mustapha. Trinidadian. Born in Trinidad, 17 December 1939. Educated at Belmont Boys Roman Catholic Intermediate School, for ten years. Married Mary Margaret Walsh in 1964; has two children. Worked as an Office Boy, in a solicitor's firm, 1954–57, Stocktaker in a hotel, 1958–59, Insurance Salesman, 1959–60, and Tally Clerk on the docks, 1960–61, all in Trinidad; Hospital Porter, England, 1961–62; Display Assistant, cosmetic factory, England, 1962–65; Stockroom Assistant, garment factory, England, 1966–70. Recipient: Arts Council bursary, 1971; John Whiting Award, 1971; *Evening Standard* award, 1975. Agent: Margaret Ramsay Ltd., 14a Goodwin's Court, London, WC2N 4LL. Address: 5 Mayberry Place, Surbiton, Surrey, England.

PUBLICATIONS

Plays

Black Pieces (includes *Party, Indian, Dialogue, My Enemy*) (produced London, 1970). Included in *As Time Goes By and Black Pieces*, 1972.
As Time Goes By (produced Edinburgh and London, 1971). Included in *As Time Goes By and Black Pieces*, 1972.

Bakerloo Line (produced London, 1972).
As Time Goes By and Black Pieces (includes *Party, Indian, Dialogue, My Enemy*).
   London, Calder and Boyars, 1972.
Nice (produced London, 1973).
Play Mas (produced London, 1974; New York, 1976).   London, Marion Boyars, 1976.
Black Slaves, White Chains (produced London, 1975).
Bread (produced London, 1976).

Screenplay: *Murders of Boysie Singh*, 1972.

Critical Study: by Darcus Howe, in *Race Today* (London), 1974.

Mustapha Matura comments:

  I grew up in a blissfully ignorant island called Trinidad, an ex-British colony. I began
writing after my arrival in England. My work has been an attempt to examine that state, its
effects, its advantages, and its purposes, and by doing so, to shed it, seeing it replaced by....

                                    *   *   *

  Mustapha Matura's *Black Pieces* were interesting not because they experimented "with
different aspects of the problem for blacks living in a white-dominated society," but because
they took place outside the Evening Institute orbit, in which other like-experiments had
been contained.
  All four fragments contain political set-pieces which are too self-consciously conceived to
be fully effective; but which display the most inventive Caribbean diction and patterns of
humour. But Matura is still straining after effect here. In one piece, a character, Z, in black
dashiki, high on his trip from Guinea, enters a pot party of black men and white women. Z
takes it upon himself to reclaim C, by humiliating C's white woman, Carol. As Z raises
Carol's skirt, she obligingly reverts to type with "...get your black hands off me, you, you
black bastard." Flushed with success, Z moves on to Sue (anti-Apartheid-white-liberal
believing in God) who soon threatens him with jail for his militancy. Finally, he encounters
V, inanely contemplating the purifying qualities of the Thames, and delivers his piece about
starving and ill-treated blacks on television. And the gathering end the scene on all fours
looking for pot.
  In *My Enemy*, the confrontation technique moves to the more familiar television where
Sir William Hardback, M.P., prepares to expose Mustafa Black, "self-styled P.M. of the
black nation of Britain," who is having the inevitable affair with Hardback's daughter. All
attempts to restrain the daughter (the pursuer) have failed – including the traditionally
literary one: "My dear fellow," Hardback confesses to a crony, "the days when one sends
one's daughter to Switzerland because she can't leave a black alone are over. Besides they all
have embassies all over the place now." Hardback can't raise the drug issue as that would
implicate his daughter, so he decides to expose Mustafa's pretensions to leadership. And the
stock responses come out. (Compare this play with a real TV brawl between James Baldwin
and the Assistant Editor of the *Telegraph*, printed in *Encounter*, September 72.)
  The other two *Black Pieces, Dialogue* and *Indian*, take us behind the scenes into the area
of West Indian domestic humour which is Mustapha's real strength. True, *Dialogue*, on the
dangers of materialism, is a false start, but it has one good observation – that in the TV
commercial for petrol, the black car always runs out before the white one. In *Indian*, the
types are more capable of manipulation. A fat man has to be turned off food and on to sex,
and is nearly destroyed by the white schoolteacher with a voracious sexual appetite and a
willingness to learn about "your culture and ways." Interestingly, this time, the joke is on

the man in the black dashiki who confronts the policeman with "This is typical of the white fascist oppressive imperialist totalitarian priggish Nazi forces of so called law and order in this country," since the improbable officer has only come to tell him that he's won first prize in the "Make your car your home" competition.

As Time Goes By is altogether a more successful "comedy of manners." The action revolves round Ram, a "genial muddle-headed con man" who tries to make a living by acting as "guru" and "spiritual" adviser to fellow West Indians with tricky personal problems. There are two brothers who work on London Transport – one on the buses and one on the trains – and they both wear their uniforms at home. Arnold loses his wife Una because of this foible. But she is living with his brother who deliverately wears *his* uniform to get rid of her! Difficult? This is a problem that only brother Ram could sort out, and, after much humour and improbability, he does. A West Indian skin-head is brought to Ram, and this is a difficult case as well, as it's the father who needs treatment. But Ram doesn't rush into things; he and his hippy friends take time off for a quiet but powerful joint, while Ram's wife Batee seethes in the kitchen and beats the child to work off her frustrations. It is the relationship between Ram and Batee however which adds pathos to the play. The emotional cruelty is unintentional, but there is no real communication between them. Batee is out of her depth in London, is fed up with the cold and hostility and poverty she has to endure, and merely wants to go back home to Trinidad.

Ram is a richly and accurately observed character and is able to suggest not only the mamaguy trickster of the Freddie Kassoon type of hero, but to parody the whole gallery of preachers, teachers and professional con men who wield power in the West Indies. Furthermore, he is pinned down to a social context – wife and child in an alien land, and he hasn't run out on them. We mustn't assume he hasn't got problems too.

The brilliant *Play Mas*, set during two different Carnivals in Trinidad, one before and one after Independence, focuses on an odd-job boy who becomes Chief of Police after Independence. This delightful play is a combination of comic sketches and colourful costumes against a background of power-games and off-stage gunfire.

—E. A. Markham

MAY, Elaine.   American.   Born in Philadelphia, Pennsylvania, in 1932. Studied acting with Maria Ouspenskaya. Married Marvin May (divorced); Sheldon Harnick (divorced); has one child. Actress in cabaret, on stage and television, and in films; stage and film director. Agent: David Cogan, 350 Fifth Avenue, New York, New York 10001, U.S.A.

PUBLICATIONS

Plays

An Evening with Mike Nichols and Elaine May (sketches; produced New York, 1960).
A Matter of Position (produced Philadelphia, 1962).
Not Enough Rope (produced New York, 1962).   New York, French, 1964.
Adaptation (also director: produced New York, 1969).   New York, Dramatists Play
    Service, 1971.

Screenplays: *Such Good Friends* (uncredited), 1971; *A New Leaf*, 1971; *Mickey and Nicky*, 1976.

Theatrical Activities:

Director: **Plays** – *The Third Ear* (revue), New York, 1964; *Adaptation, and Next* by Terrence McNally, New York, 1969. **Films** – *A New Leaf*, 1971; *The Heartbreak Kid*, 1972; *Mickey and Nicky*, 1976.

Actress: **Plays** – debut as child actress; also *An Evening with Mike Nichols and Elaine May*, New York, 1960; Shirley in *The Office* by María Irene Fornés, New York, 1966. **Films** – *Luv*, 1967; *Enter Laughing*, 1967; *A New Leaf*, 1971. **Television** – since 1959. **Cabaret** – at The Second City, Chicago, and The Compass, Chicago and New York, 1954–57; Village Vanguard and Blue Angel, New York, 1957; Town Hall, New York, 1959.

*　　*　　*

More fortunate than most struggling playwrights when they are very specially talented, Elaine May seems to have found other resources for recognition. This is largely due to her awesome versatility. A nationally celebrated comedienne – in partnership with Mike Nichols – she found herself beginning anew when the team dissolved and Mr. Nichols went on to great success as a stage and film director. Of her two one-act plays produced in New York, the lesser was more successful, a predictable enough occurrence given the absurdity of American commercial theater.

The better work, *Not Enough Rope*, opened off-Broadway as part of a triple bill with plays by Arnold Weinstein and Kenneth Koch. Miss May's play told the simple story of a girl frantic from loneliness, a girl whose only consolation is popular music. Seeking love from a neighbor, she finds him more existentially alienated than even she. As she prepares her suicide noose, she changes her mind and calls to the neighbor for help in getting down and putting on a record. He refuses until he realizes that she is hanging herself with twine borrowed from him and he helps her in order to get it back.

If the story borders on the maudlin, it is tremendously moving, and so, if Miss May's ideas about loneliness and human despair are somewhat superficial, her flair for the dramatic is intense. This came as no surprise, since her comic routines had always seemed conceived by a mind of profound sensitivity and executed by an actress of instinctive genius. The play did seem a writing-out of the sort of sketch she might have done with Nichols, but this was perhaps to be expected in an early work.

Her next work was the full-length *A Matter of Position*, in which she was starring under Mike Nichols' direction, but the project was abandoned before the planned opening in New York. Finally (it would seem), her one-act *Adaptation* was produced off-Broadway in 1969, and had a successful run, but this was due mainly to the very funny Terrence McNally play (*Next*) with which it shared the bill. Her own play was a not-very-funny and rather dated parody of television game shows that purported to satirize the concerns of American liberal intellectuals.

However, Miss May directed the entire production and its success surely played a great part in catapulting her into a healthy career as a movie writer and director (*A New Leaf, The Heartbreak Kid*). It seems a reasonable guess that her concentration will remain largely in the film medium.

—Martin Gottfried

McCLURE, Michael. American. Born in Maryville, Kansas, 20 October 1932. Married to Joanna McClure; has one daughter. Recipient: National Endowment for the Arts grant, 1967, 1974; Guggenheim Fellowship, 1973; Magic Theatre Alfred Jarry Award, 1973; Rockefeller grant, 1975. Agent: Sterling Lord Agency, 660 Madison Avenue, New York, New York 10021. Address: 264 Downey Street, San Francisco, California 94117, U.S.A.

PUBLICATIONS

Plays

   The Feast (produced San Francisco, 1960). Included in *The Mammals*, 1972.
   Pillow (produced New York, 1961). Included in *The Mammals*, 1972.
   The Growl, in *Four in Hand* (produced Berkeley, California, 1970). Published in *Evergreen Review* (New York), April–May, 1964.
   The Blossom; or, Billy the Kid (produced New York, 1964). Milwaukee, Great Lakes Books, 1967.
   The Beard (produced San Francisco, 1965; New York, 1967; London, 1968). San Francisco, privately printed, 1965; revised version, New York, Grove Press,1967.
   The Shell (produced San Francisco, 1970; London, 1975). London, Cape Goliard Press, 1968; in *Gargoyle Cartoons*, 1971.
   The Cherub (produced Berkeley, California, 1969). Los Angeles, Black Sparrow Press, 1970.
   The Charbroiled Chinchilla: The Pansy, The Meatball, Spider Rabbit (produced Berkeley, California, 1969). Included in *Gargoyle Cartoons*, 1971.
   Little Odes, Poems, and a Play, The Raptors. Los Angeles, Black Sparrow Press, 1969.
   The Brutal Brontosaurus: Spider Rabbit, The Meatball, The Shell, Apple Glove, The Authentic Radio Life of Bruce Conner and Snoutburbler (produced San Francisco, 1970; *The Authentic Radio Life of Bruce Conner and Snoutburbler* produced London, 1975). Included in *Gargoyle Cartoons*, 1971.
   The Meatball (produced London, 1971). Included in *Gargoyle Cartoons*, 1971.
   Spider Rabbit (produced London, 1971). Included in *Gargoyle Cartoons*, 1971.
   The Pansy (produced London, 1972). Included in *Gargoyle Cartoons*, 1971.
   Gargoyle Cartoons (includes *The Shell, The Pansy, The Meatball, The Bow, Spider Rabbit, Apple Glove, The Sail, The Dear, The Authentic Radio Life of Bruce Conner and Snoutburbler, The Feather, The Cherub*). New York, Delacorte Press, 1971.
   Polymorphous Pirates: The Pussy, The Button, The Feather (produced Berkeley, California, 1972). *The Feather* included in *Gargoyle Cartoons*, 1971.
   The Mammals (includes *The Blossom, The Feast, Pillow*). San Francisco, Cranium Press, 1972.
   The Pussy, The Button, and Chekhov's Grandmother; or, The Sugar Wolves (produced New York, 1973).
   Gorf (produced San Francisco, 1974). New York, New Directions, 1976.
   The Derby (produced Los Angeles, 1974).
   General Gorgeous (produced New York, 1975; Edinburgh, 1976).
   Sunny-Side Up (includes *The Pink Helmet* and *The Masked Choir*) (produced Los Angeles, 1976). *The Masked Choir* published in *Performing Arts Journal* (New York), August 1976.
   Two for the Tricentennial (includes *The Pink Helmet* and *The Grabbing of the Fairy*) (produced San Francisco, 1976).

   Radio Play: *Music Peace*, 1974.

   Television Play: *The Maze* (documentary), 1967.

Novels

The Mad Cub.   New York, Bantam, 1970.
The Adept.   New York, Delacorte Press, 1971.

Verse

Passage.   Big Sur, California, Jonathan Williams, 1956.
Peyote Poem.   San Francisco, Wallace Berman, 1958.
For Artaud.   New York, Totem Press, 1959.
Hymns to St. Geryon and Other Poems.   San Francisco, Auerhahn Press, 1959.
The New Book: A Book of Torture.   New York, Grove Press, 1961.
Dark Brown.   San Francisco, Auerhahn Press, 1961.
Two for Bruce Conner.   San Francisco, Oyez, 1964.
Ghost Tantras.   San Francisco, privately printed, 1964.
Double Murder! Vahroooooohr!   Los Angeles, Wallace Berman, 1964.
Love Lion, Lioness.   San Francisco, privately printed, 1964.
13 Mad Sonnets.   Milan, East 128, 1964.
Poisoned Wheat.   San Francisco, privately printed, 1965.
Dream Table.   San Francisco, Dave Haselwood, 1965.
Unto Caesar.   San Francisco, Dave Haselwood, 1965.
Mandalas.   San Francisco, Dave Haselwood, 1965.
Hail Thee Who Play: A Poem.   Los Angeles, Black Sparrow Press, 1968.
Love Lion Book.   San Francisco, Four Seasons Foundation, 1968.
The Sermons of Jean Harlow and the Curses of Billy the Kid.   San Francisco, Four Seasons Foundation, 1969.
The Surge: A Poem.   Columbus, Ohio, Frontier Press, 1969.
Hymns to St. Geryon and Dark Brown.   London, Cape Goliard Press, 1969.
Lion Fight.   New York, Pierrepont Press, 1969.
Star.   New York, Grove Press, 1971.
99 Theses.   Lawrence, Kansas, Tansy Press, 1972.
The Book of Joanna.   Berkeley, California, Sand Dollar Press, 1973.
Rare Angel (writ with ravens blood).   Los Angeles, Black Sparrow Press, 1974.
September Blackberries.   New York, New Directions, 1974.
Solstice Blossom.   Berkeley, California, Arif Press, 1974.
Jaguar Skies.   New York, New Directions, 1975.

Other

Meat Science Essays.   San Francisco, City Lights, 1963; revised edition, San Francisco, Dave Haselwood, 1967.
Freewheelin' Frank, Secretary of the Angels, as Told to Michael McClure by Frank Reynolds.   New York, Grove Press, 1967.

Editor, with James Harmon, *Ark II/Moby I.*   San Francisco, Editorial Offices, 1957.
Editor, with David Meltzer and Lawrence Ferlinghetti, *Journal for the Protection of All Beings.*   San Francisco, City Lights, 1961.

Bibliography: *A Catalogue of Works by Michael McClure, 1956–1965* by Marshall Clements, New York, Phoenix Book Shop, 1965.

Manuscript Collection: Simon Fraser University, Burnaby, British Columbia.

Critical Studies: "This Is Geryon," in *Times Literary Supplement* (London), 25 March 1965; interview in *San Francisco Poets*, edited by David Meltzer, New York, Bantam, 1971.

Michael McClure comments:

Theatre is an organism of poetry – weeping, and laughing, and crying, and smiling, and performing superhuman acts – on a shelf in space and lit with lights.

* * *

Michael McClure's plays aren't to be seen as much as they're to be tasted, rubbed against, lapped up, snuggled into, chewed, immersed in. These aren't plays, they're hallucinations; they waver somewhere between art and food, somewhere between food and dreams, between waking and sleeping. These plays are seizures, fevers, impossible structures in the air of the world. No way to connect with them except to open the door.

A sample. From *The Feast*:

Aynak – GOWER! NORTITHYATAP! NHT!
Boondoo – DOOOOOOOOBOOOOOON! DOOOOOOOBOOOOON! (A wail.)
Dooboon – Booooooooondoooooo! BOOOOOOOONDOOOOO! (A wail in response.)
Ohtake – THITARTARANTAK GEEEORR NORABSHY GOOOOOOOOR!
    NEEEREMGT.
Yeorg – YEORG.
Shereb – DOOOOOOOOOB! SHEE ERATT AI.
Retorp – NYOR.
Raytar – WHEET NYEEEE!
Yeorg – The light of Blessing is meaningless there's no light in the closed rose but a tiny
    black cherub sleeps there and sings to the creatures that walk in the cliffs of the
    Lily's pollen, moving from shadow to light in the drips of rain. The seen is as black
    as the eye seeing it. What is carved in air is blank as the finger touching it.
    All is the point touched and
THE RELEASE. Caress.
!
Valeth – SHOOOOOOOOWEEEE
(Yeorg places his hands upon the table and they are the dark paws of a lion.)

Or from *The Meatball*:

Geek – YIPEEEEEEEE! WOW! OH-WOWEEEE! (Tearing off plaid beret and
    waving it in air.) YEEEEEEEEEEEE-OWW-EEEEEEEEEE!
Sleek – (Almost interested.) What, Man? (Starts to nod out.)
Geek – (Waving beret frantically. Tries to stand up. Slumps back into chair.) YIP-
    EEEEEEEEEEEEE! (Pants.) YOWWWWWW! YOOOOOOODLE! OHH!
    OOOOOOOOOOOOOOOO!! WOWEEEEEEEEEEEEEEEEEEEEEEEE!!
Sleek – (Interested but non-committal.) Yeh?
Geek – OHH! AHHHH! OOOOH! (Strugglingly manages to rise. Waves beret.)
Sleek – (Slightly impatient.) Yeh?
Geek – (Ecstatically.) WE ARE THE LAST MAGICIANS!
    YOWEEEEEEEEEEEEEEEE!
Sleek – YEAH! (Pretty interested.) Yeah.
Geek – WE ARE THE LAST MAGICIANS AND WE ARE IN A SECRET FORT
    HOVERING OVER THE CITY...WITH ALL OF OUR SECRET CARVED

ANTLER TOOLS IN FRONT OF US...We are the last ones who know the RITES!
(Waving the beret. Choking.) GULG! GULG! GULG!

or The Kid's speech from *The Blossom; or, Billy the Kid*:

LIFE IS BLASPHEMY, AND ITSELF AN END
IN COLDNESS, IN COLDNESS. OH
    all to burst, I shall burst. Free,
       FREE   FREE   FREE.
Oh secret black hunger blossoming to what is unseen,
That all is pain reaching to pain, and the
HOT ACT IS A COOLNESS WITHIN IT!
THAT I AM CAUGHT TWISTING BETWEEN.
I SEE INTO THE BEAUTY THAT IS ETERNAL.
    It is light by flashes; it is not
    beauty as you know it. It is beyond
all. A CONFUSION. LOVELINESS!!!!!!!!!
THE HUGE HORROR HORROR HORROR HORROR
    HORROR HORROR HORROR HORROR (Flash of lights.)
HORROR HORROR HORROR HORROR HORROR
    HORROR BLACK ACT.

To understand McClure, you must understand him the way you understand a toothache. Even when "rational" language is used, the plays aren't *about* what the language may sometimes speak of, but the plays are *in* the language, immersed in the essence not of what the language *means* but of what it *is*.

The Beard, McClure's most popular play to date, deals with two essential figures, Billy the Kid and Jean Harlow. The Kid is a meteor, a driven streak of energy whose concern is to set the heavens afire. Harlow is a potential conflagration dampened by middle-class instincts, resisting her better nature until The Kid combusts her. But even here the play is not so much a battle, in the story sense, as a long pulsation which finally changes its nature into conflagration. Though The Kid would appear to be pursuing an argument, what we feel is not head logic but the growing body pulsations. Just as McClure speaks of his meat poems, so *The Beard* and *The Blossom* and *The Feast* and most of the *Gargoyle Cartoon* plays are meat plays.

—Arthur Sainer

McGRATH, John (Peter).   British.   Born in Birkenhead, Cheshire, 1 June 1935. Educated at Alun Grammar School, Mold; St. John's College, Oxford (Open Exhibitioner). Conscripted into the British Army, 1953–55. Married Elizabeth MacLennan in 1962; has two sons. Stage, Television, and Film Director; Founder, 7:84 Theatre Company, 1971. Agent: Margaret Ramsay Ltd., 14a Goodwin's Court, London WC2N 4LL, England.

PUBLICATIONS

Plays

A Man Has Two Fathers (produced Oxford, 1958).

The Invasion, with Barbara Cannings, adaptation of a play by Arthur Adamov (produced Edinburgh, 1958).

The Tent (produced London, 1958).

Why the Chicken (produced Edinburgh, 1959).

Basement in Bangkok (produced Bristol, 1963).

Events While Guarding the Bofors Gun (produced London, 1966).   London, Methuen, 1966.

Bakke's Night of Fame, adaptation of the novel A Danish Gambit by William Butler (produced London, 1968).   London, Davis Poynter, 1973.

Comrade Jacob, adaptation of the novel by David Caute (produced Falmer, Sussex, 1969).

Random Happenings in the Hebrides; or, The Social Democrat and the Stormy Sea (produced Edinburgh, 1970).   London, Davis Poynter, 1972.

Unruly Elements (includes Angel of the Morning, Plugged In to History, They're Knocking Down the Pie-Shop, Hover Through the Fog, Out of Sight) (produced Liverpool, 1971; Plugged In to History, produced London, 1971; Out of Sight, Angel of the Morning, They're Knocking Down the Pie-Shop, Hover Through the Fog, produced London, 1972).   Angel of the Morning, Plugged In to History and They're Knocking Down the Pie-Shop, published as Plugged In, in Plays and Players (London), November 1972.

Trees in the Wind (also director: produced Edinburgh and London, 1971; New York, 1974).

Soft or a Girl (produced Liverpool, 1971; revised version, as My Pal and Me, also director: produced Edinburgh, 1975).

Underneath (also director: produced Liverpool, 1972).

Serjeant Musgrave Dances On, adpatation of the play Serjeant Musgrave's Dance by John Arden (produced on tour, 1972).

Fish in the Sea (produced Liverpool, 1973; London, 1975).   Published in Plays and Players (London), April–May 1975.

The Cheviot, The Stag, and the Black, Black Oil (also director: produced on tour, 1973). Kyleakin, Scotland, West Highland Free Press, 1973.

The Game's a Bogey (also director: produced Edinburgh, 1974).   Edinburgh, Edinburgh University Student Publications, 1975.

Boom (also director: produced on tour, 1974).   Published in New Edinburgh Review, 1975.

Lay-Off (also director: produced on tour and London, 1975).

Oranges and Lemons (also director: produced Amsterdam, 1975).

Little Red Hen (also director: produced on tour, 1975; London, 1976).

Yobbo Nowt, music by Mark Brown (also director: produced London, 1975).

The Rat Trap, music by Mark Brown (also director: produced London, 1976).

Screenplays: Billion Dollar Brain, 1967; The Bofors Gun, 1968; The Virgin Soldiers, 1969; The Reckoning, 1970.

Television Plays: Diary of a Young Man series, with Troy K. Martin, 1964; The Day of Ragnorok, 1964; Mo, 1965; Shotgun, 1965; The Bouncing Boy, 1972; Orkney, 1973.

Other

Translator, with Maureen Teitelbaum, *Rules of the Game*, by Jean Renoir.   London, Lorrimer, 1970.

Theatrical Activities:

Director: **Plays** – many of his own plays, and *Bloomsday* by Allan McClelland, Oxford, 1958; *The Birds* by Aristophanes, Oxford, 1959; Live New Departures series of plays, 1961–64; *The Eccentric* by Dannie Abse, London, 1961. **Television** – *Z Cars* series (eight episodes), 1962; *The Compartment* by Johnny Speight, 1962; *The Fly Sham* by Thomas Murphy, 1963; *The Wedding Dress* by Edna O'Brien, 1963; *The Entertainers* (documentary), 1963; *The Day of Ragnorok*, 1964; *Mo* and *Shotgun*, 1965; *Double Bill* by Johnny Speight, 1972.

John McGrath comments:

My plays, I now realize, have been from the beginning about the relationship of the individual to other individuals and thence to history. They have pursued this theme in many ways, poetic, comic, tragic, realistic, and latterly more and more freely. Music is now coming to play a more important part in my plays, to help break through the barriers of naturalism which I can no longer tolerate. My work has never suited London (West End) audiences or ways of thinking: it is now being seen by working-class audiences from Orkney to Plymouth, and by young audiences all over the country in the new university theatres and art labs and studio theatres, via the 7:84 Theatre Company. I have also benefited from a thriving relation with the Everyman Theatre, Liverpool, under the direction of Alan Dosser, as previously from working with directors as perceptive and helpful as Ronald Eyre, Anthony Page, and Richard Eyre in Edinburgh.

My plays are not difficult to approach, although they tend to have many levels of meaning embedded fairly deeply under them as well as on the surface. The key, if key is needed, is a growing political consciousness allied to a growing feeling for individual human beings, with all the contradictions that alliance involves.

*   *   *

No one in Britain today expects playwrights to devote the whole of their time to writing for the theatre, but, if that is the central track in John McGrath's career, he has driven into more sidetracks than most, not only writing for television and the cinema but taking a full-time job with the BBC to direct and produce, and, more recently, running his own Fringe theatre company. But the question of whether he would be a better playwright if he spent more of his time writing plays is probably academic and certainly unanswerable. His company is called the 7:84 Theatre Company because 84 per cent of Britain's wealth is said to be in the hands of 7 per cent of its population. The company's declared objective is "raising consciousness. Primarily of the working class and its potential allies." It is open to doubt whether this is feasible, but there can be no doubt that the same obsessions and the same commitment run through John McGrath's work as a writer and a theatrical activist.

Events While Guarding the Bofors Gun and *Bakke's Night of Fame*, derived from William Butler's novel *A Danish Gambit*, both had their London premieres at the Hampstead Theatre Club, both directed by Ronald Eyre, and both failed to transfer to the West End, though they are both far better than most plays which are seen there. Both develop themes treated in *Why the Chicken*, which was originally produced by the Oxford University Dramatic Society in Edinburgh in 1959. The basic confrontation in it is between an individual and a group, a middle-class girl trying to get herself accepted by a crowd of working-class youngsters. In spite of the plot's dependence on an off-stage climbing incident (in which she causes the death of a boy who has tried to rape her) the action is effectively developed to penetrate quite deeply into the girl's almost loving involvement with a class that must reject her, however bravely she commits herself, and however close she comes to winning the love of the ringleader.

The equivalent role in the all-male *Events While Guarding the Bofors Gun* is a well-meaning young Lance-Bombardier, with mild, middle-class manners, who sacrifices his chances of becoming an officer by compromising with the men who are in his charge, letting them break the rules by going to a Naafi canteen while on guard duty and depending partly on their goodwill, partly on a half-hearted attempt at imposing his authority, to keep them sufficiently under control to satisfy the officer who comes around to inspect the guard. In *Why the Chicken* McGrath was already showing skill in the art of bringing a group of characters to life both collectively and individually. There was clear but economical differentiation between the members of the group, with their varying degrees of aggressiveness, while the theme of aggression which turns into self-destructiveness was given its trial run. It will feature again in *Events While Guarding the Bofors Gun* and *Bakke's Night of Fame*. The twenty-nine-year-old Gunner O'Rourke in *Events While Guarding the Bofors Gun* is described as "tall, wild and desperate. An Irish bandit with a terrifying deathwish, a desperado whose humour, viciousness, drunkeness and ultimate despair come from deep within. To say he is bitter is to underestimate his scorn for himself and all life. He is uncontrollable, manic." After taking a savage delight in exposing the weakness and inconsistency of Lance-Bombardier Evans, he jumps drunkenly out of a window and finally kills himself by falling onto a bayonet. The play's final irony is that Evans, his chances of promotion ruined by the suicide, is belatedly provoked to an act of useless aggression. Kicking the dead body, fully aware that it is dead, he tells O'Rourke he is on a charge.

A great deal of dialogue in *Bakke's Night of Fame* comes straight out of William Butler's novel, and McGrath's characterisation is loose enough to allow the part to be played either by a coloured actor, as it was at Hampstead Theatre Club, or a white actor, as in the 1972 revival at the Shaw Theatre. But he injects considerable vitality into the figure of the prisoner who is going into the electric chair. Whether or not he is guilty of the murder for which he has been condemned becomes almost irrelevant. From his behavior with the guards, the priest, the prison governor and the executioner (when he manages to secure a preliminary meeting with him), one gleans all one needs to know about how he has compulsively got himself to the situation he is now in.

Something of the same theme survives in *Plugged In to History*, the central one-act play of the three in the bill *Plugged In*, which was performed by the 7:84 Theatre Company in 1972, and the only one of the three plays in which the fusion of personal and political themes was wholly successful. A masochistic middle-class wife is involved in a park-bench encounter with an aggressive labourer who has been jilted by a middle-class girl. The climax comes when she shows that she would like him to inflict pain on her, as he has on the girl-friend who hurt him. The device of having her read imaginary news from invisible papers suspended in mid-air succeeds in planting her private agony in the public context of contemporary history's wholesale infliction of pain on masses of people who in no way need it, as she does. "When I read my papers, I feel plugged in to history. I fell the course of events coursing through my veins. I feel taken over, crushed, by many many men.... I need pain. It stops me suffering."

His recent work has been more didactic and more eclectic. His main concern has been in making the largest possible contribution to the destruction of capitalism: art must be subordinated to agitprop, characterisation to caricature. His talent can still be seen flickering through his dogmatism, particularly in scenes depicting family life. In *Fish in the Sea* and *Yobbo Nowt*, for instance, there are flashes of warmth, tenderness and humour in his dramatisation of working-class suffering. But he has come to lean heavily on other playwrights. *Serjeant Musgrave Dances On* sharpens the political edge and blunts the subtlety of John Arden's play. *Fish in the Sea* borrows from Brecht's *The Caucasian Chalk*

Circle and Arden's *Island of the Mighty. Yobbo Nowt* is about the political education of a working-class mother, and McGrath is patently indebted to Brecht's dramatisation of Gorki's *The Mother*. But *Yobbo Nowt* is incomparably thinner in dramatic texture, less effective as a play, less efficient as propaganda.

—Ronald Hayman

McNALLY, Terrence. American. Born in St. Petersburg, Florida, 3 November 1939. Educated at Columbia University, New York (Evans Traveling Fellowship, 1960), 1956–60, B.A. in English 1960 (Phi Beta Kappa). Stage Manager, Actors Studio, New York, 1961; Tutor, 1961–62; Film Critic, *The Seventh Art*, 1963–65; Assistant Editor, *Columbia College Today*, New York, 1965–66. Recipient: Stanley Award, 1962; Guggenheim Fellowship, 1966, 1969; Obie award, 1974; National Institute of Arts and Letters award, 1975. Agent: Howard Rosenstone, William Morris Agency, 1350 Avenue of the Americas, New York, New York 10019. Address: 218 West 10th Street, New York, New York 10014, U.S.A.

PUBLICATIONS

Plays

The Roller Coaster, in *Columbia Review* (New York), Spring 1960.
And Things That Go Bump in the Night (as *There Is Something Out There*, produced New York, 1962; revised version, as *And Things That Go Bump in the Night*, produced Minneapolis, 1964; New York, 1965). Published in *Playwrights for Tomorrow: A Collection of Plays, Volume 1*, edited by Arthur H. Ballet, Minneapolis, University of Minnesota Press, 1966.
The Lady of the Camellias, adaptation of a play by Giles Cooper based on the novel by Dumas (produced New York, 1963).
Next (produced Westport, Connecticut, 1967; New York, 1969; London, 1971). Included in *Sweet Eros, Next, and Other Plays*, 1969.
Tour (produced Los Angeles, 1967; New York, 1968; London, 1971). Published in *Collision Course*, New York, Random House, 1968.
Botticelli (televised, 1968; produced Los Angeles, 1971; London, 1972). Included in *Sweet Eros, Next, and Other Plays*, 1969; in *Off-Broadway Plays 2*, London, Penguin, 1972.
Sweet Eros (produced Stockbridge, Massachusetts, and New York, 1968; London, 1971). Included in *Sweet Eros, Next, and Other Plays*, 1969; in *Off-Broadway Plays*, London, Penguin, 1969.
¡Cuba Si! (produced Provincetown, Massachusetts, and New York, 1968). Included in *Sweet Eros, Next, and Other Plays*, 1969.
Witness (produced New York, 1968; London, 1972). Included in *Sweet Eros, Next, and Other Plays*, 1969.
Noon (produced New York, 1968). Published in *Morning, Noon and Night*, New York, Random House, 1968.
Apple Pie (includes *Next, Tour, Botticelli*). New York, Dramatists Play Service, 1969.
Last Gasps (televised, 1969). Included in *Three Plays*, 1970.
Bringing It All Back Home (produced New Haven, Connecticut, 1969; New York,

1972).   Included in *Three Plays*, 1970.

Sweet Eros, Next, and Other Plays (includes *Sweet Eros, Next, Botticelli, ¡Cuba Si!,* and
   Witness).   New York, Random House, 1969.

Three Plays: ¡Cuba Si!, Bringing It All Back Home, Last Gasps.   New York,
   Dramatists Play Service, 1970.

Where Has Tommy Flowers Gone? (produced New Haven, Connecticut, and New York,
   1971).   New York, Dramatists Play Service, 1972.

Bad Habits: Ravenswood and Dunelawn (produced East Hampton, New York, 1971;
   New York City, 1973).   New York, Dramatists Play Service, 1974.

Let It Bleed, in *City Stops* (produced New York, 1972).

Whiskey (produced New York, 1973).   New York, Dramatists Play Service, 1973.

The Ritz (as *The Tubs*, produced New Haven, Connecticut, 1973; revised version, as
   The Ritz, produced New York, 1975).   Included in *The Ritz and Other Plays*, 1976.

The Ritz and Other Plays (includes *Bad Habits, Where Has Tommy Flowers Gone? And
   Things That Go Bump in the Night, Whiskey, Bringin It All Back Home*).   New York,
   Dodd Mead, 1976.

Screenplay: *The Ritz*, 1976.

Television Plays: *Botticelli*, 1968; *Last Gasps*, 1969.

*   *   *

Terrence McNally is rightly bemused when he is referred to as having arrived from off-
Broadway. In truth, his career is a chronicle of recent American theatrical action – starting
off with some ill-fated Broadway productions, removing them to phenomenally successful
runs off-Broadway, and eventually into the mainstream of collegiate and regional theatre in
the United States. Finally – even at long last and deservedly – the process is reversing, and a
major American dramatist is making his way back to the Big Time – this time with triumph.

McNally has never really had much to do with the so-called "experimental theatre"
which rather more satisfies its own vanities and eccentricities than it does any true theatrical
needs or impulses. While others of his generation were busy trying to outrage their elders
and to impress their peers, McNally has steadfastly grown as a writer whose vision has been
not so much of the Main Chance as of the Major Chord.

Of all the "new writers," it is safe to say that none is more charming as a person, more
dedicated to the drums which he quite clearly hears beating, more brightly alert and
intelligent, and less an off-Broadway presence than Terrence McNally. While The Angry
Pack of modern young writers is off howling at the wind and the windmills, McNally has
been perfecting his art and his craft. Whereas that generation of playwrights seems to be
more concerned with social action than art, with politics than playmaking, McNally, so far
as I can tell at all, is a-political or at best political by implication only – both personally and
in his writing. In fact, Terrence McNally is a very private person.

As the years have swiftly moved by, bringing considerable attention and success and
fame, one particular trait has emerged in McNally the man and McNally the playwright:
he's finally smiling and enjoying himself. My earliest impressions of him were that of a Phi
Beta Kappa, which he is, and a very solemn, serious, defensive, even worried young man,
which he was. I rather thought that he was worried that people might not understand that
he was a terribly bright guy. Somehow his youth did indeed belie the intelligence, but the
seriousness of the façade also belied the wonderfully humorous man beneath.

Now, having begun to arrive in the fullest theatrical sense, he admits that he had once
taken himself and his work so seriously that he had missed his own and his work's real
import. For McNally is blessed with a true comic talent, and that talent is now shining
brightly in his plays. He is still quick to note, though, that the plays have "serious hearts,"
but he finally owns up to the laughter that those plays purposefully generate. There is a
wondrous joy in McNally's plays – not gags and gag lines but honest character comedy
which probes deeply and earnestly at where McNally is and where the world he inhabits is.

As with any significant writer, McNally's plays are deceptive: they point in one direction but go in quite another. They are not what they seem to be, and in that mystery lies the potential of greatness. In that split between the laughing surface and the puzzling center rests theatrical excitement.

Raised in Texas, and yet as un-Texas as anyone around, McNally is today at the sophisticated, attractive, dazzling core of New York theatre society without being part and parcel of its grubbier aspects. The kid who adored Kukla, Fran and Ollie on television, and who created his own puppet theatre, grew into a major force and figure in American theatre – but without quite ever losing the wonder and the gladness of Kukla and Ollie. Perhaps, too, because of an early love for opera and his predilecton for making tiny theatrical sets for those beloved operas, McNally soon turned his antennae to musical order. To this day, his work has a precision and an organisation closer to music than to the meanderings of much modern writing. It's as if he were creating a kind of personal, private opera each time – without music. In an absurdist, mechanistic world, what better metaphor than that of the puppet stage doing rather grand-ish opera?

At Columbia University, where he majored in journalism, he found himself fascinated by the living stage, going to every play he could. The endless panorama of Broadway stimulated a need, and eventually, that need burst forth into a frenzy of creativity. He wrote a Columbia varsity show, more because no one else could than because of any intention on his part to become a playwright. But then he suddenly discovered the almost indescribable joy of "making people laugh." He loved it.

Looking back now on his early short stories and journalistic pieces, one sees that he always had been more concerned with action and dialogue than with reporting and narration. He filled his earliest writing with dialogue rather than with the usual telling about what happened. In fact, one supposes, he was always a dramatist, but only in the excitement of New York did he formally accept the role. As he continued to write and be produced, he created a repertoire of talented, intensely loyal actors for whom he wrote and who loved what he wrote for them. Through them, McNally more and more has discovered that theatre is after all action, and that action reveals. A good playwright doesn't *tell*, he shows. He doesn't preach; he does indeed reveal. So the circle has gone around: from the puppets through rather pompous speechifying to theatrical pieces full of action.

But McNally's niche in the pantheon of dramatists is rightly as a comic writer – never a buffon grinding out cheap little jokes, but rather a most perceptive participant in one of the most exciting adventures of them all: theatre in the United States today. His perception has become a simile which he uses again and again to probe and prod both sensitivities and sensibilities, to stab at shibboleths, to expose fears and pretences.

Only a few short years ago, McNally seemed destined to be the sex writer of the seventies, just as Tennessee Williams seemed doomed to that unholy category in the forties. Williams has survived as a poet and chronicler of an age, and McNally has learned to laugh heartily, readily, generously – and his audiences enjoy very much laughing with him.

But the heart is indeed serious. McNally's work – and perhaps even McNally the man – are still earnest, even frightened, and above all somewhat mysterious. I have a feeling both as I see his plays and laugh delightedly, and as I talk to the man and admire the perceptions and charm, that I really don't know either the plays or the playwright at all. Both are unfathomable. I say this with admiration, for finally it is the mystery of the smile, the hidden question, the lurking glance which fascinate and call one back to art, again and again. McNally, I think, is never enigmatic deliberately but finally is enigmatic always because this is the nature of the man and his art. His enormous fondness for very old and for very young people is a reflection not of indecision but of insight and loving, but – careful, now – the bond is fragile and will not reveal itself.

McNally's work then may prove more of his time than others more flagrantly "experimenting." McNally's mystery is the mystery of living at the edge of a precipice, and perhaps that precipice is the end of the Age of the Renaissance. Perhaps. Perhaps not.

—Arthur H. Ballet

MEDNICK, Murray. American. Born in Brooklyn, New York, 24 August 1939. Educated at Fallsburg Central School, New York; Brooklyn College, 1957–59. Playwright-in-Residence and Co-Artistic Director, Theatre Genesis, New York, 1970–73. Vice-President, New York Theatre Strategy. Fellow, Florida State University, Tallahassee. Recipient: National Endowment for the Arts grant, for poetry, 1967; Rockefeller grant, 1968, 1972; Obie Award, 1970. Agent: Howard Rosenstone, William Morris Agency, 1350 Avenue of the Americas, New York, New York 10019, U.S.A. Address: Calle 19, 148A, Progreso, Yucatan, Mexico.

PUBLICATIONS

Plays

The Box (produced New York, 1965).
The Mark of Zorro (produced New York, 1966). Included in Cartoon and Other Plays, 1973.
Guideline (produced New York, 1966). Included in Cartoon and Other Plays, 1973.
Sand (produced New York, 1967; London, 1970). Included in Cartoon and Other Plays, 1973.
The Hawk: An Improvisational Play, with Tony Barsha (produced New York, 1968). Indianapolis, Bobbs Merrill, 1968.
Willie the Germ (produced New York, 1968). Included in Cartoon and Other Plays, 1973.
The Hunter (produced New York, 1968). Indianapolis, Bobbs Merrill, 1969.
The Shadow Ripens (produced San Diego, California, and New York, 1969). Indianapolis, Bobbs Merrill, 1973.
The Deer Kill (produced New York, 1970). Indianapolis, Bobbs Merrill, 1972.
Cartoon (produced New York, 1971). Included in Cartoon and Other Plays, 1973.
Cartoon and Other Plays (includes The Mark of Zorro, Guideline, Sand, Willie the Germ). Indianapolis, Bobbs Merrill, 1973.
The Last Resort (produced New York, 1973).
Are You Lookin'? (also director: produced New York, 1973).
The Black Hole in Space (produced New York, 1975).

Screenplay: Ringaleevio, with Sam Shepard, 1971.

Verse

3 Poets, with others. Indianapolis, Bobbs Merrill, 1973.

Theatrical Activities:

Director: **Plays** – Are You Lookin'?, New York, 1973; Blue Bitch by Sam Shepard, New York, 1973.

*   *   *

Murray Mednick is one of the most important younger American dramatists. In just over a decade he has produced more than a dozen plays, developing increasing technical strength, clarity, and complexity and extending his vision with passionate conviction. His plays and the worlds they evoke are a far cry from the mannered middle-class realities of contemporary commercial theatre. Mednick is Jewish and grew up in poverty, and in his writing he is concerned with ugly, crushing economic and personal pressures that lie behind the American myth of equality and social justice. He writes out of cruel experience. His humor is often bitter. His plays have not found a wide public; yet their skill, force, and struggle toward truth are undeniable, and his reputation is likely to grow.

Most of Mednick's plays have had their first productions at Theatre Genesis, a church-sponsored theatre on the lower East Side in New York. A poet before turning to drama, he wrote several one-act plays in the mid-60's, then moved on to larger forms. *Sand* shows an aging, used-up American couple who are visited by a formal Ambassador, their horrible regressive stupor unbroken by the news that their son is dead in the war. The dead soldier's body is brought in at the end on a meat hook. *Willie the Germ* is about a down-and-out man working as dishwasher for a grotesque family of Coney Island freaks who endlessly involve him in incomprehensible machinations that always get him in trouble. He yearns to escape but is kept in his place by put-downs and an invisible electric force field operated by an anonymous Button-Pusher in the audience. At the end he is destroyed and castrated by the monstrous representatives of "society."

Mednick has created two plays working with groups of actors, using improvisation to draw material from their lives and imaginations into a form he has devised. *The Shadow Ripens* was based on an Eskimo legend and embodied the idea of descending to dangerous non-rational depths of being in quest of wisdom and authenticity. *The Hawk* is a play about a drug pusher and his victims. The victims' self-revealing monologues were developed by the actors and framed by a formal, ritualistic structure. The play employed a novel and experimental set of technical acting devices and was remarkably successful in shaping very loose, idiosyncratic material within an elegantly disciplined and cohesive form.

The Hunter, a play in three acts, shows a hip, tight friendship between two men. They are united by a common enemy, a middle-aged hunter obsessed with the Civil War, whom they nail to a tree; and driven to mutual mistrust by a woman. Though the play has a contemporary setting, its place in space and time is kept ambiguous. The events of the play are spare, elusive, mysterious, moving always toward a visionary plane of perception. *The Deer Kill*, another long play, focuses on a sincere, honest young man trying to live virtuously and simply, having moved from the city to an old farm. His good nature and well-being are assaulted from all sides – by crazed friends from the city, one of whom kills himself, by his unfaithful wife, and by the local authorities, because his dog has killed a deer. The play is more realistic than Mednick's previous work, a clear, rich, and affecting study of a struggle to live morally in contemporary America.

—Michael Smith

MEDOFF, Mark (Howard).   American.   Born in Mt. Carmel, Illinois, 18 March 1940. Educated at the University of Miami, 1958–62, B.A. 1962; Stanford University, California, 1964–66, M.A. 1966. Married Stephanie Medoff in 1972; has two daughters. Supervisor of Publications, Capitol Radio Engineering Institute, Washington, D.C., 1962–64; Associate Professor of English, 1966–75, and since 1975, Dramatist-in-Residence, New Mexico State University, Las Cruces. Recipient: Drama Desk Award, 1974; Obie Award, 1974; Outer Circle John Gassner Award, 1974; Joseph Jefferson Award, for acting, 1974; Guggenheim Fellowship, 1974. Agent: Gilbert Parker, Curtis Brown Ltd., 60 East 56th Street, New York, New York 10022. Address: 800 Conway, Las Cruces, New Mexico 88001, U.S.A.

Plays

> The Wager (produced Las Cruces, New Mexico, 1967; New York, 1974).   New York, Dramatists Play Service, 1975.
> Doing a Good One for the Red Man (produced Las Cruces, New Mexico, 1969). Included in The Wager..., Doing a Good One for the Red Man, and The War on Tatem, 1976.
> The Froegle Dictum (produced Albuquerque, New Mexico, 1971).   Included in Four Short Plays, 1974.
> The War on Tatem (produced Las Cruces, New Mexico, 1972).   Included in The Wager..., Doing a Good One for the Red Man, and The War on Tatem, 1976.
> The Kramer (produced San Francisco, 1972).   New York, Dramatists Play Service, 1976.
> The Odyssey of Jeremy Jack, with Carleene Johnson (produced Las Cruces, New Mexico, 1975).   New York, Dramatists Play Service, 1973.
> When You Comin Back, Red Ryder? (produced New York, 1973).   New York, Dramatists Play Service, 1974.
> Four Short Plays (includes The Froegle Dictum, Doing a Good One for the Red Man, The War on Tatem, The Ultimate Grammar of Life).   New York, Dramatists Play Service, 1974.
> The Wager: A Play, and Doing a Good One for the Red Man, and The War on Tatem: Two Short Plays.   Clifton, New Jersey, James T. White, 1976.
> The Halloween Bandit (produced Huntington, Long Island, New York, 1976).

Theatrical Activities:

Director: **Plays** – When You Comin Back, Red Ryder; Waiting for Godot by Samuel Beckett; The Effect of Gamma Rays on Man-in-the-Moon Marigolds by Paul Zindel; Jacques Brel Is Alive and Well and Living in Paris; The Birthday Party by Harold Pinter; One Flew over the Cuckoo's Nest by Dale Wasserman.

Actor: **Plays** – Andrei Bolkonski in War and Peace; Marat in Marat/Sade by Peter Weiss; Pozzo in Waiting for Godot by Samuel Beckett; Teddy in When You Comin Back, Red Ryder?; Harold Gorringe in Black Comedy by Peter Shaffer; Bro Paradock in A Resounding Tinkle by N. F. Simpson.

Mark Medoff comments:

My work is simply a reflection of my own spirit, my fears, sorrows, and fires.

*   *   *

"The gun is the ambiance of our society," Mark Medoff confessed in a recent interview. His published plays (3 full-length plays, 4 one-acts and 1 play for children) tend to bear out his allegation.

> The Froegle Dictum: "A one room apartment...marked most noticeably by broken destruction devices – guns, rifles, knives, swords, empty medicine bottles."
> "Al enters...and has a suicidal look about him."

> *Doing a Good One for the Red Man*: "The Indian comes into view slowly. He's carrying a beaten shotgun...there is a blaze of shotgun fire into the hut..."
>
> *The Ultimate Grammar of Life*: "A coat rack with a revolver and holster and a madras sports jacket hanging from it."
>
> *The War on Tatem*: "...the *coup de grace*, a cap gun whack to Myron's nose...."
>
> *The Wager*: "He wears a turtle-neck sweater and a shoulder holster and revolver strapped over it."
>
> *When You Comin Back, Red Ryder?*: "Teddy pulls a small caliber revolver from his jacket."

The gun, usually a revolver, becomes Medoff's way of setting atmosphere, building tension, revealing character, developing plot. The critical question which his works raise is to what degree is the gun a useful symbol of the world Medoff sees, and how much is it a facile solution to the melodramatic problems which his frequently imperfect dramaturgy poses?

With the New York opening of *When You Comin Back, Red Ryder?*, Medoff became a young playwright to take seriously. The play enjoyed a long off-Broadway run, had many productions outside New York, received lavish critical praise, and introduced to the American theater a writer near the crest of his powers. Shortly thereafter, a large number of his earlier works were published and produced, and while they reveal his development as a writer and reinforce critical understanding of his thematic concerns and his dramaturgical practices, none has proven of comparable interest, although *Doing a Good One for the Red Man* was anthologized as one of the best one-acts of 1974, and both *The Wager* and *The Kramer* had New York production.

Medoff's plays are in the mainstream of American realistic dramaturgy. The locations are always recognizable. Sometimes they are highly selected almost to the point of stylization, as in *Red Man*; sometimes they are multiple, as in the two apartments and office that are required for the cinematically structured *The Kramer*; and sometimes they are as conventionally realistic as the diner in *When You Comin Back, Red Ryder?*, a setting as reminiscent of the diner in *The Petrified Forest* as the characters and action are of that 1930's version of this same story. Medoff's characters are also realistic life-studies. Some are observations of regional types, like Jaime in *The Ultimate Grammar of Life* and the Indian in *Red Man*. Others, usually the pivotal characters, seem manifestations of selected fragments of Medoff's own self-image. There is the pipe-smoking and aggressively tidy intellectual (Kramer, Leeds from *The Wager*, Richard from *Red Ryder*, Nabors from *The Froegle Dictum*). And there is the potentially violent and self-excoriating hedonist (Ward in *The Wager*, Al in *The Froegle Dictum*, and, best realized, Teddy in *Red Ryder*). The motivations for these characters are always analyzable in contemporary, psychological terms. Perhaps this is the result of Medoff's having been raised by a physician-father and psychologist-mother, perhaps it is because he is conscious of writing in the tradition of American realism, and perhaps it is because he is exploring characters who are externalizations of himself. Kenneth Frankel, the New York director of *Red Ryder* and *The Kramer*, has suggested the latter work is Medoff's seminal play in that it presents his major characters and themes in clearest light.

The language of Medoff's characters is also recognizably realistic. Too frequently it reflects Medoff's interest in academic word-play (he is a professor of English in New Mexico) and becomes too self-consciously "witty." On other occasions he is successful in fusing regionalisms, slang, philosophy and precision, as in Teddy's speech from *Red Ryder*:

> My God, the unspeakable audacity of a punk like you wearin' a tattoo like that. The real Red Ryder would've hung 'em up if anyone were to tell him he was associated with pigshit like that. And I'll tell you somethin' else: You *never* would've found the real Red Ryder sittin' about a dump like this starin' at some tourist lady's tits. I swear to goddam Christ I'm tempted to take those eyes out of your head and cut that tattoo off your arm. (*Pause.*) Now I wanna see you ride the range. You just start ridin' the range around this room till I tell you to stop.

This theatrical diction is normally harmonious with Medoff's structural configurations. The plays are typically derived from the well-made play although he will frequently jumble the sequence of the scenes, as in *The Wager* and *The Kramer*, to reflect the cinema-oriented modes of contemporary writing. His most effective work to date, *Red Ryder*, abandons the self-consciousness of that fragmented structure and opts for the tension-building structure of a direct, sequential narrative.

In most of his plays Medoff explores two inter-locking themes. The first is the plight of the disaffected alien. Usually that character, best typified by Teddy in *Red Ryder*, is young, given to philosophizing ("you make me just as sick as the rest of us do"), and dissatisfied with himself and his world. There is a continual lament for the imagined glories of by-gone days. The very use of the comic strip hero of the old west, Red Ryder, as a pervasive image for the play reveals Medoff's concern for this theme. It is made even denser by his continual introduction of yesteryear's heroes (John Kennedy, Duke Snider) into the dialogue. The second theme is the individual's quest for power which takes either a sexual form, as explored in the one-act *The Ultimate Grammar of Life*, or an intellectual form, as revealed in the manipulative game-playing of the pivotal character Leeds in *The Wager*.

In *Red Ryder*, the two quests for power merge to create Teddy, a character disturbing to audiences and critics alike because he seems, initially, to act gratuitously. The terror he perpetrates on the undeserving people at the roadside diner is motivated out of his own self-loathing and his disgust with the world. This is a perverse drive, yet it strikes close to our sensibilities because we find a note of truth about ourselves in it. Teddy wants all his captives to recognize the "truth" about themselves and, like Hickey in *The Iceman Cometh*, he expects that to bring enlightenment. But the final moment of the play brings a childishly romantic resolution – Stephen Ryder's departure from the diner, his first step towards realizing his dreams – instead of the truly moving defeat of O'Neill's denizens of Harry Hope's bar. That romantic indulgence conflicts with the realistic cynicism that has dominated the play to that point, and while it may bring temporal gratification to the audience, it makes the play an imperfect expression of Medoff's perception of contemporary life and values. In a world in which the gun is an ambiance, heroic quests seem incongruous. Indeed, the gun which is so prominent in *Red Ryder* disappears down the road with Teddy. Perhaps it will strike again (at us?). But for Medoff to resolve his play by facile removal of the catalysts is to subvert his image, his narrative, and his vision.

The gun has been present, but when it fires it only wounds. It does not resolve the action, not does it clarify the situation of the play's world. It functions dishonestly as symbol, and self-consciously as a theatrical device. The question of its place in Medoff's writing remains unanswered, although one is tempted to reflect that no symbol that is so crammed with the ammunition of significance can hope to fire accurately.

—Thomas B. Markus

MELFI, Leonard. American. Born in Binghamton, New York, 21 February 1935. Educated at Binghamton Central High School; St. Bonaventure University, New York. Worked as a waiter and a carpenter. Recipient: Eugene O'Neill Memorial Theatre Foundation Award, 1966; Rockefeller grant, 1966, 1967. Agent: Helen Harvey, Harvey and Hutto Inc., 110 West 57th Street, New York, New York 10019, U.S.A.

PUBLICATIONS

Plays

Lazy Baby Susan (produced New York, 1965).

Sunglasses (produced New York, 1965).

Pussies and Rookies (produced New York, 1965).

Ferryboat (produced New York, 1965).   Included in Encounters, 1967.

Birdbath (produced New York, 1965; Edinburgh, 1967; London, 1969).   Included in Encounters, 1967; in A Methuen Playscript, London, Methuen, 1968.

Times Square (produced New York, 1966; Edinburgh and London, 1967).   Included in Encounters, 1967.

Niagara Falls (produced New York, 1966; revised version, produced Los Angeles, 1968; London, 1976).   Published in New Theatre for Now (New Theatre in America, Volume 2), edited by Edward Parone, New York, Dell, 1971.

Lunchtime (produced New York, 1966; London, 1969).   Included in Encounters, 1967.

Halloween (produced New York, 1967; London, 1969).   Included in Encounters, 1967.

The Shirt (produced New York, 1967).   Included in Encounters, 1967.

Encounters: 6 One-Act Plays (includes Birdbath, Lunchtime, Halloween, Ferryboat, The Shirt, Times Square).   New York, Random House, 1967.

Disfiguration (produced Los Angeles, 1967).

Night (produced New York, 1968).   Published in Morning, Noon and Night, New York, Random House, 1969.

Stars and Stripes, in Collision Course (produced New York, 1968).   New York, Random House, 1968.

Stimulation (produced New York, 1968; London, 1969).

Jack and Jill (produced New York, 1968; revised version, produced as part of Oh! Calcutta!, New York, 1969; London, 1970).   New York, Grove Press, 1969.

The Breech Baby (produced New York, 1968).

Having Fun in the Bathroom (produced New York, 1969).

The Raven Rock (produced New York, 1969).

Wet and Dry, and Alive (produced New York, 1969).

The Jones Man (produced Provincetown, Massachusetts, 1969).

Cinque (produced London, 1970; New York, 1971).   Published in Spontaneous Combustion: Eight New American Plays, edited by Rochelle Owens, New York, Winter House, 1972.

Ah! Wine! (produced New York, 1974).

Beautiful! (produced New York, 1974).

Horse Opera, music by John Braden (produced New York, 1974).

Sweet Suite (produced New York, 1975).

Porno Stars at Home (produced New York, 1976).

Taffy's Taxi (produced New York, 1976).

Eddie and Susanna in Love (produced New York, 1976).

Screenplay: Mortadella, 1971.

Televison Plays: Puck! Puck! Puck!, The Rainbow Rest, 1969–70; What a Life!, 1976.

Theatrical Activities:

Actor: Plays – Knute Gary in Beautiful!, New York, 1974; Room Service in Sweet Suite, New York, 1975. Film – Mortadella, 1971.

*   *   *

"I always wanted to be on Broadway," Leonard Melfi confessed to an interviewer at the time his one-act contribution to *Morning, Noon and Night* was being prepared for its Broadway opening in October of 1968. That was an unlikely admission from the most prolific of the off-off-Broadway playwrights whose first produced play, *Lazy Baby Susan*, was done at the Cafe La Mama in 1965, who had had five plays presented at the Theatre Genesis in 1966 and who that same year had been selected as Outstanding New Playwright of the Year by the Eugene O'Neilll Memorial Theatre Foundation. Between 1965 and 1971 Melfi had productions of seventeen one-act plays, two TV dramas, and two productions of his only full-length play, *Niagara Falls*. He had nine plays published and was also discovered by the Italian film community and engaged to write screenplays of his fantastical *Times Square* (for Antonioni as a vehicle for Monica Vitti), his realistic *Birdbath* (Carlo Ponti), and an original screenplay, *Mortadella* (Ponti again, as a vehicle for Sophia Loren). Despite this apparent success, Melfi's only Broadway credit is the one act *Night*, his only critical success the realistic one-act *Birdbath*, and the early promise suggested by the O'Neill accolade remains unfulfilled. In 1970 the Cafe La Mama produced his one-act *Cinque* during its European tour; the play was not done in America until the spring of 1971. This suggests a career which is something less than meteoric and an artistic growth which is far less than visible.

Melfi's plays fall into two disparate forms: realistic dialogues which are best described as *Encounters*, the title given the 1967 published volume of his six best regarded works; and post-surrealist fantasies which reflect a strong influence from his fellow writers at the Cafe La Mama, particularly Sam Shepard. Of the former group, the most successful is unquestionably *Birdbath*. The play, which was transferred successfully to TV (for N.E.T., starring Patty Duke and James Farentino), is the encounter of a young writer and a teenage girl with a fantastical story about the murder of her mother which proves to be true in an exciting and surprising ending. The play's strengths, and Melfi's trademarks, are the simplicity of situation and environment and the vitality of the monologues which seem to be the essential moments of the play – each character has an aria. These aspects of dramaturgy are perhaps the result of conceiving plays for production in a cafe theatre context, where minimal settings and small casts are imperative considerations. It also explains why the play(s) would convert readily to the TV or film media – the close-up is the common bond between these media and the off-off-Broadway writing style reflected in Melfi's work. The sentimentality and gosh-American tone of Melfi's realistic plays was described by critic Jerry Tallmer as "an old-fashioned romantic philosophy...sex should be good and true."

Niagara Falls, Melfi's full-length script, is a clumsily well-made drama in the *Hotel Universe* tradition. It is set in a motel garden overlooking the falls on the day the American side is turned off – and the play's symbols are all as ponderous as this central one. *Niagara Falls* contains some gratuitous sex, a concluding episode of irrelevant violence, and has not even brevity to commend it. It was performed first in three acts in New York and then in two acts in Los Angeles and was published in the latter version. No amount of re-writing, however, could compensate for the banality of the situation and thesis, the poverty of the language and the incredible characters. The play seems a one-act idea which cannot support greater length.

Melfi's fantastic playlets seem derivative from the works of other writers whose impulse in this mode is more immediate. *Cinque* has a setting in the American west which is reminiscent of Shepard's *Cowboys* or *Operation Sidewinder*, and *Horse Opera* does not seem to have a matured use for that setting. *Times Square* is without the searing images found in the works of van Itallie or Adrienne Kennedy. Melfi writes in this mode almost as if he felt he were supposed to.

His most recent works show a fusing of his two earlier styles into inconsequential and frequently short pieces which use music to support their stage life. Many of the plays (*Ah! Wine!*, *Horse Opera*, and *Sweet Suite*) are stylistically "pop art" (some five years after the fad has waned) and have been described by reviewers as "crayon doodling" and "comic strip." None of the plays has enjoyed commercial production and (more significantly) none appears to have been influential in the avant-garde circles of off-off-Broadway.

Melfi appears to be a minor writer who was catapulted into the public's eye as a fragment of that explosion of "new theatre" in the mid-1960's. He has had wonderful opportunities to grow into a writer of significance, but perhaps old-line critic Stanley Kauffmann best saw his work in perspective when he wrote in a review of an early off-Broadway offering called *Six from La Mama*, "one expects work that is more adventurous in concept and method."

—Thomas B. Markus

MERCER, David. British. Born in Wakefield, Yorkshire, 27 June 1928. Educated at King's College, Newcastle upon Tyne, B.A. (honours) in fine art (Durham University) 1953. Served as laboratory technician in the Royal Navy, 1945–48. Divorced; has one child. Worked as a laboratory technician, 1942–45; Supply Teacher, 1955–59; Teacher Barrett Street Technical College, 1959–61. Full-time Writer since 1962. Recipient: Writer's Guild Award for television play, 1962, 1967, 1968; *Evening Standard* award, 1965; British Film Academy Award, 1966. Agent: Margaret Ramsay Ltd., 14a Goodwin's Court, London WC2N 4LL. Address: 37 Hamilton Gardens, London N.W.8, England.

PUBLICATIONS

Plays

> *The Governor's Lady* (broadcast, 1960; produced London, 1965).   London, Methuen,
>   1968; in *Best Short Plays of the World Theatre 1958–1967*, edited by Stanley
>   Richards, New York, Crown, 1968.
> *The Buried Man* (produced Manchester, 1962).
> *The Generations: Three Television Plays* (includes *Where the Difference Begins, A
>   Climate of Fear, The Birth of a Private Man*).   London, John Calder, and New York,
>   Fernhill, 1964.
> *Ride a Cock Horse* (produced Nottingham and London, 1965).   London, Calder and
>   Boyars, and New York, Hill and Wang, 1966.
> *Belcher's Luck* (produced London, 1966).   London, Calder and Boyars, and New
>   York, Hill and Wang, 1967.
> *Three TV Comedies* (includes *A Suitable Case for Treatment, For Tea on Sunday, And
>   Did Those Feet*).   London, Calder and Boyars, 1966.
> *In Two Minds* (televised, 1967; produced London, 1973).   Included in *The Parachute
>   with Two More TV Plays*, 1967.
> *The Parachute with Two More TV Plays: Let's Murder Vivaldi, In Two Minds*.
>   London, Calder and Boyars, 1967.
> *Let's Murder Vivaldi* (televised, 1968; produced London, 1972).   Included in *The
>   Parachute with Two More TV Plays*, 1967; in *The Best Short Plays 1974*, edited by
>   Stanley Richards, Radnor, Pennsylvania, Chilton, 1974.
> *On the Eve of Publication and Other Plays* (television plays: includes *The Cellar and the
>   Almond Tree* and *Emma's Time*).   London, Methuen, 1970; *On the Eve of
>   Publication* published in *Scripts 8* (New York), June 1972.
> *White Poem* (produced London, 1970).
> *Flint* (produced Oxford and London, 1970; Buffalo, New York, 1974).   London,
>   Methuen, 1970.

After Haggerty (produced London, 1970).   London, Methuen, 1970.

Blood on the Table (produced London, 1971).

Duck Song (produced London, 1974).   London, Eyre Methuen, 1974.

The Bankrupt and Other Plays (includes *You and Me and Him, An Afternoon at the Festival, Find Me*).   London, Eyre Methuen, 1974.

Screenplays: *Morgan! A Suitable Case for Treatment*, 1965; *Ninety Degrees in the Shade* (English dialogue), 1965; *Family Life*, 1970.

Radio Plays: *The Governor's Lady*, 1960; *Folie à Deux*, 1974.

Television Plays: *Where the Difference Begins*, 1961; *A Climate of Fear*, 1962; *A Suitable Case for Treatment*, 1962; *The Birth of a Private Man*, 1963; *For Tea on Sunday*, 1963; *The Buried Man*, 1963; *A Way of Living*, 1963; *And Did Those Feet*, 1965; *In Two Minds*, 1967; *Let's Murder Vivaldi*, 1968; *The Parachute*, 1968; *On the Eve of Publication*, 1968; *The Cellar and the Almond Tree*, 1970; *Emma's Time*, 1970; *The Bankrupt*, 1972; *You and Me and Him*, 1973; *An Afternoon at the Festival*, 1973; *Barbara of the House of Grebe*, from a story by Hardy, 1973; *Find Me*, 1974; *The Arcata Promise*, 1974; *Huggy Bear*, 1976.

Short Story

The Long Crawl Through Time, in *New Writers 3*.   London, John Calder, 1965.

Bibliography: *The Quality of Mercer: Bibliography of Writings by and about the Playwright David Mercer*, edited by Francis Jarman, Brighton, Smoothie Publications, 1974.

Critical Study: *The Second Wave* by John Russell Taylor, London, Methuen, 1971.

*   *   *

David Mercer is a prolific writer who established himself first as a television playwright and then as a dramatist of considerable power and originality. Best known in his television work for two trilogies – *The Generations* (*Where the Difference Begins, A Climate of Fear, The Birth of a Private Man*), and *On The Eve of Publication* (*On the Eve of Publication, The Cellar and the Almond Treet, Emma's Time*) – Mercer brought to his early plays not merely a serious political consciousness but a conviction that television could sustain plays which confronted social issues in an articulate and compelling way. At first he largely conformed to the naturalistic style which television in the early and middle sixties seemed to encourage, the style, indeed, of early Wesker and Osborne. But as he came to realize the flexibility of the medium and in particular its power to evoke fantasy and dream, to jump backwards in time, to reveal the internal tensions and wanderings of the mind, his stress began to change from the realistic portrayal of class conflict to a stylistically complex examination of the anguished mind. This movement was prefigured in an early television play subsequently made into a film (*A Suitable Case for Treatment*) and his first stage play (*The Governor's Lady*). Although he has always been concerned with projecting the human dimension of social problems, his central concern became the plight of the individual out of tune with his times, and pitting his personality against a social and metaphysical reality too complex or simply too opaque to understand. Thus, despite the political element which has continued to play an important, if subdued, role in his work, his real heroes are not the politically committed. The real heroes are men like Morgan (*A Suitable Case*) and the eponymous hero of *Flint*, men to whom "life became baffling as soon as it became comprehensible" but who impose their own idiosyncratic personalities on the world around them, striking out, albeit for the most part ineffectually, at those who wish to contain their energy and anarchism. As

Morgan says, "violence has a kind of dignity in a baffled man." The response of such men is to stamp their identities on life as Morgan imprints his personal cipher on everything from his mother-in-law's sheets to, in the film version, the flower bed of a mental institution. And though society conspires to extinguish such anarchic spirits their cheerful disregard for authority in any form leaves their personal rebellions intact and their irreverence a possible strategy for those similarly baffled by a world apparently eager to submit to the demands of competing ideologies and to embrace the ready to wear identities designed to subvert individuality.

Mercer wishes to release the individual not only from degrading labour, from serving the interests of a class which rules by virtue of its inhumanity no less than its wealth, but from a slavish acceptance of any mode of thought, way of life or organisational principle which will limit the real expression of his individuality. The difficulty, in his early work, lies in the fact that he feels instinctively that the individual should express something more substantial than a simple selfhood. A generation before, the issues had been clear enough but now the choice seems to lie between the mindless repression of Eastern Europe and the equally mindless trivialities of Western society. In his early plays, and particularly in his first television trilogy, he is still looking for some cause to which he can legitimately commit his characters. In his second play it is the campaign for nuclear disarmament and in his third the difficulty of re-establishing the integrity of communism. Yet he is not unaware that commitment may signify the evasion of self; that a public life may conceal a private anguish.

The flash-back in Mercer's work becomes something more than a stylistic mannerism. The past has an irrevocable hold on the present, defining identity, shaping experience and holding a sibyline clue to the central question which haunts all his work – the nature of the connection between private and public worlds. The need for commitment of some kind is expressed in most of his plays but a failure to understand the nature of that commitment or the relationship between it and the vital pressures of their inner lives leaves some of his protagonists mentally unhinged, like Morgan in *A Suitable Case*, Peter in *Ride a Cock Horse* or Anthony in *For Tea on Sunday*; suicidal, like Colin in *The Birth of a Private Man*; or simply asking plaintively, with Robert Kelvin in *On the Eve of Publication*, "Where am I going. Where?" Like Mercer many of his protagonists are the middle class offspring of working class parents – a situation which neatly unites social and psychological tensions. And this mixture has characterised Mercer's work as, in laying private ghosts, he has come close to expressing the essential dilemma of a generation which, like a character in his first play, *Where the Difference Begins*, woke up suddenly to find itself materially better off but with nothing more to do than shout "Where do we go from here? where do we go when the cities aren't fit to live in, when we have everything to live with and nothing to live for?"

Confronted with this situation Mercer has increasingly come to feel that the prime responsibility is to defend one's individuality against what his most splendidly individualistic hero, Flint, quoting from Ephesians, calls "principalities, against powers, against the rulers of the darkness of this world, against spiritual wickedness in high places." And this list can be taken to include not merely the capitalist system, but fascism, Stalinism, a schematic Freudianism, nuclear zeal and, finally, anyone who wishes to control and subdue the irrational, the emotional and the vital in man. Hence his heroes tend to take their pleasures where they may with scarcely a hint of the guilt which would be an expression of their conformity to social and moral dogma. And by the same token he is drawn to the deranged because, as he has explained, "the 'lunatic'...is the man who, almost by definition, escapes from categories." Morgan and Flint both pitch their anarchic vitality against a disciplined but ultimately sterile society.

What Mercer says of the artist applies equally well to his conception of individuality which can animate his vision of a new life – an individuality built on the spontaneous vitality of human responses rather than the anguished self-abnegation of political commitment. "He's got to be everything he's capable of being and that involves violence and brutality and outrage and despair and all kinds of things. Otherwise you're trapped in a kind of conceptual structuring of the world that makes experience." His description of himself as a communist without a party expresses his simultaneous belief in the need for a social system which could transcend the ethics of the market place and suspicion of a political organisation which has crushed the individual in the name of the very principles which it has abrogated most consistently. If this is a paradox which has haunted a generation of intellectuals, if this tension lies behind the work of a number of important post-war European writers, this serves to explain both his own sense that he was trying to work within an identifiable European tradition and also the importance which has been conceded to Mercer as a playwright both on television and the stage. His belief that "the only possible revolution is the individual revolution; any expression of individuality, however small, is a revolutionary gesture" is a long way removed from the Marxist convictions with which he started as a writer but brings him in one respect at least very close to the work of Pinter or Orton or even the Wesker of *The Old Ones*. Yet he is not unaware that individualism may bring us to the very verge of solipsism. In *On the Eve of Publication* we are shown a man who has seen his early beliefs undermined and destroyed and who is left with no resource beyond his own faltering mind. Despite the splendid inventiveness of his imagination he is a weak man. And the self-centredness which blinds him to the real value of those who surround him leaves him no real consolation for his own massive sense of failure as a man. The individual, in other words, needs a connection with other people, and the nature of that connection is the reason for political faiths and the link between the two parts of Mercer's world.

If the possibility of sustaining such a connection seems more remote in his most recent work, as the oppressive weight of modern existence threatens the collapse of personal vision (*An Afternoon at the Festival*) and even of social reality itself (*The Bankrupt; Duck Song*), for the most part there still remain the human gesture, the moment of hope, to redeem betrayal and despair.

Mercer's weaknesses are perhaps inevitable consequences of his virtues. His faith in language is sometimes sustained at the cost of dramatic invention (one stage direction simply reads, "as much lively stage business as possible") and at the risk of a wit which while agile and astringent is not always entirely appropriate. Dialogue is apt to become an exchange of aphorisms, as it does in *Ride a Cock Horse* and *Let's Murder Vivaldi*, or a mannered set-piece, as in *On the Eve of Publication* or *After Haggerty*. Words have a tendency to get out of control, as they do on occasion with Orton and Stoppard, while there is a constant temptation to devolve into interior monologue. Yet, the other side of this coin reveals an articulate writer with a clear sense of the potential and limitations of language and of the theatre itself. If the humour of *Ride a Cock Horse* is contrived and too obviously derivative of Albee and Osborne, that of *A Suitable Case* and *Flint* is the authentic voice of a writer with a clear conception of the ineluctable relationship between style and content. Though some of his stylistic experiments have not been particularly successful (*And Did Those Feet, Belcher's Luck*) his determination to experiment both in subject and form makes him one of the more interesting of contemporary dramatists. If, at times, one prays that he would dispense with what are in danger of becoming his stock characters – the illiterate and ageing ex-train driver father, the politically connected but confused writer who anguishes over each display of European revolution and counter revolution – there is no denying the skill with which he constructs his parables of public and private pain nor the compelling quality of dialogue which, if undisciplined, is articulate and moving.

—C. W. E. Bigsby

MILLAR, Ronald.   British.   Born in Reading, Berkshire, 12 November 1919. Educated at Charterhouse School, Surrey; King's College, Cambridge. Agent: Herbert de Leon Ltd., 13 Bruton Street, London W.1. Address: 7 Sheffield Terrace, London W.8, England.

PUBLICATIONS

Plays

Murder from Memory (produced London, 1942).

Zero Hour (produced London, 1944).

The Other Side, adaptation of the novel by Storm Jameson (produced London, 1946).

Frieda (produced London, 1946).   London, English Theatre Guild, 1947.

Champagne for Delilah (produced London, 1949).

Waiting for Gillian, adaptation of the novel *A Way Through the Wood* by Nigel Balchin (produced London, 1954).   London, French, 1955.

The Bride and the Bachelor (produced London, 1956).   London, French, 1958.

A Ticklish Business (produced Brighton, 1958; as *The Big Tickle*, produced London, 1958).   London, French, 1959.

The More the Merrier (produced London, 1960).   London, French, 1960.

The Bride Comes Back (produced London, 1960).   London, French, 1961.

The Affair, adaptation of the novel by C. P. Snow (produced London, 1961; Washington, D.C., 1964).   London, French, and New York, Scribner, 1962.

The New Men, adaptation of the novel by C. P. Snow (produced London, 1962). Included in *The Affair, The New Men, The Masters*, 1964.

The Masters, adaptation of the novel by C. P. Snow (produced London, 1963). Included in *The Affair, The New Men, The Masters*, 1964.

The Affair, The New Men, The Masters: Three Plays Based on the Novels and with a Preface by C. P. Snow.   London, Macmillan, 1964.

Robert and Elizabeth, music by Ron Grainer, lyrics by Ronald Millar, adaptation of the play *The Barretts of Wimpole Street* by Rudolph Besier (produced London, 1964). London, French, 1967.

On the Level, music by Ron Grainer (produced London, 1966).

Number 10, adaptation of the novel by William Clark (produced Glasgow and London, 1967).   London, Heinemann, 1967.

They Don't Grown on Trees (produced London, 1968).   London, French, 1969.

Abelard and Heloise, based on *Peter Abelard* by Helen Waddell (produced Exeter and London, 1970; New York, 1971).   London and New York, French, 1970.

Parents' Day, adaptation of the novel by Edward Candy (produced London, 1972).

Odd Girl Out, adaptation of the novel by Elizabeth Jane Howard (produced Harlow, Essex, 1973).

The Case in Question, adaptation of the novel *In Their Wisdom* by C. P. Snow (produced London, 1975).   London, French, 1976.

Screenplays: *Frieda*, 1947; *So Evil My Love*, 1948; *The Miniver Story*, 1950; *The Unknown Man*, 1950; *Scaramouche*, 1951; *Train of Events*, 1952; *Never Let Me Go*, 1953; *Rose Marie*, 1954; *Betrayed*, 1954.

Theatrical Activities:

Actor: **Plays** – in *Swinging the Gate* (revue), London, 1940; Prince Anatole Kuragin in *War and Peace* by David Lucas, London, 1943; Cully in *Mr. Bolfry* by James Bridie, London, 1943; David Marsden in *Murder for a Valentine* by Vernon Sylvaine, London, 1944; Flight Lieutenant Chris Keppel in *Zero Hour*, London, 1944; Penry Bowen in *Jenny Jones* by Ronald Gow, London, 1944; Colin Tabret in *The Sacred Flame* by W. Somerset Maugham, London, 1945; Smith in *Murder on the Nile* by Agatha Christie, London, 1946. **Films** – *The Life and Death of Colonel Blimp*, 1943; *Beware of Pity*, 1945.

*   *   *

Ronald Millar was born at Reading in 1919. When he was a small boy his mother, an actress, wishing him to be protected from the glamorous uncertainties of stage life, sent him to a good preparatory school to receive a classical education. At the end of his time there he sat for scholarships at several of the great public schools. He was offered one at Harrow, but refused it on the advice of his headmaster, who had his eye on Winchester. At the Winchester examination, however, he happened to be out of sorts and narrowly missed an award; but he did gain one at Charterhouse.

From his mother's point of view this was an unhappy accident; for at that time Charterhouse, of all the great public schools, had the closest connection with the theatre and the largest number of old boys who were actors. And from there young Ronald went on to King's, which of all the colleges in Cambridge had the strongest theatrical tradition.

The outcome was fairly predictable. Ronald Millar joined various University acting clubs, showed talent, gained experience – incidentally, he was given the leading part in the triennial Greek play which is traditionally a great dramatic event at Cambridge – and was inevitably attracted to the professional stage. Then outbreak of the 1939 war and service in the Royal Navy delayed his final decision; but by the time he was invalided out of the Service he had made up his mind. He did not return to Cambridge to take his degree, but turned actor at once.

However, the years spent with the classics were not wasted. There are many worse forms of training for a writer, and Millar's ambition to be a dramatist was at least as strong as his desire to act, and was to prove much more lasting. His second play, *Zero Hour*, was produced at the Lyric in June, 1944, with himself in the cast, and his third, *Frieda* (about a girl escaped from Nazi Germany) at the Westminster in 1946. This had a fair success on the stage and a bigger one as a film.

In 1949 he suffered a deep disappointment. Returning to England after an interlude spent writing film-scripts in Hollywood, he brought with him a light comedy, *Champagne for Delilah*, which was instantly accepted for West End production. To all the experts who handled it, it seemed certain to have a huge success, and it was received with acclaim on its prior-to-London tour. But on arrival at the New Theatre it proved a dead failure, and nobody has ever been able to suggest why. Seven years later, however, the author must have felt compensated by an ironic twist of fate when another play, *The Bride and the Bachelor*, ran for more than 500 performances after having been given a hostile reception by nearly all the critics. Later still, in 1960, a sequel to this piece, *The Bride Comes Back*, also ran very well.

By this time, Millar had enough successful work to his credit to prove that one of his outstanding qualities was his versatility. From the seriousness of *Frieda* to the frivolity of the two "Bride" plays was a far step and a vivid contrast in styles; and he now proceeded to demonstrate further uses to which his versatility might be put.

The year 1961 saw the beginning of a whole series of plays made by him from novels or other literary sources, the first of them being a stage version of C. P. Snow's story of college life at Cambridge, *The Affair*. As a Cambridge man himself, Millar was familiar with the atmosphere so truthfully rendered by the book, and, given a free hand, matched that atmosphere quite perfectly. Then came a set-back. Manager after manager refused to believe that a play so local in its application could interest the general public. At last Henry Sherek, who had been Millar's backer for *Frieda* and *Champagne for Delilah*, accepted the risk, and was rewarded with critical favour and a year's run.

A second play from a Snow novel, *The New Men*, followed in 1962 and had no success; but a second Cambridge piece, *The Masters*, was staged in 1963 and ran even longer than *The Affair* had done, and in 1975 yet another, *The Case in Question*, ran very well.

The particular talent which carries Millar to his notable successes in this field is an ability to turn a novelist's narrative prose into dialogue without losing his personal flavour, added to which is an ability where necessary to write in scenes of his own invention in a style to fit in with the rest.

This was perhaps not a specially difficult task in the case of the two Cambridge plays, where novelist and adapter had in common a detailed knowledge of and feeling for the atmosphere they wished to convey; but it became a problem of much delicacy in the case of Millar's next, and much more serious play, *Abelard and Heloise*. The main materials for this play were Helen Waddell's book about Peter Abelard and the famous letters, and the task was to find an idiom which would convey both these elements. This was done with such skill that the play drew not only the more serious playgoers but also the general public. Produced in May 1970, it ran into 1972.

One other proof of Millar's versatility may be added. In 1964 he wrote both the "book" and the lyrics for *Robert and Elizabeth*, the musical version of *The Barretts of Wimpole Street*, which ran for two years and a half.

—W. A. Darlington

MILLER, Arthur.   American.   Born in Manhattan, New York, 17 October 1915. Educated at the University of Michigan, Ann Arbor (Hopwood Award, 1936, 1937), 1934–38, A.B. 1938. Married Mary Slattery in 1940 (divorced, 1956); the actress Marilyn Monroe, 1956 (divorced, 1961); Ingeborg Morath, 1962; has three children. Member of the Federal Theatre Project, 1938. Writer for CBS and NBC Radio Workshops. International President, P.E.N., London and New York, 1965–69. Recipient: Theatre Guild Award, 1938; New York Drama Critics Circle Award, 1947, 1949; Tony Award, 1947, 1949, 1953; Pulitzer Prize, 1949; National Association of Independent Schools Award, 1954; American Academy of Arts and Letters Gold Medal, 1959; Brandeis University Creative Arts Award, 1969. D.H.L.: University of Michigan, 1956. Member, American Academy of Arts and Letters, 1971. Agent: International Creative Management, 40 West 57th Street, New York, New York 10019, U.S.A.

PUBLICATIONS

Plays

Honors at Dawn (produced Ann Arbor, Michigan, 1936).
No Villains (They Too Arise) (produced Ann Arbor, Michigan, 1937).
The Pussycat and the Expert Plumber Who Was a Man, in *100 Non-Royalty Radio Plays*, edited by William Kozlenko.   New York, Greenberg, 1941.
William Ireland's Confession, in *100 Non-Royalty Radio Plays*, edited by William Kozlenko.   New York, Greenberg, 1941.
The Man Who Had All the Luck (produced New York, 1944).   Published in *Cross-Section 1944*, edited by Edwin Seaver, New York, Fischer, 1944.
That They May Win (produced New York, 1944).   Published in *Best One-Act Plays of 1944*, edited by Margaret Mayorga, New York, Dodd Mead, 1945.
Grandpa and the Statue, in *Radio Drama in Action*, edited by Erik Barnouw.   New York, Farrar and Rinehart, 1945.
The Story of Gus, in *Radio's Best Plays*, edited by Joseph Liss.   New York, Greenberg, 1947.
The Guardsman, radio adaptation of a play by Ferenc Molnar, in *Theatre Guild on the Air*, edited by H. William Fitelson.   New York, Rinehart, 1947.
Three Men on a Horse, radio adaptation of the play by George Abbott and John Cecil

Holm, in *Theatre Guild on the Air*, edited by H. William Fitelson.   New York, Rinehart, 1947.

All My Sons (produced New York, 1947; London, 1948).   New York, Reynal and Hitchcock, 1947; in *Collected Plays*, 1957.

Death of a Salesman: Certain Private Conversations in Two Acts and a Requiem (produced New York and London, 1949).   New York, Viking Press, and London, Cresset Press, 1949.

An Enemy of the People, adaptation of a play by Ibsen (produced New York, 1950; Lincoln, 1958).   New York, Viking Press, 1951; London, Macmillan, 1960.

The Crucible (produced New York, 1953; Bristol, 1954; London, 1956).   New York, Viking Press, 1953; London, Cresset Press, 1956.

A View from the Bridge, and A Memory of Two Mondays: Two One-Act Plays (produced New York, 1955).   New York, Viking Press, 1955; revised version of *A View from the Bridge* (produced London, 1956), London, Cresset Press, 1956.

Collected Plays (includes *All My Sons, Death of a Salesman, The Crucible, A Memory of Two Mondays, A View from the Bridge*).   New York, Viking Press, 1957; London, Cresset Press, 1958.

After the Fall (produced New York, 1964; Coventry, 1967).   New York, Viking Press, 1964; London, Secker and Warburg, 1965.

Incident at Vichy (produced New York, 1964; London, 1966).   New York, Viking Press, 1965; London, Secker and Warburg, 1966.

The Price (produced New York, 1968; also director: produced London, 1969).   New York, Viking Press, and London, Secker and Warburg, 1968.

Fame, and The Reason Why (produced New York, 1970).   *Fame* published in *Yale Literary Magazine* (New Haven, Connecticut), March 1971.

The Creation of the World and Other Business (produced New York, 1972; Edinburgh, 1974).   New York, Viking Press, 1973.

Up from Paradise (produced Ann Arbor, Michigan, 1974).

The Archbishop's Ceiling (produced New Haven, Connecticut, 1976).

Screenplays: *Story of G.I. Joe*, with others, 1945; *The Misfits*, 1961.

Radio Plays: *The Pussycat and the Expert Plumber Who Was a Man, William Ireland's Confession, Grandpa and the Statue*, and *The Story of Gus*, in early 1940's.

Novels

Focus.   New York, Reynal and Hitchcock, 1945; London, Gollancz, 1949.

The Misfits (screenplay in novel form).   New York, Viking Press, and London, Secker and Warburg, 1961.

Short Stories

I Don't Need You Anymore: Stories.   New York, Viking Press, and London, Secker and Warburg, 1967.

Other

Situation Normal.   New York, Reynal and Hitchcock, 1944.

Jane's Blanket (juvenile).   New York, Crowell Collier, and London, Collier Macmillan, 1963.

In Russia, with Inge Morath.   New York, Studio Publications, and London, Secker and Warburg, 1969.

The Portable Arthur Miller, edited by Harold Clurman. New York, Viking Press, 1971.
The Theatre Essays of Arthur Miller, edited by Robert Martin. New York, Viking Press, 1977.
In the Country, with Inge Morath. New York, Studio Publications, 1977.

Bibliography: "Arthur Miller: The Dimension of His Art: A Checklist of His Published Works" by Tetsumaro Hayashi, in *The Serif* (Kent, Ohio), June 1967.

Manuscript Collections: University of Texas, Austin; Library of Congress, Washington, D.C.

Critical Study: Introduction by Harold Clurman to *The Portable Arthur Miller*, 1971.

Theatrical Activities:

Director: **Play** – *The Price*, London, 1969.

Arthur Miller comments:

I have, I think, provided actors with some good things to do and say. Beyond that I cannot speak with any certainty. My plays seem to exist and that's enough for me. What people may find in them or fail to find is not in my control anymore; I can only that life has not been made less for what I've done, and possibly a bit more.

* * *

There are two different, yet related, patterns of concern in Arthur Miller's theatre. The first dominates the plays written through *A View from the Bridge* (1955), and the second emerged in *The Misfits* and is increasingly manifest in his last plays.

The central conflict in the plays of the first period grows out of a crisis of identity. The protagonist in these plays is suddenly confronted with a situation which he is incapable of meeting and which eventually puts his "name" in jeopardy. In the ensuing struggle it becomes clear that he does not know what his name really is, and, finally, his inability to answer the question "Who am I?" produces calamity and his downfall. Miller presents this crisis as a conflict between the uncomprehending self and a solid social or economic structure. The drama emerges either when the protagonist breaks his connection with society or when unexpected pressures reveal that such a connection has in fact never even existed. For Miller the need for such a connection is absolute and the failure to achieve and/ or maintain it is bound to result in catastrophe.

Thus, each of his early plays is a judgment of a man's failure to maintain a viable connection with this surrounding world because he does not know himself. The verdict is always guilty, because of Miller's belief that if each man faced up to the truth about himself he could be fulfilled as an individual and still live within the restrictions of society. But while Miller's judgments are absolute they are also complex. There is no question that he stands on the side of the community, but until the moment when justice may be served his sympathies are directed towards those ordinary little men who never discovered who they really were.

Miller's second period is concerned with the dramatic possibilities of otherness. Beginning with *The Misfits* we see that his protagonists are not so much concerned with themselves as they are with finding a way to relate to each other. Gay and Rosalyn move from two extremes of isolation until they meet and make a promise with full respect for the "otherness" of the other. The symbol of this promise is their decision to have a child. Only when they have learned that true freedom can only be found in relationship, do they discover that they have "touched the whole world." Then they can make the deepest of human promises: to have a child.

In each of Miller's last plays he has been primarily concerned with the implications of otherness, and such a concern inevitably leads him to come to grips with those conflicts which are inherent in the crisis of generativity. The identity crisis is a crisis of consciousness; the generativity crisis is one of conscience. Beginning with *After the Fall* (1964), his protagonist is someone who knows and accepts his identity and is conscious of his unique relationship to other people. Miller's early heroes struggled unsuccessfully to discover who they were. In his last plays, Miller is concerned with the effect his protagonists have had on others and their capacity to accept full responsibility for what they have or have not done.

After the Fall is a dramatic revelation of a man who has come to realize that each one of us has, indeed, been born after the fall of man and that, if we are to know ourselves, we must recognize and accept the fact that we not only share in the fall, we perpetuate it. Only when we become aware of other people as separate identities who exist in and for themselves, and not merely as extensions of our own needs and concerns, can we be capable of seeing how our deeds can and do affect them. With such awareness we come to recognize that we are responsible for what happens, not only to ourselves, but, insofar as we relate to others, to them as well. As the play ends Quentin meets Holga with the knowledge that he is a murderer – that he bears the mark of Cain. Significantly, the play ends with a beginning ("Hello"), just as *The Misfits* did. However, now there is a knowing. The big question we are left with at the end of the plays is "Is the knowing all?" His next two plays deal with this question.

In the climactic speech of *Incident at Vichy*, the Jewish psychiatrist Leduc says to Prince Von Berg:

> ...I have never analyzed a gentile who did not have, somewhere hidden in his mind, a dislike if not a hatred for the Jews.... Until you know it is true of you, you will destroy whatever truth can come of the atrocity. Part of knowing who we are is knowing we are not someone else. And Jew is only the name we give to that stranger, that agony we cannot feel, that death we look at like a cold abstration. Each man has his Jew; it is the other. And the Jews have their Jews. And now, now above all, you must see that you have yours – the man whose death leaves you relieved that you are not him, despite your decency. And that is why there is nothing and will be nothing – until you face your own complicity with this...your own humanity.

The major theme of the play is that responsibility is not just a question of personal relationships; it must also extend to the world. What was implied by the projection of the concentration camp in *After the Fall* becomes the subject of *Incident at Vichy*. The most significant realization of the theme occurs when Von Berg comes out of the Nazi office, having been cleared, and gives his pass (the means to freedom) to Leduc. The doctor is horrified by this. The real mark of Cain is that the murderer within us cannot stand the thought that someone else could and would give up his life for our sake. Such an act makes our guilt unbearable by destroying that balance of payments which we have created in an effort to justify our guilt. We cannot permit ourselves to be in someone's debt. There must always be a price. That is why there must also always be a Jew. The ending of *Incident at Vichy* reveals that otherness is an ambiguous reality. Without it there can be no promises, and hence no love; but its very existence calls forth the murderer which each of us carries within himself.

In *The Price* Miller explores this theme. The play is essentially the confrontation of two estranged brothers. As they face each other – and their past – each of them discovers that he represents a different aspect of the same dilemma: the structure of their lives is one in which all of the positive qualities of otherness have been excluded. They have touched neither each other nor the world because they were not brought up to believe in one another but to succeed. The play is about absence, and especially the absence of love.

The central *agon* between the brothers hinges on the assumption that "there is such a thing as moral debt." Each justified everything he had or had not done, as well as everything that has or has not happened to him in terms of this imperative. Here Miller challenges the whole idea of moral debt based on "price." For whenever people relate to each other in terms of the price to be paid, they will always get less than they bargained for; the price is never enough. Both the brothers have been wrong; in life there can be no question of success or failure, or I gave more than you. And this is the significance of Gregory Solomon, the used furniture dealer who has come to purchase the junk heap of their past.

Solomon's wisdom is that it is silly for them to worry about the price since it will always be fair. He is a wise man who has lived his life fully. He has learned that the murder/suicide in each of us can never adequately explain or justify what we have or have not done to others. We must accept our guilt knowing that it is just, but also with the full awareness that any attempt to seek revenge on others for the guilt for which we are responsible is to choose the road of nothingness. That is why otherness is such an ambiguous reality. Unless we can accept a person as another we can never really touch him, and without such contact we can never touch the world of all men. Yet since we can never really know another, he will always be the Jew, the stranger. Here is an absurd contradiction that the intellect can never resolve. To live in relationship is to make the Kierkegaardian leap. This is the meaning of Solomon's laughter as the curtain falls.

Miller described one of his characters as "a lover of things, of people, of sheer living...[one who] will not compromise for less than God's own share of the world." While Miller has no such promethean ambitions, he might well be describing himself. Certainly few playwrights write with such moral earnestness or have a greater sense of moral responsibility. The dominant tone of the theatre in the mid-twentieth century has been one of despair, but Miller continually demands more. He seeks "a theatre in which an adult who wants to live can find plays that will heighten his awareness of what living in our times involves."

—Robert W. Corrigan

MILLER, Jason. American. Born in Scranton, Pennsylvania, in 1932. Educated at St. Patrick's High School, Scranton; Scranton University; Catholic University, Washington, D.C. Married Linda Gleason in 1963; has three children. Stage and film actor. Recipient: New York Drama Critics Circle Award, 1972; Tony Award, 1973; Pulitzer Prize, 1973. Address: c/o Dramatists Play Service, 440 Park Avenue South, New York, New York 10016, U.S.A.

PUBLICATIONS

Plays

Three One-Act Plays (includes *Lou Gehrig Did Not Die of Cancer, Perfect Son, The Circus Lady*) (produced New York, 1970). *The Circus Lady* published in *The Best Short Plays 1973*, edited by Stanley Richards, Radnor, Pennsylvania, Chilton, 1973.

Nobody Hears a Broken Drum (produced New York, 1970).   New York, Dramatists
Play Service, 1971.

That Championship Season (produced New York, 1972; London, 1974).   New York,
Atheneum, and London, Davis Poynter, 1973.

Theatrical Activities:

Actor: **Plays** – Champlain Shakespeare Festival, Vermont; Cincinnati Shakespeare
Festival; New York Shakespeare Festival; Edmund in *Long Day's Journey into Night* by
O'Neill; Tom in *The Glass Menagerie* by Tennessee Williams; Pip in *Pequod* by Roy S.
Richardson, New York, 1969; Assistant in *The Happiness Cage* by Dennis J. Reardon,
New York, 1970; Rogoshin in *Subject to Fits* by Robert Montgomery, New York, 1971;
in *Juno and the Paycock* by O'Casey, Washington, D.C., 1971. **Films** – *The Exorcist*, 1972;
Nickle Ride; Home of Our Own. **Television** – *Fitzgerald in Hollywood*, 1975.

*   *   *

Jason Miller's *That Championship Season* is a solid, vibrant play. The solidity comes in
part from the familiar structure of the play – too familiar, at points – but Miller's freshness
of detail saves the evening.

The event that occasions the drama has been used a lot: It is a reunion, in this case of four
members of a champion high-school basketball team of twenty years ago. The fifth man on
stage is the now-retired coach who has taught them that winning is all that counts – in
basketball and in life. As Walter Kerr has pointed out, the set itself is familiar – limp lace
curtains and a steep staircase that recalls the conventional naturalism of William Inge's *The
Dark at the Top of the Stairs*.

In fact, the experienced play-goer knows within two minutes what the arc of things will
be: The men have come together to celebrate and live again their triumph, but before the
night is out it will be revealed how everything has gone rotten somehow. And so it turns
out. One of the players is now mayor of the small Pennsylvania town, and he is proud of it.
But underneath he is a loser – and indeed it is obvious he will be thrown out in the
forthcoming election.

Another team-mate has been his chief financial backer – a man made rich through strip-
mining that ecologists condemn. But now he sees the mayor will lose, so he wants to shift
his backing to another candidate.

A third player is now a school principal who wants to be superintendent. When the
mayor tells him that he can't back him because it will hurt his own candidacy, the
superintendent angrily blurts out that the strip-miner is sleeping with the mayor's wife, and
he says he'll tell the whole town if they don't support him. But he is a mediocrity; he knows
it, his own young son knows it, and everyone on stage knows it. The coach calls his bluff,
knowing he is even too much of a mediocrity to do something so substantial as tell the town
about the mayor's wife.

The fourth player is now an alcoholic but he nevertheless sees things more clearly than
the rest. It is he who brings up Martin. In basketball there are five players; Martin was the
fifth, and at first he is mourned as if dead. Ultimately it is revealed that he has simply gone
away, turning his back on the coach and his dogmas. It was Martin who, at the coach's
direction, broke the ribs of the "nigger" who was the star of the other team, and it's clear
that's the only reason our boys won.

The play uncovers the dark underside of that old triumph and the abject failure beneath
any gloss of current success. The coach is shown to be a bigot, a right-wing supporter of Joe
McCarthy, a champion of the ugly ethic that to win is to be good.

So the route of the play is familiar and so are the figures. But the figures are not cardboard
– Miller fills in their dimension with the rich detail of an orthodox novelist. And the play is
not without surprises. In particular it is verbally surprising. Lines are fresh and newly

honed. And the humor is painfully superb. Cautioning the mayor not to exploit the fact of his handicapped child, the alcoholic says, "You lose the mongoloid vote right there." And he denies he has a liquor problem: "I can get all I want."

Miller's limitation, at least in this play, is his conventionality, his predictability. But on the American scene recently almost all experimentation has been unrewarding, and other traditionalists have lost the vitality that Miller has found. It's a somber comment on American theatre that one of the most promising plays of the early 1970's could have been written in the early 1950's.

—Thomas J. McCormack

MILNER, Ron(ald).   American.   Born in Detroit, Michigan, 29 May 1938. Educated in Detroit public schools; Columbia University, New York. Writer-in-Residence, Lincoln University, Pennsylvania, 1966–67; taught at Michigan State University, East Lansing, 1971–72. Founding Director, Spirit of Shango theatre company, Detroit. Recipient: Rockefeller grant; John Hay Whitney fellowship. Address: c/o New American Library, Box 120, Bergenfeld, New Jersey 07621, U.S.A.

PUBLICATIONS

Plays

Who's Got His Own (produced New York, 1966).   Published in *Black Drama Anthology*, edited by Woodie King and Ron Milner, New York, New American Library, 1971.
The Monster, in *Drama Review* (New York), Summer 1968.
The Warning: A Theme for Linda (produced New York, 1969).   Published in *Black Quartet: Four New Black Plays*, New York, New American Library, 1970.
What the Wine Sellers Buy (produced Los Angeles, 1973; New York, 1974).   New York, French, 1974.

Other

Editor, with Woodie King, *Black Drama Anthology*.   New York, New American Library, 1971.

*   *   *

Ron Milner, a black American playwright, has written fiction and essays but is primarily distinguished as a dramatist in the Black Arts Theatre movement in America. Believing that significant art must be functional rather than merely entertaining or diverting, dramatists of Black Arts Theatre propose to educate Afro-Americans – particularly urban Afro-Americans – to awareness of their condition and needs. In a broad sense, one can distinguish two forms of Black Arts Theatre: 1) Theatre of Black Experience, in which the dramatist, creating realistic, multi-dimensional characters, examines but does not resolve problems of black life;

2) Black Revolutionary Theatre, in which the dramatist, using allegorical figures, adumbrates a solution to a problem of Afro-American existence. Ron Milner is identified with both varieties of Black Arts Theatre.

Milner's dramas can be typified by three: *The Monster, Who's Got His Own,* and *The Warning: A Theme for Linda. The Monster,* a one-act example of Black Revolutionary Theatre, presents a confrontation between Afro-American students and a Negro dean at a college. The students personify the new "black" spirit – pride in racial identity and determination to develop their own value system. The Dean personifies those Negroes who disguise themselves in the symbols of black identity but continue to worship the values of a white-oriented society while they sacrifice black people to their own quests for prestige, status, security, and acceptance by white society. Attempting to use the Dean as a spokesman for a good cause, the students administer a serum and teach him a speech which stresses the need of black people to think, feel, and work for their own race. As soon as he encounters two white instructors, however, the drug wears off and the Dean can remember only the cliché-ridden speeches in which he instructs black students to surrender their identity for the good of mankind. Convinced that he cannot be changed, the students hang him. In that moment of truth which supposedly precedes death, the Dean remembers the message which the students taught him.

Who's Got His Own, a three-act play first presented at the American Place Theatre in New York City, was the premiere production of Harlem's New Lafayette Theatre, which is a center for the production of Black Arts drama. *Who's Got His Own* focuses on an intrafamily confrontation on the day of the funeral of Tim Bronson, who smashed his car into a wall while returning from the factory where he had a job cleaning toilets. Having returned to the house which he left four years earlier, Tim Bronson, Jr., denounces the hypocrisy of publicly mourning a father who never attended the church from which he was buried, who brutally beat his wife and children, and who cringed and cowered from white people. When Tim Jr.'s mother and sister protest, he insists that, for once, they face the truth about themselves. He accuses his mother of submitting to Bronson, Sr., hiding herself blindly in her religion, and neglecting her children. To prove that the mother is living in a fantasy world, Tim insists that his sister Clara reveal the truth about herself.

Reluctantly, Clara tells how during the first year in college she met a white youth who impressed her with his education, his words of rebellion against bourgeois life, and his need for her strength and courage. Most of all, he impressed her because, being white, he seemed free from "that black thing" which makes Negro men, like her father, attack their wives. Disillusioned by her eventual realization that her white lover cannot rid himself of guilt about sexual relationships, she considered ending the affair but became pregnant. Taken to an abortionist and abandoned by her father who acted "insane" when he heard that a white youth was responsible, rejected by the white church which previously seemed the only true religion, shocked by the pain and blood of the abortion, she returned to her mother's home to hide from the world and men.

Leaving the house after he has forced Clara to tell her story, Tim Jr. returns later with the news that he has killed a white college classmate to whom he had previously turned for consolation. This time he saw only a white face he must destroy. His mother then reveals the truth about Tim's father. Having been forced as an eight-year-old to watch a mob torture, lynch, and castrate his father for beating a white man who attempted to rape his wife, Tim, Sr., tried to isolate himself from whites for fear that he would kill one. His attacks on his family were merely frustrated ventings of his effort to subdue his murderous hatred of whites. Discovering that Tim Jr.'s victim is not critically injured, Clara assures him that revelation of the truth about their weakness has united them as a family and has solved their problem. Tim is less certain; he knows only that he finally respects his father.

In *The Warning: A Theme for Linda,* a one-act play, Milner again concerned himself with the image of black manhood. In dreams, images of black men come to seventeen year old Linda: nostalgic dreams about the grandfather she idolizes, nightmares about the man who attempted to seduce her when she was a child, sexual fantasies about the strength and power of her boyfriend Donald, who plans to be a writer. Questioning her mother about the love

559

between man and wife, she is answered by her grandmother, who, assuring her that men are no good, destroys her illusion about her grandmother: Their youngest child died because the grandfather who was too intoxicated to administer the necessary medicine. Rejecting her grandmother's suggestion that Donald resembles Linda's grandfather, Linda insists that Donald consummate their relationship and that he prove himself to be a man strong enough for the strong woman she plans to be.

—Darwin T. Turner

MITCHELL, Adrian. British. Born in London, 24 October 1932. Educated at Dauntsey's School, Wiltshire; Christ Church, Oxford (Editor, *Isis* magazine, 1954–55), 1952–55. Served in the British Army, 1951–52. Reporter, *Oxford Mail*, 1955–57, and *Evening Standard*, London, 1957–59; Columnist and Reviewer, *Daily Mail, Woman's Mirror, The Sun, The Sunday Times, Peace News, The Black Dwarf*, and *The Guardian*, all in London. Instructor, University of Iowa, Iowa City, 1963–64; Granada Fellow in the Arts, University of Lancaster, 1967–69; Fellow, Wesleyan University Center for the Humanities, Middletown, Connecticut, 1971. Recipient: Eric Gregory Award, 1961; P.E.N. Translation Prize, 1966; Tokyo Festival Television Film Award, 1971. Agent: Fraser and Dunlop Scripts Ltd., 91 Regent Street, London W1R 8RU. Address: c/o Jonathan Cape Ltd., 30 Bedford Square, London WC1B 3EL, England.

PUBLICATIONS

Plays

> *The Ledge* (libretto), music by Richard Rodney Bennett (produced London, 1961).
> *The Persecution and Assassination of Jean Paul Marat as Performed by the Inmates of the Asylum of Charenton under the Direction of the Marquis de Sade*, adaptation of the play by Peter Weiss (produced London, 1964; New York, 1965).   London, John Calder, 1965; New York, Atheneum, 1966.
> *The Magic Flute*, adaptation of the libretto by Schikaneder and Giesecke, music by Mozart (produced London, 1966).
> *US*, with others (produced London, 1966).   Published as *US: The Book of the Royal Shakespeare Production US/Vietnam/US/Experiment/Politics...*, London, Calder and Boyars, 1968; as *Tell Me Lies: The Book of the Royal Shakespeare Production US/Vietnam/US/Experiment/Politics...*, Indianapolis, Bobbs Merrill, 1968.
> *The Criminals*, adaptation of a play by José Triana (produced London, 1967; New York, 1970).
> *Tyger: A Celebration of the Life and Work of William Blake* (produced London, 1971). London, Cape, 1971.
> *Tamburlane the Mad Hen* (for children; produced Devon, 1971).
> *Man Friday* (televised, 1972; produced London, 1973).   Included in *Man Friday, and Mind Your Head*, 1974.
> *Mind Your Head: A Return Trip, with Songs*, music by Mike Westbrook (produced Liverpool, 1973; London, 1974).   Included in *Man Friday, and Mind Your Head*, 1974.

The Inspector General, adaptation of a play by Gogol (produced Nottingham, 1974).
Man Friday, and Mind Your Head: A Return Trip, with Songs, music by Mike
   Westbrook.   London, Eyre Methuen, 1974,

Screenplays: *Marat/Sade*, 1967; *Tell Me Lies* (lyrics only), 1968; *The Body*
(commentary), 1969; *Man Friday*, 1976.

Radio Play: *The Island* (libretto), music by William Russo, 1963.

Televison Plays: *Animals Can't Laugh*, 1961; *Alive and Kicking*, 1971; *William Blake*
(documentary), 1971; *Man Friday*, 1972; *Something Down There Is Crying*, 1975; *Daft
As a Brush*, 1975; *The Fine Art of Bubble Blowing*, 1975; *Silver Giant, Wooden Dwarf*,
1975.

Initiated and helped write several student shows: *Bradford Walk*, Bradford College of
Art; *The Hotpot Saga, The Neurovision Song Contest*, and *Lash Me to the Mast*,
University of Lancaster; *Move Over Jehovah*, National Association of Mental Health;
Poetry Circus, Wesleyan University; *Kardiff Rules, OK?*, University College, Cardiff,
1975.

Novels

If You See Me Comin'.   London, Cape, 1962; New York, Macmillan, 1963.
The Bodyguard.   London, Cape, 1970; New York, Doubleday, 1971.
Wartime.   London, Cape, 1973; New York, Doubleday, 1975.
Man Friday.   London, Futura, 1975.

Verse

(Poems).   Oxford, Fantasy Press, 1955.
Poems.   London, Cape, 1964.
Peace Is Milk.   London, Peace News, 1966.
Out Loud.   London, Cape Goliard Press, and New York, Grossman, 1968.
Ride the Nightmare: Verse and Prose.   London, Cape, 1971.
Cease-Fire.   London, Medical Aid Committee for Vietnam, 1973.
Penguin Modern Poets 22, with John Fuller and Peter Levi.   London, Penguin, 1973.
The Apeman Cometh.   London, Cape, 1975.

Recording: *Poems*, with Stevie Smith, Argo, 1974.

Other

Editor, with Richard Selig, *Oxford Poetry 1955*.   Oxford, Fantasy Press, 1955.
Editor, *Jump, My Brothers, Jump: Poems from Prison*, by Tim Dale.   London, Freedom
   Press, 1970.
Editor, with Brian Elliott, *Bards in the Wilderness*.   Melbourne, Nelson, 1971.

Translator with Joan Jara, *Victor Jara: His Life and Songs*.   London, Hamish
   Hamilton, 1976.

*   *   *

Because Adrian Mitchell's plays never lose the touch of the poet, it is appropriate that he should describe the form of his two longest stage pieces, *Tyger* and *Mind Your Head*, with a characteristically apt but improbable image: "A patchwork quilt being waved vigorously." The label applies to all of Mitchell's writings for the theatre, which are all collages of the poet's concerns and images.

Patchwork has no need of rare or refined materials, and Mitchell's dramatic concerns are drawn from the late 1960's common fund of excoriation and celebration: wars, pollution, racial bigotry, sexual repression, private property, schools, armies, organised religions, and other products and preservers of compartmentalised inhumanity get attacked; while life, liberation and the proximity of happiness for the entire Family of Man get affirmed. Such an ahistorical and unsystematic programme for Apocalypse probably baffles its own political purposes. It does, however, encourage satirical caricature and sustain short but splendid spurts of lyric; and Mitchell's dramatic writings are dense with these. The images which carry them are extremely particular (product names, place names, company names, famous names), topical (newspaper headlines, phrases from popular songs), and banal (ordinary objects, everyday activities, primary colours). In Mitchell's best poetry, these are assembled with exact and economical attention to contrasting associations and rhythmic patterns. The sharp combinations and short cadences are peculiarly Mitchell's own, but their constituents are so accessible that the reader or audience can accompany him on a mad flight of fantasy or in an intimate expression of emotion.

Something of this lyric style may be observed in his early libretto, *The Ledge*, where the merits of suicide are debated in images from modern urban life. Mitchell then made his theatrical reputation as a lyricist for Royal Shakespeare Company productions, with his English adaptations of the verse texts in Peter Weiss's *Marat/Sade* in 1964, and with the songs which he and the composer Richard Peaslee contributed to the collaborative venture of *US* in the following year. The songs were of enormous structural importance for both productions, the second especially. Here, as subsequently in the songs for his own shows, Mitchell's lyric practice is usually to pile up disparate images drawn from the ordinaria of existence, weld them with catchphrases, meter and wordplay, and shape them with a chorus or refrain line which becomes more sharply pointed at each recurrence.

Songs are still more crucial to Mitchell's independent works for the stage. None of these could be termed "drama" in any strict sense. The closest approximations are *Tamburlane the Mad Hen* and *Man Friday*, short pieces originally written for schools and televison performance respectively. Both aim at a maximum amount of audience involvement in an "action" which mixes song and debate. *Tyger* has for a first act a scrambled account of Mitchell's favourite poet, and gives over its second half to an all-poets birthday party for Blake, followed by a trip to the moon for a vision of the Children of Albion. *Mind Your Head* follows a No. 24 bus from Hampstead to Victoria Station (Act I) and part-way back before heading off for Wales (Act II). Fantastic passengers come and go and sometimes return en route, while a parody *Hamlet* is worked out among the three London Transport employees on board. *Tyger* and *Mind Your Head* both abandon all pretenses of dramatic action after their intervals, and throughout both it is the songs which are the principles of organisation. Around them a vast array of formal elements and styles are played off against each other. The procedure is not that of opera or musical comedy so much as of pantomime or even music hall. As in the music hall, the songs are interspersed with jokes, mime, story-telling, and tag lines. Other routines are brought in from contemporary popular culture: comic strip business, advertising jargon, sales patter, parodies of public and entertainment figures. As for action and dialogue, so too for characterization: the players are a college of caricatures, impressionistic pastiches, walking anachronisms, grotesques, and the odd spasm of psychological coherence.

It adds up to a variegated lot of good fun in the irreverent high spirits of late-blooming Flower Power. But it is as evanescent as it is ebullient. The shows elude analysis — and probably reconstitution as well. The published texts are one-dimensional records of celebrations among specific groups in particular times and places, and to some extent they are also rough notes for how other people might throw a similar party elsewhere sometime. But the party itself is over, not to be preserved in published texts and accompanying scores and recordings.

The television plays are another critical matter in a more permanent medium: the best of them are of durable dramatic value. Perhaps because they cannot count on the audience of initiates and utter innocents presupposed by the stage shows, they are much more conventional in plot, idiom, and characterisation. They present a sequence of causally connected actions, maintain stylistic consistency and formal coherence, and are arranged around the consciousness of one character – usually a figure of great sensitivity and sometimes simplicity.

The satiric and lyric techniques of Mitchell's poetry do carry over into his television plays, but here they work as supplements to drama instead of, as in the stage shows, substitutes for it. The finest of Mitchell's television scripts take full cognisance of the television camera and arrange rhythmic amalgams of visual images and patterns to work in conjunction with the verbal ones. Mitchell's increasingly imaginative mastery of the medium is apparent from a comparison of his first television script, *Animals Can't Laugh* (1961), with the more recent *Daft As a Brush* (1975). The earlier play is packed with prose poems and fables but, ignoring the camera, falls flatter than a fourth wall. *Daft As a Brush* speaks another, richer language. The play takes a military prison veteran into a Yorkshire village where he becomes a postman, marries, and gradually transforms his back garden into an enormous gallery of the *objets trouvés* in his life. Mitchell uses successions of short scenes on the postman's rounds to establish the rhythms of village life and the character's part in them. These sequences are in turn worked into patterns with scenes developing the postman's changing relations with his wife, his environment, his past, and his project. Towards the end of the play, when the viewer and the character's wife are finally allowed to see that he's been assembling, the camera wanders slowly through the exhibition, taking in every object, and creating an exact visual analogue of one of Mitchell's lyrics.

Daft As a Brush gives promise that Mitchell has found in the television play the particular dramatic form which most completely and concretely accomodates his best poetic practice.

—Marion O'Connor

MITCHELL, Loften.   American.   Born in Columbus, North Carolina, 15 April 1919. Educated at DeWitt Clinton High School, Bronx, New York, graduated 1937; City College of New York, 1937–38; Talladega College, Alabama, B.A. 1943; Columbia University, New York, 1947–51. Served as a Seaman Second Class in the navy during World War II. Married Helen Marsh in 1948; has two children. Editor, *NAACP Journal*, 1964. Recipient: Guggenheim Fellowship, 1958. Address: 368 Floral Avenue, Johnson City, New York 13790, U.S.A.

PUBLICATIONS

Plays

   Blood in the Night (produced New York, 1946).
   The Bancroft Dynasty (produced New York, 1948).
   The Cellar (produced New York, 1952).

A Land Beyond the River (produced New York, 1957).   Cody, Wyoming, Pioneer
   Drama Service, 1963.
Tell Pharaoh (televised, 1963; produced on stage, 1967).   New York, Emersòn Hall,
   1974.
Ballad for Bimshire, with Irving Burgie (produced New York, 1963; revised version,
   produced Cleveland, 1964).
Ballad of the Winter Soldiers, with John Oliver Killens (produced New York, 1964).
Star of the Morning: Scenes in the Life of Bert Williams, in Black Drama Anthology,
   edited by Woodie King and Ron Milner.   New York, New American Library, 1971.

Screenplays: Young Man of Williamsburg, 1955; Integration Report One, 1959.

Radio Writer: Tribute to C. C. Spaulding, 1952; Friendly Advisor program, 1955; The
Later Years program, 1959–62.

Television Play: Tell Pharaoh, 1963.

Other

Black Drama: The Story of the American Negro in the Theatre.   New York, Hawthorn
   Books, 1967.

Editor, Voices of the Black Theatre.   Clifton, New Jersey, James T. White, 1975.

Theatrical Activities:

Actor: **Plays** – with the Rose McClendon Players, New York; Victor in Cocktails, and
Aaron in Having Wonderful Time by Arthur Kober, 1938; Angel in The Black Messiah by
Denis Donoghue and James H. Dunmore, 1939.

                              *   *   *

Loften Mitchell, an American Negro dramatist who won a Guggenheim award for creative
writing in 1958, surely must exemplify the fact that a productive black playwright can
remain relatively unknown in the United States of America. Although he has written
screenplays, radio broadcasts, a television play, and stage plays during a writing career of a
quarter of a century, Mitchell is probably best known for an informal history, Black Drama:
The Story of the American Negro in the Theatre.
   As he has explained in the "introduction" to Black Drama, Mitchell's interest in the theatre
began when as a boy he attended vaudeville theatres in Harlem – the Lafayette, the Lincoln,
and the Alhambra. The interest flamed when, as a newsboy during the early 1930's, he talked
with such notable Negro performers as Ethel Waters, Muriel Rahn, Dick Campbell, and
Canada Lee, who told him stories of earlier black performers and writers and who
encouraged him to go into the theatre.
   While still in high school, he wrote sketches for a church group and the Pioneer Drama
group; and he acted with the Rose McClendon Players in New York in the late 1930's. After
World War II, Mitchell began writing plays in earnest. In 1946 Blood in the Night was
produced, and two years later The Bancroft Dynasty.
   Mitchell's first commercially successful dramatic production was The Cellar, produced in
Harlem by The Harlem Showcase. Scheduled for three weekends, the play ran from
November 1952 until late April 1953. The Cellar is a melodrama about a Negro blues singer,
the fugitive she befriends, and her fiancé, a brutal detective who hounds the fugitive.
   A Land Beyond the River is a realistic drama based on an actual incident in the life of the

Reverend Dr. Joseph DeLaine, a pastor and schoolteacher in Clarendon County, South Carolina, who petitioned to provide Negro children with bus transportation to rural schools. Later, the petition was changed to a suit for equal education for Negro children. In 1954 it was combined with other suits and became part of the case identified as *Brown vs. Board of Education of Topeka, Kansas*. After hearing the combined cases, the United States Supreme Court ruled that it was unconstitutional to deny black Americans the right to attend any school supported by public funds. Despite the success of the suit, Dr. DeLaine suffered personally from economic sanctions and arson in which his home burned to the ground while the Fire Department looked on. After he moved to another city, his home was repeatedly fired upon by nightriders. After he shot back in self-defense, he fled to New York, where he succeeded in defeating efforts to return him to South Carolina to stand trial for defending himself against a mob.

Mitchell's next works were collaborations. With Irving Burgie, he wrote the musical *Ballad for Bimshire*, a romantic story of a seventeen-year-old girl growing up in Barbados, and with John Oliver Killens he wrote *Ballad of the Winter Soldiers*, a pageant-like story of freedom fighters throughout history. During these years, Mitchell, writing alone, reached his artistic heights as a dramatist in *Tell Pharaoh*, an eloquent "theatre-at-the-lectern" history of black people. Another significant work of the period is *Star of the Morning*, the story of the struggle of Bert Williams, the most famous Negro stage entertainer of the first two decades of the twentieth century.

Although Mitchell would want to be judged primarily on his merits as a dramatist, scholars value him as much for his contributions as a historian of Afro-American drama. As Mitchell describes his "accidental" career as a drama historian, it began with Maurice A. Lee, his freshman English teacher at Talladega, who encouraged him to expand a term paper about Harlem's Negro performers into a book. Later, when required to write a master's thesis, he prepared a history of the groups that attempted to build a permanent theatre in Harlem. Subsequent articles on Afro-American theatrical history in *Theatre Arts Monthly, Enciclopedia Della Spettacolo*, the *Oxford Companion to the Theatre*, and the *Amsterdam News* led finally to *Black Drama*, an invaluable informal history of blacks in the New York theatre. It is presented in twelve essays which extend from the images of blacks in seventeenth and eighteenth century American plays through Broadway drama of the 1960's. Mitchell concludes the work with a brief consideration of the future of black playwrights and performers in America's entertainment world.

—Darwin T. Turner

MOLLOY, Michael (Joseph).   Irish.   Born in Milltown, County Galway, 3 March 1917. Educated at St. Jarlath's College and in a seminary for four years. Farmer.

PUBLICATIONS

Plays

Old Road (produced Dublin, 1943).   Dublin, Progress House, 1961.
The Visiting House (produced Dublin, 1946).   Published in *Seven Irish Plays, 1946–1964*, edited by Robert G. Hogan, Minneapolis, University of Minnesota Press, 1967.

The King of Friday's Men (produced Dublin, 1948; New York, 1951).   Dublin, James Duffy, 1953.

The Wood of the Whispering (produced Dublin, 1953; New York, 1975).   Dublin, Progress House, 1961.

The Paddy Pedlar (produced Dublin, 1953).   Dublin, James Duffy, 1954.

The Will and the Way (produced Dublin, 1955).   Dublin, P. J. Bourke, 1957.

A Right Rose Tree (produced Dublin, 1958).

Dughter from over the Water (produced 1962; produced Dublin, 1964).   Dublin, Progress House, 1963.

The Bitter Pill, in *Prizewinning Plays of 1964*.   Dublin, Progress House, 1965.

*   (*   *

Michael J. Molloy may be Ireland's most genuine folk-dramatist. He is certainly the most distinguished contributor to this genre since Synge. Unlike Synge, who was a stranger to rural Ireland and had to be educated about its culture, Molloy is a native of County Galway and still lives there, in simple circumstances very like those he describes in his plays. Nine of his ten plays have been produced either at the Abbey Theatre or by the Abbey Theatre Company. They represent a thirty-year effort to provide for the Irish theater the sort of play Yeats said was needed to make Irish people conscious of their own history. Molloy has singlemindedly written plays which deal with the experience of the Irish countryman. A broadly educated man himself, he has witnessed and understood the changes which in the past thirty years have moved rural Ireland away from what Molloy regards as its feudal traditions and toward a society less certain of its values and more vulnerable to the exploitation of its land and its people.

In all of Molloy's plays there is nostalgia for a time when men had a proper regard for each other and for the land, a time when depopulation had not reduced rural Ireland to a gaggle of testy and self-righteous bachelors, a time before technology and an unscrupulous middle class purloined the land. Not surprisingly, since he is a dramatist rather than an historian, Molloy's plays do not deal with that ancient age of social order, but rather with periods of conflict, of moments when one can observe the old order passing. A self-confessed romantic, Molloy can see no good coming out of this change.

Two of Michael J. Molloy's early plays, *The King of Friday's Men* and *The Visiting House*, might be regarded as paradigms of the worlds that have been lost. Set in late 18th-century Mayo and Galway, *The King of Friday's Men* reveals a large society still responsive to the old feudal structure of lord and peasant. The play concerns a lord's obsession with his right to have as his mistresses the unmarried daughters of his tenant farmers. His exploitation of a feudal right provokes disorder in the land and leads ultimately to the violent death of the lord. Molloy is not naive in his romantic attachment to Ireland's feudal past. As a Catholic, he believes that human nature has been self-seeking and violent since the Fall and can never change. Nevertheless, all the characters in *The King of Friday's Men* share the same social and moral values. Lord and tenant both know when privilege has been exploited.

The Visiting House has a contemporary setting and reveals a shrunken social order. Unlike *The King of Friday's Men* in which action ranges all over Galway and Mayo, and an heroic Bartley Dowd wipes out a contingent of the lord's men with a few swipes of his shillelagh, *The Visiting House* is confined to the single setting which Molloy has used for most of his plays. The heroics are rhetorical rather than physical as characters called The Man of Learning and The Verb-to-Be nightly take their positions by the fire and engage in a merry flyting match. Within these narrowed circumstances, however, *The Visiting House* does reveal a social order based on ownership of the land. A once flourishing institution barely more than a memory when Molloy wrote his play, the visiting house was the place where small farmers gathered and where each had respect and a social identity.

Molloy's other plays deal more directly with the breakdown of traditional Irish rural life. *Old Road* is about the depopulation caused by farmers being unable to divide their small farms any further. Only the oldest son may inherit the land. Others must leave the community for Dublin or England. *The Wood of the Whispering* also has depopulation for its theme. Molloy assembles an array of zany and impotent old bachelors who lust after the one or two girls left in the village. Their lives pass in the shadow of ancient Castle D'Arcy, a reminder to Molloy's audience of a time when society was stable. *The Will and the Way* has to do with a rural community whose visiting house is threatened by the arrival of a city-type who has no feeling for community life and who nearly succeeds in destroying it.

In his more recent plays Molloy has been unable to maintain the gentle comic spirit and ironic distance which characterize his earlier work. The last traces of genuine rural Irish life are being destroyed by technology, especially by television which gives the Irish a false sense of being a national community while at the same time imposing a radical isolation of one man from another. *A Right Rose Tree* presents a rural Ireland so fraught with social problems that the play is more like documentary than drama. It deals with the period 1921–23, when the Irish countryside rises up against the English only to witness even more bloody battles of brother against brother when the Black and Tans have left. The utter lawlessness which results permits the base to inherit the earth. The lines from Yeats which give the play its title assert the purposefulness of violence – "There's nothing but our own red blood/Can make a right Rose tree." For Michael Molloy violence has no such creative energy. The final horror of *A Right Rose Tree*, the symbolic killing of a landlord by insensitive, ignorant, and cowardly men, leaves nothing of value after it.

—Arthur E. McGuinness

MOORE, (James) Mavor. Canadian. Born in Toronto, Ontario, 8 March 1919. Educated at University of Toronto secondary schools, graduated 1936; University of Toronto, 1936–41 (Leonard Foundation Scholar), B.A. (honours) in philosophy and English 1941. Served as a Captain (Psychological Warfare) in the Canadian Army Intelligence Corps, 1941–45. Married Darwina Faessler in 1943 (divorced); the writer Phyllis Grosskurth, 1969; has four daughters. Feature Producer, Toronto, 1941–42, Chief Producer for the International Service, Montreal, 1944–45, and Pacific Region Producer, Vancouver, 1945–46, CBC Radio; Teacher, Academy of Radio Arts, Toronto, 1946–49; Managing Producer, New Play Society, Toronto, 1946–50, 1954–57; Radio Director, 1946–50, and Executive Television Producer, 1954–60, United Nations Information Division, New York; Chief Producer, CBC Television, Toronto, 1950–54; Drama Critic, Toronto *Telegram*, 1958–60; Stage Director, Canadian Opera Company, Toronto, 1959–61, 1963; General Director, Confederation Centre, Charlottetown, Prince Edward Island, 1963–65; Founder and Artistic Director, Charlottetown Festival, 1964–67; General Director, St. Lawrence Centre for the Arts, Toronto, 1965–70. Since 1961, President, Mavor Moore Productions Ltd., Toronto; since 1970, Professor of Theatre, York University, Toronto. Member of the Board of Directors, since 1953, later Senator, Stratford Festival, Ontario; Chairman, Canadian Theatre Centre, 1957–58; since 1958, Member of the Board of Governors, National Theatre School, Montreal; since 1974, Member of Canada Council. Recipient: Peabody Award, 1947, 1949, 1957; Canadian Association of Authors and Artists televison award, 1955; Canadian Centennial Medal, 1967. D.Litt.: York University, 1969. Order of Canada, 1973. Agents: (Canada) Canadian Speakers and Writers Service, 44 Douglas Crescent, Toronto, Ontario; (United Kingdom and United States) ACTAC Ltd., 16 Cadogan Lane, London S.W.1, England. Address: 147 Spruce Street, Toronto, Ontario M5A 2J6, Canada.

PUBLICATIONS

Plays

> *Spring Thaw* (revue; produced Toronto, 1947, and later versions).
> *Who's Who* (also director: produced Toronto, 1948).
> *Sunshine Town*, music and lyrics by Mavor Moore, adaptation of *Sunshine Sketches of a Little Town* by Stephen Leacock (as *The Hero of Mariposa*, televised, 1954; as *Sunshine Town*, also director: produced Toronto, 1956).
> *The Best of All Possible Worlds*, music and lyrics by Mavor Moore, adaptation of *Candide* by Voltaire (as *The Optimist*, produced Toronto, 1954; as *The Best of All Possible Worlds*, televised, 1956).
> *The Ottawa Man*, adaptation of *The Inspector General* by Gogol (produced Toronto, 1958; revised version, also director: produced Charlottetown, 1966; revised version, produced Lennoxville, 1972).
> *Louis Riel*, music by Harry Somers (produced Toronto, 1967).
> *Yesterday the Children Were Dancing*, translation of a play by Gratien Gélinas (also co-director: produced Charlottetown, 1967).   Toronto, Clarke Irwin, 1969.
> *Johnny Belinda*, lyrics by Mavor Moore, musical version of the play by Elmer Harris (produced Charlottetown, 1968).
> *Getting In* (televised, 1970).   New York, French, 1972.
> *The Pile* (broadcast, 1970).   Included in *A Collection of Canadian Plays*, 1973.
> *Inside Out* (televised, 1971).   Included in *A Collection of Canadian Plays*, 1973.
> *The Store* (televised, 1972).   Included in *A Collection of Canadian Plays*, 1973.
> *Come Away, Come Away* (televised, 1972).   Toronto, Methuen, 1973.
> *A Collection of Canadian Plays, Volume II*, edited by Rolf Kalman (includes *The Pile, Inside Out, The Store*).   Toronto, Simon and Pierre, 1973.
> *The Roncarelli Affair* (televised, 1974).   Published in *The Play's the Thing: Four Original Television Dramas*, edited by Tony Gifford, Toronto, Macmillan, 1976.

Radio Plays: *Fast Forward*, 1968; *The Pile*, 1970; *The Argument*, 1970; *A Matter of Timing*, 1971; *Customs*, 1973 (USA); *Time Frame*, 1974; *Freak*, 1975.

Television Plays: *The Hero of Mariposa*, 1954; *Catch a Falling Star*, 1956; *The Well*, 1960; *The Man Who Caught Bullets*, 1961; *The Man Born to Be King*, 1961; *Mary of Scotland*, 1966; *Getting In*, 1970; *Inside Out*, 1971; *The Store*, 1972; *Come Away, Come Away*, 1972; *The Roncarelli Affair*, 1974.

Verse

> *And What Do You Do? A Short Guide to the Trades and Professions*.   Toronto and London, Dent, 1960.

Other

> *Four Canadian Playwrights*.   Toronto, Holt Rinehart, 1973.

> Editor, *The Awkward Stage: The Ontario Theatre Study*.   Toronto, Methuen, 1969.
> Editor, *An Anthology of Candadian Plays*.   Toronto, New Press, 1973.

Theatrical Activities:

Director: **Plays** – *Who's Who*, Toronto, 1948; *King Lear*, Toronto, 1948; *Heartbreak House* by G. B. Shaw, Toronto, 1948; *The Circle* by Somerset Maugham, Toronto, 1948; *The Government Inspector* by Gogol, Toronto, 1948; *Macbeth*, Toronto, 1949; *The Tempest*, Toronto, 1949; *Sunshine Town*, Toronto, 1956; *The Ottawa Man*, Toronto, 1963, Charlottetown, 1966; *The Fourposter* by Jan de Hartog, Halifax, Nova Scotia, 1963; *Dial M for Murder* by Frederick Knott, Halifax, 1963; *Floradora*, Vancouver, 1964; *Julius Caesar*, Vancouver, 1964; *An Evening with Wayne and Shuster*, Charlottetown, 1965; *Laugh with Leacock*, Charlottetown, 1965; *Yesterday the Children Were Dancing*, Charlottetown, 1967. **Television and Radio** – productions for CBC, United Nations (New York), CBS and NBC (USA).

Actor: **Plays** – roles with the New Play Society, Toronto, the Crest Theatre, the Charlottetown and Vancouver Festivals, and other theatre companies, including title role in *King Lear*, Toronto, 1948, 1963; title role in *Riel*, Toronto, 1948; Escalus in *Measure for Measure*, Stratford, Ontario, 1954; Caesar in *Caesar and Cleopatra* by G. B. Shaw, Toronto and Vancouver, 1962; Undershaft in *Major Barbara* by G. B. Shaw, Halifax, 1963. **Television** – starring roles for all the major Canadian drama series. **Radio** – roles in numerous CBC productions, CBS and NBC (USA), etc.

*   *   *

Mavor Moore is Canada's most ubiquitous man-about-theatre. In the last 25 years, he has had great success as actor, producer, director, festival impresario and theatre administrator. Now, as professor of theatre at York University in Toronto, he has a period of relative calm in which he can once more concentrate on writing. For most of his career as a playwright for the stage, he has mainly adapted other men's work and adapted it very often for his own direction. Or, he has worked as a librettist in cooperation with composers and others.

In the area of musical drama, he has created a lively version of Mariposa, that sleepy little town which Stephen Leacock wrote about in *Sunshine Sketches*. In *Sunshine Town*, Moore wrote a book, music and lyrics which had the right period feeling; it has had several revivals.

On another occasion, for his Charlottetown Festival, he wrote a musical version of *Johnny Belinda* based on the Broadway play by Elmer Harris. Again, the quality of the writing and the success of his director, Alan Lund, made even the story of a deaf-mute who is raped a good and satisfying musical.

In *Louis Riel*, he created an opera rather than a musical. With a score composed by Harry Somers, *Louis Riel* was a notable addition to the Canadian Opera Company's repertoire for the Centennial Year of 1967. Moore went to history – Riel is a key-figure in the French-English debate which still is a central part of Canada's polity – and managed to create around it a full-blooded set of characters, even though from time to time the dialogue was more operatic than dramatic.

Moore's greatest gift as a dramatist is his skill in dialogue. Perhaps because he has written so much for radio – a purely verbal medium – he is adept at spinning out dialogue in a way which has become very fashionable now with playwrights like Pinter and Albee.

His best-known play is *The Ottawa Man*, an adaptation of Gogol's *The Government Inspector*. Only Moore's talent for dialogue could have made it the success it is because the central situation, which is firmly rooted in the official corruption of czarist Russia, cannot be easily transplanted to the relative honesty of nineteenth century pioneer Manitoba. But the fact is that one doesn't question this while the play is being acted; nor is one too aware of the fact that the characters are all stereotypes rather than people. What one is aware of is the farcical encounter between two Irishmen, a French-Canadian Catholic, a German immigrant and an English remittance man – all of whom speak in an uncannily accurate style and accent.

Now Mavor Moore has shifted into a different area. He is writing one-act plays, some of

569

which have already been seen on television and heard on radio, but which are very much in the modern English tradition. Character is not important in them but ideas and the verbal play on those ideas are. In fact, so little character is necessary for the showing of the ideas that in all that he has so far written, none of the characters has a name.

In *Come Away, Come Away*, which is about an old man facing death and a little girl fascinated by the encounter, the characters are merely labelled Old Man and Little Girl.

In *The Pile*, a fable about modern business and ecology, the characters are merely X and Y, just as in *Getting In*, a play with really strange resonance, P is the official and T is an applicant.

Perhaps the most significant of these plays is *The Argument* which, through its dialogue alone, begins to create characters who are only identified as M – a man – and W – a woman. But their dialogue, their argument, creates an interaction of character which leads one to hope that Mavor Moore is about to write a longer and more solid work than his multifarious activities up to now have allowed him the time for.

Moore certainly has the talent, and now, with the time, he may produce some first-rate work with deeper psychological insight than he has so far been able to do. When he does that, it will be the crown of what has even so far been a most successful theatrical career.

—Arnold Edinborough

* * *

MORTIMER, John (Clifford).   British.   Born in Hampstead, London, 21 April 1923. Educated at Harrow School, Middlesex, 1937–40; Brasenose College, Oxford, 1940–42, B.A. 1947; called to the Bar, 1948; Queen's Counsel, 1966. Served with the Crown Film Unit as scriptwriter during World War II. Married the writer Penelope Dimont in 1949 (divorced, 1971); Penny Gollop, 1972; has three children. Drama critic, *New Statesman, Evening Standard, Observer*, 1972, all in London. Chairman, League of Dramatists. Recipient: Italia Prize, for radio play, 1958; Screenwriters Guild Award, for television play, 1970. Agent: A. D. Peters, 10 Buckingham Street, London WC2N 6BU. Address: Turville Heath Cottage, Henley on Thames, Oxfordshire, England.

PUBLICATIONS

Plays

> *The Dock Brief* (broadcast, 1957; produced London, 1958; New York, 1961). Included in *Three Plays*, 1958.
> *I Spy* (broadcast, 1957; produced Salisbury, Wiltshire, 1959).   Included in *Three Plays*, 1958.
> *What Shall We Tell Caroline?* (produced London, 1958; New York, 1961).   Included in *Three Plays*, 1958.
> *Three Plays: The Dock Brief, What Shall We Tell Caroline?, I Spy*.   London, Elek, 1958; New York, Grove Press, 1962.

Call Me a Liar (televised, 1958; produced London, 1968).   Included in *Lunch Hour and Other Plays*, 1960; in *The Television Playwright: Ten Plays for B.B.C. Television*, edited by Michael Barry, New York, Hill and Wang, 1960.

Sketches in *One to Another* (produced London, 1959).   London, French, 1960.

The Wrong Side of the Park (produced London, 1960).   London, Heinemann, 1960.

Lunch Hour (broadcast, 1960; produced Salisbury, Wiltshire, 1960; London, 1961).   London and New York, French, 1960.

David and Broccoli (televised, 1960).   Included in *Lunch Hour and Other Plays*, 1960.

Lunch Hour and Other Plays (includes *Collect Your Hand Baggage, David and Broccoli, Call Me a Liar*).   London, Methuen, 1960.

Collect Your Hand Baggage (produced Wuppertal, Germany, 1963).   Included in *Lunch Hour and Other Plays*, 1960.

Sketches in *One over the Eight* (produced London, 1961).

Two Stars for Comfort (produced London, 1962).   London, Methuen, 1962.

A Voyage round My Father (broadcast, 1963; produced London, 1970).   London, Methuen, 1971.

Sketches in *Changing Gear* (produced Nottingham, 1965).

A Flea in Her Ear, adaptation of a play by Feydeau (produced London, 1966).   London and New York, French, 1967.

A Choice of Kings (televised, 1966).   Published in *Playbill Three*, edited by Alan Durband, London, Hutchinson, 1969.

The Judge (produced London, 1967).   London, Methuen, 1967.

Desmond (televised, 1968).   Published in *The Best Short Plays 1971*, edited by Stanley Richards, Philadelphia, Chilton, 1971.

Cat among the Pigeons, adaptation of a play by Feydeau (produced London, 1969; Milwaukee, 1971).   New York, French, 1970.

Come As You Are: Four Short Plays (includes *Mill Hill, Bermondsey, Gloucester Road, Marble Arch*) (produced London, 1970).   London, Methuen, 1971.

Five Plays (includes *The Dock Brief, What Shall We Tell Caroline?, I Spy, Lunch Hour, Collect Your Hand Baggage*).   London, Methuen, 1970.

The Captain of Köpenick, adaptation of a play by Carl Zuckmayer (produced London, 1971).   London, Methuen, 1971.

Conflicts, with others (produced London, 1971).

I, Claudius, adaptation of the novels *I, Claudius* and *Claudius the God* by Robert Graves (produced London, 1972).

Knightsbridge (televised, 1972).   London, French, 1973.

The Collaborators (produced London, 1973).   London, Eyre Methuen, 1973.

Heaven and Hell (includes *The Fear of Heaven* and *The Prince of Darkness*) (produced London, 1976).

Screenplays: *Ferry to Hong Kong* (additional dialogue), 1959; *The Innocents*, with others, 1961; *Guns of Darkness*, 1962; *I Thank a Fool*, 1962; *The Dock Brief*, 1962; *The Running Man*, 1963; *Lunch Hour*, 1963; *Bunny Lake Is Missing*, with Penelope Mortimer, 1964; *A Flea in Her Ear*, 1967; *John and Mary*, 1969.

Radio Plays: *Like Men Betrayed*, 1955; *No Hero*, 1955; *The Dock Brief*, 1957; *I Spy*, 1957; *Three Winters*, 1958; *Call Me a Liar*, 1958; *Lunch Hour*, 1960; *The Encyclopedist*, 1961; *A Voyage round My Father*, 1963; *Personality Split*, 1964; *Education of an Englishman*, 1964; *A Rare Device*, 1965; *Mr. Luby's Fear of Heaven*, 1976.

Television Plays: *Call Me a Liar*, 1958; *David and Broccoli*, 1960; *A Choice of Kings*, 1966; *The Exploding Azalea*, 1966; *The Head Waiter*, 1966; *Hughie*, 1967; *The Other Side*, 1967; *Desmond*, 1968; *Infidelity Took Place*, 1968; *Married Alive*, 1970; *Swiss Cottage*, 1972; *Knightsbridge*, 1972; *Rumpole of the Bailey*, 1975; *A Little Place off*

Edgware Road, The Blue Film, The Destructors, The Case for the Defence, Chagrin in Three Parts, The Invisible Japanese Gentlemen, Special Duties, and *Mortmain,* all from stories by Graham Greene, 1975–76.

Ballet Scenario: *Home,* 1968.

Son et Lumière script: *Hampton Court,* 1964.

Novels

Charade.   London, Lane, 1947.
Rumming Park.   London, Lane, 1948.
Answer Yes or No.   London, Lane, 1950; as *The Silver Hook,* New York, Morrow, 1950.
Like Men Betrayed.   London, Collins, 1953; Philadelphia, Lippincott, 1954.
The Narrowing Stream.   London, Collins, 1954.
Three Winters.   London, Collins, 1956.

Other

No Moaning at the Bar (as Geoffrey Lincoln).   London, Bles, 1957.
With Love and Lizards, with Penelope Mortimer (travel).   London, Joseph, 1957.

Manuscript Collection: Boston University.

Critical Study: *Anger and After* by John Russell Taylor, London, Methuen, 1962.

*   *   *

John Mortimer's whole career as a playwright can be seen in terms of a series of affairs with Naturalism. He has never made an honest woman of her and he has often made resolute efforts to give her up altogether, but he has never managed to stay away for very long.

He worked in films (as an assistant director and then as a script-writer) before he became a barrister, but the verbal element in his plays has the upper hand over the visual. Writing for radio has been an important formative influence on his style, and one which has tended to draw him away from naturalism. *The Dock Brief,* his first play and still one of his best, started its life on the radio in 1957, when he was 34, and was then adapted for television, before being staged in a double-bill with his first play he wrote specially for the stage, *What Shall We Tell Caroline?* Neither of these is a conventional piece of play-making, but his first full-length stage play, *The Wrong Side of the Park* (1960), did not depart in any way from Shaftesbury Avenue conventions.

More than most contemporary naturalists, Mortimer has concentrated on comedy. In his introduction to *Three Plays* he called it

the only thing worth writing in this despairing age, provided the comedy is truly on the side of the lonely, the neglected, the unsuccessful, and plays its part in the war against established rules and against the imposing of an arbitrary code of behaviour upon individual and unpredictable human beings.

In the Introduction to his 1970 collection, *Five Plays,* he added:

The Macmillan era was a time for low comedy in high places. Pre-war attitudes still lingered. The middle-aged formed hopeless and isolated pockets of resistance, in law-courts and seaside hotels and private schools.... So I have attempted, in these comedies, to chart the tottering course of British middle-class attitudes in decline.

He did largely succeed in capturing the flavour of the faded and fraying middle-class gentility which he went on satirising in most of his sixties comedies. The one-act ones, particularly, have great charm, which is no disadvantage when the observation is accurate enough, as in the characterisations of the pathetic barrister and the amiable henpecked murderer in *The Dock Brief*. It is a disadvantage, though, when it tilts a play towards sentimentality, as often happens when he infuses a very similar likeableness into types he seems less familiar with. His private detectives, his shabby schoolteachers, his publicans, waitresses, speculators and con men are all entertaining but unlike Morganhall and Fowle in *The Dock Brief* they are not distinctive as individuals. Remembered afterwards, the plays' identities all merge into an inchoate mass of lovableness: John Mortimer has endowed them with too much of his own charm. Meanwhile the artificial twists he has used to keep the narrative alive have obscured the social comment he intended.

The one-act plays *I Spy, Lunch Hour* and *Collect Your Hand Baggage*, and the full-length plays *The Wrong Side of the Park, Two Stars for Comfort* and *The Judge* all give the impression that Mortimer would be an excellent after-dinner speaker. The relish for words and whimsy is irrepressible: the characters often co-operate with each other to blow up enormous bubbles of fantasy. But he cannot resist delaying for too long over pricking the bubble, and the opportunity is lost of focusing the verbal self-indulgence as being that of the character.

Mannered dialogue often goes with arch, anecdotal plots. *I Spy* is about a detective who takes a job as a waiter in order to keep watch on a waitress whose husband suspects her of infidelity. Frute, the detective, finds so little to put in his reports that in desperation he makes a date with her himself. He only takes her to the cinema, but to satisfy the husband's jealousy he tells an exaggerated story of what happened, and he ends up promising the waitress to give evidence against her in court and to marry her when the divorce comes through.

Frute –   I don't know what to say.... If you *would* consider life as Mrs.
                Frute.
Mrs. Morgan –   Give that clear, oath evidence! Give them the worst of me, Mr.
                Frute! Give them misconduct *and* adultery!
Frute –   Mrs. Morgan, I will. You're a truly remarkable woman, quite
                outstanding. I loved you from the moment I first had you under
                observation.

In the full-length plays there is a less verbal self-indulgence, less mannered dialogue, but the pull towards naturalism is accordingly stronger. In *The Wrong Side of the Park* the comedy is equally dependent on the elaboration of fantasies, which seem to be imposed on the characters rather than to grow organically out of them, but the tone and style of the play derive less from the method of using words. The two central characters have enormous charm – exuberant in the men, wistful in the women – but it does not bring them fully to life. The plot is cleverly but predictably organised. Because her second husband seems so uninterested in anything but work, the attractive wife remembers her first marriage as being more exciting than it was, mentally reassigning incidents to it that have actually occurred in the second. There is a happy end when, just as she is being forced to face up to the facts, the husband suddenly becomes less dull and less preoccupied with work.

Two Stars for Comfort is a much better play, equally well-made, more touching, equally funny, and not rigged to end happily. Sam Turner, the owner of a riverside pub, is no less charming or vital than any of the earlier characters, but he is developed in greater depth. Attractive, friendly, easy-going, he is generous enough to take a girl to bed because he feels sorry for her and then capable of becoming far more deeply involved than he wanted to be. Mortimer had by now freed himself of the compulsion to make every single character lovable, and the unsympathetic neighbours in *Two Stars for Comfort* introduce a polarity — which is to figure again in *The Judge* — between the life-enhancers and the life-deniers. In both plays repressiveness is associated with the Law. Sam Turner, who knows how to enjoy life and how to share fun with other people, is taken to court and destroyed by people who are secretly jealous of his capacity for *joie de vivre*. In *The Judge*, which is less naturalistic, the anonymous Judge (who is rather like the penitent judge in Camus' last novel *La Chute*), is guiltily obsessed with the desire to *be* judged by the woman he abandoned when he thought she was pregnant. She still lives in the Northern town where he grew up, and, unlike him, she still enjoys life, running a junky antique shop, chatting about old friends and still making new ones. Thanks to her, the Judge's young Marshall, who started out with admiration for the old man and his attitudes, gravitates towards a more hedonistic view of life, but the themes never quite come into focus. Snared by the naturalistic habit into a plot which depends far too heavily on its pre-history for the style he was now trying to write in, Mortimer found himself unable to bring most of the pre-history to the surface until the Judge's only scene with his ex-girlfriend which comes right at the end of the play, and culminates in a melodramatic showdown.

A writer's most serious play does not need to be his least comic, but this was; and, as if to compensate, Mortimer swung back to a revue-sketch style in *Come As You Are*, a quartet of one-act plays about middle-aged sexual tangles. One of them, *Gloucester Road*, picks up the theme of *What Shall We Tell Caroline?* — a marriage which needs a semblance of infidelity in order to survive.

A Voyage round My Father was written first for the radio, then television. Then it was staged at Greenwich in 1970 and in the West End, slightly rewritten, in 1971. It is more autobiographical than any of the other plays, but the main focus is on the barrister father, who, like John Mortimer's, went blind during his son's boyhood and continued his career and his family life without paying any more attention to the disability than was absolutely necessary. He was obviously a fascinating man, but the play holds back from exploring him in depth or developing him as a character. It has great charm, though, as a theatrical memoir, and the old man is so vivid that the playwright-son seems almost colourless beside him.

John Mortimer's two adaptations for the National Theatre, Feydeau's *A Flea in Her Ear* and Zuckmayer's *The Captain of Köpenick*, were both well done and extremely successful. But his adaptation of Robert Graves's novel *I,Claudius* seems to have been written too hastily. The anti-naturalistic device of having a character talk directly to the audience, which Mortimer had previously used awkwardly in *The Judge* and more neatly in *A Voyage round My Father*, works awkwardly again here, and the Romans are trivialised, not altogether deliberately, by being given jokes in Mortimer's after-dinner-speech style.

—Ronald Hayman

MOSEL, Tad. American.   Born in Steubenville, Ohio, 1 May 1922. Educated at Amherst College, Massachusetts, B.A. 1947; Yale University, New Haven, Connecticut, 1947–49; Columbia University, New York, M.A. 1953. Served in the United States Army Air Force, 1943–46: Private to Sergeant. Visiting Critic in Television Writing, Yale University Drama School, 1957–58. Member of the Executive Board, *Television Quarterly*; Member of the Executive Council, Writers Guild of America. Recipient: Pulitzer Prize, 1961; New York Drama Critics Circle Award, 1961. D.Litt.: College of Wooster, Ohio, 1963. Agent: William Morris Agency, 1350 Avenue of the Americas, New York, New York 10019. Address: 400 East 57th Street, New York, New York 10022, U.S.A.

Plays

The Happiest Years (produced Amherst, Massachusetts, 1942).
Jinxed (televised, 1949). New York, French, n.d.
The Lion Hunter (produced New York, 1952).
Madame Aphrodite (televised, 1953; revised version, music by Jerry Herman, produced New York, 1962).
My Lost Saints (televised, 1955). Published in *Best Television Plays*, edited by Gore Vidal, New York, Ballantine, 1956.
Other People's Houses: Six Television Plays (includes *Ernie Barger Is Fifty, The Haven, The Lawn Party, Star in the Summer Night, The Waiting Place*). New York, Simon and Schuster, 1956.
The Out-of-Towners (televised, 1956). Published in *Television Plays for Writers: Eight Television Plays*, edited by A. S. Burack, Boston, The Writer, 1957.
The Five-Dollar Bill (televised, 1957). Chicago, Dramatic Publishing Company, 1958.
Presence of the Enemy (televised, 1958). Published in *Best Short Plays, 1957–1958*, edited by Margaret Mayorga, Boston, Beacon Press, 1958.
All the Way Home, adaptation of the novel *A Death in the Family* by James Agee (produced New York, 1960). New York, Obolensky, 1961.
Impromptu (produced New York, 1961). New York, Dramatists Play Service, 1961.
That's Where the Town's Going (televised, 1962). New York, Dramatists Play Service, 1962).

Screenplays: *Dear Heart*, 1964; *Up the Down Staircase*, 1967.

Television Plays: *Jinxed*, 1949; *The Figgerin' of Aunt Wilma*, 1953; *This Little Kitty Stayed Cool*, 1953; *The Remarkable Case of Mr. Bruhl*, 1953; *Ernie Barger Is Fifty*, 1953; *Other People's Houses*, 1953; *The Haven*, 1953; *Madame Aphrodite*, 1953; *The Lawn Party*, 1955; *Star in the Summer Night*, 1955; *Guilty Is the Stranger*, 1955; *My Lost Saints*, 1955; *The Waiting Place*, 1955; *The Out-of-Towners*, 1956; *The Five-Dollar Bill*, 1957; *The Morning Place*, 1957; *Presence of the Enemy*, 1957; *The Innocent Sleep*, 1958; *A Corner of the Garden*, 1959; *Sarah's Laughter*, 1959; *The Invincible Teddy*, 1960; *That's Where the Town's Going*, 1962.

* * *

Tad Mosel gained attention as one of the leading American writers for live television in the 1950's. His scripts were ideally suited for the medium in their restricted scope, focus on intimate details, and near-Chekhovian naturalism within a thoroughly contemporary American suburban milieu. An earlier one-act play written for the stage, *Impromptu*, has become a minor classic in its treatment of illusion and reality by means of a theatrical metaphor. A group of actors find themselves on a stage to which they have been summoned in order to improvise a play. Their groping efforts point up the recognition that life itself is essentially an improvisation in which roles are assumed and identity is elusive. Mosel handles this potentially trite and sentimental concept with wit and restraint.

His most successful work, however, was a stage adaptation of James Agee's novel, *A Death in the Family*. Mosel's play, which bears the title *All the Way Home*, captures the essence of the subjective, introspective novel while providing it with an external, theatrical form. In its depiction of several generations of a family and its compassionate rendering of death. birth, and the process of emotional maturing, the work has echoes of Thornton Wilder, an impression that is reinforced by Mosel's fluid handling of time and space. Especially noteworthy is Mosel's economy of dialogue, which is related to his sure sense of the power of the stage to communicate in unverbalized, visual terms.

Since the early 1960's Mosel has been occupied primarily in film and TV, although he declares the theatre to be his first love and is currently working on a full-length play.

—Jarka M. Burian

MOWAT, David. British. Born in Cairo, Egypt, 16 March 1943. Educated at Bryanston School, 1956–60; New College, Oxford, 1961–64, B.A. (honours) in English language and literature 1964; University of Sussex, Falmer, 1964–66. Recipient: Arts Council bursary, 1970, 1971. Agent: Michael Imison, Dr. Jan Van Loewen Ltd., 81–83 Shaftesbury Avenue, London W1V 8BX. Address: 20 Highfield Avenue, Headington, Oxford OX3 7LR, England.

PUBLICATIONS

Plays

> *Jens* (produced Falmer, Sussex, 1965; London, 1969). Included in *Anna-Luse and Other Plays*, 1970.
> *Pearl* (produced Brighton, 1966).
> *1850* (produced London, 1967).
> *Anna-Luse* (produced Edinburgh, 1968; London, 1971; New York, 1972). Included in *Anna-Luse and Other Plays*, 1970.
> *Dracula*, with others (produced Edinburgh, 1969; London, 1973).
> *Purity* (produced Manchester, 1969; London, 1970; New York, 1972). Included in *Anna-Luse and Other Plays*, 1970.
> *Anna-Luse and Other Plays* (includes *Jens* and *Purity*). London, Calder and Boyars, 1970.
> *The Normal Woman, and Tyyppi* (produced London, 1970).
> *Adrift*, with others (produced Manchester, 1970).
> *The Others* (produced London, 1970). London, Calder and Boyars, 1973.
> *Most Recent Least Recent* (produced Manchester, 1970).
> *Inuit* (produced London, 1970).
> *Liquid* (produced London, 1971).
> *The Diabolist* (produced London, 1971).
> *John* (produced London, 1971).
> *Amalfi*, based on *The Duchess of Malfi* by Webster (produced Edinburgh, 1972).
> *Phoenix-and-Turtle* (produced London, 1972). Published in *The London Fringe Theatre*, edited by Victor Mitchell, London, Burnham House, 1975.
> *Morituri* (produced London, 1972).
> *My Relationship with Jayne* (produced London, 1973).
> *Come* (produced London, 1973).
> *Main Sequence* (produced Bristol, 1974).
> *The Collected Works* (produced London, 1974).
> *The Memory Man* (produced Bristol, 1974).
> *The Love Maker* (produced Bristol, 1974).
> *X to C* (produced Bristol, 1975).

Short Stories

Four Stories, in *New Writers 11*.   London, Calder and Boyars, 1973.

David Mowat comments:

I wrote my first play in 1955, and since then have written about 50, some 20 of which have been performed in Britain, Europe, and the U.S.A. In most of my work my intention has been to enlarge people's notion of reality, and in doing so to extend the dimensions and potential of the field known as "theatre."

The most widely-performed of my plays so far, *Anna-Luse*, written in 1966, is concerned with blindness and the treatment of the physically and mentally handicapped. *Purity*, from the same year, considers the phenomenon of censorship and the plight of the casualities of the "permissive society."

Recent work of mine, from about 1973, looks at questions relating to science (a field strangely neglected by theatre), notably time and gravitation (*Come*), light and astrophysics (*Main Sequence*), memory and amnesia (*The Memory Man*). By contrast, *Phoenix-and-Turtle* and *The Collected Works* are centred on poems of Shakespeare and Wyatt respectively for their formal and thematic content. I have written musical scores for my most recently performed plays, *The Memory Man, The Love Maker*, and *X to C*.

*   *   *

The name of David Mowat is familiar to those who frequent experimental fringe theatres. He is one of the band of young writers who provide much of the repertoire of short plays produced on the lunch-time circuit.

Many of these young playwrights are almost indistinguishable from each other: indeed, some half dozen of them indulge occasionally in corporate efforts. Their methods are free-wheeling, their subject matter often sensational, and their intention to subvert the existing social structure by means of shock effects. They command respect on account of their talent and seriousness of purpose, although their playing out of sadistic and erotic fantasies induces doubt as often as cheers.

From these writers, David Mowat stands conspicuously apart. There is present in his work an obsessive search for truth: "What information, useful information for the living of our lives, are we getting from this person?" asks the Narrator in a direct address to the audience in *Phoenix-and-Turtle*. In the same play, he also observes "There's no obscenity so obscene as the horrid spectre of untruth lurking in the centre of one's home." The speaker is a Lecturer in English who has been sacked as a result of a liaison with a student; who has just burnt the manuscript of his book on the subject of the eponymous Shakespeare poem; who feels compelled to tell his wife that she has not long to live; and who – after an incestuous attack on his daughter – discovers that the latter is already pregnant. All these lies are brought into the open but, characteristically, the very act of telling the truth by means of the basic lie of theatre is also questioned. The author likens art to putting a frame around lies and, by making them scan or rhyme, pretending to give them a moral purpose.

The preceding play, *Fat-Man* (not yet produced), deals allegorically with the rifts in the political Left. Using as a motto a dictum of Mao Tse-Tung's – "When the body is healthy, the feelings are correct" – the scene is set in a gymnasium, threatened with demolition. The name of three of its four characters – Fatman, Cripple, and Little-Boy – indicate the satirical nature if the problem: each one has passionate convictions regarding the desired use of the gymnasium. The play is sub-titled "the exercise of power"; needless to say, Mowat offers no easy solutions. His recent adaptation of *The Duchess of Malfi* and his approving quotation of Webster's remark that all life is a torture chamber may point to a vein of pessimism, but this, too, could be misleading. There is a quality of nagging obsession in Mowat's plays. His zeal for uncovering the truth has an echo of Ibsen, his haunted, nightmarish fantasies remind one of Strindberg. Of living authors, only Pinter comes to mind: Mowat, too, is a master of mystery and economy and his plays, though often difficult to comprehend at first sight, share with Pinter's the power to keep an audience spellbound.

He has travelled a long way since he wrote *Jens*: a comparatively straightforward piece of symbolism in which animals and humans mingle surrealistically. His most impressive early play was *Anna-Luse*. Here, a blind young girl gets up in the morning, goes through a ritual of stock-taking of her body and her possessions, and is visited by a girl-friend (also blind), a confused young man, and a dubious P.T. instructor. The last was the victim of a gang of thugs on the way over. Drenched but undaunted, he proceeds to give the girls some strange therapy, which induces in Anna-Luse a phantom pregnancy and childbirth. It is, however, the Instructor who is revealed most surprisingly: he ends, curled up like a baby, at Anna-Luse's breast.

Mowat's plays are by no means solemn. In *The Diabolist*, for example, a worried mum is introduced to her daughter's new boy friend. He is the epitome of the ordinary bloke, but turns out unexpectedly to be a devil-worshipper. Apart from a macabre and not altogether unsuccessful ending, this sketch is as funny as anything produced by the Absurdists.

The surface of these plays is in most cases shabbily suburban and lower middle class. They gain from being staged with absolute naturalism; the tension between manner and matter becomes then increasingly menacing. The rug is slowly and unnervingly pulled from under our feet, and we leave the theatre with our heads buzzing with questions which have no easy or formal solutions but which demand to be asked, if not answered.

His full-length play, *John*, belongs in this category. Its hero spends the entire play in a catatonic trance. The unease engendered by his silence, and its effect on the other, superficially "ordinary" characters, provides an exciting evening. Sudden irruptions of extreme violence occur regularly in Mowat's work, but they never appear gratuitously.

His short play *Come* seemed to me wilfully enigmatic. Here a distraught father attempts to persuade his estranged daughter to return to him. He lies in wait for her in a room adjoining an intellectual party which becomes an orgy. Nothing is achieved, and neither the motives nor the narrative makes any comprehensible sense.

Fortunately, his subsequent full-length play, *The Collected Works*, turned out to be his most lucid and fully realized to date. The setting is a library; the books, like the eyes of accumulated wisdom and disillusion, stare down at the turbulent emotional tangle involving a researcher, a love-sick girl, the sterile Chief Librarian, and his beautiful wife. Taking as his theme the tensions between life and art, Mowat contrasts the messiness and unexpectedness of the former with the unalterable composure of the latter. There is much sly comedy as the characters explain themselves in lengthy monologues. Once again, he writes in a deliberate undertone, but the surface simmers with unease and bubbles with incipient volcanic explosions.

With his sensitivity, his depth, and his increasing technical assurance, there is every chance that he will emerge from his present, somewhat esoteric, milieu and give us a play of real significance, with "useful information for the living of our lives." There is no more ambitious and necessary purpose in the field of playwriting.

—Frank Marcus

MURDOCH, (Jean) Iris.   British.   Born in Dublin, Ireland, 15 July 1919. Educated at Froebel Education Institute, London; Badminton School, Bristol; Somerville College, Oxford, 1938–42, B.A. 1942; Newnham College, Cambridge (Sarah Smithson Student in

Philosophy), 1947–48. Married the writer John Bayley in 1956. Assistant Principal in the Treasury, London, 1942–44; Administrative Officer with the United Nations Relief and Rehabilitation Administration (UNRRA), in London, Belgium and Austria, 1944–46. Fellow and University Lecturer in Philosophy, 1948–63, and since 1963 Honorary Fellow, St. Anne's College, Oxford. Lecturer, Royal College of Art, London, 1963–67. Recipient: Black Memorial Prize, for fiction, 1974; Whitbread Literary Award, for fiction, 1974. Honorary Member, American Academy of Arts and Letters, 1975. C.B.E. (Commander, Order of the British Empire), 1976. Address: Cedar Lodge, Steeple Aston, Oxford, England.

Publications

Plays

A Severed Head, with J. B. Priestley, adaptation of the novel by Iris Murdoch (produced Bristol and London, 1963; New York, 1964).   London, Chatto and Windus, 1964.
The Italian Girl, with James Saunders, adaptation of the novel by Iris Murdoch (produced Bristol, 1967; London, 1968).   London, French, 1969.
The Servants and the Snow (produced London, 1970).   Included in *The Three Arrows and The Servants and the Snow*, 1973.
The Three Arrows (produced Cambridge, 1972).   Included in *The Three Arrows and The Servants and the Snow, 1973*.
The Three Arrows, and The Servants and the Snow: Two Plays.   London, Chatto and Windus, 1973; New York, Viking Press, 1974

Novels

Under the Net.   London, Chatto and Windus, and New York, Viking Press, 1954.
The Flight from the Enchanter.   London, Chatto and Windus, and New York, Viking Press, 1956.
The Sandcastle.   London, Chatto and Windus, and New York, Viking Press, 1957.
The Bell.   London, Chatto and Windus, and New York, Viking Press, 1958.
A Severed Head.   London, Chatto and Windus, and New York, Viking Press, 1961.
An Unofficial Rose.   London, Chatto and Windus, and New York, Viking Press, 1962.
The Unicorn.   London, Chatto and Windus, and New York, Viking Press, 1963.
The Italian Girl.   London, Chatto and Windus, and New York, Viking Press, 1964.
The Red and the Green.   London, Chatto and Windus, and New York, Viking Press, 1965.
The Time of the Angels.   London, Chatto and Windus, and New York, Viking Press, 1966.
The Nice and the Good.   London, Chatto and Windus, and New York, Viking Press, 1968.
Bruno's Dream.   London, Chatto and Windus, and New York, Viking Press, 1969.
A Fairly Honourable Defeat.   London, Chatto and Windus, and New York, Viking Press, 1970.
An Accidental Man.   London, Chatto and Windus, 1971; New York, Viking Press 1972.
The Black Prince.   London, Chatto and Windus, and New York, Viking Press, 1973.
The Sacred and Profane Love Machine.   London, Chatto and Windus, and New York, Viking Press, 1974.
A Word Child.   London, Chatto and Windus, and New York, Viking Press, 1975.
Henry and Cato.   London, Chatto and Windus, 1976; New York, Viking Press, 1977.

Other

Sartre: Romantic Rationalist.   London, Bowes, and New Haven, Connecticut, Yale University Press, 1953.

The Sovereignty of Good over Other Concepts (lecture).   Cambridge, University Press, 1967.

The Sovereignty of Good (essays).   London, Routledge, 1970; New York, Schocken Books, 1971.

Manuscript Collection: University of Iowa, Iowa City.

*   *   *

Iris Murdoch emerged as a dominating novelist during the middle 1950's with a succession of novels (still continuing) that combined a deep seriousness with a flashing sense of comedy. Her early novels seem clear-cut and decisive, but the later ones become more complex and more fantastic. Miss Murdoch herself never attempted to write for the theatre until 1970, but much earlier (and with hindsight) it was inevitable that her work could be translated for the stage. And (again with hindsight) the choice of novel for this treatment − *A Severed Head* − seems equally inevitable. With a firmly defined, neatly interlocked set of characters, a fairly limited range of scene and, most important, an entertaining plot, this novel is ideal for dramatisation. (Its subsequent success merely underlines this view.) J. B. Priestley, an experienced playwright himself, collaborated on the adaptation to produce a neat drama.

A Severed Head has been described as "a metaphysical examination of love" and "a penetrating comment on the British character." Both observations may be true, but what audiences relished was the speed, elaboration and stylisation of the comedy which relates it firmly to the accomplished (and similarly literary) comedies of the Restoration. The characters are all upper-middle-class English, with the exception of an American psychiatrist and his mysterious, catalystic half-sister. These odd siblings cause chaos, force the others to break out of the straight-jacket of Englishness, with comic result. One significant effect of this play was to clarify the intent of the novel itself. Miss Murdoch does not always signal her comedy: on the stage the confrontations, ironies and shocks are unmistakable.

Another established playwright, James Saunders, was the collaborator on the second novel to be dramatised. *The Italian Girl*, though also a comedy in many ways, is a darker, more brooding piece than *A Severed Head*. A middle-aged son returns to the sombre family house in the north of England to attend his mother's funeral. This son is a pillar of rectitude, or perhaps sexually repressed, and the morass of passion and inter-personal chaos he uncovers tests him at every turn. Again we find a well-tailored series of characters, their symbolism this time only thinly disguised by their personalities. But once more the purpose and weight of a rich but complex novel are made very clear.

Miss Murdoch's first solo attempt at an original stage play, *The Servants and the Snow*, was followed by *The Three Arrows*, produced in the provinces in 1972. *The Three Arrows* is set in medieval Japan and this location is immediately mined for its formal and complex elements, and also for some superficial comedy derived from these elements and from a judicious use of anachronism. Prince Yorimitsu is a political prisoner and a potential danger to both the effete Imperial family and to the Shogun, the general who really rules. Through a series of schemes and plots designed to render the Prince harmless, Miss Murdoch debates the question of the individual's relation to the state and also the questions of personal choice and spontaneity of action. Two of Yorimitsu's spontaneous desires (to become a monk and then to marry the Crown Princess) are pre-empted by his captors and turned into political expediency. The central debate is compelling, but the play tends to lose power by its static nature.

—Roger Baker

MURPHY, Arthur Lister. Canadian. Born in Dominion, Nova Scotia, 8 February 1906. Educated at St. Mary's High School, Halifax; Dalhousie University, Halifax (Malcolm Honor Award, 1930), B.A. 1926, M.D., C.M. 1930; Montreal General Hospital. Married Mary Sylvia Shore in 1932; has three children. Assistant and Attending Surgeon, Halifax Infirmary, 1933–60, and Victoria General Hospital, Halifax, 1934–70; Assistant, then Associate Professor of Surgery, Dalhousie University, 1934–70; Part-time Member, 1963–68, and Chairman, 1968–74, University Grants Committee, Province of Nova Scotia. Since 1974, Advisor in Higher Education to the Minister of Education, Province of Nova Scotia. Director, Nova Scotia Trust Company. Founding President, Neptune Theatre Foundation, Halifax, 1963–66. Past Director, National Theatre School. Past President, Halifax Medical Society and the Nova Scotia Medical Society. Recipient: *Canadian Drama* award, 1962; Dominion Drama Festival Shield, 1963. LL.D.: St. Francis Xavier University, Antigonish, Nova Scotia, 1966. Agent: Ray Johnson, Alex Jackinson Agency, 55 West 42nd Street, Suite 658, New York, New York, 10019, U.S.A. Address: 6369 Coburg Road, Apartment 1406, Halifax, Nova Scotia, Canada.

PUBLICATIONS

Plays

> *The Sleeping Bag* (produced Halifax, 1966).
> *The Breadwinner* (produced St. John, New Brunswick, 1967.)
> *The First Falls on Monday* (produced Lindsay, Ontario, 1967).   Toronto, University of
>   Toronto Press, 1972.
> *Charlie* (produced Halifax, 1967).
> *Tiger! Tiger!* (produced Halifax, 1970).
> *A Virus Called Clarence* (produced Saskatoon, Saskatchewan, 1974).   Toronto,
>   Playwrights Co-op, 1974.

> Television Plays: *Ben Casey* and *Dr. Kildare* series, 1964–67 (USA).

Other

> *The Story of Medicine.*   Toronto, Ryerson Press, 1954.

Arthur Lister Murphy comments:

The First Falls On Monday and *Tiger! Tiger!* are historical plays, the first based on 48 crucial hours in the birth of Canada as a nation; the second based on the conflict between the Hunter brother, William and John.

In both of these the history has been made subservient to the drama because, if it were the other way round, it would be better to stay home from the theatre and read about it, But in presenting history on the stage there are unwritten rules the honest dramatist observes: he must re-create his characters in truth, as the Lord originally created them (in-so-far-as he is able). He may not transgress the main facts of history. He may limit or develop the facts to show the depths or the growth of a character. He may modify the facts for better plot structure and dramatic impact.

Most important, the dramatist peers into the minds of his characters in the hope of learning what history does not record. As with the biographer, it is the depth, the accuracy, and especially the perceptiveness of his probing that will largely determine the value of his finished work.

A Virus Called Clarence is set in a medical research laboratory where the staff is seeking, and in the end, discovering the viral cause of human breast cancer. The brilliant worker, the plodding worker – the many characters that make up a research lab work and battle together, but unite against the threat of a rival lab trying by means sometimes dubious, to beat them to the discovery. A love theme threads its way through the research.

*   *   *

Dr. Arthur Lister Murphy's scripts for the popular *Ben Casey* and *Dr. Kildare* medical series have diverted millions of American television viewers. In Canada his non-commercial radio and television dramas have been broadcast to national audiences on the CBC network. His theatre output, however, is less well-known although his record of six professionally-produced plays is matched by few other Canadian dramatists.

The Sleeping Bag, which premiered at Halifax's Neptune Theatre 19 July 1966, was an instant hit with local audiences, and in 1967 was selected as one of two productions taken by the Neptune company on its national tour. A situation comedy, tottering on the brink of farce, the play is set in the Arctic where a dispassionate physicist, a bluff explorer, and an alluring secretary find themselves marooned. The girl, with commendable domesticity, fashions herself a sleeping-bag; and, with equally laudable alacrity, intellectual and man of action vie for a place within it. Although the plot is simply a variation on the "desert island" device, the characters are no mere stereotypes. All three are highly individualized and credible in both motivation and action. The dialogue is frequently clever, and the play moves well. The idea can sustain a good hour's theatrical romp; but, forced to do duty for twice that time, it wears a trifle thin by the final curtain.

The surgeon-dramatist's only other comedy, *The Breadwinner*, was staged in the summer of 1967 at the Rothesay Playhouse near St. John, New Brunswick, Like Neil Simon, Murphy here exploits the comic potential of a topsy-turvy social situation. The action treats the heartwarming, if unconventional, capers of two pairs of newly-weds when the wives – one rich and one poor – assume financial responsibility for their impoverished student-husbands. The play succeeds well enough for what it is meant to be – a frothy midsummer frolic.

Charlie, commissioned by Neptune for its Centennial-year repertory and first performed on 4 August 1967, represents Murphy's sole attempt thus to treat seriously a contemporary subject. Here he sets out to document the plight of Cape Breton miners stripped of their livelihood and self-respect in the name of economic efficiency. The desperate protest of the protagonist, Charlie MacLean – "Up in the sun I'd melt away" – epitomizes a way of life where identity and fulfilment are inseparable from a daily struggle with death in the dark. The topic has particular poignancy for Nova Scotians, but it evokes a sympathetic resonance wherever human aspirations take second place to fiscal advantage. Although his material is admirably-chosen, Dr. Murphy's craftsmanship proves regrettably unequal to its demands. Possibly his own sympathies temporarily get the better of his artistic objectivity. In any event, the characters frequently lack depth and conviction. Intense emotion, which should struggle with silence, bubbles away in bombast and sentimentality. The movement of the plot is heavy-handed, and almost embarrassingly gauche at times. Nevertheless, a few trenchant moments and a splendid portrait of MacLean's wife, Martha, hint of an inherent dynamism the piece might reveal with searching revision and a fresh production.

The First Falls on Monday, undoubtedly Murphy's best effort to date, premiered at the Karwartha Festival in Lindsay, Ontario, in the summer of 1967. Unfortunately the Festival was poorly patronized and the play missed the public notice it merits. Perhaps its recent publication (in a revised version) by the University of Toronto Press will prompt a more timely revival.

This drama finds Murphy engaged in a reconstruction of the somewhat obscure week-end events which preceded the Monday, July 1st, of Canadian Confederation. With the founding fathers and their wives as *dramatis personae*, he creates a convincing, if largely unheroic, account of the political and social manoeuvres, domestic infighting, and disinterested sacrifice which attended the birth-pangs of the Dominion. For much of the time, Murphy relies upon letters, diaries, and other historical documents; but when history is silent, he wades in with informed conjecture. And so convincing is his tale that critic Herbert Whittaker, in the *Toronto Globe and Mail* (27 June 1967), considers it "worthy to impose itself on our history as firmly as Shakespeare's view of Richard II."

The play is remarkably well constructed. An immense amount of historical data is incorporated without interruption of the narrative flow. The dialogue is consistently powerful and natural; and the glimpses offered into the wellsprings of human conduct are shrewd and enduring. The portraits of Sir Charles Tupper, his conniving wife, Agnes, and Sir John A. Macdonald are masterly.

Murphy's recent venture, *Tiger! Tiger!*, opened at Neptune Theatre on 17 March 1970, and played to 89.4% capacity houses throughout its run. Drawing now upon medical rather than national history, he chronicles several decades in the career of the eighteenth-century anatomist, John Hunter. Although impressive as dramatic biography, the play is marred by its rather episodic structure. Some overall unifying factor beyond the character of Hunter himself is needed to give focus to the action. Nevertheless, the irascible iconoclast emerges as a monumental figure, dwarfing everything and everyone else in the drama. Dr. Murphy evidences a fine sense of period, and his insights into the medical mind are enlightening, and even, perhaps, unique.

Unlike many of his confreres, Murphy is not primarily a social critic. His interest lies rather in the exploration of private motivation and its fruition in personal action and reaction. People matter for themselves, not for what they represent either as embodiments of ideologies or as social or political groupings. On this individual level, his observation is swift and his understanding acute. "As a physician," he said (in a conversation in August 1971), "you must put yourself on terms of intimacy with your patient in a matter of minutes." This heightened sensitivity to the human condition underlies all of Murphy's dramatic output, and may well constitute his major contribution to the Canadian stage.

—John D. Ripley

MURPHY, Thomas. Irish. Born in Tuam, County Galway, 23 February 1935. Educated at Vocational School, Tuam; Vocational Teachers' Training College, Dublin. Married to Mary Hippisley; has two children. Apprentice Fitter and Welder, Tuam, 1953–55; Engineering Teacher, Vocational School, Mountbellew, 1957–62. Actor/Director, 1951–62. Member of the Board of Directors, Irish National Theatre (The Abbey Theatre). Recipient: Irish Academy of Letters Award, 1972. Agent: Robin Dalton, Robin Dalton Associates, 11-12 Hanover Street, London W.1, England; or, Bridget Aschenberg, International Creative Management, 40 West 57th Street, New York, New York 10019, U.S.A. Address: Danesmoate, Rathfarnham, County Dublin, Ireland.

PUBLICATIONS

Plays

On the Outside, with Noel O'Donoghue (produced Cork, 1961; New Haven, Connecticut, 1976). Dublin, Gallery Press, 1976.

A Whistle in the Dark (produced London, 1961; New York, 1969).   New York, French, 1971.

Famine (produced Dublin, 1966; London, 1969).

The Orphans (produced Dublin, 1968; Newark, Delaware, 1971).   Newark, Delaware, Proscenium Press, 1974.

The Fooleen: A Crucial Week in the Life of a Grocer's Assistant (produced Dublin, 1969; California, 1971).   Dixon, California, Proscenium Press, 1970.

The Morning after Optimism (produced Dublin, 1971; New York, 1974).   Cork, Mercier Press, 1973.

The White House (produced Dublin, 1972).

On the Inside (produced Dublin, 1974; New Haven, Connecticut, 1976).   Dublin, Gallery Press, 1976.

The Vicar of Wakefield, adaptation of the novel by Goldsmith (produced Dublin, 1974).

The Sanctuary Lamp (produced Dublin, 1975).   Dublin, Poolbeg Press, 1976.

Screenplays: *The Sin-Eaters,* 1971; *Wrack,* 1972.

Television Plays: *The Fly Sham,* 1963; *Veronica,* 1963; *Snakes and Reptiles,* 1968; *Young Man in Trouble,* 1970; *The Moral Force, The Policy, Relief* (trilogy), 1973; *Conversations on a Homecoming,* 1976; *Speeches of Farewell,* 1976.

Critical Studies: review in *Time* (New York), 17 October 1969; Abbey Theatre programme, October 1975.

Thomas Murphy comments:

My plays attempt to produce something that can be identified with or recognised rather than understood or explained. Rather than developing lines that progress to a conclusion or point to a problem, details are conglomerated to re-create a mood of the human condition. The mood's the thing.

*   *   *

Thomas Murphy is best known for his still frightening study of an Irish hooligan family, *A Whistle in the Dark*, which reminded British and American audiences that not all Irish writers share Behan's joviality, Synge's melancholy or O'Casey's socialism. *A Whistle in the Dark* has all the qualities of American naturalistic drama in the 1930's – and some of the defects. The story is compelling: and the main theme – about the way in which violence is bred from a profound sense of inferiority – was journalistically relevant in the early sixties and has since seemed prophetic. The dialogue is straightforward and convincing, without any literary artifices but not without subtlety: the characterization is sure, though a little superficial in the portraits of Iggy, a tough guy, and Betty, Michael Carney's wife: and the whole play accelerates to a powerful climax in the second and third acts, which fails only perhaps at the very end, when the killing of Des seems unnecessarily melodramatic. *A Whistle in the Dark* established Murphy's reputation as an assured writer of naturalistic drama, fully aware of his background as an Irishman but determined not to be swamped by it.

The story concerns Michael Carney, an Irish immigrant to the English industrial town, Coventry. Michael is industrious and hardworking: and he has managed to establish himself in the area, living with his English wife, Betty, in a small surburban house, but he retains a loyalty and a sense of responsibility toward his five Irish brothers and his father, who come to stay with him. The other members of the Carney family are known as the Fighting Carneys, an emblem which his father, Dada, relishes: and as soon as they arrive, the Carneys try to dominate the hooligan world of thuggery and prostitution in Coventry as they have done in their Irish home town. Michael believes that his peaceful example, his reasoning will quieten them down to a more orderly way of life: and in particular, he wants to separate his youngest brother, Des, from the family violence. But he has to argue not only with his brothers but with the far more formidable influence of his father: who is still prepared to take off his belt to his sons, whose cocky assertiveness reveals a profound self-hate. Dada is disgusted by the world, by himself and by his failure in life: and this disgust becomes a violent determination to prove that the Carneys can destroy any other gang in town. In Coventry, a fight is arranged with the Mulryans, and the Carneys are victorious. Michael tries to stop the fight: but eventually, out of sheer family loyalty, he tries to join in. His indecision causes him to be a figure of fun in the family: and Dada baits him to fight young Des. Michael is so taunted that he does so – and hits his brother over the head with a bottle. Des is killed: and Dada solemnly accuses Michael of being a troublemaker.

Murphy's great achievement was to make Michael's indecision the connecting link to the play. Michael is indeed a tragic hero, torn between conflicting loyalties and eventually destroyed by refusing to listen to the voice of conscience, represented by Betty, his long-suffering wife, who leaves him. Murphy manages to analyze skilfully the causes of violence: not only the obvious ones such as the Carney's childhood humiliations at the hands of priests and teachers, but the more subtle ones, such as the treatment of women. The Carneys want to prove their masculinity whenever they can: and it is the taunt that Michael is too submissive to Betty which goads him into joining his brothers. Michael insults and strikes Betty: and by doing so he loses his main ally and his inner certainty that his ways are right. From this moral disintegration, the tragic culmination to the plot becomes inevitable, although the final killing may be too obvious a conclusion. The real tragedy was after all not the physical death, but the general acceptance of violence even by the man who has stood out against violence. The holocaust sweeps away the liberal and the fanatic together.

Murphy's later plays have not greatly added to his early reputation although they indicate that his talents are more varied than his first success implied. *Famine* was performed at the Dublin Festival and then in a rudimentary one-night production at the Royal Court in London. The story is set in the great Irish potato famine of 1846: and deals with the defiance of an Irish peasant family against physical starvation and political exploitation by English landlords. The play is tense and contains one magnificent central role, a resolute, bitter farmer: but it was considered to be over-written and somewhat humourless by some critics. Two subsequent plays, *The Orphans* and *The Morning after Optimism*, were also premiered at the Dublin Festival and were more lighthearted in their subject matter and treatment.

The orphans of the first play are two members of an Irish immigrant family, who have settled down in an English country house in Kent and amassed a small fortune. One is a poet and his sister is a painter. They live in a world of English permissiveness and have become idle dilettantes. They marry a reformed prostitute and an ex-priest: and the theme illustrates the way in which the superimposed culture fails to eradicate the centuries of physical self-hate and religious stock reactions of their Irish origins. The priest doesn't forget his priestly functions, when he loses his faith: nor does the reformed whore lose her sense of shame or her memories of innocence. The second play, *The Morning after Optimism*, tackles a somewhat similar theme in a more allegorical style: four characters meet in a wood – a Poet, an Orphan, a Whore and a Ponce. Two represent an idealized, over-romantic view of love: and two its debased, sexual equivalent. The Whore falls in love – and eventually destroys – the Poet, while the Ponce debases the virgin Orphan. The moral of the story seems to be that idealized love cannot survive contact with animal sex: and despite the brilliantly written single part of the Ponce, the downright comedy and occasional bursts of lyricism, the play was considered to be too clichaic in its subject matter and too whimsical in its treatment to survive a transference from Dublin.

Perhaps Murphy's most successful play (after *A Whistle in the Dark*) was *The White House*, produced at the 1972 Dublin Festival. In *The White House*. he returns to the naturalistic style of his first plays, but with one difference: he reverses the expected chronology of the first and second acts. The first act is set in the present – in an Irish pub, where four former friends, each suffering from the despair of early middle age, meet to discuss old times. One is a successful actor whose career has been established in England. On his return, he finds the provincial atmosphere of his home town stultifying: and his former friends resent and yet reluctantly accept his unwilling condescension. The second act takes place nine years before, at the time of President Kennedy's assassination. The news of the murder arrives on a day when the pub throbs with an unexpected pride. Kennedy is the great hero, the man whose international presence justifies the Irish heritage. The pub is run by a landlord, JJ, who models himself physically and spiritually on Kennedy: his pub is even known as the White House. The second act derives its power from the realization that all the original hopes have been dashed and that the optimism was based on shallow foundations. But it also stresses the essential self-delusion of the society – that its inhabitants are not trying to justify their lives by creating industry, products and a more equitable distribution of wealth, but by reflected glory. Their very pride underlines the sense of defeat.

Mruphy's naturalistic plays reveal an acute social awareness, a carefully organized dramatic technique and a willingness to attempt the difficult but necessary complexities of a modern political play. He is the best Irish dramatist since Sean O'Casey. But sometimes, like O'Casey, he moves away from his surefooted skills towards a more tentative allegory: and when he does so, the plays suffer from too superficial a treatment of the chosen themes. The dialogue becomes whimsical, the stories less interesting, and the characters without substance. Murphy has also written widely and successfully for television.

—John Elsom

MUSAPHIA, Joseph. New Zealander. Born in London, England, 8 April 1935. Educated at primary school in Australia, and at Christchurch Boys' High School, New Zealand. Married Marie Musaphia in 1966; has two children. Shop assistant, Ballintyne's Christchurch, 1950–51; motor mechanic, David Crozier's, Christchurch, 1951–54; commercial artist, Stuart Wearn, Christchurch, 1954–55, Wood and Braddock, Wellington, 1955, John Haddon, London, England, 1956–57, and for agencies, Wellington, 1958–60; cartoonist for the New Zealand *Listener*, Wellington, 1958–60; fish and chip shop owner, Wellington, 1971–73. Since 1974, columnist, *The Dominion* and *Sunday Times*, Wellington. Free-lance radio and television writer. Recipient: New Zealand State Literary Fund grant, 1963; New Zealand Arts Council grant, 1974, 1976. Agent: Playmarket, P.O. Box 9767, Wellington. Address: 293 Karaka Bay Road, Wellington 3, New Zealand.

PUBLICATIONS

Plays

Free (produced Wellington, 1960). Published in *Landfall 68* (Christchurch), December 1963.
Virginia Was a Dog (produced Wellington, 1968).
The Guerrilla (produced Sydney, 1971). Sydney, Currency Press, 1976.
Victims (produced Wellington, 1973). Published in *Act 20* (Wellington), August 1973.
Obstacles (produced Wellington, 1974). Published in *Act 25* (Wellington), 1974.
Mothers and Fathers (produced Wellington, 1975).

Screenplay: *Don't Let It Get You*, 1966.

Radio Plays: more than 120 plays, including *The Listener with the Pop-up Toaster; Think; Has Anybody Here Seen Christmas?; Jolly Roger; Sounds Furious.*

Television Plays: *Joe's World* series; *In View of the Circumstances* series.

Joseph Musaphia comments:

While I have tried both serious and comedy writing and acting, I prefer comedy. Receiving an immediate, vocal response from the members of an audience is the one vital peculiarity comedy has that allows its creator conclusive proof that his effort was worthwhile. By the same token, I hope that what they initially laughed at supplies them with food for thought for some time after their amusement has died down. If I had to describe my attitude towards my writing, it would probably be best summed up by a description used by a local critic in reviewing *Mothers and Fathers*. Michael Dean referred to me in the New Zealand *Listener* as a "moral democrat." Having checked out this description in as many tomes as are available to me, I have decided that it just might be inoffensive enough to be acceptable to this playwright, who is not at all happy to be categorized or to write about his own work. I don't enjoy being asked what a play of mine "was getting at," because if the play worked on stage the question should not have to be asked. I can say that after a preposterously varied existence, I count myself very lucky indeed to be making such an enjoyable living out of a typewriter. If audiences continue to get half the pleasure out of watching my plays as I get writing them, I have no complaints.

*   *   *

The development of Joseph Musaphia's plays parallels fairly closely the pattern for indigenous writing for the theatre in New Zealand in recent years. His first play, *Free*, was performed by the New Zealand Players Company as part of its workshop programme. The collapse of this company spelled the end of ambitious plans for national touring companies. While the theatre generally gathered strength, and a policy of encouragement for regional development of professional theatre evolved, would-be playwrights had radio drama as a regular outlet for their work, and the very occasional glimmer of interest from the amateur theatre. During this time Musaphia wrote and directed *Virginia Was a Dog* for the first production at Stagecraft, Wellington's amateur theatre. He also began to write and perform in television revues. A one-act play, *The Guerrilla*, was well received and ran for two and half months at Hayes Gordon's Ensemble Theatre in Sydney. An Auckland production was less well received. At this stage Musaphia's work had an over-contrived air and he was not at ease in writing for the theatre.

Theatres were founded and began to consolidate in the late 1960's and early 1970's in New Zealand, but comparatively little space was found in the programming for local playwrights. However, the wealth of locally written work on radio, the short burst of new work at Downstage, Wellington, in its early years and the interest in a Gulbenkian-sponsored workshop series of commissioned new plays all showed that conditions were coming right for theatres and audiences to accept the work of local writers on their own terms.

Musaphia's play *Victims* was his first to achieve real popularity. It was revived for a second season, given a regional tour and produced in Dunedin. *Victims* has all the hallmarks of Joseph Musaphia's style. His first concern is with shape and plot structure. He is also a collector of intriguing ideas. Snippets from old newspapers, memories, and stories that are related to him are all salted away. When a particular idea is selected he works it through before beginning to write. In *Victims* two stories of 19th century colonial New Zealand are woven together. One concerns a well-known Canterbury gentleman who shocked his family by leaving his fortune to an illegitimate daughter whose existence was unknown to the family. The second borrowed some of the colour of the history of Amy Bock, whose escapades as a confidence trickster included masquerading as a man in order to marry a young woman of comfortable means. Musaphia developed a neat and highly satisfactory plot. As part of it the young woman who inherits the money turns out to be a crusader for moral purity. (The satire on a contemporary New Zealand organisation and its founder was much enjoyed.) The play has a tendency to be overwritten and some passages are clumsy and do not quite manage the dialogue, which aims to stride this century as well as the previous one, but there are ten good comic roles, and some magnificently funny scenes in a play woven strongly together and balanced by themes of sex and death.

In writing his next play, *Obstacles*, Musaphia clearly had an eye to local conditions and was writing with a theatre and even actors in mind. The play has a strong sense of present-day Wellington. The three characters are grotesques, but credible as dregs of a recognisable society. In this play his skills in building and extending comic situations acquire a depth and an independence of revue techniques.

Since his local success with *Victims*, Musaphia has settled down to a play-a-year routine and has become a columnist for a Wellington newspaper, so earning a full-time living from writing. His most recent play, *Mothers and Fathers*, explores the proposition that a well-to-do childless couple hire the womb of a third party to produce a child. The idea is developed through well-shaped and paced first and second acts. In the third act the pressures built by the satire on New Zealand's monied suburbia and by the reversal in balance of power between the sexes almost burst the shape that the writer has fashioned. At this time Musaphia is sensing with accuracy the things that his contemporaries are willing to laugh at in themselves.

—Nonnita Rees

NAUGHTON, Bill. British. Born in Ballyhaunis, County Mayo, Ireland, 12 June 1910; grew up in Lancashire, England. Educated at St. Peter and St. Paul School, Bolton, Lancashire. Civil Defence Driver in London during World War II. Married to Ernestine Pirolt. Has worked as a lorry driver, weaver, and coal-bagger. Recipient: Screenwriters Guild Award, 1967, 1968; Prix Italia, for radio play, 1974. Agent: Dr. Jan Van Loewen Ltd., 81–83 Shaftesbury Avenue, London W1V 8BX. Address: Kempis, Orrisdale Road, Ballasalla, Isle of Man, United Kingdom.

PUBLICATIONS

Plays

    Spring and Port Wine (as *My Flesh, My Blood*, broadcast 1957; as *Spring and Port Wine*, produced Birmingham, 1964; London, 1965; as *Keep It in the Family*, produced New York, 1967). London, French, 1967.
    June Evening (broadcast, 1958; produced Birmingham, 1966). London, French, 1973.
    Alfie (as *Alfie Elkins and His Little Life*, broadcast 1962; as *Alfie*, produced London, 1963). London, French, 1963.
    All in Good Time (produced London, 1963; New York, 1965). London, French, 1964.

He Was Gone When We Got There, music by Leonard Salzedo (produced London, 1966).
Annie and Fanny (produced Bolton, Lancashire, 1967).
Lighthearted Intercourse (produced Liverpool, 1971).

Screenplays: *Alfie*, 1966; *The Family Way*, 1966; *Spring and Port Wine*, 1969.

Radio Plays: *Timothy*, 1956; *My Flesh, My Blood*, 1957; *She'll Make Trouble*, 1958; *June Evening*, 1958; *Late Night on Watling Street*, 1959; *The Long Carry*, 1959; *Seeing a Beauty Queen Home*, 1960, *On the Run*, 1960; *Wigan to Rome*, 1960; *'30-'60*, 1960; *Jackie Crowe*, 1962; *Alfie Elkins and His Little Life*, 1962; *November Day*, 1963; *The Mystery*, 1973.

Television Plays: *Nathaniel Titlark* series, 1957; *Jim Batty* (story), 1957; *Starr and Company* series, 1958; *Yorky* series, with Alan Prior, 1960; *Somewhere for the Night*, 1962; *Looking for Frankie*, 1963; *It's Your Move*, 1967.

Novels

Rafe Granite.   London, Pilot Press, 1947.
One Small Boy.   London, MacGibbon and Kee, 1957.
Alfie.   London, MacGibbon and Kee, and New York, Ballantine, 1966.
Alfie Darling.   London, MacGibbon and Kee, 1970; New York, Simon and Schuster, 1971.

Short Stories

Late Night in Watling Street and Other Stories.   London, MacGibbon and Kee, 1959; New York, Ballantine, 1966.
The Goalkeeper's Revenge.   London, MacGibbon and Kee, 1961.
The Goalkeeper's Revenge and Spit Nolan.   London, Macmillan, 1974.

Other

A Roof over Your Head (autobiography).   London, Pilot Press, 1945.
Pony Boy (autobiography).   London, Harrap, 1966.
A Dog Called Nelson (juvenile).   London, Dent, 1976.

*   *   *

Bill Naughton's emergence in the 1960's as a major writer for the theatre has been primarily seen as a revival of the spirit of the Manchester School, and indeed his two biggest successes − *All in Good Time* and *Spring and Port Wine*, concentrating on the detailed exploration of family crises in working-class Bolton − recall the world of Harold Brighouse. In fact, in these plays, Naughton emerges more as the natural successor of intermediary writers in the Manchester tradition such as Walter Greenwood, while to concentrate only on this side of his talents is to overlook the wider range and theatrical development away from realism such as in *Alfie* and even work derived from his favourite Bolton background such as *June Evening*, derived from a radio original, an episodic play covering the stream of life in a Bolton street in 1921 during a pit strike (one of Naughton's most interesting plays, it never achieved commercial success, and has had to date only an abortive provincial tour).

Naughton's earlier work in television and in radio documentary plays such as *The Long Carry* (about coal picking) and *Wigan to Rome* (following a coach-party of Northern tourists) provided much of the content and style of his work in the theatre, although his first stage play, *All in Good Time*, indicates an attempt to establish a more formal construction in contrast with his TV and radio plays, which largely avoided orthodox frameworks. However, it similarly examines a basic truth of human behaviour in a context of carefully-observed community life. Its basis, the non-consummation of a young couple's marriage, could be the core of any routine Northern comedy, even opening with the familiar situation of a wedding-party, but the human elements in the play outweigh conventionality, and already apparent is the great strength of Naughton's gentle but ironically affectionate and therefore basically unsentimental attitude towards his characters. He is particularly adroit in handling changes of mood as an initial comedy-situation graduates into a wider examination of parental problems as well as those of the younger generation. The play suffers somewhat by its rather abruptly-contrived final disclosures, revealing a certain lack of tension between Naughton's discursive manner and the demands of the three-act play format, and the same pattern occurs in the second of his Bolton comedies, *Spring and Port Wine*. A similarly warm-hearted comedy, it likewise focuses on family stress, with an even stronger paterfamilias central character in Rafe Crompton, a Hobson-like domestic tyrant. Naughton once wrote of the Bolton he knew – "I remember the smells in the homes, the jobs, and everything about the people" – an attitude reflected in the detail of the play and an understanding of his characters giving them the stamp of authenticity, just as his acute ear for the occasional deflating truth saves them from overwhelming sentimentality. Again, however, the fabric of the play tends to dissolve at the close, in a contrived happy ending of reconciliation, as Crompton crumbles in a surprisingly sudden change of heart.

Alfie reveals further Naughton's gift of creating a dynamic central character and also that he is not necessarily a playwright of Lancashire comedy only. This history of the amorous adventures of a Cockney "spiv" Don Juan had its origin in one of Naughton's best radio plays, *Alfie Elkins and His Little Life*, and its greatest strength, Naughton's extraordinary ability to get under the skin of his protagonists, remains in the stage version. Although the surroundings of his main character and the counterpoint of Alfie's monologues with action at times seem rather thin, and the transitions in the opening-out of the play occasionally somewhat stiff, Alfie himself remains a superbly-realised figure as Naughton explores all his meretricious charm and essential bleak loneliness, especially in a striking scene as Alfie thinks of fatherhood, an idea he finds at once appealing and appalling.

Naughton's work since these three successes has been sporadic. *He Was Gone When We Got There* was in a markedly different vein, a neo-Orwellian social satire probing the clash between computerised bureaucracy and anarchic individualism in the shape of Badger Brown, the last "Free unit" in a Britain entangled in red tape. A promising core is dissipated by the lumbering obviousness of the satire and even more by the surprisingly lukewarm sub-Ealing Films quality of Naughton's comedy. *Lighthearted Intercourse* (seen in Liverpool in 1971) marked a return to the surer background of his Bolton plays; a gentle, two-character comedy of married life, it has a great deal of poignancy and charm. Its loose structure and use of a shifting time-scale suggest a possible new departure for Naughton in the use of his staple Lancashire material within a freer technique, but to date no new play has been forthcoming.

—Alan Strachan

NGUGI, James T. (Ngugi Wa Thiong'o). Kenyan. Born in Limuru in 1938. Educated at University College, Makerere; Leeds University, Yorkshire. Editor, *Penpoint* magazine, Makerere. Literary and Political Journalist: Regular Contributor to the *Sunday Nation*, Nairobi. Recipient: East African Literature Bureau award, 1964. Address: c/o William Heinemann Ltd., 15 Queen Street, London W1X 8BE, England.

PUBLICATIONS

Plays

> *The Black Hermit* (produced Nairobi, 1962).   Kampala, Màkerere University Press,
>   1963; London, Heinemann, 1968.
> *This Time Tomorrow* (broadcast, 1966).   Included in *This Time Tomorrow* (collection),
>   1970.
> *This Time Tomorrow* (includes *The Rebels* and *The Wound in the Heart*).   Nairobi, East
>   African Literature Bureau, 1970.

> Radio Play: *This Time Tomorrow*, 1966.

Novels

> *Weep Not, Child.*   London, Heinemann, 1964.
> *The River Between.*   London, Heinemann, 1965.
> *A Grain of Wheat.*   London, Heinemann, 1967.

Short Stories

> *Secret Lives and Other Stories.*   London, Heinemann, and New York, Lawrence Hill,
>   1975.

Other

> *Homecoming: Essays on African and Caribbean Literature, Culture and Politics* (as
>   Ngugi Wa Thiong'o).   London, Heinemann, 1972.

*   *   *

James T. Ngugi is a better novelist than he is a dramatist. If there is any reason for his inclusion in this work other than his reputation in that field, it is that for several years after its production in 1962, *The Black Hermit* was the only full-length play in English from East Africa.

Written as a response to Uganda's achieving independence in that year, the play is a pessimistic look at the rival claims of traditional and modern ways of life, traditional and Christian religions, public service and private fulfilment. Unfortunately, as Gerald Moore said of the original production, the claims of nation, ideology, family, and love are only touched upon, not explored. The shuffling of the different issues – now one, now another held before us – produces melodrama.

Remi, the first of his tribe to go to college, loved Thoni, who married his brother while he was away. On the death of his brother, his father urged him to follow tradition and marry his brother's wife. This he did, though he felt that he could never love one who was another's. He fled from her, and from the expectations of the tribe that he would be their political leader, to the city and the love of a white girl. The play opens with the efforts of his mother and wife to get him to return; the pastor will visit Remi on their behalf. Meanwhile, the elders also send emissaries, bearing "medicine." Weighing the bible in one hand, the "medicine" in the other, Remi is moved by these "pieces of superstition" and returns home. He holds a successful political rally, against tribalism, but while he discusses future plans a woman enters with a letter from

> She who was kind.
> She who was true.
> A tender sapling growing straight.
> Though surrounded by weed.

His wife had loved him, and deep down he had loved her, but she had heard him say that he had been wrong to follow custom in marrying her, and so committed suicide, leaving the letter to state that she had always loved him. The play ends with Remi kneeling beside her body and declaring

> I came back to break Tribe and Custom,
> Instead, I've broken you and me.

More interesting is a short radio play, broadcast on the BBC African Service in 1966, *This Time Tomorrow*. A slum, ironically named Uhuru Market (Uhuru, Freedom, was a slogan of the nationalists against the British), is to be bulldozed because "tourists from America, Britain, and West Germany are disgusted with the dirt that is slowly creeping into a city that used to be the pearl of Africa." In the slum live Njango, widow of a freedom fighter, and her dreaming daughter Wanjiro. During the play, Wanjiro's lover persuades her to move into his house, and Njango attends a protest meeting, led by the Stranger, a former freedom fighter who is arrested. A bulldozer razes the huts as Njango ends the play: "If only we had stood up against them! If only we could stand together!"

Against the actualities of the situation, caught in a soliloquy of Wanjiro's − "How often have I leaned against this very post, and watched the city awake. Just now, noise is dead in the city. It is so dark outside − the crawling maggots in the drains are hidden" − are set the bland phrases of the journalist, with which the play opens − "The filthy mushrooms − inhabited by human beings − besieging our capital city, came tumbling down yesterday." *The Black Hermit* is reminiscent of Soyinka's *A Dance of the Forests* in the caution and pessimism with which it greets independence. His later play reflects an increase in bitterness, a disgust at official cant, a sense that Uhuru has brought nothing to the common people, that parallels Soyinka's development. Unfortunately, Ngugi does not have Soykinka's knowledge of the theatre, nor his ability to give vital energy to his characters.

—Anthony Graham-White

NICHOLS, Peter (Richard).   British.   Born in Bristol, 31 July 1927. Educated at Bristol Grammar School, 1936–44; Bristol Old Vic Theatre School, 1948–50; Trent Park Teachers' Training College, Hertfordshire, 1955–57. Served in the Royal Air Force, 1945–48. Married Thelma Reed in 1959; has four children (one deceased). Actor, in repertory, television and films, 1950–55. General subjects teacher in primary and secondary schools, 1957–59. Has also worked as a park keeper, English language teacher in Italy, cinema commissionaire and clerk. Visiting Playwright, Guthrie Theatre, Minneapolis, 1976. Governor, Greenwich Theatre, London, since 1970. Member of the Arts Council Drama Panel, 1972–75. Recipient: Arts Council bursary, 1961; *Evening Standard* award, 1967, 1969; John Whiting Award, 1969. Agent: Margaret Ramsay Ltd., 14a Goodwin's Court, London WC2N 4LL. Address: 9 Highbury Terrace, London N.5, England.

PUBLICATIONS

Plays

> *Promenade* (televised, 1959).   Published in *Six Granada Plays*, London, Faber, 1960.
> *Ben Spray* (televised, 1961).   Published in *New Granada Plays*, London; Faber, 1961.
> *The Hooded Terror* (televised, 1963; produced Bristol, 1964).
> *The Gorge* (televised, 1965).   Published in *The Television Dramatist*, edited by Robert
>   Muller, London, Elek, 1973.
> *A Day in the Death of Joe Egg* (produced Glasgow and London, 1967; New York, 1968).
>   London, Faber, 1967; as *Joe Egg*, New York, Grove Press, 1967.
> *The National Health; or, Nurse Norton's Affair* (produced London, 1969; Chicago, 1971;
>   New York, 1974).   London, Faber, 1970; New York, Grove Press, 1975.
> *Heart and Flowers* (televised, 1970).   Published in *The Television Play*, edited by Robin
>   Wade, London, BBC, 1976.
> *Forget-Me-Not Lane* (produced London, 1971; New Haven, Connecticut, 1973).
>   London, Faber, 1971.
> *Neither Up nor Down* (produced London, 1972).
> *Chez Nous* (produced London, 1974).   London, Faber, 1974.
> *The Freeway* (produced London, 1974).   London, Faber, 1975.
> *Harding's Luck*, adaptation of the novel by E. Nesbit (produced London, 1974).
> *Privates on Parade* (produced London, 1977).

> Screenplays: *Catch Us If You Can (Having a Wild Weekend)*, 1965; *Georgy Girl*, 1966; *A
> Day in the Death of Joe Egg*, 1972; *The National Health*, 1972.

> Television Plays: *Walk on the Grass*, 1959; *After All*, with Bernie Cooper, 1959;
> *Promenade*, 1959; *Ben Spray*, 1961; *The Big Boys*, 1961; *The Reception*, 1961; *The
> Heart of the Country*, 1962; *Ben Again*, 1962; *The Hooded Terror*, 1963; *The Continuity
> Man*, 1963; *The Brick Umbrella*, 1964; *When the Wind Blows*, 1965; *The Gorge*, 1965,
> *Majesty*, from a story by F. Scott Fitzgerald, 1968; *Winner Takes All*, from a story by
> Evelyn Waugh, 1968; *Daddy Kiss It Better*, 1969; *Hearts and Flowers*, 1970; *The
> Common*, 1973.

Critical Studies: *The Second Wave* by John Russell Taylor, London, Methuen, 1971;
interview in *Playback 2* by Ronald Hayman, London, Davis Poynter, 1973.

Theatrical Activities:

Director: **Play** – *A Day in the Death of Joe Egg*, London, 1971.

*   *   *

Few dramatists have been more successful than Peter Nichols in making their characters
reveal their attitudes towards a problem, towards each other, towards society, and in this day
of multi-media assault, where everyone's opinion is known and categorized, the writer who
is an artist at encapsulating attitude is bound to be in a position of pre-eminence.

In, for example, *A Day in the Death of Joe Egg* Nichols demonstrates admirably his ability
to deal with a forbidden subject, that of the paraplegic, the spastic, the "vegetable" (referred
to in many ways during the course of the play). There was, at the time it was performed, a
sudden rush of approval as a new barrier of inhibition was swept away: for this is very
flattering to an audience. Nichols manages to present us with an uncomfortable subject in a

593

kind of hectic, hectoring way so that it never manages to offend. He incorporates as well, cleverly, every possible range of emotional response. We come away feeling that there is something in the problem for all of us.

Nichols' jokes always cut near the bone, and in the revival of *Joe Egg* directed by the author himself one sometimes had the feeling there was no bone left to cut near. Possibly there may be something too quiescent at the back of the parents Bri and Sheila's games. They are constantly exercising their instantly dismissable feelings at the expense of their "problem." Sometimes, one feels, a good sustained heartfelt cry of pain might be more cathartic – but pain is not an attitude. One's main reservation, however, concerns the plot. Plot is the soul of a play, and in comedy such as *Joe Egg* one looks for some form to capture the imagination. Here and there Nichols throws in the possibility, as when, for instance, he points out that we are all cripples in some way, all limited. But while the peripheries of the problem never relax their hold, a central issue fails to materialize. Nichols' method is to touch upon all, and to move on with brittle and lightening force in case he loses his audience.

As in the comedies of Jean Anouilh, especially his most recent ones, it is a formula for success of the broadest kind. *The National Health* (produced by the National Theatre in 1969) has the same combination of qualities and shortcomings. Half is wry and unextended comic comment on the human race – the conclusion being that each of us is entitled to his own death – half a gallop through every known attitude to health. The result is a lively documentary, extremely well organized, but ultimately, possibly, a little thin.

In *Forget-Me-Not Lane* the debt to Anouilh appears even greater, as a middle-aged man asks himself what went wrong in his marriages, and re-examines his childhood and his life with his parents during World War Two. The device of shuttling the action back and forth between past and present results in much high comedy and some sharp theatrical moments.

Chez Nous presents the much-trodden situation of two friendly married couples, Dick and Liz, Diana and Phil, on holiday in the Dordogne, who are driven to the brink of splitting up. It is undoubtedly Nichols' best play to date. The marital tug of war that we have already seen in *Joe Egg* and *Forget-Me-Not Lane* is organized in greater depth and comic intensity than Nichols has used previously, and in his presentation of the boulevard twist of fate – that Dick's daughter has given birth to Phil's son – Nichols pulls off a memorable *coup de théâtre*. Some critics found this highly improbable, but I believe the combination of artificiality and the earthy, direct, everyday – even squalid – way the couples express themselves towards each other produces an eminently enjoyable, if not exactly profound, sense of truth.

In so far as Nichols sees human nature as a mixture of cynical and redeeming factors (which again relates him closely to Anouilh), he has hit upon an excellent formula for a well-deserved success. The parts in *Chez Nous* cry out for outstanding performance, and Nichols has always been able to tempt the very best available acting talent (in *Chez Nous*, Denholm Elliott, Albert Finney, Geraldine McEwan).

In *The Freeway* Nichols has gone back to the episodic comic style of *The National Health*, but with far less success. A great wide motor-way (the F1) has been built running from North to South, and in a week-end jam, a number of marooned motorists commingle in a form of glorified variety entertainment. Though there is some glorious satire, and some sharply observed social comment, we seem, like the cars themselves, not to arrive anywhere in particular.

Harding's Luck is a straight-forward adaptation of E. Nesbit's children's novel, using the author as narrator. The central character is Dickie, the crippled urchin from Deptford. He is elevated by the hospitality of a genteel family, finds out he is well connected, and finally he is submitted to a magical transformation backwards in time – from an Edwardian childhood into a Jacobean youth.

—Garry O'Connor

NKOSI, Lewis. British (adopted). Born in Durban, South Africa, 5 December 1936. Educated in public schools in Durban; Zulu Lutheran High School; M.L. Sultan Technical College, Durban, 1961–62; Harvard University, Cambridge, Massachusetts (Nieman Fellow), 1962–63. Married Bronwyn Ollerenshaw in 1965; has twin daughters. Staff member of the Zulu newspaper *Ilanga Lase Natal*, Durban, 1955–56; *Drum* magazine and *Golden City Post*, Johannesburg, 1956–60; *South African Information Bulletin*, Paris, 1962–68; Radio Producer, BBC Transcription Centre, London, 1962–64; National Education Television Interviewer, New York, 1963; Literary Editor, *New African* magazine, London, 1965–68; Regents Lecturer on African Literature, University of California, Irvine, Spring 1971. Recipient: Dakar World Festival of the Negro Arts prize, for essays, 1965. Agent: Deborah Rogers Ltd., 29 Goodge Street, London W.1. Address: Flat 4, Burgess Park Mansions, Fortune Green Road, London N.W.6, England.

PUBLICATIONS

Plays

> *The Rhythm of Violence* (produced London, 1963). London and New York, Oxford University Press, 1964.
> *Malcolm* (televised, 1967; produced London, 1972).

Screenplay: *Come Back Africa*, 1959.

Radio Plays: *The Trial*, 1969; *We Can't All Be Martin Luther King*, 1971.

Television Play: *Malcolm*, 1967 (Sweden).

Other

> *Home and Exile* (essays). London, Longman, 1965.

Critical Studies: review of *The Rhythm of Violence* by Naomi Mitchison, in *Venture* (London), 1965; reviews of *Malcolm* in *The Guardian* (London), 18 August 1972, and in the *Shepherds Bush Gazette* (London), 25 August 1972.

*   *   *

When Lewis Nkosi's *The Rhythm of Violence* was published in 1964 it was hailed as the first play by a black South African to appear in print since Herbert Dhlomo's *The Girl Who Killed to Save* (1935). Because of its sensitive handling of the explosive issues of South African racism the play was widely acclaimed and Nkosi was seen by some as being in the vanguard of a new black South African theatre. Since then Nkosi has published short stories and essays (a form in which he seems to excel), but his visible dramatic output has been limited to three radio and television plays.

There are several possible explanations for this, one of which might be the relative youth of Nkosi. At thirty-six he still has a great deal ahead of him. It might also be noted that the immediacy of the South African situation, the terrific tensions it creates (which Nkosi himself has noted in his speculations on the dearth of recent plays and novels from South Africa) have made it difficult for the black South African writer to do anything other than the personal forms of essay, short story and autobiography. Drama is written for an audience, and the stricter, though more subtle, laws which developed after the Sharpeville Massacre have made it impossible for a mixed audience to come together in South Africa.

Thus we are left with only one major work in theatre on which to judge Nkosi, *The Rhythm of Violence*, an outstanding first play, an important one. There are some weaknesses in the play. Certain of the scenes tend to drag and some of the characters seem static, almost unreal — especially Tula and Sarie, the Zulu boy and Boer girl who are caught in the web of destruction. Nkosi's moral, however, that violence is mindless, that it destroys both the guilty and the innocent and that violence begets more violence, is effectively acted out. Nkosi also does an excellent job in presenting the two Boer policemen, Jan and Piet, in such a way that we see beyond the harshness of their exterior into their confused souls. They are the most fully realized characters in the play and in one masterful scene, when Jan pretends to be a black politician and is carried away in his part ("You spoke just like a native communist," says Piet in a shocked voice), Nkosi makes it clear that the possibility for understanding between men does exist — unless the rhythm of violence prevents such understanding from developing.

Lewis Nkosi shows great promise as a dramatist. If his future works develop along the lines of potential indicated by his first and thus far only published play he may well turn out to be an important figure not just in the drama of South Africa but in the English speaking world as a whole.

—Joseph Bruchac

NOONAN, John Ford. American. Born in New York City, 7 October 1943. Educated at Fairfield Preparatory School, Connecticut, graduated 1959; Brown University, Providence, Rhode Island, A.B. in philosophy 1964; Carnegie Institute of Technology, Pittsburgh, M.A. in dramatic literature 1966. Married Marcia Lunt in 1962 (divorced, 1965); has three children. Taught Latin, English, and history at Buckley Country Day School, North Hills, Long Island, New York, 1966–69; stagehand, Fillmore East Rock Theatre, New York, 1969–71; Stockbroker, E.F. Hutton Company, New York, 1971–72; Professor of Drama, Villanova University, Pennsylvania, 1972–73. Recipient: Rockefeller grant, 1973. Agent: Joan Scott Inc., 162 West 56th Street, New York, New York 10019. Address: Apartment 5, 233 West 4th Street, New York, New York 10014, U.S.A.

PUBLICATIONS

Plays

The Year Boston Won the Pennant (produced New York, 1969). New York, Grove Press, 1970.
Lazarus Was a Lady (produced New York, 1970).
Rainbows for Sale (produced New York, 1971). Published in *The Off-Off-Broadway Book*, edited by Albert Poland and Bruce Mailman, Indianapolis, Bobbs Merrill, 1972.
Concerning the Effects of Trimethylchloride (produced New York, 1971).
Monday Night Varieties (produced New York, 1972).
Older People (also director; produced New York, 1972).
Good-By and Keep Cold (produced New York, 1973).

A Noonan Night (produced New York, 1973).
A Sneaky Bit to Raise the Blind, and Pick Pack Pock Puck (produced New York, 1974).

Screenplays: *Septuagenarian Substitute Ball*, 1970; *The Summer the Snows Came*, 1972.

Manuscript Collection: Lincoln Center Library of the Performing Arts, New York.

Critical Studies: "Theatre as Mystery" by John Lahr, in *Evergreen Magazine* (New York), December 1969; reviews by John Lahr, in *Village Voice* (New York), May 1971, May 1972.

Theatrical Activities:

Director: **Play** – *Older People*, New York, 1972.

Actor: since 1947, in summer stock, regional and off-Broadway theatres, and in television and movies.

John Ford Noonan comments:

In *The Year Boston Won the Pennant*, Marcus Sykowski, a once legendary baseball pitcher who has mysteriously lost his glove arm and is now in search of a chrome limb to take its place, discusses pitching as follows:

> I am a pitcher. Pitching is my job. I have lost an arm, but I will earn it back. I have science on my side. I'm no college man. I never got a degree. I am no thinker, no man whose job it is to lead or be understood. I am a pitcher. I stand on the mound. I hold the ball, smile, get the feel I'm ready. I rear, I fire, and that ball goes exactly where I tell it 'cause I tell it to, 'cause it was me who threw it, the great Sykowski. What else must they know....One strike, two strikes, three strikes, four, five, six, seven, eight, nine...the whole side, 'cause when you're pouring rhythm sweet, when you got it, really got it, they can't see it, they can't smell it, they can't touch it, they can't even believe it....It's yours, all yours...it's magic.

I believe Marcus is speaking of more than throwing a baseball.

* * *

John Ford Noonan is a very large young man, the son of a doctor, who attended a Catholic preparatory school in one of New York City's Connecticut suburbs and then went to Brown University on a basketball scholarship, until a severe knee injury forced him to give up sports. He majored in philosophy, did an honors thesis on ideas about death, and subsequently took an M.A. in theatre at Carnegie Tech. While living in New York, he has worked primarily as a stagehand and stage manager at rock concerts, and he once starred in a short movie about a rock singer. It can be seen that all of these interests appear in his works. The first full-length play, *The Year Boston Won the Pennant*, opened at the Forum Theatre of New York's Lincoln Center in 1969, and subsequent dramas have since established him as one of America's most promising young playwrights.

Noonan's plays have been stylistically conservative, its author avowedly subscribing to Aristotelian esthetics; and convention-minded critics, such as Walter Kerr, Harold Clurman and John Lahr, have especially praised his talent. Preferring to introduce his characters swiftly, he even lets a stereotype carry much of the burden of clarification. The figures in his earlier plays tended to be theatrically familiar – a baseball star, an ambitiously disingenuous wife, ethnic types – because Noonan was then less interested in character than in conflicts that had mythic overtones. The initial plays tells of a star pitcher, Marcus Sykowski, who mysteriously loses his fielding arm and thus finds his athletic career, and much else in his life, jeopardized. Determined to regain his heroic public image, he visits family and old friends, who, instead of helping, try to exploit his misfortune (as they had previously exploited his fame), and the plot follows the disintegration of a great and courageous man. Noonan's point, which seems to be human vulnerability, is nailed down by the final scene, where Sykowski is mysteriously assassinated. Another theme, which recurs in later Noonan plays, is the hysteria of rather mundane people (those around Sykowski) in an extreme situation. His second preserved play, *Lazarus Was a Lady*, deals with a dying young woman who uses her sickness as a lever to manipulate people; and in 1973 he released a text, *Good-By and Keep Cold*, that deals with familial conflict among the rich and seems stylistically closer to his earlier work. *Rainbows for Sale* (1971) represents a transition, embodying a prominent myth (in this case, Oedipal) and yet introducing two subjects Noonan would later explore at length – the madnesses of the aged and the human penchant for fantasy. In addition to portraying characters that are unfamiliar to most of us – firemen (rather than, say, policemen) – *Rainbows for Sale* contains glimmers of the truly distinguished writing that has marked Noonan's more recent drama.

The best drama so far has been *Older People*, a cycle of fifteen plays about aging, a subject which is rarely treated in theatre. They were presented in a slightly abridged form at the Public Theatre in New York City, in 1972, with six actors, three male and three female, assuming the many roles on a sparsely propped stage. In scene after scene, the play vividly, if not cruelly, illustrates that age is a determining factor in human life. Resisting the pitfalls of sentiment, Noonan portrays agedness as an extreme situation that not only influences behavior directly but also shapes mental attitudes that in turn affect behavior. "It's no sin," one character says early in the play, "but somehow I still can't forgive myself for getting old." In one sketch, a couple acknowledge that they are too old to make love any more, repeatedly nagging each other about the fact. (This echoes a Samuel Beckett novel that compares love-making of the aged to putting a pillow into a pillow-slip.) In another, two aging homosexual lovers agree to split, after many years together, one of them planning, not without anxiety, to join a commune of kids on the Oregon coast. In a third, two aging sophisticates, who were once lovers, compulsively compare notes on their current infidelities – "as good as me?" One of the juster criticisms objects to the characters' – and thus the play's – excessive preoccupation with sex.

Two pairs of sketches are related, in that the same sets of characters appear twice. The weaker of these concerns Fay, May and Kay, who seem reminiscent of Shakespeare's three witches, especially in their unison chantings. The better pair, which also belongs among the play's most successful, portrays two former pop singers, a self-styled "pair of pussy-old farts," who are now apparently resident in an old folks' home. They repeatedly rehearse their greatest hit, "Penny Arcade," until they come to a passage whose words they can no longer remember. Their predicament is solved in a subsequent scene by the arrival of the song's inspiration, Penny herself, who is now also old enough to come to the institution. (All Noonan plays except the first have interludes of song.) One scene cut from the New York production involves a woman listening to a cassette tape from her lover who subsequently appears live; and the other portrays a man recently returned from heart surgery whose wife quickly nags him to death onstage. The effect was too devastating, it seems, for those spectators with heart conditions.

The tour-de-force of *Older People* is the conclusion, originally performed in 1971 as a one-act play entitled *Concerning the Effects of Trimethylchloride*, in which a chemistry professor's widow comes to give the final lecture in his course. Although she boasts of her own contribution to his work, it becomes clear that she has been his willing guinea-pig, for all kinds of atrocious experiments; and what sustains her extended monologue is not only the horror of her revelations but the increasing excellence of Noonan's writing. Especially for the quality of his characterizations and his prose, he ranks among the best American dramatists of that generation now about thirty.

—Richard Kostelanetz

NORMAN, (John) Frank. British. Born in Bristol, 9 June 1930. Educated at St. Mary's Church School, Kingston, Surrey; Dr. Barnardo's Homes, 1937–46. Married Geraldine Norman in 1971; has one daughter by previous marriage. Worked as a farm labourer and with a travelling fair; served various prison sentences for minor crimes, including three years at Camp Hill Prison, Isle of Wight, 1954–57; after release worked as a van driver. Free-lance Writer since 1958. Recipient: *Evening Standard* award, 1960. Agent: Richard Simon Ltd., 36 Wellington Street, London W.C.2. Address: 5 Seaford Court, 222 Great Portland Street, London W.1, England.

PUBLICATIONS

Plays

> *Fings Ain't Wot They Used T'Be*, songs by Lionel Bart (produced London, 1959). London, Secker and Warburg, 1960; New York, Grove Press, 1962.
> *A Kayf Up West*, music by Stanley Myers (produced London, 1964).
> *Insideout* (produced London, 1969). Published in *Plays and Players* (London), February 1970.
> *Costa Packet*, songs by Lionel Bart and Alan Klein (produced London, 1972).

> Screenplay: *In the Nick*, 1960.

> Television Plays: *Just Call Me Lucky*, 1965; *The Sufferings of Peter Obnizov*, 1967; *Incorrigible Rogue*, 1976.

Novels

> *The Monkey Pulled His Hair*. London, Secker and Warburg, 1967, as *Only the Rich*, New York, Avon, 1969.
> *Barney Snip: Artist*. London, Secker and Warburg, 1968.
> *Dodgem-Greaser*. London, Hodder and Stoughton, 1971.
> *One of Our Own*. London, Hodder and Stoughton, 1973.
> *Much Ado about Nuffink*. London, Hodder and Stoughton, 1974.
> *Down and Out in High Society*. London, Hodder and Stoughton, 1975.

Other

> *Bang to Rights: An Account of Prison Life*. London, Secker and Warburg, 1958.
> *Stand on Me: A True Story of Soho* (autobiography). London, Secker and Warburg, 1960; New York, Simon and Schuster, 1961.

The Guntz (autobiography).   London, Secker and Warburg, 1962.
Soho Night and Day.   London, Secker and Warburg, 1966.
Banana Boy (autobiography).   London, Secker and Warburg, 1969.
Norman's London.   London, Secker and Warburg, 1969.
Lock 'em Up and Count 'em (penal reform).   London, Charles Knight, 1971.
The Lives of Frank Norman (anthology).   London, Penguin, 1972.
Why Fings Went West.   London, Lemon Tree Press, 1975.

Manuscript Collection: University of Indiana, Bloomington.

Frank Norman comments:

The notion of writing a play came to me almost by accident, during the autumn of 1958. During the summer of that year my essay on London slang had appeared in *Encounter*; at the time of writing the piece it came to me that the best and most effective way of handling the subject would be to present it in dialogue, in the form of several short playlets accompanied by brief glossaries and explanations. Stephen Spender, who was at that time co-editor of the magazine, thought it a novel idea and suggested to me one day that I should try my hand at a play. I had at that time published my first two books (*Bang to Rights* and *Stand on Me*); I knew nothing whatever about the theatre and had seen very few plays. Indeed I can only recall two: they were the musical *Annie Get Your Gun* and *The Monkey's Paw* produced by the boys in the orphanage one year. I was vaguely aware that a straight play was in three acts, and that was the format in which I laid out my forty-eight pages of dialogue. I entitled the play *Fings Ain't Wot They Used T'Be*. A friend suggested that I should send it to Joan Littlewood at the Theatre Workshop, Stratford East. This I promptly did and to my amazement she wrote to me several months later saying that she would like to produce the play on her stage at the Theatre Royal. I originally saw *Fings* as a straight play, but Miss Littlewood suggested to me that it would make a far better musical that it would a drama. She then introduced me to Lionel Bart. The rest is history. The show ran for more than two years at the Garrick Theatre.

My second play, *A Kayf Up West*, was also produced by Joan Littlewood at the Theatre Workshop (1964) and though in many ways it was a far better play than *Fings* it was not a popular success.

Insideout was originally commissioned by The Royal Shakespeare Company. Some two years after I had delivered the manuscript I was advised that a production of the play could not be scheduled. I then revised the text and sent it to the Royal Court who staged a production in November 1969.

                              *   *   *

Frank Norman's first play, *Fing's Ain't Wot They Used T'Be*, was one of the most successful Joan Littlewood productions at the Theatre Royal, Stratford East. It is a Cockney musical set in Soho, in many ways a London counterpart to the Damon Runyon stories. The action takes place in a shpieler, a gambling den; the mood varies from the brash and bawdy to the nostalgic and sentimental. Slang comes so thick and fast that at times the dialogue is almost incomprehensible. "Grass," "jacks," "snout," "guntz," "leary," "swedes," "chokey": the audience might have been puzzled by some of the jargon but they could feel confident of its authenticity. Like Brendan Behan, whose plays preceded his at Stratford East, Norman wrote a prison autobiography, *Bang to Rights*, and he has since drawn up a guide to the territory described in this first play, a book called *Soho Night and Day*.

The hero of *Fings* is Fred Cochran, a down at heel gangster trying to make a comeback, "at one time the governor of this manor but now dead skint" as the stage directions put it. Lil Smith is his loyal moll, a tart with a heart of gold, who longs for respectability and keeps a marriage licence ready for her lucky day. They are a couple who might have stepped straight out of an English *Guys and Dolls*. Fred's shpieler provides a refuge for the failures of the underworld: Paddy the gambler, Tosher the ponce with his girls Betty and Rosey, and Redhot, a sad little burglar who never manages to get warm. They all look to Fred for a living and when he wins on the horses it seems the gang may be back in business; the Horrible Percy Fortesque comes to gamble and a rival leader, Meatface, is beaten in a razor fight. At this point the play ends, somewhat lamely, with a wedding; Lil and Fred are giving up crime and handing over the shpieler to P.C. Collins, a bent cop. The glamorous bad old days will be left behind for ever; the last song laments their passing and complains of a threat to villains and heroes alike:

> Monkeys flyin' rahnd the moon—
> We'll be up there wiv'em soon.
> Fings ain't wot they used t'be.

Like most musicals at Stratford East, *Fings* grew out of a close collaboration between producer, lyricist and writer. The script was at first an eighteen-page outline which Norman worked on alongside Joan Littlewood and the cast. Lionel Bart's tunes still sing out of the text; he created the perfect complement to that mixture of tough guys and tears which made the show such successful theatre.

Frank Norman has a Dickensian fascination for those he has described as "so-called criminals: the hopelessly deprived, the misunderstood and the over-punished." Many of his books deal with the problems of crime and penal reform. Perhaps this interest ensured the spontaneity and vitality of his first play; certainly, his 1972 musical *Costa Packet* lags a long way behind *Fings*. It chronicles the joys, perils and horrors of a package tour: gigolos, Spanish food, even a Bavarian who has been misdirected on the way to the Edinburgh Festival. The mood is saucy, insular and many of the jokes could have been borrowed from a selection of seaside postcards. Nevertheless, it was received with great enthusiasm at Stratford; the Cockney playwright has not lost touch with his audience.

—Judith Cooke Simmons

NUGENT, Elliott (John).   American.   Born in Dover, Ohio, 20 September 1899, son of the playwright and actor J. C. Nugent. Educated at Dover High School, graduated 1915; Ohio State University, Columbus, A.B. 1919. Served in the United States Naval Reserve, 1918–19. Married Norma Lee in 1921; has three children. Recipient: New York Drama Critics Circle Award, for acting, 1944. D.L.: Ohio State University, 1965. Address: 333 East 57th Street, New York, New York 10022, U.S.A.

PUBLICATIONS

Plays

Kempy: A Comedy of American Life, with J. C. Nugent (produced New York, 1922). New York, French, 1922.

A Clean Town, with J. C. Nugent (produced New York, 1922).

The Dumb-Bell, with J. C. Nugent (produced New York, 1923).

The Breaks, with J. C. Nugent (produced New York, 1923).

Money to Burn, with J. C. Nugent (produced New York, 1923).   New York, French, 1930.

The Rising Son, with J. C. Nugent (produced New York, 1924).   New York, Co-National Plays, 1930.

The Poor Nut, with J. C. Nugent (produced New York, 1925).   New York, French, 1925.

Human Nature, with J. C. Nugent (produced New York, 1925).

The Trouper, with J. C. Nugent (produced New York, 1926).

Apartments to Let, with Howard Lindsay, in *The Appleton Book of Short Plays*, edited by Kenyon Nicholson.   New York, Appleton, 1926.

Nightstick, with others (produced New York, 1927).

By Request, with J. C. Nugent (produced New York, 1928).

A Fast One, with J. C. Nugent (produced San Francisco, 1931; as *Fast Service*, produced New York, 1931).

The World's My Onion, with J. C. Nugent (produced Pasadena, California, 1935).

The Fight's On, with Hagar Wilde and Ernest V. Heym (produced Richmond, Surrey, 1937).

The Male Animal, with James Thurber (produced New York, 1940, London, 1949). New York, Random House, 1940.

A Place of Our Own (also director: produced New York, 1945).

Screenplay: *Enter Madam*, 1935.

Novel

Of Cheat and Charmer.   New York, Simon and Schuster, 1962.

Other

Events Leading Up to the Comedy: An Autobiography.   New York, Simon and Schuster, 1965.

Theatrical Activities:

Director: **Plays** – *All in Favor* by Louis Hoffman and Don Hartman, New York, 1942; *Tomorrow the World* by James Gow and Arnaud D'Usseau, New York, 1943; *A Place of Our Own*, New York, 1945; *The Big Two* by L. Bush-Fekete and Mary Helen Fay, New York, 1947; *Darling, Darling, Darling*, Princeton, New Jersey, 1947; *Message for Margaret* by James Parrish, New York, 1947, *The Greatest Man Alive* by Tony Webster, New York, 1957. **Films** – *The Mouthpiece*, 1932; *Whistling in the Dark*, 1933; *Three-Cornered Moon*, 1933; *If I Were Free*, 1934; *Strictly Dynamite*, 1934; *She Loves Me Not*, 1934; *Enter Madam*, 1935; *Love in Bloom*, 1935; *Splendor*, 1935; *And So They Were Married*, 1936; *Wives Never Know*, 1936; *It's All Yours*, 1938; *Professor, Beware*, 1938; *Give Me a Sailor*, 1938; *Never Say Die*, 1939; *The Cat and the Canary*, 1939; *Nothing But the Truth*, 1941; *The Male Animal*, 1942; *Crystal Ball*, 1943; *Up in Arms*, 1944; *My Favorite Brunette*, 1947, *Welcome Stranger*, 1947; *My Girl Tisa*, 1948; *Mr. Belvedere Goes to College*, 1949; *The Great Gatsby*, 1949; *The Skipper Surprised His Wife*, 1950; *My Outlaw Brother*, 1951; *Just for You*, 1952.

Actor: **Plays** – debut in vaudeville, 1904; Tom Skerrett in *Dulcy* by Marc Connelly and George S. Kaufman, New York, 1921; title role in *Kempy*, New York, 1922, 1927; Jim Dolf in *The Breaks*, New York, 1923; Eddie Hudson in *The Wild Westcotts* by Anne Morrison, New York, 1923; Ted Alamayne in *The Rising Son*, New York, 1924; John Miller in *The Poor Nut*, New York, 1925; in *Hoosiers Abroad* by Booth Tarkington, Chicago and tour, 1927; Walter Meakin in *Good Boy* by Oscar Hammerstein II and others, New York, 1928; William Abbott in *By Request*, New York, 1928; Bing Allen in *Fast Service*, New York, 1931; Tommy Turner in *The Male Animal*, New York, 1940, 1952; Patrick Jamieson in *Without Love* by Philip Barry, New York, 1942; Bill Page in *The Voice of the Turtle* by John Van Druten, New York, 1943; George Hunter in *The Fundamental George*, toured, 1947–49; Ambrose Atwater in *Not for Children* by Elmer Rice, New York, 1951, Richard Sherman in *The Seven Year Itch* by George Axelrod, New York, 1954; Dr. Brothers in *Build with One Hand* by J. Kramm, New Haven, Connecticut, 1956. **Films** – *So This Is College*, 1929; *Not So Dumb*, 1930; *The Unholy Three*, 1930; *Sins of the Children*, 1930; *Romance*, 1930; *Virtuous Husband*, 1931; *The Last Flight*, 1931; *Stage Door Canteen*, 1943; *My Outlaw Brother*, 1951.

*   *   *

Perhaps best known as a successful actor and director, Elliott Nugent also wrote some fifteen plays, most of them in collaboration with his father, J. C. Nugent. The plays follow a classic comic pattern in their focus on love and money. Marked by a tone of genteel satire and mild farce, they reflect the manners and values of suburban bourgois America during the 1920's and 30's. Domestic finances, property, college life, post-adolescent love, and marital contretemps are recurrent motifs. The characters tend to be engaging types who are often mildly eccentric misfits trying to maintain a measure of integrity in a world of material values. A boulevard realism dominates the form of the plays: fairly standard plot complications, character entanglements, and idiomatic dialogue are handled with a skill born of long familiarity with the commercial theatre.

Although most of Nugent's plays have been more notable for their facile theatricality than for distinction in thought or style, some exceptions should be noted. One of his last plays, *The Male Animal* (a collaboration with James Thurber, a friend of long standing), reveals both grace and wit, as well as a genuine note of social concern in depicting the stubborn resistance of a diffident intellectual against pressures of social and political conformity. A much earlier collaboration with his father, *Money to Burn* (1923), though in many ways a stilted mixture of farce and melodrama, confronts issues of the class system and the financial basis of marriage with a degree of frankness and intensity unusual for its day. In *A Place of Our Own* (1945), Nugent consciously sought to deal with serious issues relating to Woodrow Wilson's role in founding the League of Nations; the play was a flat failure and strengthened the impression that his forte was light comedy.

—Jarka M. Burian

O'NEILL, Michael.   British.   Educated at Northampton Grammar School; Cambridge University. Teacher. Agent: Clive Goodwin, 79 Cromwell Road, London S.W.7, England.

PUBLICATIONS

Plays

Life Price, with Jeremy Seabrook (produced London, 1969).
Morality, with Jeremy Seabrook (produced London, 1971).
Millenium, with Jeremy Seabrook (produced London, 1973).
Our Sort of People, with Jeremy Seabrook (produced London, 1974).
Sex and Kinship in a Savage Society, with Jeremy Seabrook (produced London, 1975).

Radio Play, with Jeremy Seabrook: The Bosom of the Family, 1975.

Television Plays, with Jeremy Seabrook: A Clear Cut Case, 1973, Soap Opera in Stockwell, 1973, Children of the Sun, 1975; Beyond the Call of Duty (Crown Court series), 1976.

*   *   *

It was Genet who had his beliefs about society entirely shattered when he found out that, according to the most advanced and accurate statistics available, the percentage of criminals remained the same whichever class or system held power at a particular moment. Michael O'Neill and Jeremy Seabrook still suffer from the widespread delusion that it is only the result of capitalism, the "ceaseless gutting of their body and spirit in name of enterprise, profits, efficiency," that there is a social sediment at the bottom of society, providing both aggressors and victims for horrible crime.

For in their first performed play, Life Price, the predestined victim, Debbie, and the typical child murderer, George Reginald Dunkley, are both observed against a landscape of "neglected mounds of detritus, crumbling terraces, derelict buildings, and the housing estate itself, all cabbage-stalks and dilapidated creosote fences, maculated concrete, rusting bedsprings and motor-bikes, dead chrysanthemums and dingy paintwork."

The whole picture these authors realize is one of despondency and hopelessness, and social historians in the future will, I am sure, come to see such work as typical of an intellectual reaction against consumer affluence. Whether they will find it a truthful picture of life as lived is another matter, for the types generally found living on council estates do not, at least in my experience, conform to what the house style of the Royal Court propagated at the time as a true image.

A State of Welfare, a television play, is a much better organized work about an American Scent Spray firm moving into England, and its impact on the household of an average worker. Here the theme of the working class man's son bettering himself, by taking French lessons with an executive's wife, and so coming into conflict with his father – the two sides of industry get together over dinner in a powerful scene reminiscent of a notable climax in Ibsen's The League of Youth – forms a substantial and colourful central thread.

Morality is an even more domestic story than A State of Welfare. A family called the Pargeters are trying to make their son Nick "get on" by passing his A-level exams and winning a place at university. When it is discovered that Nick is having a homosexual affair with his progressive and sensitive teacher, Larry, the family is up in arms at the scandal this will cause in the neighbourhood. However, when Nick's parents manage to summon up the courage to go and see Larry, Larry calms them down with a hypocritical assertion of "morality." The psychology – and morality – is crude compared with other plays about divided loyalty with strong homosexual overtones (Montherlant's The Town in Which the Prince Is a Child is similarly concerned with an "altruistic" – and self-interested – teacher).

Morality is a lively portrayal of family conflict, and, as in Life Price, it is society which is to blame, the authors would seem to be saying, for the cynicism and destructiveness of young people towards their elders. This is an attitude supported by lively, factual, almost documentary writing, not by the continual assertion of a doctrinaire point of view.

In *Millenium*, there is a gap of 53 years between the first part and the second, set in a semi-detached on a Northampton housing estate. The gap achieves a neat and forceful comparison of the attitudes of the same family in the same class background. The authors find analogies in the life style of Florrie's family, and that of Doll, her granddaughter, which have a sentimental, in the best sense, ring of truth.

In Florrie's family one of the girls is dying of scarlet fever, while about her rage the violences of poverty, the stringencies of life caused by the father's status as a hired man. The rebel son, common to both generations, merely burns his sister's boots (cost, 8/6), while in the second he has, as part of a gang, tied up a boy, cut his hair, and tried to extort money from his parents. The boot-burning satisfies the instinct for anger at the circumstances, and it is punished and purged within the family unit. The second misdemeanour is a matter for the courts, showing the impersonality of justice, and how the family has broken down.

Dramatically striking is the Pirandellesque twist by which Florrie's family advance on their petty-minded materialist descendents, and engage in a battle of wits. The authors' sympathies strongly lie with the earlier brood, on whom a huddled statuesque dignity is conferred. Grim and monochrome as they appear, they have the virtue of discipline, and look to the after-life for their reward.

Sex and Kinship in a Savage Society is a less successful treatment of the same theme of family disintegration. The theme as conceived in *Millenium* is a magnificent one, though one remains with the impression that the authors, possibly because there are two of them, do not quite allow characters to become characters in their own right. As in much playwriting which is closely allied to social anthropology, the scheme comes to dominate.

—Garry O'Connor

OSBORNE, John (James).   British.   Born in London, 12 December 1929. Educated at Belmont College, Devon. Married Pamela Lane in 1951 (marriage dissolved, 1957); the actress Mary Ure, 1957 (marriage dissolved, 1963); the writer Penelope Gilliatt, 1963 (marriage dissolved, 1968); the actress Jill Bennett, 1968; has one child. Has worked as a tutor and as an assistant stage manager. Since 1958, Co-Director, Woodfall Films; since 1960, Director, Oscar Lewenstein Plays Ltd., London. Member of the Council, English Stage Company, London, since 1960. Recipient: *Evening Standard* award, 1956, 1965, 1968; New York Drama Critics Circle Award, 1958, 1965; Tony Award, 1963; Academy Award, 1964. Honorary Doctor: Royal College of Art, London, 1970. Member, Royal Society of Arts. Agent: Margery Vosper Ltd., Suite 8, 26 Charing Cross Road, London WC2H 0DG. Address: 27 Curzon Street, London W.1, England.

PUBLICATIONS

Plays

> *The Devil Inside Him*, with Stella Linden (produced Huddersfield, Yorkshire, 1950).
> *Personal Enemy*, with Anthony Creighton (produced Harrogate, Yorkshire, 1955).
> *Look Back in Anger* (produced London, 1956; New York, 1957).   London, Faber, and
>   New York, Criterion Books, 1957.

The Entertainer (produced London, 1957; New York, 1958).   London, Faber, 1957; New York, Criterion Books, 1958.

Epitaph for George Dillon, with Anthony Creighton (produced Oxford, 1957; London and New York, 1958).   London, Faber, and New York, Criterion Books, 1958.

The World of Paul Slickey, music by Christopher Whelan (also director: produced Bournemouth, Hampshire, and London, 1959).   London, Faber, 1959; New York, Criterion Books, 1961.

A Subject of Scandal and Concern (as *A Matter of Scandal and Concern*, televised 1960; as *A Subject of Scandal and Concern*, produced Nottingham, 1962; New York, 1965). London, Faber, 1961; in *The Best Short Plays of the World Theatre, 1958–1967*, edited by Stanley Richards, New York, Crown, 1968.

Luther (produced Nottingham and London, 1961; New York, 1963).   London, Faber, and Chicago, Dramatic Publishing Company, 1961.

Plays for England: The Blood of the Bambergs, Under Plain Cover (produced London, 1963; New York, 1964–65).   London, Faber, 1963; New York, Criterion Books, 1964.

Tom Jones: A Film Script.   London, Faber, and New York, Grove Press, 1964.

Inadmissible Evidence (produced London, 1964; New York, 1965).   London, Faber, and New York, Grove Press, 1965.

A Bond Honoured, adaptation of a play by Lope de Vega (produced London, 1966). London, Faber, 1966.

A Patriot for Me (produced London, 1966; New York, 1969).   London, Faber, 1966; New York, Random House, 1970.

The Hotel in Amsterdam (produced London, 1968).   Included in *Time Present, The Hotel in Amsterdam*, 1968; in *Four Plays*, 1973.

Time Present (produced London, 1968).   Included in *Time Present, The Hotel in Amsterdam*, 1968; in *Four Plays*, 1973.

Time Present, The Hotel in Amsterdam.   London, Faber, 1968.

The Right Prospectus: A Play for Television (televised, 1969).   London, Faber, 1970.

Very Like a Whale (televised, 1970).   London, Faber, 1971.

West of Suez (produced London, 1971).   London, Faber, 1971; in *Four Plays*, 1973.

Hedda Gabler, adaptation of the play by Ibsen (produced London, 1972).   London, Faber, 1972; Chicago, Dramatic Publishing Company, 1974.

The Gift of Friendship (televised, 1972).   London, Faber, 1972.

A Sense of Detachment (produced London, 1972).   London, Faber, 1973.

Four Plays: West of Suez, A Patriot for Me, Time Present, The Hotel in Amsterdam. New York, Dodd Mead, 1973.

A Place Calling Itself Rome, adaptation of the play *Coriolanus* by Shakespeare. London, Faber, 1973.

The Picture of Dorian Gray: A Moral Entertainment, adaptation of the novel by Oscar Wilde (produced London, 1975).   London, Faber, 1973.

Jill and Jack (as *Ms.; or, Jill and Jack*, televised, 1974).   Included in *The End of Me Old Cigar, and Jill and Jack*, 1975.

The End of Me Old Cigar (produced London, 1975).   Included in *The End of Me Old Cigar, and Jill and Jack*, 1975.

The End of Me Old Cigar, and Jill and Jack: A Play for Television.   London, Faber, 1975.

Watch It Come Down (produced London, 1976).   London, Faber, 1975.

Screenplays: *Look Back in Anger*, 1959; *The Entertainer*, 1960; *Tom Jones*, 1963; *Inadmissible Evidence*, 1968.

Television Plays: *For the Children* series: *Billy Bunter*, 1952, and *Robin Hood*, 1953; *A Matter of Scandal and Concern*, 1960; *The Right Prospectus*, 1969; *Very Like a Whale*, 1970; *The Gift of Friendship*, 1972; *Ms.; or, Jill and Jack*, 1974.

Critical Studies: *Anger and After* by John Russell Taylor, London, Methuen, 1962; *Look Back in Anger: A Casebook*, edited by John Russell Taylor, London, Macmillan, 1968; *Osborne* by Martin Banham, Edinburgh, Oliver and Boyd, 1969; *The Plays of John Osborne* by Simon Trussler, London, Gollancz, 1969.

Theatrical Activities:

Director. **Plays** – with the Huddersfield Repertory Company, 1949; *Meals on Wheels* by Charles Wood, London, 1965; *The Entertainer*, London, 1974.

Actor: **Plays** – Mr. Burrells in *No Room at the Inn* by Joan Temple, Sheffield, 1948; on tour and in repertory in Ilfracombe, Bridgwater, Camberwell, Kidderminster, Derby, 1948–56; with the English Stage Company, London: Antonio in *Don Juan* by Ronald Duncan, 1956, Lionel in *The Death of Satan* by Ronald Duncan, 1956, The Ancient Keeper of the Badgers in *Cards of Identity* by Nigel Dennis, 1956, Lin To in *The Good Woman of Setzuan* by Brecht, 1956, The Commissionaire in *The Apollo de Bellac* by Giraudoux, 1957, and Donald Blake in *The Making of Moo* by Nigel Dennis, 1958, Claude Hicket in *A Cuckoo in the Nest* by Ben Travers, London, 1964. **Films** – *First Love*, 1970; *Carter*, 1971. **Television** – *The Parachute* by David Mercer, 1968; *The First Night of Pygmalion* by Richard Huggett, 1969.

*   *   *

John Osborne's first fortune, and first misfortune, was the tag "angry young man." Fortune because in 1956 it helped to make new writing, and new drama in particular, a talking point, news, in a way it had never been before in the modern British theatre. Misfortune because once landed with such a label it is difficult to grow out of it and even more difficult to convince the public or the critics that you have done so.

Nevertheless, Osborne continued to develop right from the first production of *Look Back in Anger* on 8 May 1956, which was also his first appearance as a dramatist on the London stage, though two earlier plays, written in collaboration, had been briefly shown out of town. At the time he was an actor, 26, and considered something of a juvenile prodigy, at least in comparison with the largely middle-aged strength of the British theatrical establishment. The play had been quite simply sent through the post to the newly founded English Stage Company, a group idealistically devoted to new theatrical writing, and was their first new British play to be produced. It had mixed but on the whole favourable reviews: everyone at least seemed agreed that Osborne's was a distinctive new voice, and before long his hero, Jimmy Porter, became a kind of folk hero for a young generation puzzled by the Hungarian revolution, unhappy about Britain's last imperialist fling at Suez, and dedicated to protest about the Bomb and all manner of questions social and political.

Not that Jimmy Porter, or Osborne himself it would seem, was particularly interested in the larger issues: his contribution was rather a tone of voice, an attitude of private bloody-mindedness which set people wondering what exactly he was angry about. Jimmy's marital problems and social contracting-out (he is the graduate keeper of a sweet stall) were acted out in a form which Osborne himself rapidly characterized as "formal, rather old-fashioned," as were the somewhat similar difficulties of George Dillon in *Epitaph for George Dillon* (written in collaboration with Anthony Creighton), a writer with a will to failure as the only thing which will adequately motivate his sense of dissatisfaction. But Osborne was already moving on to new things technically and emotionally in *The Entertainer*, which placed a realistically treated story of a failed comedian and hollow man's last moments of contact with real emotion at the news of his son's death in Cyprus in a non-realistic context of allegorically significant sketches and numbers ostensibly from the tatty show Archie Rice is starring in, but actually reflecting on the present state of Britain and relating Archie's personal emotional failure to a wider loss of nerve and purpose. The play also, incidentally, marked the first important marriage of old theatre and new: Sir Laurence Olivier played the lead in its first production.

In the works which followed it sometimes seemed that Osborne was suffering himself from a certain loss of direction. *The World of Paul Slickey*, an ambitious satirical musical about a gossip columnist with a dual personality, was an almost unredeemed failure, and the two historical pieces which followed, *A Subject of Scandal and Concern* (television) and *Luther*, both seemed rather like academic exercises in the dramatisation of pre-existent material rather than original creations, though in the latter Osborne did succeed in making over the character of Luther (magnetically played by Albert Finney) into a figure somewhat after the image of Jimmy Porter — or rather, perhaps (since the historical sources were fairly scrupulously adhered to), managed to find in the outlines of the character someone after his own heart. In *Plays for England* some of the best of Osborne and some of the worst were juxtaposed. One of the two plays, *The Blood of the Bambergs*, a feeble satire about a royal wedding, was generally regarded as Osborne's poorest play, but the other, *Under Plain Cover*, opened up an interesting new area by embarking directly on the world of private neurosis, in this case the strange shared fantasy world of a married couple who turn out to be brother and sister.

What had worried some critics about *Look Back in Anger* was that Osborne seemed in it to be dealing with a neurotic character whom he did not fully realize to be neurotic, and any way he allowed him to win all the arguments and take on an heroic role by virtue of his sheer biting eloquence. *Under Plain Cover* might almost be a fourth act to *Look Back in Anger*, showing what could have happened to Jimmy and Alison a few years after they were reunited. Osborne's next play, and still in many ways his best, *Inadmissible Evidence*, pursues this line of dramatic thinking further. Its central character, Bill Maitland, is a lawyer who could also be Jimmy some years later. But this time he is allowed centre stage for his monologues simply because nobody bothers to listen to him any more; he rails at a world which doesn't care, and his deep sense of dissatisfaction is seen no longer as an objectively justified response to the ills of the world, but as the expression of a mind at the end of its tether. One of an accidental group of "male menopause" dramas of the 1960's (others were Arthur Miller's *After the Fall* and Fellini's $8^1/_2$), *Inadmissible Evidence* retains the extra kick of a kind of personal anguish expressed with all the lucidity and technical skill of a born dramatist working at the height of his powers.

Perhaps no play Osborne has written since has quite achieved the same happy balance, but at least there is no doubt possible about his being a born dramatist, one to whom dramatic expression comes with perfect naturalness and ease; it is fair to say that whatever the successes of other dramatists of his generation (and they have been many and varied), he is the only one who has contrived to win through consistently to an ampler public utterance, to remain defiantly a popular dramatist capable of speaking to a mass public, even if some of his plays may individually fail. *A Patriot for Me* failed, if it may be said to have failed, primarily because of a belated tangle with the moribund theatrical censorship over its homosexual theme: a large-scale period drama, it recounted the strange history of Alfred Redl, master double spy for Austria and Russia in the period immediately before the First World War. *A Bond Honoured* was in comparison a minor work, a long one-act fantasy on themes from Lope de Vega's *La Fianza Satisfecha* which made Lope's God-defying hero into almost a parody of Osborne's earlier railers; it was commissioned by the National Theatre.

In 1968 Osborne returned to the wider public stage with two new plays, presented in the first instance together although they have little or no thematic connection, *Time Present* and *The Hotel in Amsterdam*. Both represented in some respects new departures: *Time Present* was Osborne's first play to have a female protagonist, though Pamela, a "resting" actress, could not unfairly be described as a Jimmy Porter in skirts, a feminine variation of the familiar pattern, considering it her right, if not her duty, to bitch everyone in sight to compensate in some way for her gnawing sense of dissatisfaction. *The Hotel in Amsterdam* seems on the contrary like some sort of answer by Osborne to those of his critics who have complained that he tends to write monologue plays, plays in which only one character is really given a chance to speak. It is much more of an ensemble play, with several characters of almost equal weight, all of them refugees from the unseen presence of the dreaded "K.L.," a film producer around whom, in one fashion or another, all their lives revolve, who have holed up for a weekend of respite/holiday/group therapy in *the* hotel in Amsterdam.

Osborne's major subsequent play, *West of Suez*, for all its untidiness, its eagerness to pack everything possible into a form suggested by *Heartbreak House* and already bursting at the seams, does all the same have passages of Osborne's best writing, a surprising range of rounded, believable characters (in a sense it is another ensemble play), and brings us up to date on many of Osborne's pet themes, from the decline of imperialist Britain through homosexuality and nostalgia for the settled values of the past to a wary acceptance of a new, irrational order of things which may be coming to birth. In this play more than any other, Osborne seems to be deliberately siding with the conservatives, the old values. It is a long way from *Look Back in Anger*, but also by the look of it something very like a new beginning. Since *West of Suez* he has written several slight television plays, adaptations, and a couple of almost defiantly lightweight stages plays. But still we may continue to expect a further development of a dramatist who has through triumph and disaster never ceased to change and grow.

—John Russell Taylor

OSGOOD, Lawrence. American. Born in Buffalo, New York, 24 January 1929. Educated at Harvard University, Cambridge, Massachusetts, B.A. (cum laude) 1950; University of Michigan, Ann Arbor, M.A. 1952. Founding Member, Poets' Theatre, Cambridge, Massachusetts, 1950, and director of experimental productions, 1956; Member of Playwrights Unit, 1960–66, and Member of Playwrights Committee, 1962–64, Actors Studio, New York; Member of Richard Barr-Edward Albee Playwrights Unit, New York, 1962–1965; Member of the Loft Theatre Workshop, New York, 1970–71, and Director of Teenage Theatre Workshop, 1971. Head of the English Department, Haithcock School, Greenwich, Connecticut, 1958–59; Librarian, Bard College, Annandale-on-Hudson, New York, 1959–60; Editor, McGraw-Hill Book Company, New York, 1960–63; free-lance editor for New York publishers, 1964–71; Assistant Professor, Department of Dramatic Arts, University of Connecticut, Storrs, 1971–73. Agent: Samuel French Inc., 25 West 45th Street, New York, New York 10036. Address: Germantown, New York 12526, U.S.A.

PUBLICATIONS

Plays

The Ox on the Roof (produced Annandale-on-Hudson, New York, 1960).
Pigeons (produced New York, 1963).   Published in *New American Plays*, edited by
    Robert W. Corrigan, New York, Hill and Wang, 1965.
The Rook (produced New York, 1964).   Published in *New Theatre in America*, edited
    by Edward Parone, New York, Dell, 1965.
Soap (produced Stockbridge, Massachusetts, 1970; New York, 1971).

Television Plays: *Love of Life* series, 1966.

Critical Study: "Writing a Play" by the author, in *How I Write*, New York, Harcourt Brace, 1972.

Theatrical Activities:

Director: **Plays** – Poets' Theatre, Cambridge, Massachusetts, 1956; *Krapp's Last Tape* by Samuel Beckett, *Les Batisseurs d'Empire* by Boris Vian, and *The Double Dealer* by Congreve, Storrs, Connecticut, 1971–72.

Lawrence Osgood comments:

Thematically, my plays are concerned with the uses of personal power – how and why people gain, lose, exercise, and want control over other people. I see comedy as a moral instrument, theatre as illumination, and my plays as exercises in the logical pursuit of the irrational. My favorite playwrights are William Congreve and Samuel Beckett.

*   *   *

Lawrence Osgood's disturbing comedies call the expectation of violence into play – into the chessgame of *The Rook* and the dance of *Pigeons*. These published companion pieces establish his idiom. His characters seem comically familiar as theatrical types and everyday acquaintances, though freakishly or theatrically exalted by the psychological pressures around them. Offstage, society's violence is real. Characters can exert power onstage by invoking and controlling the working myth of this violence. Even the dominant find themselves caught in the dance or game they imposed. The disturbing music of violence penetrates all.

The fine, elderly lady in *Pigeons* proposes, "I'm simply going to stop her. And when I have, I'll let her go." This is the victory sought. The Old Lady and her Companion have pursued a colorfully aggressive Woman through New York to this empty lot. The Old Lady knows that any "natural order of things is an invention of the simpleminded" for evading "Them." Confronting her enemy she breaks out of her "natural order" and warns her Companion to do the same. Players who can't, like her Companion or Alf in *The Rook*, always lose their chance. They end up dancing the pigeon-dance for old ladies, or lose the game to Rico and must be shown the proper move by Edna who does not know chess, who despises and resents the game. Still, the Old Lady must dance round the other two, Alf's wife must make the move for him and return to fourteen chessboards at home, and next morning Alf's son-in-law must begin a new game with his wife Adèle. Something has happened to the manipulators too. Osgood analyzes *Rook*'s power-games in his essay on writing.

The threatening device itself normally remains vague and out of sight. Typically, the Old Lady in *Pigeons* threatens to "use what's in my purse." Is the box in *Rook* even Rico's? In one play an assumption of suicide stirs a crowd; in another an unnamed "antique piece" under Charles' "tiny bathing suit" threatens fortunes and households. The "Electroencephaloprobe" does appear onstage in *Soap*. Though often a mere assumption by the intimidated, the threat of violence akin to death is real: madness, physical force, unspecified operations, suicide, sex....Television, a mode of perceiving reality, supplies images for invoking its violence. In *Rook* Edna speaks of the "drop" used in crime shows and Adele of the depersonalization used in quiz shows. *Soap* burlesques the hospital soap-operas throughout.

Soap does humorous violence even to the exaggerated form and images of afternoon TV. As though, by its pathetic flickerings, Joe Orton and Charles Ludlam rewrote Pinero. Former stripper Billie Bombshell as the Second Mrs. Rackaman Slicer is the unacceptable wife of a famous neurosurgeon and neurotic who resents anyone's happiness and runs Maidenhead

610

Asylum. Billie, secretly embroidering something for young intern Sal Zabaglione, happily hums a blues. To discover his wife's secret of happiness Slicer probes his mentally deficient 14-year-old till Henrietta regresses to gurgling infantility: "You can't spend all day probing a brain that size and have much left." The intern and Nurse Gonad wrap Slicer up in the straitjacket Billie monogrammed "Z" and leave him for Billie. Strindberg? Now she's "gonna be happy." Like other Osgood heroines, Billie first seemed a little slow. Somehow the bizarre excesses have not excluded the wisps of real feeling that linger around afternoon television, literate allusion, and these cartoon characters. Affections have developed, and Billie's working out a future that includes the outrageous but disposable Slicer is oddly disturbing. As though Osgood had simply heightened the usual pattern of his plays by using gaudier colors and escalating the violence onstage beyond belief.

Osgood prefers suppressed violence glowing through the language. Alf laments, "If that son-of-a-bitch only hadn't taken my [white] knight." The loss of dignity crumbles the will and identity. Alf's line adds significance to Queens and Castles in his imaginary land and in the real world of every Osgood play. Talk at the subdued level of polite conversation can rip at another's dignity.

The title-music of *The Ox on the Roof* accompanies the cocktail talk in Osgood's first play. A defeated oaf leaves this civilized arena by a window and is presumed to have jumped. Upon his infuriating return, the violence almost emerges into a fight before it's smoothed over. Modulation sustains twelve characters' conversations without losing continuity. A song in each play acknowledges musical movement and rhythm in Osgood's compositions.

His latest script returns to the strain of keeping conversation polite amid violence. Still revising with working titles, he places this "Critical Comedy" in the home of an "*Old Buffalo*" Family. Mother Pauline would restore the castle and protect the fortune. To get both her share and her fiance Charles, daughter Allie must learn "*The Winning Way*" of the World. The epigraph quotes Lady Wishfort: "Ah Marwood, what's integrity to an opportunity?" Pauline enlists Sally, Allie's best friend, to help "redecorate." Sally finds pleasure in the prospect; Charles survived by servicing ladies in the Virgin Islands. At the dinner-party Sally gives the jealous mother a delicious report about an "antique piece" (cf., Wycherley's china scene) – while Charles cringes, Allie begins to comprehend, and Sally's professor husband talks on about the sociometrics of conversational assumptions. Having found sharp contemporary equivalents for the Restoration characters and situation, Osgood develops them to the concluding proviso scene between Allie and Charles. Osgood is writing comedies of humours and manners, and prefers to keep the china offstage – from where the sound of breakage comes into his plays.

—John G. Kuhn

OWEN, Alun (Davies).   British.   Born in Liverpool, Lancashire, 24 November 1926. Educated at Oulton High School, Liverpool; Cardigan Grammar School, Wales. Married Mary O'Keeffe in 1942; has two sons. Worked as a stage manager, director and actor, 1942–59. Recipient: Screenwriters and Producers Script of the Year Award, 1960; Screenwriters Guild Award, 1961; *Daily Mirror* award, 1961; Golden Star, 1967. Lives in Dublin. Address: c/o Felix de Wolfe and Associates, 1 Robert Street, Adelphi, London WC2N 6BH, England.

PUBLICATIONS

Plays

The Rough and Ready Lot (broadcast, 1958, produced London, 1959).   London, Encore, 1960.

Progress to the Park (broadcast, 1958; produced London, 1959).   Published in *New English Dramatists 5*, London, Penguin, 1962.

Three T.V. Plays (includes *No Trams to Lime Street, After the Funeral, Lena, Oh My Lena*).   London, Cape, 1961.

The Rose Affair (televised, 1961; produced Cardiff, 1966).   Included in *Anatomy of a Television Play*, London, Weidenfeld and Nicolson, 1962.

Dare to Be a Daniel (televised, 1962).   Published in *Eight Plays: Book 1*, edited by Malcolm Stuart Fellows, London, Cassell, 1965.

A Little Winter Love (produced Dublin, 1963; London, 1965).   London, Evans, 1964.

Maggie May, music by Lionel Bart (produced London, 1964).

The Game (includes *The Winner* and *The Loser*) (produced Dublin, 1965).

The Goose (produced Dublin, 1967).

The Wake (televised, 1967).   Published in *Theatre Choice: A Collection of Modern Short Plays*, edited by Michael Marland, London, Blackie, 1972.

Shelter (televised, 1967; produced London, 1971).   London, French, 1968.

George's Room (televised, 1967).   London and New York, French, 1968.

There'll Be Some Changes Made (produced London, 1969).

Norma, in *We Who Are About to...*, later title *Mixed Doubles* (produced London, 1969).   London, Methuen, 1970.

Doreen (televised, 1969).   Published in *The Best Short Plays 1971*, edited by Stanley Richards, Philadelphia, Chilton, 1971.

The Male of the Species (televised, 1969; produced Brighton and London, 1974).   Published in *Camera Three*, New York, Holt Rinehart, 1972.

Screenplays: *The Criminal (The Concrete Jungle)*, 1960; *A Hard Day's Night*, 1964; *Caribbean Idyll*, 1970.

Radio Plays: *Two Sons*, 1957; *The Rough and Ready Lot*, 1958, *Progress to the Park*, 1958; *It Looks Like Rain*, 1959.

Television Plays: *No Trams to Lime Street*, 1959; *After the Funeral*, 1960; *Lena, Oh My Lena*, 1960; *The Ruffians*, 1960; *The Ways of Love*, 1961; *The Rose Affair*, 1961; *The Hard Knock*, 1962; *Dare to Be a Daniel*, 1962; *You Can't Win 'em All*, 1962; *The Strain*, 1963; *Let's Imagine* series, 1963; *The Stag*, 1963; *A Local Boy*, 1963; *The Other Fella*, 1966; *The Making of Jericho*, 1966; *The Winner*, 1967; *The Loser*, 1967; *The Fantasist*, 1967; *The Wake*, 1967; *Shelter*, 1967; *George's Room*, 1967; *Stella*, 1967; *Thief*, 1967; *Charlie*, 1968; *Gareth*, 1968; *Tennyson*, 1968; *Ah, There You Are*, 1968; *Alexander*, 1968; *Minding the Shop*, 1968; *Time for the Funny Walk*, 1968; *The Ladies*, 1969; *Joan*, 1969; *Doreen*, 1969; *Spare Time*, 1969; *Park People*, 1969; *You'll Be the Death of Me*, 1969, *Male of the Species* (U.S. title: *Emlyn, MacNeil, Cornelius*), 1969; *Hilda*, 1970; *And a Willow Tree*, 1970; *Just the Job*, 1970; *Female of the Species*, 1970; *Joy*, 1970; *Ruth*, 1971; *Funny*, 1971; *Pal*, 1971; *Giants and Ogres*, 1971; *The Piano Player*, 1971; *The Web*, 1972, *Ronny Barker Show* (3 scripts); *Buttons*, 1973; *Flight*, 1973; *Lucky*, 1974; *Left*, 1975; *Forget-Me-Not* (6 plays), 1976.

Other

Bewin y Bél (juvenile).   Denbigh, Wales, Gwasg Gee, 1957.

Theatrical Activities:

Actor: **Plays** – with the Birmingham Repertory Company, 1943–44; Jepson in *Humoresque* by Guy Bolton, London, 1948; Rolph in *Snow White and the Seven Dwarfs*, London, 1951; with Sir Donald Wolfit's Company at the Old Vic, London, 1953: in *Tamburlaine the Great* by Marlowe, Charles in *As You Like It*, Curan and Herald in *King Lear*, Officer in *Twelfth Night*, Salarino in *The Merchant of Venice*, Sexton in *Macbeth*, Gonzales Ferera in *The Wandering Jew* by J. Temple Thurston, a Lord and Joseph in *The Taming of the Shrew*; with the English Stage Company at the Royal Court, London, 1957; Clifford in *Man with a Guitar* by Gilbert Horobin, Smith in *The Waiting of Lester Abbs* by Kathleen Sully; Reader in *The Samsom Riddle* by Wolf Mankowitz, Dublin, 1972. **Films** – *Every Day Except Christmas*, 1957; *I'm All Right Jack*, 1959; *Jet Storm*, 1959; *The Servant*, 1963.

*   *   *

The main strengths of Alun Owen's work have always been its accuracy of observation, its depth of characterization and the power and fluency of its dialogue, sometimes reaching the level of poetry. *Progress to the Park*, set in the pre-Beatles Liverpool of the late fifties, is a vivid and detailed portrait of working-class life in that town at that period. The play's central theme is the vice-like grip that religious intolerance has on the city's inhabitants; and is expressed through the central relationship between Bobby Laughlin, a Protestant boy, and Mag Keegan, a Catholic girl. Their potential love is stifled and destroyed by the bigoted attitudes of their elders. There are a number of sharply-defined character studies, including members of the Laughlin and Keegan families; and of Teifion Davies, the detached, ironic young Welshman who has a love-hate relationship to his home town, which is reflected in his commentary on the action. The play teems with vitality and power, each episode flowing effectively and relentlessly into and out of each other but related strongly to the central theme.

The Rough and Ready Lot is set in a monastery in a Spanish colony in South America a few years after the end of the U.S. Civil War and revolves around four "soldiers of fortune" – Kelly, O'Keefe, Morgan and the Colonel. They are in a lull between fighting, ostensibly on the side of the Indians in their bid to free themselves from their Spanish oppressors; in the meantime, the four men talk. O'Keefe is a fanatical Catholic; Morgan an equally fanatical political revolutionary; the Colonel is a "realist," who thinks he knows the motives for people's actions but is, in fact, incredibly blinkered; while Kelly just takes life as it comes. They argue and try to impose their views on the others, sometimes in burst of magnificent rhetoric; but in the end only Kelly survives. As Irving Wardle said in reviewing the play for the now-defunct magazine *Encore*, "Its dialogue flows beautifully; its characters are conceived in depth and, as embodiments of conflicting principles, they are disposed in a pattern of geometric symmetry; the plot is constructed solidly and attaches itself tenaciously to the governing theme."

In the musical *Maggie May*, written with Lionel Bart, he returns to the Liverpool scene and gives us another teeming, vital slice of life. The early and mid-sixties was also the time of his award-winning TV plays, also set on Merseyside, *No Trams to Lime Street*, *Lena, Oh My Lena* and *After the Funeral*; and his sharp and witty script for the Beatles' first and best film, the semi-documentary *A Hard Day's Night*. By contrast, *The Rose Affair*, also a TV award-winner, was a modernised version of the fairy-tale, *Beauty and the Beast*, the Beast-figure an isolated, high-powered businessman, the Beauty a girl he falls in love with from afar; stylistically, it had some bold innovations for its time and also had some pithy things to say on the split between being a public and a private person.

In recent years, most of his work has been for television, and includes *Shelter*, a play about the confrontation between an aggressive working-class man and an alienated young middle-class woman, and *Dare to Be a Daniel*, in which a young man with a grudge against his former schoolteacher returns to the small town where he comes from to gain his revenge.

After some years' lapse, Owen returned to the theatre in 1974 with *The Male of the*

Species. Consisting of three short plays, the play purports to show how women are exploited by men. Mary MacNeil is shown in her encounters with three crucial male figures: her father, a master carpenter; her employer, a suave, urbane barrister; and the "office cad." The trouble is, however, that the men are all depicted as attractive, while Mary is portrayed as a willing victim. The perhaps unconscious male chauvinism of the play is disappointing in a writer of Owen's talent.

—Jonathan Hammond

OWENS, Rochelle. American. Born in Brooklyn, New York, 2 April 1936. Educated at Lafayette High School, Brooklyn, graduated 1953; Herbert Berghof Studio; New School for Social Research, New York. Married the poet George Economou in 1962. Worked as clerk, typist, telephone operator. Member, Playwrights Unit, Actors Studio; Member, The New Dramatists Committee; Founding Member, New York Theatre Strategy. Recipient: Rockefeller Office for Advanced Drama Research grant, 1965; Ford grant, 1965; Creative Artists Public Service grant, 1966; Yale University Drama School Fellowship, 1968; Obie Award, 1968, 1971; Guggenheim Fellowship, 1971; National Endowment for the Arts grant, 1974; Rockefeller grant, 1975. Agent: Michael Imison, Dr. Jan Van Loewen Ltd., 81-83 Shaftesbury Avenue, London W1V 8BX, England. Address: 606 West 116th Street, No. 34, New York, New York 10027, U.S.A.

PUBLICATIONS

Plays

> *Futz* (produced Minneapolis, 1965; New York, Edinburgh and London, 1967). New York, Hawk's Well Press, 1961; revised version in *Futz and What Came After*, 1968; in *New Short Plays 2*, London, Methuen, 1969.
> *The String Game* (produced New York, 1965). Included in *Futz and What Came After*, 1968.
> *Istanboul* (produced New York, 1965). Included in *Futz and What Came After*, 1968.
> *Homo* (produced Stockholm and New York, 1966; London, 1969). Included in *Futz and What Came After*, 1968.
> *Beclch* (produced Philadelphia and New York, 1968). Included in *Futz and What Came After*, 1968.
> *Futz and What Came After* (includes *Beclch, Homo, The String Game, Istanboul*). New York, Random House, 1968.
> *The Karl Marx Play*, music by Galt MacDermot, lyrics by Rochelle Owens (produced New York, 1973). Included in *The Karl Marx Play and Others*, 1974.
> *The Karl Marx Play and Others* (includes *Kontraption, He Wants Shih, Farmer's Almanac, Coconut Folksinger, O.K. Certaldo*). New York, Dutton, 1974.
> *He Wants Shih* (produced New York, 1975). Included in *The Karl Marx Play and Others*, 1974.
> *Emma Instigated Me*, in *Performance Arts Journal 1* (New York), 1976.
> *The Widow and Me Colonel*, in *Best Short Plays 1977*, New York, Crown, 1977.

Screenplay: *Futz* (additional dialogue), 1969.

614

Short Stories

The Girl on the Garage Wall.   Mexico City, El Corno Emplumado, 1962.
The Obscenities of Reva Cigarnik.   Mexico City, El Corno Emplumado, 1963.

Verse

Not Be Essence That Cannot Be.   New York, Trobar Press, 1961.
Four Young Lady Poets, with others, edited by LeRoi Jones.   New York, Corinth
   Books, 1962.
Salt and Core.   Los Angeles, Black Sparrow Press, 1968.
I Am the Babe of Joseph Stalin's Daughter.   New York, Kulchur Press, 1972.
Poems from Joe's Garage.   Providence, Rhode Island, Burning Deck, 1973.
The Joe 82 Creation Poems.   Los Angeles, Black Sparrow Press, 1974.
The Joe Chronicles II.   Los Angeles, Black Sparrow Press, 1977.

Recordings: *A Reading of Primitive and Archaic Poetry*, with others, Broadside; *From a
Shaman's Notebook*, with others, Broadside.

Other

Editor, *Spontaneous Combustion: Eight New American Plays.*   New York, Winter
   House, 1972.

Manuscript Collection: Mugar Memorial Library, Boston University.

Critical Studies: by Harold Clurman and Jerome Rothenberg in *Futz and What Came After*,
1968. "Rochelles Owens Symposium" in *Margins 24–26* (Milwaukee) 1975.

*   *   *

Rochelle Owens, a poet-playwright, came to the attention of the theatre public with her
first play, *Futz*. Its shocking subject and inventive language launched Ms. Owens on her
theatrical career. The plays are conceived in the tradition of a completed script, but they are
distinguished by intense poetic imagery that springs from primordial human impulses of the
subconscious. Owens' plays are sensual explorations of themes of eating and sex, power and
death. Though Owens professes not to be a conscious feminist, superwoman and androgynous
creatures abound in her drama.
   Futz is preceded by a quotation from the Corinthians: "Now concerning the things
whereof ye wrote to me: It is good for a man not to touch a woman." Cyrus Futz loves his
pig, Amanda, and is relentlessly persecuted by the rural community. Marjorie Satz lusts for
all men and compels Futz to allow her to share his sexual relationship with Amanda.
Marjorie panics and tells. Oscar Loop is driven to madness and murder when he and Ann
Fox inadvertently witness the Futz-Amanda-Marjorie orgy. Oscar is condemned to hang,
Futz is imprisoned and stabbed by Marjorie's brother. Innocent sensuality is punished in a
puritanical society.
   The String Game also explores the conflict between puritanism and natural impulse.
Greenland Eskimos play the string game to ward off the boredom of long winters. They are
admonished for creating erotic images by their Italian priest, Father Bontempo, who has his
own sensual image of warm spaghetti with tomatoes and olive oil. Cecil, half German and
half Eskimo, tempts Father Bontempo with a promise of fulfillment of his longing for his
native food in exchange for the priest's support of his commercial plans. Repulsed by the

priest's gluttony, Cecil strikes him and causes his death by choking. The saddened Eskimos refuse to comply with Cecil's business venture and return to their string game.

Istamboul dramatizes a cultural clash and *Homo* a class struggle. In *Istanboul* Norman men are fascinated by hirsute Byzantine women, and their wives by the sensual Byzantine men. In a madness of religous frenzy St. Mary of Egypt murders insensitive Godfrigh, amd sensual Leo makes love to Alice as they wait for the Saracens. *Homo* presents the mutual greed and contempt of Nordic and Asiatic. An exploration of racial and class conflict provides the dramatic energy of the play in which revolution comes and goes, and middle-class workers continue their brutality.

Human perversion prevail in Owen's most savage play, *Beclch*. In a fantasy Africa, four white adventurers intrude upon the natural innocence of a village. Beclch, a monster of excess, takes on the dimension of an earth-goddess. She tantalizes an old woman and murders a preacher woman and her son. After sentimentally professing her love for young Jose, Beclch introduces him to the cruelty of cock-fighting. She seduces her male companion, Yago, with promises of power if he will become infected with elephantiasis. King Yago cannot transcend his pain and is forced by both Blacks and Whites to strangle himself. Queen Beclch moves further into excess, and Jose flees in disgust. Since a queen cannot rule without a male consort, Beclch prepares herself for death as voluptuously as she lived.

A promise of social progress resides in Owens' most anbitious work, *The Karl Marx Play*, and her first attempt to use historical subject matter. Her Marx is drained by illness, poverty, his friend Engels, lust for his aristocratic Prussian wife, and a 20th century American Black, Leadbelly. All those who surround Marx demand the completion of *Das Kapital*, but it is finally Leadbelly who actively ignites Marx to fulfill his mission. Linear time is ignored, and the play is laced with song (the music was composed by Galt MacDermot).

He Wants Shih employs ritual chants, masks, superstition and pseudo-Chinese dialect. Set in China, the play is concerned with Lan, son of the last Empress of the Manchu dynasty. Lan abdicates so as to play with the adoring princess Lang, seduce his step-brother Bok, and philosophize with his tutor Feng. The dismembered head of the Empress continues to speak on the stage while Western imperialists decimate the Chinese. In the final scene Lan-he transforms into Lan-she. Total renunciation of sex and empire ends this fantastic play.

Owens returns to historical biography in *Emma Instigated Me*. The life of Emma Goldman, the 19th century anarchist, is juxtaposed against a contemporary Author, Director and female revolutionaries. As in *The Karl Marx Play*, linear time is dissolved. The characters change from one to another, from character into actor into bystander. The theatricality of the play becomes its most important objective.

Owens continues to experiment with form and content. Her strength lies in her strong poetic imagination and violent fantastic imagery. She dares to confront the subconscious impulse and projects through language raw, uncivilized passions.

—Elaine Shragge

PATRICK, John. American.   Born in Louisville, Kentucky, 17 May 1907. Educated at Holy Cross College, New Orleans; St. Edward's College, Austin, Texas; St. Mary's Seminary, LaPorte, Texas; Columbia University, New York; Harvard University, Cambridge, Massachusetts. Served as a Captain in the American Field Service in India and Burma, 1942–44. Radio Writer, NBC, San Francisco, 1933–36; Free-lance Writer, Hollywood, 1936–38. Recipient: Pulitzer Prize, 1954; New York Drama Critics Circle Award, 1954; Tony Award, 1954; Donaldson Award, 1954; Foreign Correspondents Award, 1957; Screen Writers Guild Award, 1957. D.F.A.: Baldwin Wallace College, Berea, Ohio, 1972. Agent:

Jonathan Clowes Ltd., 20 New Cavendish Street, London W1A 3AH, England. Address: Fortuna Mill Estate, Box 3537, St. Thomas, Virgin Islands 00801, U.S.A9

PUBLICATIONS

Plays

> *Hell Freezes Over* (produced New York, 1935).
> *The Willow and I* (produced New York, 1942).   New York, Dramatists Play Service, 1943.
> *The Hasty Heart* (produced New York and London, 1945).   New York, Random House, 1945.
> *The Story of Mary Surratt* (produced New York, 1947).   New York, Dramatists Play Service, 1947.
> *The Curious Savage* (produced New York, 1950; Derby, 1966).   New York, Dramatists Play Service, 1951.
> *Lo and Behold!* (produced New York, 1951).   New York, French, 1952.
> *The Teahouse of the August Moon*, adaptation of a novel by Vern Sneider (produced New York, 1953; London, 1954).   New York, Putnam, 1954; London, Heinemann, 1955; revised version, as *Lovely Ladies, Kind Gentlemen*, music and lyrics by Stan Freeman and Franklin Underwood (produced New York, 1970), New York, French, 1970.
> *Good as Gold*, adaptation of a work by Alfred Toombs (produced New York, 1957).
> *Juniper and the Pagans* (produced Boston, 1959).
> *Everybody Loves Opal* (produced New York, 1961; London, 1964).   New York, Dramatists Play Service, 1962.
> *Everybody's Girl* (produced Miami, 1967).   New York, Dranatists Play Service, 1968.
> *Scandal Point* (produced Paramus, New Jersey, 1968).   New York, Dramatists Play Service, 1969.
> *Love Is a Time of Day* (produced New York, 1969).   New York, Dramatists Play Service, 1970.
> *A Barrel Full of Pennies* (produced Paramus, New Jersey, 1970).   New York, Dramatists Play Service, 1971.
> *Opal Is a Diamond* (produced Flat Rock, North Carolina, 1971).   New York, Dramatists Play Service, 1972.
> *Macbeth Did It* (produced Flat Rock, North Carolina, 1972).   New York, Dramatists Play Service, 1972.
> *The Dancing Mice* (produced Berea, Ohio, 1972).   New York, Dramatists Play Service, 1972.
> *The Savage Dilemma* (produced Long Beach, California, 1972).   New York, Dramatists Play Service, 1972.
> *Anybody Out There?*   New York, Dramatists Play Service, 1972.
> *Roman Conquest* (produced Berea, Ohio, 1973).   New York, French, 1973.
> *The Enigma* (produced Berea, Ohio, 1973).   New York, Dramatists Play Service, 1974.
> *Opal's Baby: A New Sequel* (produced Flat Rock, North Carolina, 1973).   New York, Dramatists Play Service, 1974.
> *A Bad Year for Tomatoes* (produced North Royalton, Ohio, 1974).   New York, Dramatists Play Service, 1975.
> *Opal's Husband.*   New York, Dramatists Play Service, 1975.
> *Noah's Animals* (produced Berea, Ohio, 1975).   New York, French, 1976.

Screenplays: *Educating Father*, 1936; *36 Hours to Live*, 1936; *Fifteen Maiden Lane*,

1936; *High Tension*, 1936; *Midnight Taxi*, 1937; *Look Out, Mr. Moto*, 1937; *Dangerously Yours*, 1937; *The Holy Terror*, 1937; *Time Out for Romance*, 1937; *Sing and Be Happy*, 1937; *Born Reckless*, 1937; *One Mile from Heaven*, 1937; *Big Town Girl*, 1937; *International Settlement*, 1938; *Battle of Broadway*, 1938; *Mr. Moto Takes a Chance*, 1938; *Five of a Kind*, 1938; *Up the River*, 1938; *Enchantment*, 1948; *The President's Lady*, 1953; *Three Coins in the Fountain*, 1954; *Love Is a Many-Splendored Thing*, 1955; *High Society*, 1956; *Teahouse of the August Moon*, 1956; *Les Girls*, 1957; *Some Came Running*, 1958; *Parrish*, 1960; *The World of Susie Wong*, 1960; *Gigot*, 1962; *The Main Attraction*, 1963; *The Shoes of the Fisherman*, 1968.

Television Play: *The Small Miracle*, 1972.

*   *   *

John Patrick, born John Patrick Goggan, began his career as an NBC script writer who became noted for radio dramatizations of novels. He first reached Broadway in 1935 with *Hell Freezes Over*, an unsuccessful and short-lived melodrama concerning polar explorers whose dirigible crash-lands in Antarctica. Patrick continued writing, primarily Hollywood film scripts. Again unsuccessful was his next play, *The Willow and I*, a forced but sensitively-written psychological drama about two sisters competing for the love of the same man and destroying each other in the struggle.

During World War II, the writer served as an ambulance driver with the British Army in North Africa, Syria, India and Burma. His experience furnished the background for *The Hasty Heart*. Set in a military hospital behind the Assam-Burma front, the action centers on a dour Scottish sergeant sent to the convalescent ward unaware that a fatal illness condemns him to early death. His wardmates, knowing the prognosis, extend their friendship. But the Scot's suspicious nature and uncompromising independence nearly wrecks their good intentions. He gradually warms to his companions until he discovers his fatal condition and concludes that their proffered fellowship is merely pity. Ultimately he comes to accept his wardmates' goodwill, poignantly demonstrating the author's premise: "the importance of man's acknowledgement of his interdependency." Although some critics disbelieved that the stubbornly misanthropic protagonist could be capable of change, the majority found the play's effect credible and warming. It enjoyed a substantial run before being made into a motion picture, and evinced its author's growth as a dramatist in dealing more incisively with plot structure, characterization, and the effect of inner states of mind on conduct and character.

Patrick's next three plays failed to win popular approval. Based on historical events, *The Story of Mary Surratt* depicts the trial and conviction of the Washington landlady sentenced to the gallows by a vindictive military tribunal for complicity in the assassination of Abraham Lincoln. The author's view was that Mrs. Surratt, whose misguided son had become involved in Booth's plot, was an innocent victim of 1865 postwar hysteria. Although the drama was a compassionate protest against injustice and the vengeful concept of war guilt, playgoers did not want to be reminded of a probable miscarriage of justice in their own history at a time when war crime trials were a present reality. Critical opinion was divided, and the production failed. The drama, despite some turgidity of dialogue and the minor portrait of its title character, still emerges as a substantial work which deserved a better fate.

Patrick turned to comedy in *The Curious Savage*. The story focuses on a charmingly eccentric wealthy widow, insistent on spending her millions on a foundation financing people's daydreams, whose mendacious stepchildren commit her to a sanitorium where she finds her fellow inmates more attractive than her own sane but greedy family; with the help of the former she outwits the latter. While admitting the play's affectionate humor, critics fairly faulted the author for treating his rational "villians" too stridently and his irrational characters too romantically. Although experiencing only a brief existence on Broadway, *The Curious Savage* has been popular with regional theatres. A sequel, *The Savage Dilemma*, was published in 1972, but not presented in New York.

Other comedies followed. *Lo and Behold!* introduces a rich, solitude-loving writer who dies, having stipulated in his will that his house be kept vacant as a sanctuary for his spirit, and returns in ghostly form to find the premises occupied by three incompatible ghosts whom he untimately persuades to leave after all join forces to resolve a stormy courtship between a lingering housemaid and the estate's executor. The humor of the comedy-fantasy did not earn sufficient praise to support success.

In 1953, Patrick achieved a Broadway triumph with *Teahouse of the August Moon*, based on a novel by Vern Sneider. The play is a satire on the American Army of Occupation's attempts following World War II to bring democracy to the people of Okinawa. Amidst amusing clashed of mores and traditions, a young colonel with a past record of failure abandons standard Occupation procedure, builds the teahouse the villagers have longed for rather than a schoolhouse, and a distillery producing a local brandy which brings them prosperity. His obtuse commanding officer visits the village and hotly orders an end to such unorthodox practices but is overridden by Congressional declaration that the colonel's methods are the most progressive in Okinawa. Critic John Mason Brown accurately commented that "no plea for tolerance between peoples, no editorial against superimposing American customs on native tradition has ever been less didactic or more persuasive." The comedy captivated audiences and critics alike to become one of America's most successful plays, winning both the Pulitzer Prize and the New York Drama Critics Award. Patrick rewrote it as a screenplay and later as a short-lasting musical called *Lovely Ladies, Kind Gentlemen* with music and lyrics by Stan Freeman and Franklin Underwood.

Other comedies by Patrick include *Good as Gold* and *Everybody Loves Opal*. The former, a dramatization of a novel by Alfred Toombs, concentrates on a botanist who discovers a formula for changing gold into soil which will grow enormous vegetables but who cannot persuade Congress to give him the contents of Fort Knox. The farcical satire on politics constructed on one joke failed to find support. The title character of *Everybody Loves Opal* is a kindly recluse, living in a dilapidated mansion, who reforms three intruding petty crooks with her faith in the goodness of man. The comedy's fun was intermittent and its run short. Patrick has written several sequels.

Several other Patrick plays, mostly comedies, have been published, but not produced on Broadway. A prolific writer of radio, film, and play scripts whose *Teahouse of the August Moon* stands among the most successful American comedies, John Patrick merits attention as a major craftsman of the American theatre.

—Christian H. Moe

PATRICK, Robert. American. Born in Kilgore, Texas, 27 September 1937. Educated at Eastern New Mexico University, Portales, three years. Host, La Mama, 1965, Secretary to Ruth Yorck, 1965, and Doorman, Caffe Cino, 1966–68, all New York. Features Editor and Contributor, *Astrology Magazine*, 1971–72. Recipient: *Show Business* Award, 1969; Creative Artists Public Service grant, 1976. Agent: James Bohan, 27 West 96th Street, New York, New York. Address: 153 First Avenue, New York, New York 10003, U.S.A.

PUBLICATIONS

Plays

The Haunted Host (produced New York, 1964; London, 1975).   Included in *Robert*

Patrick's Cheep Theatricks!, 1972; in *Homosexual Acts*, London, Inter-Action
  Imprint, 1976.
Mirage (produced New York, 1965).
Sketches (produced New York, 1966).
The Sleeping Bag (produced New York, 1966).
Halloween Hermit (produced New York, 1966).
Indecent Exposure (produced New York, 1966).
Cheesecake (produced New York, 1966).   Published in *Off-Off Magazine* (New York),
  1969.
Lights, Camera, Action (produced New York, 1967).   Included in *Robert Patrick's
  Cheep Theatricks!*, 1972.
Warhol Machine (produced New York, 1967).
Still-Love (produced New York, 1967).   Published in *Intermission* (Chicago), 1967.
Cornered (produced New York, 1967).   Included in *Robert Patrick's Cheep
  Theatricks!*, 1972.
Un Bel Di (produced New York, 1967).
Help, I Am (produced New York, 1967).   Included in *Robert Patrick's Cheep
  Theatricks!*, 1972.
See Other Side (produced New York, 1968).   Published in *Yale/Theatre Magazine*
  (New Haven, Connecticut), 1969.
Absolute Power over Movie Stars (produced New York, 1968).
Preggin and Liss (produced New York, 1968).   Included in *Robert Patrick's Cheep
  Theatricks!*, 1972.
The Overseers (produced New York, 1968).
Angels in Agony (produced New York, 1968).
Salvation Army (produced New York, 1968).
Dynel (produced New York, 1968).
Camera Obscura, in *Collision Course* (produced New York, 1968).   New York,
  Random House, 1968.
Fog (produced New York, 1969).   Published in *Now: Theater der Erfahrung: Material
  zur neuen amerikanischen Theaterbewegung*, edited by Jens Heilmeyer and Pia
  Frolich, Cologne, Verlag M. Dumont Schauberg, 1971.
I Came to New York to Write (produced New York, 1969; Edinburgh, 1975).   Included
  in *Robert Patrick's Cheep Theatricks!*, 1972.
Joyce Dynel (produced New York, 1969).   Included in *Robert Patrick's Cheep
  Theatricks!*, 1972.
Oooooooops! (produced New York, 1969).
Lily of the Valley of the Dolls (produced New York, 1969; Edinburgh, 1972).
One Person (produced New York, 1969; London, 1975).   Included in *Robert Patrick's
  Cheep Theatricks!*, 1972.
Silver Skies (produced New York, 1969).
Tarquin Truthbeauty (produced New York, 1969).
Presenting Arnold Bliss (produced New York, 1969; as *The Arnold Bliss Show*, produced
  Edinburgh, 1972).   Included in *Robert Patrick's Cheep Theatricks!*, 1972.
The Actor and the Invader (produced New York, 1969; Edinburgh, 1972).
The Golden Circle (produced New York, 1972).   Published in *New American Plays 3*,
  edited by William M. Hoffman, New York, Hill and Wang, 1970.
Hymen and Carbuncle (produced New York, 1970).
La Repetition (produced New York, 1970; Edinburgh, 1972).
A Bad Place to Get Your Head (produced New York, 1970).
Bead-Tangle (produced New York, 1970).
Sketches and Songs (produced New York, 1970).
I Am Trying to Tell You Something (produced New York, 1970).
Angel, Honey, Baby, Darling, Dear (produced New York, 1970).
The Golden Animal (produced New York, 1970).

Picture Wire (produced New York, 1970).

The Richest Girl in The World Finds Happiness (produced New York, 1970).   Included in *Robert Patrick's Cheep Theatricks!*, 1972.

A Christmas Carol (produced New York, 1971).

Shelter (produced New York, 1971).

Ludwig and Warner (produced New York, 1972).

Songs (produced New York, 1972).

Robert Patrick's Cheep Theatricks! (includes *I Came to New York to Write,' The Haunted Host, Joyce Dynel, Cornered, Still-Love, Lights, Camera, Action, Help, I Am, The Arnold Bliss Show, One Person, Preggin and Liss, The Richest Girl in the World Finds Happiness*).   New York, Winter House, 1972.

The Arnold Bliss Show (includes *The Arnold Bliss Show, The Actor and the Invader, La Repetition, Arnold's Big Break*) (produced Edinburgh, 1972).

Play-by-Play: A Spectacle of Ourselves (also director: produced New York, 1972; London, 1975).

Something Else (produced New York, 1973).   Published in *Hub* (New York), 1972.

The Twisted Root (produced New York, 1973).

Simultaneous Transmissions (produced New York, 1973).   Published in *The Scene/2 (Plays from Off-Off-Broadway)*, edited by Stanley Nelson, New York, The Smith/New Egypt, 1974.

Judas (produced New York, 1973).

Mercy Drop (produced New York, 1973).

Hippy as a Lark (produced New York, 1973).

Imp-Prisonment (produced New York, 1973).

Kennedy's Children (produced New York, 1973; London, 1974).   London, French, 1975; New York, Random House, 1976.

Fred and Harold, and One Person (produced London, 1975).   Published in *Homosexual Acts*, London, Inter-Action Imprint, 1976.

My Dear It Dosn't Mean a Thing (includes *Lights, Camera Obscura, Action, Something Else*) (produced London, 1976).

Screenplays: *The Haunted Host*, 1969; *The Credit Game*, 1972.

Theatrical Activities:

Director: **Plays** – *Wonderful, Wonderful*, by Douglas Kahn, and excerpt from *The Approach* by Jean Reavey, La Mama, New York, 1965; Artistic Director of *BbAaNnGg!!!*, New York, 1965; created Comic Book Shows at the Caffe Cino, New York, 1966; Assistant Director to Tom O'Horgan and Jerome Savary, Brandeis University, Waltham, Massachusetts, 1968; originated *Dracula*, Edinburgh, 1968; reopened *Bowery Follies*, New York, 1972; *Silver Queen* by Paul Foster, New York, 1973; directed many of his own plays.

Actor: **Plays** – at Caffe Cino, La Mama and Old Reliable in his own plays, and plays by Powell Shepherd, Soren Agenoux, John Hartnett, Stuart Koch, H. M. Koutoukas, William M. Hoffman.

Robert Patrick comments:

My plays are dances with words. The words are music for the actors to dance to. They also serve many other purposes, but primarily they give the actors images and rhythms to create visual expressions of the plays' essential relationships. The ideal production of one of my plays would be completely understandable even without sound, like a silent movie. Most of my plays are written to be done with a minimum of scenery, although I have done some fairly lavish productions of them. My plays fall into three general classes: (1) Simple histories, like *I Came to New York to Write*; (2) Surrealistic metaphors, like *The Arnold Bliss Show, Lights, Camera, Action*, and *Joyce Dynel*; and (3) Romances, like *Fog, Female Flower*, and both *The Golden Animal* and *The Golden Circle*. Basically, I believe the importance of a play to be this: A play is an experience the audience has together; it is stylized to aid in perception and understanding; and, above all, it is done by live players, and it is traced in its minutest particulars, so that it can serve as a warning (if it is a tragedy or comedy) or as a good example. Nothing must be left out or it becomes merely ritual. The time of ritual is over. The essential experience must replace it.

*   *   *

Robert Patrick, off-off-Broadway's most prolific and most frequently produced playwright, once told a playwright friend writing the introduction to a collection of his plays that his works could be best described as "stars shooting across the cobalt night sky – snowflakes that for a second enhance the eyelashes of the somber Muse!" It's a true, but rather heavy, description of Patrick's plays, each of which develops the playwright's lively pop-art imagination and is full of freewheeling forms, true feelings, and very funny jokes. He could almost be termed off-off-Broadway's Neil Simon or Jean Kerr. Patrick's output of plays has been staggering. In just nine years he has written literally hundred of plays and has had over fifty productions off-off-Broadway.

Patrick's plays come in an unending variety of flavors – the realistic plays, the New York apartment plays, the mini-plays (which he invented), comic book plays (the start of the *Story Theatre* conception), love-quarrel plays, biological plays (plays where obscure patterns in human behavior are recorded), romantic plays, pop plays, monologues, real live plays and musicals and farces written for special occasions.

The styles of these plays are eclectic and individual. Most were written for special theatres or specific actors. They were all written when there were no critical or economic pressures off-off-Broadway. It was a time when theatre was free to be an art form. The plays were mostly presented in self-supporting bars or cafes where style of production and acting was as important as the script. The one unique thing off-off-Broadway had in its early days was freedom, and Patrick is a perfect example of a playwright who took advantage of this. Today, off-off-Broadway has mostly become a showcase for future commercial ventures, and one finds the off-off-Broadway of the late sixties moving out into the campuses and coffee houses of colleges throughout the United States.

Only two of Patrick's plays, *Camera Obscura* and *The Haunted Host*, have been produced on commercial off-Broadway. *Camera Obscura* (the original mini-play) was first produced as part of an evening of mini-plays at La Mama and eventually became part of *Collision Course* off-Broadway. It is a technological fantasy in which two pen pals are trying to talk with each other over a videophone which has a five second delay that makes communication impossible.

The Haunted Host is a mystery play about Jay (the host), an older homosexual playwright whose lover Ed has just been killed or committed suicide. On the scene appears a young playwright (the guest) who looks just like Ed. The play is well-constructed and probes an interesting if complex relationship between the boy and the playwright and the ghost of his former lover. The repartee is full of Patrick's very funny epigrammatic wit.

Kennedy's Children, an international and eventually a Broadway success, has elevated Patrick's reputation. Strictly speaking, the play consists of a series of monologues spoken in a Greenwich Village bar by a group of 1960's types – hippie, John F. Kennedy fanatic, Vietnam veteran. Village homosexual, and blonde beauty with a Marilyn Monroe problem. Without ever speaking to each other, the five speakers seem to gain depth from the presence of the others.

Patrick's potpourri of plays and playwriting styles is fine proof of the way a creative talent can flourish in a non-commercial artistic milieu like off-off-Broadway. May he continue.

—Bernard Carragher

PERELMAN, S(idney) J(oseph).   American.   Born in Brooklyn, New York, 11 February 1904. Educated at Brown University, Providence, Rhode Island, 1921–25, B.A. 1925. Married Laura West in 1929; has two children. Writer, and artist, for *Judge* magazine, 1925–29, and for *College Humor* magazine, 1929–30. Contributor to *The New Yorker*, since 1930. Recipient: New York Fim Critics Award, 1956; Academy Award, 1956. Member, National Institute of Arts and Letters. Lived in London, 1970–72. Address: c/o Simon and Schuster, 630 Fifth Avenue, New York, New York 10020, U.S.A.

PUBLICATIONS

Plays

Sketches in *The Third Little Show* (produced New York, 1931).
Sketches, with Robert MacGunigle, in *Walk a Little Faster* (produced New York, 1932).
All Good Americans, with Laura Perelman (produced New York, 1933).
Sketches in *Two Weeks with Pay* (toured, 1940).
The Night Before Christmas, with Laura Perelman (produced New York, 1941).   New York, French, 1942.
One Touch of Venus, with Ogden Nash, music by Kurt Weill, based on *The Tinted Venus* by F. Anstey (produced New York, 1943).   Boston, Little Brown, 1944.
Sweet Bye and Bye, with Al Hirschfield (produced New Haven, Connecticut, 1946).
The Beauty Part, with Ogden Nash (produced New Hope, Pennsylvania, 1961; New York, 1962).   New York, French, 1963.

Screenplays: *Monkey Business*, 1931; *Horse Feathers*, 1932; *Paris Interlude*, 1934; *Florida Special*, with Laura Perelman, 1936; *Ambush*, with Laura Perelman, 1939; *Boy Trouble*, with Laura Perelman, 1939; *The Golden Fleecing*, with Laura Perelman, 1940; *Larceny, Inc.*, 1942; *One Touch of Venus*, 1948; *Around the World in Eighty Days*, with others, 1956.

Television writer: *Omnibus* series, 1957–58; *Lively Arts* series; and various specials.

Other

Dawn Ginsbergh's Revenge.   New York, Liveright, 1929.
Parlor, Bedlam and Bath, with Q.J. Reynolds.   New York, Liveright, 1930.
Strictly from Hunger.   New York, Random House, 1937.
Look Who's Talking.   New York, Random House, 1940.
The Dream Department.   New York, Random House, 1943.
Crazy Like a Fox.   New York, Random House, 1944; London, Heinemann, 1945.
Keep It Crisp.   New York, Random House, 1946; London, Heinemann, 1947.
Acres and Pains.   New York, Reynal and Hitchcock, 1947; London, Heinemann, 1948.
The Best of S.J. Perelman.   New York, Modern Library, 1947.
Westward Ha! or, Around the World in Eighty Clichés.   New York, Simon and Schuster, 1947; London, Reinhardt and Evans, 1949.
Listen to the Mocking Bird.   New York, Simon and Schuster, 1949; London, Reinhardt and Evans, 1950.
The Swiss Family Perelman.   New York, Simon and Schuster, 1950; London, Reinhardt and Evans, 1951.
A Child's Garden of Curses: Containing Crazy Like a Fox, Keep It Crisp, Acres and Pains.   London, Heinemann, 1951.

The Ill-Tempered Clavicord.   New York, Simon and Schuster, 1952; London, Max Reinhardt, 1953.

Perelman's Home Companion: A Collector's Item (the Collector Being S.J. Perelman) of 36 Otherwise Unavailable Pieces by Himself.   New York, Simon and Schuster, 1955.

The Road to Miltown; or, Under the Spreading Atrophy.   New York, Simon and Schuster, 1957; as *Bite on the Bullet; or, Under the Spreading Atrophy*, London, Heinemann, 1957.

The Most of S.J. Perelman.   New York, Simon and Schuster, 1958; London, Heinemann, 1959.

The Rising Gorge.   New York, Simon and Schuster, 1961; London, Heinemann, 1962.

Chicken Inspector No. 23.   New York, Simon and Schuster, 1966; London, Hodder and Stoughton, 1967.

Baby, It's Cold Inside.   New York, Simon and Schuster, and London, Weidenfeld and Nicolson, 1970.

Monkey Business.   New York, Simon and Schuster, 1973.

Vinegar Puss.   New York, Simon and Schuster, 1975; London, Weidenfeld and Nicolson, 1976.

*   *   *

Ah Mr. Perelman! How many would-be wits have thrown in the facecloth on hearing your jests in the theatre, or upon reading your cool little entrapments on the pages of the *New Yorker*? I was first introduced to your work on a theatrical tour trundling through Manitoba fourteen years ago. Wild giggles coming from a plump little actress in the back of the bus caused me to wonder if she wasn't in her cups at that early morning hour – which perhaps wouldn't have been too surprising in that winter country with a minus-thirty-degree wind cutting straight down from the white wastes of the Arctic like a razor blade dipped in lemon juice. But she wasn't, she was reading one of your anecdotes, stuck like a mesmerized fly in your web, helpless but happy. I read you, remembered you, saw you on the boards, and ever since then have thanked heaven for your humour....

I've only written one or two fan letters in a longish history of theatre-going and only twice during that time has my emotion overcome my embarrassment to the point at which I could shout "bravo" at a public performance. But one feels that if all the laughs, snorts, giggles, yelps of joy and shouts of merriment, privately uttered after reading Perelman's works, could be recorded the ensuing roar would be louder than a football crowd. For S.J. Perelman has a way with words and human situations that defies description.

Born in 1904 the voice of Sidney Joseph P. was first notably heard in a New York theatre in 1932 in a revue at the Music Box called *Walk a Little Faster*. It featured Beatrice Lillie, who was, bless her, already a Family Name. One might think that the saucy talents of Miss Lillie and Mr. Perelman would have been engagingly engaged – but the wise old sage of the *New York Times*, Brooks Atkinson, while glowing on about Bea's "blowsy, coquettish, low-comedy antics," hardly mentioned the material, stating: "The truth of the matter is that *Walk a Little Faster* does not put her through her funniest paces."

In other words the two comic talents clashed rather than complemented. Critic Atkinson went on to comment that "sketches are mostly silly," nor did the combined writing cannonade of Mr. *and* Mrs. (Laura) Perelman give him much pleasure a year later. About *All Good Americans*, a play about Americans living in Paris, he wrote: "Mr. and Mrs. Perelman have written a second-rate Barry comedy with a trying scene of whimsical pantomime toward the end." But although he complains that the plot is hardly profound he gave the jokes something of a warm notice.

Eight years were to pass before another Perelman comedy and for the second time its lack of success seemed to stem from lack of plot, for even the maddest farces depend sternly on a certain logic. Sections and sequences of *The Night Before Christmas* were hilarious but they did not make a satisfying whole. The *New York Times* headed its Atkinson notice "The Perelmans Crack Safes and Jokes in Sixth Avenue" but in obvious regret the critic could not give approval. "Since Mr. Perelman is one of the most insane wags of his time, and his wife must be slightly mad at least by association, it would be a service to humanity to find out why their Sixth Avenue scuffle is not one of the most hilarious escapades of the season."

One Touch of Venus, the Kurt Weill musical which enlivened the Broadway of 1943, brought Perelman into partnership with that other word-wizz, Ogden Nash. 'Although it was a slow starter their book received warm comment. In 1956 the writer received awards for his collaboration on *Around the World in Eighty Days* and New York saw no stage work until after a twenty-one year hiatus *The Beauty Part* arrived at the Music Box. This could be called a solo effort by S.J. Perelman in five characterizations – for the comedy featured the marvellous talents of the late Bert Lahr, American clown extraordinary. Here the play worked, perhaps because Perelman was allowed to create his own menagerie for an actor who understood their possibilities and made them his own. Is this sort of partnership for Perelman the secret of stage success? As Howard Taubman of *The Times* wrote: "Standing on its own the Perelman muse would not transpose easily and smoothly from the printed page to the theatre. But guided by a chap like Bert Lahr, it begins to adapt itself to the stage. Presently he helps to make it at home there."

During his stage life it becomes increasingly obvious that although the writer can spin off stories and articles like sleight-of-hand tricks he is not at home with a play. He can write clever and playable dialogue but it goes nowhere. His humour is instant and it is his own, not another character's. With Perelman the trimming is so right but the foundations of plot and characterization are often either shaky or non-existent. No comedy can stand up on only a joke-a-minute basis, however clever the cracks, for, when the fun dries for a moment, so does the play. Sadly S.J. Perelman is not a dramatist; his is the rare and marvellous talent for satire on the printed page, the kind of lush, mad phrasing that one treasures, laughs at, returns to and laughs again. Somehow his onstage writing is in the wrong style – it doesn't change for different characters unless that one character, like Mr. Lahr, happens to have an ability to dance to the same zany tune, and how much was Lahr and how much Perelman in that happy marriage of 1962 was anyone's guess.

Since the humorist only rarely turns to the theatre it may be years before he does so again – but still, one hopes not. The words of someone who knows and enjoys language and can awake the wildest eccentricities in the most mundane of minds are something of great value. Maybe Mr. Perelman's next idea may hang together with a plot that is worthy of his wit. One hopes so, for laughter is a salvation in this cracked and wild world we inhabit. If Mr. Perelman can keep us giggling, whether on the page or in the pit, he deserves our profound thanks.

—Michael T. Leech

PINNER, David. British. Born in Peterborough, Northamptonshire, 6 October 1940. Educated at Deacon's Grammar School, Peterborough; Royal Academy of Dramatic Art, London. Married the actress Catharine Henry Griller in 1965; has two children. Has acted with repertory companies in Sheffield, Coventry, Windsor and Farnham, and on the London stage. Playwright in Residence, Peterborough Repertory Theatre, 1974. Address: 18 Leconfield Avenue, London S.W.13, England.

PUBLICATIONS

Plays

Dickon (produced Hornchurch, Essex, 1966). Published in *New English Dramatists 10*, London, Penguin, 1967.

Fanghorn (produced Edinburgh and London, 1967).   London, Penguin, 1966.
Lightning at a Funeral (televised, 1967; produced Stanford, California, 1971).
The Drums of Snow (televised, 1968).   Published in *New English Dramatists 13*,
    London, Penguin, 1968; (revised version, produced Stanford, California, 1970;
    Oxford, 1974), in *Plays of the Year 42*, London, Elek, 1972.
The Potsdam Quartet (produced Guildford, Surrey, and London, 1973).
Cartoon (produced London, 1973).
An Evening with the GLC (produced London, 1974).
Hereward the Wake (produced Peterborough, 1974).
Shakebag (produced London, 1976).
Lucifer's Fair (produced London, 1976).

Radio Plays: *Lightfall*, 1967; *Cardinal Richelieu*, 1976.

Television Plays: *The Bonfire Boy*, 1966; *Eiderdown*, 1967; *Goodbye and Then*, 1967;
Lightning at a Funeral, 1967; *The Drums of Snow*, 1968; *Void*, 1969; *Strange Past*,
1974; *Juliet and Romeo* (Germany).

Novels

Ritual.   London, Hutchinson, 1967.
With My Body.   London, Weidenfeld and Nicolson, 1968.

Theatrical Activities:

Actor: **Plays** – Hornbeck in *Inherit the Wind* by Jerome Lawrence and Robert E. Lee,
Perth, Scotland, 1960; Ross in *Macbeth* and Magpie in *Naked Island* by Russell Bladdon,
Coventry, 1961; Gratiano in *The Merchant of Venice*, Newcastle upon Tyne, 1963; title
role in *Billy Liar* by Waterhouse and Hall, Windsor, 1964; Laertes in *Hamlet*, Bassanio in
The Merchant of Venice, and Edmund in *King Lear*, Sunderland, 1964–65; Lopahin in *The
Cherry Orchard*, by Chekhov, Hornchurch, Essex, 1965; Sergeant Trotter in *The
Mousetrap* by Agatha Christie, London, 1966. **Film** – *Robbery*, 1967.

*   *   *

David Pinner's *Dickon* – originally written as a radio play – was first produced at the
Hornchurch Repertory Theatre in 1966. *Fanghorn* received a West End production in 1967,
and a historical play, *The Drums of Snow* (about John Lilburne, the leader of the Levellers,
who became a powerful democratic force during 1647–49) has been published by Penguin.
But a later play, *The Potsdam Quartet*, was done at the Yvonne Arnaud Theatre, Guildford.
    Fanghorn may have misfired in the 1967 production and it may fail to sustain the comic
impact and inventiveness of the first two acts in the third, but the talent is unmistakable.
What is remarkable about the writing is its energy. It begins with a middle-aged man
beheading roses with a sword, then fencing flirtatiously with his sixteen-year-old daughter,
before switching to making her jump by slashing at her legs. And it sustains a brisk pace in
visual surprises and twists in the plot. Occasionally, an uncertain note is struck with
deliberately over-written lines like "Look at that gull battering his whiteness against the
hooks of the wind!" But there are also some very funny lines and plenty of intriguing
changes of direction in the dialogue, which builds up to the entrance of Tamara Fanghorn, a
tough-talking, leather-clad sophisticate, who arrives before she is expected, and from
upstairs. Subsequent developments make it look as though she is in league with the wife to
humiliate the husband, who is First Secretary to the Minister of Defence. Act Two ends with
him naked except for his pants, his hands tied with his belt and his feet with the telephone

wire. As the curtain falls Tamara is brandishing a cut-throat razor and threatening "Now I am going to cut off what offends me most!" When the curtain rises on Act Three, we find him denuded only of his moustache. The crucial twist comes when his disillusioned wife has walked out on him and we find that this is what he and Tamara had wanted all along.

Dickon is centred more ordinarily on family relationships. It is vitiated by perfunctoriness and superficiality in most of its characterisation, but there is a glowingly affectionate portrait of a lower-middle class father trying to fight off the awareness of cancer, and then later fighting with the pain. But the end piles on the drama too heavily, with one son powdering morphine tablets to put the dying man out of his agony, the other son giving them to him and then the two of them fighting and laughing hysterically.

There is a curious reprise of these themes in *The Potsdam Quartet*. Act One ends with the leader revealing to the cellist that for ten years he has been suffering from Parkinson's Disease, and the cellist, who had thought he was going mad, reacts with a joyful demonstration of relief. How he could have remained ignorant of his own condition is never adequately explained and there are only cursory references to the illness in Act Two, in which the biggest climax is provided by a quarrel between the second violin and the viola player, who are lovers. John (second violin) threatens Ronald (viola) that he is going to have the boyfriend of the leader's daughter, and Ronald responds by swallowing a succession of sleeping pills.

The play is set in an ante-room at the Potsdam Conference in 1945. The string quartet (which is based on the Griller Quartet) play two quartets to Churchill, Stalin and Truman. Act One takes place immediately after the first quartet and Act Two immediately after the second. Apart from the four musicians the only character is a Russian guard who hardly ever speaks. The characters are well contrasted and there is some amusing dialogue, but it is a realistic play in which the action is limited to what can go on in one room between four men who know each other extremely well. Act One cannot always avoid the pitfall of making them tell each other things they all know in order to give information to the audience and Act Two resorts to making them all drunk in order to increase the ratio of action to talk.

It lacks the energy and the courage of *Fanghorn* but after writing many unproduced plays in the six intervening years, Pinner cannot be blamed for playing safe, though the theatre can be blamed for failing to nourish the talent he originally showed.

Perhaps his two best plays are two one-acters produced at the Soho Poly. *Cartoon* is about an alcoholic cartoonist drying out in a clinic just up the road from the pub where he regularly spends his lunch-hour drinking grapefruit juice and weeping as he regularly wins money out of the fruit machine. *An Evening with the GLC* is set in a television studio where a Labour Councillor and his wife are exposed to a live interview conducted by their son. They both walk a little too willingly into the traps which are set for them, but the exposure of political dishonesties is nonetheless effective. Written when David Pinner was Resident Playwright at Peterborough, *Hereward the Wake* is another historical play with dialogue in the modern idiom.

—Ronald Hayman

PINTER, Harold. British. Born in Hackney, London, 10 October 1930. Educated at Hackney Downs Grammar School, 1943–47; Royal Academy of Dramatic Art, London, 1948. Conscientious objector: no military service. Married the actress Vivien Merchant in 1956; has one son. Professional actor, 1949–60; has acted some roles since then. Recipient: *Evening Standard* award, 1961; Newspaper Guild of New York Award, 1962; Italia Prize, for television play, 1962; Screenwriters Guild award, for television play, 1963, for screenplay, 1963; Guild of Television Producers and Directors Award, 1963; New York Film Critics Award, 1964; British Film Academy Award, 1965, 1971; Tony Award, 1967; Whitbread Award, 1967; New York Drama Critics Circle Award, 1967; Shakespeare Prize, Hamburg, 1970; Writers Guild Award, 1971. Member of the Drama Panel, Arts Council. C.B.E. (Companion, Order of the British Empire), 1966. Agent: ACTAC Ltd., 16 Cadogan Lane, London S.W.1. Address: 7 Hanover Terrace, London N.W.1, England.

PUBLICATIONS

Plays

    The Room (produced Bristol, 1957; London, 1962; New York, 1964).   Included in *The Birthday Party and Other Plays*, 1960.

    The Birthday Party (produced Cambridge and London, 1958; San Francisco, 1960; New York, 1967).   London, Encore, 1959; included in *The Birthday Party and Other Plays*, 1960; revised version, London, Methuen, 1965.

    Sketches in *One to Another* (produced London, 1959).   London, French, 1960.

    Sketches in *Pieces of Eight* (produced London, 1959).   Included in *A Slight Ache and Other Plays*, 1961; in *The Dwarfs and Eight Revue Sketches*, 1965.

    A Slight Ache (broadcast, 1959; produced London, 1961; New York, 1962).   Included in *A Slight Ache and Other Plays*, 1961; in *Three Plays*, 1962.

    The Dwarfs (broadcast, 1960; also director: produced London, 1963; revised version produced Edinburgh, 1966; Boston, 1967; New York, 1974).   Included in *A Slight Ache and Other Plays*, 1961; in *Three Plays*, 1962. '

    The Dumb Waiter (produced Frankfurt and London, 1960; Madison, Wisconsin, and New York, 1962).   Included in *The Birthday Party and Other Plays*, 1960.

    The Birthday Party and Other Plays (includes *The Dumb Waiter* and *The Room*). London, Methuen, 1960; as *The Birthday Party and The Room* (includes *The Dumb Waiter*), New York, Grove Press, 1961.

    The Caretaker (produced London, 1960; New York, 1961).   London, Methuen, 1960; in *The Caretaker and The Dumb Waiter*, 1961.

    Night School (televised, 1960).   Included in *Tea Party and Other Plays*, 1967; in *Early Plays*, 1968.

    A Night Out (broadcast, 1960; produced Dublin and London, 1961).   London, French, 1961; in *Early Plays*, 1968.

    The Collection (televised, 1961; also co-director: produced London, 1962; New York, 1963).   London, French, 1962; included in *Three Plays*, 1962.

    The Caretaker and The Dumb Waiter.   New York, Grove Press, 1961.

    Three Plays: A Slight Ache, The Collection, The Dwarfs.   New York, Grove Press, 1962.

    The Lover (televised, 1963; also director: produced London, 1963; New York, 1964). New York, Dramatists Play Service, 1965; in *The Collection and The Lover*, 1966.

    Tea Party (televised 1965; produced New York, 1968; London, 1970).   London, Methuen, 1965; New York, Grove Press, 1966; revised version, London, H. Karnac, 1968.

    The Homecoming (produced London, 1965; New York, 1967).   London, Methuen, 1965; New York, Grove Press, 1966; revised version, London, H. Karnac, 1968.

    The Dwarfs and Eight Revue Sketches.   New York, Dramatists Play Service, 1965.

    The Collection and The Lover (includes the prose piece *The Examination*).   London, Methuen, 1966.

    The Basement (televised, 1967; produced New York, 1968; London, 1970).   Included in *Tea Party and Other Plays*, 1967; in *The Lover, The Tea Party, The Basement*, 1967.

Tea Party and Other Plays (includes *The Basement* and *Night School*).   London, Methuen, 1967.

The Lover, The Tea Party, The Basement.   New York, Grove Press, 1967.

Early Plays: A Night Out, Night School, Revue Sketches.   New York, Grove Press, 1968.

Sketches by Pinter (produced New York, 1969).   Included in *Early Plays*, 1968.

Landscape (broadcast, 1968; produced London, 1969; New York, 1970).   London, Pendragon Press, 1968; included in *Landscape and Silence*, 1970.

Silence (produced London, 1969; New York, 1970).   Included in *Landscape and Silence*, 1969.

Landscape and Silence (includes *Night*).   London, Methuen, 1969; New York, Grove Press, 1970.

Night, in *Mixed Doubles* (produced London, 1969).   Included in *Landscape and Silence*, 1969.

Five Screenplays (includes *The Caretaker, The Servant, The Pumpkin Eater, Accident, The Quiller Memorandum*).   London, Methuen, 1971; modified version, omitting *The Caretaker* and including *The Go-Between*, New York, Grove Press, 1973.

Monologue (televised, 1973; produced London, 1973).   London, Covent Garden Press, 1973.

No Man's Land (produced London, 1975; New York, 1976).   London, Eyre Methuen, and New York, Grove Press, 1975.

Pinter Plays 1 (includes *The Tea Party, The Room, A Slight Ache, A Night Out*, and stories).   London, Eyre Methuen, 1975.

Screenplays: *The Servant*, 1963; *The Guest (The Caretaker)*, 1964; *The Pumpkin Eater*, 1964; *The Quiller Memorandum*, 1966; *Accident*, 1967; *The Birthday Party*, 1968; *The Go-Between*, 1971; *The Homecoming*, 1971.

Radio Plays: *A Slight Ache*, 1959; *The Dwarfs*, 1960; *A Night Out*, 1960; *Landscape*, 1968.

Television Plays: *Night School*, 1960; *The Collection*, 1963; *The Lover*, 1963; *Tea Party*, 1965; *The Basement*, 1967; *Monologue*, 1973.

Verse

Poems, edited by Alan Clodd.   London, Enitharmon Press, 1968; revised edition, 1970.

Other

Mac (on Anew McMaster).   London, Pendragon Press, 1968.

Editor, with others, *New Poems 1967: A P.E.N. Anthology.*   London, Hutchinson, 1968.

Bibliography: *Pinter, A Bibliography: His Works and Occasional Writings with a Comprehensive Checklist of Criticism and Reviews of the London Productions* by Rudiger Imhof, London, TQ Publications, 1975.

Theatrical Activities:

Director: **Plays** – *The Collection* (co-director, with Peter Hall), London, 1961; *The Lover*, London, 1963; *The Dwarfs*, London, 1963; *The Birthday Party*, London, 1964; *The Man* *in the Glass Booth* by Robert Shaw, London, 1967, New York, 1968; *Exiles* by James Joyce, London, 1970; *Butley* by Simon Gray, London, 1971; *Next of Kin* by John Hopkins, London, 1974; *Otherwise Engaged* by Simon Gray, Oxford and London, 1975; *Blithe Spirit* by Noël Coward, London, 1976.   **Film** – *Butley*, 1973.

Actor (as David Baron and Harold Pinter): **Plays** – with Anew McMaster's theatre company in Ireland, 1950–52; with Donald Wolfit's theatre company, Kings Theatre, Hammersmith, London, 1953; numerous provincial repertory companies, 1953–60; Mick in *The Caretaker*, London, 1964; Goldberg in *The Birthday Party*, Cheltenham, 1964; Lenny in *The Homecoming*, Watford, Hertfordshire, 1969. **Radio** – *Monologue*, 1975; *Rough for Radio* by Samuel Beckett, 1976. **Films** – *The Servant*, 1963; *Accident*, 1967; *The Rise and Rise of Michael Rimmer*, 1970. **Television** – *Rogue Male*, 1976.

*   *   *

Harold Pinter's early works have justifiably been referred to as "comedies of menace." In *The Room, The Birthday Party* and *The Dumb Waiter*, he invests the conventional one room setting with an almost tangible sense of threat. The security which grows out of banal routine is undermined by a disruption of the pattern; the physical and psychological protection afforded by a familiar environment is destroyed by the existence of outside forces which may intrude at any moment. Hence the play's humour, which derives in part from characters who employ linguistic registers and express social pretensions hopelessly at odds with their social class and in part from the manner in which they respond to bizarre and paradoxical events in which they find themselves involved, is constantly balanced by a fear which is barely sublimated in physical activity (Stanley whistles nervously while McCann tears paper into strips in *The Birthday Party*; the protagonists of *The Dumb Waiter* respond frantically to requests for exotic culinary dishes).

The Birthday Party, perhaps the best of these early plays, is concerned with the subjugation of Stanley Webber, a man living an apparently mundane existence in a seaside guest house. Two intruders, Goldberg and McCann, who act as agents for an unknown individual or organisation, succeed in intimidating Stanley, quickly exerting their authority over him as he had earlier over his landlady. Yet, as they effectively reduce him to an impotent silence and remove him from the house, it is apparent that they too are locked in a struggle for dominance and feel the same fear of the unknown which had gripped Stanley. This fear clearly has social and political as well as metaphysical implications. As Pinter himself has remarked, the threat implicit in the sudden arrival of two unknown men who assume an air of authority is scarcely unknown in the recent history of Europe. Nor, for that matter, one might add, are the pressures which reduce the autonomous individual to mindless subservience nor the sense of guilt which makes that individual collaborate in his own destruction. As has been pointed out before, Pinter's sensibility seems remarkably close to that of Franz Kafka.

When one character in Pinter's next play, *The Caretaker*, remarks that "I can take nothing you say at face value. Every word you speak is open to any number of interpretations," he offers a clue both to Pinter's method and to a theme which has become central to his work. The ambiguity of reality and the inadequacy of language provide the context for a play which also concerns itself with the problem of sustaining identity in a world which seems to demand conformity as the price of survival. Like Beckett, in *Waiting for Godot*, Pinter chooses as his protagonist a tramp, a man whose isolation and social insecurity are implied in his situation. Yet, despite his sense of fear and his precarious hold on experience his desire for refuge is matched by a human need to see relationships as a battle for dominance and by an unwillingness to acknowledge an identity which may define the limit of his possibility. Notwithstanding an explicitness foreign to his earlier plays, *The Caretaker* is a subtle and compelling work which advances his concern with human insecurity while probing still further his fascination with the communication of meaning on a non-verbal level.

The Homecoming is, in many senses, a transitional play and critical reaction has been sharply divided. To some it represents a considerable achievement and its somewhat arbitrary shifts of direction are seen as expressions of a subtle and complex perception of human relations; to others it is a regrettable lapse of taste in which Pinter's usual control is surrendered in the interest of easy effects and a fashionable scatology. It is transitional in that while he is no longer so concerned with exposing the fears of those who dread the disruption of private existence or who act as agents of mysterious forces, the play does not yet show evidence of that fascination with the substance of reality and the significance of memory which has become his central concern in his more recent work. *The Homecoming* is in some ways a parody of drawing room drama. It is Ibsen through a distorting mirror. As Pinter has said, it is a play about love and the lack of love, the way in which passions are bartered and relationships brutalised. His concern with the battle for dominance here gains a specifically sexual dimension which he has retained in subsequent work such as *Landscape, Silence, Night* and *Old Times*. If Pinter's suggestion that the play is "quite realistic" is manifestly absurd on one level, in that such impulses as those described in the play (a professor's wife agrees to become a prostitute at the request of her in-laws) rarely surface in language, on another level it is arguably accurate enough, for the notion of human relationships as expressions of inner violence and competing needs, conducted in terms of self-interest, is familiar enough in the modern world.

The work which Pinter has produced since *The Homecoming* has a static quality about it. His characters, for the most part, remain seated, often not recognising each other's existence. The dynamic of his work no longer relies on the physical activity of *The Room* and *The Birthday Party*, but rests on the differing perspectives of individuals who have shared experiences without sharing their perceptions of those experiences. In part this static quality derives from the fact that the world with which he has chosen to concern himself in recent years, the world of *Landscape, Silence, Night* and *Old Times,* is that created by memory. His preoccupation has been with the process whereby action is subsumed in character, refracted by individual perception and reconstructed to serve private needs. The effect is to pose questions which are in many ways antecedent to those posed in his earlier plays, questions about the nature of reailty, which do a great deal to explain the inadequacies of communication and menacing mystery of his early work. After all, if our perception of reality is faulty, if people sharing a relationship interpret it differently, if there is no agreed truth, then we are indeed adrift in a threatening world in which the desire for verification, the need for full knowledge and genuine communication, is necessarily frustrated.

The disjunction between social class and language is the source of much of the humour in Pinter's work; it is also an indication of the inadequate control which his characters maintain over the world which they inhabit. Language is presumed to be a primary instrument for social and psychological control and in the early plays reveals itself to be precisely that. In his later work, however, and more especially in *Monologue* and *No Man's Land*, its essential ambivalence is underlined. In both plays individuals fill the silence with words, constructing worlds whose meaning has nothing to do with truth and everything to do with survival, with sanity. Despite the conviction of the solitary unnamed protagonist of *Monologue* that "the ones that keep silent are the best off," it is clear that for him, as for the writer who created him and whose plight he in some degree reflects, articulateness is a necessary if dangerous strategy – dangerous because it invokes destructive as well as consoling memories, because, as in *No Man's Land*, the fictions spun out of desperation may breed their own doubts and terrors. Moreover, the stasis which they have chosen, the solipsism into which they have retreated, leaves them permanently immured in subjectivity. The imagination creates its own tomb.

In a sense all of Pinter's plays have taken place in a no man's land, a special place largely outside time, unaffected by specific and definable external realities. In his most recent work, however, that territory has been internalised, embraced until its ironies become the substance rather than the setting. When Spooner, in *No Man's Land*, says, "You are in no man's land, which never moves, which never changes, which never grows older, but which remains forever, icy and silent," and when Hirst replies, "I'll drink to that," we are closer to the mood of Beckett's work than ever we were in *The Caretaker* or *The Birthday Party*. Yet, while

Beckett sees human responses as merely ironic and the bleak landscape as a comment on human insignificance, Pinter is concerned less with mocking his characters than with dispassionately observing the impulses, fears, pleasures and psychic compulsions which determine human relationships in a world which is half refuge and half prison. Pinter's characters have devised strategies for dealing with experience, but these remain strategies. In Beckett's world communication is impossible; in Pinter's it is avoided in an attempt to escape the pain which may result from human contact.

Pinter is not primarily a social dramatist, but it is clear from *The Birthday Party, The Dumb Waiter*, and *The Caretaker* that his work has a social dimension. The struggle for supremacy is, after all, not only conducted on a personal level, nor is the threat of violence merely a detail of psychology or even an element of metaphysical unease. But obviously his central concern is with documenting the unexpressed fears and tensions which provide the axial lines for human activity. His fundamental theme is the struggle for survival, the battle to sustain oneself in the face of others similarly committed to protecting themselves or sustaining the integrity of memory.

—C.W.E. Bigsby

PLATER, Alan (Frederick).   British.   Born in Jarrow on Tyne, County Durham, 15 April 1935. Educated at Pickering Road Junior and Infant School, Hull, 1940–46; Kingston High School, Hull, 1946–53; King's College, Newcastle upon Tyne (University of Durham), 1953–57; qualified as an architect, 1961. Married Shirley Johnson in 1958; has three children. Worked in an architect's office, Hull, 1957–60. Free-lance Writer since 1961. Regular Contributor to *Architects' Journal*, London, and *Yorkshire Post*, Leeds, 1959–63. Associated with the BBC programme *Northern Drift*; co-founder of Humberside Theatre (formerly Hull Arts Centre), 1970. Agent: Margaret Ramsay Ltd., 14a Goodwin's Court, London WC2N 4LL. Address: 5 Hull Road, Cottingham, Yorkshire HU16 4PA, England.

PUBLICATIONS

Plays

    The Referees (televised, 1961; produced Stoke on Trent, 1963).
    The Mating Season (broadcast, 1962; produced Stoke on Trent, 1963).   Published in
        Worth a Hearing: A Collection of Radio Plays, edited by Alfred Bradley, London,
        Blackie, 1967.
    A Smashing Day (televised, 1962; revised version, music by Ben Kingsley and Robert
        Powell, produced Stoke on Trent, 1965; London, 1966).
    The Rainbow Machine (broadcast, 1962; produced Stoke on Trent, 1963).
    Ted's Cathedral (produced Stoke on Trent and London, 1963).
    A Quiet Night (televised, 1963).   Published in *Z Cars: Four Scripts from the Television
        Series*, edited by Michael Marland, London, Longman, 1968.
    See the Pretty Lights (televised, 1963; produced London, 1970).   Published in *Theatre
        Choice: A Collection of Modern Short Plays*, edited by Michael Marland, London,
        Blackie, 1972.
    The Nutter (televised, 1965; revised version, as *Charlie Came to Our Town*, music by
        Alex Glasgow, produced Harrogate, Yorkshire, 1966).

Excursion (broadcast, 1966).   Included in *You and Me*, 1973.

The What on the Landing? (broadcast, 1967; produced Coventry, 1968; London, 1971).

On Christmas Day in the Morning (*Softly, Softly* series; televised, 1968).   Included in *You and Me*, 1973.

Hop Step and Jump (produced Scarborough, Yorkshire, 1968).

Close the Coalhouse Door, music by Alex Glasgow, adaptation of stories by Sid Chaplin (produced Newcastle upon Tyne and London, 1968).   London, Methuen, 1968.

Don't Build a Bridge, Drain the River!, music by Michael Chapman and Mike Waterson (produced Hull, 1970).

Simon Says!, music by Alex Glasgow (produced Leeds, 1970).

And a Little Love Besides (produced Hull, 1970).   Included in *You and Me*, 1973.

King Billy Vaudeville Show, with others (produced Hull, 1971).

Seventeen Per Cent Said Push Off (televised, 1972).   Included in *You and Me*, 1973.

The Tigers Are Coming − O.K.? (produced Hull, 1972).

You and Me: Four Plays, edited by Alfred Bradley (includes *Excursions, On Christmas Day in the Morning, And a Little Love Besides, Seventeen Per Cent Said Push Off*). London, Blackie, 1973.

Swallows on the Water (produced Hull, 1973).

When the Reds Go Marching In (produced Liverpool, 1973).

Tales of Humberside, music by Jim Bywater (produced Hull, 1975).

Trinity Tales, music by Alex Glasgow (televised, 1975; produced Birmingham, 1975).

Our Albert (produced Hull, 1976).

Screenplays: *The Virgin and the Gypsy*, 1970; *Juggernaut* (additional dialogue), 1975; *All Things Bright and Beautiful*, 1976; *It Shouldn't Happen to a Vet*, 1976.

Radio Plays: *The Smokeless Zone*, 1961; *Counting the Legs*, 1961; *The Mating Season*, 1962; *The Rainbow Machine*, 1962; *The Seventh Day of Arthur*, 1963; *Excursions*, 1966; *The What on the Landing?*, 1967; *Fred*, 1970; *The Slow Stain*, 1973; *5 Days in '55 (The Gilberdyke Diaries)*, 1976.

Television Plays: *The Referees*, 1961; *A Smashing Day*, 1962; *So Long Charlie*, 1963; *See the Pretty Lights*, 1963; *Z Cars* series (18 episodes), 1963–65; *Ted's Cathedral*, 1964; *Fred*, 1964; *The Incident*, 1965; *The Nutter*, 1965; *Softly, Softly* series (30 episodes), 1966–76; *To See How Far It Is* (trilogy), 1968; *The First Lady* series (4 episodes), 1968–69; *Rest in Peace, Uncle Fred*, 1970; *Seventeen Per Cent Said Push Off*, 1972; *The Reluctant Juggler* (*The Edwardians* series), 1972; *Tonight We Meet Arthur Pendlebury*, 1972; *The Land of Green Ginger*, 1973; *It Must Be Something in the Water* (documentary), 1973; *Brotherly Love*, 1973; *The Needle Match*, 1974; *Goldilocks and the Three Bears*, 1974; *Wish You Were Here* (documentary), 1974; *Annie Kenney* (*Shoulder to Shoulder* series), 1974; *The Loner* series, 1975; *The Stars Look Down*, from the novel by A.J. Cronin, 1975; *Trinity Tales* series, 1975; *Willow Cabins*, 1975; *Practical Experience*, 1976; *Three-Fifths of the World Loves a Lover*, 1976; *Oh No − It's Selwyn Froggit* series, 1976; *A Tyneside Entertainment* (documentary), 1976; *Seven Days That Shook Young Jim* (*Goimg to Work* series), 1976.

Other

The Trouble with Abracadabra (juvenile).   London, Macmillan, 1975.

Critical Studies: introduction by the author to *Close the Coalhouse Door*, 1968; "What's Going On Behind the Coalhouse Door" by the author in *Sunday Times* (London), 9 February 1969, "The London Show" by Yorick Blumenfeld, in *Atlantic* (Boston), August 1969; *The*

Second Wave by John Russell Taylor, London, Methuen, 1971; "The Playwright and His People" by the author, in *Theatre Quarterly 2* (London), April–June 1971; "One Step Forward, Two Steps Back" by the author, in *New Statesman* (London), 3 November 1972; "Views" by the author, in *Listener* (London), 29 November 1973; "Trinity Collage" by Peter Fiddick, in *The Guardian* (London), 12 December 1975.

Alan Plater comments:

(1973) Authors introducing their work fill me with gloom, like people explaining jokes: if I didn't laugh or cry before the explanation, nothing is likely to change afterwards. Therefore all I can do is look down the laundry list of my work to date and try to work out why I bothered, apart from what Mr. Perelman calls "the lash of economic necessity."

The clue lies in the place of birth and the present address: I was born and have always lived in industrial communities. I live in a place that works for a living. I never ran barefoot other than from choice. I have always eaten well and have never been deprived of anything that mattered; but I have always been close enough to the inequalities and grotesque injustices of our society to get angry about them.

(1977) Essentially I am writing a segment of the history of a society that was forged by the Industrial Revolution. This is less earnest and painful than it sounds; if an idea is important enough it is worth laughing at and one professional associate defined my method as taking fundamentally serious concepts like Politics and Religion and Life and Death and kicking the Hell out of them with old jokes. At any rate, the evidence of the more-or-less knockabout shows we've done around the regions is that people laugh the louder if the fun is spiced with a couple of centuries of inherited prejudice.

The other thought prompted by the laundry list is that not many writers have tangled with as rich and diverse a company of people and subjects: D. H. Lawrence, Mrs. Pankhurst, Sandy Powell and Les Dawson would look good on any music-hall poster, though there might be some dispute over billing. At any rate, it underlines my feeling that it is the job of the writer at all times to head for the nearest tightrope and, in the words of Max Miller, Archie Rice or both: "You've got to admit, lady, I do have a go."

*   *   *

Alan Plater is one of several dramatists whose work has done much to further the cause of British regional theatre. Although two of his plays have transferred to London and he has written widely for national television and the cinema, Plater still lives where he was brought up, in Hull, Yorkshire: and his energies are largely directed towards ensuring the success of the ambitious Hull Arts Centre, a small 150-seat theatre. His physical home is also apparently his spiritual one: for his plays are set in the North-East of England and are largely concerned with the particular problems and history of the area. "Central to the greater part of my writing," he once stated, "is man's relationship to his work": and work in this context means particularly coal-mining and deep-sea fishing, two regional industries. Plater admires the "genuine solidarity and craft-consciousness" of those whose jobs involve "hideous physical working conditions": and he has captured the sheer pride in overcoming fear and danger, which distinguishes the miners in his highly successful musical documentary, *Close the Coalhouse Door.* Nor is this admiration a skin-deep enthusiasm, for Plater identifies wholeheartedly with the community he describes: he shares the passion for football, and once, when he was asked about his literary influences, he replied by mentioning the popular music-hall names of his youth – Norman Evans, Mooney and King. He also expresses with great fire many of the social and political attitudes (some might call them prejudices) which characterize the region: a hatred of the bosses, who are usually portrayed as effete Southerners, a respect for Trade Union tradition, a somewhat over-generalized call for revolution which is coupled with a suspicion of change, a brashly extrovert dismissal of all forms of theatre which lack working-class appeal and a socialism which refuses to accept that

Labour politicians are better than stooges for capitalistic con-men.

His work falls into two main categories. Plater has written several carefully-observed naturalistic plays: such as *See the Pretty Lights* and *A Smashing Day*, which were both rewritten for the stage from television scripts. In 1966, Plater met the composer and song-writer, Alex Glasgow, and together they have collaborated on several musical documentaries, among them *Charlie Came to Our Town*, and *Close the Coalhouse Door*. The documentaries, unlike the naturalistic plays, combine many styles of writing – cross-talk sketches, songs, impassioned oratory, summaries of historical incidents and much satire – which are all loosely brought together by a general theme, the history of Hull or the struggle of miners to gain decent living standards.

These two styles reveal different qualities. *See the Pretty Lights* is a gentle, warm and moving account of a meeting between a middle-aged man and a teenage girl at the end of a pier. Both lead dull lives: and the bright lights of the seaside and their momentary friendship helps to relieve – but also to underline – their social frustrations. The hero of *A Smashing Day* is a young man, Lennie, who suffers from bored aimlessness: he meekly accepts his job, the odd nights at the palais with his mates who never become friends, and the routine drink. But he senses that a more exciting life awaits him somewhere if only he could find out where. He goes steady with a girl, Anne, and drifts towards marriage, which he doesn't want: and the social pressures are such that he persists in marrying her even after meeting Liz, an independent and sensitive girl with whom he falls in love. Many critics felt that the increased length of the stage play failed to achieve the concentrated power of the television script: and *A Smashing Day* was not successful in London. But it did provide an excellent part for the then unknown actor, Hywel Bennett, and revealed Plater's ability to describe an apparently uninteresting person in some depth. Lennie is never allowed to be either a pathetic person or an angry young man: and despite his shy insecurity which leaves an impression of spinelessness, his situation is both moving, credible and strong enough to hold the play together.

If the naturalistic plays are distinguished by restraint and accuracy, the documentaries have entirely the opposite qualities: panache, a cheerful display of class bias and a loose, anything-goes technique. The best known is *Close the Coalhouse Door*, which was remarkably successful in Newcastle but received only a limited run in London: a fact which could be interpreted several ways. The episodes of mining history are told within the context of a golden "wedding" reception in the Milburn family, who step out of a photograph to tell stories of strikes and hardships. Some scenes were particularly powerful: the death of a miner, the rivalry between families and men, the bitterness against the blackleg miners who went back to work too soon after the General Strike. Plater stressed the complicated mixture of affection and fear for the pits: together with a scorn of modernization programmes whose effect was to send miners back on the dole. The songs by Alex Glasgow caught the friendly liveliness of music halls and pubs: and in Newcastle, the whole show became a cult. "Workers turned up in their thousands once the word got round," recalled Plater: the large Playhouse Theatre was filled to capacity night after night – the audiences would sit in the aisles, even on the steps to the stage.

Why did the show receive such a tepid reception in London? The answer is a complex one, revealing much about Plater's work. Plater has offered two reasons – that London audiences are prejudiced against working-class plays and that in any case they could not be expected to share the associations of the North. Both may be true: but isn't it the job of a dramatist to convey the importance of his theme to those who do not belong to the background? London critics generally commented on the superficial characterization of the play, on the rather simplistic dialogue and form and on the one-sided interpretations of history. These objections to Plater's documentaries were confirmed by two subsequent shows which didn't come to London: *Simon Says!*, a wholesale attack on the British ruling classes represented by Lord Thing, the Chairman of the MCC (the governing board of English cricket), and *And a Little Love Besides*, a scathing account of the uncharitable Church. The critical charge against both these plays was that the satire was too sweeping and naive to hit any real targets. Plater's documentaries are seen at their best perhaps either when the subject contains real and deeply felt observations or when the general sense of fun takes over. *Charlie Came to Our Town*, Plater's first documentary with Alex Glasgow, is a delightfully light-hearted musical about an eccentric anarchist.

Plater's two styles complement each other: and it is sad perhaps that they haven't been combined in one play. The naturalistic plays are small-scale and lack the passionate energy of the documentaries: the documentaries are too vaguely polemical and lack the construction of the naturalistic plays. Plater is a prolific writer, whose talents seem hard to control. But his adaptability is shown by the skill with which he has adjusted to the various media: his contributions to the *Z Cars* detective series on television and his screenplay for D. H. Lawrence's *The Virgin and the Gypsy* have been rightly praised. This energetic eagerness to tackle any task which interests him has already re-vitalized the theatre in the North-East and suggests that in future his many abilities may be contained within undeniably good plays.

—John Elsom

POLIAKOFF, Stephen.   British.   Born in 1953. Recipient: *Evening Standard* award, 1976. Agent: Margaret Ramsay Ltd., 14a Goodwin's Court, London WC2N 4LL, England.

PUBLICATIONS

Plays

    Granny (produced London, 1969).
    Bambi Ramm (produced London, 1970).
    A Day with My Sister (produced Edinburgh, 1971).
    Pretty Boy (produced London, 1972).
    Theatre Outside (produced London, 1973).
    Berlin Days (produced London, 1973).
    The Carnation Gang (produced London, 1973).
    Clever Soldiers (produced London, 1974).
    Heroes (produced London, 1975).
    Hitting Town (produced London, 1975).   Included in *City Sugar, and Hitting Town*, 1976.
    City Sugar (produced London, 1975).   Included in *City Sugar, and Hitting Town*, 1976.
    Join the Dance (produced New York, 1975).
    City Sugar, and Hitting Town.   London, Eyre Methuen, 1976.

*   *   *

The ingredients of Stephen Poliakoff's plays are class, violence, sex, and the breakdown of society. If that sounds over-colourful, it does not give an altogether false impression. Although he writes straightforward, contemporary stories whose setting, characterization and dialogue are more or less naturalistic and which are told chronologically – without flashbacks, dream sequences, narration or other distorting devices – Poliakoff's characteristic effect is nightmarish. One seems to be looking at nothing more than an ordinary slice of life, but as it were in a lurid light; it is like seeing familiar faces and buildings turned slightly ghastly by neon.

The ingredients I have listed are most clearly — also perhaps most crudely — discernible in *Clever Soldiers*. Set in 1914 (without any attempt at period), the first scene is a brief vignette of a public-school changing-room and creates a strong opening atmosphere of class complacency, hierarchy, barbarism, and homosexuality. Nothing much happens and both main characters are in their various ways fighting the atmosphere. Yet it persists; they secrete it and diffuse it in spite of themselves. This is typical of all Poliakoff's central characters — they are Dostoyevskian figures, irresistibly attracted to what they fear and despise, passive by nature, yet active by desire, hopelessly contaminated by their circumstances, yet curiously confident of their own individuality.

The rest of the first act of *Clever Soldiers* takes place at Oxford and adds little to the opening scene, broadening but at the same time weakening the atmosphere created there. Violence comes closer, in the shape of a mob of college "bloods," but the emphasis is on shifting relationships rather than on action. The second act is set in the Flanders trenches, an ideal locale for the full display of Poliakoff's ingredients, but for all that not quite his scene.

The reason is that he is more at home with the threat and suggestion of social and individual catastrophe than with its actuality. In *Heroes* there is a political upheaval going on off-stage, but just as the city is unnamed, so it is only the psychological effects of the upheaval on the characters and its fringe consequences — a deserted cafe, shortage of food, etc. — that we witness. In *The Carnation Gang*, an extended confrontation between upper-class twins who peddle dope and working-class teenagers who want to consume it for nothing, power ebbs and flows between the two groups without any clear issue. Violence is done to a room, but not significantly to any of the characters. Superior intelligence and education are used as weapons by one side, the threat of knives and physical strength by the other, sex by both.

Just as Poliakoff's characters are perpetually balancing their sadistic tendencies with their masochistic ones, so his plays are balanced on the struggle between the two classes, on their mutual attraction and antagonism. Nevertheless it is the upper-class characters who make the running and who chiefly occupy the foreground. They are immensely talkative, but they prefer dialogue to monologue. Hence, except in *Heroes*, where the working-class character is the upper-class character's intellectual confidant, they tend to go in pairs, working themselves up to do things, putting forward bright ideas, testing one another's reactions in a perpetual flow of enthusiastic articulacy.

In spite of their lively disgust at the conditions round them — whether of urban squalor as in *Hitting Town* or *The Carnation Gang* or the bourgeois complacency of a rich enclave as in *Pretty Boy* — their tone is persistently optimistic. The hero of *Pretty Boy* is irritated by his rich neighbours to the point of hiring a young hooligan to damage their property; he is callous towards an elderly relative and behaves like a classic male chauvinist to his long-suffering girl-friend. But he is buoyed up by his vague and baseless plans for revolution and his optimism is oddly infectious, as if his unpleasant treatment of other people were merely a temporary oversight. He is like a small child, tiresome and barbaric at one moment, prattling and charming the next. The hero of *Hitting Town* not only sleeps with his sister but insists on telling the whole of Leicester about it through a radio phone-in programme. His purpose is only partly to *épater les bourgeois*, it is also to express himself more satisfyingly in words and in public than merely in action in private.

Poliakoff's ingredients, then, are more verbal than actual. He studies feelings about class, violence, sex, and the breakdown of society rather than the things themselves. His character-range is limited and he shows little interest in the design of his plays. Everything is done through talk, for which he has a remarkable, apparently overflowing gift. Much of it would seem superfluous — it only rises occasionally and almost by accident to full intensity and it is not specially witty or memorable in detail — but it is never dull and transmits a sense of energy which is peculiar to Poliakoff among contemporary dramatists.

—John Spurling

PORTER, Hal. Australian. Born in Albert Park, Melbourne, Victoria, 16 February 1911. Educated at Kensington State School, 1917; Bairnsdale State School, Victoria, 1918–21; Bairnsdale High School, 1922–26. Married Olivia Parnham in 1939 (divorced, 1943). Cadet Reporter, *Bairnsdale Advertiser*, 1927. Schoolmaster, Victorian Education Department, 1927–37, 1940; Queen's College, Adelaide, 1941–42; Prince Alfred College, Kent Town, South Australia, 1943–46; Hutchins School, Hobart, Tasmania, 1946–47; Knox Grammar School, Sydney, 1947; Ballarat College, Victoria, 1948–49; Nijimura School, Kure, Japan (Australian Army Education), 1949–50. Director, National Theatre, Hobart, 1951–53. Chief Librarian of Bairnsdale and Shepparton, 1953–61. Full-time Writer since 1961. Australian Writers Representative, Edinburgh Festival, 1962. Lecturer for the Australian Department of External Affairs, in Japan, 1967. Recipient: Sydney Sesquicentenary Prize, 1938; Commonwealth Literary Fund Fellowship, 1956, 1960, 1964, 1968, 1972, and Subsidy, 1957, 1962, 1967; *Sydney Morning Herald* Prize, 1958; Sydney Journalists' Club Prize, for fiction, 1959, for drama, 1961; *Adelaide Advertiser* Prize, for fiction, 1964, 1970, for non-fiction, 1968; *Encyclopedia Britannica* Award, 1967; Captain Cook Bi-Centenary Prize, 1970. Address: Glen Avon, Garvoc, Victoria 3275, Australia.

PUBLICATIONS

Plays

The Tower (produced London, 1964). Melbourne, Penguin, 1963.
The Professor (as *Toda-San*, produced Adelaide, 1965; as *The Professor*, produced London, 1965). London, Faber, 1966.
Eden . House (produced Melbourne, 1969; as *Home on a Pig's Back*, produced Richmond, Surrey, 1972). Sydney, Angus and Robertson, 1969.
Parker (produced Ballarat, Victoria, 1972).

Novels

A Handful of Pennies. Sydney, Angus and Robertson, 1958; London, Angus and Robertson, 1959.
The Tilted Cross. London, Faber, 1961.
The Right Thing. Adelaide, Rigby, and London, Hale, 1971.

Short Stories

Short Stories. Adelaide, Advertiser Press, 1942.
A Bachelor's Children. Sydney and London, Angus and Robertson, 1962.
The Cats of Venice. Sydney, Angus and Robertson, 1965.
Mr. Butterfry and Other Tales of New Japan. Sydney, Angus and Robertson, 1970.
Selected Stories, edited by Leonie Kramer. Sydney and London, Angus and Robertson, 1971.
Fredo Fuss Love Life. Sydney, Angus and Robertson, 1974.

Verse

The Hexagon. Sydney, Angus and Robertson, 1956.
Elijah's Ravens. Sydney, Angus and Robertson, 1968.
In an Australian Country Graveyard and Other Poems. Sydney, Angus and Robertson, 1973.

Other

The Watcher on the Cast-Iron Balcony (autobiography).   London, Faber, 1963.
Australian Stars of Stage and Screen.   Adelaide, Rigby, 1965.
The Paper Chase (autobiography).   Sydney, Angus and Robertson, 1966.
The Actors: An Image of the New Japan.   Sydney, Angus and Robertson, 1968.
Criss-Cross (autobiography).   Sydney, Angus and Robertson, 1973.
The Extra (autobiography).   Melbourne, Nelson, 1976.

Editor, *Australian Poetry 1957.*   Sydney, Angus and Robertson, 1957.
Editor, *Coast to Coast 1961–1962.*   Sydney, Angus and Robertson, 1963.
Editor, *It Could Be You.*   Adelaide, Rigby, 1972; London, Hale, 1973.

Bibliography: *A Bibliography of Hal Porter* by Janette Finch, Adelaide, Libraries Board of South Australia, 1966.

Manuscript Collection: Mitchell Library, Sydney.

*   *   *

It is a matter of regret that, having transcended with apparent ease the provincial primitivism of most Australian drama before 1950 or thereabouts, Hal Porter should write highly polished but totally inconsequential plays: they are entertaining, stylish, and superficial, mere showcases for Porter's wit and for actors' flamboyance. Porter probably reserves his more acute perceptions and more profound conclusions for the prose fictions and autobiographies which have established his eminence in Australian letters: it is difficult to believe that the technical expertise his plays exhibit could not become the servant of his more urgent and serious creative impulses if he chose. Yet he writes drawing-room drama in which stereotyped characters, intelligent, selfish, self-deluding, vengeful, and generally unlikable, work through plots packed with incident, but in which the essential conflict is merely a battle of sharp tongues. Ultimately, it does not seem to matter much who wins and there is no real victor in a Porter play.

Between the rise of the first curtain and the drop of the final one, the audience will have been treated to brilliant repartee, startling revelations, displays of bitchiness, shocks and surprises, comedy, pathos, and melodrama in more or less equal proportions. If the plays lack substance it is because the characters displayed are, at best, two-dimensional, too obviously Porter's puppets. They come on the stage fully developed; they never grow or change. At best they drop by degrees their civilized veneers each to reveal the untamed beast within. On the surface Porter's characters are, usually, urbane, conventional middle-class and intelligent. During the course of any of his plays each is stripped of layers of pretence, and by the end, has generally been reduced to a lump of naked malice and primitive passion. However satisfying this may be to the voyeuristic impulse in the audience, it fails to impress as satire because the characters are bloodless, theatrical types, recognizable, predictable, and except for their acid tongues, boring. They belong in the land of theatrical make-believe and their connection with the real world is minimal.

Nevertheless, it is doubtful whether any Australian playwright has shown quite the same practical knowledge of stagecraft or quite the same mastery of dramatic conventions as has Porter. His published plays show a degree of control, not to say condescension, towards drama as a literary mode. They are meant to be acted rather than read, are distinguished by parts to be relished by the mannered actor, by incisive dialogue, explosive situations, and provocative curtain-lines. They have all been professionally performed in Australia and abroad, enjoy continuing success in the repertoire of amateur groups, and have, with the exception of *The Professor*, been successfully adapted for television.

This is not an accidental exception. *The Professor* is Porter's only serious attempt at theatrical experiment. It is a tragedy of manners which deals with the unbridgeable cultural gulf between east and west, specifically, Japanese and Australian. The chasm separating two civilizations is visibly demonstrated in a Noh play-within-the-play, where contrasting dramatic styles and theatrical conventions mirror societies basically irreconcilable. Their attitudes and traditions have roots in a forgotten past, are now as instinctual as breathing, and as inexplicable to the outsider as they are essential to the national identity. This exploration of the nature of theatrical experience and the way the art of the theatre reflects national cultures cannot be successfully translated into another medium without serious loss. As it is, it makes heavy demands on an audience accustomed only to traditional western theatre, and is Porter's least commercially-successful play. It is, even so, his most impressive one and may well prove to be the most enduring. It has been much underrated because its attack on modern Australians and modern Australian theatre is subtle, from within, ostentatiously non-trendy. In *The Professor* Porter's characters have unusual depth and subtlety. They are capable of passion and compassion, of joy and suffering, of vice and virtue. At the core of the play Porter is exploring the shades of menace which separate the degrees of feeling in the range between pure love and pure lust. It is often satiric in its mood, and is inescapably melodramatic in its plot, but it is much more forthright in its attack on hypocrisy and egocentricity, in its defence of honesty and selflessness than is usual in Porter's plays.

Porter's polished elegance of the dialogue and the firm control of dramatic structure were exhibited in his first play, *The Tower*, a fairly straightforward melodrama, set in colonial Hobart Town. This play mounts a stringent attack on the ruthless struggle for power and social position which engaged the energies of early administrators in Australia. More limited in theme and less complex in form than *The Professor*, *The Tower* reveals a considerable and assured talent. *The Professor* shows this talent extended to invent a dramatic structure which will underpin and demonstrate an unpalatable view of contemporary Australians.

From this point Porter seems to have abandoned drama as a challenge to his creative energies and to have concentrated on prose fiction. His later plays are the work of an accomplished craftsman with nothing much to say about characters he does not particularly care for: they are clever theatrical diversions but not the high drama to which, at moments, they seem to aspire. They have a curiously dated quality — one expects a young man in flannels to appear at French windows and say "Anyone for tennis?" at any moment. Of course Porter is much more astute than this, yet his characters show such a capacity for the riposte and the epigram, such extravagant emotional responses to trivial incidents, such flair and flamboyance in a social situation, that one is nostalgically reminded of popular stage successes of the British and American pre-war theatre: enjoyable, yes; memorable, no.

Porter customarily denigrates his plays and claims that he writes them either to fulfil promises to friends, or, more frequently, as a way of working up to, or unwinding from, a more serious literary task. This is confirmed by the plays themselves, which suggest a sophisticated, but frivolous writer. Only *The Professor* approaches the emotional power and intellectual depth of Porter's prose writing; his other plays to date reveal an impressive, professional competence in old-fashioned plays about inconsequential matters.

—Mary Lord

POTTER, Dennis (Christopher George).   British.   Born in Joyford Hill, Coleford, Gloucestershire, 17 May 1935. Educated at Christchurch Village School; Bell's Grammar School, Coleford; St. Clement Danes Grammar School, London; New College, Oxford (Editor, *Isis*, 1958), B.A. (honours) in philosophy, politics and economics 1959. Married Margaret Morgan in 1959; has three children. Member of the Current Affairs Staff, BBC

Television, 1959–61; Feature Writer, then Television Critic, *Daily Herald*, London, 1961–64; Leader Writer, *The Sun*, London, 1964; Television Critic, *New Statesman*, London, 1967, 1972, 1974–75; Book Reviewer, *The Times*, London, 1967–73. Since 1973, Book Reviewer, *The Guardian*, London. Labour Candidate for Parliament, East Hertfordshire, 1964. Recipient: Writers Guild of Great Britain award, 1965, 1969; Society of Film and Television Arts award, 1966. Agent: Clive Goodwin, 79 Cromwell Road, London S.W.7. Address: Morecambe Lodge, Duxmere, Ross-on-Wye, Herefordshire, England.

PUBLICATIONS

Plays

> *Vote Vote Vote for Nigel Barton* (televised, 1965; revised version, produced Bristol, 1968). Included in *The Nigel Barton Plays*, 1967.
> *Stand Up, Nigel Barton* (televised, 1965). Included in *The Nigel Barton Plays*, 1967.
> *The Nigel Barton Plays: Stand Up, Nigel Barton, Vote Vote Vote for Nigel Barton: Two Television Plays*. London, Penguin, 1967.
> *Son of Man* (televised, 1969; produced Leicester and London, 1969). London, Deutsch, 1970.
> *Follow the Yellow Brick Road* (televised, 1972). Published in *The Television Dramatist*, edited by Robert Muller, London, Elek, 1973.
> *Only Make Believe* (televised, 1973; produced Harlow, Essex, 1974).
> *Joe's Ark* (televised, 1974). Published in *The Television Play*, edited by Robin Wade, London, BBC, 1976.

> Television Plays: *Vote Vote Vote for Nigel Barton*, 1965; *The Confidence Course*, 1965; *Alice*, 1965; *Stand Up, Nigel Barton*, 1965; *Where the Buffalo Roam*, 1966; *Emergency Ward 9*, 1966; *Message for Posterity*, 1967; *A Beast with Two Backs*, 1968; *The Bonegrinder*, 1968; *Shaggy Dog*, 1968; *Son of Man*, 1969; *Moonlight on the Highway*, 1969; *Lay Down Your Arms*, 1970; *Angels Are So Few*, 1970; *Paper Roses*, 1971; *Traitor*, 1971; *Casanova* (series of six plays), 1971; *Follow the Yellow Brick Road*, 1972; *Only Make Believe*, 1973; *A Tragedy of Two Ambitions*, from story by Thomas Hardy, 1973; *Joe's Ark*, 1974; *Schmoedipus*, 1974; *Late Call* (serialization), from the novel by Angus Wilson, 1975; *Double Dare*, 1976; *Where Adam Stood*, from the book *Father and Son* by Edmund Gosse, 1976.

Novel

> *Hide and Seek*. London, Deutsch, 1973.

Other

> *The Glittering Coffin*. London, Gollancz, 1960.
> *The Changing Forest: Life in the Forest of Dean Today*. London, Secker and Warburg, 1962.

Critical Study: by John Ashton, S.J., in *The Month* (London), March 1970.

*   *   *

Few of the playwrights who make a considerable contribution to television drama can deny themselves the excitement of an assault on the theatre. It is difficult to adapt what they write effectively for the stage, but success in the smaller medium seems often to be only an indirect road to the greater prestige and potentially greater rewards available to the successful writer in Shaftesbury Avenue or its environs.

Vote Vote Vote for Nigel Barton, Dennis Potter's first television play, led its author to television criticism, book reviewing and the opportunity to write of social and political questions in terms other than dramatic. He had moved on to other television plays before the Bristol Old Vic, in 1968, turned his first television work into a stage play. He had gone on, in *Stand Up, Nigel Barton*, to clarify the position and attitude of a hero who was, apparently, created to reflect and clarify aspects of his author's own experience. Nigel Barton, a miner's son who began his education at an elementary school, eventually made his way through scholarships to Oxford, stood for election as a Labour candidate in a general election and failed to win the seat. By that time he had lost his faith in his party, discovered that principle is inevitably sacrificed in the pursuit of power, and gone out into an oblivion from which Potter has found it unnecessary to retrieve him. The story seems, to a considerable extent, to be Potter's own.

Its backbone is a bitter resentment of the class system as the nucleus of what is politically and socially wrong with Britain. Nigel Barton does not belong in the bourgeois world of Oxford, to the smart world in which clever young men struggle for political power; but his rise to Oxford and Parliamentary candidacy made it impossible for him to return to the class and the home in which he was born. From this springs a remarkable complex of ill effects – his own failure as a small boy to share the life of his schoolfellows (because his intelligence makes his teachers exploit him), his father's silicosis, his inability whole-heartedly to belong even to the party he hopes to serve.

Vote Vote Vote for Nigel Barton, though it can hardly be called genial, finds a good deal to laugh at in the machinery of an election and in its hero's situation as a young man trying earnestly to be simultaneously a good, responsible intellectual socialist and a faithful proletarian determined never to betray his heritage. *Stand Up, Nigel Barton*, which deals principally with the hero's background and education, is a very sour work; if the audience had not been convinced of its honesty, its almost misanthropic tone would probably have driven its viewers away, for even Nigel Barton himself begins to appear as a young man whose inadequacy in the eyes of schoolfellows and fellow students sends him off in pursuit of political eminence.

If Potter's interests had not been considerably wider than the topics which seemed at first to occupy his mind, there would have been no reason for him to write another play. *Where the Buffalo Roam* and *Beast with Two Backs*, his next pieces for television, were more sourly misanthropic than his semi-autobiographical plays. *Where the Buffalo Roam* is not concerned with a large view of society; it is the tragedy of a credible adolescent, credibly sub-normal, who lives vicariously through western films and comics, bored by everything else, unemployed and unhappy at home. His pathetically ugly revenge on his home, and his death in consequence, are written with a cold sense of disengaged pity, as though open grief would be out of place. For the first time, it seemed that Potter was thinking about actors and their contribution to his work, offering a play for their interpretation rather than a blueprint for acting. Society at its most detestable is the subject of the oddly named *Beast with Two Backs*, which manages to have nothing to do with *Othello*. Based on the story of a murder committed in Potter's native Forest of Dean in the 1890's, it is a work of unrelieved blackness. A girl is murdered by her married seducer, whom she has pursued and tormented; the village has its necessary simpleton, and everybody torments him; a wandering Italian with a performing bear excites suspicion because he is foreign, and the children torment the bear. As the climax of the play, the villagers stone the completely innocent animal to death, blaming it for the murder, and slink away in shame at what they have done. Ugly and unforgiving as the play is, it was another step forward in Potter's development; for the first time he began to be concerned about richness and expressiveness of speech.

Son of Man, which came next, is a work of remarkable audacity. To reinterpret the life of

Christ in terms of drama is to invite controversy on every front, and *Son of Man* sets the years of Christ's mission against a background of Hebrew sedition and oppressive Roman brutality. Potter sees Christ returning from his temptation in the wilderness believing that he is the Messiah but still tormented by self-doubt; his belief in himself may, he feels, be wrong, and even if it is right it can lead nowhere but to an agonising, disgusting death. Viewers and critics who expected a dramatic Christ to be a perfectly ordinary man were bothered by the idea of an unkempt fanatic whose fanaticism at times broke open into simple self-distrust. What is left of the New Testament account of Christ's teaching is as much as Potter wishes to take – egalitarian, revolutionary and pacifist; Potter's sources are Matthew and Mark, not Luke and John, and the play's religion is an attitude to man and life rather than a mystical awareness of Power beyond them; the final words of Potter's Christ are the cry of despair from the cross, "My God, why hast Thou forsaken me?" The paraphrases of passages like the Beatitudes into everyday, racily colloquial modern English reject eloquence and suggest that Christ spoke to small groups rather than to multitudes; but the play is written with great energy and conviction.

The career of Casanova naturally proved anticlimatic after this, though the six-part television series was set in an 18th century morally as squalid as Potter has shown the 20th to be. Its successors, *Follow the Yellow Brick Road* and *Only Make Believe*, though less ambitious in theme than *Son of Man*, are integral parts of Potter's irredeemable world which, visited by crazy innocence (in *Angels Are So Few*) can only deprave it. *Schmoedipus* (the title refers to the Jewish joke, "Oedipus, Schmoedipus, what does it matter so long as he's a good boy and loves his mother?") disquietingly examines the theme of personal fantasies born out of loss and insufficiently allowed to invade the actualities of life.

Potter's range of ideas has extended over a considerable area since the first appearance of Nigel Barton, but a basic misanthropy reduces his characters into mere vehicles for ideas, so that his fanatical Christ unsure of his authority is probably the most memorable personality he has created. Potter's refusal – it is probably this rather than a failure – to advance into the theatre is, perhaps, natural to a writer who has developed so total a command of the medium as a vehicle for beliefs and ideas.

—Henry Raynor

PRIESTLEY, J(ohn) B(oynton).   British.   Born in Bradford, Yorkshire, 13 September 1894. Educated at Trinity Hall, Cambridge, M.A. Served with the Duke of Wellington's and the Devon Regiments, 1914–19. Married Patricia Tempest (died, 1925); Mary Wyndham Lewis; the writer Jacquetta Hawkes in 1953. Theatrical Manager; Director of the Mask Theatre, London, 1938–39. Radio Lecturer on the BBC programme *Postscripts*, during World War II. Regular Contributor, *New Statesman*, London. President, P.E.N., London, 1936–37; United Kingdom Delegate, and Chairman, UNESCO International Theatre Conference, Paris, 1947, and Prague, 1948; Chairman, British Theatre Conference, 1948; President, International Theatre Institute, 1949; Member, National Theatre Board, London, 1966–67. Recipient: Black Memorial Prize, for fiction, 1930; Ellen Terry Award, 1948. LL.D.: St. Andrews University; D.Litt.: Birmingham and Bradford universities. Has refused three high official honours. Address: Kissing Tree House, Alveston, Stratford upon Avon, Warwickshire, England.

PUBLICATIONS

Plays

The Good Companions, with Edward Knoblock, adaptation of the novel by J.B. Priestley
    (produced London and New York, 1931).   London and New York, French, 1935.
Dangerous Corner (produced London and New York, 1932).   London, Heinemann,
    and New York, French, 1932.
The Roundabout (produced Liverpool, London, and New York, 1932).   London,
    Heinemann, and New York, French, 1933.
Laburnum Grove: An Immoral Comedy (produced London, 1933; New York, 1935).
    London, Heinemann, 1934; New York, French, 1935.
Eden End (produced London, 1934; New York, 1935).   London, Heinemann, 1934; in
    Three Plays and a Preface, 1935.
Cornelius: A Business Affair in Three Transactions (produced Birmingham and London,
    1935).   London, Heinemann, 1935; New York, French, 1936.
Duet in Floodlight (produced Liverpool and London, 1935).   London, Heinemann,
    1935.
Three Plays and a Preface (includes *Dangerous Corner*, *Eden End*, and *Cornelius*).
    New York, Harper, 1935.
Bees on the Boat Deck: A Farcical Tragedy (produced London, 1936).   London,
    Heinemann, and Boston, Baker, 1936.
Spring Tide (as Peter Goldsmith), with George Billam (produced London, 1936).
    London, Heinemann, and New York, French, 1936.
The Bad Samaritan (produced Liverpool, 1937).
Time and the Conways (produced London, 1937; New York, 1938).   London,
    Heinemann, 1937; New York, Harper, 1938.
I Have Been Here Before (produced London, 1937; New York, 1938).   London,
    Heinemann, 1937; New York, Harper, 1938.
Two Time Plays (includes *Time and The Conways* and *I Have Been Here Before*).
    London, Heinemann, 1937.
I'm a Stranger Here (produced Bradford, 1937).
People at Sea (produced London, 1937).   London, Heinemann, and New York,
    French, 1937.
Mystery at Greenfingers: A Comedy of Detection (produced London, 1938).   London,
    French, 1937; New York, French, 1938.
When We Are Married: A Yorkshire Farcical Comedy (produced London, 1938; New
    York, 1939).   London, Heinemann, 1938; New York, French, 1940.
Music at Night (produced Malvern, Worcestershire, 1938; London, 1939).   Included in
    Three Plays, 1943; in *Plays I*, 1948.
Johnson over Jordan (produced London, 1939).   Published as *Johnson over Jordan: The
    Play, And All about It (An Essay)*, London, Heinemann, and New York, Harper, 1939.
Good Night Children: A Comedy of Broadcasting (produced London, 1942).   Included
    in *Three Comedies*, 1945; in *Plays II*, 1949.
Desert Highway (produced Bristol, 1943; London, 1944).   London, French, 1944; in
    Four Plays, 1944.
They Came to a City (produced London, 1943).   Included in *Three Plays*, 1943; in
    Four Plays, 1944.
Three Plays (includes *Music at Night, The Long Mirror, They Came to a City*).   London,
    Heinemann, 1943.
The Long Mirror (produced London, 1945).   Included in *Three Plays*, 1943; in *Four
    Plays*, 1944.
How Are They at Home? A Topical Comedy (produced London, 1944).   Included in
    Three Comedies, 1945; in *Plays II*, 1949.

The Golden Fleece (as *The Bull Market*, produced Bradford, 1944).   Included in *Three Comedies*, 1945.

Four Plays (includes *Music at Night, The Long Mirror, They Came to a City, Desert Highway*).   New York, Harper, 1944; London, Heinemann, 1945.

Three Comedies (includes *Good Night Children, The Golden Fleece, How Are They at Home?*).   London, Heinemann, 1945.

An Inspector Calls (produced Moscow, 1945; London, 1946; New York, 1947).   New York, Dramatists Play Service, 1945; London, Heinemann, 1947.

Jenny Villiers (produced Bristol, 1946).

The Rose and Crown (televised, 1946).   London, French, 1947.

Ever Since Paradise: An Entertainment, Chiefly Referring to Love and Marriage (also director: produced on tour, 1946; London, 1947).   London and New York, French, 1949.

Three Time Plays (includes *Dangerous Corner, Time and the Conways, I Have Been Here Before*).   London, Pan, 1947.

The Linden Tree (produced Sheffield and London, 1947; New York, 1948).   London, Heinemann, and New York, French, 1948.

The Plays of J. B. Priestley:

    I. *Dangerous Corner, I Have Been Here Before, Johnson over Jordan, Music at Night, The Linden Tree, Eden End, Time and the Conways*.   London, Heinemann, 1948; as *Seven Plays*, New York, Harper, 1950.

    II. *Laburnam Grove, Bees on the Boat Deck, When We Are Married, Good Night Children, The Good Companions, How Are They at Home?, Ever Since Paradise*.   London, Heinemann, 1949; New York, Harper, 1951.

    III. *Cornelius, People at Sea, They Came to a City, Desert Highway, An Inspector Calls, Home Is Tomorrow, Summer Day's Dream*.   London, Heinemann, 1950; New York, Harper, 1952.

Home Is Tomorrow (produced London, 1948).   London, Heinemann, 1949; in *Plays III*, 1950.

The High Toby: A Play for the Puppet Theatre (produced London, 1954).   London, Penguin-Pollock, 1948.

Summer Day's Dream (produced Bradford and London, 1949).   Included in *Plays III*, 1950.

The Olympians, music by Arthur Bliss (produced London, 1949).   London, Novello, 1949.

Bright Shadow: A Play of Detection (produced Oldham and London, 1950).   London, French, 1950.

Treasure on Pelican (as *Treasure on Pelican Island*, televised, 1951; as *Treasure on Pelican*, produced Cardiff, 1952).   London, Evans, 1953.

Dragon's Mouth: A Dramatic Quartet, with Jacquetta Hawkes (also director: produced Malvern and London, 1952; New York, 1955).   London, Heinemann, 1952; in *The Off-Broadway Theatre*, edited by Richard A. Cordell and Lowell Matson, New York, Random House, 1959.

Private Rooms: A One-Act Comedy in the Viennese Style.   London, French, 1953.

Mother's Day.   London, French, 1953.

Try It Again (produced London, 1965).   London, French, 1953.

A Glass of Bitter.   London, French, 1954.

The White Countess, with Jacquetta Hawkes (produced Dublin and London, 1954).

The Scandalous Affair of Mr. Kettle and Mrs. Moon (produced Folkestone and London, 1955).   London, French, 1956.

These Our Actors (produced Glasgow, 1956).

Take the Fool Away (produced Vienna, 1956; Nottingham, 1959).

The Glass Cage (produced Toronto and London, 1957).   London, French, 1958.

The Thirty-First of June (produced Toronto and London, 1957).

The Pavilion of Masks (produced Bristol, 1963).   London, French, 1958.

A Severed Head, with Iris Murdoch, adaptation of the novel by Iris Murdoch (produced
   Bristol and London, 1963; New York, 1964).   London, Chatto and Windus, 1964.

Screenplays: *Sing As We Go*, 1934; *We Live in Two Worlds*, 1937; *Jamaica Inn*, 1939;
Britain at Bay, 1940; *Our Russian Allies*, 1941; *The Foreman Went to France
(Somewhere in France)*, with others, 1942; *They Came to a City*, 1943; *Last Holiday*,
1950; *An Inspector Calls*, 1954.

Radio Plays: *The Return of Jess Oakroyd*, 1941; *The Golden Entry*, 1955; *End Game at
the Dolphin*, 1956; *An Arabian Night in Park Lane*, 1965.

Television Plays: *The Rose and Crown*, 1946; *Treasure on Pelican Island*, 1951; *The
Stone Face*, 1957; *The Rack*, 1958; *Doomsday for Dyson*, 1958; *The Fortrose Incident*,
1959; *Level Seven*, 1966; *The Lost Peace* series, 1966; *Anyone for Tennis*, 1968; *Linda
at Pulteneys*, 1969.

Novels

Adam in Moonlight.   London, Heinemann, and New York, Harper, 1927.
Benighted.   London, Heinemann, 1927; as *The Old Dark House*, New York, Harper,
   1928.
Farthing Hall, with Hugh Walpole.   London, Macmillan, and New York, Doubleday,
   1929.
The Good Companions.   London, Heinemann, and New York, Harper, 1929.
Angel Pavement.   London, Heinemann, and New York, Harper, 1930.
Faraway.   London, Heinemann, and New York, Harper, 1932.
I'll Tell You Everything: A Frolic, with Gerald Bullett.   London, Heinemann, and New
   York, Macmillan, 1933.
Wonder Hero.   London, Heinemann, and New York, Harper, 1933.
They Walk in the City: The Lovers in the Stone Forest.   London, Heinemann, and New
   York, Harper, 1936.
The Doomsday Men: An Adventure.   London, Heinemann, and New York, Harper,
   1938.
Let the People Sing.   London, Heinemann, 1939; New York, Harper, 1940.
Black-Out in Gretley: A Story of – and for – Wartime.   London, Heinemann, and New
   York, Harper, 1942.
Daylight on Saturday: A Novel about an Aircraft Factory.   London, Heinemann, and
   New York, Harper, 1943.
Three Men in New Suits.   London, Heinemann, and New York, Harper, 1945.
Bright Day.   London, Heinemann, and New York, Harper, 1946.
Jenny Villiers: A Story of the Theatre.   London, Heinemann, and New York, Harper,
   1947.
Festival at Farbridge.   London, Heinemann, 1951; as *Festival*, New York, Harper,
   1951.
The Magicians.   London, Heinemann, and New York, Harper, 1954.
Low Notes on a High Level: A Frolic.   London, Heinemann, and New York, Harper,
   1954.
*Saturn over the Water: An Account of His Adventures in London, South America and
   Australia by Tim Bedford, Painter; Edited, with Some Preliminary and Concluding
   Remarks, By Henry Sulgrave and Here Presented to the Reading Public*.   London,
   Heinemann, and New York, Doubleday, 1961.
*The Thirty-First of June: A Tale of True Love, Enterprise and Progress in the Arthurian
   and ad-Atomic Ages*.   London, Heinemann, 1961; New York, Doubleday, 1962.
The Shapes of Sleep: A Topical Tale.   London, Heinemann, and New York,
   Doubleday, 1962.

Sir Michael and Sir George: A Tale of COMSA and DISCUS and the New Elizabethans.
London, Heinemann, 1964; as *Sir Michael and Sir George: A Comedy of the New
Elizabethans*, Boston, Little Brown, 1966.
*Lost Empires: Being Richard Herncastle's Account of His Life on the Variety Stage from
November 1913 to August 1914, Together with a Prologue and Epilogue.* London,
Heinemann, 1965; Boston, Little Brown, 1966.
Salt Is Leaving. London, Pan, 1966; New York, Harper, 1975.
It's an Old Country. London, Heinemann, and Boston, Little Brown, 1967.
The Image Men: Out of Town, and London End. London, Heinemann, 2 vols., 1968;
as *The Image Men*, Boston, Little Brown, 1969.
Found, Lost, Found; or, The English Way of Life. London, Heinemann, 1976.

Short Stories

Going Up: Stories and Sketches. London, Pan, 1950.
The Other Place and Other Stories of the Same Sort. London, Heinemann, and New
York, Harper, 1953.
The Carfitt Crisis and Two Other Stories. London, Heinemann, 1975; New York,
Stein and Day, 1976.

Verse

The Chapman of Rhymes (juvenilia). London, Alexander Moring, 1918.

Other

Brief Diversions: Being Tales, Travesties and Epigrams. Cambridge, Bowes and
Bowes, 1922.
Papers from Lilliput. Cambridge, Bowes and Bowes, 1922.
I for One. London, Lane, 1923; New York, Dodd Mead, 1924.
Figures in Modern Literature. London, Lane, and New York, Dodd Mead, 1924.
Fools and Philosophers: A Gallery of Comic Figures from English Literature. London,
Lane, 1925; as *The English Comic Characters*, New York, Dodd Mead, 1925.
George Meredith. London, Macmillan, and New York, Macmillan, 1926.
Talking: An Essay. London, Jarrolds, and New York, Harper, 1926.
(Essays). London, Harrap, 1926.
Open House: A Book of Essays. London, Heinemann, and New York, Harper, 1927.
Thomas Love Peacock. London, Macmillan, and New York, Macmillan, 1927.
The English Novel. London, Benn, 1927; revised edition, London, Nelson, 1935;
Folcroft, Pennsylvania, Folcroft Editions, 1974.
Too Many People and Other Reflections. New York and London, Harper, 1928.
Apes and Angels: A Book of Essays. London, Methuen, 1928.
The Balconinny and Other Essays. London, Methuen, 1929; as *The Balconinny*, New
York, Harper, 1931.
English Humour. London and New York, Longman, 1929.
The Town Major of Miraucourt. London, Heinemann, 1930.
Self-Selected Essays. London, Heinemann, and New York, Harper, 1932.
Albert Goes Through. London, Heinemann, and New York, Harper, 1933.
Four-in-Hand (miscellany). London, Heinemann, 1934.
*English Journey: Being a Rambling But Truthful Account of What One Man Saw and
Heard and Felt and Thought During a Journey Through England During the Autumn
of the Year 1933.* London, Heinemann-Gollancz, and New York, Harper, 1934.

Midnight on the Desert: A Chapter of Autobiography.   London, Heinemann, 1937; as
   *Midnight on the Desert: Being an Excursion into Autobiography During a Winter in
   America, 1935–36*, New York, Harper, 1937.
Rain upon Godshill: A Further Chapter of Autobiography.   London, Heinemann, and
   New York, Harper, 1939.
Britain Speaks (radio talks).   New York, Harper, 1940.
Postscripts (radio talks).   London, Heinemann, 1940.
Out of the People.   London, Collins-Heinemann, and New York, Harper, 1941.
Britain at War.   New York, Harper, 1942.
British Women Go to War.   London, Collins, 1943.
Here Are Your Answers.   London, Socialist Book Centre, 1944.
Letter to a Returning Serviceman.   London, Home and Van Thal, 1945.
The Secret Dream: An Essay on Britain, America and Russia.   London, Turnstile
   Press, 1946.
Russian Journey.   London, Writers Group of the Society for Cultural Relations with
   the USSR, 1946.
The New Citizen (address).   London, Committee for Education in World Citizenship,
   1946.
Theatre Outlook.   London, Nicholson and Watson, 1947.
*The Arts under Socialism: Being a Lecture Given to the Fabian Society, With a Postscript
   on What the Government Should Do for the Arts Here and Now.*   London, Turnstile
   Press, 1947.
Delight.   London, Heinemann, and New York, Harper, 1949.
A Priestley Companion: A Selection from the Writings of J. B. Priestley.   London,
   Penguin-Heinemann, 1951.
Journey down a Rainbow, with Jacquetta Hawkes (travel).   London, Cresset Press-
   Heinemann, and New York, Harper, 1955.
All about Ourselves and Other Essays, edited by Eric Gillett.   London, Heinemann,
   1956.
The Writer in a Changing Society.   Aldington, Kent, Hand and Flower Press, 1956.
Thoughts in the Wilderness (essays).   London, Heinemann, and New York, Harper,
   1957.
The Art of the Dramatist: A Lecture Together with Appendices and Discursive Notes.
   London, Heinemann, 1957; Boston, The Writer, 1958.
Topside; or, The Future of England: A Dialogue.   London, Heinemann, 1958.
The Story of Theatre.   London, Rathbone, 1959; as *The Wonderful World of the
   Theatre*, New York, Doubleday, 1959; London, Macdonald, 1969.
Literature and Western Man.   London, Heinemann, and New York, Harper, 1960.
William Hazlitt.   London, Longman, 1960.
Charles Dickens: A Pictorial Biography.   London, Thames and Hudson, 1961; New
   York, Studio Publications, 1962; as *Dickens and His World*, Thames and Hudson,
   1969.
Margin Released: A Writer's Reminiscences and Reflections.   London, Heinemann,
   1962; New York, Harper, 1963.
Man and Time.   London, Aldus Books, and New York, Doubleday, 1964.
The Moments and Other Pieces.   London, Heinemann, 1966.
All England Listened: J. B. Priestley's Wartime Broadcasts.   New York, Chilmark
   Press, 1968.
Essays of Five Decades, edited by Susan Cooper.   Boston, Little Brown, 1968; London,
   Heinemann, 1969.
*Trumpets over the Sea: Being a Rambling and Egotistical Account of the London
   Symphony Orchestra's Engagement at Daytona Beach, Florida, in July–August 1967.*
   London, Heinemann, 1968.
The Prince of Pleasure and His Regency, 1811–1820.   London, Heinemann, and New
   York, Harper, 1969.

The Edwardians.   London, Heinemann, and New York, Harper, 1970.

Snoggle (juvenile).   London, Heinemann, 1971; New York, Harcourt Brace, 1972.

Victoria's Heyday.   London Heinemann, and New York, Harcourt Brace, 1972.

Over the Long High Wall: Some Reflections and Speculations on Life, Death and Time.
   London, Heinemann, 1972.

The English.   London, Heinemann, and New York, Viking Press, 1973.

Outcries and Asides.   London, Heinemann, 1974.

A Visit to New Zealand.   London, Heinemann, 1974.

*Particular Pleasures: Being a Personal Record of Some Varied Arts and Many Different
   Artists.*   London, Heinemann, and New York, Stein and Day, 1975.

The Happy Dream (biography).   Andoversford, Gloucestershire, Whittington Press,
   1976.

Editor, *Essayists Past and Present: A Selection of English Essays.*   London, Jenkins,
   and New York, Dial Press, 1925.

Editor, *Tom Moore's Diary: A Selection.*   London, Cambridge University Press, 1925.

Editor, *The Book of Bodley Head Verse.*   London, Lane, and New York, Dodd Mead,
   1926.

Editor, *The Female Spectator: Selections from Mrs. Eliza Heywood's Periodical,
   1744–1746.*   London, Lane, 1929.

Editor, *Our Nation's Heritage.*   London, Dent, 1939.

Editor, *Scenes of London Life, From Sketches by Boz by Charles Dickens.*   London,
   Pan, 1947.

Editor, *The Best of Leacock.*   Toronto, McClelland and Stewart, 1957; as *The Bodley
   Head Leacock,* London, Bodley Head, 1957.

Editor, with O. B. Davis, *Four English Novels.*   New York, Harcourt Brace, 1960.

Editor, with O. B. Davis, *Four English Biographies.*   New York, Harcourt Brace, 1961.

Editor, *Adventures in English Literature.*   New York, Harcourt Brace, 1963.

Editor, *An Everyman Anthology.*   London, Dent, 1966.

Critical Studies: *J. B. Priestley* by Ivor Brown, London, Longman, 1957; *J.B. Priestley: An
Informal Study of His Work* by David Hughes, London, Hart Davis, 1958; *The World of J. B.
Priestley,* edited by D. G. MacRae, London, Heinemann, 1967; *J. B. Priestley: Portrait of an
Author* by Susan Cooper, London, Heinemann, 1970.

Theatrical Activities:

   Director: **Plays** – *Ever Since Paradise,* tour, 1946, and London, 1947; *Dragon's Mouth,*
   London, 1952.

                                    *   *   *

   J. B. Priestley is such a good dramatist that the problem of criticism is finding out why he is
not even better. Accomplished as his plays are, they leave a sense of deficiency when set
alongside what is known of the man's prolific literary career, the brilliance of his social
comment, the combined energy and weight of his personality, as of a genial thinking bear.
Not that any crass theatricality occurs in his unusually copious output, nor any hint of a
literary man's contempt for the public theatre. Simply it lacks the sense of total commitment
to be had not only from a genius like Strindberg but from, say, John Osborne, a playwright
with only a fraction of Priestley's education and experience. Drably functional dialogue is
part of the trouble. That and a residue of unused potential, of something held back. Why, for
example, is there no version of the 1914 war, in which Priestley fought?

   In terms of mere theatre history, of course, he can be evaluated as a dominant West End force of the nineteen-thirties, perhaps the only evolving dramatist which that brittle period of derivative conformist writing had to offer. Leaving out O'Casey, unacceptable for reasons that discredit the whole set-up, only Maugham and the short-lived Ronald MacKenzie rose above the escapist chatter. Both of them went further than Priestley in probing the human condition. He alone was set on a course likely to solve the English playwright's immediate problem, which was to reduce the insular snobbery of domestic drama without emptying the theatres. The books by Hughes and Lloyd Evans convey the excitement of his progress very well. A pity it had to be side-tracked by 1939 into expressionism, the favourite escape route of the period for writers convinced that only the box set and its furniture stood between them and a breakthrough. In fact the only thing wrong with West End stages and their decor was the written material, as has since been proved by, among others, Osborne and Pinter. Like them, Priestley is essentially a domestic dramatist. The defect of *Johnson over Jordan* and later *They Came to a City* is a lack of cohesion between abstract settings and characters not poetically stylized to fit them.

What Priestley can achieve is poetic atmosphere arising from a deep understanding of the family unit and, simultaneously, an awareness of its transience and vulnerability. In *The Linden Tree* this rueful Wordsworthian music is made explicit by an excerpt from Elgar's violin concerto. Usually it's diffused, as in *Time and the Conways*, a play geared to theories but which comes across as vivid illustration of the kind of thing time does to people. At times the disruptive factors are more sharply focused and unexpected. A prodigal daughter comes home, only to meet with conflict from a jealous sister. An elderly man caught up in a professional crisis suddenly finds his wife and son in league against him. One marriage is grimly salvaged by a stranger with claims to prophetic insight. He convinces the wife that her plan to opt out of it would end in something worse. None of these episodes or the attitude behind them would be found on the assembly line of a minor dramatist with a stake in offering comfort to escapist audiences. More than the skilled entertainment and middlebrow professionalism he excels in, this vein of uncomfortable honesty is Priestley's claim to be taken seriously.

Just how seriously? "The theatrical tradition of our time," he once wrote, "is a naturalistic tradition, and so I have in the main had to come to terms with it." The qualification covers the experimental failures and whatever surplus he got from the time theories of Dunne and Ouspensky, arguably neither more nor less than signposts to the mystery of the human condition. Otherwise he has indeed come to terms with an unpretentious behaviourist idiom, in some ways never more successfully than in *Dangerous Corner*, his first attempt. It is a play about contingency which icily demonstrates the effects of one remark alongside those of an alternative equally casual. Without character analysis or notable dialogue it has had persistent success at home and in translation. That the milieu has no tinge of the author's native Yorkshire adds an element of neutrality to the austerity and control. To dismiss all that as an essay in construction misses the point. Even the shallow characterization, more evident in reading than on stage, can be taken as social comment. It could be that Priestley, writing in a single week and better than he knew, exposed something at the core of a global public.

Time and the Conways of five years later is an ingenious, muted piece reflecting anxiety and apathy which surfaced in the Munich sell-out. The togetherness of a very English middle-class family of the period has never been better conveyed, for what that is worth. Normal sequence is reversed by placing the logical ending midway, so that the last act is enveloped in irony, the audience knowing, for example, that the youngest and most sympathetic female will be the first to die. The irony is logical without much bite and Chekhovian echoes intrude, the loss of a home through financial mismanagement, an interrupted proposal, a vulgarian interloper, a birthday party. Typical of the frustrating swing from insight to banality running through Priestley's dramatic work is an episode in which Mrs. Conway destroys rapport between a young lawyer and one of her daughters. It is a vicious incursion, with remarks about untidy hair and a shiny nose, deeply in character. Leading up to it, however, is a recital of socialist clichés and an intense quotation from Blake's *Jerusalem*, whereupon the man has to say, "Madge – you're inspired tonight." Leaving Chekhov out of it, *Time and the Conways* would have drawn on Priestley's own armoury for the relevant comedy already shown in the drunk scene in *Eden End*, for more of the ruthless probing applied to Mrs. Conway herself. Without this we are left with the faded pathos of juxtaposed photographs, accurate up to a point but lacking in definition.

A unique example of what this dramatist is capable of in uncompromising intensity with no holds barred occurs in Act II of *I Have Been Here Before*, an otherwise pedantic tribute to time and recurrence. The dramatic pressure centers on Ormund, a tycoon with a head full of marriage problems and grandiose business deals ("Who? Pensfield?...No, he won't make any trouble. I'll offer him a seat on the board"). After ensuring a hot-line to head office from this moorland pub, he selects whiskey to illuminate what he calls the darkness inside him. That, it transpires, is existential despair. The way Ormund describes his mother's death from cancer, his brothers' and those of his friends in the 1914 war, the way he reveals his own impulse to suicide, is as vivid as anything dramatized later by Sartre or Camus. Moreover, the brutal energy of Priestley's native Bradford is for once let loose on stage, as the great West Riding actor Wilfred Lawson made clear in the West End production. No English actor within living memory has rivalled Lawson in power, and here the playwright has matched him.

Both *Time and the Conways* and *I Have Been Here Before* date from 1937. There seemed no reason why the shapeliness and compassion of the first, the sudden ferocity in the second, should not combine. So much technical facility, playing over a latent gravity, points towards a maturing which did not take place. As it is, we had to wait twenty years for anything like the impact of Ormund from an English playwright. But one more of Priestley's plays came near his best and another perfected the initial approach. *The Linden Tree* builds on the *Eden End* design of a professional man's Yorkshire family, with an aging professor in place of a dying physician. Dating from 1947, the play expresses a post-war lethargy and defensiveness, the old bear cornered and wistful but ready to fight. There is indulgence for the cubs, seen as likely victims of a growing academic bureaucracy. In fact issues and conflicts which later grew to a flash-point and continue to smoulder are centered on a stubborn man of principle, recalling Ibsen.

There remains a lack of verbal exuberance and tension to inhibit Priestley from reaching the pinnacles of drama; and there is a holding back from extremes inherent to the situations and relationships invented. Instead of preferring Molière's professionalism to the "amateur" he detects in Congreve, if only he had gone to the same lengths as either of them, in artifice or in sardonic humour! If only Priestley had trusted the theatre with more of himself! Short of that, there was the return a quarter century later to the enigmatic, objective idiom of *Dangerous Corner* in *An Inspector Calls*, his masterpiece. The debt to Gogol's *Inspector General* does nothing to diminish this exploration of responsibility and guilt. Its blending of technical agility with restrained moral concern is unique, entirely Priestley's.

—Laurence Kitchin

RABE, David (William).   American.   Born in Dubuque, Iowa, 10 March 1940. Educated at Loras College, Dubuque, B.A. 1962; Villanova University, Pennsylvania, M.A. 1968. Served in the United States Army for two years. Married Elizabeth Pan in 1969. Feature Writer, *New Haven Register*, Connecticut, 1969–70. Assistant Professor, 1970–72, and since 1972, Consultant, Villanova University. Recipient: Rockerfeller grant, 1967; Associated Press Award, 1970; Obie Award, 1971; Tony Award, 1972; Outer Circle Award, 1972; New York Drama Critics Circle Citation, 1972; *Variety* award, 1972; National Institute of Arts and Letters award, 1974; New York Drama Critics Circle Award, 1976. Lives in Drexel Hill, Pennsylvania, Address: c/o Alfred A. Knopf, 201 East 50th Street, New York, New York 10022, U.S.A.

PUBLICATIONS

Plays

> *Sticks and Bones* (produced Villanova, Pennsylvania, 1969; New York, 1971).
> Included in *The Basic Training of Pavlo Hummel and Sticks and Bones*, 1973.
> *The Basic Training of Pavlo Hummel* (produced New York, 1971).   Included in *The
> Basic Training of Pavlo Hummel and Sticks and Bones*, 1973.
> *The Basic Training of Pavlo Hummel and Sticks and Bones: Two Plays*. New York,
> Viking Press, 1973.
> *The Orphan* (produced New York, 1973).   New York, French, 1975.
> *In the Boom Boom Room* (as *Boom Boom Room*, produced New York, 1973; revised
> version, as *In the Boom Boom Room*, produced New York, 1974).   New York,
> Knopf, 1975.
> *Burning* (produced New York, 1974).
> *Streamers* (produced New Haven, Connecticut, and New York, 1976).

David Rabe quotes from his introduction to *The Basic Training of Pavlo Hummel and Sticks and Bones: Two Plays* (reprinted by permission of The Viking Press, Inc.):

This statement is meant not as an introduction to my work as much as an introduction to the two plays so far made public, both of which have been labelled "anti-war" plays. I take exception to this label from the following position. An "anti-war" play is to me a play that expects, in the very fabric of its executed conception, to have political effect. I anticipated no such consequence from my plays, nor did I conceive them in the hope that they would have any such consequence. I have written them to diagnose, as best I could, certain phenomena that went on around me. It seems silly and presumptuous and pointless to call them "anti-war" plays. First of all, I believe that to think a play can have immediate, large-scale political effect is to vastly over-estimate the power that plays have. In addition, if there is, as I hope, more content in these plays than the thin line of political tract, then to categorize them as such is to diminish them. A play in which marriage looks bad is not called an "anti-marriage" play. A play in which young peoples seem not the most perfect of beings is not called an "anti-youth" play. A play about criminals is not called an "anti-crime" play. I think this is the case because Marriage, Family, Youth and Crime are all viewed as phenomena permanently a part of the eternal human pageant. I believe War to be an equally permanent part of that pageant, and will continue to do so until I see some sign in our daily activities that it is not.

*   *   *

The artistry, craftsmanship and originality of his first two plays amply prove David Rabe a major American playwright. It would be surprising, not to say disappointing, if a body of important work was not to follow.

The two, produced within six months of each other in 1971, were *The Basic Training of Pavlo Hummel* and *Sticks and Bones*, and they show Rabe a playwright in search of an American mythology. They also show him at a stylistic point between naturalism and absurdism – a point to which most contemporary playwrights have followed Strindberg. It is a style that for me is most modern and satisfying.

The Basic Training of Pavlo Hummel, though superficially about the war in Vietnam, is ultimately concerned with the wasted life of the ordinary man. Such a man, ill-equipped to understand and control his life, is conditioned to spend it in a trivial, meaningless and ultimately tragic way and he helplessly does so, though not without realizing it (too late). This is the stuff of high tragedy and Rabe's play approaches that level.

As a metaphor for such conditioning by society, Rabe has chosen the basic military training that millions of Americans experienced during army service. This was a literary and theatrical masterchoice, for basic training is a complete and familiar ritual, a real kind of theatre in itself. Pavlo Hummel, the play's anti-hero, accepts this ritual, this training, and its central equation of military achievement with masculinity. In the end, he is the victim of that preposterous equation. His is a pointless death in a useless war, wasted as are so many lives in blind obedience to learned and dubious values.

In replaying the army's training ritual, Rabe unified its comedy with its tragedy—what makes the military funny is also what makes it horrible. He also recognized that this is the stuff of which myths are made. Perhaps too aware of Greek tragedy, he introduced a chorus character who never fits into the play's reality, but that is the work's only flaw. It is a superb drama.

Sticks and Bones, though produced in New York afterward, is the earlier work. It is consistent with *The Basic Training of Pavlo Hummel* in tragic nature, bitter comedy and its mythic approach to contemporary America. In this case, the characters are named after the family in a popular American television show (*Ozzie and Harriet*) – the kind of family that has frightfully come to exemplify the ideal life situation for too many (an American political assassin wrote pathetically in his diary of dreaming to be part of such a family).

In *Sticks and Bones* a young man, blinded in war, returns home to such a family. Accustomed to bland, questionless complacency, they refuse to recognize his blindness. The play uses this loss of sense as a continuous metaphor – just as the hero is blind, so the television set has lost its sound function. Relationships are carried on with a crucial element missing. So, Rabe not only has the capacity to see the profound significance and mythic possibilities in so trivial-seeming a phenomenon as mass television. He also has awareness and command of the most classical and poetic techniques of playwriting.

Because the Broadway theatre was not at this point supporting drama, Rabe's plays had to be produced in the subsidized Public Theatre of New York's Shakespeare Festival. Although they were well produced there, they did not achieve for him the publicity essential to establish a playwright as an artist of international prominence. In fact, Rabe is one of the most important new young dramatists in America.

—Martin Gottfried

RANSLEY, Peter. British. Born in Leeds, Yorkshire, 10 December 1931. Educated at Pudsey Grammar School, Yorkshire, 1942–49; Queen Mary College, University of London, 1950–52. Married Hazel Rew in 1955 (divorced, 1970). Formerly worked as a journalist and as the development manager of a publishing company. Full-time Writer since 1971. Agent: Sheila Lemon, Spokesmen, 1 Craven Hill, London W2 3EW. Address: 33 Dordrecht Road, London W.3, England.

PUBLICATIONS

Plays

> *Disabled* (produced Manchester, 1969; as *Dear Mr. Welfare*, televised 1970; revised version, as *Disabled*, produced London, 1971). Published in *Plays and Players* (London), June 1971.

Ellen (produced Manchester, 1970; London, 1971).   Published in *Plays and Players*
   (London), April 1971.
The Thomson Report (produced London, 1972).
Runaway (produced London, 1974).

Television Plays: *Dear Mr. Welfare*, 1970; *Black Olives*, 1971; *Night Duty*, 1972;
Blinkers, 1973; *A Fair Day's Work*, 1973; *Bold Face Condensed*, 1974; *Mark Massey Is
Dead*, 1974; *Big Annie*, 1974; *Jo and Ann*, 1974; *The House on the Hill*, 1975; *The
Healing Hand*, 1975.

*   *   *

Peter Ransley's plays *Ellen* and *Disabled* are based upon actual persons. For a period
Ransley was a social worker and in his first play, *Disabled*, he writes about one particular old
man. In *Ellen*, he depicts a playwright from the North who is writing a play about Ellen, a
tramp who lives on his doorstep. When the play was staged at the Hampstead Theatre Club
the real life Ellen came to see the play about herself.

The central character in *Disabled*, Barker, is a problem case, dirty, smelly, cantankerous;
further, he is in a disputed area where three welfare districts meet, so that responsibility for
him is passed from department to department. He alienates all who try to help him, task
force, home help, male nurse. But, as Ted, a character in *Ellen*, remarks, "Help is a cruel
word." Both plays are concerned with the need to consider individuals as people, and not as
"cases." Again, as Ted says in *Ellen*, "Labels. That's what makes people acute cases. The
labels people stick on them."

At the end of the first act of *Disabled* a young man enters, an unidentified social worker
called Mike. Barker gets him to talk about his marriage, which is on the rocks. He has not had
intercourse with his wife for three years (the same length of time that Barker has been
without sex since his accident), and after her last miscarriage, Mike's wife took up social
work. Like the wife Clare in *Ellen*, she is a frigid and sterile person. When she appears at the
end of the play she says to Barker, "You are my case," to which he replies, "I am my own
case."

Disabled is about the reversal of roles; it probes and poses such questions as who is the
helper and who the helped. As Barker begins to tap Mike's dilemma we realise that it is Mike
who, psychologically, is disabled. And when at the final curtain Barker is left alone saying
"Poor bastard," it is perhaps less of himself that he is thinking than of Mike. In another sense
it is also both of them, for in this play, not wholly successfully, Ransley attempts to merge
two styles, naturalism and fantasy. In a central scene (finely directed at the Hampstead
Theatre Club by Vivian Matalon with Leonard Rossiter as Barker and Peter McEnery as
Mike), Barker gets Mike to make up his face like a woman. (Barker used to be a ventriloquist
and do an act on the halls with his wife, Maisie.) Empathetically, almost mediumistically,
Barker begins to take on the voice of Mike's wife (whom he has never met). By assuming the
persona of Mike's wife he is able to uncover Mike's neurosis. At the climax of this curious
scene he persuades Mike to lift him out of his wheel chair and to dance with him. As they
dance so "Barker's limbs come to life" (author's stage directions). The moment the wife
enters the room Barker collapses and falls to the floor.

What the author is trying to convey is that it is Mike whose psychological limbs have been
brought to life by Barker's insight and understanding. And in the process of having to think
about another human being, Barker finds a role for himself – he, too, comes to life.

Ransley described, in an audience discussion about the play, how at one point in his
relationship with the particular old man who provided the play's genesis, he lost his temper
and hit the old man. He was at once ashamed of himself but the old man laughed and
laughed. For the first time someone had responded to him not as a "case," as a disabled
person requiring a special attitude, but as a human being. By losing his temper Ransley has
revealed a true involvement with the old man, they had begun to relate to each other as
people.

In *Ellen* the author has advanced considerably in complexity and skill. While developing futher the major theme of *Disabled*, he also touches upon the dilemma of the provincial artist. At one point Ted says to the playwright "We've both come a long way since those old Brummy days. I wasn't sure it was right for you to come to London because it is more of a challenge in the provinces, and you do lose contact with the source of your material – aren't you losing contact with the source of your material – aren't you losing contact with your sources, cockalorum?" to which the playwright replies, "Trust you to go straight to the heart of my neuroses."

One of the arguments for "Drama-in-Education" is that it provides an additional teaching medium, and as such enables any subject from history to geography to English or science, to be taught, or handled, dramatically. Similarly, each one of Ransley's plays is an essay in sociology presented through the medium of drama. Carefully and sensitively he dissects aspects of our society. In *Runaway* he brings under his microscope a working class family under the shadow of cancer in a remote part of Yorkshire. The father is an old trade union man who failed to expose the risks of a dangerous chemical used in the manufacture of car tyres in the local factory. The resulting cancer which has crippled his best friend Charlie now threatens him. His eleven year old grandson, the runaway of the title, and the best written part, is at the centre of the conflicts within this family. The writing is spare, pared to the bone, and beautifully understated.

Ransley's is a quiet and thoughtful talent but it has a way of lingering on in the memory, of exercising one's conscience in every day life. Not every playwright can claim to do that.

—James Roose-Evans

RATTIGAN, Terence (Mervyn).   British.   Born in London, 10 June 1911. Educated at Harrow School (Scholar), Middlesex, 1925–30; Trinity College, Oxford, 1930–33 (history scholarship). B.A. 1933. Served as a Flight Lieutenant in the Coastal Command, Royal Air Force, 1940–45. Full-time Playwright since 1934. Recipient: Ellen Terry Award, 1947; New York Drama Critics Circle Award, 1948. C.B.E. (Commander, Order of the British Empire). 1958. Knighted, 1971. Agent: Dr. Jan Van Loewen Ltd., 81-83 Shaftesbury Avenue, London W1V 8BX, England.

PUBLICATIONS

Plays

   First Episode, with Philip Heimann (produced London, 1933; New York, 1934).
   French Without Tears (produced London, 1936; New York, 1937).   London, Hamish Hamilton, 1937; New York, Farrar and Rinehart, 1938; revised version, music by Robert Stolz, lyrics by Paul Dehn, as *Joie de Vivre* (produced London, 1960).
   After the Dance (produced London, 1939).   London, Hamish Hamilton, 1939.
   Follow My Leader, with Anthony Maurice (produced London, 1940).
   Grey Farm, with Hector Bolitho (produced New York, 1940; London, 1942).
   Flare Path (produced London and New York, 1942).   London, Hamish Hamilton, 1942.
   While the Sun Shines (produced London, 1943; New York, 1944).   New York, French, 1945; London, Hamish Hamilton, 1946.

Love in Idleness (produced London, 1944).   London, Hamish Hamilton, 1945; as *O Mistress Mine* (produced New York, 1946), New York, French, 1949.

The Winslow Boy (produced London, 1946; New York, 1947).   London, Hamish Hamilton, and New York, Dramatists Play Service, 1946.

Playbill: The Browning Version and Harlequinade (produced London, 1948; New York, 1949).   London, Hamish Hamilton, 1949; New York, French, 2 vols., 1950.

Adventure Story (produced Brighton and London, 1949).   London, French, 1950.

Who Is Sylvia? (produced Cambridge and London, 1950).   London, Hamish Hamilton, 1951.

The Deep Blue Sea (produced Brighton, London, and New York, 1952).   London, Hamish Hamilton, 1952; New York, Random House, 1953.

The Sleeping Prince (produced Manchester and London, 1953; New York, 1956). London, Hamish Hamilton, 1954; New York, Random House, 1957.

Collected Plays:

I. *French Without Tears, Flare Path, While the Sun Shines, Love in Idleness, The Winslow Boy.*   London, Hamish Hamilton, 1953.

II. *The Browning Version, Harlequinade, Adventure Story, Who Is Sylvia? The Deep Blue Sea.*   London, Hamish Hamilton, 1953.

III. *The Sleeping Prince, Separate Tables, Variation on a Theme, Ross, Heart to Heart.* London, Hamish Hamilton, 1964.

Separate Tables: Two Plays (produced Liverpool and London, 1954; New York, 1956). London, Hamish Hamilton, 1955; New York, Random House, 1957.

The Prince and the Showgirl: The Script for the Film.   New York, New American Library, 1957.

Variation on a Theme (produced Manchester and London, 1958).   London, Hamish Hamilton, 1958.

Ross: A Dramatic Portrait (produced Liverpool and London, 1960; New York, 1961). London, Hamish Hamilton, 1960; New York, Random House, 1962.

Man and Boy (produced Brighton, London and New York, 1963).   New York, French, 1963; London, Hamish Hamilton, 1964.

A Bequest to the Nation (as *Nelson*, televised 1966; revised version, as *A Bequest to the Nation*, produced London, 1970).   London, Hamish Hamilton, 1970.

All on Her Own (televised, 1968; produced Kingston on Thames and London, 1974; as *Duologue*, produced London, 1976).   Published in *The Best Short Plays 1970*, edited by Stanley Richards, Philadelphia, Chilton, 1970.

High Summer (televised, 1972).   Published in *The Best Short Plays 1973*, edited by Stanley Richards, Radnor, Pennsylvania, Chilton, 1973.

In Praise of Love: Before Dawn, and After Lydia (produced London, 1973).   London, Hamish Hamilton, 1973; (*After Lydia* produced, as *In Praise of Love*, New York, 1974), New York, French, 1975.

Screenplays: *French Without Tears*, with Anatole de Grunwald and Ian Dalrymple, 1939; *Quiet Wedding*, with Anatole de Grunwald, 1941; *The Day Will Dawn*, 1941; *The Avengers*, 1942; *English Without Tears*, 1944; *Uncensored*, with Rodney Ackland, 1944; *The Way to the Stars* (*Johnny in the Clouds*), with Anatole de Grunwald, 1945; *Journey Together*, 1946; *Brighton Rock*, with Graham Greene, 1947; *While the Sun Shines*, with Anatole de Grunwald, 1947; *The Winslow Boy*, with Anatole de Grunwald and Anthony Asquith, 1948; *Her Man Gilbey*, 1949; *Bond Street*, with Rodney Ackland, 1950; *The Browning Version*, 1951; *Breaking the Sound Barrier*, 1952; *The Final Test*, 1953; *The Deep Blue Sea*, 1955; *The Man Who Loved Redheads*, 1955; *The Prince and the Showgirl*, 1957; *Separate Tables*, 1958; *The VIPs*, 1963; *The Yellow Rolls Royce*, 1965; *Goodbye Mr. Chips*, 1969; *A Bequest to the Nation* (*The Nelson Affair*), 1973.

Radio Plays: *A Tale of Two Cities*, from the novel by Dickens, 1950; *Cause Célèbre*, 1975.

Television Plays: *The Final Test*, 1951; *Heart to Heart*, 1962; *Ninety Years On*, 1964; *Nelson*, 1966; *All on Her Own*, 1968; *High Summer*, 1972.

Critical Study: article by T. C. Worsley in *London Magazine*, September 1964.

*   *   *

Terence Rattigan is best compared with the Somerset Maugham of the short stories. This is to establish his level rather than to indicate his category. But he began his career not with narrative but as a writer of popular middle class light comedies, and he himself makes a modest claim for these: what they already exhibit is a highly developed sense of theatre, that mysterious and indefinable quality which is easily overlooked by the reader, but is unmistakable on the stage, and which is, he rightly claims, the basic *sine qua non* of the playwright.

These comedies were gay, flippant and highspirited and are worked over with a meticulous craftsmanship. But they are not, like the best of his straight plays, rooted in the social life of the times. Comedy that has a chance of living holds up a mirror to its period. It reflects that period's manners and morals, at the same time universalising them. Rattigan's comedies live in a world of make-believe, gay and bubbling but essentially unreal.

The difference in attack and effect is evident if we compare his early play, *Flare Path*, about an RAF bomber station, with the comedies. It's not only that in this play an additional gift, a gift for pathos, reveals itself. It's also that the comedy, as well, bites deeper because it is a very exact reflection of the mood of very real people at a very real time. I should not be at all surprised to find that in due course *Flare Path* could be revived brilliantly as a remarkably truthful reflection of its period in its attitudes and its characteristic use of understatement.

Picking up from *Flare Path* his next full scale narrative play was *The Winslow Boy*, founded on an Edwardian *cause célèbre* in which a young naval cadet was falsely accused of stealing a five shilling postal order, and his father ruined his health and his finances in getting the case carried to the highest possible courts to clear his name. The play is an example of his very special ability (we shall see it again in his T.E. Lawrence portrait, *Ross*) to reduce a complicated trangle of events to a thoroughly manageable shape and length. It's a small triumph of arrangement and, also, of social tone. The playwright captures effectively and unobtrusively a real sense of period.

It is with the next five narrative plays that Rattigan establishes himself as a considerable playwright – *The Browning Version, The Deep Blue Sea, Separate Tables, Variation on a Theme, Man and Boy*. The twin themes of these plays are humiliation and obsession, and in each of them the main character wins back, or at least attempts to win back, a little victory of self-respect in the face of the humiliations he or she has suffered.

Indeed I think it is generally accepted now that the dissilusioned failure of a schoolmaster in *The Browning Version* and the bogus Major in *Separate Tables* are almost perfect examples of their genre; and one must surely admire the cunning way in which a variety of quite small incidents are so built up that the denouement when it comes will have behind it the whole weight of the emotions engendered by them; and thus a comparatively simple act of self-assertion in each case, at the close, will have all the power of an explosion. Since the writer is committed by his choice of subjects to the realism of the flat language and understatement which such people use, the dramatic charge can only be sprung by this calculated use of "preparation."

The Deep Blue Sea. a full size play, traces the last stage of the obsessional love of a middle class lady (a judge's wife) for a pleasant easy-going insufficient ex-RAF officer. It is another triumph of tone, keeping with unremitting rigidity to its chosen colour of unrelenting grey. It starts as it means to go on – with an attempted suicide in a seedy North London flat, exploring nothing but the battle for survival between the woman and her lover, hers to keep him at any cost of humiliation to herself, his to get out before he finds himself responsible for more damage than he has done already.

The ending has been criticised on the grounds that after her lover had finally left her this woman had nothing to live for and that therefore the author "funked" the suicide which is in the logic of her case. But in fact the suicide solution was plainly rejected as too obvious and too easy. The playwright tries instead to redeem her by means of a most interesting minor character, a struck-off doctor who has survived disgrace and prison and has learned to live "beyond hope." Whether or not the striking duologue between him and the woman "works" the change in her is certainly arguable. I find it does.

Between these three successful plays and the next two, which were public and (mainly) critical failures, came the English theatrical revolution inaugurated by John Osborne's *Look Back in Anger* in 1956. And it is to this very thorough change-over in theatrical taste that I attribute the total failure to appreciate *Variation on a Theme* and *Man and Boy*. To me both these plays showed a marked advance in depth and range, deployed, though, with the same rigid control of tone.

Variation on a Theme may well lay a claim to be Rattigan's best play. In addition to the usual Rattigan qualities it is enclosed in a cunning literary "conceit" which to the cognoscenti gives it a special charm. Formally the play is shaped very closely scene by scene on Dumas' *La Dame aux Camélias*. It is an anti-romantic variation on this theme, and those who know the original will find all its main scenes, one by one, given a contemporary variation without any of them seeming forced or contrived. Those who are not in the know can accept the play simply for itself.

Variation on a Theme is another case of obsession. The Marguerite of this version is a tough top courtesan who has worked her way up from a Birmingham suburb via four rich husbands and is just on the point of landing her fifth and richest, a West German Millionaire. And at this point she falls victim to the charms of an equivocal little ballet dancer on the same trail. She doesn't deceive herself about the worth of the object of her passion. It is a hopeless obsession which in the end she decides not to fight.

The treatment is hard, merciless, unrelenting and absolutely modern. The whole conception is audacious, a bravura performance by a master of his particular form. The dramatist manipulates his chosen theme through to the end with its vibrant echoes and modulations of his original. One notices the brilliant duologue in which his *Armand Père* — here a father-figure, the male patron of the equivocal ballet dancer — persuades this Rose-Marguerite to give the boy up: and the splendidly theatrical device of making a tape recording for him instead of the letter of the original. Above all there is the brilliant working in of the death by consumption (sadly misunderstood at the time) in her decision to have a last fling with her ballet dancer, a fling which is calculated in her advanced state of illness as a suicidal gesture.

Man and Boy which followed it is rich in theme and ambitious in scope. It is essentially, as the title indicates, a father-son play. Antonescu is a financial tycoon in the Kruger class: and like Kruger he has reached the end of the road: he is on the run. He is humiliated by having to take refuge with the son who has intellectually rejected him, since he needs to hide up and has nowhere else to go. But if the son has rejected him intellectually, he hasn't emotionally. Being essentially weak he admires his father's strength. And part of the dark centre of the play is this clinging devotion of the weak for the strong, of the romantic for the realist, of the conscience-striken for the conscience-less.

The case is deepened by the fact that the financier has a weakness for this weak son: it is perhaps his only weakness, and when not only failure but death, too, faces the financier, it is the rejected and rejecting son who alone is prepared to see him through.

All these subtleties are there in the text. But in the actual performance the play looked rather more like a powerful and ingenious narrative of the machinations of a tycoon at the end of his tether. Whether the playwright had not brought the emotional weight to play in quite the right places, or whether the chief actor and the director were at fault, it would take another and different production to reveal. But that it remains a play of absorbing interest is certain.

I have picked out these five plays from the main body of Rattigan's work judging them to be the ones by which his reputation will probably stand. But they must be seen in the context of the other twelve highly professional and skillful plays. For Rattigan is a working dramatist – his professionalism is shown by the fact that he alone responded to the appeal for special plays for Coronation year with a delightful and appropriate *jeu d'esprit, The Sleeping Prince.* His three historical plays, *Adventure Story* about Alexander, *Bequest to the Nation* about Nelson, and *Ross* about T. E. Lawrence, all show his skillful manipulation of the material of thorough research. If *Ross* alone is wholly successful, that is because it alone presented no problem of language: the playwright's vocabulary fitted exactly with his subject's. And I would add *Ross* to the other five plays.

Too much need not be claimed for these plays. It is argued that they do not strike deep beneath the surface, and it is true they are on a small scale and their range is narrow. But within that range they are exact and true. They take a comparatively small corner of human weakness and persuade us to experience it truthfully and poignantly. They don't attempt more and they don't achieve less. When the tide of theatrical fashion (which is at present running both against the narrative play as such and, in England, against that area of middle class life where Rattigan finds his subjects) finally turns, as it will, they will be seen to stand up.

—T. C. Worsley

REANEY, James (Crerar).   Canadian.   Born near Stratford, Ontario, 1 September 1926. Educated at Elmhurst Public School, Easthope Township, Perth County; Stratford High School; University College, Toronto (Epstein Award, 1948), M.A. in English, Ph.D. 1956. Married Colleen Thibaudeau in 1951; has two living children. Member of the English Department, University of Manitoba, Winnipeg, 1949–56. Since 1960, Member of the English Department, Middlesex College, University of Western Ontario, London. Founding Editor, *Alphabet* magazine, London, 1960–71. Active in little theatre groups in Winnipeg and London. Recipient: Governor General's Award, for verse, 1950, 1959, for drama, 1963; President's Medal, University of Western Ontario, for verse, 1955, 1958; Chalmers Award, 1975, 1976. Agent: Sybil Hutchinson, Apt. 409, Ramsden Place, 50 Hillsboro Avenue, Toronto, Ontario M5R 1S8, Canada.

PUBLICATIONS

Plays

> *Night-Blooming Cereus* (broadcast, 1959; produced Toronto, 1960).   Included in *The Killdeer and Other Plays,* 1962.
> *The Killdeer* (produced Toronto, 1960; Glasgow, 1965).   Included in *The Killdeer and Other Plays,* 1962; revised version (produced Vancouver, 1970), in *Masks of Childhood,* 1972.
> *One-Man Masque* (produced Toronto, 1960).   Included in *The Killdeer and Other Plays,* 1962.
> *The Easter Egg* (produced Hamilton, Ontario, 1962).   Included in *Masks of Childhood,* 1972.

The Killdeer and Other Plays (includes *Sun and Moon, One-Man Masque, Night-Blooming Cereus*).   Toronto, Macmillan, 1962.

Sun and Moon (produced Winnipeg, Manitoba, 1972).   Included in *The Killdeer and Other Plays*, 1962.

Names and Nicknames (produced Winnigeg, Manitoba, 1963).   Included in *Apple Butter and Other Plays*, 1973.

Apple Butter (puppet play; also director: produced London, Ontario, 1965).   Included in *Apple Butter and Other Plays*, 1973.

Let's Make a Carol: A Play with Music for Children, music by John Beckwith.   Waterloo, Ontario, Waterloo Music Company, 1965.

Listen to the Wind (produced London, Ontario, 1965; Woodstock, New York, 1967).   Vancouver, Talonbooks, 1972.

Colours in the Dark (produced Stratford, Ontario, 1967).   Vancouver and Toronto, Talonbooks-Macmillan, 1970.

Three Desks (produced Calgary, 1967).   Included in *Masks of Childhood*, 1972.

Masks of Childhood (includes *The Killdeer, Three Desks, The Easter Egg*), edited by Brian Parker.   Toronto, New Press, 1972.

Apple Butter and Other Plays for Children (includes *Names and Nicknames, Ignoramus, Geography Match*).   Vancouver, Talonbooks, 1973.

The Donnellys: A Trilogy:
1. *Sticks and Stones* (produced Toronto, 1973).   Erin, Ontario, Press Porcépic, 1975.
2. *The Saint Nicholas Hotel* (produced Toronto, 1974).   Erin, Ontario, Press Porcépic, 1976.
3. *Handcuffs* (produced Toronto, 1975).   Erin, Ontario, Press Porcépic, 1976.

All the Bees and All the Keys (for children), music by John Beckwith.   Erin, Ontario, Press Porcépic, 1976.

Radio Play: *Night Blooming Cereus*, 1959.

Verse

The Red Heart.   Toronto, McClelland and Stewart, 1949.

A Suit of Nettles.   Toronto, Macmillan, 1958.

Twelve Letters to a Small Town.   Toronto, Ryerson Press, 1962.

The Dance of Death at London, Ontario.   London, Alphabet, 1963.

Poems, edited by Germaine Warkentin.   Toronto, New Press, 1972.

Selected Longer Poems, edited by Germaine Warkentin.   Erin, Ontario, Press Porcépic, 1976.

Selected Shorter Poems, edited by Germaine Warkentin.   Erin, Ontario, Press Porcépic, 1976.

Other

The Boy with an "R" in His Hand (juvenile).   Toronto, Macmillan, 1965.

Twenty Barrels.   Erin, Ontario, Press Porcépic, 1976.

Critical Studies: *James Reaney* by Alvin A. Lee, New York, Twayne, 1968; *James Reaney* by Ross G. Woodman, Toronto, McClelland and Stewart, 1971; *James Reaney* by James Stewart Reaney, Toronto, Gage, 1976.

Theatrical Activities:

Director: **Plays** − *One-Man Masque and Night-Blooming Cereus*, Toronto, 1960; *Apple Butter*, London, Ontario, 1965.

Actor: **Plays** – In *One-Man Masque and Night-Blooming Cereus,* Toronto, 1960.

James Reaney comments:

These plays are interested in telling stories. I like using choral and collage techniques. The plays, particularly the children's plays, are based on watching children play on streets and in backyards. So – Plays as play.

*   *   *

Although James Reaney is probably the best Canadian playwright writing today, his plays have been less performed than those of many other dramatists. It is easy to see Reaney's early work as outside the mainstream not only of Canadian playwriting and literature, but of modern literature generally, His debt is to a tradition of fantasy that is pre-eminently late nineteenth century. This influence comes strongly from the early Yeats, but Reaney is also indebted to the Brontës (he takes the name Branwell in his long poem *A Suit of Nettles*), and, one can't help feeling, to the Henry James of *The Turn of the Screw* and *Owen Wingrave*. Indeed, in *Listen to the Wind*, his finest play until the recent *Donnellys* trilogy, the lead is called Owen and proceeds to stage within the play another play called *The Saga of Caresfoot Court*. Reaney based this on his own childhood experience of reading Rider Haggard's *Dawn*, but it owes a good deal also to the tradition of the gothic tale out of *Wuthering Heights*.

Indeed, it is in Reaney's taste for melodrama – the sudden reversal of the last acts, for instance – that he is weakest. His attempt to justify melodrama by claiming for it another and truer world – "the patterns in it are not only sensational but deadly accurate" – is only partly successful. The "strong pattern" of melodrama can easily obscure the significant moral exploration of the play, as the exterior story of *Listen to the Wind* very nearly does.

But if the theatre of fantasy works against naturalism, it also, allied with strong lexical whimsy, works against the excesses of melodrama. The playbox of *Colours in the Dark* is not only a way of explaining the longing to get back home to childhood's Eden; it is also an outward and visible sign of those wordlists that Reaney loves – the inventory of the world. The naming of things is as important to him as it is for Eliot in *Old Possum's Book*, and shares something of that whimsical attitude to the serious matter of language. This is true in *Names and Nicknames* especially. But it is a characteristic concern of all his plays and poetry. We never forget Reaney the classicist by training. "Most of those words you've no idea of their meaning, but were sowing them in your mind anyhow," says Polly in *Easter Egg*, and elsewhere, in *Masks of Childhood*, we have a fantasia on the street names of Winnipeg, ending in a whoop – "I Winnipeg....She Winnipeggied....They Winnipugged."

Reaney's language spars with his imagery and by its whimsy prevents the apocalyptic metaphors from becoming bombastic. The verse may be Blakean but it is spoken in the dialect of John Clare. Reaney's debt to Blake, via Frye's *Fearful Symmetry,* is a stated one, but Walt Disney and Mother Goose are there as well, and a sense of the landscape that reminds us more of Palmer than of Blake, though it is the voice of the *Prophecies* that speaks in *Colours in the Dark*:

> We sit by the fire and hear the rushing sound
> Of the wind that comes from Temiskaming
> Algoma, Patricia
> Down from the north over the wilderness.

But for Reaney there is none of Blake's sense of contraries or great loss and fall. Innocence is accessible if we can but find the way or rather listen to the children who, like the children in *Burnt Norton*, know it. Their music has the apocalyptic quality of the poetry of Leonard Cohen: "I saw the sundogs barking/On either side of the sun." In that world objects have a life that is almost Dickensian (again the connection to Victorian fantasy). "I'll be the orange devil waiting in the stove/I'll be the chimney trumpeting the night," says Madam Fay in *The Killdeer*. And it is the cry of the killdeer – plaintive (like Reaney's search for the ancestors and the past that will make sense of the present) and deceiving (as Eli in that play recognizes, "It's another clock in another time") – that is a paradigm of Reaney's work. In that sense he speaks for the English Canada that he knows and loves – one of the great farmhouses surrounded by large trees on summer afternoons among musty books where "long long ago" is as real as here and now, the world of Blake and Spenser, Yeats and Rider Haggard, as immediate as the killdeer and the barnyard geese. The drift from real to fantasy is encouraged by the elements – the wind to which the children listen or the detailed catalogues of flowers and animals. It shares something of O'Neill and Miller, but its closest analogy is the late Shakesperarean romances – where Illyria is a pattern of England as Caresfoot Court becomes a way of understanding Stratford, Ontario.

This is his impetus in the long dramatic exploration of the story of the Donnellys, the family whose story Reaney has made into a sort of Canadian *Oresteia*. There can be no doubt that this trilogy – *Sticks and Stones*, *The Saint Nicholas Hotel*, and *Handcuffs* – constitutes Reaney's finest achievement so far, and perhaps the finest achievement in the Canadian theatre for that matter. Each play differs in the ritual that forms its structure, but the pattern of knowing and remembering that we think of as Faulknerian ("memory believes before knowing remembers") is common to all.

The history of the family surrounds the central event – their final murder-massacre in the last play – like dust in a sunbeam, what Eliot captures in *The Four Quartets*. We find ourselves endlessly going round events that are and must remain mysterious, with bits of evidence, voices, recollections. Shadowmaking is one of the games that Reaney uses in *Handcuffs* and it is a paradigm of our sense of the action – shadows that materialise only as they are conjured. For the plays are also a ritual. (Singing and dancing play a great part in them.) And that ritual, although Reaney intended it to be an exorcism of the "Black" Donnellys' reputation, is more a celebration of a mystery that cannot be explained, only understood. And that that understanding is possible only in dramatic terms that Reaney establishes, is a testament to his genius.

—D.D.C. Chambers

REARDON, Dennis J. American. Born in Worcester, Massachusetts, 17 September 1944. Educated at Tulane University, New Orleans, 1962–63; University of Kansas, Lawrence (Hopkins Award, 1965, 1966). 1963–66, B.A. in English (cum laude) 1966; Indiana University, Bloomington, 1966–67. Served in the United States Army, 1968–69. Married Georgia Wooldridge in 1971. Playwright-in-Residence, University of Michigan, Ann Arbor (Shubert Fellowship, 1970; Hopwood prize, 1971), 1970–71. Agent: Ellen Neuwald, 905 West End Avenue, New York, New York. Address: 106 MacDougal Street, Apartment 9, New York, New York 10012, U.S.A.

PUBLICATIONS

Plays

The Happiness Cage (produced New York, 1970). New York, French, 1971.
Siamese Connections (produced Ann Arbor, Michigan, 1971; New York, 1973).
The Leaf People (produced New York, 1975).

Manuscript Collection: Lincoln Center Library of the Performing Arts, New York.

Critical Study: *Uneasy Stages* by John Simon, New York, Random House, 1975.

Dennis J. Reardon comments:

The central dynamic in my plays exists in the tension between what is "real" and what is "made up." I often mix carefully researched and recognizably topical material with the stuff of dreams, and I am seldom precise about where one mode leaves off and the other begins. My intent is to push beyond the suffocating ephemera of journalistic fact into a more iconic realm where the only reality is a metaphor.

*   *   *

The shadow of Eugene O'Neill hangs ponderously over the shoulder of all serious young American playwrights, and Dennis J. Reardon is among those most evidently trying to cope with the master's presence. To wrestle with universal themes in the American theatre, as Reardon does in *The Happiness Cage*, is to invite comparison with the O'Neill of *The Iceman Cometh* and *Desire under the Elms*. To experiment with theatrical styles, as Reardon does in *Siamese Connections*, is to repeat the experiments of *The Hairy Ape* and *Lazarus Laughs*. To test the potentials of language in the theatre, as Reardon does in *The Leaf People*, is to re-invent *Strange Interlude* and *Mourning Becomes Electra*. To scrutinize the world through Irish-Catholic eyes is to confront *The Touch of the Poet* and *Long Day's Journey into Night*.

As the son of a lapsed Irish-Catholic father who is both a playwright and a modest scholar of O'Neill, Reardon's journey into playwriting seems almost as inevitable as the quests of the characters he writes about. In his three produced plays Reardon has grappled with the ghost of O'Neill (perhaps unknowingly) while establishing himself as one of America's most promising playwrights.

Reardon's first produced play, *The Happiness Cage*, tells the story of a notably unpleasant young man, Reese, who is unwittingly made the pawn in an experiment in which a research physician attempts to bring "happiness" to people artificially by implanting an electronic probe into the sense center of their brains. The situation of the play is based loosely on facts, which was born out by the coincidental cover-story of *Time* magazine at the time of the play's New York run. But Reardon is primarily interested in the moral implications of such actions, and the play is in part a philosophical debate between the patient, Reese, and the doctor, Freytag. Reese argues that his uniqueness is more important than his happiness; the doctor argues for the general, not the individual. Reardon's point is Augustinian: Reese seeks salvation (selfhood) through diligence (tenacious resistance to "happiness"). The play has brilliant roles, and it also has strong and carefully structured dialogue and several scenes that are maturely constructed. Indeed, a catalogue of its virtues explains why Reardon was instantly hailed as that year's "promising" playwright. But the play was only moderately successful, commercially. That is perhaps explainable by a consideration of its untraditional elements. The script is structured into short scenes, instead of single-actioned acts. That permitted Reardon to explore his thematic development discursively, instead of sequentially. Also, the play jumps back and forth between realistic melodrama and expressionistic abstraction. The final scene, for example, in which reporters question the doctor after he has performed his experiment upon Reese, greatly bothered audiences who were expecting the tidy resolution of a well-made play.

The Happiness Cage did not receive the accolades of O'Neill's first major play, *Beyond the Horizon*, but it did cause serious theatre goers and critics to hope an important career had been launched.

Siamese Connections, Reardon's second play, was a disappointment. Produced, as was *The Happiness Cage*, by Joseph Papp's New York Shakespeare Festival's Public Theatre, this play was presented in extended workshop production only. Papp never converted it to a commercial venture. The play is strongly reminiscent of *Desire under the Elms*. On a barren farm two brother vie for the land, the inheritance, the woman, and the future. The gloomy atmosphere of the play and the defeat the characters experience are intense. William Glover observed, "the intent seems to be a somber dissertation upon the unbreakable ties with which hate as well as love can bind people together." With this play Reardon continues his stylistic experiments: one of the contending brothers is a ghost who is visible on stage; the language is replete in lyricism. And he continues his thematic and structural explorations: the family is explored for the ties that truly bind it, and the play is conceived in a sequence of short scenes – several of which are compellingly powerful in performance.

The Leaf People opened the Booth Theatre season for Papp in the fall of 1975. It also lost money, and closed that entire noble adventure, cancelling the Broadway hopes for several writers. Yet the play remains an important one, as most critics understood. Clive Barnes reported, "It bombed with class. Mr. Reardon found a great theme, but made a wrong (if interesting) choice." Rarely has a failure inspired so much supportive press. Why? Clearly because the play was trying to do something important, and because the effort merited applause, if the performance did not. The O'Neill antecedents in the play are evident. A young rock singer goes on a pilgrimmage up the Amazon River (*Emperor Jones*) in quest of his father (*Mourning Becomes Electra*) who is a self-professed missionary from the Caucasian world, attempting to warn a stone-age tribe against encroaching "civilization." The Leaf People, exotic to the point of having a green man as a member of the tribe, speak Leafese, a language Reardon created, complete with etymology, syntax, and world-view. This is translated for the audience by two electronically amplified United Nations type of interpretors (shades of the linguistic explorations of *Strange Interlude*). The effect is to distance any emotional engagement (a parallel to the masks in *The Great God Brown*) and to make the audience's participation in the story, characters, or theme almost impossible. Reardon also explored something new in the American theatre. He attempted to fuse the world of rock music to that of theatre – not by laminating music to other materials (as in such pieces as *Your Own Thing*) – by structuring his play in imitaion of rock progressions, and by introducing rock songs as associative editorials upon the developing themes. This experiment is not commented upon by any of the critics of the production, through Reardon feels it is an important aspect of his play. Perhaps the integrated use of the music was obfuscated by the linguistic and structural eccentricities of the play.

Reardon is a playwright with one modest success and two failures. But his failures may prove more significant than other writers' successes, as they reveal a writer striving to come to terms with his medium – a writer with much to say, the skill with which to say it in dramatic terms, and the committment to say it in the American theatre. It can be hoped that when he has exorcized the theatrical demons (O'Neill among them) that seem to possess him at present, and when he can turn to writing honestly about what he knows closely, he may fulfill his promise.

—Thomas B. Markus

RECKORD, Barry. Jamaican. Born in Jamaica. Educated at Oxford University, 1952. Lived in London until 1970; now lives in Jamaica. Agent: International Creative Management, 40 West 57th Street, New York, New York 10019, U.S.A.

PUBLICATIONS

Plays

> *Adella* (produced London, 1954; revised version, as *Flesh to a Tiger*, produced London, 1958).
> *You in Your Small Corner* (produced Cheltenham, 1960; London, 1961).
> *Skyvers* (produced London, 1963).   Published in *New English Dramatists 9*, London, Penguin, 1966.
> *Don't Gas the Blacks* (produced London, 1969).
> *A Liberated Woman* (also director: produced New York, 1970; London, 1971).
> *Give the Gaffers Time to Love You* (produced London, 1973).
> *X* (produced London, 1974).   Incuded in *Skyvers*, 1977.
> *Skyvers* (includes *X*).   London, John Calder, 1977.

> Radio Play: *Malcolm X*, 1973.

> Television Plays: *In the Beautiful Caribbean*, 1972; *Club Havana*, 1975.

Other

> *Does Fidel Eat More Than Your Father: Conversations in Cuba.*   London, Deutsch, and New York, Praeger, 1971.

Theatrical Activities:

Director: **Play** – *A Liberated Woman*, New York, 1970.

*   *   *

Barry Reckord's studies of the effects of exploitation are thorough and broad-based. In his early play *Flesh to a Tiger* we are let in to the struggle of people in a Jamaican slum trying to emancipate themselves from superstition without falling under white domination. Della is a beautiful but poor woman, and her child is dying. She has to choose between the local "shepherd's" magic and the English doctor's medicine. Half-fearful of magic and half in love with the doctor, she encourages him only to be insulted in the end – for what he regards as his "weakness." She finally smothers the baby and stabs the shepherd.

But exploitation is basically a class evil, rather than a racial one, and Reckord illustrates this impressively in his most famous play, *Skyvers*, which is an authentic picture of students in a London comprehensive school just before they drop out. The beautifully preserved "cockney patter" is another triumph of the play. As with *Flesh to a Tiger*, it deals with the incipient violence which results from frustration and limited choice. The children are surrounded by parents and teachers who are social failures; and they dream about football stars, pop singers and big time criminals. Even if we deny that such schools are "invented" to suppress talent, the effect is the same. And the sight of "criminally ill-educated" uncertain boys suddenly acting with confidence and more than a hint of violence when they get together as a group should be a warning.

Having looked at exploitation of the group, Reckord now looks at the other side of the coin – liberation of the individual. First, in *Don't Gas the Blacks* he introduces a black lover to test the professed liberalism of a middle-class Hampstead couple, and succeeds in exposing the racialism of the one and in destroying the sexual fantasies of the white woman about the black man. In *A Liberated Woman*, the experiment is taken one stage further, where it is the husband who is black and the wife's lover white. Does the wife's liberation extend to her having a white lover?

Barry Reckord is also interested in establishing the link between social and economic exploitation and the obsession of blacks to ape white bourgeois values. The aping can be seen in a lighter vein as in *You in Your Small Corner*, where it is the black bourgeois family in Brixton who are the custodians of "culture." It is they who are educated, who "talk posh" and the English who are down-trodden and "common." The black mother (the successful owner of a club) doesn't want her son to get serious about the local girls, but to wait until he goes up to Cambridge where he will meet "people of his own class."

In his television play, though, *In the Beautiful Caribbean*, the mood is blacker. Nothing much seems to have changed in Jamaica since *Flesh to a Tiger* fourteen years earlier, except that now the class and race battles are fought to the death. The society does really seem to be in disintegration because of the many special interests hostile to each other. There's the American exploitation of bauxite, the drugs industry, the subordination of the black working classes by the black middle classes, unemployment, the generation gap and more.

This is not new in itself; what is new is the people's refusal to be abused indefinitely and this brings about the black power uprising. We trace this from One Son who is fired from his job as captain of a fishing boat, becomes interested in politics and starts selling a black power newspaper. He is thrown in jail, beaten and killed because the police think he knows where black power guns are hidden. His friend Jonathan, a barrister, and therefore middle-class, finally manages to forego white power temptations, and becomes a persuasive black power orator instead. And as so often happens, the end is bloodshed and defeat.

—E. A. Markham

REXROTH, Kenneth.   American.   Born in South Bend, Indiana, 22 December 1905. Educated at the Art Institute, Chicago; New School for Social Research, New York; New York Art Students League. Married Andree Dutcher in 1927 (died, 1940); Marie Kass, 1940 (divorced, 1948); Marthe Larsen, 1949 (divorced, 1961); has two children. Conscientious objector during World War II. Past occupations include farm worker, factory hand, insane asylum attendant. Painter: one-man shows held in Los Angeles, New York, Chicago, San Francisco, Paris. Columnist, *San Francisco Examiner*, 1958–68. Since 1953, San Francisco correspondent for *The Nation*, New York; since 1968, Columnist for *San Francisco Magazine*, and the *San Francisco Bay Guardian*. Since 1968, Lecturer, University of California, Santa Barbara. Recipient: Guggenheim Fellowship, 1948; Eunice Tietjens Award (*Poetry*, Chicago), 1957; Shelley Memorial Award, 1958; Amy Lowell Fellowship, 1958; National Institute of Arts and Letters grant, 1964; Academy of American Poets' Copernicus Award, 1975. Member, National Institute of Arts and Letters. Address: 1401 East Pepper Lane, Santa Barbara, California 93108, U.S.A.

PUBLICATIONS

Plays

> *Beyond the Mountains* (includes *Phaedra, Iphigenia, Hermaios, Berenike*) (produced New York, 1951).   New York, New Directions, and London, Routledge, 1951.

Verse

In What Hour.   New York, Macmillan, 1941.
The Phoenix and the Tortoise.   New York, New Directions, 1944.
The Art of Worldly Wisdom.   Prairie City, Illinois, Decker Press, 1949.
The Signature of All Things: Poems, Songs, Elegies, Translations, and Epigrams.   New York, New Directions, 1950.
The Dragon and the Unicorn.   New York, New Directions, 1952.
In Defence of the Earth.   New York, New Directions, 1956; London, Hutchinson, 1959.
The Homestead Called Damascus.   New York, New Directions, 1963.
Natural Numbers: New and Selected Poems.   New York, New Directions, 1963.
The Complete Collected Shorter Poems of Kenneth Rexroth.   New York, New Directions, 1967.
Penguin Modern Poets 9, with Denise Levertov and William Carlos Williams. London, Penguin, 1967.
The Collected Longer Poems of Kenneth Rexroth.   New York, New Directions, 1968.
The Heart's Garden, The Garden's Heart.   Cambridge, Massachusetts, Pym Randall Press, 1967.
The Spark in the Tinder of Knowing.   Cambridge, Massachusetts, Pym Randall Press, 1968.
Sky Sea Birds Trees Earth House Beasts Flowers.   Santa Barbara, California, Unicorn Press, 1970.
New Poems.   New York, New Directions, 1974.

Recording: *In the Cellar,* with Lawrence Ferlinghetti, Fantasy.

Other

Bird in the Bush: Obvious Essays.   New York, New Directions, 1959.
Assays (essays).   New York, New Directions, 1961.
An Autobiographical Novel.   New York, Doubleday, 1966.
Classics Revisited.   Chicago, Quadrangle Books, 1968.
The Alternative Society: Essays from the Other World.   New York, Herder, 1970.
With Eye and Ear (literary criticism).   New York, Herder, 1970.
American Poetry: In the Twentieth Century.   New York, Herder, 1971.
The Rexroth Reader, edited by Eric Mottram.   London, Cape, 1972.
The Elastic Retort: Essays in Literature and Ideas.   New York, Seabury Press, 1973.
Communalism: From Its Origins to the 20th Century,   New York, Seabury Press, and London, Peter Owen, 1975.

Editor, *Selected Poems,* by D. H. Lawrence.   New York, New Directions, 1948.
Editor, *The New British Poets: An Anthology.*   New York, New Directions, 1949.
Editor, *Four Young Women: Poems.*   New York, McGraw Hill, 1973.
Editor, *Tens: Selected Poems 1961–1971,* by David Meltzer,   New York, McGraw Hill Herder, 1973.
Editor, *The Selected Poems of Czeslav Milosz.*   New York, Seabury Press, 1973.

Translator, *Fourteen Poems,* by O. V. de L.-Milosz.   San Francisco, Peregrine Press, 1952.
Translator, *100 Poems from the Japanese.*   New York, New Directions, 1955.
Translator, *100 Poems from the Chinese.*   New York, New Directions, 1956.
Translator, *30 Spanish Poems of Love and Exile.*   San Francisco, City Lights Books, 1956.

Translator, *100 Poems from the Greek and Latin*.   Ann Arbor, University of Michigan Press, 1962.

Translator, *Poems from the Greek Anthology*.   Ann Arbor, University of Michigan Press, 1962.

Translator, *Selected Poems,* by Pierre Reverdy.   New York, New Directions, 1969; London, Cape, 1973.

Translator, *Love and the Turning Earth: 100 More Classical Poems*.   New York, New Directions, 1970.

Translator, *Love and the Turning Year: 100 More Chinese Poems*.   New York, New Directions, 1970.

Translator, *100 Poems from the French*.   Cambridge, Massachusetts, Pym Randall Press, 1970.

Translator, with Ling O. Chung, *The Orchid Boat: Women Poets of China*.   New York, Herder, 1972.

Translator, *100 More Poems from the Japanese*.   New York, New Directions, 1976.

*   *   *

A leading American poet, Kenneth Rexroth has drawn on classical prototypes for his limited dramatic output. *Beyond the Mountains*. a loosely knit tetralogy of short plays in flexible iambic meter, is based on the legends of Phaedra and the Atreidae. Taking a variety of liberties with the original plots and themes, Rexroth creates works that are rich in mythic archetypes and in poetry that makes extensive use of astronomic, animal, and sexual imagery reminiscent of the work of D. H. Lawrence and Robinson Jeffers. Rexroth's concern is with a formalized, symbolic rendering of his mystico-sexual views of love, transcendence, and history.

The philosophical themes of the tetralogy deal with an opposition between life viewed as a historically ordered series of events in which men are "marionettes of choice and consequence" and life viewed as capable of transcending necessity and circumstance by pure will and act growing from an equally pure erotic love. Most humans, Rexroth suggests, are caught in the "web of cause and effect"; very few, such as his Iphigenia, move directly to transcendence. Although Rexroth's poetry is the single most powerful element in these plays, his use of dramatic form and theatrical conventions is also noteworthy. Eschewing realism and psychological characterization, Rexroth employs a deliberately austere, highly stylized staging most nearly akin to the oriental or Yeatsian tradition. All the plays take place on a bare stage with the simplest indications of scenery and properties. The principal actors and chorus wear masks throughout, and locales are sketched on several screens. The action, too, is marked by symbolic convention: for example, the act of love is conveyed by stylized dance. The plot itself observes a cyclical pattern. The action begins with a fresh wave of barbarism (represented by Theseus' overcoming a decadent Minoan civilization), followed by the decisive turning point of the Trojan War and the eventual collapse of Greek civilization before new barbarian hordes, an event that Rexroth makes concurrent with the birth of Christ. Theatrically, Rexroth reinforces the cyclical pattern at the end of the last play by having the two leading actors (the surviving Greeks) assume the roles of the two-character chorus, a beggar and a prostitute, who had been on stage since the beginning of the action of the first play.

—Jarka M. Burian

RIBMAN, Ronald (Burt).   American.   Born in New York City, 28 May 1932. Educated at Brooklyn College, New York, 1950–51; University of Pittsburgh, B.B.A. 1954; M. Litt. 1958; Ph.D. 1962. Served in the United States Army, 1954–56. Married Alice Rosen in 1967;

has one son and one daughter. Assistant Professor of English, Otterbein College, Westerville, Ohio, 1962–63. Full–time Writer since 1963. Recipient: Obie Award, 1966; Rockefeller grant, 1966, 1975; Guggenheim Fellowship, 1970; National Endowment for the Arts grant, 1974; Creative Artists Public Service grant, 1976. Agent: Flora Roberts, 116 East 59th Street, New York, New York 10022. Address: 50 West 96th Street, New York, New York 10025, U.S.A.

PUBLICATIONS

Plays

> *Harry, Noon and Night* (produced New York, 1965).   Included in *The Journey of the Fifth Horse and Harry, Noon and Night*, 1967.
> *The Journey of the Fifth Horse,* based in part on *The Diary of a Superfluous Man* by Turgenev (produced New York, 1966; London, 1967).   Included in *The Journey of the Fifth Horse and Harry, Noon and Night*, 1967; London, Davis Poynter, 1974.
> *The Journey of the Fifth Horse and Harry Noon and Night: Two Plays.*   Boston, Little Brown, 1967.
> *The Final War of Olly Winter* (televised, 1967.)   Published in *Great Television Plays*, New York, Dell, 1969.
> *The Ceremony of Innocence* (produced New York, 1967).   New York, Dramatists Play Service, 1968.
> *Passing Through from Exotic Places* (includes *The Son Who Hunted Tigers in Jakarta, Sunstroke, The Burial of Esposito*) (produced New York, 1969).   New York, Dramatists Play Service, 1970.
> *The Most Beautiful Fish* (televised, 1969).   Published in *New York Times*, 23 November 1969.
> *Fingernails Blue as Flowers* (produced New York, 1971).   Published in *Plays of the American Place Theatre*. edited by Richard Shotter, New York, Dell, 1973.
> *A Break in the Skin* (produced New Haven, Connecticut, 1972; New York, 1973).
> *The Poison Tree* (produced Philadelphia, 1973; revised version, produced Philadelphia, 1975; New York, 1976).

Screenplay: *The Angel Levine*, with Bill Gunn, 1970.

Television Plays: *The Final War of Olly Winter*, 1967; *The Most Beautiful Fish*, 1969.

Bibliography: in *The Work of Ronald Ribman: The Poet as Playwright* by Susan H. Dietz, University of Pennsylvania, unpublished dissertation, 1974.

Manuscript Collection: New York Public Library.

Critical Studies: by Martin Gottfried, in *Women's Wear Daily* (New York) 6 May 1965, 22 April 1966, 23 December 1971; "Journey and Arrival of a Playwright" by Robert Brustein, in *New Republic* (Washington, D.C.), 7 May 1966; by Jack Gould, in *New York Times*, 30 January 1967, 12 June 1970; "Playwrights: The Inner Four" by Martin Gottfried, in *Vogue* (New York), July 1973.

*   *   *

Ronald Ribman is a difficult playwright to characterize. Although there are similarities among his plays, each of them has a voice of its own.

His first two plays – *Harry, Noon and Night* and *The Journey of the Fifth Horse* – are complicated, allusive, oblique. Although they make great demands on an audience, their vigor and inventiveness are directly appealing, their liveliness on stage unmistakable. They remain his best work for the theatre, even though as a newcomer to the stage, he tried things that a veteran dramatist would have avoided. For example, the repeated pronouns that bring down the act curtains of *Harry, Noon and Night*. At the end of Scene One (although the divisions are act length, Ribman calls them scenes), Harry is pointing to a character who is not there at all, an imaginary evocation of his brother, and shouting "Him! Him!" At the end of Scene Two when Harry's brother makes the toilet overflow, Immanuel, Harry's friend and room-mate, cries out, in triumph, "It's Harry's toilet! His! His!" At the end of the play, as Harry is carted off by the police, calling out his brother's name, Immanuel answers "*in a voice full of rage*": "Me, Harry. What about me? Me!" The use of the pronouns is a poet's trick (Ribman began as a poet), a verbal nicety that might well be missed in the theatre, but the important thing about those pronouns is their dramatic rightness; they belong in the mouths of the characters who speak them and, more than that, they identify the speaker's immediate relationship with one or both of the other main characters. I go on at length about so small a point because Ribman's usage here is symptomatic of the play of his mind as it is reflected in all of his work.

Underlying *Harry, Noon and Night* is a conventional psychological drama about a young man – a loser, "a failure clown" – perpetually in the shadow of his successful older brother. Yet, Harry can be victimizer as well as victim, and so can Immanuel, who routs the brother in Scene Two, but is himself the captive clown of Scene Three. Add the German setting with its references to the Nazis, and the play, which is very funny on the surface, becomes a black comedy with implications far beyond the standard character hidden in Harry. *The Journey of the Fifth Horse*, which grows out of Turgenev's *The Diary of a Superfluous Man* deals with two more failure clowns, Turgenev's hero and the publisher's reader who finally rejects his manuscript; the second character is only an ironic note in the original story, but Ribman creates him fully, his real and his fantasy lives, and lets him recognize and cry out against the identification he feels with the man whose diary he is reading.

With his television play, *The Final War of Olly Winter*, Ribman moved into direct social comment; it was the first of several specifically pacifist plays, which include *The Ceremony of Innocence* and the one-act *The Burial of Esposito*. There are heavy sentimental elements in both *Olly Winter* and *Esposito* which somewhat belie the tough-minded Ribman of the first two plays, but none of these works is a conventional propaganda play. *Ceremony*, for instance, is an historical drama which uses flashback scenes to explain why Ethelred will not come out of seclusion to defend England against the Danish invasion. He prefers to stand aside from a society which, mouthing the rhetoric of honor, chooses war over peace and special privilege over public welfare; still, his withdrawal is complicated by his attachment to the Danish princess – a personal, perhaps a sexual story underlying the political one – and by the fact that his refusal to fight "their" war involves a rejection of his own struggle as well.

Although *Break in the Skin*, a slapstick parable of sorts, and the short plays reflect Ribman's sense of dramatic invention, *The Poison Tree* is his most impressive work since *Fifth Horse*. It is also the play which best illustrates how difficult it is for a dramatist to walk the line between commitment and complexity. Set in prison, largely peopled by black convicts and white guards, the play can be – has been – taken as an explicit commentary on prison conditions and racial bigotry, in part because it uses stereotypes of the propaganda play and unashamedly goes for melodramatic effects. Yet behind the familiar surface, Ribman develops his titular metaphor, through which he shows all the characters as creatures of the situation, and unravels a confrontation plot in which the manipulative guard is revealed as his own victim. Although *The Poison Tree* may lack some of the richness of the early plays, it is further evidence that Ribman has no intention of simply settling into an attitude or a genre.

—Gerald Weales

RICHARDSON, Jack.   American.   Born in New York City, 18 February 1935. Educated at Columbia University, New York, B.A. 1952; University of Munich, 1958. Served in the United States Army, in France and Germany. Married Gail Roth in 1957; has one child. Recipient: Brandeis University Creative Arts Award, 1963. Address: c/o Dramatists Play Service, 440 Park Avenue South, New York, New York 10016, U.S.A.

PUBLICATIONS

Plays

The Prodigal (produced New York, 1960).   New York, Dutton, 1960.
Gallows Humor (produced New York, 1961; Edinburgh, 1964).   New York, Dutton, 1961.
Lorenzo (produced New York, 1963).
Xmas in Las Vegas (produced New York, 1965).   New York, Dramatists Play Service, 1966.
As Happy as Kings (produced New York, 1968).
Juan Feldman, in Pardon Me, Sir, But Is My Eye Hurting Your Elbow?, edited by Bob Booker and George Foster.   New York, Geis, 1968.

Novel

The Prison Life of Harris Filmore.   London, Eyre and Spottiswoode, 1961; Greenwich, Connecticut, New York Graphic Society, 1963.

*   *   *

At the outset of the 1960's four young playwrights, Edward Albee, Jack Richardson, Arthur Kopit, and Jack Gelber, held the attention of the American theatre as its best prospects for the future since the postwar emergence of Tennessee Williams and Arthur Miller. The four became acquainted, and in the season of 1962–63 at least they were simultaneously active in the Playwrights' Unit of Actors Studio in New York. Jack Richardson's particular position in this rather brilliant quartet was achieved by the success of two splendid plays produced off-Broadway, The Prodigal, his retelling in his own contemporary idiom of the Orestes story, and Gallows Humor, two linked tragicomic plays in a modern setting. In these plays Richardson stands apart from his three immediate contemporaries for certain defining characteristics unmistakably his own, characteristics that also mark his subsequent and somewhat parallel pair of Broadway plays, Lorenzo and Xmas in Las Vagas.
The plays, all vividly theatrical, are intentionally intellectual in the French tradition – somewhat unusual in American drama, although less so perhaps for a summa in philosophy from Columbia University – and for their almost neo-classical emphasis upon verbal precision and formal control. At the same time, the plays share a conscious concern for previous dramatic materials and conventions, classical, Medieval, Renaissance, and they are unified by Richardson's persistent and strongly-held view of the human predicament as man's forced participation in a destructive conflict between fundamental opposites: life, individuality, imaginative illusion but chaos on the one hand; or death, conformity, reality and order on the other.
The first pair of plays, The Prodigal and Gallows Humor, are written with an exhilarating wit and a Shavian exuberance hard to match in recent drama in English, and they are contrasting but complementary in method, with the classically inspired play modern by implication and the modern by Medieval allusion universal or timeless in intent. In the former play Richardson personifies his characteristic and paradoxically grouped opposites in

671

the figures of Aegisthus and Agamemnon, and in their conflicting views of man as either lesser or greater than he is Richardson also reflects Aristotle's definitions of comedy and tr ,gedy. Orestes, the perfect tragicomic hero, succeeds for a time in avoiding either view and the destructive oppositions Aegisthus and Agamemnon represent. He seeks instead to "walk along the shore" and adopts the detachment of "laughter." But this modern stance, interestingly prophetic of the disillusion of youth in the later 60's, proves a precarious stasis which cannot hold, and the murder of his father compels Orestes' participation in the battle of extremes he sought to avoid. The seeming inevitability of his decision is doubly reinforced in the play by the revenge theme of the myth itself and by the return motif of the Biblical reference to the prodigal son, and at the play's close Orestes identifies his own decision with the general fate of man:

> The sea will always roar with Electra's cry; the waters will always rush toward Agamemnon's vengeance. It will cleanse or wash away the earth entirely, but it will never change....I can resist these forces no longer. I will go back, murder, and say it's for a better world.

In *Gallows Humor* the two component plays are linked by their common theme and by the fact that each play exactly reverses the central characters, condemned and executioner, and the point of view of the other, and the effect of reversal is heightened by the appearance of the actors in the first play as their counterpart selves in the second. Walter, the condemned murderer, has a surprising passion for order and conformity, strives to keep his cell immaculate and to go to his death with his "number patch" in place. But in the last hours, at the imminence of death, he is seduced back toward a celebration of life, illusion, and chaos by the prison prostitute Lucy. In the second play, Phillip the executioner, properly "dressed in the trousers, shirt, and tie of his official uniform," has an irresistible attraction toward revolt and wishes for the coming solemnities "to dress up like a headsman from the Middle Ages" in "a black hood." But his cold and practical wife Martha reasons him back toward conformity and order. The hood, Lucy's face, like a "carnival mask," the essential brutality of the execution itself, and the appearance of Death from the old Moralities to deliver the Prologue, give the play its comparative time metaphor. Although modern appearances are confusing, and Death complains that it is now difficult for him to "tell the hangman from the hanged," Richardson's essential oppositions, life or death, order or disorder, conformity or individuality, illusion or reality, and hangman or hanged, are reasserted as Walter and Phillip, modern ambiguities to the contrary, do end up playing their destined roles.

To an extent *Lorenzo* is a Renaissance variation of *The Prodigal*, but with a special emphasis upon illusion and reality, and the gambling metaphor in *Xmas in Las Vegas*, with its insistence upon the either/or of winner and loser, repeats the executioner-condemned contraries of *Gallows Humor* in a zany world and manner reminiscent of Kaufman and Hart and *You Can't Take It with You*. Lorenzo, "director of the theatrical troupe 'Theatre of the First Dove,'" is caught up in the midst of a "small war of the Renaissance" in Italy, and like Orestes he tries vainly not to become involved in the destructive conflict of opposites, polarized here in the impractical Duke, Filippo, and his general, the realist Van Miessen. In *Xmas in Las Vegas* Wellspot is the inveterate gambler condemned to lose, and Olympus, the casino owner, is the financial executioner. Olympus, with his suggestion of the gods, gambling as fate or destiny, and the sacrificial connotations of Christmas all enlarge the dimension of this modern parable.

Although there are important contemporary influences and parallels in his work, Anouilh's wryly detached sense of humor, for example, Genet's concern with illusion, especially Genet's and Beckett's preoccupation with opposites, Richardson's plays (and it is their limiting strength) insist upon his own almost geometrically precise view of the human condition where everything is energized as it is drawn toward its opposite and toward its destruction, and it is this underlying and rather formulaic purity which initiates a sense of tragic inevitability beneath the comic facades of his plays.

—Gaynor F. Bradish

RIDLER, Anne (Barbara).   British.   Born in Rugby, Warwickshire, 30 July 1912. Educated at Downe House School; King's College, London, diploma in journalism 1932. Married Vivian Ridler in 1938; has four children. Member of the editorial department, Faber and Faber, publishers, London, 1935–40. Recipient: Oscar Blumenthal Prize, 1954, and Union League Civic and Arts Foundation Prize, 1955 (*Poetry*, Chicago). Address: 14 Stanley Road, Oxford, England.

PUBLICATIONS

Plays

> *Cain* (produced Letchworth, Hertfordshire, 1943; London, 1944).   London, Editions Poetry, 1943.
> *The Shadow Factory* (produced London, 1945).   London, Faber, 1946.
> *Henry Bly* (produced London, 1947).   Included in *Henry Bly and Other Plays,* 1950.
> *Henry Bly and Other Plays* (includes *The Mask* and *The Missing Bridegroom*).   London, Faber, 1950.
> *The Mask and The Missing Bridegroom* (produced London, 1951).   Included in *Henry Bly and Other Plays,* 1950.
> *The Trial of Thomas Cranmer,* music by Bryan Kelly (produced Oxford, 1956). London, Faber, 1956.
> *The Departure,* music by Elizabeth Maconchy (produced London, 1961).   Included in *Some Time After and Other Poems,* 1972.
> *Who Is My Neighbour?* (produced Leeds, 1961).   Included in *Who Is My Neighbour? and How Bitter the Bread,* 1963.
> *Who Is My Neighbour? and How Bitter the Bread.*   London, Faber, 1963.
> *The Jesse Tree: A Masque in Verse,* music by Elizabeth Maconchy (produced Dorchester, Oxfordshire, 1970).   London, Lyrebird Press, 1972.
> *Rosinda,* translation of the libretto by Faustini, music by Cavalli (produced Oxford, 1973; London, 1975.
> *Orfeo,* translation of the libretto by Striggio, music by Monteverdi (produced Oxford, 1975).
> *Eritrea,* translation of the libretto by Faustini, music by Cavalli (produced Wexford, Ireland, 1975).   London, Oxford University Press, 1976.
> *The King of the Golden River,* music by Elizabeth Maconchy (produced Oxford, 1975)

Verse

> *Poems.*   London, Oxford University Press, 1939.
> *A Dream Observed and Other Poems.*   London, Editions Poetry, 1941.
> *The Nine Bright Shiners.*   London, Faber, 1943.
> *The Golden Bird and Other Poems.*   London, Faber, 1951.
> *A Matter of Life and Death.*   London, Faber, 1959.
> *Selected Poems.*   New York, Macmillan, 1961.
> *Some Time After and Other Poems.*   London, Faber, 1972.

Other

> *Olive Willis and Downe House: An Adventure in Education.*   London, Murray, 1967.

> Editor, *Shakespeare Critism, 1919–1935.*   London and New York, Oxford University Press, 1936.

Editor, *The Little Book of Modern Verse.*   London, Faber, 1941.

Editor, *Best Ghost Stories.*   London, Faber, 1945.

Editor, *The Faber Book of Modern Verse,* revised edition.   London, Faber, 1951.

Editor, *The Image of the City and Other Essays,* by Charles Williams.   London, Oxford University Press, 1958.

Editor, *Shakespeare Criticism, 1935–1960.*   London and New York, Oxford University Press, 1963.

Editor, *Poems and Some Letters,* by James Thomson.   London, Centaur Press, and Urbana, University of Illinois Press, 1963.

Editor, *Thomas Traherne: Poems, Centuries and Three Thanksgivings.*   London, Oxford University Press, 1966.

Editor, with Christopher Bradby, *Best Stories of Church and Clergy.*   London, Faber, 1966.

Critical Study: *The Christian Tradition in Modern British Verse Drama* by William V. Spanos, New Brunswick, New Jersey, Rutgers University Press, 1967.

Anne Ridler comments:

It is a great advantage for a dramatist to know the cast and place he is writing for, the audience he is addressing. Only rarely have I had this opportunity, and this is perhaps why *Thomas Cranmer*, commissioned for performance in the church where Cranmer was tried, has been judged my best play.

Writing words for music, however, gives a rare opportunity for a contemporary poet to use his particular talents in the theatre, and it is in this field (whether by original words, or fitting a translation to a musical line) that I prefer to work at present. Libretto-writing, as W. H. Auden said, gives the poet his one chance nowadays of using the high style.

*   *   *

Anne Ridler's plays form part of the revival in blank-verse drama which began with T. S. Eliot's *Murder in the Cathedral*, and flourished immediately after the war during Martin Browne's tenure of the Mercury Theatre, Notting Hill.

The Shadow Factory was produced at the Mercury in 1945 and shows the influence of Orwell in its preoccupation with social issues and in its use of fable. The workers in Mrs. Ridler's play have become dehumanised by the tedium of their routine until they are almost part of the machine.

> You can hardly tell where the drill ends
> And the hands begin.

An artist is commissioned to paint a mural celebrating the factory but he is appalled by the quality of life there and undertakes the work only on condition that he is given a free hand and that no one sees the picture until it is finished. At Christmas the mural is unveiled; it depicts the managing director as a blind face behind a mask, playing a game of chess in which the workers are pawns. The director is at first furious but he accepts the truth of the satire after he has taken part in a nativity play, an experience which draws the whole factory together and restores harmony. The painting is allowed to stand and the artist is commissioned to create a second, more positive, view of industry.

The theme of *The Shadow Factory* is unconvincingly stated because of its implausible ending. In subsequent plays, Mrs. Ridler abandons this uneasy blend of realism and religious allegory and uses folklore as the vehicle for her ideas. *The Mask* is based on a Somerset folksong and describes the triumph of love over narcissism. *Henry Bly,* one of her most successful pieces, is a retelling of a Grimm's fairy tale, "Brother Lustig." It is the story of a likeable rogue who secures himself a place in heaven by a spontaneous act of kindness to an old tramp. The tramp is a miracle worker, a Christ figure, who pursues Bly for the rest of his life, hounding him to salvation. The verse in this play fully justifies itself as the appropriate medium of dramatic expression for a modern Everyman.

The Trial of Thomas Cranmer was written in commemoration of the 400th anniversary of the Archbishop's martyrdom. It is an imaginative reconstruction of history. Cranmer's fear of the fire is real enough; he is an old man and there is much pathos in his farewell to his wife and his ritual disrobing from the office of Archbishop. Nevertheless, the play celebrates human courage and faith. Cranmer turns on his inquisitors with calm assurance.

> Your voices seem like the nattering of grasshoppers
> On a summer afternoon. Thank God. For I trust
> In his love.

This is surely the best of Mrs. Ridler's plays and a perfect subject for a writer whose theme is often suffering but never despair.

—Judith Cooke Simmons

RUDKIN, (James) David. British. Born in London, 29 June 1936. Educated at King Edward's School, Birmingham, 1947–55; St. Catherine's College, Oxford, 1957–61, M.A. in mods and greats 1961. Served for two years with the Royal Corps of Signals. Married Sandra Thompson in 1967. Assistant Master of Latin, Greek and music, County High School, Bromsgrove, Worcestershire, 1961–64. Recipient: *Evening Standard* award, 1962; John Whiting Award, 1974. Agent: Margaret Ramsay Ltd, 14a Goodwin's Court, London WC2N 4LL, England.

PUBLICATIONS

Plays

  Afore Night Come (produced Oxford, 1960; London, 1962). Included in *New English Dramatists 7,* London, Penguin, 1963; published separately, New York, Grove Press, 1963.
  Moses and Aaron, translation of the libretto, music by Schoenberg (produced London, 1965). London, Friends of Covent Garden, 1965.
  The Grace of Todd, music by Gordon Crosse (produced Aldeburgh, Suffolk, and London, 1969). London, Oxford University Press, 1970.
  Burglars (produced London, 1970). Published in *Prompt Two,* edited by Alan Durband, London, Hutchinson, 1976.
  The Filth Hunt (produced London, 1972).
  Cries from Casement as His Bones Are Brought to Dublin (broadcast, 1973; produced London, 1973). London, BBC Publications, 1974.
  Ashes (produced London, 1974; Los Angeles, 1976). London, French, 1976.

Penda's Fen (televised, 1974).   London, Davis Poynter, 1975.
No Title (produced Birmingham, 1974).
The Sons of Light (produced Newcastle upon Tyne, 1976).

Screenplays (additional dialogue, uncredited): *Fahrenheit 451*, 1964; *Mademoiselle*, 1966.

Radio Plays: *No Accounting for Taste*, 1960; *The Persians*, from the play by Aeschylus, 1965; *Gear Change*, 1967; *Cries from Casement as His Bones Are Brought to Dublin*, 1973; *Hecuba*, from the play by Euripides, 1975.

Television Plays: *The Stone Dance*, 1963; *Children Playing*, 1967; *House of Character*, 1968; *Blodwen, Home from Rachel's Marriage*, 1969; *Bypass*, 1972; *Atrocity*, 1973; *Penda's Fen*, 1974; *Pritan* and *The Coming of the Cross* (in *Churchill's People* series), 1975; *The Ash Tree*, from the story by M. R. James, 1975.

Ballet Scenario: *Sun into Darkness*, 1966.

Theatrical Activities:

Director (amateur): **Plays** – *The Dance of Death* by Strindberg, Oxford, 1959; *Hay Fever* by Noël Coward, Birmingham, 1962; *The Birthday Party* by Harold Pinter, Birmingham, 1962; *King Lear*, Bromsgrove, 1966; *Black Mass* by Edward Bond, Bromsgrove, 1972; *The Maids* by Jean Genet, Bromsgrove, 1972.

Actor (amateur): **Plays** – Foigard in *The Beaux' Strategem* by Farquhar, 1964, Father Barre in *The Devils* by John Whiting, 1965, Feste in *Twelfth Night*, 1965, Dionysos in *The Bacchae* by Euripides, 1966, and Cornwall in *King Lear*, 1966 – all at Bromsgrove; Voltaire in *Marat-Sade* by Peter Weiss, Shrewsbury, 1973.

*   *   *

David Rudkin comes from a decidedly unlikely background for a writer who makes his mark first, and spectacularly, in the theatre. He was born in 1936 into a family of very strict evangelical Christians who regarded the theatre as a home of sin (with the grudging exception of Shakespeare) and never allowed him to go the plays, or even to films. As a teenager he became totally obsessed with music, and did not discover the theatre until he was at university. The real revelation came when he saw Pinter's *The Birthday Party*, and heavily under its influence he wrote "a blatant imitation" (unproduced). His first produced work was a short Kafkaesque fantasy for radio, *No Accounting for Taste*, about a firm of accountants run by three unseen partners who prove to be one man, and the mysterious fate of secretaries who stay on to work late at the office. After which came *Afore Night Come* in 1962.

This was produced by the Royal Shakespeare Company during an experimental season they held at the small, private Arts Theatre Club. It instantly made Rudkin's a name to conjure with, and was accepted as the most successful example in British theatre of Theatre of Cruelty as practised in France by Jean Genet. Actually, any similarity was probably coincidental: the play's antecedents could more likely be found in the novels of Thomas Hardy and D. H. Lawrence, and in the preoccupation with the "dark gods" of English writers like John Cowper Powys and a whole school of supernaturalists. The play takes place on a fruit farm somewhere in the Midlands, on the grimy fringe of industry, and the action works its way slowly but inexorably towards a ritual human sacrifice, carried out under the sinister, hovering presence of a crop-spraying helicopter, which becomes in spirit one of the dark gods impassively surveying the puny manoeuvers of mere mortals to placate them.

The effect of the play's climax is all the more startling because of the cunning way we are led into it, with an accumulation of coarse rustic humour and Zolaesque naturalistic detail: Rudkin makes us accept the seeming unreality of his conclusion as literal truth by establishing himself first of all in our minds as a scrupulous observer of things as they really are. His first television play, *The Stone Dance* (1963), worked in the same way, with dark forces as a living presence in Cornwall while the son of a fanatical itinerant preacher fights for his life and his sanity against the bigotry which surrounds him.

Of Rudkin's later plays for television, some quite short and slight, two stand out. *Children Playing* introduces us to the closed world of a group of children on holiday, subjects them to menace from two sinister young men who move in on their youth hostel, and shows how they deal with the outsiders. The pawky humour of the children's speech and fresh, unhackneyed characterisation in lighter moments show a side to Rudkin's talents not previously suspected. *House of Character* is another private-world play, this time a very strange piece showing us a series of happenings from the point of view of the person they happen to, who proves eventually to be mad, so that everything we have seen (the new home, the strange neighbours, the unexplained details) proves to be the gradually failing attempts of his deluded mind to come to terms with and make "normal" the external facts of his confinement in a lunatic asylum.

Rudkin's plays for television are absolutely of a piece with his stage work, and the best of his television plays are of scarcely less density and seriousness, but convention somehow dictates that television is less considered and less intellectually respectable than even a very marginal stage production, and regarded as an instantly dispensable form of writing. Rudkin tended, therefore, to be forgotten or regarded as to all intents and purposes inactive while he was being produced exclusively on television. Various possibilities of return to the London stage were frustrated, and he definitively returned to notice only with his full-length, more or less autobiographical play *Ashes*, first produced in 1974 and given another, more prestigious production two years later. This is a long, anguished study of a marriage breaking down, more or less unrelieved in its blackness and bringing in, with dubious dramatic relevance, the husband's complex and ambiguous reactions to the recent problems of Northern Ireland – in a way, perhaps, that has more to do with Rudkin's personal involvement in Anglo-Irish relations than with what can reasonably be managed within the confines of one play. Nevertheless, the play is a major achievement, with two big roles which offer opportunities actors obviously revel in, and it has had the admirable effect of putting Rudkin back where he belongs, in the centre of serious critical attention.

—John Russell Taylor

RYGA, George. Canadian. Born in Deep Creek, Alberta, in July 1932. Married; has five children. Worked on farms, in construction, and for a radio station in Edmonton. Full-time Writer since 1962. Address: R.R.2, Summerland, British Columbia V0H 1Z0, Canada.

PUBLICATIONS

Plays

Indian (televised, 1962; produced Winnipeg, 1974). Included in *The Ecstasy of Rita Joe and Other Plays*, 1971.

Nothing But a Man (produced Vancouver, 1966).

The Ecstasy of Rita Joe (produced Vancouver, 1967; Washington, D.C., 1973; London,
    1975).   Vancouver, Talonbooks, 1970.

Grass and Wild Strawberries (produced Vancouver, 1969).   Included in *The Ecstasy of
    Rita Joe and Other Plays, 1971.*

The Ecstasy of Rita Joe and Other Plays (includes *Indian* and *Grass and Wild
    Strawberries*), edited by Brian Parker.   Toronto, New Press, 1971.

Captives of a Faceless Drummer, music and lyrics by George Ryga (produced
    Vancouver, 1971).   Vancouver, Talonbooks, 1972.

Sunrise on Sarah, music by George Ryga (produced Banff, 1972).   Vancouver,
    Talonbooks, 1973.

A Portrait of Angelica (produced Banff, 1973).   Included in *Country and Western*,
    1976.

A Feast of Thunder, music by Morris Surdin (produced 1973).

Paracelsus, in *Canadian Theatre Review* (Toronto), Fall 1974.

Twelve Ravens for the Sun, music by Mikis Theodorakis (produced 1975).

Ploughmen of the Glacier (produced Vancouver, 1976).   Included in *Country and
    Western*, 1976.

Seven Hours to Sundown (produced Edmonton, 1976).   Included in *Country and
    Western*, 1976.

Country and Western (includes *A Portrait of Angelica, Ploughmen of the Glacier, Seven
    Hours to Sundown*).   Vancouver, Talonbooks, 1976.

Radio Plays: *A Touch of Cruelty*, 1961; *Half-Caste*, 1962; *Masks and Shadows*, 1963;
Bread Route, 1963; *Departures*, 1963; *Ballad for Bill*, 1963; *The Stone Angel*, 1965;
Miners, Gentlemen, and Other Hard Cases series, 1974–75; *Seasons of a Summer Day*,
1975; *Advocates of Danger* series, 1976.

Television Plays: *Indian*, 1962; *The Storm*, 1962; *Bitter Grass*, 1963; *For Want of
Something Better to Do*, 1963; *The Tulip Garden*, 1963; *Two Soldiers*, 1963; *The Pear
Tree*, 1963; *Man Alive*, 1965; *The Kamloops Incident*, 1965; *A Carpenter by Trade*
(documentary), 1967; *The Manipulators* series (2 scripts), 1968; *The Name of the Game*
series (1 script), 1969; *Ninth Summer*, 1972; *The Mountains* (documentary), 1973; *The
Ballad of Iwan Lepa* (documentary), 1976.

Novels

Hungry Hills.   Toronto, Longman, 1963; London, Joseph, 1965.
Ballad of a Stone-Picker.   Toronto, Macmillan, and London, Joseph, 1966.
Night Desk.   Vancouver, Talonbooks, 1976.

Critical Study: *Four Canadian Playwrights* by Mavor Moore, Toronto, Holt Rinehart, 1973.

                                *   *   *

Canada is an amorphous country, lacking a myth of national significance. George Ryga
has seen that the vacuum existing because of this is, in a way, the negative "myth" of
Canada. Possibly his own Ukrainian background has been helpful in developing his sense of
the displaced and isolated person in an alien society. In each of his stage plays he examines
the values of this individual against those of the society which has alienated him.

In his first play, *Indian*, Ryga starts by seeming to "stack the cards" against his protagonist,
whom he calls anonymously "Indian," making him drunken, undependable, and lazy, all the
sins white society conventionally attributes to Indians. Gradually, through a series of non-

sequential anecdotes, memories, and fantasies, interwoven with contemporary incident, the tragedy of the Indian's life emerges, climaxing in the account of his murdering his brother. With great subtlety Ryga shows that the source of the crime lies in the white man's cowardice and refusal to recognize the humanity and hence equality of the Indians. The murder becomes an act of mercy by Indian; and his other failings, against which white society fulminates, are seen as the despair of a degraded and dehumanized people.

Ryga sets the play in "stark non-country," grey, horizonless distance, which can symbolize Indian's non-life while at the same time representing his real world in a bare and desolate land, where he does exhausting, mindless, ill-paid work. It is this creation of the simultaneously realistic and symbolic in both "situation" and design of this play that heralds Ryga's technique in all the plays that follow.

In *Nothing But a Man* a young poet singing a ballad about the murder of Garcia Lorca is challenged as a romantic by a middle-aged man objecting from the audience. It is a slighter and less successful play than *Indian*, but of interest for its concern with the polarities of myth and reality, artist and worker, youth and age, and its balancing of lyrical ballad effects against discursive argument and the theatre's sense of real "presence."

The same themes and techniques are enlarged in *The Ecstasy of Rita Joe*, where the setting becomes totally non-realistic, and a mingling of past and present through memory, flashback, and fantasy in an associative rather than logical sequence forms the structure of the whole play. The stage directions describing a circular ramp with a cyclorama, no permanent "props," and either general highlighting or localizing spots, give great fluidity to the play. It moves from a brief realistic scene of Rita Joe before the magistrate, into her mind, mingling her six other appearances in magistrates' court with her memories of her father and sister, her childhood, incidents with Mr. Homer, and happy moments with her lover, Jamie Paul. The attitudes of the audience (white society), variously represented by Father Andrew, Mr. Homer, and the Magistrate, grow progressively more antagonistic, until the Magistrate denounces Rita Joe as a social "leper" (like Indian). The murderers, handled rather allegorically, are only faintly adumbrated at the outset, and become clearer with each successive, though brief, appearance, until at the moment when Rita Joe becomes a complete outcast (the Magistrate's accusing her of being a VD carrier), they rape and kill her. Just as the climax of *Indian* is marked by the paradox of a murder which is also an apotheosis, so in this play Rita Joe's death is her "ecstasy." Rejection by white society for her refusal to accept a non-human or degraded status results in a murder which Ryga shows as martyrdom.

The use of dance and ballad-singing as an integral part of the text, seen first in Ryga's previous play, *Nothing But a Man*, is developed ironically in *Ecstasy* where the singer functions contrapuntally with Rita Joe. The songs, naive and romantically sad, are juxtaposed to the incidents of Rita Joe's real life. The contrast points up the ignorance of even sympathetic white people and renders the true horror more acutely.

In *Grass and Wild Strawberries*, written the year after *Ecstasy*, there is even greater use of song and dance, though here, in keeping with the hippy culture which the play examines, they are used as a straight, rather than ironical, addition to the text. Again Ryga is concerned with the alienated in society, lining up the establishment against the rebel. Interestingly, it is the 30's left-wing socialist, Uncle Ted, who in this play represents the "established," as opposed to the hippies – Captain Nevada and Susan and the "chorus." The artist, Allan, is a searcher who finds drugs, vague mysticism, and non-commitment as empty as the dogma of the left, and ultimately effects a synthesis of the best of both, symbolized by the freedom of the artist's vision, which is at the same time socially and morally aware.

Technically this play continues many of the devices of the earlier ones: it uses the non-chronological episode as exposition, and again the burden of the play is moral rather than psychological. In a series of brief scenes (some only a few lines long) with non-realistic settings, the playwright focuses on the deeply felt but scarcely articulated incident in a character's life. What is new in *Grass* is Ryga's use of media – news film and recorded sound effects – to fill in history and create an environment for the non-action of the play. The folk singer of *Nothing* and *Ecstasy* here becomes a vocal group and foreshadows the chorus of Ryga's next play.

Captives of a Faceless Drummer takes as its basis the political kidnappings by the *Front de la Liberation Quebecois* (FLQ) in Montreal. It uses the technical resources of *Ecstasy*, but with the greater economy of *Indian*. And as with Indian, who is irresponsible and drunken, Ryga makes his underdogs, the FLQ members, ignorant, fanatical, and occasionally childish. At the outset most of the audience sympathy is felt for Harry, the captive, who seems decent and civilized compared with Marcel, his jailor, whose sole motive for joining the *Front* appears self-aggrandizing. However, under the pitiless probing of the guerillas' Commander, the feebleness and hypocrisy of established society represented by Harry begin to show. The Commander is even more pitiless with his own cause, recognizing the impotence of the movement and the fact that he is more a captive than Harry. (Unlike Indian, who never reaches the glory of a name, the title "Commander" is not for anonymity but for superiority, as Ryga gradually makes clear.) As a tragic hero, the Commander is fully aware of the choice he has made and actively seeks his own destruction. Like Rita Joe, his death is an apotheosis. When he offers the gun to Harry, he grants him the vision of truth that Harry, entrusted with the security and hypocrisy of established society, and enfeebled by lethargy, has never been able to see. Though Harry walks away with his rescuers, the Commander's tragic triumph is clear when it is through Harry's mouth that the Commander's death screams issue, in a way rather like the situation i Albee's *Zoo Story*.

The staging effects which create the breadth an fluidity of *Ecstasy* and *Grass* are reversed in *Captives* to achieve the claustrophobia of a single locked room. Even the flashbacks, which produce openness in the earlier plays, contribute to the sense of Harry's captivity by the memory characters constantly running against the invisible wall that separates them from Harry. The narrow focus in this play greatly intensifies its dramatic power, and marks a return to the simplicity of *Indian* from the diffuse theatricality of *Grass*.

This movement towards simplicity is continued in *Sunrise on Sarah*. a psychological monodrama of a still young, but aging and frustrated teacher. It consists solely of her reveries and reflections as, ready for bed, she begins brushing her hair when the play opens and completes it by the final curtain. Characters from her past along with figures of her imagination drift through, establishing less of a plot than a case history, with all the jerks and gaps that this implies. The play's only serious defect is that Sarah is too solidly stereotyped, with no individually vivifying personal details or presentation.

Ryga's recent play, *Paracelsus*, is clearly influenced by Brecht in theme, and retains many of his earlier techniques in lighting, use of multiple stages, and radical shifts in time scheme. It is these shifts from the medieval plot to the modern subplot which give the play its rhythm and point up the central irony. Unfortunately, the language of the medieval sections is "poeticized," resulting often in bombast. In *Paracelsus*, genius is shown to be persecuted and rejected as much as the ignorant social non-entities of his previous plays. Ryga's chief concern throughout all of his work is with the reductions of mankind – outcasts, often poverty-stricken, diseased, ignorant – but human beings suffering discrimination, humiliated by charity, demanding something better than condescension or contempt. His protagonists choose evil with eyes wide open, more aware of the opposite good than the merely lukewarm and conventionally pious are. And out of the nothingness of these unheroic heroes, Ryga creates a genuine mythology.

—Dorothy Parker

SACKLER, Howard.   American.   Born in New York City, 19 December 1929. Educated at Brooklyn College, New York, B.A. 1950. Married Greta Lynn Lungren in 1963; has two children. Director, Caedmon records, New York, 1953–68. Recipient: Rockefeller grant,

1953; Littauer Foundation grant, 1954; Maxwell Anderson Award, 1954; Sergel Award, 1959; Pulitzer Prize, 1969; New York Drama Critics Circle Award, 1969; Tony Award, 1969. Agent: ICM, 8899 Beverly Boulevard, Los Angeles, California, U.S.A. Address: Sta. Eulalia del Rio, Ibiza, Spain.

PUBLICATIONS

Plays

> *Uriel Acosta* (produced Berkeley, California, 1954).
> *Mr. Welk and Jersey Jim* (produced New York, 1960).   Included in *A Few Enquiries.* 1970.
> *The Yellow Loves* (produced Chicago, 1960).
> *A Few Enquiries* (produced Boston, 1965).   Included in *A Few Enquiries, 1970.*
> *The Nine O'Clock Mail* (televised, 1965; produced Boston, 1967).   Included in *A Few Enquiries, 1970.*
> *The Pastime of Monsieur Robert* (produced London, 1966).
> *The Great White Hope* (produced Washington, D.C., 1967; New York, 1968).   New York, Dial Press, 1968; London, Faber, 1971.
> *A Few Enquiries* (includes *Sarah, The Nine O'Clock Mail, Mr. Welk and Jersey Jim, Skippy*).   New York, Dial Press, 1970.

Screenplays: *Desert Padre* (documentary), 1950; *Killer's Kiss,* 1952; *Fear and Desire,* 1953; *A Midsummer Night's Dream,* adaption of Czech version, 1961; *The Great White Hope,* 1970; *Bugsy,* 1973; *Jaws II,* 1976.

Television Play: *The Nine O'Clock Mail,* 1965 (Canada).

Verse

> *Want My Shepherd: Poems.*   New York, Caedmon Publishers, 1954.

Manuscript Collection: University of Texas, Austin.

Critical Study: Introduction by Martin Gottfried to *A Few Enquiries, 1970.*

Theatrical Activities:

Director: **Plays** − *King John,* New York, 1953; *The Family Reunion* by T. S. Eliot, New York, 1954; *Women of Trachis* by Sophocles, New York, 1954; *Purgatory* and *The Words upon the Windowpane* by Yeats, New York, 1955; *Hamlet,* Dublin, 1957; *Krapp's Last Tape* by Samuel Beckett, Ireland and European tour, 1960; *Chin-Chin* by François Billetdoux, London, 1960; *Suzanna Andler* by Marguerite Duras, Guildford, Surrey, 1971, 1972, London, 1973; *The Duchess of Malfi* by Webster, Los Angeles, 1976. **Film** − *A Midsummer Night's Dream,* English version, 1961. **Television** − *Shakespeare: Soul of an Age,* 1964.

*   *   *

Written in a rapid, tumbling free verse, Howard Sacker's *The Great White Hope* is clearly designed as an epic − a big play on a big subject, turbulent race relations in America as reflected in the rise and fall of a Black world heavyweight champion. The play is not equal to its subject; its points are made easily, and all its color and pageantry cannot disguise the threadbare intellectual conception which is its central impulse. As a metaphor for Black-White hostilities, the prize fight ring is sure-fire but facile.

Sackler's Jack Jefferson wants to play the game his own way. He doesn't want to be the symbolic victor for his oppressed people; if he wins, he wins for himself. He doesn't want to live according to the law of either White man or Black: he flaunts his white girlfriend; he rejects his too-Black former girlfriend; he sets up a speakeasy business; he's loud, violent, in trouble with the law. But for all his stature and his heroic determination, Jefferson is defeated by his opponents – the machinery of the white establishment. After his initial victory, his triumphant defeat of the great White hope, Jefferson is thwarted, hounded, challenged by group power against which his loudly proclaimed and insisted-upon independence proves insufficient. He leaves America only to meet repeated defeats abroad, and he winds up, rock-bottom at a German café where he enacts a burlesque version of *Uncle Tom's Cabin*. His only escape is to agree to a fixed fight; in return for his agreed-upon defeat, he receives a considerable lightening of his sentence (a trumped-up charge in the first place).

Jefferson is a towering character, and Sackler has outfitted him with salty, earthy, "ethnic" dialogue. But the frame in which Sackler has placed his character is not nearly so capacious as the character himself. The playwright has used his character in the service of a standard liberal tract that bears all the marks of apologetic White liberal guilt. The play offers nothing remotely new about elemental tensions between White and Black; it settles instead for clichés of Black pride and Black sexual superiority to repressed and therefore vindictive Whites. Sackler's sources are historical, but none the less he has made Jefferson's defeat too neat a thing; his indictment of avaricious whites and his sympathy for oppressed Blacks are altogether too schematic. The play has visceral impact (given its subject, it could hardly fail in this) but it is never searching enough to compel our full intellectual commitment.

After the popular success enjoyed by *The Great White Hope*, Sackler published, under the collective title, *A Few Enquiries*, four one-act plays which he had written about ten years earlier. The plays suggest no real connection to the flamboyant epic that was to follow except, perhaps, in their theatricality, and in their interest in dialect and period. *Sarah* is set backstage at a Victorian ballet company; *Mr. Welk and Jersey Jim* takes place in a dilapidated turn-of-the-century law office; *Skippy* is set in a liquor store run by a husband and wife who might have stepped out of Bernard Malamud's *The Assistant*; significantly, the one unaccented and contemporary play, *The Nine O'Clock Mail*, is the least flavorful and the least convincing.

The plays share loose thematic connections. The characters are engaged in quests; they want either to discover more about each other or to resolve unsettling puzzles, and their "enquiries" are treated as rituals. In *Sarah*, the characters re-enact the mysterious circumstances surrounding a ballerina's death by fire; in *The Nine O'Clock Mail*, a compulsive man makes a ritual of waiting for the mail as his neglected wife tries to no avail to reason with him; in *Mr. Welk and Jersey Jim*, a lawyer rehearses his foolish and guilty client in ways of gaining sympathy in court; and in *Skippy*, a wife discovers her husband's long-withheld secret of his responsibility for the death of his kid brother. Sackler's manner in these plays is pleasing elliptical. His style is realism heightened by theatrical proportions. These four short plays are modest enough, inconsequential enough, but they hint of thematic complexities that make them more tantalizing and more promising than the bloated and oversimplified pageant of *The Great White Hope*.

—Foster Hirsch

<hr>

SAINER, Arthur.   American.   Born in New York City, 12 September 1924. Educated at Washington Square College, New York University (John Golden Award, 1946), 1942–46,

B.A. 1946; Columbia University, New York, 1947–48, M.A. in philosophy 1948. Married
Stefanie Janis in 1956 (divorced, 1962). New York Editor, *TV Guide* magazine, New York,
1956–61; Film Critic, *Show Business Illustrated* magazine, Chicago, 1961; Founding Editor,
Ikon Magazine, New York, 1967. Book Critic since 1961, Book Editor, 1962, and Drama
Critic, 1961–65 and since 1969, *Village Voice,* New York. Member of the English
Department, C.W. Post College, Brookville, New York, 1963–67; Member of the Drama
Department, Bennington College, Vermont, 1967–69; Instructor in the Fiction Workshop,
Chatauqua Writers' Workship, New York, 1969. Since 1971, Member of the Academic
Council and Programme Advisor, Campus-Free College, Boston. Co-Producer, The Bridge
Theatre, New York, 1965–66. Recipient: Office for Advanced Drama Research grant, 1967.
Agent: Ellen Levine, Curtis Brown Ltd., 60 East 56th Street, New York, New York 10022.
Address: 79 Sullivan Street, New York, New York 10012 U.S.A.

PUBLICATIONS

Plays

The Bitch of Waverly Place (produced New York, 1964).
The Game of the Eye (produced Bronxville, New York, 1964).
The Day Speaks But Cannot Weep (produced Bronxville, New York, and New York
    City, 1965).
The Blind Angel (produced New York, 1965).
Untitled Chase (produced New York, 1965).
God Wants What Men Want (also director: produced New York, 1966).
The Bombflower (also director: produced New York, 1966).
The Children's Army Is Late (produced Brookville, New York, 1967; New York City,
    1974).
The Thing Itself (produced Minneapolis, 1967; New York, 1972).   Published in
    Playwrights for Tomorrow: A Collection of Plays, Volume 6, edited by Arthur H. Ballet,
    Minneapolis, University of Minnesota Press, 1969.
Noses (produced New York, 1967).
OM: A Sharing Service (produced Boston, 1968).
Boat Sun Cavern (produced Bennington, Vermont, 1969).
Van Gogh (produced New York, 1970).
I Piece Smash (produced New York, 1970).   Published in The Scene/2 (Plays from Off-
    Off-Broadway), edited by Stanley Nelson, New York, The Smith/New Egypt, 1974.
I Hear It Kissing Me, Ladies (produced New York, 1970).
Images of the Coming Dead (produced New York, 1971).
The Celebration: Jooz/Guns/Movies/The Abyss (produced New York, 1972).
Go Children Slowly (produced New York, 1973).
The Spring Offensive (produced New York, 1974).
Charley Chestnut Rides the I.R.T., music by Arthur Sainer (produced New York, 1975).
Day Old Bread: The Worst Good Time I Ever Had (produced New York, 1976).
The Rich Man, Poor Man Play (produced New York, 1976).

Television Plays: The Dark Side of the Moon, 1957; A Man Loses His Dog More or Less,
    1972.

Other

The Sleepwalker and the Assassin: A Study of the Contemporary Theatre.   New York,
    Bridgehead Books, 1964.
The Radical Theatre Notebook.   New York, Avon, 1973.

Theatrical Activities:

Director: **Plays** – *God Wants What Men Want*, New York, 1966; *The Bombflower*, New York, 1966; *The Bitch of Waverly Place*, New York, 1971.

Actor:**Plays**–*OM: A Sharing Service*, Boston, 1968; *The Children's Army Is Late*, Parma, Italy 1974.

Arthur Sainer comments:

I like to believe I write plays to find out something – about self, about self in cosmos, about the cosmos. I try to make something in order to understand something.

But they're not thinking plays as much as feeling plays. I understand primarily through feeling. So I try to shape something into being so I can feel it, so others can feel it. Sometimes the plays use ideological material but they aren't ideological plays. Ultimately if they work they work as felt experience.

For some time I was fascinated by the juxtaposition of live performers and visual projections, concerned with an enlarged arrested image operating on a level other than that of the "real" performer. That period ran from *The Game of the Eye* (1964) through *Boat Sun Cavern* (written in '67, produced in '69). But I've lost interest in projections, I want the magic to be live, immediate, home-made. And I want the mistakes to be live ones.

Language – I've gone from many words, *God Wants What Men Want* (written in '63), to few words, *The Blind Angel* (1965), *The Bombflower* (1966), to some words, *Images of the Coming Dead* (1971). None of these approaches is superior to the others. It depends on what the play needs and what the playwright needs at that time. Bodies are no more or less useful than the utterances that emerge from them. Only truth is useful.

Words are useful, but so is everything else. I don't hold with Grotowski's belief that every conceivable element other than the performer ought to be stripped away. Everything on God's earch, everything designed or decimated by the hands of man is potentially viable and important, all of it is a testament to this life. But I've come lately (in *The Spring Offensive*) to believe in an economy of means – forget the lights, forget the setting – to believe in the magic of what is obviously being put together by hand before our eyes.

Much theatre leaves me cold, and most audiences disturb me. I don't want to make audiences happy particularly or excite them anymore. I also don't want them to be sitting there judging the play, to be weighing its excellences and faults. I want the audience to be seized and ultimately to become the play. We like to say that a really fine play changed its audience, but a really fine play also creates the condition where its audience can change it. The play ultimately is the product of this mutual vulnerability.

*   *   *

Arthur Sainer's plays are best described as uncompromising. "Unproducible," "impossible," and "demanding" might also be applied to his work but "uncompromising" is, I think, most suitable. It indicates some of the problems and some of the challenge inherent in his work.

There are but a handful of theatres in the States capable of producing his visions theatrically. At the same time, Sainter is fully trusting of the very companies which should but will not stage his plays. He leaves the physical realization of the play to the company but implicity demands without quarter full measure of talent and creative imagination from those theatres. They generally decline the invitation, more's the pity, and some of his finest work is "unproducible."

I should explain that Sainer's work is uncompromising, or demanding or even unproducible, in the same way that the best of Strindberg's plays are. No more, no less.

I suspect the heart of the difficulty with Sainer is that his *style* is what style is supposed to be: the core of the work, the spine, the form *and* the content wrapped into a theatrical package called a play. Most producing organizations cannot read this kind of style, let alone visualize and realize it for the stage. All of the easy, theatrical ways out are insistently ruled against by the playwright.

And yet the characters are compelling: their language is remarkably indicative of what and who they are and what drives them. Almost with pure poetic license, Sainer creates characters through the words they say as well as the deeds they do.

At the same time, these are *plays*, by which I mean they are not literary works *per se*, intended to be read and remembered. They demand stages and companies and audiences together in order to become whole, for that moment.

Thus the circle is dishearteningly completed: a new style demands a new kind of experimental theatre but the theatre doesn't exist and the style remains dormant. Not entirely. But almost.

The most produced of Arthur Sainer's plays is *The Bitch of Waverly Place*. In the last ten years, it has had a number of distinguished actresses essay the central role: Jenny Hecht, Sally Kirkland, Jean Armstrong, and so on. A monologue, it obviously appeals to actresses challenged by and entranced by the possibility of holding the stage alone. As with most such dramas, actors are more often fascinated by such character plays than are the audiences. Be that as it may, it represents an early but fairly typical Sainer effort. It is a play of discovery and rediscovery: the actress and the role, the character and the audience. It is a play in which stories are told directly to the audience. While it permits enormouse histrionic range for the performer and while it may be terribly interesting to the audience, it can only be judged in a theatre rather than on a page. And in a theatre it is completely at the mercy of the actress playing the role, creating the theatrical viability of the whole piece. Compared to great single-role dramas (*Krapp's Last Tape* comes most immediately to mind as does *The Stronger*), it is, for me, the least appealing of Sainer's plays. I admit to a bias against this kind of solo effort on stage but compared to other, representative plays by the same playwright, *The Bitch of Waverly Place* is somewhat shallow despite its popularity. Maybe that's why it's popular.

Boat Sun Cavern, written in 1967 in Minneapolis while he was working with the Firehouse Theatre on *The Thing Itself*, explores the hidden recesses of a boy and girl's world, real and imaginary. Almost indescribable, the play seems to me to contain an exploration *in* the play and *of* the theatre's limits itself. It is as if Sainer were denying any limits to the form and the physical presence of the theatre. It comes closer to multi-media drama than most: it moves the audience about, in and out of the theatre while it flashes at the audience film, music, and undefined images. The play moves *inside* the characters and *inside* theatre itself. It offers stream of consciousness as the theatrical machine by which the play will work; it takes a simple (almost simplistic) action and moves *into* the shaping of that action to the point where the effect is almost unbearable. I'd like to *see* (I'm tempted to say "bear witness" to) the play some day. Right now, I'd have to join most directors and say I'm not sure I'd know how to get it into a theatre and make it work. But I'd like to try.

In 1968, Sainer wrote the still unproduced *Rites*, which seems to me the most complete, total play of the lot. Again, he tries to create a relationship between the audience and the characters on stage which permits a full exploration *within* the characters. Again, Sainer uses every conceivable means (poems, music, newspaperism) and again he is concerned with the innards of the characters. But here he creates both the world within and the world outside of those characters, and so the play is more accessible (if not less demanding) to most of us. Also working for *Rites*, perhaps most brilliantly of all the plays, is Sainer's incredible ear for what can only be described as "character language." One has to see or at least read the plays to know what that means, but it might be thought of as language which defines character. A number of more prominent writers have thought they were doing just that, but Sainer really accomplishes it. The man and the woman in *Rites* who enter a new relationship are extraordinary not only because of what they see and understand, but because what they are is made manifest in the words they speak and the action they perform. What an incredible challenge for the right company, the right actors.

China Takes Eleven Hours is a handsomely constructed argument but may be *too* demanding and cold; it asks that the audience know a helluva lot about what Sainer is debating. The capture of Debray and the death of Che Guevara is the central action, but the play is really "about" the world which created these men and men like them. Sainer quotes, uses, examines and creates. Unfortunately, I just don't "get" the people, perhaps because they strike no chord of recognition in *my* life – no fault of the play that I've been sheltered from the revolutionaries! Sainer himself has called it "one of my most significant works," and I cannot quarrel with his evaluation. But I can sympathize a bit with the theatres that won't produce Sainer's plays because they don't "get" them. A turbulent work, I think it may be so specialized and "uncompromising" that few will grab onto and ride with *China Takes Eleven Hours*, but that is not to diminish its importance.

Images of the Coming Dead was finished in 1971 and performed at the Open Space Ensemble in New York under various directors. The title in a number of ways is a most adequate summary of the play, which shows us sets of people at varying stages of creating life between themselves. The most interior of Sainer's works, it should make an astounding film-stage presentation. Novelistic in structure, it provides avenues into the interior of the characters but the audience must participate fully if it is to get there. He trusts the actors to provide worlds without words, and I'm not sure that that confidence is a safe one.

Finally (and I'll have dealt here only with the work that Sainer, himself a critic for the *Village Voice*, has indicated are "representative"), the 1972 production of *The Celebration: Jooz/Guns/Movies/The Abyss* brought an enormous amount of attention to bear on Arthur Sainer. Twenty-seven in the cast, plus musicians, it took three hours on stage, and lasted an unprecedented six weeks in the West Village space where it came to life. It got at least one overwhelming rave, and a couple of damnations. It won an Obie for one of the actors, and it has been videotaped in Paris and excerpted (sanitized?) for radio in New York. And, in honesty, I must admit that for me it seems a retrogression in *style* for Sainer. It's as if he took several leaps forward (ahead of the game) and then shyly stepped back a bit. Such may be necessary for him as an artist. I don't know.

Where does he go next? I think he needs major productions. Himself a good director, he needs to have others realize his plays for him rather than stage them himself. The visions must grow theatrically. But above all, Sainer is a poet in the theatre, who uncompromisingly demands that the theatre and its inhabitants stretch far beyond their puny, present "experiments." He will be a major force to be reckoned with if we can learn to cope with his demands. We must.

—Arthur H. Ballet

SAROYAN, William.   American.   Born in Fresno, California, 31 August 1908. Educated in Fresno public schools. Served in the United Stages Army, 1942–45. Married Carol Marcus in 1943 (divorced, 1949); remarried Carol Marcus, 1951 (divorced, 1952); has two children, including the poet Aram Saroyan. Past occupations include grocery clerk, vineyard worker, post office employee; clerk, telegraph operator, then office manager of the Postal Telegraph Company, San Francisco, 1926–28. Co-Founder, Conference Press, Los Angeles, 1936. Founder and Director, Saroyan Theatre, New York, 1942. Writer-in-Residence, Purdue University, Lafayette, Indiana, 1961. Recipient: New York Drama Critics Circle Award, 1940; Pulitzer Prize, 1940 (refused). Member, National Institute of Arts and Letters. Address: 2729 West Griffin Way, Fresno, California 93705, U.S.A.

PUBLICATIONS

Plays

The Man with the Heart in the Highlands, in *Contemporary One-Act Plays*, edited by William Kozlenko. New York, Scribner, 1938; revised version, as *My Heart's in the Highlands* (produced New York, 1939), New York, Harcourt Brace, 1939; in *Three Plays*, 1940.

The Time of Your Life (also co-director: produced New York, 1939). New York, Harcourt Brace. 1939; in *Three Plays*, 1940.

The Hungerers (produced New York, 1945). New York, French, 1939.

A Special Announcement (broadcast, 1940). New York, House of Books, 1940.

Love's Old Sweet Song (also co-director: produced Princeton, New Jersey, and New York, 1940). Included in *Three Plays*, 1940.

Three Plays: My Heart's in the Highlands, The Time of Your Life, Love's Old Sweet Song. New York, Harcourt Brace, 1940; London, Faber, 1942.

Subway Circus. New York, French, 1940.

Something about a Soldier (produced in stock, 1940).

Hero of the World (produced in stock, 1940).

The Great American Goof (ballet scenario; produced New York, 1940; London, 1970). Included in *Razzle Dazzle*, 1942.

Radio Play (broadcast, 1940). Included in *Razzle Dazzle*, 1942.

The Ping Pong Game (produced New York, 1945). New York French, 1940.

Sweeney in the Trees (produced in stock, 1940). Included in *Three Plays*, 1941.

The Beautiful People (also director: produced New York, 1941; London, 1947). Included in *Three Plays*, 1941.

Three Plays: The Beautiful People, Sweeney in the Trees, Across the Board on Tomorrow Morning. New York, Harcourt Brace, 1941; London, Faber 1943.

Across the Board on Tomorrow Morning (produced Pasadena, California, 1941; New York, 1942; London, 1962). Included in *Three Plays*, 1941.

The People with Light Coming Out of Them (broadcast, 1941). Published in *The Free Company Presents...*, New York, Dodd Mead, 1941.

There's Something I Got To Tell You (broadcast, 1941). Included in *Razzle Dazzle*, 1942.

Hello, Out There (produced Santa Barbara, California, 1941; New York, 1942; London, 1962). Included in *Razzle Dazzle*, 1942.

Jim Dandy (produced in stock, 1941). Cincinnati, Little Man Press, 1941; as *Jim Dandy: Fat Man in a Famine*, New York, Harcourt Brace, 1947; London, Faber, 1948.

Talking to You (also director: produced New York, 1942; London, 1962). Included in *Razzle Dazzle*, 1942.

Razzle Dazzle; or, The Human Opera, Ballet, and Circus; or, There's Something I Got to Tell You: Being Many Kinds of Short Plays As Well As the Story of the Writing of Them (includes *Hello, Out There, Coming Through the Rye, Talking to You, The Great American Goof, The Poetic Situation in America, Opera, Opera, Bad Men in the West, The Agony of Little Nations, A Special Announcement, Radio Play, The People with Light Coming Out of Them, There's Something I Got to Tell You, The Hungerers, Elmer and Lily, Subway Circus, The Ping Pong Players*). New York, Harcourt Brace, 1942; as *Razzle Dazzle: The Human Opera, Ballet, and Circus* (includes all the above plays except *The Ping Pong Players*), London, Faber, 1945.

Opera, Opera (produced New York, 1955). Included in *Razzle Dazzle*, 1942.

Get Away Old Man (produced New York, 1943). New York, Harcourt Brace, 1944; London, Faber, 1946.

Sam Ego's House (produced Los Angeles, 1947–48). Included in *Don't Go Away Mad and Two Other Plays*, 1949.

Don't Go Away Mad (produced New York, 1949).   Included in *Don't Go Away Mad and Two Other Plays*, 1949.

Don't Go Away Mad and Two Other Plays: Sam Ego's House; A Decent Birth, A Happy Funeral.   New York, Harcourt Brace, 1949; London, Faber, 1950.

The Son (produced Los Angeles, 1950).

The Slaughter of the Innocents (produced The Hague, 1957).   Chicago, Theatre Arts, 1952.

The Oyster and the Pearl: A Play for Television (televised, 1953).   Published in *Perspectives USA* (New York), Summer 1953; in *Theatre Today*, edited by David Thompson, London, Longman, 1965.

Once Around the Block (produced New York, 1956).   New York, French, 1959.

The Cave Dwellers (produced New York, 1957).   New York, Putnam, and London, Faber, 1958.

Ever Been in Love with a Midget (produced Berlin, 1957).

Cat, Mouse, Man, Woman; and The Accident, in *Contact 1* (Sausalito, California), 1958.

Settled Out of Court, with Henry Cecil, adaptation of the novel by Henry Cecil (produced London, 1960).   London, French, 1962.

The Dogs; or, The Paris Comedy (as *Lily Dafon*, produced Berlin, 1960).   Included in *The Dogs; or, The Paris Comedy and Two Other Plays*, 1969.

Sam, The Highest Jumper of Them All; or, The London Comedy (also director: produced London, 1960).   London, Faber, 1961.

High Time along the Wabash (produced Lafayette, Indiana, 1961).

Ah Man, music by Peter Fricker (produced Aldeburgh, Suffolk, 1962).

Four Plays: The Playwright and the Public, The Handshakers, The Doctor and the Patient, This I Believe, in *Atlantic* (Boston), April 1963.

Dentist and Patient, and Husband and Wife, in *The Best Short Plays 1968*, edited by Stanley Richards.   Philadelphia, Chilton, 1968.

The Dogs; or, The Paris Comedy and Two Other Plays: Chris Sick; or, Happy New Year Anyway, Making Money, and Nineteen Other Very Short Plays.   New York, Phaedra, 1969.

The New Play, in *The Best Short Plays 1970*, edited by Stanley Richards.   Philadelphia, Chilton, 1970.

Armenians (produced New York, 1974).

The Rebirth Celebration of the Human Race at Artie Zabala's Off-Broadway Theatre (produced New York, 1975).

Screenplay: *The Good Job*, 1942.

Radio Plays: *Radio Play*, 1940; *A Special Announcement*, 1940; *There's Something I Got to Tell You*, 1941; *The People with Light Coming Out of Them*, 1941.

Television Plays: *The Oyster and the Pearl*, 1953; *Ah Sweet Mystery of Mrs. Murphy*, 1959; *The Unstoppable Gray Fox*, 1962.

Ballet Scenario: *The Great American Goof*, 1940.

Novels

The Human Comedy.   New York, Harcourt Brace, and London, Faber, 1943.

The Adventures of Wesley Jackson.   New York, Harcourt Brace, 1946; London, Faber, 1947.

The Twin Adventures: The Adventures of William Saroyan: A Diary; The Adventures of Wesley Jackson: A Novel.   New York, Harcourt Brace, 1950.

Rock Wagram   New York, Doubleday, 1951; London, Faber, 1952.

Tracy's Tiger. New York, Doubleday, 1951; London, Faber, 1952.
The Laughing Matter. New York, Doubleday, 1953; London, Faber, 1954; reprinted at *The Secret Story*, New York, Popular Library, 1954.
Mama I Love You Boston, Little Brown, 1956; London, Faber, 1957.
Papa You're Crazy. Boston, Little Brown, 1957; London, Faber, 1958.
Boys and Girls Together. New York, Harcourt Brace, and London, Davies, 1963.
One Day in the Afternoon of the World. New York, Harcourt Brace, 1964; London, Cassell, 1965.

Short Stories

The Daring Young Man on the Flying Trapeze and Other Stories. New York, Random House, 1934; London, Faber, 1935.
Inhale and Exhale. New York, Random House, and London, Faber, 1936.
Three Times Three. Los Angeles, Conference Press, 1936.
Little Children. New York, Harcourt Brace, and London, Faber, 1937.
A Gay and Melancholy Flux: Short Stories. London, Faber, 1937.
Love, Here Is My Hat. New York, Modern Age Books, and London, Faber, 1938.
A Native American. San Francisco, George Fields, 1938.
The Touble with Tigers. New York, Harcourt Brace, 1938; London, Faber, 1939.
Peace, It's Wonderful. New York, Modern Age Books, 1939; London, Faber, 1940.
3 Fragments and a Story. Cincinnati, Little Man Press, 1939.
My Name Is Aram. New York, Harcourt Brace, 1940; London, Faber, 1941.
Saroyan's Fables. New York, Harcourt Brace, 1941.
The Insurance Salesman and Other Stories. London, Faber, 1941.
48 Saroyan Stories. New York, Avon, 1942.
31 Selected Stories. New York, Avon, 1943.
Some Day I'll Be a Millionaire: 34 More Great Stories. New York, Avon, 1943.
Dear Baby. New York, Harcourt Brace, 1944; London, Faber, 1945.
The Saroyan Special: Selected Short Stories. New York, Harcourt Brace, 1948.
The Fiscal Hoboes. New York, Press of Valenti Angelo, 1949.
The Assyrian and Other Stories. New York, Harcourt Brace, 1950; London, Faber, 1951.
The Whole Voyald and Other Stories. Boston, Little Brown, 1956; London, Faber, 1957.
Love. New York, Popular Library, 1959.
After Thirty Years: The Daring Young Man on the Flying Trapeze (includes essays). New York, Harcourt Brace, 1964.
Best Stories of William Saroyan. London, Faber, 1964.
My Kind of Crazy Wonderful People: 17 Stories and a Play. New York, Harcourt Brace, 1966.
The Tooth and My Father. New York, Doubleday, 1974.

Other

The Time of Your Life (miscellany). New York, Harcourt Brace, 1939.
Harlem as Seen by Hirschfeld. New York, Hyperion Press, 1941.
Hilltop Russians in San Francisco. Palo Alto, California, Stanford University-James Delkin, 1941.
Why Abstract?, with Henry Miller and Hilaire Hiler. New York, New Directions, 1945; London, Falcon Press, 1948.
The Bicycle Rider in Beverly Hills (autobiography). New York, Scribner, 1952; London,

William Saroyan Reader.   New York, Braziller, 1958.

Here Comes, There Goes, You Know Who (autobiography).   New York, Simon and Schuster, 1961; London, Davies, 1962.

A Note on Hilaire Hiler.   New York, Wittenborn, 1962.

Me (juvenile).   New York, Crowell Collier, 1963.

Not Dying (autobiography).   New York, Harcourt Brace, 1963; London, Cassel, 1966.

Short Drive, Sweet Chariot (autobiography).   New York, Phaedra, 1966.

Look at Us: Let's See: Here We Are: Look Hard: Speak Soft: I See, You See, We All See; Stop, Look, Listen; Beholder's Eye; Don't Look Now But Isn't That You? (us? U.S.?).   New York, Cowles, 1967.

Horsey Gorsey and the Frog (juvenile).   Eau Claire, Wisconsin, E. M. Hale, 1968.

I Used to Believe I Had Forever; Now I'm Not So Sure.   New York, Cowles, 1968.

Letters from 74 rue Taitbout; or, Don't Go But if You Must Say Hello to Everybody.   Cleveland, World, 1969; as *Don't Go But If You Must Say Hello to Everybody*, London, Cassell, 1970.

Days of Life and Death and Escape to the Moon.   New York, Dial Press, 1970; London, Joseph, 1971.

Places Where I've Done Time.   New York, Praeger, 1972; London, Davis Poynter, 1973.

Famous Faces and Other Friends: A Personal Memoir.   New York, McGraw Hill, 1976.

Morris Hirshfield.   New York, Rizzoli, 1976.

Sons Come and Go, Mothers Hang In Forever (memoirs).   New York, McGraw Hill, 1976.

Editor, *Hairenik, 1934–1939: An Anthology of Short Stories and Poems.*   Boston, Hairenik Association, 1939.

Bibliography: *A Bibliography of William Saroyan, 1934–1963* by David Kherdian, San Francisco, Roger Beachum, 1965.

Theatrical Activities:

Director: **Plays** – *The Time of Your Life* (co-director, with Eddie Dowling), New York, 1939; *Love's Old Sweet Song* (co-director, with Eddie Dowling), Princeton, New Jersey, and New York, 1940; *The Beautiful People*, New York, 1941; *Across the Board on Tomorrow Morning, and Talking to You*, New York, 1942; *Sam, The Highest Jumper of Them All*, London, 1960.

*   *   *

William Saroyan is the wild man of the modern American Theatre. From the beginning of his career as a writer in the 1930's he professed not to recognize any categories or any formulas or any principles. In *Three Times Three*, for example, he wrote, "Plot, atmosphere, style, and all the rest of it may be regarded as so much nonsense." Or again, in *Razzle Dazzle*, "a play has a plot, a locale, an atmosphere, a leading character, many supporting characters, suspense, mystery, and all those other things you can buy for ten cents at any novelty or drug store." In both these statements, and countless others, we note a contempt for artifice of any kind, a contempt which has been Saroyan's stock in trade since the beginning. Saroyan has this profound distrust of artifice because he believes a great gap exists between the dramatic representation of life as it is found in the theatre and the drama of life itself. For this reason he has always avoided, as if they were leprous, orderly sequences of events, neat conflicts and resolutions, conventional play structures. He wrote as he pleased, because he wanted his plays to appear, as one editor put it, "as wayward and formless as life itself."

It would be a mistake, however, to conclude that Saroyan's objections to artifice and his insistence upon "truth" rather than "story telling" made him a photographic naturalist, for all of his plays are a kind of fantasy. He has a fine feeling for the odd, the unfamiliar, the unexpected, and the curious. At his best, Saroyan succeds in making the fantasy credible. His characters are fantastic but also, imaginably, quite human. They perform their fantastic acts, and write their fantastic novels, and live on nothing a year by a kind of economic magic. They do all this while at the same time doing the most commonplace everyday things. And their humanity is enhanced by Saroyan's insistence upon avoiding any appearance of contrivance and art in their actions. They are not going anywhere. Their dreams don't come to much. Their fantasy life, which is considerable, does not alter the major fact of their life: that they are living in a very plain house on a very plain street, eating very plain food – just living. This is the secret of Saroyan's theatre: his ability to combine the fantastic with the commonplace and have it come off.

This is no mean trick; but on reconsidering Saroyan's work today it would appear that his success is as much attributable to the mere fact that he *opposed* the conventional techniques of the theatre, as to the techniques he adopted. The very rebelliousness of his spirit breeds enthusiasm, excitement, intensity, and life. This enthusiasm is the dominant characteristic of his best work, and particularly the early plays *My Heart's in the Highlands* and *The Time of Your Life*. It is notably absent in his more recent work. The difference is clearly revealed when one examines the language of his dialogue. Compare, for example, Nick's attack on the cynical Blick in *The Time of Your Life*:

Why should I get worked up over a guy like that? Why should I hate *him*? H nothing. He's nobody. He's a mouse. But every time he comes into this place I get burned up. He doesn't want to drink. He doesn't want to sit down. He doesn't want to take things easy.

with a similar speech from *Jim Dandy*:

What unholy science and mischief is in this man to mock the hopes of all who live. This unbeliever whose enemy is miracle who in the very seed blights beauty and befouls the blessed accident of grace....

Not only is the rhetoric of *Jim Dandy*, and more recently *The Cave Dwellers*, more ponderously rhetorical, but what is being said in *Jim Dandy* is more general and less detailed; the sentiments are lofty but one is not sure where they are going to be applied. One has the feeling that the speeches are not being made in any context which matters very much to the author; they are being made instead from a pulpit.

It would seem that after a while Saroyan got so carried away with rebelling that he forgot to write plays. He forgot the first tenet of his own creed that the writer has to be in touch with life, has to feel life, has to create a living world. In the 1930's he wrote: "Nothing is trite, if you chose to be vigorous. You can imply that life is sad, which is a platitude, and if you give the implication sufficient fullness there will be no platitude: you will have implied that life is sad." And in the preface of his first collection of stories he wrote:

The most solid advice for a writer is this, I think: Try to learn to breathe deeply, really to taste food when you eat, and when you sleep, really to sleep. Try as much as possible to be wholly alive, with all your might, and when you laugh, laugh like hell, and when you get angry, get good and angry. Try to be alive. You will be dead soon enough.

If the playwright is to avoid platitudes there must be sufficient fullness; you must be able to taste and feel and smell and touch; the playwright must make a world of the play. In his early plays there is such a world most of the time, and Saroyan's feelings about life and love and

691

happiness – and they are considerable – become flesh and blood in his characters.

But Saroyan has changed. This change first became apparent in his preface to *Razzle Dazzle* where he writes disparagingly about the theatre as an art form. The substance of his objection can be reduced to the fact that he couldn't talk enough in the theatre; it imposed too many limitations; there were too many people involved; it was too artificial; and since, for him, "writing is living," the theatre was no place for him. His more recent plays, and particularly *Jim Dandy* and *The Cave Dwellers*, show he was right. He still had his wonderful felicity for the great scene, but the context, the place, the fullness of the world was gone. He no longer implied anything. He wanted to talk.

This is understandable. A writer who has from the beginning insisted that he is more interested in telling the truth than in telling a story is apt sometimes to abandon story-telling entirely, abandon the notion of having characters speaking lines which are in *character*, and abandon all the props, all the contrivances which help to make a world of the stage, in favour of getting up on the stage himself and holding forth. Saroyan did a lot of this in *My Heart's in the Highlands* and *The Time of Your Life*, but when he did it in these plays he did at the same time supply, consciously or not, a fantastic but human fictional world of sorts into which his truths readily fitted. He does not supply such a world in the plays that followed.

It was Walter Kerr who pointed out that when we attach Saroyan for his lack of discipline, we are looking for the wrong skeletons in the wrong closets. "Mr. Saroyan's irreverence for tidy theatrical forms," he says, "is probably a virtue; most of the conventions are breaking up these days, anyway. Where Saroyan is indulging himself is in the pretentious and intrusive language of the sponsor's commercial." The old actress known as The Queen in *The Cave Dwellers* is more sensible in her theatrical instincts than the man who created her. "When you're cold," she says, "it's better to have a fire than a philosophy." One of the virtues of *The Time of Your Life* and *My Heart's in the Highlands* is that the champagne still has its kick and it flows more readily than the talk.

—Robert W. Corrigan

SAUNDERS, James A.   British.   Born in Islington, London, 8 January 1925. Educated at Wembley County School; University of Southampton. Married Audrey Cross in 1951; has three children. Formerly taught English in London. Full-time Writer since 1962. Recipient: Arts Council bursary, 1960; *Evening Standard* award, 1963. Agent: c/o Margaret Ramsay Ltd., 14a Goodwin's Court, London, WC2N 4LL, England.

PUBLICATIONS

Plays

 Cinderella Comes of Age (produced London, 1949).
 Moonshine (produced London, 1955).
 Dog Accident (broadcast, 1958; revised version, produced London, 1969).   Included in
  Six of the Best, London, Inter-Action Imprint, 1976.
 Barnstable (broadcast, 1959; produced Dublin and London, 1960).   London, French,
  1961.
 Alas, Poor Fred: A Duologue in the Style of Ionesco (produced Scarborough, 1959;
  London, 1966).   Scarborough, Studio Theatre, 1960.

The Ark, music by Geoffrey Wright (produced London, 1959).

Ends and Echoes: Barnstable, Committal, Return to a City (produced London, 1960). *Return to a City* included in *Neighbours and Other Plays*, 1968.

A Slight Accident (produced Nottingham, 1961; London, 1971).   Included in *Neighbours and Other Plays*, 1968.

Double, Double (produced London, 1962).   London, French, 1964.

Next Time I'll Sing to You, suggested by a theme from *A Hermit Disclosed* by Raleigh Trevelyan (produced London and New York, 1963).   London, Deutsch, and New York, Random House, 1963.

Who Was Hilary Maconochie? (produced London, 1963).

The Pedagogue (broadcast, 1964; produced London, 1964).   Included in *Neighbours and Other Plays*, 1968.

Neighbours (produced London, 1964; New York, 1969).   Included in *Neighbours and Other Plays*, 1968.

A Scent of Flowers (produced London, 1964; New York, 1969)   London, Deutsch, and New York, Random House, 1965.

Triangle, with others (produced Glasgow, 1965).

Trio (produced Edinburgh, 1967).   Included in *Neighbours and Other Plays*, 1968.

The Italian Girl, with Iris Murdoch, adaptation of the novel by Iris Murdoch (produced Bristol, 1967; London, 1968).   London, French, 1969.

Neighbours and Other Plays (includes *Trio, Alas, Poor Fred, Return to a City, A Slight Accident, The Pedagogue*).   London, Deutsch, 1968.

Haven, later called *A Man's Best Friend*, in *We Who Are about to...*, later called *Mixed Doubles* (produced London, 1969).   London, Methuen, 1970.

The Travails of Sancho Panza, based on the novel *Don Quixote* by Cervantes (produced London, 1969).   London, Heinemann, 1969.

The Borage Pigeon Affair (produced London, 1969).   London, Deutsch, 1970.

Savoury Meringue (produced London, 1971).   Included in *Six of the Best*, London, Inter-Action Imprint, 1976.

After Liverpool (broadcast, 1971; produced Edinburgh and London, 1971; New York, 1973).   London, French, 1973.

Games (produced Edinburgh and London, 1971; New York, 1973).   London, French, 1973.

Opus (produced Loughton, Essex, 1971).

Hans Kohlhaas, adaptation of the story by Heinrich Von Kleist (produced London, 1972).

Bye Bye Blues (produced Richmond, Surrey, 1973).

Poor Old Simon, in *Mixed Blessings* (produced Horsham, Sussex, 1973).

Journey to London, adaptation of the play by Vanbrugh (produced London, 1975).

Play for Yesterday (produced Richmond, Surrey, 1975).

The Island (produced London, 1975).

Radio Plays: *Love and a Limousine*, 1952; *The Drop Too Much*. 1952; *Nimrod's Oak*, 1953; *Women Are So Unreasonable*, 1957; *Dog Accident*, 1958; *Barnstable*, 1959; *Gimlet* (version of *Double, Double*), 1963; *The Pedagogue*, 1964; *It's Not the Game It Was*, 1964; *Pay As You Go*, 1965; *After Liverpool*, 1971; *Random Moments in a May Garden*, 1974.

Television Plays: *Just You Wait* (version of *Double, Double*), 1963; *Watch Me I'm a Bird*, 1964; *The White Stocking* and five other adaptations of the works of D. H. Lawrence, 1966; *Beast in the Jungle*, 1969; *Plastic People*, 1970; *The Unconquered*, 1970; *Craven Arms*, 1972; *The Mill*, 1972; *The Black Dog*, 1972.

*   *   *

James Saunders' position, judging from his plays, is that of a liberal humanist, someone who values the virtues of common humanity, tolerance and understanding above everything else, and would like society organised in such a way that these qualities would be encouraged.

Next Time I'll Sing to You, his first major play, revolves around a real-life hermit, Jimmy Mason, who died in 1942 at the age of eight-four. By the dramatic means of other characters investigating him, the play examines sympathetically the various pressures, family, phychological and economic, that made the man chose a life of isolation in a hovel in the Essex countryside. The actor playing the hermit disputes the characters' opinions of him from time to time, and, by this dialectical method, something approaching the truth about him is discovered. Rudge, one of the investigators, comes to the conclusion that his self-imposed loneliness was remarkably lacking in hypocrisy: "The manner of his existence was a posing of the question we manage to avoid: who or what is it that is so obsessed with me that he makes it necessary for me to live out my long life in this dank slowly-decaying cell to no apparent purpose?"

The core of the play is contained in a later speech of Rudge's, where he ponders on the gap between conception and execution, and considers that life contains no neat answers to neat problems but is "a zoo with all the cage doors left open by an idiot keeper, where the animals roam at will, devouring one another, leaving exotic and unlovely messes on the neat concrete footpaths."

The play is also interesting in terms of of form, in that its structure reflects the basic artificality of theatre and of "a play." Actors play actors playing characters, so that what we get is truth at least three times removed from reality. This Pirandellian preoccupation with the very nature of theatre lies at the heart of nearly all of Saunder's work.

A Scent of Flowers is an equally sympathetic study of another kind of outcast, a young middle-class girl called Zoe, who at the beginning of the play has committed suicide because of lack of understanding and compassion by members of her family. Her father, David, an emotionally reserved and rather selfish man, has refused to discuss with her a disastrous affair she has been having with a university lecturer on the grounds that it is none of his business. Her stepmother Agnes is well-meaning but cold, and tries to impose her own standards of conduct on her stepdaughter. There is an awkwardness in the relationship between her and Godfrey, her stepbrother, as he is in love with her but not she with him. Consequently, when she and the university lecturer split up, she has no-one to turn to.

The play's form is again interesting, the dead girl entering into retrospective conversations with members of her family and the undertaker's men. We learn gradually about her character and about how no-one accepts her on her own terms. At times, also, the play is tremendously moving.

The Borage Pigeon Affair is a tilt at the sheer squalor and hypocrisy of much of our present society. Borage is a small provincial town, where a local councillor, Makepeace Garnish, keeps pigeons as a hobby, causing considerable distress to some members of the community, while others vehemently support his right to. Everyone in the play, councillor, public health officer, ordinary citizen and a television director aptly named Loathing (who has come to make a programme out of the hoo-ha caused by the pigeons) is shown to be on the make, with no real concern or feeling for the welfare or well-being of others. The play is Brechtian in a sense, as the actors are invited by the author to comment on and exaggerate the nasty, selfish traits in their characters. It contains a strong implied plea for a return to values of honesty and compassion.

His short plays vary a great deal in quality. *Neighbours* examines a confrontation between two young people, a black man and a white woman, lodgers in the same house. It explodes myths about white liberals with skin-deep tolerance and about blacks being necessarily more sexually potent than whites, is convincing in its characterisation, tautly plotted and with pungent dialogue. *The Pedagogue* is a truthful portrait in depth of a schoolmaster, his own personality stifled by the demands of his job, pleading with his pupils to respect authority, while, outside the classroom, society is audibly collapsing. *Dog Accident*, revised for Ed Berman's Inter-Action, examines passers-by's reactions to a dog being hit by a car and contains an oblique criticism of our desires not to get involved with things that don't immediately concern us. Written for the open air, it was very successfully performed at Marble Arch, London. But some of his earlier pieces, like *A Slight Accident, Trio* and *Alas, Poor Fred*, though showing flashes of his later quality, are best left decently interred.

His dramatic qualities of compassion, honesty and concern fused remarkably well with the group TOC's theatrical explorations of psychic and emotional hang-ups, under the direction of the late Naftali Yavin, when they combined to produce *Games/After Liverpool*. There are two plays. In *After Liverpool*, four actors, equally divided sexually, go through several variations on the basic steps leading to a serious emotional relationship. It is consummately well written and entertaining. *Games* is a more ambitious, complicated, Pirandellian exercise depicting four actors rehearsing a play on the My Lai massacre and disputing between themselves and with the audience as to what attitudes they can take toward their material and how they can convey the reality of those attitudes through the basically artificial form of a play. On one level, it is a return to his early preoccupation with the nature of theatre as a means of communication; and, on another, the whole relationship between theatre and major political and social events, and whether it can really exist in a dramatic sense. In performance, I found it less successful than the other; the actors' dispute with the audience is, perhaps intentionally, very irritating, being essentially phoney, as nothing the audience says really changes what the actors do. But this may be a subtle, implied comment on Saunders' part that there can be no such thing as a genuine, direct actor-audience relationship.

Saunders has always been concerned essentially with the same themes; but his desire for experiment is likely to lead him into exciting new forms of writing.

—Jonathan Hammond

SCHARY, Dore. American.   Born in Newark, New Jersey, 31 August 1905. Educated at Central High School, Newark. Married Miriam Svet in 1932; has three children. Little theatre director, actor, publicity director, newpaper writer, 1926–32. Screenwriter for Paramount, Warner Brothers, and Columbia, 1933–37; Writer, 1938–41, Executive Producer, 1941–46, and Executive Vice-President in Charge of Productions and Studio Operations, 1948–56, MGM, Hollywood: associated with more than 350 films. Producer, David O. Selznick Productions, 1943–46. Since 1956, Independent Producer, and since 1959, Director, Schary Productions and Schary Television Productions. Currently, President and Chief Executive Officer of Telepremiere International and their proprietary system of pay TV, TheatreVision. Associated with the Theatre Guild, 1956–60. President, Dramatists Guild Fund, since 1962. National Chairman, 1963–69, now Honorary Chairman, Anti-Defamation League; Commissioner of Cultural Affairs of the City of New York, 1970–71. Trustee, Eleanor Roosevelt Memorial Foundation; Trustee, Brandeis University; Sponsor, New York Shakespeare Festival; Patron, University of Judaism; Member of the Advisory Council, United States Committee for the United Nations; Member, President's Committee on Employment of the Handicapped; Member of the Board, Jewish Theological Seminary of America; Member of the Board, Authors League. Recipient: Academy Award, 1938; Tony Award, for play and production, 1958; National Association of Independent Schools Award, 1959. D.H.L.: College of the Pacific, Fresno, California, 1951; Wilberforce University, Ohio, 1951; D.F.A.: Lincoln College, Nebraska, 1960. Address: 340 West 57th Street, New York, New York 10019, U.S.A.

PUBLICATIONS

Plays

> *Too Many Heroes* (produced New York, 1937).
> *Sunrise at Campobello* (produced New York, 1958).   New York, Random House,
>   1958.
> *The Highest Tree* (also director: produced New York, 1959).   New York, Random
>   House, 1960.
> *The Devil's Advocate*, adaptation of the novel by Morris West (also director: produced
>   New York, 1961).   New York, Morrow, 1961.
> *Banderol* (also director: produced New York, 1963).
> *Storm in the West* (screenplay), with Sinclair Lewis.   New York, Stein and Day, 1963.
> *One by One* (also director: produced New York, 1964).
> *Brightower* (produced New York, 1970).
> *Antiques*, music and lyrics by Alan Greene and Laura Manning (televised; produced
>   New York, 1973).

> Screenplays: *Young and Beautiful*, 1934; *Let't Talk It Over*, 1934 *Murder in the Clouds*,
> 1934; *Chinatown Squad*, 1935; *Silk Hat Kid*, 1935; *Your Uncle Dudley*, 1935; *Her
> Master's Voice*, with Harry Sauber, 1936; *Mind Your Own Business*, 1936; *Outcast*,
> 1937; *The Girl from Scotland Yard*, 1937; *Big City*, 1937; *Boys Town*, 1938; *Edison the
> Man*, 1940; *Young Tom Edison*, 1940; *Broadway Melody of 1940*, 1940; *Married
> Bachelor*, 1941; *Behind the News*, 1941; *It's a Big Country*, 1952; *Battle of Gettysburg*,
> 1956; *Lonelyhearts*, 1959; *Sunrise at Campobello*, 1960; *Act One*, 1963; *Storm in the
> West*, with Sinclair Lewis, 1963.

> Television Play: *Antiques*.

Other

> *Case History of a Movie*, by Dore Schary as told to Charles Palmer.   New York,
>   Random House, 1950.
> *For Special Occasions* (autobiography).   New York, Random House, 1962.

Theatrical Activities:

> Director: **Plays** – *A Majority of One* by Leonard Spigelgass, New York, 1959; *The Highest
> Tree*, New York, 1959; *The Unsinkable Molly Brown* by Richard Morris and Meredith
> Willson, New York, 1960; *The Devil's Advocate*, New York, 1961; *Something about a
> Soldier* by Ernest Kinoy, New York, 1962; *Banderol*, New York, 1963; *Love and Kisses* by
> Anita Rowe Black, New York, 1963; *One by One*, New York, 1964; *The Zulu and the
> Zayda* by Howard da Silva and Felix Leon, New York, 1965. **Film** – *Act One*, 1963.

> Actor: **Plays** – Jake in *Four Walls* by George Abbott and Dana Burnett, New York, 1928;
> Reporter in *The Last Mile* by John Wexley, New York, 1930. **Television** – *MGM Story*,
> 1954.

Dore Schary comments:

> Obviously *Campobello* was my most rewarding play. It came at a crucial point in my life
> and career and because my argument at M.G.M. was based on my political activities, the

subsequent success of *Campobello* was particularly satisfying. Also the work itself renewed my confidence and restored some part of my reputation.

The Highest Tree, even though it was a commercial failure, said many things that became more popular to say later on. It also introduced Robert Redford to the theatre.

Brightower was a disaster. Much of it was my fault. Also it was ineptly directed, but that too was my fault because I chose the director. If I had produced the play I would have closed it in rehearsal. If ever I could find a company which would be interested in re-staging a failure I would jump at the chance to rewrite the play and direct, because it remains one of my favorite pieces of work.

*   *   *

In the modern theatre Dore Schary is that dramatist whose intellect and imagination are dominated by strong humanitarian impulses. There is something of the idealist in his plays, something of the hero-worshipper, something of the serious reformer. He has a purpose in writing his plays, an objective quite apart from either artistic creativity or material reward as his message to society absorbs his attention. Although two of his plays were selected as "Best Plays" during particular years, only one Schary play was successful in the theatre – *Sunrise at Campobello*. The others were acknowledged failures despite the integrity of the author or his high purpose. Although the theatre can be a remarkably effective medium for presenting opinions, Schary has not shown either the theatrical talent or the intellecual subtlety to recreate his humanitarian questions or statements upon the stage.

The themes and plots of Schary's plays show very clearly his attitude toward the theatre. In *Sunrise at Campobello*, which ran for 556 performances, he dramatized that portion of Franklin Delano Roosevelt's personal life from the summer of 1921 when he first realized that he had infantile paralysis through June, 1924, when he was able to walk with crutches across the convention platform to make his speech nominating Al Smith as the Democratic candidate for the Presidency. It is the strong emotional story of a man determined to use his talents as best he can, and Schary showed himself thoroughly devoted to FDR for whom the play is an effective tribute. Yet for all of its emotional showmanship, the success of the play depends to a considerable degree upon an audience that knows FDR and his subsequent accomplishments. *The Highest Tree* played for only twenty-one performances. It was a preachy play with stilted language and obvious editorializing. The central figure, an atomic scientist, recently stricken with leukemia who wanted to end all nuclear bonb testing, provided the conflict in numerous arguments with colleagues, soldiers, relatives, and doctors. Although *The Devil's Advocate* lasted for 116 performances, it was considered a commercial failure. A dramatization of Morris West's novel, the play takes place in Italy where a man killed after World War II is being considered for Beatification. Meredith, a priest dying of cancer and "empty of God," without pride in his past service, is sent as the devil's advocate to investigate the man's worthiness. Unfortunately, the play loses both direction and focus. Should the audience be concerned with Meredith's spiritual growth or the result of his investigation? There are interesting theological discussions, but the play is poorly structured and plotted. In *Banderol* Schary failed to dramatize a situation he must have understood very well: the struggle of two people to control a major film studio. In *One by One*, another failure, he told the story of two paraplegics who find a way to live full lives despite their handicaps. Clearly, Schary believed in the themes he dramatized, and five plays in a half-dozen years show both determination and a burst of energy. His latest play, *Brightower*, examining the role of privacy in the life of a writer who is driven to suicide, closed after its opening night on Broadway. By this time, however, Schary had additionally demonstrated his intense concern for the arts by accepting the newly-created post of Commissioner of Cultural Affairs of New York.

Besides being only occasionally effective, Schary's dramaturgy is traditional and low-keyed. He can build to good scenes of strong emotional drama as he does with FDR's paralysis and Meredith's growing involvement in man's problems. He is not innovative, however, and only an occasional flashback breaks the forward movement of a realistic play.

One of his strong points would be the creation of characters, particularly minor characters. When he becomes too involved in his message, his major characters, such as Meredith, slip out of his control while his dialogue becomes excessively preachy and undramatic. Although Schary would seem to be an unpretentious dramatist, his determined humanitatianism and devoted idealism not only detract from his dramaturgy but create problems for the person who would take him seriously. *Sunrise at Campobello* will probably remain a title in the list of American biographical plays; otherwise, Schary's works are of very minor significance in American drama.

—Walter J. Meserve

SCHEVILL, James (Erwin).   American.   Born in Berkeley, California, 10 June 1920. Educated at Harvard University, Cambridge, Massachusetts, B.S. 1942. Served in the United States Army, 1942–46. Married Margot Helmuth Blum in 1967; has two children by an earlier marriage. Member of the Faculty, California College of Arts and Crafts, Oakland, 1950–59; Member of the Faculty, 1959–68, and Director of the Poetry Center, 1961–68, San Francisco Stage College. Since 1969, Professor of English, Brown University, Providence, Rhode Island. Recipient: National Theatre Competition prize, 1945; Dramatists Alliance Contest prize, 1948; Fund for the Advancement of Education Fellowship, 1953; Phelan Biography Competition Prize, 1954; Phelan Playwriting Competition prize, 1958; Ford grant, for work with Joan Littlewood's Theatre Workshop, 1960; Rockefeller grant, 1964; William Carlos Williams Award, for verse (*Contact Magazine*), 1965; Roadstead Foundation award, 1966. Agent: Bertha Case, 42 West 53rd Street, New York, New York 10019; or, Dr. Suzanne Czech, International Copyright Bureau Ltd., 53a Shaftesbury Avenue, London W.1, England. Address: English Department, Brown University, Providence, Rhode Island 20912, U.S.A.

PUBLICATIONS

Plays

    High Sinners, Low Angels, music by James Schevill, arranged by Robert Commanday (produced San Francisco, 1953).   San Francisco, Bern Porter, 1953.
    The Bloody Tenet (produced Providence, Rhode Island, 1956; Shrewsbury, Shropshire, 1962).   Included in *The Black President and Other Plays,* 1965.
    The Cid, adaptation of the play by Corneille (broadcast, 1963).   Published in *Classic Theatre Anthology*, edited by Eric Bentley, New York, Doubleday, 1961.
    Voices of Mass and Capital A, music by Andrew Imbrie (produced San Francisco, 1962). New York, Friendship Press, 1962.
    The Master (produced San Francisco, 1963).   Included in *The Black President and Other Plays*, 1965.
    American Power: The Space Fan and The Master (produced Minneapolis, 1964). Included in *The Black President and Other Plays*, 1965.
    The Black President and Other Plays (includes *The Bloody Tenet* and *American Power: The Space Fan and The Master*).   Denver, Swallow, 1965.
    The Death of Anton Webern (produced Fish Creek, Wisconsin, 1966).   Included in *Violence and Glory: Poems 1962–1968*, 1969.

This Is Not True, music by Paul McIntyre (produced Minneapolis, 1967).
The Pilots (produced Providence, Rhode Island, 1970).
Oppenheimer's Chair (produced Providence, Rhode Island, 1970).
Lovecraft's Follies (produced Providence, Rhode Island, 1970).   Chicago, Swallow
   Press, 1971.
The Ushers (produced Providence, Rhode Island, 1971).
The American Fantasies (produced New York, 1972).
Emperor Norton Lives!, music by James Schevill (produced Salt Lake City, Utah, 1972).
Fay Wray Meets King Kong (produced Providence, Rhode Island, 1974).
Sunset and Evening Stance; or, Mr. Krapp's New Tapes (produced Providence, Rhode
   Island, 1974).
The Telephone Murderer (produced Providence, Rhode Island, 1975).
Cathedral of Ice (produced Providence, Rhode Island, 1975).
Naked in the Garden (produced Providence, Rhode Island, 1975).
Year after Year (produced Providence, Rhode Island, 1976).

Radio Plays: *The Sound of a Soldier*, 1945; *The Death of a President*, 1945; *The Cid*,
from the play by Corneille, 1963 (Canada).

Novel

The Arena of Ants.   Providence, Rhode Island, Copper Beech Press, 1976.

Verse

Tensions.   San Francisco, Bern Porter, 1947.
The American Fantasies.   San Francisco, Bern Porter, 1951.
The Right to Greet.   San Francisco, Bern Porter, 1956.
Selected Poems 1945–1959.   San Francisco, Bern Porter, 1959.
Private Dooms and Public Destinations: Poems 1945–1962   Denver, Swallow, 1962.
The Stalingrad Elegies.   Denver, Swallow, 1964.
Release.   Providence, Rhode Island, Hellcoal Press, 1968.
Violence and Glory: Poems 1962–1968.   Chicago, Swallow Press, 1969.
The Buddhist Car and Other Characters.   Chicago, Swallow Press, 1973.
Pursuing Elegy: A Poem about Haiti.   Providence, Rhode Island, Copper Beech Press,
   1974.

Other

Sherwood Anderson: His Life and Work.   Denver, University of Denver Press, 1951.
The Roaring Market and the Silent Tomb (biographical study of the scientist and artist,
   Bern Porter).   Oakland, California, Abbey Press, 1956.
Breakout! In Search of New Theatrical Environments.   Chicago, Swallow Press, 1972.

Editor, *Six Historians,* by Ferdinand Schevill.   Chicago, University of Chicago Press,
   and London, Cambridge University Press, 1956.

James Schevill comments:

   My early plays were verse plays. Recently, my plays have been written in prose. However,
as a poet, I still believe in poetry as the roots of the theatre, and do my best to upend a theatre

that is too literal and prosaic. I want an action that is both theatrical and poetic, that can use the disturbing images of our time to create a new vitality on stage. To achieve this vitality, I like to use dramatic, historical contrasts to give a play depth and perspective. Today the great possibilities of playwriting lie in the recognition that a play can range in time and space as widely as a film, that it can be as exciting in movement as a film, and that the great advantage it continues to have over film is the live actor who is capable of instantaneous, extraordinary transformations in character and situation.

*   *   *

A lyric poetic, James Schevill has been consistently drawn to the theatre, but his plays are written largely in prose. Composed of history, current events, and fantasy, they theatricalize injustice in contemporary America.

The Bloody Tenet, Schevill's first published play, takes its title from the self-defense of Roger Williams when he was persecuted for religious unorthodoxy. Schevill's play sets Williams' story as a play within a play, and the outer frame is a dialogue between a middle-aged Journalist and a voluptuous Evangelist. As the inner play dramatizes Williams' condemnation by orthodox authority, the frame play dramatizes a facile orthodoxy playing lip service to liberty. Schevill's play finally confronts his moderns with Williams himself, who refuses to choose between the Journalist's critique of his inadequacies and the Evangelist's idolization of him. In verse Roger Williams re-emphasizes his belief in individual paths to God.

Moving from religion to politics, Schevill paired his next two plays under the title *American Power.* The first play, *The Space Fan,* is subtitled a play of escape, and the second one, *The Master,* a play of commitment. The titular Space Fan is a zany lady who communicates with beings in outer space, and a suspicious government therefore assigns an Investigator to spy on her activities. Through the course of the play the Space Fan converts the Investigator to her free way of life, and as they join in a dance the Investigator declares: "For the first time in my life, I feel that I've become a real investigator."

In the companion play, *The Master,* investigation is more insidious. An attractive young woman, the Candidate, is guided by the Master in examinations which will culminate in a degree of General Mastery. During the examination the Master imposes upon the Candidate various roles, such as Army Officer, Indian squaw, Minute Man, Southern rebel, and finally corpse. Master and Candidate then oppose each other with their respective autobiographies. which erupt into scenes that glorify American power. The subtitles of both plays emerge as ironic: *The Space Fan* is a play of escape from American power, and *The Master,* a play of commitment, satirizes (and implicitly condemns) commitment to American power.

Schevill's next play, *The Black President,* is rooted in American oppression of Blacks, but it reaches out to indict the whole white racist world. Moses Jackburn, an American Black, is captain of a facsimile slaveship that is manned by the Blacks of many countries. He sails the ship up the Thames to London, demanding to speak with the British Prime Minister. He is met with pious platitudes, then mercantile bargaining, and finally threats of force. Rather than surrender the ship, Jackson orders his crew to blow it up. While awaiting extradition to America, he is visited by Spanish Carla with whom he shares a fantasy life in which she helps him campaign for the presidency, to become the first "Black President." Back in the reality of his prison, Jackburn denounces his dream, but still hopes for "a little light."

In *Lovecraft's Follies* Schevill indicates his concern about man's enslavement by technology. H. P. Lovecraft, a Rhode Island recluse, was one of the first science fiction writers to stress its Gothic horrors. The protagonist of Schevill's play, Stanley Millsage, is a physicist at a space center, who has developed a Lovecraft fixation-fear of the horrors that science can perpetrate, which are theatricalized scenically to serve as a cathartic journey for the protagonist. Thus freed from his Lovecraft fixation, Millsage declares: "Well, that's the end of Lovecraft's follies...." But the figure of Lovecraft, alone on stage, says mockingly to the audience: "Maybe!"

That "Maybe" leads to Schevill's next major play, *Cathedral of Ice,* in which technology again brings horror. On stage is a dream machine: "With our machine's modern computer device/ We conjure up a vast Cathedral of Ice./...I become Dream-Fuehrer, power to arrange." The drama fancifully traces the results of Hitler's power mania; in seven scenes he confronts historical and imaginary figures. Inspired by Napoleon and Charlemagne, Hitler summons an architect to "create for eternity our famous German ruins." Converting people's weaknesses into cruel and theatrical strengths, Hitler builds on the legends of Karl May and Richard Wagner. He refuses to tarnish his own legend by marrying Eva Braun. Above all he harnesses science to his monstrous destructive dreams. But Night and Fog, actual characters, erode his structures. Even as the gas chambers destroy their multitudes, the Nazis are destroyed by their own manias, so that Hitler finally seeks glory in a *Liebestod* in the Cathedral of Ice.

In fantastic theatrical shapes Schevill's drama explores the realities of power and politics. Using music, dance, ritual, projections, Schevill the poet has reached out to embrace many possibilities of theatre.

— Ruby Cohn

SCHISGAL, Murray (Joseph).   American.   Born in Brooklyn, New York, 25 November 1926. Educated at Long Island University, New York; Brooklyn Law School, LL.B. 1953; New School for Social Research, New York, B.A. 1959. Served as a Radioman in the United States Navy, 1944–46. Married Reene Schapiro in 1958; has two children. Jazz musician in 1940's; practiced law 1953–55; taught English, Cooper Junior High School, East Harlem, and elsewhere in New York, 1955–60. Since 1960, Full-time Writer. Recipient: Vernon Rice Award, 1963; Outer Circle Award, 1963. Agent: International Creative Management, 40 West 57th Street, New York, New York 10019. Address: 275 Central Park West, New York, New York 10024, U.S.A.

PUBLICATIONS

Plays

The Typists and The Tiger (as *Schrecks: The Typists, The Postman, A Simple Kind of Love*, produced London, 1960; revised versions of *The Typists* and *The Postman* produced as *The Typists and The Tiger*, New York, 1963; London, 1964).   New York, Coward McCann, 1963; London, Cape, 1964.

Ducks and Lovers (produced London, 1961).

Knit One, Purl Two (produced Boston, 1963).

Luv (produced London, 1963; New York, 1964).   New York, Coward McCann, 1963.

Windows (produced Los Angeles, 1965).   Included in *Fragments, Windows and Other Plays*, 1965.

Reverberations (produced Stockbridge, Massachusetts, 1965; as *The Basement*, produced New York, 1967).   Included in *Fragments, Windows and Other Plays*, 1965.

Fragments, Windows and Other Plays (includes *Reverberations, Memorial Day, The Old Jew*).   New York, Coward McCann, 1965.

The Old Jew, Fragments, and Reverberations (produced Stockbridge, Massachusetts, 1966).   Included in *Fragments, Windows and Other Plays*, 1965.

Fragments (includes *The Basement*) (produced New York, 1967).   Included in
   Fragments, Windows and Other Plays, 1965.
Memorial Day (produced Baltimore, 1968).   Included in *Fragments, Windows and
   Other Plays*, 1965.
Jimmy Shine, music by John Sebastian (produced New York, 1968).   New York,
   Athenuem, 1969.
A Way of Life (produced New York, 1969).
The Chinese, and Dr. Fish (produced New York, 1970).   New York, Dramatists Play
   Service, 1970.
An American Millionaire (produced New York, 1974).   New York, Dramatists Play
   Service, 1974.
All over Town (produced New York, 1975).   New York, Dramatists Play Service, 1975.
Roseland (produced Berlin, 1975).

Screenplay: *The Tiger Makes Out*, 1967.

Television Play: *The Love Song of Barney Kempenski*, 1966.

*   *   *

Murray Schisgal is one of the few playwrights to have survived the abrupt rise and fall of absurdism. Having begun in that vein, apparently an American cross between Beckett and Ionesco, he went on to find a personal, tremendously comic and compassionate, original style of his own. This style evolved from the two dimentional primary colored cartoon into a fantasy of reality. Schisgal's plays are set in dreamlike places, their stories free of the outer restrictions of time and place, their characters free of the inner restrictions of propriety and self control. They are almost all about the artist as a man – a peculiar, creative animal who must live among others; who wants to like people and be liked by them, but somehow cannot; who is expected to fit the artist stereotype; who is no type at all. The artist as a self-deceptive, pompous, unhappy, silly but special and original man.

Invariably, the Schisgal artist is a justified failure, dedicated but talentless. In the early one-act play, *The Tiger* (off-Broadway, 1963), he is half intellectual and half infant, unaware of any art medium through which he can pour his feelings, sensitivities and pain. Frustrated and vengeful, he kidnaps the first girl he can, only to find her a middle-class housewife. The combination is comic but, at its core, *The Tiger* is a case of type-meets-type, a full act of mocked clichés. The author was lucky – the play (on a bill with *The Typists*, an even lesser work) received enthusiastic notices and so he was encouraged to develop a palpable playwriting ability.

His next work, *Luv* (Broadway, 1964), was even luckier. A five minute sketch padded to full length, the play was an enormous New York success. In this case the artist is a poet, involved in a romantic triangle with a businessman and his clinically sexual wife. Once more, Schisgal depended on his amazing memory for clichés, mocking them ("Where there is love there can be no trust," "Give love a chance," etc.) while providing little else in story, character development or complexity to justify the play's length.

Ironically, as Schisgal's talent and craftsmanship grew, his rewards dwindled. *Fragments* (off-Broadway, 1967) was his first American failure though in fact it included his best produced work till that time – the one-act *The Basement*. In this play, the artist is an ex-science teacher trying to revive a frozen chimpanzee. His wife, a decent, efficient but unimaginative lady, prefers real if everyday life to the artist's dreams. The play is her tragedy and it is most moving. The titular play of this twin bill was still another story of failed artists – three unpublished novelists who look and talk the way writers are supposed to but never write their books.

In all these cases, Schisgal's mocked clichés grew ever more compulsive, self-destructive and less funny. (No doubt too, this encyclopedic mimickry of American jargon contributed to his problems with foreign productions.) With *Jimmy Shine* (Broadway, 1968), he finally rid himself of the mannerism. The play was his most well-crafted, most sensitive, most mature, funny and compassionate work to date.

Again, the hero is an artist – now a painter – again he isn't very good. A residue of the author's cliché compulsion remains – this painter lives in a loft in Greenwich Village and he paints in whatever style happens to be fashionable at the moment. But he is now a success as a human being. He has learned that it is all right for people you dislike not to like you either. And Schisgal himself apparently learned that being an artist is a state of mind. Rathar than laugh at such people, he has come to appreciate them.

Structurally, *Jimmy Shine* is a complicated proposition, fulfilled through mature technique. It flows back and forth through time, from youth to early manhood, and moves from place to place in a way that a designer and a director can handle. Rare is the playwright with a knowledge of practical stagecraft. Schisgal, by this point, had matured as a playwright with imagination and technique, while retaining his original genuis for the essentially theatrical story and setting.

This genius showed again in the one-act *The Chinese* (Broadway, 1970), produced on a twin bill with *Dr. Fish*, a minor satire of psychiatry. *The Chinese* is set in a Chinese laundry, a typical choice by the playwright of a place that is everyday and yet ultratheatrical. Its hero appears Caucasian though his parents are Oriental, and this unaccountable difference is both funny and relevant. For the play is about the silly desire of minority groups to be like everybody else. Like all of Schisgal, the play champions difference. Though the play did not succeed, its author did. The artistic comedy has nearly disappeared, much to the detriment of our theatre and its audiences. Murray Schisgal is the rare – and certainly the most accomplished – practitioner of it.

—Martin Gottfried

SEABROOK, Jeremy.   British.   Born in Northampton, 1939. Educated at Northampton Grammar School; Gonville and Caius College, Cambridge; London School of Economics, diploma in social administration 1967. Taught in a secondary-modern school for two years; Social Worker for the Inner London Education Authority, 1967–69. Agent: Clive Goodwin, 79 Cromwell Road, London S.W.7, England.

PUBLICATIONS

Plays

   Life Price with Michael O'Neill (produced London, 1969).
   Morality with Michael O'Neill (produced London, 1971).
   Millenium with Michael O'Neill (produced London, 1973).
   Our Sort of People with Michael O'Neill (produced London, 1974).
   Sex and Kinship in a Savage Society with Michael O'Neill (produced London, 1975).

   Radio Plays, with Michael O'Neill: *Birds in a Gilded Cage* (Seabrook only), 1974; *The Bosom of the Family*, 1975.

   Television Plays, with Michael O'Neill: *A Clear Cut Case*, 1973; *Soap Opera in Stockwell*, 1973; *Children of the Sun*, 1975; *Beyond the Call of Duty* (*Crown Court* series), 1976.

Other

*The Unprivileged: A Hundred Years of Family Life and Tradition in a Working-Class
    Street.* London, Longman, 1967.
City Close-Up. London, Allen Lane, 1971.
Loneliness. London, Temple Smith, 1971; New York, Universe Books, 1975.
The Everlasting Feast. London, Allen Lane, 1974.
A Lasting Relationship: Homosexuals and Society. London, Allen Lane, 1976.

*   *   *

See the essay on Michael O'Neill and Jeremy Seabrook on p. 604.

SELBOURNE, David. British. Born in London, 4 June 1937. Educated at
Manchester Grammar School; Balliol College, Oxford; trained as a lawyer. Currently, Tutor
in Political Theory, Ruskin College, Oxford. Recipient: Aneurin Bevan Memorial
Fellowship, 1975. Address: c/o Unna and Durbridge Ltd., 14 Beaumont Mews, Marylebone
High Street, London, W1N 4HE, England.

PUBLICATIONS

Plays

The Play of William Cooper and Edmund Dew-Nevett (produced Exeter, 1968).
    London, Methuen, 1968.
The Two-Backed Beast (produced Liverpool, 1968). London, Methuen, 1969.
Dorabella (produced Edinburgh, 1969). London, Methuen, 1970.
Samson (produced London, 1970). Included in *Samson and Alison Mary Fagan*, 1971.
Alison Mary Fagan (produced Auckland, New Zealand, 1972). Included in *Samson
    and Alison Mary Fagan*, 1971.
Samson and Alison Mary Fagan. London, Calder and Boyars, 1971.
The Damned (produced London, 1973). London, Methuen, 1971.
Class Play (produced London, 1972). London, Hutchinson, 1973.

Other

An Eye to China. London, Black Liberator Press, 1975.
Brook's Dream: The Politics of Theatre. London, Action Books, 1974.

Critical Studies: Introduction by John Russell Brown to *The Play of William Cooper and
Edmund Dew-Nevett*, 1968; introduction by Stuart Hall to *An Eye to China*, 1975.

*   *   *

David Selbourne writes with consistent strategy. He choses simple actions that involve
basic motives with the minimum of complication through story or the representation of the

processes of everyday living. So he is free to move his characters into ever-changing relationships with each other, and with their own reactions. In the one-act *Samson*, a boy tries to break away from his father in twelve short scenes. In *Dorabella*, a spinster is attracted to the boyfriend of her hairdresser. In *The Play of William Cooper and Edmund Dew-Nevett*, a simpleton and would-be artist seeks happiness and finds corruption.

They are intellectual plays in that they are based on a clear view of how time, power, imagination, thought and passions work together. But they are realized with a sensual awareness that seeks to create brilliant juxtapositions, activity and language that can take actors and audience directly to total, undisguised confrontations.

Almost all the dialogue is in a verse form that serves to accentuate thrust and concision. It also holds attention for the echoes from mystical poets and the Old Testament that play a large part in creating the overall impression of the plays. The echoes are purposefully easy to catch and, more than this, they live together with a lively response to ordinary talk and thought. David Selbourne forges his own prophetic language to pierce his audience's habitual responses. This style with its radiant images offsets the restricted nature of the play's actions, where man is repeatedly shown caught by his own conditions of living. *The Damned* presents self-deception and domination with calculated ruthlessness, but even in this painful drama the words spoken show how the hope of free life is still the characters' true source of energy. At the end of *William Cooper*, the simpleton can "fly no more," but he has only just recognized again "Light blazing into my head."

Two plays are in a spearate category, for in the one-act *Alison Mary Fagan* and the short *Class Plays* David Selbourne has placed real people in dramatic forms, in the first an actress who faces herself, her life and her career, and in *Class Plays* three pupils and a teacher facing school and life. These are difficult plays to perform, for the dialogue is still shockingly direct and the situations continually changing, but at the centre of the drama is a person who performs or children who are manipulated, and these are to be seen without artifice, recognized as if outside a theatre.

David Selbourne is a writer of teeming imagination and clear determination. He has never fallen in with a fashionable mode of writing for the stage. He has worked on his own, confident in the validity of his purpose. He stakes everything he knows; to share that risk is an exhilarating and demanding enterprise that leaves a permanent mark on one's self.

—John Russell Brown

SEYMOUR, Alan.   Australian.   Born in Perth, Western Australia, 6 June 1927. Educated at Fremantle State School and Perth Modern School. Free-lance Film and Theatre Critic and Educational Writer, Australian Broadcasting Commission, late 1940's and 1950's. Script Editor and Producer, BBC Television, London, 1974–77. Theatre Critic, *London Magazine*, 1963–65, and contributor to *Overland*, Melbourne, *Meanjin*, Melbourne, and *Bulletin-Observer*, Sydney. Recipient: *Observer* Play Competition finalist, 1957; Sydney Journalists' Club prize, 1960; Australian Council for the Arts grant, 1974. Address: c/o Laurence Fitch Ltd., 113 Wardour Street, London W1V 4EH, England.

PUBLICATIONS

Plays

Swamp Creatures (produced Canberra, 1958).
The One Day of the Year (produced Sydney and London, 1961).   Sydney, Angus and

Robertson, 1962; included in *Three Australian Plays*, London, Penguin, 1962.
The Gaiety of Nations (produced Glasgow, 1965; London, 1966).
A Break in the Music (produced Perth, 1966).
The Pope and the Pill (produced London, 1968).
Oh Grave, Thy Victory (produced Canberra, 1973).
Structures (produced Perth, 1974).
The Wind from the Plain, adaptation of the novel by Yashar Kemal (produced Turku, Finland, 1974–75).

Radio Plays: *Little Moron*, 1956; *A Winter Passion*, 1960; *Donny Johnson*, 1965 (Finland).

Television Plays: *The Runner*, 1962 (Australia); *Lean Liberty*, 1962 (UK); *Auto-Stop*, 1964 (UK); *And It Wasn't Just the Feathers*, 1964 (UK); *The Trial and Torture of Sir John Rampayne*, 1965 (UK); *Stockbrokers Are Smashing But Bankers Are Better*, 1965 (UK); *Fixation*, from work by Miles Tripp, 1973 (UK); *The Lotus, Tigers Are Better Looking*, and *Outside the Machine*, from stories by Jean Rhys, 1973–74 (UK).

Novels

The One Day of the Year.   London, Souvenir Press, 1967.
The Coming Self-Destruction of the U.S.A.   London, Souvenir Press, 1969; New York, Grove Press, 1971.

Manuscript Collection: Mitchell Library, Sydney.

Critical Studies: "Seymour's Anzac Play" by Max Harris, in *Nation* (Sydney), April 1961; Introduction by Harry Kippax to *Three Australian Plays*, 1962; *Profile of Australia* by Craig McGregor, London, Hodder and Stoughton, 1966; Introduction by Charles Higham to *Australian Writing Today*, London, Penguin, 1968; essay in *On Native Grounds: Australian Writing from Meanjin Quarterly*, Sydney, Angus and Robertson, 1968; *The Great Australian Stupor* by Ronald Conway, Melbourne, Sun Books, 1971.

Theatrical Activities:

Director: **Plays** – *The One Day of the Year*, Australia tour, 1961. Operas for the Sydney Opera Goup, 1953–57.

Alan Seymour comments:

(1973) As a theatre critic and student of theatre history and especially modern theatre experiments, I am concerned with the research for new forms. Paradoxically, the play of mine most widely performed in Australia and other countries, *The One Day of the Year*, is least typical of my work and intentions, its simple neo-realist form stemming from a conscious artistic choice as the best means to communicate my feelings on the subject of lingering militarism and a need of national self criticism, in the Australian theatre situation of the late 1950's.

Like many Australian playwrights I have in the last decade lived abroad, although the wisdom of this decision is obviously arguable. It is generally held that writers from theatrically under-developed countries need to live abroad because the more open possibilities in, for instance, London make their professional life easier. In my view, life abroad is more difficult. My creative life had I stayed at home would have developed more smoothly, though on more predictable lines. In London, though moderately successful as a television playwright and critic during the first half of the 1960's, I found that, as a playwright for the theatre, I had lost my national voice and not found a new "international" one to replace it.

By '65 this and other problems drove me to live a more isolated life, to think things through, and after five years in Izmir, Turkey, I feel I have a more complex understanding of contemporary life. Certainly some creative problems have been unblocked. Now returned at least temporarily to London, I am interested in the developing Fringe Theatre and the perennial problem of how to reinvigorate the traditional theatre. Radical politics and social problems are a continuing preoccupation.

In 1973 I revisited Australia as a guest of the first Australian National Playwrights' Conference.

*   *   *

Born in Australia, now living in England, Alan Seymour is a cosmopolitan rather than a specifically "Australian" playwright. His earliest plays were for the most part set nominally in Australia, but the setting might have been anywhere. The swamp where two elderly sisters and their servant perform weird experiments in *Swamp Creatures* is supposedly "a dank and fertile part of the Australian bush," but there is no hint of gum leaves, however rank and decayed, in the grim setting. Donny Johnson, the Don Juan hero of the play *Donny Johnson* (the Sydney Journalists' Club Play Competition prize-winning entry in 1960), could be a pop singer anywhere; it just happens that the play moves from a country town in New South Wales to Sydney. Since Alan Seymour left Australia in 1961, one stage play, *A Break in the Music*, has returned to Australia to deal with family memories of life there in the nineteen thirties and forties, but for the rest he has ranged widely. His short play, *The Gaiety of Nations*, took up the theme of Vietnam; his novel, *The Coming Self-Destruction of the U.S.A.*, deals with race conflicts in the U.S., and his television plays have covered a wide range of countries and situations.

Risking over-simplification, one might say that Alan Seymour's plays fall into two broad categories, sometimes of course overlapping: on the other hand, compassionate but comic-satiric observation of ordinary people, plays that are convincingly "real"; and on the other hand, plays which are grotesque, macabre, occasionally bordering on the grand guignol, and with characters larger than life. Included in the first type would be the delightful televison drama, *And It Wasn't Just the Feathers*, about the short-lived relationship between a frightened, lonely old woman with a passion for feathers, and a tough, drifting young man, and the two specifically Australian plays, *A Break in the Music*, and *The One Day of the Year*.

The One Day of the Year, though an early play, is still probably Seymour's most important work, and it has become part of Australian theatrical and social history. "The one day of the year" is Anzac Day, 25 April, when Australians traditionally mourn their war dead. For Alf Cook, returned soldier, the day is sacred, fraught with implications of courage, mateship, masculinity; it is the day when, marching with old comrades, he is no longer an ordinary little man who drives a lift but someone of importance, once more part of a group, "They make a fuss of y' for once. The speeches and the march...and y're all mates." For his son Hughie, now a university student and ironically becoming estranged from his parents by the education they have struggled to give him, the Day is also, though he only half comprehends this, a symbol — a symbol of all that he is struggling to free himself from in his working class backgound. Hughie comes into violent conflicts with his father when he and Jan, a girl-friend from a higher social level, collaborate to produce an article and pictures for the university newspaper; the subject is Anzac Day, and the message, loud and clear through Hughie's photographs of drunken "old diggers," is that the real significance of the so-called day of mourning is that it is an excuse for an almost national booze-up. The play comes to a slightly sentimental conclusion, suggesting that though Alf cannot change, he has gained greater insight into himself, and Hughie for his part has learned a little more tolerance of the father he loves and in some ways resembles. Seymour presents with great insight the strengths and weaknesses of each point of view: the dream as well as the drunkenness in Alf's concept of Anzac Day, and, in Hughie's, idealism combined with lack of understanding and compassion for what he has not experienced, and, of course, the need of youth to assert itself and its values. *The One Day of the Year* is basically not a play about Anzac Day or even conflicting ideas of nationalism, but the conflict of generations, heightened by disparity in education. *The One Day of the Year* on its first production roused considerable indignation, mostly from older Australians who felt with some justice that the sacred nature of Anzac Day had been assailed. In fact, *The One Day of the Year* is dramatically weighted in favour of the older, more colourful "lower class" characters, Alf, his taciturn wife Dot, and Wacka, the only real Anzac in the play; against these, the better-educated Hughie is pallid and almost priggish, his socially superior girl-friend Jan frankly unreal. Alf, Wacka and Dot have the advantage of a colourful idiom – Alf with his intolerable reiteration of "I'm a bloody Australian..." which, with all its implications of unthinking complacency, is turned against him when Jan tells him sweetly, "You're so right, Mr. Cook." The automatic invitation, "'ave a cuppa tea" has comedy, kindliness – and finally the horrors of strangling, inescapable banality.

The second category of Seymour plays could be represented by such dramas as *The Shattering, Donny Johnson*, and *Swamp Creatures*. In *Swamp Creatures*, two sisters and their servant mate different species of animals, producing obscene monsters which prowl through the swamps at night and finally turn on the human beings who made them. It is a slow, highly theatrical revelation of horrors which also carries a message, clearly embedded in the symbolism, a message a good deal less hackneyed when Seymour wrote the play than it is now: that science may in the end turn and rend its creator.

As with most writers, certain characteristic themes and forms of expression recur in Alan Seymour's plays. There is for instance a touch of caricature about many of his best characters, a suprising number of whom are older women, very like Dot Cook in *The One Day of the Year*. Seymour's plays for the most part end in one of two ways: with the main characters trapped unwillingly in some painful situation (*The One Day of the Year, Donny Johnson, Swamp Creatures, Screams from a Dark Cellar*) or else in Pinter-like isolation (*The Shattering, A Winter Passion, And It Wasn't Just the Feathers*). Alan Seymour has himself pointed out two recurring motifs, the conflict of generations which occurs in most of his plays, and the less frequent but still observably repeated situation of someone being kidnapped.

Some of Alan Seymour's best drama writing has been for television, and particularly noteworthy are his sensitive adaptations of the Jean Rhys stories *The Lotus, Tigers are Better Looking*, and *Outside the Machine*. He is also a novelist, a knowledgeable and perceptive drama critic, and the author of many short stories and articles.

—Alrene Sykes

SHAFFER, Anthony. British. Born in Liverpool, Lancashire, 15 May 1926; twin brother of Peter Shaffer, *q.v.* Educated at St. Paul's School, London; Trinity College, Cambridge (editor, *Granta*), graduated 1950. Married to Carolyn Soley; has two daughters. Worked as barrister, journalist. Lives in Wiltshire. Agent: Fraser and Dunlop Scripts Ltd., 91 Regent Street, London W1R 8RU, England.

PUBLICATIONS

Plays

The Savage Parade (produced London, 1963).
Sleuth (produced London and New York, 1970).   New York, Dodd Mead, 1970;
    London, Calder and Boyars, 1971.
Murderer (produced Brighton and London, 1975).   London, Marion Boyars, 1976.

Screenplays: *Black Comedy; Forbush and the Penguins; Absolution*, 1970; *Frenzy*,
1972; *Sleuth*, 1973; *The Wickerman; The Goshawk Squadron*, 1973; *Masada*, 1974;
The Moonstone, 1975; *Evil Under the Sun*, 1976.

Television Play: *Pig in the Middle.*

Novels

How Doth the Crocodile?, with Peter Shaffer (as Peter Anthony).   London, Evans,
    1951; as Peter and Anthony Shaffer, New York, Macmillan, 1957.
Woman in the Wardrobe, with Peter Shaffer (as Peter Anthony).   London, Evans,
    1952.
Withered Murder, with Peter Shaffer.   London, Gollancz, 1955; New York,
    Macmillan, 1956.

*   *   *

The author of three novels, a television play, and several screenplays, Anthony Shaffer is
primarily known for his stage play, *Sleuth*. A parody of detective fiction, it simultaneously
mocks and exploits the techniques of the thriller. The play is set in a Norman Manor House of
the kind beloved of writers of the Agatha Christie school. Andrew Wyke, who appears first
dressed in the requisite smoking jacket and black tie, is himself a thriller writer of a somewhat
dated kind, having created an implausible hero called St. John Lord Merridew, an amateur
sleuth of astounding perspicacity if little credibility. In the course of the play Wyke sets out to
revenge himself on his wife's lover, Milo Tindle, by first persuading him to engage in a fake
robbery while dressed in a clown's costume and them shooting him as an intruder when he
complies. Though the bullet is a blank and Milo is shocked into unconsciousness – precisely
the object of the cruel charade. But Milo subsequently reverses the situation until, beaten at
his own game, Wyke finally kills his rival – only to hear the police arrive as he sinks to the
ground gasping the words "Game, set and match."
    The clever twists of the plot, the urbane humour, the absolute command of mood make
this a distinctive work which, as a parody, is far more effective than Stoppard's *The Real
Inspector Hound* and, as a thriller, more compelling than Agatha Christie's *The Mousetrap*,
whose record run it could perhaps come to rival. Yet there is a paradox here of course not
unlike that which attaches itself to "fearless parodies of pornography" in that Shaffer is
obviously more than a little attracted to the genre which he so tellingly satirises while the
play's effectiveness turns on the brilliant exploitation of the very techniques which he derides.
This is a conjuring trick of a particularly effective kind, but a trick nonetheless and as such
subject to the criticisms which he allows his characters to level at the genre. Wyke's world of
games and puzzles, of easily resolvable complexities, of characters which devolve inevitably
into caricature, is indeed the world of crime fiction and Milo clearly has a point when he
denounces the detective story as "a world of coldness and class hatred, and two dimensional
characters who are not expected to communicate; it's a world where only amateurs win, and
where foreigners are automatically figures of fun....To be puzzled is all....To put it shortly, the

detective story is the normal recreation of snobbish, out-dated, life-hating, ignoble minds." Since Shaffer himself has employed precisely the same conventions and created a similarly dehumanised universe he might indeed seem to be vulnerable to his own criticisms, yet if he is so he fully implicates an audience which has responded to those conventions and to that universe. And the very neatness of the ending, with a police car arriving as the fatal shot is fired, is an indication both of his own keen sense of parody and, even more ironically, his command of the form which he is satirising. *Sleuth* is, perhaps, the supreme example of having one's dramatic cake and eating it.

— C. W. E. Bigsby

SHAFFER, Peter (Levin). British. Born in Liverpool, Lancashire, 15 May 1926; twin brother of Anthony Shaffer, *q.v.* Educated at St. Paul's School, London; Trinity College, Cambridge, 1947–50, B.A. 1950. Conscripted: coalminer, 1944–47. Worked in the acquisition department of the New York Public Library, 1951–54; worked for Boosey and Hawkes, music publishers, London, 1954–55; Literary Critic, *Truth*, 1956–57; Music Critic, *Time and Tide*, 1961–62. Recipient: *Evening Standard* award, 1958; New York Drama Critics Circle Award, 1960, 1975; Tony Award, 1975. Address: 18 Earl's Terrace, London W.8, England.

PUBLICATIONS

Plays

> *Five Finger Exercise* (produced London, 1958; New York, 1958). London, Hamish Hamilton, and New York, Harcourt Brace, 1958.
> *The Private Ear and The Public Eye* (produced London, 1962; New York, 1963). London, Hamish Hamilton, 1962; New York, Stein and Day, 1964.
> *The Merry Roosters Panto*, with the Theatre Worship (produced London, 1963). Sketch in *The Establishment* (produced New York, 1963).
> *The Royal Hunt of the Sun: A Play Concerning the Conquest of Peru* (produced Chichester and London, 1964; New York, 1965). London, Hamish Hamilton, and New York, Stein and Day, 1965.
> *Black Comedy* (produced Chichester, 1965; London, 1966; New York, 1967). Included in *Black Comedy, Including White Lies*, 1967; London, French, 1967.
> *A Warning Game* (produced New York, 1967).
> *White Lies* (produced New York, 1967). Included in *Black Comedy, Including White Lies*, 1967; as *The White Liars* (produced London, 1968), London, French, 1967 (revised version, produced London and New York, 1976).
> *Black Comedy, Including White Lies: Two Plays.* New York, Stein and Day, 1967; as *The White Liars, Black Comedy: Two Plays*, London, Hamish Hamilton, 1968.
> *It's about Cinderella* (produced London, 1969).
> *Shrivings* (as *The Battle of Shrivings*, produced London, 1970). London, Deutsch, 1974; in *Equus and Shrivings*, 1974.
> *Equus* (produced London, 1973; New York, 1974). London, Deutsch, 1973; in *Equus and Shrivings*, 1974.
> *Equus and Shrivings: Two Plays* New York, Atheneum, 1975.

Screenplays: *Lord of the Flies*, with Peter Brook, 1963; *The Public Eye (Follow Me!)*, 1972.

Radio Play: *The Prodigal Father*, 1957.

Television Plays: *The Salt Land*, 1955; *Balance of Terror*, 1957.

Novels

How Doth the Little Crocodile?, with Anthony Shaffer (as Peter Anthony).   London, Evans, 1951; as Peter and Anthony Shaffer, New York, Macmillan, 1957.

Woman in the Wardrobe, with Anthony Shaffer (as Peter Anthony).   London, Evans, 1952.

Withered Murder, with Anthony Shaffer.   London, Gollancz, 1955; New York, Macmillan, 1956.

*   *   *

Peter Shaffer is one of the few British dramatists to have acheived major successes, both critically and with the public, without the benefit of ever being exactly fashionable, Indeed he stood aside from the enthusiasms of the 1950's and 1960's, insisting that "labels aren't for playwrights." In 1958, when the "angry young men" at the Royal Court Theatre in London were expressing a mood of social and class frustration, Shaffer's tightly-knit domestic drama, *Five Finger Exercise*, opened in the West End: a play much in the style of Pinero and Rattigan, about the emotional problems of a wealthy middle-class family. The sheer skill of the writing, couples with a sophisticated awareness of the sexual and cultural tensions of the middle-classes, caused British and American critics to hail *Five Finger Exercise* as the best new play of the season, despite the prevailing theatrical mood. In the mid-sixties, confronted by many epic plays in the style of Brecht and productions influenced by Artaud, Shaffer incorporated some of the new techniques into his magnificent epic play, *The Royal Hunt of the Sun*, but without being drawn into the dogmatisms of either school. When many of his contemporaries were either committedly left or right wing, Shaffer maintained a sturdy liberal independence: "the greatest tragic factor in history," he once wrote, "is man's apparent need to mark the intensity of his reaction to life by joining a band; for a band, to give itself definition, must find a rival, or an enemy." The same freedom from shibboleths marks his flexible craftsmanship as a dramatist, neither avant-garde nor stolidly conservative. Almost alone among the writers of the post-war renaissance of British drama, Shaffer retains a loving regard for the traditions of middle-class theatre without closing his mind to alternatives.

This open-mindedness is reflected by the variety of his achievements. Peter Shaffer has written perhaps the best modern farce, *Black Comedy*, one of the best epics, *The Royal Hunt of the Sun*, one of the best domestic dramas, *Five Finger Exercise*, together with several absorbing but light-weight one-act plays and an ambitious philosophical drama, *The Battle of Shrivings*. This versatility was only achieved because his technique as a dramatist rests on sure foundations. It is however a somewhat self-effacing technique. His dialogue lacks the obvious wit and brilliance of, say, David Mercer's; but it rarely fails to hold the attention and, more importantly, to rise to the demands of the story. He often writes brilliantly for particular actors, catching their style and the sort of lines which only they can make funny. Kenneth Williams, the outrageously camp English comedian, scored a personal triumph in Shaffer's *The Public Eye*, but he only did so because the part of Julian Cristoforou was exactly right for him. On a more ambitious level, however, Shaffer manages to make credible extraordinary men, such as Pizarro, the gnarled, determined Spanish fighter, and Atahuallpa, the God/King of the Incas. The language of his plays – the style, intonation and nuances – almost always seem carefully planned and fails only when it becomes too conscious, too literary and a little sententious, as in *The Battle of Shrivings*. With the verbal quality of his plays, Shaffer combines an assured handling of stories and plots. The intricate interplay of the emotional themes in *Five Finger Exercise* offers one example of his ability to sustain many apparently low-powered ideas until they combine together in one critical scene – where Stanley the father dismisses Walter the German tutor – of great impact. This delicate strength was inappropriate for *The Royal Hunt of the Sun*, which required a broader, bolder treatment: and here again Shaffer triumphed. From the early recruitment scenes in Spain to the horrific denouement, Shaffer manages to evoke in a series of vivid episodes the whole desperate enterprise of the conquest of Peru: the forced marches through fever-ridden jungles, the ascent of the Andes, the fear of the Spanish hopelessly isolated in the heart of the Inca Empire and the terrible consequences of this fear. *Five Finger Exercise* requires a box-set, a cast of five and traditional British techniques of naturalistic acting: *The Royal Hunt of the Sun* demands an open stage, a huge cast trained not in naturalistic skills, but in mime, music and all forms of stylized acting. Few dramatists could write with equal assurance for such totally different genres: and the secret of Shaffer's ability to do so lies in his capacity to tell a good story, using whatever dramatic means seem appropriate.

But the versatility and open-mindedness have left Peter Shaffer with a curiously negative image, as if his sheer competence has erased his personality. John Russell Taylor, in *Anger and After*, states that "the most interesting quality of his work is its impersonality." This back-handed compliment under-rates the continuity of Shaffer's style, which persists despite the many external variations. His plays are almost always held together by strong basic conflicts, which are illustrated by his leading characters – Arieh and Jo in the television play *The Salt Land*, Louise and Stanley in *Five Finger Exercise*, Pizarro and Atahuallpa in *The Royal Hunt of the Sun,* and Mark and Gideon in *The Battle of Shrivings*. These characters are not eccentrics nor are their struggles merely personal ones. They represent opposing cultural, emotional and social forces, apparently irreconcilable: and the crises of the plays occur when, at the very moment of apparent victory or defeat, the whole battle is suddenly placed within a wider human context, which includes understanding, forgiveness and love for both sides. A humanism, a distinctive feature of Shaffer's style, overrides the hatred on which the plots are based. Saul, in *The Salt Land*, takes command of the kibbutz where Arieh has murdered Jo – and Arieh meekly allows himself to be arrested. Stanley is appalled by Walter's attempted suicide and finally recognizes him, not as an enemy in league with Louise, but as a friend and foster son. Pizarro is overwhelmed by the finalty of Atahuallpa's death and the conquistadores are shocked into shame. His most tragic plays still end with an assertion, sometimes oblique but always present, of human dignity and faith: and this optimism also sets him apart from his contemporaries.

The development of Shaffer's creative powers can best be seen in the characterisation of these conflicting personalities. In his early epic tragedy about the birth of modern Israel, *The Salt Land*, the two immigrant brothers are almost caricatures. Arieh is a modern prophet, fierce in his faith and determination: whereas Jo is a city boy, quick to exploit the new world to his advantage. The dialogue is didactic: the conflict, too obvious to need so much stressing: the murder, a foregone conclusion. Louise and Stanley, however are credible both as representatives of different cultural forces and as people: and for this reason, Shaffer retains the audience's sympathy even for the boor of husband, Stanley. When Stanley declares a belated love for Walter, this reversal of events has been prepared for but nevertheless achieves the intended shock. A similar *coupe de théâtre* – but on a much more impressive scale – occurs at the end of *The Royal Hunt of the Sun*: where Pizarro is converted to the Inca philosophy and comes to believe in Atahuallpa's god-like powers. His faith is dashed when Atahuallpa's declared resurrection fails to take place: and the horror of the story comes not with the Sun King's death, but the endless disillusion of Pizarro who is left only with the gold he came for and not the renewed hope and vitality which he accidentally discovered. Throughout his career as a dramatist. Shaffer carefully deepens and broadens in significance the basic conflicts on which his stories are based. In *The Battle of Shrivings*, one of his less successful plays, the conflict is between an Apollonian and a Dionysian man, between the super-ego and the id; but in this case, the characters are rather too obviously representative of their opposite types. A more profound and searching conflict is to be found in *Equus*, first performed by the national theatre in 1973. *Equus* is concerned with the relationship between an analyst and one of his patients, a young boy, Alan Strang, who has committed an extraordinary and grotesque crime. He has speared the eyes of six horses in a riding stable, where he was employed as a groom. In trying to understand why this happened, Dysart, the analyst, discovers that the boy has an almost religious obsession with horses. They represent god-like qualities for him, the sufferings of a Christ, nobility of movement and the rhythms of nature itself. Because he felt shame in their eyes, as the result of his first experience of sexual love, the boy sought to destroy their accusing gazes. The crime is the other side of his devotion. Dysart cannot feel this passion; and his treatment of the boy presents a moral dilemma to him. Should he, an arid, loveless, middle-aged man try to tamper with an emotion which he cannot replace or create, only perhaps destroy? Is not the destruction of a guiding passion worse even than the boy's crime, for without such a holy love, which can be perverted but nevertheless exists, the soul itself withers away.

In one sense, Shaffer is an optimistic writer, an instinctive humanist. His plays usually end with a firm statement of the importance of love and human understanding. Even in *Black Comedy*, that gorgeous one-act farce which rests on the idea that, when the lights fuse in the drawing room and the characters grope around in darkness, the audience can watch the blind fumblings in full light, there is a scene which is obviously less frivolous than the others. Brindsley has got himself engaged to Carol, the daughter of a stuffy Colonel, whom he wants to impress; but his former girl friend, Clea, returns and hides herself in the darkness of the flat where the lights have fused. But Carol cannot distinguish Brindsley's hand in the darkness, although she is engaged to him. Whereas Clea can – and so can Harold, Brindsley's homosexual neighbour. Love is not a matter of words or vows, the argument goes, but of feelings which cannot be simulated or disguised. The sudden discovery of love in this sense is the crisis of *Five Finger Exercise* as well, and also *The Royal Hunt of the Sun*. This observation may seem sententious, perhaps even naive: but Shaffer reserves pride of place in his plays for its affirmation. It is not a startling idea – nor an exceptional one, except perhaps in the controlled insistence with which it is presented. Perhaps too this affirmation accounts for the mixed reputation which Shaffer currently enjoys: some consider him a complacent dramatist, whose abilities are too often concealed between a meretricious mask and a sentimental face. Other – that his plays are satisfying precisely because they do not disdain or forget the ordinary felt loyalties on which social life is based.

—John Elsom

SHAW, Irwin.   American.   Born in New York City, 27 February 1913. Educated at Brooklyn College, New York, B.A. in English 1934. Served in the United States Army Signal Corps, in North Africa, the Middle East, Britain, France and Germany, 1942–45. Married Marian Edwards in 1939 (divorced); has one child. Radio Writer, 1934–36; Drama Critic, *New Republic*, New York, 1947–48; taught Creative Writing, New York University, 1947–48. Has lived in Europe since 1951. Recipient: O. Henry Award, for fiction, 1944, 1945; National Institute of Arts and Letters grant, 1946; *Playboy* Award, 1970. Address: P.O. Box 39, Klosters, Switzerland.

PUBLICATIONS

Plays

Bury the Dead (produced New York, 1936).   New York, Random House, 1936; in

713

Famous Plays of 1936, London, Gollancz, 1936.

Siege (produced New York, 1937).

Second Mortgage, in *One-Act Play Magazine* (New York), May 1938.

The Gentle People: A Brooklyn Fable (produced New York, 1939).   New York, Random House, 1939.

Quiet City (produced New York, 1939).

Retreat to Pleasure (produced New York, 1940).

The Shy and the Lonely (produced Los Angeles).   Published in *American Scenes*, edited by William Kozlenko, New York, Day, 1941.

Sons and Soldiers (produced New York, 1943).   New York, Random House, 1943.

The Assassin (produced London and New York, 1945).   New York, Random House, 1945.

The Survivors, with Peter Viertel (produced New York, 1948).   New York, Dramatists Play Service, 1948.

Patate, adaptation of a play by Marcel Achard (produced New York, 1958).

Children from Their Games (produced New York, 1963).   New York, French, 1962.

A Choice of Wars (produced Salt Lake City, Utah; Glasgow, 1967).

Screenplays: *The Big Game*, 1936; *The Hard Way*, 1942; *The Talk of the Town*, 1942; *Commandoes Strike at Dawn*, 1942; *Take One False Step*, 1942; *I Want You*, 1951; *Act of Love*, 1954; *Ulysses*, 1955; *Fire Down Below*, 1957; *Desire under the Elms*, 1958; *The Big Gamble*, 1961; *In the French Style*, 1963; *Survival 1967*, 1968.

Novels

The Young Lions.   New York, Random House, 1948; London, Cape, 1949.

The Troubled Air.   New York, Random House, 1950; London, Cape, 1951.

Lucy Crown.   New York, Random House, and London, Cape, 1956.

Two Weeks in Another Town.   New York, Random House, 1959; London, Cape, 1960.

Voices of a Summer Day.   New York, Delacorte Press, and London, Weidenfeld and Nicolson, 1965.

Rich Man, Poor Man.   New York, Delacorte Press, and London, Weidenfeld and Nicolson, 1970.

Evening in Byzantium.   New York, Delacorte Press, and London, Weidenfeld and Nicolson, 1970.

Nightwork.   New York, Delacorte Press, and London, Weidenfeld and Nicolson, 1975.

Short Stories

Sailor off the Bremen and Other Stories.   New York, Random House, and London, Cape, 1940.

Welcome to the City and Other Stories.   New York, Random House, 1942.

Act of Faith and Other Stories   New York, Random House, 1946.

Mixed Company: Collected Stories.   New York, Random House, 1950; as *Mixed Company: Selected Short Stories*, London, Cape, 1951.

Selected Short Stories.   New York, Modern Library, 1961.

In the French Style (screenplay and stories).   New York, MacFadden, 1963.

Love on a Dark Street and Other Stories.   New York, Delacorte Press, and London, Cape, 1965.

Retreat and Other Stories.   London, New English Library, 1970.

Whispers in Bedlam.   London, Weidenfeld and Nicolson, 1972.

God Was Here, But He Left Early.   New York, Arbor House, 1972.

Other

Report on Israel.   New York, Simon and Schuster, 1950.
In the Company of Dolphins (travel).   New York, Geis, 1964.

Manuscript Collections: Boston University; Morgan Library, Brooklyn College, New York.

*   *   *

Irwin Shaw's first play, *Bury the Dead*, exploded on the New York left-wing stage, then in the depths of the Depression. Shaw was twenty-three years old at the time. For much of his ensuing career as a playwright, he tried to convince himself and his audience that the pacifist message of this one-act play needed some modification.

Bury the Dead was first presented under the auspices of the left-wing New Theatre League for two off-Broadway performances in March 1936. So powerful was the production that it was moved to broadway by Alex Yokel, an impressario who had recently made a fortune on *Three Men on a Horse*, one of the Depression farces delightfully untouched by social significance. Not only did the Shaw play attract the commercial interests of Broadway, but it attracted enough star interest in Hollywood for a public reading by such famous actors as Frederic March, Florence Eldridge, James Cagney, and Francis Lederer. It was one of the radically chic events of the 1930's.

Set "during the second year of the war that is to begin tomorrow night," *Bury the Dead* tells the fantastic story of six soldiers who rise from their mass grave and refuse to be buried. Despite pleas by their women and the establishment leaders, the "dead" men go off to speak against war, followed by the grave-diggers who desert the army.

As staged by Worthington Miner, the play was semi-expressionistic in its fast succession of episodic scenes, in its spectacular use of spotlights on the darkened stage, in its offstage voices, and even in its use of the orchestra pit as the grave. Since each scene served to illustrate the anti-war thesis, the play was also related to such agitprops as Odets' *Waiting for Lefty* (1935) and to such epic theatre productions as Brecht's *Die Mutter* (seen as *Mother* in New York in 1935). But Shaw's play was much subtler as a propaganda piece.

Though *Bury the Dead* created pathos, anger, and horror, its special appeal was in the eerie resurrection of the soldiers. Though this device was not new − it had been used in Hans Chlumberg's full-length fantasy, *Miracle at Verdun*, in 1931 − Shaw achieved greater theatrical impact in his compressed one-act form.

In 1936, after seeing *Bury the Dead*, an enthusiastic admirer asserted that Irwin Shaw had supplanted Clifford Odets as America's first playwright. One year later, after seeing Shaw's *Seige*, another critic proclaimed that Shaw was written out. Though the dramatist never produced anything so electrifying as his first work, he continued to write plays − largely in the realistic vein − and to wrestle with his anti-war theme, modifying it as the political and military situation changed. In this respect, he was typical of many sensitive young men of the thirties and forties who were faced with the personal prospect of fighting in the Second World War.

In *Seige*, a realistic drama set in Civil War Spain, Shaw told the story of a pacifist who turns out to be more militant than the leader of a group of beseiged Loyalists. Pacifists should fight, Shaw implied, if the cause is worthy.

He pursued the limits of pacifism further in his next play, *The Gentle People*, which was presented by the Group Theatre in 1939. Subtitled "A Brooklyn Fable," this drama depicts two peaceful elderly men − one Greek and one Jew − who murder an extortionist and get away with it. Shortly before the outbreak of World War II, Shaw warned that gentle people − pacifists − had to use violence against the fascist bullies of the world.

In *Retreat to Pleasure*, which the Group Theatre produced in 1940, a year after war broke out in Europe, Shaw suggested that young Americans should pursue pleasure before the United States entered the war. The hero, a radical young man, rejects the girl he wanted to marry and goes off in search of fun. Shaw's youthful pacifism gave way to hedonism But because he recognized that American intervention was inevitable, the pursuit of happiness was temporary.

During the war Shaw continued working on his military theme in two plays. The first, *Sons and Soldiers*, a partial return to the fantasy of *Bury the Dead*, concerned a woman's vision of the future. Told that she may die in childbirth, she decides to risk becoming a mother even though she foresees that her sons will become soldiers. The production, set on a revolving stage designed by Norman Bel Geddes, was directed by Max Reinhardt. But the spectacle did not conceal the fashionably commonplace theme, and the drama faltered. So did *The Assassin*, a sensational account of the assassination of Admiral Jean Darlan in Algiers. For Shaw, who was serving in the U.S. Army at this time, the war was a simple struggle between good Allies and an evil Axis.

Since the end of the Second World War, Shaw's dramatic works have been negligible. For example, he adapted Marcel Achard's Parisian farce *Patate*, in 1958, and he wrote a play about misanthropy, *Children from their Games*, in 1963. After the success of his 1948 novel, *The Young Lions*, which concerned American and German soldiers, he devoted most of his writing energy to fiction.

As a dramatist, Irwin Shaw pursued his war theme with such intensity that it overwhelmed his theatricality, his stories, and even his characters − none of whom is really memorable. In *Bury the Dead*, his first and best drama, he achieved the fine balance between theme and theatricality that he was not able to match in his later plays.

—Morgan Y. Himelstein

SHAW, Robert (Archibald). British.   Born in Westhoughton, Lancashire, 9 August 1927. Educated at the Truro School, Cornwall; the Royal Academy of Dramatic Art, London. Married Jennifer Bourke in 1952 (divorced); the actress Mary Ure, 1963 (died, 1975); Virginia Jansen, 1976; has eight children. Stage and Film Actor. Recipient: Hawthornden Prize, for fiction, 1962. Agent: John French Artistes Agency Ltd., 10 Gilbert Place, London W.C.1, England.

PUBLICATIONS

Plays

> *Off the Mainland* (produced London, 1956).
> *The Man in the Glass Booth* (produced London, 1967; New York, 1968).   London, Chatto and Windus, 1967; New York, Grove Press, 1968.
> *Cato Street* (produced London, 1971).   London, Chatto and Windus, 1972.

> Screenplays: *Situation Hopeless−But Not Serious*, 1965; *Figures in a Landscape*, 1970.

> Television Plays: *For the Children* series, 1948, 1952; *The Pets*, 1960; *The Florentine Tragedy*, 1964.

Novels

> *The Hiding Place.*   London, Chatto and Windus, and Cleveland, World, 1959.
> *The Sun Doctor.*   London, Chatto and Windus, and New York, Harcourt Brace, 1961.

The Cure of Souls:
  I. *The Flag.*   London, Chatto and Windus, and New York, Harcourt Brace, 1965.
The Man in the Glass Booth.   London, Chatto and Windus, and New York, Harcourt
Brace, 1967.
A Card from Morocco.   London, Chatto and Windus, and New York, Harcourt Brace,
1969.

Theatrical Activities:

Actor: **Plays** – with the Royal Shakespeare Company, Stratford upon Avon: Angus in
Macbeth, Jupiter in *Cymbeline*, and Suffold in *Henry VIII*, 1949, Messenger in *Julius
Caesar*, Conrade in *Much Ado about Nothing*, and Burgundy in *King Lear*, 1950, Edmund
in *King Lear*, Dolabella in *Antony and Cleopatra*, Tranio in *The Taming of the Shrew*, and
Gratiano in *The Merchant of Venice*, 1953; toured Australia, 1949–50; with the Old Vic
Company, London: Rosencrantz in *Hamlet*, Cassio in *Othello*, and Lysander in *A
Midsummer Night's Dream*, 1951, toured South Africa in these roles and Malcolm in
Macbeth, 1952; George Lamb in *Caro William* by William Douglas Home, London, 1952;
Lazlo Rimini in *Off the Mainland*, London, 1954; Topman in *Tiger at the Gates* by
Giraudoux, London, 1955; Blackmouth in *Live Like Pigs* by John Arden, London, 1958;
Lazlo Rajk in *Shadow of Heroes* by Robert Ardrey, London, 1958; Sergeant Mitchem in
The Long and the Short and the Tall by Willis Hall, London, 1959; Sewell in *One More
River* by Beverley Cross, London, 1959; Watson in *A Lodging for the Night* by Patrick
Kirwany, London, 1960; De Flores in *The Changeling* by Middleton and Rowley, London,
1961; Aston in *The Caretaker* by Harold Pinter, New York, 1961; Mobius in *The
Physicists* by Dürrenmatt, New York, 1964; title role in *Gantry* by Peter Bellwood, New
York, 1970; Deeley in *Old Times* by Harold Pinter, New York, 1971; Edgar in *The Dance
of Death* by Strindberg, New York, 1974. **Films** – *The Dambusters*, 1955; *Sea Fury*, 1959;
The Valiant, 1961; *Tomorrow at Ten*, 1962; *From Russia with Love*, 1963; *The Caretaker*,
1963; *The Luck of Ginger Coffey*, 1964; *The Battle of the Bulge*, 1965; *A Man for All
Seasons*, 1966; *Custer of the West*, 1967; *The Birthday Party*, 1968; *Battle of Britain*,
1969; *Royal Hunt of the Sun*, 1969; *Figures in a Landscape*, 1970; *A Town Called Bastard*,
1971; *Labyrinth*, 1971; *Young Winston*, 1972. *The Hireling*, 1973; *The Sting*, 1973; *The
Taking of Pelhan 123*, 1975; *Jaws*, 1975; *Diamonds*, 1975. **Television** – roles since 1953,
including *The Buccaneer* series, *Rupert of Henzau*, *Hindle Wakes*, *The Winter's Tale*,
Hamlet; *The Florentine Tragedy*, 1964; *Luther*, 1968.

                               *   *   *

Robert Shaw is one of the growing tribe of British actor-dramatists. As an actor he has
some outstanding screen performances to his credit including his mad, bluff bully-boy of a
Henry VIII in *A Man for All Seasons* and his syphilitic Lord Randolph Churchill in *Young
Winston*; as a novelist he has won both critical acclaim and (for *The Hiding Place*) the
Hawthornden prize; and as a dramatist he has written three plays all of which aim to debate
serious issues within a popular format and all of which, at the very least, possess a strong
degree of theatricality.
    The first, *Off the Mainland* (presented in the Arts Theatre in 1956), is undeniably the
weakest of the three: an artificial cold-war melodrama, heavily influenced by Ugo Betti,
encasing an emotional story of a woman who deceives her husband with his own brother.
The trouble is the play contains too many stock characters (a sinister dark-glassed girl
Interrogator, a sterile cuckold) for its ideas to make much impact.
    However, Shaw's next play, *The Man in the Glass Booth* (staged at the St. Martin's in 1967
and based on Shaw's own novel of the same title), managed fairly skilfully to encompass the
Nazi persecution of the Jews within a whodunnit framework. The play hinges on the
character of Arthur Goldman, a New York millionaire property tycoon, who is utterly

appalled by the Vatican's official forgiveness of the Jews in 1964 for the murder of Jesus. A Jew, he decides, must show Christendom what forgiveness really means; so he allows himself to be arrested by Israeli agents as Adolf Dorf, an ex-SS mass-murderer. In the second act Goldman-Dorf is brought to trial, placed in an Eichmann-like glass booth and, before being detected as an impostor, exposes both Dorf's personal sadism and the collective German guilt.

Shaw's point is that forgiveness must be accompanied by a total recognition of brute fact: only when the realities of Nazi Germany have been fully comprehended can we hope to start afresh. And the strength of the play is that Goldman's impersonation of Dorf allows him to put across many shocking, enraging ideas (such as that the Jews, had they been chosen by Hitler, would also have followed him) that give a severe jolt to all our received attitudes. Where Shaw goes astray is in relying too much on the whodunnit format: during the trial scene our constant uncertainty as to whether Goldman might not really be Dorf after all distracts our attention from the argument and too much hinges on the surprise element in the denouement. For all that, it's a vigorously theatrical piece of work and it contains, in the first act, a definitive portrait of a New York Jewish tycoon, kept going by power, steam baths and hormone injections and ruling his subordinates with a whim of iron.

Shaw's next play, *Cato Street* (presented at the Young Vic in 1971), had both the virtues and vices of its predecessor: plenty of strong, sinewy drama and a dispassionate, clear-eyed view of history on the one hand, too great a reliance on detective story suspense and surprise plot-twists on the other.

The play deals with a relatively little-known episode in English history: the Cato Street Conspiracy of 1820 in which a group of poverty-racked radicals plotted to murder the whole Cabinet as they dined at Lord Harrowby's in Grosvenor Square. Shaw falsifies history to the extent of making the leader of the group Susan Thistlewood rather than her husband, Arthur. But otherwise he brings out very well the combination of social victimisation and muddled thinking that gave rise to the conspiracy in the first place; and he skilfully keeps the balance between the radical militants, who wanted nothing less than assassination, and the moderates like William Cobbett who argued for the gradual reform of existing parliamentary institutions.

Once again, however, Shaw's gift for theatre seems a double-edged weapon. He puts too much stress on the unmasking of the government informer within the Cato Street gang. And by failing to make clear the conspiracy's long-termed historical consequences, he makes it seem like a unique aberration in English working-class history. In fact it considerably aided the government in the short-term but in the long run helped the whole tide of proletarian protest. Still it's a bold, direct, unsentimental play and one that confirms the impression that if Shaw can ally his concern with important politico-historical themes with a more scrupulous technical control, he has it in him to write a really major work.

—Michael Billington

SHAWN, Wallace.   American.   Born in New York City, 12 November 1943. Educated at the Dalton School, New York, 1948–57; Putney School, Vermont, 1958–61; Harvard University, Cambridge, Massachusetts, 1961–65, B.A. in history 1965; Magdalen College, Oxford, 1966–68, B.A. in philosophy, politics, and economics 1968, M.A.; studied acting with Katharine Sergava, New York, 1971. Lives with Deborah Eisenberg. Taught English, Indore Christian College, India, 1965–66; taught English, Latin, and drama, Day School, New York, 1968–70; Shipping Clerk, Laurie Love Ltd., New York, 1974–75; Xerox Machine Operator, Hamilton Copy Center, New York, 1975–76. Recipient: Obie award, 1975. Agent: Audrey Wood, International Creative Management, 40 West 57th Street, New York, New York 10019, U.S.A.; or, Margaret Ramsay Ltd., 14a Goodwin's Court, London WC2N 4LL, England.

PUBLICATIONS

Plays

Play in Seven Scenes (also director: produced New York, 1974).
Our Late Night (produced New York, 1974).
In the Dark, music by Allen Shawn (also director: produced Lenox, Massachusetts,
   1976).
Three Short Plays (*Summer Evening, The Youth Hostel, Mr. Frivolous*) (produced New
   York, 1976).

Theatrical Activities:

Director: **Plays** – *Play in Seven Scenes,* New York, 1974; *In the Dark,* Lenox,
Massachusetts, 1976.

Wallace Shawn comments:

My first play, *Four Meals in May* (1967–1969), shows, in the first scene, an old man having
breakfast alone. Then his son, in the second scene, is having lunch in the back room of an art
gallery. The third scene shows us about twenty-five monks – one of them the son of the man
from the gallery – all having their supper in a monastery. And in the final scene – set several
years after the first three scenes – we discover the mother of that particular young monk
bumping into the young monk's former fiancée quite unexpectedly in a rather expensive
restaurant. Actually, when I wrote this, I felt it was my statement about the war in Vietnam. I
also felt that if people saw this play the effect of those four seasons following one after the
other would be to induce in them a sort of an enlightenment.
   Then I wrote a short play about an old man thinking in a hospital bed, *The Old Man* (1969).
Then I wrote a play with sixty characters about a hotel in the tropics, *The Hotel Play* (1970);
there is a sort of malevolent hotel clerk at the center of this rather swirling tropical work.
Then I wrote another short play, *Play in Seven Scenes* (1970), in which a rather strange and
passionate family – mother, father, and two daughters – live far away from everyone, in the
mountains.
   The Hospital Play (1971) has a lot of weeping and vomiting. *Our Late Night* (1972) shows
perhaps a rather elegant social evening, but weeping and vomiting have their place there too.
It's hard to describe these things. My latest plays (*Summer Evening, The Youth Hostel,* and
Mr. Frivolous) are grouped together under the title *Three Short Plays.* In the first, in a foreign
hotel room, a young woman tries on a lot of dresses she's bought, while her companion
watches. In the second, young people spend a moonlit night eating and fighting on beds and
floors. In the third, a man drinks coffee in an attractive room. In the opera *In the Dark* by my
brother Allen Shawn, for which I wrote the libretto, a young man breaks a lot of dishes in a
woman's apartment.
   One thing that I think I can say about my plays (to date) is that I always seem to write about
imaginery situations and places and characters, but only about those that truly and totally
absorb me. I think that perhaps at each moment in one's life there is only one such totally
fascinating imaginery thing (one picture, let us say, of one unknown person in one unknown
room), and to find that one thing inside my head is always incredibly difficult, because it is
always something I have never really seen or thought of before, and often it is something that
I don't really want to see or think about too much at all. But there is really no hope, no
chance, of changing myself before I write; I have to take myself as I am, and if what I care
about at that certain time is two elderly woman having their tea, then that must be my

subject, and if what it is at another time is a strange group masturbating in a dingy room, then I must write about that. And about each scene, there is always one true story to tell, I think; there is always one and only one thing which happened. I may not understand why my characters do what they do (and I usually don't, just as in the same sense I usually don't understand why real people do what they do in life), but I can still, at least, watch, listen, and tell the story. And I always rather boldly assume – in fact, it's an article of faith with me – that if such a story is important to me it must therefore be important to other people too, whether they know it or admit it at first or not, because I'm not that different from other people, and I'm shaped by the same things that shape them. I'm not sure whether it's vanity or modesty that makes me assume that when I'm telling the most truth I can possibly tell about the thing that truly seems most important to me, I'm giving people something that they need to know.

I must say, though, I don't truly think that the world really needs more plays, in general. I mean, the world needs to be saved, actually. I mean, when you consider the suffering that surrounds everybody, and the evil, and the murder, and the threats of murder, and when you consider the fact that our own minds seem to be under some terrible assault, so that we feel our minds are dying, so that it seems people have completely forgotten how to live, I really don't think there is very much honor in a life devoted to writing, unless that writing can do something awfully unusual, something awfully necessary. Personally, I would rather work to alleviate human misery in some simple and direct way. I would rather devote my working hours to meditation and at least achieve for myself a sense of one-ness with the universe. Because writing is not only usually a waste of one's own precious time, but it's usually so harmful to others as well, and just adds to the heap of stupidity and confusion and lies by which we are oppressed. I really do hope I'll stop writing, if I ought to.

*   *   *

Wallace Shawn's *Our Late Night* was directed in New York by André Gregory, with a cast experienced in working together, and a set dominated by a large white bed. The text makes unusual demands. On a first level most of the play is a series of encounters between variously mixed couples at a party. The characters are all young and all intelligent, although with differing powers of verbalization. They talk of other encounters of cooking, eating, lovemaking, clothes, games, childhood and, in a single sustained narrative, of the jungle. The action includes various regroupings, caresses, visits to the bathroom, vomitting, weeping and departures. All this, however, is framed by a much simpler action showing two young people going to bed, eating cereal and, in the last resort, lying or sitting up in bed, awake and silent. The party is not a real party, but a precipitation in explicit drama of the free-moving consciousness of the two central characters. In this way *Our Late Night* presents both the outward facts of living and also the tireless, sexual, fantastic inner facts of being.

The double vision of Wallace Shawn's play is achieved by bold invention and by dialogue that is musically delicate at all times. If the writer had less control his play would have been indulgently sensational; if he had played more safely, it would have been merely ingenious. As it is, *Our Late Night* is a truly original debut, extending the scope of our theatre.

—John Russell Brown

————————————

SHEPARD, Sam.   American.   Born in Fort Sheridan, Illinois, 5 November 1943. Educated at Duarte High School, California. Married O-Lan Shepard in 1969; has one son. Worked as a "hot walker" at the Santa Anita Race Track, a stable hand, sheep shearer, herdsman and orange picker, all in California; car wrecker, Charlemont, Massachusetts; busboy at the Village Gate, a waiter at Marie's Crisis Cafe, and musician with the Holy Modal Rounders, all in New York. Recipient: Obie Award, 1967; Rockefeller grant; Guggenheim Grant, 1968; Office for Advanced Drama Research Grant; Yale University fellowship; National Institute of Arts and Letters award, 1974. Address: c/o Toby Cole, 234 West 44th Street, New York, New York 10036, U.S.A.

PUBLICATIONS

Plays

Cowboys (produced New York, 1964).
Rock Garden (produced New York, 1964; excerpt produced in Oh! Calcutta!, New York, 1969, London, 1970).   Included in The Unseen Hand and Other Plays, 1971.
Up to Thursday (produced New York, 1964).
Dog (produced New York, 1964).
Rocking Chair (produced New York, 1964).
Chicago (produced New York, 1965; London, 1976).   Included in Five Plays, 1967.
Icarus's Mother (produced New York, 1965; London, 1970).   Included in Five Plays, 1967.
4-H Club (produced New York, 1965).   Included in Mad Dog Blues and Other Plays, 1967.
Fourteen Hundred Thousand (produced Minneapolis).   Included in Five Plays, 1967.
Red Cross (produced New York, 1966; Glasgow, 1969; London, 1970).   Included in Five Plays, 1967.
La Turista (produced New York, 1966; London, 1969).   Indianapolis, Bobbs Merrill, 1968; London, Faber, 1969.
Forensic and the Navigators (produced New York, 1967).   Included in The Unseen Hand and Other Plays, 1971.
Melodrama Play (produced New York and London, 1967).   Included in Five Plays, 1967.
Five Plays: Chicago, Icarus's Mother, Red Cross, Fourteen Hundred Thousand, Melodrama Play.   Indianapolis, Bobbs Merrill, 1967; London, Faber, 1969.
Cowboys #2 (produced Los Angeles, 1967; New York, 1973).   Included in Mad Dog Blues and Other Plays, 1971.
Shaved Splits (produced New York, 1969).   Included in The Unseen Hand and Other Plays, 1971.
The Unseen Hand (produced New York, 1970; London, 1973).   Included in The Unseen Hand and Other Plays, 1971; in Action, and The Unseen Hand, 1975.
Operation Sidewinder (produced New York, 1970).   Indianapolis, Bobbs Merrill, 1970.
Holy Ghostly (produced New York, 1970; London, 1973).   Included in The Unseen Hand and Other Plays, 1971.
Back Bog Beast Bait (produced New York, 1971).   Included in The Unseen Hand and Other Plays, 1971.
Mad Dog Blues (produced New York, 1971).   Included in Mad Dog Blues and Other Plays, 1971.
Cowboy Mouth (produced New York, 1971; London, 1972).   Included in Mad Dog Blues and Other Plays, 1971.
The Unseen Hand and Other Plays (includes Forensic and the Navigators, Back Bog Beast Bait, Shaved Splits, Holy Ghostly, and Rock Garden).   Indianapolis, Bobbs Merrill, 1971.
Mad Dog Blues and Other Plays (includes Cowboy Mouth, and Cowboys #2).   New York, Winter House, 1971.

The Tooth of Crime (produced London, 1972; Oswego, New York, and New York City,
     1973).   Included in *The Tooth of Crime, and Geography of a Horse Dreamer*, 1974.
Nightwalk, with Megan Terry and Jean-Claude van Itallie (produced New York, 1973).
Blue Bitch (produced New York, 1973; London, 1975).
Little Ocean (produced London, 1974).
Geography of a Horse Dreamer (produced New Haven, Connecticut, and London, 1974).
     Included in *The Tooth of Crime, and Geography of a Horse Dreamer*, 1974.
The Tooth of Crime, and Geography of a Horse Dreamer.   New York, Grove Press, and
     London, Faber, 1974.
Action (produced London, 1974; New York, 1975).   Included in *Action, and The
     Unseen Hand*, 1975.
Action, and the Unseen Hand.   London, Faber, 1975.
Killer's Head (produced New York, 1975).
Angel City, Curse of the Starving Class, and Other Plays.   New York, Urizen Books,
     1976.

Screenplays: *Me and My Brother*, with Robert Frank, 1967; *Zabriskie Point*, with
others, 1970; *Ringaleevio*, with Murray Mednick, 1971.

Short Stories

Hawk Moon.   Los Angeles, Black Sparrow Press, 1972.

Theatrical Activities:

    Actor: **Plays** – with the Bishops Company, Burbank, California; in *Cowboy Mouth*, New
    York, 1971. **Film** – *Brand X*, 1970.

Sam Shepard comments:

    I'm interested in exploring the writing of plays through attitudes derived from other forms
such as music, painting, sculpture, film, etc., all the time keeping in mind that I'm writing for
the theatre. I consider theatre and writing to be a home where I bring the adventures of my
life and sort them out, making sense or non-sense out of mysterious impressions. I like to
start with as little information about where I'm going as possible. A nearly empty space
which is the stage where a picture, a sound, a color sneaks in and tells me a certain kind of
story. I feel that language is a veil hiding demons and angels which the characters are always
out of touch with. Their quest in the play is the same as ours in life – to find those forces, to
meet them face to face and end the mystery. I'm pulled toward images that shine in the
middle of junk. Like cracked headlights shining on a deer's eyes. I've been influenced by
Jackson Pollock, Little Richard, Cajun fiddles and the Southwest.

                                    *   *   *

    In spite of his prolific output – some thirty plays since the mid-1960's – Sam Shepard's
invention never flags, and his achievements sometimes tower high. More than any
contemporary American playwright, he weaves into his own dramatic idiom the strands of a
youth culture thriving on drugs, rock music, astrology, science fiction, old movies, detective
stories, cowboy films, and races of cars, horses, dogs.
    Growing up in Southern California, Shepard fell almost accidentally into playwriting
when he went to New York City: "The world I was living in was the most interesting thing
to me, and I thought the best thing I could do maybe would be to write about it, so I started
writing plays." Since the time was the 1960's and the place was the lower East Side,

Shepard's short plays were produced Off Off Broadway. Today he finds it difficult to remember these early efforts, the best of which are published as *Five Plays*. They tend to focus on a single event, the characters often talking past one another or breaking into long monologues. However puzzling the action, these plays already ring out with Shepard's deft rhythms.

Within three years of these first efforts, in 1967, 23-year old Shepard produced his first full-length play, *La Turista*, punning on the Spanish word for tourist and the diarrhea that attacks American tourists in Mexico. Perhaps influenced by Beckett's *Godot*, *La Turista* is also composed of two acts in which the second virtually repeats the first. However, questionable identities and mythic roles are at once more blatant and more realistic than in Beckett. In both of Shepard's acts Kent is sick, and his wife Salem (both named for cigarette brands) send for a doctor, who, more or less aided by his son, essays a cure. But the first act is set in a Mexican hotel-room and the illness is *la turista*, whereas the second act is set in an American hotel-room and the illness is sleeping sickness.

Other plays followed swiftly, some published in 1971 in two volumes aptly named for the first and longest play in each book. In the six plays of *Unseen Hand* almost all the main characters are threatened by unseen hands. Two plays of *Mad Dog Blues* camp the popular arts they embrace affectionately. In the title play two friends, Kosmo, a rock star, and Yahoudi, a drug pusher, separate to seek their respective fortunes. Kosmo takes up with Mae West, and Yahoudi with Marlene Dietrich. Each pair becomes a triangle when Kosmo annexes Waco, Texas, and Yahoudi Captain Kidd, for whose treasure they all hunt. Tumbling from adventure to adventure, Yahoudi shoots Captain Kidd, Marlene goes off with Paul Bunyan, Kosmo and Mae West find the treasure, but Jesse James makes off with treasure and Mae West. Finally, Mae suggests that they all go to the Missouri home of Jesse James, and the play ends in festive song and dance.

A 1969 longer play also ends in comic celebration. The punning title *Operation Sidewinder* refers to an American army computer in the shape of a sidewinder rattlesnake. By the play's end, however, it becomes an actual snake and Hopi Indian religious symbol through whose symbiotic power a disoriented young couple is integrated into an organic society – even as in New Comedy. To attain this, the pair has to disown a revolutionary conspiracy, military backlash, several corpses, and their own highly verbal confusion.

It is generally agreed that *The Tooth of Crime* is Shepard's most impressive play. He has commented: "It started with language – it started with hearing a certain sound which is coming from the voice of this character, Hoss." And the play's strength remains in language, a synthesis of the slangs of rock, crime, astrology, and sports. Hoss has played by the code and moved by the charts, but he senses that he is doomed. Gradually, that doom takes the shape and name of Crow, a gypsy killer. Alerted through Eyes, warned by the charts of Galactic Jack, doped by his doctor, comforted by his moll, Hoss prepares for his fate, "Stuck in my image." In Act II, Hoss and Crow, has-been and would-be, duel with words and music – "Choose an argot" – as a Referee keeps score. In the third Round the Ref calls a TKO, and Hoss kills the Referee. Unable to bend to Crow's ways, Hoss prefers to die, in the manner of classical heroes but in contemporary idiom: "A true gesture that won't never cheat on itself 'cause it's the last of its kind."

Ironically, this American tragedy was written when Shepard was in London, where his *Geography of a Horse Dreamer* sprang from English dog-racing. Back in California, Shepard has completed *Action*, about two American couples, *Killer's Head*, about a cowboy in the electric chair, *Angel City*, about Hollywoodians obsessed with the movies on which they work, and *The Curse of the Starving Class*.

The Off-Off-Broadway attitude tends to be anti-intellectual, and Sam Shepard springs from the same autodidactic milieu. However, he has absorbed American pop art, media myths, and the Southwestern scene to recycle them in many – perhaps too many – image-focused plays in which the characters speak inventive idioms in vivid rhythms. At his best – *La Turista*, *Mad Dog Blues*, *The Tooth of Crime* – Shepard achieves his own distinctive coherence through beautifully bridled fantasy.

—Ruby Cohn

SIMON, (Marvin) Neil.   American.   Born in the Bronx, New York, 4 July 1927.
Educated at DeWitt Clinton High School, New York, graduated 1943; New York University,
1946; University of Denver. Served in the United States Army Air Force, 1945–46. Married
Joan Simon in 1953 (died, 1973), two children; the actress Marsha Mason, 1973. Recipient:
Evening Standard award, 1967; Shubert Award, 1968. Agent: Christopher Mann Ltd., 140
Park Lane, London W.1, England. Address: c/o Random House Inc., 201 East 50th Street,
New York, New York 10022, U.S.A.

PUBLICATIONS

Plays

> Sketches (produced Tamiment, Pennsylvania, 1952, 1953).
> Sketches, with Danny Simon, in *Catch a Star* (produced New York, 1955).
> Sketches, with Danny Simin, in *New Faces of 56* (produced New York, 1956).
> *Adventures of Marco Polo: A Musical Fantasy*, with William Friedberg, music by Clay
>   Warnick and Mel Pahl.   New York, French, 1959.
> *Heidi*, with William Friedberg, music by Clay Warnick, adaptation of the novel by
>   Johanna Spyri.   New York, French, 1959.
> *Come Blow Your Horn*, with Danny Simon (produced New York, 1961; London, 1962).
>   New York and London, French, 1961.
> *Little Me*, music by Cy Coleman, adaptation of the novel by Patrick Dennis (produced
>   New York, 1962; London, 1964).
> *Barefoot in the Park* (as *Nobody Loves Me*, produced New Hope, Pennsylvania, 1962; as
>   *Barefoot in the Park*, produced New York, 1963; London, 1965).   New York,
>   Random House, 1964; London, French, 1967.
> *The Odd Couple* (produced New York, 1965; London, 1966).   New York, Random
>   House, 1966.
> *Sweet Charity*, music and lyrics by Cy Coleman and Dorothy Fields, based on the
>   screenplay *The Nights of Cabiria* by Fellini (produced New York, 1966; London,
>   1967).   New York, Random House, 1966.
> *The Star-Spangled Girl* (produced New York, 1966).   New York, Random House,
>   1967.
> *Plaza Suit* (produced New York, 1968; London, 1969).   New York, Random House,
>   1969.
> *Promises, Promises*, music and lyrics by Burt Bacharach and Hal David, based on the
>   screenplay *The Apartment* by Billy Wilder and I. A. L. Diamond (produced New
>   York, 1968; London, 1969).   New York, Random House, 1969.
> *Last of the Red Hot Lovers* (produced New York, 1969).   New York, Random House,
>   1970.
> *The Gingerbread Lady* (produced New York, 1970; Windsor, Berkshire, and London,
>   1974).   New York, Random House, 1971.
> *The Prisoner of Second Avenue* (produced New York, 1971).   New York, Random
>   House, and London, French, 1972.
> *The Sunshine Boys* (produced New York, 1972; London, 1975).   New York, Random
>   House, 1973.
> *The Comedy of Neil Simon* (includes *Come Blow Your Horn; Barefoot in the Park; The
>   Odd Couple; The Star-Spangled Girl; Plaza Suite; Promises, Promises; Last of the Red
>   Hot Lovers*).   New York Random House, 1972.
> *The Good Doctor*, adaptation of stories by Chekhov (produced New York, 1973).   New
>   York, Random House, 1974; London, French, 1975.
> *God's Favorite* (produced New York, 1974).   New York, Random House, 1975.
> *California Suite* (produced Los Angeles, New York and London, 1976).

Screenplays: *After the Fox*, 1966; *Barefoot in the Park*, 1967; *The Odd Couple*, 1968; *The Out-of-Towners*, 1970; *The Heartbreak Kid*, 1972; *The Last of the Red Hot Lovers*, 1972; *The Prisoner of Second Avenue*, 1975; *The Sunshine Boys*, 1975; *Murder by Death*, 1976.

Television Writing: *Phil Silvers Show*, 1948, 1958–59; *Tallulah Bankhead Show*, 1951; *Sid Caesar Show*, 1956–57; *Garry Moore Show*, 1959–60; *A Quiet War*, 1976.

*   *   *

Neil Simon must be reckoned with if only because he is the most popular playwright in the history of the American theatre. By 1972, he had written eight plays and three musicals in eleven years, all but two of them *smash hits*. Although he is not the first playwright to double as librettist for musicals, he is the only one to have had such consistent commercial success in both fields. But despite this breathtaking record, Simon is generally dismissed as a hack and may well be forgotten as quickly as his plots. His writing style is closer to advertising copy writing than literature. His stories are merely situations naturalistic in the cardboard style of standard Broadway comedy (and drama, for that matter). His stage world represents the worst of suburban America – a homogenized world of middle class materialists. A real reason why Simon has been so successful is that his plays reflect and support the life of his white, middle class audiences. But a suburban mentality is not the only reason for his success. Simon can be extremely funny, as in *Promises, Promises*:

Waiter –   You like to order dinner now?
Woman – No. No dinner.
Man –   Bring us two more drinks.
Woman – No more drinks either.
Waiter –   Very good. That's no dinner and no more drinks.

That isn't just a sarcastic waiter joke. That's a weird kind of humor, a humor that sets easy colloquialism against objective reality, and Simon sometimes undercoats it with the brutal, as in *Last of the Red Hot Lovers*:

Woman – You don't think there are worse things than death?
Man –   Like suffering and pain? They're bad, but they're second and third after death. Death is first.

When Simon takes such humor and mixes it with pain, his plays achieve a real depth, using the laugh as an escape valve for the cry. The trouble, and also the really interesting thing about his plays, is their vacillation between such quirky, intense, bitter humor and the gags into which he invariably retreats. For he consistently sacrifices his best qualities to win the laughter of audiences who want only to be entertained and have their values confirmed. He is a potential artist struggling against himself and the bourgeois ethic. That is a mouthful to say of a writer who is commonly dismissed, and one must be careful not to praise him out of sheer eccentricity or reaction. Those warning noted, Simon's artistic qualities are as palpable as his shortcomings.

His plays deal with domestic problems. Growing up (*Come Blow Your Horn*), getting married (*Barefoot in the Park*) and divorced (*The Odd Couple*), sexual attraction (*The Star-Spangled Girl*), marital problems (*Plaza Suit*), middleage and sexual frustration (*Last of the Red Hot Lovers*), loneliness (*The Gingerbread Lady*) and personal world collapse (*Prisoner of Second Avenue*). This last play, a middle class *Job* – man loses job – showed Simon closer than ever before to an outright challenge of middle class values by a middle class hero.

This has been the consistent theme of his plays, invariably submerged beneath the wisecracks. Simon's characters are people intimidated by middle class standards of morality into a lifelong emotional constipation. They cannot imagine life without material comforts or such norms as employment, marriage and parenthood. Occasionally, these conventions are challenged by a rebel, but the rebellion is mild and the challenge unsuccessful. Simon is obviously aware of the inhumanity of the middle class ethic and realizes that it is observed at the price of frustration and hypocrisy, but he cannot bring himself to dismiss it. Perhaps he feels that anarchy and chaos would ensue, but he never says so. He seems less concerned with change and more with the victims of this constriction, reaching out to them with a compassion and a grasp of life's misfortune so heartfelt he approaches high theatre. But at this moment his plays drop down from the walls they have climbed in laugh-riddled desperation. Like their characters, they straighten their ties, pick up their briefcases and head for home and office.

Simon could well continue as a writer of ephemeral entertainments which, history and academe notwithstanding, is a perfectly respectable life's work (and certainly a comfortable one). But were he to overcome his inhibitions and slosh knee deep in the American middle class tragedy, he might well go to the sea floor beneath that oiled walnut surface. Domestic and personal frustration – suburbanism of existence – far from being superficial concerns, are America's most real problem. Could Simon combine his spectacular comic gift with his understanding of and compassion for the middle class, and resist the cheap success of the gag and the bromide, he might well realize the equality of comedy with drama and become the most important American playwright of his generation.

—Martin Gottfried

SIMONS, Beverley.   Canadian.   Born in Flin Flon, Manitoba, 1938. Educated at McGill University, Montreal; University of British Columbia, Vancouver, B.A. 1959. Married; has three children. Recipient: Canada Council bursary, 1967, and award, 1972. Address: 5202 Marine Drive, West Vancouver, British Columbia V7W 2P8, Canada.

PUBLICATIONS

Plays

The Elephant and the Jewish Question (produced Vancouver, 1968).   Vancouver, New
    Play Centre, n.d.
Green Lawn Rest Home (produced Burnaby, British Columbia, 1969). Toronto,
    Playwrights Co-op, 1973.
Crabdance (produced Seattle, 1969).   Vancouver, In Press, 1969; revised version
    (produced Vancouver, 1972), Vancouver, Talonbooks, 1972.
Preparing (produced Burnaby, British Columbia, 1973).   Included in Preparing
    (collection), 1975.
Preparing (includes Prologue, Triangle, Crusader, Green Lawn Rest Home).
    Vancouver, Talonbooks, 1975.
Prologue, Triangle, Crusader (produced Toronto, 1976).   Included in Preparing, 1975.
If I Turn Around Quick, in Capilano Review (North Vancouver), Summer 1976.
Leela Means to Play, in Canadian Theatre Review 9 (Downsview, Ontario), Winter
    1976.

Television Play: *The Canary*, 1968.

Bibliography: in *Canadian Theatre Review* 9 (Downsview, Ontario), Winter 1976.

* * *

Crabdance is Beverley Simons' best-known work and remains her outstanding achievement to date. In it, the commonplace world is transformed by Sadie Golden's hyper-sensitive perceptions, salesmen becoming sons, lovers, and husband as Sadie projects onto them her feelings about sex, motherhood, and her femaleness. At the critical hour of 3 p.m. she dies out of the lacerating existence in which "Mama's gone a-hunting/ She's taken off her own white skin...." The salesmen are recognizably objective figures as well as emanations from Sadie, and the play's relation to experience is powerfully present through distorted images. The great success of *Crabdance* lies in the perilous balance between observation and feeling, the known world and Sadie's vision of it.

In an earlier, one-act play, *Green Lawn Rest Home*, less ambitious than *Crabdance* but the most finished and unified of her plays, Simon also makes the internal perceptions of the characters modify the presentation of outward reality and brilliantly fuses lyrical and satirical perspectives. Society's prettification of senility and dying is critically observed while, at the same time, the mortifications before death, the leaking away of life in anguish, the tiny passions of the geriatrics, are seen and felt from within. A "date" which consists of a walk to the gate of the rest home becomes, for the old couple subjectively presented, the equivalent of the most violent adolescent exuality. Simons conveys feelingly the real hardness of the green pebbles which, from a little distance away, give the illusion of lawns.

Leela Means to Play presents, sporadically, clear moral views of the operations of legal justice through a kind of trial-by-encounters of a judge. The play is a full-length aggregation of very short scenes, related in theme but not through plot or sequence – gobbets of allegory in which the representation of modern life is distorted by an intensely feeling consciousness. There is no equivalent ot Sadie Golden, however, to give focus and coherence in this play. In this work Simons relies too naively on her audience's recogniton of the personality *behind* it. The play seems to have been untimely snatched from the authorial womb, still trailing unsynthesized bits of Beckett, Genet, Albee and Noh-via-Yeats, unfinished though very much alive.

The title piece of *Preparing* gives us (like *Crabdance*) a dramatization of the passionately sensitive perceptions of Simons. This monologue requires an actress skilled in mime and with a set of voices adequate to portray the several ages of woman. From adolescence to womanhood the monologuist undertakes preparations for imposed sexual roles ending with ultimate resistance ("fuck 'em all") to all the impositions. Two other short pieces in this collection are too clamantly "experimental"; one, *Crusader*, employs masks in a novel but clumsy way; in the other, *Triangle*, light and movement give us the geometry of bonding and victimage in the relationships of three characters. In both the moral view is rather heavily imposed and not offset by studious "theatricality."

In an earlier play, *The Elephant and the Jewish Question* (published only in mimographed form), Simons showed herself capable of handling a conventional structure and natural speech, though the piece is rather stickily embedded in "Jewish atmosphere." The great development from this to *Crabdance* is an indication of Beverley Simons' great promise, and this development is so far marked by the discovery of various ways of presenting lyrical, internalized characters within an objective framework. But her genuine distinctiveness seems to be still overlayed and obscured by studious imitation and anxiety about form

—Michael Sidnell

SIMPSON, N(orman) F(rederick).   British.   Born in London, 29 January 1919.
Educated at Emanuel School, London, 1930–37; University of London, 1950–54, B.A.
(honours) 1954. Served in the Royal Artillery, 1941–43, and the Intelligence Corps, 1943–46.
Married Joyce Bartlett in 1944; has one child. Teacher, City of Westminster College, London,
and extra-mural lecturer, 1946–62. Lives in London. Address: c/o Robin Dalton Associates,
11–12 Hanover Street, London W.1, England.

PUBLICATIONS

Plays

> *A Resounding Tinkle* (produced London, 1957; Bloomington, Indiana, 1961).
> Published in *The Observer Plays*, London, Faber, and New York, French, 1958;
> shortened version included in *The Hole and Other Plays and Sketches*, 1964.
> *The Hole* (produced London, 1958).   London and New York, French, 1958.
> *One Way Pendulum* (produced London, 1959; New York, 1961).   London, Faber,
> 1960; New York, Grove Press, 1961.
> Sketches in *One to Another* (produced London, 1959).   London, French, 1960.
> Sketches in *You, Me and the Gatepost* (produced Nottingham, 1960).
> Sketches in *On the Avenue* (produced London, 1961).
> Sketches in *One over the Eight* (produced London, 1961).
> *The Form* (produced London, 1961).   New York and London, French, 1961
> *Oh* (produced London, 1961).   Included in *The Hole and Other Plays and Sketches*,
> 1964.
> *The Hole and Other Plays and Sketches* (includes shortened versions of *A Resounding
> Tinkle, The Form, Gladly Otherwise, Oh, One Blast and Have Done*).   London,
> Faber, 1964.
> *The Cresta Run* (produced London, 1965; Louisville, Kentucky, 1968).   London,
> Faber, 1966; New York, Grove Press, 1967.
> *We're Due in Eastbourne in Ten Minutes* (televised, 1967; produced London, 1971).
> Included in *Some Tall Tinkles*, 1968; in *The Best Short Plays 1972*, edited by Stanley
> Richards, Philadelphia, Chilton, 1972.
> *Some Tall Tinkles: Television Plays* (includes *We're Due in Eastbourne in Ten Minutes,
> The Best I Can Do by Way of a Gate-Leg Table Is a Hundredweight of Coal, At Least
> It's a Precaution Against Fire*).   London, Faber, 1968.
> *Playback 625*, with Leopoldo Maler (produced London, 1970).
> *How Are Your Handles?* (includes *Gladly Otherwise, Oh, The Other Side of London*)
> (produced London, 1971).
> *Was He Anyone?* (produced London, 1972).   London, Faber, 1973.

Screenplay: *One Way Pendulum*, 1964.

Radio Plays: *Something Rather Effective*, 1972; *Sketches for Radio*, 1974.

Television Plays: *Make a Man*, 1966; *Three Rousing Tinkles* series: *The Father by
Adoption of One of the Former Marquis of Rangoon's Natural Granddaughters, If Those
Are Mr. Heckmondwick's Own Personal Pipes They've Been Lagged Once Already*, and
The Best I Can Do by Way of a Gate-Leg Table Is a Hundredweight of Coal, 1966; *Four
Tall Tinkles* series: *We're Due in Eastbourne in Ten Minutes, In a Punt with Friends
Under a Haystack on the River Mersey, A Row of Potted Plants*, and *At Least It's a
Precaution Against Fire*, 1967; *World in Ferment* series, 1969; *Charley's Grants* series,
1970; *Thank You Very Much*, 1971; *Elementary, My Dear Watson*, 1973; *Silver
Wedding*, 1974.

Novel

Harry Bleachbaker.   London, Harrap, 1976; as *Man Overboard: A Testemonial to the High Art of Incompetence,* New York, Morrow, 1976.

Critical Studies: *Curtains* by Kenneth Tynan, London, Longman, 1961; *Dramatic Essays* by Nigel Dennis, London, Weidenfeld and Nicolson, 1962; *Theatre of the Absurd* by Martin Esslin, London, Eyre and Spottiswoode, 1962.

N. F. Simpson comments:

The question that, as a writer, one is asked more frequently than any other is the question as to why of all things it should be plays that one has chosen to bring forth rather than, say, novels or books about flying saucers. The answer in my own case lies, I think, in the fact that there is one incomparable advantage which the play, as a form, has over the novel and the book about flying saucers; and this is that there are not anything like as many words in it. For a writer condemned from birth to draw upon a reservoir of energy such as would barely suffice to get a tadpole from one side of a tea-cup to the other, such a consideration cannot be the decisive. Poetry admittedly has in general fewer words still, and for this reason is on the face of it an even more attractive discipline; but alas I have even less gift for that than I have for writing plays, and if I had the gift for it, it would be only a matter of weeks before I came up against the ineluctable truth that there is just not the money in it that there is in plays. Not that, the way I write them, there is all that much money in those either.

As for methods of work, what I do is to husband with jealous parsimony such faint tremors of psychic energy as can sometimes be coaxed out of the permanently undercharged batteries I was issued with at birth, and when I have what might be deemed a measurable amount, to send it coursing down the one tiny channel where with any luck it might do some good. Here it deposits its wee pile of silt, which I allow to accumulate, with the barely perceptible deliberation of a coral reef, to the point where it may one day recognise itself with a start of suprise as the small and unpretentious magnum opus it had all along been tremulously aspiring to.

As for why one does it, there are various reasons – all of them fairly absurd. There is one's ludicrously all-embracing sense of guilt mainly. I walk the streets in perpetual fear and trepidation, like someone who expects, round the very next corner, to meet his just deserts at the hands of a lynch mob carried away by fully justified indignation. To feel *personally* responsible not only for every crime, every atrocity, every act of inhumanity that has ever been perpetrated since the world began, but for those as well that have not as yet been so much as contemplated, is something which only Jesus Christ and I can ever have experienced to anything like the same degree. And it goes a long way to account for what I write and why I write it. For not only must one do what one can by writing plays to make amends for the perfidy of getting born; one must also, in the interests of sheer self-preservation, keep permanently incapacitated by laughter as many as possible of those who would otherwise be the bearers of a just and terrible retribution. One snatches one's reprieve quite literally laugh by laugh.

My plays are about life – life as I see it. Which is to say that they are all in their various ways about a man trying to get a partially inflated rubber lilo into a suitcase slightly too small to take it even when *un*inflated. Like most Englishmen, of which I am proud to be one, I have a love of order tempered by a deep and abiding respect for anarchy, and what I would one day like to bring about is that perfect balance between the two which I believe it to be peculiarly in the nature of English genius to arrive at. I doubt very much whether I ever shall, but it is nevertheless what I would like to do.

*   *   *

By now N. F. Simpson must have grown wary of books on the modern drama in which his special quality – an inexhaustible surge of anarchic verbal invention – is relentlessly over-analysed. In the theatre most audiences are amused by the Simpsonian absurdity without seeking to explain it. Among sterner students this work is part of the Theatre of the Absurd which is by no means what it sounds.

Any discussion of his plays that goes too far into motive and method can make Simpson sound tedious whereas, both in performance and in the text, he is among the most cheerfully original dramatists of his time. One may thing of Carroll, Lear, and Gilbert, but Simpson is blissfully his own master.

True, this particular line of humour, depending as it does on the non-sequitur and on the carrying of logic as far as it will go (and further) can worry some of Simpson's listeners and readers. They find him too clever, and they became embarrassed. In *A Resounding Tinkle*, his first play, which was later revised, he makes the dramatist say:

> It is together that we must shape the experience which is the play we shall all of us have shared. The actors are as much the audience as the audience themselves, in precisely the same way that the audience are as much the actors as the actors themselves. We are all spectators of one another, mutual witnesses of each other's discomfiture.

Simpson, a Londoner and a former bank clerk, became a teacher after Intelligence Corps service during the war. He was noticed first when his earlier version of *A Resounding Tinkle* won a prize in a competition organised by *The Observer*, a London Sunday newspaper. Another treatment was staged later at the Royal Court; and in 1958 the play returned, this time in company with a one-acter, *The Hole*. It was an evening of wreathing verbal smoke-rings, and nothing is less profitable than to try and fix these in a grave dissertation.

A Resounding Tinkle is presented with the straightest of faces – never an incautious gleam in the eye, a trembling of the lip. The principal characters, who are a suburban couple, the Paradocks, keep an elephant but they think it ought to be exchanged for a snake. Agreed, a snake may be too short; still, they can have it lengthened, though then, of course, they will lose on the thickness. Somebody telephones, bothered by the eyesight of her eagles. "Uncle Ted" drops in and proves to be a charming young woman. And so on. The piece, in any version, is exceedingly funny which seems to be cause enough for its appearance. Here we have to quote the author who observes (as a character in the play): "The retreat from reason means precious little to anyone who has never caught up with reason in the first place. It takes a trained mind to relish a non-sequitur." Maybe; but there is no reason to discuss it in detail, and some critics have become almost like Simpsonian parodies in their endeavour to find every fleck of meaning in the text.

The Hole, which shared the double bill, sounded rather more laboured in performance. But most playgoers remember something from the debate among people who gather speculatively round a hole in the ground, and what they remember is usually different. An early speech may be reminiscent of Lucky's monologue in *Godot*, and a wild sporting medley can remain us of Q's *Famous Ballad of the Jubilee Cup*. But we should always beware of suggesting influences, for Simpson is very much himself: hunt as we may for resemblances and possible questions, he remains in the long run among the truest originals in the theatre of his period, even if his form of humour – and who can be dogmatic? – must sometimes be an acquired taste.

His major play is *One Way Pendulum* which he called, alarmingly, "an evening of high drung and slarrit." Later he changed this, more recognisably, to "a farce in a new dimension." Here, too, writers have been eager to explain. One has said that the play is "a ferocious comment on contemporary British life." We can doubt whether many of its watchers have seen it like that. Simpson himself has said that, as drama, *One Way Pendulum*, "with its turrets and its high pointed gables, should have a particular appeal for anyone approaching it for the first time with a lasso." Not, perhaps, helpful, but extremely Simpsonian. This dramatist of the non-sequitur governed by absolute logic is either irresistible or one sits unmoved: to explain either reaction is like trying to drain the ocean with the leaky limpet-shell Tregeagle, the Cornish giant, was given for Dozmary Pool.

Briefly, *One Way Pendulum* is set in the living-room of the Groomkirbys at an address given as 93 Chundragore Street, Suburbia, a space occupied for most of the night by a replica of an Old Bailey court. Arthur Groomkirby, passionate about the law, has put the court together with a do-it-yourself set. It takes a lot of space; when it is up, there is no room for Aunt Mildred who believes, obsessively, that she is in the Outer Hebrides waiting for a train to St. Pancras. Never mind; there will always be room for Myra who drops in professionally to finish any food left in the house – as the author puts it, to practise "incessant eating in a vocational capacity."

When the Old Bailey is set up, it needs a Judge; it acquires one at once, though not a jury ("They are here in spirit, m'Lord" the usher says). It seems that we are at the trial of the younger Groomkirby for forty-three murders – "he has been fairly regularly taking life," a prosecuting council, also on the spot, observes. But Simpson is most engaged with the evidence of Groomkirby senior. After all, it is his own Old Bailey, and he ought to have a good chance to play with it. Having therefore sworn (by Harriet Beecher Stowe) that he will speak nothing but the truth, he proposes to lie to the Court ("a frank and honest answer" the Judge observes), but wilts under cross-examination. Denying that is is a geographer, he yet admits that, to have been in Chester-le-Street on a given date, he had absented himself from most of the places "only an expert geographer could have thought of." The play goes on like this. There is no reason now to speak of the weighing-machines that must sing the Hallelujah Chorus; the woman who wears her pearls "round her waist for the tightness"; the curious nightmare quality of a game of three-handed whist for two players without cards in the dark; and a line (for Mrs. Groomkirby) that became celebrated: "We've nothing against apes. As such."

Simpson has suggested that the Groomkirbys talk and behave very much as any family might which has been harried for months on end by "a runaway drawbridge in slow motion." Excellent; but a redoubtable commentator has insisted that the play "hints at the connexion between . . . the mutual tolerance that allows each of the Groomkirbys to plant his weird preoccupations in the middle of the living-room, and the deep undercurrents of cruelty and sadism that lie behind such a society."

Each to his choice. In his next full-length play, *The Cresta Run* (which did not arrive for six years) the most wayward of intellectuals continued to work a rich vein, though he added – probably to the annoyance of expert analysts – that his plays in which some had claimed to see the hand of Edward the Confessor were in fact "the work of a little old lady in Dunstable." *The Cresta Run* is, more or less, about the "grim and sinister drama of international espionage" which provokes the author to quite irreverent laughter. It is indeed the type of piece in which someone concludes very seriously – because everyone here is very serious – "I doubt whether they'd send ostriches all the way to Scarborough by submarine to spy upon the Head of Security in London." The movement of the play can loiter; but Simpsonians (far fewer of them for this piece than for *One Way Pendulum*) can applaud passages when the dramatist lets his fancy billow out round him. Just why were sixteen-and-a-half million people out of the country at the time of the Norman Conquest? What causes the wife of the trainee spy to say: "A whole grandfather clock squandered, and nothing to show for it but a wall safe we don't know how to open – and now, chiropody." And again: "People are very funny about having the secret service run by someone who needs naturalising. Bad for the image."

We may have a feeling that Simpson's later appearances as a television dramatist were bad for the image. In an interview before the first of three short plays in 1966, he said with a kind of mild despair: "I'd never even heard of Ionesco when I first began to write plays." These brief new pieces took us back to the first *Resounding Tinkle*. Here again were the Paradocks; here again the ferociously logical and straight-gazing absurdity. "Can I interest you," asked a canvasser, "in a collapsible canoe in the form of an ocean-going liner?" "No," Middie Paradock replies, "we're too high above sea-level for that." The name of the play is, simply, *The Father by Adoption of One of the Former Marquis of Rangoon's Natural Granddaughters.*

Although Simpson's latest full-length work, *Was He Anyone?*, had well over thirty characters, it seemed faint in comparison with the earlier plays. Possibly the Simpson form of absurdity, defying all analysis, needs at the moment to be refreshed. It will undoubtedly return at full strength. At its best, in the words of one of the earlier plays, it has been "like some unspecified milk of Paradise." It is no good attempting to specify the exact brand; and probably the graver writers are recognising this.

— J. C. Trewin

SMITH, Dodie (Dorothy Gladys Smith).   British.   Born in Whitefield, Lancashire, 3 May. Attended Manchester Girls School; St. Paul's School for Girls, London; studied acting at Royal Academy of Dramatic Art, London, 1914–15. Married Alec Macbeth Beesley in 1939. Actress, 1915–22; worked as a buyer for Heal and Son, London. Address: The Barretts, Finchingfield, Essex, England.

PUBLICATIONS

Plays

British Talent (as C. L. Anthony) (produced London, 1924).
Autumn Crocus (as C. L. Anthony) (produced London, 1931; New York, 1932).
  London, Gollancz, 1931.
Service (as C. L. Anthony) (produced London, 1932).   London, Gollancz, 1932.
Touch Wood (as C. L. Anthony) (produced London, 1934).   London, Gollancz, 1934.
Call It a Day (produced London, 1935; New York, 1936).   London, Gollancz, and
  New York, French, 1936.
Bonnet over the Windmill (also co-director; produced London, 1937). London,
  Heinemann, 1937.
Dear Octopus (also co-director; produced London, 1938; New York, 1939). London,
  Heinemann, 1938; New York, French, 1939.
Lovers and Friends (produced New York, 1943).   New York, French, 1947.
Letter from Paris, adaptation of the novel *The Reverberator* by Henry James (produced
  Brighton and London, 1952).   London, Heinemann, 1954.
I Capture the Castle, adaptation of her own novel (produced Blackpool and London,
  1954).   London, Heinemann, 1954.
These People, Those Books (produced Leeds, 1958).
Amateur Means Lover (produced Liverpool, 1961).   London, French, 1962.

Screenplays: *Schoolgirl Rebels* (as Charles Henry Percy), 1915; *The Uninvited*, with
Frank Partos, 1944; *Darling, How Could You!*, with Lesser Samuels, 1951.

Novels

I Capture the Castle.   Boston, Little Brown, 1948; London, Heinemann, 1949.
The New Moon with the Old.   London, Heinemann, and Boston, Little Brown, 1963.

The Town in Bloom.   London, Heinemann, and Boston, Little Brown, 1965.
It Ends with Revelations.   London, Heinemann, and Boston, Little Brown, 1967.
A Tale of Two Families.   London, Heinemann, and New York, Walker, 1970.

Other

The Hundred and One Dalmatians (juvenile).   London, Heinemann, 1956; New York,
   Viking Press, 1957.
The Starlight Barking: More about the Hundred and One Dalmatians (juvenile).
   London, Heinemann, and New York, Simon and Schuster, 1967.
Look Back with Love: A Manchester Childhood.   London, Heinemann, 1974.

Theatrical Activities:

Director: **Plays** – *Bonnet over the Windmill* (co-director, with Murray Macdonald),
London, 1937; *Dear Octopus* (co-director, with Glen Byam Shaw), London, 1938.

Actress: **Plays** – in the sketch *Playgoers* by A. W. Pinero, London, 1915; *Kitty Grey* by
J. S. Piggott and *Mr. Wu* by H. M. Vernon and Harold Owen, tour, 1915; *Ye Gods* by
Stephen Robert and Eric Hudson, and *Jane and Niobe,* 1916–17; *When Knights Were
Bold* by Charles Marlowe, London, 1917; in music-hall sketches, in the Portsmouth
Repertory Company, and in a concert party in Dieppe, 1918; Claudine in *Telling the
Tale,* 1919–20; *French Leave* by Reginald Berkeley, 1921; *The Shewing Up of Blanco
Posnet* by G. B. Shaw, London, 1921; with the Everyman Company, Zurich, 1922.

*   *   *

Cynthia –   Is that a teddy-bear there? (*Taking it.*) Why, it's Symp.
Scrap –   (*Following Her.*) Symp?
Cynthia –   We called him that because he was extra sympathetic. We used to hug
            him whenever we were miserable – when we were in disgrace or the
            rabbits died or when nobody understood us.

The quotation is from Dodie Smith's best-known play, *Dear Octopus,* a play about a family,
its feuds and friendships, first performed in 1938 with one of those casts publicists call
"glittering" (with good reason – included in the Queen's Theatre company were Marie
Tempest, John Gielgud, Madge Compton, Angela Baddeley, among other). The theme of
sympathy, in fact, might be Dobie Smith's principal key – in all her plays she seems to
comprehend the very well-springs of her characters. She builds them surely and with
understanding; they emerge as palpable beings, ordinary people who are more-than-
ordinarily believable. And that's quite a talent.
    Starting with an early screenplay written wild studying at R.A.D.A. (*Schoolgirl Rebels* –
written under a male pseudonym) the playwright first went on stage in 1915 at the age of 19,
but it did not bring her the golden fruits her pen was later to harvest for her – after a series of
depressing tours she left the stage and became a buyer for Heal's. Fortunately while shopping
for toys and pictures for middle class kids she did not stop writing, and in 1924 *British Talent*
was given an amateur airing. In 1931 came *Autumn Crocus* – a huge success – and she was
launched. The 1930's produced a number of plays in that gilded era when old-fashioned style
and construction were of supreme value and audiences expected a well-made play. Dodie
Smith constructed her plays like boxes, solid, secure, each line leading to another line, each
situation growing and blossoming within the classic three-act mold. In fact as one reads them
now it is the strong sense of craftsmanship that still comes across – a professional and

enviable ability to forge a story so that the shape of the play, from opening curtain to closing line, is all of a piece. You can read her plays like novels – and with a little imagination see the situations developing before you. It isn't suprising that she turned to novel writing, and her first, *I Captured the Castle*, was later turned into a play. (In all she has written five novels and two books for children.) She also adapted a Henry James story, *The Reverberator*, to become *Letter from Paris*. It is a play that, unlike some of the others, has a musty air of datedness and seems more suited to the cozy home-screen than the stage, and the characters, although still firmly handled and well presented, have a slight edge of melodrama – which may of course be a Jamesian legacy.

It's not just a lucky chance that makes Dodie Smith's work so often the choice of enthusiastic amateur groups, for perhaps more than professional actors they seize quickly onto these ready-formed characters which are so near completion on the printed page. Dodie Smith likes to write about good middle-class home and people with values – taking that sensible but often ignored advice, to write about what one knows. She undoubtedly knows her people and she puts them into human situations which cleverly avoid being sentimental. Her ear for the comfortably-off family in *Dear Octopus* is very sound; indeed her dialogue has an authentic natural running ring that rarely bogs down.

—Michael Leech

SMITH, Michael (Townsend).   American.   Born in Kansas City, Missouri, 5 October 1935. Educated at the Hotchkiss School, Lakeville, Connecticut, 1951–53; Yale University, New Haven, Connecticut, 1953–55. Married Michele Marie Hawley in 1974; has one son. Theatre Critic, 1959–74, and Associate Editor, 1962–65, *Village Voice,* New York (Obie Award judge, 1962–68 and 1972–74). Taught at the New School for Social Research, New York, 1964–65; Project Radius, Dalton, Georgia, 1972; Hunter College, New York, 1972. Manager, Sundance Festival Theatre, Upper Black Eddy, Pennsylvania, 1966–68; Producer, Caffe Cino, New York, 1968; Director, Theatre Genesis, New York, since 1971. Stage lighting designer; musician. Recipient: Brandeis University Creative Arts Citation, 1965; Obie Award, for directing, 1972; Rockefeller award, 1975. Address: 40 Gold Street, Stonington, Connecticut 06378, U.S.A.

PUBLICATIONS

Plays

> *I Like It* (also director: produced New York, 1963).   Published in *Kulchur* (New York), 1963.
> *The Next Thing* (produced New York, 1966).   Published in *The Best of Off-Off-Broadway*, edited by Michael Smith, New York, Dutton, 1969.
> *More! More! I Want More!*, with Jonny Dodd and Remy Charlip (produced New York, 1966).
> *Vorspiel nach Marienstein*, with Jonny Dodd and Ondine (also director: produced New York, 1967).
> *Captain Jack's Revenge* (also director: produced New York, 1970; London, 1971). Published in *New American Plays 4*, edited by William M. Hoffman, New York, Hill and Wang, 1971.

A Dog's Love, music by John Herbert McDowell (produced New York, 1971).
Tony (produced New York, 1971).
Peas (also director: produced Denver, 1971).
Country Music (also director: produced New York, 1971).   Published in *The Off-Off-Broadway Book*, edited by Albert Poland and Bruce Mailman, Indianapolis, Bobbs Merrill, 1972.
Double Solitaire (also director: produced Denver, 1973).
Prussian Suite (also director: produced New York, 1974).
A Wedding Party (also director: produced Denver, 1974).
Rose Has an Idea (also director: produced Denver, 1976).

Other

Theatre Journal, Winter 1967.   Columbia, University of Missouri Press, 1968.
Theatre Trip (critical journal).   Indianapolis, Bobbs Merrill, 1969.

Editor, with Nick Orzel, *Eight Plays from Off-Off-Broadway.*   Indianapolis, Bobbs Merrill, 1966.
Editor, *The Best of Off-Off-Broadway.*   New York, Dutton, 1969.
Editor, *More Plays from Off-Off-Broadway.*   Indianapolis, Bobbs Merrill, 1972.

Theatrical Activities:

Director: **Plays** − many of his own plays, and *Three Sisters Who Are Not Sisters* by Gertrude Stein, New York, 1964; *Icarus's Mother* by Sam Shepard, New York, 1965; *Chas. Dickens' Christmas Carol* by Soren Agenoux, New York, 1966; *Donovan's Johnson* by Soren Agenoux, New York, 1967; *With Creatures Make My Way* by H. M. Koutoukas, New York, 1967; *The Life of Juanita Castro* by Ronald Tavel, Denver, 1968; *Dr. Kheal* by María Irene Fornés, Denver, 1968; *Hurricane of the Eye* by Emanuel Peluso, New
                                                                                                                     XX
york, 1969; *Eat Cake* by Jean-Claude van Itallie, Denver, 1971; XXX by William M.
                                                                                                                      X
Hoffman, Denver, 1971; *Bigfoot* by Ronald Tavel, New York, 1972; *Tango Palace* by María Irene Fornés, New York, 1973.

*   *   *

> It all seems to refer to something else, but it is difficult to figure out what that something else is.
>
> —*Country Music*

I offer the following tale as a model for the unconscious process that seems to underlie the plays of Michael Smith:

He has gone to a lot of trouble to arrange his materials. The plantain was picked while Venus was ascendant, the hair was surreptitiously cut from the sleeping girl, the circle was drawn in clean sand by the flowing stream, and now the words so carefully memorized are pronounced correctly. All these elements must be in order to produce the *event*.

Dutifully he summons demons to aid him. From the inner recesses of his consciousness and the stream, from his spinal column and the beech tree, from his shoulder and his dog, demons fly to him. He is protected from danger by the limits of his circle.

He perceives the demons as scraps of old arguments, flashes of relived emotions, a slight feeling of unease. Is he coming down with a cold? Why did he think of his mother? Will he stay with his lover?

His experience tells him to say "Get ye hence" to the demon-thoughts. He must go further. He's tired of emotion, bored with dialectic. "There must be something else," he thinks.

What does he want tonight? To be loved? To hate? Make fertile? Kill? None of these. Tonight he wants to be *wise*. He does not want information; he has plenty of facts. He knows that hens lay eggs, soldiers kill, lovers love. No, he wishes to know how and where to stand in relation to all his knowledge.

He throws a little something on the fire. It flares briefly, and suddenly a similar flare lights his mind. He thinks of nothing at all for some moments of eternity. The muscles of his neck relax.

After which he addresses the world as the wind makes his hair fly: "Who are you, Moon? Who are you, Stream? Who are you, Dog? Who are you, Man?"

I certainly do not wish to say that Michael Smith is a practitioner of black or white arts. What I do mean to suggest is that Smith, like many other artists of this time, wants to explore lines of inquiry that in earlier times might have been called religious.

As the magician or priest juxtaposes disparate and often illogical elements toward a magical goal, Michael Smith arranges his material without the superficially logical glue that audiences since Ibsen have come to expect.

Smith's stories often seem discontinuous in characterization and time. The actress playing the daughter in *Peas* is also asked to play her own mother, grandmother, and lover's other girlfriend. In *Country Music* costumes and make-up are changed drastically and abruptly. In *The Next Thing* the sequence of events is arranged aesthetically; reaction does not necessarily follow action, although within any small section time is "normal." In *Point Blank* (as yet unproduced) the opening stage direction reads, "This is a loop play. Begin anywhere, repeat several times, stop anywhere."

Thus in spite of fairly naturalistic dialogue the audience is somewhat disoriented by a Smith play. In fact because the dialogue is so "normal" Smith creates enormous tension by letting his characters play freely with role and time.

Smith's homely subject matter, which is most often the family, also is at variance with his treatment. Unlike most playwrights who write about the family, Smith is uninterested in commenting either unfavorably or favorably about his subject.

As the priest or witch places such ordinary elements as bread, wine, and plants in the context of the cosmos, so Michael Smith exposes his characters to time, nature, and politics.

In *Country Music* two couples are exposed to the vagaries of time and weather. Their loves seem more affected by these elements than by psychology. Change seems to occur the same way buds grow. In *Captain Jack's Revenge* the characters are subject to art and politics. In the first act the people consciously try to order their awareness by means of television, radio, stereo, slide and movie projectors, telephone, and the doorbell. In the second act we see how the minds of these same people have been shaped by the actions of remote figures in American history.

Yet Smith does not tell us that we are doomed by weather, time, politics, psychology, or the media. He is pointing two ways at once, both at the solidity of certain facts, the bread and the wine, and at the cosmic context of these facts.

Yes, the couple in *Country Music* are subject to powerful forces outside their control, but look at the stars, look at the different kinds of light we can see – candlelight, sunshine, moonlight, twilight, dawn. The actors prepare food on stage and then eat it. All these experiences are called for by the author as his characters love, grow apart, leave.

Yes, the white people in *Captain Jack's Revenge* are doomed to the Indians' revenge for the crimes of their ancestors, but notice the beauty of the revenge, the glorious but mind-numbing media, the alluring but confusing drugs.

From Smith's magical (I might say "objective") point of view comes the curiously unemotional language. Rarely do his people lose their cool. They love passionately, they hate, they murder, but their language does not often reflect this. Does the playwright feel that emotion is such a heavy element on stage that the total stage picture would be unduly dominated by it? As the son says in *Peas*, "I want other people to be there without making a point of it."

Michael Smith's plays are not designed to weigh ten tons of emotions. The audience must not be distracted from being aware they are seeing a model, not a slice, of life. The altar or voodoo dolls are not naturalistic representations either. Perhaps the logic of a Smiths play is: If you can portray a situation objectively, with the freedom to be playful, if you can see the total picture, if you can arrange the elements of existence, you can induce a state of mind that allows us to see the magic of everyday life.

—William M. Hoffman

SNYDER, William (Hartwell, Jr.).   American   Born in Memphis, Tennessee, in 1929. Educated at the Daycroft School, Stamford, Conneticut; Principia College, Illinois; Yale University Drama School, New Haven, Connecticut, M.F.A.Currently, Member of the Department of English, University of Tennessee, Martin. Agent: Leah Salisbury, 790 Madison Avenue, New York, New York. Address: Department of English, University of Tennessee, Martin, Tennessee 38237, U.S.A.

PUBLICATIONS

Plays

> *Another Summer* (produced New Haven, Connecticut, 1953).   Published in *The Best Short Plays 1953–1954*, edited by Margaret Mayorga, New York, Dodd Mead, 1954.
> *The Departing*, in *The Best Short Plays 1957–1958*, edited by Margaret Mayorga. Boston, Beacon Press, 1958.
> *The Days and Nights of Beebee Fenstermaker* (produced New York, 1962).   New York, Dramatists Play Service, 1963.
> *Birthday* (produced Swarthmore, Pennsylvania, 1964).

*   *   *

William Snyder's protagonists are young, imaginative, tense, and usually Southern. Each is the only son or dauther of a middle-class family, sometimes with a crotchety or senile grandmother, usually with a hard-working, somewhat remote father, almost always with an earnest, affectionate mother named Melinda. The protagonist has trouble communicating, even with her; she wants a "normal" life for her offspring, who has undisclosed hopes and feares of idiosyncratic intensity. With other characters, worse *malentendus* may occur: Southern society has definite ideas of how one should feel and act towards family and friends. But the consequent problems, comic or serious, are only incidentally regional, for the underlying fears – of inadequacy, of meaningless life, of mindless old age, or of sudden death – are found everywhere.

In *Another Summer* (one of several plays Snyder wrote at the Yale Drama School), seven-year-old Petey, on his annual summer visit to grandparents and maiden aunt, enjoys endless games with his grandfather, and is desperately reluctant to leave. Though Grandfather dies that winter, Petey is anxious to return the next summer, and his aunt to have him, but he is so paralyzed by the sense of mortality emanating from his grandfather's death-room, the cook's folk-fears, a neighbor's death, and an inopportune thunderstorm that his relatives think him sullen and ungrateful, and he returns with frantic eagerness to home and "safety."

The Departing shows Petey, now fifteen (and with a different last name) suffering a less serious attack of nerves before going North to prep-school, in the family tradition. His one "friend" jealously harps on the disadvantages and dangers of going away, particularly for anyone with Petey's antisocial addictions to Lewis Carroll and Gilbert and Sullivan. Petey's last night is poisoned until at last the family achieves that moment of warm, unifying good humor they had all been querulously seeking.

In The Days and Nights of Beebee Fenstermaker, Snyder's only New York production to date, Beebee, fresh from a Southern University, comes to New York determined to achieve both a career, preferably as a writer, and a perfect marriage. Her autobiographical novel bogs down in endless re-writes of the beginning and decreasing empathy for her teen-aged self as subject. Having taken a "temporary" office job, she tries art; each time she goes to a new teacher she starts well, then gets worse as she tries harder. A semi-intellectual lover, full of pop-psychology, moves in and revives her writing by prescribing non-stop writing stints, sans re-reading. But Beebee's very exhilaration at thus overriding her inhibitions while unloading all responsibility on Ed makes her so afraid of losing him she both asks and gives too much; he is overwhelmed and almost paralyzed by the time she herself goads him into breaking free. She slumps into aimless desperation until a resilient boy, fresh from the South, with small education but a large sense of humor, proves to be, if far from the "perfect" lover she once demanded, the essential "someone who can bear me and [whom] I can bear. At least for a little while."

Reviews ranged from enthusiastic to lukewarm, but agreed that Snyder's dialogue was lively and real, and Beebee's scenes with her two lovers very effective; less so her long monologues and the alternating episodes in which her mother and two aunts bicker while their own lives deteriorate.

Subsequent plays for stage and screen (mostly in the limbo of "properties" purchased but not yet produced) include Birthday, a three-character one-acter in which a monstrously self-indulgent seeker of eternal youth discovers with horror that his once-energetic, long-neglected mother has grown amiably senile, and a haunting script, The Dream and the Game. In this, ten-year-old Jimmy's mother has died; he moves into a weed-surrounded farmhouse with a senile grandmother and elderly housekeeper. He suffers recurrent nightmares but joins other boys in a semi-ritual game of "knighthood" and "cathedral"-building; at last, driven by dreams, rituals, and his grandmither's death, he gets himself buried alive as a "sacrifice."

Here, as in a screen-play of The Moviegoer (the novel by his fellow-Southener, Walker Percy), Snyder cuts dialogue to a minimum, showing a flair for visual narration and imagery which it would be interesting to see filmed.

—George McElroy

SOYINKA, Wole (Akinwande Oluwole Soyinka).   Nigerian.   Born in Abeokuta, 13 July 1934. Educated at Government College, Ibadan; University of Leeds, Yorkshire, 1954–57, B.A. (honours) in English. Married; has children. Play Reader, Royal Court Theatre, London, 1958–59; Research Fellow in Drama, University of Ibadan, 1960–61; Lecturer in English, University of Ife, 1962–63; Senior Lecturer in English, University of Lagos, 1964–67; Director of the School of Drama, University of Ibadan, 1969–72. Research Professor in Drama, 1972–75, and since 1975, Professor of Comparative Literature,

University of Ife. Founding Director of the Orisun Theatre and the 1960 Masks theatre, Lagos and Ibadan. Political Prisoner, Lagos and Kaduna, 1967–69. Recipient: Dakar Negro Arts Festival award, 1966; John Whiting Award, 1966; Jock Campbell Award (*New Statesman*), for fiction, 1968. D.Litt.: University of Leeds, 1973. Agent: Morton Leavy, Katz, Leavy Rosenberg, and Sindle, 437 Madison Avenue, New York, New York 10022, U.S.A. Address: Department of Literature, University of Ife, Ile-Ife, Nigeria.

PUBLICATIONS

Plays

> *The Swamp Dwellers* (produced Ibadan and London, 1958; New York, 1968). Included in *Three Plays*, 1963; *Five Plays*, 1964.
> *The Lion and the Jewel* (produced Ibadan, 1959; London, 1966).   London, Ibadan, and New York, Oxford University Press, 1963.
> *The Invention* (produced London, 1959).
> *A Dance of the Forests* (produced Ibadan, 1960).   London, Ibadan, and New York, Oxford University Press, 1963.
> *The Trial of Brother Jero* (produced Ibadan, 1960; Cambridge, 1965; London, 1966; New York, 1967).   Included in *Three Plays*, 1963; *Five Plays*, 1964.
> *Camwood on the Leaves* (broadcast, 1960).   London, Eyre Methuen, 1972.
> *Three Plays: The Trials of Brother Jero, The Swamp Dwellers, The Strong Breed.* Ibadan, Mbari, 1963.
> *The Strong Breed* (produced Ibadan, 1964; London, 1966; New York, 1967). Included in *Three Plays*, 1963; *Five Plays*, 1964.
> *Kongi's Harvest* (produced Ibadan, 1964; New York, 1968).   London, Ibadan, and New York, Oxford University Press, 1967.
> *Five Plays: A Dance of the Forests, The Lion and the Jewel, The Swamp Dwellers, The Trials of Brother Jero, The Strong Breed.*   London, Ibadan, and New York, Oxford University Press, 1964.
> *Before the Blackout* (produced Ibadan, 1964).   Lagos, Orisun Editions, 1971; in *Camwood on the Leaves, and Before the Blackout*, 1974.
> *The Road* (produced London, 1965).   London, Ibadan, and New York, Oxford University Press, 1965.
> *Madmen and Specialists* (produced Waterford, Connecticut, and New York, 1970; revised version, produced Ibadan, 1971; London, 1972).   London, Methuen, 1971; New York, Hill and Wang, 1972.
> *The Jero Plays: The Trials of Brother Jero and Jero's Metamorphosis.*   London, Eyre Methuen, 1972.
> *The Bacchae: A Communion Rite*, adaptation of the play by Euripides (produced London, 1973).   London, Eyre Methuen, 1973; New York, Norton, 1974.
> *Collected Plays:*
> > I. *A Dance of the Forest, The Swamp Dweller, The Strong Breed, The Road, The Bacchae.*   London and New York, Oxford University Press, 1974.
> > II. *The Lion and the Jewel, Kongi's Harvest, The Trials of Brother Jero, Metamorphosis, Madmen and Specialists.*   London and New York, Oxford University Press, 1974.
> *Camwood on the Leaves, and Before the Blackout: Two Short Plays.*   New York, Third Press, 1974.
> *Death and the King's Horseman.*   London, Eyre Methuen, 1975; New York, Norton, 1976.

Screenplay: *Kongi's Harvest*, 1970.

Radio Play: *Camwood on the Leaves*, 1960 (UK).

Television Documentaries: *Joshua: A Nigerian Portrait*, 1962 (Canada); *Culture in Transition*, 1963 (USA).

Novels

The Interpreters.   London, Deutsch, 1965; New York, Macmillan, 1970.
Season of Anomy.   London, Rex Collings, 1973; New York, Third Press, 1974.

Verse

Idanre and Other Poems.   London, Methuen, 1967; New York, Hill and Wang, 1968.
A Shuttle in the Crypt.   London, Eyre Methuen-Rex Collings, and New York, Hill and Wang, 1972.

Other

The Man Died: Prison Memoirs.   London, Eyre Methuen-Rex Collings, 1972.
In Person: Achebe, Awoonor, and Soyinka at the University of Washington.   Seattle, University of Washington African Studies Program, 1975.
Myth, Literature and the African World.   London, Cambridge University Press, 1976.

Editor, *Poems of Black Africa.*   London, Secker and Warburg, and New York, Hill and Wang, 1975.

Translator, *The Forest of a Thousand Daemons: A Hunter's Saga*, by D. A. Fagunwa. London, Nelson, 1968; New York, Humanities Press, 1969.

Critical Studies: *The Writing of Wole Soyinka* by Eldred Jones, London, Heinemann, 1972; "Théâtre et Nationalisme: Wole Soyinka et LeRoi Jones" by Alain Ricard, in *Présence Africaine* (Paris). 1972; *Wole Soyinka* by Gerald Moore, London, Evans, 1972.

Theatical Activities:

Director: **Plays** – by Brecht, Chekhov, Clark, Easmon, Eseoghene, Ogunyemi, Shakespeare, Synge, and his own works; *L'Espace et la Magie*, Paris, 1972.

*   *   *

There are few living writers who can match Wole Soyinka in those areas on which all good drama is built – language and vision. One of Africa's better poets, Soyinka has consistently brought a language of muscular imagery to the theatre, enriching it with a mythical structure which is an integral part of both the action in his plays and the writer's own background and beliefs. His brutally honest portrayals of gods, heroes, and common men are characteristic of even the earliest of his works, yet that brutal honesty never completely excludes the possibilities for both courage and hope.

Soyinka's early devotion to the writings of J. M. Synge, another playwright who used a second language while living in a culture affected by a colonial presence to forge new directions in theatre, is obvious in many aspects of Soyinka's plays. A frequent use of flashbacks, narrators who provide both framework and continuity, and an "arrangement of English" (as Gerald Moore puts it) which suggests the presence of another tongue beneeath it, revitalizing and forging the language anew, are all reminiscent of the Irish playwright – though Soyinkamakes such things very much his own. Soyinka's awareness of other African writers is also a part of his genius, and the influence of Yoruba Concert Parties (such as were made popular by Hubert Ogunde) and other of his contemporaries writing in the Yoruba language (such as Duro Ladipo and Obotunde Ijimere) may also be seen in his work – though it should be remembered that all of these writers are drawing from the same rich tradition.

Born in the Western Nigerian town of Abeokuta, Soyinka has taken the god Ogun, a masculine deity who seems to represent for the artist an aggressive devotion to creativity, as his patron saint. Thus Soyinka has found no need, as has been the case with some Western writers, to create new mythologies or revive ones long dead. He has immersed himself in the mythology which still strongly exists (so strongly that a former god of Iron has now also become the patron deity of lorry drivers) and the Yoruba pantheon and the rich possibilities for both action and imagery which it suggests are found at the center of some of Soyinka's most powerful efforts, including *The Road* and *A Dance of the Forests*. Eldred Jones, in a fine essay entitled "The Essential Soyinka" has described Soyinka's use of his heritage in the following words: "Few writers have used the totality of African experience to better purpose or with more effect. No African writer has been more successful in making the rest of the world see humanity through African eyes."

In addition to his highly successful use of traditional beliefs and natural imagery, Soyinka has also managed to combine dance, music and action in many of his recent works in such a manner as to enliven and make more effective the play as a whole. Even Soyinka's darkest vision, that brilliant parable of war, power and their attendant corruption, *Madmen and Specialists*, makes use of music and dance.

All this may seem to counter the one aspect of Soyinka which has been so overpublicized – his "hostility" to Negritude. What Soyinka's objections point out, it seems (especially when one considers how his life and work are one of the finest testaments to the African greatness which Negritude is supposed to stand for) is a characteristic unwillingness on the writer's part to accept an oversimplified view of any aspect of human experience. For Soyinka the past is not more to be worshipped than the present. In an unpublished thesis for the University of Ghana, Robert Maccani makes the important point that for Soyinka there is a crucial difference between history and tradition. History can all too easily be distorted for nationalistic purposes. Tradition, on the other hand, can be used as a guide and inspiration for both artist and society. In nearly every play which Soyinka has written we find this dichotomy – history versus tradition – at the center of the action. In *A Dance of the Forests* (which was commissioned for the Nigerian Independence celebrations) Adenebi, an orator for the council, has the idea of summoning spirits from the glorious past: "Perhaps a descendant of the great Lisabi. Zimbabwe. Maybe the legendary Prester John himself....I was thinking of heroes like they." What he gets are two very nondescript dead people who are all too truthful about the great empire which callously destroyed them. In refusing to recognize the reality of the past, Adenebi also does not accept his own responsibility for the present – where his corrupt licensing of a ramshackle motor lorry has led to the deaths of sixty-five people. Without a true vision of the past, its evils will only be repeated again. In one of the great ironies of history, the words spoken by the ancient court historian in reference to one of the Dead people Adenebi brings back were applied almost exactly to Soyinka himself when he was imprisoned for his protests against the Nigerian Civil War: "Soldiers have never questioned bloodshed...this man is a traitor. He must be in the enemy's pay."

Wole Soyinka is, in the truest sense of the word, a committed writer. In some ways he resembles the character in his play *The Strong Breed* who chooses to be the ritual carrier of the sins of his society, a scapegoat, one of the "strong breed." A theme which runs consistently through his plays is that of the false prophet, sometimes a political figure (as in *Kongi's Harvest*), sometimes a religious one (as in *The Swamp Dwellers*). In each of these plays where a false prophet appears (with the exception of *The Trials of Brother Jero*, a comedy in which the roguish prophet comes out on top) there is a scene of unmasking in which some member of Soyinka's "strong breed" engineers the debunking. Soyinka's hilariously vitriolic sketches in his revue *Before the Blackout*, the before-mentioned *Madmen and Specialists* (in which the main character is a doctor who has become Head of Intelligence during the war, presumably because he knows where to put the electrodes), even his collection of essays, *The Man Died*, all further attest to the fact that he views the role of the artist as that of a man with a responsibility to take action through his art.

In speaking of Soyinka, however, one should avoid oversimplification. He is one of the most complex and cerebral of modern playwrights. This in no way means that his works are impenetrable. Quite the contrary, they are characterized by a clarity of action and message matched by few. However, they exist on so many levels at the same time, that there is great richness – and the very real possibility that while a play of Soyinka's may mean one thing for everyone in his audience it may also mean something else in addition to those who are African or at least familiar with the subtleties of Yoruba culture and belief which he handles so masterfully. *The Road*, one of Soyinka's most impressive pieces of theatre, has at its heart certain intricacies of Yoruba religion and its tenets concerning life, death and sacrifice which may well go over the heads of some Western viewers, yet the search on the part of Professor for the meaning of the word, his "part psychic, part intellectual grope...towards the essence of death," as Soyinka puts it in his note for the producer, is as meaningful for a "universal" audience as are the actions of the characters in Beckett's *Waiting for Godot*. Soyinka's real theme is the human condition. Because he explores it so well, in both comedy and tragedy, truimph and defeat, he is more than just an African playwright (even as a certain long-dead Englishman was more than just a dramatist from Stratford) – he is a writer for everyone.

—Joseph Bruchac

SPEIGHT, Johnny. British. Born in Canning Town, London, in 1921. Left school at fourteen. Served in the army, 1939–45. Married to Constance Barrett; has three children. Worked in a factory; as a jazz drummer; insurance salesman, 1952–55. Radio and television scriptwriter for the BBC since 1955. Agent: A.L.S. Management Ltd., 67 Brook Street, London W.1 Address: 9 Orme Court, London W.2, England.

PUBLICATIONS

Plays

　　Mr. Venus, with Ray Galton, music and lyrics by Trevor H. Stanford and Norman Newell (produced London, 1958).
　　Sketches in *The Art of Living* (produced London, 1960).
　　The Compartment (televised, 1961; produced Pitlochry, Perthshire 1965).
　　The Knacker's Yard (produced London, 1962).
　　The Playmates (televised, 1962; as *Games*, produced London, 1971).
　　If There Weren't Any Blacks You'd Have to Invent Them (televised, 1965; produced Loenersloot, Holland, and London, 1965). Loenersloot, Holland, Mickery Books, 1965; London, Methuen, 1970.
　　Sketches in *In the Picture* (produced London, 1967).

The Salesman (televised, 1970; produced London, 1970).
Till Death Us Do Part.   London, Woburn Press, 1973.
The Thoughts of Chairman Alf (produced London, 1976).

Screenplays: *Privilege*, 1967; *The Garnett Saga*, 1972; *Till Death Us Do Part*, 1973.

Radio Writing: for the *Edmondo Ros, Morecambe and Wise*, and *Frankie Howerd* shows, 1956–58; *Early to Braden* show, 1957–58; *The Deadly Game of Chess*, 1958; *The April 8th Show* (*7 Days Early*), 1958; *Eric Sykes* show, 1960–61.

Television Writings: for the *Arthur Haynes* show; *The Compartment*, 1961; *The Playmates*, 1962; *Shamrot*, 1963; *If There Weren't Any Blacks You'd Have to Invent Them*, 1965; *Till Death Us Do Part* series, 1966–75; *To Lucifer a Sun*, 1967; *Curry and Chips* series, 1969; *The Salesman*, 1970; *Them* series, 1972; *Speight of Marty* series, 1973; *For Richer... For Poorer*, 1975.

Other

It Stands to Reason.   London, Joseph-Hobbs, 1973.
*The Thoughts of Chairman Alf: Alf Garnett's Little Blue Book; or, Where England Went
    Wrong: An Open Letter to the People of Britain.*   London, Robson Books, 1973.
Pieces of Speight.   London, Robson Books, 1974.

*   *   *

Johnny Speight is one of those writers whose success in television has become a trap. Unlike almost every other writer of comic series for peak-hour viewers, he is a source of controversy, scandal and outrage as well as rewarded with a popularity which has proved to be less than totally advantageous to him. Born in 1921, he was a factory worker before World War II, and it was not until 1955 that his determination to succeed as a writer bore any fruits. His first work was the writing of scripts for such comedians as Frankie Howerd, Arthur Askey, Cyril Fletcher, Eric Sykes and others. When he began to write for Arthur Haynes, he began to show an ability to create unusual material rather than the power to exploit the familiar gifts of an established comedian. For Haynes, Speight created the character of a tramp whose aggressive, rebarbative personality had a striking originality.

It was through a series of programmes for BBC television, *Till Death Us Do Part*, that Speight became a household word. His work, for a number of reasons most of which were irrelevant, became a battle ground over which "permissive" liberals fought the old-fashioned viewers who believe in verbal restraint, the importance of good taste and the banishment of certain topics, notably religion, from light entertainment. What Speight wrote was originally in essence a cartoon, a cockney version of the north country Andy Capp, in which attitudes almost everybody would condemn as anti-social were derided. Four people – husband and wife, their daughter and their son-in-law – inhabit the sitting-room of a slum house; they have nothing in common except their bitter dislike for each other. The father, Alf Garnett, is barely literate, full of misconceived, misunderstood and ignorant prejudices about race, politics and religion; his language is atrocious. His wife is reduced almost to the stage of a vegetable, coming to life only when her detestation of her husband finds some opportunity of expressing itself. The son-in-law, as ignorantly and stupidly of the left as Garnett is of the right, is a Liverpool-Irish Roman Catholic, who dresses flamboyantly, wears his hair long and does no work whatever; his only spell of activity was an inefficient attempt to swindle social security officials. The daughter agrees in all things with her husband, but it is plain that her agreement is the result of his effectiveness as a lover rather than of any intellectual processes of argument.

Through these appalling people, Speight was able for time to lambast senseless racial and political prejudices while making cheeky fun of the Royal Family, the church and anything else which drifted into what passes in the Garnett household for conversation, and Garnett for a time was a very effective weapon against bigotry and stupidity. Unfortunately, his effectiveness as a vehicle for satire tended to diminish as the monstrous energy with which he was created slipped out of control and allowed him to take possession of each episode of a series which continued long after the original impetus has exhausted itself and which began to show something dangerously ambivalent in Speight's attack on racialism. The creation of two Garnett films demonstrated that Speight's monsters were at their most popular when there was nothing left to say about them, so that *Till Death Us Do Part* seemed to turn into an incubus from which the author was unable to escape.

Curry and Chips, another effort to stifle racial prejudice by allowing it to be voiced in its most extreme forms by the stupid, lacked the vitality of *Till Death Us Do Part*, and a later series, *Them*, in which two tramps dreamed of grandeur, their dreams contrasted sharply with the reality of their way of life, was notable only for the gentleness of its comedy, proving that Speight was capable of more than the stridency of life with the Garnett family.

Such work, for all the energy of Garnettry, and the strength with which the leading monster had been created, made it seem that Speight had moved a long way in the wrong direction. In 1961, his first television play proper, *The Compartment*, had nothing to do with the sort of writing which later made him notorious. In a compartment of an old-fashioned train which has no corridor, a businessman is alone with a practical joker who persecutes him for the length of the journey; it becomes the joker's amusement to convince his pompous, easily frightened companion that he is helpless in the company of an armed, murderous psychopath. There are no motives, no explanations, no rationalisations; the events simply happen with a sort of uneasy humour. A year later, the same joker, selling "jokes" and tricks from door to door, finds himself sheltered for a night by a strange, psychopathic girl who is a big house's only inhabitant. *The Playmates* – for the girl wants to join in fun with the traveller's samples – shares the disregard for motives and explanations already shown by *The Compartment*. A third play, offering, it seems, another aspect of the experience of the joker, was equally effective. The ideas were fashionable at the time when it was *avant garde* and exciting to offer allegiance to "The Theatre of the Absurd," but Speight produced his genuine shocks and *frissons*.

Both *The Compartment* and a later television play, *If There Weren't Any Blacks You'd Have to Invent Them*, were adapted for stage performances but, despite some success, proved to belong to the screen rather than the stage. *If There Weren't Any Blacks* exploited Speight's reputation, won from the Garnett series, as a passionate opponent of racialism, and makes its point amusingly and convincingly with none of the ambivalence which crept into *Till Death Us Do Part* when Garnett took control of the series and began to speak as a character in his own right rather than as an instrument designed by his creator to ridicule the politically idiotic. Speight's only genuine play for the theatre, not adapted from television material, *The Knacker's Yard*, won some praise for the vigour and imaginativeness of its dialogue.

It is impossible not to think of Speight as a creator of grotesque, disturbing characters trapped by television into a situation which demands that he continuingly repeat, in series after series of *Till Death* with diminishing returns, a success which rapidly lost its inventiveness. Thus, he pays the penalty of his originality.

—Henry Raynor

SPENCER, Colin.   British.   Born in London, 17 July 1933. Educated at Brighton Grammar School, Selhurst; Brighton College of Art. Served in the Royal Army Medical Corps, 1950–52. Married Gillian Chapman in 1959; has one child. Paintings exhibited in

Cambridge and London; costume designer. Agent (plays) Margaret Ramsey Ltd., 14a Goodwin's Court, London, WC2N 4LL; (novels) Richard Scott Simon, 36 Wellington Street, London W.C.2. Address: 44 Lonsdale Square, London N1 1EW, England.

PUBLICATIONS

Plays

> *The Ballad of the False Barman*, music by Clifton Parker (produced London, 1966).
> *Spitting Image* (produced London, 1968; New York, 1969).   Published in *Plays and Players* (London), September 1968.
> *The Trial of St. George* (produced London, 1972).
> *The Sphinx Mother* (produced Salzburg, Austria, 1972).
> *Why Mrs. Neustadter Always Loses* (produced London, 1972).

Television Plays: *Flossie*, 1975; *Vandal Rule OK?* (documentary), 1976.

Novels

> *An Absurd Affair.*   London, Longman, 1961.
> *Anarchists in Love.*   London, Eyre and Spottiswoode, 1963; as *The Anarchy of Love*, New York, Weybright and Talley, 1967.
> *Asylum.*   London, Blond, 1966.
> *Poppy, Mandragora and the New Sex.*   London, Blond, 1966.
> *The Tyranny of Love.*   London, Blond, and New York, Weybright and Talley, 1967.
> *Lovers in War.*   London, Blond, 1970.
> *Panic.*   London, Secker and Warburg, 1971.
> *How the Greeks Kidnapped Mrs. Nixon.*   London, Quartet, 1974.

*   *   *

Harold Hobson, reviewing Colin Spencer's musical play *The Ballad of the False Barman* in *The Sunday Times*, referred to "Mr. Spencer's great and complicated skill . . . unified by [his] overwhelming sense of evil. This is its aesthetic strength." Certainly there is something in the play that both attracts and alienates. I recall that, as artistic director of the Hampstead Theatre Club where it was premiered, I sent it to nine directors before the tenth, Robin Phillips, accepted it. Yet re-reading it now for what must be about the twelfth time I find that my first impression is unchanged. The play still seems to me like an impassioned sermon by John Donne, written with the sensuality of Genet, the cogency (especially in the lyrics) of Brecht, and the high camp of Ronald Firbank. If this sounds like mirroring too many influences it should be remembered that it is, after all, a play about disguises. The setting is a bar in Brighton to which come all the so-called "dregs of society." They are welcomed by an enigmatic barman (played by a woman) who fulfills their needs:

> Give me the right to exploit you,
> Tell me your private dream,
> I can fix anything, just leave it to me.

The play's central theme is the opposition of corruption, in the person of the barman, and goodness, in the person of Josie. As the Barman says to Josie, "Your goodness is a thorn in our flesh."

When Josie's lover, a gigolo and burglar called Bill, is thrown into prison, Josie is thrown out of the bar. No one will help her. (*En route* Spencer makes a scathing attack on conventional morality, on the inhumanity of the professional clergyman, the police and the judiciary.) Josie is driven to accept the hospitality of a mysterious Duke whose advances she has long resisted. But now she says, "I am too tired to do anything else."

She enters the Duke's house with its many rooms. "Explore them," says the Duke, "I will give you thoughts like new children. I will uncover areas of feeling, of rhythm, and motion, which will astonish, amaze, excite ...," to which Josie replies, "You have shown me things in myself that I never dreamt were there.... You have shown me mirrors." The Duke answers, "The more you know, the greater you will grow."

No critic at the time realized what Spencer was doing here. Brilliantly, more alarmingly than in any Mystery play of York or Wakefield, he has updated the story of the serpent in the Garden of Eden, the temptation to eat of the Tree of Knowledge of good *and* evil. The death of Josie's baby comes in this context as a brutal, dream-potent image of the death of innocence, the expulsion from Eden. At the end of the play Josie says to the Duke, "You are all the terror in my soul. You are the darkness that I have always feared but when I was laid in your arms I knew such peace." Throughout Spencer is dealing with the metaphysic of evil, with what Jung calls the *shadow* side of experience. Anyone who has read Jung's *Answer to Job* will recognise that ultimate goodness cannot be separated from the question of ultimate evil. And though there is undoubtedly a force of evil, the powers of darkness, just as there is a force of good, Spencer questions whether what we call evil is necessarily always evil. And whether what we call good is necessarily always good. We have first to come to terms with our shadow side and only then is a transformation possible. It is only when Prospero ceases to call Caliban "a devil, a demi-devil," and says "This thing of darkness I acknowledge as my own," that Caliban, his shadow side, is enabled to say, "Henceforth I'll seek for grace."

Josie comes to see that her goodness was no more than "simplicity, easily destroyed and now quite worthless." She becomes a whore. "I began to do what you all do because I thought you'd understand. How does sin destroy what's good?" Yet she is not corrupted. She merely sheds the shell of naivety which we, all too often and mistakenly, call innocence. For, as Amanda, the militant Christian in the play, remarks, "It's difficult to go naked in this world."

What Josie finally learns is that "You can't act being good. It just exists in itself. Goodness is a thing apart. It is itself." And because she believes this she will not accept the only society she knows, that of the Bar. She cries out, "Are we in this modern world trapped so vilely in our flesh? No, no, no, no!"

It is with this affirmation that the play ends. And it seems to me in retrospect that no production has yet done the play credit. It is all too easy to be carried away by the surface camp (admittedly a part of the play's fabric) and to neglect its deep moral purpose.

For, fundamentally, Colin Spencer is a moralist. What he does, more urgently than any other contemporary writer, more wittily and with refreshing humour, is to question accepted conventions. In a new play, *The Sphinx Mother* (a modern version of the Oedipus story) there is a moving scene at the beginning of the second act between Clare (the Jocasta figure) and Owen (the Oedipus figure):

Clare – There has never been such a partnership of power and goodness.
Owen – How can that be! Goodness based on corruption?
Clare – Where was the corruption? I have experienced no cruelty or violence
        from you, nor given you any. We trod softly through each other's lives
        and gave freely.

Clare challenges Owen's terrible self-mutilation, "all that he showed was his pathetic weakness." Through her, Spencer challenges.

our abstract ideas of what life and love ought to be. It is these abstract ideas that
cause violence and aggression. Can you not accept that we did love each other,
totally? If a son has lain with his mother for a quarter of a lifetime is that as
grotesque as we think it is?

In other plays, notably the comedies, *The Fruiting Body* (not yet produced) and *Spitting Image*, Spencer continues to question and probe. *Spitting Image*, a "happy play" as Spencer had it billed, revealed as John Russell Taylor observed in a brilliant review of the play, that the author has learnt from a writer like Firbank that camp nonsense can sometimes cut deep. And though, on the surface, *Spitting Image* is about two homosexuals one of whom gives birth to a baby by the other, he has used this fantastic particular instance in order to illuminate a believable, disturbing reality. "If the birth is fantastic," writes Taylor,

> the opposition Gary and Tom encounter, the ways and means by which the authorities seek to supress the akward individual, the special case which obstinately refuses to fit into the nearest convenient pigeon-hole, are all too unforgettably credible. The fantastic particular is made to stand effectively for the host of less eye-catching realities, and the social comment reaches its target unerringly.

If sometimes, as in certain passages from *The Sphinx Mother*, or *The Ballad*, Spencer seems almost florid, baroque in his writing, it is because in these passages (*vide* Bill's loneliness speech in prison, and the Duke's long arias) he is trying to pierce below the external observable reality to that anguish of spirit that cannot really be put into words. In these passages he employs, deliberately, a convoluted, imagistic, surreal style of writing, digging out the kind of uncomfortable and embarrassing images that perhaps occur only in dreams. He is concerned to articulate the lost areas of human experience. In the unproduced *Summer at Camber − 39* (the setting is the outbreak of World War II) he has Hester say,

> I feel trapped, Maud. I'm thirty-nine and I feel trapped. I don't think I'll ever get free...so many things there are battering begging to speak, not just from inside of me, but...so much... I don't quite understand. You don't understand. Eddy can't understand, ever...what am I doing? How long must I stay without...being able to know...more?

The intensity of emotion conveyed by those dots, those broken phrases, is what increasingly concerns theatre in the seventies. As Constantin Stanislavsky wrote at the turn of the century, "It is necessary to picture not life itself as it takes place in reality, but as we vaguely feel it in our dreams, our visions, our moments of spiritual uplift." Virginia Woolf said that she wanted to write "books about silence; about the things people do not say," but because she, like Spencer, was a writer, she had to try and use words. I, myself, am trying to create a form of visual poetry for the theatre, in which visual images will convey the intensity and complexity of experience. How to reach the centre is the shared concern of many different artists in this decade. One cry rings through all these explorations, the cry of Josie in *The Ballad of the False Barman*, "Who among you cares enough? Stop all this deceit, please, oh, please. Stop all these disguises!"

—James Roose-Evans

SPURLING, John. British. Born in Kisumu, Kenya, 17 July 1936. Educated at Dragon School, 1946–49; Marlborough College, 1950–54; St. John's College, Oxford, 1957–60, B.A. 1960. National Service Commission in Royal Artillery, 1955–57. Married Hilary Forrest in 1961; has one daughter and one son. Plebiscite Officer for the United Kingdom in Southern Cameroons, 1960–61; Announcer, BBC Radio, London, 1963–66; Radio and Book Reviewer, *The Spectator*, London, 1966–70, and other publications. Henfield Fellow,

University of East Anglia, Norwich, 1973. Lives in London. Address: c/o Patricia Macnaughton, M.L.R., 194 Old Brompton Road, London SW5 OAS, England.

PUBLICATIONS

Plays

Char (produced Oxford, 1959).
MacRune's Guevara As Realised by Edward Hotel (produced London, 1969; New York, 1975).   London, Calder and Boyars, 1969.
Romance, music and lyrics by Charles Ross (produced Leeds and London, 1971).
In the Heart of the British Museum (produced Edinburgh and London, 1971).   London, Calder and Boyars, 1972.
Shades of Heathcliff (produced Sheffield, 1971; London, 1972).   Included in Shades of Heathcliff, and Death of Captain Doughty, 1975.
Peace in Our Time (produced Sheffield, 1972).
Death of Captain Doughty (televised, 1973).   Included in Shades of Heathcliff, and Death of Captain Doughty, 1975.
McGonagall and the Murderer (produced Edinburgh, 1974).
On a Clear Day You Can See Marlowe (produced London, 1974).
Shades of Heathcliff, and Death of Captain Doughty.   London, Marion Boyars, 1975.

Television Plays: Hope, 1970; Faith, 1971; Death of Captain Doughty, 1973; Silver, 1973.

Other

Samuel Beckett: A Study of His Plays, with John Fletcher.   London, Eyre Methuen, and New York, Hill and Wang, 1972.

John Spurling comments:

MacRune's Guevara was written from a desire to create an event in space rather than to turn out something recognisable as a play (I imagined it being performed in an art gallery rather than a theatre); at the same time I wanted to represent to myself my own conflicting reactions to Che Guevara and to attack certain forms of artistic and political cant which were dominant in the theatre at the time – perhaps still persist.

I found the idea for the more complex structure of In the Heart of the British Museum in Francis Yates's book on Renaissance theories of The Art of Memory, but after completing five scenes I put the play away. I took it up again as a commission for the Traverse Workshop Theatre, under Max Stafford-Clark's direction. The piece, with its emphasis on song and dance, was finished with this particular company in mind, but since I had felt the need for just such a company to perform it even before I knew of the company's existence, the original structure did not have to be altered. The subject-matter comprises Aztec and Chinese legend, the recent Chinese Cultural Revolution, the exile of the Roman poet Ovid, and some of the subject-matter of Ovid's own poems. The central theme is also Ovid's, the idea of Metamorphosis, and this is an important element in the structure.

Shades of Heathcliff grew directly out of being commissioned for Ed Thomason's Crucible Vanguard Theatre in Sheffield. A play for Sheffield seemed to call for a version of Wuthering

Heights; the company consisting only of three actors and one actress, and performing in a small space, dictated that it be a chamber piece and that the characters of the four Brontë children and of the novel itself be melted together.

Peace in Our Time was commissioned by the Crucible Theatre, Sheffield. It is the first part of a larger work called *Ghosts and Monsters of the Second World War*, which I have yet to finish. This first part is set in Hell, where the characters (Hitler, Stalin, Mussolini, Chamberlain, etc.) replay some of the political games of 1935–39.

McGonagall and the Murderer is a short play commissioned by the Pool Theatre, Edinburgh. A man who has failed to assassinate Queen Victoria and is now confined in Broadmoor tries to win a second chance by entering the mind of the poet McGonagall, himself on the road to Balmoral. *On a Clear Day You Can See Marlowe* was first written in 1970 and revised in 1974 for the Major Road Company. The play is something of a companion piece to *MacRune's Guevara* – a collage of the few known facts about the playwright Marlowe, much speculation (both reasonable and ludicrous), and versions of his own work in modern rehearsal.

* * *

John Spurling's play, *MacRune's Guevara*, is a pioneering example of what has come to be known as "multi-viewpoint" drama, where a character (in this case Che Guevara) is shown simultaneously as he appears in the minds of different people. Spurling's mechanism is imaginative. He gives us a narrator. Edward Hotel, who is also the supposed dramatist. Hotel has lately taken a room occupied in the period immediately before his death by an impecunious, unsuccessful Marxist Scottish artist, MacRune. The room's walls are covered all over with graffiti in which MacRune has depicted in graphic detail the events of Guevara's Bolivian champaign.

Hotel, overcome with admiration, determines to realise these drawings in dramatic terms. This raises two difficulties: one, that the drawings are often unclear and difficult to separate from other marks on the wall; and two, that while MacRune was a Marxist who had (so Hotel believes) progressed to a heretical belief in armed revolution in the Thirld World, Hotel himself is by temperament a supporter of established governments.

The Guevera who appears in the sequence of scenes that comprise the play is therefore a complex character whose multiple origins come from history (as reported in the Press), from MacRune's view of history, Hotel's view of history, and occasional errors due to misinterpretation of the marks on the wall. An extra dimension is added to the play by Spurling's casting the episodes in the form of a series of parodies of established theatrical forms – musical, drawing-room comedy, television drama, and so on. The result is not only ingenious and comic; it is also an object-lesson in the assessment of contemporary heroes.

Since *MacRune's Guevara*, Spurling has not yet succeeded in touching an equally fertile note. His work oscillates wildly from end to end of the dramatic spectrum. *Romance* is a sentimental comedy with music, so redolent of the clichés of the "little English musical" that one would have taken it as satirical had not its London production in 1971 been presented purely as a little English musical: unless of course it was a parody so faithful as to be indistinguishable from the real thing.

At the Edinburgh Festival of 1971 the Traverse Workshop Company put on Spurling's *In the Heart of the British Museum*. This is a fantasy in which there are three interwoven narratives dealing with the disgrace and rehabilitation of a Chinese professor under the Cultural Revolution, the exile and death of Ovid, and the temptation and fall of the god Quetzalcoatl and his succession by the grimmer god Texcatlipoca. Its conclusion is that power can lead only to war and to the death of culture.

Like *MacRune's Guevara* this is also written in a series of short scenes, but they range further afield, into the realms of mime, dance and song. The effect, though often pleasing to the senses, is to distract attention from the argument, and *In the Heart of the British Museum* cannot be rated as a significant success.

Peace in Our Time is an ambitious work in several parts dealing with the events leading up to World War II. Only the first part has been produced at the time of writing, and discussion of it should perhaps be postponed until the whole sequence is ready.

—B. A. Young

STARKWEATHER, David. American. Born in Madison, Wisconsin, 11 September 1935. Educated at the University of Wisconsin, Madison, 1953–57, B.A. 1957. Editor of a visitors newspaper in New York. Recipient: Creative Artists Public Service grant, 1975. Address: 340 West 11th Street, New York, New York 10014, U.S.A.

PUBLICATIONS

Plays

Maggie of the Bargain Basement, music by David Starkweather (ballad opera; produced Madison, Wisconsin, 1956).
Excuse Me, Pardon Me (produced Madison, Wisconsin, 1957).
You May Go Home Again (produced New York, 1963). Published in *The Off-Off-Broadway Book*, edited by Albert Poland and Bruce Mailman, Indianapolis, Bobbs Merrill, 1972.
So Who's Afraid of Edward Albee? (produced New York, 1963).
The Love Pickle (produced New York, 1963; Edinburgh, 1971).
The Family Joke (produced New York, 1965).
The Assent (produced New York, 1967).
Chamber Comedy (produced Washington, D.C., 1969).
A Practical Ritual to Exorcise Frustration after Five Days of Rain, music by Allan Landon (also co-director; produced New York, 1970).
The Poet's Papers: Notes for an Event (produced Boston, 1971). Published in *New American Plays 3*, edited by William M. Hoffman, New York, Hill and Wang, 1970.
The Straights of Messina (produced New York, 1973).
Language (also director; produced New York, 1974).

Theatrical Activities

Director: **Plays** – *A Practical Ritual to Exorcise Frustration after Five Days of Rain* (co-director, with Rob Thirkield), New York, 1970; *The Family Joke*, New York, 1973; *Language*, New York, 1974.

David Starkweather comments:

Two mirrors facing what do they reflect?
Slice the mind in fives Conciousness stage center. One way wings of Memory, staging areas of attention seeking self-ordering re-experience, detouring terror into ritual belief:

Subconscious. Opposite wings of Appetite, senses drawn to sources of actuation, pulled always into foreign homes: Superconscious. Deeper still surrounding wings as well as centers, forms in the mind's structure beneath conception, containing all potential concepts like the possibilities of a medium: Unconscious. Facing Other Consciousness awareness of other centers of awareness, the possibilities of union/conflict with/within all potential spectators. The boundaries between these modes of mindworks the symbol, always blocking one way, all ways disappearing another.

My current vision of theatre is a head, the bodies of the audience resonating chambers like the jugs beneath the stage in the classic Noh, feeling their behavioral imaginations. Sound surrounds but the eyes are in front perceiving SENSES in terms of each other. Vision is figure to sound's ground and vice versa because each word has an aural and visual component. A noun is a picutre (visual/spatial) and a verb is a melody (aural/temporal) relation. The split between being and doing dissolves when nouns are just states verbs are in at a given moment. The central human art form is the spoken word.

We laugh at people who are out of control. We laugh with people who are shoulder to shoulder. And we call it tragedy when a hero who is behind us loses.

If you write a play and do it badly that play is about incompetence. My plays in their forms hope to suggest what competence is. Moving toward an ideal, And I deal this round. Place your bets. It's a show of competence. All plays are about knowing. Being is where they're at. What I seek in a word is Order. In a feeling release of energy.

For themes I have recognized a clear line of development in my last three plays: 1. There is nothing you can know without limiting your ability to know something equally true; 2. The only thing we need to believe is that there is nothing we need to believe; and 3. The only taboo is on taboos.

I write consistently about changing minds.

A number of works, my most ambitious, are as yet unproduced: *Owey Wishey Are You There?*, 1965, *The Wish-House*, 1967.

*   *   *

Ham – And where are you?
Noah – I am here and it is now. And all
    around is mystery.

—A Practical Ritual to Exorcise Frustration
after Five Days of Rain.

It's not that he hates his family, his religion, or the rest of society; it's just that he can't stand their noise. Most people he knows participate in the trivia of family life and the charades of state. They believe that somewhere there is *one* person who will solve the riddle of their emotional needs, that the state must be protected, especially from within, that there is a god who sits on a throne, somewhere.

So the young man leaves his home, not to be mean or ornery, but because he'll go crazy if he stays. He goes Downtown, where there are so many people that no one will notice him, or Downtown to the wilderness, where there are no people. And now he is in the Downtown part of his mind, where memories of his former life rise and beckon him to return and resume the old ties. He replies to their telephone calls and to his dreams that their lives are meaningless and their ways are mindless and hold no allure.

But the old ways are alluring to him in his solitude, and part of him wants to go home. However, gradually, painfully, he withdraws into the land of light, and now he's totally alone with his mind. Soon he *is* his mind and alone he's together. At this still point fears arise in their pure form and threaten his sanity. Fears: of pain, of people, of death, of body functions.

He discovers that these fears cannot be conquered in their essence but must be met in their actuality, and so, here he goes, folks, back to the "real world" to conquer his fears. But this time he's armed: around his waist he carries self-containment; his vest is armored with enlightenment; his helmet is pure reason.

There are no trumpets on his return. People have scarcely noticed he's been gone, so busy have they been with their own wars and marriages. When he approaches the natives he finds that things are as they've always been between him and them: they don't see what he sees. So he withdraws again, and returns again, armed with new weapons. The cycle is endless, the man in lonely, but filled with love. His attitude is increasingly ironic.

This portrait of the saintly exile is a composite of the heroes and mock heroes that form the core of David Starkweather's work, the recalcitrant lover Colin of *So Who's Afraid of Edward Albee?*, the errant son David of *You May Go Home Again*, the would-be suicide Alan of *The Assent*, the wandering Poet of *The Poet's Papers*, and both Sonny and Pittsburgh, who together form the hero of *Language*. They are all versions of the Odysseus/Christ/dropout antiheroes of our time.

Colin, one of Starkweather's earliest creations, is merely disgusted by the System and puzzled by his disgust. David, created later, overwhelmed by his ambiguous feelings toward his family, goes into exile. Alan, guilty in exile, longs for death. The Poet, more comfortable in his separation from society, wanders the earth watching it destroy itself. And Sonny and Pittsburgh, in the playwright's play to date, who have in different ways plumbed the mysteries of isolation, now seek a way back into the society they have left.

In all of his plays, but especially in *The Family Joke* and *The Wish-House*, Starkweather provides ample reason for self-exile, and incidentally offers savage but concerned criticism of Western society. In *The Family Joke* the nuclear family is seen as the System's breeding factory. Children must be raised, no matter what the cost to the parents. *The Wish-House* presents an almost paranoid view of the methods of mind control that the System is willing to employ. For the enemy, here represented by a Dr. Brill, is in possession of the same knowledge that Starkweather's exile-heroes have struggled so hard to obtain: "All that you consider yourself to be is merely the stopper to contain what you really are. All that you do most easily, by habit and without thought, is only to avoid your most beautiful and dangerous nature.

In conterpoint to some of the most glorious abstractions in contemporary theatre, architectural visions that spring from contemplation of the basic dualities of thought, Starkweather weaves the anxieties that often accompany advanced thought: fears of death, impotence, blood, piss, and shit.

In *The Poet's Papers* the war between the two divisions of mankind, the Orals and the Anals, is conducted in lyrical language. In *The Assent* the System prefers control of urination to control of theft: "Petty theft raises the living standard of the worker . . . and stimulates cash flow. Whereas urine . . . involves the production of a non-salable commodity and is therfore a general drain on the corporate effort." In *Language* Sonny, a virgin admits: "I think that potency has something to do with murder."

In the plays of David Starkweather we have a most complete view of what in olden times would have been called a saint: the man who leaves his society, goes into physical and psychical exile, searches for his god, and brings back the golden fleece to an indifferent world. In play after play, in growing clarity, Starkweather shows us the dangerous yet exciting journey, the abandoned society, and the funny, heartbreaking return. He even allows us glimpses of the fleece:

> He goes away within
> miles from the common road
> to bring back for this world
> something lovely something pure
> Thank you, man.

—William M. Hoffman

STAVIS, Barrie. American. Born in New York City, 16 June 1906. Educated at New Utrecht High School, Brooklyn, New York, graduated 1924; Columbia University, New York, 1924–27. Served in the Army Signal Corps, Plans and Training section, 1924–45: Technical-Sergeant. Married Leona Heyert in 1925 (divorced, 1939); Bernice Coe, 1950; has two children. Foreign Correspondent, in Europe, 1937–38; Free-lance Journalist after World War II. Co-Founder, and member of the Board of Directors, New Stages theatre group, 1947. Member of the Board of Directors, United States Institute for Theatre Technology, 1961–64, and since 1969. Visiting Fellow, Pennsylvania State University, University Park, 1971. Recipient: Yaddo Fellowship, 1939; National Theatre Conference award, 1948, 1949. Agent: Jill Dargeon, 160 East 84th Street, New York, New York. Address: 70 East 96th Street, New York, New York 10028, U.S.A.

PUBLICATIONS

Plays

    The Sun and I (produced New York, 1933; revised version, produced New York, 1937).
    Refuge: A One-Act Play of the Spanish War (produced London, 1938). New York,
      French, 1939.
    Lamp at Midnight: A Play about Galileo (produced New York, 1947; Bristol, 1956).
      New York, Dramatists Play Service, 1948; revised version, South Brunswick, New
      Jersey, A.S. Barnes, and London, Yoseloff, 1966; shortened version (produced
      Chicago, 1972), Chicago, Dramatic Publishing Company, 1973; shortened church
      version (produced New York, 1973).
    The Man Who Never Died: A Play about Joe Hill (produced St. Paul, 1955; New York,
      1958). New York, Haven Press, 1954; revised version, music by Alan Bush
      (produced Berlin, 1970); revised version, South Brunswick, New Jersey, A.S. Barnes,
      and London, Yoseloff, 1972.
    Banners of Steel: A Play about John Brown (produced Carbondale, Illinois, 1962; New
      York, 1964); revised version, as *Harpers Ferry: A Play about John Brown* (produced
      Minneapolis, 1967). South Brunswick, New Jersey, A.S. Barnes, and London,
      Yoseloff, 1967.
    Coat of Many Colors: A Play about Joseph in Egypt (produced Provo, Utah, 1966).
      South Brunswick, New Jersey, A.S. Barnes, and London, Yoseloff, 1968.

Novels

    The Chain of Command. New York, Ackermann, 1945.
    Home Sweet Home! New York, Sheridan House, 1949.

Other

    Notes on Joe Hill and His Time, in *The Man Who Never Died,* 1954.
    John Brown: The Sword and the Word. South Brunswick, New Jersey, A.S. Barnes,
      and London, Yoseloff, 1970.

    Editor, with W. Frank Harmon, *The Songs of Joe Hill.* New York, People's Artists,
      1955.

Manuscripts Collections: Lincoln Center Library of the Performing Arts, New York; Pennsylvania State University, University Park.

Critical Study: "Barrie Stavis: The Epic Vision" by Herbert Shore, in *Educational Theatre Journal* (Washington, D.C.), October 1973.

Barrie Stavis comments:

I wrote my first full-length play when I was nineteen years old. I had my first production when I was twenty-six. Fortunately there are no scripts in existence. About a dozen plays followed – all since destroyed.

The material and form of these early plays were derivative, echoing closely the dominant writing and production modes of the American stage. I refer to the Theatre of Illusion where the play is naturalistic in concept and style, generally romantic in approach. The physical envelope of such plays consists of a box set, usually a four-walled room with the fourth wall removed so that the audience can "peek in" and see what happens to those "real" people on the stage.

I was gradually becoming dissatisfied with this kind of stage and its "imitation of life." It could not contain the statements I was trying to make in the theatre. But at that time I did not know how to break away from the narrow restrictions of the romantic-naturalism and the pseudo-realism of the Theatre of Illusion. I knew (though certainly not as clearly as I know it now) that I was concerned with writing plays where the driving force of the characters was the clash of their *ideas*, not their subjective emotions.

Form is dictated by content and should grow out of function. Thus, I was also searching for a form which would be consonant with my material. I was seeking a freedom and a plastic use of the stage which the box set could not give me. I began studying Shakespeare intensively. Shakespeare was, and remains even to this day, my major theatre influence, followed by the Bible for its style, and its ruthlessly candid and objective way of telling a story. My study of the Elizabethan theatre, along with Greek theatre and the Roman amphitheatre, gradually led me to devise what I designated (1933–34) as "Time-Space Stage" – a stage where both time and space could be used with fluidity.

In 1939 I began to work on *Lamp at Midnight*. It took three years to complete. It was in this play that I first achieved a successful synthesis of content and form. The characters in the play are embattled over basic philosophic concepts; and the plastic use of time and space on the stage proved to be the perfect medium for expressing the conflict of ideas.

It was then that I realized I wanted to write further plays exploring this use of the stage. Although all the plays in the series would have the same major theme, each play would be independent unto itself with the common theme developed from a different axis of observation.

The series proved to be a tetralogy exploring the problems of men who have ushered in new and frequently drastic changes in the existing social order – men who are of their time and yet in advance of their time. And I have been concerned with examining the thrust they exercise on their society, and the counter-thrust society exerts on them.

It is the essence of nature and of man to undergo continual change. New forms evolve from old, mature, and, as the inevitable concomitant of their maturation, induce still newer forms which replace them. This is the historical process.

This process of change is gradual. It is not always perceived nor clearly apparent. Yet it is constant and inexorable. At a given moment when historical conditions are ripe, a catalyst enters and fragments the existing culture, setting into motion a new alignment of forces, a new series of relationships, which gradually become stabilized, codified.

It is this process of change that I endeavor to capture in my plays: the precise moment in history when society, ripe for change, gives birth to the catalyst who sets the dynamics of change into accelerated motion.

The four plays in their order are: *Lamp at Midnight* (Galileo Galilei), *The Man Who Never Died* (Joe Hill), *Harpers Ferry* (John Brown), *Coat of Many Colors* (Joseph in Egypt). In the first of these plays, *Lamp at Midnight*, I dramatize the story of Galileo Galilei, the first human being to turn his new, powerful telescope to the night skies, there to discover the true motion of our solar system, a discovery unleashing a host of scientific and social consequences which heralded the coming Industrial Age. In *The Man Who Never Died*, I dramatize the story of Joe Hill, troubador, folk poet and trade union organizer, who was framed on a murder charge and who, during the 22 months of his prison stay, grew to heroic proportions. In *Harpers Ferry*, I dramatize the story of John Brown's raid on Harpers Ferry, a raid which was the precursor to the Civil War. In *Coat of Many Colors*, I dramatize the story of Joseph in Egypt, the world's first great agronomist and social planner, and I explore the theme of power and its uses....These four plays have been so designed that they can be performed by a single basic acting company. Further, all four plays can be produced on the same basic unit set.

Galileo Galilei, Joe Hill, John Brown, Joseph – these men have certain things in common. They were put on trial for their thoughts and deeds, found guilty and punished. Yet their very ideas and acts achieved their vindication by later generations. Thus does the heresy of one age become the accepted truth of the next.

I have chosen to write plays about men who have an awareness of social and moral responsibility, plays that have faith in man's capacity to resolve his problems despite the monumental difficulties facing him. Why? Because I believe in ethical commitment. I believe that man is capable of ultimately solving the problems of the Nuclear Age.

Today, much theatre writing is obsessed with frustration and defeat. One trend of such playwriting deals with personality maladjustments and sexual aberration. This theatre is preoccupied with such matters as who goes to bed with whom, the gap in communication between parent and adolescent, the need to show that sex is either rape or submission. There is intense concern with subjective, neurotic problems, very little concern with the objective and social conditions of the world in which the characters live and the impact of the world upon them. It is as though the characters were living in a vacuum tube. Outside is the pulsating, throbbing world, but within the tube they function only insofar as their psyches collide with one another. Of the outside world, there is barely a reflection. A second contemporary trend is the writing of plays which explore the thesis that the human condition is hopeless because man is utterly dislocated in his society, that rational thought is a snare, that human life is purposeless, that action is without point for it will accomplish no result. There is in such plays no release for the affirmative emotion of an audience.

However, I believe with Chekhov, that "Every playwright is responsible not only for what man is, but for what man can be." With Aristophanes, I seek to banish the "little man and woman affair" from the stage and to replace it with plays which explore ideas with such force and clarity as to raise them to the level of passion. Today especially, it should be the responsibility of the playwright to search out those situations which, by the inherent nature of the material, will capture the emotions and the intellect of an audience and focus it on men and women striving creatively for a positive goal.

*   *   *

A mere glance at the men Barrie Stavis has chosen to write about is indicative of his own passions, goals, intentions: John Brown, Joe Hill, Galileo, the Biblical Joseph, and now in various stages of completion, works about George Washington, Hidalgo, and Bolivar.

There is about Stavis an almost Talmudic fury when he discusses his work and when he writes. This is in strange contrast to the man himself: warm, friendly, hopeful, and eager. Stavis is intellectually always aware ("conscious" might be an even better word) of what he is doing, dramaturgically and theatrically. His experience in theatre goes back further than most, and he has worked with almost every kind of theatre – getting his plays on to stages everywhere.

Beyond grass roots experiences, there is a playwright, Stavis, who is very like the protagonists in his own plays: a man with a vision. It is a driving, almost monomaniacal vision which he, the artist, holds in careful, classical check.

He promises that the new trilogy (Washington, Hidalgo, Bolivar), which obviously will deal with American liberators, will explore in depth the "processes of throwing off to gain freedom." Knowing Stavis at all is to know that his plays indeed will deliver. Just as his earlier works dealt with, in his words, "four aspects of mankind," all of his plays are precisely predjcated. *Lamp at Midnight* (seen by twenty million in one night on a Hallmark Hall of Fame telecast) is "about Truth" (no small feat to undertake in a single play); *The Man Who Never Died* is "about Human Dignity"; *Harpers Ferry* is "about Freedom"; and *Coat of Many Colors* is "about Power." Stavis writes that kind of play deliberately, and there are abundant audiences and theatres in the United States and abroad eagerly seeking these plays: they have something to say, say it clearly, and are "about" something. As with good textbooks (*good* textbooks, mind), his work is pedantic, fascinating, and satisfying.

As with any conscientious teacher, Stavis is a superb researcher, who reads and studies about and around the men he will put on stage. Eventually, out of that research comes the spine of the play, the direction dictated by the material. His own humanistic background, of course, controls the aesthetics and even the politics of the play, and his experience controls the shape of the work, but the man and the artist avoid the merely pedantic, the narrowly polemic, the purely didactic. The five years he works on any single play make it fairly inevitable as a work: big, intellectual, more than a little "preachy" but almost always theatrical.

Stavis is a grassroots playwright. Middle America listens to the voice of history, and it is history that Stavis purveys most astutely and clearly. Grandeur and pageantry are second nature to the themes and the shapes of his work. His best work, I think, is *The Man Who Never Died*. It is no small accident that the play deals with an early "liberal," an American labor leader martyred and misplaced in time and place. That this play comes most successfully to the stage finally in the form of a German opera is really no surprise to those most familiar with Stavis' work.

He denies a tendency to romanticism and insists on the classical nature of his work. As did Brecht, Stavis claims to be more concerned with the *how* of an action than with the *why*. And in fact, his plays (the Joseph play possibly excepted) tend to Seriousness, with a capital S. There is generally little to amuse one in a Stavis play; the solemnity of the central figure is reflected in the almost complete lack of humor in the play itself. Even love is dealt with clinically and analytically. He leaves it to the total action to *move* his audiences: the themes that last, the appeal to noble if belated stances, the hero out of time.

Stavis, quite seriously and realistically, sees his own work as primarily influenced by both Shakespeare and the Holy Bible. If there are more rabbinic research and prophetic polemicism than there are lyricism and joy, Stavis cannot be faulted: he is after all very much a writer of his own time and place, with a keen eye on the lessons of the past.

He is a "pro." Methodical, organized, enthusiastic, and almost pristinely professional as he is, there is a double irony in the fact that he has never really "hit" on Broadway. Yet he represents professional theatre to literally dozens of colleges and repertory companies not only in the States but around the world. To non-Americans, particularly, as the late Sir Tyrone Guthrie indicated, Barrie Stavis represents the clearest and "most American" voice of the time. As perhaps is still true with O'Neill, Stavis seems most American to those who are least American, and he seems most "universal" to his American audiences.

There is, in any event, no mistaking Stavis' intent and purpose. If heroic drama has gone out of fashion in an era of the anti-hero, Barrie Stavis persistently views history and man's passage through that history as essentially Heroic with a capital H.

Finally, Barrie Stavis is quite the opposite in one crucial aspect from the heroes of his plays. While each of them is a man *out* of joint with his own time, Stavis is *of* his time and writes for that broadest, most fundamental of audiences: people, not critics.

—Arthur H. Ballet

STEWART, Douglas (Alexander).   Australian.   Born in Eltham, New Zealand, 6 May 1913. Educated at New Plymouth Boys High School; Victoria University College, New Zealand. Married Margaret Coen in 1946; has one daughter. Literary Editor, *The Bulletin*, Sydney, 1940–61. Literary Adviser, Angus and Robertson Ltd., publishers, Sydney, 1961–72. Recipient: Encyclopedia Britannica Award, 1968; Wilke Award, for non-fiction, 1975. Agent: Custis Brown (Australia) Pty. Ltd., P.O. Box 19. Paddington, New South Wales 2021. Address: 2 Banool Avenue, St. Ives, New South Wales 2075, Australia.

PUBLICATIONS

Plays

> *The Fire on the Snow* (broadcast, 1941).   Included in *The Fire on the Snow and The Golden Lover*, 1944.
> *The Golden Lover* (broadcast, 1943).   Included in *The Fire on the Snow and The Golden Lover*, 1944.
> *Ned Kelly* (produced Sydney, 1944).   Sydney and London, Angus and Robertson, 1943.
> *The Fire on the Snow and The Golden Lover: Two Plays for Radio.*   Sydney and London, Angus and Robertson, 1944.
> *Shipwreck* (produced Sydney, 1948).   Sydney, Shepherd Press, 1947.
> *Four Plays* (includes *The Fire on the Snow, The Golden Lover, Ned Kelly, Shipwreck*). Sydney and London, Angus and Robertson, 1958.
> *Fisher's Ghost: The Historical Comedy* (produced Sydney, 1961).   Sydney, Wentworth Press, 1960.

> Radio Plays: *The Fire on the Snow*, 1941: *The Golden Lover*, 1943; *The Earthquake Shakes the Land*, 1944.

Short Stories

> *A Girl with Red Hair and Other Stories.*   Sydney and London, Angus and Robertson, 1944.

Verse

> *Green Lions: Poems.*   Auckland, Whitcombe and Tombs, 1937.
> *The White Cry: Poems.*   London, Dent, 1939.
> *Elegy for an Airman.*   Sydney, Frank C. Johnson, 1940.
> *Sonnets to the Unknown Soldier.*   Sydney and London, Angus and Robertson, 1941.
> *The Dosser in Springtime.*   Sydney and London, Angus and Robertson, 1946.
> *Glencoe.*   Sydney and London, Angus and Robertson, 1947.
> *Sun Orchids.*   Sydney and London, Angus and Robertson, 1952.
> *The Birdsville Track and Other Poems.*   Sydney and London, Angus and Robertson, 1955.
> *Rutherford and Other Poems.*   Sydney and London, Angus and Robertson, 1962.
> *The Garden of Ships: A Poem.*   Sydney, Wentworth Press, 1962.
> *(Poems)*, selected and introduced by the author.   Sydney, Angus, and Robertson, 1963; as *Selected Poems*, 1969, 1973.
> *Collected Poems, 1936–1967.*   Sydney and London, Angus and Robertson, 1967.

Other

The Flesh and the Spirit: An Outlook on Literature.   Sydney and London, Angus and
    Robertson, 1948.
The Seven Rivers (on angling).   Sydney, Angus and Robertson, 1966.
The Broad Stream (criticism).   Sydney, Angus and Robertson, 1975.
Norman Lindsay: A Personal Memoir.   Melbourne, Nelson, 1975.

Editor, Coast to Coast: Australian Stories.   Sydney, Angus and Robertson, 1945.
Editor, with Nancy Keesing, Australian Bush Ballads.   Sydney, Angus and Robertson,
    1955.
Editor, with Nancy Keesing, Old Bush Songs and Rhymes of Colonial Times, Enlarged
    and Revised from the Collection of A.B. Paterson.   Sydney, Angus and Robertson,
    1957.
Editor, Voyager Poems.   Brisbane, Jacaranda Press, 1960.
Editor, The Book of Bellerive, by Joseph Tischler.   Brisbane, Jacaranda Press, 1961.
Editor, Modern Australian Verse: Poetry in Australia II.   Sydney, Angus and
    Robertson, 1964; Berkeley, University of California Press, 1965.
Editor, Selected Poems, by Hugh McCrae.   Sydney, Angus and Robertson, 1966.
Editor, Short Stories of Australia: The Lawson Tradition.   Sydney, Angus and
    Robertson, 1967.
Editor, with Nancy Keesing, The Pacific Book of Bush Ballads.   Sydney, Angus and
    Robertson, 1967.
Editor, with Nancy Keesing, Bush Songs, Ballads, and Other Verse.   Penrith, New
    South Wales, Discovery Press, 1968.
Editor, with Beatrice Davis, Best Australian Short Stories.   Hawthorne, Victoria,
    Lloyd O'Neil, 1971.
Editor, The Wide Brown Land: A New Selection of Australian Verse.   Sydney, Pacific
    Books, 1971.
Editor, Australia Fair.   Sydney, Ure Smith, 1976.

Manuscript Collection: National Library, Canberra.

Critical Studies: Douglas Stewart by Nancy Keesing, Sydney, Oxford University Press, 1967;
Douglas Stewart by Clement Semmler, New York, Twayne, 1975.

*   *   *

Douglas Stewart is not only a playwright but critic, short story writer, for many years
literary editor of The Bulletin — and one of Australia's major poets. He is in fact primarily a
poet, and for this reason his highest achievement in drama has been with radio rather than
stage plays.

To date, Stewart has looked to the past, and usually to the romantic past, for the subjects of
his verse plays. These plays come in a burst of dramatic creativity beginning with The Fire on
the Snow (completed in 1939) and ending with Shipwreck in 1947. (Fisher's Ghost, published
in 1960, is a short, delightfully amusing entertainment rather than a serious play.) The Fire on
the Snow is a radio play about the expedition by Scott and his party to the Antarctic in 1912,
ending with the deaths of all of them. In this play Stewart encompassed in their simplest and
most straightforward form most of the themes that also shape his later work, and in
particular the vision of man as a heroic dreamer who risks everything and suffers everything
for a dream that is doomed to fail. In spite of the heroism of Scott and his party, they fail to
reach the Pole first, beaten at the end by the Norweigan, Amundsen. The Fire on the Snow
accepts uncritically the intrinsic worth of endurance for its own sake, even when in practical
terms it achieves very little; in the end, the play is a celebration of man's courage in a hostile

universe, outstanding for the visual beauty of its imagery, with the counterpoint of fire and ice, and the music of the verse, the five male voices contrasting with the cooler tones of the Announcer, since the first broadcast traditionally played by a woman.

In his next play, *Ned Kelly*, Stewart turned to the stage, and a more complex and critical approach to his theme of the failure of a heroic dream. This time his hero was Australia's favourite and most disreputable folk hero, the bushranger Ned Kelly who, after a short and exciting career highlighted by holding up banks, was captured in 1880 and hanged. The real Ned Kelly was close enough in memory to make the thought of a presentation of him as traditional romantic highwayman ridiculous, and so Douglas Stewart shared the centre of the stage between two characters: Ned Kelly himself, tough, courageous, very much the leader of men, driven by a dream of power and acclamation; and Joe Byrne, the "brains of the gang," handsome, a successful lover with a dream of "a brumby mare called Freedom" – and speaking most of the romantic and beautiful poetry of the play. Stewart recognises the loneliness of the "free" life of the Kelly gang that becomes finally "empty and barren and stony" for Joe at least; he accepts its destruction of the innocent (the names of three murdered policemen, Kennedy, Scanlon, Lonergan, sound through the play like a knell); he recognises the appeal that the heroic Kelly image has for so many of the law-abiding little men who, in the end, bring Kelly down. With drastic cuts, the play has been successfully performed on stage, but is too repetitive, too much inclined to hold up the action while people simply talk, in isolated conversations that frustratingly do not lead to any further action. In spite of the violence of Stewart's plots, his technique is usually "talk against a background of violence," and he tends to hurry over any forceful action which he cannot avoid presenting on stage – e.g., the scene in which Ned, in his grotesque armour, is finally shot down. *Ned Kelly* is really notable for passages of magnificent verse, much of it describing Australia "the violent country," and the heroic dream seen through the eyes of Ned Kelly and Joe Byrne.

The Golden Lover, a radio play based on a Maori legend from Stewart's native New Zealand, seens on first glance less serious and less ambitious than its predecessors; but with *The Fire on the Snow* it marks the height of Douglas Stewart's dramatic achievement. In spite of its subject and its considerable poetic charm *The Golden Lover* is perhaps the least romantic of Stewart's plays, and, like *Fisher's Ghost* after it, gives scope for his rather wry humour. Tawhai, a self-confidently beautiful young Maori woman, is married to fat, lazy, cowardly Ruarangi. All her life Tawhai has dreamed of a "golden lover haunting the fringe of [her] dreams," so when she is suddenly carried off by auburn-haired Whana, one of the legendary faery people of the mists, she is less indignant than she suggests. In the end, Tawhai has to choose between life with her golden lover in the cold and mist of the forest, or life with her dull husband in the warm and comfortable village, surrounded by family and the friends of her childhood. Tawhai is the first of Stewart's dreamers to reject the dream, deliberately, rather than see it torn from her grasp; perhaps Stewart suggests that woman are the more practical sex. Tawhai at any rate turns her back on the forest and·

> the golden hawk
> Who hangs in the sky of my dreams.

Stewart has said in the introduction of the published play that its theme is "acceptance of life."

While *The Golden Lover* examined the failed dream on a domestic scale. *Shipwreck*, his latest full-length stage play, takes it to its final limits of violence and animal brutality. *Shipwreck* is more disciplined and technically sophisticated play than *Ned Kelly*, but it is less attractive, partly because it lacks a sympathetic protagonist. The physical appearance of the characters comes through the dialogue quite precisely, as in most good radio plays, but one has no feeling of understanding them at any depth. In 1629, a Dutch ship under Commander Pelsart was wrecked off the West Coast of Australia, on a small, waterless island; Pelsart and a handful of his men set off to seek help. The result is bloodshed, rape and murder among those left behind. The "dream" this time is the dream of the mis-shapen supercargo Cornelius, who takes command of the mutineers and of the beautiful but unwilling Lucretia, who accepts him only that she may survive. Cornelius's dream ends in death with the return of Pelsart. Values made attractive in *Ned Kelly* arouse horror in *Shipwreck*.

A comment once made by Stewart (in "The Playwright in Australia" in *The First Year*, 1956) throws light on his aims as a dramatist. He said:

> The playwright, I think, creates the myths by which the people live: the heroic, gigantic, legendary figures, fathers of the race, ancestors spiritual or actual, to which the living man can point and say, "That is what I am made of; that is what makes us different from other people; that is what I believe in; those are my gods and my devils.

Stewart's myths have an assured place in Australian drama.

—Alrene Sykes

STOPPARD, Tom. British. Born in Zlin, Czechoslovakia, 3 July 1937; emigrated to Singapore in 1938, and to England in 1946. Educated abroad, and at Dolphin School, Nottinghamshire, and Pocklington School, Yorkshire. Married Jose Ingle in 1965; Miriam Moore-Robinson, 1972; has four children. Journalist, *Western Daily Press*, Bristol, 1954–58; *Bristol Evening World*, 1958–60; Free-lance Journalist, 1960–63. Recipient: John Whiting Award, 1967; *Evening Standard* award, 1967, 1973, 1975; Prix Italia, 1968; Tony Award, 1968, 1976; New York Drama Critics Circle Award, 1968, 1976. Address: c/o Fraser and Dunlop Scripts Ltd., 91 Regent Street, London W1R 8RU, England.

PUBLICATIONS

Plays

A Walk on the Water (televised, 1963; produced Hamburg, 1964); revised version, as
   The Preservation of George Riley (televised, 1964); as Enter a Free Man (produced
   London, 1968; New York, 1974).   London, Faber, 1968, New York, Grove Press,
   1972.
The Gamblers (produced Bristol, 1965).
Tango, adaptation of a play by Slawomir Mrozek, translated by Nicholas Bethell
   (produced London, 1966).   London, Cape, 1968.
A Separate Peace (televised, 1966).   Published in Playbill 2, edited by Alan Durband,
   London, Hutchinson, 1969.
Rosencrantz and Guildenstern Are Dead (produced Edinburgh, 1966; revised version,
   produced London, 1967; New York, 1968).   London, Faber, and New York, Grove
   Press, 1967.
Albert's Bridge (broadcast, 1967; produced New York, 1975).   Included in Albert's
   Bridge and If You're Glad I'll Be Frank, 1969.
The Real Inspector Hound (produced London, 1968; New York, 1972).   London,
   Faber, 1968; New York, Grove Press, 1969.
Albert's Bridge and If You're Glad I'll be Frank: Two Plays for Radio.   London, Faber,
   1969.

After Magritte (produced London, 1970; New York, 1972).   London, Faber, 1971;
   New York, Grove Press, 1972.
Dogg's Our Pet (produced London, 1971).   Published in *Six of the Best*, London, Inter-
   Action Imprint, 1976.
Jumpers (produced London, 1972; Washington, D.C., and New York, 1974).
   London, Faber, and New York, Grove Press, 1972.
The House of Bernarda Alba, adaptation of the play by Lorca (produced London, 1973).
Artist Descending a Staircase, and Where Are They Now? Two Plays for Radio.
   London, Faber, 1973.
Travesties (produced London, 1974; New York, 1975).   London, Faber, and New
   York, Grove Press, 1975.
Dirty Linen, and New-found-land (produced London, 1976).   London, Faber, 1976.

Screenplays: *The Engagement*, 1969; *The Romantic Englishwoman*, 1975.

Radio Plays: *The Dissolution of Dominic Boot*, 1964; *M Is for Moon among Other Things*,
   1964; *If You're Glad I'll Be Frank*, 1965; *Albert's Bridge*, 1967; *Where Are They Now?*,
   1970; *Artist Descending a Staircase*, 1972.

Television Plays: *A Walk on the Water*, 1963 (as *The Preservation of George Riley*,
   1964); *A Separate Peace*, 1966; *Teeth*, 1967; *Another Moon Called Earth*, 1967; *Neutral
   Ground*, 1968; *One Pair of Eyes* (documentary), 1972; *Boundaries*, with Clive Exton,
   1975; *Three Men in a Boat*, from the novel by Jerome K. Jerome, 1975.

Novel

Lord Malquist and Mr. Moon.   London, Blond, 1966; New York, Knopf, 1968.

Short Stories

Introduction 2, with others.   London, Faber, 1964.

Theatrical Activities:

Director: **Play** – *Born Yesterday* by Garson Kanin, London, 1973.

*   *   *

Tom Stoppard's *Rosencrantz and Guildenstern Are Dead* was described by *The Observer*
theatre reviewer as "the most brilliant debut of the sixties" and by Harold Hobson in *The
Sunday Times* as "the most important event in the British professional theatre of the last nine
years." First performed by the Oxford Theatre Group as part of the "fringe" of the
Edinburgh Festival in 1966, it appeared in London, in a longer version, the following year as
a production of the National Theatre Company. The play itself is a brilliant examination of
the effect of placing the two nonentities of Shakespeare's play at the centre of dramatic
attention. It is a witty but penetrating look at two men who grudgingly recognise that they are
the mainspring of neither historical process nor creation itself. The central situation of the
play, as of Stoppard's plays in general, is that outlined by the Player when he says that "we
pledged our identities, secure in the conventions of our trade, that someone would be
watching. And then, gradually, no one was. We were caught high and dry...habit and
stubborn trust that our audience spied upon us from behind the nearest bush, forced our
bodies to blunder on long after they had emptied of meaning." Man, in other words, is a

minor character in a drama which he cannot understand, dependent for recognition on people who do not even control their own fate and forces which may not even exist. Critics recognised his debt to Beckett and certainly the situation of two characters waiting for meaning to crystallise while passing their time in circuitous conversations and pointless games was familiar enough to audiences brought up on *Waiting for Godot.* Yet Stoppard's world is not the reified one of Samuel Beckett and, despite the feeling, common to so many of his characters, that they have been ignored and passed by, his focus is less on the abandonment of man than the humour and perverse vitality which men generate even in despair; less on the absence of truth or its terrifying implications than its relativity. It is not surprising to learn that Magritte is Stoppard's favourite artist for both men secure their particular effects by essentially the same method. The wrenching of object from setting, of events from context, results not merely in a revealing absurdity but in a perception of the contingent nature of truth. Stoppard has suggested that this is one of his main subjects and it is certainly of central concern in *Rosencrantz and Guildenstern Are Dead, Enter a Free Man, The Real Inspector Hound, After Magritte* and *Jumpers.*

Stoppard's radio plays, *The Dissolution of Dominic Boot, M Is for Moon among Other Things,* and, more importantly, *If You're Glad I'll be Frank* and *Albert's Bridge,* though admirably adapted to the medium, are not by any means his most compelling work. *If You're Glad I'll Be Frank* is an absurdist drama about two star-crossed lovers kept apart by the vicissitudes of their work, one being a bus driver and the other the voice of the speaking clock (shades once again of N. F. Simpson). *Albert's Bridge* recounts the plight of an ex-philosophy student who undertakes the job of painting a railway bridge single-handed. Due to a mathematical error by the local council he has to be given a thousand assistants in order to complete the job before the old paint deteriorates too severely. The massed march of the painters is more than the bridge can bear and the play ends with the collapse of the entire structure. Essentially elaborations of a single joke like his television dramas, *A Separate Peace* and *Boundaries,* neither play approaches the achievement of his best theatre work, though both pursue that fascination with the construction of flawlessly logical sequences resting on totally absurd premises which has been the basis of his work.

Despite the initial impact of *Rosencrantz and Guildenstern Are Dead,* the plays which subsequently appeared in the West End were not particularly impressive and secured little critical response. *Enter a Free Man* was a much rewritten version of an early television play originally entitled *A Walk on the Water. After Magritte* was a delightful but slight piece of work written for the Ambiance Theatre Club.

However, in February 1972 the National Theatre produced what remains clearly his best play and a work which confirmed him as a major talent in the contemporary theatre. *Jumpers* takes place immediately after an election victory by the Radical-Liberal alliance and a disastrous British landing on the moon. Neither event is untouched by absurdity but they do both suggest a hard-minded rationality, as one astronaut abandons another on the moon following a mechanical break-down (a decision which ironically inverts the famous Scott/ Oates incident from Scott's last expedition to the Antarctic), and as the State sets out to rationalise the Church. Opposing this capitulation to pragmatism and rational process are George, a professor of moral philosophy, and his ex-show-business wife, Dottie. Like Rosencrantz and Guildenstern, they play visual and verbal games to maintain their sanity and to substantiate their frail vision of a moral, romantic and intuitive world. George remains convinced that "nothing can be created out of nothing, that my moral conscience is different from the rules of my tribe, and that there is more to me than meets the microscope." And because of this he is "lumbered" with an "incredible, undesirable and definitely shifty God," who defies logical explanation but remains the final sanction and justification for his vision of man's potential. Dottie, dismayed at the collapse of her emotionally structured life, strays to the verge of breakdown. As a singer of popular ballads which usually turn on the romantic potential of the moon, she has been shattered by a moon landing which has simultaneously served to destroy the elaborate and reassuring imagery of the unattainable and to reveal a new perspective on man who stands revealed suddenly as an apparently insignificant creation whose most profound convictions seem little more than expedient illusions. The jumpers of the title are a team of philosophers who have combined philosophical enquiry with gymnastics but who find their carefully constructed human pyramids no more secure than the logical theories which they adduce and which they employ to pin man to metaphysical absurdity. The whole action is characterised by a deliberately wild excess while Stoppard launches a display of baroque wit and verbal agility only rivalled by his own first play. His usual themes of the relativity of truth, man's apparent need to divert himself from painful realities, the failure of language to do more than parody conviction, the inability of the rational mind to adequately explain man to himself – all these coalesce in a play which unites the very best of Stoppard's characteristics as a playwright – a mastery of language, a clear sense of style and rhythm, and a wit which has both a verbal and visual dimension. His vices as a dramatist are largely aspects of his virtues. His painstaking demonstrations of logic are sometimes conducted with more single-mindedness than dramatic effect, while wit is at times permitted to displace insight. Indeed, Stoppard will go a considerable distance out of his way in order to achieve a single linguistic flourish – George's pet tortoise, which is to play an important role in his elaborate demolition of his academic opponents, is surely named Pat only so that he may later parody the graceless line from *Hamlet*, "now might I do it, Pat." His work is in fact littered with ironic quotations from other plays – more especially in *Rosencrantz and Guildenstern Are Dead* which quotes obliquely from Edward Albee and John Osborne as well as from Shakespeare. The avowed theatricalism of his plays (*Rosencrantz and Guildenstern Are Dead*, *The Real Inspector Hound*, *Jumpers*, and *Travesties* all incorporate theatrical events) is itself a clue to his concern with the difficulty of defining reality with any real conviction and the confusion between role and identity which seems to grip his heroes as they try to distinguish the mechanism which lies behind a bewildered world.

Travesties actually use Wilde's *The Importance of Being Earnest* as a skeletal structure. In this play Stoppard conducts a debate about the role of art and the nature of reality – a debate in which he remains heroically uninvolved, while pressing a judicious thumb onto both sides of the scales in turn. Turning James Joyce into a music hall comedian and disguising the Dadaist Tristan Tzara as a Wildean hero, he creates a brilliantly funny and perceptive farce which only shatters when it encounters the granite inflexibility of the political revolutionary, Lenin. And here is the root of the problem, for the tone of sustained levity cannot adapt itself to the ponderous realities of politics. In a world of fiction-makers some fictions are more equal than others, and that knowledge nestles unavoidably in the consciousness of any audience – a fact which seems to unnerve even the unflappable Stoppard. As a consequence the second act lacks something of the detached irony which gives the first its pace and humour.

Once again he chooses to refract his debate through the mind of a marginal man, in this case Henry Carr, a modern Rosencrantz suddenly asked to write the history of Hamlet. Not unnaturally he sees himself as the hub around which the wheel of history turned – a conviction which in some degree or other is a familiar enough delusion. And this is a clue both to Stoppard's method and his subject. For beneath his baroque style and irresistible wit, his consummate technical finesse, is a serious man asking questions in what he clearly feels to be the only form available to a putative philosopher in the second half of the twentieth century – the ironic joke designed to penetrate to the marrow, a farce in which discussions about art and life are subordinated to questions about the nature of reality itself.

—C. W. E. Bigsby

STOREY, David (Malcolm). British. Born in Wakefield, Yorkshire, 13 July 1933; brother of the novelist Anthony Storey. Educated at Queen Elizabeth Grammar School,

Wakefield, 1943–51; Wakefield Art School, 1951–53; Slade School of Fine Art, London, 1953–56, Diploma in fine arts. Played professionally for the Leeds Rugby League Club, 1952–56. Fellow, University College, London. Recipient: Macmillan Fiction Award, 1959; Rhys Memorial Award, for fiction, 1961; Maugham Award, 1963; *Evening Standard* award, 1967, 1970; Variety Club of Great Britain Writer of the Year Award, 1971; New York Drama Critics Circle Award, 1971, 1973, 1974; Faber Memorial Prize, 1973; Obie Award, 1974. Agent: International Famous Agency, 11/12 Hanover Street, London W.1, England.

PUBLICATIONS

Plays

> *The Restoration of Arnold Middleton* (produced Edinburgh, 1966; London, 1967). London, Grove Press, 1975.
> *In Celebration* (produced London, 1969; Los Angeles, 1973). London, Cape, 1969; New York, Grove Press, 1975.
> *The Contractor* (produced London, 1969; New Haven, Connecticut, 1970; New York, 1973). London, Cape, 1970; New York, Random House, 1971.
> *Home* (produced London and New York, 1970). London, Cape, 1970; New York, Random House, 1971.
> *The Changing Room* (produced London, 1971; New Haven, Connecticut, 1972; New York, 1973). London, Cape, and New York, Random House, 1972.
> *The Farm* (produced London, 1973; Washington, D.C., 1974; New York, 1976). London, Cape, 1973.
> *Cromwell* (produced London, 1973). London, Cape, 1973.
> *Life Class* (produced London, 1974). London, Cape, 1975.
> *Mother's Day* (produced London, 1976). London, Cape, 1977.

Screenplays: *This Sporting Life*, 1963; *In Celebration*, 1974.

Television Play: *Grace*, from the story by James Joyce, 1974.

Novels

> *This Sporting Life.* London, Longman, and New York, Macmillan, 1960.
> *Flight into Camden.* London, Longman, and New York, Macmillan, 1961.
> *Radcliffe.* London, Longman, 1963; New York, Coward McCann, 1964.
> *Pasmore.* London, Longman, 1972; New York Dutton, 1974.
> *A Temporary Life.* London, Allen Lane, 1973; New York, Dutton, 1974.
> *Saville.* London, Cape, 1976.

Other

> *Writers on Themselves*, with others. London, BBC Publications, 1964.
> *Edward*, drawings by Donald Parker. London, Allen Lane, 1973.

Critical Studies: in *The Cambridge Quarterly*, Summer 1966, Autumn 1970; *The Second Wave* by John Russell Taylor, London, Methuen, 1971; in *Theatre Quarterly 1* (London), April-June, 1971; in *Books and Bookmen* (London), March 1972; in *Plays and Players*

(London), September 1973; in *Modern Drama* (Toronto), December 1973 ; *David Storey* by John Russell Taylor, London, Longman, 1974.

Theatrical Activities:

Director: **Television** – *Portrait of Margaret Evans*, 1963; *Death of My Mother* (D. H. Lawrence documentary), 1963.

*   *   *

David Storey is a Yorkshireman, the son of a miner; he is also highly educated and lives in the south of England. The effects of his social, topographical, intellectual, and (perhaps) moral uprooting are everywhere to be seen in his work, as they are in that of his friend and fellow working-class Yorkshireman, David Mercer. But he has achieved a greater degree of detachment than Mercer, and his plays, consequently, tend to be more universal in their implications. One theme that runs through them is the power the past has over the present: it takes a man of exceptional (indeed, impossible) strength to break away from his background and life a full, first-hand life. Another related theme is implicit in a remark in *The Restoration of Arnold Middleton*, that "disintegration is inimical to the soul." Storey's plays, it may be argued, tacitly build up a vison of integration, of human and social wholeness, by openly concentrating on twentieth century deviations from this ideal: man alienated from his family, his roots, his class, his work, his language, and even from himself – a dissociation of sensibility that divides mind from emotion and hands from mind.

Arnold Middleton, Storey's first play, wasn't performed until 1967, but was actually written in 1959 between two of the novels which originally brought him fame. It was widely praised, and remains an impressive debut: rich and intricate, if also sometimes confused and obscure. We are never sure what has driven the provincial schoolmaster, Arnold Middleton, to the brink of madness. Presumably a combination of factors is responsible: his own immaturity and inability to sustain relationship; female pressure, from a demanding, jealous wife and a mother-in-law with a more than maternal interest in him; the northern parents he rarely sees; the mediocrity and moral listlessness of his milieu, "the passivity of modern society." What cannot be missed, however, is the splendidly humorous rhetoric with which Middleton defends himself. It carries one along, whether he is imagining himself in the part of Robin Hood (the archetypal outsider he is representing in the school play), or pretending he is actually a king (symbol, to him, of moral authority and sure social purpose), or, finally confessing his own irradicable weaknesses ("scars...they inhabit the skin. They grow there after a while like natural features....Remove them, and you remove life itself"). The conclusion seems to be that, assert his individuality as he may, a man must substantially reconcile himself to what experience has made him. "Everything has to be defined. Yet how can you define anything except by its limitations?"

This sort of resilient stoicism also emerges from *In Celebration*, which deals more explicitly with the background Storey himself knows. The Shaws are visited on their fortieth wedding anniversary by their three sons: one a teacher, another a solicitor turned artist, the third an industrial relations expert, and all clearly live markedly less adequate and fulfilling lives than their father, though neither he nor Storey attempts to sentimentalise the pits in which he works. As Steven, the unhappiest of the uprooted three, declares: "His work actually has significance for him...while the work he's educated us to do...is nothing...at the best a pastime, at the worst a sort of soulless stirring of the pot...honestly, what hope has any of us got?" There is more to the play than this suggests, since Storey is at pains to show the complexities of the participants' motives. Old Shaw wanted the boys to be successful in order to appease his wife, who married beneath her, and whom he impregnated, before them, with a son who later died. Andrew is cynical and angry because they rejected him on his brother's death. Under the skilfully sustained surface of the "celebration" of the title, a dark drama of sin, guilt, and atonement begins to untravel – only to be checked by Steven, the nearest to

Storey's mouthpiece in the play. There is, he says, "this feeling of disfigurement, this crushing, bloody sense of injury"; but it was "inflicted by innocent hands." Like Middleton, they must accept their scars and learn to make the best of them.

Storey's career has been much helped by the devotion of Lindsay Anderson, who has directed all his plays with a marvellous feeling for detail and the nuance of character. Nowhere was this more evident than with *The Contractor*, a much more visual and less dramatically explicit play than those before it. In the first half a tent is painstakingly and precisely raised, and in the second lowered: what would be the central event in a more conventional piece (a wedding and a reception) occurs in the interval. The "family" wanders in and out, notably Ewbank, the bride's father, a tenting contractor and self-made Yorkshireman; but the action mainly involves the seemingly aimless backchat and banter of the men putting up the tent.

The workmen are obvious misfits, "those that nobody else'll employ," but almost everyone else is out of love with society. Ewbank's son tries hopelessly to identify with the men; Ewbank's father bores them with stories of the good old days before machines; Ewbank himself reverberates with unease beneath a tough exterior. Everything is allusive, understated, and, as Storey himself said, the metaphor of the tent "contains the possibility" of many interpretations. In the light of his previous writing, however, it seems best to regard it primarily as a symbol of the frivolity of contemporary work and the impermanence of its achievement.

Home continues the process, both stylistic and moral. The subject is a still deeper alienation; but its expression is oblique, tentative, and even vague. Two old men exchange smalltalk, using dated expressions like "my word" and "by Jove"; two women join them, talking of sex and suffering; and it becomes apparent that this "home" is in fact an asylum. These people could not function in a scarcely saner outside world, and they are not at peace in this secluded one. And Storey goes further, dropping hints that the madhouse is an impressionistic picture of contemporary Britain, deprived of a secure, authoritative place in the world. In other words, *Home* evokes a more total dislocation than any Storey play to date. Indeed, alienation has gone so far that the old men cannot even approximately say what they mean. Their language is all social form, without personal content; speech is separated from feeling. All they can do to express themselves is to let fall the occasional tear − as both do, with great dramatic effect.

The Changing Room is a play so lacking in overt significance that it might be mistaken for pure documentary − and, as such, proved compulsorily watchable in the theatre. But, as always with Storey, more occurs than appears on the surface. Not only is there considerable opportunity to speculate on the rugby footballers: there are also moments when individuality disappears, and we are able to see the team as a team, each member giving his all to a cooperative enterprise. On the field, 13 minds, hearts, and pairs of hands have worked as one. Man may be alienated from his work: he is not, it seems, always alienated from his play. There is *some* hope.

—Benedict Nightingale

STOTT, Mike.   British.   Born in Rochdale, Lancashire, 2 January 1944. Attended Manchester University. Stage manager at the Scarborough Library Theatre, and play-reader for the Royal Shakespeare Theatre, three years; Script Editor, BBC Radio, London 1970–72; Thames Television Resident Writer, Hampstead Theatre Club, London, 1975. Agent: Michael Imison, Dr. Jan Van Loewen, 81–83 Shaftesbury Avenue, London W1V 8BX, England.

Plays

> *Mata Hari* (produced Scarborough, 1965).
> *Erogenous Zones* (produced London, 1969).
> *Funny Peculiar* (produced Bochum, Germany, 1973; Liverpool, 1975; London, 1976).
>   Published in *Plays and Players* (London), April–May 1976.
> *Lenz*, adaptation of the story by Georg Büchner (produced London, 1974).
> *Plays for People Who Don't Move Much* (produced London, 1974).
> *Midnight* (produced London, 1974).
> *Other People* (produced London, 1974).
> *Men's Talk (Hard Slog, The Force, Fixtures)* (produced Edinburgh and London, 1974).
> *Ghosts*, adaptation of a play by Wolfgang Bauer (produced London, 1975).
> *Lorenzaccio*, adaptation of the play by Alfred de Musset (produced Exeter, 1976).

> Radio Plays: *Lucky*, 1970; *When Dreams Collide*, 1970; *Early Morning Glory*, 1972; *Lincoln*, 1973; *Richard Serge*, 1973; *The Bringer of Bad News*, 1973; *The Doubting Thomases*, 1973.

> Television Plays: *The Flaxton Boys*, 1969; *Susan*, 1973; *Thwum*, 1975.

*   *   *

Mike Stott's 1976 West End success with his comedy *Funny Peculiar* is the culmination, or climax, of his search for the ideal, or at least clinching, formula for the permissive sex comedy.

This search began with *Erogenous Zones*, a collection of sketches for performance by a company of six, centred round the twin themes of love and homicide. The mixture here is one of strip cartoon wit and woman's magazine cliché, the main charm residing in the way all passion is reduced to absurdity by being couched in dumb and deadpan phrases. The types are instantly recognizable – the doughy sweetheart, the sadistic cop, the clean-limbed officer doing press-ups, the big beefy success, the mad gunman, the obsessive lawyer – and the point is always clear before the pay-off. The ideas are absorbing in their manner of catching the comedy of the obvious, while managing to avoid repetition.

In *Other People* the form is sometimes laboured, though the dialogue is often sharp. It begins with an arresting image of a "flasher" naked under his plastic see-through mac, and a pretty Czech girl who frightens him away by her eagerness to participate in anything he might suggest.

But an arresting image does not make a play, and the web of relationships Stott establishes – between a successful business man, Dave, who ends by taking an overdose of sleeping pills, an out-of-work Italian father-of-five who is given a cheque by the dying man to solve all his problems, a lonely widow of 51 who lacks love, and her daughter, married to Dave's friend Geoff – fails to form a very coherent pattern of comic interest. The mood also varies too strongly, sometimes hilarious, sometimes melodramatic. The theme of sexual permissiveness is provocatively explored, with the sound of couples making love upstairs, and one couple attempting to initiate group sex; but it is hard to make out what Stott's intention is – merely an exploitation of current fashion, or an attempt at genuine and social observation. But the characters are strong, and the dialogue is lively and full of unexpected development. Enrico the Italian's fantasy of selling underwear to Arabs in hair-covered boxes – "We buy the hair, we comb it, shampoo, and we stick it on the boxes. And those Arabs, those Greeks, they go CRAZY in the shops, just to stroke our sexy hairy boxes. Believe me, Mr. Brock, I know those men, the foreigners, the Aristotles, the Ahmeds. They KILL each other to be stroking a hairy English box" – provoked some brilliant and subtle playing from Tom Conti in the

Hampstead Theatre Club production.

Funny Peculiar has a very moral ending. The hero, Trevor, a North country grocer proclaiming the virtues of sexual freedom, falls down into his cellar, pursued by a sex-hungry puritan lady of advanced years, and is consequently rendered helpless in plaster and straps on a hospital bed. There he becomes the passive object of wife and mistress's simultaneous oral lust. A new and up-to-date variation of the "tu l'a voulu, Georges Dandin" syndrome, this may well be, and the degree of obsessiveness in Trevor's obsession with sex is certainly kept beautifully simmering in his naked cavorting among the council estate flower beds, and in his attempting to preach to the unconverted customers of his shop (losing his custom as a result).

The best writing is found in the scenes when he tries to convince his wife to leap onto the freedom bandwagon, and when he upbraids her for her sexual ordinariness: her defence is so heartfelt and real that it is hard not to feel her subsequent conversion is engineered for the sake of the plot. There is one piece of slapstick business — a fight with confectionary between a visiting confectionary salesman and Trevor — which must rate as highly as any piece of comic anarchy seen recently on the West End stage. Whether Stott will move beyond formula writing — in this case the pieces all fit with dazzling professionalism—has yet to be seen.

In Büchner's *Lenz* and Wolfgang Bauer's *Ghosts* Stott demonstrates more fragmented skills as an adaptor/translator. *Lenz* was originally a short story about a Strasbourg intellectual who believes he can raise a girl from the dead; it is written in innumerable short scenes (in Büchner's own expressionistic manner) which do not really come to grips with any central issue. The original of *Ghosts* is a roughed up re-write of Brecht's satire on a lower middle class wedding party, using socially more sophisticated, though dramatically more crude, characters.

—Garry O'Connor

SUTHERLAND, Efua (Theodora).   Ghanaian.   Born in Cape Coast, 27 June 1924. Educated at St. Monica's School and Training College, Cape Coast; Homerton College, Cambridge; School of Oriental and African Studies, London. Married William Sutherland in 1954. Schoolteacher in Ghana, 1951–54. Founding Director, Experimental Theatre Players, now Ghana Drama Studio, Accra, since 1958. Founder of Ghana Society of Writers, now the University of Ghana Writers Workshop. Co-Founder, *Okyeame* magazine, Accra. Lives in Ghana. Address: c/o Longman Group, 74 Grosvenor Street, LondonW1X 0AS, England.

PUBLICATIONS

Plays

Edufa, based on *Alcestis* by Euripides (produced Accra, 1964).   London, Longman, 1967; in *Plays from Black Africa*, edited by Frederic M. Litto, New York, Hill and Wang, 1968.
Foriwa.   Accra, Ghana Publishing House, 1967; New York, Panther House, 1970.
Vulture! Vulture! and Tahinta: Two Rhythm Plays.   Accra, Ghana Publishing House, 1968; New York, Panther House, 1970.
The Marriage of Anansewa: A Storytelling Drama.   London, Longman, 1974.

Other Plays: *Anansegoro: You Swore an Oath*, 1964; *Odasani*, version of *Everyman*; adaptation of Chekhov's *The Proposal*; *The Pineapple Child*; *Ananse and the Dwarf Brigade*; *Nyamekye*; version of *Alice in Wonderland*.

Other

Playtime in Africa (juvenile).   London, Brown Knight and Truscott, 1960; New York, Atheneum, 1962.
The Roadmakers.   Accra, Ghana Information Services, and London, Neame, 1961.

                                        *   *   *

It is impossible to consider Efua Sutherland's plays apart from her work as a founder, organiser, and stimulator of theatres and troupes. This work is probably more important for the development of drama in Africa than are her plays, good as these are. I suspect, indeed, that this would be her own assessment, for several of her plays have never appeared in print.

In the mid-1950's Efua Sutherland sets up a writer's society to write for children, and her concern with children has been a continuing one. For them she has written many plays, some based upon traditional tales, one an adaptation of *Alice in Wonderland*. Of these, only *Anasegoro: You Swore an Oath* and "two rhythm plays," *Vulture! Vulture!* and *Tahinta* have been published. The rhythm plays, consisting of simple one-line statements followed by an unvarying chorus line, mean very little on the page. *Anansegoro* is based upon the common tale of a deer who turns into a woman. Ananse has shot a deer, who turns into a beautiful woman and lives with him, relieving him of his poverty with rich gifts. She has told Ananse of her identity and he has sworn never to tell another. His wife becomes jealous of the deer-woman – with reason – and keeps pressing for Ananse's "relative" to leave. Eventually, Ananse tells her the secret and is stripped of all his riches as the deer-woman departs. "If you rub the face of a blessing in the dirt, it deserts you." The events are set in a narrative framework, with a story-teller and a chorus, whose members also play minor parts. The short play is vigorous, simple, and highly theatrical. Children can take pleasure in the story, the song and the dance, adults in the sophistication of the presentation.

In 1958 Sutherland founded the Experimental Theatre Players in Accra which became the Ghana Drama Studio. In 1960 a courtyard theatre was built for it, drawing in concept upon traditional performance areas. This was, I believe, the first attempt to design an indigenous form of theatre, rather than to copy European proscenium stages. A few years later Sutherland designed another open-air theatre for experiments at blending traditional story-telling and drama. The Ghana Drama Studio has become the base for Kusum Agoromba (Kusum Players), which tours schools and training colleges, incorporating the local schoolchildren into its productions; The Studio also collaborates with the Workers Brigade Drama Group, which tours and tries to reach the ordinary man. Both touring companies play in English and in Akan.

Sutherland's concern is less with present success in Accra than with the future development of drama in Ghana as a whole: with reaching the children and the common people, particularly those outside the capital, and, at the same time, establishing the basis for the development of African styles of performance and drama.

She has published two full-length plays. *Edufa* is a re-working of *Alcestis*, in which the Admetus-figure becomes a selfish member of the *nouveau riche* and the play a tragedy, ending with the wife's death. Such a radical change necessitates a change in the Heracles-character, now a seedy intellectual who hides the emptiness of his life and his ambitions as a writer behind the image of a wandering prankster full of songs. The father, self-centered in Euripides, becomes a sympathetic character, full of dignity, knowledge, and insight. The action is set, with rather heavy irony, against an annual ceremony in which funeral songs are sung as evil is expelled from the town. This ceremony, and various omens in which Edufa, the modern man, professes to disbelieve, creates an atmosphere of foreboding. Efua

Sutherland has also adapted *Everyman* and Chekhov's *The Proposal*, but they have not been published.

Her second full-length play, *Foriwa*, impresses one with its usefulness. It is intended to be performed in the open air in a street in any of many small Ghanaian towns, and it tells how to bring life and vitality to such a place. The central characters are Labaran, a university-educated stranger who is camping in the town and "planting seeds" in the minds of those who are receptive, and Foriwa, a beautiful girl just returned from training as a teacher. By the end of the play, of course, they have fallen in love with each other (Sutherland's rejection of tribalism, since Labaran is a Hausa from the North). Yet Sutherland is careful not to present progress as pressed upon the people by the young and educated. Labaran's ally is the retired postmaster; and Foriwa's mother, the Queen-Mother of the town, has long been working for new ways. The climax of the play is her use of a traditional ceremony – again, Sutherland emphasises the alliance of new and old – to call for a re-birth in the town. The play is without villains, for the message is that all must co-operate; even the elders, Labaran says, "have come as far as they are able."

The tone of the play is set in Labaran's opening soliloquy:

> ...The town has slept itself to raggedness.
> I am keeping vigil here, placing my faith in some daybreak after this long night,
> when the townsmen shall wake and shake my soul with vibrant talk....
> I was impatient at the beginning; in haste. Seeing the raggedness of my people's
> homes, I was ashamed, even angry. I heard it screamed: Progress! Development! I
> wanted it far and everywhere.

As she says later in the speech, "This is my office, this street; the people who use it are my work and education." Such patently utilitarian drama may be valuable to contemporary Ghana. But Efua Sutherland's talent as a writer has been subordinated to her theatrical projects and the laudable aims they serve, and it is her endeavour as a whole for which one's admiration is greatest.

—Anthony Graham-White

TABORI, George. British. Born in Budapest, Hungary, 24 May 1914. Served in the British Army Middle East Command, 1941–43. Married the actress Viveca Lindfors in 1954; has three children. Artistic Director, Berkshire Theatre Festival. Recipient: British Film Academy Award, 1953; Best Foreign Film Award (France and Italy), 1969. Agent: Bertha Case, 42 West 53rd Street, New York, New York 10019, U.S.A.; or, Kiepenheuer Verlag, Schweinfurtherstrasse 60, Berlin 33, West Germany; or, Marta Andras, Martonplay, 33 Champs Elysees, Paris 8, France.

PUBLICATIONS

Plays

Flight into Egypt (produced New York, 1952). New York, Dramatists Play Service, 1953.

The Emperor's Clothes (produced New York, 1953).   New York, French, 1953.
Miss Julie, adaptation of the play by Strindberg (also director: produced New York, 1956).
Brouhaha (produced London, 1958; New York, 1960).
Brecht on Brecht (produced New York and London, 1962).   New York, French, n.d.
The Resistible Rise of Arturo Ui: A Gangster Spectacle, adaptation of the play by Brecht (produced New York, 1963; Edinburgh, 1968; London, 1969).   New York, French, 1972.
Andorra, adaptation of the play by Max Frisch (produced New York, 1963).
The Guns of Carrar, adaptation of the play by Brecht (produced Syracuse, New York, 1963; New York City, 1968).   New York, French, 1970.
The Niggerlovers (produced New York, 1967).
The Cannibals (produced New York, 1968).   London, Davis Poynter, 1973.
Mother Courage, adaptation of the play by Brecht (produced Washington, D.C., 1970).
Pinkville (produced Stockbridge, Massachusetts, 1970; New York, 1971).
Clowns (also director: produced Tübingen, 1972).
Talk Show (produced Bremen, 1976).
Changes (produced Munich, 1976).

Screenplays: *Young Lovers*, 1952; *I Confess*, 1953; *The Journey*, 1959; *No Exit*, 1962; *Secret Ceremony*, 1968; *Insomnia*, 1975.

Novels

Beneath the Stone the Scorpion.   London, Boardman, and Boston, Houghton Mifflin, 1945.
Companions of the Left Hand.   London, Boardman, and Boston, Houghton Mifflin, 1946.
Original Sin.   London, Boardman, and Boston, Houghton Mifflin, 1947.
The Caravan Passes.   London, Boardman, and New York, Appleton Century Crofts, 1951.
The Journey: A Confession.   New York, Bantam, 1958; London, Corgi, 1959.
The Good One   New York, Pocket Books, 1960.

Theatrical Activities:

Director: **Plays** – *Miss Julie* by Strindberg, New York, 1956; *Brecht on Brecht*, toured, 1962; *Hell Is Other People*, New York, 1964; *The Cannibals* (co-director, with Marty Fried), Berlin, 1970; *Pinkville*, Berlin, 1971; *Clowns*, Tübingen, 1972; *Kohlhaas*, Bonn, 1974; *Emigrants*, Bonn, 1975; *Afore Night Come* by David Rudkin, Bremen, 1975; *The Trojan Women* by Euripides, Bremen, 1976.

*   *   *

George Tabori's world recalls the Sherwood Anderson title, *Dark Laughter*. What a world – betrayal, repression, violence, cannibalism, and, unlike the Greeks', no redemption. And envisioned more and more these last years as a black comedy. But not quite. The flavor is sardonic, tongue-in-cheek, but beneath this is absolutely no acceptance of the world as is. Beneath the sardonic tone we can apprehend the eyes of an anguished, lacerated soul who has seen mankind in one perversion, one degradation after another, seen Hungary in its fascistic period earlier in the century, Germany in the time of its Nazidom, and America in its growing role as police-butcher of the world, has seen it all, and yet whose outcry marks him as one who still believes in the impossible dream of brotherhood. I have the sense that Tabori is too angry, too disgusted to *want* to believe, but that past his disgust, past his disillusionment, there is a tremendous yearning, a cavernous yearning to believe in the possibility of a decent society.

Early Tabori is represented by *The Emperor's Clothes*, the tale of a "fuzzy-headed idealist" intellectual (my quotes) in Budapest who appears to renounce all his beliefs when he falls into the hands of the secret police but emerges as a man with backbone. Under torture he rediscovers his manhood. In short, Tabori at his most idealistic.

But then the world grows darker and Tabori begins to shift from naturalism toward a more abstract, less lyrical and far harsher theatre. He has been adapting Brecht, e.g. *Brecht on Brecht* and *Arturo Ui*, and his own work becomes more detached, more sardonic, more abstract, more song-and-dance oriented. By the time of *The Cannibals* in 1968, the work is very dry, very dark, very bitter, very removed. In a Nazi concentration camp, the prisoners decide to cook and eat their friend Puffi, the fat man who has just died. Hirschler says:

> (To Uncle who is protesting the cannibalism) Listen, Uncle, let's have some perspective. The cake is too small. Whenever you eat, you take a crumb out of someone else's mouth. At this very moment, while you're making such a fuss, millions are starving to death in India; but today we may have stumbled on the most elegant solution. The graveyards are full of goodies; the chimneys are going full blast, and nice fat suicides come floating down every river and stream. All that perfectly good stuff going to waste.

Shades of Swift's *Modest Proposal*. And the cannibalism, which Tabori treats both literally and as a metaphor, is painted as inexorable. At the end of the play, The Loudspeakers place the action in historic context:

> ...some savages eagerly desire the body of a murdered man
> So that his ghost may not trouble them,
> For which reason I recommend, dear brethren in Christ,
> The Jew's heart, in aspic or with sauce vinaigrette,
> So soft it will melt in your mouth.

In *The Niggerlovers*, Tabori views the racial tensions that afflict the U.S., but any sympathy is sublimated. No one comes off with any saving grace, the White liberals are stupid or saccharine or slightly perverted, the Blacks are corroded with cynicism. No action seems to be of any help, there is no way out.

Pinkville, several years after *The Cannibals* and *The Niggerlovers*, studies the development of an American killer – specifically how the U.S. army takes a non-violent, righteous young man and, using his very righteousness, subverts him into the killer it needs to massacre Vietnamese. Again the action is inexorable. Everything becomes grist for the army's purpose. Again the world is so self-enclosed that there is no way out.

And yet the way out is through the action of Tabori's art. For the very work is a cry. The sardonic element has within it a taint of satisfaction, as if the worst is always somehow satisfying, but the worst is also an indictment of us, ultimately a call. For the early heroes are gone, no heroes left in the later plays, nothing for us to emulate. You and I become the only possible heroes left to Tabori and to the world.

—Arthur Sainer

TAVEL, Ronald. American. Born in New York City, 17 May 1941. Studied at American universities: B.A., M.A. in philosophy and literature. Screenwriter, Andy Warhol Films Inc., New York, 1964–66; Playwright-in-Residence, Play-House of the Ridiculous, New York, 1965–67; Literary Adviser, *Scripts* magazine, New York, 1971–72; Playwright-in-Residence, Theatre of the Lost Continent, New York, 1971–73; Actors Studio, New York, 1972, and Yale University Divinity School, New Haven, Connecticut, 1975. Currently, Lecturer, New York State Council on the Arts; Adviser-Contributor, Subplot Theatre; Member, New York Theatre Strategy. Recipient: Obie Award, 1969; American Place Theatre grant, 1970; Rockefeller grant, 1972; Creative Artists Public Service grant, 1972, 1974; Guggenheim Fellowship, 1973; National Endowment for the Arts grant, 1974. Agent: Helen Merrill, 337 West 22nd Street, New York, New York 10011. Address: 438 West Broadway, Apartment 1, New York, New York 10012, U.S.A.

PUBLICATIONS

Plays

Christina's World, in *Chicago Review*, Winter-Spring 1963.
The Life of Juanita Castro (produced New York, 1965). Included in *Bigfoot and Other Plays*, 1973.
Shower (produced New York, 1965). Included in *Bigfoot and Other Plays*, 1973.
Tarzan of the Flicks (produced Plainfield, Vermont, 1965). Published in *Blacklist* (Maplewood, New Jersey), no. 6, 1965.
Harlot (scenario), in *Film Culture* (New York), Spring 1966.
The Life of Lady Godiva (produced New York, 1966). Published in *The New Underground Theatre*, edited by Robert Schroeder, New York, Bantam, 1968.
Indira Gandhi's Daring Device (produced New York, 1966). Included in *Bigfoot and Other Plays*, 1973.
Screen Test (produced New York, 1966).
Vinyl (produced New York, 1967). Published in *Clyde* (New York), ii, 2, 1966.
Kitchenette (produced New York, 1967). Included in *Bigfoot and Other Plays*, 1973.
Gorilla Queen (produced New York, 1967). Published in *The Best of Off-Off-Broadway*, edited by Michael Smith, New York, Dutton, 1969.
Canticle of the Nightingale (produced Stockholm, 1968).
Cleobis and Bito (oratorio; produced New York, 1968).
Arenas of Lutetia (produced New York, 1968). Published in *Experiments in Prose*, edited by Eugene Wildman, Chicago, Swallow Press, 1969.
Boy on the Straight-Back Chair, music by Orville Stoeber (produced New York, 1969). Included in *Bigfoot and Other Plays*, 1973.
Vinyl Visits an FM Station (produced New York, 1970). Published in *Drama Review* (New York), September 1970.
Bigfoot (produced New York, 1970). Included in *Bigfoot and Other Plays*, 1973.
Words for Bryan to Sing and Dance (produced New York, 1971).
Secrets of the Citizens Correction Committee (produced New York, 1973). Published in *Scripts 3* (New York), January 1972.
Arse Long – Life Short (produced New York, 1972).
Bigfoot and Other Plays (includes *Boy on the Straight-Back Chair, The Life of Juanita Castro, Indira Gandhi's Daring Device, Kitchenette, Shower*). New York, Winter House, 1973.
Queen of Greece (produced New York, 1973).
The Last Days of British Honduras (produced New York, 1974).

Screenplays: *Harlot*, 1964; *Philip's Screen Test*, 1965; *Screen Test*, 1965; *Suicide*, 1965; *The Life of Juanita Castro*, 1965; *Horse*, 1965; *Vinyl*, 1965; *Kitchen*, 1965; *Space*, 1965; *Hedy; or, The 14-Year-Old Girl*, 1966; *Withering Sights*, 1966; *The Chelsea Girls*, 1966; *More Milk Evette*, 1966.

Novel

Street of Stairs.   New York, Olympia Press, 1968.

Manuscript Collections: Mugar Library, Boston University; Lincoln Center Library of the Performing Arts, New York; University of Wisconsin Center for Theatre Research, Madison.

Critical Studies: "The Pop Scene" by Peter Michelson, in *Tri-Quarterly 6* (Evanston, Illinois), 1966; in *Film Culture 45* (New York), 1967; "Pop Goes America" by Peter Michelson, in *New Republic* (Washington, D.C.), 9 September 1967; "Ronald Tavel: Ridiculous Playwright" by Dan Isaac, in *Drama Review* (New York), Spring 1968; "Toward Eroticizing All Thought" by Gino Rizzo, in *The New York Times*, 5 January 1969; "Ronald Tavel: Celebration of a Panic Vision" by Gino Rizzo, in *Village Voice* (New York), 6 March 1969; "A Kid Named Toby" by Jack Kroll, in *Newsweek* (New York), 24 March 1969.

Theatrical Activities:

Director: **Plays** − *The Life of Juanita Castro*, New York, 1967; *Arenas of Lutetia*, New York, 1968. **Films** − many of his own screenplays.

Actor: **Play** − *In Search of the Cobra Jewels*, New York, 1972. **Films** − in all his own films, and in *Fifty Fantasticks*, 1964; *Bitch*, 1965; *Jail*, 1967; *Suicide Notations: Fire Escape*, 1972; *Infinity*, 1974.

Ronald Tavel comments:

My earliest tales were delivered Homerically. At the age of six or seven I took the first step toward giving them permanent form: comic books. While these comics were shameless imitations of the pictorial styles featured in the funnies we read at that time, there was, I fancy, something more urgent in my stories and characterizations. I wrote my first (verse) play (or fragment of one) in my sophomore year in high school and ten verse plays (or fragments of ones) followed that effort. The last of these have reached print but only one (*Cleobis and Bito*) was ever produced. In 1965, after two years of writing, directing, and acting in films, I turned again to playwriting. These were the one-acters that inaugurated The Theatre of the Ridiculous movement − a term I invented to catch the attention of critics and lower them into a category in order to facilitate their work. The term "Ridiculous" should not be taken too seriously (!) unless you want to re-define that word as Professor Peter Michelson did in his essay on the new American absurdity (*The New Republic*, 9 September 1967). I sought in these abstract satires to find a distinctly American language for the stage and that is a continuing preoccupation in my later and mercilessly longer "tragedies." In the early plays I also attempted to destroy plot and character, motivation, cause, event, and logic along with their supposed consequences. The word was All: what was spoken did not express the moment's preoccupation; rather, the preoccupation followed the word. In *The Life of Lady Godiva* I reached, cynically, for the Aristotelian principles of playmaking. While cynicism is the major thrust of *Godiva*, a near decade of concern with *The Poetics* was worming its way, re-evalued, to the core of my chores. *Gorilla Queen* progresses by building and abolishing, rebuilding and reabolishing, etc., the Aristotelian constructs. The full-length plays after *Gorilla Queen* obey, I believe, without too much objection, the Greek's difficult insights. While I have no single favorite, I am particularly fond of *Shower* because it continues to mystify me, am protective of *Arenas of Lutetia* because no one else will be, and consider *Bigfoot* (if you will allow me to play critic) my most ambitious and best play to date.

*   *   *

It has been said that to approach the aesthetic behind Ronald Tavel's work for theater, you must reread Susan Sontag's essays on pop art, camp, the revival of Art Nouveau, the underground film, and especially her critique of Jack Smith's film *Flaming Creatures*. The reason being that Ronald Tavel, poet, novelist, and scenarist, is a playwright born out of the mainstream of the sixties' pop culture who writes plays in the language of a poet.

After writing screenplays for Andy Warhol (including *The Chelsea Girls*), Tavel turned to playwriting and with director John Vaccaro founded the Play-House of the Ridiculous. At the Play-House Tavel wrote many pop-art plays, the funniest and most successful being *The Life of Juanita Castro*, a political-sexual joke about the pros and cons of contemporary Cuban life.

In 1967 Tavel left his Ridiculous Company for the Judson Poets Theater where he presented his *Gorilla Queen*, an avant-garde *Hellzapoppin* that became a watershed in off-off-Broadway entertainments.

Gorilla Queen is a spoof on all late show 1940's movies, covering everything from King Kong to Busby Berkeley to Astaire and Rogers and Clyde Beatty. It had songs by Al Carmines, a pseudo Greek chorus dressed as monkeys and full of monkeyshines and sexual variations in 28 flavors (men and women, men and men, women and women, men and apes, apes and queens, queens and queens). As with all Tavel plays, the heart of *Gorilla Queen* does not lie with its seemingly endless campy playfulness but rather with the playwright's unique use of language.

In my mind, Tavel's most interesting play is *Boy on the Straight-Back Chair* which, like *Gorilla Queen*, was devised and inspired by the mass media as well as 30's and 40's movies. The writing of the play was in part stimulated by the series of violent mass murders that took place all over America during the late 60's. Tavel's hero, Toby, is a composite of the characteristics of such American killers as Starkwater, Richard Speck, Charles Whitman, and the murderers of Theresa Genovese and Jane Britton.

The countryside in the play is referred to with a typical Tavel pun as "the lie of the land." According to Tavel's program notes for the American Place Theatre production, this phrase best describes the play: "It is what the play is about: the lie of the land, the lies that create ritualistic killers, the lies that have made government the foundation of pop culture."

"All my things begin and end in words," Tavel has noted. "In the beginning was the word; at the end there is only the word," says the hero of Tavel's novel *Street of Stairs*. Ultimately Tavel's "lie of the land" is the lie of our contemporary language. Our mass media and Madison Avenue today work overtime to destroy meaning in words. "But," according to Tavel, "poetic revelation can leap beyond the words. The word is the ground for truth, not truth itself."

—Bernard Carragher

TAYLOR, Cecil P(hilip).   British   Born in Glasgow, Scotland, 6 November 1929. Educated at Queen's Park Secondary School. Married Irene Diamond in 1955; Elizabeth

Screen, 1967; has four children. Worked as an electrician, engineer, salesman, journalist. Literary Adviser, since 1968, for the Northumberland Youth Theatre Association, Shiremoor, and since 1971, for the Tyneside Theatre Trust and the Everyman Theatre, Liverpool. Since 1969, Director of the Writers' Workshop, Northumberland. Script Editor, *Burns* series of television plays; writer for BBC Educational Television. Recipient: Arts Council bursary, 1965; Scottish Television Theatre Award, 1969. Agent: Clive Goodwin, 79 Cromwell Road, London S. W. 7. Address: 2 Smallburn Road, Longhorsley, Northumberland, England.

PUBLICATIONS

Plays

> *Aa Went te Blaydon Races*, music by Cecil P. Taylor (produced Newcastle upon Tyne, 1962).
> *Happy Days Are Here Again* (produced Edinburgh, 1965).   Published in *New English Dramatists 12*, London, Penguin, 1968.
> *Of Hope and Glory* (produced Edinburgh, 1965).
> *Fable* (produced Glasgow, 1965).   Edinburgh, Edinburgh University Drama Society, 1967.
> *Allergy* (produced Edinburgh and London, 1966; New York, 1974).   Published in *Traverse Plays*, London, Penguin, 1966.
> *Bread and Butter* (produced Edinburgh and London, 1966; Washington D.C., 1969). Published in *New English Dramatists 10*, London, Penguin, 1967.
> *Who's Pinkus? Where's Chelm?*, music by Monty Norman (produced Edinburgh, 1966; London, 1967).
> *Mister David* (produced Warsaw, 1967).
> *The Ballachulish Beat: A Play with Songs*, music by Cecil P. Taylor.   London, Rapp and Carroll, 1967.
> *Oil and Water* (televised, 1967; produced on tour, Scotland, 1972).
> *What Can a Man Do* (produced Newcastle upon Tyne, 1968).
> *Happy Anniversary* (televised, 1968; produced Edinburgh, 1972).
> *Thank You Very Much* (produced Shiremoor, Northumberland, 1969).   London, Methuen, 1970.
> *Lies about Vietnam/Truth about Sarajevo* (produced Edinburgh, 1969).   Published as *The Truth about Sarajevo: A Play for the Traverse Theatre*, Kirknewton, Midlothian, Scottish Theatre Editions, 1970.
> *Brave* (produced Shiremoor, Northumberland, 1970).
> *Revolution* (televised, 1970).   Section entitled *Charles and Cromwell*, included in *Making a Television Play*, 1970.
> *The Cleverness of Us* (produced Liverpool, 1971).
> *Bloch's Play* (televised, 1971; produced Edinburgh, 1971).   Kirknewton, Midlothian, Scottish Theatre Editions, 1971.
> *Grace Darling Show* (produced Newcastle upon Tyne, 1971).
> *Passion Play*, in *Christmas Present* (produced Edinburgh, 1971).
> *Em'n Ben* (produced Shiremoor, Northumberland, 1971).
> *Ginger Golly and the Fable Men* (for children; produced Newcastle upon Tyne, 1972).
> *The Black and White Minstrels* (produced Edinburgh, 1972).
> *Me* (produced Glasgow, 1972).
> *Words* (televised, 1972).   Published in *Second Playbill 2*, edited by Alan Durband, London, Hutchinson, 1973.
> *Peer Gynt*, adaptation of the play by Ibsen (produced Newcastle upon Tyne, 1972; as *Gynt*, produced Edinburgh, 1975).

Antigone, adaptation of the play by Sophocles (produced Newcastle upon Tyne, 1972).

Threepenny Opera, adaptation of a play by Brecht, music by Kurt Weill (produced Newcastle upon Tyne, 1972).

You Are My Heart's Delight (produced London, 1973).

The Grand Adultery Convention (produced London, 1973).

Next Year in Tel Aviv (produced Edinburgh, 1973).

Drums in the Night, adaptation of a play by Brecht (produced Edinburgh and London, 1973).

5P Opera (produced Newcastle upon Tyne, 1973).

Waiting for Lefty, adaptation of the play by Clifford Odets (produced Newcastle upon Tyne, 1973).

Apples (produced Newcastle upon Tyne, 1973).   Published in *Prompt One*, edited by Alan Durband, London, Hutchinson, 1976.

Columba (produced Edinburgh, 1973).

Carol O.K. (produced Newcastle upon Tyne, 1974).

Schippel, adaptation of the play by Carl Sternheim (produced Edinburgh, 1974; as *The Plumber's Progress*, produced London, 1975).

So Far So Bad (produced Newcastle upon Tyne, 1974).

Spital Tongue Plays (produced Newcastle upon Tyne, 1974).

Pilgrim (produced Newcastle upon Tyne, 1975).

The Killingworth Play (produced Killingworth, 1975).

All Change, with Alex Glasgow (produced Newcastle upon Tyne, 1975).

Aladdin (produced Newcastle upon Tyne, 1976).

Bandits (produced Newcastle upon Tyne, 1976).

Goldberg (produced London, 1976).

Radio Play: *Love Story*, 1966.

Television Plays: *Lone Rider*, 1966; *Myopia*, 1967; *Oil and Water*, 1967; *Friends*, 1967; *Happy Anniversary*, 1968; *Thank You Very Much for the Family Circle*, 1968; *In Case*, 1969; *Street Fighter*, 1969; *Revolution* (trilogy: *Charles and Cromwell, Lenin, Castro*), 1970; *Bloch's Play*, 1971; *Adam Smith* series, 1972; *Words*, 1972; *King and Cuthbertson*, 1974; *Izzie* (*Nightingale's Boys* series), 1975; *The First Train Now Arriving*, from work by Hunter Davies, 1975; *For Services to Myself*, 1976.

Other

Making a Television Play: A Complete Guide from Conception to B.B.C. Production, Based on the Making of the Play "Charles and Cromwell" for B.B.C. "Thirty Minute Theatre." Newcastle upon Tyne, Oriel Press, 1970.

Manuscript Collections: National Library, Edinburgh; Central Library, Newcastle upon Tyne.

Critical Studies: *Anger and After* and *The Second Wave* by John Russell Taylor, London, Methuen, 1962, 1971; prefaces to *New English Dramatists 10, 12, 14*, London, Penguin, 1967, 1968, 1969; "The Plays of Cecil P. Taylor" by Alastair Cording, in *Scottish Theatre* (Inverkeithing, Fife), iii, 4, 1971.

Cecil P. Taylor comments:

A gradual scaling down of ambition is the best description of my development as a playwright. Starting with the aim of the theatre as a potent instrument of the revolution, I have been beaten down to theatre as another of the communication arts. I used to write plays, such as *Blaydon Races*, genuinely convinced they would move the workers, by the insights the plays gave into great political truths, to the revolution. I now write plays as a novelist writes novels or a poet poetry – to communicate my narrow, odd vision of the world as I am seeing it at the time of writing. Always in the hope that my hang-ups, flaws, insecurities and so on will cross at times those of my audience and they might feel a bit less on their own in this big world, as I do when I read a real book or see a real play.

I don't accept categories in writing, "expressionist," "naturalist," etc. The content, if it is a real play, determines the form. I don't like to see actors acting or "plays" in the theatre. I have to be caught up completely in the world of the play, or the play has failed. I suppose it's an arbitrary kind of rule but I tend to think and work to it: if it's true, it's good, if it's false, it's bad.

*   *   *

Cecil P. Taylor is perhaps the most gifted of several outstanding young Scottish dramatists whose work has been particularly associated with the little Traverse Theatre Club in Edinburgh. His best plays are naturalistic comedies, often set in the Gorbals district of Glasgow, Taylor's home town: but the implications of these stories are neither local nor particularly Scottish. Taylor is a socialist by political conviction: but his plays derive their distinctive humour from the wry recognition that people who profess socialist ideals are rarely able to carry them out in daily life. Taylor has a wonderful ear for inappropriate political jargon. In *Allergy*, his one-act play, Jim, the editor of *Socialist Reflection* (circulation: 150 copies), seduces Barbara by saying that "you're the first woman I've met who's sparked off insights in me" – insights (that is) about the course of world revolution. Morris (in *Bread and Butter*) is convinced that Hitler (in the early 1930's) is really taking part in the glorious class struggle by only menacing rich Jews. Taylor's comedies have sometimes been interpreted as concealed attacks on socialism, simply because the characters who talk most about the revolution are obviously incapable of running anything – either an affair, a small newspaper or a car. When a journalist like Christopher (in *Allergy*) gets a decent job, his revolutionary fervour dwindles away. Taylor (it has been suggested) celebrates a sell-out to capitalism: and for this reason his plays in Glasgow – such as *Me* at the Citizens Theatre – have suffered from two types of attack, from those who are distressed by the "bad language" and "immorality" of his plays and from those who deplore the images of comic self-deception among socialists, from the political left and right.

But Taylor is not primarily a political dramatist – in the sense that his plays are not concealed polemic. "The first thing a play has to be about....," he once write, "is people: their relationships to one another and to the society they live in." *Bread and Butter*, his first major success, concerns two Scottish-Jewish couples, Morris and Sharon, and Alec and Miriam, as they grow up and grow old together in Glasgow. The play covers a time-span from 1931 to 1965, a fact which suggests that *Bread and Butter* is a historical documentary. But, in fact, the external history is incidental to the main story which is about the way in which they adjust to one another and to life. Morris, the son of a rich man, is an incurable optimist, believing that the socialist revolution is round the corner: Alec is his working-class friend, poor but doggedly surviving through dreary jobs, until by the end of the Second World War their financial situations have changed. Morris is ruined: Alec is doing well, although Miriam his wife keeps a tight hand on the purse. From these slight biographies of apparently uninteresting people, Taylor manages to construct a play which is both funny and absorbing: and his skill is shown by the way in which the superficial incidents of the first act gain a depth of significance in the second. The play moves with an easy relaxation towards greater profundity. Morris's optimism becomes a domineering control over his wife: Alec's peaceful acceptance of hardship becomes a sort of masochism, from which he makes only tentative efforts to escape. The dialogue throughout contains this gentle irony, somewhat similar to Bernard Malamud's style, which pokes fun at hope without disavowing it.

The Black and White Minstrels is again an ambitious play which moves from small incidents to major themes. It does not however spread over a wide span of time. Two couples live together in a Glasgow house, sharing partners by rota system to prove their togetherness. A black girl, renting a room in the same house, causes trouble: and the couples gang up against her, partly because she's a puritan and aggressive and partly out of sheer loyalty to each other. But they're socialists too, and therefore to defend the landlord (who is one of them) against a black tenant in a Rent Tribunal court causes them much private anguish. Their cause succeeds: but from the tension between the ideals they profess and the problems they face, the community spirit, fragile enough at the best of times, starts to disintegrate. Taylor manages to balance many themes around this pivot – the impotency of Harry, the harassment of Cyril, an impoverished writer, the earnest maternalism of Pat, and the quieter affection of Gil: and the play accumulates meanings and interest as it progresses, always the sign of a good play.

Allergy is a delightful one-act play: about a journalist, Christopher, who is allergic to adultery but can't avoid seducing girls, and an editor, Jim, who takes over his unconsummated affairs. In *Gynt*, 1975, his adaptation of Ibsen's *Peer Gynt*, performed by the Traverse, Taylor presents three different stages in Peer Gynt's life as three characters, each of whom alternately playing the scenes and watching the others doing so. By that means, Taylor tries to show that Gynt is continually making the choices which lead to his death at the hands of the button-moulder. Death is present in the first scene, as well as the last: and so is Gynt's youth. Time does not pass, but rather repeats itself. *Gynt* is perhaps the most successful of Taylor's allegories. He has, however, written several non-naturalistic plays: notably a documentary for the Northumberland Youth Theatre, *Thank You Very Much*, and several allegories, *Happy Days Are Here Again, Who's Pinkus? Where's Chelm?* and his first play, *Mr David* (written in 1962). But Taylor's great talent for discovering humour and relevance within small totally plausible incidents tends to get lost in the broader, more slapdash style of his documentaries and allegories. In one scene from *Thank You Very Much*, a father meets his daughter's suitor believing that the young man wants to buy his greyhound, and the cross-talk between them provides a good revue sketch – but quite without the Glasgow-Yiddish humour of his naturalistic plays. In *Who's Pinkus? Where's Chelm?*, a fool leaves a city of fools to seek his fortune in the neighbouring town of Mazeltov (Yiddish for good luck): he fails in his quest, but returns to his home town with tales of success, thus establishing a legendary reputation for business acumen. Pinkus is an amusing central character: but the play seems loosely strung together and rather superficial. Taylor's best political plays, such as *Lies about Vietnam*, are basically naturalistic and two-edged in their attacks. The campaign against Vietnam – though necessary – contains as many self-deceptions as the American war effort itself.

When Taylor remains within the social situations which he knows and relishes – and within the technical range of his idiosyncratic comedy style – he is one of the most rewarding dramatists currently writing. When he is attracted away from this far from narrow scope, he is a competent and intelligent journalist-playwright, to rank with (say) Alan Plater, but lacking his particular originality and charm.

—John Elsom

TERRY, Megan. American. Born in Seattle, Washington, 22 July 1932. Educated at Banff School of Fine Arts, Alberta, Summers 1950–52, 1956; University of Alberta, Edmonton, 1952–53; University of Washington, Seattle, B.Ed. 1956. Taught drama at the Cornish School of Allied Arts, Seattle, 1954–56; Writer-in-Residence, Yale University

Drama School, New Haven, Connecticut, 1966–67. Founding Member, 1963, and Director of the Playwrights Workshop, 1963–68, Open Theatre, New York. Founding Member and Treasurer, New York Theatre Strategy, 1971; Founding Member, Women's Theatre Council, New York, 1971. Recipient: Stanley Drama Award, 1965; Office of Advanced Drama Research Award, 1965; ABC-Yale University Fellowship, 1966; Rockefeller grant, 1968; Obie Award, 1970. Agent: Elisabeth Marton, 96 Fifth Avenue, New York, New York 10011, U.S.A.

PUBLICATIONS

Plays

Beach Grass (also director: produced Seattle, 1955).
Seascape (also director: produced Seattle, 1955).
Go Out and Move the Car (also director: produced Seattle, 1955).
New York Comedy: Two (produced Saratoga, New York, 1961).
Ex-Miss Copper Queen on a Set of Pills (produced New York, 1963).   Published in Playwrights for Tomorrow: A Collection of Plays, Volume 1, edited by Arthur H. Ballet, Minneapolis, University of Minnesota Press, 1966.
When My Girlhood Was Still All Flowers (produced New York, 1963).
Eat at Joe's (produced New York, 1964).
Calm Down Mother (produced New York, 1965; London, 1969).   Indianapolis, Bobbs Merrill, 1966.
Keep Tightly Closed in a Cool Dry Place (produced New York, 1965; London, 1968). Included in Four Plays, 1967.
The Magic Realists (produced New York, 1966).   Included in Three One-Act Plays, 1972.
Comings and Goings (produced New York, 1966; Edinburgh, 1968).   Included in Four Plays, 1967.
The Gloaming, Oh My Darling (produced Minneapolis, 1966).   Included in Four Plays, 1967.
Viet Rock: A Folk War Movie (also director: produced New York, 1966).   Included in Four Plays, 1967.
Four Plays: Viet Rock; Comings and Goings; Keep Tightly Closed in a Cool Dry Place; The Gloaming, Oh My Darling.   New York, Simon and Schuster, 1967.
The Key Is on the Bottom (produced Los Angeles, 1967).
The People vs Ranchman (produced Minneapolis, 1967; New York, 1968).   With Ex-Miss Copper Queen on a Set of Pills, New York, Dramatists Play Service, 1968.
Home (televised, 1968).   New York, French, 1972.
Jack-Jack (produced Minneapolis, 1968).
Massachusetts Trust (produced Waltham, Massachusetts, 1968).   Published in The Off-Off-Broadway Book, edited by Albert Poland and Bruce Mailman, Indianapolis, Bobbs Merrill, 1972.
Sanibel and Captiva (broadcast, 1968)   Included in Three One-Act Plays, 1972.
One More Little Drinkie (televised, 1969).   Included in Three One-Act Plays, 1972.
Approaching Simone (produced Boston and New York, 1970).   Old Westbury, New York, Feminist Press, 1972.
The Tommy Allen Show (also director: produced Los Angeles and New York, 1970). Published in Scripts 2 (New York), December 1971.
Grooving (produced New York, 1972).
Choose a Spot on the Floor, with Jo Ann Schmidman (produced Omaha, Nebraska, 1972).
Three One-Act Plays (includes Sanibel and Captiva, The Magic Realists, One More Little Drinkie).   New York, French, 1972.

Couplings and Groupings (Theatre Verité).   New York, Pantheon, 1973.
Susan Perutz at the Manhattan Theatre Club (produced New York, 1973).
Thoughts (lyrics only), book by Lamar Alford (produced New York, 1973).
Nightwalk, with Sam Shepard and Jean-Claude van Itallie (produced New York, 1973).
St. Hydro Clemency; or, A Funhouse of the Lord: An Energizing Event (produced New York, 1973).
The Pioneer, and Pro-Game (produced New York, 1974).
Hothouse (produced New York, 1974).   New York, French, 1975.
Babes in the Big House (produced New York, 1974).
All Them Women, with others (produced New York, 1974).

Radio Plays: *Sanibel and Captiva*, 1968; *American Wedding Ritual Monitored/ Transmitted by the Planet Jupiter*, 1972.

Television Plays: *The Dirt Boat*, 1955; *Home*, 1968; *One More Little Drinkie*, 1969; *Brazil Fado: You're Always with Me*, 1972.

Critical Study: "Who Says Only Words Make Great Drama" by the author, in *New York Times*, 10 November 1968.

Theatrical Activities:

Director: **Plays** – with the Cornish Players, Seattle: *Beach Grass, Seascape*, and *Go Out and Move the Car*, 1955; with the Open Theatre's Playwrights Workshop, New York, 1962–68; *Viet Rock*, New York, 1966; *The Tommy Allen Show*, Los Angeles, 1970; and other plays. **Television:** *The Dirt Boat*, 1955.

*   *   *

America as victim. Megan Terry sees the country as a vast, smiling ice-cream exterior hiding a dark, cancerous interior. But the interior can't be hidden and the exterior always gives evidence of its being a vessel of malady.

In *The Tommy Allen Show*, Terry's anti-hero is a four-faceted, smiling affable, baby-faced television star.

> Tommy I enters and flashes his famous warm smile: Hello, folks. Hi, folks. Ladies and gentlemen. You look good to me. You're there. I like to see you there every night, five nights a week, fifty-two weeks a year. I say to myself: Tommy, all you have to do is walk around the corner of that curtain right into the arms of the audience. Look at that smile.

The point is made blatantly but nevertheless made. America is lonely, her stars are lonely, she is sick from not knowing or being able to accept who she is, sick from an obsessional need for solace. And the very blatancy is poignant. It is as if the sickness of the personality is so pervading that subtleties cannot be coped with and appear to be irrelevant. And as if it isn't possible for America to have a private life while the public life is so cancerous. Again from *Tommy Allen*:

> I've got to get to the post office. They's been sending me yellow messages, and I don't like it. They want me to come in there and sign up, and then they'll know what my signature looks like. When I get there they'll arrest me. There's one letter I'm interested in though. It has postage due of twenty-five cents. A big fat letter. A big fat letter that means somebody loves me.

The private life is threatened either by paranoia, which drives it further into a kind of empty privacy, or drives it into the arms of officialdom where, seeking a fat love letter, it will have its life arrested.

The early transformation plays, e.g. *Calm Down Mother*, which were inspired by and developed with the Open Theatre, also militate against a private world. The nature of the transformation play is that people and situations are rapidly transformed into other people and situations, that no private residue of character is allowed to accumulate, that people as function, people as symbol of certain American conditions wipe out all possibilities of people as people. Certain quivering traits are exposed and then through a magical twist they become other traits.

The plays have a certain business, a certain raucousness that seems to echo the need of the characters, e.g. Tommy Allen, not to be alone with self. The air is like a perpetually self-charging circus, things are constantly in motion, tremors and little explosions are constantly taking place or are constantly about to take place. Again it is as if the public life will not allow the private life a little peace to become itself.

And we come to *Approaching Simone*, and a breakthrough for Terry. For in this tribute to the life of the French philosopher, Simone Weil, Terry finally confronts a private life which is tremulously charged with character. Weil is constantly challenging herself, looking into her life, tearing at herself in the fight to become a better, more responsible being. Here is no victim but an existential heroine who is making her life through moral and intellectual bravery, through harrowing insights she refuses not to see. She wants to see deeper and in seeing deeper use her life for the good of humanity. And appropriately, the play slows down the quivering business that is so much a part of Terry's earlier work, slows down significantly. For she is looking into a breathing life, not a symbol, into a courageous being, not a victim, and the richness of this challenging being demands a new measure of tranquility.

—Arthur Sainer

TERSON, Peter. Pseudonym for Peter Patterson.   British.   Born in Newcastle upon Tyne, 24 February 1932. Educated at Heaton Grammar School; Newcastle upon Tyne Technical College; Bristol Training College, 1952–54. Served in the Royal Air Force, 1950–52. Married; has children. Worked as a games teacher for ten years. Associated with the Victoria Theatre, Stoke on Trent, and the National Youth Theatre. Recipient: Arts Council bursary, 1966; John Whiting Award, 1967; Writers Guild of Great Britain award, 1971. Agent: Margaret Ramsay Ltd., 14a Goodwin's Court, London WC2N 4LL, England.

PUBLICATIONS

Plays

    A Night to Make the Angels Weep (produced Stoke on Trent, 1964; London, 1971).
       Published in *New English Dramatists 11*, London, Penguin, 1967.
    The Mighty Reservoy (produced Stoke on Trent, 1964; London, 1967).   Published in
       New English Dramatists 14, London, Penguin, 1970.
    The Rat Run (produced Stoke on Trent, 1965).

All Honour Mr. Todd (produced Stoke on Trent, 1966).

I'm in Charge of These Ruins (produced Stoke on Trent, 1966).

Sing an Arful Story, with others (produced Stoke on Trent, 1966).

Jock-on-the-Go, adaptation of the story "Jock-at-a-Venture" by Arnold Bennett (produced Stoke on Trent, 1966).

Holder Dying (extracts produced Stoke on Trent, 1966).

Mooney and His Caravans (televised, 1966; produced London, 1968). Included in *Zigger Zagger and Mooney and His Caravans*, 1970.

Zigger Zagger (produced London, 1967). Included in *Zigger Zagger and Mooney and His Caravans*, 1970.

Clayhanger, with Joyce Cheeseman, adaptation of the novel by Arnold Bennett (produced Stoke on Trent, 1967).

The Ballad of the Artificial Mash (produced Stoke on Trent, 1967).

The Apprentices (produced London, 1968). London, Penguin, 1970.

The Adventures of Gervase Beckett; or, The Man Who Changed Places (produced Stoke on Trent 1969). Edited by Peter Cheeseman, London, Eyre Methuen, 1973.

Fuzz (produced London, 1969).

Inside-Outside (produced Nottingham, 1970).

Zigger Zagger, and Mooney and His Caravans. London, Penguin, 1970.

The Affair at Bennett's Hill, (Worcs.) (produced Stoke on Trent, 1970).

Spring-Heeled Jack (produced London, 1970). Published in *Plays and Players* (London), November 1970.

The 1861 Whitby Lifeboat Disaster (produced Stoke on Trent and London, 1971).

The Samaritan, with Mike Butler (produced Stoke on Trent and London, 1971). Published in *Plays and Players* (London), July 1971.

Cadium Firty (produced London, 1971).

Good Lads at Heart (produced London, 1971).

Slip Road Wedding (produced Newcastle upon Tyne and London, 1971).

Prisoners of the War (produced Newcastle upon Tyne, 1971).

But Fred, Freud Is Dead (produced Stoke on Trent, 1972). Published in *Plays and Players* (London), March 1972.

Moby Dick (produced Stoke on Trent, 1972).

The Most Cheerful Man (produced Stoke on Trent, 1973).

Geordie's March (produced London, 1973).

The Trip to Florence (produced London, 1974).

Lost Yer Tongue? (produced Newcastle upon Tyne, 1974).

Vince Lays the Carpet, and Fred Erects the Tent (produced Stoke on Trent, 1975).

The Ballad of Ben Bagot, in *Prompt Two*, edited by Alan Durband. London, Hutchinson, 1976.

Love Us and Leave Us, with Paul Joyce (produced London, 1976).

The Bread and Butter Trade (produced London, 1976).

Radio Play: *The Fishing Party*, 1971.

Television Plays: *Mooney and His Caravans*, 1966; *The Heroism of Thomas Chadwick*, 1967; *The Last Train Through the Harecastle Tunnel*, 1969; *The Gregorian Chant*, 1972; *The Dividing Fence*, 1972; *Shakespeare – or Bust*, 1973; *Three for the Fancy*, 1973; *Dancing in the Dark*, 1974; *The Rough and the Smooth*, 1975; *The Jolly Swagman*, with Paul Joyce (*Crown Court* series), 1976.

*   *   *

Peter Terson has been called a "primitive," a term which (in its complimentary sense) is intended to mean that his technique is artless, his observation fresh and original and his naturally prolific talents untainted by too much sophistication. This somewhat backhanded tribute, however, belittles his ability. Few dramatists have the sheer skill to write successfully for both the small "in the round" theatre company at the Victoria, Stoke on Trent, and the large casts of the British National Youth Theatre, whose London productions take place in conventional proscenium arch theatres. Nor is Terson unknowledgeable about current trends in the theatre. He insisted, for example, that Harry Philton in *Zigger Zagger*, the boy who escapes from the mindless enthusiasms of a football crowd to learn a trade, should not "mature or have a *Roots*-like vision of himself" – thus pushing aside one cliché of contemporary naturalistic drama. One under-rated aspect of Terson's style is the way in which he either avoids an idea which has become too fashionable or twists it to his own ends. In *The Mighty Reservoy*, he plays with the Lawrentian theme of the dark, elemental forces of nature and makes it seem both credible as a psychological obsession and (through this haunting power over the mind) a force indeed to be feared. Terson is however ruthless with the pretentiousness of middle-class theatre: on receiving a Promising Playwright's Award from Lord Goodman, he enquired whether Green Shield stamps went with it. This latent cheekiness is also part of his plays. Although he rarely ventures into the class polemic of some of Plater's documentaries, he usually caricatures people in authority: magistrates and social workers (in *Zigger Zagger*), scientists and business tycoons (in *The Ballad of the Artificial Mash*) and the paternalistic firm (in *The Apprentices*). He chooses working-class rather than middle-class, themes and environments: and writes with particular passion about his own childhood in Newcastle upon Tyne, the poverty and unemployment of the 1930's. This refusal to accept the normal attitudes of the West End, his strong regional loyalties, may help to account for his reputation as a "primitive": but for this very reason the term is misleading. He doesn't write popular West End comedies because he doesn't choose to do so; he doesn't write about middle-class families in the grip of emotional dilemmas because the problems which he tackles seem to him more important. He is a highly skilled writer with a particular insight into Northern working class societies and whose plays have, at best, a richness of imagination and an infectious humour.

Terson's first plays were produced at the Victoria Theatre, Stoke on Trent, a pioneering Midlands company directed by Peter Cheeseman whose work concentrates on "in the round" productions, on plays with local associations and documentary plays. Terson caught immediately the company style and became their resident playwright in 1966. His first plays, *A Night to Make the Angels Weep* and *The Mighty Reservoy*, were naturalistic comedies, but with strong underlying themes. *The Mighty Reservoy* is set in the Cotswolds, on a large reservoir built on a hill, which is guarded by Dron. The reservoir is presented as a passionate force of water, which might at any time swamp the surrounding villages. Dron has an affectionate pride towards it: and he introduces his friend Church to its mysteries, among them that the water demands one human sacrifice before it will be satisfied. Church eventually becomes this sacrifice. But the dialogue between the two men ranges from intimate, slightly drunken chat about their dissatisfactions about life to a passionate yearning for union with nature. *Mooney and His Caravans*, another two-person play written for the Victoria Theatre represents a different type of "drowning": a couple on a caravan site are gradually driven away from their home by the aggressive commercialism of Mooney, whom they admire and who owns the site. With these small cast, tightly-knit naturalistic plays, Terson also wrote several looser, more flexible and easy-going works, such as *Jock-on-the-Go*, a picaresque tale about a lad on the make in nineteenth-century Yorkshire, and *The Ballad of the Artificial Mash*, a horror story about the effect of hormone poultry foods on a salesman, one of the first and most effective plays about environmental pollution. Both these plays were in the style of the Stoke documentaries: short scenes, mainly satirical, brought together by songs and dances written and performed by the company. Although Terson left the Victoria Theatre in 1967, the influence of its informal atmosphere, the economy of means and the easiness of story-telling (using a narrator and props to indicate change of locale) remained with Terson as a formative inspiration. He has since written other plays for the company, including *But Fred, Freud Is Dead*, an amusing Northern comedy.

In 1966, Michael Croft, the director of the National Youth Theatre, invited Terson to write a play for his largely amateur group of schoolchildren and young adults. Terson's first play for the company, *Zigger Zagger*, was enormously successful, although its story seems flimsy and episodic. Harry Philton leaves school without distinction, and drifts from one job to another, from his unhappy home to his well-intentioned brother-in-law, sustained at first by his love of football. Eventually however this craze for football leaves him and he settles down to a proper apprenticeship to a trade. Terson sets this story against a background of a football terrace, with fans whose songs and attitudes comment on the main events of the story. The exuberance of the production, the nostalgia and fervour of the football crowds provided an unforgettable image of surging humanity, charged with a youthful energy which only heightened the sad frustrations of Harry's career. *The Apprentices* tackled a somewhat similar theme, but more naturalistically. Bagley, a young tearaway, works reluctantly in a local factory – playing football whenever he has the opportunity. He deliberately scorns all opportunities for promotion, determined to leave the town and his job as soon as he can: but he is trapped into an unwise marriage and at the end of the play, he is resigned to a dull frustrating future. *Spring-Heeled Jack* and *Good Lads at Heart*, two other plays written for the National Youth Theatre, explore the frustrations of the misfits in an impoverished society.

Although Terson's plays have a much greater variety and range than is often supposed, he usually limits himself to social surroundings with which he is familiar: and perhaps the least satisfactory part of this limitation is that he shares some stock reactions, say, about the awfulness of progress and the craftsmanship of the past which are expressed rather too often in his plays. He also fails to pare down his documentary plays to the dramatic essentials. But his influence in British regional theatre has been considerable and more than any other contemporary dramatist he carries forward the ideas of social drama pioneered by Joan Littlewood in the past.

—John Elsom

THOMAS, Gwyn.   British.   Born in Porth, Rhondda, Wales, 6 July 1913. Educated at Porth Grammar School; St. Edmund Hall, Oxford, B.A. (honours) 1934; University of Madrid. Married Eiluned Thomas in 1938. University Extension Lecturer, 1934–40; schoolmaster in modern languages, 1940–62. Recipient: *Evening Standard* award, 1961. Agent: Curtis Brown Ltd., 1 Craven Hill, London W2 3EW, England. Address: Cherry Trees, Pwll-y-Min Crescent, Wyndham Park, Peterston-Super-Ely, Cardiff CF5 6LR, Wales.

PUBLICATIONS

Plays

> *The Keep* (produced London, 1960).   London, Elek, 1962.
> *Loud Organs* (produced Blackpool, 1962).
> *Jackie the Jumper* (produced London, 1963).   Published in *Plays of the Year 26*, London, Elek, 1963.
> *The Loot*, in *Eight Plays: Book 2*, edited by Malcolm Stuart Fellows.   London, Cassell, 1965.
> *The Councillor* (produced London, 1972).
> *Sap* (produced Cardiff, 1974.

Radio Plays: *Gazooka*, 1952; *Forenoon*, 1953; *The Deep Sweet Roots*, 1953; *The Singers of Meadow Prospect*, 1954; *Vive L'Oompa*, 1955; *Up the Handling Code*, 1955; *To This One Place*, 1956; *Merlin's Brow*, 1957; *The Long Run*, 1958; *Noise*, 1960; *The Walk-Out*, 1963; *The Entrance*, 1964; *The Alderman*, 1966; *The Giving Time*, 1968; *He Knows, He Knows*, 1972; *The Worriers*, 1974.

Television Plays: *The Slip*, 1962; *The Dig*, 1963; *Up and Under*, 1974; *The Ghost of Adelphi Terrace*, 1975.

Novels

The Dark Philosophers, in *Triad One*, edited by Jack Aistrop.   London, Dobson, 1946; published separately, Boston, Little Brown, 1947.
The Alone to the Alone.   London, Nicholson and Watson, 1947; as *Venus and the Voters*, Boston, Little Brown, 1948.
All Things Betray Thee.   London, Joseph, 1949; as *Leaves in the Wind*, Boston, Little Brown, 1949.
The World Cannot Hear You: A Comedy of Ancient Desires.   London, Gollancz, 1951; Boston, Little Brown, 1952.
Now Lead Us Home.   London, Gollancz, 1952.
A Frost on My Frolic   London, Gollancz, 1953.
The Stranger at My Side.   London, Gollancz, 1954.
A Point of Order.   London, Gollancz, 1956.
The Love Man.   London, Gollancz, 1958; as *A Wolf at Dusk*, New York, Macmillan, 1959.
The Sky of Our Lives.   London, Hutchinson, 1972.

Short Stories

Where Did I Put My Pity? Short Stories.   London, Progress Publishing Company, 1946.
Gazooka and Other Stories.   London, Gollancz, 1957.
Ring Delirium 123.   London, Gollancz, 1960.
The Lust Lobby: Stories.   London, Hutchinson, 1971.

Other

A Welsh Eye.   London, Hutchinson, 1964; Brattleboro, Vermont, Greene Press, 1965.
A Few Selected Exits: An Autobiography of Sorts.   London, Hutchinson, and Boston, Little Brown, 1968.

*   *   *

The world of Gwyn Thomas is inhabited by exploiters and exploited. The exploited are not simply people at the mercy of a pathetic weakness in their economic position, though poverty and unemployment weaken their ability to resist those whose aim is to make use of them; they lack a special ingredient, the combination of ruthless ambition with unimaginative humourlessness which makes it possible for exploiters to make life intolerable for their fellows. The power to exploit comes from a sad poverty of spirit. Everything Thomas has written presents some aspect of the powerlessness of those who are open to life and emotion when attacked by grey-spirited people who, in the name of capitalist finance, efficiency, organisation or Puritan religion, are determined to take the colour out of life and harness other people to the service of their mean ideals.

These concerns seem to belong naturally to a writer born into industrial South Wales and growing up in the Great Depression of the 1930's. So, too, does Thomas's wild adoration of language and the things it can do. The preface to *The Keep*, the first of his stage plays, mentions his uncertainty about the nationality of his *dramatis personae*, but no one else can doubt their complete Welshness; these people have the natural eloquence, the care for words, the belief in education as the was of escape from industrial oppression, the inherited strain of religious revivalism and an inborn fantasy – qualities which reveal their nationality. Their humour, like their creator's, is the defensive derision of the underdog, and it is lifted into fantastic absurdity by its delight in verbal elaboration; Thomas, it may be, develops the Welsh literary tradition by submitting to it the vocabularies of psychology, sociology and politics.

Obviously, even when in *Jackie the Jumper* he writes about Wales in the 1830's or thereabouts, when the spoliation of the Rhondda Valley was only beginning, Thomas is a Welsh writer by nature, not by any desire to restrict his attention to his native land. In his work, his nation, his people and their problems epitomise the problems of industrial society, and he considers these problems in the accent and style of a Welsh tradition; Welshness is, so to speak, incidental but not irrelevant. *Sap*, produced in Cardiff in 1974, remains a hope for the future in which Thomas's vivid hilarity and social passion will not have lost its point.

The struggle in which all his writing – plays and novels alike – is rooted is not the class war or the combat of socialism against capitalism; it is the struggle of the life-enhancers against the life-deniers. In the nature of things the life-deniers – the exploiters, the bosses, the preachers of hell-fire – are almost sure to win; the people who achieve worldly success do so because their minds are too cramped and their spirits too poverty-stricken to enjoy excitement, fun, sensual pleasure, endless speculative talk and the day-dreams which come to the rich in mind to make them richer. Jackie Rees, "Jackie the Jumper," is not the political or theological enemy of his uncle, the Reverend Richie Rees, who preaches restraint, discipline, obedience and raw revivalism with an inextinguishable celtic fervour; his is not the political enemy of the English iron-master, who knows himself to be as hopelessly trapped as any of his workers; he has no doctrinaire answer to the Sheriff and the Colonel who impose an alien, English authority on his homeland. He is against them because they oppose ease, friendliness, liberty and the warmth of the sensual life. Only his preacher uncle bothers about his libertinage as an affront to conventional morality, for Jackie is the great lover, the totally irresponsible preacher of wine, women and song as facets of the naturally good; the others object to him only because people cannot devote their lives to pleasure and at the same time make money for themselves and their masters. Granted a little time in which to organise his Utopia, Jackie rules with a quaint poetic justice. He believes that, without political authority, such people can say and do what is natural to them without becoming more than figures of fun. He is wrong: their concentration on what he believes to be worthless gives them the power to destroy him and his dream world.

Jackie the Jumper was Thomas's conscious effort, so his preface declares, to get away from the proletarian, industrial world symbolised by the chip shop run by a philosophical Italian exile; it attempts to force an entry into the emotional freedom and melodrama of Verdian opera; it asks for song, dancing and symbolic movement. For all its eloquence, it does not meet the audience with the same impact as *The Keep* and the less ambitious radio and television plays which belong to the contemporary world. *The Keep* is one of the funniest plays ever to send its audience home in a mood of gentle melancholy. The Morton family – five brothers, their father and their sister – live under the domination of Con, the second brother. The eldest son is an ardent trades unionist, the third a schoolmaster who once wrote a successful novel, the fourth a doctor, and the fifth, a pathetically neurotic young man, is a railway station ticket office clerk but also conductor of a male voice choir. The play chronicles the rise of Con, a local government official, from the day on which he belatedly qualifies as a solicitor and future Town Clerk to the day on which his *hubris* is punished and his brothers, who have accepted his dreams of glory, fall with him. The family is united only by its devotion to the mother whom they believe to have been killed in a railway accident. Con's fall coincides with the discovery that she had used the railway accident as a way of escape from them all. Apart from the sad complexities of its theme, every line of *The Keep* is a comic delight, bursting into ridiculous imagery or fantastications of the obvious. To these people, there is no such thing as a plain statement; every thought in their minds is accompanied by a multitude of conditions and implications, most of them self-mocking. The play is a continuous verbal fireworks display.

The Keep is Thomas at his most individual. *Loud Organs* is like *Jackie the Jumper* in its attempt to reject the naturalism that *The Keep* transfigures. But the radio and television pieces succeed. In *Gazooka*, the unemployed form a gazooka band as an effort in self-help to which even the stalwart intellectuals of the Working Men's Institute adhere. Occasionally, as in *The Slip*, the exploiters are defeated by sheer obstinate refusal to submit to interference. In *The Walk-Out* (which contains some of Thomas's richest, most absurd eloquence) a tyrannical headmaster is brought low by the spontaneous departure of his scholars from the building he rules.

—Henry Raynor

TRAVERS, Ben. British   Born in Hendon, London, 12 November 1886. Educated at the Abbey School, Beckenham, Surrey; Charterhouse, Surrey. Served in the Royal Naval Air Service, 1914–17: Squadron Commander; transferred to the Royal Air Force as Major, 1918: Decorated with the Air Force Cross, 1920; rejoined the Royal Air Force in 1939: Squadron Leader, 1940. Married Violet Mouncey in 1916 (died, 1951); has three children. Prime Warden of the Fishmongers Company, 1946. President, Dramatists Club, 1956–60. Recipient: *Evening Standard* award, 1976. C.B.E. (Commander, Order of the British Empire), 1976. Agent: Spokesmen, 1 Craven Hill, London W2 3EW; or, Robin Dalton, 11 Hanover Street, London W.1. Address: Flat 3C, Artillery Mansions, 75 Victoria Street, London SW1H 0HZ, England.

PUBLICATIONS

Plays

> *The Dippers*, adaptation of his own novel (produced Liverpool and London, 1922).
> *The Three Graces*, adaptation of the play by Carl Lombardi and A. M. Willner, music by Franz Lehar (produced London, 1924).
> *A Cuckoo in the Nest*, adaptation of his own novel (produced Liverpool and London, 1925).   London, Bickers, 1939.
> *Rookery Nook*, adaptation of his own novel (produced London, 1926).   London, Bickers, 1930.
> *Thark* (produced Southsea and London, 1927; New York, 1950).   London, Bickers, 1932.
> *Mischief*, adaptation of his own novel (produced London, 1928).
> *Plunder* (produced London, 1928).   London, Bickers, 1931.
> *A Cup of Kindness* (produced London, 1929).   London, Bickers, 1934.
> *A Night Like This* (produced London, 1930).
> *Turkey Time* (produced London, 1931).   London, Bickers, 1934.
> *Dirty Work* (produced London, 1932).

A Bit of a Test (produced London, 1933).
Chastity, My Brother (produced London, 1936).
Nun's Veiling (as *O Mistress Mine*, produced London, 1936; revised version, as *Nun's Veiling*, produced Bromley, Kent, 1953).   London, French, 1956.
Banana Ridge (produced London, 1938).   London, Bickers, 1939.
Spotted Dick (produced London, 1939).
She Follows Me About (produced Birmingham and London, 1943).   London, French, 1945.
Outrageous Fortune (produced London, 1947).   London, French, 1948.
Runaway Victory (produced Brighton, 1949).
Wild Horses (produced Manchester and London, 1952).   London, French, 1953.
Corker's End (produced Guildford, Surrey, 1968).
The Bed Before Yesterday (produced London, 1975).

Screenplays: *Rookery Nook*, 1930; *A Chance of a Night-Time*, 1931; *Mischief*, 1931; *Plunder*, 1931; *A Cuckoo in the Nest*, 1932; *Thark*, 1932; *A Night Like This*, 1932; *Just My Luck*, 1933; *Turkey Time*, 1933; *Lady in Danger*, 1934; *A Cup of Kindness*, 1934; *Fighting Stock*, 1935; *Stormy Weather*, 1935; *Foreign Affairs*, 1935; *Pot Luck*, 1936; *Dishonour Bright*, 1936; *For Valour*, 1937; *Second Best Bed*, 1937; *Old Iron*, 1938; *Up to the Neck*, 1938; *Uncle Silas*, 1947.

Television Plays: *Potter*, 1948; *Picture Page*, 1949.

Novels

The Dippers.   London and New York, Lane, 1920.
A Cuckoo in the Nest.   London, Lane, 1922; New York, Doubleday, 1925.
Rookery Nook.   London, Lane, 1923.
Mischief.   London, Lane, and New York, Doubleday, 1925.
The Dippers, Together with Game and Rubber and The Dunkum Jane.   London, Lane, 1932.
Hyde Side Up.   London, Lane, 1933.

Short Stories

The Collection Today.   London, Lane, 1929.

Other

Vale of Laughter (autobiography).   London, Bles, 1957.

Editor, *The Leacock Book.*   London, Lane, 1930.
Editor, *Pretty Pictures: Being a Selection of the Best American Pictorial Humour.* London, Lane, 1932.

*   *   *

Of three great writers of farce, the Englishman Arthur Wing Pinero had a few concentrated and fruitful years during the 1880's; the Frenchman Georges Feydeau wrote throughout his life; and the Englishman Ben Travers, coming to the theatre relatively late after success as a novelist − he had worked in a publisher's office − produced a line of plays, known now as "the Aldwych farces," within the years between 1925 and 1933. His fame rests upon the Aldwych sequence and upon the parts he created then for an ensemble that has not been matched in this exceedingly difficult form of theatre.

He never liked the Feydeau style which he regarded as mechanical. Always a devoted adherent of Pinero, he believed in founding his plays on a solid and reasonable basis before letting them take off suddenly into an upper air of the most cheerful lunacy. He knew, none better, that farce needs a cracking pace, a fuming last-act rally – no wavering there – and dialogue that, though it snows down in whirling flakes of nonsense, never freezes into the cold glitter of epigram.

Invariably he insisted that his characters, whatever maze they might find themselves in, should be immediately recognisable, plausible types. Once he had got them into a farcical imbroglio he was as verbally inventive as Pinero had been. He seldom troubled to tie up the ends of his plays artificially. A good farce, he thought, should simply stop. So we have the end of *Thark* – the title of this is the name of a haunted manor-house in Norfolk – in which curtains are blown across the room, there is a violent thunderclap, blankets and quilts fly off the bed, a great portrait topples from the mantlepiece, and the curtain falls to the furious beating of a gong. When it rises again for the curtain call an immense tree-branch has fallen through the window and on the stage the full cast has somehow assembled.

The famous run of farces opened with *A Cuckoo in the Nest*, Traver's own version of his novel about the mistakes of a night in a Somerset inn. (He was then living in the West Country himself.) The parts he wrote for such players of his period as Ralph Lynn, Tom Walls, and Yvonne Arnaud – though she was in only one Aldwych farce – have proved eminently durable in revivals by other companies. They are durable because Travers has a sharply visual sense. At the Aldwych he knew exactly how his characters would look when he had suitably tangled them, and he could offer the kind of dialogue to match their embarrassments: the farce of situation fortified by a steady verbal cross-fire.

This dialogue may not often look much on paper; but it has been tested steadily in performance. Observe only that prelude to the haunted-bedroom scene in *Thark* where the sinister butler, who admits that his name is Death, brings the last post, tells a waiting manservant that he will follow with the sheets, and inquires when the gentlemen would like their call.

Travers has never failed to go on like this. Though we are far now from the old Aldwych – and of his famous company few survive – playgoers continue, as a critic has said, to laugh at his knowledge of the art of gibbering. No dramatist in our day has gibbered to so much effect. True, he was lucky to have the quicksilver response of that flickering zany Ralph Lynn, the ruthless timing of Tom Walls, Mary Brough in unquenchable ire, and Robertson Hare as a sepulchral bittern; but all of them testified to the quality of the Travers scripts, his constant attention (something he had learned from Pinero) to the importance of climax.

The plays had such titles as *Rookery Nook, Plunder, A Night Like This*, and *Turkey Time.* All of these were in the Aldwych run, peopled by characters with such names as D'Arcy Tuck, Mrs. Bugle, Toome, and Connie Pepper. But there were other later farces as well, and especially Travers's own favourite, *Banana Ridge*, which he wrote for Robertson Hare and Alfred Drayton. Here Travers himself appeared in London as a Malayan house-boy. He had once worked in Malaya where he read for the first time the plays of Pinero that would have so vigorous an influence on him.

He has not been entirely a writer of farce. In 1936 he wrote (originally it was anonymous) a play about St. Paul called *Chastity, My Brother*; received with some appreciation at a London fringe theatre, the Embassy, in 1936, it got no further, and it still surprises researchers to find it in the Travers list. One cannot blame them, for a dramatist who specialised as he did, and who was labelled irrevocably, was unlikely to get a new public for work so far out of his line. Many-sided though he is, and as his autobiography, *Vale of Laughter*, shows, he will live in stage history as the amplest and gayest of twentieth-century farceurs, the theatre's Lords of Misrule.

Travers always insisted that he wanted to write comedy, as distinct from farce; and in his ninetieth year the veteran had a great London success with *The Bed Before Yesterday*. The play's title was its key. This, Travers said, was something he would have liked to write more than forty years earlier when the Censorship prevented him from doing so. Now, in the "permissive" world of the mid-1970's, he presented a comedy, frank, witty, and civilised, about a mature woman who, for the first time, realised delightedly what sex could be. In its mood, the piece – directed by Lindsay Anderson – was a triumph; Travers went straight from it to a National Theatre revival (January 1976) of one of his central Aldwych farces, *Plunder*. Though he remained our first Lord of Misrule, he was aware now that historians would think of him in another stage dimension.

—J. C. Trewin

TREVOR, William. Pseudonym for William Trevor Cox. Irish. Born in Mitchelstown, County Cork, 24 May 1928. Educated at St. Columba's College, Dublin, 1942–46; Trinity College, Dublin, B.A. 1950. Married Jane Ryan in 1952; has two children. History Teacher, Armagh, Northern Ireland, 1951–53; Art Teacher, Rugby, England, 1953–55. Sculptor, in Somerset, 1955–60. Advertising Copywriter, London, 1960–64. Recipient: *Transatlantic Review* prize, for fiction, 1964; Hawthornden Prize, for fiction, 1965; Society of Authors Travelling Fellowship, 1972; Allied Irish Banks Prize, for fiction 1976; Heinemann Award, for fiction, 1976. Member, Irish Academy of Letters. Address: Stentwood House, Dunkeswell, near Honiton, Devon, England.

PUBLICATIONS

Plays

The Elephant's Foot (produced Nottingham, 1965).
The Girl (televised, 1967; produced London, 1968).
A Night with Mrs. da Tanka (televised, 1968; produced London, 1972).   London, French, 1972.
Going Home (broadcast, 1970; produced London, 1972). London, French, 1972.
The Old Boys, adaptation of his own novel (produced London, 1971).   London, Davis Poynter, 1971.
A Perfect Relationship (broadcast, 1973; produced London, 1973).   London, Burnham House, 1976.
The 57th Saturday (produced London, 1973).
Marriages (produced London, 1973).   London, French, 1974.

Radio Plays: *The Penthouse Apartment*, 1968; *Going Home*, 1970; *The Boarding House*, from his own novel, 1971; *A Perfect Relationship*, 1973; *Scenes from an Album*, 1975.

Television Plays: *The Baby-Sitter*, 1965; *Walk's End*, 1966; *The Girl*, 1967; *A Night with Mrs. da Tanka*, 1968; *The Mark-2 Wife*, 1969; *The Italian Table*, 1970; *The Grass Widows*, 1971; *O Fat White Woman*, 1972; *The Schoolroom*, 1972; *Access to the Children*, 1973; *The General's Day*, 1973; *Miss Fanshawe's Story*, 1973; *An Imaginative Woman*, from story by Thomas Hardy, 1973; *Love Affair*, 1974; *Eleanor*, 1974; *Mrs. Acland's Ghosts*, 1975; *The Statue and the Rose*, 1975; *Two Gentle People*, from story by Graham Greene, 1975; *The Nicest Man in the World*, 1976; *Afternoon Dancing*, 1976.

Novels

A Standard of Behaviour.   London, Hutchinson, 1958.
The Old Boys.   London, Bodley Head, and New York, Viking Press, 1964.
The Boarding House.   London, Bodley Head, and New York, Viking Press, 1965.
The Love Department.   London, Bodley Head, 1966; New York, Viking Press, 1967.
Mrs. Eckdorf in O'Neill's Hotel.   London, Bodley Head, 1969; New York, Viking Press, 1970.
Miss Gomez and the Brethren.   London, Bodley Head, 1971.
Elizabeth Alone.   London, Bodley Head, 1973; New York, Viking Press, 1974.
The Children of Dynmouth.   London, Bodley Head, 1976.

Short Stories

The Day We Got Drunk on Cake and Other Stories.   London, Bodley Head, 1967; New York, Viking Press, 1968.
Penguin Modern Stories 8, with others.   London, Penguin, 1971.
The Ballroom of Romance and Other Stories.   London, Bodley Head, and New York, Viking Press, 1972.
The Last Lunch of the Season.   London, Covent Garden Press, 1973.
Angels at the Ritz and Other Stories.   London, Bodley Head, 1975; New York, Viking Press, 1976.

*   *   *

A successful novelist and prolific television and radio dramatist before turning in any real measure towards the theatre, William Trevor has been somewhat unlucky in his career as far as his full-length plays are concerned. *The Elephant's Foot* closed during its prior-to-London tour, and *The Old Boys* had a particularly unfortunate opening in London with its star's first-night nerves hindering the flow of a play whose full effect depended on the subtleties of its verbal nuances; and although the central performance improved immeasurably during its original limited Mermaid Theatre run and throughout a subsequent provincial tour, sadly the play did not find a West End theatre.

The Elephant's Foot (along with his early one-acter *The Girl*) represents something of a false start for Trevor. Both reveal his unusual gift for dialogue, particularly that of characters enmeshed in their own sense of failure and for those verging on the sinister or seedy, but both remain somewhat inert, heavily relying as they do on a central situation, of strange intruders entering domestic scenes, itself something of a cliché-situation in the theatre of the early 1960's. In *The Girl*, set in suburban London (one of Trevor's favourite locales, both in novels and plays), a mysterious teenage girl descends on the Green household, convincingly claiming to be Mr. Green's daughter, the result of a single drunken escapade with a prostitute. Her arrival, not surprisingly, divides the family, until it is revealed, with the near-curtain arrival of the girl's violent young friends, that Green is only the latest in a long list of the prostitute mother's clients, to be descended on and terrorised in turn by the loutish teenage gang. It is adroit and suspenseful enough to sustain its length, although the ghost of Pinter looms heavily over the play, even to some extent over the dialogue, particularly in the opening sections between the Green family, laden with pauses and the reiteration of the clichés of suburban small-talk. *The Elephant's Foot* is similarly burdened with a top-heavy plot and reliance on a closing "surprise"; an elderly couple, Colonel and Mrs. Pocock, who live apart except for their Christmas reunion with their twin children, in the midst of preparing their Christmas meal are invaded by the bizarre stranger Freer (first-cousin to the splendid con-man Swingler in *The Old Boys*) and his mute associate Tiger. Freer gradually unsettles the Pococks, frightening them by anticipating the non-arrival of their children, but the fails to insinuate Tiger into the household in the twins' place and the play closes with the

Pococks again alone preparing to reassume their old domestic battle. After a promising opening, with a very funny verbal tussle between the Pococks over the unfortunate selection of the Christmas brussels sprouts, the play collapses in the second act, only sustaining itself to the final curtain by resorting to coincidence and unconvincing metaphysical overtones. Nevertheless, *The Elephant's Foot* revealed that Trevor was capable of an individual dramatic verbal style (which his early novels, largely in dialogue, had pointed towards), a stylized counterpointing of the colloquial with the rhetorical which owes a little to Ivy Compton-Burnett but essentially remains very much his own.

This was further developed in *The Old Boys*, his own adaptation of his Hawthornden Prize-winning novel of the same name, which revealed too Trevor's special understanding of elderly characters, particularly in those scenes set in a London residential hotel populated entirely by old boys of the same minor public-school and tyrannised over by a dragoness of a Matron-surrogate. In its study of an old schoolboy rivalry extending from out of the past to influence a struggle over the presidency of the Old Boys' Association, the play is by turns hilarious and deeply touching, although the first act never satisfactorily solves some problems of construction in the adaptation-process. But the climactic scene as old Mr. Jaraby at last realises the futility of his grudges and ambitions and, now a widower preparing to join the other old men at the Rimini Hotel, launches into a speech of life-affirming anarchy at the expense of the bullying proprietrix, stands as one of Trevor's finest achievements. No full-length play has appeared since *The Old Boys*, but in recent years Trevor has enjoyed considerable success on the London lunchtime-theatre circuit, mainly with one-act plays often adapted from previous television and radio plays or from short stories. Most of these are acutely-observed and tightly written duologues between different kinds of victim – the lonely, deserted or repressed characters Trevor reveals so compassionately. Some of these, such as *A Night with Mrs. da Tanka*, a hotel-encounter between a sad drunken divorcée and a shy bachelor, suffer in the transition to the stage and seem curiously artificial, but the best of them, especially *Going Home*, in which a precocious schoolboy and a spinster Assistant Matron, travelling in a train-compartment together for the holidays, painfully realise their mutual loneliness, capture moments of crisis in their characters' lives and give them a genuine life on stage beyond the confines of the original medium from which they were adapted. Likewise, some of the best scenes in *The Old Boys* are those not in or most freely adapted from the original novel; hopefully before long Trevor may emerge with a new full-length play original in all senses of the word.

—Alan Strachan

TSEGAYE GABRE-MEDHIN.   Ethiopian.   Born in Boda, Showa, 17 August 1936. Educated at Zema and Kine Ethiopian Orthodox Church Schools, 1945–48; Ambo Elementary School; General Wingate and Commercial Secondary Schools, 1952–56; Blackstone School of Law, Chicago, LL.B. 1959. Married Laketch Bitew in 1961; has two daughters. Studied British theatre at the Royal Court Theatre, London, and French theatre at the Comédie Française, Paris, 1959–60. Director, Haile Selassie I National Theatre, Addis Ababa, 1961–71. Editor, Oxford University Press, Addis Ababa. Since 1971, Research Fellow, University of Dakar, Senegal. Art Adviser to the Haile Selassie I National Theatre, to the Fine Arts Department of the Ministry of Education, and to the Creative Arts Centre, Haile Selassie I University. General Manager, Ethiopian National Theatre. Permanent Secretary, Ministry of Culture, Sports, and Youth Affairs. Delegate to the First World Negro Arts Festival, Dakar, 1964; the Afro-Scandinavian Cultural Conference, Copenhagen, 1967; the International Poets Night, Belgrade, 1968; the First Pan-African Cultural Festival, Algiers,

1969; the Afro-European Dialogue, Rome, 1969; the African Studies Association Meeting, Denver, 1971; and African Ministers of Culture Meeting, Addis Ababa, 1976. Government Guest at the Republic Day of Tanzania, 1964; Independence Day of Kenya, 1964; and in Israel, 1964, the United States, 1965, 1971, West Germany, 1966, U.S.S.R., 1968, France, 1971, Senegal, 1972, and Congo, 1972. Recipient: UNESCO Fellowship, 1959, Haile Selassie I Prize, 1965. Commander of the Senegal National Order, 1972. Address: P.O. Box 1907, Addis Ababa, Ethiopia.

PUBLICATIONS

Plays

    Belg (Autumn) (produced Addis Ababa, 1957).   Addis Ababa, Berhanena Selam, 1962.

    Yeshoh Aklil (Crown of Thorns) (produced Addis Ababa, 1958).   Addis Ababa, Berhanena Selam, 1959.

    Askeyami Lijagered (The Ugly Girl) (produced Addis Ababa, 1959).

    Jorodegif (Mumps) (produced Addis Ababa, 1959).

    Listro (Shoe Shine Boy) (produced Addis Ababa, 1960).

    Igni Biye Metahu (Back with a Grin) (produced Addis Ababa, 1960).

    Chulo (Errand Boy) (produced Addis Ababa, 1961).

    Kosho Cigara (Cheap Cigarettes) (produced Addis Ababa, 1961).

    Yemama Zetegn Melk (Mother's Nine Faces) (produced Addis Ababa, 1961).

    Tewodros (in English; produced Addis Ababa, 1962).   Published in *Ethiopia Observer* (Addis Ababa), 1965.

    Othello, adaptation of the play by Shakespeare.   Addis Ababa, Oxford University Press, 1963.

    Tartuffe, adaptation of the play by Molière (produced Addis Ababa, 1963).

    The Doctor in Spite of Himself, adaptation of the play by Molière (produced Addis Ababa, 1963).

    Oda Oak Oracle: A Legend of Black Peoples, Told of Gods and God, Of Hope and Love, Of Fears and Sacrifices (produced Addis Ababa, 1964).   London and New York, Oxford University Press, 1964.

    Azmari (in English; produced Addis Ababa, 1964).   Published in *Ethiopia Observer* (Addis Ababa), 1965.

    Yekermo Sew (The Seasoned) (produced Addis Ababa, 1966).   Addis Ababa, Berhanena Selam, 1967.

    King Lear, adaptation of the play by Shakespeare (produced in part, Addis Ababa, 1968).

    Kirar Siker (Kirar Tight-Tuned) (produced Addis Ababa, 1969).

    The Cry of Petros at the Hour (produced Addis Ababa, 1969).

    Macbeth, adaptation of the play by Shakespeare.   Addis Ababa, Oxford University Press, 1972.

    Hamlet, adaptation of the play by Shakespeare.   Addis Ababa, Oxford University Press, 1972.

    Ha Hu Besidist Wer (A-B-C in Six Months) (produced Addis Ababa, 1974). Addis Ababa, Berhanena Selam, 1975.

    Enat Alem Tenu (Mother Courage), adaption of the play by Brecht (produced Addis Ababa, 1975).   Addis Ababa, Berhanena Selam, 1975.

    Atsim Beyegetsu (Skeleton in Pages) (produced Addis Ababa, 1975).

    Collision of Altars.   London, Rex Collings, 1976.

Theatrical Activities:

    Director: **Plays** – almost all the above plays and others.

Tsegaye Gabre-Medhin comments:

I do not think in English or French but in Ethiopian first. My cultural personality is formed out of a background which consciously resists being re-created in the image of any and all supremacist alien values. I write for a people who for many thousands of years have developed a conscious taste for their own poetic heritage, in one of their own scripts, and in one of their own indigenous languages. In the literature of one of the children of Kam: of Meroe, of Nubia, of Egypt, of Ethiopia – of the cradles of the world's earliest civilization. The people are still the judges of my plays which mirror them. They are still the critics of the poetry and culture that make them, and which in turn they themselves make.

If for instance a British poet *naturally* felt hard put to think or dream his verse in Chinese it is because (a) Chinese is not the natural expression of British culture, (b) Chinese literature forms the Chinese personality, makes and develops first a Chinese universal man and not first a Briton or a British personality, and (c) the said British poet is not yet re-created in the image of the Chinese. Can any African artist-poet or playwright (unless of course his culture is already killed in him and replaced by something else) afford to think or dream his verse in anything less than what is his indigenous African expression FIRST? Just like *no* Chinese literature can make a truly British culture, so there is *no* English, French, Dutch or Portuguese, etc., literature which can make a truly African culture.

*   *   *

Tsegaye Gabre-Medhin has written plays in Amharic, and written and directed Amharic versions of *Othello, Macbeth, Hamlet, Tartuffe,* and *The Imaginary Invalid.* In the three plays he has written in English, both the phrasing and the poetic conception suggest that he is experimenting with the transferral into English of devices alien to it. For instance, in *Oda Oak Oracle,* Goaa has this speech:

> It is not easy, Ukutee.
> To speak
> Of the gloomy path
> Of a lone walker.
> Loneliness is
> When the ripe fruit fails,
> To make the bird
> Aware of its existence.
> Loneliness is
> When the avoided heart,
> Growing stale every night,
> Wears a mask of bitterness,
> While the tense veins
> Growing frantic and mad
> Scratch at the mask
> Of a stricken heart.
> Loneliness is
> When the aged mule
> Rubs its flank
> Against the deserted trunk
> Of a dead bush.
> Loneliness is
> When the moon is left cold
> Among a glowing
> Jungle of stars.

The richness of elaboration and repetition, together with heavy rhetoric and (in two of the three plays) musical accompaniment, contributes to florid, torrid melodrama.

Only *Oda Oak Oracle* is easily available in English. The oracle has decreed marriage between Shanka and Ukutee, and the sacrifice of their first-born to the ancestors. To avoid this, Shanka refuses to consummate the marriage. In humiliation and frustration she offers herself to Shanka's friend, Goaa. He brings to the play the perspective of another society, for he had once been taken away by strangers and instructed by them in the Gospel. His criticism of the oracle and traditional beliefs feeds Shanka's doubts. By the last act Ukutee is in labour. Cloud darkens the valley and there is perturbation among the elders at the lack of sun. The oracle commands a combat between Goaa and Shanka, the victor to be flogged from the valley by Ukutee. Goaa is killed and Ukutee consents to whip out Shanka because the oracle has promised that she will then bear a fine son. In fact, she dies giving birth to a daughter and the play ends with Shanka holding the child as a mob approaches to stone both of them to death.

This doom-laden play Albert Gerard, in his *Four African Literatures* (1971), finds to be "one of the finest plays to have been written in Africa." Personally, I find the extremely short lines awkward and their divisions of little help to the speaker; moreover the climax of the play seems to pile up punishments over-ingeniously.

More interesting, I believe, are two plays which appeared in a 1965 issue of the *Ethiopia Observer*. *Tewodros* is an account of a mid-nineteenth century purgative dealer's son who rose to be Emperor. He had a vision of uniting Ethiopia, but his rule was troubled by various revolts and ended by British invasion. Showing both concern for the welfare of the common people and bloody ruthlessness, Tewodros is an ambiguous figure, and the interest of Tsegaye's play lies not in his Tamburlaine-like career, but in the doubts expressed by his first and second wives and by others around him:

> Washing my hands in other's blood and watching mine flow out has occupied the best years of my life. The one exciting activity I can remember of my only son is the lashing of his paper sword and his shouting of the war-cry "zeraf"...until finally I heard him repeat the same thing on the battlefield once and for all...then he bled to death in my arms. What has the poor peasant to live for, Princess, if he can't afford to question why his children should sing war songs and not read the Book of Life?

Most successful of his plays, I believe, is *Azmari*. *Azmaris* are professional singers, and female *azmaris* are considered little better than courtesans. Tsegaye's play portrays the tensions in a family, in each generation of which a member is called to be "the expressive medium for Nature's passions" – and so Lulu considers herself. The centre of the play is her clash with her mother, who resents her being "out with that moaning harp of hers day and night, and never lifting a finger to help the family," and maintains that a minstrel's is "no decent folk's way of life." Who is betraying whom, the member of the family who rejects the call of music, or the artist who does not help support it?

Unlike Tsegaye's other plays, *Azmari* has only one violent action, the smashing of her harp. As in Chekhov, the significant action takes place offstage – Lulu has played at the marriage of the man she loved, who has jilted her for a socially acceptable bride – and no resolution is offered. The use of music as an emotional punctuation of the scenes is dramatically relevant. Grandiloquence, too, is used dramatically, for it is set off against the everyday speech of those in the family who refuse music's call.

—Anthony Graham-White

TURNER, David. British. Born in Birmingham, Warwickshire, 18 March 1927. Educated at Moseley Grammar School; Birmingham University, B.A. 1950. Served in an army educational theatre unit, 1945–47. Taught for nine years. Agent: Harvey Unna Ltd., 14 Beaumont Mews, Marylebone High Street, London W1N 4HE, England.

PUBLICATIONS

Plays

The Bedmakers (produced Coventry, 1962).
Semi-Detached (produced Coventry and London, 1962; New York, 1963). London, Heinemann, 1962; New York, Dramatists Play Service, 1964.
Believe It or Not, with Edward J. Mason (produced Coventry, 1962).
Trevor (produced London, 1963).
The Antique Shop (produced Coventry, 1963).
Slap in the Middle, with others (produced Birmingham, 1965).
Bottomley (produced Coventry, 1965).
Way Off Beat (televised, 1966). Published in *Conflicting Generations: Five Television Plays*, edited by Michael Marland, London, Longman, 1968.
The Beggar's Opera, music edited by Benjamin Pearce Higgins, adaptation of the opera by John Gay (produced London, 1968).
The Servant of Two Masters, with Paul Lapworth, music by Benjamin Pearce Higgins, adaptation of the play by Carlo Goldoni (produced London, 1968).
Quick Quick Slow, music and lyrics by Monty Norman and Julian More (produced Birmingham, 1969).
The Prodigal Daughter (produced Colchester, 1973).
The Miser, adaptation of a play by Molière (produced Birmingham, 1973).
The Only True Story of Lady Godiva, with Paul Lapworth (produced Coventry, 1973).
The Girls (produced London, 1975).

Radio Plays: *Grantham's Outing*, 1956; *...And Tomorrow*, 1956; *Change of Plan*, 1957; *Me, Me Dad and His'n*, 1957; *Mind Your Own Business*, 1958; *Family Business*, 1959; *Come Back Jack*, 1959; *Any Other Business*, 1961; *Now More Than Ever*, 1961.

Television Plays and Serializations: *Fresh as Paint*, 1956; *The Train Set* 1961; *Cry from the Depths*, 1961; *The Final Result*, 1961; *On the Boundary*, 1961; *Summer, Autumn, Winter, Spring*, 1961; *Choirboys Unite!*, 1961; *The Chem Lab Mystery*, 1963; *Swizzlewick*, 1964; *This Man Craig* series, 1966; *Way Off Beat*, 1966; *North and South*, from the novel by Mrs. Gaskell, 1966; *Angel Pavement*, from the novel by J. B. Priestley, 1967; *Treasure Island*, from the novel by Robert Louis Stevenson, 1968; *Père Goriot*, from the novel by Balzac, 1968; *Cold Comfort Farm*, from the novel by Stella Gibbons, 1968; *Cambridge Footlights Revue*, 1969; *Olive*, 1970; *Germinal*, from the novel by Zola, 1970; *The Roads to Freedom*, from the novels by Jean-Paul Sartre, 1972; *Daisy* (*The Edwardians* series), 1973; *Neighbours*, 1973; *Father*, 1973; *Requiem for a Crown Prince*, 1974; *Harold*, 1975; *Prometheus*, from the novel by André Maurois, 1975.

*   *   *

David Turner's plays are all firmly rooted in the Midlands, where he lives, and nearly all are closely-observed pictures of lower middle-class life and values. *Semi-Detached* is his best-known play and satirises those values accurately and cruelly. Fred Midway is a middle-aged insurance agent, living with his family in a semi-detached in a Midlands town, absolutely obsessed with his status in life and "what the neighbours think." He imposes these preconceptions with near-disastrous results on his wife Hilda, his son Tom and his daughters Eileen and Avril. Eileen is knocking about with a married man, while Avril's husband, Nigel Hadfield, is in disgrace because he went with a prostitute on his visit to London for a football match.

The play is Jonsonian in almost every particular. The author has an unmitigated loathing and contempt for his characters, whose real-life prototypes he has clearly spent many hours observing, and portrays them as caricatures with a grotesquerie arising from their essential social and individual truth. The names of the characters are a clear guide to their personalities – *Mid*way, *Free*man, Make*piece* – and the plot is beautifully constructed and worked out. The play is also excoriatingly witty and funny; witness lines like Fred's "If only I could have a grandchild who actually went to a Public School" and the behaviour of everyone involved in the row between Avril and Nigel, pretending to be acmes of morality but actually basing their behaviour on the most sordidly commercial considerations.

Bottomley is a portrait of another character from the same social and class background as Midway, this time the real-life Horatio Bottomley, the notorious early twentieth century swindler. Bottomley rises meteorically to fame as a businessman and as a politician. A right-wing populist with a strong appeal to the working-class, not unlike Enoch Powell in some aspects, he comes unstuck only because of his tendency to megalomania. The play convincingly reveals Bottomley within his particular political and social context and, by implication, shows how easy it is for a cunning right-wing demagogue to carve a very powerful niche for himself in our society.

The Bedmakers is a sad picture of an elderly workman, Bill Summers, left behind by the march of technology, unable to adjust himself to the new, more sophisticated demands of society for more trendy goods, geared to a quick obsolescence. He determines to make an old-fashioned iron bed for his grandson and the grandson's wife-to-be, fatally unaware that it will be totally useless to them. Both the bed and Bill end up symbolically on the scrapheap. The play is occasionally moving in the ways it depicts the conflicts between Bill, his family and his bosses (who are keeping him on for sentimental reasons); but overall it is a little too heavy-handed and obvious.

By contrast, *The Antique Shop* is a study in corruption. A successful young shop-owner, Don Newman, is corrupted by his desire for money without really realising the source of his infection. He has three girlfriends in tow and plays off one against the other. Predictably, two of them ditch him and the third, the Jonsonianly-named Judy Trader, only makes a fresh start with him when he inadvertently ruins himself and has to start all over again. The play is an ironic picture of the dehumanising effect of the narrow, commercially-based attitudes of lower middle-class capitalism, which is both witty and pointful.

Come Back Jack, a television play, shows Jack, a lower middle-class man, unsuccessfully struggling to keep his family firm from going bust, hampered by his idle, useless partner, his brother-in-law Donald. Jack married into the family essentially because his shrewd father-in-law realised his potential as a businessman. The basically commercial attitudes of the family towards Jack distort their inter-relationships, twisting Jack's character and desires, so that he spends his life fulfilling their objectives and not his. It is only when an ex-girlfriend forces Jack to face up to the cipher that he has become that he manages to free himself, breaking away from the doomed family firm and starting afresh on a new basis with his wife.

Of his other plays, *The Train Set* is a wry, well-observed study of the relationship between a working-class father and his young son and how it can be affected and twisted by lack of money, while *Quick Quick Slow*, a musical written with Monty Norman and Julian More, is a satirical tilt at the ersatz cultural values, in this case represented by ballroom dancing, brought about by the industrial capitalism of the Midlands.

At his best, David Turner is a keen and truthful observer of the narrowing, repressive effects that the values of modern industrial capitalism have on human beings, and can express them in suitably socially-based styles.

—Jonathan Hammond

USTINOV, Peter (Alexander).   British.   Born in London, 16 April 1921. Educated at Westminster School, London, 1934–37; London Theatre Studio, 1937–39. Served in the Royal Sussex Regiment, Royal Army Ordnance Corps, 1942–46; Army Kinetograph Service, 1943. Married Isolde Denham in 1940 (marriage dissolved, 1950); Susanne Cloutier, 1953 (marriage dissolved, 1971); Helene du Laud-Allemans, 1972; has four children. Co-Director of the Nottingham Playhouse, 1963. Rector, University of Dundee, 1968–73. Goodwill Ambassador, UNICEF, since 1969. Recipient: Golden Globe Award, 1952; New York Drama Critics Circle Award, 1953; *Evening Standard* award, 1956; Benjamin Franklin Medal, 1957; Emmy Award, for acting, three times; Academy Award, for acting, 1961, 1965. D.L.: University of Dundee, 1969; D.M.: Cleveland, 1970; D.F.A.: La Salle University, Philadelphia, 1971; D.Litt.: University of Lancaster, 1972. Fellow, Royal Society of Arts. C.B.E. (Commander, Order of the British Empire), 1975. Agent: Christopher Mann, 140 Park Lane, London W.1, England.

PUBLICATIONS

Plays

The Bishop of Limpopoland (sketch; produced London, 1939).

Sketches in *Diversion* and *Diversion 2* (produced London, 1940, 1941).

Fishing for Shadows, adaptation of a play by Jean Sarment (also director: produced London, 1940).

House of Regrets (produced London, 1942).   London, Cape, 1943.

Beyond (produced London, 1943).   London, English Theatre Guild, 1944; in *Five Plays*, 1965.

Blow Your Own Trumpet (produced Liverpool and London, 1943).   Included in *Plays about People*, 1950.

The Banbury Nose (produced London, 1944).   London, Cape, 1945.

The Tragedy of Good Intentions (produced Liverpool, 1945).   Included in *Plays about People*, 1950.

The Indifferent Shepherd (produced London, 1948).   Included in *Plays about People*, 1950.

Frenzy, adaptation of a play by Ingmar Bergman (also director: produced London, 1948).

The Man in the Raincoat (produced Edinburgh, 1949).

Plays about People (includes *The Tragedy of Good Intentions, Blow Your Own Trumpet, The Indifferent Shepherd*).   London, Cape, 1950.

The Love of Four Colonels (also director: produced Birmingham and London, 1951; New York, 1953).   London, English Theatre Guild, 1951; New York, Dramatists Play Service, 1953.

The Moment of Truth (produced Nottingham and London, 1951).   London, English Theatre Guild, 1953; in *Five Plays*, 1965.

High Balcony (produced London, 1952).

No Sign of the Dove (also director: produced Leeds and London, 1953).   Included in *Five Plays*, 1965.

Romanoff and Juliet (produced Manchester and London, 1956; New York, 1957).   London, English Theatre Guild, 1957; New York, Random House, 1958; revised version, as *R Loves J*, music and lyrics by Alexander Faris and Julian More (produced Chichester, 1973).

The Empty Chair (produced Bristol, 1956).

Paris Not So Gay (produced Oxford, 1958).

Photo Finish: An Adventure in Biography (also director: produced Dublin and London,

1962; New York, 1963).   London, Heinemann, 1962; Boston, Little Brown, 1963.
The Life in My Hands (produced Nottingham, 1963).
Five Plays: Romanoff and Juliet, The Moment of Truth, The Love of Four Colonels,
    Beyond, No Sign of the Dove.   London, Heinemann, and Boston, Little Brown, 1965.
The Unknown Soldier and His Wife: Two Acts of War Separated by a Truce for
    Refreshment (produced New York, 1967; also director: produced Chichester 1968;
    London, 1973).   New York, Random House, 1967; London, Heinemann, 1968.
Halfway up the Tree (produced Germany, 1967; also director: produced New York and
    London, 1967).   New York, Random House, 1968; London, English Theatre Guild,
    1970.
Who's Who in Hell (produced New York, 1974).

Screenplays: *The New Lot* (documentary), 1943; *The Way Ahead*, with Eric Ambler,
1944; *The True Glory*, 1944; *School for Secrets*, 1947; *Vice Versa*, 1947; *Private Angelo*,
1949; *The Secret Flight*, 1952; *School for Scoundrels*, 1960; *Romanoff and Juliet*, 1961;
Billy Budd, with Robert Rossen, 1962; *Lady L.*, 1965; *Hot Millions*, with Ira Wallach,
1968; *Hammersmith Is Out*, 1972.

Radio Plays: *In All Directions* series.

Television Play: *Ustinov ad lib*, 1969.

Novels

The Loser.   London, Heinemann, and Boston, Little Brown, 1961.
Krumnagel.   London, Heinemann, and Boston, Little Brown, 1971.

Short Stories

Add a Dash of Pity: Short Stories.   London, Heinemann, and Boston, Little Brown,
    1959.
The Frontiers of the Sea.   London, Heinemann, and Boston, Little Brown, 1966.

Other

Ustinov's Diplomats: A Book of Photographs.   New York, Geis, 1961.
We Were Only Human (caricatures).   London, Heinemann, and Boston, Little Brown,
    1961.
The Wit of Peter Ustinov, edited by Dick Richards.   London, Frewin, 1969.
Rectorial Address Delivered in the University, 3rd November 1972.   Dundee,
    University of Dundee Press, 1972.

Bibliographies: *Peter Ustinov* by Geoffrey Willans, London, Peter Owen, 1958; *Ustinov in
Focus* by Tony Thomas, London, Zwemmer, and Cranbury, New Jersey, A. S. Barnes, 1971.

Theatrical Activities:

Director: **Plays** – *Fishing for Shadows*, London, 1940; *Squaring the Circle* (revue),
London, 1941; *Frenzy*, London, 1948; *The Love of Four Colonels*, London, 1951; *No Sign
of the Dove*, London, 1953; *Photo Finish*, London, 1962; *Halfway up the Tree*, New York,

1967; *The Unknown Soldier and His Wife*, Chichester, 1968, London, 1973. **Television** – *A Quiet War* by Neil Simon, 1976 (USA). **Operas** – *L'Heure Espagnol, Erwartung*, and *Gianni Schicchi* (triple bill), London, 1962; *The Magic Flute*, Hamburg, 1968.

Actor: **Plays** – Waffles in *The Wood Demon* by Chekhov, Sherre, Surrey, 1938; in *The Bishop of Limpopoland*, London, 1939; Aylesbury Repertory Company: in *French Without Tears* by Terence Rattigan, *Pygmalion* by G. B. Shaw, *White Cargo* by Leon Gordon, *Rookery Nook* by Ben Travers, and *Laburnum Grove* by J. B. Priestley, 1939; Reverend Alroy Whittingstall in *First Night* by Reginald Denham, Richmond, Surrey, 1940; *Swinging the Gate* (revue), London, 1940; M. Lescure in *Fishing for Shadows*, London, 1940; *Diversion* and *Diversion 2* (revues), London, 1940, 1941; Petrovitch in *Crime and Punishment* by Rodney Ackland, London, 1946; Caligula in *Frenzy*, London, 1948; Sergeant Dohda in *Love in Albania* by Eric Linklater, London, 1949; Carabosse in *The Love of Four Colonels*, London 1951; The General in *Romanoff and Juliet*, London, 1956, New York, 1957; Sam Old in *Photo Finish*, London, 1962, New York, 1963; Archbishop in *The Unknown Soldier and His Wife*, Chichester, 1968, London, 1973. **Films** – *Hello Fame*, 1941; *Let the People Sing*, 1941; *Mein Kampf, My Crimes*, 1941; *The Goose Steps Out*, 1941; *One of Our Aircraft Is Missing*, 1941; *The Way Ahead*, 1943; *The True Glory*, 1944; *The School for Secrets*, 1947; *Vice Versa*, 1947; *Private Angelo*, 1949; *Odette*, 1950; *Quo Vadis*, 1951; *Hotel Sahara*, 1952; *The Magic Box*, 1952; *The House of Madame Tellier*, 1954; *The Egyptian*, 1954; *Beau Brummell*, 1954; *We're No Angels*, 1954; *Lola Montès*, 1955 (released, 1967); *An Angel over Brooklyn* (*The Man Who Wagged His Tail*), 1957; *Les Espions* (*The Spies*), 1957; *Spartacus*, 1960; *The Sundowners*, 1960; *Romanoff and Juliet*, 1961; *Billy Budd*, 1962; *Women of the World*, 1963; *Topkapi*, 1964; *John Goldfarb, Please Come Home*, 1964; *Lady L.*, 1965; *The Comedians*, 1967; *Bluebeard's Ghost*, 1968; *Hot Millions*, 1968; *Viva Max*, 1969; *Hammersmith Is Out*, 1972; *Big Truck and Sister Clare*, 1973; *One of Our Dinosaurs Is Missing*, 1976; *Logan's Run*, 1976. **Television** – *The Life of Dr. Johnson*, 1957; *A Storm in Summer*, 1970 (USA); *Lord North*, 1972; *The Mighty Continent* (narrator), 1974; *A Quiet War*, 1976 (USA).

Peter Ustinov comments:

I believe that theories should emerge as a logical consequence of practice, and not be formulated in a coldly intellectual climate for eventual use. I therefore regard myself as a practical writer who began to write in the period of the proscenium arch, but who survived into the epoch of the arena and platform stages. The theatre, to survive, must do what film and television cannot do, and that is to exploit the physical presence of the audience. Naturalism was the logical reaction against romanticism, but the poetry inherent in all valid works of any school emerges more easily on film and even more easily on television than on the stage, and the time of the "fourth wall" has passed. Also, with the extraordinarily graphic quality of current events diffused by the news media, and the growing public sense of irony and scepticism about the nature and possibilities of government, tragedy and comedy have been chased for ever from their ivory towers. This is the time of the tragic farce, of the comic drama, of the paradox, of the dramatized doubt. In my plays as in my non-dramatic works I have always been interested in the comic side of things tragic and in the melancholy of things ribald. Life could not exist without its imperfections, just as the human body could not survive without germs. And to the writer, the imperfections of existence are life-blood.

*   *   *

Peter Ustinov's early career seemed to mark him out as a younger version of Noël Coward. With a versatility similar to Coward's he turned with apparently effortless facility from acting in revue, to playwriting, to film and stage appearances, to the novel and short story, to scriptwriting and later directing films. His talent, however, is very different from Coward's, and whereas Coward, despite the occasional excursion into other media, has remained firmly loyal to the theatre, Ustinov, after a prolific early stage output, has concentrated more on the cinema in recent years while his plays have appeared at increasingly iinfrequent intervals.

Like Coward with *The Vortex*, Ustinov had a dazzling early break in his career. While he was appearing in a Herbert Farjeon revue, Farjeon gave one of Ustinov's plays to James Agate, then at the height of his influence on *The Sunday Times*. Following Agate's lavish praise of the play – *House of Regrets* – it was produced in 1942. It is very much a young man's play; its story of Russian emigrés living in genteel poverty in London during the war is an at times over-consciously "atmospheric" piece, but it shows already Ustinov's extraordinary sympathetic identification with eccentrics and the aged in his picture of the old Admiral and General planning their coup to re-enter Russia. In the years following Ustinov's plays appeared with bewildering frequency, perhaps too frequently for their own good. Too many of them could be described in the terms he uses to label *Blow Your Own Trumpet*, a fantasy set in an Italian restaurant, a refuge for souls too weak for the outer world – "An idea rather than a play in the ordinary sense of the word." *The Tragedy of Good Intentions*, a chronicle-play about the Crusades, is unfocused and verbose; *The Indifferent Shepherd*, Ustinov's closest approach to a conventional West End well-made play, turning on a clergyman's crisis of conscience, is somewhat lacklustre for all its sincerity; and *No Sign of the Dove*, his most resounding critical failure, a modern re-working of the Noah legend, despite a fine opening with some splendid neo-Firbankian lines, dwindles into a strange mixture of *Heartbreak House* and bedroom-door farce. Too often the initial impetus in these earlier plays, packed with good ideas as they are, is simply not sustained through their length.

At the same time, however, his unique gift for the fantastic was developing more surely. *The Banbury Nose*, a kind of *Milestones* viewed backwards, tracing a great military family through three generations in reverse, is technically an accomplished *tour-de-force*, but more than that, in the scenes between the wife and the men who have loved her, Ustinov reveals a sure understanding of the threads of response between people. And although his work in the fifties saw some oddly muffled efforts – such as *The Moment of Truth*, an over-inflated political drama – he also produced two of his best and most successful plays. Both *The Love of Four Colonels* and *Romanoff and Juliet* saw him at his inventive best. *The Love of Four Colonels*, set in a European state disputed by the Allies, brilliantly satirizes national characteristics as the four colonels try to awaken the Sleeping Beauty's love in pastiche scenes in which they play out their own hopes and ideals, while *Romanoff and Juliet* adapts the Romeo and Juliet story in the context of the Cold War between rival Russian and American embassies in "the smallest country in Europe." Both plays demonstrate that fantastic quality of Ustinov's best work, which underneath the fairy-tale and Ruritanian trappings reveals a shrewd core of humanist understanding of contemporary problems, although with Ustinov's polyglot ancestry this inevitably emerges in an international rather than local context.

His output more recently has been to some extent a development and fuller exploration of earlier themes and ideas. *Photo Finish* recalls *The Banbury Nose* in its flashback time-sequence; it is a deep and often subtly disturbing play, presenting an old and famous writer in confrontation with his younger selves, looking back in a mirror of the past to find a portrait of eighty years with an infinity of other portraits underneath. *The Unknown Soldier and His Wife* is to a certain extent a further exploration of some material in *The Tragedy of Good Intentions*, but its scope and assurance come from a dramatist at the height of his powers. An indictment of war throughout the centuries, it sweeps in time from ancient Rome to medieval England, to the eighteenth century to modern times, linked by the same recurring characters who emerge whenever war comes and who control its course – the forces of the Church and the Army. What could have been a series of admittedly amusing sketches becomes a complex and multi-layered play of great wit and insight which must rank with his best work.

The standard complaint against Ustinov is that his abundance of good ideas rarely finds a satisfactory form, and it is true that few of his best plays have a tight plot-progression; as in his novels, he is happiest in a kind of picaresque style. But this is to look for the wrong things in Ustinov. His origin draws on that Russian literary tradition, unrooted in a classical context, which inextricably blends tragedy and comedy. His best plays have a strong tension between the two, and he is a master of a light touch which underneath contains a profounder channel. He once wrote of the influence music had had on his work, and there is indeed an almost Mozartian strain which informs his most enduring plays – *The Love of Four Colonels* and *The Unknown Soldier and His Wife* in particular – which, despite an apparent surface plotlessness, have an internal pattern and rhythm which gave them a strong theatrical movement. Some of his recent work, such as *Halfway up the Tree*, has been disappointingly conventional by comparison, but still not quite so distressingly feeble as his latest piece, *Who's Who in Hell*. Again, it has a splendid initial idea; it is set in an anteroom of hell, where a Judge-figure decides the ultimate destination of new arrivals, who include the U.S. President, the Russian Premier and the young American radical who assassinated both before his own death by Secret Service bullets. But the sharp political discussion-piece it sets out to be crashes before it gets off the ground; the level of intellectual argument is woefully jejune and, surprisingly from Ustinov, there is not even the compensation of good jokes, since he humour in the main consists of would-be epigrams strangled by clumsy phrasing.

—Alan Strachan

---

van ITALLIE, Jean-Claude. American. Born in Brussels, Belgium, 25 May 1936; emigrated to the United States in 1940. Educated at Great Neck High School, New York; Deerfield Academy, Massachusetts; Harvard University, Cambridge, Massachusetts, B.A. 1958; New York University, 1959; studied acting at the Neighborhood Playhouse, New York. Editor, *Transatlantic Review*, New York, 1960–63; Playwright-in-Residence, Open Theatre, New York, 1963–68; Free-lance Writer on public affairs for NBC and CBS television, New York, 1963–67; taught playwriting at the New School for Social Research, New York, 1967–68, 1972, and Yale University Drama School, New Haven, Connecticut, 1969. Since 1973, Visiting Lecturer, Princeton University, New Jersey, and summers since 1974. Instructor, Naropa Institute, Boulder, Colorado. Visiting Mellon Professor, Amherst College, Massachusetts, Fall 1976. Recipient: Vernon Rice Award, 1967; Outer Circle Award, 1967; Obie Award, 1968; Creative Artists Public Service grant, 1975. Agent: Janet Roberts, William Morris Agency, 1350 Avenue of the Americas, New York, New York 10019, U.S.A.

PUBLICATIONS

Plays

War (produced New York, 1963; Edinburgh, 1968; London, 1969). Included in *War and Four Other Plays*, 1967; in *America Hurrah*, 1967.

Almost Like Being (produced New York, 1964). Included in *War and Four Other Plays*, 1967; in *America Hurrah*, 1967.

I'm Really Here (produced New York, 1964). Included in *War and Four Other Plays*, 1967.

The Hunter and the Bird (produced New York, 1964). Included in *War and Four Other Plays*, 1967.

Interview (as *Pavane*, produced Atlanta, 1965; revised version, as *Interview*, produced New York, 1966; London, 1967). Included in *America Hurrah*, 1967.

Where Is de Queen? (as *Dream*, produced New York, 1965; revised version, as *Where Is de Queen?*, produced Minneapolis, 1965). Included in *War and Four Other Plays*, 1967.

Motel (as *America Hurrah*, produced New York, 1965; revised version, as *Motel*, produced New York, 1966; London, 1967). Included in *America Hurrah*, 1967.

America Hurrah (includes *Interview, TV, Motel*) (produced New York, 1966; London, 1967). New York, Coward McCann, 1967; with *War* and *Almost Like Being*, London, Penguin, 1967.

The Girl and the Soldier (produced Los Angeles, 1967). Included in *Seven Short and Very Short Plays*, 1975.

War and Four Other Plays (includes *Where Is de Queen?, Almost Like Being, The Hunter and the Bird, I'm Really Here*). New York, Dramatists Play Service, 1967.

Thoughts on the Instant of Greeting a Friend on the Street, with Sharon Thie (produced Los Angeles, 1967; in *Collision Course*, produced New York, 1968). New York, Random House, 1968.

The Serpent: A Ceremony, with the Open Theatre (produced Rome, 1968; New York, 1970). New York, Atheneum, 1969.

Take a Deep Breath (televised, 1969). Included in *Seven Short and Very Short Plays*, 1975.

Photographs: Mary and Howard (produced Los Angeles, 1969). Included in *Seven Short and Very Short Plays*, 1975.

Eat Cake (produced Denver, 1971). Included in *Seven Short and Very Short Plays*, 1975.

Mystery Play (produced New York, 1973). New York, Dramatists Play Service, 1973; revised version, as *The King of the United States*, music by Richard Peaslee (also director: produced New York, 1973), New York, Dramatists Play Service, 1975.

Nightwalk, with Megan Terry and Sam Shepard (produced New York, 1973).

The Sea Gull, adaptation of a play by Chekhov (produced Princeton, New Jersey, 1973; New York, 1975). New York, Dramatists Play Service, 1974.

A Fable (produced New York, 1975). New York, Dramatists Play Service, 1976.

Seven Short and Very Short Plays (includes *Photographs, Eat Cake, The Girl and the Soldier, Take a Deep Breath, Rosary, Harold, Thoughts on the Instant of Greeting a Friend in the Street*). New York, Dramatists Play Service, 1975.

Television Plays: *Hobbies; or, Things Are All Right with the Forbushers*, 1967; *Take a Deep Breath*, 1969; adaptations for *Look Up and Live* series.

Manuscript Collections: Kent State University, Ohio; Harvard University Library, Cambridge, Massachusetts.

Critical Studies: by Walter Kerr, in *New York Times*, 11 December 1966; "Three Views of America" by Robert Brustein, in *The Third Theatre*, New York, Simon and Schuster, 1970; *Up Against the Fourth Wall* by John Lahr, New York, Grove Press, 1970; "Jean-Claude van Itallie" issue of *Serif* (Kent, Ohio), Winter 1972.

Theatrical Activities:

Director: **Play** – *The King of the United States*, New York, 1973.

Jean-Claude van Itallie comments:

I seem to have been most intent on playing with and exploring new forms that might express theatre with validity, at least to me. I have worked as a playwright in solitude. I have adapted into English from a foreign language. I have worked as a poet in collaboration with a theatre director and actors, and with actors alone. I have written for puppets. I have written screenplays and specifically for television. I have written and directed a pornographic film. I am not entirely comfortable in any of these forms. I question theatre but I remain married to it, more or less. I agree that language itself helps to keep us isolated but I continue to write. I want to write with greater clarity; to write more for the theatre, or at least that little sector of it to which I belong. I like to work with other artists in the theatre, and to imagine the audience as a community of friends.

*   *   *

Jean-Claude van Itallie's first published play, *War*, employs the basic technique which governs his later, often much more complex works: a fundamental term or theme is introduced, then illustrated metaphorically and applied to a shifting series of particular instances. There is no plot or character development in any conventional sense; rather the essence of the theme is made manifest by an accumulation of poetic illustrations. Thus in *War* two actors meet by appointment to improvise for an acting class. The scene is charged with hostilities: the older actor resents his youthful partner, and the younger man, unproved and inexperienced, is ill at ease in the atmosphere of the big city. Their mounting resentments are twice dissipated by the appearance of a dreamlike Lady in Edwardian dress who represents a "remembered ideal," but a regressive, infantile ideal which cannot be brought into the present or shared. Aggression reasserts itself and the final stage direction underlines the dominant image of conflict:

> The actors march in towards each other. They kneel at the center of the stage. They put their inner arms around each other but with their free arms they continue to hit each other. The Lady steps up from behind them ... and stands above them: this tableau forms a hieroglyph, an emblem, the two-headed eagle of war.

The Hunter and the Bird is a brief but highly poetic statement, this time posing and then inverting the basic metaphor of the hunter and the hunted. The hunter stalks his prey, but from a sense of incompleteness, motivated by a desire to possess something his victim has (in this case, the power to fly); and the essential dependence of the hunter upon the hunted, of predator upon victim, is revealed when the bird in turn shoots the hunter. The play lasts only a few moments, but like the best of van Itallie's work makes an indelible impression.

Almost Like Being and *I'm Really Here* are cabaret sketches, easy caricatures of the empty, sniggering Doris Day movie romances of the 1950's, hardly worth the poetic skill or indignation of a writer as sophisticated as van Itallie. *Thoughts on the Instant of Greeting a Friend on the Street* (written with Sharon Thie) and *Where Is de Queen?*, however, are fresh experiments with the device which traditionally has shaped the dramatic presentation of theme, the linear unfolding of a time sequence. In *Thoughts* the moment of greeting between two friends is held in suspension: the conventional greeting, "Hi, how are you?" and response, "Fine thanks, how are you?" penetrate the minds of the speakers, who then explore briefly their private associations with the idea of danger, safety and well-being. The responses are presented as simultaneously as stage action will permit, an experiment carried even further in *Where Is de Queen?* "The entire play takes place," van Itallie tells us, "in the instant of the man's beginning to awake when his wife calls him on the telephone." As the man comes back to consciousness and the realities of wife, home and job, the remnants of his dreamlife appear and disappear – a childhood nanny, a poet, among others, and three menacing blacks who start out as vaudeville comics but gradually threaten and overpower the "queen," the principle, perhaps, of daylight, order and control. "Plays should be instruments for getting into people's dreams," van Itallie has remarked, but the particular meanings of these dream images are as ambiguous as they are troubling. Do the blacks represent the dreamer's anarchic unconscious, or some suppressed racial guilt? It is impossible to tell, and the questions themselves are finally irrelevant to the charged, fading nightmare atmosphere van Itallie conjures up so quickly and effectively.

The trilogy *America Hurrah* (*Interview, TV* and *Motel*) and *The Serpent* confirmed van Itallie's position as a poetic dramatist of unmistakable power and inventiveness. *Interview* is a complex verbal fugue, with overlapping statements and metaphors which change with dazzling speed. The theme, however, is clear: "can I help you?" It appears first in the embarrassing impersonality of the job interview situation, then reappears in the analogous relationships between priest and parishioner, analyst and patient, politician and public. But with each manifestation the possibility of help seems further attenuated; the speakers drift apart, isolated and increasingly at the mercy of the "authorities." The three television researchers of *TV* are gradually drawn into the banalities of the programs they monitor. Their lives are admittedly small and inconsequential, but they are at least human and touching; the programs which absorb them are depersonalizing clichés which destroy any sense of reality which may exist beyond the stereotypes. In the final play, *Motel*, a grotesque motel-keeper doll mechanically lists the virtues of an endless series of rooms and guests while two equally grotesque customer dolls enter, undress, couple and systematically destroy the motel room. As Robert Brustein comments, the play "becomes an image of our violence, our insanity, our need to defile ... a metaphor so powerful that it may well become the objective correlative of the Johnson age."

The Serpent is van Itallie's most ambitious play to date. The earlier works are vivid but essentially static explorations of a central theme restated metaphorically, but unsustainable, perhaps, because they float free of any definable "plot." In *The Serpent*, however, van Itallie takes up the dominant myth of the west – the garden of Eden, the temptation (the invitation to an expanded awareness of good and evil), the fall and the primal murder. The play opens with tableaux-like representations of the Kennedy and King assassinations, compelling emblems of evil in our time, and then pushes back to the archetypal explanation of how such evil came into the world. The conclusion of *The Serpent* is stunningly unexpected and revitalizing, as John Lahr has observed:

> Theatrically ... guilt and death have been acted out. Actors, posing in decrepit age, stare at the audience. Suddenly the actors break into somber rhythm – jumping, chanting, churning with determined energy. In the final beats of the performance, they move out into the audience singing "Moonlight Bay." The moment is a leap of faith. As Joseph Chaikin [the producer] explains, "The intention is a moment of celebration. The stillness of Cain's waiting, the fact of death – you can really get dragged down by that and die from it. Or you can just go another way." The Open Theatre opts for action, not resignation, a life force instead of a death wish. This is, in itself, a gesture beyond the Absurd.

The Serpent is a kind of therapeutic experience, a ceremony and religious rite which establishes the fundamental connection between van Itallie's highly experimental work and the most ancient conception of the function of dramatic representation.

—Elmer Borklund

VIDAL, Gore.   American.   Born in West Point, New York, 3 October 1925. Educated at Phillips Exeter Academy, New Hampshire. Served in the United States Army, 1943–46. Full-time Writer since 1944. Member, Advisory Board, *Partisan Review*, New Brunswick, New Jersey, 1960–71. Democratic-Liberal Candidate for Congress, 1960. Member, President's Advisory Committee on the Arts, 1961–63. Co-Chairman, The New Party, 1968–71. Address: 21 Via di Torre Argentina, Rome, Italy.

PUBLICATIONS

Plays

Visit to a Small Planet (televised, 1955).   Published in *Visit to a Small Planet and Other Television Plays*, 1957; revised version (produced New York, 1957; London, 1960), Boston, Little Brown, 1957; in *Three Plays*, 1962.

Honor (televised, 1956).   Published in *Television Plays for Writers: Eight Television Plays*, edited by A. S. Burack, Boston, The Writer, 1957; revised version, as *On the March to the Sea: A Southron Comedy* (produced Bonn, Germany, 1962), in *Three Plays*, 1962.

Visit to a Small Planet and Other Television Plays (includes *Barn Burning, Dark Possession, The Death of Billy the Kid, A Sense of Justice, Smoke, Summer Pavilion, The Turn of the Screw*).   Boston, Little Brown, 1957.

The Best Man: A Play of Politics (produced New York, 1960).   Boston, Little Brown, 1960; in *Three Plays*, 1962.

Three Plays (Visit to a Small Planet, The Best Man, On the March to the Sea).   London, Heinemann, 1962.

Romulus: A New Comedy, adaptation of the play by Friedrich Dürrenmatt (produced New York, 1962).   New York, Dramatists Play Service, 1962.

Weekend (produced New York, 1968).   New York, Dramatists Play Service, 1968.

An Evening with Richard Nixon (produced New York, 1972).   New York, Random House, 1972.

Screenplays: *The Catered Affair*, 1956; *I Accuse*, 1958; *The Scapegoat*, 1958; *Suddenly Last Summer*, with Tennessee Williams, 1959; *The Best Man*, 1964; *Is Paris Burning?*, with Francis Ford Coppola, 1966; *Last of the Mobile Hot-Shots*, 1970; *Gore Vidal's Caligula*, 1977.

Television Plays: *Barn Burning*, 1954; *Dark Possession*, 1954; *Smoke*, 1954; *Visit to a Small Planet*, 1955; *The Death of Billy the Kid*, 1955; *A Sense of Justice*, 1955; *Summer Pavilion*, 1955; *The Turn of the Screw*, 1955; *Honor*, 1956; *The Indestructible Mr. Gore*, 1960.

Novels

Williwaw.   New York, Dutton, 1946; London, Heinemann, 1970.

In a Yellow Wood.   New York, Dutton, 1947.

The City and the Pillar.   New York, Dutton, 1948; London, Heinemann, 1949; revised edition, Dutton, 1965; Heinemann, 1966.

The Season of Comfort.   New York, Dutton, 1949.

A Search for the King: A Twelfth Century Legend.   New York, Dutton, 1950.

Dark Green, Bright Red.   New York, Dutton, and London, Heinemann, 1950.

The Judgment of Paris.   New York, Dutton, 1952; London, Heinemann, 1953.

Messiah.   New York, Dutton, 1954; London, Heinemann, 1955; revised edition, Boston, Little Brown, 1965.

Three: Williwaw, A Thirsty Evil, Julian the Apostate.   New York, New American Library, 1962.

Julian.   Boston, Little Brown, and London, Heinemann, 1964.

Washington, D.C.   Boston, Little Brown, and London, Heinemann, 1967.

Myra Breckinridge.   Boston, Little Brown, and London, Blond, 1968.

Two Sisters: A Novel in the Form of a Memoir.   Boston, Little Brown, and London, Heinemann, 1970.

Burr.   New York, Random House, 1973; London, Heinemann, 1974.
Myron.   New York, Random House, 1974; London, Heinemann, 1975.
1876.   New York, Random House, and London, Heinemann, 1976.

Novels (as Edgar Box)

Death in the Fifth Position.   New York, Dutton, 1952; London, Heinemann, 1954.
Death Before Bedtime.   New York, Dutton, 1953; London, Heinemann, 1954.
Death Likes It Hot.   New York, Dutton, 1954; London, Heinemann, 1955.

Short Stories

A Thirsty Evil: 7 Short Stories.   New York, Zero Press, 1956; London, Heinemann, 1958.

Other

Rocking the Boat (essays).   Boston, Little Brown, 1962; London, Heinemann, 1963.
Reflections upon a Sinking Ship (essays).   Boston, Little Brown, and London, Heinemann, 1969.
Homage to Daniel Shays: Collected Essays, 1952–1972.   New York, Random House, 1972; as *Collected Essays, 1952–1972*, London, Heinemann, 1974.

Editor, *Best Television Plays.*   New York, Ballantine, 1956.

Critical Studies: *Gore Vidal* by Ray Lewis White, New York, Twayne, 1968; *Vidal* by Bernard F. Dick, New York, Random House, 1973.

*   *   *

Eschewing all consideration of Gore Vidal as a novelist and short story writer (we recall the novels, *The City and the Pillar, Messiah, Julian*, and about eight others) the critic must associate his theatrical production with its kinship to cinema and television, i.e., Vidal's plays are quite stageable yet are intrinsically cinematographic or televisionistic. They have a modernity about them that facilitates their being restructured for each medium – because they are thematically and linguistically hinged loosely but integrally, and the characters drawn in such a manner that in displacing a character, in changing a tempo, or shifting psychology for a particular medium, Vidal does not violate the play's integrity. Critics have envied Vidal's facile success on TV and stage; but his success would not be forthcoming were he not an extremely proficient stylist. True, Vidal has a grudge against a complacent "bourgeois" society and likes to jab at sensitive and vulnerable spots, and he succeeded cinematographically in *Suddenly Last Summer*. The film *Lefthanded Gun* (based on his television play on the Billy the Kid legend) succeeded; but *Myra Breckinridge* failed because the producers were not faithful to Mr. Vidal.

His themes – extreme and tabooistic in his novels – are more traditional in his plays, mainly war and politics. But the persistent leitmotiv in all his works is man bereft in the modern world. Should man relinquish certain values? Find new ones? Vidal assigns satire for the first alternative, irony for the second. Vidal the person seems to opt for relative values, and creates types (as do all playwrights) to epitomize these values; yet Vidal the writer, in creating the antagonistic types to exemplify certain absolutes, finds himself with characters possessing more dramatic qualities and effectiveness – which indicates that Vidal the writer is instinctively more sage than Vidal the person. Since the antagonist stands well in his own defence he wins dramatic or tragic sympathy; hence, the thesis comes to no social conclusion and the spectator is left with the unresolved futility of modern life. This is good dramaturgy.

Let us analyse several of Vidal's plays beginning with *Weekend*, the least effective of his plays. It is an attempt to profit from the topical concern about miscegenation which the author encrusts on a political campaign (not unlike *The Best Man*); but the situation and the characters are not real enough for good satire, nor exaggerated enough to make good farce. Vidal's merit as a playwright, however, is best demonstrated in his Trilogy: *Visit to a Small Planet, On the March to the Sea, The Best Man.*

Visit to a Small Planet is the story of a one-man invasion from outer space – an extraterritorial being who is intent on creating a state of war between his world and ours. This "man" is called Kreton (may all warmongers bear this epithet!) and almost succeeds in creating a war hysteria on earth through certain well-conceived comic situations. It was because of these situations that his play became a very successful television series. However, its anti-war theme is ineffective because we cannot associate the Kreton's world with our own cretin world. After all, it was they who wanted war, not us humans. The audience can't help but feel self-righteous at the end when Kreton is led off to his celestial kindergarten. In attempting a satire on war Vidal created an excellent science fiction farce with characterizations that are memorable – the pixie Kreton, the prototype of the war-loving general, Tom Powers, and Roger Felding, an equally ambitious television commentator.

Although the theme of *On the March to the Sea* is shopworn – the disasters wrought on Southern families, particularly that of John Hinks', by the ravages of Civil War – this play is poignant and highly dramatic. The characters are all believable, with the possible exception of Captain Taylor of the Union Army – flamboyant, too philosophic (war participants, i.e. soldiers, are never introspective nor contemplative, at least about ethical or social problems, during bellicose engagements). Vidal thought a lot of this character and gave him the final words of the play; but the character really caught in the maelstrom of life and war, John Hinks, was the authentic tragic figure of the play. The play is in a war setting and the war pervades all. Yet as the title aptly indicates, the main theme is not Sherman's march to the sea, but a series of incidents that take place *on* the march to the sea. The question of what is human dignity (the answer to one's own conscience) and honor (the answer to social conscience) is put literally through a trial of fire. The characters, even though typified (intentionally so) are all quite well drawn, except for Colonel Thayer, who is the "heavy."

But Colonel Thayer is too celluloidish a character to be really cruel. The cruelty prize goes to Clayton, son of John Hinks, too young and self-centered to understand his father's anguish. Though *Visit to a Small Planet* was intended as a satire on war, *On the March to the Sea* is infinitely more effective as an anti-war drama.

The Best Man is the struggle between two Presidential aspirants, jockeying, scratching and grubbing for the nomination of their Party. The play is a well-wrought urn, perfectly structured, containing political characters that emulate Hollywoodian stereotypes (Vidal had every intention of doing this), effective dialogue, with each character keeping to his prose program. The suspenseful outcome of the nomination is solved by an honorable, classical, and justified theatrical technique: President ex-machina. The solution is not only theatrically perfect, but thematically perfect, in that the person eventually to be nominated is of little importance.

The main theme – Does one have to be a demogogue to be successful in political life? Vidal gives us such a selection of Presidential aspirants that they seem *inverosimil* and incredible. But as the old Italian quip says, "If it's not a wolf, it's a dog." This is ingeniously planted in the mind of the spectator and this is why *The Best Man* is extremely good satire.

—John V. Falconieri

VONNEGUT, Kurt, Jr. American Born in Indianapolis, Indiana, 11 November 1922. Educated at Cornell University, Ithaca, New York, 1940–42; University of Chicago, 1945–47. Served in the United States Army Infantry, 1942–45; awarded Purple Heart. Married Jane Marie Cox in 1945; has three children. Police Reporter, Chicago City News Bureau, 1946; worked in public relations for the General Electric Company, Schenectady, New York, 1947–50. Free-lance Writer since 1950. Since 1965, Teacher, Hopefield School, Sandwich, Massachusetts. Visiting Lecturer, Writers Workshop, University of Iowa, Iowa City, 1965–67; Harvard University, Cambridge, Massachusetts. 1970–71. Recipient: Guggenheim Fellowship, 1967; National Institute of Arts and Letters grant, 1970. Litt. D.: Hobart and William Smith Colleges, Geneva, New York, 1974. Member, National Institute of Arts and Letters, 1973. Address: Scudder's Lane, West Barnstable, Massachusetts 02668, U.S.A.

PUBLICATIONS

Plays

    The Very First Christmas Morning, in *Better Homes and Gardens* (Des Moines, Iowa), December 1962.
    Fortitude, in *Playboy* (Chicago), September 1968.
    Happy Birthday, Wanda June (produced New York, 1970). New York, Delacorte Press, 1971; London, Cape, 1973.
    Between Time and Timbuctoo; or, Prometheus-5: A Space Fantasy (televised, 1972; produced New York, 1976). New York, Delacorte Press, 1972.

    Television Play: *Between Time and Timbuctoo,* 1972.

Novels

    Player Piano. New York, Scribner, 1952; London, Macmillan, 1953; as *Utopia 14,* New York, Bantam, 1954.
    The Sirens of Titan. New York, Dell, 1959; London, Gollancz, 1962.
    Mother Night. Greenwich, Connecticut, Fawcett, 1961; London, Cape, 1968.
    Cat's Cradle. New York, Holt Rinehart, and London, Gollancz, 1963.
    God Bless You, Mr. Rosewater; or, Pearls Before Swine. New York, Holt Rinehart, and London, Cape, 1965.
    Slaughterhouse-Five; or, The Children's Crusade: A Duty-Dance with Death, by Kurt Vonnegut, Jr., A Fourth-Generation German-American Now Living in Easy Circumstances on Cape Cod [and Smoking Too Much] Who, as an American Infantry Scout Hors de Combat, as a Prisoner of War, Witnessed the Fire-Bombing of Dresden, Germany, the Florence of the Elbe, a Long Time Ago, and Survived to Tell the Tale: This Is a Novel Somewhat in the Telegraphic Schizophrenic Manner of Tales of the Planet Tralfamadore, Where the Flying Saucers Come From. New York, Delacorte Press, 1969; London, Cape, 1970.
    Breakfast of Champions; or, Goodbye, Blue Monday. New York, Delacorte Press, and London, Cape, 1973.
    Slapstick; or Lonesome No More. New York, Delacorte Press, and London, Cape, 1976.

Short Stories

    Canary in a Cathouse. Greenwich, Connecticut, Fawcett, 1961.

Welcome to the Monkey House: A Collection of Short Works.   New York, Delacorte Press, 1968; London Cape, 1969.

Other

The Vonnegut Statement, edited by Jerome Klinkowitz and John Somer.   New York, Delacorte Press, 1973.
Wampeters, Foma, and Granfalloons: Opinions.   New York, Delacorte Press, 1974; London, Cape, 1975.

Bibliography: *Kurt Vonnegut, Jr.: A Descriptive Bibliography and Annotated Secondary Checklist* by Asa B. Pieratt, Jr., and Jerome Klinkowitz, Hamden, Connecticut, Shoe String Press, 1974.

*   *   *

In his first short drama, Kurt Vonnegut designed a morality playlet about selfishness and sharing for children. His subsequent dramatic productions have followed in the morality mode, though now directed to the adolescent sensibility. Reducing fashionable liberal doctrines to simplest terms, the popular author sets his Jonsonian humours or similar stereotypes at odds in lightly satirical plots. Mixing whimsy, wit, and generous dollops of heavy irony, he depicts the present-day psychomachia, the identity crisis. The modern Everyman is lonely, confused, divided against himself; hampered by atavistic habits and haunted by the spectre of a dehumanized future, he finds himself caught within an increasingly schizoid society. Naïve faith in Progress is not redemption, and the long hope of liberation is not forthcoming. For Mankind has been outwitted, or is about to be, by Science. Curiously enough, Vonnegut's responses to the absurdities and paradoxes of modern life are rather conservative. While he seldom offers solutions to the social predicaments he discerns, he does suggest that amelioration lies in return to fundamentals: common sense, good humor, and feeling. In his entertainments, however, these qualities bear close resemblance to facile resignation, cleverness, and sentimentality. Though somewhat ingenious, his dramas are less revelations of the present human condition or predictions about its future state than confirmations and reinforcements of popular prejudices and fears concerning both.

Thus, in *Fortitude* he expresses a widely shared criticism of modern medicine's unreasonable attempts to prolong life. While the world's poor starve and seldom visit a doctor, a 100-year-old multi-millionairess endures "the latest wonders science has to offer" as the sole patient of "a crass medical genius" named Dr. Norbert Frankenstein, lest the point be missed. Awakened, put to sleep, energized, and tranquilized by machines and drugs, Sylvia Lovejoy is a travesty of a human being, but a triumph of engineering. The brief sparks of humanity left in her, the infrequent expressions of free will cry out to be allowed to die. With a friend's help, Mrs. Lovejoy gets partial revenge, by shooting the mad scientist and taking him with her, literally. According to his master's plan, assistant Tom Swift connects Frankenstein to Mrs. Lovejoy's apparatus, and to the strains of "Ah, Sweet Mystery of Life" the doctor awakens to at least 500 years of technologically-sustained existence. Subtlety is not Vonnegut's forte.

Vonnegut deals with rôle-playing and the need for human feeling in *Happy Birthday, Wanda June,* and here his characteristic simplification, sentimentality, and perceptive wit produce an effective satire. He up-dates the story of Odysseus's homecoming by translating the epic figures into modern equivalents, caricatures which reveal the absurdities of the myth of male superiority and the traditional, aggressive means by which it is manifested. He makes Harold Ryan a parody of masculinity: an egomaniacal big-game hunter, swaggering seducer, and sniggering bully. He also makes him – and most of the other characters, despite their faults – quite likable. During his eight-year absence – for most of which Harold was drugged and rendered harmless by jungle "savages" – Penelope has progressed from the teen-aged car-hop that Ryan married to a liberated woman with an M.A. in English and two antagonistic suitors whom she tolerates. In them Vonnegut presents other images of the modern man. Herb Shuttle proved himself by making Eagle Scout and has become a successful vacuum cleaner salesman; he, of course, idolizes the great Harold. In contrast, Dr. Norbert Woodly is an effete, smooth-talking amateur violinist, who delights in denigrating the idol and all his works.

When Harold returns most unexpectedly with his indecisive sidekick, Col. Looseleaf Harper (*he* has the distinction of having dropped the bomb on Nagasaki), he immediately proceeds to set things to rights. With supreme self-assurance, he asserts his male authority by ordering Penelope to the kitchen, humiliating the sycophantic Shuttle, smashing Woodly's two-hundred-year-old fiddle, and beginning the initiation of his adolescent son into the rites of manhood. But Harold's ruthlessness backfires. It brings out the sensitivity in Col. Harper, who looks with regret upon his life and makes telling comments upon the games American men are forced to play. Son Paul is intimidated. Penelope gives a stern, elementary lecture to Harold on the psychopathology of heroes, and then walks out. Harold is left alone with his trophies. It is left to Woodly, as the voice of civilization, to deliver the final blow, by making Harold realize that he is a menace in a fragile world, a walking fossil, a mock hero, an anachronistic joke.

Here, as in other satires, comic exposure and ridicule offer no real solutions to cultural problems. Vonnegut himself points out "the intolerable balancing of characters and arguments" in the play. Certainly difficulties arise with the scenes set in Heaven, where he has Jesus and Judas, innocent little Wanda June and Harold's drunken former wife, the Beast of Yugoslavia and his victims all live happily ever after – though this sentimental vision disturbs the moral and comic balance of the piece. In doing this, however, Vonnegut has made the comedy reflect his personal feelings: "I felt and I still feel," he explains, "that everybody is right, no matter what he says." The statement also helps explain his success as a spokesman of popular opinion for the younger set.

—Joseph Parisi

WALCOTT, Derek (Alton).   British.   Born in Castries, St. Lucia, West Indies, 23 January 1930. Educated at St. Mary's College, St. Lucia; University of the West Indies, Kingston, Jamaica, B.A. 1953. Married; has three children. Taught at St. Mary's College and Jamaica College. Formerly, Feature Writer, *Public Opinion*, Kingston, and *Trinidad Guardian*, Port-of-Spain, Trinidad. Since 1959, Founding Director, Trinidad Theatre Workshop. Recipient: Rockefeller Fellowship, 1957; Guinness Award, 1961; Heinemann Award, for verse, 1966. Cholmondeley Award, 1969; Order of the Humming Bird, Trinidad and Tobago, 1969; Obie Award, 1971; Jock Campbell Award (*New Statesman*, London), 1974. Address, 165 Duke of Edinburgh Avenue, Diego Martin, Trinidad.

PUBLICATIONS

Plays

    Henri Christophe: A Chronicle (produced St. Lucia, 1950; London, 1951). Bridgetown, Barbados Advocate, 1950.
    Henri Dernier: A Play for Radio Production.   Bridgetown, Barbados Advocate, 1951.
    Sea at Dauphin (produced Trinidad, 1954; London, 1960)   Mona, University College of the West Indies Extra-Mural Department, 1954; in *The Dream on Monkey Mountain and Other Plays*, 1971.

Ione: A Play with Music (produced Trinidad, 1957).   Mona, University College of the
   West Indies Extra-Mural Department, 1954.
Drums and Colours (produced Trinidad, 1958).   Published in *Caribbean Quarterly*
   (Kingston), vii, 1 and 2, 1961.
Ti-Jean and His Brothers, music by André Tanker (produced Port-of-Spain, Trinidad,
   1958; also director: produced New York, 1972).   Included in *The Dream on Monkey
   Mountain and Other Plays*, 1971.
Malcochon; or, Six in the Rain (produced St. Lucia, 1959; as *Six in the Rain*, produced
   London, 1960; as *Malcochon*, produced New York, 1969).   Included in *The Dream
   on Monkey Mountain and Other Plays*, 1971.
The Dream on Monkey Mountain (produced Toronto, 1967; Waterford, Connecticut,
   1968; New York, 1971).   Included in *The Dream on Monkey Mountain and Other
   Plays*, 1971.
In a Fine Castle (produced Jamaica, 1970; Trinidad, 1971; Los Angeles, 1972).
The Dream on Monkey Mountain and Other Plays (includes *Ti-Jean and His Brothers,
   Malcochon, Sea at Dauphin,* and the essay "What the Twilight Says").   New York,
   Farrar Straus, 1971; London, Cape, 1972.
The Charlatan, music by Galt MacDermot (produced Los Angeles, 1974).

Verse

Twenty-Five Poems.   Port-of-Spain, Trinidad, Guardian Commercial Printery, 1948.
Epitaph for the Young.   Bridgetown, Barbados Advocate, 1949.
Poems.   Kingston, City Printery, 1953.
In a Green Night: Poems 1948–1960.   London, Cape, 1962.
Selected Poems.   New York, Farrar Straus, 1964.
The Castaway and Other Poems.   London, Cape, 1965.
The Gulf and Other Poems.   London, Cape, 1969; as *The Gulf*, New York, Farrar
   Straus, 1970.
Another Life.   London, Cape, and New York, Farrar Straus, 1973.
Sea Grapes.   London, Cape, and New York, Farrar Straus, 1976.
Selected Verse.   London, Heinemann, 1976.

*   *   *

It may seem surprising that one of the more perceptive and lucid speakers for modern man
should emerge from the island of Trinidad in the West Indies. But it is nonetheless true. As a
man of the theatre Derek Walcott is that sensitive poet-dramatist who contends with the
questions that have concerned thoughtful man since time began. What is man? What is his
relationship with God? Always aware of the culture and society which produced the present
situation, Walcott also relates man to man and seriously questions the values that modernity
has brought to man. Although he is particularly conscious of what he calls the present
"African phase," his art at its best – his fears, his fire, his compassion – treats and yet
transcends what he describes as "one race's quarrel with another's God" and may be
associated with the writing of Camus, Sophocles, and the philosophy found in the Noh and
Kabuki drama. He writes of man as well as men.
   Both in dramaturgy and expressed ideas Walcott's plays provide levels of audience
experience ranging from the simplicity of folk drama to the intellectual and emotional
entanglements of highly sophiisticated discussion. Essentially, he is a poet concerned with
language – its dialectual expression, its varying rhythm, its imagery. Nature is ever present
and forceful for him. There is the "sea grinding his teeth" or God, "a big fish eating small
ones." Contingent upon his use of nature is that folk quality which in his plays is also
illustrated by his frequent use of a *conteur* who directs the action of a play. People, characters,
are of greatest importance in his plays, while his presentation of their actions and his ideas

may appear as manipulated as the work of the Greek dramatists or the writers of traditional Japanese drama. Music and song add to the folk or fable dimension of his plays. He also uses soliloquies, dreams, fantasies, or varied experimental techniques such as masks, symbols or symbolic figures, or disguises to express his ideas. In these ways he achieves his theatrical change of pace, interspersing light touches of humor through dialect or folk action. During the action of his plays on stage his use of language and his innovative structure provide theatrical entertainment while his serious concern for man becomes overwhelmingly apparent through his carefully drawn characters and the conflicts in which they are involved.

Not all of Walcott's plays are published, but the few that have been suggest his range. In *Sea at Dauphin* two fishermen argue about taking to sea with them an old man who commits suicide when he is refused. It is a fearful life for fisherman where "God is a white man" and "his spit on Dauphin people is the sea." People work hard, have nothing, and see only death in a circular despair shown in the play by the fisherman's acceptance of a boy for their trip the next day. *Ti-Jean and His Brothers* is a fable in which three brothers representing physical strength, academic wisdom, and "man-wit, common sense" try to unmask the devil. The Devil fights and even the third brother, Ti-Jean, who argues and therefore defeats the devil by refusing to obey him, is "a fool like all heroes" and must be helped by God. In *Malcochon; or, Six in the Rain* Walcott brings six people together in various confessions that show their frailty and humanity while exposing views of God and justice. His best play is *Dream on Monkey Mountain.* "In the beginning was the ape, and the ape had no name, so God called him man." In an epic fashion set within a mock trial, Walcott equates man's search for identity, his dream, with a present desire for black brotherhood. Following a Christian theme, the hero of the play is betrayed, confesses that "God dead," and is condemned for attempting to escape from the prison of his life. Materialized for his defense, even the best minds of the past cannot help him. He must personally destroy his God and his dream. But the argument and conflict of the play are also only a dream as the action before the final curtain reverts to the opening scene of the simple man in his squalid life.

Themes involving God and justice are most persistent in Walcott's plays as he writes about the condition of the common man. God is always a factor in the lives of his characters, but his own despair at both the God of his characters and the social conditions with which they must contend is dominant in his plays. Although the hero's "dream touch everyone" in *Monkey Mountain*, it was only a dream, a bitter irony. Yet Walcott's plays must also "touch everyone" as he makes use of a long career in the theatre to provide the innovative dramaturgy which transfers his thoughtful concern for man to the public theatre.

—Walter J. Meserve

WALKER, George F. Canadian. Born in Toronto, Ontario, 23 August 1947. Married to Stephanie Walker. Dramaturge, 1972–73, and Resident Playwright, 1972–76, Factory Theatre Lab, Toronto. Recipient: 4 Canada Council grants. Agent: Great North Agency, 345 Adelaide Street West, Toronto, Ontario M5V 1R5, Canada.

PUBLICATIONS

Plays

The Prince of Naples (produced Toronto, 1971). Toronto, Playwrights Co-op, 1972.
Ambush at Tether's End (produced Toronto, 1971). Toronto, Playwrights Co-op, 1972.

Sacktown Rag (produced Toronto, 1972).   Toronto, Playwrights Co-op, 1972.
Bagdad Saloon (produced Toronto and London, 1973).   Toronto, Playwrights Co-op, 1973.
Demerit (produced Toronto, 1974).
Beyond Mozambique (produced Toronto, 1974).   Toronto, Playwrights Co-op, 1975.
Ramona and the White Slaves (produced Toronto, 1976).

Radio Play: *The Private Man*, 1973.

Television Plays: *Microdrama*, 1975; *Strike*, 1976.

Critical Studies: *Factory Lab Anthology*, Vancouver, Talonbooks, 1974; "Playnotes" by Richard Horenblas, in *Scene Changes* (Toronto), October 1975.

George F. Walker comments:

I think all I am trying to do with my plays is find a form which allows my ideas and obsessions free and creative expression. Theatre today must clearly separate itself from film and television – must do something that no other medium can do as well. My plays combine large doses of the verbal and the visual in an attempt to realize this separation. The best examples are my last three plays: *Bagdad Saloon, Beyond Mozambique,* and *Ramona and the White Slaves*. Together they form a sort of trilogy: highly theatrical parables – words and images built specifically for the theatre.

*   *   *

George Walker's world is post-Beckett, but the scene enacted within that world is his own highly comic invention. The characters Bush and Galt in *Ambush at Tether's End* conduct a Godot-like conversation about the virtues of hanging themselves. Galt's fear that "all this" is "just a plot" is capped by Bush's that it is "just a joke." But the play hovers always on the edge of slapstick – talking corpses and verbal jokes. "Stop telling me to watch my step and stay on my toes," says Galt. We run the gamut from *Harold and Maude* through the *Goon Show* to *Rosencrantz and Guildenstern*. Walker gives us the ambience in the introduction: "Bush and Galt are ordinary men, businessmen, a comedy team, a couple of lost souls."
    The world of comic pathos is one that Walker sharpens by context. "Surely," says Soyer, the pedagogue in *Prince of Naples*, "you must realize that this novel was written in the Italian semi-surrealist vein." Significantly, it is when, as in *Sacktown Rag*, Walker comes closest to what (mistakenly) we should call realism that he is weakest. The insistence of the past (the burden of that play) is less forceful than the necessary absurdity of the present. In a world where what is called "communication" is in fact gibberish, the playwright's business is to present *The Dunciad* alive and kicking. "You're a cold-blooded killer," says Sara to Doc Halliday in *Bagdad Saloon*. "Yeah. It doesn't matter though, does it?" he replies. "'Cause I'm still whatyacallit. Just like the rest of them. Whatyacallit? Eternal?"
    Walker's temptation is to gravel this enterprise in the one-liners for which he has a talent. "I've always believed that evasiveness is next to godliness," says Max in *Ambush*, a sentiment that could sit well with the priest Liduc's advice to the whore Rita in *Beyond Mozambique*: "Jesus doesn't mind losers but he has no patience for idiots."
    But perhaps the one-liners are the play and the rest is the context for their delivery. Certainly the world of the later plays (*Bagdad Saloon, Beyond Mozambique,* and *Ramona and the White Slaves*) is one in which any grip on mundane reality is extremely tenuous. The cartoon sense of reality that is manifested at length in *Bagdad Saloon* is prepared for in *Sacktown Rag* where one of the characters describes the rest as "cartoon, comic book."

The peri-realism of Walker's manner continually circles the central mystery that is taking its course. "You have to look behind the words to read the truth of the matter," says Soyer in *Prince of Naples*. And in the later play, *Beyond Mozambique*, an interchange between the ex-Fascist doctor Rocco and the failed priest Liduc explores the same tension.

Rocco – My wife believes that she is a character from that play [*The Three Sisters*]. Her namesake. The eldest sister.
Liduc – How does she reconcile this belief with reality?
Rocco – Which reality?
Liduc – I understand.
Rocco – Do you?
Liduc – No.

"Personality," says Liduc, falling back later into a coke trance, "is a dangerous illusion." But then so, in Walker's plays, is "reality." The plays surround other realities without enclosing them or subscribing to them. The grey-face make-up of *Beyond Mozambique* suggests the film ambience that Rita at least makes explicit.

The usefulness of cartoon is that it cannot be mistaken for naive verisimilitude and reminds the facile viewer, as Soyer says, that "this isn't yesterday, it's almost tomorrow and an entire school of philosophy has been discarded since then." Beyond the self-parody and perpetual déjà-vu that characterize the highly wrought surface of these plays is the only felt design of darkness that gives them their lurking force. The act of seeing is the reality.

—D. D. C. Chambers

WALKER, Joseph A.   American.   Recipient: Obie Award, 1973. Address: c/o Hill and Wang, 19 Union Square West, New York, New York 10003, U.S.A.

PUBLICATIONS

Plays

The Believers, with Josephine Jackson, music and lyrics by Benjamin Carter and others (produced New York, 1968).
The Harangues (produced New York, 1970).
Ododo (also director: produced New York, 1970).
The River Niger (produced New York, 1972).   New York, Hill and Wang, 1973.
Yin Yang, music by Dorothy A. Dinroc (also director: produced New York, 1973).

Theatrical Activities

Director: **Plays** – *Ododo*, New York, 1970; *Yin Yang*, New York, 1973.

*   *   *

Black impotence, frustration, internecine strife, and frequent self-defeat form recurring themes in Joseph A. Walker's highly emotional though rather erratic dramas. The playwright sets many lives and varieties of consciousness in conflict, and the tensions between young and old, militant and resigned, idealistic and pragmatic erupt in heated quarrels which end in physical violence. For all the richness of detail, however, his people do not always emerge from the patterns of stereotype and perhaps unconscious caricature which Walker's heavy handed theses set up. Too often his spectrum of characters remains merely representative, figures convenient for pointing to pre-drawn conclusions. Thus, since hhis plays beg the question and telegraph their predictable conclusions far in advance, dramatic action is weakened by excessive and clumsy plotting. Though many of his lines are now dated with the propaganda of the turbulent last decade, Walker's true strength lies in pungent dialogue which captures the accents of tenement and street and sometimes aspires to the vision and music of poetry.

Throughout his work Walker reiterates that survival depends upon the strength of family and community ties and upon the hope that future generations will find material success and true liberation. This hope cannot be realized, however, so long as Blacks betray it, through lack of self-respect, parasitic crime, and divisive rage. Although he reveals the internal struggles of his more complex characters, Walker generally divides his casts into opposing camps along simplistic, ideological lines. This attempt at artistic control provides some clarity but also results in self-consciousness. The artifice accentuates the irrationality of climactic outbursts and, ultimately, the arbitrary manner by which his overwrought plots are resolved.

In *The Harrangues*, Walker pairs two plays in which desperate men, driven by hatred to revenge, fall victim to their own plans. The themes of exploitation and hopelessness are announced by way of a prologue, in which an African father during the time of the slave trade kills his infant rather than surrender him to the ships. In the first play, a young Black plots to murder his pregnant fiancée's stepfather to prevent her disinheritance, but meets that fate himself at the hands of the White man and his Black minions. In the second, a range of defective personalities reveals the sickness of the present time: a thrill-seeking White girl whose Black lover is ashamed of his race, a homosexual pimp, and a deranged old Black man who rants against them and against White liberals and Uncle Toms. Both sections illustrate the bleak message of the opening, that the ancient anger and despair continue, leading to madness and the perpetuation of primitive and suicidal cruelty.

In his well-received and most ambitious work, *The River Niger*, Walker attempts a complex and realistic portrait of the hopes and frustrations of a Black family in Harlem, a story which resonates beyond its topical details for universal appeal. But in trying to convey a large number of concepts and to depict several contrasting personalities, the author does not always succeed: characters have not the leisure to develop naturally, plot lines are not always clear, and we are told more than we are shown. Again, structure is arbitrary, with juxtapositions more convenient than credible. The idealistic but failed paterfamilias, Johnny Williams, seeks refuge in poetry and the bottle, while still clinging to the hope of a better life which is possible for his son Jeff. But here too he is disappointed. His son's commission in the Air Force represents to Daddy Johnny a sign of success and a cause for pride. But to Jeff, a disillusioned member of the new generation, the uniform is but a reminder of his failure and another instance of subjugation to forces of bigotry and an unfair power structure; Jeff has left the Service not only for philosophical reasons but because he cannot make the grade. Ironically, though the son has more opportunity than his father had, he does not have the same talents as Johnny. Further, Jeff's new plans may be frustrated by his past as a gang leader. The new leader, Mo, is in the midst of a vendetta, and as he and his dope-addicted and perverted henchmen thrust themselves forcibly into Jeff's life, the newly liberated man is nearly dragged back into their vicious, suicidal world.

As representatives of the social diseases of the ghetto and the forces which make the patterns of crime and betrayal and failure so difficult to break, the function of the gang in the play is clear. But the details of the gang war are needlessly complicated, not to say confusing, and the reason the traitor should be homosexual is not made clear. So too, Grandma Brown represents additional tensions between the generations, but mainly provides awkward comic relief through the very hackneyed joke of an unsuccessful secret drunk. Likewise, Johnny's cynical old friend, Dr. Dudley Stanton, not only offers clever retorts to the poet's romantic opinions, but, in his capacity as a physician, is conveniently on hand to dress wounds and to announce that Johnny's wife Mattie is dying of cancer. While this fact compounds the tragedy, the effect seems gratuitous, and this melodramatic handling of plot detracts from the genuine power of Mattie's character. For the relationship of Johnny and Mattie, replicated in Jeff's girlfriend's fierce loyalty, forms the vital core of a heart-felt and potentially affecting drama. The fears, desires, strengths, and weaknesses which husband and wife and son and lover share speak not only to the hard life in the ghetto but to the universality of the human condition.

—Joseph Parisi

WALTER, Nancy.   American   Born in St. Paul, Minnesota, 28 June 1939. Attended the University of Minnesota, Minneapolis. Married Marlow Hotchkiss in 1959; Sydney Walter, 1968; has three children. Associated with the Firehouse Theatre, Minneapolis and San Francisco, since 1965. Recipient: Office for Advanced Drama Research Fellowship, 1969–72. Address: c/o Firehouse Theatre, 1563 Page Street, San Francisco, California; or, 881 Lowell Avenue, Mill Valley, California 94941, U.S.A.

PUBLICATIONS

Plays

> *Trunity* (produced Minneapolis, 1968).
> *Rags* (produced Minneapolis, 1969; New York, 1970).   Minneapolis, University of
>   Minnesota Press, 1971.
> *Blessings* (produced San Francisco, 1970).
> *Still Falling* (produced San Francisco, 1971).
> *The Window* (produced San Francisco, 1972).
> *Traveling Light* (produced San Francisco, 1972).
> *Stab and Dance* (produced San Francisco, 1974).
> *Something Funny* (produced San Francisco, 1976).

Nancy Walter comments:

On the Theatre:
Speaking of the common body

We couldn't keep him alive
through the wars
through the hierarchies of waste and survival,
our sense of him was hidden
in our private cries
for new ways to be born
and the calling of distant seclusions.

When I look back
to find him
I imagine that we met without edges
that our ceremonies
touched his quick spirit
and invited the slow drowning of our senses
in the stuff of his elusive world
at once
all of us together.

If we meet here now
strangers
in the theatre
it is to unwrap the mummy
of our common self.

And if we are to go beyond his painted portrait
if the windings are to be continuously undone
it is time
to share the secret field of our natural singular acts:
together to
call down its holes
to clamber over its rocks
to speak without shame of the times we lost ourselves there.

If we succeed
disclose
the transparent material of the flesh itself
still sweet and unfolding:
the dancer himself
a presence we must surely
be nourished by
for we have seen too long
only the shadow of the dancer's dance.

If we succeed
he moves
we circulate his substance among us
and it doesn't diminish,
his blood
challenges the walls
making them shiver,
his eyes
move the curtains.

From behind
the lost origins of the words
he speaks into his hand
the ground on which we stand,
we receive the image he can't keep.

In the richness
of our interconnexion
and attention
he transforms through

an infinite series of world illusions
through countless falls beyond balance
and the exhilaration of recoveries
that contradict
the waste and disillusion
of the easy gesture
and the lonely heave within.

*   *   *

Nancy Walter has created her works originally for one ensemble, The Firehouse Theatre, formerly of Minneapolis, more recently of San Francisco. But it would be more accurate to say that while she began writing for the ensemble several years ago, she now writes for the active participation both of the ensemble and its audiences. More and more, her work is concerned with the psychic and tactile awareness of the performer and the spectator.

Rags, one of her first produced works for The Firehouse, remained primarily in the hands of the performers and stuck closely to the written text. But the plays since then have more and more demanded that the performer, through improvisation, search his own psyche, and have offered the spectator a similar chance through physical participation in the proceedings. In fact, by the time of *Still Falling*, it was possible for the spectator to take over one of the principal roles from a performer and radically alter the character of that night's drama.

Given the growing openness of the action, the written text is nevertheless *precisely* written, in fact normally structured in verse, and the images concrete. The dialogue tends to be highly lyrical, and is usually introspective and philosophical. Nancy Walter's people are always conjecturing about where they are in the cosmos and trying to get a mental foothold on states of being. For instance, Glaber in *Blessings*:

> Listen to me. There was nothing.
> There was suffering and discontent.
> But there was no way to look at it.
> There was blood and disorder.
> But there was no way to hold it.
> I was not there,
> all my cells had gone into the woods, each
> one separately, I thought
> I was running with them but I was wrong

Or Yublom in *Still Falling*:

> Can you stretch me into a world?
> can you let the others out?
>   just to stay alive is an ordeal
> I never thought
> I could come back to this place
> another bowl of worms
> now I'm the bowl and the worms too
> I'm pretty sure this place wasn't meant for me.

The events in the plays are events only in the sense that dreams are events. More and more they take on an interior life, they seem to be happening in someone's head, perhaps our own. They are set up without designated locales, deepening one's uncertainty about the level of reality. There is no real feeling of time, only the sense sometimes of initiation, sometimes of recurrence. No real feeling of place, but of being sometimes lodged, sometimes confined, sometimes free, sometimes adrift. If events have primarily an interior life, characters exist not as people but as certain propensities in the natural order of things. Yublom, for example, is first seen in a mudhole, "raging around, his hair is matted, he's half-naked and dirty. His behavior is compulsive in the extreme: he rocks, sucks, strokes himself. He is often on his hands and knees or his haunches. He screams a couple of loud warning screams, battlecries, and begins to throw shit at the audience." The aura of Yublom is strongly that of primitive consciousness being dragged from the primeval sludge towards some refinement of consciousness. But really, the sense is that Yublom is being dragged *back*, that he has been there before. Pop, the father in *Rags*, represents rather than is certain authoritarian and heavily masculine traits. Others are fools, saints, stricken angels. But still others can't be so readily seen, their traits are murkier, more complex. It's almost as if they are attempting to get their traits in order.

Many of the names suggest mythic qualities, Yublom, Astruth, Karun, Marmo, prehistoric or metaphysical figures moving through the cosmos before the dawn of man. But they are also very much creatures of our own urban disorder, righteous, confused, lustful, looking down the road for the next high. Yublom:

> Someone will come and get me soon, in the evening when it's dark those people will come again. Some will be dumped in here with me, those recent victims — those who killed their best selves, who were found hanging in the broom closet and put away, who were killed accidentally or on purpose, who were put away by the state, you know, jonathan jackson, caryl chesman, Charles Manson, janis joplin, Dag Hammersjkold, Martin Luther King, Sharon Tate, Medgar Evars, Al Capone, people who hurt themselves, jimi hendrix, billy the kid, teddy kennedy, my brother Ted too, and that kid who shot himself in the school washroom, I don't remember his name, Marcel Proust and Julius Caesar, Paul the Absurd and Yoko Ono ....

The plays are nothing if not impassioned. In Nancy Walter's plays, humanity is obstinately seeking out its own wounds, trying to understand, trying to be whole. "Someday," says Glaber,

> when I am loosed from this knot
> I will sing one clear note, one clear word
> I will be released to one single act
> How sweet the world will be to me then.
> Then when I lay down
> I will not crush the grass
> Then when I speak I will
> know my voice
> My burning brain and my skeleton will meet the air.

—Arthur Sainer

WARD, Douglas Turner.   American.   Born in Burnside, Louisiana, 5 May 1930. Educated at Xavier University Preparatory School, 1941–46; Wilberforce University, Ohio, 1946–47; University of Michigan, Ann Arbor, 1947–48; Paul Mann's Actors Workshop, New York, 1955–58. Married Diana Hoyt Powell in 1966; has two children. Co-Founder, 1965, and since 1967, Artistic Director, Negro Ensemble Company, New York. Recipient: Vernon Rice Award, 1966; Obie Award, 1966, 1970, for acting, 1973; Drama Desk Citation, for acting, 1969. Agent: Gilbert Parker, Curtis Brown Ltd., 60 East 56th Street, New York, New York 10022. Address: 222 East 11th Street, New York, New York 10003, U.S.A.

PUBLICATIONS

Plays

> *Happy Ending, and Day of Absence* (produced New York, 1965).   New York,
>   Dramatists Play Service, 1966.
> *The Reckoning* (produced New York, 1969).   New York, Dramatists Play Service,
>   1970.
> *Brotherhood* (also director: produced New York, 1970).   New York, Dramatists Play
>   Service, 1970.

Critical Study: Introduction by Sheila Rush, to *Two Plays* by Douglas Turner Ward, New
York, Third Press-Viking Press, 1971.

Theatrical Activities:

Director: **Plays** – *Daddy Goodness* by Richard Wright and Louis Sapin, New York, 1968;
Man Better Man by Errol Hill, New York, 1969; *Contribution* by Ted Shine, New York,
1969; *Brotherhood and Day of Absence*, New York, 1970; *Ride a Black Horse* by John
Scott, New York, 1971; *Perry's Mission* by Clarence Young III, New York, 1971; *The
River Niger* by Joseph A. Walker, New York, 1972; *The Great MacDaddy* by Paul Carter
Harrison, New York, 1974; *The First Breeze of Summer* by Leslie Lee, New York, 1975.

Actor: as Douglas Turner and Douglas Turner Ward: **Plays** – Joe Mott in *The Iceman
Cometh* by O'Neill, New York, 1957; in *Lost in the Stars* by Maxwell Anderson, New
York; Moving Man, then Walter Younger, in *A Raisin in the Sun* by Lorraine Hansberry,
New York, 1959, then tour, 1960–61; Archibald in *The Blacks* by Jean Genet, New York,
1961; Porter in *Pullman Car Hiawatha* by Thornton Wilder, New York, 1962;
understudied Fredericks in *One Flew over the Cuckoo's Nest* by Dale Wasserman, New
York, 1963; Zachariah Pieterson in *The Blood Knot* by Athol Fugard, New York, 1964 and
tour; Fitzroy in *Rich Little Rich Girl* by Hugh Wheeler, Philadelphia, 1964; Roman Citizen
in *Coriolanus*, New York, 1965; Arthur in *Happy Ending*, New York, 1965; Mayor and
Clan in *Day of Absence*, New York, 1965; with the Negro Ensemble Company, New
York: Oba Danlola in *Kongi's Harvest* by Wole Soyinka, 1968, in *Summer of the
Seventeenth Doll* by Ray Lawler, 1968, Thomas in *Daddy Goodness* by Richard Wright and
Louis Sapin, 1968, Russell B. Parker in *Ceremonies in Dark Old Men* by Lonne Elder III,
1969, Scar in *The Reckoning*, 1969, Black Man and Asura in *The Harangues* by Joseph A.
Walker, 1970, in *Frederick Douglass in His Own Words*, 1972, Johnny Williams in *The
River Niger* by Joseph A. Walker, 1972, and Harper Edwards in *The First Breeze of
Summer* by Leslie Lee, 1975. **Film** – *Man and Boy*, 1971. **Television** – roles since 1958, in
Studio One, East Side/West Side, The Edge of Night series, and *Look Up and Live*.

Douglas Turner Ward comments:

I am a black playwright, of black sensibilities, primarily utilizing the devices of satire,
exaggeration and mordant humor to explore and express themes of contemporary life,
particularly as they relate to black survival.

*   *   *

Douglas Turner Ward, an American Negro, is one of those rare individuals who have successfully combined careers as actor, writer, and director. He has twice won Obie awards for plays which he wrote and in which he performed. In 1966, he was awarded an Obie for writing and for acting in *Happy Ending* and *Day of Absence*, and in 1970 he earned another for *The Reckoning*. In 1966 he received the Vernon Rice Award for writing *Happy Ending* and *Day of Absence*. Since 1967 he has been Artistic Director of the Negro Ensemble Company, an important repertory company which he and actor-director Robert Hooks founded.

Despite his success as an actor, Ward is better known as a dramatist, particularly for his first two plays, *Happy Ending* and *Day of Absence*, in which he revealed a talent for satirical treatment of the relationships between blacks and whites. The history of these award-winning one-acts is almost as ironic as their subject matter. Although both plays were completed by 1960, Ward could not find a producer until, five years later, the Negro actor Robert Hooks, operating on limited financing, arranged to have them produced at St. Mark's Theatre.

As *Happy Ending* opens, two female Negro domestics are lamenting their employer's decision to divorce his promiscuous wife. Their sorrow is interrupted by their dapper nephew, who rebukes them for pitying people who have overworked and underpaid them. This, he informs them, is their chance to escape from domestic labor. Then, they educate hhim to the ironies of life: as middle-aged Negro women, with limited formal education (four strikes against them), they can expect only low paying jobs which will barely provide subsistence. In contrast, as domestic laborers, though they have received little money, they have provided their nephew with fashionable clothes not missed from the employer's wardrobe and with food smuggled from the employer's larder. As the nephew joins in their sorrows, they receive the happy news that the employers have become reconciled.

Day of Absence is a one-act satirical fantasy about the turmoil in a Southern city on a day when all blacks disappear. White couples begin to argue as they discover that they have no experience tending the house or caring for their children. The Ku Klux Klan is bitter because, with Negros gone, it no longer has a pretext for existence and victims for sadistic practices. Elected repeatedly on a campaign of keeping Negroes in their places, the mayor proves incompetent to manage the affairs of the town. In the midst of the despair, the reappearance of one Negro reassures the whites that others will return. The play ends, however, with the question of whether the whites have fully learned how much they depend upon blacks.

Ward's first full-length play, *The Reckoning*, produced by the Negro Ensemble Company in 1969, focuses on a confrontation between a Negro pimp and a Southern governor. Ward continued his satire in the one-act *Brotherhood* (produced in 1970), in which a white husband and wife try to mask their anti-Negro sentiments from a middle-class Negro couple whom they have invited to their house. The Negroes are not deceived. In 1966, in an article published in the Sunday *New York Times*, Ward adumbrated the need for a predominantly Negro audience "to readily understand, debate, confirm, or reject the truth or falsity" of the creations of the black playwright. Ward insisted that whenever a black playwright writes for a predominantly white audience — "least equipped to understand his intentions, woefully apathetic or anesthetized to his experience, often prone to distort his purpose" — that writer must restrict himself to the rudimentary re-education of that audience. Consequently, he has no opportunity to develop artistically. Although he admitted that a black playwright could gain the necessary "theatre of Negro identity" in a Negro community, Ward saw no possibility for such a theatre prior to massive reconstruction of the urban ghettos.

His hope of such a Negro-oriented theatre inspired the founding of the Negro Ensemble Company, which, since 1968, has been housed at the St. Mark's Theatre in New York City. The company, which won Tony awards in 1969 and 1974, probably achieved its greatest success to date with the 1969 production of Lonne Elder's *Ceremonies in Dark Old Men*.

—Darwin T. Turner

WATERHOUSE, Keith (Spencer).   British.   Born in Leeds, Yorkshire, 6 February 1929.
Educated at Osmondthorpe Council School, Leeds. Married Joan Foster in 1950 (divorced,
1968); has three children. Free-lance Journalist and Writer, in Leeds and London, since
1950. Currently, Columnist, *Daily Mirror*, London. Governor, Leeds Theatre Trust. Agent:
London Management, 235-241 Regent Street, London W1A 2JT. Address: 70 St. Paul Street,
London N.1, England.

PUBLICATIONS

Plays

    Billy Liar, with Willis Hall, adaptation of the novel by Keith Waterhouse (produced
        London, 1960; Los Angeles and New York, 1963).   London, Joseph, and New
        York, Norton. 1960.
    Celebration: The Wedding and The Funeral, with Willis Hall (produced Nottingham
        and London, 1961).   London, Joseph, 1961.
    England, Our England, with Willis Hall, music by Dudley Moore (produced London,
        1962).   London, Evans, 1964.
    Squat Betty, with Willis Hall (produced London, 1962; New York, 1964).   Included in
        The Sponge Room and Squat Betty, 1963.
    The Sponge Room, with Willis Hall (produced Nottingham and London, 1962; New
        York, 1964).   Included in *The Sponge Room and Squat Betty*, 1963; in *Modern Short
        Plays from Broadway and London*, edited by Stanley Richards, New York, Random
        House, 1969.
    All Things Bright and Beautiful, with Willis Hall (produced Bristol and London, 1962).
        London, Joseph, 1963.
    The Sponge Room and Squat Betty, with Willis Hall.   London, Evans, 1963.
    Come Laughing Home, with Willis Hall (as *They Called the Bastard Stephen*, produced
        Bristol, 1964; as *Come Laughing Home*, produced Wimbledon, 1965).   London,
        Evans, 1965.
    Say Who You Are, with Willis Hall (produced London, 1965).   London, Evans, 1967;
        as *Help Stamp Out Marriage* (produced New York, 1966), New York, French, 1966.
    Joey, Joey, with Willis Hall, music by Ron Moody (produced London, 1966).
    Whoops-a-Daisy, with Willis Hall (produced Nottingham, 1968).
    Children's Day, with Willis Hall (produced Edinburgh and London, 1969).   London,
        French, 1975.
    Who's Who, with Willis Hall (produced Coventry, 1971; London, 1973).   London,
        French, 1974.
    Saturday, Sunday, Monday, with Willis Hall, adaptation of a play by Eduardo de Filippo
        (produced London, 1973).   London, Heinemann, 1974.
    The Card, with Willis Hall, music and lyrics by Tony Hatch and Jackie Trent, adaptation
        of the novel by Arnold Bennett (produced Bristol and London, 1973).

Screenplays, with Willis Hall: *Whistle Down the Wind*, 1961; *A Kind of Loving*, 1961;
The Valiant, 1962; *Billy Liar*, 1963; *West Eleven*, 1963; *Man in the Middle*, 1964; *Pretty
Polly (A Matter of Innocence)*, 1968; *Lock Up Your Daughters*, 1969.

Radio Plays: *The Town That Wouldn't Vote*, 1951; *There Is a Happy Land*, 1962; *The
Woolen Bank Forgeries*, 1964; *The Last Phone-In*, 1976.

Television Plays: *The Warmonger*, 1970; with Willis Hall: *Happy Moorings*, 1963; *How
Many Angels*, 1964; *Inside George Webley* series, 1968; *Queenie's Castle* series, 1970;
Budgie series, 1971–72; *The Upper Crusts* series, 1973; *Three's Company* series, 1973;
By Endeavour Alone, 1973; *Billy Liar* series, 1973–74.

Novels

There Is a Happy Land.   London, Joseph, 1957.
Billy Liar.   London, Joseph, 1959; New York, Norton, 1960.
Jubb.   London, Joseph, 1963; New York, Putnam, 1964.
The Bucket Shop.   London, Joseph, 1968; as *Everything Must Go.* New York, Putnam, 1969.
Billy Liar on the Moon.   London, Joseph, 1975, New York, Putnam, 1976.

Other

The Cafe Royal: Ninety Years of Bohemia, with Guy Deghy.   London, Hutchinson, 1955.
How to Avoid Matrimony, with Guy Deghy (as Herald Froy).   London, Muller, 1957.
Britain's Voice Abroad, with Paul Cave.   London, Daily Mirror Newspapers, 1957.
The Future of Television.   London, Daily Mirror Newspapers, 1958.
The Joneses: How to Keep Up with Them, with Guy Deghy (as Lee Gibb).   London, Muller, 1959.
The Higher Jones, with Guy Deghy (as Lee Gibb).   London, Muller, 1961.
The Passing of the Third Floor Buck (*Punch* sketches).   London, Joseph, 1974.
Mondays, Thursdays (*Daily Mirror* columns).   London, Joseph, 1976.

Editor, with Willis Hall, *Writers' Theatre.*   London, Heinemann, 1967.

*   *   *

See the essay on Willis Hall and Keith Waterhouse on page 348.

WEBB, Leonard.   British.   Born in Bow, London, 21 August 1930. Educated at Attlee Road Elementary School and the Coopers' Company's School, London; St. Catherine's College, Oxford (Spender Memorial Prize, 1953), B.A. (honours) 1954. Served in the Royal Army Service Corps, 1950–51: Corporal Instructor. Has two children. Lektor, British Centre, Sweden, 1955–57; Tutor, City Literary Institute and the Workers Educational Association, London, 1968–70. Since 1967, Tutor, Morley College, London; since 1968, Lecturer, Chelsea College, London; since 1969, Lecturer, American Institute for Foreign Studies, London. Visiting Playwright, Baldwin-Wallace College, Berea, Ohio, 1971. Comedian, Windmill Theatre, London, 1955; Television Interviewer and Panelist. Recipient: Allied Theatre Grant, 1967–69. Agent: Margaret Ramsay Ltd., 14a Goodwin's Court. London WC2N 4LL. Address: 20 Thurloe Road, London N.W.3, England.

PUBLICATIONS

Plays

Charade for Seven (produced Oxford, 1954).
Chance a Cockney (produced London, 1960).
The Spiral Bird (produced Bristol, 1965).
So What about Love? (produced Cambridge and London, 1969).

For What We Are about to Conceive (produced London, 1969).
Stag Party (produced Dublin, 1972).
Not Drowning But Waving (produced London, 1973).

Radio Plays: *Murder Can Lead to Divorce*, 1967; *Taking the Plunge*, 1968.

Television Plays: *Oxford Accents*, 1954; *Cheerio Lou*, 1961; *Maggie*, 1964; *Do What You Want To*, 1973; *Poppy and Her*, 1976.

Theatrical Activities:

Actor: **Plays** – understudied all four roles in *Beyond the Fringe*, London, 1961; roles in London, Edinburgh, Glasgow, and on television.

Leonard Webb comments:

Although I have been an obsessional writer of seriously-comic plays since student days, and a certain body of moderately distinguished approval is beginning to cluster around my work, my achievement is still too diffuse, my development too tortuous, to warrant the Olympian indulgence of self-criticism.

*   *   *

Leonard Webb is a rare kind of writer to find in modern England: someone who seriously explores the relationship between sex and love within the framework of conventional West End comedy. But then several things about Mr. Webb are unusual. He must be the only Oxford graduate in English ever to have worked at the old Windmill Theatre as a stand-up comic doing a 15-minute spot six times a day, and he also has the unique distinction of having understudied the whole London cast of *Beyond the Fringe* during its run at the Fortune Theatre.

His writing career began at Oxford where he was a prominent performer in university revues; he had some television plays done during the Sixties, including *Maggie* on BBC 1 with Vanessa Redgrave; and he had a comedy, *The Spiral Bird*, presented at Bristol Old Vic in 1965. But it was only with *So What about Love?* at the Criterion in 1969 that he came to public attention; and not the least surprising thing about the play was that a young writer should have chosen the seemingly outmoded form of traditional Shaftesbury Avenue comedy in which to express his ideas.

In retrospect one can see why, for Mr. Webb's point is that sex without love is not enough, and the light comedy form, with its concentration on private rather than public life, fits this kind of theme perfectly. Thus the central figure in *So What about Love?* is a divorced biology teacher from Battersea who can't make up her mind whether or not to settle down with Dicky, a dithering poetry lecturer from Chelsea. The problem is that she already has four other lovers gently simmering on the quiet and he is living with the success-worshipping daughter of a Home Counties stockbroker-father. And just to complicate matters there is a smoothly assured lawyer floating around desperately in love with Dicky's upper-class girl.

Simple enough fare, you might think. But not really, for Mr. Webb pins down with some accuracy the aimless misery of the new-style London singles who all sleep around quite freely but who are really hungering for some permanent relationship or for marriage or for, quite simply, love. It might be too much to call Mr. Webb an old-fashioned moralist; but the truth is that, no less than Malcolm Muggeridge, he obviously believes that random physical attachments without any element of love are ultimately rather joyless and destructive. He also has the essential gift of writing individually funny lines: "That's real class," says the heroine at one point observing candles alight in the afternoon, "having things you don't need." The weakness of the play is that, although he endows the characters with perfectly believable desires and emotions, he doesn't pay enough attention to the social background: you completely accept, for instance, the biology teacher's enthusiastic enjoyment of sex but the mind boggles at the thought of her in a classroom. Still it remains an impressive play in that it tries to give substance and depth to a genre that, as a rule, offers little more than lightweight escapism.

So far Webb's recent play, *Stag Party*, has only been seen at the 1972 Dublin Theatre Festival; but, like its predecessor, it too is concerned with the interlocking emotional and sexual lives of a contemporary foursome. The hero here is a 39-year-old wine-dealer who has been married for 15 years but who has been in love with Freddie, his old school-army-and-business chum, for more than 20 years. He also wants to bed a girl called Rose who wants to bed Freddie who in turn cannot make any positive commitment towards anyone because of his emotional atrophy.

It sound like a complex bedroom farce but in point of fact it's one of those strange tragi-comic plays in which the laughs are usually dependent on someone else's pain. It is also very much an extension of the previous play in that no-one wants sex without love; and as a result all the characters end up without either. Once again, in fact, Mr. Webb's thesis seems to be that physical desire and emotional fulfilment should ideally go hand in hand and that to emphasise one at the expense of the other leads to an unhealthy imbalance.

So far Mr. Webb has handled this one theme with a good deal of insight, wit and theatrical flair. The question now is to see how far he can extend his theatrical territory to take in the public as well as the private world and to see whether he can get beyond the relatively confined stylistic space in which he has so far successfully operated.

—Michael Billington

WEIDMAN, Jerome. American. Born in New York City, 4 April 1913. Educated at the City College of New York, 1930–33; Washington Square College, New York, 1933–34; New York University Law School, 1934–37. Served with the United States Office of War Information, 1942–45. Married Elizabeth Ann Payne in 1943; has two children. Since 1967, President, Authors League of America. Recipient: Pulitzer Prize, 1960; New York Drama Critics Circle Award, 1960; Tony Award, 1960. Agent: Brandt and Brandt, 101 Park Avenue, New York, New York 10017. Address: 1390 South Ocean Boulevard, Pompano Beach, Florida 33062, U.S.A.

PUBLICATIONS

Plays

Fiorello!, with George Abbott, music and lyrics by Sheldon Harnick and Jerry Bock (produced New York, 1959; Bristol and London, 1962). New York, Random House, 1960.
Tenderloin, with George Abbott, music and lyrics by Sheldon Harnick and Jerry Bock, adaptation of the work by Samuel Hopkins Adams (produced New York, 1960). New York, Random House, 1961.

I Can Get It for You Wholesale, music by Harold Rome, adaptation of the novel by
Jerome Weidman (produced New York, 1962).   New York, Random House, 1963.
Cool Off!, music by Howard Blackman (produced Philadelphia, 1964).
Pousse Café, music by Duke Ellington (produced New York, 1966).
Ivory Tower, with James Yaffe (produced Ann Arbor, Michigan, 1968).   New York,
Dramatists Play Service, 1969.
The Mother Lover (produced New York, 1969).
Asterisk! A Comedy of Terrors (produced New York, 1969).   New York, Dramatists
Play Service, 1969.

Screenplays: *The Damned Don't Cry*, 1950; *The Eddie Cantor Story*, 1953; *House of
Strangers*, 1955; *Slander*, 1957.

Television Plays: *The Reporter* series, 1964.

Novels

I Can Get It for You Wholesale.   New York, Simon and Schuster, 1937; London,
Heinemann, 1938.
What's in It for Me?   New York, Simon and Schuster, 1938; London, Heinemann,
1939.
I'll Never Go There Anymore.   New York, Simon and Schuster, 1941; London,
Heinemann, 1942.
The Lights Around the Shore.   New York, Simon and Schuster, 1942; London, Hale,
1948.
Too Early to Tell.   New York, Reynal, 1946.
The Price Is Right.   New York, Harcourt Brace, 1949, London, Hammond Hammond,
1950.
Give Me Your Love.   New York, Harcourt Brace, 1949.
The Hand of the Hunter.   New York, Harcourt Brace, 1951; London, Cape, 1952.
The Third Angel.   New York, Doubleday, 1953; London, Cape, 1954.
Your Daughter, Iris.   New York, Doubleday, 1955, London, Cape, 1956.
The Enemy Camp.   New York, Random House, 1958; London, Heinemann, 1959.
Before You Go.   New York, Random House, 1960, London, Heinemann, 1961.
The Sound of Bow Bells.   New York, Random House, 1962; London, Heinemann,
1963.
Word of Mouth.   New York, Random House, 1964; London, Bodley Head, 1965.
Other People's Money.   New York, Random House, and London, Bodley Head, 1967.
The Center of the Action.   New York, Random House, 1969; London, Bodley Head,
1970.
Fourth Street East.   New York, Random House, and London, Bodley Head, 1971.
Last Respects.   New York, Random House, and London, Bodley Head, 1972.
Tiffany Street.   New York, Random House, and London, Bodley Head, 1974.
The Temple.   New York, Simon and Schuster, 1975; London, Boadly Head, 1976.

Short Stories

The Horse That Could Whistle "Dixie" and Other Stories.   New York, Simon and
Schuster, 1939; London, Heinemann, 1941.
The Captain's Tiger.   New York, Reynal, 1947.
A Dime a Throw.   New York, Harcourt Brace, 1957.
Nine Stories.   New York, Random House, 1960.
My Father Sits in the Dark and Other Selected Stories.   New York, Random House,

1961; London, Heinemann, 1963.
Where the Sun Never Sets and Other Stories.   London, Heinemann, 1964.
The Death of Dickie Draper and Nine Other Stories.   New York, Random House, 1965.

Other

Letter of Credit (travel).   New York, Simon and Schuster, 1940.
Back Talk (essays).   New York, Random House, 1963.

Editor, *A Somerset Maugham Reader.*   New York, Garden City Books, 1943.
Editor, *Traveler's Cheque.*   New York, Doubleday, 1954.
Editor, with others, *The First College Bowl Question Book.*   New York, Random
    House, 1961.

Manuscript Collection: Humanities Research Center, University of Texas, Austin.

*   *   *

The best of Jerome Weidman's musical comedies are concerned with some aspect of New
York life: *Fiorello!*, which traces the rise of the city's illustrious mayor, deals with problems
of politics, *Tenderloin* with vice and corruption in a particular area of New York, and *I Can
Get It for You Wholesale* with the trials, tribulations and ethos of the garment district. Yet, the
plays are far from parochial, because character and theme transcend the narrow confines of
their specific period and geographic location. Fiorello's "little tin box" is not far removed
from political life in America today and the problems of the Reverend Brock in *Tenderloin*
are reminiscent of certain news from England. Nor is there any question that such themes are
appropriate for the musical stage. They are, after all, part of a tradition which dates back at
least as far as Gay's *Beggar's Opera* via Gilbert and Sullivan's "intellectual comedies."

The protagonist of these three plays are men of considerable ambition. But there is a
difference between the aspirations of La Guardia, the moral fervor of Reverend Brock and
Harry Bogan's crooked deals which Weidman, in his equally sympathetic treatment of all
three, tends to obscure and thereby undermines the moral dimension on which he insists.
Both La Guardia and Brock are lively and sympathetic, but Harry Bogan's shady operations –
breaking a strike, unloading a trusting partner, blowing the firm's money on a "fashion
consultant" and throwing the blame for a bankruptcy on another partner – are neither
exhilarating matter for the musical theater, nor treated with the cynicism of Brecht.

With *Ivory Tower*, Weidman moves from musical comedy to drama. Although Weidman
and his collaborator, James Yaffe, explicitly disclaim any specific identification with historical
personages, the fate of the protagonist strongly resembles that of Ezra Pound. Simon Otway is
a famous expatriate poet who broadcast propaganda for the German army during World War
II; the intended subject is the relationship between the artist and society and the action
involves his trial for sedition after the armistice. All this should make for an interesting play
but, unfortunately, the authors' use of the material does not measure up to its potential.

The dramatis personae include an array of stereotypes, such as Harold Gutman, the Jewish
prosecutor, Wendel Drew, an English professor in charge of the "Save Otway Committee,"
and Vincent Rimini, the young defense attorney who stakes his career on this case. There is
the pseudo-Freudian exploration of Otway's childhood and early marriage to a waitress. But
the main problem with the play is that we are meant to see Simon Otway as a major artist,
even if politically irresponsible. We are told, for example, that his work embodies "the
greatest experiment with language this century has seen," and even one of his critics calls
him "the finest master of the short story in this century." Otway, however, spouts little more
than literary and philosophical clichés. In the end he breaks under the pressure of Gutman's

questions and, his megalomania and paranoia no longer disguised, suffers a psychotic episode.

Weidman is generally most successful in musical comedy where his talent to dramatize the big city atmosphere can be augmented by music and lyrics.

—Erica Aronson

WEINSTEIN, Arnold. American. Born in New York City, 10 June 1927. Educated at Hunter College, New York, B.A. in classics 1951 (Phi Beta Kappa); University of London, 1949–50; Harvard University, Cambridge, Massachusetts, M.A. in comparative literature 1952; University of Florence (Fulbright Fellowship), 1958–60. Served in the United States Navy, 1944–46. Married Suzanne Burgess in 1969. Visiting Lecturer, New York University, 1955–56; University of Southern California, Los Angeles; United States Information Service Lecturer, Italy, 1958–60; Director of Drama Workshop, Wagner College, Staten Island, New York, Summers 1964, 1965; Visiting Professor, Hollins College, Virginia, 1964–65; Professor of Dramatic Literature, New School for Social Research, New York, 1957–66; Chairman of the Department of Playwriting, Yale University, New Haven, Connecticut, 1966–69; Visiting Professor, University of Colorado, Boulder, Summer 1969; Chairman of the Department of Drama, Columbia College, Chicago, 1969–70. Co-Director, with Paul Sills, Second City, and other improvisational groups; Director, Free Theatre, Chicago; Actors Studio, New York and Los Angeles; Rock Theatre and Guerilla Theatre, Los Angeles. Recipient: Guggenheim Fellowship, 1965. Agent: Audrey Wood, International Creative Management, 40 West 57th Street, New York, New York 10019. Address: Pitcher Pond, Lincolnville, Maine, U.S.A.

PUBLICATIONS

Plays

Red Eye of Love (produced New York, 1958). New York, Grove Press, 1961.
White Cap (produced New York, 1960).
Fortuna, music by Francis Thorne, adaptation of a play by Eduardo de Filippo and Armando Curcio (produced New York, 1962).
The Twenty Five Cent White Hat, in 3x3, with Elaine May and Kenneth Koch (produced New York, 1962).
Food for Thought: A Play about Food, with Jay and Fran Landesman (produced St. Louis, 1962).
Dynamite Tonite, music by William Bolcom (produced New York, 1963; revised versions, produced New York, 1964, New Haven, Connecticut, 1966). New York, Trio Music, 1964.
Party (produced New York, 1964).
They (produced Philadelphia, 1965).
Reg. U.S. Pat. Off., in Pardon Me, Sir, But Is My Eye Hurting Your Elbow, edited by Bob Booker and George Foster. New York, Geis, 1968.
Story Theatre (produced New Haven, Connecticut, 1968).
Greatshot, music by William Bolcom (produced New Haven, Connecticut, 1969).
Ovid, adaptation of Metamorphoses by Ovid (produced Chicago, 1969; New York, 1971).

Mahagonny, adaptation of the libretto by Brecht, music by Kurt Weill (produced New York, 1970).   Excerpts published in *Yale/Theatre* (New Haven, Connecticut), 1969.

The American Revolution, with Paul Sills, music by Tony Greco, lyrics by Arnold Weinstein (produced Washington, D.C., 1973).

More Metamorphoses, adaptation of the work by Ovid (produced Spoleto, Italy, 1973).

Gypsy New York (produced New York, 1974).

Lady Liberty's Ice Cream Cone (produced New York, 1974).

Captain Jinks, adaptation of the play by Clyde Fitch, music arranged by William Bolcom (produced New York, 1976).

Party, music by Laurence Rosenthal (produced New York, 1976).

Street Opera, music by William Russo (produced San Francisco, 1976).

Improvisational Material: *Second City*, New York, 1963–64.

Television Plays:*Improvisation; Story Theatre; The Last Ingredient*, music by David Amram.

Verse

Different Poems by the Same Author.   Rome, United States Information Service, 1960.

Manuscript Collection: Yale University, New Haven, Connecticut.

Critical Studies: *American Drama since World War II* and *The Jumping-Off Place* by Gerald Weales, New York, Harcourt Brace, 1962, 1969; *A Theatre Divided* by Martin Gottfried, Boston, Little Brown, 1967; *Opening Nights* by Martin Gottfried, New York, Putnam, 1969; *Common and Uncommon Masks* by Richard Gilman, New York, Random House, 1971.

Theatrical Activities:

Director: **Plays** − *Second City* (co-director, with Paul Sills), and other improvisational groups; his own and other plays at the Free Theatre, Chicago, Actors Studio, New York and Los Angeles, and the Rock Theatre and the Guerilla Theatre, Los Angeles.

Arnold Weinstein comments:

I try to write the history and mythology of today. I believe in the trinity of reading and righting and reaching; the schoolroom, the churchroom, the theatre are one, or all are lost. Drama and karma are one. Look them up. Look them up and down. The audience is half the action, the actors the other half; the author starts the fight. Power. The passing of power. It really is life there in the dark, here. The lightning of television terrifies most. Right in the word the intrusion of fear − fear of loss of control, loss of sale, loss of sorcery. Loss of power. Our fear sends us through the channels, puts us on our tracks. If the trinity does not control the power, what's left? Only everything. Everything running around in formless rampant ranks waiting for daring brutes to pick up the wire reins.

*   *   *

The generation of American playwrights that followed Arthur Miller and Tennessee Williams was a troubled one, reflecting a country that was emerging from a history of brute domination into a future of questions and complexities. These playwrights were similarly trapped between the theater styles and values of an outgoing past and the uncertainty of a fast-approaching future. Such men as Jack Gelber and Jack Richardson never fulfilled their early promise, but Arnold Weinstein's inability to find himself as a playwright is perhaps the most painful, for he is the most artistic, talented and original of the lot. But he has been hurt by a combination of critical rejection and changing taste, and though the author of charming plays and libretti, his career seems frustrated.

His New York professional debut was a production by The Living Theatre of *Red Eye of Love*, which remains his only full length play. The Living Theatre at the time was in its Brecht stage and so was Weinstein, who was to prove too affected by changing fashion and too insecure in his own style. The play is a romantic fable about American capitalism. Its hero is a toy-inventor in love with a girl who feels it her "duty to marry money." She turns to the owner of a 13-story meat market, which grows beyond 40 stories as the play progresses. This girl vacillates between the inventor (artist) and the butcher (capitalist) while the play does vaudeville turns to Joycean word games with a whimsicality that would prove a Weinstein signature. The author's stage energy, his antic humor, his feel for America and his deep love of cheap sentiment are established as they would persist through his subsequent work, but the play is too often precious and almost blatantly Brechtian.

In 1962 he wrote the libretto for an off-Broadway musical of inspired zaniness – *Fortuna* (Weinstein was to become involved with many musical projects, one of America's rare artistic playwrights to appreciate their value, but though several were planned, none reached Broadway). *Fortuna*, adapted from an Italian comedy, told of the impoverished and luckless title character who inherits a fortune on the condition that he have no sons. After a series of farcical complications, Fortuna gets his fortune. Once again, Weinstein was dealing with a Schweikian hero-victim (Expressionist and absurdist influences would for too long influence his work and keep him from self-discovery).

His one-act absurdist play, *The Twenty Five Cent White Hat*, opened and closed off-Broadway, unappreciated by New York's critics. Though the play tritely pled the importance of individuality, it was filled with Weinstein's lively and poetic comedy writing.

The turning point in the playwright's career, I feel, came with *Dynamite Tonite*, his "comic opera for actors" written with composer William Bolcom. Though not without relation to Brecht, the work had a brisk originality of its own. For though it was a legitimate opera, it was indeed written for actors – that is, non-singers. Weinstein's libretto was intensely pacifist, yet romantic and comic, tender and suffused with affection for a vulnerable mankind. Its operetta-style hero and heroine sang hilarious Wagnerian parodies in counterpoint to flatfooted soldiers doing soft shoe dances, and set as the work was on the battleground of a neverneverland it had an odd mixture of Expressionism and Americana that somehow worked.

Dynamite Tonite is a superb theater work, but it was so brutally criticized that it closed on its first night. Several attempts were made to revive it, first by the Repertory Theatre at Yale Drama School and once more off-Broadway, but it seemed doomed to rejection despite (or perhaps because of) its artistic superiority.

Weinstein wrote another musical work with Bolcom – *Greatshot*, also produced at Yale – this time in the style of the then-popular self-creative companies (such as his friends at The Living Theatre had developed), but there was no soul to the work, nor clarity of intention. The structured, verbal theater to which the playwright naturally inclined did not mesh with physical, improvisational, antiverbal theater he was emulating.

Meanwhile, he had been long preparing a new translation of the great Brecht-Weill opera, *Mahoganny*, and when it was finally produced after many years of effort, his work proved mediocre, though hardly showcased by the disastrous production.

Weinstein's history, then, is one of victimization by the American theater's commercialism, which leaves little room for so creative, artistic and poetic a playwright; it is a victimization by British-American theater generally, with its overwhelming sense of trend (absurdism, once hailed as *the* style for moderns, was obsolete after no more than five years of fashion); and it is a victimization by rejection. His past shows some fulfillment and great promise; his present is in limbo; his future depends on his own resolve and his treatment at the hands of both the theater and circumstance.

—Martin Gottfried

WELLER, Michael. American. Born in New York City, in 1942. Attended Brandeis University, Waltham, Massachusetts; Manchester University, Lancashire, 1964. Recipient: Creative Artists Public Service grant, 1976. Agent: Michael Imison, Dr. Jan Van Loewen Ltd., 81-83 Shaftesbury Avenue, London W1V 8BX, England.

PUBLICATIONS

Plays

Fred, music by Michael Weller, adaptation of the novel *Malcolm* by James Purdy (produced Waltham, Massachusetts, 1965).

How Ho-Ho Rose and Fell in Seven Short Scenes, music by Michael Weller (produced Exeter, 1968; London, 1972).

The Making of Theodore Thomas, Citizen, adaptation of the play *Johnny Johnson* by Paul Green (produced London, 1968).

Happy Valley (produced Edinburgh, 1969).

The Bodybuilders, and Now There's Just the Three of Us (produced London, 1969). Included in *The Bodybuilders, and Tira*, 1972; in *Off-Broadway Plays 2*, London, Penguin, 1972.

Poison Come Home (produced London, 1970).

Cancer (produced London, 1970). London, Faber, 1971; as *Moonchildren* (produced Washington, D.C., and New York, 1972), New York, French, 1971.

Grant's Movie (produced London, 1971). Included in *Grant's Movie, and Tira*, 1972.

Tira Tells Everything There Is to Know about Herself (produced London, 1971). Included in *The Bodybuilders, and Tira*, 1972; as *Tira* (produced New York, 1975), in *Grant's Movie, and Tira*, 1972.

The Bodybuilders, and Tira Tells Everything There Is to Know about Herself. New York, Dramatists Play Service, 1972.

Grant's Movie, and Tira. London, Faber, 1972.

More Than You Deserve, music by Jim Steinman, lyrics by Michael Weller and Jim Steinman (produced New York, 1973).

Twenty-Three Years Later (produced Los Angeles, 1973).

Fishing (produced New York, 1975; London, 1976). New York and London, French, 1975.

Dwarfman (produced New York, 1976).

*   *   *

In his introduction to the second Penguin collection of Off-Broadway plays, Charles Marowitz characterised Michael Weller's work as opening up a new kind of realism – unmundane, untrivial, unlike the pallid reproductions of "real life" which abound in both the American and English theatre; a realism which, still linked to the characteristics of its style, manages to extend itself into what I can only call "operatic" areas....His plays are an attempt to bring hyperbole back into the theatre...a kind of contemporary rhetoric in which the intensity of a character's feeling – no matter how inarticulate he may be – wells up in a loftiness of utterance which is simultaneously incongruous and inevitable.

In terms of the progress of his career so far, these judgments are particularly apt. His early plays all have in common dominating figures who burst in on a situation and radically alter, by their actions and attitudes, the preoccupations and life-styles of the people in that situation. *Now There's Just the Three of Us* revolves around two young American guys sharing a flat, both of whom are virgins and afflicted by a deep sexual timidity. Perry is at least honest about his hang-ups; but Frank tries to conceal his by bluff and bluster. A sexual athlete called Deke suddenly appears in their flat and both by his own actions and his perceptive exposure of the reasons for the boys' problems helps Perry, at least, to start overcoming them. Weller takes care not to establish Deke's background in too much naturalistic detail, so his existence as a kind of "alter ego" to the other two can be implied, not necessarily dependent on his physical reality. The play is distinguished by sharp characterisation, an ear for the nuances of dialogue and a zappy rhythm that is one of the author's hallmarks.

The Bodybuilders has many of the same qualities of dialogue and characterisation, but is rather less convincing, as the central relationship – between Keith, a frustrated young writer, and his shrewish wife, Kate, who is sucking his life blood – is observed from too prejudiced and subjective a fiviewpoint. Flash and Powie, the two "bodybuilders" of the title who sort everything out to Keith's satisfaction, are, as their names imply, wish-fulfilment figures who are scarcely credible even as projections of Keith's suppressed ego.

How Ho-Ho Rose and Fell is a bright, episodic little piece about fascism. A group of disoriented young people gather around a leader, Ho-Ho, who demands and gets unquestioning obedience. He leads them into several murderous escapades until, faced with the prospect of annihilation, they start to rebel against him and eventually abandon him. However, they have been so corrupted by his fascist values that, once they have got rid of him, they immediately start to look for someone among themselves to take his place. As in the other plays, the protagonist who alters the direction of the other characters – in this case, Ho-Ho – exists on a psychological and spiritual level outside his surface naturalism.

The experiments in a fresh, uncluttered kind of realism that these plays attempt reach a maturity in his three most accomplished pieces to date – *Cancer, Grant's Movie* and *Tira Tells Everything There Is to Know about Herself. Cancer* is a painfully funny and truthful confrontation between two life-styles – a group of young American college kids, living together in the same flat, with fashionably liberal and anarchic attitudes, opposite authoritarian figures like their landlord, cops and uncle of one of them, who form part of President Nixon's "silent majority." The relationships within the group are beautifully and accurately observed; every character's individual identity is strongly defined and evoked and is expressed through heightened prose whose effect is described so well by Mr. Marowitz. But the authoritarian figures are also living human beings in their own right, not just the one-dimensional caricatures they might so easily have been. The vacillating landlord who likes the kids but is under pressure from his more conformist tenants to do something about them; the cops who start by being brutal and are charmed into a more sympathetic attitude; and the uncle who comes to break the news to his nephew that his mother is dying of cancer – all these balance perfectly the hopefulness, rebelliousness and liveliness of the kids. In its entirety, the play is an elegiac, perhaps slightly over-romanticised impressionistic picture of the life of young people at university in the late sixties, but it is so exquisitely constructed, so essentially truthful to anyone who has been through a similar experience, that its faults are not important.

The hero of *Grant's Movie*, if such he can be called, never makes an appearance till right at the end of the play; but any similarities with Beckett and *Godot* end there. Three young

Californian hippies – Gug, Zig and Morning Glory – kidnap a cop who may or may not have shot Grant's brother dead at a demonstration. They indulge a prolonged fantasy of revenge according to a scenario planned by the absent Grant. As in *Cancer*, two different life-styles are brought into conflict, this time in an atmosphere of harsh brutality. The play tells us a great deal about the late sixties' political and cultural division between the "freaks" and the "straights" in U.S. society; and is riveting as a purely theatrical exercise, having all Weller's qualities of rhythm and characterisation.

Tira is a young working-class girl who goes through affairs with several men, none of which satisfies her. They are either very boring or very queer or very brutal. The play marks something of a departure, both in content and style, and is a subtle and sensitive character study.

Weller has also written an unperformed epic play about the first Kennedy assassination, entitled *The Greatest Little Show on Earth*. It is a cynical, satirical tilt at the strong tendency of the U.S. political system to reduce complex issues to comic-strip, *Boy's Own Paper* levels – epitomised by the election of Kennedy as President, not for his political qualities, but for his glamour and the fact that that quality was supported by considerable family wealth. An ironical look at the events of his short Presidency is juxtaposed with an increasingly fatuous debate between Gerald Ford, a Republican senator, and Joachim Joesten, writer of a book doubting the Warren Commission's verdict on Kennedy's death. Both conservative and radical are so unwittingly obsessed by Kennedy's personality, and that of Lee Oswald, that they fail properly to look at what values, if any, they stood for. This play is an encouraging development, as Weller has all the intellectual equipment, and ability to work on many levels simultaneously, to tackle overtly political themes.

—Jonathan Hammond

WESKER, Arnold.   British.   Born in Stepney, London, 24 May 1932. Educated at Upton House School, Hackney, London, 1943–48; London School of Film Technique, 1956. Served in the Royal Air Force, 1950–52. Married Doreen Bicker in 1958; has three children. Worked as furnituremaker's apprentice, carpenter's mate, bookseller's assistant, plumber's mate, farm labourer's seed sorter, kitchen porter, pastry cook, chef. Founder-Director, Centre 42, 1961–71. Recipient: Arts Council grant, 1958; *Evening Standard* award, 1959; Encyclopedia Britannica Award, 1959; Marzotto Prize, 1964. Address: 27 Bishops Road, London N.6, England.

PUBLICATIONS

Plays

The Wesker Trilogy.   London, Cape, 1960; New York, Random House, 1961.
   Chicken Soup with Barley (produced Coventry and London, 1958; Cleveland, 1962).
      Published in *New English Dramatists*, London, Penguin, 1959.
   Roots (produced Coventry and London, 1959; New York, 1961).   London,
      Penguin, 1959.
   I'm Talking about Jerusalem (produced Coventry and London, 1960).   London,
      Penguin, 1960.
The Kitchen (produced London, 1959; New York, 1961).   Published in *New English
   Dramatists 2*, London, Penguin, 1960; expanded version, London, Cape, and New

York, Random House, 1962.

Chips with Everything (produced London, 1962; New York, 1963).   London, Cape, 1962; New York, Random House, 1963.

The Nottingham Captain: A Moral for Narrator, Voices and Orchestra, music by Wilfred Josephs and Dave Lee (produced London, 1962).   Included in *Six Sundays in January*, 1971.

Menace (televised, 1963).   Included in *Six Sundays in January*, 1971.

Their Very Own and Golden City (produced Brussels, 1965; London, 1966).   London, Cape, 1966; revised version (produced Aarhus, Denmark, 1974).

The Four Seasons (produced Coventry and London, 1965; New York, 1968). London, Cape, 1966.

The Friends (also director: produced Stockholm and London, 1970).   London, Cape, 1970.

The Old Ones (produced London, 1972; New York, 1974).   London, Cape, 1973; revised version, edited by Michael Marland, London, Blackie, 1974.

The Wedding Feast, adaptation of story by Dostoevsky (produced Stockholm, 1974).

The Journalists .   London, Writers and Readers Publishing Cooperative, 1975.

The Plays of Arnold Wesker.   New York, Harper, 1976.

Screenplay: *The Kitchen*, 1961.

Television Plays: *Menace*, 1963; *Love Letters on Blue Paper*, from his own story, 1976.

Short Stories

Love Letters on Blue Paper.   London, Cape, 1974; New York, Harper, 1975.

Other

Labour and the Arts: II, or, What, Then, Is to Be Done?   Oxford, Gemini, 1960.

The Modern Playwright; or, "O Mother, Is It Worth It?"   Oxford, Gemini, 1961.

Fears of Fragmentation (essays).   London, Cape, 1970.

Six Sundays in January (miscellany).   London, Cape, 1971.

Say Goodbye − You May Never See Them Again: Scenes from Two East-End Backgrounds, paintings by John Allin.   London, Cape, 1974.

Critical Studies: *The Writer and Commitment* by John Mander, London, Secker and Warburg, 1961; *Midcentury Drama* by Laurence Kitchin, London, Faber, 1962; *Anger and After* by John Russell Taylor, London, Methuen, 1962; "Two Romantics: Arnold Wesker and Harold Pinter" by Clifford Leech, in *Contemporary Theatre*, London, Edward Arnold, 1962; in *New Theatre Magazine* (Bristol), viii, 3, 1968, and xi, 2, 1971; "Casebook on Wesker" by Garry O'Connor in *Theatre Quarterly* (London), April 1971; *The Plays of Arnold Wesker* by Glenda Leeming and Simon Trussler, London, Gollancz, 1971; "Profile" by Margaret Drabble, in *New Review* (London), March 1975.

Theatrical Activities:

Director: **Plays** − *The Four Seasons*, Havana, 1968; *The Friends*, Stockholm and London, 1970; *The Old Ones*, Munich, 1973; *Their Very Own and Golden City*, Aarhus, Denmark, 1974.

*   *   *

A *Punch* illustration of the period shows an audience in evening dress intent on some play acted out in a working-class setting. That neatly summarized what happened to English drama in the nineteen-fifties, with Arnold Wesker prominent. It was confusing to many, but to anyone not identified with West End values or those of the current literary establishment, Wesker's achievement was evident at once. First he reversed the former role of underprivileged characters and insisted that they be taken seriously. Second, he responsibly dramatized history from the Depression to 1955 in terms of an East End Jewish family like his own. Third, he detected the contradictions of mass education and media persuasion, still a key issue thirteen years later, and in *Roots* expressed them definitively. Finally, in a flawed but powerful play, he explored the English ruling caste's method of absorbing rebels. To have the National Anthem rendered satirically with the audience seated was a uniquely subversive coup.

Chicken Soup with Barley, which first put Wesker in the mainstream of new drama in 1958, stands up to rigorous examination. The author's admitted debts to Miller and O'Casey are visible in the background, no more, without dependence on idiom or local setting. There is the familiar Jewish immigrant pattern of harassed father, in this case a natural loser, sensitive son, and enveloping extrovert mother, and there is the impact of political violence on working-class families. What Wesker makes of this in transplanting the themes to London's East End is original and important. Some idea of his achievement can be had from comparing *Chicken Soup* with the cult of the same locality emerging at about the same time from Joan Littlewood's Theatre Workshop. *Fings Ain't Wot They Used T'Be, Sparrers Can't Sing* – the titles point well enough to a homely celebration of Cockney humour and vitality derived from the music halls, anachronistic and sentimental. The well-publicized affluence of a composer like Lionel Bart came as a reminder that this kind of entertainment was conformist. Like the decaying music halls, mourned most of all by the Establishment, it offered benign stereotypes instead of East End realities. That it was toothlessly traditional is confirmed by the way it faded out, in the middlebrow success of *Oliver* and the failure of Bart's musical about, of all people, Robin Hood. The reality was surviving anti-Semitism, social disruption, union activity, and the Rock culture flexing its muscles.

Nothing Wesker has written has anything to do with the showbiz Cockney syndrome. *Chicken Soup* has both the resilience and the defeatism you might expect from a man of emigré Russian and Hungarian parentage. It looks back, yes, but to a political not a histrionic tradition, and precisely to the confrontation between Mosley's Fascists, the police and East Enders on 4 October 1936. We are made aware that it could and did "happen here" in a way not to be forgotten, as a television documentary of the late nineteen-sixties was to underline. The way this climactic event is rendered in domestic terms on a single set amounts to construction of a very high order, to O'Casey's example austerely digested. Another theme is interwoven, that of the Kahn parents, explored meticulously within the main action, as when the battles in Spain are mentioned and Sarah comments, "Casa del Campo! Madrid! Such beautiful names and all that killing!"

All this is done in the masterly first act. The militant locals escape from stereotype by exact placing in relation to job, crisis, and the Kahn family. What follows calls for less intense yet unwavering imagination. The time span from 1936 to 1955 bristles with dangers for the over-ambitious, and what time accomplishes is the controlling theme. It reduces Harry Kahn to an incontinent invalid, his son from literary ambitions to work in a restaurant kitchen; it develops his daughter towards a critique of the socialism absorbed at home, and her soldier husband towards contempt for the working-class. The episodes are mostly downbeat, but spaced in a way to focus the group against changes outside. Far from being diffuse, the ten-year intervals result in clarity and economy. The briefest of exchanges, for example, charts one member's progress from Cable Street hero to conformist shopkeeper. Sarah's defiance of the Mosleyites is redirected against Welfare State bureaucrats. There is mature social and political insight, always in a personal context, and no sentimentality or cheating.

At one point only in *Chicken Soup* – where even the title is placed with dramatic effect – is there disturbance of the steady, selective focus. And that is the author-surrogate Ronnie, frankly a drip. Well, it has been the same with many others, O'Neill included. Wesker's admitted enthusiasm for D. H. Lawrence foreshadows an excusable obscurity in the mother-and-son relationship. Sarah Kahn is uncompromisingly realized, magnificent. Her son's intellectual growing pains, as commonly on stage, do not register. Indeed, there is no stronger proof of Wesker's artistic instinct than what is done to Ronnie in *Roots*, the following play. Ronnie is suppressed, suppressed but not eliminated. Both his personal weakness and his intellectual growth are made use of to determine the action by proxy. The device gives a seemingly unadventurous domestic drama, quickly seized on by provincial reps, technical originality geared to a purpose.

Reasons given at the time for assessing *Roots* as a masterpiece can be repeated without qualification. It deals essentially with the alienation from home environment caused by mass education, with the growing away from it. In this case the setting is rural Norfolk at a time when vestigial feudal values are crumbling under the impact of TV and commercialism generally. The layers of such a community are embodied, as the political ones are in *Chicken Soup*, but with brutal authenticity. Into them is introduced a daughter migrated to London, now groping under her boyfriend's influence towards enlightenment. Conflict arises with her mother, the half-educated at odds with the unteachable ("Turn that squit off" on hearing Mendelssohn). The ebb and flow of the relationship is varied and subtle. But Beatie's discovery of a new identity goes well beyond rejecting her family. She brands ignorance, not poverty, as the people's major enemy. She attacks not only vested interests but popular apathy. No dramatist other than Wesker has drawn such an indictment from grass roots material.

In the interests of the very high estimate he deserves, it is best to regard *Chicken Soup* and *Roots* as independent, for *I'm Talking about Jerusalem* does not work its passage in a trilogy. The comic potentialities of "Two Jews in the Fens," to quote Ronnie's earlier comment on the situation, give way to the flavour of William Morris, exhausted Chekhov, and the F.R. Leavis of "organic society." The introduction of a superb East End aunt merely underlines a drop into facile cynicism which was to be repeated in altered terms in *The Four Seasons*, *Their Very Own and Golden City*, and *The Friends*. These three explorations of what Leeming and Trussler aptly define as "private pain" date from the second half of the nineteen-sixties. What had happened to the dramatist? Success, its rewards and consequent stresses. Without the framework afforded by a broadly imagined political and social context, the tortured self is less than dramatic in Wesker. The political self miscalculated (Centre Forty-Two) in aiming to base a popular arts revival on trade union support. It was a time-consuming episode as misguided as Ronnie Kahn's enthusiasm for his sister's rural experiment.

Alongside the domestic, ruefully disillusioned Wesker, there is another who generates furious theatrical power. The range is unique among his contemporaries. As *The Times* critic remarked, *Chips with Everything* has something to say about intellectual fellow-travellers. Unfortunately the public school R.A.F. rebel is crudely sketched. On the other hand, the victimization of a handicapped recruit by impersonal training is set forth with genius. Also in a violent ritual mode, *The Kitchen* met with stubborn critical resistance. As a coherent masterpiece, why? One can only point to England's half-century neglect of Gorky after a snobbish review by Max Beerbohm. And there are some who prefer an executive office to a cooking area for a symbol of capitalism.

When personal pain is digested great things can be expected from Wesker. The later sixties, in the grip of visceral and literary fantasy, were never his scene. But responsible stagings of East End issues and the countryside in transition are his alone. The exploitation of conscripts and urban workers is increasingly debated abroad. *I'm Talking about Jerusalem* parallels the aspirations of a California commune, just as it was Cambridge undergraduates who instantly got the message of *The Kitchen*. In 1969 a Japanese scholar on a British Council grant arrived in England. His research interests were the Tudor dramatists and Arnold Wesker. Straws in the wind?

—Laurence Kitchin

WHEELER, Hugh (Callingham).   American.   Born in London, England, 19 March 1912; naturalized American citizen, 1942. Educated at Clayesmore School; University of London, B.A. in English 1932. Served in the United States Army Medical Corps during World War II. Recipient: Edgar Allan Pole Award, for fiction, 1961, 1973; Tony Award, 1973; New York Drama Critics Circle Award, 1973; Drama Desk Award, 1973. Address: Twin Hills Farm, Monterey, Massachusetts 01245, U.S.A.

PUBLICATIONS

Plays

   Big Fish, Little Fish (produced New York, 1961; London, 1962).   New York, Random
      House, and London, Hart Davis, 1961.
   Look: We've Come Through! (produced New York, 1961).   New York, Dramatists
      Play Service, 1963.
   Rich Little Rich Girl, adaptation of a play by Miguel Mihura and Alvaro deLaiglesia
      (produced Philadelphia, 1964).
   We Have Always Lived in the Castle, adaptation of the novel by Shirley Jackson
      (produced New York, 1966).   New York, Dramatists Play Service, 1967.
   A Little Night Music, music and lyrics by Stephen Sondheim, adaptation of a film by
      Ingmar Bergman (produced New York, 1973; London, 1975).
   Irene, with Joseph Stein, adaptation by Harry Rigby, music by Harry Tierney, lyrics by
      Joseph McCarthy, adaptation of the play by James Montgomery (produced New
      York, 1973; London, 1976).
   Candide, music by Leonard Bernstein, lyrics by Richard Wilbur, adaptation of the novel
      by Voltaire (produced New York, 1973).
   Pacific Overtures, with John Weidmann, music and lyrics by Stephen Sondheim
      (produced New York, 1976).

   Screenplays: *Five Miles to Midnight*, with Peter Viertel, 1962; *Something for Everyone*,
   1969; *Cabaret*, 1972; *Travels with my Aunt*, 1973.

Novel

   The Crippled Muse.   London, Hart Davis, 1951; New York, Rinehart, 1952.

Novels (with Richard Webb until 1948)

   Death Goes to School (as Q. Patrick).   London, Cassell, and New York, Smith and
      Haas, 1936.
   A Puzzle for Fools (as Patrick Quentin).   London, Gollancz, and New York, Simon and
      Schuster, 1936.
   Grindle Nightmare.   New York, Hartney Press, 1936; as *Darker Grows the Valley*,
      London Gollancz, 1936.
   Murder Gone to Earth (as Jonathan Stagge).   London, Joseph, 1936; as *The Dogs Do
      Bark*, New York, Doubleday, 1937.
   Death for Dear Clara (as Q. Patrick).   London, Cassell, and New York, Simon and
      Schuster, 1937.
   File on Fenton and Farr (as Q. Patrick).   New York, Morrow, 1937; London, Jarrolds,
      1938.
   Murder or Mercy (as Jonathan Stagge).   London, Joseph, 1937; as *Murder by*

Prescription, New York, Doubleday, 1938.

Puzzle for Players (as Patrick Quentin).   New York, Simon and Schuster, 1938;
    London, Gollancz, 1939.

File on Claudia Cragge (as Q. Patrick).   London, Jarrolds, and New York, Morrow,
    1938.

Death and the Maiden (as Q. Patrick).   London, Cassell, and New York, Simon and
    Schuster, 1939.

The Stars Spell Death (as Jonathan Stagge).   New York, Doubleday, 1939; as *Murder
    in the Stars*, London, Joseph, 1940.

Turn of the Table (as Jonathan Stagge).   New York, Doubleday, 1940; as *Funeral for
    Five*, London, Joseph, 1940.

Return to the Scene (as Q. Patrick).   New York, Simon and Schuster, 1941; as *Death in
    Bermuda*, London, Cassell, 1941.

The Yellow Taxi (as Jonathan Stagge).   New York, Doubleday, 1942; as *Call a Hearse*,
    London, Joseph, 1942.

The Scarlet Circle (as Jonathan Stagge).   New York, Doubleday, 1943; as *Light from a
    Lantern*, London, Joseph, 1943.

Puzzle for Puppets (as Patrick Quentin).   New York, Simon and Schuster, and London,
    Gollancz, 1944.

Death, My Darling Daughters (as Jonathan Stagge).   New York, Doubleday, 1945; as
    Death and the Dear Girls, London, Joseph, 1946.

Puzzle for Wantons (as Patrick Quentin).   New York, Simon and Schuster, 1945;
    London, Gollancz, 1946.

Puzzle for Fiends (as Patrick Quentin).   New York, Simon and Schuster, 1946;
    London, Gollancz, 1947.

Death's Old Sweet Song (as Jonathan Stagge).   New York, Doubleday, 1946; London,
    Joseph, 1947.

Puzzle for Pilgrims (as Patrick Quentin).   New York, Simon and Schuster, 1947;
    London, Gollancz, 1948.

Run to Death (as Patrick Quentin).   New York, Simon and Schuster, and London,
    Gollancz, 1948.

The Three Fears (as Jonathan Stagge).   New York, Doubleday, and London, Joseph,
    1949.

The Follower (as Patrick Quentin).   New York, Simon and Schuster, and London,
    Gollancz, 1950.

Danger Next Door (as Q. Patrick).   London, Cassell, 1951.

Black Widow (as Patrick Quentin).   New York, Simon and Schuster, 1952; as *Fatal
    Woman*, London, Gollancz, 1953.

The Girl on the Gallows (as Q. Patrick).   New York, Fawcett, 1954.

My Son, The Murderer (as Patrick Quentin).   New York, Simon and Schuster, 1954; as
    The Wife of Ronald Sheldon, London, Gollancz, 1954.

The Man with Two Wives (as Patrick Quentin).   New York, Simon and Schuster, and
    London, Gollancz, 1955.

The Man in the Net (as Patrick Quentin).   New York, Simon and Schuster, and
    London, Gollancz, 1956.

Suspicious Circumstances (as Patrick Quentin).   New York, Simon and Schuster, and
    London, Gollancz, 1957.

Shadow of Guilt (as Patrick Quentin).   New York, Simon and Schuster, and London,
    Gollancz, 1959.

The Green-Eyed Monster (as Patrick Quentin).   New York, Simon and Schuster, and
    London, Gollancz, 1960.

Short Stories

The Ordeal of Mrs. Snow and Other Stories (as Patrick Quentin).   London, Gollancz,

1961; New York, Random House, 1962.
Family Skeletons (as Patrick Quentin).   New York, Random House, and London,
Gallancz, 1965.

*   *   *

Hugh Wheeler's reputation as a playwright – not at all the same thing as his current high
visibility as a musical-comedy librettist – rests with two plays produced in 1961 – *Big Fish,
Little Fish* and *Look: We've Come Through!* Neither of them was very successful
commercially, but in the fifteen years since it was first presented *Big Fish, Little Fish* has
developed an underground reputation as a small classic of sorts and has found its way into
Broadway's Beautiful Losers, a collection of neglected plays edited by Marilyn Stasio. In the
face of this belated recognition, it is tempting to overrate the play if only to make up for the
lack of appreciation it received first time around. To do so would be a mistake, however, for
overinflation would tend to hide the fact that *Big Fish, Little Fish* is simply a good bittersweet
comedy (with more emphasis on *bitter* than that genre usually allows). It shows that Wheeler
has a genuine talent for characterization in which satire and pathos struggle for supremacy,
or work together, a combination that helps explain why he was particularly suited to do the
book of a musical like *A Little Night Music*. The protagonist of *Big Fish, Little Fish* is a man in
his forties, working at a dull and routine job in a textbook publishing house and getting
through life on a diet of bridge, double-crostics, and too much liquor; he is sustained by a
band of the lost and lonely – a suburban grandmother who has been his mistress for almost
twenty years, a homosexual teacher with an undeclared love for him, a drunken ex-publisher
so pugnacious that almost no-one will give him house room. A charming and totally selfish
novelist passes through, disrupting the group by dangling the possibility of a new job, a new
life for the hero, and then, when the offer falls through, what remains of the group closes in
around him for the pathetic final curtain. In retrospect, one realizes that the events of the play
are imposed from outside, except in so far as a certain kind of personality invites being used,
but the external action is of minor importance in any case; what is likely to stay with an
audience is the bitchily affectionate portrait of the group. *Look: We've Come Through!*, a
somewhat caustic variation on the standard play in which adolescents, discovering one
another, discover themselves, has some of the dark comic tone of *Big Fish, Little Fish*, but –
perhaps because Wheeler was almost fifty when he first came to the theater – the playwright
seems surer of himself with the older characters in his first play than with the young people
in the second.

After his first two attempts, in which he seemed to be trying to find a dramatic voice of his
own, Wheeler turned to adaptation and, then, to the collaborative business of musical
comedy. This is hardly surprising. For the first twenty-five years of his writing life, he
worked with Richard Webb as a team which turned out mystery stories under the
pseudonyms of Q. Patrick, Patrick Quentin, and Jonathan Stagge. Of his adaptations, *Rich
Little Rich Girl*, based on a play by Miguel Mihura and Alvaro deLaiglesia, never reached
Broadway, and *We Have Always Lived in the Castle*, a dramatization of the Shirley Jackson
novel of the same name, stayed for only nine performances. Jackson's novel uses a murder to
set up one of her confrontations – compare her story, "The Lottery" – between a brutally
self-protective village and an element the villagers see as defiling, but Wheeler – ignoring the
substance of Jackson's work – turns it into a conventional melodrama about a stage crazy.
With *A Little Night Music* Wheeler found his place in American theater; working with
Stephen Sondheim, who did the music and lyrics, and Harold Prince, a producer-director
celebrated for taking an active hand in the creation of the works he puts on, Wheeler
borrowed from the Ingmar Bergman film *Smiles of a Summer Night* and constructed an
efficient book, a skeleton on which Sondheim was able to hang an interesting experiment that
– in the absence of the usual musical-comedy chorus – might be called a chamber musical.
Wheeler has moved from success to success – *Irene, Candide*, the film version of *Cabaret* –

which must be very pleasant for him, but the group games of these endeavors seem to have stilled the small, authentic voice of *Big Fish, Little Fish*.

—Gerald Weales

WHITE, John (Sylvester).   American.   Born in Philadelphia, Pennsylvania, 31 October 1919. Educated at Gonzaga High School, Washington, D.C., 1933–37; University of Notre Dame, Indiana, 1937–41, A.B. in English 1941. Actor for fifteen years: Charter Member, Actors' Studio, New York. Lives in California. Address: c/o Ninon Tallon Karlweis, 250 East 65th Street, New York, New York 10021, U.S.A.

PUBLICATIONS

Plays

> *Twist* (produced New York, 1963).
> *Bugs* (produced New York, 1964).   Included in *Bugs and Veronica*, 1966.
> *Sand* (produced New York, 1964).
> *Veronica* (produced New York, 1965).   Included in *Bugs and Veronica*, 1966.
> *Bugs and Veronica: Two Plays.*   New York, Dramatists Play Service, 1966.
> *Bananas* (produced New York, 1968).
> *The Dog School* (produced New York, 1969).
> *Lady Laura Pritchett, American* (produced Southampton, New York, 1969).
> *Mirage* (produced Hanover, New Hampshire, 1969).
> *The Passing of Milldown Muldern* (produced Los Angeles, 1974).
> *Ombres* (produced Paris, 1975).
> *Les Punaises* (produced Paris, 1975).

> Screenplay: *Skyscraper*, 1959.

Other

> American Adaptor, *Report from Palermo*, by Danilo Dolci.   New York, Orion, 1958.

Manuscript Collection: Lincoln Center Library of the Performing Arts, New York.

Theatrical Activities:

> Actor: **Plays** – as John Sylvester: roles in *Richard III*, New York, 1943; *Sundown Beach* by Bessie Brewer, New York, 1948; *Danny Larkin* by James V. McGee, New York, 1948; *All You Need Is One Good Break* by Arnold Manoff, New York, 1950. Also actor in radio and television plays.

John White comments:

Unless writing for hire, I write privately, from within, using for material the backwash of fifty years of existence, sometimes even living. I cannot work from the daily paper or the latest vogue. Indeed, I am turned off by the world. When I think about it, I can't write. I have been accused of being formless and have been applauded, on the other hand, for good form. I detest critics (in the main; there are a few splendid exceptions) and professional "knowershow." Lonely is the word.

*   *   *

Though represented by professional productions of just one full-length and two one act plays, John White in the 1960's established himself as one of the freshest and most talented playwrights in America. Writing in a strikingly idiosyncratic style – the hallmark of any artist – he applied modern surrealism (less than absurdist, more than naturalist) to find a mythology in American roots. His small body of work is uneven – *Bugs* a good one act play, *Veronica* a superlative one, and *Bananas* a prematurely produced full length play that, with polishing, would have been a major work. But like too many playwrights producing in New York during this period, White was hurt by a powerful and ignorant fraternity of critics (it was an era when *Waiting For Godot, Entertaining Mr. Sloane* and *The Homecoming* by Beckett, Orton and Pinter were rejected). The playwright fled to Hollywood to seek a living wage at least. Ironically, the style that he plumbed has since become familiar (and therefore palatable) through the work of playwrights from Pinter to Sam Shepard.

Bugs (American vernacular for mad) is about a disturbed young man who has escaped from a hospital and returned to a home where things aren't much saner. His mother and girl friend are respectively and insanely cheerful and stupid. His father, when not hidden behind a newspaper, is a ranting menace. Though the play might have been more, it gave clear promise of the author's specialness.

Veronica fulfilled the promise. Its central characters are a popular songwriting team of America's Thirties. They are holed up in a hotel room, trying desperately to repeat the huge success they had with a song called "Veronica." They are interrupted by a most peculiar burglar whose very philosophy of life, as it turns out, was inspired by the lyrics of that song.

These lyrics, in accurate satire of period popular music, spell out the passé, nostalgic, American dream as once advertised – a dream of beautiful blonds and money and trips to tropical islands. But has this sweet, silly dream now grown obsolete, only to be superseded by mundane social responsibility? One of the songwriters is too absorbed by war and disease to write again about June and moon. His partner is furious – "People haven't changed – a kiss is still a kiss, a sigh is still a sigh."

This yearning for a country once foolish and lovable – this choice of innocence over sophistication – was more deeply explored in the ambitious *Bananas* that was presented at Lincoln Center in 1968. The play is set in a period burlesque house during a rehearsal by three comics and an actress. A critic arrives. A series of sketches begins in which the author relates the techniques of burlesque to those of absurdism, suggesting that in a nostalgic, truthful-sardonic way, everything is bananas (another American slangword for madness, obviously White's view of existence). As the play continues, the metaphor of a show as life changes from the burlesque theater to a modern television studio, but everyday conversation remains as a replica of dialogue we have heard on some stage, somewhere.

The idea is excellent and much of the technique is virtuosic, but the play was produced prematurely, and is ultimately confusing, though its argument seems clear enough – a preference for the innocence of actors, entertaining, over the hopeless attempts by intellectuals to make sense of life. Without being repetitive, White – like most fine playwrights – had from the start a consistency to his style and content.

But sadly, a start seems to be all that his playwrighting career will have. Like too many in the brutal, competitive, business controlled and mindlessly commercial and anti-artistic

American theater, his sensitivity as a playwright seems to have been beaten down by senseless rejection and unappreciation.

—Martin Gottfried

WHITE, Patrick (Victor Martindale).   Australian.   Born in London, England, 28 May 1912. Educated in schools in Australia, 1919–25; Cheltenham College, Gloucestershire, 1925–29; King's College, Cambridge, 1932–35, B.A. 1935. Served as an Intelligence Officer in the Royal Air Force, in the Middle East, 1940–45. Recipient: Australian Literary Society Gold Medal, 1956; Miles Franklin Award, Conference of Christians and Jews' Brotherhood Award, 1962; Nobel Prize for Literature, 1973. Address: 20 Martin Road, Centennial Park, Sydney, New South Wales 2021, Australia.

PUBLICATIONS

Plays

Return to Abyssinia (produced London, 1947).
The Ham Funeral (produced Adelaide, 1961; Crewe, Cheshire, 1969).   Included in
    Four Plays, 1965.
The Season at Sarsaparilla (produced Adelaide, 1962).   Included in Four Plays, 1965.
A Cheery Soul (produced Melbourne, 1963).   Included in Four Plays, 1965.
Night on Bald Mountain (produced Adelaide, 1964).   Included in Four Plays, 1965.
Four Plays (includes The Ham Funeral, The Season at Sarsaparilla, A Cheery Soul,
    Night on Bald Mountain).   London, Eyre and Spottiswoode, 1965; New York,
    Viking Press, 1966.

Novels

Happy Valley.   London, Harrap, 1939; New York, Viking Press, 1940.
The Living and the Dead.   London, Routledge, and New York, Viking Press, 1941.
The Aunt's Story.   London, Routledge, and New York, Viking Press, 1948.
The Tree of Man.   New York, Viking Press, 1955; London, Eyre and Spottiswoode,
    1956.
Voss.   New York, Viking Press, and London, Eyre and Spottiswoode, 1957.
Riders in the Chariot.   New York, Viking Press, and London, Eyre and Spottiswoode,
    1961.
The Solid Mandala.   New York, Viking Press, and London, Eyre and Spottiswoode,
    1966.
The Vivisector.   New York, Viking Press, and London, Cape, 1970.
The Eye of the Storm.   London, Cape, 1973; New York, Viking Press, 1974.
A Fringe of Leaves.   London, Cape, 1976; New York, Viking Press, 1977.

Short Stories

The Burnt Ones.   New York, Viking Press, and London, Eyre and Spottiswoode, 1964.

The Cockatoos: Shorter Novels and Stories. London, Cape, 1974; New York, Viking Press, 1975.

Verse

The Ploughman and Other Poems. Sydney, Beacon Press, 1935.

Bibliography: *A Bibliography of Patrick White* by Janette Finch, Adelaide, Libraries Board of South Australia, 1966.

*   *   *

Patrick White is better known as a novelist and winner of the Nobel prize for literature than as a playwright. A special difficulty in assessing his four published plays (*The Ham Funeral, The Season at Sarsaparilla, A Cheery Soul*, and *Night on Bald Mountain*) is that, fascinating though the plays are, they have not been performed very often, and few critics would have seen all of them on stage – which is perhaps one reason why judgements on their theatrical qualities seem more than usually personal and idiosyncratic. Each play has its own defenders, but probably most people would settle for the earliest of them, *The Ham Funeral* (written in London in 1947, and first performed 1961) as the most successful and least flawed.

Patrick White is one of the few Australian playwrights to have attempted large-scale themes. He deals with the fundamentals of life and death, with the life force, and the ways it is channelled – and perverted – in human lives. In his latest play, *Night on Bald Mountain*, he essays tragedy, though the play fails for most people, in spite of a few fine scenes, because characterisation and motivation remain unconvincing. *A Cheery Soul*, which White himself describes as being about "the destructive power of good," has a painfully superb central character in Miss Docker, the relentless do-gooder and devout church-goer who wreaks havoc in the lives around her. Miss Docker is almost a tragic character, but the play blurs half way through, and becomes, partly because of its chaotic scene shifts, dauntingly difficult to produce.

In technique also Patrick White stood outside the mainstream of Australian drama. At a time when Australian drama was wedged relentlessly in unbroken naturalism, White was writing plays close to expressionism, plays designed to dissolve the barriers between the inner and external lives of the characters. One play in particular, *The Season at Sarsaparilla*, prefigures the "cartoon" style currently very popular with Australian playwrights. Sarsaparilla is middle-class Australian suburbia, temporarily bedevilled by the howling of a pack of dogs pursuing a bitch on heat; the town is represented by the kitchens of three adjoining houses in Mildred Street. The action moves in counterpoint between these three houses, and the passing of time is indicated by a whirling razzle-dazzle. The characters are for the most part deliberate stereotypes, primarily different aspects of sexuality; one character, Nola Boyle, is as much a stereotype as the rest, but so far surpasses the other characters in warmth and vitality that one loses any sense that the interest of the play is balanced equally between the three households. Like Alma Lusty in *The Ham Funeral*, Nola Boyle, the one naturally sensuous character, is partly crippled by her need for love; she is childless, and her promiscuity is destroying her marriage. The only whole character in the play seems to be the alert, curious child Pippy; and she too in the course of the action suffers disillusionment. However, White's comments on suburbia in *The Season at Sarsaparilla* are more superficial than the comments on suburbia of his novels, and his sympathies seem too obviously weighted – particularly in the lack of apparent compassion for the unattractive characters, in particular Girlie Pogson, whose dimples have disappeared and whose sexuality has faded into social pretensions.

The Ham Funeral is poetic, symbolic, and Patrick White's most optimistic play. The Young Man, who is both narrator and central character (we see the action primarily though not wholly from his point of view) announces at the beginning that it is "as usual...a piece about eels," and indeed the play defies precise, point by point interpretation; but *The Ham Funeral* is generally accepted as a kind of parable about the growth of a human psyche, one step at least, on the road to maturity. The play was inspired by William Dobell's painting *The Dead Landlord*, by Dobell's reminiscence of the experience which led him to paint the picture (he had been a lodger in a house in London where the landlord had died suddenly, and the landlady had "taken down her hair announcing that there would be a ham funeral and that he must go and fetch the relatives"), and presumably Patrick White's own memories of life in London as a young writer. When the Landlord, Will Lusty, dies, the Young Man (a poet) faces his first brutal involvement with death, and then with life, when the Landlady, Alma Lusty (life force, overpowering sexuality, frustrated maternalism) assaults him, after the ritual ham funeral. The Landlord and the Landlady live in the basement; a third character, the Girl, lives behind the closed door of the bedroom next to that of the Young Man. She is his anima, and possibly also the unattractively catarrhal "real" young woman, Phyllis Pither. The Girl seems to be that part of the Young Man's nature which drives him to fresh exploration and discovery, essential in the growth of an artist. At one point in the play he tells her, through the closed door which always separates them, "...if you remain on the other side of the door, we can never complete each other." Her stern comment on the word "complete" is: "For you, death in two syllables."

The Ham Funeral is a vital play, coherent with the surreal coherence of a dream, sometimes very funny; its perceptions about the inner life of the young poet are a good deal more profound than White's comments on the society of Sarsaparilla.

—Alrene Sykes

WHITEHEAD, E(dward) A(nthony). British. Born in Liverpool, Lancashire, 3 April 1933. Educated at St. Francis Xavier's Jesuit College; Christ's College, Cambridge, B.A. (honours) in English 1955. Served in the Infantry, 1955–57. Worked as a milkman, postman, bus conductor, sales promotion writer, drug salesman, teacher, advertising copywriter, and, from 1966 to 1971, as an advertising account executive. Resident Dramatist, Royal Court Theatre, London, 1971–72. Recipient: George Devine Award, 1971; *Evening Standard* award, 1971. Agent: Margaret Ramsay Ltd., 14a Goodwin's Court, London WC2N 4LL, England.

PUBLICATIONS

Plays

   The Foursome (produced London, 1971; Washington, D.C., 1972; New York, 1973). London, Faber, 1972.
   Alpha Beta (produced London, 1972; New York, 1973). London, Faber, 1972.
   The Punishment (televised, 1972). Published in *Prompt Three*, edited by Alan Durband, London, Hutchinson, 1976.
   The Sea Anchor (produced London, 1974). London, Faber, 1975.
   Old Flames (produced Bristol, 1975; London, 1976). London, Faber, 1976.
   Mecca (produced London, 1977).

Television Plays: *Under the Age*, 1972; *The Punishment*, 1972; *The Peddler*, 1976.

*   *   *

E. A. Whitehead's *The Foursome* is more successful within the limits it sets for itself than *Alpha Beta*, a two-character play studying the breakdown of a marriage by spreading its three acts over a nine-year period. *The Foursome* is about a sexual relationship which lasts less than 24 hours between two boys and two girls. With two couples and a less predictable progress to chart, it provides more opportunities for variety, counterpoint, comedy and surprise. The relationship may be more physical and more superficial, but Whitehead's style is more suited to this sort of subject-matter. He does not have deep insight into character or deep interest in it. In both plays his concern to make general statements about working-class morality and sex or marriage tilts him towards characterising his people more as representatives than individuals. It is characteristic that Mr. and Mrs. Elliott in *Alpha Beta* are never given Christian names. Personalities and motivation are not what interest him. But he has an excellent ear for Liverpool dialogue and a sense of humour which comes into its own when he detects insecurity under the cocky badinage that goes on between boys and girls to cover the fact that they are sniffing each other over sexually. The best dialogue he has written is in the first act of *The Foursome* and in a television play he wrote for the BBC's Thirty Minute Theatre about boys at a loose end chatting up girls in a Liverpool pub.

The opening of *The Foursome* is written with a superb control over its material. The male striptease is not just a calculated piece of audience provocation. The ways in which the two boys do it are amusingly contrasted, but instead of using this as a starting point for a psychological exploration of the difference between them, Whitehead is theatricalising a semi-sociological study of the courting behaviour of the young working-class male. The girls, equally, are representatives of a kind of behaviour. Tight-sweatered and mini-skirted, with lacquered hair piled up high, they are seen more as products of a particular environment than as particular personalities. The progress of the elaborate game leading up to love-making has an irresistible fascination for an audience. More even than in *Alpha Beta*, Whitehead is picking on raw and under-exposed areas of the sexual relationship and exposing the contradictions both relentlessly and funnily. He is good at handling the changes of mood that lead up to the climax in which the aggressions come right out into the open, but the final climax in which the boys decide to abandon the girls does not quite bring the action to a satisfactory resolution. Of course it is part of the play's point that the final decision has less to do with what has happened between the four of them than with Tim's misogynist disgust which surfaces in his long speech at the end of Act Two describing the smell and the graffiti in a women's lavatory, and the used Tampax he found on the floor. But the speech reaches into a strong, if rancid emotion; the present-tense relationships between the boys and girls involve only appetites and sensations. The play never quite finds its level between the two.

But at least we are left to take sides as we wish – to pity the jilted girls, cheated of their promising evening in the pub, or to be as nauseated by their realistically portrayed behaviour as Tim is by his memories of a smell. *Alpha Beta* is in many ways a more compassionate play, probing the wounds and showing the pain of both victims caught in the trap of monogamy, but it is also making a general statement which nearly overbalances the structure. Naturalism is also more of a weakness than in *The Foursome*, which was set in a hollow of the sandhills at Freshfield: the sand provided a minimal but realistic and unusual setting. In *Alpha Beta* we are inside a house with changes in the furniture helping to indicate the passage of time, and toys and bicycles to indicate that children are also living there. But one never quite believes in them.

However much one sympathizes with all the points Whitehead is making against everything that marriage does to reduce freedom and legitimize jealousy, one cannot want the play to suffer as much as it does from being imprisoned within the marital battle. Even Strindberg found it necessary to bring in other characters to set off against his warring husbands and wives, but Whitehead, knowing some surprises and variations are necessary to relieve the tedium of a predictable downhill journey, has recourse to melodramatic poison when Mrs. Elliott's threat to kill the children and herself is made the peg on which the whole of Act Three is hung. There are passages where unexaggerated realism is extremely telling, but they neither come to life quite sufficiently as individuals nor bring enough of their lives into their dialogue to carry the play.

One sign of the greater depth, subtlety and complexity in *The Sea Anchor* is that only two of the four characters form a couple. One is married to a fifth, Nick, who never appears, though by the end of the play we know as much about him as about the others. He thinks he's achieved something every time he beds a new girl. He treats his wife as badly as his steady girlfriend treats her husband, and she is no more generous to Nick than his wife is in allowing him the liberty he'd take anyway to sleep around.

We are in Dublin Bay, sharing the edgy anxiety of the four characters as they scan the horizon with binoculars, worried about Nick's non-arrival. They are asserting their freedom by means of a dirty weekend, while he has daringly asserted his by sailing from Liverpool, alone in a dinghy. Some of the dialogue is rather laboured in its reconstruction of offstage events, but for most of the time the tension is well sustained by the dawning certainty that Nick's bravado has been suicidal. Desperate to escape the other traps, he has fallen into the ultimate one.

Old Flames is another play about the sex war. Invited to dinner by the girl he fancies, a man is disconcerted to be told that she has also invited friends, more disconcerted to discover that they are his two ex-wives and his mother, and more disconcerted still to be told that they are going to eat him. The skilfully sprung surprises keep the first act taut, but our uncertainty about whether they are serious is not enough to sustain the wordy second act, in which the four women discuss their grievances against the other sex. Spiced though it is with confessions about masturbation, Lesbianism and promiscuity, the dialogue is too much like a series of monologues. It lacks dramatic flavour and interaction.

Certainly there is much that needs to be said about the human damage still being done by obsolescent sexual and marital conventions, but it is not enough to let characters argue and reminisce. That E.A. Whitehead is capable of verbal economy is demonstrated by his one-act television two-hander *The Punishment*, which shows a sanctimonious Jesuit headmaster indulging himself by using his power over a boy whom he finally beats. The full-length plays will improve if, like this, they subordinate the words to the statement made by the action.

—Ronald Hayman

WILDER, Thornton (Niven).   American.   Born in Madison, Wisconsin, 17 April 1897. Educated at Oberlin College, Ohio, 1915–17; Yale University, New Haven, Connecticut, A.B. 1920; American Academy in Rome, 1920–21; Princeton University, New Jersey, A.M. 1926. Served in the United States Coast Artillery Corps, 1918–19; in United States Army Air Intelligence, rising to the rank of Lieutenant-Colonel, 1942–45, honorary M.B.E. (Member, Order of the British Empire), 1945. Teacher, 1921–28, and House Master, 1927–28, Lawrenceville School, New Jersey. Full-time Writer since 1928. Lecturer in Comparative Literature, University of Chicago, 1930–36; Visiting Professor, University of Hawaii, Honolulu, 1935; Charles Eliot Norton Professor of Poetry, Harvard University, Cambridge, Massachusetts, 1950–51. United States Delegate: Institut de Cooperation Intellectuelle, Paris, 1937; with John Dos Passos, International P.E.N. Club Congress, England, 1941; UNESCO Conference of the Arts, Venice, 1952. Recipient: Pulitzer Prize, for fiction, 1928, for drama, 1938, 1943; National Institute of Arts and Letters Gold Medal, 1952; Friedenpreis des Deutschen Buchhandels, 1957; Austrian Ehrenmedaille, 1959; Goethe-Plakette, 1959; Brandeis University Creative Arts Award, for drama, 1959; Edward MacDowell Medal,

1960; Presidential Medal of Freedom, 1963; National Book Committee's National Medal for Literature, 1965; Century Association Art Medal; National Book Award, for fiction, 1968. D.Litt.: New York University, 1930; Yale University, 1947; Kenyon College, Gambier, Ohio, 1948; College of Wooster, Ohio, 1950, Northeastern University, Boston, 1951; Oberlin College, 1952; University of New Hampshire, Durham, 1953; Goethe University, Frankfurt, 1957; University of Zurich, 1961; LL.D.: Harvard University, 1951. Chevalier, Legion of Honor, 1951, Member, Order of Merit, Peru; Order of Merit, Bonn, 1957; Honorary Member, Bavarian Academy of Fine Arts; Mainz Academy of Science and Literature. Member, American Academy of Arts and Letters. Address: 50 Deepwood Drive, Hamden, Connecticut 06517, U.S.A. *Died 7 December 1975.*

PUBLICATIONS

Plays

> *The Trumpet Shall Sound* (produced New York, 1927).
> *The Angel That Troubled the Waters and Other Plays* (includes *Nascuntur Poetae, Proserpina and the Devil, Fanny Otcott, Brother Fire, The Penny That Beauty Spent, The Angel on the Ship, The Message and Jehanne, Childe Roland to the Dark Tower Came, Centaurs, Leviathan, And the Sea Shall Give Up Its Dead, Now the Servant's Name Was Malchus, Mozart and the Gray Steward, Hast Thou Considered My Servant Job?, The Flight into Egypt*).   New York, Coward McCann, and London, Longman, 1928.
> *The Long Christmas Dinner* (produced New Haven, Connecticut, 1931; Liverpool, 1932).   Included in *The Long Christmas Dinner and Other Plays*, 1931; libretto, music by Paul Hindemith (produced Mannheim, Germany, 1961, New York, 1963), libretto published, Mainz and New York, B. Schotts Söhne, 1961.
> *The Happy Journey to Trenton and Camden* (produced New Haven, Connecticut, 1931). Included in *The Long Christmas Dinner and Other Plays*, 1931; revised version, as *The Happy Journey*, New York, French, 1934; London, French, 1947.
> *Such Things Only Happen in Books* (produced New Haven, Connecticut, 1931). Included in *The Long Christmas Dinner and Other Plays*, 1931.
> *Love and How to Cure It* (produced New Haven, Connecticut, 1931; Liverpool, 1932). Included in *The Long Christmas Dinner and Other Plays*, 1931.
> *The Long Christmas Dinner and Other Plays in One Act* (includes *The Happy Journey to Trenton and Camden, Love and How to Cure It, Queens of France, Such Things Only Happen in Books*, and *Pullman Car Hiawatha*).   New York and New Haven, Connecticut, Coward McCann-Yale University Press, 1931; as *The Long Christmas Dinner and Other Plays*, London, Longman, 1931.
> *Queens of France* (produced Chicago, 1932).   Included in *The Long Christmas Dinner and Other Plays*, 1931.
> *Pullman Car Hiawatha* (produced New York, 1962).   Included in *The Long Christmas Dinner and Other Plays*, 1931.
> *Lucrece*, adaptation of a play by André Obey (produced New York, 1932; London, 1948).   Boston, Houghton Mifflin, and London, Longman, 1933.
> *A Doll's House*, adaptation of a play by Henrik Ibsen (produced Central City, Colorado, 1937).
> *The Merchant of Yonkers*, adaptation of a play by Johann Nostroy, based on *A Well-Spent Day* by John Oxenford (produced Boston and New York, 1938; London, 1951). New York and London, Harper, 1939; revised version, as *The Matchmaker* (produced Edinburgh and London, 1954; Philadelphia and New York, 1955), New York, Harper, 1955; London, French, 1957.

Our Town (produced Princeton, New Jersey, and New York, 1938; London, 1946).
New York, Coward McCann, 1938, London, Longman, 1956.
The Skin of Our Teeth (produced New Haven, Connecticut, and New York, 1942;
London, 1945).   New York and London, Harper, 1942.
Our Century.   New York, Century Association, 1947.
The Victors, adaptation of a play by Jean-Paul Sartre (produced New York, 1949).
A Life in the Sun (produced Edinburgh, 1955); as *The Alcestiad*, music by L. Talma
(produced Frankfurt, Germany, 1962).   Published as *Die Alkestiade*, Frankfurt, S.
Fischer Verlag, 1958.
The Drunken Sisters.   New York, French, 1957.
Bernice (produced Berlin, 1957).
The Wreck of the 5:25 (produced Berlin, 1957).
Plays for Bleecker Street (includes *Infancy, Childhood*, and *Someone from Assisi*)
(produced New York, 1962; *Infancy and Childhood* produced London, 1972).   New
York, French, 3 vols., 1960, 1961.

Screenplays: *Our Town*, 1940; *Shadow of a Doubt*, 1943.

Novels

The Cabala.   New York, Boni, and London, Longman, 1926.
The Bridge of San Luis Rey.   New York, Boni, and London, Longman, 1927.
The Woman of Andros.   New York, Boni, and London, Longman, 1930.
Heaven's My Destination.   London, Longman, 1934; New York, Harper, 1935.
The Ides of March.   New York, Harper, and London, Longman, 1948.
The Eighth Day.   New York, Harper, and London, Longman, 1967.
Theophilus North.   New York, Harper, 1973; London, Allen Lane, 1974.

Other

The Intent of the Artist, with others.   Princeton, New Jersey, Princeton University
Press, 1941.
Kultur in einer Demokratie.   Frankfurt, S. Fischer Verlag, 1957.
Goethe une die Weltliteratur.   Kassel, privately printed, 1958.

Theatrical Activities:

Actor: **Plays** – Stage Manager in *Our Town*, New York, 1938, and on other occasions; Mr.
Antrobus in *The Skin of Our Teeth*, Cohasset, Massachusetts, 1946, and on other
occasions.

*   *   *

Thornton Wilder's literary career has been divided between fiction and drama, which he
distinguishes: "The novel is pre-eminently the vehicle of the unique occasion, the theater of
the generalized one." However, generalization is not evident in his first volume of sixteen
three-minute playlets for three actors, *The Angel That Troubled the Waters*. Drawing upon
history and legend, these literary exercises nevertheless predict Wilder's consistent anti-
realism in the theater. As Tyrone Guthrie wrote: "Wilder uses the stage not to imitate nature,
but to evoke, with the utmost economy of means, a series of images."
Economical images dramatize generalized occasions in Wilder's 1931 volume of six plays.
Three of these play in Pirandellian fashion with the problematical relation of fiction to reality.

More substantial are three plays that experiment with stage space and time in order to make a statement about the human condition, the most general of occasions. In these three plays Wilder deliberately spurns elaborate staging to focus on the simple and the functional. *The Long Christmas Dinner* centers on a dinner table, stage entrance is birth, and stage exit is death. In *Pullman Car Hiawatha* and *The Happy Journey to Trenton and Camden* a railroad car and an automobile are presented by a few chairs, so that the journeys demand metaphoric extension. At the center of *The Happy Journey* and *The Long Christmas Dinner* is the American family; indeed, one might say an American dynasty in the latter play, whose fictional duration is ninety years. *Pullman Car Hiawatha* involves towns, planets, and archangels in the destiny of human passengers, who are manipulated by a Stage Manager. He sets the scene, plays minor parts, regulates the dialogue, and orchestrates a wordless harmony: "The human beings murmur their thoughts; the hours discourse; the planets chant or hum." Less pretentious, *The Happy Journey* also uses a Stage Manager to describe the homey quality of the Kirby family. In all three plays, human beings know joy and sorrow, birth and death, living in an inscrutable but benevolent universe.

Wilder's most popular play, *Our Town*, rests on the techniques of these shorter plays. "Our town" is Grover's Corners, New Hampshire, but Wilder's intention in entitling it *our* town has been fulfilled by generations of American high school students who have been taught to regard this town as theirs, with its simple middle-class all-American inhabitants. Crucial to the idealized portrait of a turn-of-the-century American small town is the spare staging, to emphasize the generalized picture. Focusing on two families, Editor Webb's and Dr. Gibbs', the act titles indicate the universalizing intention: I Daily Life, II Love and Marriage, III Death. A Stage Manager presides over events, evoking comedy with his statistics and pathos with his prescience about death.

The "Daily Life" of Act I is conveyed through novel staging: a newspaper boy delivers imaginary newspapers, a milkman delivers imaginary bottles of milk, Mrs. Gibbs feeds imaginary chickens, Mrs. Webb strings imaginary beans, characters from the audience question the Stage Manager, two ladders represent the upper stories of the Webb and Gibbs houses, where Emily Webb and George Gibbs are more interested in one another than in their home work. Significantly, Act II is entitled "Love *and* Marriage"; the two are inseparable in Grover's Corners. But Emily as George's wife dies in childbirth, and in Act III she returns to earth. Her realization – "Do any human beings ever realize life while they live it? – every, every minute?" – seems to be Wilder's climactic point, as expressed in his words: "[*Our Town*] is an attempt to find a value above all price for the smallest events in our daily life."

Skirting philosophy in his first full-length play, Wilder turned to farce for his second, *The Merchant of Yonkers*, which is based on a farce by Johann Nestroy, which was in turn based on a farce by John Oxenford. When first produced, Wilder's farce was a failure on Broadway, but it succeeded in its revised version, *The Matchmaker*, and went on to record-breaking fame in its musical adaptation *Hello Dolly*.

The plot is appropriately preposterous. A widow, Dolly Gallagher Levi, pretends to arrange a match between a merchant of Yonkers, Horace Vandergelder, and a rich young heiress. Dolly has actually marked him for herself because she cannot bear the thought of his money lying fallow. Moving with rapid physicality, the play abounds in traditional devices of farce: disguises, lost (and found) purses, mistaken identity, concealment and chases, complexities which are compounded and then dissolved. But whereas the characters of Labiche and Feydeau rush through their plots with frantic earnestness, those of Wilder wink knowingly at their audience, and Dolly prompts young Barnaby to enunciate a moral, delivered directly to the audience: "that in your lives you have just the right amount of – adventure."

The anti-realistic universals of *Our Town* and the farcical adventures of *The Merchant of Yonkers* contribute to Wilder's next play, *The Skin of Our Teeth*, whose colloquial title contains its meaning: the human race has weathered all crises by "the skin of our teeth," and the possibility is strong that it will continue to do so.

The play centers on the Antrobus family, at once primitive cave-dwellers, the first humans of Genesis, suburbanites of modern America, and actors playing roles. In three successive acts Wilder's Antrobus family survives three disasters – glacier, tempest, and war. In the first act the Antrobus family resists freezing with cultural achievements – invention of the wheel, the Muses and Moses, the multiplication table – while the maid Sabina converts into firewood chairs passed up from the audience. In the second act, Mr. Antrobus and Sabina have an affair, the Antrobus son Henry is murderously hostile, the Antrobus daughter Gladys seems to imitate Sabina rather than her mother. As a second flood pours forth, Mr. Antrobus-Noah mans his ark, *pater familias* in the crisis. In Act III universal war has broken out between aggressive humans: "Henry *is* the enemy." One actor nearly chokes another, but the family triumphs again, and Sabina finally assures the audience: "Mr. and Mrs. Antrobus! Their heads are full of plans and they're as confident as the first day they began – and they told me to tell you: goodnight." After all, they live in Excelsior.

After revising *The Merchant of Yonkers* into *The Matchmaker*, Wilder wrote a tetralogy of plays about the Greek Alcestis story, which has been performed in English but published only in German translation. Euripides' play is the basis for Wilder's second play, whereas his third shows an older Alcestis accepting a death which is an eternal life. Wilder's indomitable optimism penetrates his classically based tetralogy, which ends with a satyr-play. For over a decade there have been rumors that Wilder is working on two cycles of one-act plays, *The Seven Deadly Sins* and *The Seven Ages of Man*, from which three were staged in 1962.

Thornton Wilder is a cultured man who has written perceptively on Gertrude Stein and James Joyce, but his plays have appealed to a wide popular audience. Consistently, he has rejected illusionist theater and accepted the simplified surface of human experience. In his more ambitious plays he has attempted to show that stereotyped characters speaking in colloquial Americanese are embedded in a wider context of inscrutable cosmic forces as well as in the cultural history of the human race. He himself has most accurately summarized his dramatic accomplishment: "The theater has lagged behind the other arts in finding the 'new ways' to express how men and women think and feel in our time. I am not one of the new dramatists we are looking for."

—Ruby Cohn

WILKINSON, Christopher.   British.   Born 4 May 1941. Address: 12 Hanover Square, Sheffield S3 7UA, England.

PUBLICATIONS

Plays

Their First Evening Alone Together (produced Sheffield, 1969; London, 1971).
Wally, Molly and Polly (produced Sheffield, 1969).
Teasdale's Follies, with Frank Hatherly, music by Jeremy Barlow (produced Sheffield, 1970).
Strip Jack Naked (produced Sheffield, 1970; London, 1971).
Dynamo (produced London, 1971).
Plays for Rubber Go-Go Girls (produced London, 1971).
I Was Hitler's Maid (also director: produced Sheffield and London, 1971).

Theatrical Activities:

Director: **Play** – *I Was Hitler's Maid*, Sheffield and London, 1971.

*   *   *

Christopher Wilkinson is best known for his work with two fringe companies – the touring Portable Theatre, and the Vanguard Theatre Club, which is attached to Sheffield's main repertory theatre, the Crucible. These close associations have influenced his work. Wilkinson has written ordinary playscripts, such as *Strip Jack Naked*, which revealed his wit, his ear for a good line of dialogue and his delight in a Grand Guignol situation. But more recently he has chosen not to write formal scripts, but rather to suggest themes and games for the acting companies to explore – in improvisation and other ways. *I Was Hitler's Maid* was an example of this non-scripted play. Wilkinson offered the actors some stories taken from semi-pornographic men's magazines: blood, sex and action. These magazines were of a type distributed to American troops in Vietnam, and were therefore considered to relate in some way to a real political situation. The stories were all exceptionally violent. Some were set in the Second World War – among SS officers and patriots of the French resistance: others in South America – among guerilla bands and the forces of Law and Order. But the settings were almost irrelevant, for the situations were pointedly similar. A girl was tortured and repeatedly raped by the Enemy, before being rescued by the Hero. In the opening scene, she is whipped by "Hitler": in a later scene, she becomes "Calamity Jane," the whipping Wild West heroine. The dialogue is based on the clichés of the genre: and the actors were encouraged to break up the story patterns, the snatches of rehearsed scenes, even the moments of violence, in order to emphasize the arbitrary lack of logic of the fantasies. The production progresses towards two main climaxes – an orgy scene (three men raping one girl) and a disembowelling scene, where three soldiers attack a lifelike (female) doll hanging in a cupboard.

Some critics considered *I Was Hitler's Maid* was not so much a comment on pornography, as pornography itself: while others deplored the deliberate lack of play construction. But few productions could have achieved such a telling diatribe against sex-and-violence comics without seeming lofty and puritanical. Wilkinson, by presenting the stories on stage – where actors leapt up in astonishing health after being beaten senseless – and by denying the elementary logic which kept the stories credible, brought out the full sado-masochistic absurdity of the genre. A somewhat similar production, *Dynamo*, was less successful perhaps because Wilkinson's moral intentions had to be more overtly expressed. *Dynamo* is set in a strip club: and the first section consists of ordinary dull strip routines performed by gum-chewing, bored girls. We watch them preparing to go on stage, collecting their props and records, adjusting their hair: then we see the routines. But after a time the strip club becomes an interrogation cell, where a girl is tortured by a police chief, kicked around the floor and finally hung up naked. Wilkinson wished to draw the parallel between ordinary pornographic fantasies and the political torture of an Algerian suspect by the French police: but the play failed because the association between the two events seemed at best clichaic and at worst tenuous and unconvincing. If Wilkinson meant to imply that in both cases women were treated like mere objects of male desire, the theme is convincing enough but rather obvious and could have been developed in many other ways. If he was suggesting that pornography leads to political violence, then the fact that there was no logical connecting link between the scenes damaged his argument.

Wilkinson's most successful work, however, is *Plays for Rubber Go-Go Girls*. These are sketch sequences, loosely linked by an attack on American imperialism and on the sexual fantasies supporting repression. The first half of the production consists of various sex-and-violence stories in the style of *I Was Hitler's Maid*: but the deliberate disorganization of the earlier play is replaced by a solemn burlesque treatment – high camp. The stories could come from an outrageous adventure story, in the style of James Bond, with beautiful girls from Vietnam and Latin America, submitting with delight to Commie-hating G.I.s. The second half is an amusing skit on childhood training in the States. An American cop warns his daughter, Fuzz Child, against everything, from drugs to long hair, which might threaten the purity of American middle-class life. The juxtaposition of the repressed fantasies with the formal teaching are related to the Vietnam War, until the war itself is shown to be an effect of various cultural forces. Among these forces is perhaps Wilkinson's most typical preoccupation – the maltreatment of women by men. Women are presented as rubber girls who can be endlessly stabbed either with a phallus or a bayonet. This serious theme is treated with an immense satirical verve and accuracy: the fantasies are funny, familiar and, shocked out of their usual contexts, have been presented to the public as grotesque art objects, as representative of our civilization as the pyramids were of ancient Egypt. Wilkinson's great achievement as a writer is to make us look afresh at the clichés surrounding our lives.

—John Elsom

WILLIAMS, (George) Emlyn. British.   Born in Mostyn, Flintshire, Wales, 26 November 1905. Educated at Holywell County School, Flintshire; Christ Church, Oxford, M.A. 1927. Married Molly O'Shann in 1935 (died, 1971); has two sons. Actor and Director. Recipient: New York Drama Critics Circle Award, 1941. LL.D.: University College of North Wales, Bangor, 1949. C.B.E. (Commander, Order of the British Empire), 1962. Address: 123 Dovehouse Street, London S.W.3, England.

PUBLICATIONS

Plays

> *Vigil* (produced Oxford, 1925).   Published in *The Second Book of One-Act Plays*,
>   London, Heinemann, 1954.
> *Full Moon* (produced Oxford, 1927; London, 1929).
> *Glamour* (produced London, 1928).
> *A Murder Has Been Arranged: A Ghost Story* (also director: produced London, 1930).
>   London, Collins, 1930; New York, French, 1931.
> *Port Said* (produced London, 1931; revised version, as *Vessels Departing*, produced
>   London, 1933).
> *The Late Christopher Bean*, adaptation of the play by Sidney Howard, based on a play by
>   René Fauchois (produced London, 1933).   London, Gollancz, 1933.
> *Josephine*, adaptation of a work by Hermann Bahr (produced London, 1934).
> *Spring 1600* (produced London, 1934; revised version, produced London, 1945).
>   London, Heinemann, 1946.
> *Night Must Fall* (produced London, 1935; New York, 1936).   London, Gollancz,
>   1935; New York, Random House, 1936.
> *He Was Born Gay: A Romance* (also co-director: produced London, 1937).   London,
>   Heinemann, 1937; in *Collected Plays*, 1961.
> *The Corn Is Green* (also director: produced London, 1938; New York, 1940).
>   London, Heinemann, 1938; New York, Random House, 1941.
> *The Light of Heart* (also director: produced London, 1940).   London, Heinemann,
>   1940; in *Collected Plays*, 1961.

The Morning Star (also director: produced London, 1941).   London, Heinemann, 1942.

Yesterday's Magic (produced New York, 1942).

Pen Don (produced Blackpool, 1943).

A Month in the Country, adaptation of a play by Turgenev (produced London, 1943; revised version, produced Chicago, 1956; Guildford, Surrey, and London, 1965). London, Heinemann, 1943; New York, French, 1957.

The Druid's Rest (also director: produced London, 1944).   London, Heinemann, 1944.

The Wind of Heaven (also director: produced London, 1945; Westport, Connecticut, 1963).   London, Heinemann, 1945.

Thinking Aloud: A Dramatic Sketch (produced London, 1945; New York, 1975). London, French, 1946.

Trespass: A Ghost Story (also director: produced London, 1947).   London, Heinemann, 1947.

Pepper and Sand: A Duologue (broadcast, 1947).   London, Deane, 1948.

Dear Evelyn, adaptation of a play by Hagar Wilde and Dale Eunson (produced Rutherglen, Lanarkshire, 1948).   London, French, n.d.

The Corn Is Green, with Two Other Plays (includes *The Wind of Heaven* and *The Druid's Rest*).   London, Pan, 1950.

Accolade (produced London, 1950).   London, Heinemann, 1951.

Emlyn Williams as Charles Dickens, based on writings by Dickens (produced London, 1951; New York, 1952).   Published as *Readings from Dickens,* London, Folio Society, 1953.

Bleak House, dramatic reading based on the novel by Dickens (produced Edinburgh and London, 1952; New York, 1953).

Someone Waiting (produced Liverpool and London, 1953; New York, 1956). London, Heinemann, 1954; New York, Dramatists Play Service, 1956.

A Boy Growing Up, dramatic reading based on works by Dylan Thomas (produced London, 1955, New York, 1957).

Beth (also director: produced Brighton and London, 1958).   London, Heinemann, 1959.

The Collected Plays I (includes *The Corn Is Green, He Was Born Gay, The Light of Heart, Night Must Fall*).   New York, Random House, 1961.

The Master Builder, adaptation of a play by Ibsen (produced London, 1964).   New York, Theatre Arts Books, 1967.

Screenplays: *Friday the Thirteenth,* 1933; *Evergreen,* 1934; *This England,* 1941; *The Last Days of Dolwyn,* 1948.

Radio Script: *Emlyn,* from his own book, 1974.

Television Plays: *A Month in the Country,* 1947; *Every Picture Tells a Story,* 1949; *In Town Tonight,* 1954; *A Blue Movie of My Own True Love,* 1968; *The Power of Dawn,* 1975.

Other

George: An Early Autobiography.   London, Hamish Hamilton, 1961; New York, Random House, 1962.

Beyond Belief: A Study in Murder.   London, Hamish Hamilton, 1967; New York, Random House, 1968.

Emlyn: An Early Autobiography 1927–1935.   London, Bodley Head, 1973; New York, Viking Press, 1974.

Theatrical Activities:

Director: **Plays** – *A Murder Has Been Arranged*, London, 1930; *He Was Born Gay* (co-director, with John Gielgud), London, 1937; *The Corn Is Green*, London, 1938; *The Light of Heart*, London, 1940; *The Morning Star*, London, 1941; *The Little Foxes* by Lillian Hellman, London, 1942; *Watch on the Rhine* by Lillian Hellman, London, 1942; *The Druid's Rest*, London, 1944; *The Wind of Heaven*, London, 1945; *Trespass*, London, 1947; *Beth*, Brighton and London, 1958. **Film** – *The Last Days of Dolwyn*, 1948.

Actor: **Plays** – Pelling's 'Prentice in *And So to Bed* by J. B. Fagan, London, 1927; Pepys' Boy in *And So to Bed* by J. B. Fagan, New York, 1928; Rev. Yorke and Billy Saunders in *The Pocket-Money Husband* by John Gliddon, London, 1928; Jack in *Glamour*, London, 1928; Camille in *Thérèse Raquin* by Emile Zola, London, 1929; Beppo in *Mafro, Darling* by Naomi Ryde-Smith, London, 1929; Berthold in *The Mock Emperor* by Pirandello, London, 1929; The Trumpeter in *The Silver Tassie* by O'Casey, London, 1929; Captain Sandys in *Tunnel-Trench* by Hubert Griffith, London, 1929; Jules Varnier in *French Leave* by Reginald Berkeley, London, 1930; Giovanni d'Amora in *La Piccola* by Massimo Bontempelli, London, 1930; The Usher in *The Fire at the Opera House* by Georg Kaiser, London, 1930; Angelo in *On the Spot* by Edgar Wallace, London, 1930; Adolph in *Devant la Porte* by Henri Duvernois, London, 1930; Commissar Neufeld in *The Mouthpiece* by Edgar Wallace, London, 1930; title role in *Etienne* by Jacques Deval, London, 1931; Lord Lebanon in *The Case of the Frightened Lady* by Edgar Wallace, London, 1931, as *Criminal at Large*, New York, 1932; Youssef el Tabah in *Port Said*, London, 1931; The Young Frenchman in *The Man I Killed* by Reginald Berkeley, London, 1932; Jack in *Man Overboard* by Sutton Vane, London, 1932; Branwell Brontë in *Wild Decembers* by Clemence Dane, London, 1933; Piers Gaveston in *Rose and Glove* by Hugh Ross Williamson, London, 1934; Eugene Beauharnais in *Josephine*, London, 1934; Dan in *Night Must Fall*, London, 1935, New York, 1936, and toured, 1943; Lambert in *He Was Born Gay*, London, 1937; Oswald in *Ghosts* by Ibsen, Buxton, 1937; Angelo in *Measure for Measure*, London, 1937; Duke of Gloucester in *Richard II*, London, 1937; Morgan Evans in *The Corn Is Green*, London, 1938; Maddoc Thomas in *The Light of Heart*, London, 1940; Cliff Parrilow in *The Morning Star*, London, 1941; toured the Middle East for overseas forces in *Night Must Fall*, *Blithe Spirit* by Noël Coward, and *Flare Path* by Terence Rattigan, 1944; Ambrose Ellis in *The Wind of Heaven*, London, 1945; Sir Robert Morton in *The Winslow Boy* by Terence Rattigan, London, 1946; Saviello in *Trespass*, London, 1947; Izquierdo in *Montserrat* by Lillian Hellman, New York, 1949; Will Trenting in *Accolade*, London, 1950; *Emlyn Williams as Charles Dickens*, London, 1951, New York, 1952; Reader in *Bleak House*, Edinburgh and London, 1952, New York, 1953; Fenn in *Someone Waiting*, London, 1953; Reader in *A Boy Growing Up*, London, 1955, New York, 1957; Hjalmar Ekdal in *The Wild Duck* by Ibsen, London, 1955; Shylock in *The Merchant of Venice*, Iago in *Othello*, and Angelo in *Measure for Measure*, Stratford upon Avon, 1956; The Author in *Shadow of Heroes* by Robert Ardrey, London, 1958; The Man in *Lunch Hour* by John Mortimer, Mr. Chacterson in *The Form* by N.F. Simpson, and Edward in *A Slight Ache* by Harold Pinter (triple bill), London, 1960; Ascolini in *Daughter of Silence* by Morris West, New York, 1961; Sir Thomas More in *A Man for All Seasons* by Robert Bolt, New York, 1962; Pope Pius XII in *The Deputy* by Rolf Hochhuth, New York, 1964; Ignaty Illyich in *A Month in the Country* by Turgenev, London, 1965; The Headmaster in *Forty Years On* by Alan Bennett, London, 1969. **Films** – *The Case of the Frightened Lady (Criminal at Large)*, 1932; *Friday the Thirteenth*, 1934; *Evensong*, 1934; *The Iron Duke*, 1935; *Men of Tomorrow*, 1935; *My Love for You*, 1935; *Loves of a Dictator*, 1935; *Broken Blossoms*, 1937; *The Citadel*, 1938; *Dead Men Tell No Tales*, 1939; *Jamaica Inn*, 1939; *The Girl in the Mews*, 1941, *Major Barbara*, 1941; *The Stars Look Down*, 1941; *This England*, 1941; *Hatter's Castle*, 1948; *The Last Days of Dolwyn*, 1948; *Three Husbands*, 1951; *The Scarf*, 1951; *Another Man's Poison*, 1952; *Ivanhoe*, 1952; *The Deep Blue Sea*, 1955; *I Accuse!*, 1958; *Beyond This Place*, 1958; *The*

Wreck of the Mary Deare, 1959; *The L-Shaped Room*, 1963; *The Eye of the Devil*, 1967; *The Walking Stick*, 1969; *David Copperfield*, 1969. **Television** – *Every Picture Tells a Story*, 1949.

*   *   *

Emlyn Williams, born in a small Flintshire village in 1905, has been for many years an outstanding figure in the English theatre, both as dramatist and as actor.

He comes of Welsh peasant stock, and there is in his make-up a great deal more of the imaginative Celtic than the more solid Anglo-Saxon breed. His father was an attractive but rather raffish character who was by turns merchant seaman, greengrocer, village innkeeper, and foreman in an ironworks; his mother was a stern Puritan whose one purpose in life besides her Wesleyanism, was to keep her home above the poverty line. When her eldest son George (always his name in the family) proved good at his books she was unsympathetic. Instead of going to work and helping with upkeep, he cost money.

Good at his books, however, George certainly was. His family was entirely Welsh-speaking, and though he learnt English at school he never heard it used as a spoken language until he was 11. The ease with which he then took to it caught the interest of his French teacher, Miss S. G. Cooke, who realised that she had a born linguist on her hands and set herself to shape a career for him.

She perfected his English, taught him French, paid his expenses for a term at a French school, arranged lessons in Italian for him. He won scholarship after scholarship, which took him not only to Oxford, but to Paris and Rome as well. Yet in the end he went his own way, not Miss Cooke's. He did indeed take his degree, but it was not the brilliant affair she had hoped for. Somewhere along the line he had discovered the theatre and his own aptitude for it; and it was the O.U.D.S., not the lecture-room, which became the scene of his university life.

In the 1920's the Drama Society at Oxford took itself very seriously as a nursery for the professional stage, and George (who now assumed his less ordinary second name and became known as Emlyn Williams) gained some useful experience both as actor and as dramatist.

He was still only 21 when he made his debut on the London stage in 1927, and the fact that his services were at once in constant demand proved that his choice of the theatre as a profession had been a wise one. This became clearer still in 1935, when his play *Night Must Fall* enjoyed a triumph in London, repeated in New York, and Williams himself won high praise in both cities for his playing of the key part of a sinister young killer.

In 1938 there followed another notable and popular piece – *The Corn Is Green*. This was in essence a gesture of gratitude to Miss Cooke for all that she had done for him; and though Williams was now 33 years old he was still youthful-looking enough to appear as the boy (in the play, a miner's son) to whom the teacher devoted her talent and her savings.

Drama was not of much interest to Miss Cooke, and it may be doubted whether the idea of being made the model for a threatrical character appealed to her; but it is scarcely to be doubted that the affection with which the portrait was made or the sincerity and understanding with which Sybil Thorndike brought it to life must have been some reward to her for love's labour partly lost.

The outbreak of war in 1939 drove the London theatre out of existence for a time; but when the German air-attacks had been beaten off in 1940 Williams' next play, *The Light of Heart*, with its moving study of an old actor, drew eager audiences. In the following year another play, *The Morning Star*, raised his reputation as a serious dramatist still higher.

This latter piece had a curious history. It was intended by Williams as a tribute to the gallantry with which the people of London, his adopted city, has behaved under the bombing. He never expected it to have commercial success, because it was not to be thought that people who had so recently had to endure the real thing would care to subject their nerves to imitation air-raids. He wished to make his gesture of admiration while memory of the events was still fresh in mind, and therefore his play, though deeply felt, was rather too hastily put together. In the event, the nerves of London proved equal to this extra test. Very much to the author's surprise, the play proved very popular.

With the war ending, he added in 1945 one more to his group of serious comedies, *The Wind of Heaven*; but after that the theatre moved against him, as it did against most of the established dramatists. A new young generation of play-goers, who had discovered the living theatre while in the forces or the wartime factories, was more interested in revivals than in contemporary drama. Except for the poetic work of T.S. Eliot and Christopher Fry, few new plays of quality reached the stage during the post-war decade, and after that came the New Wave of dramatists who were in revolt against the so-called "well-made" play.

Many of the established writers were reduced to silence by this development, but not so Williams. In his orthodox plays he had usually included a part for himself – not necessarily a leading part, but always one worth acting. Now he switched his talent as dramatist to the resuscitation of an art-form which had been immensely popular 100 years earlier – the "recital" or "reading" – which was virtually a play with a part for himself and nobody else.

The great exponent of this kind of entertainment had been Charles Dickens, whose readings from his own works had been immensely popular. Williams now set himself to bring back to the stage a replica of one of Dickens' performances, with himself in the part of the novelist. Strictly speaking, this was not play-writing, but only a playwright of experience and skill could have done it.

He launched this enterprise in 1951, and when it turned out to be immensely popular he added a one-man version of *Bleak House* to his repertoire in 1952 and a Dylan Thomas programme in 1955. He has carried these activities almost over the whole of the globe and they have replaced almost entirely his normal career both as dramatist and as actor.

—W. A. Darlington

WILLIAMS, Heathcote. British. Born in Helsby, Cheshire, 15 November 1941. Associate Editor, *Transatlantic Review*, London and New York; Founding Editor, *Suck*, Amsterdam. Recipient: *Evening Standard* award, 1970; George Devine Award, 1970; John Whiting Award, 1971; Obie Award, 1971. Agent: Emanuel Wax, ACTAC, 16 Cadogan Lane, London, S.W.1. Address: Transatlantic Review, 33 Ennismore Gardens, London, S.W.7, England.

PUBLICATIONS

Plays

   The Local Stigmatic (produced Edinburgh, 1965; London, 1966; Boston, 1967; New
      York, 1968).   Published in *Traverse Plays*, London, Penguin, 1965; in *AC/DC, and
      The Local Stigmatic*, 1973.
   AC/DC (produced London, 1970; New York, 1971).   London, Calder and Boyars,
      1972; in *AC/DC, and The Local Stigmatic*, 1973.
   AC/DC, and The Local Stigmatic: Two Plays.   New York, Viking Press, 1973.
   Remember the Truth Dentist (produced London, 1974).
   Very Tasty – A Pantomime (produced London, 1975).

Screenplay: *Malatesta*, 1969.

Other

The Speakers.   London, Hutchinson, 1964; New York, Grove Press, 1967.
Manifestoes, Manifesten.   Rotterdam, Cold Turkey Press, 1975.

*   *   *

Heathcote Williams imperatively demands inclusion in any cyclopedia of contemporary dramatists on the strength of, essentially, one play, *AC/DC*. But that play, obviously, is very exceptional, both as a piece of sustained writing and as a theatrical experience. Up to the time of its appearance in 1970 he was known as the author of a very strange book, *The Speakers*, a remarkably successful attempt to enter into the world of some of the more evidently demented of the regular speakers at Speakers' Corner, and a one-act play of almost unrelieved verbal and physical violence, *The Local Stigmatic*, which has no noticeable plot, just a succession of savage encounters composed with the utmost care and precision of style in mustering an extraordinary battery of insults and threats.

AC/DC is in the direct succession of these works. Obviously Williams, who was born in 1941 and has apparently lived with the mental oddities he evokes in *The Speakers* (whether in a spirit of research or from voluntary choice is not clear), has an absorbing, even obsessive interest in schizophrenia and various kinds of mental disorder. Also, a considerable sympathy with sufferers, even to the extent of wondering – and he is not the first – whether they may not be somehow hooked into a kind of cosmic connection which the conventionally "sane" have allowed themselves to cut off but which may neverthelss be the means of conveying some useful truths about human existence, if only we would or could listen.

Hence, *AC/DC* is in effect an evening with two schizophrenics and three other characters they draw more or less into their own private world. In the first act, which is called "Alternating Current," an empty-headed, deeply conventional hippy couple wander into an amusement arcade with a black girl called Sadie, who seems to be a sort of third member of the ménage. Here they meet Maurice and Perowne, two apparent lunatics who move in on Sadie and draw her away from the other couple, whom she and they recognize as Mr. and Mrs. America 1970, just the latest incarnation of bourgeois convention. This act has patches of tedium as well as vividly gripping sections like Maurice's monologue in which he describes how he dealt with a couple of psychologists eager to use hypnotism in order to demonstrate the reality of reincarnation. But the feeling persists of some powerful talent at work behind the façade; it even seems possible that in so far as this act tests an audience's powers of endurance to the utmost, it may be meant to – part of the theatrical experience this play offers is that of an obstacle course which may lead one, rightly negotiated, to some outstanding theatrical reward.

This does in fact materialize in the second act, "Direct Current," in which, Mr. and Mrs. America once disposed of, we get down to the private obsessions of Maurice, his use of Perowne as a sort of friend/lover doctor/patient master/slave, and his successful attempts to engulf Sadie in the world he inhabits. There is much wild and vivid talk about the conservation and right use of energy in the universe, the waste and misuse of energy through the adulation of pop stars, the vampiric effects of the mass media, sapping spectators of their essential energy. There are also magical moments of theatrical action, like Sadie's progressive destruction of a vast collage of mind-eating figures out of the pop culture pantheon, or her trepanning of Perowne (ritual theatre at its best, this) and orgasmic exorcism of Maurice's fantasies.

Even despite its looseness, its occasional infatuation with words for their own sake, above and beyond any kind of dramatic functionalism, its dangerous hovering on the border of something so private as to be beyond communication at all, *AC/DC* is a rare tour de force, without any close parallel in British or world theatre today. William Gaskill, who directed its first production at the Royal Court, said curiously during a radio interview that Heathcote Williams is like Congreve. Weird as the comparison sounds, one can see what he means.

—John Russell Taylor

859

WILLIAMS, Tennessee (Thomas Lanier Williams).   American.   Born in Columbus, Mississippi, 26 March 1911. Educated at the University of Missouri, Columbia, 1930–32; Washington University, St. Louis, 1936–37; University of Iowa, Iowa City, 1938, A.B. 1938. Clerical Worker and Manual Laborer, International Shoe Company, St. Louis, 1934–36; held various jobs, including waiter and elevator operator, New Orleans, 1939; teletype operator, Jacksonville, Florida, 1940; worked at odd jobs, New York, 1942, and as a Screenwriter for MGM, 1943. Full-time Writer since 1944. Recipient: Rockefeller Fellowship, 1940; National Institute of Arts and Letters grant, 1944, and Gold Medal, 1969; Pulitzer Prize, 1948, 1955; New York Drama Critics Circle Award, 1945, 1948, 1955, 1962; Brandeis University Creative Arts Award, 1964. Member, National Institute of Arts and Letters. Lives in Key West, Florida, and New York. Address: c/o Audrey Wood, International Creative Management, 40 West 57th Street, New York, New York 10019, U.S.A.

PUBLICATIONS

Plays

   Cairo! Shanghai! Bombay! (produced Memphis, 1936).
   The Magic Tower (produced St. Louis, 1936).
   Headlines (produced St. Louis, 1936).
   Candles in the Sun (produced St. Louis, 1936).
   Fugitive Kind (produced St. Louis, 1937).
   Spring Song (produced Iowa City, 1938).
   The Long Goodbye (produced New York, 1940).   Included in *27 Wagons Full of Cotton*, 1946.
   Battle of Angels (produced Boston, 1940; New York, 1974).   Murray, Utah, Pharos-New Directions, 1945; revised version, as *Orpheus Descending* (produced New York, 1957; London, 1959), published as *Orpheus Descending, with Battle of Angels*, New York, New Directions, 1958; as *Orpheus Descending*, London, Secker and Warburg, 1958.
   At Liberty (produced New York, 1968).   Published in *American Scenes*, edited by William Kozlenko, New York, Day, 1941.
   Stairs to the Roof (produced Pasadena, California, 1944).
   You Touched Me, with Donald Windham, suggested by the story by D. H. Lawrence (produced Cleveland, 1944; New York, 1945).   New York, French, 1947.
   The Glass Menagerie (produced Cleveland, 1944; New York, 1945; London, 1948). New York, Random House, 1945; London, Lehmann, 1948.
   27 Wagons Full of Cotton and Other One-Act Plays (includes *The Purification, The Lady of Larkspur Lotion, The Last of My Solid Gold Watches, Portrait of a Madonna, Auto-da-Fé, Lord Byron's Love Letter, The Strangest Kind of Romance, The Long Goodbye, Hello from Bertha*, and *This Property Is Condemned*).   New York, New Directions, 1946; London, Grey Walls Press, 1947; augmented edition (includes *Talk to Me Like the Rain and Let Me Listen* and *Something Unspoken*), New Directions, 1953.
   This Property Is Condemned (produced New York, 1946; London, 1953).   Included in *27 Wagons Full of Cotton*, 1946.
   Portrait of a Madonna (produced Los Angeles, 1946; New York, 1959).   Included in *27 Wagons Full of Cotton*, 1946.
   The Last of My Solid Gold Watches (produced Los Angeles, 1946).   Included in *27 Wagons Full of Cotton*, 1946.
   Lord Byron's Love Letter (produced New York, 1947).   Included in *27 Wagons Full of Cotton*, 1946; revised version, music by Raffaello de Banfield (produced London, 1964); libretto published, Milan and New York, Riccordi, 1955.

Auto-da-Fé (produced New York, 1947; Bromley, Kent, 1961).   Included in *27 Wagons Full of Cotton*, 1946.

The Lady of Larkspur Lotion (produced New York, 1947; London, 1968).   Included in *27 Wagons Full of Cotton*, 1946.

The Purification (produced Dallas, 1954; Cambridge, England, 1955; New York, 1959). Included in *27 Wagons Full of Cotton*, 1946.

27 Wagons Full of Cotton (produced New Orleans and New York, 1955).   Included in *27 Wagons Full of Cotton*, 1946.

Hello from Bertha (produced Bromley, Kent, 1961).   Included in *27 Wagons Full of Cotton*, 1946.

The Strangest Kind of Romance (produced London, 1969).   Included in *27 Wagons Full of Cotton*, 1946.

Mooney's Kid Don't Cry (produced Los Angeles, 1946; New York, 1947; London, 1971). Included in *American Blues*, 1948.

A Streetcar Named Desire (produced New York, 1947; London, 1949).   New York, New Directions, 1947; London, Lehmann, 1949.

Summer and Smoke (produced Dallas, 1947; New York, 1948; London, 1952).   New York, New Directions, 1948; London, Lehmann, 1952; revised version, as *The Eccentricities of a Nightingale* (produced Nyack, New York, 1964; Guildford, Surrey, 1967), published as *The Eccentricities of a Nightingale, and Summer and Smoke*, New York, New Directions, 1965.

American Blues: Five Short Plays (includes *Mooney's Kid Don't Cry, The Dark Room, The Case of the Crushed Petunias, The Long Stay Cut Short; or, The Unsatisfactory Supper*, and *Ten Blocks on the Camino Real*).   New York, Dramatists Play Service, 1948.

Ten Blocks on the Camino Real, in *American Blues*, 1948; revised version, as *Camino Real* (produced New York, 1953; London, 1957), New York, New Directions, 1953; London, Secker and Warburg, 1956.

The Case of the Crushed Petunias (produced Cleveland, 1957; New York, 1958; Glasgow, 1968).   Included in *American Blues*, 1948.

The Dark Room (produced London, 1966).   Included in *American Blues*, 1948.

The Long Stay Cut Short; or, The Unsatisfactory Supper (produced London, 1971). Included in *American Blues*, 1948.

The Rose Tattoo (produced New York, 1951; London, 1959).   New York, New Directions, 1951; London, Secker and Warburg, 1955.

I Rise in Flame, Cried the Phoenix: A Play about D. H. Lawrence (produced New York, 1953; London, 1971).   New York, New Directions, 1951.

Talk to Me Like the Rain and Let Me Listen (produced Westport, Connecticut, 1958; New York, 1962).   Included in *27 Wagons Full of Cotton*, 1953.

Something Unspoken (produced New York and London, 1958).   Included in *27 Wagons Full of Cotton*, 1953.

Cat on a Hot Tin Roof (produced New York, 1955; London, 1958).   New York, New Directions, 1955; London, Secker and Warburg, 1956; revised version (produced West Springfield, Massacusetts, 1973), New York, New Directions, 1975.

Three Players of a Summer Game (produced Westport, Connecticut, 1955).

Sweet Bird of Youth (produced Coral Gables, Florida, 1956; New York, 1959; Watford, Hertfordshire, 1968).   New York, New Directions, 1959; London, Secker and Warburg, 1961.

Baby Doll: The Script for the Film, Incorporating the Two One-Act Plays Which Suggested It: 27 Wagons Full of Cotton and The Long Stay Cut Short; or, The Unsatisfactory Supper.   New York, New Directions, 1956; as *Baby Doll: The Script for the Film*, London, Secker and Warburg, 1957.

Garden District: Something Unspoken, Suddenly Last Summer (produced New York and London, 1958).   New York, New Directions, 1958; London, Secker and Warburg, 1959.

The Fugitive Kind: Original Play Title: Orpheus Descending (screenplay).   New York,
   New American Library, 1958.
A Perfect Analysis Given by a Parrot (produced New York, 1976).   New York,
   Dramatists Play Service, 1958.
The Enemy: Time, in *Theatre* (New York), March 1959.
The Night of the Iguana (produced Spoleto, Italy, 1959; revised version, produced New
   York, 1961; London, 1965).   New York, New Directions, 1962; London, Secker
   and Warburg, 1963.
Period of Adjustment: High Point over a Cavern: A Serious Comedy (produced Miami,
   1959; New York, 1960; Bristol, 1961; London, 1962).   New York, New Directions,
   1960; London, Secker and Warburg, 1961.
To Heaven in a Golden Coach (produced Bromley, Kent, 1961).
The Milk Train Doesn't Stop Here Anymore (produced Spoleto, Italy, 1962; revised
   versions, produced New York, 1962; Abington, West Virginia, 1963; New York,
   1964; London, 1968).   New York, New Directions, and London, Secker and
   Warburg, 1964.
Slapstick Tragedy (*The Mutilated* and *The Gnädiges Fräulein*) (produced New York,
   1966).   New York, Dramatists Play Service, 2 vols., 1967; revised version of *The
   Gnädiges Fräulein,* as *The Latter Days of a Celebrated Soubrette* (produced New
   York, 1974).
Kingdom of Earth, in *Esquire* (New York), February 1967; revised version, as *Kingdom
   of Earth: The Seven Descents of Myrtle* (produced New York, 1968).   New York,
   New Directions, 1968.
The Two Character Play (produced London, 1967; revised version, produced London,
   1969).   New York, New Directions, 1969; revised version, as *Out Cry* (produced
   Chicago, 1971, New York, 1973), New Directions, 1973; revised version (produced
   New York, 1974).
In the Bar of a Tokyo Hotel (produced New York, 1969; London, 1971).   New York,
   Dramatists Play Service, 1969.
I Can't Imagine Tomorrow (televised, 1970; produced London, 1976).   Included in
   Dragon Country, 1970.
Dragon Country: A Book of Plays (includes *In the Bar of a Tokyo Hotel, I Rise in Flame,
   Cried the Phoenix, The Mutilated, I Can't Imagine Tomorrow, Confessional, The
   Frosted Glass Coffin, The Gnädiges Fräulein,* and *A Perfect Analysis Given by a
   Parrot*).   New York, New Directions, 1970.
Small Craft Warnings (produced New York, 1972; London, 1973).   New York,
   Dramatists Play Service, 1972; London, Secker and Warburg, 1973.
The Theatre of Tennessee Williams:
   I. *Battle of Angels, A Streetcar Named Desire, The Glass Menagerie.*   New York,
      New Directions, 1972.
   II. *The Eccentricities of a Nightingale, Summer and Smoke, The Rose Tattoo, Camino
      Real.*   New York, New Directions, 1972.
   III. *Cat on a Hot Tin Roof, Orpheus Descending, Suddenly Last Summer.*   New
      York, New Directions, 1972.
   IV. *Sweet Bird of Youth, Period of Adjustment, Night of the Iguana.*   New York,
      New Directions, 1972.
   V. *The Milk Train Doesn't Stop Here Anymore; Kingdom of Earth,* revised version;
      Small Craft Warnings; The Two Character Play, revised version.   New York,
      New Directions, 1976.
The Red Devil Battery Sign (produced Boston and New York, 1974; revised version,
   produced Vienna, 1976).
Demolition Downtown: Count Ten in Arabic − Then Run (produced London, 1976).
This Is an Entertainment (produced San Francisco, 1976).

Screenplays: *Senso (The Wanton Countess,* English dialogue, with Paul Bowles), 1949;

The Glass Menagerie, with Peter Berneis, 1950; *A Streetcar Named Desire*, with Oscar Saul, 1951; *The Rose Tattoo*, with Hal Kanter, 1955; *Baby Doll*, 1956; *Suddenly Last Summer*, with Gore Vidal, 1959; *The Fugitive Kind*, with Meade Roberts, 1960; *Boom*, 1968.

Television Play: *I Can't Imagine Tomorrow*, 1970.

Novels

The Roman Spring of Mrs. Stone. New York, New Directions, and London, Lehmann, 1950.
Moise and the World of Reason. New York, Simon and Schuster, 1975; London, W. H. Allen, 1976.

Short Stories

One Arm and Other Stories. New York, New Directions, 1948.
Hard Candy: A Book of Stories. New York, New Directions, 1954.
Three Players of a Summer Game and Other Stories. London, Secker and Warburg, 1960.
Grand. New York, House of Books, 1964.
The Knightly Quest: A Novella and Four Short Stories. New York, New Directions, 1967; augmented edition, as *The Knightly Quest: A Novella and Twelve Short Stories*, London, Secker and Warburg, 1968.
Eight Mortal Ladies Possessed: A Book of Stories. New York, New Directions, 1974; London, Secker and Warburg, 1975.

Verse

Five Young American Poets, with others. New York, New Directions, 1944.
In the Winter of Cities: Poems. New York, New Directions, 1956.

Other

Memoirs. New York, Doubleday, 1975; London, W. H. Allen, 1976.

*   *   *

Tennessee Williams is probably the most productive writer in the contemporary American theatre. Since the opening of *The Glass Menagerie* in 1945, he has written almost twenty full-length plays, a large number of one-acts, several screenplays, a novel, and four collections of short stories.

Everything he has written springs from his continuing preoccupation with the extremes of human aspiration and frustration. His plays deal with the war perpetually waged within the hearts of men between death and desire, the public and the private, the real and the ideal, the need for faith and the inevitability of inconstancy, the love of life and the overpowering urge towards self-destruction. But we discover that, underneath these dualities, all his characters are searching or meaningful relationships with their fellow men. In pursuing this quest, Blanche DuBois may be Williams' most representative character. Having lost the stability of the "Beautiful Dream" of her ancestral society, she has been exiled into a world in which she cannot exist. In her confusion she gives herself to desire not realizing that beauty and desire often lead to destruction. Innocently, she depends on the "kindness of strangers" unaware that these strangers are, in fact, the surrogates of that Death which haunts both Williams' imagination and the world of his plays.

Many people accuse Williams of being morbidly obsessed with violence and perverted sexuality; but this is to misread him and forget one of his most significant insights. In an interview given shortly after *Sweet Bird of Youth* was produced, Williams commented: "Desire is rooted in a longing for companionship, a release from the loneliness which haunts every individual." Like the writers whom he most admires — Chekhov, D. H. Lawrence, Giraudoux, and Beckett — Williams is primarily interested in dramatizing the anguish of solitude, a solitude which is made increasingly unbearable as the individual feels cut off from all the old securities, as he becomes conscious of the disparity between the outer life of one way of living and the inner life of a different way of dreaming. His is a drama of lost souls.

There has, nonetheless, been a discernible development in Williams' work. In it he has traced a chart of the fevers that he has experienced in looking at the world outside and within himself. From *The Glass Menagerie*, which dramatized man's tendency and need to escape the snares and dualities of a misfit world, through the maze of violence, brutality, and desire of such plays as *A Streetcar Named Desire* and *Cat on a Hot Tin Roof*, Williams has come increasingly toward an interest in the condition of man's spiritual life. With only a few exceptions, the characters in all of Williams' plays written prior to 1960 are lost souls because they are, as Harold Clurman put it,

> torn between the godseeking impulse and the pull of desire. In the shambles of our civilization, desire has been debased into raw carnality. Sex without the blessedness of love is death-dealing corruption. In this corrupt atmosphere — always captivatingly colorful in Williams, even to the very names of the vicinities in which his dramas take place — his men and women are destroyed by the poisons which emanate from it. The lacerations they suffer are the result of their bodies and souls being at odds. The sharpness of this division is a characteristic of [Williams'] Puritan consciousness.

But in *Night of the Iguana*, written in 1961, we notice a profound change. For the first time we find him confronting directly the anguished condition of man's spiritual life with the result that in this play the continuing theme of all his work has an added dimension of depth. All of the well-known Williams trademarks are still present, but they have been recast. The sexuality and violence so characteristic of his earlier plays have been softened and moved to the play's outer edges; and the sense of human fragility has taken on a new and steely strength. The central action of *Night of the Iguana* takes place in the world of inner disturbance and the dominant force in that world turns out to be the fantastic, that mysterious chemistry in human encounters which, to use theological terms, has the transforming power of grace. Both Shannon and Hannah, the play's central characters, have been brought to the last outpost of human possibility and in their different ways they discover and earn a moment of peace.

I believe it is worth noting that while so many European playwrights were protesting against the impossibility of meaningful human communication, America's most productive playwright was celebrating man's capacity — admittedly hesitant and crippled — to achieve a situation in which there need be no limits, a place where a "little understanding" between two people can exist. (Significantly, this union is not sexual. Nothing underscores the growth in Williams' perspectives more forcefully than the realization that Shannon and Hannah have clearly evolved from Stanley Kowalski and Blanche DuBois of *A Streetcar Named Desire*.) But there is nothing easy about this achievement, nor is the playwright sentimental in his treatment of it. The play ends at a moment of repose when all is in balance; but as Hannah speaks the final lines ("Oh, God, can't we stop now? Finally? Please let us. It's so quiet here, now") there is panic in her heart. Like the iguana of the title, man may be set free briefly from the "continual rush of time," but we and the characters know the still moment will not last. However, that moment, surrounded as it is by perils and impermanence, nonetheless reveals not only the possibilities of human experience but also intimations of the eternal. No one writing for the contemporary theatre is more conscious of how difficult it is for people to communicate and thus discover a meaning for their lives, than is Tennessee Williams. However, unlike so many of his Continental colleagues, he has not capitulated before this difficulty but rather, like the wise men of old, he has sought out new ways, with the result that his work celebrates the capacity of the human spirit to triumph, if only briefly, over what had seemed to be insuperable odds.

However, in this development it is clear that all of the characteristics of his earlier work are very much present: the fluidity and mercurial instability of all emotion, the haunting imminence of death, the specters of violence and disease, the attraction to and guilt in sex, nostalgia for the past and hope for the future, a childlike humor even in the most morbid situations, and the conviction that "we're all of us sentenced to solitary confinement inside our own skins."

It is also clear from his more recent plays, particularly the bewildering and disturbing *In the Bar of a Tokyo Hotel* and the unjustly neglected romance of the entertainment world, *The Gnädiges Fräulein*, that that dichotomy of spirit which lead to so many breakdowns in Williams' personal life, is also the source of his rebirth and renewal as an artist. Like the bedevilled Swede, August Strindberg, with whom he has so much in common, Tennessee Williams may be justly accused of having a limited perspective on the alternatives of the human condition, but within the limits of the world he has chosen he has probably achieved more than any other living American dramatist.

—Robert W. Corrigan

WILLIAMSON, David (Keith).   Australian.   Born in Melbourne, Victoria, 24 February 1942. Educated at Monash University, Clayton, Victoria, B.E. 1964; Melbourne University. Married Carol Anne Cranby in 1965 (marriage dissolved), two children; Kristin Ingrid Green, 1974, two foster children. Design Engineer, General Motors, Melbourne, 1965; Lecturer, Swinburne College of Technology, Melbourne, 1966–72. Member, Australian Council of the Arts. Recipient: George Devine Award, 1971; Australian Writers Guild award, 1972, 1973; *Evening Standard* award (London), 1974; Australian Film Institute award, 1975. Agent: Curtis Brown (Australia) Pty. Ltd., 38 Stafford Street, Paddington, New South Wales 2021. Address: P.O. Diamond Creek, Victoria 3089, Australia.

PUBLICATIONS

Plays

    The Coming of Stork (produced Melbourne, 1970).   Included in *The Coming of Stork, Jugglers Three, What If You Died Tomorrow,* 1974.

    The Removalists (produced Melbourne, 1971; London and Cleveland, 1973; New York, 1974).   Sydney, Currency Press, 1972; London, Eyre Methuen, 1973.

    Don's Party (produced Melbourne, 1971; London, 1975).   Sydney, Currency Press, and London, Eyre Methuen, 1973.

    Jugglers Three (produced Melbourne, 1972).   Included in *The Coming of Stork, Jugglers Three, What If You Died Tomorrow,* 1974.

What If You Died Tomorrow (produced Melbourne, 1973; London, 1974).   Included in
   The Coming of Stork, Jugglers Three, What If You Died Tomorrow, 1974.
The Coming of Stork, Jugglers Three, What If You Died Tomorrow: Three Plays.
   Sydney, Currency Press, and London, Eyre Methuen, 1974.
The Department (produced Adelaide, 1974).   Sydney, Currency Press, and London,
   Eyre Methuen, 1976.
A Handful of Friends (produced Adelaide, 1976).

Screenplays: *Stork*, 1971; *The Family Man* (episode in *Libido*), 1972; *Petersen*, 1974;
The Removalists, 1974; *Don's Party*, 1976; *Eliza Fraser*, 1976.

Critical Studies: "Mask and Cage: Stereotype in Recent Drama" by Margaret Williams, in
Meanjin (Melbourne), September 1972; in *Southerly* (Sydney), June 1973; "*The Removalists*:
A Conjunction of Limitations" by the author, in *Meanjin* (Melbourne), vol. 4, 1974;
"Australian Bards and British Reviewers" by Alrene Sykes, in *Australian Literary Studies*
(Hobart, Tasmania), May 1975.

David Williamson comments:

I would regard my early plays as mounting a satiric-ironic attack, albeit with a modicum of
ambivalent affection, on the comformist philistine, materialist, sexist, and aggressive aspects
of the Australian social ethos. In my later plays (*The Department* and *A Handful of Friends*)
the personal as distinct from the sociological observations are accorded more weight but the
ironic-satiric stance of the earlier plays is, I think, maintained.

*   *   *

David Williamson's plays probably owed their almost instant popularity with Australian
audiences to two things: their forceful and amusing dialogue, and the fact that audiences
could readily recognise themselves in the characters on stage – oddly, until the late 1960's,
Australian dramatists had very little success in portraying urban, middle-class Australia. Like
most Australian dramatists since then, Williamson is fascinated by the patterns and pressures
of society. Talking of the group which later became the Australian Performing Group he
said: "What brought us together...was a desire to write about this Australia we all grew up
in. No one had got it right before." Williamson did indeed get it right; but – as is not always
recognised when the plays are performed outside Australia – his plays are heightened
naturalism, rather than the literal transcript of slice-of-life. Few in the audiences of his early
plays would use quite so many four-letter words or as much violence as they observed on
stage, but they would certainly recognise beneath this dramatic heightening their own
tensions and frustrations. Williamson is interestingly aware of much Australian speech and
manner as a deliberate style. Speaking of *Don's Party*, he said: "The fact that most of the
characters in the play are patently aware of the un-English bluntness of their social manners
and are using this bluntness as a *style* is quite clear....The scene in which Don and Mal shout
abuse at each other in apparent fury, dissolves into laughter. They have been using an
archetypal Australian style. Belligerence without real resentment. Real resentment in this
country tends to be wreathed in polite smiles."
   The first Williamson play to reach a wide audience was *The Removalists* (later made into a
film) in which a young policeman goes beserk and beats a man to death. The play is not,
Williamson says, an attack on the police force, but a drama about authoritarianism and its
effects, and it shows clear-sighted understanding of both the policemen and their victim,
understanding of the pressures and problems on both sides which lead inevitably to murder.
This refusal by the author to make overt moral judgements on his characters was to prove

one of the constant distinguishing characteristics of the Williamson play; nevertheless, there is an implied judgment on the society which has conditioned their violent, primitive reactions, and for this reason *The Removalists* comes closer to taking a visible moral stance than most Williamson plays.

David Williamson's portrayal of individual characters is normally perceptive and soundly based, but his real interest seems to be in group interaction rather than the individual. In most of the plays performed since *The Removalists*, a group of people are brought together, and the subtle threads of communication (and some not so subtle) are revealed, the past relationships and the present pressures. One of the joys of a Williamson play can be the uncanny rightness of the ways in which the characters react to each other. *Don's Party* is an interaction play; with almost no plot or forward movement, it remains from moment to moment theatrically vibrant, gripping the attention. The party of the title is held on election night, and the guests are mostly university graduates, one time radicals now in their thirties, aware of the failed promise of their youth and caught up in a world of bigger houses, larger swimming pools. Needless to say, the political party for which all except two of the guests have voted (Labor) is defeated. Closest to *Don's Party* in its almost total lack of any real plot is the recent and brilliant *The Department*, a mirror look at a departmental committee meeting in a tertiary institution.

David Williamson's plays over the last five years have modified and matured, just as the characters he writes about have become older, more successful – though they are still coping with insecurities, still looking for the best way to shape their lives. In some of the earlier and middle plays (*The Coming of Stork, Jugglers Three*, and *What If You Died Tomorrow*) one sometimes felt that exuberant theatricality had taken over, and a lively character or scene had been allowed to take the reins and gallop the play almost off its track. In almost every Williamson play there is at least one extrovert character; in *Jugglers Three* and *What If You Died Tomorrow*, it has been suggested, extrovert characters (Gunter and Dennis) are almost clown figures, not fully integrated with the central action and themes. Williamson's later plays are more disciplined; in *A Handful of Friends* there are five characters only, and the progression of the play is our increased awareness of the links between them as they make use of each other, love each other, and maim each other; each scene is part of the wider pattern of the whole.

It is inarguable that David Williamson's plays work in the theatre; critics have therefore argued whether or no he is also a "serious" playwright. To me he is far from superficial in his observation of man, woman and society. (The two women in *The Removalists* were justly criticised as stock figures, but Williamson has since then written much more perceptively about women in several plays.) A difficulty in assessing the depth of Williamson's plays is that if one is familiar with the situations and the characters about which he is writing, the plays have reverberations that do not seem to exist for anyone meeting the characters for the first time. There are several reasons why a hasty assessment might underestimate Williamson's seriousness of purpose. They include his refusal to make clear-cut moral judgements; his habit of sketching with a light hand, often giving only bare – if accurate – outlines; and above all, the quiet irony (very typically Australian) which plays over Williamson's work, and draws him away from portraying deep emotion seriously and unselfconsciously. He comes closest to portraying emotion "straight" in his latest play, *A Handful of Friends*, but for the most part, the author tends to remain slightly detached from his characters, aware of inherent comedy in even tragic situations – for instance, Gunter, the suicidal jilted lover in *What If You Died Tomorrow*; though Gunter is perhaps such an extreme example that it is not quite fair to cite him. Williamson's irony is not, however, cynicism; it very often covers, to use one of his own phrases, "heavily disguised compassion."

—Alrene Sykes

WILLIS, Ted (Edward Henry Willis); Baron Willis of Chislehurst.   British.   Born in Tottenham, Middlesex, 13 January 1918. Educated at state schools, 1923–33. Served in the Royal Fusiliers, 1940; Writer for the War Office and Ministry of Information. Married Audrey Hale in 1944; has two children. Artistic Director, Unity Theatre, London, 1945–48. Since 1967, Director, World Wide Pictures. Executive Member, League of Dramatists, London, 1948–74. Chairman, 1958–63, and President, 1963–68 and since 1976, Writers Guild of Great Britain; President, International Writers Guild, 1967–69. Member of the Board of Governors, National Film School, London; since 1964, Governor, Churchill Theatre Trust, Bromley, Kent. Recipient: Berlin Festival Award, for screenplay, 1957; Edinburgh Festival Award; Writers Guild award, 1964, 1967. Life peer, 1963. Agent: Elaine Greene Ltd., 31 Newington Green, London N16 9PU, England.

PUBLICATIONS

Plays

Sabotage (as John Bishop) (produced London, 1943).
Buster (produced London, 1943).   London, Fore Publications, n.d.
All Change Here (produced London, 1944).
"God Bless the Guv'nor": A Moral Melodrama in Which the Twin Evils of Trades Unionism and Strong Drink Are Exposed, "After Mrs. Henry Wood" (produced London, 1945).   London, New Theatre Publications, 1945.
The Yellow Star (also director: produced London, 1945).
What Happened to Love? (produced London, 1947).
No Trees in the Street (produced London, 1948).
The Lady Purrs (produced London, 1950).   London, Deane, 1950.
The Magnificent Moodies (produced London, 1952).
The Blue Lamp, with Jan Read (produced London, 1952).
A Kiss for Adele, with Talbot Strothwell, adaptation of the play by Barillet and Grédy (produced London, 1952).
Kid Kenyon Rides Again, with Allan Mackinnon (produced Bromley, Kent, 1954).
George Comes Home.   London, French, 1955.
Doctor in the House, adaptation of the novel by Richard Gordon (produced London, 1956).   London, Evans and New York, French, 1957.
Woman in a Dressing Gown (televised, 1956).   Included in Woman in a Dressing Gown and Other Television Plays, 1959; (revised version, produced Bromley, Kent, 1963; London, 1964); London, Evans, 1964.
The Young and the Guilty (televised, 1956).   Included in Woman in a Dressing Gown and Other Television Plays, 1959.
Look in Any Window (televised, 1958).   Included in Woman in a Dressing Gown and Other Television Plays, 1959.
Hot Summer Night (produced Bournemouth and London, 1958).   London, French, 1959.
Woman in a Dressing Gown and Other Televisions Plays (includes The Young and the Guilty and Look in Any Window).   London, Barrie and Rockliff, 1959.
Brothers-in-Law, with Henry Cecil, adaptation of the novel by Cecil (produced Wimbledon, Surrey, 1959).   London, French, 1959.
When in Rome, with Ken Ferry, music by Kramer, lyrics by Eric Shaw, adaptation of a play by Garinei and Giovannini (produced Oxford and London, 1959).
The Eyes of Youth, adaptation of the novel A Dread of Burning by Rosemary Timperley (as Farewell Yesterday, produced Worthing, Sussex, 1959; as The Eyes of Youth, produced Bournemouth, 1959).   London, Evans, 1960.

Mother, adaptation of the novel by Gorky (produced Croydon, Surrey, 1961).
Doctor at Sea, adaptation of the novel by Richard Gordon (produced Bromley, Kent,
    1961; London, 1966).   London, Evans, and New York, French, 1961.
The Little Goldmine.   London, French, 1962.
A Slow Roll of Drums (produced Bromley, Kent, 1964).
A Murder of Crows (produced Bromley, Kent, 1966).
The Ballad of Queenie Swann (televised, 1966; revised version, music by Dick Manning
    and Marvin Laird, lyrics by Ted Willis, produced Guildford, Surrey, 1967; as
    Queenie, produced London, 1967).
Dead on Saturday (produced Leatherhead, Surrey, 1972).

Screenplays: *The Waves Roll On* (documentary), 1945; *It's Great to Be Young*, 1946,
Holiday Camp, 1947; *Good Time Girl*, 1948; *A Boy, A Girl, and a Bike*, 1949; *The
Huggetts Abroad*, 1949; *The Undefeated* (documentary), 1950; *The Blue Lamp*, 1951;
The Wallet, 1952; *Burnt Evidence*, 1952, *Top of the Form*, 1953; *Trouble in Store*, 1953;
One Good Turn, 1954; *Up to His Neck*, 1954, *The Skywalkers*, 1956; *Woman in a
Dressing Gown*, 1957; *The Young and the Guilty*, 1957; *No Trees in the Street*, 1959; *Six
Men and a Nightingale*, 1961; *Flame in the Streets*, 1961; *The Horsemasters*, 1961;
Bitter Harvest, 1963; *Last Bus to Banjo Creek*, 1968; *Our Miss Fred*, 1972; and other
documentaries.

Radio Play: *Big Bertha*, 1962.

Television Plays: *The Handlebar, The Pattern of Marriage, Big City, Dial 999, The
Sullavan Brothers, Lifeline*, and *Taxi* series; *The Young and the Guilty*, 1956; *Woman in
a Dressing Gown*, 1956; *Look in Any Window*, 1958; *Strictly for the Sparrows*, 1958;
Scent of Fear, 1959; *Dixon of Dock Green* series, 1960 and later; *Days of Vengeance*,
with Edward J. Mason, 1960; *Flowers of Evil* series, with Mason, 1961; *Outbreak of
Murder*, with Mason; *Sergeant Cork* series, 1963; *The Four Seasons of Rosie Carr*,
1964; *Dream of a Summer Night*, 1965; *Mrs. Thursday* series, 1966; *The Ballad of
Queenie Swann*, 1966; *Virgin of the Secret Service* series, 1968; *Crimes of Passion* series,
1970–72; *Copper's End* series, 1971; *Hunter's Walk* series, 1973, 1976; *Black Beauty*
series, 1975; *Barney's Last Battle*, 1976.

Novels

The Blue Lamp.   London, Convoy, 1950.
The Devil's Churchyard.   London, Max Parrish, 1957.
Dixon of Dock Green: My Life, with Charles Hatton.   London, William Kimber, 1960.
Dixon of Dock Green: A Novel, with Paul Graham.   London, Mayflower, 1961.
Seven Gates to Nowhere.   London, Max Parrish, 1962.
Dead on Saturday.   London, Odanti Script Services, 1970.
Black Beauty.   London, Hamlyn, 1972.
Death May Surprise Us.   London, Macmillan, 1974; as *Westminster One*, New York,
    Putnam, 1975.
The Left-Handed Sleeper.   London, Macmillan, 1975, New York, Putnam, 1976.
Man-Eater.   London, Macmillan, 1976; New York, Morrow, 1977.

Other

Fighting Youth of Russia.   London, Russia Today Society, 1942.
Whatever Happened to Tom Mix? The Story of One of My Lives.   London, Cassell,
    1970.

Theatrical Activities:

Director: **Plays** – Unity Theatre, London: *The Yellow Star*, 1945; *Boy Meets Girl* by Bella and Samuel Spewack, 1946; *All God's Chillun Got Wings* by Eugene O'Neill, 1946; *Golden Boy* by Clifford Odets, 1947; *Anna Christie* by Eugene O'Neill.

Ted Willis comments:

I am a good example of what can be done by hard work. I've taken a small talent, honed and sharpened it into a good professional instrument. Might have been a better writer if I'd stuck to one area and kept out of politics (both writing and national) but that's the way I am.

*   *   *

There is no doubt in my mind that Ted Willis owes his success in life to his quite extraordinary power of concentration. At a very early age he decided that he was going to be a writer. When he left school finally at 15 and confided to the Headmaster his determination to write, the crisp comment was "Don't be a fool. You've no literary gift whatever. Much better learn a trade." But to waste time and energy in learning a trade was no part of the Willis plan. He was teaching himself one, and making progress. His intensive study of the cinema was encouraging him to try his hand at that medium, and television; so he took the kind of ill-paid jobs that were open to an unskilled man, and went on writing.

His pen was by now a very well-tempered instrument; but it was through his politics, not his fiction, that this first became publicly known. His views were of the extreme left-wing order, and he expressed them with a force and pungency that made him a valuable asset to the Labour Party. But when he was 21, the 1939–45 war broke out, and it was in the Army that he was given the chance to write his first film-scripts. This decided his future – for when he went back into civil life in 1945 and was invited to stand for a safe Labour seat in Parliament, he refused. He was still a writer.

He is an inventive story-teller, and his high standard of craftsmanship and severe self-discipline have lead inevitably to success, especially in such compositions as his television series *Dixon of Dock Green* and *Mrs. Thursday*. What it does not necessarily lead to is artistry; and one gathers that Ted knows this very well himself, for he once said modestly to an interviewer, "There are hundreds of better writers with much greater talent than mine. But less ability to work hard."

That honest, if overstated, attempt at self-assessment has a modicum of truth in it, and it is remarkable that not one of his productions has ever induced West End audiences to show much enthusiasm. Even *Woman in a Dressing Gown* (by common consent his best play) caused little stir.

So evident an effect must have a definable cause; but to say simply that Ted Willis has a better talent for film-scripts than for stage-plays is merely to define the matter without explaining it. There could be a dozen explanations but one is fundamental. The world of the living theatre was unknown to the boy who played truant from school to revel in the glories of the cinema. When Ted first encountered the stage in his mid-twenties it was in the spirit not of a lover but of an immensely industrious student. He learned much; but it is not thus that a dramatist acquires that mysterious sense of the theatre which enables him to serve the art of the actor. The hard-working student may well deserve success, but in the theatre he cannot command it.

—W. A. Darlington

WILSON, Lanford.   American.   Born in Lebanon, Missouri, 13 April 1937. Educated at Ozark High School, Missouri; Southwest Missouri State College, Springfield, 1955–56; San Diego State College, California, 1956–57; University of Chicago, 1957–58. Director, actor and designer for Caffe Cino and Cafe La Mama theatres, New York, and other theatres. Since 1969, Co-Founder and Resident Playwright, Circle Repertory Company, New York. Recipient: Rockefeller grant, 1967, 1974; Vernon Rice Award, 1968; ABC-Yale University Fellowship, 1969; New York Drama Critics Circle Award, 1973; Obie Award, 1973, 1975; Outer Circle Award, 1973; National Institute of Arts and Letters award, 1974. Agent: Bridget Aschenberg, International Creative Management, 40 West 57th Street, New York, New York 10019. Address: Box 891, Sag Harbor, New York 11963, U.S.A.

PUBLICATIONS

Plays

> *So Long at the Fair* (produced New York, 1963).
> *No Trespassing* (produced New York, 1964).
> *Home Free!* (also director: produced New York, 1964; London, 1968).   Included in *Balm in Gilead and Other Plays*, 1965; in *The Madness of Lady Bright, and Home Free!*, 1968.
> *Balm in Gilead* (produced New York, 1964).   Included in *Balm in Gilead and Other Plays*, 1965.
> *The Madness of Lady Bright* (also director: produced New York, 1964; London, 1968). Included in *The Rimers of Eldritch and Other Plays*, 1967; in *The Madness of Lady Bright, and Home Free!*, 1968.
> *Ludlow Fair* (produced New York, 1965; Edinburgh, 1967).   Included in *Balm in Gilead and Other Plays*, 1965.
> *Balm in Gilead and Other Plays* (includes *Home Free!* and *Ludlow Fair*).   New York, Hill and Wang, 1965.
> *Sex Is Between Two People* (produced New York, 1965).
> *The Rimers of Eldritch* (also director: produced New York, 1965).   Included in *The Rimers of Eldritch and Other Plays*, 1967.
> *This Is the Rill Speaking* (also director: produced New York, 1965).   Included in *The Rimers of Eldritch and Other Plays*, 1967.
> *Days Ahead* (produced New York, 1965).   Included in *The Rimers of Eldritch and Other Plays*, 1967.
> *The Sand Castle* (produced New York, 1965).   Included in *The Sand Castle and Three Other Plays*, 1970.
> *Wandering: A Turn* (produced New York, 1966).   Included in *The Rimers of Eldritch and Other Plays*, 1967.
> *The Rimers of Eldritch and Other Plays* (includes *This Is the Rill Speaking, Wandering, Days Ahead, The Madness of Lady Bright*).   New York, Hill and Wang, 1967.
> *Miss Williams: A Turn* (produced New York, 1967).
> *Untitled Play*, music by Al Carmines (produced New York, 1967).
> *The Madness of Lady Bright, and Home Free!*   London, Methuen, 1968.
> *The Gingham Dog* (produced Washington, D.C., 1968; New York, 1969; Manchester, 1970).   New York, Hill and Wang, 1970.
> *The Great Nebula in Orion* (produced Manchester, 1970; New York, 1972).   Included in *The Great Nebula in Orion and Three Other Plays*, 1973.
> *Lemon Sky* (produced Buffalo and New York, 1970).   New York, Hill and Wang, 1970.
> *Serenading Louie* (produced Washington, D.C., 1970; New York, 1976).   New York,

Dramatists Play Service, 1976.

The Sand Castle and Three Other Plays (includes *Wandering, Stoop: A Turn, Sextet (Yes): A Play for Voices*).   New York, Dramatists Play Service, 1970.

Sextet (Yes): A Play for Voices (produced New York, 1971).   Included in *The Sand Castle and Three Other Plays*, 1970.

Summer and Smoke, music by Lee Hoiby, adaptation of the play by Tennessee Williams (produced St. Paul, 1971, New York, 1972).   New York, Belwin Mills, 1972.

Ikke, Ikke, Nye, Nye, Nye (produced New Haven, Connecticut, 1971; New York, 1972).   Included in *The Great Nebula in Orion and Three Other Plays*, 1973.

The Family Continues (produced New York, 1972). Included in *The Great Nebula in Orion and Three Other Plays*, 1973.

The Great Nebula in Orion and Three Other Plays (includes *Ikke, Ikke, Nye, Nye, Nye, The Family Continues, Victory on Mrs. Dandywine's Island*).   New York, Dramatists Play Service, 1973.

The Hot l Baltimore (produced New York, 1973; London, 1976).   New York, Hill and Wang, 1973.

The Mound Builders (produced New York, 1975).   New York, Hill and Wang, 1976.

Screenplay: *One Arm*, 1970.

Television Play: *The Migrants*, 1974.

Theatrical Activities:

Director: **Plays** – many of his own plays, including *Home Free!*, New York, 1964; *The Madness of Lady Bright*, New York, 1964; *The Rimers of Eldritch*, New York, 1965; *This Is the Rill Speaking*, New York, 1965; *Indecent Exposure* by Robert Patrick, New York, 1968; *Not to Worry* by A. E. Santaniello, New York, 1975.

Actor: **Plays** – in *The Clown*, New York, 1968; *Wandering*, New York, 1968; *Him* by E. E. Cummings, New York, 1974.

*   *   *

Lanford Wilson's plays are peopled, they are populated with the idea of people, whole crops, schools, covies, bands. They announce, ruminate, declare, soliloquize, confess, blaspheme. The words scurry about, often backtrack, often appear in exultant banners. The people are busy as puppies, making words or witnessing with eternal patience the making Baltimore, in *The Madness of words by others*.

There is such a proliferative sense of peopleness and such a cluster and constant humming of words that events hardly seem possible, such absorption in verbal byplay, in declaration or rumination that there is hardly space for events. And the outside world is seldom looked to: "*...our father was killed in the war,*" says Kenny in The Sand Castle, "but you don't have to worry about that because it doesn't have anything to do with the play." What has to do with the play is primarily *play* itself, spirit in partial disembodiment, the play as playfulness. The outside world, when it exists at all, exists as some kind of exotic, inexplicable creature, treated with the kind of incredulity reserved for Martians.

There is also a sense of innocence about life. If events seem both doubtful and exotic, evil events and evil forces seem non-existent. There are no evil forces in *The Sand Castle*, in *Lemon Sky*, in *Hot l Baltimore*, in *The Madness of Lady Bright*. White Vincent and black Gloria in *The Gingham Dog* break up because of inherited social values that can't be reconciled, they don't want to harm one another, they don't want to get the best of one another. (It's the only Wilson play I'm aware of in which the society of the present day *is* prevalent and affects the characters.) There are not only no agents of foreign powers or insensitive domestic interests in the plays, there is little grappling (with *Lady Bright* a notable exception) with one's own devils, with the subconscious powers of darkness. It there is not always sunlight, there is always at least a wan light. No sharp teeth, no malevolent beasts hiding in the bush, but a long, virtuous, vegetable afternoon.

The absence of evil goes hand in hand with an absence of eroticism, again discounting the homosexual agitation of *Lady Bright*. In *The Sand Castle* Reen and her lover seem more like buddies than lovers, good companions for a camping trip. The young men in *Lemon Sky* and *The Sand Castle* give off no sense of erotic longing. Owen, in the latter play, idealizes the young wife of a friend; she is pregnant and her state is seen as holy. No hint that the adorer can accept the obvious physical circumstances that created the pregnancy.

In *The Hot l Baltimore*, the presence of hookers simply indicates the presence of a certain business enterprise; the air is charged with as much sensuality as that of a brokerage house.

The adolescent world bears the central, psychic thrust and the most striking offstage props are the old copies of Batman comics which crowd Owen's bedroom. Through Batman, one partakes of the energy of the miraculous hero, one enters his body. Batman copes with all contingencies but Owen, coming into legal maturity, forced to leave the early miracles in the closet, seems adrift and uncomprehending in the glare of the everyday world.

Wilson's relationship to his characters is one of tender observer, painfully aware that all is not working out, that the world *is* out there if seemingly remote. If outer events are barely possible, there is still the growing vulnerability of the soul and the critical eye which will not let things alone. Vincent and Gloria have a line on one another and the relationship withers under mutually scorching criticism. The hero's father in *Lemon Sky* senses, without understanding, the latent homosexuality in his son, he indicts what seems to him male inadequacy without truly seeing his son, and this relationship also withers. Lady Bright, the screaming queen, is seen only by Wilson and us, prancing and preening in growing hysteria about his apartment, unable to come to terms with his own homosexuality. Rootlessness is a strong motif in *The Hot l Baltimore*. The hotel itself houses transients. The brother and sister who buy farmland soon learn that nothing will grow there, that the earth cannot support them.

Since any behavior in the outside world seems difficult, since the actions of the characters are circumscribed, most of their time – certainly most of their *stage* time – is spent in chatter or ruminations about the nature of things. And often Wilson has them performing, breaking into conscious theatrical structures. Both *Lemon Sky* and *The Sand Castle* employ characters as narrators. The young hero in *Lemon Sky* offers the audience biographical and spiritual information. Kenny, the 12-year-old in *The Sand Castle*, offers the audience information they would soon glean anyway. "I get to begin the play now, and I get to close it later on with little narrations – little scenes, little speeches. And I sing in one of the songs too, later. I'm Kenny, the younger son...." Characters will burst into play attitudes, imitating archetypal theatrical figures, or burst into song. It is a way of getting on in the world, of getting through the day, of being in the theatre. Wilson obviously loves the theatre, loves the play, and over and over again he veers from the concerns of his people to the attitudes of theatrical frolic.

In *The Gingham Dog*, a later play, the world is a little darker. Small talk becomes recognized for what it is. The spaces between talk can no longer so easily be reconciled, the relationship between Vincent and Gloria cannot be cemented with chatter or a chorus from a drinking song. Some better understanding of how to live in the world is needed. And it isn't there for these two. The play ends with Gloria alone, the marriage definitely at an end. And as Gloria sits by the window waiting for morning, there is nothing in the room but uncreative silence.

—Arthur Sainer

WILSON, Robert M. Pseudonym: Byrd Hoffman.   American.   Born in Waco, Texas, 4
October 1944. Educated at Pratt Institute, New York, B.F.A.; studied painting with George
McNeil, Paris, 1962; apprenticed to Paolo Soleri, Phoenix, Arizona, 1966. Artistic Director,
Byrd Hoffman Foundation, 1970–75. Conducted workshops at the University of Iowa, Iowa
City, Fall 1970, and at Royaumont, France, Spring 1972. Artist: one-man-shows – Willard
Gallery, New York, 1971, and Musée Galliera, Paris, 1972, 1974. Designed outdoor
environment-theatre, Loveland, Ohio, 1967. Recipient: Guggenheim Fellowship, 1971; Obie
Award, for directing, 1974. Address: 147 Spring Street, New York, New York 10012, U.S.A.

PUBLICATIONS

Plays

>   *Dance Event* (also director: produced New York, 1965).
>   *Solo Performance* (also director: produced New York, 1966).
>   *Theatre Activity* (also director: produced New York, 1967).
>   *The King of Spain* (also director: produced New York, 1969).   Published in *New
>   American Plays 3*, edited by William M. Hoffman, New York, Hill and Wang, 1970.
>   *The Life and Times of Sigmund Freud* (also director: prc ʝuced New York, 1969).
>   *Deafman Glance* (also director: produced Iowa City, 1970; New York, 1971).
>   *Program Prologue Now, Overture for a Deafman* (also director: produced Paris, 1971).
>   *Overture* (also director: produced New York, 1972).
>   *Ka Mountain and Gardenia Terrace: A Story about a Family and Some People Changing*
>   (also director: produced Shiraz, Iran, 1972).
>   *King Lyre and Lady in the Wasteland* (also director: produced New York, 1973).
>   *The Life and Times of Joseph Stalin* (also director: produced Copenhagen and New
>   York, 1973).
>   *A Mad Man a Mad Giant a Mad Dog a Mad Urge a Mad Face* (also director: produced
>   Rome and Washington, D.C., 1974).
>   *The Life and Times of Dave Clark* (also director: produced Sao Paulo, 1974).
>   *"Prologue" to A Letter for Queen Victoria* (also director: produced Spoleto, Italy, 1974).
>   *A Letter for Queen Victoria* (also director: produced Spoleto, Italy, and tour, 1974; New
>   York, 1975).   Paris, privately printed, 1974.
>   *The $ Value of Man* (also director: produced New York, 1975).

Critical Study: "L'Art de Robert Wilson (Le Regard du sourd)" by Stephan Brecht, in *Le
Theatre 1972: 1*, edited by Arrabal, Paris, Christian Bourgeois, 1972.

Theatrical Activities:

>   Director: **Plays** – all his own plays. **Films** – *The House*, 1963; *Slant*, 1963; *Overture for a
>   Deafman*, 1971.

>   Set Designer: **Play** – *America Hurrah* by Jean-Claude van Itallie, New York, 1963.

                              *   *   *

Robert Wilson's marathon spectacles defy classification. Reminiscent of the experimental
Happenings of the 1960's, they seem to have scripts written by Sterne, casts assembled by
Fellini, and productions devised by The Living Theatre. Employing elements of drama,

ballet, opera, and primitive ritual, these elaborate constructs seem designed to probe the premises of the theater as they test the preconceptions, psyches, or endurance-levels of the audience. Through images both universal and personal, he and his company project surrealistic visions which simultaneously state and deny reality. They force re-examination of ordinary concepts of time and motion by pushing these fundamental aspects of reality to extremes, mainly by non-verbal, non-rational means. Wilson charts the topography of the subconscious, abandoning conventional plotting for the logic of the dream world. Slow motion and repetition evoke a non-temporal realm in which symbolic figures play out the compulsive fantasies of the neurotic (that is, modern) mind. And as the several hours of performance pass – not without large stretches of ennui – both the actors and the spectators who remain seem engaged as much in a therapeutic as in a theatrical experience.

Like Fellini, Wilson is drawn to the extraordinary and the grotesque. To fill his imaginative landscapes, he requires huge casts composed principally of non-professionals – friends, interesting people encountered on the street, his octagenarian grandmother – and a core of familiar performers, called the Byrd Hoffman School of Byrds, some of whom create their own material. Truly corporate enterprises, Wilson's works place almost maniacal emphasis upon "body language." Contrary to conventional dramatic practice, which truncates time and pares action to essentials, Wilson deliberately elongates these elements to focus upon minute, commonplace, apparently irrelevant but ultimately individualizing details which habit causes to be overlooked. As "real-life" people (some of them handicapped and most of them unusual in other ways) join with dancers and actors to impersonate historical figures and animals, distinctions between appearance and reality begin to blur. Almost imperceptibly, props descend upon and characters inch across the stage, forming strange *tableaux vivants*. These trance-like states alternate with periods of free-form dancing or eternities of whirling. Wilson's theatricals are processes, where improvization and chance occurrences operate within formal arrangements; and the gradual unfolding of each unique presentation demands exorbitant sums of time. (*A Letter for Queen Victoria* ran for three and one-half hours, *The Life and Times of Joseph Stalin* for twelve; it took seven days and nights to create *Ka Mountain and Gardenia Terrace*.) But this luxurious inflation of time, not to mention tedium, may drive the viewer to study personal thoughts, if it does not send him to sleep and private dreams.

Because his short-lived productions are not primarily literary but psychological experiences expressed through impressionistic techniques, Wilson's works encourage multiple, highly individual interpretations. Some idea of his concepts and methods of execution can be gained, however, from a short view of *The Life and Times of Joseph Stalin*, which incorporates and is a culmination of elements from previous pieces. Through the several sections of its seven acts, *Stalin* (its title, as in the others, bears scant relation to the content) presents a great variety of movement. Dozens of stout "mammies" in black face waltz to "The Blue Danube"; other dancers spin and perform ritualistic steps. A chair takes three hours to descend from on high; a giant turtle crawls at its accustomed rate across the stage. Characters run, leap, hop backwards, play in slow motion. Freud, Ivan the Terrible, the Pope, Washington, Marie Antoinette, and other historical agents of good or ill enter and depart. Queen Victoria mourns, shrieks, releases (perhaps) a primal scream. Other figures appear to deliver unintelligible monologues; the disjointed phrases rise in crescendo, clash, stop.

Various segments of the action continue at great length or are repeated. Stretches of silence induce an atmosphere of reverie, only to be suddenly broken by violent outbursts of cacaphony. Figures from myths or fables or nightmares summon up haunting images from the universal and personal subconscious. The mother murders her children. Animal-people, the lion, the fox, the ape, the bear, lie down together. One by one bars descend, turning the (Platonic) cave into a prison. Innocence decays with experience; primitive freedom gradually ends in the deadening rigidity of civilization. And as the hours pass and exhaustion sets in, the scenes become almost hallucinatory, more disturbing, then oddly tranquil, perhaps bringing about a catharsis.

Through a kind of controlled madness, Wilson pushes the possibilities of the theater nearer to their realization. Whatever the significance of their content and form, his works provoke a reassessment of the nature and limits of the stage, and of its powers to communicate and perhaps enlighten.

—Joseph Parisi

WILSON, Snoo (Andrew Wilson). British. Born in Reading, Berkshire, 2 August 1948. Educated at Bradfield College, Berkshire, 1962–66; the University of East Anglia, Norwich, 1966–69, B.A. (upper second) in English and American studies, 1969. Since 1969, Associate Director, Portable Theatre, London; since 1975, Director, Scarab Theatre. Agent: Clive Goodwin Associates, 79 Cromwell Road, London S.W.7, England.

PUBLICATIONS

Plays

Girl Mad As Pigs (produced Norwich, 1967).
Ella Daybellfesse's Machine (produced Norwich, 1967).
Between the Acts (produced Canterbury, 1969).
Charles the Martyr (produced Southampton, 1970).
Device of Angels (produced Edinburgh and London, 1970).
Pericles, The Mean Knight (also director: produced London, 1970).
Pignight (also director: produced Leeds and London, 1971). Included in *Pignight and Blow Job*, 1975.
Blow Job (produced Edinburgh and London, 1971). Included in *Pignight and Blow Job*, 1975.
Lay By, with others (also director: produced Edinburgh and London, 1971). London, Calder and Boyars, 1972.
Reason the Sun King (produced Edinburgh, 1972); as *Reason: Boswell and Johnson on the Shores of the Eternal Sea*, in *Point 101* (produced London, 1972).
England's Ireland, with others (also director: produced Amsterdam and London, 1972).
Vampire (produced London, 1973). Published in *Plays and Players* (London), July 1973.
The Pleasure Principle: The Politics of Love, The Capital of Emotion (produced London, 1973). London, Eyre Methuen, 1974.
The Beast (produced London, 1974). Published in *Plays and Players* (London), December 1974-January 1975.
The Everest Hotel (produced London, 1975). Published in *Plays and Players* (London), March 1976.
Pignight and Blow Job. London, John Calder, 1975.
Soul of the White Ant (produced London, 1975).

Screenplays: *Sunday for Seven Days*, 1971; *Pignight*, with Dusty Hughes, 1975.

Television Plays: *The Good Life*, 1971, *Swamp Music*, 1972; *More about the Universe*, 1972; *The Barium Meal*, 1974; *The Trip to Jerusalem*, 1975; *A Greenish Man*, 1975; *Don't Make Waves*, 1975.

Manuscript Collection: Mme. Duvé, 7 rue des Bêtises, Vichy sur Loire, France.

Critical Study: "Pig in a Poke" by Leslie Bamber, in *Honey* (London), February 1971.

Theatrical Activities:

Director: **Plays** – *Pericles, The Mean Knight*, London, 1970; *Pignight*, Leeds and London, 1971; *Lay By*, Edinburgh and London, 1971; *England's Ireland*, Amsterdam and London, 1972; *Bodywork* by Jennifer Phillips, London, 1974.

Actor: **Play** – *Lay By*, London, 1971.

Snoo Wilson comments:

More than anything else the proscenium arch theatre suggests the success of drawing room conversation as a mirror for a mature civilisation. In these mirrors, the even keel of the state slices through the waters of unconsciousness, and very few playwrights have managed to knock any holes in the boat, though a number have suggested that the ship was sinking without their assistance, and others, like the stewards on the *Titanic*, bicycle gaily round the first-class gym, declaring that there is no list to the ship. These last are the ones most likely to be rewarded by the first-class passengers for their élan vital, even while the bilge water is rising round the ankles of the steerage families. The bicycling stewards are most likely to be able to command support that is quite independent of anything except people's gratitude at being amused, and many of them die peacefully in their beds declaring that there was always a slight list to port anyhow, and their reward was plainly a just one since people came and gave willingly, and were briefly happy.

A different brand of steward feels considerable unease at the condition of the ship, and his actions are likely to be much less popular at first than the bicyclists, though as time passes and his costume becomes charmingly archaic his pieces will be revived as Art, safe now from the Life he tried to redirect, which will have moved on in a lateral, unexpected direction. Television in this country created a brand of "responsible" playwrights whose reputations at first were large and abrasive but now have stabilised in characteristic and therefore unsurprising because recognisable positions of social dynamism, and there the matter rests, a compromise acceptable both to producers who would like to produce more radical plays but have taken "Grandmother's footsteps" as far as they think the head of drama will let them, and an audience stunned by tedium and kept alive by a feeling they ought to watch plays, sustained by tiny whiffs of excellence that occur in the smog of apathy. Both television and the theatre with one or two exceptions had failed to either make any formal advances in technique or investigate areas of emotion which would force advances on them: I say "failed" because I believe that there must always be a technical evolution in theatre if only to remind audiences that they are watching a particular genre: playwrights who are adept at naturalism can take the edge off the most workmanlike oeuvre by making its naturalism subliminal.

The small groups who started with very little assistance at first – sometimes none – from the Arts Council in the late 1960's had a different sort of audience, a different sort of motive, and were a growth outside the conventional structure of theatre in this country largely because it was dull and extremely conservative and did not provide outlets for the sort of things they wanted to do, or in the case of Portable Theatre, a writer's theatre first, to write. Since there was very little money anyway the opportunity to write what the writer wanted to write and put it on in the way he wanted it was possible, and a series of one night stands provided continuous platforms for plays which in the beginning we were prepared to take anywhere.

Now, there are a large number of studio theatres, almost a circuit, round the country. The success of *Lay By*, a group play written round a newspaper story, at the Edinburgh Festival, suggested that it was desirable and possible to launch a play about contemporary events to tour large theatres round England and Scotland. After six months of extreme difficulty we managed to set up a tour of a play about Northern Ireland, called *England's Ireland*, which had its first three weeks in Holland because we were unable to find theatres in England in sufficiently large numbers prepared to take the risk of an unknown play by a previously, quote, experimental group.

When we did bring the play to England, sadly it was in Chalk Farm at the Roundhouse rather than in Glasgow where it drew a significant response, and Lancaster and Nottingham were the only large repertory companies which would have it.

This demonstrates, among other things, the self stultifying conservatism of the control of British theatre boards who believe that their audiences should be fed what they are accustomed to consume, either the costume drama of Ibsen's Choice, or on plays which by ignoring all but the most trivial of human difficulties and miseries close minds rather than open them in a stuffy two hours at the theatre.

The title I would choose for this essay, *The Freudian Landscape and the Proscenium Mind*, suggests that the middle class mind is firmly ensconced on stage; this is true only by its being a self perpetuating situation: it is not true that if we want to widen the range of theatrical experience we have to abandon the theatre. The theatre has always been a whore to safe fashion, but at the moment there is a pressure for a particular sort of awareness and articulacy which hopefully may lead to the good lady opening her legs to a different position, and a renewed and enlarged clientele being the result. The plangent cries of either the affronted audience or management should not be an invitation to a secondary dialogue, whose end is respectability. Nor should this secondary dialogue be mistaken for a play, for the theatre is not that self-sufficient, being old, and bloated with the worst vices of time serving and sycophancy: and these will show through shallow devices. It is ourselves, finally, rather than the civilisation, who we have to prove mature; so, paradoxically, the struggle for exposure which shapes the ideas must not dent them, any more than an achieved articulacy within theatrical convention supplants the need for further thought.

*   *   *

Snoo Wilson's *Pignight* is a brilliant and disturbing little play. Set on a Lincolnshire farm, it revolves around a psychopathic German farm labourer, Smitty, inherited by the new owner, Mr. Bravington, who has bought the farm from a couple who have left for Australia. Smitty has killed the farm dog, Robby, and entered into an almost affectionate relationship with its corpse, and takes delight in butchering pigs. There are also Ray Gibbs, manager of the farm for Bravington, brutal and callous in a more conventional way, and his whore girlfriend, Jasmine.

Violence and brutality form the play's central image, the exigencies of society forming different psychological perversions in each of the characters. The play is almost Swiftian in its emphasis on the physical, sexual and pathological details of violence, as is evidenced by the symbolic scenes between the pigs, where they threaten to take over from the humans.

Blow Job is an even more violent exercise in the alienations and hang-ups caused by modern society. Two young skinhead crooks plan to blow a safe in a factory. The opening of the play juxtaposes them in a working men's club with a queer security guard trying to pick them up, unsuccessfully, and follows them through on different sides of the law. Both the crooks and the security guard suffer from psychological kinks caused by the roles they are forced to play in society, one of the crooks, in a memorable image, dressing up in women's clothes to carry out the crime. Another character, symbolically sitting on the fence between the two sides, is a girl university student, totally at odds with her situation, as she is alienated by what she is supposed to be studying and the whole university scene.

Like *Pignight*, the play is about how the basic perversion of society's organization causes different kinds of tensions in characters of varying outlooks and degrees of intelligence. The play's resolution, where the two crooks blow the safe and themselves to bits, seriously wounding the security officer in the process, is a symbolic one; by extension, it shows society beginning to blow itself apart. The play is also remarkable, like *Pignight*, for the emphasis it gives to the physical, sensual details of decay and violence.

Vampire is a quite extraordinary piece of work. Conventionally structured in three acts, it is a surrealistic exploration of the baneful effects of Victorian morality on our inner, sexual and imaginative selves. The first act revolves around three daughters of a Welsh Presbyterian parson. After one of them weds Reuben, he confesses that he slept with her sister Joy. As a penance, he shoots himself, blinding himself in the process. Many years pass; he joins a clairvoyant parlour with Joy. The repressive parson visits the parlour, not knowing that Joy and Reuben are there, and makes love to Joy, believing that she is his long-lost wife. The second act shows Sarah, an upper-class young lady, being wooed by Henry, a handsome young cricketer. He is killed in the First World War and returns in his astral body to try and make love to Sarah. She is frightened of being seen. Freud and Jung then come on the scene on stilts and discuss her hang-ups in their own particular psychoanalytic jargon, while a talking ox grunts "Let's go to my place and fuck." The third act whisks us to the early 1970's where we see three bored young bisexual transvestites in a secular funeral parlour, each trying to grab psychic juices from the others. The play ends with Enoch Powell arising out of a coffin and spouting his notorious "Rivers of Blood" speech.

The Pleasure Principle has a similar structure to *Vampire* and is also about the effects of external codes of morality on our internal freedoms. The play focuses on an almost unspoken relationship between two characters, Robert and Gale, whose opposing ideas of pleasure prevent them from actually making love until the final act. Robert is an aggressive businessman who believes that rampant capitalism is the only thing that can rescue Ireland from the effects of religious fanaticism. After having a mental breakdown, he enters an asylum and then withdraws into a circus tent. Gale acquires a husband, with whom she makes rather apathetic love while burglars strip her flat bare. The final act takes place in the circus tent, where Robert seduces Gale in a cardboard swan. A dance rounds off the play.

The Beast is an examination of the life of satanist Aleister Crowley, the "wickedest man in the world," and the effects of what he represents on the alternative culture that has grown up since the mid-sixties. We see him first of all in a seedy hotel in mid-1920's Belgium, outwitting a pompous policeman trying to arrest him for passport irregularities. A flashback shows his Plymouth Brethren parents and implies the effect their repressions must have had on the young Aleister. The action cuts to the "community" he created on the island of Cefalu to pursue the ideal of self-knowledge. As Wilson himself says in an interview, the "community" is just like the Manson Family, though not quite as nasty. *The Beast* never quite fulfils the promise of its central concept as a play, possibly because the high degree of spuriousness in Crowley's make-up comes across, despite the author's skilful attempts to conceal it.

Wilson's talent as a playwright is to explore in surrealistic ways the juxtaposition between the kind of behaviour demanded by civilised society and the subterranean ideas, images and impulses, frequently destructive, that constantly threaten to undermine that society. As Peter Ansorge says in his valuable study *Disrupting the Spectacle*, normal conversation in Wilson's plays "is forever being broken up by more bizarre kinds of communication." This quality makes his plays both strikingly original and threatrically compelling.

—Jonathan Hammond

WOOD, Charles. British. Born in Guernsey, Channel Islands, 6 August 1933. Educated at Chesterfield Grammar School, 1942–45; King Charles I School, Kidderminster, 1945–48;

Birmingham College of Art, 1948–50. Served in the 17/21st Lancers, 1950–55: Trooper. Married Valerie Elizabeth Newman in 1954; has two children. Designer and Scenic Artist; Stage Manager. Recipient: *Evening Standard* award, 1963, 1973; Screenwriters Guild award, 1965. Agent: Fraser and Dunlop Scripts Ltd., 91 Regent Street, London W1R 8RU. Address: The Manor House, Milton, Banbury, Oxfordshire, England.

PUBLICATIONS

Plays

    Cockade (includes *Prisoner and Escort, John Thomas, Spare*) (produced London, 1963). Published in *New English Dramatists 8*, London, Penguin, 1965; published separately, New York, Grove Press, 1967.

    Tie Up the Ballcock (produced Bristol, 1964). Published in *Second Playbill 3*, edited by Alan Durband, London, Hutchinson, 1973.

    Don't Make Me Laugh (produced London, 1965).

    Meals on Wheels (produced London, 1965; shortened version, produced Liverpool, 1971).

    Fill the Stage with Happy Hours (produced Nottingham, 1966; London, 1967). Published in *New English Dramatists 11*, London, Penguin, 1967.

    Dingo (produced Bristol and London, 1967). London, Penguin, and New York, Grove Press, 1969.

    Labour (produced Bristol, 1968).

    H: Being Monologues at Front of Burning Cities (produced London, 1969). London, Methuen, 1970.

    Colliers Wood (produced Liverpool, 1970; London, 1971).

    Welfare (includes *Tie Up the Ballcock, Meals on Wheels, Labour*) (produced Liverpool, 1971).

    Veterans; or, Hairs in the Gates of the Hellespont (produced Edinburgh and London, 1972). London, Eyre Methuen, 1972.

    The Can Opener, adaptation of a play by Victor Lanoux (produced London, 1974).

    Jingo (produced London, 1975).

    The Script (produced London, 1976).

Screenplays: *The Knack*, 1965; *Help!*, 1965; *Tie Up the Ballcock*, 1965; *The Long Day's Dying*, 1967; *How I Won the War*, 1967; *The Charge of the Light Brigade*, 1968; *The Long Day's Dying*, 1968; *The Bed-Sitting Room*, with John Antrobus, 1969; *Fellini Satyricon* (English dialogue), 1969.

Radio Plays: *Prisoner and Escort*, 1962; *Cowheel Jelly*, 1962; *Next to Being a Knight*, 1972.

Television Plays: *Traitor in a Steel Helmet*, 1961; *Not at All*, 1962; *The Drill Pig*, 1964; *Drums along the Avon*, 1967; *A Bit of a Holiday*, 1969; *The Emergence of Anthony Purdy, Esq.*, 1970; *A Bit of Family Feeling*, 1971; *A Bit of Vision*, 1972; *Death or Glory Boy*, 1974; *Mützen ab*, 1974; *A Bit of an Adventure*, 1974; *Love Lies Bleeding*, 1976; *No*, 1976.

Critical Studies: *The Second Wave* by John Russell Taylor, London, Methuen, 1972; *Revolution in Modern English Drama* by Katherine J. Worth, London, Bell, 1973; *The Modern Actor* by Michael Billington, London, Hamish Hamilton, 1973.

*   *   *

All art is presumably the transmutation of personal experience; but, in the case of Charles Wood, the two are unusually closely linked. He served in the army: two of his major plays, and two of his shorter ones, concern it. He worked in the theatre: *Fill the Stage with Happy Hours* takes place in and around the bar and offices of a small-town rep. He has written scripts for, and worked on the sets of, several films: *Veterans*, his most recent play, is reportedly based on the shooting of *The Charge of the Light Brigade*, and its main character bears an uncanny likeness to Sir John Gielgud, who in fact starred in both film and play. Such a method of functioning has its advantages, notably a more thorough comprehension of the subject in question, and its obvious dangers, notably the lack of perspective that often results from an author being emotionally too close to his material. But Wood is very far from being an unreflective, impetuous writer, and, as it turns out, succumbs to no such danger. In all, or nearly all, his plays, we can safely say that he has transmuted autobiography into art, "art" being tentatively defined in this context as work of some general validity, speaking effectively to the minds, hearts and spirits of more than the odd, isolated individual.

Wood first came to notice with *Cockade*, and, particularly, with *Prisoner and Escort*, the principal of the three short plays that constituted it. The other two, *John Thomas* and *Spare*, were intellectually fuzzier, linguistically less striking and generally less memorable: this was clearly the voice of a young writer with an individual command of language and a strong sense of theatre. Briefly, it concerns two crude and disagreeable soldiers escorting a third, Jupp, in a train back to the prison from which he has apparently absconded, having apparently disgraced himself and his unit by publicly urinating on the boots of a visiting German general. They handcuff him to the luggage rack: he bears the discomfort stoically, but is clearly not altogether the righteous and sympathetic figure we might believe him, as is suggested not only by what is rightly diagnosed as his "high and mighty" manner, but by the instinctive disgust with which he hears that a girl fellow-traveller is in fact sexually attached to a black. There is a moral ambivalence about Jupp and his situation characteristic of Wood, and several other idiosyncracies which make the piece helpful as an introduction to his later work. There is the strong, fascinated grasp of a particular milieu, in this case, military, with its distinctive manners and slang, and, in the fascination, some evidence of nostalgia and affection, notwithstanding its ugliness. There is the transformation of informal English, including (and perhaps especially) the slang, into a distinctive dramatic poetry, imaginative, metaphoric, rhythmic and yet persuasively "real," even naturalistic. And there is a hint of what may be seen as the overriding theme of his work to date, that of the gulf between pretension and fact. By humiliating a German general in so decided a fashion, Jupp (and his author) is not only drawing attention to the supposed hypocrisy of feting a recent enemy: he is, he says, "shooting it up the kilt of every stupid bastard as braces up to the beat of a drum...every twat as thinks it's more than just a great carve-up." He is, if you like, protesting against the ceremony and sentiment that make some forget that an army is essentially designed to kill people.

Such ideas are most evident, however, in *Dingo*, which was described by a major critic as "one of those milestones at which a younger generation overthrows the taste and beliefs of an older one." It is a bitter play, poised, calculated and yet fiercer than anything written in the period of the "angry young men," ten years earlier; an attack on all who would tend to glamourize, not just war, but a particular war that most of us still think justified, World War II. Satiric scenes are juxtaposed with painfully real ones. On the one hand, we catch a British officer in the act of doltishly hero-worshipping Rommel, as many actually did, a parody of General Montgomery describing the war as a tennis match, and prisoners, dressed as chorus girls for a camp concert, tunnelling out of German territory in a burlesque of British escape films. On the other, we see soldiers kicked to death by their fellow-soldiers, bayonetted by guards, and screaming as they burn in tanks. "That's enemy," says the cynical protagonist, Dingo, as a crazed private cuddles the charred corpse of his friend, "You won't find a photograph, a statue, a painting of a British soldier like that"; and he and his mate take bets on the time of the death of an officer they direct into a minefield, and then they masturbate. Once again, the gulf between what has been called "the aftermyth of war" and the truth about it is shown to be total; and so captivated by this aperçu is Wood that he neglects to answer satisfactorily what seems a vital question, whether it was right to fight Hitler at all Churchill, says Dingo, "pissed" on us; the war was fought "for all the usual reasons"; and that is that.

The piece does, however, have the power of its overstatement, and proved more theatrically gripping than the thematically somewhat similar *H* did, though this may have been partly due to the latter's awkward first production at the National Theatre. *H* is ambitious and prolix, taking us, as it does, from the beginning of the Indian mutiny to the evacuation of Lucknow: it is beautifully written, in dialogue that capitalizes on the concreteness, the slight primness and the marginally incorrect grammar the author finds in idiomatic Victorian speech: it is also considerably subtler than *Dingo*. General Havelock, the "H" of the title, is warmer, more humane and considerate, than General Neill, the ferocious "scourge of the Lord," who would slaughter every Sepoy if he could. Nevertheless, he allows his troops to revel and loot, he shoots rebels from guns, and he is, as Wood sees it, fighting a palpably unjust colonial war: all of which is hard to reconcile with his high principles, religious convictions, and tendency to use most human encounters for a proselytizing homily. His way of life is designed to disprove "the vile falsehood that it is never possible to be a soldier and a Christian at the once"; the sad irony is that it tends to prove exactly that. The truest (because most open and unpretentious) representative of British military might is probably not New Testament Havelock, nor even Old Testament Neill, but the character Wood has said the play is "about": a genial, rather stupid, totally unselfquestioning Welsh captain who idealises the war as much as any, but is mainly interested in securing himself a higher rank and more pay. The "holy" crusade against the mutineers was really about the advancement of the British nation and of individual members of the British army. Anything else is mere camouflage and self-deception.

Self-deception is also the theme of one of Wood's most successful pieces, *Fill the Stage with Happy Hours*. Its characters are the members and hangers-on of a run-down theatre, desperate for its next Arts Council grant; and most of them speak a theatrical language all their own, full of the obvious "loves" and "darlings," but put together by Wood with his usual style and imagination. These people no longer know what, if anything, they feel, and they have constructed a rhetoric which rarely does more than approximate to emotions either true or untrue. "You bitch; you're talking about our son; have a heart, love," says the manager's wife to the actress who is supposed to have seduced her son, and it is as if she were experimenting with three different methods of expressing the same, vague anger. First, there is melodrama, "bitch"; then something straighter and more factual; then a sentimental appeal; and all in the same sentence. Some people in the play are taken in by these verbal mishits, and a few correctly diagnose them as "slab emotions – you can only laugh at them." The trouble, of course, is that not all "slab emotions" deserve laughter. Every now and then the manager's wife mentions she has had cancer confirmed, and may only have a short time to live, and by the end, it is clear that this may indeed be the case. But who can take it seriously? Even she seems to find it difficult to do so, having lived too far from reality for too long a time. The moral, which would seem to be that pretension rots the mind and heart, is put sadly and sympathetically by Wood, who is (as before) half in love with the verbose, chaotic, pathetic milieu he is so carefully recording.

Of his other plays, two deserve mention: *Meals on Wheels*, unusual in that it is not about the army or show business, but about old age, and *Veterans*, which touches on all three of these subjects. The first, which is repetitive, ill-organised and generally agreed to be the least successful of the longer plays, does, however, have a certain vigour and ebullience in its satiric attempts to dispose (characteristically) of some of the myths that attach to the aged and supposedly venerable. Its characters spend their waning years shut away and full of vague resentments, pretending to one another they look more spry and youthful than they do and, mainly, expressing impotent lust in a salacious rhetoric which, as always, Wood handles with invention and wit. Indeed, it is possible that the piece is most memorable for the extraordinary variety of idiom with which the sexual act is invoked.

Veterans is slighter, but better: an entertaining account of life on location, and marked by a genuine affection for the main character, Sir Geoffrey Kendle, a kindly, gentle man, given to upsetting those around him with a devastating, but entirely unintended, tactlessness. Possibly the play is best seen as an act of homage to him, or rather to Sir John Gielgud, with whom he appears to have more than coincidental affinities. Most of the other characters are vulgar, selfish and tedious by comparison, and the actual process of filming what seems to be a screenplay of Wood's own *H* is shown to be indescribably enervating, very far from the image of such events put about by the fan magazines. The horses are made of wood, and the young male heroes are neurotically concerned with their own uncertain virility. Yet, finally, the play does not achieve that general validity most of Wood's others do. The milieu, far from proving a satisfactory metaphor for human illusion and disillusion, as in *H* and *Fill the Stage with Happy Hours*, remains simply a well-depicted milieu: the insistence on its detail seems tantamount to a sustained in-joke about the British film industry: the total effect is nearer memoir than "art" in the sense postulated earlier. It goes without saying that a writer who has proved himself at once so intellectually questioning, verbally gifted and dramatically assured is capable of much more than this.

—Benedict Nightingale

WYMARK, Olwen (Margaret).   American.   Widow of the actor Patrick Wymark. Recipient: Zagreb Drama Festival Prize, 1967. Agent: Felix De Wolfe and Associates, 1 Robert Street, Adelphi, London WC2N 6BH, England.

PUBLICATIONS

Plays

Lunchtime Concert (produced Glasgow, 1966).   Published in *The Best Short Plays 1975*, edited by Stanley Richards, Radnor, Pennsylvania, Chilton, 1975.

Triple Image (includes *Coda, Lunchtime Concert, The Inhabitants*) (produced Glasgow, 1967).   Published as *Three Plays*, London, Calder and Boyars, 1967.

The Gymnasium (produced Edinburgh, 1967; London, 1971).   Included in *The Gymnasium and Other Plays*, 1972.

The Technicians (produced Leicester, 1969; London, 1971).   Included in *The Gymnasium and Other Plays*, 1972.

Stay Where You Are (produced Edinburgh, 1969; London, 1973).   Included in *The Gymnasium and Other Plays*, 1972; in *The Best Short Plays 1972*, edited by Stanley Richards, Philadelphia, Chilton, 1972.

No Talking (produced London, 1970).

Neither Here Nor There (produced London, 1971).   Included in *The Gymnasium and Other Plays*, 1972.

Speak Now (produced Edinburgh, 1971; revised version, produced Leicester, 1975).

The Committee (produced London, 1971).

Jack the Giant Killer (produced Sheffield, 1972).   Included in *The Gymnasium and Other Plays*, 1972.

The Gymnasium and Other Plays (includes *The Technicians, Stay Where You Are, Jack the Giant Killer, Neither Here Nor There*).   London, Calder and Boyars, 1972.

Tales from Whitechapel (produced London, 1972).

Chinig Chinich (produced London, 1973).
Watch the Woman (produced London, 1973).
The Bolting Sisters (produced London, 1974).
The Inhabitants (produced London, 1974).
Starters (produced London, 1975).
The Twenty-Second Day (produced London, 1975).
Three for All (includes *Box Play, Family Business, Extended Play*) (produced London, 1976).

Television Plays: *Mrs. Moresby's Scrapbook*, 1973; *Vermin*, 1974; *Marathon*, 1975; *Mother Love*, 1975; *Dead Drunk*, 1975.

Olwen Wymark comments:

Since 1973, I have had occasion to do a good deal of writing for television as well as work on several projects involving collaborating with school children on producing their own original dramatic texts. Consequently I have been obliged to learn a great deal about structure and technique. This has, I think, helped me to move on from the territory of fantasy and games-playing of my early plays toward more accessible "external" work. With the rewriting of my first full-length play, *Speak Now*, I have become increasingly interested in the use of comedy in exploring serious themes. Although I am still concerned with short plays involving interior explorations, I find myself attracted and challenged by work on long plays in a more structured and naturalistic tradition.

*   *   *

A sense of reality comes and goes in Olwen Wymark's plays, but it bites sharply and stimulates unexpected reactions. The settings for the plays are sparse, such as a bench, a rope or a tree. Their characters are frequently called simply "Man," "Boy" and "Woman," or "He" and "She." When they have names, like William and Lenny, they still have no address, and no purpose beyond what they show in the play's action. We never see them work, or live in any way that is a recognizable image of social or family life. These characters are usually, but not always, distinguished by age, sex or physique, and they all play games or charades, tell stories and engage in inquisitions or small rituals. They fight and fondle each other, and they break away in silence or anger. They play along together, usually with some marked degree of unwillingness; they bare their fangs and deliberately perplex each other. They are like self-aware wilful children, exultant and defeated, possessive and mystifying, giggling and weeping. Then suddenly, the dramatist springs the last trick and the "play" is over.

These fantastic plays have the reality of nightmare. In these strange, subtle and complicated contrivances, we catch echoes of our own half-conscious thoughts. This is partly because the dialogue uses ordinary fashionable phrases, that make the fiction suddenly recognizable; partly because when the dialogue has run smoothly for a time it then cracks, splutters or explodes and we are left piecing together the fragments in our own attempt to comprehend, and then some pun or echo seems to betray an underlying futility, guilt or desperation.

Perhaps the most unusual quality of these bizarre, intense plays is the sense they give of their own playfulness. The author has played with her fantasies and the audience joins in the short though urgent game of cat and mouse, aware at the end that although she may cheat in order to close the play, there is an acknowledgement of that device and an earnest will still remains beyond the game to hold attention. So the cruelty implicit in *Lunchtime Concert*, is tidied away out of mind as the birdwatcher takes playful refuge in despising other people's litter. At the end of *Coda*, a "Voice" is heard, *"Discreet, female and efficient over loudspeaker"*: "Ladies and Gentlemen, the curtain is about to fall." The audience has shared a restless, unappeased awareness of mutual need and distrust; an intelligent game has been played on those elements of our inward lives that intelligence cannot command. In performance Olwen Wymark's plays can be both deeply rewarding and unsatisfying.

—John Russell Brown

YANKOWITZ, Susan. American. Born in Newark, New Jersey, 20 February 1941. Educated at Sarah Lawrence College, Bronxville, New York, B.A. 1963; Yale University Drama School, New Haven, Connecticut, M.F.A. 1968. Recipient: Joseph E. Levine Fellowship in Screenwriting, 1968; Vernon Rice Award, 1970; MacDowell Colony Fellowship, 1971, 1973; National Endowment for the Arts Fellowship, 1972; Rockefeller grant, 1973; Guggenheim Fellowship, 1974; Creative Artists Public Service Grant, 1974. Agent: Gloria Loomis, A. Watkins Inc., 77 Park Avenue, New York, New York 10016. Address: 463 West Street, No. 960, New York, New York 10014, U.S.A.

PUBLICATIONS

Plays

The Cage (produced New York, 1965).
Nightmare (produced New Haven, Connecticut, 1967; New York, 1968).
Terminal (produced New York, 1969). Published in Scripts 1 (New York), November 1971.
The Ha-Ha Play (produced New York, 1970). Published in Scripts 10 (New York), October 1972.
The Lamb (produced New York, 1970).
Slaughterhouse Play (produced New York, 1971). Published in New American Plays 4, edited by William M. Hoffman, New York, Hill and Wang, 1971.
Transplant (produced Omaha, Nebraska, 1971).
Basics in Tabula Rasa (produced New York, 1972).
Positions in Up (produced New York, 1972).
Boxes (produced New York, 1972). Published in Playwrights for Tomorrow: A Collection of Plays, Volume 11, edited by Arthur H. Ballet, Minneapolis, University of Minnesota Press, 1973.
Acts of Love (produced Atlanta, Georgia, 1973).
Monologues for Wicked Women Revue (produced New York, 1973).
Wooden Nickles (produced New York, 1973).
America Piece, with the Provisional Theatre (produced Los Angeles, 1974).

Screenplays: Danny AWOL, 1968; The Land of Milk and Funny, 1968.

Radio Plays: Rats' Alley, 1969; Kali, 1969.

Television Play: The Prison Game, 1976.

Novel

Silent Witness.   New York, Knopf, 1976.

Critical Studies: interview with Erika Munk in *Performance* (New York), December 1971, and with Arthur Sainer in *The Radical Theatre Notebook*, New York, Avon, 1975.

Susan Yankowitz comments:

Most of my work for the theatre has been an attempt to explore what is intrinsically unique in the theatrical situation. That is, I've been interested in sound, gesture and movement as a corollary to language; in the interation between the visual and verbal elements of stage life; in the fact of live performers engaged with live audience members in an exchange; and in the development of a theatrical vocabulary. My work has been generally informed by the social and political realities which impinge on all our lives; these, to a large extent, influence and shape my plays. In addition, I have been interested in a collective or collaborative approach to evolving works for the theatre and in working improvisationally with actors and directors to "find" a play which is a creative expression of our shared concerns.

At present, I am growing more concerned with the question of language – its limits and possibilities – and am moving into the realm of fiction which I feel is a more appropriate medium for that adventure.

*   *   *

Susan Yankowitz's concerns: politics and the moral life of the race. With some exceptions, where the rearguard head of naturalism crops up, the impulse is toward ritual, toward rhetorical and even choral language, toward allegory, toward fluid action dictated by the unconscious. But all grounded in a moral base.

Terminal, on which Yankowitz participated as writer with the Open Theatre, has as one of its underlying beliefs the notion that society must learn to face the reality of death and must face its life with dignity in part by facing its death with dignity. *Wooden Nickels*, one of Ms. Yankowitz's full-length plays, takes a hard and disfavorable look as Uncle Sam and the Statue of Liberty (man and wife), whose well-being has been nurtured by the blood of its young, who in their own saccharine manner have built an acquisitive and murdurous society in the name of God and liberty. *Slaughterhouse Play* also criticizes American society. Here the U.S. is seen as a greedy culture that enslaves and butchers its minorities. In *Slaughterhouse Play*, minorities are victimized. In *Wooden Nickels*, the mainstream, as represented by the youth in the armed forces, becomes its own victim. So that the picture of American culture that emerges is of an acquisitive, blood-thirsty society that victimizes the weak, bleeds the young, murders in the name of liberty and quails at the idea of its own death.

Nor is there the sense that this society contains the seeds for its own salvation. *Terminal* depicts a condition, in its most positive sense is a cry of conscience; but nothing in the play answers the cry. In *Slaughterhouse Play*, the black victims rise up at the end but they rise to revolt, not to reform. There is no awakened conscience in the air, only bullets. In *Boxes*, a recent play, the culture is stratified, there is no sense of cohesion, everyone is out for himself.

Slaughterhouse Play maintains a Brechtian stance. Its air is didactic and it is pervaded with irony. The butchers who hack away at what we come to learn is human flesh do so with a sense of ghoulish righteousness. They are, they insist, only performing a public service, giving the customers what they want, fulfilling a civic need. In fact, they are both lying and telling the truth, for while they are truly responding to a demand, they do so with gusto and are guilty of perpetuating the demand. Nor are they really trying to convince us of their position. They are indulging in a game; if they are cats, we are allied with their mice, seemingly as helpless as their victims. But condemnation is seen through a thick film of irony.

Except in certain and then very few naturalistic moments which seem out of keeping with the aesthetic design of *Slaughterhouse Play*, Yankowitz creates considerable distance between the spectator and any personal sense of the characters. The latter are not allegorical figures, as Sam and Liberty are, not really traits but rather evil possibilities in society. Sam and Liberty are frozen in their roles, but these butchers make the existential choice each day to continue being butchers. Still, the distance is marked by their representing tendencies rather than existing as beings with full moral tensions.

The recent *Boxes* recalls the ensemble sense of *Terminal*. Roles are interchangeable. The play, which is about city life, about people in interchangeable boxes (apartment dwellings), gives off the sense of humanity interchangeably buzzing away about nothing in particular, affecting nothing very much, energetically determining nothing very much. If *Terminal* is a cry in the face of a mortality no one can come to terms with, *Boxes* is a constant hum in the face of this same mortality. In both cases, humanity doesn't face it and doesn't make it.

—Arthur Sainer

ZINDEL, Paul.   American.   Born in Staten Island, New York, 15 May 1936. Educated at Wagner College, New York, B.S., M.A. Married Bonnie Hildebrand in 1973. Chemistry Teacher, Tottenville, New York, 1960–69. Recipient: Obie Award, 1970; Vernon Rice Drama Desk Award, 1970; New York Drama Critics Circle Award, 1970; Pulitzer Prize, 1971. D.H.L.: Wagner College, 1971. Agent: Gilbert Parker, Curtis Brown Ltd., 60 East 56th Street, New York, New York. Address: c/o Harper and Row, 10 East 53rd Street, New York, New York 10022, U.S.A.

PUBLICATIONS

Plays

   Dimensions of Peacocks (produced New York, 1959).
   Euthanasia and the Endless Hearts (produced New York, 1960).
   A Dream of Swallows (produced New York, 1962).
   The Effect of Gamma Rays on Man-in-the-Moon Marigolds (produced Houston, 1965;
      New York, 1970; Guildford, Surrey, 1972; London, 1973).   New York, Harper,
      1971; in *Plays and Players* (London), December 1972.
   And Miss Reardon Drinks a Little (produced Los Angeles, 1967; New York, 1971;
      London, 1976).   New York, Random House, 1972.
   The Secret Affairs of Mildred Wild (produced New York, 1972).

Screenplays: *Up the Sandbox*, 1973; *Mame*, 1974.

Novels

   The Pigman.   New York, Harper, 1968; London, Bodley Head, 1969.
   My Darling, My Hamburger.   New York, Harper, 1969; London, Bodley Head, 1970.

I Never Loved Your Mind. New York, Harper, 1970; London, Bodley Head, 1971.
Pardon Me, You're Stepping on My Eyeball! New York, Harper, and London, Bodley Head, 1976.

Other

I Love My Mother (juvenile). New York, Harper, 1975.

*   *   *

When *The Effect of Gamma Rays on Man-in-the-Moon Marigolds* opened off-Broadway to excellent critical notices in April, 1970, Paul Zindel overnight became one of America's most promising young playwrights. Prior to its New York success various mutations of *Marigolds* had been displayed at regional theatres in Houston, Texas, and Cleveland, Ohio, and on National Educational Television.

The play is a straight-forward domestic drama about a domineering misfit, Beatrice Hunsdorfer, and her two teenage daughters, Ruth, subject to epileptic fits, and Tillie, a plain, shy scientific prodigy. It is Tillie's ingenious experiment determining the effects of atomic rays on the growth of marigolds that wins first prize in the high school science fair and which gives the play its title. Beatrice holds dictatorial sway over her ramshackle household, wandering around in a shabby bathrobe with a cigarette in one hand and a glass of whiskey in the other. Her energies have been turned to angry frustration, her ambition stifled by the chore of bringing up two daughters. She is greedy, impulsive, cynical, vicious and, most of all, lost. We learn that the only man she ever loved was her father and that her husband never amounted to anything and left her penniless, her only source of income being a mere $50 a week she receives from a geriatric woman boarder.

Zindel constructs his play in a series of vignettes and conversations: Beatrice, all offhand — iron courtesy and cutting explanations, talking on the telephone to a science teacher who is looking for Tillie; the girl herself, clutching her pet rabbit, listening to the conversation in frozen apprehension; Beatrice berating her daughter for not doing the housework; Beatrice impulsive and loving, soothing her edgy Ruth, who has been frightened by a midnight thunderstorm.

In the play's last sequence we hear Tillie's timid but determined lecture on the effects of radiation. Here Zindel neatly contrasts the fate of the poor marigolds with the fate of this tortured family. We are all the product of our environment, all the product of our particular "gamma rays," but some survive and some are destroyed. She voices, tremulously, but insistently, her own stubborn confidence that "man will someday thank God for the strange and beautiful energy of the atom."

The theme of *Marigolds* is realistic and at times poetic and comes quite close in tone to Tennessee Williams' *The Glass Menagerie.* The lacerating family abuses that all but extinguish any love at all reminds one of Eugene O'Neill's tortured Tyrone family in *Long Day's Journey into Night.*

At all times Zindel's writing in this play is first-rate. His dialogue reveals an ear attuned sensitively and faithfully to the language of his people. It is very easy for an audience to listen to and for actors to read; it has been tightened to a lean and compact point. There is a vulnerable and open quality to this play that overcomes its occasional slips into melodrama and the basic slimness of the story. *Marigolds* played for over two years off-Broadway and garnered such kudos as the New York Drama Critics Circle Award as the best American play of 1970 and the 1971 Pulitzer Prize.

Zindel followed *Marigolds* with *And Miss Reardon Drinks a Little*, produced on Broadway at the Morosco Theater in February, 1971, for an engagement of 108 performances. Once again in the play Zindel shows that he has a keen ability to write very funny and witty dialogue, but despite this quite obvious talent the play is seriously flawed.

The basic problem of *Miss Reardon* is that the plot simply does not go forward as the play progresses. The action takes place in the New York apartment of the two unmarried Reardon sisters, whose mother has recently died. Both have been schoolteachers and both are now deeply troubled. Anna recently disgraced herself by having a sexual encounter with a young boy at her school and now appears teetering on the edge of insanity (echoes of Blanche DuBois from Williams' *Streetcar*). Her sister Catherine drinks a good deal more than a little, a weakness that is certainly not helped by Anna's bizarre behavior.

Into this unhappy menage enters a third sister, Ceil, who is married to an old boyfriend of Catherine. She arrives with papers that would commit Anna to a mental institution. The question whether the papers should be actually signed drags on through the play's three acts. At the end they still haven't been signed. Catherine's final lines declare that she does intend to sign them and have Anna sent away.

Despite the stilted and fabricated plot Zindel manages to tough some profound questions. You sense, for instance, that just possibly it is poor demented Anna who is sanest. She won't touch meat, eats only vegetables, shrinks from fur and leather and cherishes that bit of sex she had with a student. Her sister, Ceil, the prestigious school supervisor, exemplifies proper behavior, but is obviously a frustrated, unhappily married woman. The question arises: who's sane and who's insane in a world where little animals, as Anna notes, are raised in boxes so eventually pretentious women can decorate themselves in fur. There are occasional bright spots in *Miss Reardon*, and Zindel displays, as he did in *Marigolds*, a talent for drawing strong female characters, but overall it is a disappointing endeavor by a playwright who clearly possesses ability.

Recently I spoke with Zindel and he commented on his past works and what he hopes to do in the future as a playwright:

> When I first started writing plays I relied totally upon my instincts. *Marigolds* was written ten years ago, and *Miss Reardon* seven, and both were bound by the fabric woven out of myself at that time when my talent was not fully aligned. They are not the plays I'd write today, because I've grown and changed a lot since then. At the time I was working without any knowledge of the classical structuring of a play. Since then I've made up for that deficiency. In my future works I hope to be able to render most of the theatre of the last century obsolete. My next play, I hope, will embrace theatre totally as Shakespeare did, and will make use of the stage, of language and wit in a new way. I know this sounds arrogant, but the situation did not come about because of me. It became possible because at this particular point of civilization we find ourselves ripe for this innovation. If I don't become the founding talent for this revolution, then there will be someone else very soon who will.

—Bernard Carragher

SCREEN
WRITERS

Fashion and convention tend to govern our assumptions about the balance of power in any artistic medium which depends to some significant extent on collaboration and teamwork. And for some historical reason which is not altlltogether clear (it may have something to do with the beginnings of film as a silent, primarily non-verbal medium) the standing of the writer in the cinema has never been very high. Certainly not in the English-language cinema. There has always been a three-way split of opinion. To the average regular filmgoer the most important element was the cast: stars were the only names of all those recorded somewhere on a film's credits which meant anything. In the commercial world of the cinema the essential was the producer and the production company responsible for putting together the package. And for highbrow critics, theorists of the film as an art form, the artist of the film was from very early on taken to be the director. Writers, despite some determined propaganda on their own behalf, have never managed to rate much with anyone as more than one of the team, contributors to the whole but seldom if ever the determining factor in overall judgment of a film's quality.

Inevitably this question of standing has affected the attitude writers have tended to adopt to work in the cinema. The history of the film is littered with famous cases of once-famous, once-talented writers (like F. Scott Fitzgerald) trying on their way down to scrape a living in the, to them, demeaning circumstances of the commercial film grind; with distinguished birds of passage (Maugham, Maeterlinck) who left the studios perhaps a mite richer and totally dissatisfied; and with important writers (Huxley, Faulkner, Isherwood) who earned money in films from time to time by exercising their craft and consciously leaving their art at home, as something obviously not wanted on voyage. And meanwhile those writers who chose for some reason to work almost entirely within the cinema seemed fated to have their contribution to famous films underrated (when people talk of *Citizen Kane* everyone remembers Orson Welles, who directed it; no one remembers Herman Mankiewicz, who wrote it), or have to graduate to the ranks of directors, bringing their own scripts to the screen, before they can hope for any serious attention.

In the contemporary cinema we can find examples of all these attitudes and situations. Many of the dramatists who feature elsewhere in this volume have had at least a flirtation or two with the cinema. Sometimes it will have been simply in their being called on to adapt, or help to adapt, their own stage works to the film. Sometimes it will be to adapt some other pre-existent work – John Osborne and *Tom Jones*, Harold Pinter and *The Servant*, *The Pumpkin Eater* or *The Go-Between*, Christopher Fry and *The Bible*. Rarely are established writers actually asked to create an original screenplay, and when they are the results (witness, for example, Terence Rattigan's *The V.I.P.s* and *The Yellow Rolls-Royce* are unlikely to be among their more characteristic or substantial works. There are a few exceptions, of course, like Graham Greene's screenplay for *The Third Man* or Paddy Chayefsky's for *The Goddess*, but it is notable that Samuel Beckett's strange genius could be accommodated to the screen only in the very special, non-commercial circumstances in which his *Film* was made.

Of more interest in the present context are those writers who have chosen to exercise their talents largely or entirely in the cinema. There is, of course, a very large number of such writers. Most of them have done other things as well, since few begin fully fledged as film writers; they probably come to films on the strength of at least one novel or play, and maybe continue to write from time to time in other media, if only to keep their hand in and perhaps ensure that measure of respect which for the majority of film writers only comes from success, or at any rate some attempt, elsewhere than in the cinema. With writers functioning primarily or wholly in the cinema we encounter special problems when it comes to discussing the body of their work. Particularly is it difficult to assess the precise nature and quality of their own individual contribution to any specific film, not to mention the degree of choice and control they have had in their careers as a whole. For in the nature of things most films, especially in America, are adaptations of pre-existent plays or stories. Moreover, many film scripts are avowedly collaborations, and many more have gone through several drafts by different writers before they reach the version we finally see.

This situation creates difficulties for those critics who seek to emphasize the importance of the writer as an autonomous creator in the cinema, if not the dominant influence on films.

While rejecting the excesses of the "auteur" theory of film direction, which treats films as though they are the work of one man in just the same way that novels or paintings are, with continuity of theme, philosophical consistency, etc., which can be traced from film to film, such critics fall into exactly the same sort of special pleading about writers. One such, for instance, has found in the scripts of Howard Koch (born 1902) an obsessive preoccupation with the subject of letters as determining factors in life on the strength of his having scripted, among other films, *The Letter, Letter from an Unknown Woman* and *The Thirteenth Letter* – but without making any mention at all of these each being a close adaptation of a respectable literary original. Obviously to assess the importance of the "letter" theme to Howard Koch we would have to know a lot more than we reasonably can, not only about how far the subject had been played up or played down in adaptation, but also about whether these were subjects Koch himself chose to work on, or merely material assigned to him to work on. In other words, we can often hope, at best, to assess only the sheer craftsmanship of leading film writers, but must accept that we are on much more dangerous ground if we try to go further, into their more personal creative qualities.

All the same, there are a number of film writers, mostly those who have managed to gradute to the position of being their own producers and directors, whose work can profitably (and realistically) be studied in such terms. The classic example in American cinema, creator of a whole body of original comedies marked in every part by his own idiosyncratic personality and approach, was the late Preston Sturges. Among currently active film-makers Billy Wilder (born 1906) comes nearest to the same ideal. Though most of his screenplays have been written in collaboration, first with Charles Brackett (*Lost Weekend, Sunset Boulevard, Ace in the Hole*) then with I. A. L. Diamond (*Some Like It Hot, The Apartment*, and *Kiss Me, Stupid*), and few of them have not been at least "inspired" by some already written novel, play or film-script, there is a very obvious consistency of vision in the films' mordant sense of humour, occasional sentimentality, and studied disregard for the normally accepted canons of good taste which mark them all as being essentially the creation of one man, one intelligence which makes over everything very much in its own image. Significant, when Wilder came to make a film on such a sacrosanct subject as Sherlock Holmes (*The Private Life of Sherlock Holmes*) that he should substitute for Conan Doyle's creation his own half-romantic, half-cynical fantasy, and curiously enough do so without even getting the Holmes devotees up in arms.

Another veteran writer-director, Joseph L. Mankiewicz (born 1909) achieved a recognisable style and tone in a succession of long, rather stagy, to some tastes over-talkative films he made in the late 1940's and early 1950's. The most famous of them were *A Letter to Three Wives* and *All about Eve*, both sophisticated comedies full of witty dialogue and meaty roles for actors. Curiously enough, Mankiewicz was a film man from way back, having started at the age of twenty writing titles for silent films and functioned throughout the latter half of the 1930's as a busy producer. Otherwise one might have supposed that his obvious romance with the Broadway stage (*All about Eve* gets as near as any film to catching the contradictory magic of the theatre) and the histrionic style of high stage comedy might be put down to the ill-concealed nostalgia of a theatre-man out of his element. Mankiewicz's equivalent study of film milieux, *The Barefoot Contessa*, unfortunately allowed personal bitterness to overbalance its ironic detachment, and most of his subsequent films have been more in the nature of directorial exercises with Mankiewicz's distinctive writing gifts as dialogue writer and creator of character kept in abeyance.

The only figure in the British cinema to achieve a similar standing as a writer-director with a similarly coherent body of original films to his credit is Michael Powell (born 1905). For some eighteen years at the height of his career Powell worked in regular collaboration with the Hungarian writer Emeric Pressburger, with whom he shared writer, producer and director credits. All the same, his own work before and after the collaboration is perfectly consistent with what he did with Pressburger – the luxuriant romanticism, the mixture of sometimes extravagantly perverse cruelty and rampant sentimentality, the preoccupation with the continuing power of myth, the lasting virtues of a military approach to life. In any case, whoever contributed whatever to the actual writing of the films Powell unarguably directed, they constitute one of the largest and most exceptional bodies of original writing in the British cinema, mingling a few relatively straightforward adaptations of sympathetic material from other media (*Black Narcissus, Gone to Earth, The Tales of Hoffmann*) with many screen originals. Films like *The Life and Death of Colonel Blimp*, with its acute and curiously ambivalent dissection of the role of the military in twentieth-century British history, was an extraordinary document to appear in 1943; *A Matter of Life and Death*, with its somewhat pretentious yet enthralling cosmic debate around the head of a British flier on the operating table, summed up many of the contradictory, sometimes crazily idealistic notions about postwar Ango-American cooperation which were in the air in 1946; and *The Red Shoes*, for all its oversimplifications, brought the world of the ballet and much of its magic and mystery into the awareness of millions who had never before given it a serious thought.

Hardly any other writers in the British cinema have achieved a comparable standing or freedom of action, which may explain why very few suggest themselves for individual consideration. Robert Boolt's plaace is in any case primarily in the theatre, even though of late he has devoted most of his time to the cinema; most of his work there has been done in tandem with the director David Lean (*Lawrence of Arabia, Doctor Zhivago*, and the screen original *Ryan's Daughter*), but it seems possible after *Lady Caroline Lamb* (1972), which he wrote and directed, that he may graduate into the class of total creators for the cinema. The only writer who has established a name and an image entirely as a writer of scripts for other people to direct is T. E. B. Clarke (born 1907), whose fame resides principally in the series of whimsical comedies based on the quirks and quaintnesses of English character and the English way of life which he created for Ealing Films during their postwar heyday. It could be urged against *Hue and Cry, Passport to Pimlico, The Lavender Hill Mob* and *The Titfield Thunderbolt* that they are altogether too cosy, peopled exclusively with amiable eccentrics of a kind that never existed even in the most comfortable reaches of the prosperous home counties. But then where is it laid down that the vision of a dramatist, or a film writer, has to be ruthlessly realistic? Clarke has created his own comic world, with its own special flavour, its own secret geography.

These are the principal creators of a body of original works specially written for the screen in the by now senior generation. Though there are many other writers of note at work, particularly in the American cinema, with nearly all the rest we run into the problem of apportioning responsibility in an adaptation or deciding how far the decisions involved were really those of the writer credited on the screen credits. There are several Hollywood writers of a slightly junior generation who have also managed to assume overall control of their work by becoming, at least occasionally, directors (though this tends to be a vicious circle, in that writers so promoted often find that they do not have time to write their own scripts any more). One might instance from this group Garson Kanin (born 1912), Abraham Polonsky (born 1910) and Richard Brooks (born 1912).

Kanin has had a curious career, beginning as a young prodigy writing and directing his own films in the later 1930's, then in his middle years going through a phase of scriptwriting, mostly in collaboration with his wife Ruth Gordon and mostly for director George Cukor, only to return of late to writer-director status. Most of his most memorable work as a writer belongs to the middle period, when he created original screen comedies such as *Adam's Rib* (1949) and *Pat and Mike* (1951), the definitive expressions of the Spencer Tracy-Katharine Hepburn tug-of-war on screen, and some sadder, more off-beat comedy-dramas like *The Marrying Kind* (1952). Polonsky began with a strange and personal kind of proletarian poetry in *Body and Soul* (1947) and *Force of Evil* (1948), which he also directed, then languished for some years under an un-American cloud, to return in full force in 1969 with *Tell Them Willie Boy Is Here*, an off-beat Western which he wrote and directed. Richard Brooks has chosen in his directorial career to work mainly with adaptations, but his recent works include two originals, *$*, an ingeniously constructed perfect-robbery thriller, and, more important, *The Happy Ending*, a thoroughly personal observation about the effect the falling-short of reality relative to the romantic fictions of the cinema may have on a film-bred generation; one of the very few original screenplays of the last few years to make some kind of new and valuable statement which can be applied beyond the immediate confines of its dramatic expression.

Though determined attempts have been made in the new, television-dominated era of Hollywood (and by extension the British cinema) to recruit young writing talent, most of the newcomers have been content to extract from the cinema whatever they could get quickly, without too much involvement, and make a rapid escape. True, some of the biggest successes of late years have been based on original screenplays from this generation of writers – films like *Butch Cassidy and the Sundance Kid* and *Bonnie and Clyde*. But William Goldman, the author of *Butch Cassidy* and otherwise a reputed novelist and commentator, shows little signs of wanting to involve himself more deeply in the cinema, and has since written nothing of comparable interest for the screen. On the other hand David Newman and Robert Benton, who wrote *Bonnie and Clyde*, have followed it up with several more scripts, leading to the perhaps inevitable conclusion of their both becoming directors (on separate films, both written by the two of them as a team). And in the present muddled, one might almost say desperate, stage of film history, there is a certain spirit abroad of try anything once, so that complete outsiders may well find themselves given the chance to write originals and direct their own scripts straight away, on the strength of a reputation gained in some completely different field. Yet puzzles remain. Take the case of Elaine May, who scored an unexpected success with her first one-woman effort, *A New Leaf*. So what happens? Her next screenplay, *Such Good Friends*, is directed by someone else, while she, for her second directorial enterprise, ends up directing a screenplay by Neil Simon, of all people, *The Heartbreak Kid*. But then with writing for the screen, nothing is ever simple. The new big names, like Willard Huyck and Gloria Katz (*American Graffiti*) and Adrien Joyce (*Five Easy Pieces*), may fade into insignificance on unsuitable assignments or have subsequent scripts butchered to no purpose. The only wonder is that as much good writing manages to reach the screen, and so many writers, mentioned above and in the appended listing, despite all the obstacles the system places in their way, do from time to time succeed in breaking through to some sort of personal expression. The only shame is that there are not more of them.

—John Russell Taylor

*   *   *

BENTON, Robert.   Screenplays, with David Newman: *Bonnie and Clyde*, 1967; *There Was a Crooked Man*, 1970; *What's Up, Doc?*, with Buck Henry, 1972; *Bad Company*, 1972; *Money's Tight*, 1973.

BOLT, Robert.   See his dictionary entry.

BROOKS, Richard.   Screenplays include: *Men of Texas*, with Harold Shumate, 1942; *Don Winslow of the Coast Guard*, with others, 1942; *White Savage*, 1943; *Cobra Woman*, 1944; *My Best Gal*, 1944; *Swell Guy*, 1946; *Brute Force*, 1947; *To the Victor*, 1948; *Key Largo* with John Huston, 1948; *Any Number Can Play*, 1949; *Mystery Street*, 1950; *Crisis*, 1950; *Storm Warning*, with Daniel Fuchs, 1951; *The Light Touch*, 1951; *Deadline – USA (Deadline)*, 1952; *Battle Circus*, 1953; *The Last Time I Saw Paris*, with Julius J. Epstein, 1954; *The Blackboard Jungle*, 1955; *The Last Hunt*, 1956; *Something of Value*, 1957; *The Brothers Karamazov*, 1957; *Cat on a Hot Tin Roof*, with James Poe, 1958; *Elmer Gantry*, 1960 (Academy Award); *Sweet Bird of Youth*, 1962; *Lord Jim*, 1965; *The Professionals*, 1966; *In Cold Blood*, 1967; *The Happy Ending*, 1969; *$*, 1971. Books: *The Boiling Point*; *The Brick Foxhole*.

CASSAVETES, John.   Screenplays: *Shadows*, 1959; *Too Late Blues*, 1962; *Faces*, 1968; *Husbands*, 1970; *Minnie and Moscowitz*, 1971; *A Woman under the Influence*, 1974. Film director and actor.

CHAPLIN, Charlie.   Films since 1930: *City Lights*, 1931; *Modern Times*, 1936; *The Great Dictator*, 1940; *Monsieur Verdoux*, 1947; *Limelight*, 1952; *A King in New York*, 1957; *A Countess from Hong Kong*, 1967.

CHAYEFSKY, Paddy.   See his dictionary entry.

CLARKE, T. E. B.   Screenplays include: *For Those in Peril*, 1944; *Johnny Frenchman*, 1945; *Dead of Night*, 1945; *Half-Way House*, 1945; *Hue and Cry*, 1946; *Passport to Pimlico*, 1948; *The Blue Lamp*, 1948; *Against the Wind*, 1949; *The Magnet*, 1951; *The Lavender Hill Mob*, 1951 (Academy Award); *Encore*, 1952; *Train of Events*, 1952; *The Titfield Thunderbolt*, 1953; *All at Sea*, 1957; *A Tale of Two Cities*, 1958; *Law and Disorder*, 1958; *Gideon's Day (Gideon of Scotland Yard)*, 1958; *Sons and Lovers*, with Gavin Lambert, 1960; *The Horse Without a Head*, 1963; *A Man Could Get Killed*, 1966.

DASSIN, Jules.   Screenplays: *Rififi*, 1954; *He Who Must Die*, 1957; *Where the Hot Wind Blows*, 1958; *Never on Sunday*, 1959; *Phaedra*, 1962; *10.30 P.M., Summer*, with Marguerite Duras, 1966; *Uptight*, with Ruby Dee and Julian Mayfield, 1968; *Promise at Dawn*, 1970.

FORBES, Bryan.   Screenplays, in collaboration: *The Black Knight*, 1954; *The Cockleshell Heroes*, 1956; *House of Secrets*, 1956; *Triple Deception*, 1957; *The Black Tent*, 1957; *The Baby and the Battleship*, 1957; *I Was Montie's Double*, 1958; *The Captain's Table*, 1959; *The Angry Silence*, 1960; *The League of Gentlemen*, 1960; *Man in the Moon*, 1960; *Only Two Can Play*, 1961; *The L-Shaped Room*, 1962; *Seance on a Wet Afternoon*, 1964; *Station 6 – Sahara*, 1964; *Of Human Bondage*, 1964; *The High Bright Sun (McGuire Go Home)*, 1965; *King Rat*, 1965; *The Whisperers*, 1967; *Deadfall*, 1968; *The Raging Moon*, 1971. Film director and actor.

FOREMAN, Carl.   Screenplays: *Spooks Run Wild*, 1941; *Rhythm Parade*, 1942; *Dakota*, 1945; *So This Is New York*, 1948; *Champion*, 1949; *The Clay Pigeon*, 1949; *Home of the Brave*, 1949; *Young Man with a Horn*, 1950; *The Men*, 1950; *Cyrano de Bergerac*, 1950; *High Noon*, 1952; *The Sleeping Tiger* (co-writer, as Derek Frye), 1954; *The Bridge on the River Kwai* (uncredited), with Michael Wilson, 1957; *The Key*, 1958 ; *The Guns of Navarone*, 1961; *The Victors*, 1963; *MacKenna's Gold*, 1969; *Young Winston*, 1972.

FRY, Christopher.   See his dictionary entry.

GOLDMAN, William.   Screenplays: *Masquerade*, 1965; *Harper (The Moving Target)*, 1966; *Butch Cassidy and the Sundance Kid*, 1969; *Hot Rock (How to Steal a Diamond)*, 1972; *The Great Waldo Pepper*, 1974; *The Stepford Wives*, 1975. Stage Plays: *Blood, Sweat and Stanley Poole*, with James Goldman, 1961; *A Family Affair*, with James Goldman and John Kander, 1962. His most recent novels are *Marathon Man*, 1974, and *The Princess Bride*, 1975.

GREENE, Graham.   See his dictionary entry.

HENRY, Buck.   Screenplays: *The Troublemaker*, with Theodore Flicker, 1964; *The Graduate*, with Calder Willingham, 1967; *Candy*, 1968; *Catch-22*, 1970; *The Owl and the Pussycat*, 1970; *What's Up, Doc.?*, with Robert Benton and David Newman, 1972; *The Day of the Dolphin*, 1973. Film actor.

HUSTON, John.   Screenplays: *A House Divided*, 1931; *Murders in the Rue Morgue*, 1932; *The Amazing Dr. Clitterhouse*, 1938; *Jezebel*, with Clements Ripley and Abem Finkel, 1938; *Juarez*, with Wolfgang Reinhart and Aeneas MacKenzie, 1939; *The Story of Dr. Ehrlich's Magic Bullet* (co-writer), 1940; *High Sierra*, with W. R. Burnett, 1941; *Sergeant York*, with Howard Koch, Abem Finkel, and Harry Chandlee, 1941; *The Maltese Falcon*, 1941; *In This Our Life*, with Howard Koch, 1942; *Across the Pacific*, 1942; *Report from the Aleutians*, 1943; *The Battle of San Pietro*, 1944; *Let There Be Light* (co-writer), 1945; *Three Strangers*, with Howard Koch, 1946; *The Stranger* (uncredited), with Orson Welles, 1946; *The Killers* (uncredited), with Anthony Veiller, 1946; *The Treasure of the Sierra Madre*, with Robert Rossen (uncredited), 1948; *Key Largo*, with Richard Brooks, 1948; *We Were Strangers*, 1949; *The Asphalt Jungle*, with Ben Maddow, 1950; *The Red Badge of Courage*, 1951; *The African Queen*, with James Agee, 1951; *Moulin Rouge*, with Anthony Veiller, 1953; *Beat the Devil*, with Truman Capote, 1954; *Moby Dick*, with Ray Bradbury, 1956; *Heaven Knows, Mr.*

Allison, with John Lee Mahin, 1957; *Freud* (co-writer), 1962; *Night of the Iguana*, with Anthony Veiller, 1964; *The Kremlin Letter* (co-writer), 1970.

ISHERWOOD, Christopher.   See his dictionary entry.

KANIN, Garson.   See his dictionary entry.

KOCH, Howard.   Screenplays: *The Letter*, 1940; *The Sea Hawk*, with Seton I. Miller, 1940; *Shining Victory*, 1941; *Sergeant York*, with John Huston, Abem Finkel, and Harry Chandlee, 1941; *In This Our Life*, with John Huston, 1942; *Mission to Moscow*, 1943; *Casablanca*, with Julius J. Epstein and Philip G. Epstein, 1943 (Academy Award); *In Our Time*, 1944; *Rhapsody in Blue*, with Elliot Paul, 1945; *Three Strangers*, with John Huston, 1946; *Letter from an Unknown Woman*, with Max Ophüls, 1948; *The Rules of the Game*, 1950; *No Sad Songs for Me*, 1950; *The Thirteenth Letter*, 1951; *The Greengage Summer (Loss of Innocence)*, 1961; *The War Lover*, 1962; *633 Squadron*, 1964; *The Fox*, with Lewis John Carlino, 1967. Stage plays: *Give Us This Day* and *In Time to Come*. Radio play: *War of the Worlds*, 1940.

KUBRICK, Stanley.   Screenplays: *Killer's Kiss*, 1955; *The Killing*, 1956; *Paths of Glory*, 1957; *Dr. Strangelove; or, How I Learned to Stop Worrying and Love the Bomb*, with Terry Southern and Peter George, 1963; *2001: A Space Odyssey*, with Arthur C. Clarke, 1968; *A Clockwork Orange*, 1971; *Barry Lyndon*, 1975. Early documentaries: *Day of the Fight* and *Flying Padre*, 1951.

MANKIEWICZ, Joseph L.   Screenplays: *Close Harmony*, 1929; *The Man I Love*, 1929; *Thunderbolt*, 1929; *Slightly Scarlet*, 1930; *Finn and Hattie*, with Norman MacLeod, 1931; *Skippy*, with Norman MacLeod, 1931; *Million Dollar Legs* (co-writer), 1932; *This Reckless Age*, 1932; *Alice in Wonderland*, with William Menzies, 1933; *Manhattan Melodrama*, with Oliver H. P. Garrett, 1934; *Our Daily Bread*, 1934; *Forsaking All Others*, 1934; *I Live My Life*, 1935; *Keys of the Kingdom*, with Nunnally Johnson, 1944; *Dragonwyck*, 1946; *Somewhere in the Night* (co-writer), 1946; *A Letter to Three Wives*, 1949 (Academy Award); *All about Eve*, 1950 (Academy Award); *No Way Out*, with Lesser Samuels, 1950; *People Will Talk*, 1951; *Julius Caesar*, 1953; *The Barefoot Contessa*, 1954; *Guys and Dolls*, 1955; *The Quiet American*, 1958; *Cleopatra*, with others, 1963; *The Honey Pot*, 1967; *Sleuth*, 1974.

MAY, Elaine.   See her dictionary entry.

NEWMAN, David.   See list for Robert Benton above.

OSBORNE, John.   See his dictionary entry.

PERRY, Eleanor.   Screenplays: *David and Lisa*, 1962; *Ladybug, Ladybug*, 1963; *The Swimmer*, 1967; *Trilogy*, 1969; *Last Summer*, 1969; *Diary of a Mad Housewife*, 1970; *The Lady in the Car with Sunglasses and a Gun* (co-writer), 1970; *La Maison sous les Arbres* (co-writer), 1972.

PINTER, Harold.   See his dictionary entry.

POLONSKY, Abraham.   Screenplays: *Body and Soul*, 1947; *Golden Earrings*, 1947; *Force of Evil* (co-writer), 1948; *I Can Get It for You Wholesale* (co-writer), 1951; *Madigan* (co-writer), 1968; *Tell Them Willie Boy Is Here*, 1969.

POWELL, Michael.   Screenplays: *My Friend the King*, 1931; *The Fire-Raisers*, 1933; *Red Ensign* (co-writer), 1933; *The Edge of the World*, 1937; *Contraband (Blackout)* (co-writer), 1940; with Emeric Pressburger: *One of Our Aircraft Is Missing*, 1942; *The Life and Death of Colonel Blimp*, 1943; *The Volunteer*, 1943; *A Canterbury Tale*, 1944; *I Know Where I'm Going*, 1945, *A Matter of Life and Death (Stairway to Heaven)*, 1946, *Black Narcissus*, 1947, *The Red Shoes*, 1948, *The Small Back Room (Hour of Glory)*, 1948, *The Elusive Pimpernel (The Fighting Pimpernel)*, 1950, *Gone to Earth (The Wild Heart)*, 1950, *The Tales of Hoffmann*, 1951, *The Battle of the River Plate (Pursuit of the Graf Spee)*, 1956, and *Ill-Met by Moonlight (Night Ambush)*, 1957; *Honeymoon* (co-writer), 1958.

RAPHAEL, Frederic. Screenplays: *Bachelor of Hearts*, 1958; *Don't Bother to Knock (Why Bother to Knock)*, with Denis Cannon, 1961; *Nothing But the Best*, 1964; *Darling*, 1965; *Two for the Road*, 1967; *Far from the Madding Crowd*, 1967; *How about Us?*, 1971; *A Severed Head*, 1971; *Daisy Miller*, 1974. Television: *Rogue Male*, from the novel by Geoffrey Household, 1976. Stage plays: *Lady at the Wheel*, with Lucienne Hill, music and lyrics by Leslie Bricusse and Robin Beaumont, 1958; *A Man on the Bridge*, 1961. His most recent books are the novels *Richard's Things*, 1973, and *California Time*, 1975, and *Somerset Maugham and His World*, 1975.

RATTIGAN, Terence. See his dictionary entry.

SIMON, Neil. See his dictionary entry.

SOUTHERN, Terry. Screenplays: *Candy Kisses*, 1955; *Dr. Strangelove; or, How I Learned to Stop Worrying and Love the Bomb*, with Stanley Kubrick, 1963; *The Loved One*, with Christopher Isherwood, 1965; *The Cincinnati Kid*, with Ring Lardner, Jr., 1965; *Barbarella*, 1967; *Easy Rider*, with Peter Fonda and Dennis Hopper, 1969; *End of the Road*, 1969; *The Magic Christian*, 1970; *Electric Child*, 1970. Books: *The Journal of "The Loved One,"* 1965, and several novels, the most recent being *Blue Movie*, 1970.

STERN, Stewart. Screenplays: *Teresa*, 1951; *Benjy*, 1951; *Rebel Without a Cause*, 1955; *The Rack*, 1956; *The James Dean Story*, 1957; *Thunder in the Sun*, 1958; *The Outsider*, 1961; *The Ugly American*, 1963; *Rachel, Rachel*, 1968.

TRUMBO, Dalton. Screenplays: *Jealousy*, 1934; *Love Begins at Twenty*, 1936; *Road Gang*, 1936; *The Story of Isadora Bernstein*, 1936; *Devil's Playground*, 1937; *Fugitives for a Night*, 1938; *A Man to Remember*, 1938; *Sorority House*, 1939; *Career*, 1939; *Five Came Back*, with Nathanael West and Jerry Cady, 1939; *The Flying Irishman*, with Ernest Pagano, 1939; *Heaven with a Barbed Wire Fence*, 1939; *Kitty Foyle*, 1940; *Half a Sinner*, 1940; *We Who Are Young*, 1940; *A Bill of Divorcement*, 1940; *Curtain Call*, 1940; *You Belong to Me*, 1941; *The Remarkable Andrew*, 1942; *Tender Comrade*, 1943; *A Guy Named Joe*, 1943; *Thirty Seconds over Tokyo*, 1944; *Our Vines Have Tender Grapes*, 1945; *The Brave One* (as Richard Rich), 1957; *Spartacus*, with Howard Fast, 1960; *Exodus*, 1960; *The Last Sunset*, 1961; *Lonely Are the Brave*, 1962; *The Sandpiper*, 1965; *Hawaii*, 1966; *The Fixer*, 1970; *Johnny Got His Gun*, 1970; *The Horseman*, 1971. Stage play: *The Biggest Thief in Town*, 1949. Books: several novels and *Additional Dialogue* (letters), 1970.

WELLES, Orson. Screenplays: *Citizen Kane*, with Herman J. Mankiewicz, 1941; *The Magnificent Ambersons*, 1942; *Journey into Fear*, 1943; *The Stranger*, with John Huston (uncredited), 1946; *Macbeth*, 1948; *The Lady from Shanghai*, 1948; *Othello*, 1952; *Confidential Report*, 1958; *Touch of Evil*, 1958; *Mr. Arkadin*, 1962; *The Trial*, 1963; *Chimes at Midnight*, 1966; *The Immortal Story*, 1968. Stage and film actor and director.

WILDER, Billy. First film: *Menschen am Sonntag* (co-writer), 1929, then other German films; *Mauvaise Graine*, with Alexander Esway, 1934; *Music in the Air*, 1934; with Charles Brackett: *Bluebeard's Eighth Wife*, 1938, *Midnight*, 1939, *Ninotchka*, with Walter Reisch, 1939, *Arise My Love*, 1940, *Hold Back the Dawn*, 1941, *Ball of Fire*, 1941, *The Major and the Minor*, 1942, *Five Graves to Cairo*, 1943, *The Lost Weekend*, 1945, *The Emperor Waltz*, 1948, *A Foreign Affair*, 1948, and *Sunset Boulevard*, with D. M. Marshman, Jr., 1950; *Double Indemnity*, with Raymond Chandler, 1944; *Ace in the Hole (The Big Carnival)*, with L. Samuels and W. Newman, 1951; *Stalag 17*, with Edwin Blum, 1953; *Sabrina*, 1954; *The Seven Year Itch*, with George Axelrod, 1955; *The Spirit of St. Louis*, with Wendell Mayes, 1957; *Witness for the Prosecution*, with Harry Kurnitz, 1957; with I. A. L. Diamond: *Love in the Afternoon*, 1957, *Some Like It Hot*, 1959, *The Apartment*, 1960, *One, Two, Three*, 1961, *Irma La Douce*, 1963, *Kiss Me, Stupid*, 1964, *The Fortune Cookie (Meet Whiplash Willie)*, 1966, *The Private Life of Sherlock Holmes*, 1970, *Avanti*, 1971; *The Front Page*, 1975.

RADIO
WRITERS

At a rough count something over eighty of the authors listed in this book have had plays performed on radio. About half that number are what might be termed *radio* playwrights in the sense that they have written specifically for sound, though not by any means all of that half can be called active – "active" signifying that a writer has provided a new script sometime in the last two years and had it performed. By those tokens, less than a score of the names to be found here refer to radio authors.

This may well suggest a dire state of affairs, but the truth of it is rather different. Two years is an arbitrary limit: add another and the list would grow – whereas if we measured activity by rate of submission it would increase like a population curve. In short, by a criterion of selectivity alone, current radio drama is alive and well: many may call, but comparatively few get chosen.

Perhaps a word or two of background is in order here. One refers to "radio drama," portmanteau fashion, as if it were a unity: nothing could be further from the truth. Radio is a purchaser for several different "theatres," each of different character, their output ranging from the relatively difficult work to be found on Radio 3 to the less demanding repertoire of the afternoons on Radio 4. Even this is a gross generalisation: wherever you look the audience is heterogeneous and on Radio 4 alone its taste in plays embraces very nearly everything – from detective thrillers through domestic or social problem dramas to a bit of Pinter or Terson. It was not always thus: when I first began professional listening in the mid-sixties, the Pinters and the Tersons were generally in purdah on the Third and there were many weeks when old Home Service standards suggested that, far from selecting anyone at all, the drama department had been obliged to tour the literary highways and hedges, compelling contributions from a job lot of the poor, the maimed, the halt and the blind. We have come along a bit since then.

However, despire such improvements, it is still to Radio 3 that I shall be turning for most of my illustrations: the great majority of writers who in the last few years have put in interesting and/or original work have had their "first nights" there and this is perhaps the moment to explain that even if only a dozen of them are entered in these pages, the total roll call runs without the slightest effort to very nearly fifty names. Radio drama has its own stable, largely dependent of the theatre, independent – though less markedly – of television: by that criterion too it is in good condition and it continues, as it has always done, to school playwrights for other media. James Saunders, Harold Pinter, Tom Stoppard are some of its more distinguished old boys and it is noticeable that without any apparent condescension established writers return – or turn for the first time – to radio.

Again this marks a slight but evident change: in the excitement of television's blast-off it seemed as if the notion were abroad that radio was played out. By now it is clear that dramatically, imaginatively TV has its limitations, and radio's power to suggest, the extraordinary freedom it offers to those who know how to use it, once again begin to seem attractive. To some extent this goes for the theatre too: no one who saw Stoppard's *Jumpers* and then heard his *Artist Descending a Staircase* will be in any doubt that the radio play was the next major work in the opus, that without the possibilities of sound neither this play nor any other quite like it would have been written. Stoppard has his own entry here, so I do not want to dwell on his work except to say that of all living writers whose major reputation rests elsewhere, he is probably the most accomplished when it comes to radio; he illustrates the point that to write a good radio play an author must do something quite different from writing one for stage or television. He must master different skills and techniques and he finds himself working for a medium capable of starting on the threshold of a country which, in other media, he would first have to reach.

Things being what they are, however, radio in most people's eyes is the disregarded poor relation of the drama, so before getting down to further instances, I think it would be worthwhile to examine what it is that makes a radio – as opposed to any other kind of – playwright. The question is best illustrated by a paradox: one of the most expert radio writers of them all is dead and gone and never saw or heard a radio – Shakespeare. Not by any means every classic giant profits from being played in sound alone, but in some cases the action migrates quite happily. Shakespeare's is one of them and possibly this happens *because* he wrote for the stage – wrote for a stage whose technical limitations were so narrow that a writer who restricted his action only to what could convincingly be represented to the eyes would end up with very little to represent. His alternative – and quite obviously this was Shakespeare's – was largely to ignore the trammels and instead to count on the most profound imaginative cooperation from his audience. This, you will observe, is precisely what the radio playwright has to do and in both cases it gives the writer freedom to enter any realm at all: supernatural, fantastic, intimately psychological – and he can leap around in time and space as well. This, to a considerable extent, accounts for Shakespeare's success on radio and those living writers who make a mark are in my view doing the same sort of thing. In fact you could say that the playwright who ignores this freedom will never make an interesting mark at all.

Although things were worse in the mid-sixties, it remains true that in radio as a whole there are many playwrights who do ignore – or seem never to have heard of – their opportunities. Perhaps this is symptomatic: if we are talking about imaginative cooperation, then it goes without saying that the writer must offer his listeners something worth imagining and the fact is that the majority of radio plays offer their audiences nothing of the sort. Those involved will probably contest this: the argument goes that since the listener cannot actually see the scene in progress, ergo he is exercising the holy power of his imagination, and that, per se, is good. Ponder the exercise imagination gets from conjuring up pictures or recreating emotions which are in every respect as commonplace as those in which the hearer spends the greater part of what passes for his waking life....

I am not saying that plays with this low level of imaginative content should not exist; in many instances they are what an immense body of listeners seems to want and looks to the BBC to provide. Good luck all round, but I would like to distinguish this kind of commercial transaction in which one party sells the other the dramatic equivalent of a couple of aspirin from the truly creative one. This is to provide an element which not only on the air but in all drama takes us into states of mind we do not normally inhabit – states of insight, of intuition, of reflection, of laughter, of uncertainty, of self-recognition. Without that we have literally only pastimes – plays for passing the next hour or so without noticing a thing.

Natural technique apart, it is obvious that Shakespeare provides his audience with vast opportunities for entering other states of mind: much of his time is spent exploring the kind of interior country I have been referring to – although even old-established Shakespearians who heard the newest radio productions of *Hamlet* and *Othello* may have been surprised to discover just how much time he spends. This again is an effect of radio: it will locate and intensify interior landscapes if they exist; on the other hand, if they do not it is remorseless in exposing the horrible gap – and it is not only the most obvious pastime plays which turn out to be vacant at the centre. Of course, faced with any approximations to Shakespeare's mix of technique and inward looking, the listener needs to be on his guard for radio will penetrate and persuade him whether he likes it or not. God knows on what bleak and sterile promontory of the soul Samuel Beckett's famous *All That Fall* is played out: such is Beckett's power that the listener, in sound as by no other means, takes in the geography and may well end up inclined to believe that it alone exists. Imagination has its limits: because a vision swims into the head and the head's possessor has the gift to set it down, that does not prove any other reality.

Beckett in fact is one of those Olympians of radio who continue to contribute, although his recent works can hardly be called plays: *Lessness* (1971) was a reading for six solo voices, evoking a cold, grey and sterile interior landscape; *The Lost Ones* (1973) was an immensely powerful monologue using the metaphor of a large cylinder with no way out to represent the world and the condition of mankind. Both scripts harped upon the unremitting repetitiveness of human existence and its inescapability; in *The Lost Ones* absolute cessation of the restless search for fulfilment is seen as the final, desirable end. After this what can follow, unless it be a 40-minute silence punctuated by low moans? Another Olympian, Harold Pinter, has done nothing new since an 8-minute sketch, *Night* (1970), but interestingly it is he and Beckett who seem to have handed down the prevailing palette of radio playwriting: black, grey, sepia, white, pale olive. The brighter, bolder colours of Dylan Thomas, Louis MacNeice or Henry

Reed have been very largely put aside.

Of the playwrights now known chiefly for their radio work two have reputations going back over many years: Rhys Adrian is one – he has been productive since at least 1956; Don Haworth – nothing to do with the author of *Lily in Little India* who is Howarth – is the other. Both men – and radio of course encourages this – are highly individual stylists in the matter of dialogue. Adrian is reminiscent in style and treatment of that other lamented master of radio drama, the late Giles Cooper. He has been prolific – not as prolific as Cooper who, with all the respect due to his many exceptional plays, wrote more than he had to say – but there is by now an impressive collection of skilful, sensitively written, highly characteristic scripts.

One of the best known, *Evelyn*, won an Italia Prize in 1970, suggesting what is indeed the case, that the cutting edge of this slightly absurd, near-black style of comedy draws blood just as freely on the continent. *Evelyn* is instantly recognisable as an original Adrian, a dialogue between some subtle female innocent, voiced like a turtle dove and about as implacable, and her temporary lover (all her lovers are temporary) whom she bullies into inventing another women (Evelyn). She does it by manipulating his self-esteem and then, all saucer-eyed, assumes his invention to be true: it enables her to cast him off with that much less compunction. Adrian achieves his effect in part by the careful placing of commonplace phrases in slightly bizarre situations. He is also a master of the formal repetition: hearers of *Evelyn* must have some problems nowadays with the words "remarkable person," there used and reused to suggest depths of human ordinariness previously unsuspected. It was noticeable, by the way, that when this play subsequently turned up on television it lost a very great part of its suggestive power.

Don Haworth's natural talents are for radio but with the years his work there has undergone a change, the course of which can be followed in the six scripts recently issued by BBC Publications. Without much doubt the most attractive as well as the most memorable of them is the title play of the collection, *We All Come to It in the End*. This, like *Evelyn*, went in for an Italia Prize but without success: Haworth's is much less the type of work to appeal to international juries – it is rooted in the North of England and written for preference in that mixture of the colloquial and the portentous which singles out Northern speech. This, in the mouth of a resigned innocent like his George, takes on a sharpness which always, as it makes you laugh, cuts to a stratum below laughter. But as I say, there have been changes: *We All Come to It* and the plays close to it in time rode on a pneumatic cheerful pessimism, were filled with wonder at the sheer oddity of mankind. Latterly the bounce has departed, the loving characterisation – like that of George's Uncle Percy – has been set aside in favour of shorter plays for two or three voices (*The Illumination of Mr. Shannon, The Enlightenment of the Strawberry Gardener*), presenting situations every bit as absurd but in which the innocent party ends up not as was George, acceptant of his lot, but thoroughly, even harshly, duped.

One might mention in company with Adrian and Haworth another long-standing contributor whose work, it seems to me, has recently taken on new stature: Frederick Bradnum first appears in the play catalogue in 1947; my own first encounters with him were much later and made only a moderate impression, but the last couple of years have thrown up some things that stick in the memory, notably *You Are Not Alone in the House*, a telling fantasy about an old woman dying, with Death portrayed as a pair of jokey, talkative housebreakers.

F. C. Ball has been a rarer contributor, but his few scripts (*A Breath of Fresh Air, A Grotto for Miss Maynier* – based on a novel, this – and *From Oblivion to Obscurity*) possess qualities which root them in the hearer's mind: they are limpid, tender, slightly melancholy, with a sharp eye for character and an ear for visual evocation. It is a matter for regret that we do not hear from Mr. Ball more often. No glance at the older guard of active radio writers should overlook Gwyn Thomas, better known perhaps as a novelist, but a reliable provider of small, rich comedies – Welsh to the last comma and packed to bursting with large, gusty turns of phrase.

With some of radio's newer writers, there is a problem though one, I hope, which time will cure: most of them – Bill Morrison, Jonathan Raban, Piers Paul Read and others – are represented by only one or two plays. On this basis I can form very little judgement except to say – in these instances at least – that I hope there will be more and I shall take good care to hear them. This would apply particularly to Bill Morrison (resident playwright at Stoke-on-Trent) whose *The Love of Lady Margaret* was memorable for its sensitivity in the handling of intimate sexual matters as well as for its grip on irony and structure.

For more substantial output one turns to three names: Susan Hill, Caryl Churchill and Michael Sadler. Miss Hill has already won a brilliant reputation for her novels and in some respect her plays for radio are very much those of the novelist: technically not very adventurous – remarkable, however, for their unostentatious probing of relationships, not simply of one person to another, but of the individual to something other-worldly. *The End of Summer* appeared one afternoon on Radio 4 – it was about two people in a house in the country and torrential rain and the death of a cat; *Lizard in the Grass* told of a rather idiosyncratic little girl at school near sunken Dunwich and how she was visited by the spirit of John Skelton. *The Cold Country*, more dramatic by these standards, was about the failure of a disastrous polar expedition, but it, like each of these plays, said far more than can be accounted for by its not very eventful story line. There is something cool and deep about Miss Hill's work for radio. Like a river under trees.

Caryl Churchill is a very different matter and I have to confess that I do not greatly enjoy her work. Her plays are brighter, quick and clever in their writing, and from *Lovesick* on through *Identical Twins, Abortive, Schreber's Nervous Illness* (more case history than play) and *Henry's Past* they revolve round characters who all in some degree appear to have sustained pretty crippling psychological damage. A variation, *Not, Not, Not Enough Oxygen* was a fantasy set in a world so polluted that everybody gasped for breath: comic in intention – slightly bleak and unfunny in invention. For me the most successful Churchill play by far was the tiny 20-minute long *Abortive* where she explored with subtlety and feeling a situation giving less evidence than usual of a taste for psychopathology. *Henry's Past* was also her most ambitious – attempting and to a high degree succeeding in making its hearers understand what it is like to live a prisoner to the past and suddenly to comprehend the present, the Now. I suspect that both here and in *Abortive* the essential difference was a greater measure of compassion.

In comparison with these two ladies, in comparison with almost anyone now writing for radio, Michael Sadler is the possessor of a large and colourful talent. His three plays so far, *Gulliver's Way, The Bull of La Plata* and *Hopcraft into Europe*, are arranged not only chronologically but in descending order of luxuriance – *Gulliver* being a wild and improbable fantasy with a strong taste of Firbank, *The Bull* seeming to be about the Man of Mind's failure to subdue the awful Female Principle. In both works the invention ran wild and glorious, but here I fear we had examples of that slight gap at the centre which radio is so quick to detect; one felt that the lines and the bizarre situations had occurred first and their inventor had been hard put to it to provide the bone structure sufficient to support them. *Hopcraft* is less ephemeral; it boasts a small and by earlier comparisons prosaic plot to which, in the manner of Feydeau, Sadler has applied his talents to produce a genuinely farcical situation; there is also a development of interest in character somewhat beyond the demands of farce. Yet the whole remains airborne.

If Michael Sadler is the nearest radio comes to full colour, one must remember that this is in relation to radio drama's prevailing low-key palette. In style or technique today there is little or nothing to be heard which would have astonished or even mildly surprised Thomas or MacNeice. John George with *Sad and True and Sealed For Ever* follows Thomas but at a distance and looking down my list there is only David Halliwell who in *Bleats from a Brighouse Pleasure Ground* has done anything to tax production resources; this was an attempt – and an entertaining one – to impart the idea of the multi-dimensional moment, but in retrospect it has the flavour of an exercise and if any one should resurrect me for the Corporation's Centenary, I shall be amazed if that gets resurrected also.

I want to give a general impression and it is that in the time I have been in the gamekeeping business radio drama has improved vastly; nevertheless – and in the perfect realisation that general standards at the time may have been less impressive – it seems to me that one must still look back to the so-called "golden years" if one wants distinction. In the realm of drama and the related one of features, radio then touched heights, demonstrated capacities which it has not since exceeded and to which it only infrequently returns. Those who heard *Under Milk Wood* repeated in the autumn of 1972 may well have reflected: "They don't write things like that any more." Unfortunately it is impossible to say such a thing without being branded as a reactionary, so let me make it clear – there is no going back. At the same time the force of the reflection is undeniable.

What distinguishes *Under Milk Wood* is a certain unquenchable cheerfulness and good humour. In today's drama there may be talent and sensitivity and many other virtuous things, but there is precious little cheer. Pessimism prevails and this, on radio, is what the palette taken on from Beckett and Pinter is ideally suited to portray.

In his preface to *The Dark Tower* MacNeice wrote: "In an age which precludes the simple and militant faith of a Bunyan, belief (whether consciously formulated or not) still remains a *sine qua non* of the creative writer. I have my beliefs and they permeate *The Dark Tower*." This makes my point as well as anything, for I cannot easily see any of today's writers subscribing to it – at least not if by "belief" MacNeice meant what *The Dark Tower* suggests. There might be one exception, one who is a radio playwright only now and then: John Arden. His *Life of Man* and *The Bagman of Muswell Hill* stand outside the present mood of radio writing; they display that touch of myth and magic and of fire. Of the others some might smile and some might sneer; some – Don Haworth perhaps – might look back on a view they held to once but lost. The move from near optimism to near pessimism is the difference between *We All Come to It* and the later Haworth plays.

It seems to me that belief, cheerfulness, good humour – all these suggest a certain basic optimism, though by no means, as MacNeice makes clear, a simple-minded one. Optimism in radio invites a large, exploratory, colourful technique, a search for new effects because there seems to be more to say and it will be worth saying: with this there goes – dare one write it? – a touch of romanticism. If by contrast today's radio plays are cool and pale and unexuberant (or if highly-coloured then the work of miniaturists), perhaps this reflects not so much the state of radio drama as of a nation – a nation whose answer to the question "What is it all about?" ranges from "Don't Know" to "Nothing."

I suppose that if I had to express a hope for radio drama in the coming years it would be for a shift in mood. How this might happen I do not know: the factors contributing to the present one are so interlocked and it is hard for any organisation, let alone one small drama department, to go against the society of which it forms a part. I am not saying that there are greater grounds for optimism – I doubt if there are, but it seems to me that we have every bit as much capacity for it as for pessimism, that we need to keep the two in equilibrium and have gone too far the way of gloom.

Perhaps a starting point is to allow that a change is desirable and could happen; or to remember the story of the king who, in confusion of mind, asked his councillors how he could find stability. They thought and then they handed him a ring, telling him to look at it whenever he felt sad or happy – on it was inscribed the words "This too will pass"; or else we might bear in mind the catchphrase of a once renowned radio pessimist: "It's being so cheerful as keeps me going." Which of course it is.

(1977) It is some three years since I wrote the last few pages; how do they look now? Has there been the hoped-for shift in mood? Given the trend of national and international affairs, it would have been amazing if there had: all one can say with any certainty is that the mood is no more pessimistic than it was. Time may see to that. On the other hand I am inclined to think that, for example, Beckett's several contributions in this period, though sombre as ever, are not quite as characteristic of the prevailing tone as once they might have been.

If Beckett has been productive, from Pinter there has been no new radio work at all; indeed from many of the names I mentioned there is little to report – Rhys Adrian, Piers Paul Read, F. C. Ball, Caryl Churchill, John George, Michael Sadler. Some have added nothing at all; such new things as there were have provoked no particular response. Michael Sadler is a negative exception: his *South Coast Twilight Serenade* lost all the weight of *Hopcraft into Europe* and reverted to the empty-decorative.

Of the others who have been productive, Susan Hill has added half a dozen titles to her list, but, with the possible exception of *Consider the Lilies*, I cannot say that I have had much pleasure from them. It continues to be a cold country in which Miss Hill is working; the sun does not often shine, nor is much laughter heard – a state of affairs not really altered by her comedy *The Summer of Giant Sunflowers*, which in an effort to change mood lost character.

Two plays from Jonathan Raban, *At the Gate* and particularly *The Anomaly*, gave cause for hope, but there have been no successors. One encouraging event in the last year or so has been to hear Don Haworth, in his two most recent scripts, re-emerge into what may well be a new area of creativity. Tom Mallin's *Rooms* and above all his *Vicar Martin* marked a strong advance on previous work.

Fortunately there are names to add: I cannot satisfactorily explain how it was possible to omit R. C. Scriven from the first edition – it appears to have come home to me only since that here is one of radio's best talents, a man who has found in his own blindness and deafness a rich and powerful impetus toward some of the most vivid writing currently to be heard. Gabriel Josipovici is another individual but very different voice, by no means to everybody's taste, but I find his use of sound and way of dipping into the labyrinth of human consciousness exceedingly effective.

These are two of whom I have some expectations between now and the next postscript. Likewise of Fay Weldon as long as she maintains the imaginative tension of *The Doctor's Wife*. John Fletcher's *Wandering in Eden* bids fair for nomination as the most original contribution of the time I am reviewing – although some people might prefer to put up Philip Oxman's *The Origins of Capital and the Descent of Power*: it is not a question I can discuss, since the latter left me utterly uncomprehending.

Who else shall I be looking to? Shirley Gee if she will build on *Stones*; David Rudkin if only he would bring to radio the voice he found for television in *Penda's Fen*, or could approach on his own the grandeur of his cooperation with Euripides's *Hecuba*; Peter Cator if he can follow up his prize-winning *The Search for Hamilton Stiggs* and not in Sadler fashion lose substance; Derek Raby, on the strength of *Tiger*. Let us hope.

Whether the mood of radio drama has shifted is, as I say, unclear; but this postscript is evidence of another much less arguable change: the examples I have quoted are now drawn not just from Radio 3, but to a great extent from Radio 4 as well. So much the better – it is a healthy trend. What of the whole state of the nation, however, the present health or otherwise of radio plays? There is no room for an analysis, but feeling plays a part in this so let me lean on that: how do I feel about the number and the names of those who have been silent or said nothing much? There are more than I should like. And for the hopes of those still active or new upon the scene? With rare exceptions, there is a want of stature.

—David Wade

* * *

ADRIAN, Rhys. Radio plays include *The Man on the Gate*, 1956; *The Passionate Thinker*, 1957; *The Prizewinner*, 1960; *Betsie*, 1960; *The Bridge*, 1961; *Too Old for Donkeys*, 1963; *A Room to Let*, 1963; *A Nice Clean Sheet of Paper*, 1963 (published in *New Radio Drama*, 1966); *Sunday, The First of May*, 1964; *Helen and Edward and Henry*, 1966; *Between the Two of Us*, 1967; *Ella*, 1968; *Echoes*, 1969; *Evelyn*, 1969; *I'll Love You Always, Always*, 1970; *The Gardeners of My Youth*, 1970 (staged, 1976); *Mr. and Mrs. Squirrel*, 1971; *A Chance Encounter*, 1972; *Memoirs of a Sly Pornographer*, 1972; *Angle*, 1975; and others. Television plays include *The Protest*, 1960 (published in *New Granada Plays*, 1961); *Helen and Edward and Henry*, 1965; *Stan's Day Out*, 1967; *The Drummer and the Bloke*, 1968; *The Fox Trot*, 1971; *No Charge for Extra Service*, 1971; *Thrills Galore*, 1972; *The Withered Arm*, from story by Thomas Hardy, 1973; *The Joke* and *The Cafeteria*, from stories by Isaac Bashevis Singer, 1974; *Tea at Four*, 1975; *Buffet*, 1976.

ARDEN, John. See his dictionary entry.

BALL, F. C. Radio plays include *A Breath of Fresh Air*, 1964 (published, 1961); *A Grotto* *for Miss Maynier*, 1967 (published, 1965); *From Oblivion to Obscurity*, 1969. Books: *Tressell of Mugsborough*, 1951; *One of the Damned*, 1972.

BARKER, Howard.   See his dictionary entry.

BECKETT, Samuel.   See his dictionary entry.

BRADNUM, Frederick.   Radio plays include *No Commemorating Stone*, 1954; *The Pity of Love*, 1955; *No Going Home*, 1957; *Private Dreams and Public Nightmares*, 1957; *Chloroform for Mr. Bartlett*, 1957; *Mr. Goodjohn and Mr. Badjack*, 1958; *The Cave and the Grail*, 1959; *Hedgehog*, 1961; *The Fist*, 1963; *The Crack of Doom*, 1964; *Appearances Deceive*, 1964; *Rimbaud at Harar*, 1965; *Pennicotte's Truth*, 1966; *A Lonely Place in a Dark Wood*, 1967; *The Pallingham Depression*, 1969; *Goose with Pepper*, 1970; *Alive and Well and Living in London*, 1971; *A Terribly Strange Man*, 1971; *The Recruiter*, 1971; *A Putney Christmas*, 1971; *Enigmatic Conversations with Eminent Sociologists*, 1972; *You Are Not Alone in the House*, 1972; *The Final Solution*, 1973; *The Questionable Child*, from work by Terence Tiller, 1973; *The Young Lady from Midhurst*, 1974; *A Dead Man on Leave*, 1974; *Degas, Cellini, Ming*, 1975; *Who Am I Now?*, 1975; and many radio adaptations of plays and novels. Television play: *The Defector*, 1975. Stage plays: *In at the Kill*, 1963; *Minerva Alone*, 1963; *Liselotte*, from work by Duchesse d'Orleans, 1973. Book: *The Long Walks: Journeys to the Sources of the White Nile*, 1969.

CATOR, Peter.   Radio play: *The Search for Hamilton Stiggs*, 1974.

CHURCHILL, Caryl.   See her dictionary entry.

DOUGALL, Ian.   Radio plays: *The Immortal Young Ladies of Avignon*, 1970; *Extra-Terrestrial Objects*, 1974.

FLETCHER, John.   Radio plays include *Wandering in Eden*, 1974; *The View from the Mountain*, 1975. Television play: *Silence*, 1974.

GEE, Shirley.   Radio play: *Stones*, 1974.

GEORGE, John.   Radio plays: *Sad and True and Sealed for Ever*, 1969; *The Lady and the Saint*, 1970; *Cadwallader Rides Again*, 1972; *All the Prizes*, 1972; *Just Beyond the Bay*, 1974; *So Favourite a Son*, 1976.

HALLIWELL, David.   See his dictionary entry.

HARRISON, John.   Radio play: *Unaccompanied Cello*, 1971. Television plays: *Windmill near a Frontier*, 1959; *Any Number Can Play*, 1967. Stage plays: *Farewell Content*, 1948; *Sylvie and the Ghost* (for children), 1953; *Gone to Ground*, 1968.

HAWORTH, Don.   Radio plays include *The Man with the Red Door*, 1965; *There's No Point in Arguing the Toss*, 1966 (published, 1972); *We All Come to It in the End*, 1968 (published, 1972); *A Time in Cloud Cuckoo Land*, 1969; *The Prisoner*, 1969 (published, 1972); *Where Is This Here Building – By What Route Do I Get There?*, 1970 (published, 1972); *Simcocks Abound Across the Earth*, 1971; *The Illumination of Mr. Shannon*, 1971 (published, 1972; staged 1973); *The Enlightenment of the Strawberry Gardener*, 1972 (published, 1972; staged, 1974); *The Eventful Deaths of Mr. Fruin*, 1972; *A Damsel and Also a Rough Bird*, 1974; *Mr. Bruin Who Once Drove the Bus*, 1975; *Events at the Salamander Hotel*, 1975; *On a Day in Summer in a Garden*, 1975; *Memories of a Childhood Friendship*, 1976. Television plays: *Ein Haus Voll Zeit*, 1972 (Germany); *A Brisk Dip Sagaciously Considered*, 1974. Stage play: *A Hearts and Mind Job*, 1971 (published, 1971).

HILL, Susan.   Radio plays include *Miss Lavender Is Dead*, 1970; *Taking Leave*, 1971; *A Change for the Better*, 1971; *The End of Summer*, 1971 (published, 1975); *Lizard in the Grass*, 1971 (published, 1975); *The Cold Country*, 1972 (published, 1975); *White Elegy*, 1973; *Consider the Lilies*, 1973 (published, 1975); *A Window on the World*, 1974; *Strip Jack Naked*, 1974 (published, 1975); *The Summer of the Giant Sunflowers*, 1975. Her most recent novels are *The Bird of Night*, 1972, *In the Springtime of the Year*, 1974, and *The Land of Lost Content*, 1976; short stories: *A Bit of Singing and Dancing*, 1973.

JOSIPOVICI, Gabriel.   Radio plays: *Playback*, 1973; *Words*, 1973; *A Life*, 1973. Stage plays: *Dreams of Mrs. Frazer*, 1972; *Evidence of Intimacy*, 1972; *Flaws*, 1973; *Echo*, 1975.

LIVINGS, Henry.   See his dictionary entry.

MALLIN, Tom.   Radio plays: *Curtains*, 1971 (published, 1971); *Downpour*, 1972; *Rooms*, 1973; *Vicar Martin*, 1975; *The Lodger*, 1976. Stage plays: *As Is Proper*, 1971; *The Novelist*, 1971; *Cot*, in *Christmas Present*, 1971; *Mrs. Argent*, 1973. Novel: *Knut*, 1971.

MARTIN, Philip.   Radio plays: *Negatives*, 1972; *Lord Nelson Lives in Liverpool 8*, 1974. Television plays: *Gun Play*, 1971; *About a Bout*, 1973. Stage plays: *A Minor Operation*, 1969; *The Gunner's Daughter*, 1970; *Theatre of Death*, 1970; *Duel*, 1970; *The Deed*, 1971; *Window in the Roof of the Sky*, 1971; *One Long Hunt; or, How Would You Like It?*, 1972; *The Rapist*, 1973; *A Tide in the Affairs of Women*, 1975.

MORRISON, Bill.   Radio plays: *The Love of Lady Margaret*, 1972; *The Great Gun-Running Episode*, 1974; *Ellen Cassidy*, 1974; *Crime and Punishment*, from the novel by Dostoevsky, 1975; *The Emperor of Ice-Cream*, from the novel by Brian Moore, 1975 (staged, 1975); *Crow's Flight*, 1975; *The Game of Dice*, from play by Dimitri Kehaidis, 1975. Television play: *McKinley and Sarah*, 1973. Stage plays: *Sam Slade Is Missing*, 1969 (published, 1973); *Please Don't Shoot Me When I'm Down*, 1970; *Tess of the D'Urbervilles*, from the novel by Thomas Hardy, 1971; *Conn and the Conquerors of Space* (for children), 1971; *Flying Blind*, 1975.

OXMAN, Philip.   Radio play: *The Origins of Capital and the Descent of Power*, 1974.

PINTER, Harold.   See his dictionary entry.

RABAN, Jonathan.   Radio plays: *A Game of Tombola*, 1972; *At the Gate*, 1973; *The Anomaly*, 1974. Television plays: *Snooker*, 1975; *Water Baby*, 1975. Books: *Mark Twain's "Huckleberry Finn,"* 1968; *The Technique of Modern Fiction*, 1968; *The Society of the Poem*, 1971; editor, *Poems* by Robert Lowell, 1974.

RABY, Derek.   Radio plays: *The Office*, 1973; *Tiger*, 1974; *A Cat Called Willie*, 1974; *Bandstand*, 1975.

READ, Piers Paul.   Radio plays: *The Family Firm*, 1970; *The House on Highbury Hill*, music by Julian Slade, 1971. Television plays: *Coincidence*, 1968; *The Childhood Friend*, 1974. Stage play: *The Class War*, in *Colloquialisms*, 1964. His most recent novels are *The Professor's Daughter*, 1971, and *The Upstart*, 1973; also author of *Alive! The Story of the Andes Survivors*, 1974.

REED, Henry.   Radio plays: *Noises On*, 1947; *Noises – Nasty and Nice*, 1947; *Moby Dick*, from the novel by Melville, 1947 (published, 1947); *Pytheas*, 1947; *Leopardi: The Unblest, The Monument*, 1949–50 (published, 1971); *A By-Election in the Nineties*, 1951; *The Dynasts*, 1951; *Malatesta*, 1952; *The Streets of Pompeii*, 1952 (published, 1971); *The Great Desire I Had*, 1952 (published, 1971); *Return to Naples*, 1953 (published, 1971); *All for the Best*, 1953; *A Very Great Man Indeed*, 1953 (published, 1971); *The Private Life of Hilda Tablet*, 1954 (published, 1971); *Hamlet; or, The Consequences of Filial Piety*, 1954; *The Battle of the Masks*, 1954; *The Queen and the Rebels*, from a play by Ugo Betti, 1954 (staged, 1955; published, 1956); *Emily Butler*, 1954; *Vincenzo*, 1955 (published, 1971); *A Hedge, Backwards*, 1956 (published, 1971); *Don Juan in Love*, 1956; *Alarica*, 1956; *Irene*, 1957; *Corruption in the Palace of Justice*, from a play by Ugo Betti, 1958 (staged, 1963); *The Primal Scene, As It Were*, 1958 (published, 1971); *The Auction Sale*, 1958; *The Island Where the King Is a Child*, 1959; *One Flesh*, 1959; *Not a Drum Was Heard*, 1959; *Musique Discrète*, with Donald Swann, 1959; *The House on the Water*, 1961; *A Hospital Case*, 1961; *The America Prize*, 1964; *Zone 36*, 1965; *Summertime*, 1969; *The Two Mrs. Morlis*, 1971; *Like* *the Leaves*, from play by Giuseppe Giacosa, 1976. Stage adaptations: *The Burnt Flower-Bed*, from a play by Ugo Betti, 1955 (published, 1956); *Summertime*, from a play by Ugo Betti, 1955 (published, 1956); *Island of Goats*, from a play by Ugo Betti, 1955 (published as *Crime on Goat Island*, 1960); *The Advertisement*, from a play by Natalia Ginzburg, 1968 (published, 1969). Other books: *A Map of Verona*, 1946, and *Lessons of the War*, 1970, both verse, and *The Novel since 1939*, 1947.

RUDKIN, David.   See his dictionary entry.

SADLER, Michael.   Radio plays: *Gulliver's Way*, 1970; *The Bull of La Plata*, 1970; *Hopcraft into Europe*, 1972; *South Coast Twilight Serenade*, 1975. Television plays: *Mrs. Pool's Preserves*, 1973; *Pigeon-Hawk or Dove?*, 1974; *Cork and Bottle*, 1976. Stage play: *And Was Jerusalem*, 1967.

SAUNDERS, James.   See his dictionary entry.

SCRIVEN, R. C.   Radio plays: *The Peacock City of P'Tzan King*, 1947; *A Single Taper*, 1948 (published, 1953); *The Inward Eye: Boy – 13*, 1948 (published, 1953); *The Island of White Birds*, 1948; *Baron Bear and the Little Prince*, with Phyllis Scriven, 1949; *Little Jan Pandrum*, with Phyllis Scriven, 1950; *Vi'lets Sweet Vi'lets*, with Phyllis Scriven, 1950; *The Snow Queen*, with Phyllis Scriven, 1950; *Poet and Englishman*, 1950; *One Man's City: Leeds*, 1951; *The Runaway Rocking Horse*, with Phyllis Scriven, 1952; *Bluecap and the Singing Wheel*, with Phyllis Scriven, 1953; *Joy of Angels*, 1954; *The Night and the Shadow*, 1955; *The Year of the Phoenix*, 1955 (published, 1959); *The Lamp and the Flame*, 1956; *Writing a Pantomime – The Babes in the Wood*, 1961; *Reynard the Fox*, 1965; *The Blue Cloak*, 1966; *Jack and the Beanstalk*, 1968; *The Prospect of Whitby*, 1968 (published, 1971); *Fiddler's Green*, 1968; *The Seasons of the Blind*, 1968 (published, 1974); *The Poltergoose*, 1969 (published, 1973); *All Early in the April*, 1970 (published, 1974); *The Peacock Screamed One Morning*, 1970 (published, 1974); *Dandelion and Parsnip, Vintage 1920*, 1971 (published, 1974); *The House of Houses*, 1971; *Summer with Flowers That Fell*, 1972 (published, 1974); *Give Me London Weather*, 1974; *A Measure of Sliding Sand*, 1974; *Nocturne of a Provincial Spring*, 1975. Other books: *The Year of the Phoenix and Other Poems*, 1959; *The Thingummy Jig*, 1973; *The Fairy Tale Cook Book*, 1974.

SIMPSON, N. F.   See his dictionary entry.

STOPPARD, Tom.   See his dictionary entry.

TAYLOR, Don.   Radio plays: *At Nunappleton House*, 1971; *Rudkin's Dream*, 1973. Television plays: *Prisoners*, 1971; *The Excursion*, 1972; *Actor I Said*, 1972; *The Exorcism*, 1972; *The Agreement of the People*, 1975. Stage plays: *Grounds for Marriage*, 1967; *The Roses of Eyam*, 1972; *Out on the Lawn*, 1975; *Dad*, 1976.

TERSON, Peter.   See his dictionary entry.

THOMAS, Gwyn.   See his dictionary entry.

TREVOR, William.   See his dictionary entry.

WELDON, Fay.   See her entry in Television Writers section.

TELEVISION
WRITERS

To the dramatist television presents a bewildering array of contradictions. It offers an enormous audience and at the same time a tiny audience, of one or two or three people. His play can be watched with an absorption beyond anything dreamed of in the theatre or cinema; equally it may have to contend with the telephone ringing, a child crying, someone coming late for supper or a clamour for football on the other channel. Television can bring him quick renown but apparent oblivion for his handiwork, expended in a night. It may reward him well but if he can turn out umpteen episodes of some thick-ear crime serial it will probably reward him much better.

In some respects the géneral classification "fiction" is more accurate than "drama." Television has taken over from the cinema, radio, lending libraries and magazines the task of supplying the majority of people with the commodity they have hungered for since the days of the Saxon story-tellers. In almost every television system in the world fiction accounts for the bulk of programming, especially during peak hours when the audience is greatest. In Britain the five-hour period between seven and midnight will usually accommodate about three hours of fiction on the commercial channel, perhaps a little less on the BBC channels. That it ranges from the feeble daily doings of a serial like *Crossroads* – the equivalent of leaving the drama tap dribbling – via an assortment of retired feature films to, say, a new play by John Osborne is one of the inconsistencies and also, I would suggest, one of the joys. The context in which a play takes place is bound to affect it. If it follows some enormously popular comedy show it may inherit millions who might not normally have switched over. If it follows some vivid actuality from Ulster or Angola it has to run the risk of seeming artificial by contrast.

It would be a mistake to discount all the mass-produced series and serials which swell the flood of television fiction on both sides of the Atlantic. The philosophy behind them is frankly commercial – it is clearly easier to guarantee audiences and sell advertising time over a future period with stories about known characters in established, not to say predictable, situations. It is only too evident that nearly all series, and especially infinite serials like *Coronation Street*, go on too long, so that any original flavour becomes stale, the characters are increasingly indulged and whatever sociological novelty there may have been is lost. Yet it is also clear that the series can attain standards of writing and performance as high as anything on television, and accommodate themes as important; indeed, since it reaches an audience which might fight shy of a more overt declaration of the subject matter it is arguably of greater value. Proclaim a play to be about care of the aged or conservation of natural resources and it will produce anticipatory yawns, not without some justification; slip it into *Doomwatch* or transpose it for *Star Trek* and the message infiltrates home.

At its best, as T. C. Worsley has tirelessly argued, the series is in fact an elongated play, taking advantage of the weekly pattern, and the week-to-week anticipation which can build up, to tell a fuller story than would otherwise be possible, to explore character in more directions and pursue a greater number of subsidiary plots. *A Family at War* was – or should have been – a play by John Finch on a Tolstoyan scale, a forty-hour chronicle of the experiences of one English family between 1938 and 1945. Where it failed was where it departed from this ideal: because one man couldn't write it all in the time available, other hands had to be brought in, with inevitable inconsistencies and duplications – no less than four episodes turned on mine warfare and/or booby traps. When the same author embarked on *Sam*, a further marathon concerned ultimately with social changes brought about by the war, he allowed himself time to write it single-handedly. The result was much more personal, if rather stretched.

From the creative point of view the single or "one-off" play remains the purest and most prestigious form of television drama. This is where reputations are made, frontiers advanced and new idioms tried out (though in the matter of actual techniques the series has been just as much to the forefront, *Z Cars* having developed for instance the elliptical narrative style which is commonplace today). Here, in theory, the writer's lone voice is least subject to the predications of producer and story-editor. In practice, unfortunately, the single play has declined in both influence and quantity. At the time of writing the three British channels carry an average of three plays a week, often fewer, compared with six on two channels at the height of the television play craze in 1961; and of the three it is likely that at least one will have had to conform to some loopy generic title like *Trapped* or *Love Story* or *What Would You Do?*

It may well be that over-production in earlier days caused the slide: there simply wasn't enough talent and originality around to maintain the supply. Moreover there was a tradition dating from the short-lived golden era of television drama in the United States that the television play should concern itself only with the mundane, the ordinary, the untheatrical. It yielded famous results in the hands of Paddy Chayefsky, Tad Mosel and Horton Foote but the very ordinariness is said to have contributed to the virtual disappearance of the play from American television within a few years. Here it resulted, as J. B. Priestley once grumbled, in an endless succession of anecdotes about Fred losing his job or Bill his girl.

Looking back, how grateful one was for the exercises of the imagination demonstrated by Nigel Kneale or that most original and inventive of all television writers, the late Giles Cooper. Today it is still depressing to note how much television drama is content to remain within the traditional confines. The commonest arena is still the living room (with the bedroom a close second), the commonest subject marriage – especially the middle-distance, middle-class marriage of the kind of people most conveniently to hand for a writer flogging away at his fourth script of the year: in other words, writers or journalists or television executives or advertising men. There is a reluctance, admittedly reinforced by the economics of television production which encourage the use of small casts in compact settings, to venture beyond a simple domestic parable. The language may be ten times franker, the attitudes brightly up to date, the narrative clicking sophisticatedly between past and present tenses, or between the story as seen by one participant and as seen by another, but in essence the television play by such admired authors as Fay Weldon, Alun Owen or Donald Churchill is the equivalent of the mild domestic dramas, 3m, 3f, one set, which circulated thirty years ago in Messrs. French's acting editions.

If an isolated packet of drama is to stand out from the great flood it must surely have particularity before anything else. To be fair, Donald Churchill often achieves this by being very funny, which is rare in television drama, and Mrs. Weldon by being sharp, and Alun Owen by the exactness of his characterisation, but one is more grateful than ever for some freshness of subject matter. John Bowen took the kind of old pagan rite than might just linger on in a rural community and spun from it a wonderfully chilling anthropological thriller, *Robin Redbreast*. John Osborne turned the familiar schooldays play upside down for the dream-like *The Right Prospectus* in which it was unblinkingly accepted by all concerned, including the audience, that a married couple in middle years should enrol at a boys' public school. Colin Welland charted a day in the routine of a northern secondary school with the opposite degree of unwavering realism for *Roll On Four O'Clock*. It was Welland who also rediscovered the dramatic potential of sports and pastimes with *Bangelstein's Boys*, about a Rugby team, and paved the way for Arthur Hopcraft's *The Mosedale Horseshoe* (fell walking), *The Panel* (bowling) and *The Birthday Run* (cycling), Jack Rosenthal's *Another Sunday and Sweet F. A.* (trials of an embattled Sunday morning soccer referee), and eventually his own full series about a rugby club, *The Wild West Show*. Robert Holles and Charles Wood drew on their experience in the ranks of the regular army for plays like *The Discharge of Trooper Lusby* and *Death or Glory Boy*. Brian Clark made a powerful debut with *Whose Life Is It, Anyway?*, a plea for cabbage-like existence to be terminated if the victim so chose. Another gifted newcomer, Peter McDougall, won the Italia Prize for the BBC in 1975 with *Just Another Saturday*, about a young Glasgow Orangeman suffering a change of heart as he twirls his mace through the streets at the head of a march.

If there is one word to convey what I mean it is "aboutness" – what the play is about and how the author goes about its presentation. Arthur Barron's *Orville and Wilbur* and Hans Gottschalk's *The Assassin* which the BBC bought from National Education Television (USA) and Bavarian Television respectively, were of immediate interest because the Wright brothers and Georg Elser, who tried to kill Hitler in 1939, were fascinating historical figures who had never previously been portrayed on TV, though without Fritz Hollenback's stumpy, bristle-headed impersonation or the painstaking detail with which Gottschalk and the director,

Rainer Erler, reconstructed Elser's plot the latter wouldn't have sustained interest, just as *Orville and Wilbur* owed much to the performances of Stacy and James Keach and some superb flying sequences by Jack Lambie. Dennis Potter enshrined the subject of death quaintly but movingly in a pet-shop for *Joe's Ark*. The shifting tensions of class distinction underlay several plays of the 1970's, but it was the writer who could frame them in an effective dramatic metaphor who best made his point: Brian Clark again, with *The Saturday Party*, and Peter Nichols, whose haves and have-nots in *The Common* were separated by the very piece of land that both were supposed to enjoy. With Michael Frayn, Willis Hall and Donald Churchill, Nichols is incidentally one of the handful of dramatists who have shown that it is possible – even in the absence of the shared enjoyment and infectious laughter of a cinema or theatre house – to achieve very funny comedy on television.

As I said earlier, the context in which a play reaches the screen is important to it. Despite some dull patches at one extreme and some periods, at the other, when it strove too consciously to be shocking, the BBC's Play for Today – previously Wednesday Play – is simply the premier drama outlet. Anything under its umbrella is likely to be watched more attentively and discussed more heatedly. If it's the work of a new writer it will gain in stature by the company it keeps. Nothing on the commercial network has comparable standing; the regular outlets are turned over to series or thematic anthologies, with single plays bobbing up only intermittently. BBC2 offers the only avowed opportunity for new writers and experimental work, unfortunately without justifying much clamour for either.

Bound up with any consideration of context is the physical means of production, which itself is bound up with things like budgets and resources. The great innovation of the past few years is the wholly filmed play, as heralded in the mid-sixties by *Up the Junction* and advanced by the progressive (in both senses) writers and directors associated with the independent Kestrel group. Film permits freely ranging stories, "actual" backgrounds and sharper editing. But it's more expensive than videotape, the emphasis begins to shift from words to pictures and, as in the cinema, the director shapes the final product as much as the author. *Mad Jack*, about Siegfried Sassoon's ineffectual anti-war protest, and *Stocker's Copper*, a china-clay workers' strike in 1913, are identified with Jack Gold and only in the next breath with Tom Clarke, who wrote them.

Other threats to a writers' theatre include the BBC's institution of the Play of the Month, which diverts a substantial part of the drama budget towards the exercise of old war horses from the classic repertory for the benefit of favourite actors; a periodic craze for documentary drama or dramatised documentaries; and a growing interest in co-production with television systems abroad, which has economic advantages but curiously only within a lavish context, e.g., some dreadful epic with a supposedly international cast and a part somewhere for Richard Burton.

Can the lone voice survive? If it does, how can it make itself heard above the rising clamour of the series and serials? How can one isolated hour or so compete for attention with something which is going to be there week after week? It's an easy answer, but the only one, to say that every single play should strive to be an event, every season of plays a season of events, and that the word "routine" applied to drama should be a very dirty word indeed. Meanwhile a specific recourse which is beginning to appeal to a number of writers is the short (six or seven part) series which offers all the advantages of T. C. Worsley's "long-play" – including a build-up in renown and audience-expectation over the weeks – while remaining comfortably within the compass of one author.

The most famous (or infamous) venture in this field lately has been *Days of Hope*, which is a rather special case. Not only was Jim Allen's interpretation of Socialist history between 1916 and 1926 challenged, but the four episodes were deliberately classed as films rather than plays, and identified with Ken Loach (director) and Tony Garnett (producer) as much as with Allen. A better example is Arthur Hopcraft's *The Nearly Man*, a seven-part sage of an embattled Labour M.P. developed from a single play of the same title. Perhaps the most versatile demonstration of the possibilities has come from Philip Mackie, first with *The Caesars*, recently with *Good Girl*, and in between with *The Organisation*, an elegant and witty satire about the public relations department of a large company in which two characters came to the forefront each episode while the grand design continued in the background. The acknowledged masterpiece, admittedly extended over only four episodes but in total playing time on the same scale, remains John Hopkins' *Talking to a Stranger*, first transmitted in 1966. Hopkins took a suburban family and pored over the events of one fateful weekend, as seen by each member of it in turn. As lines of dialogue recurred and recurred, but taking on a fresh significance each time, as the veils of pretence were systematically stripped away, as the terrible climax approached again, television was accomplishing something uniquely its own, something which has no equivalent in any other branch of drama.

—Philip Purser

* * *

ALLEN, Jim. Television plays include *The Lump*, 1966; *The Man Beneath*, 1967; *The Pub Fighter*, 1968; *The Big Flame*, 1969; *The Talking Head*, 1969; *Rank and File*, 1971; *Walt King of the Dumper*, 1971; *Punchy and the Fairy*, 1973; *In the Heel of the Hunt*, 1973; *Days of Hope*, 1975; *The Hard Word*, 1975; *The Extremist*, 1975, and *Tell the Truth and Shame the Devil*, 1976 (*Crown Court* series); *Willie's Last Stand*, 1976. Book: *Days of Hope*, 1975.

BARRON, Arthur. Television play: *Orville and Wilbur*, 1972.

BOWEN, John. See his dictionary entry.

CHAYEFSKY, Paddy. See his dictionary entry.

CHURCHILL, Donald. Television plays include *Always Something Hot*, 1962; *Sharp at Four*, 1964; *The Cherry on the Top*, 1964; *The Hothouse*, 1964; *The Paraffin Season*, 1965; *The Man Without a Mortgage*, 1966; *Comrades in Arms*, 1966; *The Happy Sacking*, 1967; *Floating Population*, 1967; *A Second Look*, 1968; *Never a Cross Word*, 1968; *Return Match*, 1968; *Room in Town*, 1970; *The Loving Lesson*, 1971; *You Don't Know Me But...*, 1972; *A Fluid Arrangement*, 1972; *The Leftovers*, 1972; *Feeling the Pinch*, 1973; *Harriet's Back in Town*, 1973; *A Bit of a Lift*, 1974; *A Girl's Best Friend*, 1974; *Moody and Peg* series, with Julia Jones, 1974, 1975; *Feeling His Way*, 1975; *The Five Pound Orange*, 1975; *Pie in the Sky*, 1975; *Distant Islands*, with Julia Jones, 1975; *Ron*, 1975; *Our Mutual Friend*, with Julia Jones, from the novel by Dickens, 1976. Radio plays: *The Expenses*, 1967; *The Party Piece*, 1969; *Lines from My Grandfather's Forehead*, with others. Stage plays: *Gestures; A Woman on Friday; Performing Husband*, 1972; *A Far Better Husband*, with Peter Yeldham, 1975; *Fringe Benefits*, with Peter Yeldham, 1976.

CLARK, Brian. Television plays: *The Torrey Canyon*, 1972; *Play in a Manger*, 1972; *Whose Life Is It, Anyway?*, 1972; *Operation Magic Carpet*, 1973; *Achilles Heel*, 1973; *Easy Go*, 1974; *A Follower for Emily*, 1974; *The Saturday Party*, 1975; *Parole*, 1975; *The Eleventh Hour*, with others, 1975; *An Evil Influence*, 1975; *Post Mortem*, 1975 (staged, 1975); *Or Was He Pushed*, 1976. Stage plays: *Truth or Dare?*, 1972; *Campion's Interview*, 1976.

CLARKE, Tom. Television plays include *The Escape of RD.7*, 1961; *A Matter of Conscience*, from a work by Tolstoy, 1962; *A Little Temptation*, 1965 (published 1966); *Don't Go Down The Bingo, Mother, Father's Home to Tea*, 1966; *A Brilliant Future Behind Him*, 1967; *Haven't You People Got Homes*, 1967; *Mad Jack*, 1970 *The Moonlighers*, 1971; *A Settled Sort of Life*, 1971; *Stocker's Copper*, 1972 (published in *The Television Play*, 1976); *Feet Together, Hands to the Sides*, 1973.

EXTON, Clive. Television plays: *No Fixed Abode*, 1959; *The Silk Purse*, 1959; *Kipps* series, 1960; *Where I Live*, 1960; *Some Talk ; The Big Eat*, 1962; *The Trial of Doctor Fancy*, 1963; *The Land of My Dreams*, 1964; *The Close Prisoner*, 1964; *The Boneyard*, 1966; *Are You Ready for the Music?*, 1966; *The Dream of Timothy Evans*, 1970; *Mother and Child*, 1970; *Conversation Piece*, 1970; *The Rainbirds*, 1971; *Legacies* (3 plays), 1973; *The Boundary*, with Tom Stoppard, 1975; *Breakthrough*, from story by Daphne du Maurier,

1975; *When Greek Meets Greek* and *The Root of All Evil*, 1975, and *A Chance for Mr. Lever* and *The Overnight Bag*, 1976, from stories by Graham Greene; *The Killers* series, 1976. *The Creez* series, 1976. Stage play: *Have You Any Dirty Washing, Mother Dear?*, 1969 (published, 1970). Screenplays: *Night Must Fall*, 1963; *Isadora*, with Melvyn Bragg, 1968; *Entertaining Mr. Sloane*, 1969; *Ten Rillington Place*, 1970; *Doomwatch*, 1971; *Running Scared*, with David Hemmings, 1971; *Nightmare Park*, with Terry Nation, 1973.

FINCH, John. Television plays include *Dark Pastures*, 1963; *The Villains* series, 1964; *The Old Man of Chelsea Reach*, 1965; *Brothers*, 1966; *Wanted*, 1967; *Victims*, 1968; *The Visitors*, 1968; *Them Down There*, 1968; *It's Dearer after Midnight*, 1968; *The House That Jigger Built*, 1968; *A Family at War* series, 1970; *Sam* series, 1973; *Spivvy*, 1975. Stage play: *Brigade*, 1976.

FOOTE, Horton. Television plays include *A Young Lady of Property, The Dancers, The Old Beginning, John Turner Davis, The Death of the Old Man, The Oil Well, Tears of My Sister, Midnight Caller, Old Man, Tomorrow, Roots in a Parched Ground, Flight*. Collected television plays: *Harrison, Texas*, 1956. Stage plays: *The Chase*, 1952 (published, 1952); *The Trip to Bountiful*, 1953 (published, 1954); *The Traveling Lady*, 1954 (published, 1955); *Gone with the Wind*, music by Harold Rome, from the novel by Margaret Mitchell, 1972. Screenplays: *To Kill a Mocking Bird*, 1963; *Baby the Rain Must Fall*, 1965; *Hurry Sundown*, 1967; *Tomorrow*, 1973.

FRAYN, Michael. See his dictionary entry.

GREATOREX, Wilfred. Television plays include *The Power Game* series, 1965; *The Curtis Affair*, 1968; *The Eleventh Commandment*, 1970; *Dying Gets You Nowhere*, 1970; *Hine* series, 1971; *Night of the Tanks*, 1972; *Man from Haven* series, 1972; *The Inheritors*, 1974; *Did Machiavelli Have Welch Blood*, 1974. Screenplays: *Nobody Runs Forever (The High Commissioner)*, 1968; *Battle of Britain* 1969.

HOLLES, Robert. Television plays include *The Mating Age*, 1961; *Behind the Line*, 1962; *June Fall*, 1963; *Andersen*, 1963; *The Wedding of Smith Seven-Nine*, 1963; *Across the Border*, 1964; *The Big Toe*, 1964; *The Apprentices*, 1964; *The Taming of Trooper Tanner*, 1965; *The Reluctant Witness*, 1966; *Conduct to the Prejudice*, 1966; *The Hunting of Aubrey Hopkiss*, 1966; *The Education of Corporal Holliday*, 1967; *First of the Nightingales*, 1967; *The Wind in a Tall Paper Chimney*, 1968; *Natural Justice*, 1968; *Night of Talavera*, 1968; *The Discharge of Trooper Lusby*, 1969; *There's Always a First Time*, 1970; *Brown Skin Gal Stay Home*, 1971; *Michael Regan*, 1971; *Old Comrades*, 1972; *The Birdwatcher*, 1972; *Bye Bye Mrs. Bly*, 1972; *The Breaking of Colonel Keyser*, 1972; *The Sterile Weapons*, 1973; *Death of Glory*, 1973; *A Little Local Knowledge*, 1973; *Comrades in Arms*, 1973; *Cherryripe and the Lugworm Digger*, 1974. Stage play: *The Siege of Battersea*, 1962. Screenplay: *Guns at Batasi*, 1964. His most recent novels are *Religion and Davey Peach*, 1962, and *The Nature of the Beast*, 1965.

HOPCRAFT, Arthur. Television plays include *The Mosedale Horseshoe*, 1971; *The Panel*, 1971; *The Birthday Run*, 1971; *The Reporters*, 1972; *Said the Preacher*, 1972; *Buggins' Ermine*, 1972; *Katapult*, 1973; *Humbug, Finger or Thumb?*, 1973; *Jingle Bells*, 1973; *Baa Baa Blacksheep*, from a story by Rudyard Kipling, 1974; *The Nearly Man*, 1974, and series, 1975; *Nightingale's Boys* series (2 episodes), 1975; *A Journey to London*, completion of the play by John Vanbrugh, 1975; *Wednesday Love*, 1975; *Hard Times*, from the novel by Dickens, 1976. Books: *Born to Hunger*, 1968; *The Football Man*, 1968; *The Great Apple Raid*, 1970.

JONES, Julia. Television plays include *The Navigators*, 1965; *Common Ground*, 1965; *The Spoken Word*, 1965; *A Designing Woman*, 1966; *Up and Down*, 1966; *Trapped*, 1966; *First Catch Your Hare*, 1966; *Two's Company*, 1966, and *As You Were*, 1973 (*Love Story* series); *Tickle Times*, 1967; *Love with a Few Hairs*, from the novel by Mohammed Mrabet translated by Paul Bowles, 1967; *Give and Take*, 1967; *A Bit of a Crucifixion Father*, 1968;

Penny Wise, 1968; *The Piano Tuner*, 1969; *Faith and Henry*, 1969; *Devon Violets, Heart's Ease, Sweet Basil,* and *Roses round the Door* (*Take Three Girls* series), 1970; *The Piano*, 1971; *Home and Away* (7 plays), 1972; *Still Waters*, 1972; *Anne of Green Gables* (serialization), from the novel by L. M. Montgomery, 1972; *The Stretch*, 1973; *This Quiet Half Hour*, 1973; *Hearty Crafty*, 1974; *Back of Beyond*, 1974; *Moody and Peg* series, with Donald Churchill, 1974, 1975; *Shouts and Murmurs* (*Churchill's People* series), 1975; *A Free Woman* (*Within These Walls* series), 1975; *Old Fogey*, 1975; *Nuts and Bolts*, 1975; *Our Mutual Friend* (serialization), with Donald Churchill, from the novel by Dickens, 1976. Radio plays: *The H'arrogance of Youth*, 1965; *Honey and Bread* and *A Time to Laugh*, from stories by Rhys Davies, 1969; *The Piano Tuner*, 1970; *Hobble de Hoys*, 1973; *The Day of the Tortoise*, 1973. Stage plays: *Sleeping Partners*, 1967; *Had We Never Loved So Kindly*, 1969; *The Garden*, 1972; *A Few Kind Words* (*Dear Winnie*), 1973.

KNEALE, Nigel.   Television plays include *Mrs. Wickers in the Fall*, 1957 (published, 1971); the *Quatermass Plays* (*The Quatermass Experiment, Quatermass II, Quatermass and the Pit*) (published 1959–60); *The Road*, 1963 (published, 1976); *The Crunch*, 1964; *1984*, from the novel by George Orwell, 1965; *The Year of the Sex Olympics*, 1969 (published, 1976); *Bam Pow Zapp*, 1969; *Wine of India*, 1970; *The Chopper*, 1971; *The Stone Tape*, 1972 (published, 1976); *Back of Beyond*, 1974; *Jack and the Beanstalk*, 1974; *Murrain*, 1975. Screenplays: *Quatermass II* (*Enemies From Space*), 1957; *H.M.S. Defiant* (*Damn the Defiant*), 1962; *First Men IN the Moon*, 1964; *The Witches* (*The Devils Own*), 1966; *Quatermass and the Pit* (*Five Million Years to Earth*), 1967; *The Plumed Serpent*, 1973. Short Stories: *Tomato Cain*, 1961.

MACKIE, Philip.   Television plays include *The Hole in the Wall*, 1955; *Drink Doggie Drink*, 1956; *A Death in the Family*, 1956; *The Girl at the Next Table*, 1957; *The Money*, 1961; *Paris 1900* (6 plays), 1965; *The Liars* series, with Hugh Leonard, 1966; *Mr. Rose* series, 1967; *The Caesars* (6 plays), 1968; *The Rivals of Sherlock Holmes* series (5 plays), 1970; *A Marriage*, 1971; *The Organisation* (7 plays), 1971 (published, 1974; stage version, as *The Chairman*, 1975); *Conjugal Rights* (trilogy), 1972; *Dolly* (3 plays), 1973; *The Middle-of-the-Road Show*, 1973; *Napoleon and Love* (9 plays), 1974 (published, 1974); *Good Girl* (6 plays), 1974; *Raffles*, from the novel by E. W. Hornung, 1975; *Cheap in August*, 1975, and *A Drive in the Counntry*, 1976, from stories by Graham Greene; *The Naked Civil Servant*, from the book by Quentin Crisp, 1975. Stage plays: *The Right Person*, 1954 (published, 1955); *The Whole Truth*, 1955 (published, 1956); *Open House*, 1957 (published, 1958); *The Key of the Door*, 1958 (published, 1959); *The Big Killing*, 1962 (published, 1962); *Maigret and the Lady*, 1965. Screenplays: *Clue of the Twisted Candle*, 1960, *The Share Out*, 1962, *Vengence* (*The Brain*), 1963; *The £20,000 Kiss*, 1963. *All the Way Up*, 1970. Books: *Hurrah! The Flag*, 1957; *All the Way Up*, 1970

McDOUGALL, Peter.   Television plays: *Just Another Saturday*, 1975; *The Elephants' Graveyard*, 1976; *A Wily Couple*, 1976.

MOSEL, Tad.   See his dictionary entry.

NICHOLS, Peter.   See his dictionary entry.

OSBORNE, John.   See his dictionary entry.

OWEN, Alun.   See his dictionary entry.

POTTER, Dennis.   See his dictionary entry.

ROSENTHAL, Jack.   Television plays include *Green Rub*, 1963; *Pie in the Sky*, 1963; *The Night Before the Morning After*, 1966; *Compensation Alice*, 1967; *There's a Hole in Your Dustbin, Delilah*, 1968; *The Dustbinmen* series, 1969; *Your Name's Not God, It's Edgar*, 1969; *The Lovers* series, 1971; *Another Sunday and Sweet F.A.*, 1972; *And for My Next Trick*, 1973; *Hot Fat*, 1974; *Polly Put the Kettle On*, 1974; *Mr. Ellis Versus the People*, 1974; *There'll Almost Always Be an England*, 1974; *Sadie, It's Cold Outside* series, 1975; *Big Sid*,

1975; *The Evacuees,* 1975 (published in *The Television Play,* 1976); *Ready When You Are, Mr. McGill* and *Well, Thank You, Thursday* (*Red Letter Day* series), 1976. Screenplay: *The Lovers,* 1973.

WELDON, Fay.   Television plays include *Wife in a Blonde Wig,* 1966; *What about Me,* 1967; *Dr. De Waldon's Therapy,* 1967; *Goodnight Mrs. Dill,* 1967; *The 45th Unmarried Mother,* 1967; *Fall of the Goat,* 1967; *Ruined Houses,* 1968; *Venus Rising,* 1968; *The Three Wives of Felix Hull,* 1968; *Hippy Hippy Who Cares,* 1968; *£13083,* 1968; *The Loophole,* 1969; *Who Cares,* 1969; *Poor Mother,* 1970; *Office Party,* 1971; *On Trial* (*Upstairs, Downstairs* series), 1971; *Old Man's Hat,* 1972; *A Splinter of Ice,* 1972; *Hands,* 1972; *The Lament of an Unmarried Father,* 1972; *A Nice Rest,* 1972; *Comfortable Words,* 1973; *Desirous of Change,* 1973; *In Memoriam,* 1974; *Poor Baby,* 1975; *Poor Mother,* 1975; *The Tale of Timothy Bagshott,* 1975; *Aunt Tatty,* from the story by Elizabeth Bowen, 1975. Radio plays: *Spider,* 1972; *Mr. Fox and Mr. First,* 1974; *The Doctor's Wife,* 1975. Stage plays: *The Fat Woman's Joke,* 1967 (US title: *And the Wife Ran Away,* 1968); *Permanence,* in *Mixed Doubles,* 1970; *Words of Advice,* 1974 (published, 1975); *Friends,* 1975; *Moving House,* 1976; *Second Chance,* in *Bundles of Joy,* 1976. Novels: *Down among the Women,* 1973; *Female Friends,* 1974; *Remember Me,* 1976.

WELLAND, Colin.   Television plays include *Bangelstein's Boys,* 1968; *Slattery's Mounted Foot,* 1970; *Say Goodnight to Your Grandma,* 1970 (as *Say Goodnight to Grandma,* staged, 1971; published, 1973); *Catherine Wheel,* 1970; *Roll On Four O'Clock,* 1970; *The Hallelujah Handshake,* 1970; *A Roomful of Holes,* 1971; *Kisses at Fifty,* 1973 (published in *The Television Play,* 1976); *Jack Point,* 1973; *Leeds − United!,*1974; *The Wild West Show* series, 1975. Stage, television, and film actor.

MUSICAL
LIBRETTISTS

Gilbert and Sullivan notwithstanding, the librettist (the book writer, as he is still called outside histories of musical comedy) seldom gets equal billing with the composer. There are contemporary instances of shared eminence (Rodgers and Hammerstein), some of which, as in the case of Gilbert and Sullivan, put the librettist first — Lerner and Loewe. I suspecct that euphony, as much as a judicious consideration of importance, decides the order in this last example; in any case, where the librettist is considered half a famous team, he is always the lyricist as well, and it is that function that elevates him to an equal position with the composer. It is, after all, the music, the songs, by which musical comedies are known, celebrated, remembered. That does not mean that the book is unimportant, but that it is the librettist's job to provide the skeleton for the show and, then, to get out of the way and let the musical numbers do their work. As the musical has become more serious in its dramatic intentions, particularly since World War II, it has tried to introduce believable characters in recognizable milieus and — following the conventional drama of the period — to provide psychological studies, social commentary, satiric significance. Although the new seriousness of the musical has attracted many writers with a reputation in drama and in fiction, the librettist, unlike the playwright, must forego the most telling lines and the best scenes because, in a good musical, the songs do the exposition, provide the characterization, embody the conflict. For instance, "Rose's Turn," the musical number that brings *Gypsy* to a close, is a moment of revelation as dramatically important as the one in Arthur Laurent's *Home of the Brave* in which the paralyzed veteran is forced to walk. Yet, Laurents, as librettist, had to step back and let Jule Styne and Stephen Sondheim, as composer and lyricist, do the scene. The total effect of *Gypsy*, however — and it is one of the best American musicals — depends on a carefully conceived book which provides the occasion for the songs that define Rose, one of the most fully realized characters in musical comedy.

Librettos were not always so impressive. In the good old days, they were little more than excuses for a collection of vaguely related songs, although they did provide occasional farce bits for comics who worked in words instead of music. The movement toward a coherent libretto — hence, an integrated musical — began early, and the impulse toward, as well as the backsliding from, coherence can be found in the work which Guy Bolton did with P. G. Wodehouse. Although Jerome Kern's *Leave It to Jane* (1917) and George Gershwin's *Oh, Kay!* (1926) are not the most successful shows that Wodehouse and Bolton wrote, they have both been revived in recent years, a fact that suggests that they have a continuing vitality. The first is one of the earliest shows set on a college campus — a setting that continues to haunt the musical — in which the manipulations of the titular Jane provide a recognizable plot line; but the second, an exercise in lack of logic involving a notorious ladies' man and a cache of bootleg whiskey, seems to have been designed to show off its star (Gertrude Lawrence) and to make room for good irrelevant Gershwin tunes.

During the 1930's the musical turned political. Although *Johnny Johnson*, the Kurt Weill show that the Group Theatre produced in 1936, was not a success at the time, it can be seen now as a good example both of the political attitudes of the decade and of the influence of the German musical theatre from which Weill had come. It was, however, a mixture of styles because the librettist, Paul Green, was an established American playwright who used indigenous materials to create a pacifist fable with the sainted fool as central figure. The importance of the book (some would say that it weighs down the score) can be seen in the fact that it was published — and still is — as a Paul Green play. In 1936, it was still unusual for a playwright of Green's reputation to turn to the musical, but since then a great many serious dramatists have become librettists. Lillian Hellman and Arthur Laurents have been most successful artistically. The Hellman book for *Candide* (1956) not only sets up the situations which allow the musical numbers to work satirically, but it contributes dramatic juxtapositions and occasional strong lines that strengthen the effect of the satire. Despite the obvious quality of Hellman's work, some admirers of the musical blamed her book for the commercial failure of the show, and Harold Prince, when he revived — recreated rather — *Candide* in 1973, turned to another playwright, Hugh Wheeler, for a new libretto. Wheeler had already used Ingmar Bergman's film *Smiles of a Summer Night* as the basis for *A Little Night Music* (1973), one of the most innovative musicals of recent years, and had helped

Joseph Stein piece together a nostalgic pastiche on the 1919 musical *Irene* (1973). Although Laurents has sometimes come a cropper as a librettist – the over-elaborate *Anyone Can Whistle* (1964) – with *Gypsy* (1959) and with *West Side Story* (1957), in which he uses *Romeo and Juliet* as a jumping-off place for his own romantic story of lovers beset by the conventions and prejudices of their society, he has written two musical books that are more effective dramatically than any of his straight plays.

A playwright of a different kind but of equal eminence in her own genre is Bella Spewack, who with her husband Sam wrote the book for Cole Porter's *Leave It to Me!* (1938), a more light-hearted satire than *Johnny Johnson*. For the show, the Spewacks, leading American farceurs, turned out a libretto which, at least in setting (a slapstick Soviet Russia), suggests their earlier farce, *Clear All Wires*. Their best-known libretto, however, is the one for the postwar Porter show, *Kiss Me, Kate* (1948), in which they mix *The Taming of the Shrew* with a fairly typical backstage story. The Spewacks, working in farce and the musical at the same time, were following a Broadway tradition that is still carried on by Neil Simon, the most successful comic writer of the postwar period. His libretti are a great deal less tightly written than his plays; the best of them, *Promises, Promises* (1968) owes as much to the Billy Wilder-I. A. L. Diamond film *The Apartment*, on which it is based, as it does to Simon's invention. Another adaptation from film, *Sweet Charity* (1966), an Americanization of *Nights of Cabiria*, has unhappily none of the quality of the Fellini original. Garson Kanin, whose work falls somewhere near the serious side of Simon's kind of comedy, wrote *Do Re Mi* (1960), based on his own novella, a musical which begins as broad caricature but which collapses as the central figure demands that we take him seriously as a victim of the American success dream.

Active 1930's librettists whose real home was the musical comedy include Morrie Ryskind, Howard Dietz, and E. Y. Harburg. Ryskind, who later became a conservative voice on the *National Review*, was a leftist satirist in his Broadway days; he revised an earlier George S. Kaufman script for the anti-war *Strike Up the Band* (1930); with Kaufman, he wrote *Of Thee I Sing* (1931), a satire on presidential politics that became the first musical to win the Pulitzer Prize for drama, and *Let 'em Eat Cake* (1933), its even tougher sequel; and, after these Gershwin shows, he wrote, for Irving Berlin, *Louisiana Purchase* (1940), a gentler satire about a political boss vaguely suggesting Huey Long. Dietz, who usually worked as lyricist for Arthur Schwartz, is best known for his contribution to revues such as *Three's a Crowd* (1930) and *The Band Wagon* (1931), but he did two book shows with Schwartz, *Revenge with Music* (1934) and *Between the Devil* (1937); neither seduction in Spain nor bigamy in England led him to libretti as effective as his revue sketches. Harburg's work in the 1930's was primarily as a lyricist although he did provide the idea from which Howard Lindsay and Russel Crouse wrote the book for *Hooray for What!* (1937), in which a toughly satirical antiwar play is sacrificed to the nonsense expected of a show starring Ed Wynn. It was not until after the war that Harburg emerged as a librettist when, with Fred Saidy, he wrote *Finian's Rainbow* (1947), an antiracist fantasy with satire reminiscent of the 1930's. A second attempt at fantasy-satire, *Flahooley* (1951), proved unsuccessful. Saidy was also Harburg's co-author on that show as well as on the more conventional and hence more acceptable *Jamaica* (1957); with Sig Herzig, Saidy wrote *Bloomer Girl* (1944), one of the first of the post-*Oklahoma!* shows to mix successfully an exploration of the American past with a contemporary attraction to Agnes de Mille ballet.

Another librettist who worked in the 1930's is George Abbott, but – as an actor, as director, as author – he has been around the theatre almost as long as Guy Bolton and he has been so busy with the postwar musical that he obviously cannot be hidden behind a decade label. He wrote *The Boys from Syracuse* (1938), an adaptation of *The Comedy of Errors, Where's Charley?* (1948), based on *Charley's Aunt*, and *New Girl in Town* (1957), a version of *Anna Christie*. Although he may have had William Shakespeare, Brandon Thomas and Eugene O'Neill as silent collaborators on those shows, he worked directly with the authors of the original material when he helped Betty Smith write *A Tree Grows in Brooklyn* (1951), Richard Bissal convert *7½ Cents* into *Pajama Game* (1954) and Douglass Wallop turn *The Year the Yankees Lost the Pennant* into *Damn Yankees* (1955). Jerome Weidman joined Abbott in two musicals which looked back at an innocently corrupt New York, *Fiorello!* (1959) and the less successful *Tenderloin* (1960); perhaps emboldened by his work with Abbott, Weidman went solo and adapted his novel *I Can Get It for You Wholesale* (1962) for the musical stage.

The image of the director turned author, or more often co-author, is hardly an unusual one on the Broadway musical stage. As early as 1940, Joshua Logan joined Gladys Hurlbut to provide the book for the Rodgers-and-Hart show *Higher and Higher*. His most famous collaboration is with Oscar Hammerstein II on *South Pacific* (1949), which in its day was considered the last word in serious musical books, particularly by critics for whom seriousness is equated with liberal sentiments and solemn sentimentality. No such artistic claims were, or can be, made for Logan's commercial successes such as *Wish You Were Here* (1952), which he and Arthur Kober adapted from Kober's *Having Wonderful Time*, and *Fanny* (1954), which he and S. N. Behrman carved out of the Marcel Pagnol trilogy, *Marius, Fanny* and *César*. More impressive is the best work of Abe Burrows: *Guys and Dolls* (1950), written with Jo Swerling, which caught some of the tough sweetness of the original Damon Runyon story and mocked it and embraced it at once; and *How to Succeed in Business Without Really Trying* (1961), written with Jack Weinstock and Willie Gilbert, a satire on American business which lets no one off unscathed. On the other hand, *Can-Can* (1953), which plays around with the conventional idea of wicked France, is more cunning than clever. Michael Bennett not only directed and choreographed *Seesaw* (1973), but wrote the maudlin book based on William Gibson's *Two for the Seesaw*; he is credited with having "conceived" (whatever that means) *A Chorus Line* (1975), but the book – biographical confessions of dancers at an audition – is by James Kirkwood and Nicholas Dane. John-Michael Tebelak, another director-cum-conceiver, is presumably responsible for the book of *Godspell* (1971), unless that cheerful essay in adolescent theology be blamed on St. Matthew, whose Gospel gets credit in the program. Bob Fosse, another director-choreographer often praised for imposing final shape on a show – for instance, *Pippin* (1972), which has a book by Roger O. Hirson – emerged as co-author, with Fred Ebb, of *Chicago* (1975), "a musical vaudeville" based on Maurine Watkin's popular 1920's comedy melodrama about Roxie Hart. Ebb, best known as a lyricist, had already turned librettist, with Norman L. Martin, on *70 Girls 70* (1971), a tough-minded, much underrated musical about American attitudes toward aging and death.

Perhaps the most impressive librettists – in industry if not always in final product – are those jack-of-all-musical-trades who insist on writing music, lyrics and book. Several English writers who fall into this category have achieved transoceanic success in recent years: Sandy Wilson, who is best known for *The Boy Friend* (1953), a delightful parody of the 1920's musical at its most fatuous; Lionel Bart, whose *Oliver!* (1960) tried at least to hold on to some of the scariness of the Dickens original; and Leslie Bricusse and Anthony Newley, whose pretentious and sentimental excursions into symbolic parable – *Stop the World – I Want to Get Off* (1961) and *The Roar of the Greasepaint – The Smell of the Crowd* (1965) – found audiences that were willing to take them at their mask value. There were American composers who wrote their own books, of course, Meredith Willson being the most successful. His *The Music Man* (1957), ostensibly the story of a raunchy traveling salesman domesticated by a librarian, is actually a nostalgic celebration of the mythical American small town as it is supposed to have been before the first world war. Willson used a librettist, Richard Morris, in his second show, *The Unsinkable Molly Brown* (1960), but the composer's influence is clear in a musical that sentimentalized a fascinating real woman as the earlier one softens the traditional conman. More recently, Peter Link and C. C. Courtney shared credit for book, music and lyrics of a rock examination of the ways toward and need for *Salvation* (1969), although Link's more recent work suggests that he was the composer of the show. In *Ain't Supposed to Die a Natural Death* (1971) and *Don't Play Us Cheap* (1972), Melvin Van Peebles drew affectionate caricatures of Harlem life which have, among other things, helped to change the character of American audiences by drawing large numbers of blacks into the theatres. Al Carmines, the singing clergyman, has been touted as a latter-day Noël Coward, off-off-Broadway variation, but his best works are not those like *Joan* (1972), for which he did his own book, but those in which he had the help of librettists such as María Irene Fornés, whose *Promenade* (1969) is a full-length version of an earlier play, and Tim Reynolds, who went to Aristophanes for *Peace* (1969).

At this point, pressed by lack of space, I had best resort to a catalogue of sorts:

Alan Jay Lerner, although he wrote a clever book for Kurt Weill's *Love Life* (1948), did his best and most celebrated work as half of Lerner and Loewe, particularly in the shows following their romantic fantasy *Brigadoon* (1947). In *Paint Your Wagon* (1951) and *Camelot* (1960), he displays a textual density that would have wrecked shows with weaker scores as his contribution to Burton Lane's *On a Clear Day You Can See Forever* (1965) indicates. His best and leanest work is *My Fair Lady* (1956), thanks in part to the Shaw original, *Pygmalion*. In 1973, he and Loewe tried, unsuccessfully, to make a stage musical of their earlier film *Gigi*.

Betty Comden and Adolph Green, having begun as lyricists and performers, wrote their first book for Leonard Bernstein – *On the Town* (1944), a wartime salute to New York. They are at their most characteristic – sly, wry and a little soft-hearted – when they stick to New York – *Bells Are Ringing* (1956) – or to show business – *Applause* (1970) – but the same two subjects can go soft in their hands, as in *Subways Are for Sleeping* (1961) and *Fade Out – Fade In* (1964).

Jerome Chodorov and Joseph Fields, after turning their *My Sister Eileen* into Leonard Bernstein's *Wonderful Town* (1953) – lyrics inevitably by Comden and Green – tried, with less success, to create an earlier New York by building *The Girl in Pink Tights* (1954) around the story of America's first musical, *The Black Crook*.

Joseph Stein has tried, with varying degrees of failure, to be convincingly Pennsylvania Dutch in *Plain and Fancy* (1955) and black in *Mr. Wonderful* (1956), both with Will Glickman's help, and, on his own, Irish in *Juno* (1959) and Greek in *Zorbá* (1968). His best book is clearly *Take Me Along* (1959), adapted with Robert Russell from O'Neill's *Ah, Wilderness!*, but he is most famous for having reduced Sholom Aleichem's Tevye to a lovable figure with a message in *Fiddler on the Roof* (1964).

Michael Stewart's best book is *Bye Bye Birdie* (1960), a tough and funny satire on American taste; his most celebrated, *Hello, Dolly!* (1964), a flaccid adaptation of Thornton Wilder's *The Matchmaker*.

Peter Stone, after having written a very workable libretto, *1776* (1969), in which American history shares space with stereotypical comedy as the United States is born, went on to make very weak adaptations of Clifford Odets's *The Flowering Peach – Two by Two* (1970) – and the Wilder-Diamond film *Some Like It Hot – Sugar* (1972).

Burt Shevelove, having, somewhat incredibly, made Plautus live on the contemporary stage in *A Funny Thing Happened on the Way to the Forum* (1962), written with Larry Gelbart, went on to rewrite the Otto Harbach-Frank Mandel book for *No, No, Nanette* (1925) and – as director as well as adapter – to polish the Vincent Youmans show into the nostalgia hit of the early 1970's.

Tom Jones' best libretto and the phenomenal musical success of the 1960's is *The Fantasticks* (1960), a bittersweet adaptation of Rostand's *Les Romanesques. I Do! I Do!* (1966), his adaptation of Jan de Hartog's *The Fourposter*, is a much more conventional libretto. Recently, he and composer Harvey Schmidt have been experimenting with small studio musicals – *Portfolio Revue* (1974), *Philemon* (1975) – which, although they have not been well received, suggest a return to the production intimacy that led to *The Fantasticks*.

Beverley Cross, who is known in the United States primarily for *Half a Sixpence* (1963), an adaptation of H. G. Wells's *Kipps* which retained much of the charm but little of the social comment of the original, has written libretti for almost a dozen musicals, including the opera *The Mines of Sulphur* (1965) and *The Great Society* (1974).

Philip Rose and Peter Udell, who helped Ossie Davis turn his caricature comedy *Purlie Victorious* into *Purlie* (1970), joined James Lee Barrett on *Shenandoah* (1975), an occasionally sentimental, sometimes serious musical with a Civil War setting.

Mention should be made of a number of authors whose reputations, as librettists at least, depend on a single show, sometimes because they worked on no more than one. Here they are, alphabetically. Don Appell used a cross-the-cultures romance in *Milk and Honey* (1961), but it was the Israeli setting that made the show. William F. Brown wrote *The Wiz* (1975), a black version of *The Wizard of Oz* that turned out to be more Broadway show-biz than American fantasy. Truman Capote adapted his story about a Caribbean brothel for Harold Arlen's *House of Flowers* (1954), a show with an underground reputation much more substantial than its original commercial success. Nevill Coghill, who once held the Merton Chair of English Literature at Oxford, helped his former student Martin Starkie turn four of Chaucer's naughtier anecdotes into a musical *Canterbury Tales* (1968). Gretchen Cryer used a hapless hero to make comments, mostly amiable, on contemporary social phenomena in *The Last Sweet Days of Isaac* (1970). Donald Driver gave a vaguely mod touch to *Twelfth Night* as the title *Your Own Thing* (1968) indicates. George Furth examined and finally recommended marriage in the occasionally satiric *Company* (1970). William Gibson was presumably largely responsible for *Golden Boy* (1964), which, not very satisfactorily, transferred Clifford Odets's play to a Harlem setting. James Goldman imposed soap-opera romance on showbusiness reminiscence in *Follies* (1971). Jim Jacobs and Warren Casey made the profitable discovery, with *Grease* (1972), that the 1950's were ready for the nostalgia treatment. Jerome Lawrence and Robert E. Lee turned a very successful pig's ear into a still more successful pig's ear when they carpentered *Mame* (1966) out of their earlier play *Auntie Mame*. Stephen Longstreet used his novel *Some Like Them Handsome* as the basis for *High Button Shoes* (1947), one of the most charming of the nostalgia-for-the-American-past shows so popular just after World War II. Joe Masteroff fashioned a libretto from Christopher Isherwood's *Berlin Stories* and John Van Druten's *I Am a Camera*, spongey in plot and character, but distinguished in its presentation of the titular *Cabaret* (1966), the setting for the most acid of the Fred Ebb-John Kander songs. Robert Nemiroff, with Charlotte Zaltzberg, continued his theatrical resurrection of Lorraine Hansberry's literary remains, this time by softening her *A Raisin in the Sun* into *Raisin* (1973). S. J. Perelman, with Ogden Nash, wrote *One Touch of Venus* (1943), an intricately plotted yet rather haphazard story of Venus's disruptive return to earth – largely an excuse for one of Kurt Weill's best American scores. Gerome Ragni and James Rado wrote a conventional pacifist plot for *Hair* (1967), but they increased its popularity by decorating it with the minutiae of high-school hippie acts and attitudes. Bob Randall concocted a tacky backstage story for *The Magic Show* (1974), an excuse to bring a talented magician on stage. Tim Rice working in the tradition that retells the Bible stories in slang, redid the Gospels for a rock generation in *Jesus Christ Superstar* (1970). Budd Schulberg, with his brother Stuart, made a workable but less astringent libretto of the novel that made his reputation as a writer, *What Makes Sammy Run?* (1964). Samuel Taylor wrote an interracial love story for *No Strings* (1962) which was unusual only in that the libretto, on the page, gives no indication that the girl is Negro. Dale Wasserman, working from his own television adaptation of *Don Quixote*, wrote an essay in uplift called *Man of La Mancha* (1965), beloved by everyone except admirers of Cervantes. Aubrey Woods, perhaps because he is primarily a performer and perhaps because the Victorian theater specialist George Rowell had a hand in the show, saw that his *Trelawney* (1972) not only borrowed the sentimental love-across-the-classes plot of *Trelawney of the Wells* but retained the serious point about changing theatrical conventions that was so important in the Arthur Wing Pinero original.

For some historians of the musical, such as composer Alec Wilder (*American Popular Song*), the musical's best days came before the second world war when a group of talented and witty composers regularly turned out sophisticated scores. If one thinks in terms of complete shows rather than songs, however, the richest years are almost certainly the late 1940's and early 1950's in which the librettos moved away from the pre-war formulas in search of more complicated material. In the 1960's and early 1970's, the musical was suffering the consequences of that move. There was something exciting, at first, when the librettists turned to other genres – novels, plays – in search of adaptable stories. The borrowing which began as a release for the writer's imagination has become a trap, a crutch. A look at the current musical listings in New York or London will turn up one adaptation after another; even the most successful of these shows, commercially, tend to be pedestrian. It is not simply that the surprise has gone out of adaptation as a device, but that other elements which helped define the musical – irreverence and a sense of fun – have disappeared almost completely. The formula writing now lies in the feel, the tone of the librettos rather than in their plots and their comic devices. Now that the Broadway musical – and its West End counterpart, to a lesser extent – has become so expensive to produce, each one is an institution before the curtain rises with all the heaviness of heart that the word *institution* implies. There is as yet a minimum of evidence, but I suspect that the hope for the libretto, for musical comedy itself, lies in the small musical which is a reaction, often of young writers and composers, to the overstuffed output of their elders. After all, isn't the history of theatre a string of small revolutions?

—Gerald Weales

* * *

ABBOTT, George.   See his dictionary entry.

APPELL, Don.   *Milk and Honey*, music and lyrics by Jerry Herman, 1961. Other plays: *This Too Shall Pass*, 1946; *Lullaby*, 1954 (as *And Mama Makes Three*, 1962); *A Girl Could Get Lucky*, 1964. Stage and television director.

BART, Lionel.   *Fings Ain't Wot They Used T'Be* (lyrics and music only), book by Frank Norman, 1959; *Lock Up Your Daughters* (lyrics only), book by Bernard Miles, music by Laurie Johnson, 1959; *Oliver!*, music and lyrics by Lionel Bart, 1960; *Blitz*, with Joan Maitland, music and lyrics by Lionel Bart, 1962; *Merry Roosters Panto*, book by Peter Shaffer, music and lyrics by Lionel Bart, 1963; *Maggie May*, book by Alun Owen, music and lyrics by Lionel Bart, 1964; *Twang*, with Harvey Orkin, music and lyrics by Lionel Bart, 1965; *La Strada*, book by Charles K. Peck, Jr., music and lyrics by Lionel Bart, 1969.

BENNETT, Michael.   Musicals: *Seesaw*, music by Cy Coleman, lyrics by Dorothy Fields, from the play *Two for the Seesaw* by William Gibson, 1973; "conceived" *A Chorus Line*, book by James Kirkwood and Nicholas Dane, music by Marvin Hamlisch, lyrics by Edward Kleban, 1975.

BOLTON, Guy.   *Ninety in the Shade*, music by Jerome Kern, 1915; *Nobody Home*, with Paul Rubens, music by Jerome Kern, 1915; *Very Good, Eddy*, with Philip Bartholomae, music by Jerome Kern, lyrics by Schuyler Green and P. G. Wodehouse, 1915; *Miss Springtime*, with P. G. Wodehouse, music by Emmerich Kalman, 1916; *Have a Heart*, with P. G. Wodehouse, music by Jerome Kern, 1916; *Oh, Boy*, with P. G. Wodehouse, music by Jerome Kern, 1917 (as *Oh, Joy*, 1919); *Leave It to Jane*, with P. G. Wodehouse, music by Jerome Kern, 1917; *The Rose of China*, with P. G. Wodehouse, music by Armand Vecsey, 1917; *The Riviera Girl*, with P. G. Wodehouse, music by Emmerich Kalman, 1917; *Miss 1917*, with P. G. Wodehouse, music by Jerome Kern, 1917; *Oh, Lady, Lady*, with P. G. Wodehouse, music by Jerome Kern, 1917; *The Girl Behind the Gun*, with P. G. Wodehouse, music by Ivan Caryll, 1918; *Oh My Dear*, with P. G. Wodehouse, music by Louis A. Hirsch, 1918; *See You Later*, with P. G. Wodehouse, music by J. Szulc, 1918; *Sally*, music by Jerome Kern, lyrics by Arthur Grey, 1920; *Tangerine*, with Philip Bartholomae, music by Carlo Sanders, lyrics by Howard Johnston, 1921; *The Hotel Mouse*, music by Armand Vecsey and Ivan Caryll, lyrics by Clifford Grey, 1922; *Daffy Dill*, with Oscar Hammerstein II, music by Herbert Stothart, lyrics by Oscar Hammerstein II, 1922; *Primrose*, with George Grossmith, music by George Gershwin, 1924; *Lady Be Good*, with Fred Thompson, music by George Gershwin, lyrics by Ira Gershwin, 1924; *Sitting Pretty*, with P. G. Wodehouse, music by Jerome Kern, 1924; *Tip-Toes*, with Fred Thompson, music by George Gershwin, 1925; *The Bamboula*, with H. M. Vernon, music and lyrics by Albert Sirmay, Harry Rosenthal, Douglas Furber, and Irving Caesar, 1925; *Oh, Kay*, with P. G. Wodehouse, music by George Gershwin, lyrics by Ira Gershwin, 1925; *The Ramblers*, with Bert Kalmar and Harry Ruby, music and lyrics by Bert Kalmar and Harry Ruby, 1926; *Rio Rita*, with Fred Thompson, music by Harry Tierney, lyrics by Joseph McCarthy, 1927; *Five O'Clock Girl*, with Fred Thompson, music and lyrics by Bert Kalmar and Harry Ruby, 1927; *She's My Baby*, with Bert Kalmar and Harry Ruby, 1927; *Rosalie*, with W. A. McGuire, music by George Gershwin and Sigmund Romberg, lyrics by Ira Gershwin and P. G. Wodehouse, 1928; *Blue Eyes*, with Graham John, music by Jerome Kern, 1928; *Top Speed*, with Bert Kalmar and Harry Ruby, 1929; *Simple Simon*, with Ed Wynn, music by Richard Rodgers, lyrics by Lorenz Hart, 1930; *Girl Crazy*, with John McGowan, music by George Gershwin, lyrics by Ira Gershwin, 1930; *The Song of the Drum*, with Fred Thompson, music and lyrics by Vivian Ellis and Herman Finck, 1931; *Give Me a Ring*, with R. P. Weston and Bert Lee, music by Martin Broones, 1933; *Seeing Stars*, with Fred Thompson, music by Martin Broones, lyrics by Graham John, 1935; *This'll Make You Whistle*, with Fred Thompson, music and lyrics by Sigler, Goodhart, and Hoffman, 1935; *At the Silver Swan*, with Clifford Grey, music by Edmond Grey, 1936; *Swing Along*, with Fred Thompson and Douglas Furber, music by Martin Broones, 1936; *Going Places*, with Fred Thompson, music and lyrics by Vivian Ellis, 1936; *Going Greek*, with Douglas Furber and Fred Thompson, music and lyrics by Goodhart, Hoffman, and Lerner, 1937; *Hide and Seek*, with Fred Thompson and Douglas Furber, music and lyrics by Vivian Ellis, Lerner, Goodhart, and Hoffman, 1937; *The Sun Never Sets*, with Pat Wallace, music by Cole Porter and Kenneth Leslie-Smith, 1938; *The Fleet's Lit Up*, with Fred Thompson and Bert Lee, music and lyrics by Vivian Ellis, 1938; *Running Riot*, with Firth Shephard and Douglas Furber, music and lyrics by Vivan Ellis, 1938; *Bobby Get Your Gun*, with Fred Thompson and Bert Lee, music by Clifford Grey, Bert Lee, and Desmond Carter, lyrics by Jack Waller and Joseph Tunbridge, 1938; *Magyar Melody*, with Fred Thompson and Eric Maschwitz, music by George Posford and Bernard Grün, 1939; *Walk with Music*, with Parke Levy and Alan Lipscott, music by Hoagy Carmichael, lyrics by Johnny Mercer, 1940; *Hold On to Your Hats*, with Matt Brooks and Eddie Davis, music by Burton Lane, lyrics by E. Y. Harburg, 1940; *Jackpot*, with Sidney Sheldon and Ben Roberts, music and lyrics by Vernon Duke and Howard Dietz, 1944; *Follow the Girls*, with Eddie Davis, music and lyrics by Dan Shapiro, Milton Pascal, and Phil Charig, 1944; *Music at Midnight*, music by Offenbach and Hans May, lyrics by Harold Purcell, 1950; *Rainbow Square*, with Harold Purcell, music by Robert Stolz, 1951; *Ankles Aweigh*, with Eddie Davis, music by Sammy Fain, lyrics by Dan Shapiro, 1955; *Anya*, with George Abbott, music and lyrics by Robert Wright and George Forrest, 1965. Other plays: *The Drone*, with Douglas J. Wood, 1911; *The Rule of Three*, 1914; *The Fallen Idol*, 1915; *The Sea-Wolf*, with Joseph Noel, 1915; *Her Game*, 1915; *Hit-the-Trail Holiday*, with George Middleton and George M. Cohan, 1915; *Children*, with Tom Carlton, 1916; *A Happy Thought*, with George Middleton, 1916; *Polly with a Past*, with George Middleton, 1917; *Ringtime*, with P. G. Wodehouse, 1917; *The Five Million*, with Frank Mandel, 1919; *Adam and Eva*, with George Middleton, 1919; *The Light of the World*, with George Middleton, 1920; *The Cave Girl*, with George Middleton, 1920; *The Nightcap*, with Max Marcin, 1921; *Chicken Feed*, 1923; *Nobody's Business*, with Frank Mandel, 1923; *Polly Preferred*, 1924; *Grounds for Divorce*, 1924; *The Nightingale*, with P. G. Wodehouse, 1927; *Polly*, with George Middleton, 1929; *A Song of Sixpence*, with Ian Hay, 1930; *Who's Who*, with P. G. Wodehouse, 1934; *Ladies in Love*, with V. Katon, 1937; *Wise Tomorrow*, with Virginia de Lanty (as Stephen Powys), 1937; *Nuts in May*, with Sonny Miller and Steve Geray, 1938; *Three Blind Mice*, with Virginia de Lanty (as Stephen Powys), 1938; *Number Six*, with Gerald Fairlie, 1938; *Red Sky at Morning*, with Vernon Sylvaine, 1939; *Two and Two Make Five*, with Vernon Sylvaine, 1939; *Golden Wings*, with William Jay, 1941; *Another Heaven*, with John Golden, 1943; *The Shelley Story*, 1947; *Humoresque*, 1948; *Don't Listen, Ladies*, with Stephen Powys, 1948; *Larger Than Life*, 1950; *The Long Arm*, 1951; *Guardian Angel*, 1953; *Anastasia*, 1953; *Come On, Jeeves*, with P. G. Wodehouse, 1956; *A Man and His Wife*, 1974. Author of screenplays, novels, and memoirs.

BRAHMS, Caryl.   *No Bed for Bacon*, with S. J. Simon, 1959, musical version, music by Ned Sherrin, 1964; *Cindy-Ella; or, I Gotta Shoe*, music by Ned Sherrin, 1962; *The Spoils*, music by Ned Sherrin, 1968; *Sing a Rude Song*, with Ned Sherrin, additional material by Alan Bennett, music by Ron Grainer, 1970; *Nickleby and Me*, with Ned Sherrin, music by Ron Grainer, 1975. Play: *Let's Get to Bed*, with Ned Sherrin, 1976. Fiction; *A Mutual Pair*, with S. J. Simon, 1976.

BROWN, William F.   Sketches and lyrics for *Dime a Dozen*, 1962; *Baker's Dozen*, 1964; *Bits and Pieces*, 1964; *Pick a Number XV*, 1965; *Leonard Sillman's New Faces of 1968*, 1968. Musicals: *How to Steal an Election*, music and lyrics by Oscar Brand, 1968; *The Wiz*, from the novel *The Wizard of Oz* by J. Frank Baum, 1975. Other play: *The Girl in the Freudian Slip*, 1967.

BURROWS, Abe.   See his dictionary entry.

CAPOTE, Truman.   *House of Flowers*, music by Harold Arlen, 1954. Other plays: *The Grass Harp*, 1952; *The Thinksgiving Visitor*, 1968. Author of screenplays, novels, and other books.

CARMINES, Al.   Director of the Judson Poets Theatre, New York. Musicals and librettos include *The Journey of Snow White*, 1970; *Joan*, 1972; *Christmas Rappings*, 1972; *A Look at the Fifties*, 1972; *The Life of a Man*, 1972; *The Faggot*, 1973; *Religion*, 1973; *The Future*, 1974. Music and songs for many plays, the most recent being *Wanted* by David Epstein, 1972; *The Making of Americans* by Leon Katz, from the novel by Gertrude Stein, 1972.

CASEY, Michael.   Musical: *Grease*, with Jim Jacobs, 1972.

CHODOROV, Jerome.   *Pretty Penny*, music and lyrics by Harold Rome, 1949; *Wonderful Town*, with Joseph Stein, music by Leonard Bernstein, lyrics by Betty Comden and Adolph Green, 1953; *The Girl in Pink Tights*, with Joseph Fields, music by Sigmund Romberg, lyrics by Leo Robin, 1954; *I Had a Ball*, music and lyrics by Jack Lawrence and Stan Freeman, 1964; *The Great Waltz*, music by Johann Strauss adapted by Erich Korngold and others, adaptation of the book by Moss Hart and Milton Lazarus, 1965; *Dumas and Son*, music and lyrics by Robert Wright and George Forrest, 1967. Other plays: with Joseph Fields, *Schoolhouse on the Lot*, 1938, *My Sister Eileen*, 1940, *Junior Miss*, 1941, *The French Touch*, 1945, *Anniversary Waltz*, 1954, *The Ponder Heart*, 1956, and *Tunnel of Love*, 1957; *Three Bags Full*, 1966. Screenplays, with Joseph Fields, *My Sister Eileen*, 1955; *Happy Anniversary*, 1959. Stage director and screenwriter.

COGHILL, Nevill.   *Canterbury Tales*, with Martin Starkie, music by Richard Hill and John Hawkins, lyrics by Nevill Coghill, 1968. Director of *Samson Agonistes*, 1930; many Shakespeare plays; *Dr. Faustus*, 1966. Translator of *The Canterbury Tales*.

COMDEN, Betty.   With Adolph Green: *The Revuers*, 1944; *On the Town*, music by Leonard Bernstein, 1944; *Billion Dollar Baby*, music by Morton Gould, 1945; *Two on the Aisle*, with others, music by Jule Styne (revue), 1951; *Wonderful Town* (lyrics only), book by Joseph Fields and Jerome Chodorov, music by Leonard Bernstein, 1953; *Peter Pan* (some lyrics only), play by James M. Barrie, 1954; *Bells Are Ringing*, music by Jule Styne, 1956; *Say Darling* (lyrics only), book by Abe Burrows and Richard and Marian Bissell, music by Jule Styne, 1958; *Do Re Mi* (lyrics only), book by Garson Kanin, music by Jule Styne, 1960; *Subways Are for Sleeping*, music by Jule Styne, 1961; *Fade Out – Fade In*, music by Jule Styne, 1964; *Hallelujah Baby* (lyrics only), book by Arthur Laurents, music by Jule Styne, 1967; *Applause*, music by Charles Strouse, lyrics by Lee Adams, 1970; *By Bernstein*, 1975. Screenplays and film lyrics: *Good News*, 1947; *The Barkleys of Broadway*, 1949; *Singin' in the Rain*, 1952; *The Band Wagon*, 1953; *It's Always Fair Weather*, 1955; *What a Way to Go*, 1964; and others. Actress and singer.

COURTNEY, C. C.   *Salvation*, with Peter Link, 1969; *East of Ruston*, with Ragan

Courtney, music by Peter Link, 1971.

CROSS, Beverley.   See his dictionary entry.

CRYER, Gretchen.   *The Last Sweet Days of Isaac: The Elevator, and I Want to Walk to San Francisco*, music by Nancy Ford, 1970; *Shelter*, music by Nancy Ford, 1972.

DAVIS, Ossie.   See his dictionary entry.

DIETZ, Howard.   Contributor to revues: *The Little Show*, 1929; *The Second Little Show*, 1930; *Three's a Crowd*, 1930; *The Band Wagon*, 1931; *Flying Colors*, 1932; *At Home Abroad*, 1935; *Jackpot*, 1944. Musicals: *Dear Sir* (lyrics only), book by Edgar Selwyn, music by Jerome Kern, 1924; *Merry-Go-Round*, with Morrie Ryskind, music by Henry Souvaine and Jay Gorney, 1927; *Revenge with Music*, music by Arthur Schwartz, 1934; *Between the Devil*, music by Arthur Schwartz, 1937.

DRIVER, Donald.   *Your Own Thing*, music and lyrics by Hal Hester and Danny Apolinar, 1968. Play: *Status Quo Vadis*, 1973. Stage director.

EBB, Fred.   Lyrics for *From A to Z*, 1960; *Vintage 60*, 1960; *Put It in Writing*, 1963; *Flora, The Red Menace* by George Abbott and Robert Russell, music by John Kander, 1965; *Cabaret*, by Joe Masteroff, music by John Kander, 1966; *By Jupiter* (additional material) by Richard Rodgers and Lorenz Hart, 1967; *The Happy Time* by N. Richard Nash, music by John Kander, 1968; *Zorbá* by Joseph Stein, music by John Kander, 1968. Musical books: *Morning Sun*, music by Paul Klein, 1963; *70 Girls 70*, with Norman L. Martin and Joe Masteroff, music by John Kander, lyrics by Fred Ebb, 1971; *Chicago*, with Bob Fosse, music by John Kander, 1975. Television: *Lisa*, 1970 (staged, 1974).

FOSSE, Bob.   Choreographer: *The Pajama Game*, 1954; *Damn Yankees*, 1955; *Bells Are Ringing*, with Jerome Robbins, 1956; *New Girl in Town*, 1957; *Redhead* (also director), 1959; *How to Succeed in Business Without Really Trying*, 1961; *Little Me* (also co-director), 1962; *Sweet Charity* (also director), 1965; *Pippin* (also director), 1972. Musical book: *Chicago*, with Fred Ebb, music by John Kander, 1975. Stage and film actor and dancer.

FURTH, George.   *Company*, music and lyrics by Stephen Sondheim, 1970. Film, television, and stage actor since 1956.

GIBSON, William.   See his dictionary entry.

GOLDMAN, James.   See his dictionary entry.

GREEN, Adolph.   See the entry for Betty Comden above.

GREEN, Paul.   See his dictionary entry.

HARBURG, E. Y.   Contributor to revues: *Earl Carroll's Sketch Book*, 1929; *Garrick Gaieties*, 1930; *The Vanderbilt Review*, 1930; *Earl Carroll's Vanities*, 1930; *Shoot the Works*, 1931; *Americana*, 1932; *Walk a Little Faster*, 1932; *Ziegfield Follies*, 1934; *Life Begins at 8:40*, 1934; *Hooray for What!*, 1937; *Hold On to Your Hats*, 1940. Musicals: *Ballyhoo of 1932* (lyrics only), book by Norman B. Anthony, music by Lewis E. Gensler, 1932; *Bloomer Girl* (lyrics only), book by Fred Saidy and Sid Herzig, music by Harold Arlen, 1944; *Finian's Rainbow*, with Fred Saidy, music by Burton Lane, 1947; *Flahooley*, with Fred Saidy, music and lyrics by E. Y. Harburg and Sammy Fain, 1951; *Jamaica*, with Fred Saidy, music by Harold Arlen, 1957; *The Happiest Girl in the World*, with Henry Myers, music by Offenbach, lyrics by E. Y. Harburg, 1961; *Darling of the Day*, music by Jule Styne, 1968; *The Wizard of Oz* (lyrics only), book by Bill Baird and Arthur Cantor, music by Harold Arlen, 1968. Film lyrics. Book: *At This Point in Rhyme*, 1976.

HELLMAN, Lillian.   See her dictionary entry.

JACOBS, Jim.   Musical: *Grease*, with Warren Casey, 1972.

JONES, Tom.   Sketches in *Four Below*, 1956; *Shoestring '57*, 1956; *Kaleidoscope*, 1957; *Demi-Dozen*, 1958. Musical books, with music by Harvey Schmidt: *The Fantasticks*, 1959, expanded version, 1960; *110 in the Shade* (lyrics only) by N. Richard Nash, 1963; *I Do! I Do!*, 1966; *Celebration*, 1969; *Colette* (lyrics only) by Elinor Jones, 1970; *Portfolio Revue*, 1974; *Philemon*, 1975; *The Bone Room*, 1975. Television: *New York Scrapbook*, 1961.

KANIN, Garson. See his dictionary entry.

LAURENTS, Arthur. See his dictionary entry.

LAWRENCE, Jerome, and **Robert E. LEE.** See their dictionary entries.

LERNER, Alan Jay. Musicals: *What's Up* (revue), with Arthur Pierson, music by Frederick Loewe, 1943; *The Day Before Spring*, music by Frederick Loewe, 1945; *Brigadoon*, music by Frederick Loewe, 1947; *Love Life*, music by Kurt Weill, 1948; *Paint Your Wagon*, music by Frederick Loewe, 1951; *My Fair Lady*, music by Frederick Loewe, 1956; *Camelot*, music by Frederick Lowe, 1960; *On a Clear Day You Can See Forever*, music by Burton Lane, 1965; *Coco*, music by André Previn, 1969; *Gigi*, music by Frederick Loewe, based on his own film, 1973; *1600 Pennsylvania Avenue*, music by Leonard Bernstein, 1976. Play: *The Life of the Party*, 1942. Screenplays: of several of his own musicals, and *Royal Wedding*, 1951; *An American in Paris*, 1951; *Gigi*, 1958; *The Little Prince*, 1975.

LOGAN, Joshua. *Higher and Higher*, with Gladys Hurlbut, music by Richard Rodgers, lyrics by Lorenz Hart, 1940; *South Pacific*, with Oscar Hammerstein II, music by Richard Rodgers, lyrics by Oscar Hammerstein II, 1949; *Wish You Were Here*, with Arthur Kober, music and lyrics by Harold Rome, 1952; *Fanny*, with S. N. Behrman, music and lyrics by Harold Rome, 1954. Other plays: *Mister Roberts*, with Thomas Heggen, 1948; *The Wisteria Trees*, 1950. Screenplay: *Ensign Pulver*, 1964. Book: *Josh*, 1976. Stage and film director.

LONGSTREET, Stephen. Musical: *High Button Shoes*, music and lyrics by Jule Styne and Sammy Kahn, 1947. Play: *Gauguin*, 1948. Screenplays: *The Gay Sisters*, 1942; *Stallion Road*, 1943; *The Jolson Story*, 1946; *Duel in the Sun*, 1946; *Silver River*, 1948; *The Greatest Show on Earth*, 1952; *The Helen Morgan Story*, 1957; and others. Author of radio and television scripts; painter and cartoonist; journalist. His most recent books are *Chicago*, 1973; *World Cookbook*, 1973; *God and Sarah Pedlock*, 1976; *The Bank*, 1976. Since 1973, Professor of Performing Arts, University of Southern California, Los Angeles.

MASTEROFF, Joe. *She Loves Me*, music by Jerry Bock, lyrics by Sheldon Harnick, 1963; *Cabaret*, music by John Kander, lyrics by Fred Ebb, 1966; *70 Girls 70*, with Fred Ebb and Norman L. Martin, music by John Kander, lyrics by Fred Ebb, 1971. Other play: *The Warm Peninsula*, 1959.

NEMIROFF, Robert. Musicals, with Charlotte Zaltzberg: *The Sign in Sidney Brustein's Window*, music by Gary William Friedman, lyrics by Ray Errol Fox, from the play by Lorraine Hansberry, 1972; *Raisin*, music by Judd Woldin, lyrics by Robert Brittain, from the play *Raisin in the Sun* by Lorraine Hansberry, 1973. Other plays: *Postmark Zero*, 1965; *To Be Young, Gifted and Black*, from writings by Lorraine Hansberry, 1969; *Les Blancs*, adaptation of the play by Lorraine Hansberry, 1970.

NEWLEY, Anthony. Musicals: *Stop the World – I Want to Get Off*, with Leslie Bricusse, 1961; *The Roar of the Grease Paint – The Smell of the Crowd*, with Leslie Bricusse, 1965; *The Good Old Bad Old Days*, with Leslie Bricusse, 1973; *Royalty Follies*, music by Anthony Newley and John Taylor, 1974. Music and songs: for the movies *Willie Wonka and the Chocolate Factory*, 1971, and *Mr. Quilp*, 1975; *Peter Pan* (television), 1976. Stage and film actor and director.

PERELMAN, S. J. See his dictionary entry.

RADO, James. Musicals: *Hair*, with Gerome Ragni, music by Galt MacDermot, 1967; *Rainbow*, with Ted Rado, music and lyrics by James Rado, 1972.

RAGNI, Gerome. Musicals: *Hair*, with James Rado, music by Galt MacDermot, 1967; *Dude*, music by Galt MacDermot, 1972.

RANDALL, Bob.   Musical: *The Magic Show*, music by Stephen Schwartz, 1974. Play: *6 Rms Riv Vu*, 1972.

RICE, Tim.   Musicals: *Joseph and His Amazing Technicolour Dream Coat*, music by Andrew Lloyd Webber, 1968, expanded version, 1973; *Jesus Christ Superstar*, music by Andrew Lloyd Webber, 1970.

ROSE, Peter.   Musicals: *Purlie*, with Peter Udell and Ossie Davis, music by Gary Geld, lyrics by Peter Udell, from the play *Purlie Victorious* by Ossie Davis, 1970; *Shenandoah*, with James Lee Barrett, music by Gary Geld, lyrics by Peter Rose, 1975 (also director).

RYSKIND, Morrie.   Musicals: *The '49-ers* (revue), 1922; *Americana* (lyrics only), 1926; *Merry-Go-Round*, with Howard Dietz, music by Henry Souvaine and Jay Gorney, 1927; *Animal Crackers*, with George S. Kaufman, music and lyrics by Harry Ruby and Bert Kalmar, 1928; *Ned Wayburn's Gambols*, music by Walter G. Samuels, 1929; *Strike Up the Band*, music by George Gershwin, lyrics by Ira Gershwin, 1930; *The Gang's All Here*, with Russel Crouse and Oscar Hammerstein II, music by Lewis E. Gensler, lyrics by Owen Murphy and Robert A. Simon, 1931; *Of Thee I Sing*, with George S. Kaufman, music by George Gershwin, lyrics by Ira Gershwin, 1931; *Let 'em Eat Cake*, with George S. Kaufman, music by George Gershwin, lyrics by Ira Gershwin, 1933; *Louisiana Purchase*, music and lyrics by Irving Berlin, 1940. Writer of humorous verse and screenplays; director.

SAIDY, Fred.   See the entry for E. Y. Harburg above.

SCHULBERG, Budd.   *What Makes Sammy Run?*, with Stuart Schulberg, music by Ervin Drake, 1964. Other play: *The Disenchanted*, with Harvey Breit, 1958. Screenplays: *On the Waterfront*, 1954; *A Face in the Crowd*, 1958; and others. His most recent novel is *Sanctuary V*, 1970.

SHERRIN, Ned.   Musical books: *Sing a Rude Song*, with Caryl Brahms, additional material by Alan Bennett, music by Ron Grainer, 1970; *Nickleby and Me*, with Caryl Brahms, music by Ron Grainer, 1975. Play: *Lets Get to Bed*, with Caryl Brahms, 1976. Composer: *Cindy-Ella; or, I Gotta Shoe* by Caryl Brahms, 1962; *No Bed for Bacon* by Caryl Brahms and S. J. Simon, 1964; *The Spoils* by Caryl Brahms, 1968. Stage, film, and television director.

SHEVELOVE, Burt.   Contributor to the revue *Small Wonder*, 1948; *A Funny Thing Happened on the Way to the Forum*, with Larry Gelbart, music and lyrics by Stephen Sondheim, 1962; *No, No, Nanette*, music by Vincent Youmans, 1971; *The Frogs*, music and lyrics by Stephen Sondheim, 1974. Other play: *Too Much Johnson*, 1967. Screenplay: *The Wrong Box*, 1966. Television and stage director.

SIMON, Neil.   See his dictionary entry.

SPEWACK, Bella.   With Sam Spewack: *Leave It to Me!*, music by Cole Porter, 1938; *Kiss Me, Kate*, music by Cole Porter, 1948. Other plays, with Sam Spewack: *The Solitaire Man*, 1926; *Poppa*, 1928; *The War Song*, 1928; *Clear All Wires*, 1932; *Spring Song*, 1934; *Boy Meets Girl*, 1935; *Miss Swan Expects*, 1939; *Woman Bites Dog*, 1946; *My Three Angels*, 1953; *Festival*, 1955. Television play: *Enchanted Nutcracker*, 1963. Director; screenwriter.

STEIN, Joseph.   Contributor to revues: *Lend an Ear*, 1948; *Mrs. Gibbons' Boys*, 1949; *Alive and Kicking*, 1950; *Inside USA*, 1951. Musicals: *Plain and Fancy*, with Will Glickman, music by Albert Hague, lyrics by Arnold B. Horwitt, 1955; *Mr. Wonderful*, with Will Glickman, music and lyrics by Jerry Bock, Larry Holofcener, and George Weiss, 1956; *The Body Beautiful*, with Will Glickman, music by Jerry Bock, lyrics by Sheldon Harnick, 1958; *Juno*, music and lyrics by Marc Blitzstein, 1959; *Take Me Along*, with Robert Russell, music and lyrics by Robert Merrill, 1959; *Fiddler on the Roof*, music by Jerry Bock, lyrics by Sheldon Harnick, 1964; *Zorbá*, music by John Kander, lyrics by Fred Ebb, 1968; *Irene*, with Hugh Wheeler, adaptation by Harry Rigby, music by Harry Tierney, lyrics by Joseph McCarthy, adaptation of the play by James Montgomery, 1973; *So Long, 174th Street*, music and lyrics by Stan Daniels, adaptation of the novel by Carl Reiner, 1976. Play: *Enter Laughing*, 1963. Radio, television, and film writer.

STEWART, Michael.   Musicals: *Bye Bye Birdie*, music by Charles Strouse, lyrics by Lee Adams, 1960; *Carnival*, music and lyrics by Bob Merrill, 1961; *Hello, Dolly!*, music and lyrics by Jerry Herman, adaptation of the play *The Matchmaker* by Thornton Wilder, 1964; *George M!*, with John and Fran Pascal, music and lyrics by George M. Cohan, revised by Mary Cohan, 1968; *Mack and Mabel*, music and lyrics by Jerry Herman, 1975. Play: *Those That Play the Clowns*, 1968. Contributor to revues.

STONE, Peter.   *Kean*, music and lyrics by Robert Wright and George Forrest, 1959; *Skyscraper*, music by James Van Heusen, lyrics by Sammy Kahn, 1965; *1776*, music and lyrics by Sherman Edwards, 1969; *Two by Two*, music by Richard Rodgers, lyrics by Martin Charnin, 1970; *Sugar*, music by Jule Styne, 1972. Other plays: *Friend of the Family*, 1958; *Full Circle*, adaptation of play by Erich Maria Remarque, 1973. Screenplays: *Charade*, 1963; *Father Goose*, 1964; *Mirage*, 1965; *Arabesque*, 1966; *Sweet Charity,* 1969;*Skin Game*, 1971, and others; author of television plays and musicals.

TABELAK, John-Michael.   Musical: *Godspell*, music by Stephen Schwartz, 1971.

TAYLOR, Samuel.   *No Strings*, with Richard Rodgers, 1962. Other plays: *The Happy Time*, 1950; *Nina*, 1951; *Sabrina Fair*, 1953; *The Pleasure of His Company*, with Cornelia Otis Skinner, 1958; *First Love*, 1961; *Beekman Place*, 1964; *Avanti*, 1968; *A Touch of Spring*, 1975.

UDELL, Peter.   Musical: *Purlie*, with Peter Rose and Ossie Davis, music by Gary Geld, lyrics by Peter Udell, from the play *Purlie Victorious* by Ossie Davis, 1970.

VAN PEEBLES, Melvin.   Musicals (author and composer): *Ain't Supposed to Die a Natural Death*, 1971; *Don't Play Us Cheap*, 1972.

WASSERMAN, Dale.   Musical: *Man of La Mancha*, music by Mitch Leigh, lyrics by Joe Darion, 1965. Other plays: *Livin' the Play*, with Bruce Geller, 1955; *The Pencil of God*, 1961; *998*, 1962; *One Flew over the Cuckoo's Nest*, from the novel by Ken Kesey, 1963. Screenplays: *The Vikings*, 1958; *Cleopatra*, 1963; *Mister Buddwing*, 1965; *A Walk with Love and Death*, 1969; *Man of La Mancha*, 1972; and others. Author of several television plays.

WEIDMAN, Jerome.   See his dictionary entry.

WILLSON, Meredith.   *The Music Man*, with Franklin Lacey, music and lyrics by Meredith Willson, 1957; *The Unsinkable Molly Brown* (music and lyrics only), book by Richard Morris, 1960; *Here's Love*, music and lyrics by Meredith Willson, story by Valentine Davies, 1963. Film scores: *The Great Dictator*, 1940; *The Little Foxes*, 1941.

WILSON, Sandy.   Contributor to revues: *Slings and Arrows*, 1948; *Oranges and Lemons*, 1949; *See You Later*, 1951; *See You Again*, 1952; *Pieces of Eight*, 1959. Musicals (author and composer): *The Boy Friend*, 1953; *The Buccaneer*, 1953; *Valmouth*, 1959; *Call It Love* (songs only), book by Robert Tanitch, 1960; *Divorce Me, Darling!*, 1965; *As Dorothy Parker Once Said* (music only), 1969; *His Monkey Wife*, from the novel by John Collier, 1971; *Sandy Wilson Thanks the Ladies* (one-man show), 1971. Television scores: *The World of Wooster*, 1965; *Danny La Rue's "Charley's Aunt"*, 1970. Books: *This Is Sylvia*, 1954; *The Poodle from Rome*, 1962; *I Could Be Happy* (autobiography), 1975; *Ivor*, 1976.

WOODS, Aubrey.   Musical: *Trelawney*, music by Julian Slade, from the play *Trelawney of the Wells* by Pinero, 1972.

ZALTZBERG, Charlotte.   See the entry for Robert Nemiroff.

THE THEATRE
OF
MIXED MEANS

Mixed-means performances differ from conventional drama in de-emphasizing verbal language, if not avoiding words completely, in order to stress such presentational means as sound and light, objects and scene, and/or the movement of people and props, often in addition to the newer technologies of film, recorded tape, amplification systems, radio and closed-circuit television. Some mixed-means theatre incorporates spoken language; but if words are the principal means of communication, the result does not qualify as a genuinely mixed-means work. Americans dominate this art, especially within the English-speaking world; and it is my contention that the very best American theatre, especially in contrast to British, has always regarded the prerogatives of performance as more important than the literary text. (The U.S. has thus had both a lively theatre and a negligible drama.) In my judgment, most of the best theatre I saw in New York in the past decade occurred at mixed-means performances. (From our perspective, Gustav Metzger's ideas about destructive art seemed to be the most interesting British work, though no one should definitely judge mixed-means performances he has not seen.)

Consequential mixed-means performances have been done by theatrical groups (discussed in another supplement), by sometime theatrical directors (Ken Dewey, Michael Kirby), and mostly by individual Americans who were initially trained and/or involved in other arts: painting (Allan Kaprow, Jim Dine, Al Hansen, Red Grooms, Robert Rauschenberg, Carolee Schneemann), scuplture (Claes Oldenburg, Robert Whitman, Robert Watts), choreography (Merce Cunningham, Alwin Nikolais, Ann Halprin, Elaine Summers, Meredith Monk, Mimi Garrard), music (John Cage, Dick Higgins, La Monte Young, Ben Patterson), film (Stan VanDerBeek), architecture (George Maciunas, Robert Wilson, a.k.a. "Byrd Hoffman"), and poetry (Vito Acconci, Jackson Mac Low, Dan Graham). This new theatre grows out of discernible, though secondary, traditions in all the arts it encompasses; and a particular performance tends to reflect not only an individual creative style but the original artistic interests of its author.

The mixing of presentational means is probably as old as theatre itself; but whereas such post-Renaissance forms as opera and musical comedy emphasize poetic language against a background of song, setting and dance, the new theatre mixes the various media in distinctly different ways. Second, in contrast to, say, both Diaghilev's spectacular ballets and most multi-media rock concerts, where the various elements complement each other – the music clearly accompanies the singer or dancer, each coinciding with the other's beat – in nearly all mixed-means theatre the components function independently of each other in space and non-synchronously in time. Furthermore, whereas the activities in classical theatre assume the shape of a continuous flow, the relations between successive events in the new theatre are usually disconnected; and if rhythms in the old theatre march at a steady beat, in mixed-means performances the pace of a particular piece is customarily irregular. John Cage's *Imaginary Landscape IV* (1952), which consists of sound produced by twelve on-stage radios, was ostensibly a musical concert, its marvellous theatricality notwithstanding; but Cage's *Variations V* (1965), which is described ahead, clearly qualifies as a mixed-means performance. A better example of a borderline case is the Open Theatre's *Terminal* (1969), a highly choreographed performance about death that uses a rather negligible text that was composed, in collaboration with the performers, during the piece's original rehearsals.

One reason why the theatre of mixed-means seems so different from literary theatre is that most of the former's creators intentionally exclude any signs of past art. In addition to abandoning such traditional theatrical contexts as auditoria, for instance, they tend to avoid especially skilled performers, such as actors and acrobats, for more "ordinary" people. Nonetheless, even these consciously artless mixed-means pieces are still basically theatrical in that some people have agreed to perform for other people, who may not necessarily have agreed to become an audience. The new theatre announces its existence not by the environment in which it occurs but by the purpose of its participants – as the late Ken Dewey put it, "People gather together to articulate something of mutual concern." This definition successfully encompasses both certain strains of modern-dance and the street performances we have come to call "guerilla theatre."

The new movement was initially called "happenings," in acknowledgement of Allan

Kaprow's coinage for his own post-painterly performances. Although this word seemed a particularly apt description of the miscellaneous, if not chaotic, character of Kaprow's own work, it was hardly an accurate term for the entire movement. (To make matters worse, it got vulgarized to mean, as Kaprow observed, "any kind of rather casual and usually innocuous event.") First of all, all works of mixed-means theatre follow some kind of script, consisting not of dialogue but of physical directions, which reflect in turn a definable intention. Only a few allow unexpected events to occur; and even fewer attempt, as Kaprow did, to involve their audiences. Back in 1968, I preferred to call it "the theatre of mixed means" (in a book of that title), because that term isolated a crucial compositional characteristic; but more recent examples of non-literary theatre, especially in the realm of "conceptual art," have revealed the limitations of this definition. It described, for one thing, a theatre of abundance, but in the past few years minimalism has been the artistic rage. Moreover, the term hardly explained the number of new phrases that were necessary to talk sensibly about differences *within* the new theatre. In my book, I defined four distinctly separate genres, so to speak, of mixed-means performance: pure happenings, staged happenings, kinetic environments, and staged performances. What makes the genres differ from each other is that each uses time, space and material in a particular combination of ways, as well as offering audiences a specific kind of theatrical experience.

In pure happenings, the script is so unspecific that unforeseen events can be incorporated into the piece and/or prescribed events can take place in an unplanned succession. That is, although the piece's author will instruct his participants to do certain things, his directions are so approximate and autonomous that the resulting actions will occur in an unrepeatable manner and will have an unpredictable effect. This means that activities in a pure happening are not improvised but *indeterminate*. A typical instruction in Kaprow's *Calling* (1965) reads: "At the garage, a waiting auto starts up, the person is picked up from the concrete pavement, is hauled into the car, is taken to the information booth at Grand Central Station. The person is propped up against it and left." In doing this piece, Kaprow directed separate groups to perform comparably approximate specified activities all over New York City – in the streets, in telephone booths, in the major railroad terminal – and the second day's events were done in the woods of suburban New Jersey.

Here, as in other examples, a pure happening envelopes an audience of accidental spectators, initially mere bystanders on the scene, who are induced to feel that they too are participants in a significant process; and Kaprow considers their experience, and the subsequent retellings of that experience, to be post-facto parts of his piece. As pure happenings have open or unfixed dimensions, in both space and time, they are usually not performed in theatres, which function to close off a space and impose a measure of focus. Instead, these pieces have exploited natural open-space surroundings, such as a bathing beach or even an entire city. In this category also belong "events," most of which are destined for private performance, and which were particularly favored by members of the Fluxus group, an international post-Dada movement with bases in Germany, Japan and the U.S. An example is George Brecht's *Word Events* (1961), which reads, in its entirety: "*Exit." Kaprow's pure happenings are meant to be as formally disorganized and happenstance as life itself; but just as a work of representational art is considerably different from its original model, so a realized pure happening creates a heightened experience that is discernibly above the normal run of life.

Staged happenings differ from pure happenings in one crucial respect – they occur within a fixed space, usually on a theatrical stage. Otherwise, as in pure happenings, the actions and interrelations of participants can vary from performance to performance; and the script is sufficiently indeterminate to insure that events can never be precisely duplicated. Most of John Cage's post-musical concerts are staged happenings, as the performers are offered only approximate instructions for creating a predictably miscellaneous aural and visual field; yet since Cage, unlike Kaprow, does not allow his spectators to participate in creating the theatrical effects, the audience's role is more observational than participational. In *Variations V* (1965), done in collaboration with the Merce Cunningham Dance Company, the stage is filled with a network of vertical poles that, like Theremin, respond to the physical proximity of the dancers by generating autonomous electronic sound. Thus, the more figures there are on the stage, and the more frequently they move, the more chaotic is the aural mix likely to be. Meanwhile, films by Stan VanDerBeek are projected on four overhead screens, along with kinetic collages composed of changing slides and looped film footage. The result is a chaotically structured performance field – organized disorganization, rather than disorganized disorganization – that is rich in miscellaneous activity. It never loses its rhythmic and spatial irregularity and yet remains continually interesting and innovative in detail. *Variations V* is also the epitome of that peculiarly American contribution to a European tradition called "opera." The Living Theatre's *Paradise Now* (1968) would also be classified as a staged happening, though it differs from Cage's work in encouraging audience response.

Kinetic environments are, like staged happenings, fixed in space and unfixed in duration, but their components and/or activities are more exactly planned and precisely executed. Essentially, they create a constant, intrinsically interminable, enclosed field of multi-sensory activity through which a spectator can proceed at his own pace, and where he stands or sits in relation to the whole customarily determines the kinds of perception he has. In the mid-sixties, USCO, a group of artists living in Garnerville, New York, created mixed-means environments of music, taped noise, paintings, sculptural machines, electronic instruments (such as televisions or oscilloscopes), and projected images (both on slides and film), all of which induced an experience of sensory overload. In *The Theatre of Mixed Means*, I regarded kinetic environments as a kind of theatre; but in a subsequent essay on "artistic environments," which is my term for esthetically defined enclosures, I placed them as one genre within a larger form. Like so much other truly avant-garde art, such works resist precise critical classification.

The last genre of mixed-means theatre, staged performances, are as closely planned in conception and precise in execution as kinetic environments; but here the action is customarily more focused, the work's duration more fixed, and the audience's role more observational. Indeed, in all these respects, mixed-means staged performances resemble the format and structure of traditional theatre; the crucial difference is that, as noted before, speech is here de-emphasized and the means of expression are thoroughly mixed. Prominent examples of this genre include the choreography of Alwin Nikolais, who skilfully integrates sound, light, props and setting with the movements of his dancers; Robert Wilson's masterpiece, *The Life and Times of Sigmund Freud* (1969); Richard Foreman and Stanley Silverman's *Elephant Steps* (1968); Mimi Garrard's *Flux* (1968), which projects film (made in collaboration with her husband, the electronic sculptor James Seawright) on moving props and live performers; Meredith Monk's *16 Millimeter Earrings* (1966); and most live performances by the sometime poet Vito Acconci. For structural reasons, the audience's experience of a staged performance is akin to that of a dance concert, a vaudeville show, or even a rock concert. The following chart graphiccally depicts the dimensional differences of the four genres:

GENRE	SPACE	TIME	ACTION
Pure happenings	Open	Variable	Variable
Staged happenings	Closed	Variable	Variable
Staged performances	Closed	Fixed	Fixed
Kinetic environments	Closed	Variable	Fixed

The themes expressed in most mixed-means pieces relate more to how we perceive than what we think; and in this respect, its relevant "contents" *Prune, Flat* (1965), which is a staged performance, pre-filmed moving images are projected upon both a stationary screen and white-smocked live performers. Certain images on screen are duplicated live on stage and vice versa, while the texture of the theatrical light, the shape of the perceptible space, and the relations between the elements are all continually rearticulated. These strategies contribute to the piece's major theme, which is the difference between filmed images and live ones, or between kinetic activity and static information; for it endeavors to make us more aware of perceptual subtleties. Whitman himself was originally a sculptor; and like most mixed-means creators, he takes his esthetic exemplars, as well as his artistic ideals, from outside "legitimate" theatrical circles.

What the various strains of mixed-means theatre have in common, then, is a distinct distance from literary theatre; and the measure of this separation includes a rejection of the visual clichés of "dramatic" body-movement and setting; an abandonment of narrative plot; a format that is comparatively unfocused – most pieces lack a distinct introduction, a climax or a clear conclusion, as well as visual and aural foci to rivet the audience's attention. Most mixed-means performances also have a structure based upon discontinuous events or images, which usually attain their unity through repetition or incongruous relation; performers who do not play roles (others) but merely fulfill prescribed tasks (themselves), which are to varying degrees less precisely programmed than an actor's activity in theatrical drama; an unfettered attitude toward both the various materials of communication and the possibilities of theatrical situations. In contrast to the literary theatre, which is predominantly visual (even the sounds are based upon words, which are usually comprehended visually), the theatre of mixed means appeals to the total sensorium – the ears as well as the eyes, the nose as well as the receptors of touch, if not the kinesthetic senses too; and in this respect, the new movement contributes to what Marshall McLuhan has characterized as the contemporary drift out of a predominantly visual existence into a multiply aware orientation reminiscent of primitive man.

A mixed-means piece usually opens with a sound-image complex that is instantly communicated; and rather than resort to the linear techniques of variation and development, the piece generally sustains, or fills in, its opening out line. Narrative, when it exists, functions more as a convention than a revelatory structure or primary dimension, for the themes of a mixed-means piece are more likely to emerge from the repetition of certain actions and/or the coherence of successive imagery. Therefore, the comprehension of a mixed-means piece more closely resembles looking at an unfamiliar street or overhearing a distant conversation than deducing the theme of drama; for the longer and more deeply the spectator assimilates and dissects its sound-image complex and then associates the diverse elements, the more intimate becomes his understanding of an individual work.

The ways of presenting mixed-means material are nearly as various as the populace of practitioners; and since the new art's characteristics often leave the eye unsure of where it should look, and the ear unsure of what it should hear, each piece ideally challenges the perceptual capacities of its spectators. The process of understanding such an unfamiliar form of communication appears to involve three separate recognitions, which Edward T. Hall in *The Silent Language* (1959) defines as "*sets, isolates* and *patterns*. The sets (words) are what you perceive first, the isolates (sounds) are the components that make up the sets, while the patterns (syntax) are the ways in which sets are strung together in order to give them meaning." Even in miscellaneous material, the mind learns to perceive several levels of coherence; and it should be clear that any presentation that can be defined as one thing, rather than as another, is, by such definition, revealed to have an artistic structure.

Like many important tendencies in contemporary art, the theatre of mixed means emphasizes the processes of creation, rather than the final product – the esthetic values reward exploration and surprise, rather than the fulfillment of convention; and like the electronic media themselves, the new theatre creates a field of multifarious activity that appeals to more than one of the senses. Not only does the new theatre return the performance-audience situation back to its original, primitive form as a ceremony encompassing various arts, but it also endeavors to speak internationally, in the universal language of sights and movements, at a time when the old spoken languages contribute to archaic nationalisms. Mixed-means theatre denies the myth that formal education is necessary for the appreciation of art and, therefore, the tradition that theatrical arts are solely for the educated class, even though many pieces demand an experienced perception that is best inculcated by acquaintance with the art itself.

In the history of art, the theatre of mixed means represents the radical departure from nineteenth-century forms that the theatrical medium, unlike the other arts, has yet to undergo. "The theatre is always twenty or thirty years behind poetry," writes the French playwright Eugene Ionesco, "and even the cinema is in advance of the theatre." As the modern revolt in poetry overthrew post-Renaissance ideas of perception and connection, so the new theatre also implies a rejection of linearity and explanatory truth. It asks us to perceive not isolated events in space and time but accidental coherences and transforming patterns in space-time; for as life around us becomes more complex and various, so should the modes by which we perceive and arrange our experience. Perhaps the greatest purpose implicit in the new theatre is initiating that multiple awareness that enables us better to comprehend what the architectural historian Sigfried Giedion identified as "a principle which is ultimately bound up with modern life – simultaneity," as posed by our comprehensively transforming, thoroughly discontinuous environment.

The rumor is that "happenings are dead," and so do they superficially seem. While none of the visual artists that were prominently involved continue to do theatrical work, the sometime choreographers persist, as do Robert Wilson and La Monte Young. The liberating influence of the new movement also lingers, not only in the theatricality of, say, post-painterly "conceptual art" and Christo's monumental wrappings, but also in the multi-media trappings that have infiltrated more conventional stages – in the renewed emphasis upon performance-values, often at the expense of the literary. The reason for this pervasive impact is easy to identify. The theatre of mixed means epitomizes pure theatre, whose language of expression is so exclusively theatrical that no other medium can adequately reproduce the art, for only in live performance can a particular work be experienced or finally understood.

—Richard Kostelanetz

*   *   *

BRECHT, George.   Editor of *Fluxus*, New York. Performances include *Toward Events*, New York, 1959; *Card Piece for Voice, and Candle Piece for Radios*, New York, 1960; *Gossoon*, New York, 1960; *Iced Dice*, New York, 1961; *Dithyramb*, 1962; *Nectarine*, New York, 1962; *Life of George Washington*, New York, 1964; *The Book of the Tumbler on Fire*, New York, 1965; *Shake, Sit-Stand-Walk*, London, 1965; and many other events. Cards, kits, posters, etc. published by Fluxus. Books: *Chance Imagery*, 1966; *Games at the Cedilla; or, The Cedilla Takes Off*, with Robert Filliou, 1967; *Vicious Circles and Infinity*, with Patrick Hughes, 1975.

CAGE, John.   Co-Editor, *New Music*, 1943–54. Compositions include *The Seasons*, 1947; work for two pianos, 1954; *Fontana Mix*, 1958; *Atlas Eclipticalis*, 1961; *HPSCHD*, with Lejaren Hiller, 1967–69. Musical Director, Merce Cunningham, and Dance Company, 1943–67. Recorded music directly on to magnetic tape, 1951. Performances include untitled piece at Black Mountain College, North Carolina, 1952; *Water Music*, 1952; *Williams Mix*, 1952; *Suite for Toy Piano, and Imaginary Landscape No. 5*, New York, 1960; *Theatre Piece*, 1960; *Rozart Mix*, 1965; *Variations V*, 1965; *Variations VII*, 1966; *Water Walk; Sounds of Venice*. Books: *Virgil Thomson: His Life and Works*, with Kathleen Hoover, 1959; *Silence*, 1961; *John Cage* (catalogue), 1962; *A Year from Monday*, 1967; *Notations*, with Alison Knowles, 1969; *M: Writings 1967–1972*, 1974.

CUNNINGHAM, Merce.   Dancer and choreographer: with Martha Graham Company, 1940–45; first solo concert, 1944; Director, Merce Cunningham Dance Company, since 1952, Dance School, since 1959, and Dance Foundation, since 1965. Principal works choreographed: *The Seasons*, 1947; *Sixteen Dances for Soloist and Company of Three*, 1951; *Les Noces*, 1952; *Septet*, 1953; *Minutiae*, 1954; *Suite for Five*, 1956; *Nocturnes*, 1956; *Antic Meet*, 1958; *Summerspace*, 1958; *Rune*, 1959; *Crises*, 1960; *Aeon*, 1960; *Story*, 1963;

Winterbranch, 1964; *Variations V*, 1965; *How to Pass, Kick, Fall, and Run*, 1965; *Place*, 1966; *Scramble*, 1967; *Rain Forest*, 1968; *Walkaround Time*, 1968; *Canfield*, 1969; *Signals*, 1970; *Loops*, 1971; *Landrover*, 1972; *TV Rerun*, 1972; *Changing Steps*, 1973; *Solo*, 1973; *Un Jour ou Deux*, 1973; *Sounddance*, 1974; *Westbeth*, 1974; *Exercise Piece*, 1975; *Rebus*, 1975; *Torse*, 1975.

DINE, Jim.   Painter: one-man shows since 1959. Performances include *The Smiling Workman*, New York, 1960; *Car Crash*, New York, 1960; *Vaudeville Act*, New York, 1960; *A Shining Bed*, New York, 1960; *Spring Cabinet*, New York, 1961; *Natural History (The Dreams)*, New York, 1965.

FOREMAN, Richard.   See his entry on p.

GROOMS, Red.   Painter: one-man shows since 1958. Designed sets and costumes for Kenneth Koch's *Guinevere*, 1964. Performances include *Play Called Fire*, Provincetown, Massachusetts, 1958; *Walking Man*, Provincetown, Massachusetts, 1959; *Burning Building*, New York, 1959; *Fireman's Dream (The Magic Trainride)*, New York, 1960; *The Big Leap*, New York, 1960. Films include: *Unwelcome Guests*, 1961; *Shoot the Moon*, 1962; *Miracle on the BMT*, 1963; *Lurk*, 1964; *Spaghetti Trouble*, 1964; *Man or Mouse*, 1964; *Umbrellas, Bah!*, 1965; *Big Sneeze*, 1965; *Secret of Wendel Sampson*, 1965–66; *Before 'n' After*, 1966; *Washington's Wig Whammed!*, 1966; *Fat Feet*, 1966; *Meow, Meow!*, 1967.

HALPRIN, Ann.   Choreographer. Founder, San Francisco Dancers' Workshop, 1959. Founder, *Impulse* magazine. Has worked with the director Ken Dewey; the composers La Monte Young, Terry Riley, Morton Subotnick, Luciano Berio; the artists Charles Ross, Anthony Martin, Jerry Walters, and Jo Landor; the poets James Broughton and Richard Brautigan. Works choreographed include *Trunk Dance; Four Square; The Prophetess; The Lonely Ones; Visions; Birds of America, or, Gardens Without Walls* (first full-length work), 1959; *The Flowerburger*, 1960; *Rites of Women*, 1961; *Five-Legged Stool*, 1962; *Esposizione*, Venice, 1963; *Visage*, 1963; *Parades and Changes*, 1964; *Apartment 6*, 1965; *The Bath*, 1966; *Myths*, 1967; *Ceremony of US*, Watts, 1969; *Invocation of the Cement Spirit*, 1970; *Animal Ritual*, 1971; *Trance Dance* and *Totem* (improvisation pieces on-going since 1970).

HANSEN, Al.   Painter. Co-Founder, Audio-Visual Group, 1958. Owner, Third Rail Galleries, New York. Performances: *Projections*, New York, 1960; *Bibbe's Tao*, New York, 1960; *A Program of Happenings? Events! Situations?*, New York, 1960; *Hi-Ho Bibbe*, New York, 1960; *Car Bibbe*, Woodstock, New York, 1962; *Hall Street Happenings*, New York, 1962; *Silver City for Andy Warhol*, New York, 1963; *Parisol 4 Marisol*, New York, 1963; *Monica Harmonica*, New York, 1964; *Red Dog for Freddie Herko, Piano for Lil Picard, and Oogadooga*, New York, 1964; *Garbo-X-Mas-Bibbe*, New York, 1964; *The Gunboat Panay*, New York, 1965; *Happenings at the Bridge*, New York, 1965; *A McLuhan Megillah*, New York, 1966; *Event with Motor-Cycle, Paper Happening, and Coin Piece*, London, 1966; *Three Events*, New York, 1966; *Toilet Paper*, Tokyo, 1966; *Baker's Dozen*, New York, 1967; *The Hamlet of Gertrude Stein*, New York, 1969.

HIGGINS, Dick.   Founder, Something Else Press, 1964, and *Something Else Newsletter*, 1966. Performances include *Cabarets, Contributions, Einschusz*, New York, 1960; *Saint Joan at Beaurevoir*, New York, 1960; *Simultaneous Performance of Four Compositions*, San Francisco, 1960; *Two Generous Women, Graphis 24, Graphis 82*, New York, 1962; *The Broadway Opera*, Cologne, 1962; *Lots of Trouble*, New York, 1963; *Requiem for Wagner*, New York, 1964; *Danger Music No. 17*, New York, 1964; *An Evening of Opera*, New York, 1964; *The Tart*, New York, 1965; *Sounds of the Animals Dying 13 to 1*, London, 1965; *To Everything Its Season, Celestrials, Graphis 118, Gangsang*, New York, 1965; *Graphis 132*, New York, 1967; *The Thousand Symphonies*, New Brunswick, New Jersey, 1968. Books include *Jefferson's Birthday/Postface*, 1964; *FOEW £ OMBWHNW*, 1969; *A Book about Love & War & Death*, 1972; *City with All the Angels*, 1974; *Modular Poems*, 1975.

KAPROW, Allan. Painter: one-man shows since 1953. Performances include *18 Happenings in 6 Parts*, New York, 1959; *Sound Piece*, New York, 1960; *Intermission Piece*, New York, 1960; *An Apple Shrine*, New York, 1960; *A Spring Happening*, New York, 1961; *Night*, Ann Arbor, Michigan, 1961; *Yard*, New York, 1961; *Courtyard*, New York, 1962; *Coca Cola/Shirley Cannonball*, 1960; *The Big Laugh*, New York, 1960; *A Service for the Dead 1*, New York, 1962; *Sweeping*, Woodstock, New York, 1962; *A Service for the Dead 2*, Bridgehampton, New York, 1962; *Words*, New York, 1962; *Chicken*, Philadelphia, 1962; *Mushroom*, St. Paul and Minneapolis, 1962; *Push and Pull: A Furniture Comedy for Hans Hoffman*, New York, 1963; *May*, New York, 1963; *Bon Marché*, Paris, 1963; *Out*, Edinburgh, 1963; *Eat*, New York, 1964; *Birds*, Carbondale, Illinois, 1964; *Orange*, Coral Gables, Florida, 1964; *Paper*, Berkeley, 1964; *Household*, Ithaca, New York, 1964; *Calling*, New York, and New Jersey (two-day event), 1965; *Soap*, Sarasota, Florida, 1965; *Self-Service*, Boston, New York, and Pasadena, California (four-month event), 1966; *Gas*, New York (three-day event), 1966; *Fluids*, Los Angeles, 1967; *Moving*, Chicago, 1967; *Runner*, St. Louis, 1968; *Transfer*, Middletown, Connecticut, 1968; *Hello*, Boston, 1968; *Round Trip*, Albany, New York, 1968; *Record II*, Austin, Texas, 1968; *Arrivals*, Garden City, New York, 1968; *Population*, Madison, New Jersey, 1968; *Six Ordinary Happenings (Charity, Pose, Fine, Shape, Giveaway, Purpose)*, Berkeley, 1969; *Course*, Iowa City, 1969; *Level*, Aspen, Colorado, 1970. Books: *Assemblages, Environments, and Happenings*, 1966; *Some Recent Happenings*, 1966; *Untitled Essay and Other Works*, 1967; *Five Happenings*, in *New Writers 4*, 1967.

MAC LOW, Jackson. See his entry on p.498.

NIKOLAIS, Alwin. Choreographer. Director, Nikolais School of Dance, 1939–42, Henry Street Playhouse, 1948–70, and Alwin Nikolais Dance Company, since 1953. Principal works: *Kaleidoscope*, 1956; *Runic Canto*, 1957; *Allegory*, 1959; *Prism*, 1960; *Imago*, 1963; *Sanctum*, 1964; *Galaxy*, 1965; *Totem: Vaudeville of the Elements*, 1965; *Somniloquy*, 1967; *Triptych*, 1967; *Fusion*, 1967; *Tent*, 1968; *Limbo*, 1968; *Structures*, 1969; *Scenario*, 1970; *The Relay*, 1971; *Foreplay*, 1972; *Grotto*, 1973; *Cross-Fade*, 1974; *Nik: An Experiment in Sight and Sound*, for the US Information Service, 1974; *Temple*, 1974; *Tribe*, 1975.

OLDENBURG, Claes. Sculptor: one-man shows since 1959. Performances include *Snapshots from the City*, New York, 1960; *Blackouts*, New York, 1960; *Circus (Ironworks/Fotodeath)*, New York, 1961; *Ray Gun Theatre (Store Days 1 and 2, Nekropolis 1 and 2, Injun 1 and 2, World's Fair 1 and 2)*, New York, 1962; *Injun*, Dallas, 1962; *Sports*, New York, 1962; *Gayety*, Chicago, 1963; *Stars*, Washington, D. C., 1963; *Autobodys*, Los Angeles, 1963; *Washes*, New York, 1965; *Moviehouse*, New York, 1965; *Birth of the Flag*, New York, 1965; *Message*, Stockholm, 1966; *The Typewriter*, New York, 1969. Books: *Spicy Ray Gun, Ray Gun Poems*, and *More Ray Gun Poems* 1960; *The Store*, 1961; *Injuns and Other Histories*, 1966; *Store Days*, 1967; *Proposals for Monuments and Buildings*, 1969.

PATTERSON, Benjamin. Performances include *Situationen...*, Cologne, 1961; *Lemons*, Cologne, 1961; *Après John Cage*, with George Maciunas, *Duo*, and *Variation für Contrabass*, Wuppertal, 1962; *Exposition à Paris*, Paris, 1962; *Paper Piece* and *The Triumph of Egg*, London, 1962; *Night Kite*, New York, 1966.

RAUSCHENBERG, Robert. Painter: set, costume, and lighting designer. One-man shows since 1951. Performances include *Pelican*, 1963; *Spring Training*, 1965; *Map Room I*, 1965; *Map Room II*, New York, 1965; *Linoleum*, 1966; *Open Score*, 1966.

SCHNEEMANN, Carolee. "Kinetic theatre" works: *Labyrinths*, Sidney, Illinois, 1960–61; *Glass Environment for Sound & Motion*, New York, 1962; *Newspaper Event*, New York, 1962; *Chromelodeon*, New York, 1963; *Lateral Splay*, New York, 1963; *Meat Joy*, Paris, London, and New York, 1964; *Music Box Theatre*, New York, 1964; *The Queen's Dog*, New York, 1965; *Noise Bodies*, with James Tenney, New York, 1965; *Ghost Rev*, with USCO, New York, 1966; *Water Light/Water Needle*, New York, 1966; *Snows*, New York, 1967; *Night Crawlers*, Montreal, 1967; *Ordeals*, Training, 1965; *Map Room I*, 1965; *Map*

Room II, New York, 1965; *Linoleum*, 1966; *Open Score*, 1966.

SCHNEEMANN, Carolee. "Kinetic theatre" works: *Labyrinths*, Sidney, Illinois, 1960–61; *Glass Environment for Sound & Motion*, New York, 1962; *Newspaper Event*, New York, 1962; *Chromelodeon*, New York, 1963; *Lateral Splay*, New York, 1963; *Meat Joy*, Paris, London, and New York, 1964; *Music Box Theatre*, New York, 1964; *The Queen's Dog*, New York, 1965; *Noise Bodies*, with James Tenney, New York, 1965; *Ghost Rev*, with USCO, New York, 1966; *Water Light/Water Needle*, New York, 1966; *Snows*, New York, 1967; *Night Crawlers*, Montreal, 1967; *Ordeals*, New York, 1967; *Snug Harbor*, Staten Island Ferry, 1967; *Illinois Central*, Chicago, 1968; *Illinois Central Transposed*, New York state tour, 1968; *Expansions*, New York, 1969; *Thames Crawling*, London, 1970; *Schlaget-auf (Ein Gestalt)*, Berlin, 1971; *Rainbow Blaze*, London-New York, 1971; *Icestrip*, London-Edinburgh, 1972. Films: *Viet-Flakes*, 1965; *Fuses*, 1967; *Plumb Line*, 1972; *Cooking with Apes or Subtle Gardening*, 1973; *Kitch's Last Meal*, 1973; *Carl Ruggles Christmas Breakfast*, 1973. Books: *Parts of a Body House Book*, 1972; *Cezanne, She Was a Great Painter*, 1975. Painter, sculptor, lecturer, director, performer.

USCO, or US Company. Gerd Stern, Steve Der Key, Michael Callahan, poet, painter, and carpenter. Performances include *Billymaster* (tape-collage); *Verbal American Landscape*, 1964; *Afterimage*, 1965; *Lower East Side Past and Present Environment*, New York, 1967.

WHITMAN, Robert. Painter and sculptor: one-man shows since 1959. Performances include *E.G.*, New York, 1960; *Small Cannon*, New York, 1960; *Small Smell*, New York, 1960; *The American Moon*, New York, 1960; *Untitled*, New York, 1961; *Ball*, New York, 1961; *Mouth*, New York, 1961; *Movies with Sound, Movement, Song, Play*, New York, 1962; *Flower*, New York, 1963; *Water*, New York, 1963; *Hole*, New York, 1963; *Prune, Flat*, New York, 1965; *The Night Time Sky*, New York, 1965; *Two Holes of Water*, East Hampton, New York, 1966. Cinema pieces: *Cinema, Shower*, and others.

WILSON, Robert. See his entry on p.

YOUNG, La Monte. Composer; Director of the Theatre of Eternal Music. Compositions include *Octet for Brass*, 1957; *Trio for Strings*, 1958; *Vision*, 1959; *Compositions 1960; Two Sounds*, 1960; *Poems for Chairs, Table and Benches, Etc.; or, Other Sound Sources*, 1960; *The Second Dream of the High-Tension Line Step-Down Transformer*, 1962; *Piano Piece for T. Riley no. 2*, 1963; *The Well-Tuned Piano*, 1975. Performances include *Collaboration Event*, Berkeley, 1960; *Simultaneous Performance of Four Compositions*, San Francisco, 1960; *Sopranino*, East Hampton, New York, 1962; *Music*, New York, 1963; *The Tortoise, His Dream and Journeys*, 1964 (various versions); *Dream Music*, New York, 1964; *Dream House*, 1975. Books: *Composition 1961*, 1963; *Selected Writings*, 1968; Editor, *An Anthology*, 1963.

BIBLIOGRAPHY:

Ay-o, and others, editors, *Manifestos*. New York, Something Else Press, 1966.

Baxandall, Lee, "Dramaturgy of Radical Activity," in *Drama Review* (New York), Summer 1969.

Becker, Jurgen, and Wolf Vorstell, *Happenings*. Hamburg, Rowholt, 1965. (Includes texts, in German.)

Epstein, John, and others, *The Black Box*. London, Latimer, 1970.

Esslin, Martin, "The Happening," in *Reflections*. New York, Doubleday, 1969; as *Brief Chronicles*, London, Temple Smith, 1970.

Foreman, Richard, "The Life and Times of Sigmund Freud," in *Village Voice* (New York), 1 January 1970.

Henri, Adrian, *Total Art*. London, Thames and Hudson, and New York, Praeger, 1974.

Kaprow, Allan, *Assemblages, Environments and Happenings*. New York, Abrams, 1966.

(Includes scripts.)

Kirby, Michael, *The Art of Time*.   New York, Dutton, 1969.

Kirby, Michael, *Happenings*.   New York, Dutton, and London, Sidgwick and Jackson, 1965. (Includes scripts.)

Kirby, Michael, and Richard Schechner, editors, *Tulane Drama Review* (New Orleans, Louisiana), Winter 1965. (Includes scripts.)

Knowles, Alison, and others, editors, *Four Suits*.   New York, Something Else Press, 1965. (Includes scripts.)

Kostelanetz, Richard, *The Theatre of Mixed Means*.   New York, Dial Press, 1968. (Includes comprehensive bibliography.)

Kostelanetz, Richard, editor, *Moholy-Nagy*.   New York, Praeger, 1970; London, Allen Lane, 1971.

Kulterman, Udo, *Art and Life*.   New York, Praeger, 1971.

Nyman, Michael, *Experimental Music*.   New York, Schirmer, and London, Studio Vista, 1974.

Sohm, H., editor, *Happenings and Fluxus: Materialen*.   Cologne, Koelnischer Kunstverein, 1970. (Includes bibliography and performance list.)

Tomkins, Calvin, *The Bride and the Bachelors*.   New York, Viking Press, and London, Weidenfeld and Nicolson, 1965; revised edition, Viking Press, 1968.

THEATRE
COLLECTIVES

The counter culture which developed during the 1960's in the U.S.A. and England as well as other countries in Western Europe formed its own alternative theatres outside the etablishment. The structures of these groups, their working methods, and the theatre pieces they created reflected the aesthetic, social and political convictions at the heart of their dissent from traditional theatre and its culture. Although much of the political energy of the cultural movement seems to have been dissipated, many of the theatre groups have continued to function ten or fifteen years after their formation.

The mainstream of Western society since the industrial revolution had become increasingly specialized and competitive. This was reflected in an established theatre based on competition and a theatrical method involving individual specialists such as playwright, director, designer, and actor. By contrast, the alternative society focused upon the group rather than the individual or a script, and its pieces were created collectively through group cooperation rather than individual competition.

Instead of the two-process method of the traditional twentieth-century theatre − a playwright writing a script in isolation and the other artists staging it − the method of the theatre collective involves a single process wherein the group itself develops the piece from initial conception to finished performance. The typical member of such a group is not merely a performer, but a person with broader creative responsibilities who may not distinguish between the work of performer, director, designer, and playwright, but who applies his creative energies to the making of a theatre piece whatever that might involve. Some individuals may provide more leadership than others, but the works which result are truly the expression of the group, not merely of the playwright as interpreted by director and actors.

The collective method which developed was one expression of the need for wholeness in contrast with the psychic fragmentation of the individual in the established technocratic society which still believes that man's needs are fulfilled by technical means achieved by more and more specialization. Such specialization has resulted in the individual losing his view of the whole, tending to make the work he performs unfulfilling. Further, just as governments preach one ethic to their citizens while practicing another in wars and political intrigue, there is a disparity between the ethics an individual practices at home with his family and that which is operable when he goes to work where the good of the employing organization becomes the sole guide for behavior. Such fragmentation of the individual is disorienting and alienates him from self and community. In reaction many young people disassociated themselves from the established culture and its work ethic, they formed collectives of various kinds, sometimes lived in communes, and participated in numerous group activities, especially those with political, social, or artistic aims.

The alternative theatres, unlike commercial theatres, are not concerned with entertainment as a product to be sold. Instead, they are anxious to improve the quality of life for themselves and audiences, and developed their collective method and their conceptions to achieve this end. The script-oriented theatre of the absurd, the *avant-garde* of the 1950's, reflected the philosophical alienation of the individual; the alternative theatre of the 1960's reflected the social commitment of the group. This focus not only required a new collective method, but new techniques were needed to express the new theatrical conceptions which grew out of this commitment.

Because the focus was not upon the individual, there was no realistic psychological development of character. The characters became archetypes, fantastic imaginings, or undefined dance-like figures. Several figures sometimes represented one character simultaneously or at different times, and sometimes they were simply the performers who did not assume characters. There was an aversion to the traditional theatrical spaces associated with the established theatre because such theatres were too large and typically were divided into stage and auditorium. Smaller undivided spaces permit a more informal relationship between performer and spectator, thus making possible the development of a community spirit.

Words, the chief tool of established culture, were suspect, and in the alternative theatre were diminished in importance. Further, there was a belief that words, because in most usages they are limited to expressing discursive concepts, had tended to replace other modes of expression which may be the only means of expressing some experiential conceptions. The established society, having relied upon words as a nearly exclusive mode of expression, had tended to cut itself off from its experience. Furthermore, especially in the United States, the alternative culture denigrated the establishment's nationalism which in part is perpetuated by national languages. In their attempts to develop other modes of expression, some alternative theatre groups experimented with non-verbal sounds, with focusing upon the performer's body, and with a variety of visual means. There are, of course, other practical considerations which motivated some groups toward a visual emphasis. Many of them subsist from touring, often in foreign language countries, and some perform outdoors where words do not carry well.

Improvisation became the principal technique of group creation. Everyone could participate. It was used to train members of the group to work creatively and collectively, to suggest initial conceptions for new pieces and to develop them into finished productions. Sometimes the improvisational exercises themselves became the performance. Despite the use of improvisation by nearly every group, each developed its own method which could change somewhat from work to work as they experimented with new conceptions and new means of expressing them. One of the chief ways their methods differed was in the source of or the means of discovering an inceptive idea for a piece – from exercises; from a social, political, or aesthetic problem; from a text or painting; from working with an object or materials; or from a script by someone within the group.

Until the industrial revolution brought about increased specialization in most activities including the theatre, and realism seemed to make a dictatorial theatre director essential, collaboration between all theatre functionaries was common. Frequently, as with Shakespeare and Molière, the playwright was a member of a theatre company. In the first half of the twentieth century such examples are rare. Those performing in English include The Group Theatre in New York during the 1930's, directed by Harold Clurman, which fostered the young dramatist Clifford Odets. In 1945 Joan Littlewood formed the Theatre Workshop in London where playwrights could collaborate with other artists and where fledgling dramatists such as Brendan Behan and Frank Norman could come under her developing influence. These groups, however, had less impact upon the theatre collectives developing in the 1960's and 1970's than did the theories of Artaud, the political ideas and theatrical practice of Brecht, the performer-training ideas of Grotowski, and the experiments with performer-spectator interaction of the Living Theatre.

One of the earliest and most active of the alternative theatre groups providing young playwrights with opportunities to work collaboratively with other theatre artists was La Mama Experimental Theatre Club of New York founded by Ellen Stewart and Paul Foster in 1961. Its stated purpose was to develop new writers who were interested in experimenting with fresh theatrical concepts and through experimentation to develop a new acting style to express these concepts. In addition to Foster's plays, La Mama presented works by Leonard Melfi, Sam Shepard, Jean-Claude van Itallie, Lanford Wilson, Megan Terry, Julie Bovasso, and Rochelle Owens. Tom O'Horgan's association with the group began in 1964 and it was under his direction that a permanent company was formed and arduous physical training was begun. The unique acting style which resulted approached acrobatic movement, made use of transformations wherein the performer could instantaneously shift character or respond to the imaginary locale or a prop as if it had changed, and sometimes incorporated improvisatory moments during performance. In recent years, groups having varying relationships with the original La Mama, but all using the name, have been formed in Japan, Columbia, Canada, Australia, Austria, Germany, France, and England.

In some groups the director assumes the leadership in the development of a play from a variety of sources. The Pip Simmons Theatre Group in London began working in 1968. They create their own pieces under the direction of Pip Simmons in such a way as to use the performers' musical skills, both vocal and instrumental, as well as their acting ability. A style emerged which uses amplified music composed and performed by the group in combination with acrobatic movement and speech, often narrative rather than dialogue, spoken directly to the audience. According to its director, the group uses a "musical form" so as to investigate the possibility of destroying the "absurd failure of the 'literary' theatre." *Superman*, which focuses upon the disillusionment with the American dream, takes its inceptive idea from a comic strip but also includes ideas and language from other sources including Sophocles, Aeschylus, Nietzsche, Arrabal, and Ed Bullins. *Do It!* is based upon Jerry Rubin's book of that name and satirizes liberals and their romanticizing of Yippies and revolutionary ideas. In *Alice,* based upon the stories of Lewis Carroll, the title role is played simultaneously by a girl and a man. The other performers, as in their previous works, play multiple roles. Several other theatre groups developed productions based upon the Alice stories about the same time as the Pip Simmons Theatre Group. Among them were the Moving Being which considers itself a dance company, the Manhattan Project under the direction of Andre Gregory in New York, and the Toronto Workshop which in *Chicago '70* alternated Alice scenes with excerpts from the transcript of the Chicago conspiracy trial.

Another starting point for some theatre groups has been classical plays. In this they have been influenced by the practice of the Polish director Jerzy Grotowski. Work on a piece may begin with reading, discussing, and improvising upon a Greek or Elizabethan script, but the script serves neither as a guide for a production nor as a work to be elucidated or interpreted. Rather, the original work is used by the group as a point of departure, a catalyst, as material for its own unique theatre piece. Sometimes the original script is dissected and reassembled into a collage as Charles Marowitz has done with *Hamlet, Macbeth,* and *Othello* at the Open Space Theatre in London; or as Richard Schechner says of the Performance Group's *Makbeth* which he directed in New York, "we used Shakespeare the way a plasterer uses plaster, to fill in some things, to make something." *Dionysus in 69* by the Performance Group used fewer than half the lines from *The Bacchae* of Euripides; the rest of the text was made by the performers themselves. In London the Freehold under the direction of Nancy Meckler created *Antigone* which is a collage of Sophocles, added speeches written specifically for the production, and sections developed entirely through improvisation. The resulting work was so much their own accomplishment that the Freehold received the John Whiting Award for "new and distincitve development in dramatic writing," the first time the award was made to a group instead of a playwright.

The work of Jerzy Grotowski, the Freehold, and others exemplifies yet another characteristic of some alternative theatre work – a visual focus which, as in dance, is upon the body of the performer rather than his environment, objects, lighting, or costumes. In part this results from an attempt to find that which is unique to the theatre experience rather than depending upon the same visual elements as motion pictures and television. The actual physical presence of the performer is put into focus. Some dancers have thus become innovators in the alternative theatre movement. Foremost among these is Ann Halprin, director of the Dancers' Workshop of San Francisco, who tended more and more toward involving the spectator as participant, and then eliminated the spectator entirely and concentrated on therapeutic workshops. Another group, the Moving Being in London and subsequently in Cardiff, directed by Geoff Moore, has maintained the traditional separation between performer and audience and has broadened its media to include various kinds of projection.

The director of the Open Theatre, Joseph Chaikin, while not a dancer, has focused almost exclusively upon the performer, extending the range of movement and sounds to find new means of expression. Chaikin had been a member of the Living Theatre in its early days but formed his own group in 1963. He has been instrumental in collecting, developing, and disseminating psycho-physical exercises similar to those used by Grotowski, and has used them as a means of training members of the group. The Open Theatre developed its pieces improvisationally, sometimes with the collaboration of a playwright member, around universal human concerns such as death in *Terminal* and human adaptation in *The Mutation Show*. The group's last production before disbanding in 1973 was *Nightwalk* which developed out of their investigation of levels of sleep.

Mabou Mines, a group directed by Lee Breuer in New York, demonstrated that the bodies of performers can be used in yet another way. In *Red Horse Animation* the movement of the performers, as they lie on the floor viewed from above by the spectators does not *represent* the movement of people nor for that matter of a horse, but *presents* the abstract concept of a horse in motion.

Visual artists had an important influence upon the collective creation of theatre pieces through the happenings presented in the 1960's by such artists as Allan Kaprow, Claes Oldenburg, and Robert Whitman. In these happenings there was no traditional dramatic illusion of a particular place or time; they were not organized around a plot but around a series of images and tasks, and many details were left to be determined in performance. An important function of the happenings was to make poeple see in a different more direct way and to free the artist from various conventions. A theatre group in London called the People Show, formed in 1966, has made at least one piece with these characteristics. Each of eighteen spectator-participants received at his home a yellow suitcase and two bolts, with instructions to carry the suitcase around in a certain section of Soho at a particular time until he met someone else with a yellow suitcase. The two were to introduce themselves, bolt their suitcases together, and continue walking, repeating the process until all eighteen suitcases were bolted together. Then all eighteen people marched to Trafalgar Square where they separated and intentionally lost their suitcases. As with found art, everyday objects and tasks devoid of their efficacy become perceptual events.

More recent work of the People Show has centered on the five permanent members of the group each of whom develops his own character and environment. Together they devise a framework which guides the improvised performances. However, they avoid an ensemble approach because they believe it would inhibit individuality and variety. Another English group, the John Bull Puncture Repair Kit, works in a similar fashion, often designing their semi-improvised pieces for specific environments.

A further extension of this principle is evident in the work of Welfare State formed by John Fox in England in 1968. The 10–16 painters, sculptors, musicians, and dancers who call themselves Civic Magicians and Engineers of the Imagination live in several caravans on a disused municipal rubbish tip on the outskirts of Burnley where they present some of their work. They believe that art should not be separate from the rest of their lives but intrinsic. Therefore, they do not create a fictional illusion of time and place, but present their fantasies in such a way that they exist, like a painting or sculpture, in the actual time and place of the spectator. They have created outdoor ceremonies in celebration of a variety of events – the coming of winter and spring, New Year's Eve, the naming of children. Their larger performances include a one-month 150 mile pilgrimage following in reverse the legendary route of King Arthur. The journey was one continuous performance incorporating surrealistic events and images from the life of their perennial hermaphrodite hero Sir Lancelot Icarus Handyman Quail. The presentation of large images in actual space and time tend to make found art of the actual environment in which they are seen.

Similarly, when performers play themselves the focus is upon the actual time and locale of the performance. The performers of *Dionysus in 69* alternated between playing characters and being themselves, occasionally revealing their actual inner feelings in their actions as when one of the actors in the middle of a performance left the theatre with a spectator. Sometimes the image of character and performer seemed to exist simultaneously, superimposed one on the other.

The Living Theatre began working in New York in 1951, but it was only after their self-imposed exile to Europe in 1964 that they took deliberate steps toward working without a fictional illusion. In *Mysteries and Smaller Pieces* they performed some tasks involving spectators as in the section called "The Plague" when bodies of performers and spectators were placed in a pile. But this was in the context of an imagined plague. In *Paradise Now* there was another shift in reality. Performers, playing themselves, were efficacious in their confrontations with spectators, sometimes eliciting emotional responses. Spectators were encouraged to perform actions such as "flying" which involved leaping from a high point into the arms of those below. These were not fictional enactments, and the resulting emotive responses were actual symptomatic feelings, not merely representations of character emotions. There are a number of other instances in which the exercises of rehearsal become the performance when repeated for or with an audience. These breaks from the contrived linear cause-and-effect structure of traditional fictional theatre attempt to free the theatre from restricting illusionist conventions thereby making possible the creation of a community between performers and spectators.

Such interest in social utility is manifested in the work of many groups. Sometimes it aims to free the individual from self-imposed oppression, sometimes it attempts to help him to more fulfilling relationships with others, and sometimes it focuses upon increasing his political awareness.

The Company Theatre of Los Angeles in a piece called the *James Joyce Memorial Liquid Theatre* led the spectator with eyes closed through a "sensory maze" consisting of a series of tactile and taste sensations intended to awaken his senses. This voluptuous experience was intended to prepare the spectator to join the performers in the trust and sensitivity exercises that followed. In London, the Other Company (T.O.C.) of Inter-Action Trust used variations of these exercises in parts of *The Pit* and *The Journey* with audiences limited to thirty-four and fifteen respectively, so that performers and spectators could inter-relate. Another group within Inter-Action, the Dogg's Troupe, works with children, usually on playgrounds to which they attract their spectator-participants with a parade. A typical piece uses a narrative which affords many opportunities for the children to participate in theatre games focused toward developing individual sensitivity, group inter-action, and cooperation. In *Comics* the children help find the hidden Kryptonite and thus restore Superman's failing strength. Furthermore a piece such as *Moonmen* may serve to reduce fear of strangers and thereby diminish aggressive tendencies toward foreigners. At the Theatre Workshop, Boston, children have been helped to greater awareness of certain cultural and environmental problems through participation with performing leaders in narratives dealing with American Indians and environmental pollution.

A significant number of alternative theatres, comprised of those from oppressed minorities or those who oppose the established culture, concern themselves with exposing the injustices of the establishment and its institutions, raising the awareness of their audiences to these evils, and developing within oppressed people the solidarity and self esteem that will move them to political action. At the end of *Paradise Now* the Living Theatre led the audience into the street to begin the "nonviolent anarchist revolution." The Cartoon Archetypical Slogan Theatre (CAST) in London "attempts to serve the socialist revolution" through its performances for workers at union meetings. Their pieces, ranging from twenty to forty minutes, revolve around the character Muggins, a clown-like embodiment of twentieth-century urban man acted upon by capitalistic and military forces of the establishment.

Some of the politically focused groups perform outdoors in parks, streets, and at fairs so as to reach audiences that normally do not attend theatre performances. The San Francisco Mime Troupe, formed under the direction of R. G. Davis and later reorganized as a collective with rotating responsibilities, began performing outdoors in 1962. In 1965 Davis was arrested when the group performed in a park after the city refused to grant a permit. The refusal was later ruled an unconstitutional attempt at censorship. Recently the work of the group has focused exclusively upon raising political awareness. Each year its repertoire includes a long play of an hour or more on a broad political subject such as *The Dragon Lady's Revenge*, dealing with the collusion of U.S. and South Vietnamese officials in maintaining power in Vietnam, or *The Independent Female*, concerned with the domination of American women by men. In addition, short plays of perhaps twenty minutes are created in reaction to specific political events as they occur, such as a satire on President Nixon's price and wage control policies called *Frozen Wages*. The group is entirely self sufficient, subsisting financially by passing the hat at performances and fees paid for performances at universities. In the early days the plays developed by the group took the form of modern commedia dell'arte; later they combined these techniques with those of burlesqued nineteenth-century melodramas, vaudeville, and the circus. Nearly everyone in the group, in addition to acting, plays musical instruments and juggles.

The Bread and Puppet Theatre was formed in New York about the same time as the San Francisco Mime Troupe and has continued from the beginning under the direction of Peter

Schumann. Although Schumann subscribes to no political doctrine, he would persuade people from harmful ones. His productions are characteristically in the form of parables sometimes using biblical or oriental images. The pieces are usually narrated by the director and are performed by human performers, often with masks, in combination with puppets which range in height up to twenty feet and require as many as five people to operate. Several similar groups have been formed by people who have worked with the Bread and Puppet Theatre. Among them is the Beggars Theatre in California which in 1976 undertook a three-month tour of Mexican towns and villages.

In London the Red Ladder Theatre takes its plays to where people live and work – to factory gates, union meetings, community centers, pubs, and "working men's" clubs. They write their plays with the help of workers, and by setting everyday problems in an economic and political framework, they "seek to expose and demystify the operations of the Capitalist system of production." They do not provide political solutions, but raise issues and ask questions in their strikingly visual productions which serve as a basis for the discussion which follows each performance. In this way the group intends to make its contribution to "the struggle for Socialism in Britain."

Among other groups in England with similar objectives is Belt and Braces Roadshow Company formed in 1973 "to provide articulate and entertaining socialist theatre from a working class viewpoint." To enhance the entertainment value of their work they incorporate a band and songs into each of their productions.

A phenomenon which began in the United States but has since spread to England is the formation of theatre groups from racial minorities or others who do not share fully in the benefits of the established society. The principal aim of such theatre groups which may be comprised of blacks, Chicanos, gays, or women liberationists is to create an awareness of their plight among their respective constituencies, to identify the oppressor, and to raise self esteem by pointing out their unique positive qualities.

The first of the black theatres, the Free Southern Theatre, was formed in Mississippi in 1963 as part of the civil rights movement and became a new means of protesting the oppression of blacks. The group hoped that a theatrical form would emerge which would be as unique to black American culture as blues, jazz, and gospel music. By 1972 there were more than a hundred black theatres spread throughout the United States. These include two with which Imamu Amiri Baraka (LeRoi Jones) has been associated – the Black Arts Repertory Theatre in Harlem, New York, and Spirit House in nearby Newark, New Jersey. Others of importance are the New Lafayette Theatre of playwright Ed Bullins and the Negro Ensemble Company in New York, the Black Educational Theatre directed by Marvin X and the Grassroots Experience Theatre directed by John Doyle in San Francisco, and the Bodacious Buggerrilla directed by Ed Bereal in Los Angeles. In London the Black Theatre of Brixton has been the most active.

El Teatro Campesino was formed in 1965 by Luis Valdez to help articulate the issues of the grape strike in California and to help organize the Chicano workers into the National Farm Workers Association being formed by Caesar Chavez. Performing in a combination of Spanish and English the group began by presenting ten to fifteen minutes "actos" which, in the manner of the commedia dell'arte, used such stereotype characters as Huelgista (striker), Esquirole (scab), and Patroncito (grower). Subsequently the group incorporated *corridos* (traditional folk ballads) and *mitos* (myths from Aztec and Mayan religions), and have come to be guided in their agrarian living by the traditions and philosophy of the ancient Maya. Valdez says, "We will consider our job done when every one of our people has regained his sense of personal dignity and pride in his history, his culture and his race." Other Chicano theatres in the southwestern states have emulated Valdez' beginnings, and have developed their own styles.

Feminists and gays have also used theatre for political and social ends. The women's theatre groups have attempted to raise awareness of both men and women to the potentials of women in relation to their possibilities in society, to the nature of the oppression, and to the identity of the oppressor. Further, as with the blacks and Chicanos, the formation of such groups provided creative opportunities which had largely been denied them by the white male domination of the theatre. The most active groups in New York have been the New Feminist Theatre which produced some of the early plays of Myrna Lamb and the It's All Right to Be Woman Theatre which often uses the lives of its members as a basis for their collective work. In London the work of the Women's Theatre Group is directed toward "exploration of the female situation from a feminist viewpoint." *My Mother Says I Never Should*, a play concerning the sexual contradictions and problems confronting adolescent girls, toured to schools, colleges, and youth clubs in 1975. *Work to Role* exposes the clichés concerning the potential of women in family and work roles.

One of the earliest gay theatres was the Cockettes formed in San Francisco in 1970. Their intention was to give gays the courage to "come out" and dress as they like. Their collective pieces are aggressively amateurish in the style of camped Hollywood musicals of the 1930's and 1940's. They describe their work as "sexual role confusion." Some men play in drag, sometimes with decorated genitals visible, some dress as men, women dress as both females and males, often with fake over-sized phalli and real breasts swinging. Their success is perhaps indicated by the spirit of community developed among their heterogeneous audiences which include many gays in drag. Two groups in New York that frequently mix up sex roles are the Play-House of the Ridiculous directed by John Vaccaro and Charles Ludlam's Ridiculous Theatrical Company. Both of these groups work in a more disciplined way and are less concerned with immediate social impact. The Gay Sweatshop in London has given more serious attention to analyzing the problems encountered by gays. In *Mister X* they argue that homosexuals should accept themselves. It is not necessary for them to play the heterosexual roles of the established society. A male homosexual need not imitate either a masculine man or woman; he can be himself. Each performance is followed by a candid discussion of the problems of the gays in their audience.

The chief distinguishing method of the alternative theatre is that its pieces are created by theatre collectives through a single process from inception to completion somewhat as in the visual arts. This requires broader creative responsibility than is typical in the established theatre where participants are more narrowly specialized. Their work is optimistic in that it expresses the belief that the quality of life can be improved by non-material means. But the optimism of theatre collectives is not only reflected in the social and political utility of their pieces; it is also evident in the continuing vitality of the groups despite lack of facilities and inadequate or non-existent subsidies.

—Theodore Shank

*   *   *

THE ALIVE AND TRUCKING THEATRE COMPANY.   Formed in Minneapolis, Minnesota, 1971, as a socialist-feminist theatre collective. Major pieces include *Pig in a Blanket*, 1971; *The People Are a River, The Welfare Wizard of Ours*, and *Rats, Bats, Hells Bells and Son of Evil Genius*, 1972; *The Exception and the Rule* by Brecht and *Ally, Ally All Come Free*, 1973; *Battered Homes and Gardens*, 1974.

BEGGARS THEATRE.   Founded by Christopher Hardman and Laura Farabough, Venice, California, 1972; moved to San Francisco in 1973 and subsequently to Sausalito. Productions include *The Woman of Viet Nam Cries, Punch and Judy, The Burning of Beelzebub*, and *The Christmas Story*, 1972; *The Wildman Pageant, The Alienated Life of Punchinello, The Harvest Pageant, The Good Man and the Bad King*, and *The Rat Story*, 1973; *State of the Union, The Beast, The Creation and Destruction of the World, Lucifer Crowns Himself King of the World, Ivan Captures Death, Lady Chile Says No, The Death Ship Esmerelda, The Bone Show/Calaveras*, and *George Washington and the Witch*, 1974; *The Generals Send Death, Ja Ja Man, The Hunger Show, The Grand Architect and Mother Earth, The Fool Asleep, The Lunatics, Thanksgiving Play*, and *Eye of Darkness*, 1975; *Woman of Sorrow* and *The Dog with Two Sandwiches*, 1976.

BELT AND BRACES ROADSHOW COMPANY LTD.   Formed in 1973 by former members of the Ken Campbell Roadshow and 7:84 Theatre Company. Productions include *Ramsay MacDonald: The Last Ten Days, Bollix,* and *The Great Money Trick,* 1973; *The Recruiting Officer,* and *The Front Line,* 1974; *Weight,* 1975; *England Expects* and *An Eye's Top Whack,* 1976.

BREAD AND PUPPET THEATRE. Founded by Peter Schumann, Germany, then New York. Productions include Mime and Mask Plays, Giant Puppet Shows, Sidewalk Shows, Puppet Plays, Children's Shows, Political Pageants, Crankys, and Parades: *Totentanz, The Battle,* and *Fire I,* 1962; *Neither; The Cry; Dance of Death* (first U.S. play); *The Dead Man Rises; Apocalypse; Chicken Little; Johnny; The Good King; The Blue-Ribboned Beauty; Christmas Story; Death, Narrator and the Great Warrior,* 1967; *A Man Says Goodbye to His Mother; The Cry of the People for Meat,* 1969; *The Difficult Life of Uncle Fatso,* 1970; *Birdcatcher in Hell, Emilia, The Quest,* and *Attica,* 1971; *The Fourteen Stations of the Cross, Laos, Hallelujah, The Coney Island Cycle,* and *That Simple Light May Rise Out of Complicated Darkness,* 1972; *Three Yells, Trouble,* and *Attica Memorial,* 1973; *Christmas Story, Easter's Stations of the Cross,* and *Our Domestic Resurrection Fair and Circus,* 1974; *A Monument for Ishi – An Anti-Bicentennial Pageant,* 1975; *Domestic Resurrection,* 1976. References: *The Drama Review 38, 47, 55,* and *61* (New York), 1968–74; *Le Bread and Puppet Theatre* by François Kourilsky, Paris, Le Cité Editeur, 1971; *Theatre Quarterly 20–21* (London), 1975.

CARTOON ARCHETYPICAL SLOGAN THEATRE (CAST). Founded in London, 1966. First work, *John D. Muggins Is Dead,* followed by *Mr. Oligarchy's Circus, The Trials of Horatio Muggins, Muggins Awakens, Harold Muggins Is a Martyr* (with John Arden), 1969; *Sam the Man,* 1976. The group divided in 1972 and three members formed Cartoon Clowns. CAST was dormant for some time and began working again in 1975.

THE COCKETTES. Founded by the Angels of Light, San Francisco, 1969. Productions include *Tinsel Tarts in a Hot Coma, Pearls over Shanghai, Hollywood Babylon, Hell's Harlots, Les Cockettes de Paris, Elephant Shit under the Big Top, Les Etoiles de Minuit,* and *Cockettes in Clapland.* After a New York tour (1972) the group disbanded. Some members of the group moved to New York and formed a new group using the old name The Angels of Light.

THE COMPANY THEATRE. Founded, Los Angeles, 1967. Productions include *In White America* by Martin Duberman and *Johnny Johnson* by Paul Green, 1967; *Antigone, Comings and Goings* and *Keep Tightly Closed in a Cool Dry Place* by Megan Terry, *Sir!, Coney Island of the Mind* by Lawrence Ferlinghetti, *Icarus's Mother* by Sam Shepard, *The Martyrdom of Peter Ohey, The Empire Builders* by Boris Vian, 1968; *The Sport of My Mad Mother* by Ann Jellicoe, *Red Cross* by Sam Shepard, *Voyages, The Emergence,* and *Such As We Are for As Long As It Lasts,* 1969; *The James Joyce Memorial Liquid Theatre I* and *II,* 1969–70; *Narrow Road to the Deep North* by Edward Bond and *Children of the Kingdom,* 1970; *The Plague, The Gloaming, Oh My Darling* by Megan Terry, and *Meatball,* 1971; *Caliban* and *Mother of Pearl,* 1972; *Endgame* by Samuel Beckett, 1973; *The Hashish Club.* Tours of U.S. and Europe, 1972. In 1972 the group divided some continuing to work as The Company Theatre, others forming The Pro(visional) Theatre. Productions by The Pro(visional) Theatre include *Dominus Marlow/A Play on Doctor Faustus,* 1973; *America Piece,* 1974; *XA, A Vietnam Primer,* 1975; and *Voice of the People,* 1976.

THE FIREHOUSE THEATRE. Founded by James Faber and Charles Morrison, Minneapolis, 1963; the group disbanded almost immediately and reformed the same year under Marlow Hotchkiss and Sidney Walter; moved to San Francisco in 1969. Productions include *The Connection* by Jack Gelber; *Happy Days* and *Waiting for Godot* by Beckett; *A Song for All Saints* by James Lineberger; *Jack-Jack, Viet Rock,* and *Keep Tightly Closed in a Cool Dry Place* by Megan Terry; *The Brig* by Kenneth H. Brown; *The Caretaker* by Pinter; and plays by Dürrenmatt and Frisch. The group's later work was either adaptations of classics (*Faust, Woyzeck,* and *Iphigenia Transformed*), or plays written by group member Nancy Walter: *Blessings,* 1970; *Escape by Balloon* and *Still Falling,* 1971; *The Window,*

Travelling Light, and *Stab and Dance*, 1972; and its last piece, *Doomeager*, 1973. In 1973 the group disbanded. References: *The Drama Review 32* and *45* (New Orleans, New York), 1966, 1969.

THE FREE SOUTHERN THEATRE.   Founded by Gilbert Moses, John O'Neal, and Doris Derby in Mississippi, 1963; moved to New Orleans, 1965. Productions include *Purlie Victorious* by Ossie Davis and *Waiting for Godot* by Beckett, 1964; *In White America* by Martin Duberman, and *The Rifles of Senora Carrar* by Brecht, 1965; other plays by Brecht, Gilbert Moses, Ionesco, Beckett, and Douglas Turner Ward; and pieces written in the Community Workshop Program as well as poetry readings and television work. References: *The Drama Review 28* (New Orleans), 1965; *The Free Southern Theatre*, edited by Thomas C. Dent and Richard Schechner, Indianapolis, Bobbs Merrill, 1969.

THE FREEHOLD.   Formed in London, 1969, by seven former members of Wherehouse La Mama, London, as an exploratory workshop under the direction of Nancy Meckler. Productions include *Alternatives* and *Antigone*, 1969; *The Duchess of Malfi* by Webster and *Drums in the Night* by Brecht, 1970; *Pantagleize* by Michel de Ghelderode, *Harlequinade*, and *Mary, Mary* by Roy Kift, 1971; *Genesis* by Kift, *Icarus's Mother* by Sam Shepard, and *There/this/move* by Michael Kirby, 1972; *Beowulf*, 1973. The company disbanded in 1973. Reference: *The Drama Review 54* (New York), 1972.

HULL TRUCK.   Founded by Mike Bradwell, 1971. Improvisationally developed productions include *Children of the Lost Planet; The Weekend after Next; The Knowledge; Oh What!*, 1975; *Bridget's House* and *Melody Bandbox Rhythm Roadshow*, 1976.

INTER-ACTION TRUST.   Founded by Ed Berman and Naftali Yavin, as a charitable trust. Includes three separate groups: **The Ambiance Lunch Hour Theatre Club** – began in 1968, and moved to the Almost Free Theatre when it was established by Inter-Action in 1972; it performs short contemporary scripts. **The Dogg's Troupe** – directed by Ed Berman, works with children. Productions include *The Moonmen, The Comics, Technicolour Peelers, Bonkers* (a series of street performances), *Doll Shows, Father Christmas Union, Act-in, Epic*, and *Joy Scouts*. **T.O.C. (The Other Company)** – directed by Naftali Yavin until his death in 1972 after which the group became inactive. Productions include *The Pit*, 1969; *The Journey*, 1970; *Games* and *After Liverpool* by James Saunders, 1971; four Peter Handke plays, 1971–72. Reference: *Fine Arts Bus: An Inter-Action Project*, edited by Justin Wirtle, London, Eyre Methuen, 1975.

IT'S ALL RIGHT TO BE WOMAN THEATRE.   Founded in New York, 1970. Pieces include feminist vignettes, plays, crankys, poems, and songs, all written by the group. Production: *Wherever You Land, That's Who You Are*, 1974. References: *The Drama Review 54* and *63* (New York) 1972, 1974.

JOHN BULL PUNCTURE REPAIR KIT.   Formed by Michael Banks, Al Beach, John Darling, and Diz Willis, a performance art group, London, 1968. They have produced over a hundred works including *Earthprobes* and *Beachboys/Barrowboys*, 1972; *Morbid Interests*, 1973; *The John Bull Stately Home and Safari Park* and *Southern Comfort*, 1975; *Welcome to Dallas, J.C.* by David Edgar, 1976. Reference: *Travail Théâtral* (Paris), Winter 1976.

LA MAMA EXPERIMENTAL THEATRE CLUB.   Founded by Ellen Stewart and Paul Foster, New York, 1961; first permanent company formed by Tom O'Horgan, 1964. Productions include *Futz* by Rochelle Owens, *Hair* by Gerome Ragni and James Rado, *Tom Paine* by Foster, *The Room* by Pinter, and plays by Tom Eyen, Lanford Wilson, Sam Shepard, Ruth Krauss, Megan Terry, Julie Bovasso, Leonard Melfi, and Jean-Claude van Itallie. Toured Europe 1965 and later. O'Horgan left La Mama in 1969. E.T.C. Company/La Mama was formed by John Braswell and Wilford Leach in 1970. Productions include *Gertrude; or, Would She Be Pleased to Receive It, Carmilla, Renard, The Only Jealousy of Emer*, and *Demon*, 1970–72; *The Bar That Never Closes, Interior Castle* and *Corfax (Don't Ask)*, 1973; *Troyer*, 1973, 1974. Reference: *The Drama Review 34* (New Orleans), 1967.

THE LIVING THEATRE.   Founded by Judith Malina and Julian Beck, New York, 1947; formally launched in 1951, moved to Europe in the mid-1960's, returned to New York, '1968, moved to Brazil, 1970, returned to U.S. after imprisonment, 1971, worked in Brooklyn, moved to Pittsburgh in 1974. First play presented in a theatre was *Dr. Faustus Lights the Lights* by Gertrude Stein, 1951; later productions include *Beyond the Mountains* by Kenneth Rexroth, 1951; *Desire Trapped by the Tail* by Picasso, *Faustina* by Paul Goodman, *Sweeney Agonistes* by T.S. Eliot, *Ubu Roi* by Jarry, and *Ladies' Voices* by Stein, 1952; *The Age of Anxiety* by W. H. Auden and *The Heroes* by John Ashbery, 1954; *The Young Disciples* by Goodman, 1955; *Many Loves* by William Carlos Williams, 1959; *The Marrying Maiden* by Jackson Mac Low, *Women of Trachis* by Ezra Pound, and *Antigone* by Brecht, translated by Malina, 1960; *The Brig* by Kenneth H. Brown, 1963; and plays by Jack Gelber, Jean Cocteau, Yeats, Lorca, and Strindberg; later productions are *Mysteries and Smaller Pieces*, Paris, 1964; *Frankenstein*, 1965; *Paradise Now*, 1968; *The Legacy of Cain* (developing cycle) – *Christmas Cake for the Hot Hole and the Cold Hole*, Sao Paulo, 1970; *Rituals and Transformations*, Embu, Brazil, 1970; *A Critical Examination of Six Dreams about Mother*, Saramenha, Brazil, 1971; *Seven Meditations on Political Sado-Masochism*, 1973; *Strike Support Oratorium* and *The Money Tower*, 1974; *Six Public Acts*, 1975. References: *The Drama Review 43, 51*, and *62* (New York), 1969–74; *The Living Theatre/USA* by Renfreu Neff, Indianapolis, Bobbs Merrill, 1970; *We, The Living Theatre* by Aldo Rostagno, Julian Beck, and Judith Malina, New York, Ballantine, 1970; *Scripts 1* (New York), November 1971; *The Living Theatre* by Pierre Biner, New York, Avon Books, 1972; *The Life of the Theatre* by Julian Beck, San Francisco, City Lights, 1972; *The Enormous Despair* by Judith Malina, New York, Random House, 1972; *Praxis* (Berkeley, California), Spring 1975.

LUMIERE AND SON.   Formed by director Hilary Westlake and playwright-performer David Gale, London, 1974. Productions are either theatrical (indoors) or environmental, and include *Tip Top Conditioning, Jack....The Flames, The Poshingtons, The Mad Girls*, and *The Quacking Kabukis from Togoland*, 1974; *Pet Cure and Molester, Indications Leading to* (fill in name of performance site), *White Men Dancing*, and *The Sleeping Quarters of Sophia*, 1975; *Dogs*, 1976. Reference: *Travail Théâtral* (Paris), Winter, 1976.

MABOU MINES.   Founded by director Lee Breuer and composer Philip Glass, Paris, 1965; moved to New York, 1970. Productions include group-developed pieces *Red Horse Animation*, 1971, *B-Beaver Animation*, 1973, *Music for Voices, The Saint* and *The Football Players*; other works include *Play, Come and Go, The Lost Ones*, 1975, and *Cascando*, 1976, by Beckett.

THE MOVING BEING.   Founded by Geoff Moore, London, 1968; moved to Cardiff, 1971. Multi-media productions include *Dog God the Tight-Rope Walker*, 1970; *Condor; Package Deal; Signs: Sequences for the Theatre*, 1971; *Phoenix; The Real Life Attempt*, a trilogy consisting of *Signs, Angels*, and *Sun; Dreamplay*, based on a play by Strindberg; *The Journal of Anaïs Nin*, 1975.

THE NATURAL THEATRE.   Formed in Bath in 1971 as part of the Bath Arts Workshop, a community and arts organization started in 1970. Productions include *The Rocky Rickkets Show, Rocky and the Jets*, and clown and puppet shows.

NEGRO ENSEMBLE COMPANY.   Founded by Douglas Turner Ward, Robert Hooks, and Gerald S. Krone, New York, 1966. Productions include *Song of the Lusitanian Bogey* by Peter Weiss, *Kongi's Harvest* by Wole Soyinka, *Summer of the Seventeenth Doll* by Ray Lawler, *Daddy Goodness* by Richard Wright and Louis Sapin, and *God Is a (Guess What?)* by Ray McIver, 1968; *Man Better Man* by Errol Hill, *Contribution* by Ted Shine, *String* by Alice Childress, *Malcochon* by Derek Walcott, and *Ceremonies in Dark Old Men* by Lonne Elder III, 1969; *Song of Absence* by Ward and *The Harangues* and *Ododo* by Joseph A. Walker, 1970; *Ride a Black Horse* by John Scott, 1971; *Sty of the Blind Pig* by Philip Hayes Dean, 1971; *Akokawe; The River Niger* by Walker, 1972; *In the Deepest Part of Sleep* by Charles Fuller, 1974. References: *Theatre Crafts* (New York), March-April 1974.

NEW LAFAYETTE THEATRE.   Founded by playwright Ed Bullins and director Robert Macbeth, Harlem, New York, 1967. Productions include many of Bullins' over 60 plays (*A Son, Come Home; The Electronic Nigger; Clara's Ole Man; In The Wine Time; Goin' a Buffalo; The Duplex*; and *The Fabulous Miss Marie*, among others), and plays by Ron Milner, Athol Fugard, Sonny Jim, Martie Charles, Richard Wesley, and collectively-created pieces. The group disbanded in 1974.

OPEN THEATRE.   Founded by Joseph Chaikin (formerly with the Living Theatre), New York, 1963. Productions include *Viet Rock* by Megan Terry, 1966; *America Hurrah*, 1966, and *The Serpent*, 1968, by Jean-Claude van Itallie; *Ubu Cocu* by Jarry, *Endgame* by Beckett, and *Terminal* by Susan Yankowitz, 1969; *Mutation Show*, 1971; *Nightwalk* by van Itallie, Sam Shepard, and Terry, 1973. The group disbanded in 1973. References: *A Book on the Open Theatre* by Robert Pasolli, Indianapolis, Bobbs Merrill, 1970; *The Presence of the Actor* by Joseph Chaikin, New York, Atheneum, 1972; *Three Works by the Open Theatre* by Karen Malpede, New York, Drama Books, 1974.

ORGANIC THEATRE.   Founded by Stuart Gordon, Madison, Wisconsin, 1969; moved to Chicago, 1970. Productions include adaptations of *Richard III* by Shakespeare; *Animal Farm* by George Orwell and *The Tarot Cards*, 1970; *Candide* by Voltaire, *Poe*, and *WARP* (a trilogy), 1971; *The Wonderful Ice Cream Suit* by Ray Bradbury, 1973; *Bloody Bess: A Tale of Piracy and Revenge* and *Sexual Perversity in Chicago* by David Mamet, 1974; *Adventures of Huckleberry Finn* by Mark Twain, 1975.

THE PEOPLE SHOW.   Founded by Mark Long and others, London, 1966. Originally produced new scripts (several by Jeff Nuttall). Later material originates within group with all members contributing and working without a director. Each production bears a number and sometimes a subtitle. In 1976 they were up to *People Show No. 64 (Boxing)*. References: *Gambit 16* (London), 1969; *The Drama Review 52* and *62* (New York), 1971, 1974.

THE PERFORMANCE GROUP.   Founded by Richard Schechner, New York, 1967. Productions include *Dionysus in 69*, 1968; *Makbeth*, 1969; *Commune*, 1970 with subsequent changes *Commune 2*, then *Commune 3; Concert for T.P.G.*, 1971; *The Tooth of Crime* by Sam Shepard, 1972; *The Beard* by Michael McClure, 1973; *Mother Courage* by Brecht, *A Wing and a Prayer* by Ellen LeCompte, *Sakonnet Point*, and *The Marilyn Project*, 1975. References: *The Drama Review 39, 43, 50*, and *51* (New York), 1968–71; *Theatre Quarterly* (London), 1971.

PIP SIMMONS THEATRE GROUP.   Founded by Pip Simmons, London, 1968. The group disbanded in 1974 and Pip Simmons worked briefly in Holland returning to England in 1975. Productions include plays by Jean Tardieu and Arrabal and group developed pieces *The Pardoner's Tale*, 1969; *Superman*, 1970; *Do It!* and *Alice*, 1971; *George Jackson's Black and White Minstrel Show*, 1972; *Dracula*, 1974; *An die Musik* and *The Dream of a Ridiculous Man*, 1975. References: *Superman* script published in *New Short Plays 3*, London, Methuen, 1972; *Travail Théâtral* (Paris), Winter 1976; *The Drama Review 68* (New York), 1975.

THE PLAY-HOUSE OF THE RIDICULOUS.   Founded by John Vaccaro, New York, 1965. Productions include *Terrene the Terrible Tart from Terra Cotta, The Life of Juanita Castro*, and *Kitchenette* by Ronald Tavel, 1965; *The Life of Lady Godiva, Screen Test*, and *Indira Gandhi's Daring Device* by Tavel, 1966; *Big Hotel* and *Conquest of the Universe* by Charles Ludlam, 1967 (after which he left the group to form the Ridiculous Theatrical Company); *The Moke-Eater*, 1968, and *Heaven Grand in Amber Orbit* and *Night Club*, 1970, by Kenneth Bernard; *Persia; A Desert Cheapie* by Vaccaro and Bernard Roth, *Satyricon* by Vaccaro and Paul Foster, and *Sissy* by Seth Allen, 1972; *The Magic Show of Dr. Ma-Gico* by Bernard, 1973.

THE PRO(VISIONAL) THEATRE.   See **THE COMPANY THEATRE.**

RED LADDER THEATRE (or The Big Red Ladder Show, formerly Agit-Prop Theatre). Founded as a political theatre co-operative in London, 1968. Indoor and outdoor work includes *Housing Play, Race Play, Productivity Play, Unemployment Play, Happy Robots, A Woman's Work Is Never Done*, and *It Makes You Sick*. References: *The Drama Review 44* (New York), 1969; *Travail Théâtral* (Paris), Winter, 1976.

RIDICULOUS THEATRICAL COMPANY.   Founded by Charles Ludlam (formerly with the Play-House of the Ridiculous) in New York, 1967. Most productions are written by Ludlam and include *When Queens Collide* and *Big Hotel*; *Whores of Babylon* by Bill Vehr; *Turds in Hell, Grand Tarot*, and *Bluebeard*, 1970; *Eunuchs of the Forbidden City*, 1971; *Corn*, 1972; an adaptation of *Camille*, 1973; *Hot Ice*, 1974; *Stage Blood*, 1974 (based on *Hamlet*); *Caprice*, 1976. References: *The Drama Review 62* (New York), 1974.

SAN FRANCISCO DANCERS' WORKSHOP.   Founded by Ann Halprin, San Francisco, 1959. See her entry in Theatre of Mixed Means Section.

SAN FRANCISCO MIME TROUPE.   Founded by R. G. Davis, San Francisco, 1959. Reformed in 1970 as a collective. Early productions were mainly *commedia dell'arte* pieces based on Molière and Goldoni. Collectively developed pieces include *Eco-Man*, adapted from *Everyman, Telephone, Independent Female* by Joan Holden, and *Seize the Time* (based on Bobby Seale's book), 1970; *Highway Robbery, Soledad, G.I. Show*, and *The Dragon Lady's Revenge*, 1971; *Frozen Wages, The American Dreamer*, and *High Rises*, 1972; *The Mother* by Brecht and *San Fran Scandals of '73*, 1973; *The Great Air Robbery*, 1974; *Frijoles or Beans* and *Power Play*, 1975. References: *The Drama Review 32* and *61* (New Orleans, New York), 1966, 1974; *The San Francisco Mime Troupe: The First Ten Years* by R. G. Davis, Palo Alto, California, Ramparts Press, 1975.

EL TEATRO CAMPESINO (The Farmworker's Theatre).   Founded by Luis Valdez, Delano, California, 1965; moved to Fresno, California, 1969, then to permanent headquarters in San Juan Bautista, California, 1971. Early work was short improvised *actos* (political skits) in support of the United Farm Workers strikes and organizing activities. Productions include *Las Dos Garas del Patroncito* (The Two Faces of the Boss), 1965; *Quinta Temporado*, 1966; *Los Vendidos* and *The Shrunken Head of Pancho Villa*, 1967; *La Conquista de Mexico* (Puppet Show), 1968; *No Saco Nada de la Escuela* (I Don't Get Anything Out of School) and *The Militants*, 1969; *Vietnam Campesino, Bernabe*, and *Huelguistas* (Strikers), 1970; *Los Olivos Pits*, 1972; *La Carpa de los Rasquachis* (The Tent of the Underdogs) and *El Baille de los Gigantes* (The Dance of the Giants), 1973; *El Fin del Mundo* (The End of the World), 1975. References: *The Drama Review 36* and *64* (New Orleans, New York), 1967, 1974; *Actos* by Luis Valdez y El Teatro Campesino, San Juan Bautista, California, Cucaracha Press, 1971; *Performance 7* (New York), Fall 1973.

THEATRE WORKSHOP.   Founded by Joan Littlewood, Manchester, 1945; later in London, and since 1953 at the Theatre Royal, Stratford East; some gaps in the existence of the group. Productions include English, Greek, and French classics often adapted by Littlewood and Ewan MacColl, and new works: *Operation Olive Branch*, adaptation by MacColl of *Lysistrata* by Aristophanes, London, 1947; *Uranium 235* by MacColl, 1952; *The Travellers* by MacCall (first production at Stratford East), 1953; *Van Call* by Anthony Nicholson, *The Fire Eaters* by Charles Fenn, *Jupiter's Night Out*, adaptation of *Amphitrion 38* by Giraudoux, *The Flying Doctor* by Molière and *Johnny Noble* by MacColl, *Arden of Faversham, The Cruel Daughters*, adapted by Littlewood from *Père Goriot* by Balzac, *The Good Soldier Schweik* by MacColl, *The Chimes*, adaptation by Littlewood of the Dickens novel, and *The Prince and the Pauper*, adaptation by Littlewood and MacColl of the Twain novel, 1954; *The Dutch Courtesan* by Marston, 1954, 1959; *The Other Animals* by MacColl, *Volpone* by Jonson, *The Midwife* by Julya Hay, *The Legend of Pepito* by Ted Allan, *The Sheep-Well* by Lope de Vega, *The Italian Straw Hat* by Labiche and Marc-Michel, and *The Big Rock Candy Mountain* by Alan Lomax, 1955; *Edward the Second* by Marlow and *The Quare Fellow* by Brendan Behan, 1956; *You Won't Always be on Top* by Henry Chapman and *And the Wind Blew* by Edgard da Roche Miranda, 1957; *Celestina* by Fernanda de Rojas, *Unto Such Glory* by Paul Green, *The Respectable Prostitute* by Sartre, *A Taste of Honey* by

Shelagh Delaney, and *A Christmas Carol*, adaptation by Littlewood of the Dickens novel, 1958; *The Hostage* by Behan, 1958, 1972; *Make Me an Offer* by Wolf Mankowitz and *Fings Ain't Wot They Used T'Be* by Frank Norman, 1959; *Sparrers Can't Sing* by Lewis, 1960; *They Might Be Giants* by James Goldman, 1961; *Oh What a Lovely War* and *Merry Roosters Panto* by Peter Shaffer, 1963; *A Kayf Up West* by Norman, 1964; *Henry IV*, Edinburgh, 1964; *Macbird* by Barbara Garson, *Intrigues and Amours*, adaptation of *The Provoked Wife* by Vanbrugh, *Mrs. Wilson's Diary*, and *The Marie Lloyd Story*, 1967; *Forward up Your End* by Kenneth Hill and *The Projector*, 1970; *The Finest Family in the Land* by Henry Livings and *Costa Packet* by Frank Norman, 1972; *Cranford*, adaptation by Littlewood and John Wells of the Gaskell novel, 1975.

WELFARE STATE. Formed by John Fox in England, 1968; a performance art group, they call themselves Civic Magicians or Engineers of the Imagination; headquarters in Burnley. Performances include ceremonies in celebration of events such as the coming of winter or spring, halloween, marriage, or the naming of children: *The Tide Is OK for the 30th* and *The Marriage of Heaven and Hell*, 1968; *Ceremony and Ritual Play* and *Earthrise*, 1969; *Circus Time* and *Dr. Strangebrew's Plastic Hand*, 1970; *Dr. Strangebrew's Garden Fete* and *The Sweet Misery of Life Show*, 1971; *A Christmas Naming Company* and *The Travels of Sir Lancelot Quail*, 1972; *Beauty and the Beast*, 1973; *Memorial to the First Astronaut* and *Ringmaen*, 1974; *Slug City, Harbinger, Alien: A Science Fiction Rumour, Anacrucus*, and *Cook*, 1975; *Secrets of the Iron Egg* and *Island of the Lost World – A Momentary Journey into Dream Time*, 1976. References: *Theatre Quarterly* (London), October 1972; *Arts in Society* (Madison, Wisconsin), Spring 1975; *Travail Théâtral* (Paris), Winter 1976.

WOMEN'S THEATRE GROUP. Formed in London, 1973. Productions include dramatized readings from *The New Portuguese Letters* by The 3 Marias, *Fantasia, My Mother Says I Never Should*, and *Work to Role*.

—compiled by Adele Edling Shank

APPENDIX

BEHAN, Brendan (Francis).   Irish.   Born in Dublin, 9 February 1923. Educated at the French Sisters of Charity School, Dublin. Married Beatrice ffrench-Salkeld in 1955; one daughter. Joined the I.R.A. at 14; sent to a British borstal correctional school for 3 years, 1939; served 6 years of a 14-year sentence for political offences, 1942–48. Worked as a housepainter and journalist. *Died 13 May 1961.*

PUBLICATIONS

Plays

> *The Quare Fellow* (produced Dublin, 1954; London, 1956; New York, 1958). London, Methuen, and New York, Grove Press, 1956.
> *The Hostage* (produced London, 1958; New York, 1960).   London, Methuen, and New York, Grove Press, 1958; revised edition, Methuen, 1962.
> *The Big House* (broadcast, 1957; produced London, 1963).   Published in *Evergreen Review* (New York), September–October 1961.
> *Moving Out, and A Garden Party*, edited by Robert Hogan.   Dixon, California, Proscenium Press, 1967.
> *Richard's Cork Leg*, edited and completed by Alan Simpson (produced Dublin and London, 1972).   London, Eyre Methuen, 1973; New York, Grove Press, 1974.
> *Time for a Gargle* (produced Leicester, 1973).

> Radio Play: *The Big House*, 1957.

Novel

> *The Scarperer.*   New York, Doubleday, 1964; London, Hutchinson, 1966.

Verse

> *Life Styles: Poems, with Nine Translations from the Irish of Brendan Behan*, translated by Ulick O'Connor.   Dublin, Dolmen Press, and London, Hamish Hamilton, 1973.

Other

> *Borstal Boy* (autobiography).   London, Hutchinson, 1958; New York, Knopf, 1959.
> *Brendan Behan's Ireland: An Irish Sketch-Book.*   London, Hutchinson, and New York, Geis, 1962.
> *Hold Your Hour and Have Another* (articles).   London, Hutchinson, and Boston, Little Brown, 1963.
> *Brendan Behan's New York.*   London, Hutchinson, and New York, Geis, 1964.
> *Confessions of an Irish Rebel.*   London, Hutchinson, 1965; New York, Geis, 1966.
> *The Wit of Brendan Behan*, edited by Sean McCann.   London, Leslie Frewen, 1968.

Critical Studies: *My Brother Brendan Behan* by Dominic Behan, London, Leslie Frewen, 1965; New York, Simon and Schuster, 1966; *The World of Brendan Behan*, edited by Sean McCann, London, New English Library, 1965; *Brendan Behan: Man and Showman* by Rae Jeffs, London, Hutchinson, 1966; Cleveland, World, 1968; *Brendan Behan* by Ted E. Boyle,

New York, Twayne, 1969; *Brendan Behan* by Ulick O'Connor, London, Hamish Hamilton, 1970; *Brendan Behan: A Memoir* by Seamus de Burca, Dixon, California, Proscenium Press, 1971; *The Major Works of Brendan Behan* by Peter Gerdes, Bern, Herbert Lang, 1973; *My Life with Brendan* by Beatrice Behan, Des Hickey, and Gus Smith, London, Frewin, and Los Angeles, Nash, 1974.

*   *   *

Formidable obstacles bar a just appreciation of Brendan Behan as dramatist. First is his "legend," live enough to prompt a biography staged in New York as recently as 1975. Then the post-O'Casey Irish fantasies tend to assimilate a writer with a superficial relationship to them. But Behan is not reducible to publicity sprung from self-destructive alcoholism or to spin-off from Abbey Theatre tradition. A look at *The Hostage* in the context of political and terrorist activity some fifteen years later will identify an original talent.

Synge's *Playboy* provoked riots. In certain locations *The Hostage* would be likely to do so now. If not, it would be because dramatized controversy is no longer a monopoly of the theatre. "The IRA and the War of Independence are as dead as the Charleston," "The IRA is out of date." That only for starters. Equally insolent remarks are directed at: The Gaelic language, Padraic Pearse, the St. Vincent de Paul Society ("all ex-policemen"), the RAF, Irish patriots, gunmen, de Valera, Handel, Protestant bishops, puritanical Catholics, the Royal Family as reported in the popular press ("you might almost be in the yacht there with them"), Evelyn Waugh, the Queen, and as a component of cockney rhyming slang, the Holy Ghost.

These and countless equally subversive comments revolve round the inhabitants of a lodging-house and grotesque visitors ranging from a Polish Communist sailor to an evangelical whore. Its caretaker, claiming to be a survivor of the Troubles and the Easter Rising, lives on the immoral earnings of his abrasive wife. Yeats once proclaimed the birth of "a terrible beauty," and this community is its tawdry old age. Wildly farcical collisions of stereotypes occur without probing or development of character. Then what is there to mould chaotic action into shape? A catalyst, the hostage himself. In retaliation for the sentencing of a young activist due to be hanged in Belfast, the IRA has kidnapped a British soldier outside a dance hall. He arrives under escort at the end of the first act, and in view of Behan's experience of imprisonment in England it's a proof of artistic detachment that this Londoner commands more sympathy than anyone else in the play. Those lucky enough to have seen Murray Melvin's performance can attest that the role skirts "cockney sparrer" clichés without falling into them. Surprisingly from an Irish playwright, it is perhaps the most authentic working-class character in English drama. Information about the boy's social background, for example, is uncommonly precise and the same is true of Teresa, a devout Roman Catholic servant girl in the lodging-house. Between those two, one reared in a convent and the other in the Old Kent Road, a love affair of great delicacy and pathos illuminates the second act.

Parallels with the situation in Cyprus and an awareness of imperial decline, along with a prophetic sense of youth's indifference to such issues, can be had from *The Hostage* over and above its mature attitude to the conflict in Northern Ireland. That, and unflagging satirical energy, ought to preserve the play. The ending, though, defaces it. To have the young soldier killed in error during a shoot-out with government agents is evasively casual. "He died in a strange land and at home he has no one," says Teresa finely, then ruins the gravity by adding that she'll never forget him, "never till the end of time." A jaunty song by the resurrected soldier unwisely includes fragments from the burial service. These draw attention to a profundity which the action has been steadily working towards and finally shirked.

There are no such flaws in *The Quare Fellow* (1956), a durable masterpiece if ever there was one, hard-edged and classical for all its colloquial idiom and gallows humour. The play is about hanging and could serve as polemic worthy of Swift. But it more than that. An entire prison community is brought to life, from the novice alert to education in crime ("Do you think Triplex or celluloid is best for yale locks, sir?") to the Governor intent on providing a good breakfast for the hangman, who renders "The Rose of Tralee" before calculating the condemned man's weight in relation to the law of gravity. Nothing frivolous here, because the grisly ritual from night watch to burial has been realized cumulatively by convicts' and warders' conversation.

Within the austere dramatic structure there is profuse variety of incident. One warder is outspokenly disgusted; it is taboo to name the hangman other than as "himself"; an old lag bets his bacon ration against reprieve. All that and more is geared to the classical unities of action and time. Unity of place is relaxed for episodes in the prison yard, the digging and filling up of an incorrectly numbered grave. And the condemned man, though he dominates the drama, is never heard or seen.

—Laurence Kitchin

COOPER, Giles (Stannus). Irish. Born in Carrickmines, County Dublin, 9 August 1918. Educated at Lancing College, Sussex; Grenoble University; Webber-Douglas School of Drama. Served in the British Army, 1939–46, including four years with the West Yorkshire Regiment in Burma; joined the London Irish Rifles (Territorial Army), 1949. Married Gwyneth Lewis in 1947. Actor in repertory in London and in the provinces, 1946–52; Assistant Script Editor, BBC-TV, 1953, and Associated Rediffusion TV, 1955. Recipient: Guild of Television Producers Script Award, 1961; Czech International Prize for Radio Drama, 1966. O.B.E. (Officer, Order of the British Empire), 1960. Agent: Harvey Unna, 14 Beaumont Mews, Marylebone High Street, London W1N 4HE, England. *Died 2 December 1966.*

PUBLICATIONS

Plays

Never Get Out (produced Edinburgh and London, 1950).
Haddock's Eyes (produced London, 1950).
Unman, Wittering and Zigo (broadcast, 1958). London, Macmillan, 1971.
Everything in the Garden (produced London, 1962). London, Evans, 1963.
Out of the Crocodile (produced Oxford and London, 1963). London, Evans, 1964.
The Lady of the Camellias, adaptation of the play by Dumas, adapted by Terrence McNally (produced New York, 1963).
The Object (broadcast, 1964). Published in *New English Dramatists 12,* London, Penguin, 1968.
Happy Families (produced London, 1966). Published in *New English Dramatists 11,* London, Penguin, 1967.
The Spies Are Singing (produced Nottingham, 1966).
Six Plays for Radio (includes *Mathry Beacon; Unman, Wittering and Zigo; The Disagreeable Oyster; Without the Grail; Before the Monday; Under the Loofah Tree).* London, BBC, 1966.

Radio Plays: *Thieves Rush In,* 1950; *The Forgotten Rotten Borough,* 1950; *The Timbimbo Craze, or, New Games for Old,* 1950; *Small Fortune,* 1951; *The Private Line,* 1951; *The Owl and the Pussycat,* 1953; *The Sound of Cymbals,* 1955; *Mathry Beacon,*

1956; *The Volunteer*, 1956; *The Disagreeable Oyster*, 1957; *Unman, Wittering and Zigo*, 1958; *Without the Grail*, 1958; *Under the Loofah Tree*, 1958; *All for Three Days: A Story of the Hungarian Revolution* (in *With Courage* series), 1958; *Dangerous Word*, 1958; *Before the Monday*, 1959; *Caretaker*, 1959; *Part of the View*, 1959; *A Crown of Gold*, 1959; *Pig in the Middle*, 1960; *The Return of General Forefinger*, 1961; *A Perfectly Ghastly Joke*, 1962; *General Forefinger*, 1961; *I Gotta Universe*, 1963; *All the Way Home*, 1963; *The Object*, 1964; *The Lonesome Road*, 1964; *Something from the Sea*, 1966; *Brass Farthing*, from the novel by Rupert Croft Cooke, 1966; *The Day of the Triffids*, from the novel by John Wyndham, 1968; *Oliver Twist*, from the novel by Charles Dickens, 1970; *The Private Patient*, 1970; *The Wrong Box*, from the story by Robert Louis Stevenson, 1972.

Television Plays: *The No-Man*, 1955; *General Confusion*, 1955; *Liberty Hall*, 1958; *Maigret and the Lost Life*, 1959, and the *Maigret* series, 1960, from the novels by Simenon; *Point of Honour*, 1960; *Where the Party Ended*, 1960; *The Night of the Big Heat*, from the novel by John Lymington, 1960; *Love and Penguins*, 1961; *The Power of Zero*, 1962; *The Double Doll*, 1963; *True Love and Limbeck*, 1963; *Loop*, 1963; *The Freewheelers*, 1963; *A Wicked World*, 1964; *The Other Man*, 1964; *Carried by Storm*, 1964; *Madame Bovary*, from the novel by Flaubert, 1965; *The Six Napoleons*, from the story by Arthur Conan Doyle, 1965; *The Way of All Flesh*, from the novel by Samuel Butler, 1965; *The Canterville Ghost*, from the story by Oscar Wilde, 1965; *Lost Hearts*, from the story by M. R. James, 1965; *Seek Her Out*, 1965; *The Long House*, 1965; *For Whom the Bell Tolls*, 1965, and *A Farewell to Arms*, 1966, from the novels by Ernest Hemingway; *I Am Osango*, 1967; *Sword of Honour*, from the novels by Evelyn Waugh, 1967; *Kittens Are Brave*, 1967; *To the Frontier*, 1968; *A Man in the Zoo*, from the novel by David Garnett, 1975.

Novel

The Other Man.   London, Panther, 1964.

*   *   *

When the curtain rose on Giles Cooper's plays for the stage – well, they had the appearance of being the sort of plays on which curtains *would*, eternally, rise. But in the expanding imaginative universe of his work for radio and television one might find oneself transported anywhere from the ur-world spawned under his eponymous *Carboy* (unproduced) to the more prosaic but no less microcosmic bathtub of *Under the Loofah Tree*. Beneath a prosceniun arch, it was as if Cooper (not unlike those established novelists who were coerced into trying their hands for the theatre in the early days of the Royal Court) felt constrained by conventions of "well-made" construction which, in his more accustomed medium, he had long ago transcended.

Donald McWhinnie, who directed much of Cooper's work for all three media, has commented on the "drawbacks" of his stage techniques: "the audience cannot afford to take its eye, or its ear, off the machine, if it wants to see how the wheels go round." This is because Cooper's plays have "a terseness of expression, an elliptical form ... the result of years of thinking in terms of the rapid interconnections and swift, understated action" of radio and television drama. No wonder that theatre audiences, lulled into a false sense of security by the comfortable settings of the plays, found their burgeoning ambiguities not only disturbing but profoundly puzzling.

Everything in the Garden thus opens with a sunlit vignette of suburban affluence; *Out of the Crocodile* with a glimpse of bland metropolitan sophistication; and *Happy Family* in the slightly shabby gentility of the governing classes in rural retreat.

Each proceeds to expode its paricular myth, showing an acquisitive society ready to sell itself body and soul in the first play; self-deception taken to an extreme of conditioned solipsism in the second; and "breeding" turned viciously in upon itself in the third. Charges by some critics of random motivation and of arbitrary endings usually reveal only their own lulled awareness: scupulously, perhaps over scrupulously, all the causes and effects are *there* in the writing, its sheer density and comic deceptiveness tempting audiences into the half-attention the conventions seem to permit.

In the plays for television and, more especially, for radio, Cooper fashioned his own conventions. Whether in the surrealistic progress of a piece like *The Disagreeeable Oyster* (in which a night out "on the town" turns into a nightmare progressing with its own unreasonable yet irresistible momentum), or the psychological realism of the male-female encounter in *Before the Monday,* he allowed his material to forge its appropriate formal medium. Both plays, however, also typify the pessimism of his world view. It is true that his targets are almost invariably of the middle classes, or of the more ossified establishment institutions: but he does not offer even an implicit alternative, whether to the kind of facile human relationships he shows to be empty, or to the bourgeois values he reveals as a worthless facade. Even the obvious outsiders – the artist who suffers for being a social misfit in *Everything in the Garden,* for example – achieve only the enigmatic affirmation of martyrdom.

Cooper was essentially a writer for voices. Not that he was unable to handle stage pictures, or to think in televisual terms: but he was at his best when the emphasis could fall most naturally upon verbal modulation and counterpoint. Hence the insidious menace behind probably his best known work for radio, *Unman, Wittering and Zigo,* where the quasi-naturalistic struggle for authority between a schoolmaster and his pupils is constantly underpinned by that almost liturgical feeling for the force of words resonant even in the play's title. The accidental rhythm beaten out by three surnames at the end of an alphabetical roll call utters a threat at once in its arbitrariness, its elusive associative quality, and its self-sustaining assonance.

Thus Cooper worked both by highlighting the unexpectedly "normal" in the fantastic, and by exposing the absurdity of the ostensibly commonplace. Often, he was able to make one faintly ashamed of one's own laughter, as what had seemed to be no more than a ludicrous boil on society's rump was laid bare as a terminal growth. Another reason, no doubt, why theatre audiences, reluctant to laugh lest laughter echo their own poor taste, found his plays so disconcerting, while the listener to the radio plays could relate to Cooper and his world directly – and alone.

In one of those radio plays, *Without the Grail,* Cooper used a "realistic" conflict of character to expose the opposing but equal failures of imperialism, communism, tribalism, and pragmatism. Not content with creating this vacuum of communal ideals, he allowed condemnation and catastrophe also to overtake the one character totally immersed in his own self. The only redemptive feature in this as in almost all his work is its humour – which is never a matter of light relief, but itself embodies an attitude towards his material and so, surely, an attitude to life. If Cooper left humanity without a shred of illusion, at least he allowed it the gift of laughter, and the perverse relief of total comic catharsis.

—Simon Trussler

HANSBERRY, Lorraine (Vivian).   American.   Born in Chicago, Illinois, 19 May 1930. Educated at the Art Institute, Chicago; University of Wisconsin, Madison, 1948. Married Robert Barron Nemiroff in 1953 (divorced, 1964). Worked as journalist and editor. Recipient: New York Drama Critics Circle Award, 1959. *Died 12 January 1965.*

PUBLICATIONS

Plays

> A Raisin in the Sun (produced New York and London, 1959).   New York, Random
> House, 1959; London, Methuen, 1960.
> The Sign in Sidney Brustein's Window (produced New York, 1964).   New York,
> Random House, 1965; in Three Negro Plays, London, Penguin, 1969.
> Les Blancs, edited by Robert Nemiroff (produced New York, 1970).   Included in Les
> Blancs (collection), 1972.
> Les Blancs: The Collected Last Plays of Lorraine Hansberry (includes Les Blancs, The
> Drinking Gourd, What Use Are Flowers?), edited by Robert Nemiroff.   New York,
> Random House, 1972.

> Screenplay: A Raisin in the Sun, 1961.

Other

> A Matter of Colour: Documentary of the Struggles for Racial Equality in the USA.
> London, Penguin, 1965.

Theatrical Activities:

> Director: **Play** – Kicks and Co., Chicago, 1960.

*   *   *   *

"Presume no commitment, disavow all engagement, mock all great expectations," says
Sidney in The Sign in Sidney Brustein's Window, Lorraine Hansberry's second play, the last
one that she finished before her death in 1965. In contrast, the playwright, speaking at a
Negro Writers Conference shortly before the opening of her first play in 1959, stood out
against the fashionable angst of time: "man is unique in the universe, the only creature
who has in fact the power to transform the universe . . . man might just do what the apes
never will – impose the reason for life on life." A far cry from an easy optimist ("Despair?"
she once wrote, ". . . listen to the sons of those who have known little else"), she spoke in a
persistently positive voice, directly in speeches and articles, dramatically through her
protagonists.

A Raisin in the Sun is a realistic family play set on Chicago's Southside. A black play, in its
characters and its concerns, it is also a combination of two pervasive American subjects, a
maturation play containing a critique of the American Dream. The leading character, Walter
Lee Younger, is at once a product and a victim of American attitudes toward success. A
chauffeur who feels trapped by his job, his home, even his family, he is convinced that all he
needs is a little money, a push that will propel him into the big time. Using the familiar
insurance-policy plot, Hansberry gives Walter the money and a chance to lose it, reminding
the audience once again that, whatever popular mythology may say, success is not inevitable.
Nor need it be material, for at this point the other play takes over. Lena, the strong mother
figure in the play, has used part of the insurance money to make a down payment on a house
in a white neighborhood, a tentative first step on that journey out of the ghetto which Walter
expected to make in a flamboyant single leap, and, in his new despair, Walter is willing to sell
out to the white neighborhood association, to take the money and run. Or – as his Uncle Tom
routine indicates – to take the money and shuffle. When the moment comes, he cannot
demean himself; he makes a rambling, painful but effective speech on family pride and, as

Lena says, comes "into his manhood."

Sidney Brustein is unusual among plays by black dramatists in that most of its characters are white, but its middle-class Jewish hero is cousin-german to Walter, although Sidney is not so much an innocent who must find himself as a perennial loser-of-innocence who regularly refinds himself. A "modern bourgeois intellectual," as one character puts it, suffering from "the great sad withdrawal from the affairs of men," Sidney begins the play with a failed business and a failing marriage, commits himself to a reform political campaign and, after a descent into drunken and murderous despair when his white knight turns out to be conventionally tarnished, he recommits himself to social and personal possibility – to political action and his uncertain marriage.

Les Blancs, Hansberry's African play, was unfinished when she died, and the play as we have it must be taken as an attempt by Robert Nemiroff (her husband and literary executor) and Charlotte Zaltzberg to give a workable final shape to a drama that was still in process. Yet, its protagonist, Tshembe Matoseh, is so clearly a character in the Sidney Brustein mold, that the play, in its essentials, is clearly Hansberry's work. Tshembe returns from England to a fictional African colony, an ironic outsider, neither African nor European, and is claimed by the rebellion in process. A speech invoking Orestes and Hamlet and the recurrent use of the symbolic dancer suggest that, unlike Walter and Sidney, Tshembe is more chosen than choosing. Although Tshembe's commitment is the culmination of *Les Blancs*, much of its power lies in his reluctance to declare himself and in the pain of his final decision.

In discussing Hansberry's work ideationally, I have been unfair to her if I have implied that her social and philosophical concerns led her to sacrifice art to argument. Her strengths as a playwright lie in her ability to create an almost tangible milieu – particularly out of Chicago and the Greenwich Village settings that she knew so well – and in her understanding of and affection for human complexity. This last is most apparent in Walter and Sidney, her two finest creations, characters so rich that the affirmative endings, however important to the playwright, almost come as impositions – saved, of course, by the fact that Hansberry, too, knew that they were tentative.

—Gerald Weales

HUNTER, N(orman) C(harles).   British.   Born in Derbyshire, 18 September 1908. Educated at Repton School; Sandhurst Military College. Served for 3 years in the 4/7 Dragoon Guards, and in the Royal Artillery during World War II. Married Germaine Marie Dachsbeck. Staff member of the BBC, 1934–39. *Died 19 April 1971.*

PUBLICATIONS

Plays

> *The Merciless Lady*, with John Ferguson (produced Birmingham, 1934).
> *All Rights Reserved* (produced London, 1935).   London, French, 1935.
> *Ladies and Gentlemen* (produced London, 1937).
> *Little Stranger*, adaptation of a play by Katherine Hilliker and H. H. Caldwell (produced London, 1938).
> *A Party for Christmas* (produced London, 1938).   London, French, 1938.

Grouse in June (as *Galleon Gold*, produced Richmond, Surrey, 1939; as *Grouse in June*, produced London, 1939).   London, Duckworth, 1939.

Smith in Arcady (produced London, 1947).

The Affair at Assino (produced Windsor, 1950).

A Picture of Autumn (produced London, 1951).   London, English Theatre Guild, 1957.

Waters of the Moon (produced London, 1951).   London, English Theatre Guild, 1951.

Now the Serpent (produced Folkestone, Kent, 1951.

Adam's Apple: A Victorian Fairy Tale (produced London, 1952).   London, English Theatre Guild, 1953.

A Day by the Sea (produced London, 1953; New York, 1955).   London, English Theatre Guild, 1954.

A Touch of the Sun (produced London, 1958).   London, English Theatre Guild, 1958.

A Piece of Silver (produced Cheltenham, 1960).   London, English Theatre Guild, 1961.

The Tulip Tree (produced London, 1962).   London, English Theatre Guild, 1963.

The Excursion (produced Croydon, Surrey, 1964).   London, English Theatre Guild, 1964.

Adventures of Tom Random (produced Guildford, Surrey, 1967).

One Fair Daughter (produced Perth, 1970).

Radio Play: *Henry of Navarre*, 1966.

Novels

Let's Fight till Six (as Noel Nicholson).   London, Jarrolds, 1933.

The Servitors.   London, Jarrolds, 1934; as *Marriage with Nina,* New York, Morrow, 1934.

Riot.   London, Jarrolds, 1935.

The Ascension of Mr. Judson.   London, Hale, 1950.

The Romsea Romeo.   London, Hale, 1950.

The Losing Hazard.   London, Hale, 1951.

Other

Modern Trends in the Theatre (lecture).   Swansea, University College, 1969.

Translator, *The Fight in the Forest*, by Victor Eloy.   London, Hale, 1949.

*   *   *

N. C. Hunter once called himself a "majority dramatist," and with some reason. Though such plays as *Waters of the Moon* (1951) and *A Day by the Sea* (1953) were sustained Haymarket Theatre triumphs of their period, that particular form of triumph was anathema to the sterner "minority" critics, even then preparing for the break-through that came in 1956 with the consequent disintegration of traditional West End drama.

Yet Hunter's best plays of the time – and we can add a third, *The Tulip Tree*, from the early 1960's – were too good, within their own conventions, to be thrown relentlessly into the discard. What were these conventions? Here different critics have different answers. Opponents saw the plays simply as watered-down Chekhov, genteel imitations of a master's method. Supporters found them wistful, touching, and deliberately under-stated impressionist narratives in which any resemblance to Chekhov was entirely fortuitous.

It could not be denied that they gave uncommon acting parts to some of the day's principal players: Sybil Thorndike, Edith Evans, and Wendy Hiller in *Waters of the Moon*; John Gielgud, Sybil Thorndike, and Ralph Richardson in *A Day by the Sea*; Celia Johnson and

John Clements in *The Tulip Tree*, least commercially successful but a piece, maybe, that time – the final arbiter – will put above the others.

Curiously, these plays – and possibly one might include *A Touch of the Sun*, not a Haymarket piece but one in which Michael Redgrave acted during 1958 – formed a group quite out of key with the rest of Hunter's work, before or after. Nobody begins now to consider such comedies, amiable, glossy, forgettable, as *All Rights Reserved*, *Grouse in June*, or *Smith in Arcady* in which bureaucracy, in the person of Smith, was taken for an uncomfortable rural ride.

It was after the war that Hunter found himself, first with *Waters of the Moon* where Dame Edith Evans appeared as a chance visitor, sophisticated and shallow, rattling and gushing, snowed-up over New Year's Eve in a melancholy Dartmoor-fringe guest-house. There were three unexpected visitors. Like swans that skimmed a duckpond, husband, wife, and daughter turned the place for a moment into Swan Lake and then took off again. The house would not recover from their disruptive flight. "It is not kind," said a drudging girl (movingly presented by Wendy Hiller), "to make us dream of the waters of the moon, all kinds of happiness that are out of reach."

Dame Sybil Thorndike was one of the guest-house residents, "tall, spare, aristocratic-looking." As in Fitzgerald's poem, "o'er the solemn woods that bound thee/Ancient sunsets seem to die." Dame Sybil, in the early scenes, could express an entire life almost without speaking. One might not believe it in a romantic, sentimental grease-paint guest from Vienna, or in a Cockney woman who would have fled the Devon remoteness after one startled week. But the others are right, especially the decayed Colonel, a portrait sketched in soft pencil, a wraith dimming into the sleep of tired old age.

At the time it was fashionablee to attribute the play's success to its performance; but the dialogue is closely-textured, and one cannot re-read it now without recognising a dramatist in his own right. So, also, with *A Day by the Sea*. Here, under a spreading oak in a Dorset garden, or on the beach below with its lunging groynes, chalky steeps in the background and an insistent wash of the tide, we are haunted again by a longing for the unattainable, by the frustration, the melancholy that some held in the 1950's to be sub-Chekhovian. It was more than that; as much as anyone writing at that hour, Hunter was a dramatist of atmosphere.

Three of his other plays need to be recalled: *A Touch of the Sun*, a study in selfishness, with its central figure an over-worked, ill-paid, priggish idealist in a school for backward boys; *A Piece of Silver*, which did not reach London, a picture of intolerance and espionage in East Germany; and, particularly *The Tulip Tree*. A Quiet, dignified play, set in a Hampshire garden, it is basically about middle age. A husband and wife cannot come to terms. He, a publisher, hates and fears the country, seeking an escape in London and in work, while his wife clings to her country home and to the past ("What I fear most is forgetting"). Early in the play the husband has an outbreak against Nature that reminds one, again and again, of lines from another writer's Litany to Pan ("By the abortions of the teeming Spring, by Summer's starved and withered offering...").

Possibly it is the phrase, "What I fear most is forgetting," that one must now remember. Hunter's most accomplished work is too good to be forgotten. It is unfair that the changes in theatrical temperature should wither dramatic writing honestly and impressively of its period. One day, when the "middle-class" label – another unfortunate and irrelevant description – has peeled off, Hunter's plays should be heard and seen again without those references to pastiche-Chekhov in which too many of us (at one time) indulged.

—J. C. Trewin

INGE, William (Motter). American. Born in Independence, Kansas, 3 May 1913. Educated at the University of Kansas, Lawrence, A.B. 1935; Peabody Teachers College, M.A. 1936; Yale University, New Haven, Connecticut, 1940. Taught at Columbus High School, Missouri, 1937–38; Stephens College, Columbia, Missouri, 1938–43; Washington University, St. Louis, 1946–49. Arts Critic, St. Louis *Star-Times*, 1943–46. Recipient: George Jean Nathan Award, 1951; Pulitzer Prize, 1953; New York Drama Critics Circle Award, 1953; Donaldson Award, 1953; Academy Award, 1962. Agent: Audrey Wood, International Creative Management, 40 West 57th Street, New York, New York 10019, U.S.A. *Died 10 June 1973.*

PUBLICATIONS

Plays

The Dark at the Top of the Stairs (as *Farther Off from Heaven*, produced Dallas, 1947; revised version, as *The Dark at the Top of the Stairs*, produced New York, 1957; London, 1961). New York, Random House, 1958; in *Four Plays*, 1958.

Come Back, Little Sheba (produced New York, 1950; London, 1952). New York, Random House, 1950; in *Four Plays*, 1958.

Picnic: A Summer Romance (produced New York, 1953; London, 1962). New York, Random House, 1953; in *Four Plays*, 1958; revised version, as *Summer Brave* (produced Hyde Park, New York, 1962; New York City, 1973), included in *Summer Brave and Eleven Short Plays*, 1962.

Bus Stop (produced New York, 1955; Leatherhead, Surrey, 1958; London, 1976). New York, Random House, 1955; in *Four Plays*, 1958.

Four Plays (includes *Come Back, Little Sheba, Picnic, Bus Stop, The Dark at the Top of the Stairs*). New York, Random House, 1958; London, Heinemann, 1960.

Glory in the Flower (produced New York, 1959). Published in *24 Favorite One-Act Plays*, edited by Bennett Cerf and Van H. Cartmell, New York, Doubleday, 1958.

The Tiny Closet (produced Spoleto, Italy, 1958). Included in *Summer Brave and Eleven Short Plays*, 1962.

A Loss of Roses (produced New York, 1959). New York, Random House, 1960.

Splendor in the Grass: A Screenplay. New York, Bantam, 1961.

Natural Affection (produced Phoenix, 1962; New York, 1963). New York, Random House, 1963.

Summer Brave and Eleven Short Plays (includes *To Bobolink, For Her Spirit; A Social Event; The Boy in the Basement; The Tiny Closet; Memory of Summer; The Rainy Afternoon; The Mall; An Incident at the Standish Arms; People in the Wind; Bus Riley's Back in Town; The Strains of Triumph*). New York, Random House, 1962.

The Love Death Plays: Memory of Summer, The Rainy Afternoon, People in the Wind, Bus Riley's Back in Town (produced New York, 1975). Included in *Summer Brave and Eleven Short Plays*, 1962.

Where's Daddy? (as *Family Thing Etc.*, produced Falmouth, Massachusetts, 1965; as *Where's Daddy?*, produced New York, 1966). New York, Random House, 1966.

The Disposal (as *Don't Go Gentle*, produced Los Angeles, 1967–68; as *The Last Pad*, produced Phoenix, 1972). Published in *Best Short Plays of the World Theatre, 1958–1967*, edited by Stanley Richards, New York, Crown, 1968; revised version, as *The Disposal*, music by Anthony Caldarella, lyrics by Judith Gero (produced New York, 1973).

Two Short Plays: The Call, and A Murder. New York, Dramatists Play Service, 1968.

Midwestern Manic, in *Best Short Plays 1969*, edited by Stanley Richards. Philadelphia, Chilton, 1969.

Caesarian Operation (produced Los Angeles, 1972).
Overnight (produced New York, 1974).

Screenplays: *Splendor in the Grass*, 1961; *All Fall Down*, 1962.

Television Play: *On the Outskirts of Town*, 1964–65.

Novels

Good Luck, Miss Wyckoff.   Boston, Little Brown, and London, Deutsch, 1971.
My Son Is a Splendid Driver.   Boston, Little Brown, 1972.

Critical Study: *William Inge* by Robert B. Shuman, New York, Twayne, 1965.

Theatrical Activities:

Actor: **Film** – *Splendor in the Grass*, 1961.

*   *   *

> But the aristocracy of Freedom, Kansas,
> was not that of eighteenth-century France.
>
> —*Good Luck, Miss Wyckoff*

William Inge's plays epitomize the weaknesses inherent in American society. Even in those works set outside the dreary Kansas-Oklahoma area of the 1920's and 1930's that is Inge's usual world, his characters, lacking authority figures within the family or community, frequently turn to actors for models, or for emotional and aesthetic satisfaction: Bobolink, whose devotion to autograph hunting raises her to "professional" status in the early one-acter *To Bobolink, For Her Spirit*; Pinky, whose recollections of the stage performances of Ina Claire and Ethel Barrymore are indices to a vanished civilization superior to the one he inhabits in *Where's Daddy?* In general, the personal styles of the stars and the clichés of their films are criteria against which characters measure their own situations. Even the hard-boiled Rosemary Sidney in *Picnic* (and its revision *Summer Brave*) cries to her unromantic lover: "I want to drive into the sunset, Howard! I want to drive into the sunset!"

Given the pantheon of film stars and the American thrust for upward mobility and popularity, Inge's characters often aspire disastrously toward theatrical careers, or give impromptu amateur performances. In *Picnic*, Hal claims to have failed as a film star only because he would not have his teeth fixed; in *Where's Daddy?* and *Midwestern Manic* the protagonists are serious young actors who must earn their living in television commercials. Though occasionally someone like Millie in *Picnic* reads Carson McCullers, hangs a Picasso reproduction in her room, and plans on a writing career, the bartender in *Glory in the Flower* best summarizes Inge's young: "They're all ambitious but they all wanta be movie stars or bandleaders, or disc-jockeys. They're too *good* for plain, ordinary, everyday work. And what's gonna happen to us if everyone becomes a bandleader, I'd like to know."

Democratic egalitarianism, a post-frontier product of the unchallenging geography of the middle-west, created a tyranny of the majority, the female majority, that controlled every area of life, especially sexual life. Inge's women, who function within the family and the community as the standard-bearers of morality (often equated to mutilating naked statues of Roman gladiators, and making men obey the prescripts of etiquette in the bathroom), attempt to repress sex in others and, ironically, deny the drive in themselves, often with disastrous results. Mrs. Loomis in Inge's screenplay *Splendor in the Grass* convinces her daughter Deanie that "a woman doesn't enjoy these things like a man does," a conviction that helps drive Deanie into a lengthy spell of madness, like Jackie in *Bus Riley's Back in Town*.

With these problems of normal sexuality in Inge's work, it is predictable that those outside this range will suffer even further. Spencer Scranton, the middle-aged undertaker of *The Boy in the Basement*, must restrict his homosexual activities to furtive weekends in Pittsburgh, while his mother dominates his life back home and taunts him when she learns the truth. The basement suggests not only the literal headquarters of Spencer's undertaking business, but also the semi-acknowledged arena of his sexuality. The two meanings fuse when Spencer can touch the body of the delivery boy, Joker Evans, whom he loves, only in the basement when he prepares the drowned youth for burial. Similarly, *The Tiny Closet* hides the secret transvestism of another middle-aged homosexual, the floorwalker Mr. Newbold, but the play deals less with the nature of Newbold's fixation than with the repressive activities of his landlady, Mrs. Crosby, determined to invade her boarder's privacy, lest it conceal political and moral unorthodoxy. (Communism and sexual aberrations are interchangeable examples of the non-conformity in Inge's world.) Many of his characters, especially schoolteachers, lead lonely boardinghouse existences subject to the tyranny of their landladies; Inge's one-acter *A Murder* carries roominghouse restrictions to their absurd extreme, as the protagonist desperately tries to get a lock on a closet: "I have some *things* I want to keep quite safe." (Another middle-aged neurotic, in *The Call*, carries his secrets around in a suitcase.) The male desire for privacy is, of course, impossible in a world in which the unrestricted petty tyrannies of women assume enormous proportions.

Male tyrants, inside and outside the family, are rarer in Inge. Ace Stamper in *Splendor in the Grass* is a self-made oilman who dominates the town's economy and his son Bud's life. Another self-made millionaire, Del Loomis in *Bus Riley's Back in Town*, runs the community and imprisons his daughter's lover primarily because he is poor and half-Mexican: "But I guess all that money and all that power kinda went to his head. He was actin' kinda crazy around here, like he was Nero or one of those Roman emperors." Ultimately, both Stamper and Loomis lose their wealth and authority. Thus, the traditional American aspiration to rise in society produces tyrannies, however short-lived, as oppressive as those democracy supposedly replaced.

From the infantile worship of the film stars, through the submission to the petty absolutism of landladies, to the perversion of the American dream, Inge's characters dramatize the spiritual poverty and emotional repression of democratic life. Though freudianism is obviously crucial in Inge's work, and explains especially the mother-son relationships and the dangers of repressed sexuality, the psychological exploration of character seems less an end itself than a means of assessing the larger social context. Despite their greater power, even the domineering women seem more the products of this society than its ultimate shapers.

Despite Inge's frequent revisions and variant versions of his works, it is possible to assess chronologically both the development of his major dramatic concerns and the worth of individual plays. The immediate problem of *Come Back, Little Sheba* is Lola's attempt to control the drinking of her husband, Doc Delaney, with the help of Alcoholics Anonymous. What prevent the play becoming merely an A.A. tract are the garrulous Lola, simultaneously ludicrous and touching, desperately talking to whoever will listen, and Inge's deft use of a subplot involving the Delaneys' roomer, Marie, to parallel and contrast with their situation. Doc is infatuated with Marie, whose relationship with a virile college student seems a recapitulation of Lola's past, while Lola identifies childishly with Marie's affair. The Delaneys' involvement with Marie helps clarify their own lives through the illusion of two time levels; both Doc and Lola are trapped in the past as they work desperately to resolve their current dilemma. His attraction to Marie indicates that he wants to repeat the mistake that create his initial disaster. However, when Lola finally accepts the loss of her dog that has dominated her thoughts and her dreams, she is presumably ready to be an adequate wife and has conquered her desire to relive her youth: "I don't think Little Sheba's ever coming back, Doc. I'm not going to call her any more." The symbolism is effective without becoming obtrusive, though the suddenly mature Lola and sober Doc are not totally convincing. The play works best dramatizing the link between impoverished social values (puritanical sex codes, concern with job and financial status) and the impoverished lives they produce.

Picnic and its revision *Summer Brave* are Inge's most ambitious and successful works. Both plays attempt to endow the central figure Hal, an out-of-work wanderer, with mythical sexual qualities, as he changes the lives of the women he encounters in the Kansas town where he seeks help from his wealthy college friend, Alan Seymour. Hal's jeans-clad appearance transforms Millie Owens from a tomboy, while her sister Madge either runs off with Hal to a life of romantic improvidence (*Picnic*) or loses both her virtue and her chance to marry Alan (*Summer Brave*), after a dance with Hal that "has something of the nature of a primitive rite that could mate the young people." Such over-reaction to male bodies is, of course, typical of many Inge women: Jackie Loomis in *Bus Riley's Back in Town* and *Glory in the Flower* sees Bus as a kind of sexual "god" and submits appropriately, though she later frees herself from this kind of worship in *Glory*; but sometimes women like Cora, in *The Dark at the Top of the Stairs*, who is obsessed with her husband's physicality, spend their lives fighting this passion and attempt to make the male conform to female notions of "decency." Rosemary Sidney's attraction to Hal is so strong, perhaps because she tries to deny it, that in her stimulated state she gives herself to her suitor Howard and persuades him to marry her. The Labor Day setting reinforces Rosemary's now-or-never desperation, since her teaching chores will resume the next day, along with the restricted life of a teacher in a small Kansas town. Madge's mother, though she sees Hal as an obvious threat to her daughter's future, also responds to his charms in a way that recalls her reluctant emotional and physical dependence on her husband. Sixtyish Helen Potts whose unconsummated marriage had been annulled forty years before by the tyrannical mother she still serves slavishly, reacts sentimentally to Hal when he performs odd jobs for her: "Everything he did reminded me there was a man in the house, and it seemed good." Thus, all the women in the play respond to Hal's fertility god appeal, though perhaps the Fall Kansas setting explains the muted reaction of some females. The theme seems to demand the intensity and exalted language of Lorca works like *Blood Wedding*, but stifled passion and prosaic language are more suited to Kansas. *Picnic* seems a gentler version of Ugo Betti's *The Crime on Goat Island*; while Betti's stranger seduces all three women in the community he invades, and then dies in the appropriately symbolic well into which they have tricked him, Hal's behavior is comparatively guileless, and Inge's women, dominated by their feelings, if not their hormones, lack the cunning and intellectual force of Betti's and embody the very limited development their society permits. In a "dry" state like Kansas, where even adults must drink secretly, schoolteachers like Rosemary, the strongest woman in the play, deny their physical drives and study during the summer only to satisfy the Board of Education requirements. And just as the women conform to a concept of femininity that limits both body and mind, Hal lacks any real freedom – the women force him to put on his shirt, and the exploits of which he boasts, notably encounters with sexually aggressive females, have degraded him. Though he excites women, they fear this excitement so much they wish to control its source. Hal is a victim of society that can cast a well-built, but poor and not overly bright young man only as a purely physical object: his fraternity tolerated him as long as they thought his athletics would bring them prestige. Alan's attempt to use his father's power to run Hal out of town reinforces Inge's view that the perversion of democracy in American society denies the humanity of the individual.

Bus Stop brings together a group of characters in a small Kansas town to contrast various male/female encounters: Grace and the busdriver who have a brief sexual union in her apartment above the restaurant/bus stop; Elma, the young waitress, more observer than participant in the adult world she is about to join, and Dr. Lyman, failed college professor and semi-pathological pursuer of young girls, who tries to establish a bond with her by quoting Shakespeare; and, most important, Bo Decker, returning to his Montana ranch with Cherie, an unsuccessful *chanteuse*, as his unwilling companion. Having had his first sex experience with Cherie while he was in Kansas City for a rodeo, Bo tries to force her to marry him. Though she resists and tries to run away, her pathetic past and uncertain future make it inevitable that she will marry and presumably love him, especially since she acknowledges his physical appeal. With an actress capable of the right blend of toughness and pathos, the role of Cherie can be the emotional focus of the play. The easily-satisfied longings of Grace, and the terrifying loneliness of Dr. Lyman offer the only possible alternatives to marrying Bo. Because of Bo's vitality and Cherie's comic uncertainty, *Bus Stop* is the most cheerful of Inge's works, despite Dr. Lyman, and Virgil, Bo's lifelong companion and substitute father, who chooses to stay behind, once Bo has won Cherie. When Grace tells Virgil there is no place to wait after the bus stop has closed: "... you're just left out in the cold," he replies, "Well...that's what happens to some people." Though the play says nothing of Virgil's private life and presents him only as unnecessarily noble, since he could presumably work on Bo's ranch even after the wedding, the implied motivation links him with Pinky, the homosexual college professor in *Where's Daddy?*, who picks up 15-year-old Tom and raises him as a combination son and lover. Thus, Virgil's solitary stance at the climax adds another dimension to the pervasive loneliness which most of the characters confront (the bus stop offers even less permanence than Inge's familiar boardinghouse). Depending on emphases of staging and performance, Virgil's final line can turn the play into a study of those excluded from any conventional relationship, or merely suggest that Inge was unready to face this theme in the early 1950's. Since Inge provides no convincing explanation of the psychology of his characters, *Bus Stop* remains primarily a study of emotionally impoverished lower middle-class people who, like those in other Inge works, are willing to settle for less than an ideal life.

Of the four major Inge works that had successful Broadway runs and film versions, *The Dark at the Top of the Stairs* is the most persistent attempt to probe the psychology of the characters, Cora and Rubin Flood, and their children, 10-year-old Sonny, and 16-year-old Reenie, in an Oklahoma town of the 1920's. The play explores Sonny's oedipal involvement and suggests that he is rather miraculously outgrowing this attachment to his mother as "he avoids her embrace," at the climax of Act III, when he and Reenie leave for the movies, and Cora climbs the stairs for a reunion with her husband: "we see Rubin's naked feet standing in the warm light at the top." However, neither Sonny's rapid independence nor Cora's acceptance of the masculinity in Rubin that she has continously fought, seems convincing, and the ending lacks the irony to make clear the impermanence of these resolutions. What dominates the play, despite character analysis and the lengthy sexual confession of Cora's sister, Lottie, is the sense of the changing economy which caused Rubin to lose his financial and emotional bearings. Cora tells Sonny that Rubin "and his family were pioneers. They fought Indians and buffalo, and they settled in this country when it was just a wilderness." However, at the play's conclusion, Rubin confesses to his fears:

> I s'pose all this time you been thinkin' you was married to one a them movin'-pitcher fellas that jump off bridges and hold up trains and shoot Indians, and are never a scared a nothin'. Times are changin', Cora, and I dunno where they're goin'.... Men becomin' millionaires overnight, drivin' down the street in big limousines, goin' out to the country club and gettin' drunk, acting like they was lords of creation. I dunno what to think of things now, Cora. I'm a stranger in the very land I was born in.

Thus, the economic situation seems the root of the other problems in the play — Rubin's travelling job and insecurity cause his infidelities; his enforced absence from home increases Sonny's dependence on Cora, and Reenie's lack of confidence with men. The money shortage prevents Cora taking the children to Oklahoma City, as does her inadequate job training. The play makes the general inadequacy of the society more crucial than the psychology of the characters. Ironically, though Sammy Goldenbaum, the unloved son of a film actress, commits suicide, surely a sign that stars may be unworthy of the adulation and intense interest of Sonny, and even Lottie, the play ends as Sonny and Reenie leave for the movies, presumably to worship the players as well as the fantasies they enact.

A Loss of Roses, Inge's first major failure, another study of a strong mother-son relationship, seems, despite this psychological core, to link with the problem plays of the 1930's (Odets' *Paradise Lost*, for example), which stress the economic and social origins of democratic inadequacies. Kenny Baird's attachment to his mother, Helen, is more serious than Sonny's, since Kenny is 21, and Mr. Baird has been dead for a number of years, having drowned saving Kenny. The appearance of Lila Green, a 32-year-old friend of Helen's and Kenny's former baby-sitter, triggers Kenny's attempt to assert himself, ironically with a woman who is a substitute mother. When Kenny proves unable to marry her, Lila returns to a former lover and a downhill theatrical career that will continue her exploitation. Though the play seems uncertain who is the protagonist, in the revised version Inge published Lila dominates the final scene and delivers the curtain line, "No one's gonna porteck me," a speech linking her with Virgil in *Bus Stop* and Inge's world of loners and outsiders. Typically, the characters eke out near-subsistence livings (Helen is a nurse and Kenny a filling-station attendant) or perpetually face starvation, like Lila and her fellow performers. That these actors display no interest in the theater, no commitment to anything but sex and survival, reveals the intellectual vacuity of Inge's society.

Inge's last Broadway plays, both failures, seem partially attempts to keep up with trends toward violence and sexually explicit dialogue. *Natural Affection*, another mother-son study, focusing on Sue Barker and her 17-year-old son Donnie, home for Christmas from reform school, opens with Sue and her lover Bernie in bed and contains some racy dialogue, especially from their neighbor, Vince Brinkman (both he and his wife Claire are attracted to Bernie, a situation raising the already high temperature). Donnie's involvment with his mother expresses itself in ardent caresses, as he pleads with her to keep him at home so he can avoid returning to the school. Sue's refusal causes Donnie to explode in a fit of rage and kill a young woman who innocently wanders into the apartment from a holiday party and makes the mistake of flirting with him. Despite Inge's belief that "The terror of rejection seemed to me the cause of violence everywhere" (Preface), neither the characters nor the audience achieves any illumination into the nature of the society shaping violent behavior or the psychology of the violent. The characters remain personifications of an emotional flatness that never deserts them, even when they deliver long confessions or commit murder. *Where's Daddy?* tries, through the introduction of the homosexual father figure, Pinky, to make contemporary the familiar story of a young man's maturing and accepting responsibility as a parent. The Manhattan setting, the sympathetic portrayal of a Negro couple, and some peripheral banter about the state of the theater in a hip society fail to disguise the sentimentality of the material.

Despite his Hollywood activity and two late novels, Inge continued to produce new plays and rewrite old ones (a revised *Summer Brave* appeared briefly in New York in 1973). The new plays try not only to embody recent fashions in sexual frankness, but also to create characters who, unlike the trapped and inarticulate victims of the earlier works, convey political and philosophical insights. The symbolic Houseman in *A Murder*, the archetypal boardinghouse play, uses existentialist formulae to give resonance to his observations: "When we consider that the things we think are absurd are just as true as the things we don't think are absurd, then you have to belive that *everything* is absurd, or *nothing* is absurd." Predictably, the harried would-be hoarder is called simply The Man, and the landlady The Landlady, to eliminate details that might detract from the significance of the actions. *The Disposal*, an attack on capital punishment, set on death row, is more successful, despite the rambling speculations and embarrassing self-doubts of the prison chaplain. What generates the chief interest is not the plight of the condemned man, Jess, who having "absurdly" murdered his pregnant wife, awaits a meaningful, but ultimately empty meeting with his long absent father. Though "Jess loses control of his bowels," as the guards carry him off, he is upstaged by Archie, another condemned man, a homosexual, whose bitchy and obscene comments, and wide-ranging quotations, convey the pervasive hysteria absent from Jess' character. Archie, an apparent fusion of Vince in *Natural Affection* and Pinky in *Where's Daddy?*, with a touch of some Genet criminals, suggests that Inge should have devoted a play to such a character. Most successful of Inge's later plays is *Midwestern Manic*, which opens, like *Natural Affection*, with a sleeping couple who will presumably appear naked in this scene and others. The play, one of a contemplated series on life in a housing development in the East, begins with a focus on George Krimm's embarrassment, when his vulgar Oklahoman sister, brother-in-law, and nephew arrive unexpectedly at his New York appartment, while George and his mistress Diane are in bed. The play seems a traditional bedroom farce, as George tries to keep Diane's presence and his lost virginity a secret from his sister, but ultimately turns into a comic allegory of eastern liberalism versus southwestern conservatism, as Diane and the brother-in-law, Harley, clash. The two are amusing caricatures, and even the inevitability of Harley's violent seduction of Diane (liberals are traditionally stimulating) reinforces the implied meaning of the rival social philosophies. These last three plays indicate that Inge might profitably have pursued his gifts as a delineator of the bizarrely comic and foregone the serious issues.

Any appraisal of Inge's work must both acknowledge and question the immense popularity and critical acclaim he shared in the 1950's with Miller and Williams. Certainly, Inge's dialogue is undistinguished. The folksy, unstylized colloquialisms, appropriate for the characters, fail to generate much excitement or convey nuances of feeling. The many recitations from Shakespeare in the plays (Archie in *The Disposal* also quotes from Shaw, Wilde, Housman, and Millay) emphasize the inadequacies of Inge's language more than is necessary to reinforce a sense of midwestern flatness. Perhaps Inge's success stemmed from his single sets and concentrated time that produce tight, uninnovative drama, and from his technical expertise in using secondary characters to reinforce and counterpoint the protagonists' situations, as in *Bus Stop*, and *Come Back, Little Sheba*. Perhaps, more important, was Inge's confronting what were, for the period, somewhat daring themes and providing happy, though occasionally wistful, endings. Inge's world contains no Willy Loman, who escaped the weaknesses of Miller's style and sociology into the realm of authentic American myth, and Inge's plays convey little of the psychological power, often obsessive, of Williams, but perhaps Inge's schoolteachers and other forlorn seekers of privacy, if not fulfillment, will remain part of the American consciousness. Inge's bleak world does offer the comfort of dramatic control, concern for the displaced, and the limited insight that "If you expect happy endings anywhere outside the movies, you're fooled" (*Summer Brave*). Thus, it is possible to accept the shallow Howard's verdict in the same play: "It's not a very lively part of the country, but a person learns to like it."

—Burton Kendle

ORTON, Joe (John Kingsley Orton). British. Born in Leicester, 1 January 1933. Educated at Royal Academy of Dramatic Art, London (Leicester Council grant), for 2 years. Actor at the Ipswich Repertory Theatre. Recipient: *Evening Standard* award, 1967. *Died 9 August 1967.*

PUBLICATIONS

Plays

    Entertaining Mr. Sloane (produced London, 1964; New York, 1965). London, Hamish Hamilton, 1964; New York, Grove Press, 1965.
    The Ruffian on the Stair (broadcast, 1964; produced London, 1966). Included in *Crimes of Passion*, 1967.

Loot (produced Cambridge, 1965; London, 1966; New York, 1968).   London, Methuen, and New York, Grove Press, 1967.

Crimes of Passion: The Ruffian on the Stair, and The Erpingham Camp (produced London, 1967; New York, 1969).   London, Methuen, 1967.

The Good and Faithful Servant (televised, 1967; produced London, 1971).   Included in *Funeral Games, and The Good and Faithful Servant*, 1970.

Funeral Games (televised, 1968; produced London, 1970; New York, 1973). Included in *Funeral Games, and The Good and Faithful Servant*, 1970.

What the Butler Saw (produced London, 1969).   London, Methuen, 1969; New York, Grove Press, 1970.

Funeral Games, and The Good and Faithful Servant.   London, Methuen, 1970.

Complete Plays.   London, Eyre Methuen, 1976.

Radio Play: *The Ruffian on the Stair*, 1964.

Television Plays: *The Good and Faithful Servant*, 1967; *Funeral Games*, 1968.

Other

Head to Toe.   London, Blond, 1971.

*   *   *

Joe Orton made West End audiences laugh about sodomy, casual murder, nymphomania, sexual blackmail, vicarious incest, and something approaching necrophilia – all this, just a few years after the nation's jurists had deemed *Lady Chatterley's Lover* fit reading for their wives and servants. But Orton's bland outrageousness has tended to make us overlook the fact that he was actually working within very traditional forms of English comedy. Lady Wishfort in Congreve's *The Way of the World* only embodies in an ennobled form the thwarted, middle-aged sexuality of Kath in *Entertaining Mr. Sloane* – and, long before *Loot*, Ben Travers had recognized in *Plunder* that criminal self-interest was a fit subject for manipulative comedy. In between, Oscar Wilde had shown, often in more predictably inverted clichés, that the technique of the epigram lies as much in its disappointment of verbal expectation as in its own actual felicity. And, visually, the world of Joe Orton is not far from that of Donald McGill.

At the same time, it is impossible to forget that the man who wrote with such apparent brutality about being done to death was himself brutally done to death by his own longstanding homosexual partner, who then committed suicide – so far as one can understand, as a result of feeling outcast by Orton's sudden rise to fame. The fragile line that divides fantasy from reality, here so tragically breached, points to the necessity for Orton's purgative kind of art. He laughed us out of violence: those incapable of laughter had, surely, the greater capacity for violence.

Orton's first stage play, *Entertaining Mr. Sloane*, was first produced in May 1964: he was murdered in August 1967. During that brief period he had already achieved a rare combination of "serious" critical acclaim and solid commercial success. But he was, and is, overpraised. His was the assured kind of craftsmanship that matures with practice, not the instant genius that stretches thinner with the years: thus, by normal standards the three full-length and handful of shorter pieces by which we must judge him would have represented exciting but exploratory early work. Indeed, *Entertaining Mr. Sloane* is still groping to find its form: where *Loot* and *What the Butler Saw* are unashamed farces, *Sloane* keeps a hiccuping hold on naturalism, and this occasionally raises irrelevant questions for its audiences.

Poetic justice triumphs in *Sloane* – its eponymous young bitter well and truly bitten, and his attempt to manipulate poor Kath and gullible Ed for his own comfort neatly inverted, to leave him the object of their evenly apportioned sexual appetites. But poetic justice seldom has logic or probability on its side, where farce demands both — not in any pedantic sense, but in the same way that tragedy, not so far away along the generic axis, needs to be sufficient unto itself. The world of farce, as of tragedy, is one in which the circumstances and the people one instinctively keeps apart suddenly converge, and control of events is lost. Granted the coincidental conventions such a convergence assumes, if the farceur wishes to add mortality and murder to his usual themes of adultery and fraud, the loss of control is rather more likely to be tragic than comic in its implications. Orton triumphantly transcends that likelihood, and in *Loot* makes mortality (and an embarrassingly omnipresent corpse) hilariously funny — yet somehow incidental to the sense of impending catastrophe which Orton was able to evoke with an impish integrity that was all his own.

"We must keep up appearances" is the last line of *Loot*: it typifies at once the social propriety which Orton's characters are so often concerned to assert (in the face of their every action), and his turning of linguistic cliché against itself. His characters distil their speech quite unconsciously from their media-saturated experience — utilizing, say, the idiom of a holiday brochure to defend their moral probity, or of a civil-service footnote to make an amorous advance. The resulting dissonance can be very funny: there is a danger that it may also become baffling, as the prose it parodies accretes unto itself new kinds of jargon. This may be why Orton was feeling his way in *What the Butler Saw* towards a comedy in which language and action are much more closely integrated. Socially a cut above the characters of the earlier plays, his characters here are more conscious of verbal facility in the face of the multiple disasters of the action — often using it as their only defence against those disasters. The play points the way towards a quite unique blend of comedy of manners and broad farce with a richness of invention that is more reminiscent of, say, *Bartholomew Fair* than Congreve. So it is no dismissal with faint praise to suggest that Orton left us with the finest body of apprentice work in the English drama: rather, it is to mourn the lost comic masterpieces that would surely have been the products of his developing genius.

—Simon Trussler

WHITING, John (Robert).   British.   Born in Salisbury, Wiltshire, November 1917. Educated at Taunton School, Somerset; Royal Academy of Dramatic Art, London, 1934–36. Served in the Royal Artillery, 1939–44. Married Asthore Lloyd Mawson; four children. Actor in repertory and London, 1936–52. Drama Critic, *London Magazine*, 1961–62. *Died 16 June 1963.*

PUBLICATIONS

Plays

    Paul Southman (broadcast, 1946; produced London, 1965).
    A Penny for a Song (produced Wimbledon and London, 1951).   Included in *The Plays of John Whiting*, 1957; revised version (produced London, 1962), London, Heinemann, 1964.
    Saint's Day (produced London, 1951).   Included in *The Plays of John Whiting*, 1957.
    Marching Song (produced Cardiff and London, 1954; New York, 1959).   London, French, 1954.
    Sacrifice to the Wind, adaptation of a play by André Obey (televised, 1954; produced

London, 1955).   Published in *Plays for Radio and Television*, edited by Nigel
Samuels, London, Longman, 1959.
The Gates of Summer (produced Leeds, 1956).   Included in *The Collected Plays*, 1969.
The Plays of John Whiting (includes *Saint's Day, A Penny for a Song, Marching Song*).
London, Heinemann, 1957.
Madame de..., *and Traveller Without Luggage*, adaptation of plays by Jean Anouilh
(produced London, 1959).   London, French, 1959.
A Walk in the Desert (televised, 1960).   Included in *The Collected Plays*, 1969.
The Devils, adaptation of the book *The Devils of Loudon* by Aldous Huxley (produced
London, 1961; New York, 1965).   London, Heinemann, 1961; New York, Hill and
Wang, 1962.
No Why (produced London, 1964).   London, French, 1961.
Conditions of Agreement (produced Bristol, 1964).   Included in *The Collected Plays*,
1969.
The Nomads (produced London, 1965).   Included in *The Collected Plays*, 1969.
The Collected Plays, edited by Ronald Hayman.   London, Heinemann, and New York,
Theatre Arts Books, 1969.
  1. *Conditions of Agreement, Saint's Day, A Penny for a Song.*
  2. *The Gates of Summer, No Why, A Walk in the Desert, The Devils, Noman, The
  Nomads.*
No More A-Roving.   London, Heinemann, 1975.

Screenplays: *The Ship That Died of Shame*, with Michael Relph and Basil Dearden,
1954; *The Good Companions*, with T. J. Morrison and J. L. Hodgson, 1957; *The
Captain's Table*, with Bryan Forbes and Nicholas Phipps, 1959; *Young Cassidy*, 1965.

Radio Plays: *Paul Southman*, 1946; *Eve Witness*, 1949; *The Stairway*, 1949; *Love's Old
Sweet Song*, 1950.

Televison Plays: *A Walk in the Desert*, 1960; *Sacrifice to the Wind*, 1964.

Other

John Whiting on Theatre.   London, Alan Ross, 1966.
The Art of the Dramatist and Other Pieces, edited by Ronald Hayman.   London, Alan
Ross, 1969.

Critical Studies: *John Whiting* by Ronald Hayman, London, Heinemann, 1969; *The Plays of
John Whiting: An Assessment* by Simon Trussler, London, Gollancz, 1972.

*   *   *

John Whiting was and remains an enigma. Although he was consistently championed by
men of the theatre rather than by armchair critics, he only once achieved the conventional
success of a prolonged London run – and that with his least characteristic, final play, *The
Devils*. Previously he had all but abandoned working in the live theatre in order to make the
livelihood it denied him by scripting films. Yet his three early plays, together with the long
unperformed *Conditions of Agreement* and *The Gates of Summer* (which never reached
London), represent the most considerable body of writing from any British dramatist of the
immediate post-war period, Fry, Eliot and Rattigan notwithstanding.
    Not that Whiting *did* withstand them: he was a highly allusive dramatst as well as an
elusive one, and something of Eliot's metaphysical spirituality, of Fry's often downbeat
whimsy, and even of Rattigan's over-structured colloquialism is there in his plays for the

finding. These echoes are often disconcerting, but they only partially explain the opacity of his work. Whiting wrote public plays from the raw material of intensely private experience, and so occasionally gave images – or themes, or tones of voice – a significance disproportionate to their actual, dramatic function. Yet it is in part because of this that his plays take on something of the baffling totality and infinitely tangential quality of "real" life, in which any individual's experience is a sum that defies neat, objective encapsulation.

Hence, *Conditions of Agreement* and *Saint's Day* create closely felt, individual worlds of elliptic human relationships, and of occasionally warped causality: but those worlds are total, complex, and – the ultimate test – capable of being fully achieved by actors on a stage. They are, in these plays, childhood worlds – in the sense that *Conditions of Agreement* is "about" the adult struggling to repudiate adolescence, and *Saint's Day* "about" the second childhood of senility. Similarly, Whiting's last three plays, the one-acters *No Why* and *A Walk in the Desert*, and *The Devils*, are "about" apparently unmotivated cruelties which are, directly or allusively, childish.

A Penny for a Song is, in these terms, child*like* – a joyous, unequivocal celebration of happiness which is unique in Whiting's work, and which lacks (in its original, more satisfactory version) the dark corners of the adult world. Oddly, when Whiting tried to fill in those dark corners for the Royal Shakespeare Company's revival of the play, it appeared suddenly loose at the seams. Even *Marching Song* and *The Gates of Summer*, while far from childlike, are curiously innocent – their life-and-death debates somehow abstracted from the stuff of life and death.

Whiting felt that much of his work was about self-destruction. This is so, in the sense that he was characteristically concerned with the inward-turning of sensibility – a reversion, one might say, to the selfishness of infancy – that makes a man or woman a spiritual cripple. And this points to another paradox of his work: for he wrote, he claimed, for an elite, and he certainly always wrote *about* an elite, stressing the irrationality of the common people transformed into a threatening mob. Yet his aristocrats and his artists were invariably in the grip of decadence, and in the process of self-destruction, while his most nearly happy and fulfilled characters were refugees from the slums. He sought to elevate resignation into stoicism, yet affirmed that love was the only viable line of communication. He explored and created character through incongruous, sometimes ridiculous actions, yet made these actions so self-sufficient dramatically that they seemed, after all, to *matter*.

Thus, Whiting's best plays are most readily understood as parables, infinitely extensible rather than particular in reference, and paradigms of human behavior rather than enquiries into its idiosyncrasies – though these may be superficially prominent. Perhaps it is because actors and directors can fully explore the multiple possibilities during the rehearsal process, and choose the line which their own interpretation will take, that they have been so much more responsive to Whiting's work than front-of-house critics, always in search of a particular, literal-minded explanation.

Similarly, those familiar with the whole of Whiting's work will find individual plays more rewarding for their awareness of his recurrent motifs and preoccupations. Saints and nomads, cripples and clowns, childishness and self-destruction: when these continuing concerns are seen within the total context of Whiting's work, their significance, or apparent lack of it, is less baffling for the knowledge that they are a matter of personal vocabulary – of Whiting's way of seeing the world – rather than precise points of reference within a particular play. It is no more possible to take in at a first sitting a play by Whiting than *Hamlet*. This does not make Whiting a bad or, intrinsically, a difficult dramatist: it means that he demands and repays our full and continuing attention.

—Simon Trussler

TITLE
INDEX

The following list of play titles includes all stage, screen, radio, and television plays listed in the entries in the body of the book and in the Supplement and Appendix. The name(s) in parenthesis after the play title is not meant to indicate full credits for the play, but to direct the reader to the appropriate entry where full information is given. The date given is that of the first production or publication; alternative and revised titles are listed with their appropriate dates. In instances where a stage play and a screen play with the same title are included, the abbreviation "scr" indicates the author of the screen play.

A (Mario Fratti), 1965
Aa Went to Blaydon Races (Cecil P. Taylor), 1962
A-A-American (Edward Bond), 1976
Abe Burrows' Almanac (Abe Burrows), 1950
Abe Burrows Show (Abe Burrows), 1946
Abelard and Heloise (Ronald Duncan), 1960
Abelard and Heloise (Ronald Millar), 1970
Abortive (Caryl Churchill), 1971
About a Bout (Philip Martin, suppl 2), 1973
Abraham Lincoln (Denis Johnston), 1941
Absent Friends (Alan Ayckbourn), 1974
Absolute Beginners (Trevor Griffiths), 1975
Absolute Power over Movie Stars (Robert Patrick), 1968
Absolution (Anthony Shaffer), 1970
Absurd Person Singular (Alan Ayckbourn), 1972
Academic Murders, The (Kenneth Koch), 1966
Academy, The (Mario Fratti), 1963
Accademia, L' (Mario Fratti), 1964
Access to the Children (William Trevor), 1973
Accident (Harold Pinter), 1967
Accident, The (William Saroyan), 1958
Accolade (Emlyn Williams), 1950
AC/DC (Heathcote Williams), 1970
Ace in the Hole (Billy Wilder, suppl 1), 1951
Aces High (Howard Barker), 1975
Aces Wild (Thomas Hendry), 1974
Achilles Heel (Brian Clark, suppl 3), 1973
Acrobats (Israel Horovitz), 1968
Across the Board on Tomorrow Morning (William Saroyan), 1941
Across the Border (Robert Holles, suppl 3), 1964
Across the Pacific (John Huston, suppl 1), 1942
Across the River and into the Jungle (Arthur Kopit), 1958
Act of Love (Irwin Shaw), 1954
Act One (Dore Schary), 1963
Act Without Words (Samuel Beckett), 1958
Act Without Words II (Samuel Beckett), 1959
Acte (Lawrence Durrell), 1961
Acte sans Paroles (Samuel Beckett), 1957
Act-In (Inter-Action Trust, suppl 6)
Action (Sam Shepard), 1974
Action in the North Atlantic (John Howard Lawson), 1943
Actor and the Alibi, The (Hugh Leonard), 1974
Actor and the Invader, The (Robert Patrick), 1969
Actor, I Said (Don Taylor, suppl 2), 1972
Acts of Love (Susan Yankowitz), 1973
Adam (Lonnie Carter), 1966
Adam Adamant (Terence Frisby), 1966
Adam and Eva (Guy Bolton, suppl 4), 1919

Adam Smith (Cecil P. Taylor), 1972
Adam's Apple (N. C. Hunter, appendix), 1952
Adams County Illinois (Jackson Mac Low), 1963
Adam's Rib (Garson Kanin), 1949
Adaptation (Elaine May), 1969
Adelaise (James Forsyth), 1951
Adella (Barry Reckord), 1954
Admiral, The (Archibald MacLeish), 1944
Adrian (George Birimisa), 1974
Adrift (David Mowat), 1970
Adventure Story (Terence Rattigan), 1949
Adventures of Gervase Beckett, The (Peter Terson), 1969
Adventures of Huckleberry Finn (Organic Theatre, suppl 6), 1975
Adventures of Marco Polo (Neil Simon), 1969
Adventures of the Black Girl in Her Search for God, The (Christopher Isherwood), 1969
Adventures of Tom Random (N. C. Hunter, appendix), 1967
Advertisement, The (Henry Reed, suppl 2), 1968
Aeon (Merce Cunningham, suppl 5), 1960
Affair, The (Ronald Millar), 1961
Affair at Assino, The (N. C. Hunter, appendix), 1950
Affair at Bennett's Hill, (Worcs.), The (Peter Terson), 1970
Affair at Kirklees, The (Ronald Gow), 1932
Afore Night Come (David Rudkin), 1960
African Queen, The (John Huston, suppl 1), 1951
After All (Peter Nichols), 1959
After Haggerty (David Mercer), 1970
After Hours (David French), 1965
After Life, The (Barry Bermange), 1965
After Liverpool (James Saunders), 1971
After Lydia (Terence Rattigan), 1973
After Magritte (Tom Stoppard), 1970
After the Dance (Terence Rattigan), 1939
After the Fall (Arthur Miller), 1964
After the Fox (Neil Simon), 1966
After the Funeral (Alun Owen), 1960
After the Last Lamp (Henry Livings), 1967
After the Party (John Hopkins), 1958
After the Rain (John Bowen), 1966
After the Wedding Was Over (Kevin Laffan), 1975
Afterimage (USCO, suppl 5), 1965
Afternoon at the Festival, An (David Mercer), 1973
Afternoon at the Seaside (Agatha Christie), 1962
Afternoon Dancing (William Trevor), 1976
Afternoon for Antigone (Willis Hall), 1956
Against the Wind (T. E. B. Clarke, suppl 1), 1949

Bon Marché (Allan Kaprow, suppl 5), 1963
Bon-Bons and Roses for Dolly (Dorothy Hewett), 1972
Bond Honoured, A (John Osborne), 1966
Bond Street (Rodney Ackland, Terence Rattigan), 1950
Bonds of Love, The (Bruce Mason), 1953
Bone Room, The (Tom Jones, suppl 4), 1975
Bone Show/Calaveras, The (Beggars Theatre, suppl 6), 1974
Bonegrinder, The (Dennis Potter), 1968
Bones of My Toe, The (Ray Mathew), 1957
Boneyard, The (Clive Exton, suppl 3), 1966
Bonfire Boy, The (David Pinner), 1966
Bonjour Tristesse (Arthur Laurents), 1955
Bonkers (Inter-Action Trust, suppl 6)
Bonnet over the Windmill (Dodie Smith), 1937
Bonnie and Clyde (Robert Benton, David Newman, suppl 1), 1970
Boo! (David Campton), 1971
Book of Murder, The (Ron Cowen), 1974
Book of the Tumbler on Fire, The (George Brecht, suppl 5), 1965
Boom (Tennessee Williams), 1968
Boom (John McGrath), 1974
Boom Boom Room (David Rabe), 1973
Bootsie and Snudge (John Antrobus)
Borage Pigeon Affair, The (James Saunders), 1969
Born in Israel (Bernard Kops), 1963
Born of Medusa's Blood (John Herbert), 1972
Born Reckless (John Patrick), 1937
Born Yesterday (Garson Kanin), 1946
Bosom of the Family, The (Michael O'Neill, Jeremy Seabrook), 1975
Boston Story, A (Ronald Gow), 1968
Botticelli (Terrence McNally), 1968
Bottomley (David Turner), 1965
Bouncing Boy, The (John McGrath), 1972
Boundary, The (Tom Stoppard, Clive Exton), 1975
Bow, The (Michael McClure), 1971
Box, The (Murray Mednick), 1965
Box and Quotations from Chairman Mao Tse-Tung (Edward Albee), 1968
Box Car Ballet (Thomas Hendry), 1955
Box Play (Olwen Wymark), 1976
Boxes (Susan Yankowitz), 1972
Box-Mao-Box (Edward Albee), 1968
Boy, A Girl, and a Bike, A (Ted Willis), 1949
Boy Friend, The (Sandy Wilson, suppl 4), 1953
Boy Growing Up, A (Emlyn Williams), 1955
Boy in the Basement, The (William Inge, appendix), 1962
Boy Meets Girl (Bella Spewack, suppl 4), 1935
Boy on the Straight-Back Chair (Ronald Tavel), 1969
Boy Philosopher, The (Bernard Kops) 1974
Boy Ten Feet Tall, A (Denis Cannan), 1965
Boy Who Wouldn't Play Jesus, The (Bernard Kops), 1965
Boy with a Cart, The (Christopher Fry), 1938
Boychik, The (Wolf Mankowitz), 1954

Boys from Syracuse, The (George Abbott), 1938
Boys in the Band, The (Mart Crowley), 1968
Boys' Town (Dore Schary), 1938
Brace (Cecil P. Taylor), 1970
Bradford Walk (Adrian Mitchell)
Brain, The (Philip Mackie), 1963
Brain Rot (Jack Hibberd), 1967
Brainscrew (Henry Livings), 1966
Brand (James Forsyth), 1949
Brass Farthing (Giles Cooper, appendix), 1966
Brassneck (Howard Brenton, David Hare), 1973
Brave One, The (Dalton Trumbo, suppl 1), 1957
Brazil Fado: You're Always with Me (Megan Terry), 1972
Breach in the Wall, A (Ray Lawler), 1967
Bread (Mustapha Matura), 1976
Bread and Butter (Cecil P. Taylor), 1966
Bread and Butter Come to Supper (Paul Green), 1928
Bread and Butter Trade, The (Peter Terson), 1976
Bread Route (George Ryga), 1963
Breadwinner, The (Arthur Lister Murphy), 1967
Break in the Music, A (Alan Seymour), 1966
Break in the Skin, A (Ronald Ribman), 1972
Break Up (John Hopkins), 1958
Break-Down (Stewart Conn), 1961
Breakfast at Eight (Ronald Gow), 1920
Breakfast at Tiffany's (George Axelrod), 1961
Breakfast at Tiffany's (Edward Albee), 1966
Breakfast with Burrows (Abe Burrows), 1948
Breaking of Colonel Keyser, The (Robert Holles, suppl 3), 1972
Breaking Through the Sound Barrier (Terence Rattigan), 1952
Breakout (Peter Barnes), 1959
Breaks, The (Elliott Nugent), 1923
Breakthrough (Clive Exton, suppl 3), 1975
Breath (Samuel Beckett), 1970
Breath of Fresh Air, A (F. C. Ball, suppl 2), 1961
Brecht in '26 (Keith Dewhurst), 1971
Brecht on Brecht (George Tabori), 1962
Breech Baby, The (Leonard Melfi), 1968
Breeze from the Gulf, A (Mart Crowley), 1973
Brick and the Rose, The (Lewis John Carlino), 1957
Brick Umbrella, The (Peter Nichols), 1964
Bridal Dinner, The (A. R. Gurney, Jr.), 1962
Bride and the Bachelor, The (Ronald Millar), 1956
Bride Comes Back, The (Ronald Millar), 1960
Bride for the Unicorn, A (Denis Johnston), 1933
Bridegroom, The (Marc Connelly), 1929
Bridge, The (Rhys Adrian, suppl 2), 1961
Bridge, The (Mario Fratti), 1970
Bridge of Adam Rush, The (Lee Kalcheim), 1974
Bridge on the River Kwai, The (Carl Foreman, suppl 1), 1957
Bridget's House (Hull Truck, suppl 6), 1976
Brief Encounter (John Bowen), 1976
Brig, The (Kenneth H. Brown), 1963
Brigade (John Finch, suppl 3), 1976
Brigadoon (Alan Jay Lerner, suppl 4), 1947

Early Morning Glory (Mike Stott), 1972

Early to Braden (Ted Allan, John Antrobus, Johnny Speight), 1957

Earthprobes (John Bull Puncture Repair Kit, suppl 6), 1972

Earthquake Shakes the Land, The (Douglas Stewart), 1944

Earthrise (Welfare State, suppl 6), 1969

East of Ruston (C. C. Courtney, suppl 4), 1971

Easter (Kenneth Koch), 1966

Easter Egg, The (James Reaney), 1962

Easter's Stations of the Cross (Bread and Puppet Theatre, suppl 6), 1974

Easy Death (Caryl Churchill), 1962

Easy Go (Brian Clark, suppl 3), 1974

Easy Rider (Terry Southern, suppl 1), 1969

Eat (Allan Kaprow, suppl 5), 1964

Eat at Joe's (Megan Terry), 1964

Eat Cake (Jean-Claude van Itallie), 1971

Eccentric, The (Dannie Abse), 1961

Eccentricities of a Nightingale, The (Tennessee Williams), 1964

Echo (Gabriel Josipovici, suppl 2), 1975

Echoes (Rhys Adrian, suppl 2), 1969

Echoes from a Concrete Canyon (Wilson John Haire), 1975

Ecole Normale, L' (Kenneth Koch), 1973

Eco-Man (San Francisco Mime Troupe, suppl 6), 1970

Economic Necessity (John Hopkins), 1973

Ecstasy of Rita Joe, The (George Ryga), 1967

Eddie and Susanna in Love (Leonard Melfi), 1976

Eddie Cantor Story, The (Jerome Weidman), 1953

Eden (J. B. Priestley), 1934

Eden House (Hal Porter), 1969

Eden Rose, The (Robert Anderson), 1948

Edge of the World, The (Michael Powell, suppl 1), 1937

Edison the Man (Dore Schary), 1940

Editor Regrets, The (William Douglas Home), 1970

Edmondo Ros show (Johnny Speight), 1956

Educating Father (John Patrick), 1936

Education of an Englishman (John Mortimer), 1964

Education of Corporal Holliday, The (Robert Holles, suppl 3), 1967

Education of Skinny Spew, The (Howard Brenton), 1969

Edufa (Efua Sutherland), 1964

Edward: The Final Days (Howard Barker), 1971

Edwardians, The (Ronald Gow), 1959

Edwardians, The (Alan Plater), 1972

Effect of Gamma Rays on Man-in-the-Moon Marigolds, The (Paul Zindel), 1965

Ego Hugo (John Hale), 1973

Eh? (Henry Livings), 1964

Eh Jow (Samuel Beckett), 1966

Eiderdown (David Pinner), 1967

1850 (David Mowat), 1967

18 Happenings in 6 Parts (Allan Kaprow, suppl 5), 1959

1861 Whitby Lifeboat Disaster, The (Peter Terson), 1971

8th Ditch, The (LeRoi Jones), 1964

Elagabalus (Martin Duberman), 1973

Eleanor (William Trevor), 1974

Eleanor Roosevelt Story, The (Archibald MacLeish), 1965

Eleanora Duse (Mario Fratti), 1967

Election, The (Kenneth Koch), 1960

Electric Child (Terry Southern, suppl 1), 1970

Electric Map, The (Martin Duberman), 1970

Electronic Nigger, The (Ed Bullins), 1968

Elementary, My Dear Watson (N. F. Simpson), 1973

Elephant and the Jewish Question, The (Beverley Simons), 1968

Elephant Shit under the Big Top (The Cockettes, suppl 6)

Elephant's Foot, The (William Trevor), 1965

Elephants' Graveyard, The (Peter McDougall, suppl 3), 1976

Elephant-Steps (Richard Foreman), 1968

Eleventh Commandment, The (Wilfred Greatorex, suppl 3), 1970

Eleventh Hour, The (Brian Clark, suppl 3), 1975

Eliza Fraser (David Williamson), 1976

Elizabeth I (Paul Foster), 1972

Ella (Rhys Adrian, suppl 2), 1968

Ella Daybellfesse's Machine (Snoo Wilson), 1967

Ellen (Peter Ransley), 1970

Elmer and Lily (Willaim Saroyan), 1942

Elmer Gantry (Richard Brooks, suppl 1), 1960

Elusive Pimpernel, The (Michael Powell, suppl 1), 1950

Em 'n Ben (Cecil P. Taylor), 1971

Embers (Samuel Beckett), 1959

Emergence, The (Company Theatre, suppl 6), 1969

Emergence of Anthony Purdy, Esq., The (Charles Wood), 1970

Emergency Channel, The (John Bowen), 1973

Emergency Ward 9 (Dennis Potter), 1966

Emilia (Bread and Puppet Theatre, suppl 6), 1971

Emily and Heathcliff (Paul Ableman), 1967

Emily Butler (Henry Reed, suppl 2), 1954

Emlyn (Emlyn Williams), 1974

Emlyn, MacNeil, Cornelius (Alun Owen), 1969

Emlyn Williams as Charles Dickens (Emlyn Williams), 1952

Emma Instigated Me (Rochelle Owens), 1976

Emmanuel (James Forsyth), 1950

Emmanuel Xoc (Jack Gray), 1965

Emma's Time (David Mercer), 1970

Emmerdale Farm (Kevin Laffan), 1972

Emperor Jones, The (Errol Jones), 1953

Emperor Norton Lives! (James Schevill), 1972

Emperor of Ice-Cream, The (Bill Morrison, suppl 2), 1975

Emperor Waltz, The (Billy Wilder, suppl 1), 1948

Emperor's Clothes, The (George Tabori), 1953

God Bless the Guv'nor (Ted Willis), 1945
God Wants What Men Want (Arthur Sainer), 1966
Goddess, The (Paddy Chayefsky), 1958
Godiva (Jack Gray), 1967
God's Favorite (Neil Simon), 1974
Godspell (John-Michael Tabelak, suppl 4), 1971
Goin' a Buffalo (Ed Bullins), 1968
Going Greek (Guy Bolton, suppl 4), 1937
Going Home (David Campton), 1950
Going Home (William Trevor), 1970
Going Places (Guy Bolton, suppl 4), 1936
Going to Work (Alan Plater),1976
Gold Standard, The (Kenneth Koch), 1966
Gold Through the Trees (Alice Childress)
Goldberg (Cecil P. Taylor), 1976
Goldbrickers of 1944 (Ossie Davis), 1944
Golden Animal, The (Robert Patrick), 1970
Golden Boy (William Gibson), 1964
Golden Circle, The (Robert Patrick), 1970
Golden Cuckoo, The (Denis Johnston), 1938
Golden Earrings (Abraham Polonsky, suppl 1), 1947
Golden Entry, The (J. B. Priestley), 1955
Golden Fleece, The (A. R. Gurney, Jr.), 1968
Golden Fleece, The (J. B. Priestley), 1945
Golden Fleecing, The (S. J. Perelman), 1940
Golden Lover, The (Douglas Stewart), 1943
Golden Pathway Annual, The (John Burrows, John Harding), 1973
Golden West, The (Ronald Gow), 1932
Golden Wings (Guy Bolton, suppl 4), 1941
Goldilocks and the Three Bears (Alan Plater), 1974
Gone (Dannie Abse), 1962
Gone Are the Days (Ossie Davis), 1963
Gone to Earth (Michael Powell, suppl 1), 1950
Gone to Ground (John Harrison, suppl 2), 1968
Gone with the Wind (Horton Foote, suppl 3), 1972
Good and Faithful Servant, The (Joe Orton, appendix), 1967
Good as Gold (John Patrick), 1957
Good Companions, The (J. B. Priestley), 1931
Good Companions, The (scr John Whiting, appendix), 1957
Good Doctor, The (Neil Simon), 1973
Good Girl (Philip Mackie, suppl 3), 1974
Good Girl Is Hard to Find, A (LeRoi Jones), 1958
Good Grief! (Henry Livings), 1967
Good Job, The (William Saroyan), 1942
Good King, The (Bread and Puppet Theatre, suppl 6)
Good Lads at Heart (Peter Terson), 1971
Good Life, The (Snoo Wilson), 1971
Good Man and the Bad King, The (Beggars Theatre, suppl 6), 1973
Good Money (David Campton)
Good Night Children (J. B. Priestley), 1942
Good Night, I Love You (William M. Hoffman), 1966
Good Old Bad Old Days, The (Anthony Newley, suppl 4), 1973

Good Son, The (Ted Allan), 1969
Good Soup, The (Garson Kanin), 1960
Good Thing and a Bad Thing, A (Ann Jellicoe), 1974
Good Time Girl (Ted Willis), 1948
Good-By and Keep Cold (John Ford Noonan), 1973
Goodbye, The (Paul Green), 1928
Goodbye America (John Hale), 1976
Goodbye and Then (David Pinner), 1967
Goodbye Charlie (George Axelrod), 1959
Goodbye, Dan Dailey (Kenneth Bernard), 1971
Goodbye World (Bernard Kops), 1959
Goodnight Mrs. Dill (Fay Weldon, suppl 3), 1967
Goon Show, The (John Antrobus)
Goose, The (Alun Owen), 1967
Goose with Pepper (Frederick Bradnum, suppl 2), 1970
Gordon (Bridget Boland), 1961
Gordone Is a Muthah (Charles Gordone), 1970
Gore Vidal's Caligula (Gore Vidal), 1976
Gorf (Michael McClure), 1974
Gorge, The (Peter Nicholas), 1965
Gorgeous Lady Blessington, The (Denis Johnston), 1941
Gorilla Queen (Ronald Tavel), 1967
Gorillas Drink Milk (Charles Dyer), 1964
Gosforth's Fate (Alan Ayckbourn), 1974
Goshawk Squandron, The (Anthony Shaffer)
Gossoon (George Brecht, suppl 5), 1960
Government Inspector, The (Henry Livings), 1969
Government Property (Howard Brenton), 1975
Governor's Lady, The (David Mercer), 1960
Grabbing of the Fairy, The (Michael McClure), 1976
Grace (David Storey), 1974
Grace Darling Show (Cecil P. Taylor), 1971
Grace of Todd, The (David Rudkin), 1969
Graduate, The (Buck Henry, suppl 1), 1967
Grand Adultery Convention, The (Cecil P. Taylor), 1973
Grand Architect and Mother Earth, The (Beggars Theatre, suppl 6), 1975
Grand Old Opry (George Axelrod), 1950
Grand Tarot, The (Charles Ludlam), 1971
Grand Tenement/November 22nd (Tom Eyen), 1967
Grandma Faust (Edward Bond), 1976
Grandma Moses (Archibald MacLeish), 1950
Grandpa and the Statue (Arthur Miller), 1945
Grannie's a Hundred (Ronald Gow), 1 1939
Granny (Stephen Poliakoff), 1969
Granny Boling (Paul Green), 1921
Grantham's Outing (David Turner), 1956
Grant's Movie (Michael Weller), 1971
Graphis 118 (Dick Higgins, suppl 5), 1965
Graphis 132 (Dick Higgins, suppl 5), 1965
Graphis 24 and 82 (Dick Higgins, suppl 5), 1962
Grass and Wild Strawberries (George Ryga), 1969
Grass Harp, The (Truman Capote, suppl 4), 1952
Grass Is Singing, The (Doris Lessing), 1962

It's a Big Country (Dore Schary), 1952
It's a Lovely Day Tomorrow (Bernard Kops), 1975
It's a Two-Foot-Six-Inches-above-the-Ground World (Kevin Laffan), 1969
It's a Wise Child (Kevin Laffan), 1975
It's about Cinderella (Peter Shaffer), 1969
It's All for the Best (Steve Gooch), 1972
It's All in the Mind (John Hale), 1968
It's Called the Sugar Plum (Israel Horovitz), 1967
It's Dearer after Midnight (John Finch, suppl 3), 1968
It's Great to Be Young (Ted Willis), 1946
It's My Criminal (Howard Brenton), 1966
It's Not the Game It Was (James Saunders), 1964
It's Your Move (Bill Naughton), 1967
Ivan Captures Death (Beggars Theatre, suppl 6), 1974
I've Seen You Cut Lemons (Ted Allan), 1969
Ivory Tower (Jerome Weidman), 1968
Iz She Izzy or Iz He Ain'tzy or Iz They Both (Lonnie Carter), 1972
Izzie (Cecil P. Taylor), 1975

J. B. (Archibald MacLeish), 1958
Ja Ja Man (Beggars Theatre, suppl 6), 1975
Jabberwock (Jerome Lawrence, Robert E. Lee), 1972
Jack and Jill (Leonard Melfi), 1968
Jack and Jill (John Osborne), 1975
Jack and the Beanstalk (Nigel Kneale, suppl 3), 1974
Jack and the Beanstalk (Henry Livings), 1974
Jack and the Beanstalk (R. C. Scriven, suppl 2), 1968
Jack in the Box (David Cregan), 1974
Jack in the Box (Roger MacDougall), 1971
Jack Point (Colin Welland, suppl 3), 1973
Jack Shepherd (Wolf Mankowitz), 1972
Jack...The Flames (Lumiere and Son, suppl 6), 1974
Jack the Giant Killer (Olwen Wymark), 1972
Jackie Crow (Bill Naughton), 1962
Jackie the Jumper (Gwyn Thomas), 1963
Jack-Jack (Megan Terry), 1968
Jacob's Wake (Michael Cook), 1975
Jackpot (Guy Bolton, suppl 4), 1944
Jackpot Question, The (John Bowen), 1961
Jack's Horrible Luck (Henry Livings), 1961
Jake's Brigade (Trevor Griffiths), 1971
Jakey Fat Boy (Stanley Eveling), 1969
Jamaica Inn (J. B. Priestley), 1939
James Dean Story, The (Stewart Stern, suppl 1), 1957
James Joyce Memorial Liquid Theatre, The (Company Theatre, suppl 6), 1969
Jamie, On a Flying Visit (Michael Frayn), 1968
Jane (Hugh Leonard), 1970
Janitor, The (Ronald Duncan), 1955
Janitress Thrilled by Prehensile Penis (David Halliwell), 1972
Janus (Tom Galllacher), 1972

Jason (Tom Gallacher), 1972
Jason and the Argonauts (Beverley Cross), 1963
Jassy (Ronald Gow), 1947
Jaws II (Howard Sackler), 1976
Jealousy (Dalton Trumbo, suppl 1), 1934
Jeb (Robert Ardrey), 1946
Jeeves (Alan Ayckbourn), 1975
Jello (LeRoi Jones), 1965
Jenny Jones (Ronald Gow), 1944
Jenny Villiers (J. B. Priestley), 1946
Jens (David Mowat), 1965
Jero Plays, The (Wole Soyinka), 1972
Jero's Metamorphosis (Wole Soyinka), 1972
Jesse Tree, The (Anne Ridler), 1970
Jesus Christ Superstar (Tim Rice, suppl 4), 1970
Jewels of the Crown, The (James Ene Henshaw), 1957
Jezebel (John Huston, suppl 1), 1938
Jezebel Ex-UK (Hugh Leonard), 1963
Jig for the Gypsy, A (Robertson Davies), 1954
Jig Saw (Ronald Gow), 1942
Jim Batty (Bill Naughton), 1957
Jim Dandy (William Saroyan), 1941
Jimmy Shine (Murray Schisgal), 1968
Jingle Bells (Arthur Hopcraft, suppl 3), 1973
Jingo (Charles Wood), 1975
Jinxed (Tad Mosel), 1949
Jo and Ann (Peter Ransley), 1974
Jo Anne!!! (Ed Bullins), 1976
Joan (Al Carmines, suppl 4), 1972
Joan (Dorothy Hewett), 1975
Joan (Alun Owen), 1969
Joan Davis Program (Abe Burrows), 1945
Jock-on-the-Go (Peter Terson), 1966
Jockey Club Stakes, The (William Douglas Home), 1970
Joe Egg (Peter Nichols), 1967
Joe's Ark (Dennis Potter), 1974
Joe's World (Joseph Musaphia)
Joey, Joey (Willis Hall, Keith Waterhouse), 1966
John (David Mowat), 1971
John and Mary (John Mortimer), 1969
John Brown (Ronald Gow), 1934
John Bull Stately Home and Safari Park, The (John Bull Puncture Repair Kit, suppl 6), 1975
John D. Muggins Is Dead (Cartoon Archetypical Slogan Theatre, suppl 6)
John Thomas (Charles Wood), 1963
John Turner Davis (Horton Foote, suppl 3)
Johnny (Bread and Puppet Theatre, suppl 6)
Johnny Belinda (Mavor Moore), 1968
Johnny Frenchman (T. E. B. Clarke, suppl 1), 1945
Johnny Got His Gun (Dalton Trumbo, suppl 1), 1970
Johnny in the Clouds (Terence Rattigan), 1945
Johnny Johnson (Paul Green), 1936
Johnson over Jordan (J. B. Priestley), 1939
Joie de Vivre (Terence Rattigan), 1960
Join the Dance (Stephen Poliakoff), 1976
Joke, The (Rhys Adrian, suppl 2), 1974

1970

Legend of Paradiso (Ted Allan), 1960

Legend of Pepito (Ted Allan), 1955

Lemmings, The (Bernard Kops), 1963

Lemon Sky (Lanford Wilson), 1970

Lemons (Benjamin Patterson, suppl 5), 1961

Lena, Oh My Lena (Alun Owen), 1960

Lend an Ear (Joseph Stein, suppl 4), 1948

Lenin (Cecil P. Taylor), 1970

Lennon Play, The (Adrienne Kennedy), 1967

Lenny the Lion (John Antrobus), 1957

Lenz (Mike Stott), 1974

Leonard Sillman's New Faces of 1968 (William F. Brown, suppl 4), 1968

Leonardo's Last Supper (Peter Barnes), 1969

Leopardi (Henry Reed, suppl 2), 1949

Les Darcy Show, The (Jack Hibberd), 1974

Lesson in Dead Language, A (Adrienne Kennedy), 1968

Let It Bleed (Terrence McNally), 1972

Let There Be Light (John Huston, suppl 1), 1945

Let's Get a Closeup of the Messiah (Lee Kalcheim), 1969

Let's Get to Bed (Caryl Brahms, Ned Sherrin, suppl 4), 1976

Let's Hear It for the Queen (Alice Childress), 1976

Let's Imagine (Alun Owen), 1963

Let's Make a Carol (James Reaney), 1965

Let's Murder Vivaldi (David Mercer), 1967

Let's Talk It Over (Dore Schary), 1934

Letter, The (Mario Fratti), 1972

Letter, The (Howard Koch, suppl 1), 1940

Letter for Queen Victoria, A (Robert Wilson), 1974

Letter from a Soldier (Wilson John Haire), 1975

Letter from an Unknown Woman (Howard Koch, suppl 1), 1948

Letter from Colette, A (H. M. Koutoukas), 1966

Letter from Paris (Dodie Smith), 1952

Letter in the Desert, A (James Hanley), 1958

Letter to Three Wives, A (Joseph L. Mankiewicz, suppl 1), 1949

Letters for Iris, Numbers for Silence (Jackson Mac Low), 1962

Letters of a Portuguese Nun (Barry Bermange), 1966

Letters to a Lady (Paul Ableman), 1951

Level (Allan Kaprow, suppl 5), 1970

Level Seven (J. B. Priestley), 1966

Leviathan (Thornton Wilder), 1928

Liam Liar (Hugh Leonard), 1976

Liar (David Campton), 1969

Liars, The (Hugh Leonard), 1966

Liberated Woman, A (Barry Reckord), 1970

Liberated Zone (David Edgar), 1973

Liberty Hall (Giles Cooper, appendix), 1958

Libido (David Williamson), 1972

Library Raid, The (Frank Gagliano), 1961

Licensed Victualler, The (Bruce Mason), 1955

Liebelei (Frank Marcus), 1954

Liebestraum and Other Pieces (David Cregan),

1970

Lies about Vietnam/Truth about Sarajevo (Cecil P. Taylor), 1969

Life, A (Gabriel Josipovici, suppl 2), 1973

Life and Death of Almost Everybody, The (David Campton), 1970

Life and Death of Colonel Blimp, The (Michael Powell), 1943

Life and Death of Lovely Karen Gilhooley, The (Keith Dewhurst), 1964

Life and Times of Dave Clark, The (Robert Wilson), 1974

Life and Times of Joseph Stalin, The (Robert Wilson), 1973

Life and Times of Sigmund Freud, The (Robert Wilson), 1969

Life Class (David Storey), 1974

Life in My Hands, The (Peter Ustinov), 1963

Life in the Sun, A (Thornton Wilder), 1955

Life of a Man, The (Al Carmines, suppl 4), 1972

Life of George Washington (George Brecht, suppl 5), 1964

Life of Juanita Castro, The (Ronald Tavel), 1965

Life of Lady Godiva, The (Ronald Tavel), 1966

Life of Man, The (John Arden), 1956

Life of the Party, The (Alan Jay Lerner, suppl 4), 1942

Life of the Party, The (Ray Mathew), 1960

Life Price (Michael O'Neill, Jeremy Seabrook), 1969

Lifeline (Ted Willis)

Light of Heart, The (Emlyn Williams), 1940

Light of the World, The (Guy Bolton, suppl 4), 1920

Light the Blue Touch Paper (John Hale), 1966

Light Shining in Buckinghamshire (Caryl Churchill), 1976

Light Touch, The (Richard Brooks, suppl 1), 1951

Lightfall (David Pinner), 1967

Lighthearted Intercourse (Bill Naughton), 1971

Lightning at a Funeral (David Pinner), 1967

Lights, Camera, Action (Robert Patrick), 1967

Like Men Betrayed (John Mortimer), 1955

Lillibulero (Denis Johnston), 1937

Lily Dafon (William Saroyan, 1960

Lily in Little India, A (Donald Howarth), 1962

Lily of the Valley of the Dolls (Robert Patrick), 1969

Lilly Turner (George Abbott), 1932

Limbo (Alwin Nikolais, suppl 5), 1968

Limelight (Charlie Chaplin, suppl 1), 1952

Lincoln (Mike Stott), 1973

Lincoln, The Unwilling Warrior (Jerome Lawrence, Robert E. Lee), 1975

Linda at Pulteney (J. B. Priestley), 1969

Linden Tree, The (J. B. Priestley), 1947

Line (Israel Horovitz), 1967

Line of Least Existence, The (Rosalyn Drexler), 1967

Lines from My Grandfather's Forehead (Donald Churchill, suppl 3)

Lunch Hour (John Mortimer), 1960
Lunchtime (Leonard Melfi), 1966
Lunchtime Concert (Olwen Wymark), 1966
Lushly (Howard Brenton), 1972
Luther (John Osborne), 1961
Luv (Murray Schisgal), 1963

M Is for Moon among Other Things (Tom Stoppard), 1964
Macadam and Eve (Roger MacDougall), 1950
Macbeth (Tsegaye Gabre-Medhin), 1972
Macbeth (Orson Welles, suppl 1), 1948
Macbeth Did It (John Patrick), 1972
MacEnery's Vision of Pipkin (John Grillo), 1973
Machine Gun McCain (Israel Horovitz), 1970
Mack and Mabel (Michael Stewart, suppl 4), 1975
MacKenna's Gold (Carl Foreman, suppl 1), 1969
Macmillan and Wife (Oliver Hailey), 1971
Macquarie (Alexander Buzo), 1972
MacRune's Guevara (John Spurling), 1969
Mad Dog Blues (Sam Shepard), 1971
Mad Girls, The (Lumiere and Son, suppl 6), 1974
Mad Jack (Tom Clarke, suppl 3), 1970
Mad Man a Mad Giant a Mad Dog a Mad Urge a
    Mad Face, A (Robert Wilson), 1974
Madame Bovary (Robert Ardrey), 1949
Madame Bovary (Giles Cooper, appendix), 1965
Madame de...(John Whiting, appendix), 1959
Madam Senator (Mario Fratti), 1975
Madame Aphrodite (Tad Mosel), 1953
Made (Howard Barker), 1972
Made in Britain (Steve Gooch), 1976
Mademoiselle (David Rudkin), 1966
Madheart (LeRoi Jones), 1967
Madigan (Abraham Polonsky, suppl 1), 1968
Madigan's Lock (Hugh Leonard), 1958
Madly in Love (Paul Ableman), 1968
Madmen and Specialists (Wole Soyinka), 1970
Madness of Lady Bright, The (Lanford Wilson),
    1964
Madonna in the Orchard, The (Paul Foster), 1965
Mafia (Mario Fratti), 1966
Maggie May (Alun Owen, Lionel Bart), 1964
Maggie of the Bargain Basement (David Stark-
    weather), 1956
Magic Christian, The (Terry Southern, suppl 1),
    1970
Magic Flute, The (Adrian Mitchell), 1966
Magic in the Blood (James Ene Henshaw), 1964
Magic Island, The (Keith Dewhurst), 1974
Magic Realists, The (Megan Terry), 1966
Magic Show, The (Bob Randall, suppl 4), 1974
Magic Show of Dr. Ma-Gico, The (Kenneth Bernard), 1973
Magic Tower, The (Tennessee Williams), 1936
Magnet, The (T. E. B. Clarke, suppl 1), 1951
Magnificence (Howard Brenton), 1973
Magnificent Ambersons, The (Orson Welles, suppl
    1), 1942
Magnificent Moodies, The (Ted Willis), 1952
Magyar Melody (Guy Bolton, suppl 4), 1939

Mahagonny (Arnold Weinstein), 1969
Maigret (Giles Cooper, appendix), 1960
Maigret and the Lady (Philip Mackie, suppl 3),
    1965
Maigret and the Lost Life (Giles Cooper, appendix), 1959
Main Attraction, The (John Patrick), 1963
Main Sequence (David Mowat), 1974
Maison sous les Arbres, La (Eleanor Perry, suppl
    1), 1972
Majesty (Peter Nichols), 1968
Major and the Minor, The (Billy Wilder, suppl 1),
    1942
Makbeth (Performance Group, suppl 6), 1970
Make a Man (N. F. Simpson), 1966
Make Believe Man, The (John Hopkins), 1965
Make Me an Offer (Wolf Mankowitz), 1952
Making and Breaking of Splinters Braun, The
    (Israel Horovitz) 1976
Making Faces (Michael Frayn), 1975
Making Money (William Saroyan), 1969
Making of Americans, The (Al Carmines, suppl 4),
    1972
Making of Jericho, The (Alun Owen), 1966
Making of Moo, The (Nigel Dennis), 1957
Making of Theodore Thomas, Citizen, The
    (Michael Weller), 1968
Malatesta (Henry Reed, suppl 2), 1952
Malatesta (Heathcote Williams), 1969
Malcochon (Derek Walcott), 1969
Malcolm (Edward Albee), 1966
Malcolm (Lewis Nkosi), 1967
Malcolm X (Barry Reckord), 1973
Male Animal, The (Elliott Nugent), 1940
Male Armor (Martin Duberman), 1975
Male of the Species (Alun Owen), 1969
Mall, The (William Inge, appendix), 1962
Maltese Falcon, The (John Huston, suppl 1), 1941
Mame (Jerome Lawrence, Robert E. Lee), 1966
Mame (scr Paul Zindel), 1974
Mammals, The (Michael McClure), 1972
Man above Men (David Hare), 1973
Man Alive (George Ryga), 1965
Man and Boy (Terence Rattigan), 1963
Man and His Mother-in-Law, A (Hugh Leonard),
    1968
Man and His Wife, A (Guy Bolton, suppl 4), 1974
Man Behind the Gun, The (Arthur Laurents)
Man Beneath, The (Jim Allen, suppl 3), 1967
Man Better Man (Errol Hill), 1960
Man Born to Be King, The (Mavor Moore), 1961
Man for All Seasons, A (Robert Bolt), 1954
Man Friday (Adrian Mitchell), 1972
Man from Clare, The (John B. Keane), 1963
Man from Haven (Wilfred Greatorex, suppl 3),
    1972
Man Has Two Fathers, A (John McGrath), 1958
Man I Love, The (Joseph L. Mankiewicz, suppl 1),
    1929
Man in the Glass Booth, The (Robert Shaw), 1967
Man in the Green Muffler, The (Stewart Conn),

Master of Arts (William Douglas Home), 1949
Masters, The (Ronald Millar), 1963
Mata Hari (Mike Stott), 1965
Match Play (Lee Kalcheim), 1964
Match-Fit (Willis Hall), 1976
Matchmaker, The (Thornton Wilder), 1954
Mates (Peter Kenna), 1975
Mathry Beacon (Giles Cooper, appendix), 1956
Mating Age, The (Robert Holles, suppl 3), 1961
Mating Season, The (Alan Plater), 1962
Matter of Conscience, A (Tom Clarke, suppl 3), 1962
Matter of Gravity, A (Enid Bagnold), 1975
Matter of Innocence, A (Willis Hall, Keith Waterhouse), 1968
Matter of Life and Death, A (Michael Powell, suppl 1), 1946
Matter of Position, A (Elaine May), 1962
Matter of Pride, A (Frank D. Gilroy), 1957
Matter of Scandal and Concern, A (John Osborne), 1960
Matter of Timing, A (Mavor Moore), 1971
Maurice (Carol Bolt), 1974
Mauvaise Graine (Billy Wilder, suppl 1), 1934
Max (Denis Cannan), 1949
May (Allan Kaprow, suppl 5), 1963
Mayerling (Denis Cannan), 1968
Maze, The (Michael McClure), 1967
McCloud (Lonne Elder, III), 1970
McGonagall and the Murderer (John Spurling), 1974
McGuire Go Home (Bryan Forbes, suppl 1), 1965
McKinley and Sarah (Bill Morrison, suppl 2), 1973
McLuhan Megilla, A (Al Hansen, suppl 5), 1966
Me (Cecil P. Taylor), 1972
Me and My Brother (Sam Shepard), 1967
Me Mammy (Hugh Leonard), 1970
Me, Me Dad and His'n (David Turner), 1957
Me, Third (Mary Chase), 1936
Meals on Wheels (Charlie Wood), 1965
Meaning of the Statue, The (Roger Howard), 1971
Meanwhile, Backstage in the Old Front Room (Donald Howarth), 1975
Measure for Measure (Howard Brenton), 1972
Measure of Sliding Sand, A (R. C. Scriven, suppl 2), 1974
Meat Joy (Carolee Schneemann, suppl 5), 1964
Meatball (Company Theatre, suppl 6), 1971
Meatball, The (Michael McClure), 1969
Mecca (E. A. Whitehead), 1977
Mechanic, The (Lewis John Carlino), 1972
Medea (H. M. Koutoukas), 1966
Medea of Euripides, The (Ray Mathew), 1954
Medicine for Love (James Ene Henshaw), 1964
Medicine Man, The (James Forsyth), 1950
Meet Corliss Archer (Robert E. Lee), 1942
Meet My Father (Alan Ayckbourn), 1965
Meet Whiplash Willie (Billy Wilder, suppl 1), 1966
Meeting by the River, A (Christopher Isherwood), 1972
Meeting Place (Robert Lord), 1972

Melinda (Lonne Elder, III), 1972
Melodrama Play (Sam Shepard), 1967
Melody Bandbox Rhythm Roadshow (Hull Truck, suppl 6), 1976
Memento Mori (David Campton), 1957
Memoirs of a Sly Pornographer (Rhys Adrian, suppl 2), 1972
Memorial Day (Murray Schisgal), 1965
Memorial to the First Astronaut (Welfare State, suppl 6), 1974
Memories of a Childhood Friendship (Don Haworth, suppl 2), 1976
Memory Bank, The (Martin Duberman), 1970
Memory Man, The (David Mowat), 1974
Memory of Eden, A (Thomas Hendry), 1975
Memory of Summer (William Inge, appendix), 1962
Memory of Two Mondays, A (Arthur Miller), 1955
Men, The (Carl Foreman, suppl 1), 1950
Men Are Unwise (Ronald Gow), 1937
Men in White (Sidney Kingsley), 1933
Men of Iron (Keith Dewhurst), 1969
Men of Texas (Richard Brooks, suppl 1), 1942
Menace (Arnold Wesker), 1963
Ménage à Trois (Ronald Duncan), 1963
Men's Talk (Mike Stott), 1974
Menschen am Sonntag (Billy Wilder, suppl 1), 1929
Menzogna, La (Mario Fratti), 1959
Merchant of Yonkers, The (Thornton Wilder), 1938
Merciless Lady, The (N. C. Hunter, appendix), 1934
Mercy Drop (Robert Patrick), 1973
Meriel the Ghost Girl (David Halliwell), 1976
Merlin's Brow (Gwyn Thomas), 1957
Merry Roosters Panto (Lionel Bart, Peter Shaffer), 1963
Merry Stones, The (Kenneth Koch), 1966
Merry-Go-Round (Albert Maltz), 1932
Merry-Go-Round (Frank Marcus), 1953
Merton of the Movies (Marc Connelly), 1922
Message (Claes Oldenburg, suppl 5), 1966
Message and Jehanne, The (Thornton Wilder), 1928
Message for Posterity (Dennis Potter), 1967
Metamorphosis (Charles Dizenzo), 1972
Metaphors (Martin Duberman), 1968
Mhil'daim (Arthur Kopit), 1963
Micah Clarke (John Hale), 1966
Michael Regan (Robert Holles, suppl 3), 1971
Mick and Nick (Hugh Leonard), 1966
Mickey (Mary Chase), 1969
Mickey and Nicky (Elaine May), 1976
Microdrama (George F. Walker), 1975
Midas Connection (David Edgar), 1975
Middle of the Night (Paddy Chayefsky), 1954
Middle-of-the-Road Show, The (Philip Mackie, suppl 3), 1973
Midgie Purvis (Mary Chase), 1961

1968
Mrs. Palfrey at the Claremont (Ray Lawler), 1973
Mrs. Pool's Preserves (Michael Sadler, suppl 2), 1973
Mrs. Porter and the Angel (Dorothy Hewett), 1970
Mrs. Thursday (Ted Willis), 1966
Mrs. Wickers in the Fall (Nigel Kneale, suppl 3), 1957
Mo (John McGrath), 1965
Moby Dick (John Huston, suppl 1), 1956
Moby Dick (Keith Johnstone), 1967
Moby Dick (Kenneth Koch), 1973
Moby Dick (Henry Reed, suppl 2), 1947
Moby Dick (Peter Terson), 1972
Modern Times (Charlie Chaplin, suppl 1), 1931
Mojo (Alice Childress), 1971
Moke-Eater, The (Kenneth Bernard), 1968
Mole on Lincoln's Cheek, The (Marc Connelly), 1941
Moll (John B. Keane), 1971
Molly's Dream (María Irene Fornés), 1968
Moment of Truth, The (Peter Ustinov), 1951
Monday at Seven (Willis Hall), 1957
Monday Night Varieties (John Ford Noonan), 1972
Monday on the Way to Mercury Island (Julie Bovasso), 1971
Money, The (Philip Mackie, suppl 3), 1961
Money Makers, The (Ted Allan), 1954
Money to Burn (Elliott Nugent), 1923
Money Tower, The (Living Theatre, suppl 6), 1974
Money's Tight (Robert Benton, David Freeman, suppl 1), 1972
Monica Harmonica (Al Hansen, suppl 5), 1964
Monkey Business (S. J. Perelman), 1931
Monkeys of the Organ Grinder, The (Kenneth Bernard), 1970
Monologue (Harold Pinter), 1973
Monsieur Verdoux (Charlie Chaplin, suppl 1), 1947
Monster, The (Ron Milner), 1968
Month in the Country, A (Emlyn Williams), 1943
Montserrat (Lillian Hellman), 1949
Monument, The (Henry Reed, suppl 2), 1950
Monument for Ishi, A (Bread and Puppet Theatre, suppl 6), 1975
Moods of Love, The (Laurence Collinson), 1964
Moody and Peg (Donald Churchill, Julia Jones, suppl 3), 1974
Moody Tuesday (Robert Lord), 1972
Moon Ballon, The (Kenneth Koch), 1969
Moon Dreamers, The (Julie Bovasso), 1967
Moon in Capricorn (James Leo Herlihy), 1953
Moon in the Yellow River, The (Denis Johnston), 1931
Moon on a Rainbow Shawl (Errol John), 1958
Moon Section (Allen Curnow), 1959
Moonchildren (Michael Weller), 1972
Mooney and His Caravans (Peter Terson), 1966
Mooney's Kid Don't Cry (Tennessee Williams), 1946

Moonlight on the Highway (Dennis Potter), 1969
Moonlighters, The (Tom Clarke, suppl 3), 1971
Moonmen, The (Inter-Action Trust, suppl 6)
Moonshine (James Saunders), 1955
Moonstone, The (Hugh Leonard), 1972
Moonstone, The (Anthony Shaffer), 1975
Moral Force, The (Thomas Murphy), 1973
Morality (Michael O'Neill, Jeremy Seabrook), 1971
Morbid Interests (John Bull Puncture Repair Kit, suppl 6), 1973
More about the Universe (Snoo Wilson), 1972
More Deadly Than the Sword (Terence Frisby), 1966
More Metamorphoses (Arnold Weinstein), 1973
More Milk Evette (Ronald Tavel), 1966
More! More! I Want More! (Michael Smith), 1966
More Than You Deserve (Michael Weller), 1973
More the Merrier, The (Garson Kanin), 1943
More the Merrier, The (Ronald Millar), 1960
More War in Store (Lonnie Carter), 1970
Morecambe and Wise Show (Johnny Speight), 1956
Morgan! (David Mercer), 1965
Morituri (David Mowat), 1972
Morning (Israel Horovitz), 1968
Morning after Optimism, The (Thomas Murphy), 1971
Morning Place, The (Tad Mosel), 1957
Morning Star, The (Emlyn Williams), 1941
Morning Sun (Fred Ebb, suppl 4), 1963
Mortadella (Leonard Melfi), 1971
Mortification, The (Barry Bermange), 1964
Mortmain (John Mortimer), 1976
Moscow Strikes Back (Albert Maltz), 1942
Mosedale Horseshoe, The (Arthur Hopcraft, suppl 3), 1971
Moses and Aaron (David Rudkin), 1965
Moss (Bernard Kops), 1975
Most Beautiful Fish, The (Ronald Ribman), 1969
Most Cheerful Man, The (Peter Terson), 1973
Most Recent Least Recent (David Mowat), 1970
Most Unfortunate Accident, A (John Bowen), 1968
Most Wonderful Thing , A (Henry Livings), 1976
Motel (Jean-Claude van Itallie), 1966
Moth and the Star, The (Denis Cannan), 1950
Mother, The (Paddy Chayefsky), 1955
Mother, The (Steve Gooch), 1973
Mother (Ted Willis), 1961
Mother Adam (Charles Dyer), 1971
Mother and Child (Clive Exton, suppl 3), 1970
Mother Courage (George Tabori), 1970
Mother Earth (Martin Duberman), 1971
Mother Figure (Alan Ayckbourn), 1973
Mother Love (Olwen Wymark), 1975
Mother Lover, The (Jerome Weidman), 1969
Mother of Pearl (Company Theatre, suppl 6), 1972
Mothers and Fathers (Joseph Musaphia), 1975
Mother's Day (J. B. Priestley), 1953
Mother's Day (David Storey), 1976

Names for the Rivers, The (Archibald MacLeish), 1944

Nansen of the "Fram" (Denis Johnston), 1940

Napoleon and Love (Philip Mackie, suppl 3), 1974

Narrow Road to the Deep North (Edward Bond), 1968

Nascunter Poetae (Thornton Wilder), 1928

Nathan and Tabileth (Barry Bermange), 1962

Nathaniel Titlark (Bill Naughton), 1957

National Health, The (Peter Nichols), 1969

National Interest, The (David Edgar), 1971

National Theatre, The (David Edgar), 1975

National Velvet (Enid Bagnold), 1945

Native Son (Paul Green), 1941

Nativity (Robert Lord), 1973

Nativity Play (William M. Hoffman), 1970

Natural Affection (William Inge, appendix), 1962

Natural History (The Dreams) (Jim Dine, suppl 5), 1965

Natural Justice (Robert Holles, suppl 3), 1968

Navigators, The (Julia Jones, suppl 3), 1965

Nearly Man, The (Arthur Hopcraft, suppl 3), 1974

Nectarine (George Brecht, suppl 5), 1962

Ned Kelly (Douglas Stewart), 1943

Needle Match, The (Alan Plater), 1974

Negatives (Philip Martin, suppl 2), 1972

Neighbours (James Saunders), 1964

Neighbours (David Turner), 1973

Neither (Bread and Puppet Theatre, suppl 6)

Neither Here nor There (Olwen Wymark), 1971

Neither Up nor Down (Peter Nichols), 1972

Nekropolis 1 and 2 (Claes Oldenburg, suppl 5), 1962

Nelson (Terence Rattigan), 1966

Nelson Affair, The (Terence Rattigan), 1973

Nelson Cape Requests the Pleasure (Henry Livings), 1967

Network (Paddy Chayefsky), 1975

Neurovision Song Contest, The (Adrian Mitchell)

Neutral Ground (Tom Stoppard), 1968

Never a Cross Word (Donald Churchill, suppl 3), 1968

Never Forget a Face (Barry Bermange), 1961

Never Get Out (Giles Cooper, appendix), 1950

Never Let Me Go (Ronald Millar), 1953

Never on Sunday (Jules Dassin, suppl 1), 1959

Never So Good (Kevin Laffan), 1976

New Bestiary, A (Roger Howard), 1971

New Britain, The (Graham Greene), 1940

New Communion — for Freaks, Prophets and Witches, A (Jane Arden), 1971

New Faces of 56 (Neil Simon), 1956

New Girl in Town (George Abbott), 1957

New Leaf, A (Elaine May), 1971

New Lot, The (Peter Ustinov), 1943

New Men, The (Ronald Millar), 1962

New Patriots, The (R. Sarif Easmon), 1965

New Play, The (William Saroyan), 1970

New Portuguese Letters, The (Women's Theatre Group, suppl 6)

New Quixote, The (Michael Frayn), 1970

New York (Mario Fratti), 1974

New York Comedy: Two (Megan Terry), 1961

New York Scrapbook (Tom Jones, suppl 4), 1961

New Yorkers, The (Jerome Lawrence, Robert E. Lee), 1963

New-found-land (Tom Stoppard), 1976

Newsletter (Ruth Krauss)

Newspaper Event (Carolee Schneemann, suppl 5), 1962

Next (Terrence McNally), 1967

Next Half Thing, The (Mary Chase), 1945

Next of Kin (John Hopkins), 1974

Next Thing, The (Michael Smith), 1966

Next Time I'll Sing to You (James Saunders), 1963

Next to Being a Knight (Charles Wood), 1972

Next Year Country (Carol Bolt), 1971

Next Year in Tel Aviv (Cecil P. Taylor), 1973

Niagara Falls (Leonard Melfi), 1966

Nice (Mustapha Matura), 1973

Nice Clean Sheet of Paper, A (Rhys Adrian, suppl 2), 1963

Nice Girl Like You, A (Carol Bolt), 1974

Nice Rest, A (Fay Weldon, suppl 3), 1972

Nicholas and Alexandra (James Goldman), 1971

Nicholas Nickleby (Hugh Leonard), 1968

Nickleby and Me (Caryl Brahms, Ned Sherrin, suppl 4), 1975

Nigel Barton Plays, The (Dennis Potter), 1967

Nigger Hunt, The (Keith Johnstone), 1959

Niggerlovers, The (George Tabori), 1967

Night (Allan Kaprow, suppl 5), 1961

Night (Leonard Melfi), 1968

Night (Harold Pinter), 1969

Night Ambush (Michael Powell, suppl 1), 1957

Night and the Shadow, The (R. C. Scriven, suppl 2), 1955

Night Before Christmas, The (S. J. Perelman), 1941

Night Before the Morning After, The (Jack Rosenthal, suppl 3), 1966

Night Cap, The (Guy Bolton, suppl 4), 1921

Night Club (Kenneth Bernard), 1970

Night Crawlers (Carolee Schneemann, suppl 5), 1967

Night Duty (Peter Ransley), 1972

Night in the House (Rodney Ackland), 1935

Night Kite (Banjamin Patterson, suppl 5), 1966

Night Life (Sidney Kingsley), 1962

Night Like This, A (Ben Travers), 1930

Night Must Fall (Emlyn Williams), 1935

Night of Talvera (Robert Holles, suppl 3), 1968

Night of the Beast (Ed Bullins), 1971

Night of the Dunce (Frank Gagliano), 1966

Night of the Iguana (scr John Huston, suppl 1), 1964

Night of the Iguana, The (Tennessee Williams), 1959

Night of the Tanks (Wilfred Greatorex, suppl 3), 1972

Night on Bald Mountain (Patrick White), 1964

Night Out, A (Harold Pinter), 1960

Night School (Harold Pinter), 1960

Night Thoreau Spent in Jail, The (Jerome Lawrence, Robert E. Lee), 1970

Night Time Sky, The (Robert Whitman, suppl 5), 1965

Night to Make the Angels Weep, A (Peter Terson), 1964

Night Watch (Rodney Ackland), 1941

Night with Mrs. da Tanka, A (William Trevor), 1968

Night-Blooming Cereus (James Reaney), 1960

Nightcap Yarns (Jerome Lawrence), 1939

Nightcomers, The (Michael Hastings), 1971

Nightingale, The (Guy Bolton, suppl 4), 1927

Nightingale, The (Willis Hall), 1954

Nightingale in Bloomsbury Square, A (Maureen Duffy), 1973

Nightingale's Boys (Arthur Hopcraft, suppl 3), 1975

Nightlight (Kenneth H. Brown), 1973

Nightmare (Susan Yankowitz), 1967

Nightstick (Elliott Nugent), 1927

Nightwalk (Sam Shepard, Megan Terry, Jean-Claude van Itallie), 1973

Nightwalkers, The (Beverley Cross), 1960

Nik (Alwin Nikolais, suppl 5), 1974

Nil Carborundum (Henry Livings), 1962

Nimrod's Oak (James Saunders), 1953

Nina (Samuel Taylor, suppl 4), 1951

998 (Dale Wasserman, suppl 4), 1962

Nine O'Clock Mail, The (Howard Sackler), 1965

Nine Rivers from Jordan (Denis Johnston), 1969

1984 (Nigel Kneale, suppl 3), 1965

Nineteen Thirty Nine (John Grillo), 1973

Ninety Degrees in the Shade (David Mercer), 1965

Ninety in the Shade (Guy Bolton, suppl 4), 1915

Ninety Years On (Terence Rattigan), 1964

Ninotchka (Billy Wilder, suppl 1), 1939

Ninth Summer (George Ryga), 1972

Nirvana (John Howard Lawson), 1926

No (Charles Wood), 1976

No Accounting for Taste (David Rudkin), 1960

No Answer (William Hanley), 1968

No Bed for Bacon (Caryl Brahms, suppl 4), 1959

No Charge for Extra Service (Rhys Adrian, suppl 2), 1971

No Commemorating Stone (Frederick Bradnum, suppl 2), 1954

No 'Count Boy, The (Paul Green), 1925

No Exit (George Tabori), 1962

No Fixed Abode (Clive Exton, suppl 3), 1959

No Go Area (David Campton), 1976

No Going Home (Frederick Bradnum, suppl 2), 1957

No Hero (John Mortimer), 1955

No Man Can Serve Two Masters (Michael Cook), 1967

No Man's Land (Harold Pinter), 1975

No More A-Roving (John Whiting, appendix), 1975

No More in Dust (John B. Keane), 1962

No, No, Nanette (Burt Shevelove, suppl 4), 1971

No One Was Saved (Howard Barker), 1971

No Place to Be Somebody (Charles Gordone), 1969

No Quarter (Barry Bermange), 1962

No Saco Nada de la Escuela (El Teatro Campesino, suppl 6), 1969

No Sad Songs for Me (Howard Koch, suppl 1), 1950

No Sign of the Dove (Peter Ustinov), 1953

No Sirree! (Marc Connelly), 1922

No Skill or Speical Knowledge Is Required (John Hopkins), 1966

No Strings (Samuel Taylor, suppl 4), 1962

No Such Thing as a Vampire (Hugh Leonard), 1968

No Sugar for George (Laurence Collinson), 1949

No Talking (Olwen Wymark), 1970

No Telegrams, No Thunder (Dannie Abse), 1962

No Title (David Rudkin), 1974

No Trams to Lime Street (Alun Owen), 1959

No Trees in the Street (Ted Willis), 1948

No Trespassing (Lanford Wilson), 1964

No Villains (They Too Arise) (Arthur Miller), 1937

No Way Out (Joseph L. Mankiewicz, suppl 1), 1950

No Why (John Whiting, appendix), 1961

Noah's Animals (John Patrick), 1975

Nobodaddy (Archibald MacLeish), 1926

Nobody Hears a Broken Drum (Jason Miller), 1970

Nobody Home (Guy Bolton, suppl 4), 1915

Nobody Loves Me (Neil Simon), 1962

Nobody Runs Forever (Wilfred Greatorex, suppl 3), 1968

Nobody's Business (Guy Bolton, suppl 4), 1923

Noces, Les (Merce Cunningham, suppl 5), 1952

Nocturne of a Provincial Spring (R. C. Scriven, suppl 2), 1975

Nocturnes (Merce Cunningham, suppl 5), 1956

No-Good Friday (Athol Fugard), 1956

Noise (Gwyn Thomas), 1960

Noise Bodies (Carolee Schneemann, suppl 5), 1965

Noise Stopped, The (John Hale), 1966

Noises — Nasty and Nice (Henry Reed, suppl 2), 1947

Noises On (Henry Reed, suppl 2), 1947

Nomads, The (John Whiting, appendix), 1965

No-Man, The (Giles Cooper, appendix), 1955

Noman (John Whiting, appendix), 1969

Nongogo (Athold Fugard), 1957

Non-Stop Connolly Show, The (John Arden), 1975

Noon (Terrence McNally), 1968

Noonan Night, A (John Ford Noonan), 1973

Noonday Demons (Peter Barnes), 1969

Norm and Ahmed (Alexander Buzo), 1968

Norma (Alun Owen), 1969

Normal Women, The (David Mowat), 1970

Norman Conquests, The (Alan Ayckborun), 1973

North and South (David Turner), 1966

Slight Accident, A (James Saunders), 1961

Slight Ache, A (Harold Pinter), 1969

Slight Touch of the Sun, A (Stewart Conn), 1972

Slightly Scarlet (Joseph L. Mankiewicz, suppl 1), 1930

Slim John (David Campton), 1971

Slinga and Arrows (Sandy Wilson, suppl 4), 1948

Slip, The (Gwyn Thomas), 1962

Slip of a Girl, A (Mary Chase), 1941

Slip Road Wedding (Peter Terson), 1971

Slob on Friday, The (Laurence Collinson), 1969

Slow Dance on the Killing Ground (William Hanley), 1964

Slow Roll of Drums, A (Ted Willis), 1964

Slow Stain, The (Alan Plater), 1973

Slug City (Welfare State, suppl 6), 1975

Small Back Room, The (John Hopkins), 1959

Small Back Room, The (Michael Powell, suppl 1), 1948

Small Cannon (Robert Whitman, suppl 5), 1960

Small Change (Peter Gill),1976

Small Craft Warnings (Tennessee Williams), 1972

Small Explosion, A (Dannie Abse), 1964

Small Fish Are Sweet (Peter Luke), 1959

Small Fortune (Giles Cooper, appendix), 1951

Small Miracle, The (John Patrick), 1972

Small Smell (Robert Whitman, suppl 5), 1960

Small Wonder (George Axelrod, Burt Shevelove), 1948

Smashing Day, A (Alan Plater), 1962

Smashup (John Howard Lawson), 1947

Smell of Burning, A (David Campton), 1957

Smile Boys, That's the Style (John Hale), 1968

Smile of the World, The (Garson Kanin), 1949

Smiling Workman, The (Jim Dine, suppl 5), 1960

Smith in Arcady (N. C. Hunter, appendix), 1947

Smoke (Gore Vidal), 1954

Smokeless Zone, The (Alan Parker), 1961

Smoky Links (Lonnie Carter), 1972

Snake Pit, The (Arthur Laurents), 1948

Snakes and Reptiles (Thomas Murphy), 1968

Snaps (John Grillo), 1973

Snapshots from the City (Claes Oldenburg, suppl 5), 1960

Sneaky Bit to Raise the Blind, A (John Ford Noonan), 1974

Snooker (Jonathan Raban, suppl 2), 1975

Snow Queen, The (John Bowen), 1974

Snow Queen, The (R. C. Scriven, suppl 2), 1950

Snow Tiger, The (Frank Marcus), 1966

Snowangel (Lewis John Carlino), 1962

Snows (Carolee Schneemann, suppl 5), 1967

Snug Harbor (Carolee Schneemann, suppl 5), 1967

So Evil My Love (Ronald Millar), 1948

So Far So Bad (Cecil P. Taylor), 1974

So Favourite a Son (John George, suppl 2), 1976

So Long at the Fair (Lanford Wilson), 1963

So Long Charlie (Alan Plater), 1963

So Long, 174th Street (Joseph Stein, suppl 4), 1976

So Please Be Kind (Frank D. Gilroy), 1972

So This Is New York (Carl Foreman, suppl 1), 1948

So What about Love? (Leonard Webb), 1969

So Who's Afraid of Edward Albee? (David Starkweather), 1963

So You Think You're a Hero (David Campton)

Soap (Allan Kaprow, suppl 5), 1965

Soap (Lawrence Osgood), 1970

Soap Opera in Stockwell (Michael O'Neill, Jeremy Seabrook), 1973

Sociability (Charles Dizenzo), 1970

Social Event, A (William Inge, appendix), 1962

Socorro, When Your Sons Forget (Archibald MacLeish), 1944

Soft or a Girl (John McGrath), 1971

Softly, and Consider the Nearness (Rosalyn Drexler), 1964

Softly, Softly (Keith Dewhurst), 1967

Softly, Softly (Alan Plater), 1966

Soldier from the Wars Returning (David Campton), 1960

Soldier, Soldier (John Arden), 1960

Soldiers, The (George Ryga), 1963

Soldiers of No Country, The (Lawrence Ferlinghetti), 1963

Soldier's Tale, The (John Arden), 1968

Solid Gold Cadillac, The (Abe Burrows), 1956

Solitaire/Double Solitaire (Robert Anderson), 1971

Solitaire Man, The (Bella Spewack, suppl 4), 1926

Solo (Merce Cunningham, suppl 5), 1973

Solo (Maureen Duffy), 1970

Solo Performance (Robert Wilson), 1966

Some Angry Summer Songs (John Herbert), 1974

Some Came Running (John Patrick), 1958

Some Distant Shadow (John Hopkins), 1971

Some Kind of Nut (Garson Kanin), 1969

Some Like It Hot (Billy Wilder, suppl 1), 1959

Some of My Best Friends Are Husbands (Hugh Leonard), 1976

Some Place of Darkness (John Hopkins), 1966

Some Talk of Alexander (Clive Exton, suppl 3), 1960

Someone from Assisi (Thornton Wilder), 1960

Someone in the Lift (David Campton), 1967

Someone Waiting (Emlyn Williams), 1953

Something about a Soldier (William Saroyan), 1940

Something Down There Is Crying (Adrian Mitchell), 1975

Something Else (Robert Patrick), 1972

Something for Everyone (Hugh Wheeler), 1976

Something from the Sea (Giles Cooper, appendix), 1966

Something Funny (Nancy Walter), 1976

Something I'll Tell You Tuesday (John Guare), 1966

Something of Value (Richard Brooks, suppl 1), 1957

Something Rather Effective (N. F. Simpson), 1972

Something to Sing About (Garson Kanin), 1964

Something Unspoken (Tennessee Williams),

Ten Blocks on the Camino Real (Tennessee Williams), 1948

Ten Days That Shook the World (Robert E. Lee), 1972

Ten Films (Kenneth Koch), 1973

Ten Little Indians (Agatha Christie), 1944

Ten Little Niggers (Agatha Christie), 1943

Ten Million Ghosts (Sidney Kingsley), 1936

10:30 P.M., Summer (Jules Dassin, suppl 1), 1966

Tenant of Wildfell Hall, The (Christopher Fry), 1968

Tender Branch, The (David French), 1972

Tender Comrade (Dalton Trumbo, suppl 1), 1943

Tenderloin (George Abbott, Jerome Weidman), 1960

Tennyson (Alun Owen), 1968

Tent, The (John McGrath), 1958

Tent (Alwin Nikolais, suppl 5), 1968

Tenth Man, The (Paddy Chayefsky), 1959

Teresa (Stewart Stern, suppl 1), 1951

Terese's Creed (Michael Cook) 1976

Terminal (Susan Yankowitz), 1969

Terrible Day, A (James Hanley), 1973

Terrible Jim Fitch james Leo Herlihy), 1968

Terrible Veil, The (Lonne Elder, III), 1964

Terrible Strange Man, A (Frederick Bradnum, suppl 1), 1971

Tess of the D'Urbervilles (Ronald Gow), 1946

Tess of the D'Urbervilles (Bill Morrison, suppl 2), 1971

Tests (Paul Ableman), 1966

Tewedros (Tsegaye Gabre-Medhin), 1962

Texaco Star Theatre (Abe Burrows), 1939

Texas (Paul Green), 1966

Thacred Nit (Henry Livings), 1961

Thames Crawling (Carolee Schneemann, suppl 5), 1970

Thank You, Miss Victoria (William M. Hoffman), 1965

Thank You Very Much (N. F. Simpson), 1971

Thank You Very Much (Cecil P. Taylor), 1969

Thank You Very Much for the Family Circle (Cecil P. Taylor), 1968

Thanks (Jackson Mac Low), 1962

Thanksgiving Play (Beggars Theatre, suppl 6), 1975

Thanksgiving Visitor, The (Truman Capote, suppl 4), 1968

Thark (Ben Travers), 1927

That Boy—Call Him Back (Thomas Hendry), 1970

That Championship Season (Jason Miller), 1972

That Family Next Door (Douglas Archibald), 1973

That Quiet Earth (John Hopkins), 1972

That Simple Light Mayy Rise Out of Complicated Darkness (Bread and Puppet Theatre, suppl 6), 1972

That Summer—That Fall (Frank D. Gilroy), 1967

That They May Win (Arthur Miller), 1944

That Time (Samuel Beckett), 1976

That Time of Life (David Cregan), 1972

That Woman (James Hanley), 1967

That Woman Is Wrecking Our Marriage (Paul Ableman), 1969

That's Charlie George Over There (Keith Dewhurst), 1972

That's Where the Town's Going (Tad Mosel), 1962

Theatre (Alan Ayckbourn), 1976

Theatre Activity (Robert Wilson), 1967

Theatre of Death (Philip Martin, suppl 2), 1970

Theatre of Power (Obi Egbuna), 1969

Theatre Outside (Stephen Poliakoff), 1973

Theatre Piece (John Cage, suppl 5), 1960

Their First Evening Alone Together (Christopher Wilkinson), 1969

Their Very Own and Golden City (Arnold Wesker), 1965

Them (Johnny Speight), 1972

Them Damned Canadians (Ted Allan), 1973

Them Down There (John Finch, suppl 3), 1968

Then...(David Campton), 1957

There Are Humans at the Bottom of My Garden (Kevin Laffan), 1972

There Is a Happy Land (Keith Waterhouse), 1962

There Is Something Out There (Terrence McNally), 1962

There Was a Crooked Man (Robert Benton, David Newman, suppl 1), 1970

There! You Died (Maria Irene Fornés), 1963

There'll Almost Always Be an England (Jack Rosenthal, suppl 3), 1974

There'll Be Some Changes Made (Alun Owen), 1969

There's a Girl in My Soup (Terence Frisby), 1964

There's a Hole in Your Dustbin, Delilah (Jack Rosenthal, suppl 3), 1968

There's a Little Ambiguity Over There among the Bluebells (Ruth Krauss), 1968

There's a Seal at the Bottom of the Garden (Michael Cook), 1973

There's Always a First Time (Robert Holles, suppl 3), 1970

There's No Point in Arguing the Toss (Don Haworth, suppl 2), 1966

There's No Room for You Here for a Start (Henry Livings), 1963

There's Something I Got to Tell You (William Saroyan), 1941

Thermidor (Trevor Griffiths), 1971

These Our Actors (J. B. Priestley), 1956

These People, Those Books (Dodie Smith), 1958

These Three (Lillian Hellman), 1936

They (Arnold Weinstein), 1965

They Called the Bastard Stephen (Willis Hall), 1964

They Came to a City (J. B. Priestley), 1943

They Don't All Open Men's Boutiques (Willis Hall), 1972

They Don't Grow on Trees (Ronald Millar), 1967

They Knew What They Wanted (Robert Ardrey), 1940

They Live Forever (Jerome Lawrence), 1942

They Might Be Giants (James Goldman), 1961

They Shall Have Music (John Howard Lawson), 1939

They Sleep Together (John Antrobus), 1976

They're Knocking Down the Pie Shop (John McGrath), 19971

Thief (Alun Owen), 1967

Thieves Rush In (Giles Cooper, appendix), 1950

Thin Man, The (Arthur Laurents), 1939

Thing Itself, The (Arthur Sainer), 1967

Think (Joseph Musaphia)

Think of the Day (Keith Dewhurst), 1960

Thinking Aloud (Emlyn Williams), 1945

Thinking Straight (Laurence Collinson), 1975

Third Daughter, The (Mario Fratti), 1966

Third Little Show, The (S. J. Perelman), 1931

Third Man, The (Graham Greene), 1950

Thirsting Heart, The (Paul Green),1959

Thirteen Against Fate (John Hale), 1966

£13083 (Fay Weldon, suppl 3), 1968

Thirteenth Letter, The (Howard Koch, suppl 1), 1951

Thirty-First of June, The (J. B. Priestley), 1957

Thirty Seconds over Tokyo (Dalton Trumbo, suppl 1), 1944

36 Hours to Live (John Patrick), 1936

'30-'60 Bill Naughton), 1960

This Breast (Ruth Krauss)

This Breast Gothic (Ruth Krauss), 1973

This England (Bridget Boland, Emlyn Williams), 1941

This Gun for Hire (Albert Maltz), 1942

This I Believe (William Saroyan), 1963

This Is an Entertainment (Tennessee Williams), 1976

This Is New York (Abe Burrows), 1938

This Is Not True (James Schevill), 1945

This Is Our Chance (James Ene Henshaw), 1957

This Is Show Business (Abe Burrows), 1950

This Is the Rill Speaking (Lanford Wilson), 1965

This Is Your FBI (Arthur Laurents), 1945

This Jockey Drives Late Nights (Henry Livings), 1972

This Little Kitty Stayed Cool (Tad Mosel), 1953

This Man Craig (David Turner), 1966

This Man in Paris (Roger MacDougall), 1939

This Man Is News (Roger MacDougall), 1938

This Music Crept by Me upon the Waters (Archibald MacLeish), 1953

This Old Man Comes Rolling Home (Dorothy Hewett), 1966

This Play Is about Me (Israel Horovitz), 1960

This Property Is Condemned (Tennessee Williams), 1946

This Quiet Half Hour (Julia Jones, suppl 3), 1973

This Reckless Age (Joseph L. Mankiewicz, suppl 1), 1932

This Sporting Life (David Storey), 1963

This Story of Yours (John Hopkins), 1968

This Stratford Business (Ronald Gow), 1971

This Time Tomorrow (James T. Ngugi), 1966

This Too Shall Pass (Don Appell, suppl 4), 1946

This Way to the Tomb (Ronald Duncan), 1945

This'll Make You Whistle (Guy Bolton, suppl 4), 1935

Thistle and the Rose, The (William Douglas Home), 1949

Thistlewood (Stewart Conn), 1975

Thomson Report, The (Peter Ransley), 1972

Thor, With Angels (Christopher Fry), 1948

Those That Play the Clowns (Michael Stewart, suppl 4), 1968

Those We Love (George Abbott), 1930

Thoughts (Megan Terry), 1973

Thoughts of Chairman Alf, The (Johnny Speight), 1976

Thoughts on the Instant of Greeting a Friend on the Street (Jean-Claude van Itallie), 1967

Thousand Symphonies, The (Dick Higgins, suppl 5), 1968

Three Arrows, The (Iris Murdoch), 1972

Three Bags Full (Jerome Chodorov, suppl 4), 1966

Three Blind Mice (Guy Bolton, suppl 4), 1938

Three Cavaliers, The (Beverley Cross), 1960

Three Coins in a Fountain (John Patrick), 1954

Three Desks (James Reaney), 1967

Three Events (Al Hansen, suppl 5), 1966

Three for All (Olwen Wymark), 1976

Three for the Fancy (Peter Terson), 1973

Three from the Earth (Djuna Barnes), 1919

Three Graces, The (Ben Travers), 1924

Three Men for Colverton (David Cregan), 1966

Three Men in a Boat (Tom Stoppard), 1975

Three Men on a Horse (George Abbott), 1935

Three Men on a Horse (Arthur Miller), 1947

Three Minidramas (Mario Fratti), 1972

Three Months Gone (Donald Howarth), 1970

Three Musketeers, The (Robert Ardrey), 1948

Three on a Weekend (Rodney Ackland), 1937

Three People (A. R. Gurney, Jr.), 1956

Three Players of a Summer Game (Tennessee Williams), 1955

Three Sheets to the Wind (Robert E. Lee), 1942

Three Sisters, The (Edward Bond), 1967

Three Sisters from Springfield, Illinois (Tom Eyen), 1971

Three Strangers (John Huston, Howard Koch, suppl 1), 1946

Three Thousand Red Ants (Lawrence Ferlinghetti), 1963

Three to Play (Tom Gallacher), 1972

Three Tools of Death, The (Hugh Leonard), 1974

Three Winters (John Mortimer), 1958

Three Wishes for Jamie (Abe Burrows), 1952

Three Wives of Felix Hull, The (Fay Weldon, suppl 3), 1968

Three Yells (Bread and Puppet Theatre, suppl 6), 1973

Three-Fifths of the World Loves a Lover (Alan Plater), 1976

Threepenny Opera (Cecil P. Taylor), 1972

Three's Company (Willis Hall, Keith Waterhouse), 1973

Thrills Galore (Rhys Adrian, suppl 2), 1972
Through a Film Darkly (Joe DeGraft), 1966
Through the Night (Trevor Griffiths), 1975
Thunder in the Sun (Stewart Stern, suppl 1), 1958
Thunder Rock (Robert Ardrey), 1939
Thunderball (John Hopkins), 1965
Thunderbolt (Joseph L. Mankiewicz, suppl 1), 1929
Thursday's Child (Rodney Ackland), 1943
Thursday's Child (Christopher Fry), 1939
Thwarting of Baron Bolligrew, The (Robert Bolt), 1965
Thwum (Mike Stott), 1975
Ticket, The (Willis Hall), 1969
Tickle Times (Julia Jones, suppl 3), 1967
Ticklish Acrobat, The (Robert Hivnor), 1954
Ticklish Business, A (Ronald Millar), 1958
Tiddles (Henry Livings), 1970
Tide in the Affairs of Women, A (Philip Martin, suppl 2), 1975
Tide Is OK for the 30th, The (Welfare State, suppl 6), 1968
Tidy Passions (H. M. Koutoukas), 1965
Tie Up the Ballcock (Charles Wood), 1964
Tiger (Derek Raby, suppl 2), 1974
Tiger, The (Murray Schisgal), 1963
Tiger and the Horse, The (Robert Bolt), 1960
Tiger at the Gates (Christopher Fry), 1955
Tiger Makes Out, The (Murray Schisgal), 1967
Tiger! Tiger! (Arthur Lister Murphy), 1970
Tigers Are Better Looking (Alan Seymour), 1973
Tigers Are Coming—O.K?, The (Alan Plater), 1972
Ti-Jean and His Brothers (Derek Walcott),1958
Till Death Us Do Part (Johnny Speight), 1966
Tiln (Michael Cook), 1971
Timbimbo Craze, The (Giles Cooper, appendix), 1950
Time and the Conways (J. B. Priestley), 1937
Time and Time Again (Alan Ayckbourn), 1971
Time for a Change (David Campton), 1969
Time for a Gargle (Brendan Behan, appendix), 1973
Time for Doors, A (Michael Cook), 1970
Time for the Funny Walk (Alun Owen), 1968
Time Frame (Manor Moore), 1974
Time in Cloud Cuckoo Land, A (Don Haworth, suppl 2), 1969
Time Machine, The (Keith Johnstone), 1967
Time, Murderer, Please (Charles Dyer), 1956
Time of the Barracudas, The (Peter Barnes), 1963
Time of the Cuckoo, The (Arthur Laurents), 1952
Time of Wolves and Tigers, A (Hugh Leonard), 1967
Time of Your Life, The (William Saroyan), 1939
Time Out for Romance (John Patrick), 1937
Time Out of Mind (Bridget Boland), 1970
Time Out of Mind (Paul Green), 1947
Time Out of Mind (John Hopkins), 1964
Time Present (John Osborne), 1968
Time Space (Lonnie Carter), 1970

Time to Die, A (Eric Bentley), 1967
Time to Laugh, A (Julia Jones, suppl 3), 1969
Time to Live, A (Eric Bentley), 1967
Timepiece, The (Stanley Eveling), 1965
Times Square (Leonard Melfi), 1966
Timesneeze (David Campton), 1970
Timothy (Bill Naughton), 1956
Tina (David Cregan), 1975
Tinguely Machine Mystery, The (Kenneth Koch), 1965
Tinkle of Tiny Bells, A (David Campton), 1963
Tinsel Tarts in a Hot Coma (The Cockettes, suppl 6)
Tiny Alice (Edward Albee), 1964
Tiny Closet, The (William Inge, appendix), 1958
Tip Top Conditioning (Lumiere and Son, suppl 6), 1974
Tipper (David Cregan), 1969
Tip-Toes (Guy Bolton, suppl 4), 1925
Tira (Michael Weller), 1972
Tira Tells Everything There Is to Know about Herself (Michael Weller), 1971
Titfield Thunderbolt, The (T. E. B. Clarke, suppl 1), 1953
Tits (Jackie Curtis), 1971
To Be Young, Gifted and Black (Robert Nemiroff, suppl 4), 1969
To Bobolink, For Her Spirit (William Inge, appendix), 1962
To Dorothy, A Son (Roger MacDougall), 1950
To Dwell in a Place of Strangers (Arthur Kopit), 1958
To Everything Its Season (Dick Higgins, suppl 5), 1965
To Heaven in a Golden Coach (Tennessee Williams), 1961
To Inhabit the Earth Is Not Enough (Michael Cook), 1971
To Kill a Mockingbird (Horton Foote, suppl 3), 1963
To Lucifer a Sun (Johnny Speight), 1967
To Sea in a Sieve (Christopher Fry), 1935
To See How Far It Is (Alan Plater), 1968
To the Dogs (Djuna Barnes), 1923
To the Frontier (Giles Cooper, appendix), 1968
To the Ladies (Marc Connelly), 1922
To the Victor (Richard Brooks, suppl 1), 1948
To This Hard House (Brian Friel), 1958
To This One Place (Gwyn Thomas), 1956
To Wally Pantoni, We Leave a Credenza (John Guare), 1964
To Whom It May Concern (Jack Gray), 1958
Toast to Melba, A (Jack Hibberd), 1976
Toda-San (Hal Porter), 1965
Today Is Independence Day (William Hanley), 1963
Toilet, The (LeRoi Jones), 1964
Toilet Paper (Al Hansen, suppl 5), 1966
Token Gesture, A (David French), 1970
Tom (Alexander Buzo), 1972
Tom Jones (John Osborne), 1963

You and Your Wife (Denis Cannan), 1955

You Are My Heart's Delight (Cecil P. Taylor), 1973

You Are Not Alone in the House (Frederick Bradnum, suppl 2), 1972

You Belong to Me (Dalton Trumbo, suppl 1), 1941

You Can Only Buy Once (Kevin Laffan), 1969

You Can't Say Hello to Anybody (Dannie Abse), 1964

You Can't Win 'em All (Alun Owen), 1962

You Don't Know Me But... (Donald Churchill, suppl 3), 1972

You Gonna Let Me Take You Out Tonight, Baby (Ed Bullins), 1972

You in Your Small Corner (Barry Reckord), 1960

You Know I Can't Hear You When the Water's Running (Robert Anderson), 1967

You May Go Home Again (David Starkweather), 1963

You, Me and the Gatepost (David Campton, N. F. Simpson), 1960

You Smell Good to Me (Thomas Hendry), 1972

You Started It (David Campton)

You Touched Me (Tennessee Williams), 1944

You'll Be the Death of Me (Alun Owen), 1969

You'll Come to Love Your Sperm Test (John Antrobus), 1965

You'll Know Me by the Stars in My Eyes (Barry England), 1966

You'll Never Guess (Ann Jellicoe), 1973

Young and Beautiful (Dore Schary), 1934

Young and the Guilty, The (Ted Willis), 1956

Young Cassidy (John Whiting, appendix), 1965

Young Guy Seeks Part-Time Work (John Bowen), 1973

Young Lady from Midhurst, The (Frederick Bradnum, suppl 2), 1974

Young Lady of Property, A (Horton Foote, suppl 3)

Young Love (Jerome Lawrence, Robert E. Lee), 1949

Young Lovers (George Tabori), 1952

Young Man in Trouble (Thomas Murphy), 1970

Young Man of Williamsburg (Loften Mitchell), 1955

Young Man with a Horn (Carl Foreman, suppl 1), 1950

Young Tom Edison (Dore Schary), 1940

Young Winston (Carl Foreman, suppl 1), 1972

Your Fiery Furnace (Paul Green), 1926

Your Name's Not Got, It's Edgar (Jack Rosenthal, suppl 3), 1969

Your Own Thing (Donald Driver, suppl 4), 1968

Your Uncle Dudley (Dore Schary), 1935

You're Free (Henry Livings), 1967

You're Gonna Be Alright, Jamie Boy (David Freeman), 1974

Youth (Kenneth Koch), 1973

Youth Hostel, The (Wallace Shawn), 1976

Z Cars (Keith Dewhurst, John Hopkins), 1962

∠ Cars (Alan Plater), 1963

Zabriskie Point (Sam Shepard), 1970

Zelda Trio, The (Laurence Collinson), 1961

Zero (Samuel Beckett), 1960

Zero Hour (Ronald Millar), 1944

Zero Inn (Bruce Mason), 1970

Zigger Zagger (Peter Terson), 1967

Zodiac in the Establishment, The (Bridget Boland), 1963

Zone 36 (Henry Reed, suppl 2), 1965

Zonk (John Grillo), 1971

Zoo Story, The (Edward Albee), 1959

Zoo Zoo Widdershins Zoo (Kevin Laffan), 1969

Zorbá (Fred Ebb, Joseph Stein, suppl 4), 1968

Zounds! (Michael Frayn), 1957

NOTES
ON
ADVISERS
AND
CONTRIBUTORS

ARONSON, Erica.   Assistant Professor of Modern Languages at Roosevelt University, Chicago. Author of "Freedom and Determinism" in *Perspectives of Social Science*, 1970. **Essay:** Jerome Weidman.

BAKER, Roger.   Free-lance Writer. Author of *The Book of London*, 1968; *Drag: A History of Female Impersonation on the Stage*, 1968; *Binding the Devil* (on Exorcism), 1974; *Mister X* (play), with Drew Griffiths, 1976. Regular Book Reviewer for *The Times*, and *Books and Bookmen*; essays appear in *Daily Telegraph Magazine, Queen, Harper's*, and *Illustrated London News*. **Essays:** Jane Arden; Laurence Collinson; Simon Gray; Iris Murdoch.

BALLET, Arthur H.   Director, Office for Advanced Drama Research (funded by the Rockefeller Foundation), University of Minnesota, Minneapolis; Professor of Theatre, University of Minnesota; Consultant, O'Neill Theatre Center; Board Member, American Playwrights Theatre and Margo Jones Playwriting Committee. Editor, *Playwrights for Tomorrow* series, 13 vols. Contributor to *Theatre Three*, 1971. **Essays:** Lee Kalcheim; Terrence McNally; Arthur Sainer; Barrie Stavis.

BEAMS, David W.   Articles on Lotte Lenya and Brechtian theatre, Hochhuth's *The Deputy*, the critic James Huneker, Henry Ainley and other "matinee idols," and the Henry James novel from which *Berkeley Square* derives have been published in *Theatre Arts, Criticism, Boston University Journal*, and *Films in Review*. **Essay:** Mart Crowley.

BENEDIKT, Michael.   Professor and/or Poet-in-Residence at Bennington College, Vermont, Sarah Lawrence College, Bronxville, New York, Hampshire College, Amherst, Massachusetts, and Boston University, 1967–76; Poetry Editor, *Paris Review*. Editor of anthologies of French, German, Spanish, and American plays: *Modern French Theatre: The Avant-Garde, Dada, and Surrealism*, 1965; *Post-War German Plays*, 1966; *Modern Spanish Theatre*, 1968; *Theatre Experiment* (American plays), 1968; *The Poetry of Surrealism*, 1975. His own collections of verse/prose poems include *The Body*, 1968; *Sky*, 1970; *Mole Notes*, 1971; *Night Cries*, 1976.

BENTLEY, Eric.   See his own entry.

BERTRAM, James.   Professor of English, Victoria University of Wellington. Editor of *Phoenix*, 1932; associated with the founding of *Landfall*, 1946. Author of several books on China. Editor of *New Zealand Letters of Thomas Arnold the Younger*, 1966; contributor to *Student Guide to English Poetry*, 1969. **Essays:** Allen Curnow; Bruce Mason.

BIGSBY, C. W. E.   Lecturer in American Literature, University of East Anglia, Norwich. Author of *Confrontation and Commitment: A Study of Contemporary American Drama*, 1967; *Edward Albee*, 1969. Editor of *Three Negro Plays*, 1969; *The Black American Writer*, 1970; *Dada and Surrealism*, 1972; *Superculture*, 1974; *Edward Albee*, 1975. **Essays:** Edward Albee; Robert Anderson; Brian Friel; Henry Livings; David Mercer; Harold Pinter; Anthony Shaffer; Tom Stoppard.

BILLINGTON,   Michael. Drama and Film Critic, *The Times*, since 1965; writes for *The Illustrated London News, Birmingham Post, Plays and Players*; critic for the Thames Television programme *Today*. Author of *The Modern Actor*, 1972. **Essays:** Alan Ayckbourn; Denis Cannan; Nigel Dennis; Hugh Leonard; Robert Shaw; Leonard Webb.

BLAU, Herbert.   Dean of the Division of Arts and Humanities, University of Maryland, Baltimore County; Artistic Director, Kraken. Co-Founder and Co-Director of the Actor's Workshop, San Francisco, 1952–65; Co-Director, Repertory Theatre of Lincoln Center, New York, 1965–67; directed the American premieres of *Mother Courage, Serjeant Musgrave's Dance, The Condemned of Altona*, and other plays. Provost, and Dean of the School of

Theatre and Dance, California Institute of the Arts, 1968–72. Author of *The Impossible Theater*, 1964. Plays: *Telegraph Hill; A Gift of Fury;* texts for Kraken: *Seeds of Atreus; The Donner Party, Its Crossing.*

BORKLUND, Elmer. Associate Professor of English, Pennsylvania State University, University Park. Former Associate Editor, *The Chicago Review*. Articles and reviews published in *Modern Philology, Commentary, New York Herald Tribune Book Week, Journal of General Education*; literary entries in *The World Book Encyclopedia*. **Essay:** Jean-Claude van Itallie.

BOWEN, John. See his own entry. |**Essays**: John Hale; Christopher Hampton; David Lan.

BRADISH, Gaynor F. Visiting Lecturer at the State University of New York at Albany. Head of the Playwrights' Unit, Actor's Studio, New York, 1962–63; Head of the Dunster Drama Workshop, Harvard University; first director of Department of Dramatic Literature at New York University, to 1968. Director of *Asylum* by Arthur Kopit, New York, 1963. Drama Advisor, Hill and Wang publishers, 1961–67. Author of Introduction to Kopit's *Oh Dad, Poor Dad...*, 1960. **Essays:** Arthur Kopit; Jack Richardson.

BRISBANE, Katharine. Founding Editor of Currency Press Pty. Ltd., Woollahra, since 1971, and Chairman and Editor of Currency Methuen Drama Pty. Ltd., since 1973. Drama Critic for *The West Australian*, 1959–65, and *The Australian*, 1967–74. Author of introductions to the work of Alexander Buzo, Peter Kenna, Jim McNeil, Katharine Susannah Prichard, and John Romeril, of the drama section of *The Literature of Australia*, 1976, and of a chapter in Allardyce Nicoll's revised version of *World Drama*, 1976. **Essays:** Alexander Buzo; Dorothy Hewett; Peter Kenna.

BRISSENDEN, Connie. Theatre Liaison, Playwrights Co-op, Toronto. Author of a thesis at the University of Alberta on modern Canadian playwriting, and the editor of 5 anthologies of Canadian plays. **Essay:** Michael Cook.

BROWN, John Russell. Professor of English, University of Sussex, Falmer; Assistant Director, The National Theatre, London. Former Head of the Department of Drama and Theatre Arts, University of Birmingham; Director of Orbit Theatre Company. Author of *Shakespeare's Plays in Performance*, 1966; *Effective Theatre*, 1969; *Theatre Language*, 1972; *Free Shakespeare*, 1974. **Essays:** Barry Collins; David Cregan; Shelagh Delaney; David Selbourne; Wallace Shawn; Olwen Wymark.

BRUCHAC, Joseph. Editor of *The Greenfield Review*, Greenfield Center, New York. Taught in Ghana, 1966–69. Author of several collections of poetry – the most recent being *Flow*, 1975 – and a novel, *The Way to Black Mountain*, 1975. Editor of *Words from the House of the Dead: Anthology of Prison Writings from Soledad* (with William Witherup), 1971. **Essays:** Joe DeGraft; R. Sarif Easmon; Obi Egbuna; Athol Fugard; James Ene Henshaw; Lewis Nkosi; Wole Soyinka.

BURIAN, Jarka M. Professor in the Department of Theatre, State University of New York at Albany. Has been active as actor, producer, and director. Author of *The Scenography of Josef Svoboda*, 1971, and many articles. **Essays:** William Alfred; Tad Mosel; Elliott Nugent; Kenneth Rexroth.

CARRAGHER, Bernard. Free-lance Writer. **Essays:** Lonnie Carter; Charles Dizenzo; Paul Foster; Robert Patrick; Ronald Tavel; Paul Zindel.

CHAMBERS, D. D. C. Assistant Professor of English, Trinity College, Toronto. **Essays:** Carol Bolt; Jack Gray; John Herbert; James Reaney; George F. Walker.

CLURMAN, Harold. Critic and Lecturer. Member of the Greenwich Village Playhouse and the Theatre Guild in the 1920's; Founder of the Group Theatre in 1931; has produced and directed many plays since then. Consultant for the Repertory Theatre of Lincoln Center, 1963–64; Visiting Professor, Hunter College, 1967. Author of *The Fervent Years: The Story of the Group Theatre*, 1945; *Lies Like Truth: Theatre Essays and Reviews*, 1958; *All Men Are Famous: Instead of an Autobiography*, 1974. **Essay:** Lillian Hellman.

COHN, Ruby. Professor of Comparative Drama, University of California at Davis; Editor, *Modern Drama*, and Associate Editor, *Educational Theatre Journal*. Author of *Samuel Beckett: The Comic Gamut*, 1962; *Currents in Contemporary Drama*, 1969; *Edward Albee*, 1970; *Dialogue in American Drama*, 1971; *Back to Beckett*, 1973; *Modern Shakespeare Offshoots*, 1976. **Essays:** Djuna Barnes; Samuel Beckett; Edward Bond; Rick Cluchey; Lawrence Ferlinghetti; John Hawkes; Robert Lowell; Archibald MacLeish; James Schevill; Sam Shepard; Thornton Wilder.

COLOMBO, John Robert. Managing Editor, *The Tamarack Review*; Advisory Editor, *Performing Arts in Canada*. Special Lecturer, Atkinson College, York University, Toronto; contributor to CBC; producer of *Literary Evenings*, The Bohemian Embassy, Toronto; author of *The Colombo Plan*, produced at The Three Schools, Toronto. Most recent volumes of verse are *John Toronto, New Poems*, and *The Great San Francisco Earthquake and Fire*.

COOK, Albert. Professor of Comparative Literature, State University of New York at Buffalo. Author of several plays – *Double Exposure, Big Blow, Check, Arches, The Death of Trotsky* – and an adaptation of *Oedipus Rex*. Author of many books, the most recent being *Enactment: Greek Tragedy*, 1971; *Shakespeare's Enactment*, 1972; *Adapt the Living* (verse), 1976.

CORRIGAN, Robert W. Dean of the School of Fine Arts, University of Wisconsin, Milwaukee. Taught at Johns Hopkins, Tulane, and New York universities, Carleton College, University of Minnesota, Carnegie Institute of Technology, California Institute of the Arts, and the University of Michigan. Author of *Theatre in Search of a Fix*, 1973. Editor of several volumes of plays, and of volumes on comedy and tragedy, and on Arthur Miller. Founding Editor, *Tulane Drama Review* (later *Drama Review*). **Essays:** Saul Bellow; Arthur Miller; William Saroyan; Tennessee Williams.

DARLINGTON, W. A. Member of the Editorial Staff, and Chief Drama Critic, 1920–68, *Daily Telegraph*. Author of *Alf's Button*, 1919 (novel), 1924 (play); *I Do What I Like*, 1947; *The Actor and His Audience*, 1949; *Six Thousand and One Nights*, 1960. C.B.E., 1963. **Essays:** Ronald Gow, Ronald Millar; Emlyn Williams; Ted Willis.

DOUGLAS, Reid. University Teacher and Editor of *Contemporary Theatre*. **Essay:** Ray Mathew.

EDINBOROUGH, Arnold. Editor of *Performing Arts in Canada* magazine; President of The Council for Business and the Arts in Canada; President of Edina Productions Ltd.; columnist for *Financial Post* and *Canadian Churchman*; Member of the Board of Governors of the Stratford Festival. Taught at Queen's University, University of British Columbia, Cambridge University, and University of Lausanne; past editor of the Kingston *Whig-Standard, Saturday Night, Monday Morning*, and *Parallèle*. **Essay:** Mavor Moore.

ELSOM, John. Free-lance Writer. Author of *Theatre Outside London*, 1972; *Post-War British Theatre*, 1976. **Essays:** Dannie Abse; Barry Bermange; C. G. Bond; J. P. Donleavy; Ronald Duncan; Steve Gooch; John Grillo; Wilson John Haire; Willis Hall and Keith Waterhouse; Thomas Murphy; Alan Plater; Peter Shaffer; Cecil P. Taylor; Peter Terson; Christopher Wilkinson.

FALCONIERI, John V.   President of John Cabot International College, Rome; Editor of *Theatre Annual*. Editor of *Otra Orilla* by Jose Lopez Rubio and *Fuga* by Enrique Anderson. **Essays:** Robert Ardrey; Gore Vidal.

FEINGOLD, Michael.   Literary Manager, Yale Repertory Theatre, New Haven, Connecticut; Drama Critic, **Village Voice**. Productions include John Arden's *The Business of Good Government*, and Lanford Wilson's *Ikke Ikke Nye Nye Nye*. Translator of plays by Brecht, Ibsen, and Prevert. **Essay:** Kenneth Bernard.

FLEISCHER, Leonard.   Senior Executive Staff Writer, RCA, New York. Member of the New York Bar. Articles and reviews published in *Saturday Review, London Jewish Quarterly, Congress Bi-Weekly*, and other publications. **Essays:** Oliver Hailey; John Howard Lawson.

FRIEDMAN, Melvin J.   Professor of Comparative Literature, University of Wisconsin at Milwaukee; Fulbright Lecturer, University of Antwerp, 1976. Author of *William Styron*, 1974. Editor or Co-Editor, *Configuration Critique de Samuel Beckett*, 1964; *The Added Dimension*, 1966; *Configuration Critique de William Styron*, 1967; *Samuel Beckett Now*, 1970; *The Shaken Realist*, 1970; *The Vision Obscured*, 1970; *William Styron's "The Confessions of Nat Turner": A Critical Handbook*, 1970. Associated with the periodicals *Wisconsin Studies in Contemporary Literature, Comparative Literature Studies, Yale French Studies, Modern Language Journal*; currently, Advisory Editor, *Journal of Popular Culture, Renascence, Studies in the Novel*. **Essay:** Bruce Jay Friedman.

FUEGI, John.   Professor of Comparative Literature, University of Wisconsin at Milwaukee; Managing Editor, *The Brecht Yearbook*. Author of *The Essential Brecht*, 1972. Editor of *Brecht Heute/Brecht Today*, 1971. **Essays:** Eric Bentley; Robert Bolt; Marc Connelly; Christopher Isherwood.

GILBERT, S. R.   Professor of Drama and Comparative Literature and Chairperson of the Humanities Division, Capilano College, North Vancouver. Author of the play *A Glass Darkly* (published in *Dialogue and Dialectic*, 1972), "A Bibliography of British Columbia" in *Communique*, 1973, and other articles and reviews. **Essays:** David Freeman; Thomas Hendry.

GILMAN, Richard.   Literary Editor, *New Republic*; Professor of Drama, Yale University, New Haven, Connecticut. Drama Critic for *Commonweal*, 1961–64, and for *Newsweek*, 1964–68. Author of *The Confusion of Realms*, 1970; *Common and Uncommon Masks*, 1971; *The Making of Modern Drama*, 1975.

GOTTFRIED, Martin.   Drama Critic, *Women's Wear Daily* and *Vogue Magazine*. Guest Lecturer, Carnegie-Mellon University, Pittsburgh. Author of *A Theater Divided*, 1968; *Opening Nights*, 1970. **Essays:** Lewis John Carlino; Charles Ludlam; Elaine May; David Rabe; Murray Schisgal; Neil Simon; Arnold Weinstein; John White.

GRAHAM-WHITE, Anthony.   Associate Professor of Theatre, Southern Methodist University, Dallas. Editor of *Educational Theatre Journal*, 1972–75. Author of *The Drama of Black Africa*, 1976. **Essays:** Ama Ata Aidoo; John Pepper Clark; James Ngugi; Efua Sutherland; Tsegaye Gabre-Medhin.

HAMMOND, Jonathan.   Editor, Penguin Books, London. Contributor on the class and economic basis of theatre to *Culture and Agitation* and *Plays and Players*. **Essays:** Peter Barnes; Howard Brenton; John Burrows and John Harding; Stuart Conn; David Edgar; Trevor Griffiths; David Hare; Roger Howard; Alun Owen; James Saunders; David Turner; Michael Weller; Snoo Wilson.

HAYMAN, Ronald. Free-lance Writer and Director. Author of Heinemann's Contemporary Dramatists Series volumes on Beckett, Pinter, Osborne, John Arden, Whiting, Bolt, Wesker, Miller, Albee, Ionesco (1968–72), and of books on Techniques of Acting, Tolstoy, John Gielgud, and the Chichester Festival Theatre. Most recent productions include Peter Handke's *My Foot My Tutor* and Martin Walser's *Home Front*, both 1971, and Rainer Werner Fassbinder's *Bremen Coffee*, 1974. **Essays:** Ted Allan; Howard Barker; Bridget Boland; John Bowen; Brigid Brophy; David Caute; Caryl Churchill; Michael Hastings; Donald Howarth; Doris Lessing; John McGrath; John Mortimer; David Pinner; E. A. Whitehead.

HIGGINS, Dick. Founder of the Something Else Press, 1964, and the *Something Else Newsletter*, 1966. Performances of his own works include *Saint Joan at Beaurevoir*, New York, 1960; *The Tart*, New York, 1965; *The Thousand Symphonies*, New Brunswick, New Jersey, 1968. Author of *Postface/Jefferson's Birthday*, 1964; *A Book about Love and War*, 1970; *Modular Poems*, 1975. **Essay:** Jackson Mac Low.

HILL, Errol. See his own entry. **Essay:** LeRoi Jones.

HIMELSTEIN, Morgan Y. Professor of English and Director of Graduate Studies, Adelphi University, Garden City, New York. Author of *Drama Was a Weapon: The Left-Wing Theatre in New York 1929–1941*, 1963, and articles and reviews in periodicals. **Essays:** Mary Chase; Paul Green; Sidney Kingsley; Irwin Shaw.

HIRSCH, Foster. Assistant Professor of English and Film, Brooklyn College. Author of books on George Kelly, Tennessee Williams, Elizabeth Taylor, Edward G. Robinson, Laurence Olivier on film, and *The Epic Film*. **Essays:** George Abbott; Abe Burrows; Frank D. Gilroy; Charles Gordone; Howard Sackler.

HOBSON, Harold. Drama Critic, *Sunday Times*, London, 1947–76. Author of a novel, *The Devil in Woodford Wells*, 1946; *Theatre*, 1948; *Theatre II*, 1950; *The Theatre Now*, 1953; *The French Theatre of Today*, 1953. Editor, *International Theatre Annual*. **Essay:** Charles Dyer.

HOFFMAN, William M. See his own entry. **Essays:** Michael Smith; David Starkweather.

KAUFFMANN, Stanley. Film and theatre critic, *New Republic*; Distinguished Professor of English, City University of New York. Author of three collections of film criticism, *A World on Film*, 1966, *Figures of Light*, 1971, and *Living Images*, 1975, and one collection of theatre criticism, *Persons of the Drama*, 1976.

KENDLE, Burton. Associate Professor of English, Roosevelt University, Chicago. Articles on D. H. Lawrence, John Cheever, and Chekhov published in periodicals. **Essays:** Alan Bennett; Joseph Heller; James Leo Herlihy; William Inge (appendix).

KITCHIN, Laurence. Professor of Drama, City University of New York. Taught at Bristol and Tufts universities; past Drama Critic for *The Times* and BBC broadcaster; represented the United Kingdom on the Editorial Committee of *World Theatre*. Author of *Mid-Century Drama*, 1960, 1962; *Drama in the Sixties*, 1966. **Essays:** John Arden; Brendan Behan (appendix); J. B. Priestley; Arnold Wesker.

KOSTELANETZ, Richard. Poet, Critic, Visual Artist, and Cultural Historian; Co-Founding Editor, *Assembling* (an annual of otherwise unpublishable literature). Author of *The Theatre of Mixed Means*, 1968; *Master Minds*, 1969; *Visual Language*, 1970; *The End of Intelligent Writing*, 1974, and the creative works *I Articulations/Short Fictions*, 1974;

Recyclings, 1974; *Openings & Closings*, 1975; *Constructs*, 1975, *Portraits from Memory*, 1975. Co-Editor, *The New American Arts*, 1965, and editor of several anthologies. **Essays:** Jack Gelber; Robert Hivnor; Kenneth Koch; John Ford Noonan; Theatre of Mixed Means.

KUHN, John G.   Associate Professor of English, and Chairman of the Division of Language and Literature, Rosemont College, Pennsylvania. **Essay:** Lawrence Osgood.

LEECH, Michael T.   Free-lance Writer. Author of *Italy*, 1974. **Essays:** Robertson Davies; Jerome Lawrence and Robert E. Lee; S. J. Perelman; Dodie Smith.

LEWIS, Allan.   Littlefield Professor of Shakespearean Studies, and Director of The Shakespeare Institute, University of Bridgeport, Connecticut. Taught at New School for Social Research, Bennington College, Briarcliff College, National University of Mexico. Director of the National Theatre, Mexico City, 1955–57; Executive Director, New Dramatists, 1964–65; Drama Critic, New Haven *Register*. Author of *The Contemporary Theatre*, 1971; *American Plays and Playwrights*, 1971; *Ionesco*, 1972. **Essay:** Paddy Chayefsky.

LORD, Mary.   Senior Teaching Fellow, Monash University, Melbourne. Drama Critic for *The Bulletin*, 1950–54, 1963–65. Actress, producer, stage manager, composer; writer for radio and of children's plays. Author of *Hal Porter*, 1972. Editor of *Modern Australian Short Stories*, 1971. **Essays:** Ray Lawler; Hal Porter.

MARCUS, Frank.   See his own entry. **Essays:** Maureen Duffy; Peter Gill; David Mowat.

MARKHAM, E. A.   Free-lance Writer. **Essays:** Douglas Archibald; Errol John; Mustapha Matura; Barry Reckord.

MARKUS, Thomas B.   Professor of Theatre, Temple University, Philadelphia; Book Review Editor for *Educational Theatre Journal*. Editor of *Callboard* magazine, 1966–67; professional director and actor in New York and Hollywood. Author of essays on Genet and Albee. **Essays:** Ron Cowen; Martin Duberman; John Guare; Mark Medoff; Leonard Melfi; Dennis J. Reardon.

McCORMACK, Thomas J.   President of St. Martin's Press, Inc., New York. Author of the play *American Roulette*. Editor of *Afterwords*, 1969. **Essay:** Jason Miller.

McELROY, George.   Lecturer at Indiana University Northwest, Gary. Writer for the University of Chicago Home Study Department's Great Books syllabus; author of a text on drama for the University of Wisconsin's Home Study Department. Regular Contributor to *Opera News*, for 22 years. **Essay:** William Snyder.

McGUINNESS, Arthur E.   Associate Professor of English, University of California at Davis; Founding Editor of *Eighteenth-Century Studies*. Author of *George Fitzmaurice*, 1975. Articles and reviews published in *Studies in Short Fiction*, *Texas Studies in Literature and Language*, *Studies in Scottish Literature*, *Studies in Burke*, and *Philological Quarterly*. **Essays:** John B. Keane; Michael Molloy.

MESERVE, Walter J.   Professor of Theatre and Drama, Indiana University, Bloomington. Taught at the University of Kansas and Manchester University. Author of *An Outline of American Drama*, 1965, and *Robert Sherwood: Reluctant Moralist*, 1970. Editor of *The Complete Plays of W. D. Howells*, 1960; *Discussions of Modern American Drama*, 1966; *American Satiric Comedies*, 1969; *Modern Dramas from Communist China*, 1970; *The Rise of Silas Lapham* by W. D. Howells, 1971; *Studies in "Death of a Salesman,"* 1972; *Modern Literature from China*, 1974. **Essays:** George Axelford; William Hanley; Garson Kanin; Arthur Laurents; Dore Schary; Derek Walcott.

MITCHELL, Louis D.   Professor of English, University of Scranton, Pennsylvania. Author of songs and lyrics for *Star of the Morning*, published 1971, and many articles in *Theatre Notebook, Eighteenth Century Studies, Crisis,* and other publications. **Essays:** Ossie Davis; Errol Hill.

MOE, Christian H.   Professor of Theatre, Southern Illinois University, Carbondale; Member of the Advisory Board, Institute of Outdoor Drama. Publicist for the Cornell University Theatre, 1956–58; Chairman of the Publications Committee, American Educational Theatre Association, 1966–71. Fulbright Lecturer, Flinders University, Bedford Park, South Australia, 1975. Author of *Creating Historical Drama* (with George McCalmon), 1965, an essay on D. H. Lawrence as playwright, and *How Santa Claus Came to Simpson's Crossing* (play, with Cameron Garbutt), 1975. Editor of *The William and Mary Theatre: A Chronicle, 1926–56* (with others), 1968; *Six New Plays for Children* (with Darwin Payne), 1971. **Essays:** William Gibson; Albert Maltz; John Patrick.

NIGHTINGALE, Benedict.   Free-lance Writer. **Essays:** Paul Ableman; David Campton; Beverley Cross; John Hopkins; Bernard Kops; David Storey; Charles Wood.

O'CONNOR, Garry.   Free-lance Writer. Author of several plays – including *I Learned in Ipswich How to Poison Flowers, The Musicians, Different Circumstances,* and *A Dialogue Between Friends* – and *French Theatre Today,* 1975. **Essays:** Michael Frayn; Peter Nichols; Michael O'Neill and Jeremy Seabrook; Mike Stott.

O'CONNOR, Marion.   Member of the Faculty of Humanities. University of Kent, Canterbury. **Essays:** Tom Gallacher; Adrian Mitchell.

PARISI, Joseph.   Free-lance writer and teacher in Chicago. **Essays:** Kurt Vonnegut, Jr.; Joseph A. Walker; Robert Wilson.

PARKER, Dorothy.   Associate Professor of English, Victoria College, University of Toronto. **Essays:** David French; George Ryga.

PURSER, Philip.   Television Critic, *Sunday Telegraph,* London. Author of several novels, including *Night of Glass,* 1968, and *The Holy Father's Navy,* 1971, and *The Last Great Tram Race* (spurious memoirs), 1974. **Essay:** Television Writers.

RAYNOR, Henry.   Schoolmaster and Free-lance Writer. Writer on the theatre, music, and television for *The Times* and other periodicals. Author of *Joseph Haydn,* 1962; *Wagner,* 1970; *Radio and Television,* 1970; *A Social History of Music from the Middle Ages to Beethoven,* 1972; *Mahler,* 1975; *Music and Society since 1815,* 1976; *The Orchestra,* 1976. **Essays:** Clive Exton; Terence Frisby; Graham Greene; William Douglas Home; Kevin Laffan; Dennis Potter; Johnny Speight; Gwyn Thomas.

REES, Nonnita.   Free-lance Writer and Director. Taught at California State University at Humboldt, 1967–69; Editor of *Act* magazine, New Zealand, 1970–74; founder of Playmarket agency; Company Member of Downstage Theatre, Wellington, 1972–74. **Essay:** Joseph Musaphia.

REILLY, John M.   Associate Professor of English, State University of New York at Albany. Editor of *Twentieth Century Interpretations of "Invisible Man,"* 1970, and author of essays on Dos Passos, Richard Wright, Chester Himes, and radical writers of the thirties. **Essay:** Ed Bullins.

RIPLEY, John D.   Associate Professor and Director of Drama, McGill University, Montreal. **Essay:** Arthur Lister Murphy.

ROOSE-EVANS, James. Director, author, and lecturer; Founder of the Hampstead Theatre Club and the Stage Two Theatre Workshop. The plays he has directed most recently are Williams' *A Streetcar Named Desire* and Coward's *The Vortex* and *Fallen Angels*. Author of several children's books, *Directing a Play*, revised edition, 1972, and *Experimental Theatre*, revised edition, 1974. **Essays:** Agatha Christie; James Forsyth; James Hanley; Peter Luke; Peter Ransley; Colin Spencer.

SAINER, Arthur. See his own entry. **Essays:** Julie Bovasso; Rosalyn Drexler; Ruth Krauss; Michael McClure; George Tabori; Megan Terry; Nancy Walter; Lanford Wilson; Susan Yankowitz.

SCHECHNER, Richard. Founding Director, The Performance Group, since 1967; Professor of Drama, New York University, since 1967. Editor of *Tulane Drama Review* (later *Drama Review*), 1962–69. Author of *Public Domain*, 1968; *Environmental Theatre*, 1973; *Theatres, Spaces, and Environments*, with Jerry N. Rojo and Brooks McNamara, 1975. Editor, with Gilbert Moses and Tom C. Dent, *Free Southern Theatre*, 1969.

SCHNEIDER, Alan. Director. Broadway and off-Broadway productions include plays by Edward Albee, Samuel Beckett, Edward Bond, Harold Pinter, William Saroyan, Tennessee Williams, and Lanford Wilson.

SHANK, Adele Edling. Playwright and translator. Participant in group-developed theatre pieces; translator of Arrabal's *The Architect and the Emperor of Assyria*, 1969; author of several articles on collective theatres. **Essays:** Performance list of Theatres Collectives.

SHANK, Theodore. Professor of Dramatic Art, University of California at Davis. Director of group-developed theatre pieces at Davis. Author of several essays on group-theatre pieces and *The Art of Dramatic Art*, 1969. **Essay:** Theatre Collectives.

SHRAGGE, Elaine. Graduate student, University of California at Davis. **Essay:** Rochelle Owens.

SIDNELL, Michael. Professor of English, Trinity College, University of Toronto. Actor and director; most recently acted in Denis Johnston's *The Scythe and the Sunset* and directed Donagh MacDonagh's *Happy as Larry*. Author of articles on Irish and theatre subjects, and co-author of *Druid Craft* (on Yeats), 1971. **Essay:** Beverley Simons.

SIMMONS, Judith Cooke. Lecturer in the Extra-Mural Department of the University of London. **Essays:** Keith Dewhurst; Lawrence Durrell; Wolf Mankowitz; Frank Norman; Anne Ridler.

SITNEY, P. Adams. Director of Library and Publications, Anthology Film Archives, New York. **Essay:** Richard Foreman.

SMITH, Michael. See his own entry. **Essays:** George Birimisa; Jackie Curtis; Tom Eyen; María Irene Fornés; William M. Hoffman; H. M. Koutoukas; Murray Mednick.

SOGLIUZZO, A. Richard. Associate Professor of Theatre, University of Texas at Dallas; Assistant Editor, *Theatre Annual*. Author of many articles on Italian theatre, and on Miller, O'Neill, and Coward, in *A Handbook of Modern Drama, A History of the Theatre*, and in periodicals. **Essays:** Mario Fratti; Frank Gagliano; Israel Horovitz.

SPURLING, John. See his own entry. **Essays:** Rodney Ackland; Barry England; Stanley Eveling; David Halliwell; Stephen Poliakoff.

STERN, Carol Simpson.   Member of the School of Speech, Northwestern University, Evanston, Illinois. **Essays:** Kenneth H. Brown; James Goldman.

STRACHAN, Alan.   Director. Productions in London include *The Watched Pot* by Saki, 1970; *John Bull's Other Island*, 1971, and *Misalliance*, 1973, by Shaw; *The Old Boys* by William Trevor, 1971; *A Family and a Fortune* by Julian Mitchell, 1975; co-devised *Cowardy Custard*, 1972; co-devised and directed *Cole*, 1974, and *Yahoo*, 1976; devised and directed *Shakespeare's People*, 1975. **Essays:** John Antrobus; Walter Greenwood; A. R. Gurney, Jr.; Denis Johnston; Keith Johnstone; Bill Naughton; William Trevor; Peter Ustinov.

STYAN, J. L.   Andrew Mellon Professor of English, University of Pittsburgh. Author of *The Elements of Drama*, 1960; *The Dark Comedy*, 1962, 1968; *The Dramatic Experience*, 1965; *Shakespeare's Stagecraft*, 1967; *Chekhov in Performance*, 1971; *The Challenge of the Theatre*, 1972; *Drama, Stage and Audience*, 1975. **Essay:** Christopher Fry.

SYKES, Alrene.   Senior Lecturer in English, University of Queensland, St. Lucia. - Formerly Drama Department Editor for the Australian Broadcasting Commission. Author of articles on modern drama, and *Harold Pinter*, 1970. Editor of *Five Plays for Radio* and two other anthologies of Australian plays. **Essays:** Ron Hibberd; Alan Seymour; Douglas Stewart; Patrick White; David Williamson.

TAUBMAN, Howard.   Drama Critic, 1960–66, and Critic at Large, 1966–75, *The New York Times*; Advisor to the Exxon Corporation on its "Theatre in America" series and other arts programs. Author of several books on music, and *The Making of American Theatre*, 1965. Editor, *The Roosevelt I Knew* by Frances Perkins, 1946.

TAYLOR, John Russell.   Professor in the Division of Performing Arts, University of Southern California, Los Angeles. Film Critic, *The Times*, London, 1962–72, and contributor to many other periodicals. Author of many books, the most recent being *Harold Pinter*, 1969; *The Hollywood Musical*, 1970; *The Second Wave*, 1971; *Directors and Directions*, 1975. Editor of *Look Back in Anger: A Casebook*, 1968; *Graham Greene on Film*, 1972. **Essays:** Ann Jellicoe; John Osborne; David Rudkin; Heathcote Williams; Screen Writers.

THOMPSON, J. E. P.   Member of the English Department, Victoria University of Wellington. **Essay:** Robert Lord.

TREWIN, J. C.   Drama Critic, *Illustrated London News* since 1946, *The Lady* since 1949, *Birmingham Post* since 1955; Editor of *Plays of the Year* series since 1949. Past drama critic for *The Observer, The Sketch, John o' London's Weekly*, and *The Listener*. President of The Critics' Circle, 1964–65; Chairman of the West Country Writers' Association, since 1964. Author of 40 books, including *Mr. Macready*, 1955; *Benson and the Bensonians*, 1960; *Shakespeare on the English Stage, 1900–64*, 1964; *Peter Brook: A Biography*, 1971; *Theatre Bedside Book*, 1974; *The Edwardian Theatre*, 1976. Co-devised *Farjeon Reviewed*, 1975. **Essays:** N. C. Hunter (appendix); Roger MacDougall; N. F. Simpson; Ben Travers.

TRUSSLER, Simon.   Editor of *Theatre Quarterly*, London; Drama Critic, *Tribune*, London, and London correspondent, *The Drama Review*. Author of *Edward Bond*, 1976. Editor of *The Oxford Companion to the Theatre*, 1969. **Essays:** Giles Cooper (appendix); Joe Orton (appendix); John Whiting (appendix).

TURNER, Darwin T.   Professor of English, University of Iowa, Iowa City. Taught at Clark College, Florida A and M. College, North Carolina A and T State University, and the universities of Wisconsin, Michigan and Hawaii. Author of *Catharsis* (verse), 1964; *Nathaniel Hawthorne's "The Scarlet Letter,"* 1967; *Afro-American Writers*, 1970; *In a*

Minor Chord: Three Afro-American Writers of the Renaissance, 1971; *Frank Yerby: The Golden Debunker*, 1972. Editor of *Images of the Negro in America*, 1965; *Black American Literature: Essays, Fiction, and Poetry*, 3 vols., 1969; *Black Drama in America*, 1971; *Voices from the Black Experience: African and Afro-American*, 1972. **Essays:** James Baldwin; Alice Childress; Lonne Elder III; Adrienne Kennedy; Ron Milner; Loften Mitchell; Douglas Turner Ward.

WADE, David.   Radio Critic of *The Times* since 1967. Former critic for *The Listener*. Author of several plays for radio, including *The Cooker, The Guthrie Process, The Goldspinners, Three Blows in Anger, The Ogden File*, and *The Nightingale*. **Essay:** Radio Writers.

WARDLE, Irving.   Drama Critic, *The Times*.

WORSLEY, T. C.   Television Critic, *Financial Times*. Former Drama Critic of the *New Statesman*, 1948–63, and *Financial Times*, 1963–67. Author of *The Fugitive Art*, 1952; *Flannelled Fool*, 1964. **Essay:** Terence Rattigan.

YOUNG, B. A.   Drama Critic, *Financial Times*, London. Assistant Editor, *Punch*, 1949–63. Author of radio and television plays. **Essays:** Enid Bagnold; Frank Marcus; John Spurling.